Spain

written and researched by

Mark Ellingham and John Fisher
with Graham Kenyon and Jules Brown

revised and updated by

Robert Alcock, Simon Baskett, Brian Catlos, Marc Dubin, Geoff
Garvey, Phil Lee, Chris Lloyd, Iain Stewart, Gavin Thomas and
Charles Young

additional accounts by

Guy Barefoot, Hugh Broughton, Manuel Domínguez, Jan Fairley,
David Loscos, Teresa Farino and Gordon McLachlan.

ROUGH
GUIDES

www.roughguides.com

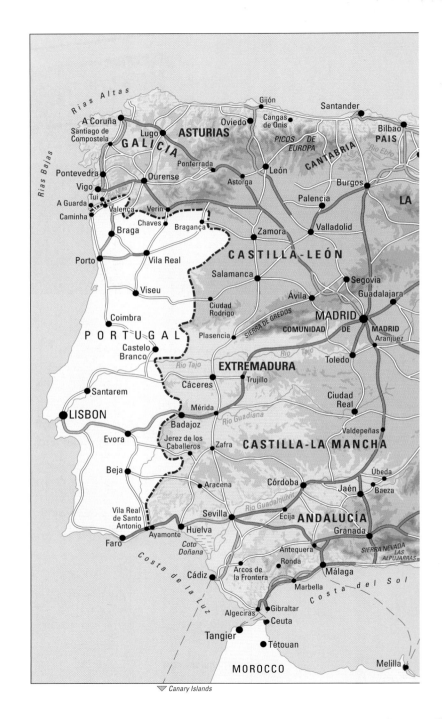

Canary Islands

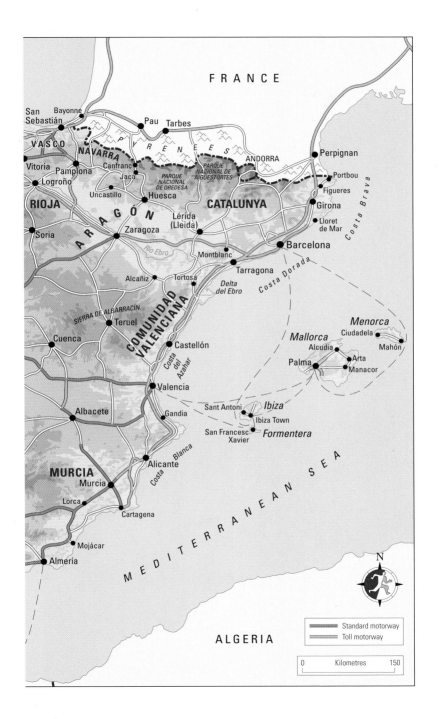

Introduction to

Spain

If you are coming to Spain for the first time, be warned: this is a country that fast becomes an addiction. You might intend to come just for a beach holiday, or a tour of the major cities, but before you know it you'll find yourself hooked by something quite different – by the celebration of some local fiesta, perhaps, or the amazing nightlife in Madrid, by the Moorish monuments of Andalucia, by Basque cooking, or the wild landscapes and birds of prey of Estremadura. And by then, of course, you will have noticed that there is not just one Spain but many. Indeed, Spaniards often speak of *Las Españas* (the Spains) and they even talk of the capital in the plural – *Los Madriles*, the Madrids.

This regionalism is an obsession and perhaps the most significant change to the country over recent decades has been the creation of seventeen *autonomías* – autonomous regions – with their own governments, budgets and cultural ministries. The old days of a unified nation, governed with a firm hand from Madrid, seem to have gone forever, as the separate kingdoms which made up the original Spanish state reassert themselves. And the differences are evident wherever you look: in language, culture and artistic traditions, in landscapes and cityscapes, and attitudes and politics.

The cities – above all – are compellingly individual. Barcelona, for many, has the edge: for Gaudí's splendid *modernista* architecture, the lively promenade of Las Ramblas, designer clubs *par excellence*, and, not least, for Barça

Fact file

- Spain's land area is around half a million square kilometres – about twice the size of the UK or Oregon. Of its 40 million-strong population some 99 per-cent declare themselves Catholic.

- Politically, Spain is a parlia-mentary monarchy – democra-cy and the monarchy having been restored in 1977, after the death of General Franco, the dictator who seized power in the Civil War of 1936–39. The current parliament is controlled by the centre-right Partido Pop-ular, under President José Maria Aznar.

- Regionalism is a major force in Spanish politics, with the country divided into seventeen autonomous regions. The most powerful are Catalunya and the Basque Country, where national-ism is a potent force. In the Basque Country, the paramilitary organization, ETA, conducts an ongoing campaign of terrorism targeted at "the Spanish state".

- Spanish (Castilian) is spoken as a first language by 74 per-cent of the population, while seventeen percent speak vari-ants of Catalan (in Catalunya, parts of Valencia and Alicante provinces, and the Balearic islands), seven percent speak Galician, and two percent Basque. As the regional lan-guages were banned under Franco, the vast majority of the people who speak them are also fluent in Castilian.

- The most important newspa-pers are *El Pais* and *El Mundo*, both of which are liberal in out-look. But Spaniards read fewer papers than almost all other Europeans – and the bestseller is *Marca*, a daily devoted purely to football.

- A minority of Spaniards attend bullfights; it doesn't rain much on the plains; and they only dance flamenco in the southern region of Andalucía.

– the city's football team. But Madrid, although not as pretty, claims as many devotees. The city and its people, immortalized in the movies of Pedro Almodóvar, have a vibrancy and style that is revealed in a thousand bars and summer terrazas. Not to mention three of the world's finest art museums. Then there's Sevilla, home of flamenco and all the clichés of southern Spain; Valencia, the vibrant Levantine city with an arts scene and nightlife to equal any Euro-pean rival; and Bilbao, a new entry on Spain's cultural circuit, due to Frank Gehry's astonishing Guggenheim museum.

Monuments range just as widely from one region to another, dependent on their history of control and occupation by Romans and Moors, their role in the "golden age" of Imperial Renaissance Spain, or their twentieth-century for-tunes. Touring Castile and León, you confront the classic Spanish images of vast cathedrals and *reconquista* castles – literally hundreds of the latter; in the northern mountains of Asturias and the Pyrenees, tiny, almost organic Romanesque churches dot the hillsides and villages; Andalucía has the great mosques and Moorish palaces of Granada, Sevilla and Córdoba; Castile has the superbly preserved medieval capital, Toledo, and the gorgeous Renaissance university city of Salamanca; while the harsh landscape of Estremadura cradles the ornate *conquistador* towns built with riches from the "New World".

Not that Spain is predominantly about buildings. For most visitors, the landscape holds just as much fascination – and variety. The evergreen estuaries of Galicia could hardly be more different from the high, arid plains of Castile, or the gulch-like desert landscapes of Almería. Agriculture makes its mark in the patterned hillsides of the wine- and olive-growing regions and the rice fields of the Levante. Spain is also one of the most mountainous countries in Europe, and there is superb walking and wildlife

Spanish time

Spanish time is notionally one hour ahead of the UK – but conceptually Spain might as well be on a different planet. Nowhere in Europe keeps such late hours. Spaniards may not take a traditional midday siesta so much as they used to, but their life cycles remain committedly nocturnal. They'll saunter out around 8pm or 9pm in the evening for a *paseo*, to greet friends and maybe have a drink and tapas, and if they're eating out, they'll commonly start at 10 or 11pm, sometimes later in Madrid. It's not unusual for someone to phone around midnight to see if you're going out for the evening.

Like everything else, practises differ somewhat by region. Madrid is famed for staying up the latest, with Andalucía a close second. In the north, particularly in Catalonia, they keep more Northern European hours. And, of course, summer nights are the real late, late shows.

in a dozen or more sierras – above all in the Picos de Europa and Pyrenees. Spain's unique fauna boast protected species like brown bears, the Spanish lynx and Mediterranean monk seals as well as more common wild boar, white storks and birds of prey.

One of Spain's greatest draws is undeniably its beaches although with infinitely more variety than you would be led to believe from the sun-and-sand holiday brochures. Long tracts of coastline – along the Costa del Sol, in particular – have been developed into concrete hotel and villa complexes but delightful pockets remain even on the big tourist costas. On the Costa Brava, the string of coves between Palamos and Begur are often overlooked, while in the south there are superb windsurfing waters around Tarifa and some decidedly low-key resorts along the Costa de la Luz. In the north, the cooler Atlantic coastline boasts the surfing sands of Cantabria and the unspoilt coves of Galicia's estuaries. Offshore, the Balearic islands have some superb sands and, if you're up for it, Ibiza also offers one of the most hedonistic backdrops to beachlife in the Mediterranean.

> **Spain is one of the most mountainous countries in Europe, and there is superb walking and wildlife in a dozen or more sierras**

Wherever you are in Spain, you can't help but notice the Spaniards' infectious enthusiasm for life. In the cities there is always something happening – in bars and clubs, on the streets, and especially at fiesta times.

Even in out of the way places there's a surprising range of nightlife and entertainment, not to mention the daily pleasures of a round of tapas, moving from bar to bar, having a beer, a glass of wine or a *fino* (dry sherry) and a bite of the house speciality.

The identity and appeal of each of the regions is explored in the chapter introductions, where you'll find a rundown on their highlights, while in the following pages you'll find a selection of the very best of Spain.

Fiestas

It's hard to beat the experience of arriving in some small Spanish village, expecting no more than a bed for the night, to discover the streets decked out with flags and streamers, a band playing in the plaza and the entire population out celebrating the local fiesta. Everywhere in Spain, from the tiniest hamlet to the great cities, devotes at least a couple of days a year to their festivals. Usually it's the local saint's day, but there are celebrations of harvests, of deliverance from the Moors, of safe return from the sea – any excuse will do. There are also the events of the Catholic calendar, most notably Semana Santa (Holy Week), which in Andalucía sees theatrical religious floats carried through the streets, accompanied by hooded penitents atoning for the year's misdeeds.

Each festival is different. In the Basque country there will often be bulls running through the streets (most famously at Pamplona in July); in Andalucía, horses, flamenco and the guitar are an essential part of any celebration; in Valencia they specialize in huge bonfires and deranged firework displays (climaxing in Las Fallas in March). But this is just the mainstream. Fiestas can be very strange indeed, ranging from parades of devils to full-blown battles with water or even tomatoes.

For more on fiestas, see p.54, and for a calendar of local events, see the listings at the beginning of each chapter.

Tapas

Tapas have become international fare in recent years – yet nothing can prepare you for the variety on offer on their home soil. That is, if you're prepared to do things properly, wandering from one bar to another to sample a particular speciality. Although many bars will have a range of tapas on display or on their menu board, most tend to be known for just one or two dishes ... and the locals would not think of ordering anything else. So you might go to one place for a slice or two of *jamon serrano* (cured ham), another for *pulpo Gallego* (deliciously tender pot-cooked octopus), a third for the bizarre *pimientos de Padron* (strange small peppers – about one in ten of which are chilli-hot), and then maybe on to a smoky old bar that serves just *fino* (dry sherry) from the barrel along with slices of *mojama* (dried, pressed roe).

When to go

Overall, spring, early summer and autumn are ideal times for a Spanish trip – though the weather varies enormously from region to region. The high central plains suffer from fierce extremes, stiflingly hot in summer, bitterly cold and swept by freezing winds in winter. The Atlantic coast, in contrast, has a tendency to damp and mist, and a relatively brief, humid summer. The Mediterranean south is warm virtually all year round, and in parts of Andalucía positively subtropical, warm enough to wear a T-shirt by day even in the winter months.

In high summer the other factor worth considering is tourism itself. Spain plays host to some thirty million tourists a year – almost one for every resident – and all the main beach and mountain resorts are packed in July and August, as are the major sights. August, Spain's own holiday month, sees the coast at its most crowded and the cities, by contrast, pretty sleepy.

Average temperatures

	Jan	March	May	July	Sept	Nov
Madrid (°C)	9	15	21	31	25	13
Castile (°F)	49	59	70	88	77	56
Málaga (°C)	17	19	23	29	29	20
Costa del Sol (°F)	63	67	74	84	84	68
Sevilla (°C)	15	21	26	35	32	20
Inland Andalucía (°F)	59	70	78	95	90	68
Pontevedra (°C)	14	16	20	25	24	16
Galicia (°F)	58	61	68	77	75	61
Santander (°C)	12	15	17	22	21	15
Cantabrian coast (°F)	54	59	63	72	70	59
Barcelona (°C)	13	16	21	28	25	16
Catalunya (°F)	56	61	70	83	77	61
Cap Bagur (°C)	14	16	20	27	25	16
Costa Brava (°F)	58	61	68	80	77	61
Alicante (°C)	16	20	26	32	30	21
Costa Blanca (°F)	61	68	78	90	86	70
Mallorca (°C)	14	17	22	29	27	18
Balearic Islands (°F)	58	63	72	84	80	65

Note that these are all **average temperatures** – and whilst Sevilla, the hottest city in Spain, can soar into the nineties at midday in summer, it is a fairly comfortable 23–27°C (75–80°F) through much of the morning and late afternoon. Equally, bear in mind that temperatures in the north, in Galicia for example, can approach freezing point at night in winter, whilst mountainous regions can get extremely cold at any time of year.

44

things not to miss

It's not possible to see everything that Spain has to offer in one trip – and we don't suggest you try. What follows is a selective taste of the country's highlights: outstanding buildings, natural wonders, spectacular festivals and unforgettable journeys. They're arranged in five colour-coded categories, which you can browse through to find the very best things to see and experience. All highlights have a page reference to take you straight into the guide, where you can find out more.

01 Wine Page **50** • Spain's formidable variety of quality wines remain little known outside the peninsula.

02 Aqueduct, Segovia Page **185** ● 800 metres long, this solid piece of Roman engineering has been spanning the Castilian town for nearly 2000 years

04 Sherry Page **51** ● There are few greater pleasures than a chilled glass of *fino* or *manzanilla* accompanied by a bite of the local speciality.

03 Las Fallas Page **881** ● In March, Valencia erupts in festivities as giant models are burnt and fireworks crackle across town to celebrate San José.

xiii

05 Paella
Page **884** •
The subtle saffron taste of this rice-based dish is best enjoyed with a sea view in its home province of Valencia.

06 Picasso
Page **106** • Picasso's portrayal of the agony of Spain's struggle and suffering against fascism in *Guernica* is considered his strongest work.

08 Cota de Doñana
Page **326** • Doñana's unique habitats enables this vast national park to host a myriad of birds and other wildlife, including the Iberian lynx.

07 Dalí Museum, Figueres
Page **768** • The egg-capped museum is as surreal as its creator – who lies in a mausoleum within.

09 Deià old town, Mallorca
Page **991** • Explore the labyrinthine alleys overlooking terraced fields tumbling down to the sea.

10 Flamenco Page **1044** • The stamp of heels and heart-rending lament of a *cante jondo* encapsulate the soul of the Spanish South.

11 Windsurfing Page **314** • Catch the wind in Tarifa at one of the world's top windsurfing spots.

12 **Paradors**
Page **43** • Converted castles and monasteries provide the atmospheric setting for many of these luxurious hotels.

13 **Las Alpujarras** Page **370** • Drive over lemons and walk old mulepaths in this picturesque region of mountain villages nestling in the southern folds of the Sierra Nevada.

14 **Seafood** Page **48** • From Galicia's *pulpo* (octopus) and *veiras* (scallops) to Andalucia's fried *boquerones* and tiny *chanquetes*, Spain's seafood is unbeatable for quality and variety.

15 Parque Nacional de Ordesa

Page **663** • This national park on the edge of the Pyrenees offers fantastic hiking, with waterfalls, canyons and birds of prey.

16 Mini-Hollywood, Almería
Page **384** • Ride into town for a shoot-out or a drink at the saloon on the set of *The Good, the Bad and the Ugly*, deep in the Almerían desert.

17 Jamón serrano
Page **202** • A few thin slices of the best cured *jamón* are a must for any carnivore.

18 El Camino de Santiago
Page **590** • The medieval pilgrim route to the shrine of Santiago left a swath of Renaissance and Gothic buildings, not least the great cathedral of Santiago de Compostela at the end of the road.

19 **Clubbing** Page **939** • Forget sleep, experience everything else to excess, on Ibiza – the ultimate party island.

21 **A night on the tiles, Madrid** Page **126** • Delight in the capital's most traditional of rituals – a night of bar hopping and clubbing rounded off by a dawn reviver of hot chocolate and *churros*.

22 **Salamanca** Page **395** • Wander the narrow streets of this ancient university town with its untouched Gothic and Renaissance buildings.

20 **Semana Santa** Pages **54 & 292** • Easter week sees processions of masked penitents parade around villages and towns across Spain, with the biggest events in Sevilla and Málaga.

23 La Liga Page **57** • Spanish football is arguably the best in Europe right now. Get to a match (or just watch in a bar) and debate the merits of Barça, Real Madrid and Deportivo La Coruña.

24 Modernisme Page **712** • The sculptural forms of Barcelona's *modernista* architects – most famously Gaudí – define the city's exuberant architectural heritage.

25 Fería de Abril Page **293** • Sevilla's week-long fiesta is Andalucía at its celebratory best, with a vast fair of flamenco dance tents, and horsemen and women dressed to kill.

26 The Rastro, Madrid Page **95** • Join the locals and spend the morning rooting out for bargains and meeting friends at the capital's flea market.

28 Alhambra, Granada Page 354
• The legendary Moorish palace complex is a monument to sensuality and contemplative decoration.

27 Goya Page 99
• The genius of this artist ranges through his light court scenes to the haunting black paintings he created near the end of his life.

29 San Fermín, Pamplona Page 500
• Join in with the celebrations but watch others run with the bulls at Spain's most famous festival.

30 Skiing Page 368
• In late spring you can ski in the Sierra Nevada in the morning and pop down to the Mediterranean for a dip in the afternoon.

31 Miró Page **710** • The bold paintings and abstract forms of the artist's work are housed in the wonderfully sympathetic building of the Fundació.

33 Carnaval Pages **559 & 848** • Take to the streets with fancy dress and floats; Avilés and Sitges throw two of the most spectacular carnival parties.

34 Parque Natural de Monfragüe Page **221** • Birds of prey, especially eagles and vultures, abound in this protected area of Estremadura.

32 Sevilla Page **287** • The quintessential Andalucian city with sun-drenched plazas, Moorish monuments and more bars than seems remotely feasible.

35 Guggenheim Museum, Bilbao Page **489** • The undulating titanium of Bilbao's flagpiece has become one of the iconic buildings of modern Spain.

36 Ibiza and Formentera's beaches Pages **945 & 948** • The islands' little-developed beaches vary from gem-like coves to sweeps of white sand.

37 Pavelló Mies van der Rohe Page **710** • Visit Barcelona for the perfect lines of this exquisite building by the father of Modernism.

38 Mezquita, Cordoba Page **335** • Nothing can prepare you for the breathtaking beauty of the Grand Mosque of Cordoba – one of the world's great buildings.

39 Velazquez Page **99** • The greatest Spanish artist? Decide for yourself in the salons of the Prado gallery in Madrid.

40 Sonár Page **737** • In June Barcelona hosts the very latest in cutting-edge electronic music and arts at the international Sonár festival.

41 Picos de Europa Page **539** • This stunning northern area of mountain peaks and gorges has superb walking, canoeing and rock-climbing.

42 Café society Page **52** • One of the enduring pleasures of Spain's terrazas is to sip a coffee, read the paper and watch the world.

43 Toledo Page **151** • The capital of Medieval Spain and a symbol of religious tolerance has changed little since its depiction in El Greco's paintings.

44 Port Aventura Page **858** • Travel through time and around the globe in a day of rides and fun at Spain's premier theme park.

contents

using the Rough Guide

We've tried to make this Rough Guide a good read and easy to use. The book is divided into five main sections, and you should be able to find whatever you want in one of them.

colour section

The front colour section offers a quick tour of Spain. The **introduction** aims to give you a feel for the place, with suggestions on where to go. We also tell you what the weather is like and include a basic country fact file. Next, our authors round up their favourite aspects of Spain in the **things not to miss** section – whether it's great food, amazing sights or a special hotel. Right after this comes the Rough Guide's full **contents** list.

basics

You've decided to go and the Basics section covers all the **pre-departure** nitty-gritty to help you plan your trip. This is where to find out which airlines fly to your destination, what paperwork you'll need, what to do about money and insurance, about internet access, food, security, public transport, car rental – in fact just about every piece of **general practical information** you might need.

guide

This is the heart of the Rough Guide, divided into user-friendly chapters, each of which covers a specific region. Every chapter starts with a list of **highlights** and an **introduction** that helps you to decide where to go, depending on your time and budget.

Likewise, introductions to the various towns and smaller regions within each chapter should help you plan your itinerary. We start most town accounts with information on arrival and accommodation, followed by a tour of the sights, and finally reviews of places to eat and drink, and details of nightlife. Longer accounts also have a directory of practical listings. Each chapter concludes with **public transport** details for that region.

contexts

Read Contexts to get a deeper understanding of what makes Spain tick. We include a brief **history**, articles about **architecture**, **wildlife** and **music**, a detailed further reading section that reviews dozens of **books** relating to the country, a **language** section which gives useful guidance for speaking Spanish, and a glossary of words and terms that are peculiar to the country.

index + small print

Apart from a **full index**, which includes maps as well as places, this section covers publishing information, credits and acknowledgements, and also has our contact details in case you want to send in updates and corrections to the book – or suggestions as to how we might improve it.

chapter map of **Spain**

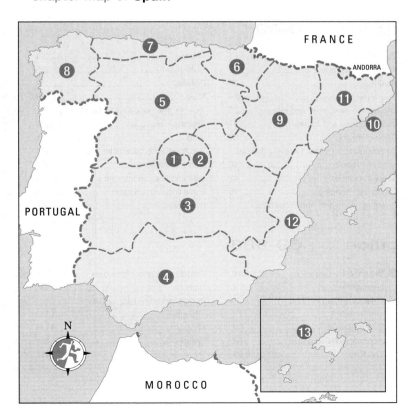

contents

colour section · i–xxiv

basics · 9–68

guide · 69–986

contexts 987–1080

index and small print 1081–1093

map symbols

symbols

maps are listed in the full index using coloured text

▬▬▬	Motorway (standard)	◆	General point of interest
▬▬▬	Motorway (tolled)	⚱	Waterfall
═══	Major road	⊥	Spa
═══	Minor road	◠	Mountain range
▭▭▭	Steps	▲	Mountain peak
‑ ‑ ‑ ‑ ‑	Track	⚡	Viewpoint
- - - - -	Footpath	⌒	Caves
▬■▬■	Railway	♜	Castle
─ ─	Ferry route	⸙	Lighthouse
───	Waterway	⚲	Ski area
▬ ▬ ▬	Chapter division boundary	⊞	Hospital
▬▬・	National border	ⓘ	Tourist office
▬・▬・	Provincial border	⊠	Post office
✈	Airport	ⓣ	Telephone
⬥	Metro station	🅿	Parking
◉	Hotel	■	Building
⌂	Campsite	⊶	Church
⛿	Mountain refuge	▦	Park
⛪	Church (regional maps)	▧	Wood/forest
♙	Monastery	▦	Beach

basics

basics

Getting there

From the United Kingdom and Ireland the most convenient way of getting to Spain from the UK and Ireland is to fly – flights from London take around two hours to Madrid and Barcelona and two and a half hours to Málaga, and the lowest-priced air fares are cheaper than tickets for the long train or bus journey. There are also direct ferry services from Plymouth to Santander and from Portsmouth to Bilbao. From North America a number of airlines fly direct to Madrid, many with onward connections to Barcelona. Occasionally, however – and especially if you're coming from Canada – you may find it cheaper to route via London, picking up an inexpensive onward flight from there. There are no direct flights to Spain from Australia or New Zealand; the quickest route is via Asia.

Air fares always depend on the **season**, with the highest being around Easter and June to the end of September, when the weather is best; fares drop during the "shoulder" seasons – October and May to mid-May – and you'll get the best prices during the low season, November to March (excluding Christmas and New Year when prices are hiked up and seats are at a premium). Note also that flying at weekends ordinarily adds £35/$50 to the round-trip fare; price ranges quoted below assume midweek travel.

You can often cut costs by going through a **specialist flight agent** – either a consolidator, who buys up blocks of tickets from the airlines and sells them at a discount, or a **discount agent**, who in addition to dealing with discounted flights may also offer special student and youth fares and a range of other travel-related services such as travel insurance, rail passes, car rentals, tours and the like. Some agents specialize in **charter flights**, which may be cheaper than anything available on a scheduled flight, but again departure dates are fixed and withdrawal penalties are high. For some of the popular holiday destinations, such as the Costa del Sol or the Balearics, you may even find it cheaper to pick up a bargain **package deal** from one of the tour operators listed below and then find your own accommodation when you get there.

If Spain is only one stop on a longer journey, you might want to consider buying a **Round-the-World (RTW) ticket**. Some travel agents can sell you an "off-the-shelf" RTW ticket that will have you touching down in about half a dozen cities; others will have to

assemble one for you, which can be tailored to your needs but is apt to be more expensive. Figure on £950/$1500 for an RTW ticket including Spain.

Booking flights online

Many airlines and discount travel websites offer you the opportunity to book your tickets online, cutting out the costs of agents and middlemen. Good deals can often be found through discount or auction sites, as well as through the airlines' own websites.

Online booking agents and general travel sites

Ⓦ **www.etn.nl/discount.htm** A hub of consolidator and discount agent web links, maintained by the nonprofit European Travel Network.

Ⓦ **www.flyaow.com** Online air travel info and reservations site.

Ⓦ **http://travel.yahoo.com** Incorporates a lot of Rough Guide material in its coverage of destination countries and cities across the world, with information about places to eat and sleep etc.

Ⓦ **www.cheaptickets.com** Discount flight specialists.

Ⓦ **www.cheapflights.com** Flight deals, travel agents, plus links to other travel sites.

Ⓦ **www.lastminute.com** Offers good last-minute holiday package and flight-only deals.

Ⓦ **www.deckchair.com** Bob Geldof's online venture, drawing on a wide range of airlines.

Ⓦ **www.expedia.com** Discount air fares, all-airline search engine and daily deals.

Ⓦ **www.travelocity.com** Destination guides, hot web fares and best deals for car rental and accommodation, as well as fares. Provides access to the travel agent system SABRE, the most comprehensive central reservations system in the US.

ⓦ www.hotwire.com Bookings from the US only. Last-minute savings of up to forty percent on regular published fares. Travellers must be at least 18 and there are no refunds, transfers or changes allowed. Log-in required.

ⓦ www.priceline.com Bookings from the US and UK only. Name-your-own-price website that has deals at around forty percent off standard fares. You cannot specify flight times (although you do specify dates) and the tickets are non-refundable, non-transferable and non-changeable.

ⓦ www.skyauction.com Bookings from the US only. Auctions tickets and travel packages using a "second bid" scheme. The best strategy is to bid the maximum you're willing to pay, since if you win you'll pay just enough to beat the runner-up regardless of your maximum bid.

ⓦ www.sydneytravel.com Australian discount air tickets agents.

ⓦ www.travel.com.au Australian website with good range of discounted air fares.

ⓦ www.travelshop.com.au Australian website offering discounted flights, packages, insurance and online bookings.

ⓦ www.uniquetravel.com.au Australian site with a good range of packages and good-value flights.

ⓦ www.gaytravel.com Gay online travel agent, concentrating mostly on accommodation.

Flights from the UK and Ireland

There are numerous flights from the UK and Ireland to Spain throughout the year, with charters and cut-price no-frills airlines generally being the least expensive. **Charters** are usually block-booked by package holiday firms, but even in the middle of August they're rarely completely full and spare seats are often sold off at discounts. For an idea of current prices and availability, contact any high-street travel agent, or a specialist agency or operator, such as Air 2000 or AVRO plc, listed below. Ads also regularly appear in local evening newspapers, as well as broadsheet weekend supplements and the *Time Out* listings magazine.

Cut-price airlines – such as easyJet, Go and Buzz – are just as inexpensive, offering mostly single fares, sold direct, on **no-frills flights**. Prices start from as little as £34 one-way from London to Madrid. It is advisable to book as far ahead as possible, as these airlines have limited cheap seats on each flight and regular seats are more than twice as expensive. Tickets can be bought over the phone or slightly discounted on the internet.

Iberia, Spain's national airline, and British Airways have the widest range of **scheduled flights**, including regular services from London to Santiago, Bilbao, Valencia and Sevilla, as well as to the main Spanish destinations. Iberia also offers direct flights from Manchester to Barcelona, while British Airways flies direct from both Manchester and Birmingham to Madrid and Barcelona. From Dublin you can fly direct with Iberia to Madrid and Barcelona. Aer Lingus also operates direct services from Dublin, but only from April to late October. There are no direct scheduled flights from Belfast to Spain: most routeings are via London or Birmingham.

A typical high-season scheduled **fare** from London to Madrid costs around £180, not including airport tax, though special offers can take the price as low as £100. In low season, reckon on paying around £135. Fares from Dublin to Madrid in high season are around €330, including tax, and €293 in low season. For non-direct flights via London, fares on Aer Lingus, BA and Iberia are basically the same.

There is also a scheduled service with Air Europa which only flies from Gatwick to Madrid and Palma, but whose six weekly services tend to be rather cheaper than either BA or Iberia.

Package holiday deals can be worth looking at, especially if you book early, late or out of season. While the cheaper, mass-market packages may seem to restrict you to some of the worst parts of the coast, remember that there's no compulsion to stick around your hotel. Get a good enough deal and it can be worth it simply for the flight – with transfer to a reasonably comfortable hotel laid on for a night or two at each end. Bargains can be found at virtually any high-street travel agent.

City breaks are often available at excellent package rates and destinations on offer include Barcelona, Madrid, Sevilla and Granada, flying from London or Manchester. Prices **from London** vary between around £250 (Madrid) and £300 (Sevilla) for three days (two nights). Prices **from Belfast** run from £300 to 350; you can book a city break from Dublin, but it basically means sorting out a city break deal from London with your travel agent, who will then be able to sell you an add-on Dublin–London flight for €76–114, depending on which London airport you fly into. Adding extra nights or upgrading your hotel is possible, too, usually at a fairly reasonable cost. The prices normally include return flights, airport transfer and bed and breakfast in a centrally located one-, two- or three-star hotel. Again, ask your travel agent for the best deal – especially for those under 26 – and check the addresses on p.14.

Fly-drive deals are well worth considering, too, as a combined air ticket and car rental arrangement can be excellent value. There are also some very good (and very attractive) deals available in **villas and apartments**, especially from companies who specialize in off-the-beaten-track farmhouses and the like. Several companies also offer a range of *casas rurales*, on a similar basis to French *gîtes*. Other specialist companies offer an enticing range of **trekking or mountain-biking holidays** or more upmarket tours based around the country's historic *paradores*.

Airlines

Aer Lingus ☻www.aerlingus.ie, UK ☎0845/973 7747, Republic of Ireland ☎01/886 8888. Direct flights from Dublin to Barcelona and Madrid.
Air Europa ☻www.aireuropa.com, ☎0870/240 1501. From Gatwick to Madrid and in summer (May–Sept) to Palma.
British Airways ☻www.britishairways.com, UK ☎0845/773 3377, Republic of Ireland ☎1800/626 747. From Heathrow or Gatwick to Madrid, Sevilla, Jerez, Bilbao, Palma, Murcia, Barcelona, Málaga, Alicante, Valencia and Gibraltar. Also has direct flights from Manchester and Birmingham to Madrid and Barcelona, with Madrid also served direct from Glasgow.
British Midland ☻www.flybmi.com, UK ☎0870/607 0555, Northern Ireland ☎08457/554 554, Republic of Ireland ☎01/283 8833. Regular scheduled flights from Belfast, Dublin, Edinburgh, Glasgow, Leeds, London Heathrow and Manchester to Madrid and Barcelona. Belfast, Dublin, Edinburgh and East Midlands also fly to Malaga and Palma. In addition, Glasgow, London Heathrow and Manchester fly to Palma.
Buzz ☻www.buzzaway.com, ☎0870/240 7070. No-frills airline with direct flights from London Stansted to Murcia, Jerez and Girona.

easyJet ☻www.easyjet.com, ☎0870/600 0000. Budget scheduled flights from London Luton and Liverpool to Barcelona, Palma, Madrid and Málaga.
Go ☻www.go-fly.com, ☎0870/607 6543. Low-cost airline offering direct flights from London Stansted Airport to Barcelona, Bilbao, Madrid, Málaga, and also Ibiza and Mallorca in summer.
Iberia Airlines ☻www.iberia.com, UK ☎0845/601 2854, Republic of Ireland ☎01/677 9846. From Heathrow and Gatwick direct to Madrid, Barcelona, Bilbao, Santiago, Sevilla, Málaga, Alicante, Valencia and Oviedo with internal connections to most other airports in Spain. Also has direct flights from Manchester to Barcelona and from Dublin to Madrid and Barcelona.
Ryanair ☻www.ryanair.com, UK ☎0870/156 9569, Republic of Ireland ☎01/609 7800. From Stansted to Biarritz and Perpignan, both useful for northern Spain.
Virgin Express ☻www.virgin-express.com, ☎0800/891199. From Heathrow to Madrid, Barcelona and Málaga. Note that all flights involve changing planes at Brussels.

Flight and travel agents

Air 2000 ☻www.firstchoice.co.uk, ☎0870/750 0001. Charter arm of First Choice Holidays.
Aran Travel International ☻www.iol.ie/~aran/aranmain.htm, Galway ☎091/562 595. Good-value flights to all parts of the world.
AVRO plc ☻www.avro-flights.co.uk, ☎020/8715 4440. UK specialists in charter and scheduled flights.
Bridge the World ☻www.bridgetheworld.com, ☎020/7911 0900. Specializing in round-the-world tickets, with good deals aimed at the backpacker market.
CIE Tours International ☻www.cietours.ie, Dublin ☎01/703 1888. General flight and tour agent.
Flightbookers ☻www.ebookers.com, ☎020/7757 2444. Low fares on an extensive selection of scheduled flights.
Joe Walsh Tours ☻www.joewalshtours.ie, Dublin ☎01/872 2555, Cork ☎021/4277 959. General budget fares agent.
Lee Travel, ☻www.leetravel.ie, Cork ☎021/4277 111. Flights and holidays.
Liffey Travel Dublin ☎01/878 8322 or 878 8063. Package-tour specialists.
The London Flight Centre ☻www.top decktravel.co.uk, ☎020/7244 6411. Long-established agent dealing in discount flights.
McCarthy's Travel ☻www.mccarthystravel.ie, Cork ☎021/4270 127. General flight agent.

Rosetta Travel ⓦ www.rosettatravel.com, Belfast
ⓣ 028/9064 4996. Flight and holiday agent.
STA Travel ⓦ www.statravel.co.uk,
ⓣ 0870/1606070. Specialists in low-cost flights and
tours for students and under-26s, though other
customers welcome.
Student & Group Travel Dublin ⓣ 01/677 7834.
Student and group specialists, mostly to Europe.
Trailfinders ⓦ www.trailfinders.com, UK
ⓣ 020/7628 7628, Republic of Ireland ⓣ 01/677
7888. One of the best-informed and most efficient
agents for independent travellers; produce a very
useful quarterly magazine worth scrutinizing for
round-the-world routes.
Usit Campus ⓦ www.usitcampus.co.uk,
ⓣ 0870/240 1010. Student/youth travel specialists,
offering discount flights.
USIT Now ⓦ www.usitnow.ie, Belfast ⓣ 028/9032
7111, Dublin ⓣ 01/602 1777 or 677 8117, Cork
ⓣ 021/4270 900, Derry ⓣ 028/7137 1888. Student
and youth specialists for flights and trains.

Tour Operators

Cox & Kings ⓦ www.coxandkings.co.uk,
ⓣ 020/7873 5018. Nature tours of the Aragonese
Pyrenees and Andalucía, staying in farmhouses.
Discover Andalucía
ⓦ www.discoverandalucia.com, ⓣ 956 447 577.
Avda. Los Remedios 45, Vejer de la Frontera, Cádiz
11150, Spain. Activity holidays including guided
bird-watching, painting and archeology breaks. Also
offers multi-adventure, mountain biking, cycling and
canyoning trips.
Exodus Travels ⓦ www.exodus.co.uk,
ⓣ 020/8675 5550. Walking and cycling in
Andalucía, Mallorca, the Picos de Europa and the
Pyrenees (and most of the other minor mountain
ranges), as well as multi-adventure (climbing, caving,
rafting etc) cultural and sightseeing trips.
Explore Worldwide Ltd ⓦ www.explore
worldwide.co.uk, ⓣ 01252/760 000. Walking in
Andalucía, Sierra Nevada and the Picos de Europa.
Hotels Abroad ⓦ www.hotelsabroad.co.uk,
ⓣ 01689/882500. Specialist operator with a wide
range of accommodation, from rustic farmhouses to
luxurious country manors. Can also arrange ferries
and car rental at discount rates.
Individual Travellers ⓦ www.indiv-
travellers.com, ⓣ 01798/869 461. Farmhouses,
cottages and village houses all over Spain. Can also
arrange flights and ferries.
Keytel International ⓣ 020/7402 8182,
ⓔ paradores@keytel.co.uk. Official UK agents for
Spain's paradores; occasionally has special offers.

Madrid and Beyond
ⓦ www.madridandbeyond.com, ⓣ 917 580 063.
Madrid-based British specialist operator offering
anything from accommodation reservations to city
breaks or tailor-made itineraries throughout Spain.
Martin Randall Travel
ⓦ www.martinrandall.com, ⓣ 020/8742 3355.
Small-group cultural tours to Madrid, Toledo and
Seville, among others; led by experts on art,
archeology or music.
Mountain Bike España ⓦ www.mountbik-
espana.co.uk, UK ⓣ 01494/870486 or Spain
ⓣ 952 491 137. Small company organizing guided
mountain-bike tours around the mountains and
national parks above Málaga.
Pilgrim Adventure ⓣ 0117/957 3997; 120
Bromley Heath Rd, Downsend, Bristol BS16 6JJ.
Religious tours.
Portland Holidays ⓦ www.portland-direct.co.uk,
ⓣ 0870/5002 200. Package holidays on Costa
Brava, Costa del Sol and Balearic Islands.
Ramblers Holidays ⓣ 01707/320226,
ⓔ info@ramblersholidays.co.uk. Walking, hiking
and sightseeing holidays throughout Spain.
Rustic Blue ⓦ www.rusticblue.com, ⓣ 958 763
381. Spain-based company specializing in rural
holidays, from traditional villages to furnished cave-
dwellings in the Sacromonte area of Granada. Also
organizes specialized and adventure tours.
Sherpa Expeditions ⓦ www.sherpa-walking-
holidays.co.uk, ⓣ 020/8577 2717. Trekking in the
Sierra Nevada, the Alpujarras, the Pyrenees, the
Picos de Europa and Mallorca.
Spanish Travel Services ⓣ 020/7387 5337.
Spanish flight, city-break and package specialists.
Time Off ⓣ 0845/733 6622 or 0870/584 6363.
City-break specialists.
Travellers Way ⓦ www.travellersway.co.uk,
ⓣ 01527/836 791. Tailor-made holidays and city
breaks all over Spain, especially Andalucía and the
northwest.
Waymark Holidays ⓦ www.waymarkholidays.
co.uk, ⓣ 01753/516 477. Walking holidays in
Andalucía, the Pyrenees, the Picos de Europa and
along the Camino de Santiago.
Winetrails ⓦ www.winetrails.co.uk,
ⓣ 01306/712111. Ten-day wine tours through
Navarra, Andalucía and La Rioja.

Flights from the USA and Canada

There is a fair variety of scheduled and charter flights from most parts of North America
to Madrid, often with connections on to
Barcelona. Occasionally, however – and

especially if you're coming from Canada – you'll find it cheaper to route via London, picking up an inexpensive onward flight from there (see "Flights from the UK and Ireland" for all the details). If Spain is part of a longer European trip, you'll also want to check out details of the Eurail pass, which must be purchased in advance of your arrival and can get you by train from anywhere in Europe to Spain. Price ranges quoted in the following sections assume midweek travel and include tax (around $50 or CAN$40–55).

Iberia flies nonstop to Madrid from New York, Miami and Chicago, and has the advantage that it offers connecting flights to almost anywhere in Spain, often very good value if booked with your transatlantic flight. Several **US airlines** fly direct from the East Coast to Madrid; Delta Airlines also operates a non-stop flight to Barcelona. Finally, you might check out **Air Europa**'s New York–Madrid flights, which are less frequent, but very competitively priced.

You may also find good deals on **routeings via other major European cities** with the airlines of those countries: KLM via Amsterdam, Lufthansa via Frankfurt, TAP via Lisbon, British Airways via London, or Sabena via Brussels, for example. Remember, though, that you may be better off continuing with a locally bought flight, or overland (especially if you plan to buy a rail pass). The widest range of deals is on the New York–London route, served by dozens of airlines. Competition is intense, so look for bargains, especially out of season.

At the time of writing, the major carriers were offering the following round-trip **fares** to Madrid: from New York $575/935 (low/high season respectively); from Chicago $757/952; from LA $820/1179; and from Miami $766/1021. With special promotional offers, round-trip fares can drop as low as $300 from New York and $500 from LA. Flying time is around seven hours from New York to Madrid.

There are no nonstop flights **from Canada** to Spain. However, you should be able to find a fairly convenient routeing using a combination of airlines – most likely via another European capital – from any of the major cities. West of the Rockies you're probably best off either flying Vancouver–London and continuing on to Madrid or another Spanish city from there, or alternatively getting a flight from Seattle.

At the time of writing, APEX round-trip **fares** to Madrid start at around CAN$984 in the low season or CAN$1338 in the high season from Toronto or Montréal, and CAN$1190/1967 from Vancouver.

Package tours may not sound like your kind of travel, but don't dismiss the idea out of hand. In addition to the fully escorted variety, many agents can put together very flexible deals, sometimes amounting to no more than a flight plus car or rail pass and accommodation; if you're planning to travel in moderate or luxury style, and especially if your trip is geared around special interests, such packages can work out cheaper than the same arrangements made on arrival. A package can also be great for your peace of mind, if only to ensure a worry-free first week while you're finding your feet on a longer tour (of course, you can jump off the itinerary any time you like). Most companies will expect you to book through a local travel agent, and since it costs the same you might as well.

Plenty of tour companies offer whirlwind itineraries around Spain. Most of these also offer independent **city breaks** or more structured **escorted tours**. Other options include **trekking** (backpacking) in the Basque Pyrenees or basking on the **beaches** of the Costa del Sol. Typical prices for a week's independent winter break in Madrid, with round-trip air fare from New York included, are US$700 per person. If you're planning to stay in Spain's historic *paradores*, then expect to pay around US$70–$100 per night for accommodation alone.

Airlines

Air Europa ⓦ www.aireuropa.com, ☏ 1-800/327-1225. Monday, Tuesday, Thursday, Friday and Saturday flights from New York to Madrid.

Air France ⓦ www.airfrance.com, ☏ 1-800/237-2747, Canada ☏ 1-800/667-2747. From New York, Chicago, Atlanta, Miami, San Francisco, Los Angeles, Washington DC, Toronto and Montréal to Madrid, Barcelona, Málaga and Sevilla, all via Paris.

American Airlines ⓦ www.aa.com, ☏ 1-800/433-7300. Daily nonstop flights from Miami and Chicago to Madrid.

British Airways ⓦ www.britishairways.com, ☏ 1-800/247-9297, Canada ☏ 1-800/668-1059. From Montréal, Toronto and Vancouver plus 21 gateway cities in the US to Madrid, Barcelona and Málaga, all via London.

Continental Airlines ⓦ www.continental.com, ☏ 1-800/231-0856. Daily nonstop flights from

Newark to Madrid.

Delta Airlines ⓦ www.delta.com, ☎ 1-800/241-4141. Daily nonstop flights from New York and Atlanta to Madrid and Barcelona with connections from most other major North American cities.

Iberia ⓦ www.iberia.com, ☎ 1-800/772-4642. From New York, Miami and Chicago nonstop to Madrid with connections to many other Spanish cities.

Lufthansa USA ⓦ www.lufthansa-usa.com, ☎ 1-800/645-3880; Canada ⓦ www.lufthansa-ca.com, ☎ 1-800/563-5954. From major US cities to Madrid, Barcelona, Valencia, Málaga, Bilbao and Palma, Mallorca, all via Frankfurt.

Northwest/KLM ⓦ www.nwa.com, ☎ 1-800/447-4747 or 1-800/374-7747. From major US and Canadian cities to Madrid and Barcelona via Amsterdam.

Sabena ⓦ www.sabena.com, ☎ 1-800/955-2000. From East Coast and Midwest cities to Barcelona, Bilbão, Madrid, Málaga, Sevilla and Palma, Mallorca, all via Brussels.

TAP Air Portugal ⓦ www.tap-airportugal.pt, ☎ 1-800/221-7370. Flights to Madrid and Barcelona via Lisbon; daily from New York and from Boston on Tuesday, Thursday & Saturday.

United Airlines ⓦ www.ual.com, ☎ 1-800/538-2929. Daily nonstop flights from Washington DC to Madrid.

Courier flights

Air Courier Association ☎ 1-800/282-1202, ⓦ www.aircourier.org. Courier flight broker. Membership (1yr $49, 3yr $98) also entitles you to twenty-percent discount on travel insurance and name-your-own-price non-courier flights.

International Association of Air Travel Couriers ☎ 561/582-8320, ⓦ www.courier.org. Courier flight broker with membership fee of $45 a year.

Now Voyager ☎ 212/431-1616, ⓦ www.nowvoyagertravel.com. Courier flight broker and consolidator.

Discount travel companies

Air Brokers International ⓦ www.airbrokers.com, ☎ 1-800/883-3273 or 415/397-1383. Consolidator and specialist in RTW tickets.

Airhitch ⓦ www.airhitch.org, ☎ 1-800/326-2009 or 212/864-2000. Standby-seat broker: for a set price, they guarantee to get you on a flight as close to your preferred destination as possible, within a week. Costs are currently $165 (plus taxes and a $29 processing fee) from or to the east coast region; $233 (plus tax & $29 reg. fee) from/to the west coast or (when available) the Pacific northwest; $199 (plus tax & $29 reg. fee) from/to the midwest; and $177 (plus tax & $29 reg. fee) from/to the southeast. Taxes for all Europe itineraries are $16 eastbound and $46 westbound.

Airtech ⓦ www.airtech.com, ☎ 1-800/575-8324 or 212/219-7000. Standby-seat broker; also deals in consolidator fares and courier flights.

Council Travel ⓦ www.counciltravel.com, ☎ 1-800 226 8624 or 617/528 2091. Nationwide organization that mostly, but by no means exclusively, specializes in student/budget travel.

Educational Travel Center ⓦ www.edtrav.com, ☎ 1-800/747-5551 or 608/256 5551. Student/youth discount agent.

High Adventure Travel ⓦ www.airtreks.com, ☎ 1-800/350-0612 or 415/912-5600. Round-the-world tickets. The website features an interactive database that lets you build and price your own RTW itinerary.

New Frontiers/Nouvelles Frontières ⓦ www.NewFrontiers.com, ☎ 1-800/677 0720 or 212/986 6006. French discount-travel firm. Other branches in LA, San Francisco and Québec City.

Skylink US ☎ 1-800/AIR-ONLY or ☎ 212/573-8980, Canada ☎ 1-800/SKY-LINK. Consolidator.

STA Travel ⓦ www.sta-travel.com, ☎ 1-800/777-0112 or 1-800/781-4040. Worldwide specialists in independent travel; also student IDs, travel insurance, car rental, rail passes, etc.

Student Flights ⓦ www.isecard.com, ☎ 1-800/255-8000 or 480/951-1177. Student/youth fares, student IDs.

TFI Tours International ☎ 1-800/745-8000 or 212/736-1140. Consolidator.

Travac ⓦ www.thetravelsite.com, ☎ 1-800/872-8800. Consolidator and charter broker.

Travelers Advantage Cendant Membership Services, Inc ⓦ www.travelersadvantage.com, ☎ 1-877/259-2691. Discount travel club; annual membership fee required (currently $1 for 3 months trial).

Travel Avenue ⓦ www.travelavenue.com, ☎ 1-800/333-3335. Full-service travel agent that offers discounts in the form of rebates.

Travel Cuts ⓦ www.travelcuts.com, Canada ☎ 1-800/667 2887, US ☎ 416/979 2406. Canadian student-travel organization.

Worldtek Travel ⓦ www.worldtek.com, ☎ 1/800-243-1723. Discount travel agency for worldwide travel.

Worldwide Discount Travel Club ☎ 305/534-2642. Discount travel club.

Tour operators

Abercrombie and Kent
ⓦ www.abercrombiekent.com, ☎ 1-800/323-7308
or 630/954-2944. Upmarket independent and fully
escorted holidays, including walking tours in
Andalucía.

Adventure Center ⓦ www.adventure-center.com,
☎ 1-800/228-8747 or 510/654-1879. Active
vacations in the Picos, Andalucía and the Sierra
Nevada.

Central Holidays ⓦ www.centralh.com, ☎ 1-
800/935-5000. Agents for Iberia's tour department,
Discover Spain Vacations. Group and independent
tours.

Delta Vacations ⓦ www.deltavacations.com,
☎ 1-800/872-7786. City breaks with optional car
rental and city tours.

Easy Rider Tours ⓦ www.easyridertours.com,
☎ 1-800/488-8332 or 978/463-6955.
Cycling/hiking tours in Andalucía and along the
pilgrim's way to Santiago de Compostela.

EC Tours ⓦ www.ectours.com, ☎ 1-800/388-
0877. Pilgrimages, historic city tours, wine and
gourmet tours.

Escapade Tours ⓦ www.isram.com, ☎ 1-
800/356-2405. City breaks and multi-city packages.

M.I. Travel Inc ⓦ www.mitravel-melia.com, ☎ 1-
800/848-2314 or 212/967-6565. City packages
and motorcoach tours.

Mountain Travel/Sobek ⓦ www.mtsobek.com,
☎ 1-888/MTSOBEK. Hiking in the Picos de Europa
and Basque Pyrenees.

Petrabax Tours ⓦ www.petrabax.com, ☎ 1-
800/634-1188. Motorcoach tours, parador bookings,
plus a variety of set packages.

Saga Holidays ⓦ www.sagaholidays.com, ☎ 1-
877/265-6862. Group travel for seniors.

Travel Go Round, Inc
ⓦ www.travelgoround.com, ☎ 1-800/293-0076.
City breaks, motorcoach tours, fly/drives, beach
vacations and *parador* bookings.

Wilderness Travel ⓦ www.wildernesstravel.com,
☎ 1-800/368-2794 or 510/558-2488. Hiking in the
Pyrenees or Basque country.

Flights from Australia and New Zealand

There are no direct flights to Spain from
Australia or New Zealand, but changing
planes once or twice can get you there within 24 hours via Asia or 30 hours via the USA
– not counting time spent on stopovers.
Flights via Asia are generally the cheaper
option.

Most regular return economy **fares** to
Spain cost between A$1800 in the low sea-
son and A$2800 in the high season from
eastern Australian gateways. From Perth
and Darwin expect to pay A$100–300 less
than this if you're travelling via Asia, or
A$400 more if routeing via the USA. Fares
from Auckland cost between NZ$2000 in
the low season and NZ$3000 in the high
season. Fares rise by about A$300/NZ$300
in the shoulder season and then by about
this much again in high season.

Alternatively, you can find a **rock-bottom
return fare** to Amsterdam, London or another European hub city with the likes of
Garuda or Sri Lanka Airlines for around
A$1400/NZ$1700 low season, and then
either pick up a cheap charter flight (see
p.13) or travel overland by road (see p.19) or
rail (see "Rail Passes" on p.33). However,
with the high living and transport costs in
northwestern Europe, this rarely works out
any cheaper in practice.

Some of the best agents for discounted
tickets are Flight Centres, STA and
Trailfinders (see p.18); these can also help
with visas, travel insurance and tours. There
are also a number of online agents worth
looking up for cheap offers; details are given
on p.11.

The cheapest **scheduled** flights **from
Australia** are via Asia and there are several
airlines that fly into both Barcelona or
Madrid. The lowest fares are offered by
Japan Airlines (to Madrid, with an overnight
stop in either Tokyo or Osaka included in the
fare), Olympic Airways (to Madrid or
Barcelona via Athens), and Alitalia (to Madrid
or Barcelona via Milan) – all from A$1500 in
the low season to A$2600 in the high sea-
son. Mid-range fares are with Thai Airways,
Air France and Lauda Air via their respective
gateway cities of Bangkok, Paris and Vienna
for A$1800–2600. A little more expensive, at
A$1900–2800, but faster – with only a short
refuelling stop or quick change of planes in
Singapore – are Singapore Airlines' flights to
Madrid.

Travelling **from New Zealand** to Spain via
Asia, Thai Airways and Alitalia (both via
Sydney) have through fares from Auckland
to both Madrid and Barcelona, and Japan
Airlines (JAL) has flights to Madrid – all with
either a transfer or overnight stop in their
carrier's home city – for between
NZ$2000–2400 (low/high season). Qantas

(via Sydney and Bangkok) and Singapore Airlines (via Singapore), both also fly to Madrid, but are more expensive at NZ$2300–3000.

Flights from New Zealand via the USA are somewhat limited, with United Airlines and Spanair teaming up to offer through flights to Madrid (with transfers in LA and Washington) for around NZ$2499–3000.

Organized tours may seem a little expensive but are well worth it, especially if your time is limited, if you're unfamiliar with the country's customs and language, have special interests or you just don't like travelling alone. Adventure tours are also worth considering, especially if you want to cover a lot of ground or get to places that could be difficult to reach independently.

Airlines

Air France ⓦ www.airfrance.fr, Australia ☎ 02/9244 2100, New Zealand ☎ 09/308 3352. Daily flights to Madrid and Barcelona from major Australian gateway cities, with transfers in Paris and either Singapore or Bangkok. Code-shares with Qantas for the first leg.

Alitalia ⓦ www.alitalia.it, Australia ☎ 02/9244 2400, New Zealand ☎ 09/ 302 1452. Three flights weekly to Madrid and Barcelona from Sydney and Auckland via Bangkok (refuelling only) and with a transfer in Milan.

Garuda ⓦ www.garuda-indonesia.com, Australia ☎ 13 1223 or 02/9334 9900, New Zealand ☎ 09/366 1862 or 1800/128 510. Several flights weekly from major cities in Australia and New Zealand to Paris, Rome and Amsterdam, with either a transfer or an overnight stop in Denpasar or Jakarta: connections to destinations in Spain.

Japan Airlines (JAL) ⓦ www.japanair.com, Australia ☎ 02/9272 1111, New Zealand ☎ 09/379 9906. Daily flights to Madrid from Brisbane and Sydney, and several flights a week from Cairns and Auckland, with either a transfer or overnight stop in Tokyo or Osaka. Code-shares with Iberia and Air New Zealand.

Lauda Air ⓦ www.laudaair.com, Australia ☎ 1800/642 438 or 02/9251 6155, New Zealand ☎ 09/308 3368. Four flights weekly to Barcelona from Sydney with transfers in Kuala Lumpur and Vienna.

Olympic Airways ⓦ www.olympic-airways.com, Australia ☎ 1800/221 663 or ☎ 02/9251 2044. One flight a week to Barcelona and three weekly to Madrid from Melbourne and Sydney with a transfer in Athens.

Qantas ⓦ www.qantas.com.au, Australia ☎ 13/13 13, New Zealand ☎ 09/357 8900 or 0800/808 767. Daily flights to Madrid from major cities in Australia and New Zealand with a transfer in either Singapore or Bangkok and London.

Singapore Airlines ⓦ www.singaporeair.com, Australia ☎ 13/10 11 or 02/9350 0262, New Zealand ☎ 09/303 2129 or 0800/808 909. Daily flights to Madrid from Brisbane, Sydney, Melbourne, Perth and Auckland with either a transfer or overnight stop in Singapore, and on some flights a transfer in Zurich.

Sri Lanka Airlines ⓦ www.srilankan.com, Australia ☎ 02/9244 2234, New Zealand ☎ 09/308 3353. Three flights a week to London, Paris and Rome from Sydney with a transfer or overnight stop in Colombo: connections to destinations in Spain.

Thai Airways ⓦ www.thaiair.com, Australia ☎ 1300/651 960, New Zealand ☎ 09/377 3886. Several flights weekly to Madrid from Sydney, Melbourne, Brisbane and Auckland with a transfer in either Rome or Frankfurt and another transfer or overnight stop in Bangkok.

United Airlines ⓦ www.ual.com, Australia ☎ 13/1777, New Zealand ☎ 09/379 3800. Several flights a week to Madrid from Sydney, Melbourne and Auckland with transfers in LA and Washington. Code-shares with Spanair from Washington.

Travel agents

All the agents listed below offer competitive discounts on air fares as well as a good selection of package holidays and tours, and can also arrange car rental and bus and rail passes.

Anywhere Travel Australia ☎ 02/9663 0411, ⓔ anywhere@ozemail.com.au.

Budget Travel New Zealand ☎ 0800/808 040.

Destinations Unlimited New Zealand ☎ 09/373 4033.

Flight Centres ⓦ www.flightcentre.com.au, Australia ☎ 02/9235 3522 or for nearest branch ☎ 13 1600, New Zealand ☎ 09/358 4310.

Northern Gateway Australia ☎ 08/8941 1394, ⓔ oztravel@norgate.com.au.

STA Travel ⓦ www.statravel.com.au, Australia ☎ 1300/360 960, New Zealand ☎ 0800/874773.

Student Uni Travel Australia ☎ 02/9232 8444, ⓔ Australia@backpackers.net.

Thomas Cook ⓦ www.thomascook.com.au, Australia ☎ 13 1771, New Zealand ☎ 09/379 3920.

Trailfinders ⓦ www.travel.com.au, ☎ 02/9247 7666.

Usit Beyond ⓦ www.usitbeyond.co.nz, ☎ 0800/788 336.

Specialist agents

Adventure Specialists Australia ☎02/9261 2927. Overland specialist and agent for numerous adventure travel operators that offer walking and camping trips through Spain.

Adventure World ⊛www.adventureworld. com.au, Australia ☎02/9956 7766 or 1300/363 055, New Zealand ☎09/524 5118. Agents for a vast array of international adventure travel companies that offer small-group tours, including Explore's 15-day trek through the High Alpujarras, staying in *hostales* and *pensiones* along the way (from A$990/NZ$1260).

Australians Studying Abroad ⊛www. asatravinfo.com.au, ☎1800/645 755 or 03/9509 1955. Offers 22-day guided study tours, focusing on Spain's art and culture; some courses can be credited towards Australian tertiary awards.

CIT ⊛www.cittravel.com.au, Australia ☎02/9267 1255. Specializes in city tours and accommodation packages, plus bus and rail passes and car rental.

IB Tours Australia ☎02/9560 6932. Villas in Spain, Portugal, and Morocco, as well as car rental, and city stays. Offers a range of 3–5 star hotel and villa accommodation and individually tailored holidays.

Ibertours ⊛www.ibertours.com.au, Australia ☎03/9670 8388 or ☎1800/500 016. Specializes in escorted small group and private tours.

IT Adventures Australia ☎1800/804 277, ⊜don@kumuku.co.uk. Extended overland camping/hostelling expeditions, including Exodus' 8-day "Picos Biking" trip through the Picos de Europa in northern Spain (from A$1090/NZ$1340 excluding flights).

Tour operators

The Adventure Travel Company New Zealand ☎09/379 9755, ⊜advakl@hot.co.nz. NZ agent for Peregrine: see below.

Contiki Holidays ⊛www.contiki.com, Australia ☎02/9511 2200 or 1300/301 835. Specializes in extended coach tours for 18–35-year-olds.

Explore Holidays ⊛www.exploreholidays. com.au, Australia ☎02/9857 6200 or 1300/731 000. Accommodation and package tours.

Kompas Holidays ⊛www.kompasholidays. com.au, Australia ☎07/3222 3333 or 1800/269 968. Packages and tours in Spain.

Peregrine Adventures
⊛www.peregrine.net.au, Australia ☎03/9662 2700 or 1300 655 433; New Zealand see Adventure Travel Company. Guided and independent walking and cycling trips in Spain.

Walkabout Gourmet Adventures Australia ☎03/5159 6556, ⊜WalkaboutAus@ compuserve.com. Classy food-and-wine walking tours in Spain.

By rail from the UK and Ireland

With the **Channel Tunnel**, you have the choice between crossing over to the continent by boat or taking the Eurostar from Waterloo International in London. Both options involve changing trains in **Paris** (from Nord to Austerlitz via Metro line 5), and again at the **Spanish border**. The standard rail and boat journey is around 27 to 29 hours from London to Barcelona, another five hours to Madrid; with the Eurostar, it's around 17 hours to Barcelona. If you're prepared to pay a good deal extra, you can take the Trenhotel from Paris to Madrid or Barcelona direct, which reduces these journeys by two to three hours.

Two exciting (but more expensive) **alternatives** are the minor routes which cross the central Pyrenees to enter Aragón at Canfranc, or Catalunya at Puigcerdà. On the first of these, Rail Europe will issue a ticket only as far as Oloron in France, from where you have to cross the border by bus. Similarly, on the Catalan route, Rail Europe fares are sold only as far as the French station at Bourg-Madame, just over the frontier from Puigcerdà, where you must change trains. Tickets bought from Connex, however, will take you through to your final destination in Spain. On both routes you may have to spend the night at either of the border towns if you want to see the mountains in daylight.

A **standard rail/boat ticket** currently costs £200 return from London to Madrid and £125 to Barcelona, is valid for two months and allows you to stop anywhere along the way. There is a slight discount for students. If you're travelling by **Eurostar**, it's £140–250 for a return to Madrid, or Barcelona (depending on age, season and time of day). Reservation charges from Paris are £3–4 for a seat or around £14 for a couchette (included in the price if you're taking the Eurostar).

Tickets are bookable through some travel agents, main Connex stations and Usit Campus; note that Rail Europe will only sell tickets using the Eurostar. It's also currently cheaper – especially if you're under-26 or a student – to buy your Eurostar tickets from an agent.

If you plan to travel extensively in Europe by train, you might consider buying a rail pass. Details of these are given on p.33.

Useful rail companies

Connex, ☎0870/001 0174. International enquiries and reservations.
Eurostar ⊛www.eurostar.com, ☎0870/1606600.
Iarnród Éireann ⊛www.irishrail.ie, Dublin ☎01/8366 6222.
Northern Ireland Railways
⊛www.nirailways.co.uk, ☎028/9089/9411.
Rail Europe ⊛www.raileurope.co.uk, ☎0870/5848 848. SNCF French Railways.
Unit Campus ⊛www.usitcampus.co.uk,
☎0870/240 1010. Can book student/youth discount train tickets and sell passes.

Eurotunnel, cross-Channel and motorail services

The fastest way to get your car across to the continent is the Eurotunnel service via the Channel Tunnel. The alternative is one of the time-honoured ferry crossings. Once across, if you don't fancy the long drive through France, you could consider putting your car on the Motorail service from Paris to Madrid.

Eurotunnel operates shuttle trains 24 hours a day and is for cars, motorcycles, buses and their passengers. The service runs continuously between Folkestone and Coquelles, near Calais, with up to four departures per hour (only one per hour midnight–6am) and takes 35min (45min for some night departure times), though you must arrive at least 30min before departure. It is possible to turn up and buy your ticket at the toll booths (after exiting the M20 at junction 11a), though at busy times booking is advisable. Rates depend on the time of year, time of day and length of stay (the cheapest ticket is for a day-trip, followed by a five-day return); it's cheaper to travel between 10pm and 6am, while the highest fares are reserved for weekend departures and returns in July and August.

The more traditional cross-Channel options are the **ferry** links between Dover or Folkestone and Calais or Boulogne, or fer-

ries to Caen, Le Havre, Cherbourg and St Malo (from Portsmouth or Poole), or even Roscoff (from Plymouth). Any of these cuts out the trek round or through Paris, and opens up some interesting detours around Brittany and the French Atlantic coast.

Ferry **prices** vary according to the time of year and, for motorists, the size of your car. The Dover–Calais/Boulogne runs, for example, start at about £100–165 one-way (£245–340 open return) for a car, two adults and two kids, but these figures can nearly double in high season. Foot passengers should be able to cross for about £15 one-way, or £20–30 open return. For both ferries and tunnel, fares are lower if you travel during the off-peak time – generally between 10pm and 6am.

Once you're across the Channel you can significantly reduce your driving time by taking the SNCF-operated **Motorail** service. Cars or motorbikes are loaded onto the special daily train at Paris – which departs Paris 10.50pm and arrives in Madrid at 8.05am the next day. For a small car (such as a Fiat Uno) the single fare is €180/£120, plus €120/£74 per adult (€98/£60 for under-26s), although prices rise around fifty percent in July and August. Information and bookings can be made only by contacting SNCF direct in France (see box), though they have English-speaking operators and accept most credit cards.

Eurotunnel, ⊛www.eurotunnel.com. Customer Services Centre ☎0870/535 3535.
SNCF (Motorail service), ⊛www.sncf.fr, ☎(+33) 836.35 35.39.

Ferry companies

Brittany Ferries ⊛www.brittanyferries.co.uk,
☎0870/901 2400, Republic of Ireland ☎021/277 705. Poole to Cherbourg; Portsmouth to Caen and St Malo; Plymouth to Roscoff and to Santander (March–Nov/Dec); Cork to Roscoff (March–Oct only).
Hoverspeed ⊛www.hoverspeed.co.uk,
☎08705/240241. Twenty-four daily departures. Dover to Calais and Ostend; Newhaven to Dieppe.
Irish Ferries ⊛www.irishferries.com,
☎0875/171 717, Republic of Ireland ☎01/661 0511. Dublin to Holyhead; Rosslare to Pembroke, Cherbourg and Roscoff. Continental services March to end Sept.
P&O European Ferries ⊛www.poportsmouth.com, ☎0870/242 4999. Portsmouth to Cherbourg, Le Havre and Bilbão.

Sea Cat ☎08705/523 523, Republic of Ireland
☎1800/551743. Belfast to Stranraer, Heysham and
Troon; Dublin to Liverpool.
Sea France ⓦ www.seafrance.com, ☎0870/571
1711. Dover to Calais.

The ferry to Bilbão and Santander

There are two direct ferry sailings to Bilbão
and Santander from Britain. See above for
ferry company addresses, or contact your
local travel agent for the latest ticket and sailing details; alternatively, you can check out
the ferries' website at ⓦ www.seaview.co.uk.

The ferry to **Santander** leaves from
Plymouth and is operated by Brittany
Ferries. It takes 24 hours and runs on
Mondays and Wednesdays during the summer (April to mid-Sept) and Wednesdays
and Sundays the rest of the year. Ticket
prices vary enormously according to the
season, the number of passengers carried
and the length of time you want the ticket to
be valid for; for example, a return ticket for a
car and two adults can cost anything from
£128 (valid for 5 days in low-season) to
£710 (for an open ticket in high-season).
Foot passengers pay around £50–80 one-
way (depending on season), and everyone
has to book some form of accommodation;
a Pullman seat is cheapest at £4–6, a berth
costs £20–25, and two- and four-berth cabins are available for £57–77 and £80–100
respectively. Tickets are best booked in
advance, through any major travel agent.

P&O operates a twice-weekly ferry service
from Portsmouth to Bilbão. The journey
takes approximately 35 hours and leaves
Portsmouth on Saturdays and Tuesdays.
Return fares for a car and two people work
out at between £310 and £720 (according to
season), with foot passengers paying
£260–400. Cabins are included in these
prices. Note that this sailing is significantly
cheaper for motorcyclists than for cars, especially if you can find one of the frequent discounts offered by motorcycling publications.

Note that both routes are often closed for
a couple of weeks in January for maintenance.

By bus

The main bus routes from Britain to Spain
are from London to Barcelona (5 weekly in

summer, 3 weekly out of season; 25hr), and
Alicante (3 weekly; 32hr) via San Sebastián
(21hr). There are also two buses a week to
Algeciras (39hr), via Paris, Madrid (27hr),
Málaga (36hr) and the Costa del Sol; at least
one a week to Pamplona (23hr); and one to
Santiago (32hr) along the north coast. Fares
start at around £65 single, £99 return (to
San Sebastián), rising to £99 single, £158
return to Alicante.

All these routes are operated by **Eurolines**
in Britain and by Iberbus/Linebus and Julia in
Spain. In both Britain and Spain tickets are
bookable through most major travel agents
and on the internet at ⓦ www.eurolines.
co.uk; Eurolines also sells tickets and
through-transport to London at all British
National Express bus terminals.

Also worth looking at is the **Busabout
Pass**, which allows unlimited travel on all of
Eurolines' routes and is available in thirty-
and sixty-day versions. The price is seasonal
with an under-26s thirty-day pass costing
£139 in low season (Nov–March), rising to
£153 in mid-season (April–May & Sept–Oct)
and £195 during the summer (June–Aug);
over-26s pay around 30 percent more. The
sixty-day version will cost an additional 50
percent or so. The pass is ideal if you're
planning a lot of travel to the major cities,
though you'll have to plan your route carefully and be prepared to see a lot of Madrid.

Bus information

Busabout ⓦ www.busabout.com, ☎020/7950
1661. Busabout runs every 2–3 days on 5 circuits in
summer, fewer in winter, taking in 70 European
cities, with add-on connections to 5 more, plus a link
to London and through tickets from elsewhere in
Britain and Ireland. Tickets are available in
increments of 15 days, 21 days, 1 month, 2 months,
or 3 months; there are also special deals on set
itineraries. Also sells Flexipasses, allowing 10 or 15
days' travel within 2 months; 21 days' travel within 3
months; or 30 days out of 4 months. The passes are
available from STA Travel in the US.
Eurolines ⓦ www.eurolines.co.uk, UK
☎0870/514 3219, Republic of Ireland ☎01/836
6111. Tickets can also be purchased from any
Eurolines or National Express agent (☎0870/580
8080, ⓦ www.gobycoach.com. As well as ordinary
tickets on its scheduled coach services to an
extensive list of over 460 European cities, Eurolines
offers a pass for Europe-wide travel, for either 15,
30, or 60 days, between 46 European cities,

including London, Barcelona and Madrid. Eurolines services to and from Ireland include Dublin–London (via Birmingham and Holyhead); Cork and Killarney–London (via Bristol and Fishguard), Limerick and Tralee–London (via Bristol and Fishguard) and Belfast–London (via Birmingham, Manchester and Stranraer).

Ulsterbus Northern Ireland ☎028/9033 7003, ⊛www.ulsterbus.co.uk. Runs services from Belfast using the Larne–Stranraer crossing to London, Birmingham (via Manchester) and Edinburgh via Glasgow. Also sells bus passes.

Red tape and visas

Citizens of most EU countries (and of Norway and Iceland) need only a valid national identity card to enter Spain for up to six months. Since Britain has no identity card system, however, British citizens have to take a passport. US, Canadian, Australian and New Zealand citizens do not need a visa for stays of up to ninety days, but this must be for tourism purposes only and not for work or study. Visa requirements do change and it is always advisable to check the current situation before leaving home.

To **stay longer**, EU nationals (and citizens of Norway and Iceland) can apply for a *permiso de residencia* (EU residence permit) once in Spain. A temporary residency permit is valid for up to a year, and you'll need an extension after that (valid for up to five years). Applications need to be made at the *Oficina de Extranjeros* in the main cities or at the police station nearest to where you'll be taking up residency. You'll either need to produce proof that you have sufficient funds (officially around €30 a day) to be able to support yourself without working – easiest done by keeping bank exchange forms every time you change money – or you'll need to have a contract of employment (*contrato de trabajo*) or become self-employed (for example as a teacher), which involves registering at the tax office.

US citizens can apply for one ninety-day extension, showing proof of funds, but this must be done from outside Spain. Other nationalities will need to get a special visa from a Spanish consulate before departure (see below for addresses).

Spanish embassies and consulates

Australia,15 Arkana St, Yarralumla, ACT 2600 ☎02/6273 3555; 24th Floor, St Martin's Tower, 31 Market St, Sydney, NSW 2000 ☎02/9261 2433, ℮consulspain@smartchat.net.au; 4th Floor, 540 Elizabeth St, Melbourne, VIC 3000 ☎03/9347 1966, ℮conspainmelb@primus.com.au.
Britain, 20 Draycott Place, London SW3 2RZ ☎020/7589 8989; Suite 1a, Brook House, 70 Spring Gardens, Manchester M2 2BQ ☎0161/236 1213; 63 North Castle St, Edinburgh EH2 3LJ ☎0131/220 1843.
Canada, 350 Sparks St #802, Ottawa, Ontario K1R 7S8 ☎613/237-2193, ⊛www.docuweb.ca/SpainInCanada; 1 Westmount Sq #1456, Ave Wood, Montréal, Quebec H3Z 2P9 ☎514/935-5235, ⊛www.total.net/~consular; 1200 Bay St #400, Toronto, Ontario M5P 2A5 ☎416/967-4949.
Ireland, 17a Merlyn Park, Ballsbridge, Dublin 4 ☎01/269 1640.
New Zealand, contact the consulate in Sydney.
USA, 2375 Pennsylvania Ave NW, Washington DC 20037 ☎202/452-0100, ⊛www.spainemb.org/ ingles/indexing.htm; 150 E 58th St, New York, NY 10155 ☎212/355-4090, ⊛www.spainconsul-ny.org; 545 Boylston St #803, Boston, MA 02116 ☎617/536-2506, ⊛www.spainconsul-ny. org/boston.html; 180 N Michigan Ave #1500, Chicago, IL 60601 ☎312/782-4588, ℮cgspain.chicago@mail.mae.es; 1800 Bering Drive #660, Houston, TX 77057 ☎713/783-6200, ℮spainconsulatehoust@prodigy.net; 5055 Wilshire

Blvd #960, Los Angeles, CA 90036 ☏ 323/938-0158, ✉ consplax@mail.mae.es; 2655 Le Jeune Rd #203, Coral Gables, Miami, FL 33134 ☏ 305/446-5511, ✉ cgspain.miami@mail.mae.es; 2102 World Trade Center, 2 Canal St, New Orleans, LA 70130

☏ 504/525-4951, ✉ conspneworleans@mail.mae.es; 1405 Sutter St, San Francisco, CA 94109 ☏ 415/922-2995, ✉ conspsfo@mail.mae.es.

Health

As an EU country, Spain has free reciprocal health agreements with other member states (you should carry form E111, available from main post offices). Even so, some form of travel insurance is still all but essential; with it, you should be able to claim back the cost of any drugs prescribed by pharmacies. European policies generally also cover your baggage/tickets in case of theft, so long as you get a report from the local police.

No **inoculations** are required for Spain, though if you plan on continuing to North Africa, typhoid and polio boosters are highly recommended. The worst that's likely to happen to you is that you might fall victim to an upset stomach. To be safe, wash fruit and avoid *tapas* dishes that look as if they were cooked last week.

For minor complaints go to a **farmacia** – they're listed in the phone book in major towns and you'll find one in virtually every village. Pharmacists are highly trained, willing to give advice (often in English), and able to dispense many drugs which would be available only on prescription in most other countries. They keep usual shop hours (9am–1.30pm & 5.30–8pm), but some open late and at weekends while a rota system keeps at least one open 24 hours. The rota is displayed in the window of every pharma-

cy, or you can check in one of the local newspapers under *Farmacias de guardia*.

In more serious cases you can get the address of an English-speaking doctor from the nearest relevant consulate, or with luck from a *farmacia*, the local police or turismo. If you have special medical or dietary requirements, it is advisable to carry a letter from your doctor, translated into Spanish, indicating the nature of your condition and necessary treatments. In **emergencies** dial ☏ 091 for the *Servicios de Urgencia*, or look up the *Cruz Roja Española* (Red Cross) which runs a national ambulance service. Treatment at hospitals for EU citizens in possession of form E111 is free; otherwise you'll be charged at private hospital rates, which can be very expensive. Accordingly, it's essential to have comprehensive travel insurance.

Insurance

Even though EU health care privileges apply in Spain, you'd do well to take out an insurance policy before travelling to cover against theft, loss and illness or injury. Before paying for a new policy, however, it's worth checking whether you are already covered: some all-risks home insurance policies may cover your possessions when overseas, and many private medical schemes include cover when abroad.

In Canada, provincial health plans usually provide partial cover for medical mishaps overseas, while holders of official student/teacher/youth cards in Canada and the US are entitled to meagre accident coverage and hospital inpatient benefits. Students will often find that their student health coverage extends during the vacations and for one term beyond the date of last enrolment.

After exhausting the possibilities above, you might want to contact a specialist travel insurance company, or consider the travel insurance deal we offer (see box). A typical travel insurance policy usually provides cover for the loss of baggage, tickets and – up to a certain limit – cash or cheques, as well as cancellation or curtailment of your journey. Most of them exclude so-called dangerous

sports unless an extra premium is paid: in Spain this can mean windsurfing, skiing and trekking. Many policies can be chopped and changed to exclude coverage you don't need – for example, sickness and accident benefits can often be excluded or included at will. If you do take medical coverage, ascertain whether benefits will be paid as treatment proceeds or only after your return home, and whether there is a 24-hour medical emergency number. When securing baggage cover, make sure that the per-article limit – typically under £500 – will cover your most valuable possession. If you need to make a claim, you should keep receipts for medicines and medical treatment, and in the event you have anything stolen, you must obtain an official statement from the police.

Rough Guide travel insurance

Rough Guides offers its own travel insurance, customized for our readers by a leading UK broker and backed by a Lloyds underwriter. It's available for anyone, of any nationality, travelling anywhere in the world.

There are two main Rough Guide insurance plans: **Essential**, for basic, no-frills cover; and **Premier** – with more generous and extensive benefits. Alternatively, you can take out **annual multi-trip insurance**, which covers you for any number of trips throughout the year (with a maximum of 60 days for any one trip). Unlike many policies, the Rough Guides schemes are calculated by the day, so if you're travelling for 27 days rather than a month, that's all you pay for. If you intend to be away for the whole year, the Adventurer policy will cover you for 365 days. Each plan can be supplemented with a "Hazardous Activities Premium" if you plan to indulge in sports considered dangerous, such as skiing, scuba-diving or trekking. Rough Guides also does good deals for older travellers, and will insure you up to any age, at prices comparable to SAGA's.

For a policy quote, call the Rough Guide Insurance Line on UK freefone ☎0800/015 09 06; US freefone ☎1-866/220 5588, or, if you're calling from elsewhere ☎+44 1243/621 046. Alternatively, get an online quote at ⊛www.roughguides.com/insurance

Information, maps and websites

The Spanish National Tourist Office (SNTO; ⓦwww.tourspain.es) produces and gives away an impressive variety of maps, pamphlets and special interest leaflets. If you can, visit one of their offices before you leave and stock up, especially on city plans, as well as province-by-province lists of hotels, *hostales* and campsites.

Information offices

In Spain itself you'll find SNTO turismos (tourist offices) in virtually every major town and from these you can usually get more specific local information. SNTO offices are often supplemented by separately administered provincial or municipal bureaus. These vary enormously in quality, but while they are generally extremely useful for regional information, and local maps, they are not always as helpful about what goes on outside their patch.

Spanish turismo **hours** are usually Mon–Fri 9am–1pm and 3.30–6pm, Sat 9am–1pm, but you can't always rely on the official hours, especially in the more out-of-the-way places. In many major cities and coastal resorts the offices now tend to remain open all day in season (Apr–Sept).

In the main cities, branches of the department store **El Corte Inglés** also provide information services and useful free maps.

SNTO offices abroad

Australia, The Spanish National Tourist Office (SNTO), 1st Floor, 178 Collins St, Melbourne, VIC ☎03/9650 7377 or 1/800 817 855.
Britain ⓦwww.tourspain.co.uk, ☎020/7486 8077; 22–23 Manchester Square, London W1U 3PX.
Canada ⓦwww.tourspain.toronto.on.ca, ☎416/961-3131. 2 Bloor St West, 34th Floor, Toronto, Ontario M4W 3E2.
New Zealand, contact the office in Australia.
USA ⓦwww.okspain.org; 666 Fifth Ave, 35th Floor, New York, NY 10103 ☎212/265-8822; San Vincente Plaza Bldg, 8383 Wilshire Blvd, Suite 956, Beverly Hills, CA 90211 ☎323/658-7188; 845 North Michigan Ave, Suite 915-E, Chicago, IL 60611 ☎312/642-1992; 1221 Brickell Ave, Suite 1850, Miami, FL 33131 ☎305/358-1992.

Maps

In addition to the maps in this book and the various free leaflets available, the one extra you'll want is a reasonable **road map**. This is best bought in Spain, where you'll find a good selection in most bookshops (*librerías*) and at street kiosks or petrol stations. Among the best are those published by Editorial Almax, which also produces reliable indexed **street plans** of the main cities.

Good alternatives, especially if you're shopping before arrival, are the 1:300,000 *Euro Road Atlas* put out by RV (Reise und Verkehrsverlag, Stuttgart; packaged in Spain by Plaza & Janes), or the slightly larger-scale but generally excellent and accurate Michelin, covering the country in six 1:400 000 regional maps sold in atlas format. Less detailed offerings from Firestone or Rand McNally are another option.

The most comprehensive **city street plans** are the fold-out *Falkplans*, covering all the suburbs and with full street indexes; they are available for Madrid, Barcelona and Sevilla. Otherwise the Spanish publisher, *Everest*, produces a range of indexed street maps for most of the other major towns and cities; these are widely available from bookshops throughout the country.

Serious **trekkers** can get more detailed maps from La Tienda Verde at c/Maudes 38, Madrid (☎91 534 32 57; ⓜPlaza de Castilla), and in Barcelona at Librería Quera at c/Petritxol 2, Barcelona (☎933 180 743, ⓦwww.llibreriaquera.com; ⓜLiceo) or the Institut Cartogràfic de Catalunya, c/Balmes 209–211 (☎932 188 758). These outlets – and many other bookshops in Spain, and a few specialists overseas – stock the full range of **topographical maps** issued by two government agencies: the IGN (Instituto Geográfico Nacional), and the SGE (Servicio

Geográfico del Ejército). They are available at scales of 1:200,000, 1:100,000, 1:50,000 and even occasionally 1:25,000. The various SGE series are considered to be more up to date, although neither agency is hugely reliable.

Internet sources for maps include In Internet, a Barcelona-based firm which has a website (圝 www.netmaps.es with a page in English) where you can buy a wide selection of different types of maps. Another (in Spanish only) web-based source is at 圝 www.verdinet.com/mapas/; here you can purchase detailed maps (including SGE maps) with postal costs included.

A Catalunya-based company, Editorial Alpina (圝 www.editorialalpina.com), produces useful 1:40,000 or 1:25,000 **map/booklet** sets for most of the Spanish mountain and foothill areas of interest, and these are also on sale in many bookshops; the relevant editions are noted in the text where appropriate.

Map outlets

UK and Ireland

Blackwell's Map and Travel Shop, 53 Broad St, Oxford OX1 3BQ ☏ 01865/792792, 圝 www.bookshop.blackwell.co.uk.
Easons Bookshop, 40 O'Connell St, Dublin 1 ☏ 01/873 3811, 圝 www.eason.ie.
Heffers Map and Travel, 20 Trinity St, Cambridge, CB2 1TJ ☏ 01223/568 568, 圝 www.heffers.co.uk.
Hodges Figgis Bookshop, 56–58 Dawson St, Dublin 2 ☏ 01/677 4754, 圝 www.hodgesfiggis.com.
John Smith and Sons, 26 Colquhoun Ave, Glasgow, G52 4PJ ☏ 0141/552 3377, 圝 www.johnsmith.co.uk.
James Thin Melven's Bookshop, 29 Union St, Inverness, IV1 1QA ☏ 01463/233500, 圝 www.jthin.co.uk.
The Map Shop, 30a Belvoir St, Leicester, LE1 6QH ☏ 0116/2471400.
National Map Centre, 22–24 Caxton St, SW1H 0QU ☏ 020/7222 2466, 圝 www.mapsnmc.co.uk.
Newcastle Map Centre, 55 Grey St, Newcastle upon Tyne, NE1 6EF ☏ 0191/261 5622, 圝 www.traveller.ltd.uk.
Ordnance Survey Service, Phoenix Park, Dublin 8 ☏ 01/820 6100, 圝 www.irlgov.ie/osi/.
Ordnance Survey of Northern Ireland, Colby House, Stranmillis Ct, Belfast BT9 5BJ ☏ 028/9066

1244, 圝 www.osni.gov.uk.
Stanfords, 12–14 Long Acre, WC2E 9LP ☏ 020/7836 1321, 圝 www.stanfords.co.uk; maps by mail or phone order are available on this number and via ✉ sales@stanfords.co.uk. Other branches within British Airways offices at 156 Regent St, W1R 5TA ☏ 020/7434 4744, and 29 Corn St, Bristol BS1 1HT ☏ 0117/929 9966.
The Travel Bookshop, 13–15 Blenheim Crescent, W11 2EE ☏ 020/7229 5260, 圝 www.thetravelbookshop.co.uk.

USA and Canada

Adventurous Traveler Bookstore, PO Box 64769, Burlington, VT 05406 ☏ 1-800/282-3963, 圝 www.AdventurousTraveler.com.
Book Passage, 51 Tamal Vista Blvd, Corte Madera, CA 94925 ☏ 415/927-0960, 圝 www.bookpassage.com.
Elliot Bay Book Company, 101 S Main St, Seattle, WA 98104 ☏ 206/624-6600 or 1-800/962-5311, 圝 www.elliotbaybook.com.
Forsyth Travel Library, 226 Westchester Ave, White Plains, NY 10604 ☏ 1-800/367-7984, 圝 www.forsyth.com.
Globe Corner Bookstore, 28 Church St, Cambridge, MA 02138 ☏ 1-800/358-6013, 圝 www.globecorner.com.
GORP Adventure Library online only ☏ 1-800/754-8229, 圝 www2.gorp.com.
Map Link Inc., 30 S La Patera Lane, Unit 5, Santa Barbara, CA 93117 ☏ 805/692-6777, 圝 www.maplink.com.
Phileas Fogg's Travel Center, #87 Stanford Shopping Center, Palo Alto, CA 94304 ☏ 1-800/533-3644, 圝 www.foggs.com.
Rand McNally, 444 N Michigan Ave, Chicago, IL 60611 ☏ 312/321-1751, 圝 www.randmcnally.com; 150 E 52nd St, New York, NY 10022 ☏ 212/758-7488; 595 Market St, San Francisco, CA 94105 ☏ 415/777-3131; around thirty stores across the US – call ☏ 1-800/333-0136 ext 2111 or check the website for the nearest store.
Travel Books & Language Center, 4437 Wisconsin Ave, Washington, DC 20016 ☏ 1-800/220-2665, 圝 www.bookweb.org/bookstore/travellers.
The Travel Bug Bookstore, 2667 West Broadway, Vancouver V6K 2G2 ☏ 604/737-1122, 圝 www.swifty.com/tbug.
World of Maps, 118 Holland Ave, Ottawa, Ontario K1Y 0X6 ☏ 613/724-6776, 圝 www.itmb.com.
World Wide Books and Maps, 1247 Granville St, Vancouver V6Z 1G3 ☏ 604/687-3320, 圝 www.worldofmaps.com.

Australia and New Zealand

The Map Shop, 6 Peel St, Adelaide ☎ 08/8231 2033, ⓦ www.mapshop.net.au.
Specialty Maps, 46 Albert St, Auckland ☎ 09/307 2217, ⓦ www.ubd-online.co.nz/maps.
Mapworld, 173 Gloucester St, Christchurch ☎ 03/374 5399, ⓦ www.mapworld.co.nz.
Mapland, 372 Little Bourke St, Melbourne ☎ 03/9670 4383, ⓦ www.mapland.com.au.
Perth Map Centre, 1/884 Hay St, Perth ☎ 08/9322 5733, ⓦ www.perthmap.com.au.

Spain on the internet

Spain is represented pretty strongly on the internet, with websites in both English and Spanish offering information on most conceivable subjects. The websites detailed below are useful starting points and most contain numerous links on to more detailed areas.

Dónde ⓦ http://donde.uji.es/ Search engine for Spanish-language websites.

Go Spain ⓦ www.gospain.org Has almost every Spain-related link; especially good for fiesta listings.

Hotel Search ⓦ www.hotelsearch.com Extensive, though not exhaustive, list of Spanish accommodation in English.

El Índice ⓦ www.//elindice.com/ Very useful Barcelona-based search engine which allows you to search Spanish sites by subject.

Interbook ⓦ www.libreria.interbook.net Major Spanish online bookstore, offering over a million titles.

Museums in Spain
ⓦ www.icom.org/vlmp/spain.html A comprehensive list of all Spain's museums and art galleries.

Paginas Amarillas ⓦ www.paginas-amarillas.es Spain's Yellow Pages online, with dedicated eating and accommodation sections. Very useful it is too, though unfortunately only available in Spanish.

El País Digital ⓦ www.elpais.es/ Impressive digital version of Spain's major newspaper.

Restaurant Menus ⓦ www.webarcelona.com/ emen.htm Excellent five-page list of translations into English of Spanish and Catalan dishes and foods – handy to print out and take along.

Soccer Spain ⓦ www.soccer-spain.com English-language news, views, fixtures and results from La Liga. Marca, the leading Spanish sports paper, also has a good and comprehensive site (ⓦ www.marca.com) which allows you to delve into the lower league stats, too.

Spanish Search Engines
ⓦ www.searchenginecolossus.com Choose the Spain entry on this site for a comprehensive list of Spanish search engines including many regional and local ones.

Travlang - Learn Spanish
ⓦ www.travlang.com/languages/ Select "Spanish". Good site for picking up a bit of the lingo (has a neat pronunciation tool) before you set off.

El Vino ⓦ www.el-vino.com A complete guide to Spanish wines – which ones to drink and where to drink them.

Yahoo España ⓦ www.//es.yahoo.com/ The Spanish cousin of Yahoo's main search engine which is excellent for digging out things Hispanic.

Costs, money and banks

Although still thought of as a budget destination, hotel prices in Spain have increased considerably over the last ten years, and if you're spending a lot of your time in the cities, you can expect to spend almost as much as you would at home. However, there are still few places in Europe where you'll get a better deal on the cost of simple meals and drink.

On average, if you're prepared to buy your own picnic lunch, stay in inexpensive *pensiones* and hotels, and stick to local restaurants and bars, you could get by on £15–20/US$20–27 a day. If you intend to upgrade your accommodation, experience the city nightlife and eat fancier meals, then you'll need more like £40/$55 a day. On £50–60/$68–80 a day and upwards you'll be limited only by your energy reserves – though of course if you're planning to stay in four- and five-star hotels or Spain's magnificent *paradores*, this figure often won't even cover your room.

Room prices vary considerably according to season. In the summer you'll find little below €12 (£8/$11) single, €15 (£9.50/$12.50) double, and €15 single, €21 double (£13.50/$18) might be a more realistic average. Campsites start at around €2.40 (£1.50/$2) a night per person (more like €3–4.20 in some of the major resorts), plus a similar charge for a tent and a car respectively.

The cost of **eating** can vary wildly, but in most towns there'll be restaurants offering a basic three-course meal for somewhere between €4.50–9 (£3–5.50/$4–7.50). As often as not, though, you'll end up wandering from one bar to the next sampling tapas without getting round to a real sit-down meal – this is certainly tastier though rarely any cheaper (see "Eating and Drinking", p.45). Drink, and wine in particular, costs ridiculously little: €6 (£3.80/$5) will see you through a night's very substantial intake of the local vintage.

Long-distance **transport**, if used extensively, may prove a major expense; although prices compare well with the rest of Europe, Spain is a very large country. Madrid to Sevilla, for example – a journey of over 500km – costs around €18 (£10/$15.30) by bus or train. Urban transport almost always operates on a flat fare of €0.75–1.50 (50p–£1/$0.65–1.30).

All of the above, inevitably, are affected by where you are and when. The big cities and tourist resorts are invariably more expensive than remoter areas, and certain regions tend also to have higher prices – notably the industrialized north, Euskal Herria, Catalunya and Aragón, and the Balearic Islands. Prices are hiked up, too, to take advantage of special events. Despite official controls, you'd be lucky to find a room in Sevilla during its April *feria*, or in Pamplona for the running of the bulls, at less than double the usual rate. As always, if you're travelling alone you'll end up spending much more than you would in a group of two or more – sharing rooms saves greatly. An ISIC student card is worth having – it'll get you free or reduced entry to many museums and sites as well as occasional other discounts – and an FIYTO youth card (available to anyone under 26) is almost as good.

One thing to look out for on prices generally is the addition of sales tax – **IVA** (usually pronounced "iba") – which may come as an unexpected extra (currently seven percent for hotels and restaurants, sixteen percent for other goods and services) when you pay the bill for food or accommodation, especially in more expensive establishments.

Money and the exchange rate

Spain is one of twelve European Union countries which have changed over to a single currency, the euro (€). Euro notes and coins were issued on January 1, 2002, with pesetas remaining in place for cash transactions, at a fixed rate of 166.386 pesetas to one euro, until they are scrapped entirely at the end of February, 2002. After this date you can exchange your pesetas in banks until June 30 2002, after which date they may only be exchanged at the Banco de España (which has branches in all provincial capitals) for a further limited period.

All prices in this book are given in euros and correct at the time of going to press. There will no doubt be some rounding off or, more probably, up of prices in the first few months after the introduction of the euro. Notes will be issued in **denominations** of 5, 10, 20, 50, 100, 200 and 500 euros, and coins in denominations of 1, 2, 5, 10, 20 and 50 cents and 1 and 2 euro.

At the time of writing the **exchange rate** for the euro was around €1.64 to the pound sterling (or £0.60 to one euro) and €1.16 to the dollar (or $0.85 to one euro). You can take into Spain as much money as you want (in any form), although amounts over €6000 must be declared, and you may only take amounts over €6000 out if you can prove that you brought more with you in the first place. Not, perhaps, a major holiday worry.

Travellers' cheques and credit cards

A safe and easy way to carry your funds is in **travellers' cheques**, though most Visa,

To cancel lost or stolen credit cards, call the following numbers:
American Express ☎915 720 303
Diners Club ☎915 474 000
Mastercard ☎900 971 231
Visa ☎900 974 445

Visa Travel Money (www.visa.com)

This is a disposable debit card prepaid with dedicated travel funds which you can access from over 457,000 Visa ATMs in 120 countries with a PIN that you select yourself. When your funds are depleted, you simply throw the card away. Since you can buy up to nine cards to access the same funds – useful for couples/families travelling together – it's recommended that you buy at least one extra as a back up in case your first is lost or stolen. There is a 24-hour visa global customer assistance services centre which you can call from any of the 120 countries toll-free. The number to call from Spain is ☎ 900 99 1124. In the UK, many Thomas Cook outlets sell the card.

Mastercard (Access) or British automatic bank cards, and US cards in the Cirrus or Plus systems, can be used for **withdrawing cash** from ATMs in Spain: check with your bank to find out about these reciprocal arrangements – the system is highly sophisticated and can usually give instructions in a variety of languages.

Leading **credit cards** are recognized, too, and are useful for car rental, hotels and restaurants, as well as for cash advances at banks. American Express and Visa, which has an arrangement with the Banco de Bilbao Vizcaya Argentaria, are the most useful; Mastercard is less widely accepted.

Changing money

Spanish **bancos** (banks) and **cajas de ahorros** (savings banks) have branches in all but the smallest villages, and most of them should be prepared to change travellers' cheques (albeit occasionally with reluctance for certain brands, and often with hefty commissions). The Banco Santander Central Hispano (BSCH) and Banco Bilbao Vizcaya Argentaria (BBVA) are two of the most efficient and widespread; both can change most brands of travellers' cheques, and give cash advances on credit cards; commissions at the Banco Central Hispano are generally the lowest.

ATM cash machines (cajeros automaticos) are now widespread throughout the country in cities, towns and even many villages and you only need a valid card with PIN number to use them; this is probably the most convenient way to get cash when you need it, although you would be wise not to rely on this method exclusively – it's not uncommon for cards to be swallowed up or, indeed, lost or stolen. **Moneychanging machines** now feature also in many larger cities and feeding in pounds or dollars will give you instant cash.

Banking hours are generally Mon–Fri 8.30am–2pm, with some city branches open

Sat 8.30am–1pm (except from June to September when all banks close on Saturday), although times can vary from bank to bank. Outside these times, it's usually possible to change cash at larger hotels (generally bad rates, low commission) or with travel agents, who may initially grumble but will eventually give a rate with the commission built in – useful for small amounts in a hurry.

In tourist areas you'll also find specialist **casas de cambio**, with more convenient hours (though rates vary), and most branches of El Corte Inglés, a major department store found throughout Spain, have efficient exchange facilities open throughout store hours, offering competitive rates and generally a much lower commission than the banks (though they're worse for cash).

Wiring money

Having money wired from home using one of the companies listed below is never convenient or cheap, and should be considered a last resort. It's also possible to have money wired directly from a bank in your home country to a bank in Spain, although this is somewhat less reliable because it involves two separate institutions. If you go this route, your home bank will need the address of the branch bank where you want to pick up the money and the address and telex number of the Madrid head office, which will act as the clearing house; money wired this way normally takes two working days to arrive, and costs around £25/$40 per transaction.

Money-wiring companies

In the UK and Ireland

Western Union Money Transfer
ⓦ www.westernunion.com, ☎ 0800/833 833.
Moneygram ⓦ www.moneygram.com,
☎ 0800/018 0104.

29

Thomas Cook @ www.thomascook.com,
☎ 01733/318922, Belfast ☎ 028/9055 0030,
Dublin ☎ 01/677 1721.

In North America

American Express Moneygram
@ www.moneygram.com, ☎ 1-800/926-9400.
Western Union @ www.westernunion.com,
☎ 1-800/325-6000.
Thomas Cook @ www.us.thomascook.com, US
☎ 1-800/287-7362, Canada ☎ 1-888 /8234-7328.

In Australia

American Express Moneygram
@ www.moneygram.com, ☎ 1800/230 100.
Western Union @ www.westernunion.com,
☎ 1800/649 565.

In New Zealand

American Express Moneygram
@ www.moneygram.com, ☎ 09/379 8243 or
0800/262 263.
Western Union @ www.westernunion.com,
☎ 09/270 0050.

Youth and student discounts

Various official and quasi-official **youth/stu-
dent ID cards** soon pay for themselves in

savings. Full-time students are eligible for the
International Student ID Card (ISIC), which
entitles the bearer to special air, rail and bus
fares and discounts at museums, theatres
and other attractions. For Americans there's
also a health benefit, providing up to $3000
in emergency medical coverage and $100 a
day for 60 days in the hospital, plus a 24-
hour hotline to call in the event of a medical,
legal or financial emergency. The card costs
£6 in the UK; $22 for Americans; Can$16 for
Canadians; AUS$16.50 for Australians; and
$NZ21 for New Zealanders.

You have to be 26 or younger to qualify for
the **International Youth Travel Card**, which
costs £7/US$22 and carries the same bene-
fits. All these cards are available in the UK
from Usit Campus and STA; in the US from
Council Travel, STA, Travel Cuts and, in
Canada, Hostelling International (see p.16
for addresses); in Australia and New Zealand
from STA or Campus Travel.

Several other travel organizations and
accommodation groups also sell their own
cards, good for various discounts. A university photo ID might open some doors, but is
not as easily recognizable as the ISIC card,
although the latter is often not accepted as
valid proof of age, for example in bars or
clubs.

Getting around

**Most of Spain is well covered by both bus and rail networks and for journeys between
major towns there's often little to choose between them in cost or speed. On shorter or
less obvious routes buses tend to be quicker and will also normally take you closer to
your destination; some train stations are several kilometres from the town or village they
serve and you've no guarantee of a connecting bus. Approximate journey times and frequencies can be found in the "Travel details" at the end of each chapter, and local peculiarities are also pointed out in the text of the Guide. Car rental may also be worth considering, with costs among the lowest in Europe. If your trip to Spain is part of a wider
European tour, then it may be worth investing in a rail pass, such as the InterRail ticket.**

By bus

Unless you're travelling on a rail pass, **buses**
will probably meet most of your transport
needs; many smaller villages are accessible
only by bus, almost always leaving from the
capital of their province. Service varies in

quality, but buses are generally reliable and
comfortable enough – especially for long distances, with prices pretty standard at around
€5 per 100km. The only real problem
involved is that many towns still have no
main bus station, and buses may leave from
a variety of places (even if they're heading in

△ Pilgrim on the Camino de Santiago

the same direction, since some destinations are served by more than one company). Where a new terminal has been built, it's often on the outer fringes of town. As far as possible, departure points are detailed in the text or the "Travel details".

One important point to remember is that all public transport, and the bus service especially, is drastically reduced on **Sundays and holidays** – it's best not even to consider travelling to out-of-the-way places on these days. The words to look out for on timetables are *diario* (daily), *laborables* (workdays, including Saturday), and *domingos y festivos* (Sundays and holidays).

By train

RENFE, the Spanish rail company, operates a horrendously complicated variety of train services, divided into three main sections. **Cercanías** are local commuter trains in and around the major cities. **Regionales** are equivalent to buses in speed and cost, and run between cities – Regional exprés and Delta trains can cover longer distances. **Largo recorrido** (long-distance) express trains have a bewildering number of names: in ascending order of speed and luxury, they are known as Diurno, Intercity (IC), Estrella (often just signified by a star *), Talgo, Talgo P(endular), Talgo 200 (T200), and Trenhotel. Anything above Intercity can cost upwards of twice as much as standard second class. There is also a growing number of super-high-speed trains from Madrid, such as AVE to Sevilla and EuroMed to Alicante; for those who can afford it, these have cut travelling times dramatically, with Madrid to Sevilla, for example, taking 2hr 30min compared with 6–9 hours on the slower trains. For budget travellers however, it can mean switching between *regional* trains to find an alternative route, and rail staff can be reluctant to work these out for you. However, you can ring the centralized RENFE information and reservation number on ☎902 240 202 – though you'll need to speak Spanish – or look on the internet at ⓦ www.renfe.es (English version available).

In recent years many bona fide train services have been phased out in favour of buses operated jointly by RENFE and a private bus company. This is particularly the case when the connection is either indirect or the daily train or trains leave at inconven-

ient times. On some routes the **rail buses** outnumber the conventional departures by a ratio of four to one. Prices are the same as on the trains, and these services usually leave and arrive from the bus stations of the towns concerned.

The Spanish tend to use *largo recorrido* trains in much the same way as aeroplanes, with **advance booking** essential for both the outward and return journey. Most RENFE train tickets can be booked in advance from **North America** through V.E. Tours (☎1-800/222-8383, Ⓕ305/477-4220); there's no RENFE representation in Britain, Ireland or Australasia.

Be aware that the different train types produce their own separate timetables; looking at just one can give the false impression that the overall service is dramatically less than it is.

Tickets and fares

RENFE offers a whole range of **discount fares** of between 25 and 40 percent for those over sixty, the disabled, children aged four to eleven years and groups of more than ten. Return fares are also discounted by ten percent on *regionales* (valid for fifteen days) and twenty percent on *largo recorridos* (valid for sixty days) – you can buy a single, and so long as you show it when you buy the return, you'll still get the discount.

Tickets can be bought at the stations between sixty days and ten minutes before departure from the *venta anticipada* window, or in the final two hours from the *venta inmediata* window. Don't leave it to the last minute, though, as there are usually long queues. There may also be separate windows for *largo recorrido* (long-distance) trains and *regionales* or *cercanías* (locals). If you board the train without a ticket the conductor may charge you up to double the normal fare; if you don't have the cash, they'll call the police. If you do get on a train without a ticket it's always best to find the conductor first and explain, rather than wait to have them find you.

A good way to avoid the queues is to buy tickets at **travel agents** which display the RENFE sign – they have a sophisticated computer system which can also make seat reservations (€3) obligatory on *largo recorrido* trains; the cost is the same as at the station. Most larger towns also have a **RENFE** office in the centre, or you can use the new centralized 24-hour **telephone reservation service** – ☎902 240 202.

You can change the departure date of an electronically issued, reserved-seat, *largo recorrido* ticket up to one hour before your originally scheduled departure with a penalty of €1.20. If you want to cancel the same sort of ticket, as long as you do so at least half an hour before departure, you'll be entitled to an 85 percent refund of the ticket price.

Rail passes

Useful timetable publications

The red-covered **Thomas Cook European Timetable** details schedules of over 50,000 trains in Europe, as well as timings of over 200 ferry routes and rail-connecting bus services. Updated and issued every month; main changes in June edition (published end of May) with details of the summer European schedules, and October (published end of Sept) for the winter schedules; some have advance summer/winter timings also.

Rail passes are worth considering if you plan to travel extensively around Spain or are visiting the country as part of a wider tour of Europe. There are a number of different passes available. Some such as the Eurail pass have to be bought before leaving home, others can only be bought in the country itself. RENFE also offers its own passes, available in advance from selected agents or from RENFE offices in Spain.

Note that **InterRail** (see p.35) and **Eurail** (p.36) **passes** are valid on all RENFE trains except EuroMed, but that there is a supplement payable for travelling on the fastest trains. The apparently random nature of these **surcharges** can be a source of considerable irritation. It's better to know what you're letting yourself in for by reserving a seat in advance, something you'll be obliged to do in any case on some trains. For €3.60 you'll get a large, computer-printed ticket which will satisfy even the most unreasonable of guards.

RENFE Tarjeta Explorerail

If you're using the trains extensively in Spain, but not outside the country, and you are under 26, you might consider a **RENFE Tarjeta Explorerail**, accepted on all trains except some *regionales* and high-speed services – and currently the only pass available within Spain itself (although it can also be purchased before arrival from selected travel agents). You can buy passes for seven-, fifteen- or thirty-day periods; a second-class seven-day pass costs €115 (£73/$105); a fifteen-day pass costs €140 (£88/$128); and a thirty-day pass costs €180 (£113/$164). Passes are available from RENFE offices and many local travel agencies.

Euro Domino pass

British and Irish citizens might also consider purchasing the **Spanish Euro Domino Pass** from Rail Europe (see p.36), Usit CAMPUS or some travel agents before arrival. The passes are available for between three and eight days' unlimited travel within a one-month period. There is a discounted youth price for those under 26, and a half-price child (age 4–11) fare. Prices for under/over 26s are three days (£52/69), five days (£80/105), eight days (£122/159). Most high-speed train supplements are also included in the price. Individual passes can be bought for any of 28 European and North African countries, and you can buy as many separate country passes as you want.

Spain Flexipass

North American and Australasian travellers can buy a Spain Flexipass, roughly equivalent to the Euro Domino pass. The **North American Spain Flexipass**, available in both first- and second-class versions, allows three days' unlimited travel in a two-month period for $200/155 (first-/second-class), with the option of buying up to seven additional rail days at $35/32 per day. North Americans considering a combination of rail and car travel might also be interested in the Spain **Rail 'n' Drive pass**, valid for three or more days' rail travel and two or more days' car rental in a two-month period. Prices vary according to the number of travel days, style of car, and number of adults sharing it. See p.36 for details of where to buy the Spain Flexipass and the Rail n' Drive pass.

The **Australasian Spain Flexipass** is issued for travel on a certain number of days within a two-month period and available in second-/first-class versions: 3 days cost (A\$250/ 320, NZ\$300/385); 5 days (A\$365/460, NZ\$435/550); and 10 days (A\$625/795, NZ\$750/1050).

Note that with all these passes you may also be stung for surcharges (see box previous page).

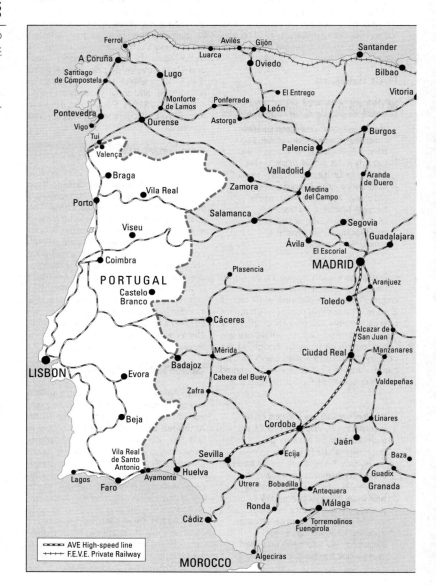

AVE High-speed line
F.E.V.E. Private Railway

InterRail pass

InterRail passes are only available to European residents, and you will be asked to provide proof of residency before being allowed to purchase one. They come in over-26 and (cheaper) under-26 versions, and cover 28 European countries (including Turkey and Morocco) grouped together in zones:

A Republic of Ireland/Britain
B Norway, Sweden, Finland

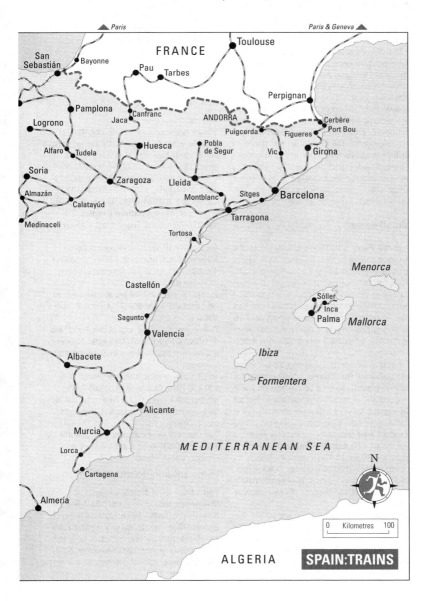

C Germany, Austria, Switzerland, Denmark
D Czech & Slovak Republics, Poland, Hungary, Croatia
E France, Belgium, Netherlands, Luxembourg
F Spain, Portugal, Morocco
G Italy, Greece, Turkey, Slovenia plus some ferry services between Italy and Greece
H Bulgaria, Romania, Yugoslavia, Macedonia

The passes are available for 22 days (one zone only), or one month and you can purchase up to three zones or a global pass covering all zones. You can save £10 by booking via the InterRail website ⓦwww.inter-rail.co.uk. InterRail passes do not include travel between Britain and the continent, although InterRail Pass holders are eligible for discounts on rail travel in Britain and Northern Ireland and cross-Channel ferries and discounts on shipping services around the Balearics. The InterRail pass also gives a discount on the London–Paris Eurostar service.

Eurail passes

A **Eurail Pass** is not likely to pay for itself if you're planning to stick to Spain, but is definitely worth considering if you're planning to do a fair amount of train travel in other European countries. The pass, which must be purchased before arrival, allows unlimited free first-class train travel in Spain and 16 other countries and is available in increments of 15 days, 21 days, 1 month, 2 months and 3 months.

If you're under 26, you can save money with a **Eurail Youthpass**, which is valid for second-class travel or, if you're travelling with 1–4 other companions, a joint **Eurail Saverpass**, both of which are available in the same increments as the Eurail Pass. You stand a better chance of getting your money's worth out of a **Eurail Flexipass**, which is good for 10 or 15 days' travel within a 2-month period. This, too, comes in first-class, under-26/second-class (**Eurorail Youth Flexipass**) and group (**Eurail Saver Flexipass**) versions.

In addition, a scaled-down version of the Flexipass, the **Europass**, is available. This allows first-class and youth (second-class) travel in France, Germany, Italy, Spain and Switzerland for any 5 days, 6 days, 8 days, 10 days or 15 days within 2 months. Up to

four "associate" countries (Austria/Hungary, Benelux, Greece, Portugal) can be included for an additional fee. The **Europass Saverpass** is a version of the Europass for people travelling in groups of two or more that offers a savings of 15 percent per person on the regular fare.

Details of prices for all these passes can be found on ⓦwww.raileurope.com, and the passes can be purchased from one of the agents listed below.

Rail contacts

In North America

BritRail Travel International
ⓦwww.raileurope.com, ☏1-888/BRITRAIL or 212/490-6688. Sells European rail passes. BritRail's British Travel Shop is at 551 Fifth Ave (at 45th Street), New York, NY 10176 ☏1-800/677-8585.
CIT Rail ⓦwww.fs-on-line.com, ☏1-800/223-7987, ☏1-800/CIT-TOUR or 212/730-2400, in Canada ☏1-800/361-7799. Eurail and Europass.
DER Travel ⓦwww.dertravel.com/Rail, ☏1-888/337-7350. Eurail, Europass and individual country passes.
European Rail Services ⓦwww.european railservices.com, Canada ☏1-800/205-5800 or 416/695-1211. Eurail, Europass, and individual country passes.
Europrail International Inc ⓦwww.europrail. net Canada, ☏1-888/667-9734. Eurail, Europass and individual country passes.
Online Travel ⓦwww.eurorail.com, Eurail Pass ☏1-800/660-5300 or 847/318-8890. Europass and individual country passes for Spain and other countries.
Rail Europe ⓦwww.raileurope.com/us, ☏1-800/438-7245, Canada ☏1-800/361-7245. Official North American Eurail Pass agent; also sells Europass, multinational passes and most single-country passes.
ScanTours ⓦwww.scantours.com, ☏1-800/223-7226 or 310/636-4656. Eurail and many other European country passes.

In the UK and Ireland

Rail Europe (SNCF French Railways)
ⓦwww.raileurope.co.uk, ☏0870/5848 848. Discounted rail fares for under-26s on a variety of European routes; also agents for InterRail, Eurostar and Euro Domino, and sells rail passes for Spain.
Usit Campus ⓦwww.usitcampus.co.uk, ☏0870/ 240 1010. Books student/youth discount train tickets and sells passes.

In Australia and New Zealand

Busabout Europe Australia ☎1300 301 776.
Hop-on hop-off bus passes.
CIT World Travel ⊛ www.cittravel.com.au,
Australia ☎02/9267 1255. Sells Eurail and
Europass.
Rail Plus, Australia ☎1300/555 003 or 03/9642
8644, ⓔ info@railplus.com.au, New Zealand
☎09/303 2484. Sells Eurail and Europass
Trailfinders ⊛ www.trailfinder.com.au, Australia
☎02/9247 7666. All Europe passes.

By car

Whilst getting around on public transport is
easy enough, you'll obviously have a great
deal more freedom if you have your **own
car**. Major roads throughout the country
are generally good, and traffic, while a little
hectic in the cities, is generally well
behaved – though Spain does have one of
the highest incidences of traffic accidents in
Europe. Equally, it also has some of the
lowest fuel prices on the continent (but still
almost double US prices). In the big cities
at least you'll probably want to pay extra for
a hotel with parking, use a guarded pay-car
park, or be prepared to strip the car of all
its contents should you park on the street
(see "Vehicle crime" below); the only alternative to this is to stay on the outskirts.

Most foreign **driver's licences** are honoured in Spain – including all EU, US and
Canadian ones – but an International
Driver's Licence (available from motoring
organizations, like the AA or RAC, in your
home country) is an easy way to set your
mind at rest. If you're bringing your own
car, you must have a green card from your
insurers, and a bail bond or extra coverage
for legal costs is also worth having, since if
you do have an accident it'll be your fault,
as a foreigner, regardless of the circumstances. Without a bail bond both you and
the car could be locked up pending investigation.

Away from main roads you yield to vehicles approaching from the right, and barring the odd "*loco*" the rules of the road are
generally adhered to. **Speed limits** are
posted – maximum on urban roads is
50kph, on other roads 90kph or 100kph
where there is an *arcén*, or hard shoulder;
the limit on *autopistas* or motorways is
120kph. On the main highways speed
traps are common, especially in the morning. If you're stopped for any violation, the
Spanish police can and usually will levy a
stiff, on-the-spot fine (which can range
from €300–600) before letting you go on
your way, especially since as a foreigner
you're unlikely to want, or be able, to
appear in court. Should you not have the
cash on you they will obligingly escort you
to the nearest cash machine and issue you
with a receipt there and then; should you
lack the ability to pay up immediately they
can impound the vehicle and take your
passport as security.

Parking laws are rigorously enforced in
cities, and any illegally parked vehicle will be
removed promptly – the authorities sometimes (but don't count on this) leave a stick-
er on the road telling you where to pay the
hefty fine (€90 upwards) to retrieve it. If your
car disappears off the street it is best to
assume that it has been towed to the local

Motoring organizations

In the UK and Ireland
RAC ⊛ www.rac.co.uk, ☎0800/550055.
AA ⊛ www.theaa.co.uk, ☎0800/444500.
AA Travel ⊛ www.aaireland.ie, Dublin ☎01/617 9988.

In North America
American Automobile Association (AAA). Each state has its own club – check the phone book for
local address and phone number (or call ☎1-800/222-4357, ⊛ www.aaa.com).
Canadian Automobile Association (CAA) ⊛ www.caa.com, ☎613/247-0117. Each region has its
own club – check the phone book for local address and phone number.

In Australia and New Zealand
Australian Automobile Association ☎02/6247 7311.
New Zealand Automobile Association ☎09/377 4660.

pound and enquiries in any hotel, government office or police station should produce the address. You will be required to pay the fine in cash. It's worth noting that it is also a towable offence to park on a taxi-rank, so study any street signs carefully wherever you park and if in doubt ask locals to be absolutely sure. The EU's new disabled parking badges will satisfy even the most pedantic of police.

Vehicle rental

Renting a car lets you out of many of the hassles, and Spain is one of the cheapest countries in Europe for this. You'll find a choice of companies in any major town, with the biggest ones – Hertz, Avis and Europcar – represented at the airports as well as in town centres. Local companies – such as Turarche in Málaga, see p.256 – can often offer excellent value for money. You'll need to be 21 or over (and have been driving for at least a year), and you're looking at from €30 (£20/$27) per day for a small car (less for the week, special rates at the weekend).

Fly-drive deals with Iberia and other operators can be good value if you know in advance that you'll want to rent a car. The big companies all offer schemes, but you'll often get a better deal through someone who deals with local agents. On the internet, **easyRentacar.com** (www.easyRentacar.com) offers car rental from Barcelona, Málaga and Madrid from as little as €14 (£9/$12) per day but with mileage restrictions and glaring company advertising on the exterior (see below). If you're going in high season try and book well in advance.

Vehicle crime is rampant in Spain, particularly in the major cities – never leave anything visible in the car, empty it if the vehicle is to be left on a city street overnight and check that all locks are fully functioning when you take delivery. It's a good idea to establish whether you have to pay extra if you remove any stickers bearing the rental company's name or logo. Many people are uncomfortable with these and regard them as a magnet for thieves but there are often siginificant financial penalties written into the small print of your car rental document.

Renting **motorcycles** and **scooters** is also possible and prices start from around €18–24 (£12–16/$16–21) a day, cheaper by the week You have to be fourteen or over to ride a machine under 75cc, eighteen for one over 75cc, and crash helmets are compulsory. Note that mopeds and motorcycles are often rented out with insurance that doesn't include theft – always check with the company first.

Car rental agencies

In the UK

Autos Abroad ⓦ www.autosabroad.co.uk, ☎ 0870/066 7788.
Avis ⓦ www.avisworld.com, ☎ 0870/606 0100.
Budget ⓦ www.go-budget.co.uk, ☎ 0800/181181.
Europcar ⓦ www.europcar.co.uk, ☎ 0845/722 2525.
National ⓦ www.nationalcar.com, ☎ 0870/536 5365.
Hertz ⓦ www.hertz.co.uk, ☎ 0870/844 8844.
Holiday Autos ⓦ www.holidayautos.com, ☎ 0870/400 0000.
Suncars ⓦ www.suncars.com, ☎ 0870/500 5566.
Thrifty ⓦ www.thrifty.co.uk, ☎ 01494/751600.

In Ireland

Atlas ⓦ www.atlascarhire.com, ☎ 01/862 0306.
Autos Abroad ⓦ www.autosabroad.com, ☎ 0870/066 7788.
Avis ⓦ www.avis.co.uk, Northern Ireland ☎ 028/9442 3333, Republic of Ireland ☎ 01/605 7555.
Budget ⓦ www.budgetcarrental.ie or ⓦ www.budget-ireland.co.uk, Northern Ireland ☎ 028/9442, Republic of Ireland ☎ 01/878 7814.
Cosmo Thrifty ⓦ www.thrifty.co.uk, ☎ 028/9445 2565.
Europcar ⓦ www.europcar.ie, Northern Ireland ☎ 028/9442 3444, Republic of Ireland ☎ 01/614 2800.
Hertz ⓦ www.hertz.co.uk; Northern Ireland ☎ 028/9442 2533, Republic of Ireland 0903/27711.
Holiday Autos ⓦ www.holidayautos.ie, ☎ 01/872 9366.
SIXT ⓦ www.irishcarrentals.ie, ☎ 061/453048.

In North America

Alamo ⓦ www.alamo.com, ☎ 1-800/522-9696.
Auto Europe ⓦ www.autoeurope.com, US ☎ 1-800/223-5555, Canada ☎ 1-888 /223-5555.
Avis ⓦ www.avis.com, US ☎ 1-800/331-1084, Canada ☎ 1-800/272-5871.
Budget ⓦ www.budgetrentacar.com, ☎ 1-800/527-0700.

Enterprise Rent-a-Car Ⓦ www.enterprise.com, ☏ 1-800/325-8007.

Europe by Car Ⓦ www.europebycar.com, ☏ 1-800/223-1516.

Hertz Ⓦ www.hertz.com, US ☏ 1-800/654-3001, Canada ☏ 1-800/263 0600.

Kemwel Holiday Autos Ⓦ www.kemwel.com, ☏ 1-800/422-7737.

National Ⓦ www.nationalcar.com, ☏ 1-800/227-7368.

Thrifty Ⓦ www.thrifty.com, ☏ 1-800/367-2277.

In Australia

Avis Ⓦ www.avis.com, ☏ 13/6333.

Budget Ⓦ www.budget.com, ☏ 1300/362 848.

Dollar Ⓦ www.dollarcar.com.au, ☏ 02/9223 1444 or 1800/358 008.

Hertz Ⓦ www.hertz.com, ☏ 1800/550 067.

National ☏ 13/1908.

Thrifty Ⓦ www.thrifty.com.au, ☏ 1300/367 227.

In New Zealand

Apex ☏ 1800/121 029.

Avis Ⓦ www.avis.com, ☏ 09/526 5231 or 0800 655 111.

Budget Ⓦ www.budget.com, ☏ 0800/ 652 227 or 09/375 2270.

Hertz, Ⓦ www.hertz.com, ☏ 09/309 0989 or 0800 655 955.

National ☏ 09/537 2582.

Thrifty Ⓦ www.thrifty.com.nz, ☏ 09/309 0111.

Hitching

As in most other countries these days, we do not recommend hitching in Spain as a safe method of getting around.

If you are determined to hitch, be warned that the road down the east coast (Barcelona–Valencia–Murcia) is notoriously difficult, and trying to get out of either Madrid or Barcelona can prove to be a nightmare (you're best off taking a bus out to a smaller place on the relevant road). Thumbing on back roads is, however, often surprisingly productive; the fewer cars there are, the more likely they are to stop.

Regionally there's considerable variation as well: the Basque country, and the north in general, often prove quite easy, whereas Andalucía tends to involve long (and very hot) waits.

By bicycle

Taking your own bike can be an inexpensive and flexible way of getting around, and of seeing a great deal of the country that would otherwise pass you by. Do remember, though, that Spain is one of the most mountainous countries in Europe and in the searing high summer temperatures, attempting to scale hills becomes an endurance test. Seasoned cycle tourists start out at dawn, covering the main part of the day's schedule by mid-morning, before the temperature peaks. That leaves the rest of the day for sightseeing, picnicking around riverbanks or dipping into the often pleasant village swimming pools, before covering a few more kilometres in the cooler hours before sunset.

The Spanish are keen cycle fans – both on and off-road – which means that you'll be well received and find reasonable facilities. There are **bike shops** in the larger towns and parts can often be found at auto repair shops or garages – look for Michelin signs. On the road, cars tend to hoot before they pass, which can be alarming at first but is useful once you're used to it. When cycling on major roads in a group always go in single file – never side by side – as this is dangerous and has resulted in several deaths in recent years. Cycle-touring guides to the better areas can be found in good bookshops – in Spanish, of course.

Getting your bike there should present few problems. Most **airlines** are happy to take them as ordinary baggage provided they come within your allowance (though it's sensible to check first and get an agreement in writing from the agent or airline as they may try to charge you up to £60/$80 at the airport); crowded charters may be less obliging. Deflate the tyres to avoid explosions in the unpressurized hold. Spanish **trains** are also reasonably accessible, though bikes can only go on a train with a guard's van (*furgón*) and must be registered – go to the *Equipajes* or *Paquexpres* desk at the station. If you are not travelling with the bike you can either send it as a package or buy an undated ticket and use the method above.

When staying in major towns and cities try not to leave your bike on the street overnight, even with a secure lock, as thieves view them as easy pickings. Most *hostales* seem able to find somewhere safe for overnight storage.

By plane

Iberia and the smaller, slightly cheaper subsidiary Aviaco, as well as the independent companies Spanair and AirEurope, operate an extensive network of internal flights. While these are quite reasonable by international standards, they still work out very pricey, and are only really worth considering if you're in a hurry and need to cross the entire peninsula. The main exceptions are the route between Madrid and Barcelona, which is very poorly serviced by public transport, or getting to, and between, the Balearic Islands, for which flights are only marginally more expensive than the ferries. In peak season you may well have to reserve long in advance for these (see "The Balearic Islands" for more details).

From North America, Central Holidays/Discover Spain Vacations (see p.17) sell the **Spain Airpass** for $165 per flight on Iberia within Spain (in conjunction with an Iberia transatlantic flight); a minimum of two passes are required but there is no limit to how many passes you may purchase. Air Europa (see p.15) is a carrier offering internal flights which can be booked from North America. In Australia, the Spain Airpass is available from Spanish Tourism Promotions in Melbourne (see p.25). The Spain Airpass isn't available in Britain and Ireland.

Communications: post, phones, internet and media

Post offices (Correos) are generally found near the centre of towns and are normally open from 8am to noon and again from 5 to 7.30pm, though big branches in large cities may have considerably longer hours and usually do not close at midday. Except in the cities there's only one post office in each town, and queues can be long: stamps are also sold at tobacconists (look for the brown and yellow Tabac sign).

You can have letters sent **poste restante** (Lista de Correos) to any Spanish post office: they should be addressed (preferably with the surname underlined and in capitals) to Lista de Correos followed by the name of the town and province. To collect, take along your passport and, if you're expecting mail, ask the clerk to check under all of your names – letters are often to be found filed under first or middle names.

Outbound mail is reasonably reliable, with letters or cards taking around five days to a week to the UK and Europe, a week to ten days to North America, New Zealand and Australia.

Phones

Spanish public **phones** work well and have instructions in English. If you can't find one, many bars also have pay phones you can use. Cabins and other phones have been adapted to take the new euro currency (see p.28) but you're best off buying a phone card (from a kiosko or tabac) of €6 or €12 which avoids hassles finding the right change. All cabins should display instructions in a variety of languages. Spanish provincial (and some overseas) dialling codes are displayed in the cabins. The **ringing tone** is long, **engaged** is shorter and rapid; the standard Spanish response is digáme ("speak to me"), often abbreviated to diga, or the even more laconic si.

For **international calls**, you can use any street cabin or go to a **locutorio**, an office where you pay afterwards. Phoning within Spain is cheaper after 6pm and all weekend for metropolitan and inter-provincial calls. International rates are slightly cheaper between midnight and 8am; the reduced rates apply all day on Saturday and Sunday. If you're using a cabin to call abroad and don't use a phone card, you're best off putting at least €2 in to ensure a connection.

Useful telephone numbers

Directory Enquiries ☎1003
International Operator ☎1008 (Europe)
International Operator☎1005 (rest of the world)
Alarm call ☎096
Time ☎093
Weather ☎906 365365

Calling home from Spain

To Britain: dial ☎00 then 44 + area code minus first 0 + number.
To Ireland: dial ☎00 then 353 + area code minus first 0 + number.
To North America: dial ☎00 then 1 + area code + number.
To Australia: dial ☎00 then 61 + area code minus first 0 + number.

Calling Spain from abroad

From Britain: dial ☎00 + 34 + number.
From North America: dial ☎011 + 34 + number.
From Australia: dial ☎0011 +34 + number.
From New Zealand: dial ☎00 +34 + number.

Mobile phones

If you want to use your **mobile phone** in Spain, you'll need to check with your phone provider whether it will work abroad, and what the call charges are. In the **UK**, for all but the very top-of-the-range packages, you'll have to inform your phone provider before going abroad to get international access switched on. You may get charged extra for this depending on your existing package and where you are travelling to. You are also likely to be charged extra for incoming calls when abroad, as the people calling you will be paying the usual rate. If you want to retrieve messages while you're away, you'll have to ask your provider for a new access code, as your home one is unlikely to work abroad. For further information about using your phone abroad, check out ⓦwww.telecomsadvice.org.uk/features/using_your_mobile_abroad.htm.

Unless you have a tri-band phone, it is unlikely that a mobile bought for use in the **USA** will work outside the States and vice versa. They tend to be very expensive to own in the US, too, as users are billed for both incoming and outgoing calls. For details

of which mobiles will work outside the US, contact your mobile service provider.

Most mobiles in **Australia and New Zealand** use GSM, which works well in Europe.

Email

One of the best ways to keep in touch while travelling is to sign up for a free internet **email** address that can be accessed from anywhere, for example YahooMail or Hotmail – accessible through ⓦwww.yahoo.com and ⓦwww.hotmail.com. Once you've set up an account, you can use these sites to pick up and send mail from any internet café or hotel with internet access.

ⓦwww.kropka.com is a useful website giving details of how to plug your laptop in when abroad, phone country codes around the world, and information about electrical systems in different countries.

The internet

The **internet** has made great inroads into Spanish life and access is widely available at internet cafés (more commonly referred to as *cibercafés* in Spanish), some computer shops and many *locutorios*. Prices vary; in cities hourly rates can be as little as €1.80, rising to around €6 in some smaller towns. For details of useful websites on Spain, see p.27.

Media

Of the **Spanish newspapers** the best are the centre-left *El País* and the centre-right *El Mundo*, both of which have good arts and foreign news coverage, including comprehensive regional "what's on" listings and supplements every weekend. Other national papers include the solidly elitist *ABC* and Barcelona's nationalist *La Vanguardia*. The regional press is generally run by local magnates and is predominantly right-wing, though often supporting local autonomy movements. Nationalist press includes *Avui* in Catalunya, printed largely in Catalan, and the Basque papers *El Correo Español del Pueblo Vasco*, *Deia* and *Gara*, the last a supporter of ETA.

British newspapers and the *International Herald Tribune* are on sale in most large cities and resorts. There are also various

English-language magazines produced by and for the expatriate communities in the main cities and on the *costas*; all are of limited interest, though occasionally they carry details of local events and entertainment.

TV and radio

You'll inadvertently catch more **TV** than you expect sitting in bars and restaurants where the set often blares away on a shelf in one corner. On the whole it's a fairly entertaining mix of films, talk and game shows, news programmes and children's TV. Sports fans are well catered for, with regular live coverage of **football** and basketball matches. In the football season, you can watch live matches from the Spanish, Italian and British leagues as they're shown in many bars.

If you have a **radio** which picks up short wave you can tune in to the BBC World Service, broadcasting in English for most of the day on frequencies between 12MHz (24m) and 4MHz (75m). You may also be able to receive Voice of America and American Forces' stations.

Accommodation

Simple, reasonably priced rooms are still very widely available in Spain, and in almost any town you'll be able to get a no-frills double for around €15–21, a single for €9–15. Only in major resorts and a handful of "tourist cities" (such as Toledo or Sevilla) need you pay more.

We've detailed where to find places to stay in most of the destinations listed in the Guide, and given a price range for each (see below), from the most basic rooms to luxury hotels. As a general rule, all you have to do is head for the cathedral or main square of any town, invariably surrounded by an old quarter full of accommodation possibilities. In Spain, unlike most countries, you don't always have to pay more for a central location (this goes for bars and cafés, too), though you do tend to get a comparatively bad deal if you're travelling on your own as there are relatively few single rooms. Much of the time you'll have to negotiate a reduction on the price of a double.

It's often worth **bargaining** over room prices, since the regulated prices don't necessarily mean much. In high season you're unlikely to have much luck (although many hotels do have rooms at different prices, and tend to offer the more expensive ones first) but at quiet times you may get quite a discount, even at fancier places, particularly if you plan to stay more than one night. If there are more than two of you, most places have rooms with three or four beds at not a great deal more than the double-room price – a bargain, especially if you have children.

Hotel vouchers (*bonos*), available from local travel agents, often give substantial discounts at medium to upmarket hotels; simply present the voucher at the hotel instead of payment.

Fondas, pensiones, hostales and hoteles

The one thing all travellers need to master is the elaborate variety of types and places to stay. Least expensive of all are **fondas** (identifiable by a square blue sign with a white **F** on it, and often positioned above a bar), closely followed by **casas de huéspedes** (**CH** on a similar sign), the more common **pensiones** (**P**) and, less frequent **hospedajes**. Distinctions between all of these are rather blurred, but in general you'll sometimes find food served at both *fondas* and *pensiones* while *casas de huéspedes* (literally "guest houses") were traditionally for longer stays. However, as Spain upgrades its tourist

Accommodation price codes

All the establishments listed in this book have been price-graded according to the following scale. The prices quoted are for the **cheapest available double room in high season**; effectively this means that anything in the ❶ and most places in the ❷ range will be without private bath, though there's usually a washbasin in the room. In the ❹ category and above you will probably be getting private facilities. Remember, though, that many of the budget places will also have more expensive rooms including en-suite facilities. Youth hostels are graded under ❶ as the price per person is less than half of the category's upper limit.

Note that in the more upmarket *hostales* and *pensiones*, and in anything calling itself a hotel, you'll pay a **tax** (IVA) of seven percent on top of the room price.

❶ Under €12	❹ €27–36	❼ €60–90
❷ €12–18	❺ €36–48	❽ €90–120
❸ €18–27	❻ €48–60	❾ Over €120

facilities, both *fondas* and *casas de huespedes* are gradually disappearing and, along the *costas* particularly, they are very rare.

Slightly more expensive but far more common are **hostales** (marked **Hs**) and **hostal-residencias** (**HsR**). These are categorized from one star to three stars, but even so prices vary enormously according to location – in general the more remote, the less expensive. Most *hostales* offer good functional rooms, usually with private shower, and, for doubles at least, they can be excellent value.

Moving up the scale you finally reach fully-fledged **hoteles** (**H**), again star-graded by the authorities (from one to five). One-star hotels cost no more than three-star *hostales* – sometimes they're actually less expensive – but at three stars you pay a lot more, at four or five you're in the luxury class with prices to match.

Near the top end of this scale there are also state-run **paradores** (ⓦwww.parador.es): usually beautiful places, often converted from castles, monasteries and other minor Spanish monuments. If you can afford them these are almost all wonderful. Even if you can't afford to stay, the buildings are often worth a look in their own right, and usually have pleasantly classy bars and restaurants.

Outside all of these categories you will sometimes see **camas** (beds) and **habitaciones** (rooms) advertised in private houses or above bars, often with the phrase *camas y comidas* ("beds and meals"). If you're travelling on a very tight budget these can be worth looking out for – particularly if you're offered one at a bus station and the owner is prepared to bargain with you.

Finally, **casas rurales** (rural houses), a scheme established along the lines of French *gîtes*, have gone from strength to strength in Spain and can offer excellent value – they are where many Spanish holiday-makers stay if they have the choice. Accommodation at these can vary from bed and breakfast at a farmhouse to half-board or self-catering in a restored manor. Local turismos have details.

Note: if you have any **problems** with Spanish rooms – overcharging, most obviously – you can usually produce an immediate resolution by asking for the *libro de reclamaciones* (complaints book). By law all establishments must keep one and bring it out for regular inspection by the authorities. Although little is ever written in them they are worth using and, as the pages are numbered, difficult to tamper with. If you do make an entry, English is acceptable but write clearly and simply; add your home address, too, as you are entitled to be informed of any action including – but don't count on it – compensation. Most establishments prefer to keep them empty, thus attracting no unwelcome attention from officialdom which, of course, works in your favour. You can also take your complaint to any local turismo, who will, if possible, attempt to resolve the matter while you wait.

Youth hostels, mountain refuges, and monasteries

Albergues Juveniles (youth hostels) are rarely very practical, except in northern Spain (especially the Pyrenees) where it can be difficult for solo, short-term travellers to find any other bed in summer. Outside Andalucía, which has recently upgraded its nineteen hostels, only about twenty Spanish *albergues* stay open all year – the rest operate just for the summer (or spring and summer) in temporary premises – and in cities they tend to be inconveniently located. The most useful are detailed in the Guide, or you can get a complete list (with opening times and phone numbers) from the YHA. Be warned that they tend to have curfews, are often block-reserved by school groups and demand production of a YHA card (though this is generally available on the spot if you haven't already bought one from your national organization). At around €8 under-26/€11 over-26 in high season per person, too, you can quite easily pay the same as for sharing a cheap double room in a *hostal* or *pension*.

In isolated mountain areas the Federación Madrileña de Montañismo, Apodaca 18, 1° Dcha, Madrid 28004 (☎915 038 074), and two Catalunya-based clubs – the Federació d'Entitats Excursionistes de Catalunya (Rambla 41 1r Pral., 08002 Barcelona; ☎934 120 777, ⓦwww.feec.es), and the Unió Excursionista de Catalunya de Gràcia (Santa Agata 30, 08012 Barcelona; ☎932 175 650, ⓦwww.gencat.es/entitats/ unexcag.htm) – run a number of **refugios**: simple, cheap dormitory-huts for climbers and trekkers, generally equipped only with bunks and a very basic kitchen, and costing around €3 per person. Again off the beaten track, it is sometimes possible to stay at Spanish **monasterios** or **conventos**. Often severely underpopulated, these may let empty cells for a small charge. You can just turn up and ask – many will take visitors regardless of sex – but if you want to be sure of a reception it's best to approach the local turismo first, and phone ahead. There are some particularly wonderful monastic locations in Galicia, Catalunya and Mallorca.

Those following the **Camino de Santiago** can also take advantage of monastic accommodation specifically reserved for pilgrims along the route; some of the best places are detailed in the text.

Youth hostel associations

England and Wales

Youth Hostel Association (YHA), Trevelyan House, 8 St Stephen's Hill, St Albans, Herts AL1 2DY ☎0870/870 8808, ⓦwww.yha.org.uk and ⓦwww.iyhf.org. Annual membership £12.50, for under-18s £6.25.

Scotland

Scottish Youth Hostel Association, 7 Glebe Crescent, Stirling, FK8 2JA ☎0870/1553 255, ⓦwww.syha.org.uk. Annual membership £6, for under-18s £2.50.

Ireland

An Óige, 61 Mountjoy St, Dublin 7 ☎01/8430/4555, ⓦwww.irelandyha.org. Adult (and single parent) membership €12.70; family (2 parents and children under 16) €25.40; under-18s €5.
Hostelling International Northern Ireland, 22–32 Donegall Rd, Belfast BT12 5JN ☎028/9032 4733, ⓦwww.hini.org.uk. Adult membership £10; under-18s £6; family £20.

USA

Hostelling International-American Youth Hostels (HI-AYH), 733 15th St NW, Suite 840, PO Box 37613, Washington, DC 20005 ☎202/783-6161, ⓦwww.hiayh.org. Annual membership for adults (18–55) is $25, for seniors (55 or over) is $15, and for under-18s is free. Lifetime memberships are $250.

Canada

Hostelling International/Canadian Hostelling Association, Room 400, 205 Catherine St, Ottawa, ON K2P 1C3 ☎1-800/663 5777 or 613/237 7884, ⓦwww.hostellingintl.ca. Rather than sell the traditional 1- or 2-year memberships, the association now sells one individual Adult membership with a 16- to 28-month term. The length of the term depends on when the membership is sold, but a member can receive up to 28 months of membership for just $35. Membership is free for under-18s and you can become a lifetime member for $175.

Australia

Australia Youth Hostels Association, 422 Kent St, Sydney ☎02/9261 1111, ⓦwww.yha.com.au. Adult membership rate A$49 for the first twelve months and then A$32 each year after.

New Zealand

New Zealand Youth Hostels Association, 173 Gloucester St, Christchurch ☎03/379 9970, ⓦwww.yha.co.nz. Adult membership NZ$40 for one year, NZ$60 for two and NZ$80 for three.

Camping

There are some 350 authorized **campsites** in Spain, predominantly on the coast. Note that the larger ones aren't very tent-friendly and you're better off sticking to the smaller sites if you're planning on spending time under canvas. Campsites usually work out at about €2.50–3 (£1.50–1.80/ US$2.27–2.72) per person plus the same again for a tent, and a similar amount for each car or caravan, perhaps twice as much for a van. Only a few of the best located or most popular sites are significantly more expensive. Again, we've detailed the most useful in the text, but if you plan to camp extensively then pick up the free *Mapa de Campings* from the National Tourist Board, which marks and names virtually all of them. A complete *Guía de Campings* (€6), listing full prices, facilities and exact locations, is available at most Spanish bookshops.

Camping outside campsites is legal – but with certain restrictions. There must be fewer than ten people in your group, and you're not allowed to camp "in urban areas, areas prohibited for military or touristic reasons, or within 1km of an official campsite". What this means in practice is that you can't camp on tourist beaches (though you can,

discreetly, nearby) but with a little sensitivity you can set up a tent for a short period almost anywhere in the countryside. Whenever possible ask locally first.

If you're planning to do a lot of camping, an **international camping carnet** may be a good investment, giving a ten-percent discount on quality campsites. In the **UK and Ireland**, the carnet costs £4.50, and is available to members of the AA or the RAC (see above), or for members only from either of the following: the **Camping and Caravanning Club**, Greenfields House, Westwood Way, Coventry, CV4 8JH (☎024/76694995, ⓦwwwcampingandcaravanningclub.co.uk), or the foreign touring arm of the same company, the **Carefree Travel Service** (☎024/ 76422024), which provides the CCI free if you take out insurance with them; they also book ferry crossings and inspect campsites in Europe.

In the **US and Canada**, the carnet is available from home motoring organizations, or from **Family Campers and RVers** (FCRV), 4804 Transit Rd, Building 2, Depew, NY 14043 (☎1-800/245-9755, ⓦwww.fcrv.org). FCRV annual membership costs $25, and the carnet an additional $10. The carnet serves as useful identification and covers you for third-party insurance when camping.

Eating and drinking

There are two ways to eat in Spain: you can go to a *restaurante* or *comedor* (dining room) and have a full meal, or you can have a succession of tapas (small snacks) or *raciones* (larger ones) at one or more bars.

At the bottom line a *comedor* – where you'll get a basic, filling, three-course meal with a drink, the **menú del día** – is the cheapest option, but they're often tricky to find, and drab places when you do. Bars tend to work out pricier but a lot more interesting, allowing you to do the rounds and sample local or house specialities.

Breakfast, snacks and sandwiches

For **breakfast** you're best off in a bar or

café, though some *hostales* and *fondas* will serve the "Continental" basics. The traditional Spanish breakfast is *chocolate con churros* – long tubular doughnuts (not for the weak of stomach) with thick drinking chocolate. But most places also serve *tostadas* (toast) with oil (*con aceite*) or butter (*con mantequilla*) – and jam (*y mermelada*), or more substantial egg dishes such as *huevos fritos* (fried eggs), which are not a typical Spanish breakfast but do tend to be on offer in tourist areas. *Tortilla* (potato omelette) also makes an excellent breakfast.

Coffee and pastries (*pasteles* or *bollos*) or doughnuts are available at most cafés, too, though for a wider selection of cakes you should head for one of the many excellent *pastelerías* or *confiterías*. In larger towns, especially in Catalunya, there will often be a *panadería* or *croissantería* serving quite an array of appetizing baked goods besides the obvious bread, croissants and pizza. For ordering coffee see p.52.

Some bars specialize in **bocadillos** – hearty French bread-style sandwiches with a choice of fillings. If you want them wrapped to take away with you, ask for them *para llevar*. Incidentally, be careful not to use the word "sandwich" to order a *bocadillo*, as an Iberian *sandwich* is usually on sad, processed white bread – often with ham and cheese or something with a lot of mayonnaise.

Tapas and raciones

One of the advantages of eating in **bars** is that you are able to experiment. Many places have food laid out on the counter, so you can see what's available and order by pointing without necessarily knowing the names; others have blackboards or "*lista de las tapas*" (see box below). **Tapas** (often called **pinchos** or **pintxos** in northern Spain) are small portions, three or four small chunks of fish or meat, or a dollop of salad, which traditionally used to be served up free with a drink. These days you often have to pay for anything more than a few olives, but a single helping rarely costs more than €1.20–2.40 unless you're somewhere very flashy. **Raciones** (costing around €6.50–9) are simply bigger plates of the same intended for sharing among a couple of people, and can be enough in themselves for a light meal. The more people you're with, of course, the better; half a dozen *tapas* or *pinchos* and three *raciones* can make a varied and quite filling meal for three or four people.

Tascas, **bodegas**, **cervecerías** and **tabernas** are all types of bar where you'll find tapas and *raciones*. Most of them have different sets of prices depending on whether you stand at the bar to eat (the

---

Tapas and other snacks

The most usual **fillings for bocadillos** are *lomo* (loin of pork), *tortilla* and *calamares* (all of which may be served hot), *jamón* (York or, much better, *serrano*), *chorizo*, *salchicha* (and various other regional sausages – such as the small, spicy Catalan *butifarras*), *queso* (cheese) and *atún* (tuna – probably canned).

Standard tapas and raciones might include:

Aceitunas	Olives	*Garbanzos*	Chick peas
Albóndigas	Meatballs	*Gambas*	Prawns
Anchoas	Anchovies	*Habas*	Broad beans
Berberechos	Cockles	*Habas con jamón*	Broad beans with ham
Boquerones	Anchovies	*Hígado*	Liver
Cabrillas	Large snails with tomato	*Huevo cocido*	Hard-boiled egg
		Jamón serrano	Dried ham (like Parma ham)
Calamares	Squid		
Callos	Tripe	*Mejillones*	Mussels
Caracoles	Snails	*Navajas*	Razor clams
Carne en salsa	Meat in tomato sauce	*Patatas alioli*	Potatoes in garlic mayonnaise
Champiñones	Mushrooms, usually fried in garlic		
		Patatas bravas	Spicy fried potatoes
Chocos	Deep fried cuttlefish	*Pimientos*	Peppers
Chorizo	Spicy sausage	*Pincho moruno*	Kebab
Cocido	Stew	*Pisto*	Ratatouille
Empanadilla	Fish/meat pasty	*Pulpo*	Octopus
Ensaladilla rusa	Russian salad (diced vegetables in mayonnaise)	*Riñones al Jerez*	Kidneys in sherry
		Salchicha	Sausage
		Sepia	Cuttlefish
Escalibada	Aubergine (eggplant) and pepper salad	*Tortilla española*	Potato omelette
		Tortilla francesa	Plain omelette

basic charge) or sit at tables (up to fifty percent more expensive – and even more if you sit out on a terrace).

Wherever you have tapas, it is important to find out what the local **special** is and order it. Spaniards will commonly move from bar to bar, having just the one dish that they consider each bar does well. A bar's "non-standard" dishes, these days, can all too often be microwaved – which is not a good way to cook squid.

Meals and restaurants

Once again, there's a multitude of distinctions. You can sit down and have a full meal in a *comedor*, a *cafetería*, a *restaurante* or a *marisquería* – all in addition to the more food-oriented bars.

Comedores are the places to seek out if your main criteria are price and quantity. Sometimes you will see them attached to a bar (often in a room behind), or as the dining room of a *hostal* or *pensión*, but as often as not they're virtually unmarked and discovered only if you pass an open door. Since they're essentially workers' cafés they tend to serve more substantial meals at lunchtime than in the evenings (when they may be closed altogether). When you can find them – the tradition, with its family-run business and marginal wages, is on the way out – you'll probably pay around €4.50–8 for a **menú del día**, **cubierto** or **menú de la casa**, all of which mean the same – a complete meal of three courses, usually with bread, wine and dessert included.

The highway equivalent of *comedores* are **ventas** which you'll be extremely glad of if you're doing much travelling by road. These roadside inns dotted along the highways between towns and cities have been serving Spanish wayfarers for hundreds of years – many of them quite literally – and the best *ventas* are wonderful places to get tasty country cooking at bargain prices. Again the *menú del día* is the one to go for and the best places usually have quite a gathering of lorries in their car park, shrewd long-distance truck drivers being among the best customers.

Replacing *comedores* to some extent are **cafeterías**, which the local authorities grade from one to three cups (the ratings, as with restaurants, seem to be based on facilities offered rather than the quality of the food). These can be good value, too, especially the self-service places, but their emphasis is more northern European and the light snack-meals served tend to be dull. Food here often comes in the form of a **plato combinado** – literally a combined plate – which will be something like egg and chips or *calamares* and salad (or occasionally a weird combination like steak and a piece of fish), often with bread and a drink included. This will generally cost in the region of €4.50–6. *Cafeterías* often serve some kind of *menú del día* as well. You may prefer to get your *plato combinado* at a bar, which in small towns with no *comedores* may be the only way to eat inexpensively.

Moving up the scale there are **restaurantes** (designated by one to five forks) and **marisquerías**, the latter serving exclusively fish and seafood. *Restaurantes* at the bottom of the scale are often not much different in price from *comedores*, and will also generally have *platos combinados* available. A fixed-price *menú del día* is often better value though: generally three courses plus wine and bread for around €4.50–9. Chinese restaurants – increasingly popular in Spain – generally have the cheapest *menús del día*: €4.50–6 is the norm. Move above two forks, however, or find yourself in one of the more fancy *marisquerías* (as opposed to a basic seafront fish-fry place), and prices can escalate rapidly. However, even here most of the top restaurants offer an upmarket *menú* called a **menú de degustación** (a sampler meal, usually including wine) which is often excellent value and allows you to try out some of the country's finest cooking for €20–30.

To avoid receiving confused stares from waiters in restaurants, you should always ask for **la carta** when you want a menu; *menú* in Spanish refers only to fixed-price meal. In addition, in all but the most rock-bottom establishments it is customary to leave a small **tip** (*propina*): Spaniards are judicious tippers, so only do so if the service merits it: the amount is up to you, though 5 to 10 percent of the bill in a restaurant is quite sufficient. Service is normally included in a *menú del día*. The other thing to take account of in medium- and top-price restaurants is the addition of **IVA**, a seven percent tax on your bill. It should say on the menu if you have to pay this.

Understanding Spanish menus

As with tapas and *raciones*, restaurant dishes vary enormously from region to region. The list below is no more than a selection, with the main Spanish dishes and a handful of local specialities. Wherever possible you'll do best by going for the latter; some are mentioned in the regional chapters that follow, others you'll simply see people eating. *Me gustaría uno así* ("I'd like one like that") can be an amazingly useful phrase.

Basics

Aceite	Oil
Ajo	Garlic
Arroz	Rice
Azúcar	Sugar
Huevos	Eggs
Mantequilla	Butter
Miel	Honey
Pan	Bread
Pimienta	Pepper
Sal	Salt
Vinagre	Vinegar

Meals

Almuerzo/Comida	Lunch
Botella	Bottle
Carta	Menu
Cena	Dinner
Comedor	Dining room
Cuchara	Spoon
Cuchillo	Knife
La cuenta	The bill
Desayuno	Breakfast
Menú del día/	Fixed-price set meal
cubierto	
Mesa	Table
Platos combinados	Mixed plate
Tenedor	Fork
Vaso	Glass

Soups (*Sopas*) and starters

Caldillo	Clear fish soup
Caldo	Broth
Caldo verde or	Thick cabbage-based
gallego	broth
Ensalada	(Mixed/green) salad
(mixta/verde)	
Gazpacho	Cold tomato and cucumber soup
Pimientos rellenos	Stuffed peppers
Sopa de ajo	Garlic soup
Sopa de cocido	Meat soup
Sopa de gallina	Chicken soup
Sopa de mariscos	Seafood soup
Sopa de pescado	Fish soup
Sopa de pasta	Noodle soup
(fideos)	
Verduras con	Boiled potatoes with
patatas	greens

Fish (*pescados*)

Anchoas	Anchovies (fresh)
Anguila/Angulas	Eel/Elvers
Atún	Tuna
Bacalao	Cod (often salt)
Bonito	Tuna
Boquerones	Small, sardine-like fish
Chanquetes	Whitebait
Lenguado	Sole
Merluza	Hake
Mero	Perch
Pez espada	Swordfish
Rape	Monkfish
Raya	Ray, skate
Rodaballo	Turbot
Salmonete	Mullet
Sardinas	Sardines
Trucha	Trout

Seafood (*mariscos*)

Almejas	Clams
Arroz con mariscos	Rice with seafood
Calamares	Squid (in ink)
(en su tinta)	
Centollo	Spider-crab
Cigalas	King prawns
Conchas finas	Large scallops
Gambas	Prawns/shrimps
Langosta	Lobster
Langostinos	Crayfish
Mejillones	Mussels
Nécora	Sea-crab
Ostras	Oysters
Paella	Classic Valencian dish with saffron rice, chicken, seafood, etc
Percebes	Goose-barnacles
Pulpo	Octopus
Sepia	Cuttlefish
Vieiras	Scallops
Zarzuela de	Seafood casserole
mariscos	

Some common terms

al ajillo	in garlic
asado	roast
a la Navarra	stuffed with ham
a la parrilla/plancha	grilled
a la Romana	fried in batter

al horno	baked
alioli	with garlic mayonnaise
cazuela, cocido	stew
en salsa	in (usually tomato) sauce
frito	fried
guisado	casserole
rehogado	sautéed

Meat (Carne) and Poultry (Aves)

Callos	Tripe
Carne de buey	Beef
Cerdo	Pork
Chuletas	Chops
Cochinillo	Suckling pig
Codorniz	Quail
Conejo	Rabbit
Cordero	Lamb
Escalopa	Escalope
Fabada asturiana/ Fabes a la catalana	Hot pot with butter beans, black pudding, etc
Hamburguesa	Hamburger
Hígado	Liver
Lacón con grelos	Gammon with turnips
Lengua	Tongue
Lomo	Loin (of pork)
Pato	Duck
Pavo	Turkey
Perdiz	Partridge
Pollo	Chicken
Riñones	Kidneys
Solomillo	Sirloin steak
Solomillo de cerdo	Pork tenderloin
Ternera	Beef/Veal

Vegetables (Legumbres)

Acelga	Chard
Alcachofas	Artichokes
Arroz a la cubana	Rice with fried egg and tomato sauce
Berenjenas	Aubergine/eggplant
Cebollas	Onions
Champiñones/Setas	Mushrooms
Coliflor	Cauliflower
Espárragos	Asparagus
Espinacas	Spinach
Garbanzos	Chickpeas
Habas	Broad/fava beans
Judías blancas	Haricot beans
Judías verdes, rojas, negras	Green, red, black beans
Lechuga	Lettuce
Lentejas	Lentils
Menestra/Panache de verduras	Mixed vegetables

Nabos/Grelos	Turnips
Patatas	Potatoes
Patatas fritas	French fries (chips)
Pepino	Cucumber
Pimientos	Peppers/capsicums
Pisto manchego	Ratatouille
Puerros	Leeks
Puré	Mashed potato
Repollo	Cabbage
Tomate	Tomato
Zanahoria	Carrot

Fruit (frutas)

Albaricoques	Apricots
Cerezas	Cherries
Chirimoyas	Custard apples
Ciruelas	Plums, prunes
Dátiles	Dates
Fresas	Strawberries
Granada	Pomegranate
Higos	Figs
Limón	Lemon
Manzanas	Apples
Melocotones	Peaches
Melón	Melon
Naranjas	Oranges
Nectarinas	Nectarines
Peras	Pears
Piña	Pineapple
Plátanos	Bananas
Sandía	Watermelon
Toronja/Pomelo	Grapefruit
Uvas	Grapes

Desserts (postres)

Arroz con leche	Rice pudding
Crema catalana	Catalan crème brûlee
Cuajada	Cream-based dessert served with honey
Flan	Crème caramel
Helado	Ice cream
Melocotón en almíbar	Peaches in syrup
Membrillo	Quince paste
Nata	Whipped cream
Natillas	Custard
Yogur	Yogurt

Cheese

Cheeses (quesos) are on the whole local, though you'll get the hard, salty queso manchego everywhere. Mild sheep's cheese (queso de oveja) from the León province is widely distributed and worth asking for.

You'll find numerous recommendations, in all price ranges, in the main body of the Guide. Spaniards generally eat very late, so most of these places serve food from around 1 until 4pm and from 8pm to midnight. Many restaurants **close on Sunday or Monday evening**. Outside these times, generally the only places open are the **fast-food** joints; *Pans & Co* and *Bocatta* serve suprisingly good *bocadillos* and often have special offers.

What to eat

It's possible to make a few generalizations about Spanish food. If you like **fish and seafood** you'll be in heaven in Spain as this forms the basis of a vast array of tapas and is fresh and excellent even hundreds of miles from the sea. It's not cheap, unfortunately, so rarely forms part of the lowest priced menus (though you may get the most common fish – cod, often salted, and hake – or squid) but you really should make the most of what's on offer. Fish stews (*zarzuelas*) and rice-based paellas (which also contain meat, usually rabbit or chicken) are often memorable in seafood restaurants. Paella comes originally from Valencia and is still best there, but you'll find versions of it all over Spain.

Meat is most often grilled and served with a few fried potatoes and a couple of salad leaves, or cured or dried and served as a starter or in sandwiches. *Jamón serrano*, the Spanish version of Parma ham, is superb, though the best varieties, from Extremadura and Huelva in the southwest, are extremely expensive. In country areas game is very much on the menu, too – you may find the baby animal specialities of central Spain, such as *cochinillo* (suckling pig) or *lechal* (suckling lamb), less appetizing.

Vegetables rarely amount to more than a few fries or boiled potatoes with the main dish (though you can often order a side dish à la carte). It's more usual to start your meal with a **salad** or, in the north especially, you may get hearty vegetable soups or a plate of boiled potatoes and greens as a starter.

Dessert in the cheaper places is nearly always fresh fruit or flan, the Spanish crème caramel, with the regions often having their own versions such as *crema catalana* in Catalunya and the Andalucian *tocino de cielo*. There are also various varieties of *pudín* – rice pudding or assorted blanc-

mange mixtures. In some fancier restaurants you may discover a chef who has a flair for desserts or who gets his *dulces* supplied by a local convent (usually excellent), but generally desserts are not a high point of Spanish cuisine and you may want to stick to fruit and cheese.

Vegetarians

Vegetarians have a fairly hard time of it in Spain: there's always something to eat, but you may get weary of eggs and omelettes (*tortilla francesa* is a plain omelette, *tortilla de patatas* comes with potatoes, *con champiñones* with mushrooms). In the big cities you'll find vegetarian restaurants and ethnic places which serve vegetable dishes. Otherwise, superb fresh produce is always available in the markets and shops, and cheese, fruit and eggs are available everywhere. In restaurants you're faced with the extra problem that pieces of meat – especially ham, which the Spanish don't seem to regard as real meat – are often added to vegetable dishes to "spice them up".

The phrases to get to know are *Soy vegetariano/a. Como sólo verduras. Hay algo sin carne?* ("I'm a vegetarian. I only eat vegetables. Is there anything without meat?"); you may have to add *y sin mariscos* ("and without seafood") and *y sin jamón* ("and without ham") to be really safe. A good resource for those with internet access is a new **website** – Ⓦ www.veg.org – which hopes to compile, with a little help from users, a guide to vegetarian restaurants in Spain.

If you're a vegan, you're either going to have to be not too fussy or accept weight loss if you're away for any length of time. Some salads and vegetable dishes are strictly vegan, but they're few and far between. Fruit and nuts are widely available, nuts being sold by street vendors everywhere.

Alcoholic drinks

Over fifty percent of the European Union's vineyards lie in Spain and **vino** (wine), either *tinto* (red), *blanco* (white) or *rosado/clarete* (rosé), is the invariable accompaniment to every meal. As a rule, wine is extremely inexpensive and while low prices used to be equated with low quality, in recent years enormous investment has been flowing into the Spanish wine trade and standards have risen dramatically. The wines to look out for are whites from Galicia and reds from Rioja, Navarra and Ribera del Duero. *Cava* (Spain's champagne) generally comes from Catalunya and is a real bargain, whilst Andalucía is noted for its sherries and brandies. One thing worth knowing about Spanish wine is the terms related to the **ageing process** which defines the best wines; *crianza* wines must have a minimum of two years ageing before sale; red *reserva* wines at least two years (of which one must be in oak barrels); red *gran reserva* at least two years in oak and three in the bottle). White *gran reserva* guarantees five years' ageing (of which six months must be in oak).

The most common bottled variety you'll encounter in the more economical restaurants and *comedores* is Valdepeñas, a good standard mass produced wine from the central plains of New Castile; most Valdepeñas is ordinary if quaffable stuff, but the Los Llanos bodega produces an outstanding and affordable *gran reserva*. Rioja, from the area round Logroño on the edge of the Basque country, is rightly Spain's best known wine and available everywhere (Cune, Berberana, Marques de Caceres and La Rioja Alta are brands to try). Another top-drawer and currently fashionable region is Ribera del Duero in Castilla-León which makes Spain's most expensive wine, Vega Sicilia, besides other outstanding reds (Pesquera, Viña Pedrosa and Senorio de Nava are names to look out for). There are also scores of local wines – some of the best are Navarra (Chivite, Palacio de la Vega) and Catalunya (Bach, Raimat, Caus Lubis and Alvaro Palacios), a region which also produces the champagne-like **cava** (Codorniu, Marques de Monistrol); Galicia too, in the temperate northwest is producing some notable white wines (Ribeiro, Fefiñanes and Albariño are prominent producers). However, in most low-budget eating places you'll rarely be offered a wide choice of Spain's better wines, which tend to appear only in the higher-class establishments.

Dining off the beaten track may mean drinking whatever comes out of the barrel, or the house-bottled special (ask for *caserío* or *de la casa*). This can be great, it can be lousy, but at least it will be distinctively local. In a bar, a small glass of wine will generally cost around €0.30–0.60; in a restaurant, if

wine is not included in the menu, prices start at around €2 a bottle although you'll be paying at least double this and more for quality wine. If it is included, you'll usually get a whole bottle for two people, a *media botella* (a third to a half of a litre) for one. Be on your guard for the odd skinflint establishment which may try to get away with serving you a single glass of wine to comply with the "including wine" offer, thus obliging you to buy a bottle on top. A polite but firm word with the waiter is usually enough to secure your rights.

The classic Andalucian wine is **sherry** – *vino de Jerez* which refers to the wines produced in a triangular-shaped area to the west of the town of Jerez de la Frontera. Served chilled or at *bodega* temperature – *fino* (the Spanish name for dry sherry) is a perfect drink to wash down tapas – and, like everything Spanish, it comes in a perplexing variety of forms. The main distinctions are between *fino* or *jerez seco* (dry sherry), *amontillado* (medium dry), and *oloroso* or *jerez dulce* (sweet), and these are the terms you should use to order. *Manzanilla* is another member of the sherry family produced in the seaside town of Sanlúcar de Barrameda; the vineyards' proximity to the sea gives it a delicate, briny tang and among Spaniards it is currently the most popular of all the dry *finos*. Similar – though not identical – is *montilla*, an excellent dry sherry-like wine from the province of Córdoba. The main distinction between this and the other *finos* is that no alcohol is added at the production stage, prompting the *cordobeses* to claim that theirs is the more natural product, but sales and popularity still lag way behind those of its rival.

Cerveza, lager-type beer, is generally pretty good, though more expensive than wine. It comes in 300-ml bottles (*botellines*) or, for about the same price, on tap – a *caña* of draught beer is a small glass, a *caña doble* larger, and asking for *un tubo* (a tubular glass) gets you about half a pint. Many bartenders will assume you want a *doble* or *un tubo*, so if you don't, say so. Mahou, Cruz Campo, San Miguel, and Victoria are all decent beers and good local brands too are worth trying, such as Estrella de Galicia or Alhambra.

Equally refreshing, though often deceptively strong, is **sangría**, a wine-and-fruit punch which you'll come across at fiestas and in

Drinks and beverages

Alcohol

Beer	*Cerveza*
Alcohol-free beer	*Sin-alcol*
Champagne	*Champán/Cava*
White wine	*Vino Blanco*
Red wine	*Vino tinto*
Rosé wine	*Vino rosado*
Red wine with soda	*Tinto de verano*
Sweet	*Dulce*
Dry	*Seco*
A shandy	*Una clara*
Gin & tonic	*Un gintonic*
Gin & Coke	*Un cubata*
Rum & Coke	*Un cubalibre*

Hot drinks

Coffee	*Café*
Espresso coffee	*Café solo*
White coffee	*Café con leche*
Decaff	*Descafeinado*
Tea	*Té*
Drinking chocolate	*Chocolate*

Soft drinks

Water	*Agua*
Mineral water	*Agua mineral*
…(sparkling)	*…(con gas)*
…(still)	*…(sin gas)*
Milk	*Leche*
Juice	*Zumo*
Tiger nut drink	*Horchata*
Milk shake	*Batido*

tourist bars. *Tinto de verano* is a similar red wine and soda or lemonade combination which is a great refresher in high temperatures; variations on this include *tinto de verano con naranja* (red wine with orangeade) or *con limón* (mixed with a Fanta lemon juice).

In mid-afternoon – or even at breakfast – many Spaniards take a *copa* of **liqueur** with their coffee. The best are *anís* (like Pernod) or *coñac*, excellent local brandy with a distinct vanilla flavour; try Magno, Soberano, or Carlos III ("tercero") to get an idea of the variety, or Carlos I ("primero"), Lepanto, or Gran Duque de Alba for a measure of the quality. Most brandies are produced by the great sherry houses in Jerez, but one equally good one that isn't is Mascaró, produced in Catalunya and resembling an armagnac.

In bars **spirits** are ordered by brand name, since there are generally less expensive Spanish equivalents for standard imports. Larios gin from Málaga, for instance, is about half the price of Gordon's. Specify *nacional* to avoid getting an expensive foreign brand. Spirits can be very expensive at the trendier bars; however, wherever they are served, they tend to be staggeringly generous – the bar staff pouring from the bottle until you suggest they stop.

Mixed drinks are universally known as *copa* or *Cubata*, though strictly speaking the latter is rum and Coke. Juice is *zumo*; orange, *naranja*; lemon, *limón*; and tonic *tónica*.

Soft drinks and hot drinks

Soft drinks are much the same as anywhere in the world, but try in particular *granizado* (slush) or *horchata* (a milky drink made from tiger nuts or almonds) from one of the street stalls that spring up everywhere in summer. You can also get these drinks from *horchaterías* and from *heladerías* (ice cream – *helados* – parlours), or in Catalunya from the wonderful milk bars known as *granjas*. Although you can drink the **water** almost everywhere it usually tastes better out of the bottle – inexpensive *agua mineral* comes either sparkling (*con gas*) or still (*sin gas*).

Café (coffee) – served in cafés, *heladerías* and bars – is invariably espresso, slightly bitter and, unless you specify otherwise, served black (*café solo*). If you want it white ask for *café cortado* (small cup with a drop of milk) or *café con leche* (made with lots of hot milk). For a large cup of weaker coffee ask for an *americano*. Coffee is also frequently mixed with brandy, cognac or whisky, all such concoctions being called *carajillo*. Iced coffee is *café con hielo*, another great high summer refresher: a *café solo* is served with a glass of ice cubes. Pour the coffee onto the cubes - it cools instantly.

Té (tea) is also available at most bars, although bear in mind that Spaniards usually drink it black. If you want milk it's safest to ask for it afterwards, since ordering *té con leche* might well get you a glass of milk with a tea bag floating on top. Perhaps a better

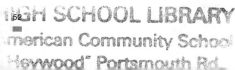

bet would be **herbal teas** and most bars keep these: *manzanilla* (camomile, not to be confused with the sherry of the same name), *poleomenta* (mint tea) and *hierba luisa* (lemon verbena) are all popular herbal infusions.

Chocolate (hot chocolate) is incredibly thick and sweet, and is a popular early-morning drink after a long night on the town. If you'd prefer a thinner cocoa-style drink ask for a brand name, like Cola Cao.

Opening hours and public holidays

Almost everything in Spain – shops, museums, churches, tourist offices – closes for a siesta of at least two hours in the hottest part of the day. There's a lot of variation (and the siesta tends to be longer in the south) but basic summer working hours are 9.30am–1.30pm and 4.30–8pm. Certain shops (mainly big chains and department stores) do now stay open all day, and there is a move towards "normal" working hours. Nevertheless, you'll get far less aggravated if you accept that the early afternoon is best spent asleep, or in a bar, or both.

Museums, with very few exceptions, follow the rule above, with a break between 1 and 4pm; watch out for Sundays (most open mornings only) and Mondays (most close all day). Admission charges vary, but there's usually a big reduction or free entrance if you show a student or pension card. Anywhere run by the Patrimonio Nacional (such as El Escorial and the Royal Palace in Madrid) is free to EU citizens on Wednesdays – you'll need to show your passport.

Note that the official beginning of **summer opening hours** for Patrimonio Nacional monuments – and some privately owned ones – varies from year to year, and is generally not announced until April/May. Where this is the case, we have given opening hours for "summer" and "winter"; contact the local Turismo for more up-to-date information.

Getting into **churches** can be a problem. The really important ones, including most cathedrals, operate in much the same way as museums and almost always have some entry charge to view valued treasures and paintings, or their cloisters. Other churches, though, are usually kept locked, opening only for worship in the early morning and/or the evening (between around 6–9pm), so you'll either have to try at these times, or find someone with a key. A sacristan or custodian almost always lives nearby and most people will know where to direct you. You're expected to give a small tip, or donation.

For all churches "decorous" dress is required, ie no shorts, bare shoulders, etc.

Public holidays

Public holidays can (and will) disrupt your plans at some stage. Alongside the national holidays (see below) there are scores of local fiestas (different in every town and village, usually marking the local saint's day); any of them will mean that everything except bars (and *hostales*, etc) locks its doors.

Spanish national holidays

January 1, *Año Nuevo*, New Year's Day

January 6, *Epifanía*, Epiphany

Good Friday, *Viernes Santo*

Easter Sunday, *Domingo de la Resureccion*

Easter Monday, *Lunes de Pascua*

May 1, *Fiesta del Trabajo*, May Day

August 15, *La Asunción*, Assumption of the Virgin

October 12, *Día de la Hispanidad*, National Day

November 1, *Todos los Santos*, All Saints

December 6, *Día de la Constitución*, Constitution Day

December 8, *Fiesta de la Hispanidad*

Christmas Day, *Navidad*

In addition, **August** is Spain's own holiday month, when the big cities – especially Madrid – are semi-deserted, and many of the shops and restaurants closed for the duration of the month. In contrast, it can prove nearly impossible to find a room in the more popular coastal and mountain resorts at these times; similarly, seats on planes, trains and buses in August should if possible be booked in advance.

Fiestas

Fiestas are an absolutely crucial part of Spanish life. Even the smallest village gives at least a couple of days a year over to partying, and happening across a local event can be huge fun, propelling you right into the heart of its culture. But as well as such community celebrations, Spain has some really major events: most famously the Running of the Bulls at Pamplona, the April Feria of Seville, and the great religious processions of Semana Santa, leading up to Easter. Any of these can be worth planning your whole trip around.

Following is a very basic **calendar of fiesta highlights**. For more detailed listings, see the boxes at the beginning of each chapter, which cover each region's best events, and consult local tourist offices. Outsiders are always welcome at fiestas, the one problem being that it can be hard to find a hotel, unless you book well in advance.

> Note that saint's day festivals – indeed all Spanish celebrations – can **vary in date**, often being observed over the weekend closest to the dates given in our listings. Contact local tourist offices for more details.

January
16–17: San Antoni's day is preceded by bonfires and processions, especially on the **Balearic Islands**.

February
Carnaval (the week preceding Ash Wednesday and Lent) is an excuse for wild partying and masques, most riotous in **Cádiz** (Andalucía), **Sitges** (Catalunya), and **Águilas** (Valencia).

March
12–19 Las Fallas in Valencia (p.881) is the biggest of the bonfire festivals held for San José, climaxing on the Night of Fire when enormous caricatures are burnt and firecrackers take over the streets.

Easter (March/April)
Semana Santa (Holy Week) is celebrated across Spain with religious processions, at their most theatrical in the cities of **Sevilla, Málaga, Murcia** and **Valladolid**, where *pasos* – huge floats of religious scenes – are carried down the streets, accompanied by hooded penitents atoning for the year's misdeeds. **Good Friday** sees the biggest processions.

April
22–24: Moros y Cristianos – mock battle between Moors and Christians – in Alcoy, Valencia. (Similar events take place throughout the year all around Spain.
23: San Jordi – Catalunya's patron saint's day is a big party across the region and is also celebrated on National Book Day throughout Spain.
Last week: Feria de Abril – spectacular week-long fair at Sevilla.

May
Early May: Horse Fair at Jerez (Andalucía).
7–22: San Isidro – Madrid's patron saint (15th) – is a signal for parades, free concerts, and the start of the bullfight season.
Pentecost (Whitsun: 7th Sunday after Easter)**:** the great pilgrimage to **El Rocío** (p.327), near Huelva (Andalucía).
Corpus Christi (Thursday after Trinity; May/June) is a focus for religious processions, accompanied by floats and penitents, notably in Toledo, Granada and Valencia. Many town fiestas also take place,

including the spectacular costumed events of the **Festa de la Patum** (Catalunya, p.809).

June

23–24: San Juan and midsummer's eve is celebrated with bonfires all over Spain – particularly in San Juan de Alicante, where a local version of Las Fallas takes place.

29: San Pedro – patron of fishermen – is honoured by flotillas of boats, and partying all along the coast.

July

7–14: San Fermin – the famed **running of the bulls** at **Pamplona** (p.498).

25: Santiago – Spain's patron saint, St James – is honoured at Santiago de Compostela, with fireworks and bonfires.

August

10–11: Elche (Valencia) hosts mock battles between Christians and Moors, ending with a centuries-old mystery play.

First/second week: Mass **canoe races** down the Río Sella in Asturias.

Third week: Toledo's main fiesta, climaxing in amazing fireworks at the weekend.

Last week: Gigantones (giant puppets) are paraded in Alcalá de Henares (Castile).

Last Wed (usually): La Tomatina in Buñol, near Valencia: the country's craziest fiesta, a two-hour tomato fight (p.889).

September

First week: Vendimia (grape harvest) celebrations at **Valdepeñas** (New Castile), **Jerez** (Andalucía) and other wine towns.

21: Rioja wine harvest celebrated in Logroño (Old Castile).

October

1: San Miguel Villages across the country celebrate their patron saint's day

12: La Virgen del Pilar – the patron saint of Aragón – is an excuse for bullfights and *jota* dancing at **Zaragoza** and elsewhere.

December

31: Nochevieja New year is celebrated by eating a grape for every stroke of the clock in Plaza del Sol in Madrid.

Bullfights

Bullfights are an integral part of many fiestas. In the south, especially, any village that can afford it will put on a corrida for an afternoon, while in big cities like Madrid or Sevilla, the main festival times are accompanied by a week-long (or more) season of prestige fights.

Los Toros, as Spaniards refer to bullfighting, is big business. It is said that 150,000 people are involved, in some way, in the industry, and the top performers, the **matadores**, are major earners, on a par with the country's biggest pop stars. There is some **opposition** to the activity from animal welfare groups but it is not widespread: if Spaniards tell you that bullfighting is controversial, they are likely to be referring to practices in the trade. In recent years, bullfighting critics (who you will find on the arts and not the sports pages of the newspapers) have been expressing their perennial outrage at the widespread but illegal shaving of bulls' horns prior to the *corrida*. Bulls' horns are as

sensitive as fingernails, and filing them a few millimetres deters the animal from charging; they affect the bull's balance, too, further reducing the danger for the *matador*.

Notwithstanding such abuse (and there is plenty more), *Los Toros* remain popular throughout the country. To *aficionados* (a word that implies more knowledge and appreciation than "fan"), the bulls are a culture and a ritual – one in which the emphasis is on the way man and bull "perform" together – in which the *arte* is at issue rather than the cruelty. If pressed on the issue of the slaughter of an animal, they generally fail to understand. Fighting bulls are, they will tell you, bred for the industry; they live a reason-

55

able life before they are killed, and, if the bull-fight went, so too would the bulls.

If you spend any time at all in Spain during the **season** (which runs from March to October), you will encounter *Los Toros* on a bar TV – and that will probably make up your mind whether to attend a *corrida*. If you decide to go, try to see a big, prestigious event, where star performers are likely to despatch the bulls with "art" and a success-ful, "clean" kill. There are few sights worse than a *matador* making a prolonged and messy kill, while the audience whistles and chucks cushions over the *barrera*. If you have the chance to see one, the most excit-ing and skilful events are those featuring **mounted matadores**, or *rejoneadores*; this is the oldest form of *corrida*, developed in Andalucía in the seventeenth century.

Established and popular matadores include the veteran Enrique Ponce, César Rincón, Victor Mendes, Joselito, Litri, David "El Rey" Silveti and José María Manzanares. Two newer stars are Sevilla's golden boy, Antonio Bareas, and the 18-year-old prodigy Julián "El Juli" López. Cristina Sánchez, the first woman to make it into the top flight for many decades, retired in 1999, blaming sex-ist organizers, crowds and fellow *matadores* – many of whom refused to appear on the same bill as a woman. A complete guide to bullfighting with exhaustive links can be found at ⊛www.mundo-taurino.org.

The corrida

The **corrida** begins with a **procession**, to the accompaniment of a *paso doble* by the band. Leading the procession are two *algauziles* or "constables", on horseback and in traditional costume, followed by the three *matadores*, who will each fight two bulls, and their *cuadrillas*, their personal "team", each comprising two mounted *picadores* and three *banderilleros*. At the back are the mule teams who will drag off the dead bulls.

Once the ring is empty, the *algauzil* opens the *toril* (the bulls' enclosure) and the first bull appears – a moment of great physical beauty – to be "tested" by the *matador* or his *banderilleros* using pink and gold capes. These preliminaries conducted (and they can be short, if the bull is ferocious), the **suerte de picar** ensues, in which the *picadores* ride out and take up position at opposite sides of the ring, while the bull is distracted by other

toreros. Once they are in place, the bull is made to charge one of the horses; the *pica-dor* drives his short-pointed lance into the bull's neck, while it tries to toss its padded, blindfolded horse, thus tiring the bull's pow-erful neck and back muscles. This is repeat-ed up to three times, until the horn sounds for the *picadores* to leave. Cries of "*fuera!*" (out) often greet the overzealous use of the lance, for by weakening the bull too much they fear the beast will not be able to put up a decent fight. For many, this is the least acceptable stage of the corrida, and it is clearly not a pleasant experience for the horses, who have their ears stuffed with oil-soaked rags to shut out the noise, and their vocal cords cut out to render them mute.

The next stage, the *suerte de banderillas*, involves the placing of three sets of *banderil-las* (coloured sticks with barbed ends) into the bull's shoulders. Each of the three *ban-derilleros* delivers these in turn, attracting the bull's attention with the movement of his own body rather than a cape, and placing the *banderillas* whilst both he and the bull are running towards each other. He then runs to safety out of the bull's vision, some-times with the assistance of his colleagues.

Once the *banderillas* have been placed, the *suerte de matar* begins, and the *matador* enters the ring alone, having exchanged his pink and gold cape for the red one. He (or she) salutes the president and then dedicates the bull either to an individual, to whom he gives his hat, or to the audience by placing his hat in the centre of the ring. It is in this part of the *corrida* that judgements are made and the performance is focused, as the *matador* displays his skills on the (by now exhausted) bull. He uses the movements of the cape to attract the bull, while his body remains still. If he does well, the band will start to play, while the crowd *olé* each pass. This stage lasts around ten minutes and ends with the kill. The *matador* attempts to get the bull into a position where he can drive a sword between its shoulders and through to the heart for a *coup de grâce*. In practice, they rarely succeed in this, instead taking a second sword, crossed at the end, to cut the bull's spinal cord; this causes instant death.

If the audience are impressed by the *mata-dor*'s performance, they will wave their hand-kerchiefs and shout for an award to be made by the president. He can award one or both ears, and a tail – the better the display, the more pieces he gets – while if the *matador* has excelled himself, he will be carried out of the ring by the crowd, through the *puerta grande*, the main door, which is normally kept locked. The bull, too, may be applauded for its performance, as it is dragged out by the mule team.

Tickets for *corridas* are €18 and up – much more for the prime seats and prestigious fights. The cheapest seats are *gradas*, the highest rows at the back, from where you can see everything that happens without too much of the detail; the front rows are known as the *barreras*. Seats are also divided into *sol* (sun), *sombra* (shade), and *sol y sombra* (shaded after a while), though these distinctions have become less crucial as more and more bullfights start later in the day, at 6 or 7pm, rather than the traditional

5pm. The *sombra* seats are more expensive, not so much for the spectators' personal comfort as the fact that most of the action takes place in the shade. On the way in, you can rent **cushions** – two hours sitting on concrete is not much fun. Beer and soft drinks are sold inside.

Anti-bullfight organizations

Spain's main opposition to bullfighting is organized by ADDA (Asociación para la defensa del animal). They co-ordinate the Anti-Bullfight Campaign (ABC) International and also produce a quarterly newsletter in Spanish and English. Their bilingual website – ⓦintercom.es/adda/ – has information about international campaigns and current actions.

Football

To foreigners, the bullfight is easily the most celebrated of Spain's spectacles. In terms of popular support in modern Spain, however, it ranks far below fútbol (soccer). If you want the excitement of a genuinely Spanish event, watching a Sunday evening game in *La Liga* usually produces as much passion as anything you'll find in the Plaza de Toros.

For many years, the country's two dominant teams have been big-spending **Real Madrid** and **F.C. Barcelona**, and these two have shared the League and Cup honours more often than is healthy. Recently, however, both teams have faced a bit more opposition, notably from **Deportivo La Coruña** (winners of La Liga in 2000) and **Valencia**. Other significant teams include **Athletic Bilbao** (who have never fielded a non-Basque), **Celta Vigo** (from Galicia), **Real Sociedad** (from San Sebastián), **Real Zaragoza**, **Deportivo Alavès** (from Vitoria in the Basque country), and the Sevilla teams **Sevilla** and **Real Betis**. Real Madrid's local rivals, **Atlético de Madrid**, should be in this list, too, but they are currently the Manchester City of Spain, having been relegated to the Division Two in 2001.

The league **season** runs from early-September until mid-June, with a short break for Christmas and the New Year. Most of the league games kick off at 5pm or 7pm on Sundays, though live TV demands that one key game kicks off at 9pm on Saturday and Sunday.

With the exception of a few big games – mainly those involving Real Madrid and Barcelona – **tickets** are not too hard to get. They start at around €15 for First Division games, with the cheapest in the *fondo* (behind the goals); *tribuna* (pitchside stand) seats are pricier. Trouble is very rare: English fans, in particular, will be amazed at the easy-going family atmosphere and mixed-sex crowds.

If you don't go to a game, the atmosphere can be pretty good **watching on TV** in a local bar, especially in a city whose team is playing away. Many bars advertise the matches they screen, and they will often feature Sunday afternoon **English league and cup games**, if they have satellite.

Two essential phrases: "¿Como va el partido?' (What's the score), and "Fuera de juego" (offside).

Music

An account of Spain's diverse music appears in the Contexts section of this guide. Enough to say, here, that you should catch all that is going on. You will see and hear plenty of regional specialities at any of the country's fiestas.

Traditional **flamenco** – the country's most famous sound – is best witnessed in its native Andalucía, and particularly at one of the major fiestas. There are also some specifically flamenco festivals in the summer, most notably at Cartagena and around Granada. Clubs and bars which feature flamenco performers tend on the whole to be expensive and tourist-oriented, while the *peñas* (clubs) are often members-only affairs. However, it is possible to find accessible places which cater for *aficionados*, and in Andalucía itself almost any flamenco guitarist you come across is likely to be extremely good. Just watch the cost of the drinks. In recent years, there has been an exciting development in the shape of new flamenco bands, some of whom have attempted introducing jazz, rock and African elements into their music. Some of the best artists in this field are to be seen in Madrid.

If you're anywhere in Spain between about December 18 and January 3, watch for performances in local churches of **villancicos**. These are Christmas carols in local style – they can be flamenco, waltz or polyphonic – and are sung by fairly large *coral/rondalla* groups of instrumentalists and vocalists of both sexes. When they're good they're extremely beautiful, and it's obviously a non-boozy, family-oriented spectacle.

Rock music in Spain may tend to follow British and American trends, but the scene is livelier – and less slavishly derivative – than in almost any other west European country, at its best drawing from a broad range of influences in which traditional Spanish and Latin American rhythms play a major part. There are some excellent home-grown bands and

regular gigs in most of the big cities, especially in the north. Both Madrid and Barcelona attract major **international concerts** from time to time, usually staged in their giant football stadiums. Wherever you are, keep an eye out for posters or check the entertainments sections in the local press – you'll find local bands airing their talents at just about any fiesta.

Two relative newcomers to the music scene are the festivals of **Sònar** (ⓦ www.sonar.ya.com) and **Benicàssim** (ⓦ www.fiberfib.com). The former held in Barcelona in June is a showpiece of electronic music and DJs (see p.737) and the latter, a 4-day alternative music festival held on the beach in Benicàssim (see p.893). The festivals attract the biggest names in their respective fields – as does the **WOMAD** (World Music) festival held in Caceres (Estremadura) over the first weekend in May..

Because of relatively large expatriate populations, Madrid and Barcelona are also good places to hear **Latin American and African** music – again, keep your eye out for posters and check the club and dance-hall listings in the local papers.

There are several excellent **jazz festivals** in the summer: notably in San Sebastián in the middle of July, and in Barcelona, Santander, Sitges and Almuñecar. Worth checking out, too, is the International Festival of Guitar in Córdoba (early July), where many of the great **classical guitarists** put in an appearance along with exponents of Latin American and flamenco styles.

All of Spain's major music festivals are listed on the **internet** at ⓦ www.festivals.com.

Trouble, the police and sexual harassment

While you're unlikely to encounter any trouble during the course of a normal visit, it's worth remembering that the Spanish police, polite enough in the usual course of events, can be extremely unpleasant if you get on the wrong side of them. There are three basic types: the Guardia Civil, the Policía Municipal, and the Policía Nacional, all of them armed.

Avoiding trouble

Almost all the problems tourists encounter are to do with **petty crime** – pickpocketing and bag-snatching – rather than more serious physical confrontations, so it's as well to be on your guard and know where your possessions are at all times. Sensible **precautions** include: carrying bags slung across your neck, not over your shoulder (although obviously no bag at all is preferable); not carrying anything in zipped pockets facing the street; having photocopies of your passport, and leaving passport and tickets in the hotel safe; and noting down travellers' cheque and credit card numbers. There are also several ploys to be aware of and situations to avoid as you do the rounds of the city:

❏ Thieves often work in pairs, so watch out for people standing unusually close if you're studying postcards or papers at stalls; keep an eye on your wallet if it appears you're being distracted. **Ploys** (by some very sophisticated operators) include: the "helpful" person pointing out birdshit (shaving cream or something similar) on your jacket while someone relieves you of your money; the card or paper you're invited to read on the street to distract your attention; the move by someone in a café for your drink with one hand (the other hand's in your bag as you react to save your drink); and the beggars who place trays under your face while rifling your bag unseen below.

❏ If you have a **car** don't leave anything in view when you park it, especially in major cities; take the radio with you. Vehicles are rarely stolen, but luggage and valuables left in cars do make a tempting target and rental cars are easy to spot. At beauty spots, beaches and out-of-the-way attractions, peruse the ground carefully when you park; if it's strewn with broken window glass it's a sure sign that thieves are frequent visitors and you'll need to park elsewhere or take appropriate action.

❏ **Looking for hotel rooms**, don't leave any bags unattended anywhere. This applies especially to blocks where the hotel or *hostal* is on the higher floors and you're tempted to leave baggage in the hallway or ground-floor lobby.

❏ The American Embassy in Madrid says it frequently receives reports of **roadside thieves** posing as "good Samaritans" to persons experiencing car and tyre problems. The thieves typically attempt to divert the driver's attention by pointing out a mechanical problem and then steal items from the vehicle while the driver is looking elsewhere. The problem is particularly acute with vehicles rented at Madrid's Barajas airport. Be cautious about accepting help from anyone other than a uniformed Spanish police officer and, if you do break down, keep your valuables in sight or lock them in the vehicle.

What to do if you're robbed

If you're robbed, you need to **go to the police** to report it, not least because your insurance company will require a police report. Don't expect a great deal of concern if your loss is relatively small – and expect the process of completing forms and formalities to take ages. In the unlikely event that you're **mugged**, or otherwise threatened, never resist; hand over what's wanted and go straight to the police, who on these occasions will be more sympathetic.

If you have your passport stolen or lose all your money, you can contact your **consulate** (see "Listings" in the Guide for individual cities), which is required to assist you to some degree.

The police

There are three main types of **police**: the Guardia Civil, the Policía Municipal and the Policía Nacional.

The **Guardia Civil**, in green uniforms, are the most officious and the ones to avoid. Though their role has been cut back since they operated as Franco's right hand, they remain a reactionary force.

If you do need the police – and above all if you're reporting a serious crime such as rape – you should always go to the more sympathetic **Policía Municipal**, who wear blue-and-white uniforms with red trim. In the countryside there may be only the Guardia Civil; though they're usually helpful, they are inclined to resent the suggestion that any crime exists on their turf and you may end up feeling as if you are the one who stands accused.

The brown-uniformed **Policía Nacional** are mainly seen in cities, armed with submachine guns and guarding key installations such as embassies, stations, post offices and their own barracks. They are also the force used to control crowds and demonstrations.

Offences

There are a few **offences** you might commit unwittingly that it's as well to be aware of:

❏ In theory you're supposed to carry some kind of **identification** at all times, and the police can stop you in the streets and demand it. In practice they're rarely bothered if you're clearly a foreigner, but given the occasional terrorist and illegal-immigrant clamp-downs it would be wise to carry some means of identification even if it's only a photocopy of your passport details.

❏ **Nude bathing** or **unauthorized camping** are activities that might bring you into contact with officialdom, though these days a warning to cover up or move on is more likely than any real confrontation. There are now nudist beaches and mixed beaches (both nudist and clothed) on all the major *costas* and **topless** tanning is commonplace at all the trendier resorts; however, in country areas where attitudes are still very traditional, you should take care not to upset local sensibilities.

❏ Spanish **drug laws** are in a somewhat bizarre state at present. After the socialists came to power in 1983, cannabis use (possession of up to 8g of what the Spanish call *chocolate*) was decriminalized. Subsequent pressures, and an influx of harder drugs, changed that policy and – in theory at least – any drug use is now forbidden. You'll see signs in some bars saying *no porros* ("no joints"), which you should heed. However, the police are in practice little worried about personal use. Larger quantities (and any other drugs) are a very different matter.

Should you be **arrested** on any charge, you have the right to contact your **consulate**, although they're notoriously reluctant to get involved. If you've been detained for a drugs offence, don't expect any sympathy or help from your consulate.

Sexual harassment

Spain's macho image has faded dramatically and these days there are relatively few parts of the country where foreign women travelling alone are likely to feel threatened, intimidated, or to attract unwanted attention.

Inevitably, the **big cities** – like any others in Europe – have their no-go areas, where street crime and especially drug-related hassles are on the rise, but there is little of the pestering and propositions that you have to contend with in, say, the larger French or Italian cities. The outdoor culture of *terrazas* (terrace bars) and the tendency of Spaniards to move around in large, mixed crowds, filling central bars, clubs and streets late into the night, help to make you feel less exposed. If you are in any doubt, there are always **taxis** – plentiful, reasonably priced, and certainly the safest way to travel late at night. Make full use of them, particularly in Madrid and Barcelona.

The major **resorts** of the *costas* have their own artificial holiday culture. The Spaniards who hang around in discos here or at fiesta fairgrounds pose no greater or lesser threat than similar operators at home. The language barrier simply makes it harder to know who to trust. *Déjame en paz* ("leave me in peace") is a fairly standard rebuff.

Predictably, it is in **more isolated regions**, separated by less than a generation from desperate poverty (or still starkly poor), that most serious problems can occur. You do need to know a bit about the land you're travelling around. In some areas you can walk for hours without coming across an inhabited farm or house. It's rare that this poses a threat – help and hospitality are much more the norm – but you are certainly more vulnerable. That said, **trekking** is becoming more popular in Spain as a whole and many women happily tramp the foot-paths, from Galicia to the Sierra Nevada. In the south, especially, though, it is worth finding rooms in the larger villages, or, if you camp out, asking permission to do so on private land, rather than striking out alone.

Work

Unless you have a particular skill and have applied for a job advertised in your home country, such as au pair work, the only real chance of long-term work in Spain is in language schools. If you intend to stay in Spain longer than three months, you'll need a *permiso de residencia* – see "Red Tape and Visas" (p.22). A word of warning: police are cracking down on people without these and may ask for passport/residence papers on the spot, especially out of the tourist season.

European Union citizens may find the EU's website for those planning to live or work abroad within the EU a useful resource; it can be found at ⓦhttp://citizens.EU.int/.

Teaching and office work

Finding a teaching job is mainly a question of pacing the streets, stopping in at every language school around and asking about vacancies. For the addresses of schools look in the Yellow Pages (*Páginas Amarillas*) under *Idiomas enseñanza* or *Academias de Idiomas*. You'll need to persevere, though, if you're to come up with a rewarding position; a TEFL (Teaching English as a Foreign Language) or ESL (English as a Second Language) certificate gives you a much better chance of success.

Other options are to try advertising **private lessons** (better paid at €10–15 an hour, but harder to make a living at) on the *Philología* noticeboards of university faculties or in local bookshops.

Another possibility, if your Spanish is excellent, is **translation work**, most of which will be business correspondence – look in the Yellow Pages under *Traductores*. If you intend doing agency work, you'll usually need access to a PC and either email or fax.

Temporary work

If you're looking for **temporary work** the best chances are in the **bars and restaurants** of the big Mediterranean resorts. This may help you have a good time but it's unlikely to bring in much money; pay (often from British bar owners) will reflect your lack of official status or work permit. If you turn up in spring and are willing to stay through the season you might get a better deal – also true if you're offering some special skill such as windsurfing (there are schools sprouting up all along the coast). Quite often there are jobs at **yacht marinas**, too, scrubbing down and repainting the boats of the rich; just turn up and ask around, especially from March until June. As an inexperienced foreigner you've no hope at all of work on harvests as most agricultural work goes to North African immigrants prepared to work for around €25 per day.

Travellers with disabilities

Spain is not exactly at the forefront of providing facilities for travellers with disabilities. That said, there are accessible hotels in the major cities and resorts and, by law, all new public buildings are required to be fully accessible. There are also a number of active groups of disabled people: ONCE, the Spanish organization for the blind, is particularly weighty, its huge lottery bringing with it considerable power.

Transport is still the main problem, since buses (outside the main cities at least) are virtually impossible for wheelchairs and trains only slightly better (though there are wheelchairs at major stations and wheelchair spaces in some carriages – especially on the more modern trains such as the AVE between Madrid and Sevilla). Hertz has cars with hand controls available in Madrid and Barcelona (with advance notice), and taxi drivers are usually helpful. The Brittany Ferries crossing from Plymouth to Santander offers good facilities if you're **driving to Spain** (as do most cross-Channel ferries).

Once out of the cities and away from the coast, the difficulties increase. Road surfaces in the mountain regions can be rough and toilet facilities for disabled motorists are a rare sight. If you've got the money, *paradores* are one answer to the problem of unsuitable **accommodation**. Many are converted from castles and monasteries and although not built with the disabled guest in mind, their grand scale – with plenty of room to manoeuvre a wheelchair inside – tends to compensate.

Here are several websites which may prove usueful when planning your holiday:
ⓦ www.everybody.co.uk – a database of wheelchair-accessible hotels and airlines.
ⓦ www.disabilityresources.org – a comprehensive interactive database with lots of information on travel and other topics.
ⓦ www.access–able.com – a site specifically geared to journey planning for elderly and disabled travellers and a section on Spain can be researched by province or city or subject (e.g. hotels, tours and trips, medical services etc.)
ⓦ www.wemedia.com – another good site for information on travel, and has useful links to other sites dealing with disabled traveller's topics.
ⓦ http://polibea.virtualave.net/guia.html – a

Spanish site with all kinds of addresses in Spain which can help and advise disabled travellers.

Contacts for travellers with disabilities

In Spain

Spanish National Tourist Office (see p.25 for addresses). Publishes a fact sheet listing a variety of useful addresses and some accessible accommodation.
ECOM (Federation of Spanish private organizations for the disabled), Gran Vía de las Corts Catalanas 562 principal, 2ª, 08011 Barcelona ☏ 934 515 550; c/Germán Pérez Carrasco, 65, Madrid ☏ 914 060 270. Produces an Access city guide for Barcelona and Madrid.
Organización Nacional de Ciegos de España (ONCE), c/Prado 24, 28014 Madrid ☏ 915 974 727; c/Calabria 66–76, Barcelona 08015 ☏ 933 259 200, ⓦ www.once.es. The national and extremely influential organization for the blind.
Comité de Representantes de Minusválidos (CERMI) c/Prim 3, Madrid (ⓜ Banco de España). Provides information and sells Braille maps and a wide range of aids for the blind.
Rompiendo Barreras Travel, c/Roncevalles 3, 28007 Madrid ☏ 915 513 622, ⓦ www.rbtravel.es. Spanish travel agency dedicated to disabled travel. Provides a wide range of information (in Spanish) and organizes hotels, tours, rural tourism and lots more all over Spain. Although operating in Spanish they will respond to communications in English.

In the UK and Ireland

Access Travel, 6 The Hillock, Astley, Lancashire M29 7GW ☏ 01942/888844, ⓦ www.access-travel.co.uk. Tour operator that can arrange flights, transfer and accommodation. This is a small business, personally checking out places before recommendation. They can guarantee accommodation standards in Florida, France, Spain, Portugal, the Balearic Islands, Lanzarote, Malaga, Malta, Rhodes and Tenerife. ATOL bonded, established seven years.

Disability Action Group, Portside Business Park, 189 Airport Road West, Belfast BT3 9ED ☎028/90297880. Information on disabled travel abroad and produces a holiday factsheet.

Holiday Care, 2nd floor, Imperial Building, Victoria Rd, Horley, Surrey RH6 7PZ ☎01293/774535, Minicom ☎01293/776943, @www.holidaycare.org.uk. Provides a free comprehensive travel pack on Spain with details of facilities in hotels, resorts etc. Information on financial help for holidays available.

Irish Wheelchair Association, Blackheath Drive, Clontarf, Dublin 3 ☎01/833 8241, ☎833 3873, ✉admin@iwa.ie. Advice and guidance about travelling abroad with a wheelchair.

Mobility International, Boulevard de Baudouin 18, Brussels B1000 ☎00322/201 5711, @www.mobility-international.org. Information, access guides, tours and exchange programmes for British disabled travellers.

RADAR (Royal Association for Disability and Rehabilitation), 12 City Forum, 250 City Rd, London EC1V 8AF ☎020/7250 3222, Minicom ☎020/7250 4119, @www.radar.org.uk. A good source of advice on holidays and travel in the UK. They produce an annual holiday guide called Holidays in Britain and Ireland for £8 in the UK, £11 to Europe and £15 to other overseas destinations (includes p&p). Their website is useful and well organized.

Tripscope, Alexandra House, Albany Rd, Brentford, Middlesex TW8 0NE ☎08457/585 641, @www.justmobility.co.uk/tripscope.This registered charity provides a national telephone information service offering free advice on UK and international transport for those with a mobility problem.

In US and Canada

Access-Able @www.access-able.com. Online resource for travellers with disabilities.

Directions Unlimited, 123 Green Lane, Bedford Hills, NY 10507 ☎1-800/533-5343 or 914/241-1700. Tour operator specializing in custom tours for people with disabilities.

Mobility International USA, 451 Broadway, Eugene, OR 97401 Voice and TDD ☎541/343-1284, @www.miusa.org. Information and referral services, access guides, tours and exchange programmes. Annual membership $35 (includes quarterly newsletter).

Society for the Advancement of Travelers with Handicaps (SATH), 347 5th Ave, New York, NY 10016 ☎212/447-7284, @www.sath.org. Nonprofit educational organization that has actively represented travellers with disabilities since 1976.

Travel Information Service ☎215/456-9600. Telephone-only information and referral service.

Twin Peaks Press, Box 129, Vancouver, WA 98661 ☎360/694-2462 or 1-800/637-2256, @www.twinpeak.virtualave.net. Publisher of the *Directory of Travel Agencies for the Disabled* ($19.95), listing more than 370 agencies worldwide; *Travel for the Disabled* ($19.95); the *Directory of Accessible Van Rentals* ($12.95); and *Wheelchair Vagabond* ($19.95), loaded with personal tips.

Wheels Up! ☎1-888/389-4335, @www.wheelsup.com. Provides discounted air fares, tour and cruise prices for disabled travellers; also publishes a free monthly newsletter and has a comprehensive website.

In Australia and New Zealand

ACROD (Australian Council for Rehabilitation of the Disabled), PO Box 60, Curtin ACT 2605 ☎ 02 6282 4333; 24 Cabarita Rd, Cabarita NSW 2137 ☎02 9743 2699. Provides lists of travel agencies and tour operators for people with disabilities.

Disabled Persons Assembly, 4/173–175 Victoria St, Wellington, New Zealand ☎04/801 9100. Resource centre with lists of travel agencies and tour operators for people with disabilities.

Senior travellers

The senior traveller market is well catered for in Spain, especially in the south, where the long summer and mild winters can mean real out-of-season bargains for older visitors who tend to be more flexible in their travel arrangements. Most public museums, galleries and archeological sites offer discounts to senior visitors (usually the same as a student discount) and it is always worth enquiring when purchasing your ticket. Similarily there are deals to be had for the over-60s on the extensive train network (see p.32).

Contacts for senior travellers

In the UK

Saga Holidays ⊛ www.sagaholidays.com, ☎ 01303/771111. The country's biggest and most established specialist in tours and holidays aimed at older people.

In the US

American Association of Retired Persons, 601 E St, NW Washington, DC 20049 ☎ 1-800/424-3410, membership hotline ☎ 1-800/515-2299 or 202/434-2277, ⊛ www.aarp.org. Can provide discounts on accommodation and vehicle rental. Membership open to US and Canadian

residents aged 50 or over for an annual fee of US $10 or $27 for three years. Canadian residents have only the annual option.
Elderhostel, 75 Federal St, Boston, MA 02110 ☎ 1/877-426-8056, ⊛ www.elderhostel.com. Runs an extensive worldwide network of educational and activity programmes, cruises and homestays for people over 60 (companions may be younger). Programmes generally last a week or more and costs are in line with those of commercial tours.
Saga Holidays, 222 Berkeley St, Boston, MA 02116 ☎ 1-877/265-6862,. Specializes in worldwide group travel for seniors. Saga's Road Scholar coach tours and their Smithsonian Odyssey Tours have a more educational slant.
Vantage Travel ⊛ www.vantagetravel.com, ☎ 1-800/322-6677. Specializes in worldwide group travel for seniors.

Gay and lesbian travellers

Gay and lesbian life in Spain has come a long way in the twenty years or so since Franco's death. There are strong lobbying movements for same-sex marriages and for same-sex couples to have equal rights; these movements are given greater strength by the suppport of some autonomous governments. The age of consent is 16 – the same as for heterosexual couples.

There are thriving gay communities in most of Spain's main cities, notably of course, Madrid and Barcelona. For gay resorts Sitges is unbeatable, and, as in Cádiz, *carnaval* is a wonderfully hedonistic time to visit. Ibiza and Torremolinos are two other popular holiday destinations.

Contacts for gay and lesbian travellers

In the UK

⊛ www.gaytravel.co.uk Online gay and lesbian travel agent, offering good deals on all types of holiday. Also lists gay- and lesbian-friendly hotels around the world.

Dream Waves, Redcot High St, Child Okeford, Blandford, DT22 8ET ☎01258/861149, ✉Dreamwaves@aol.com. Specializes in exclusively gay holidays, including skiing trips and summer sun packages.

Madison Travel, 118 Western Rd, Hove, East Sussex NN3 1DB ☎01273/202532, ⓦwww.madisontravel.co.uk. Established travel agents specializing in packages to gay- and lesbian-friendly mainstream destinations, and also to gay/lesbian destinations.

Respect Holidays, 74 Haverstock Hill, London NW3 2BE ☎020 7485 8855, ⓦwww.respect-holidays.co.uk. Offers exclusively gay packages to all popular Europan resorts.

Also check out adverts in the weekly papers Boyz and Pink Paper, handed out free in gay venues.

In USA and Canada

Damron Company, PO Box 422458, San Francisco CA 94142 ☎1-800/462-6654 or 415/255-0404, ⓦwww.damron.com. Publisher of the *Men's Travel Guide*, a pocket-sized yearbook full of listings of hotels, bars, clubs and resources for gay men; the *Women's Traveler*, which provides similar listings for lesbians; and *Damron Accommodations*, which provides detailed listings of over 1000 accommodations for gays and lesbians worldwide. All of these titles are offered at a discount on the website. No specific city guides – everything is incorporated in the yearbooks.

Ferrari Publications, PO Box 37887, Phoenix, AZ 85069 ☎1-800/962-2912 or 602/863-2408, ⓦwww.ferrariguides.com. Publishes *Ferrari Gay Travel A to Z*, a worldwide gay and lesbian guide; *Inn*

Places, a worldwide accommodation guide; the guides *Men's Travel in Your Pocket* and *Women's Travel in Your Pocket*, and the quarterly *Ferrari Travel Report*.

International Gay/Lesbian Travel Association, 4331 N Federal Hwy, Suite 304, Ft Lauderdale, FL 33308 ☎1-800/448-8550, ⓦwww.iglta.org. Trade group that can provide a list of gay- and lesbian-owned or friendly travel agents, accommodation and other travel businesses.

In Australia and New Zealand

Gay and Lesbian Travel ⓦwww.galta.com.au. Directory and links for gay and lesbian travel in Australia and worldwide.

Gay Travel ⓦwww.gaytravel.com. The site for trip planning, bookings, and general information about international travel.

Parkside Travel, 70 Glen Osmond Rd, Parkside, SA 5063 ☎08/8274 1222 or 1800/888 501, ✉hwtravel@senet.com.au. Gay travel agent associated with local branch of Hervey World Travel; all aspects of gay and lesbian travel worldwide.

Pinkstay ⓦwww.pinkstay.com. Everything from visa information to finding accommodation and work around the world.

Silke's Travel, 263 Oxford St, Darlinghurst, NSW 2010 ☎02/9380 6244 or 1800/807 860, ✉silba@magna.com.au. Long-established gay and lesbian specialist, with the emphasis on women's travel.

Tearaway Travel, 52 Porter St, Prahan, VIC 3181 ☎03/9510 6344, ✉tearaway@bigpond.com. Gay-specific business dealing with international and domestic travel.

Travelling with children

Spain is a good country to travel with children of any age; they will be well received everywhere and babies and toddlers, in particular, will be made a real fuss of. If you're travelling independently there are numerous theme parks and leisure activities specifically aimed at kids mentioned throughout the guide; in particular see Port Aventura in Catalunya (see p.858) and Mini Hollywood in Almería (see p.384). Many tourist attractions and sights have discounts or free entry for children and some cities and resorts produce pamphlets of attractions aimed at kids; Barcelona is especially well organized.

RENFE allows children under four to travel free on trains, with forty-percent discount for those between four and twelve years.

Accommodation shouldn't be a problem as *hostales* and *pensiones* generally welcome accompanied children and offer rooms with three or four beds. If you're travelling in the north, or out of season, however, bear in mind that many *hostales* (as opposed to more expensive hotels) don't have heating systems – and it can get very cold. The wide availability of self-catering options can be appealing for a family holiday and Spain has a good choice of accommodation from seaside apartments to country *casas rurales* (see p.43). There are also a myriad of package-tour companies that cater specifically for holidays with children (see below) and arrange activities for kids of all ages throughout the holiday.

As in other Mediterranean countries children stay up late in Spain, especially in the summer. It's very common for them to be running around pavement cafés or restaurants and your kids will no doubt enjoy joining in.

As far as **babies** go, food seems to work out quite well (*hostales* sometimes prepare food specially, or will let you use the kitchen to do so). Disposable nappies (*panuelos*, or more colloquially, *Dodots*) and other standard needs are very widely available. Many *hostales* will be prepared to baby-sit, or at least to listen out for trouble. This is obviously more likely if you're staying in an old-fashioned family-run place than in the fancier hotels.

Contacts for travellers with children

In the UK and Ireland

Club Med ⓦ www.clubmed.com, ☏ 0700/2582633. Specializes in purpose-built holiday resorts, with kids' club, entertainment and sports facilities on site.
Mark Warner Holidays ⓦ www.markwarner.co.uk, ☏ 020/7761 7000. Holiday villages with children's entertainment and childcare laid on.
Simply Travel ⓦ www.simply-travel.com, ☏ 020/8541 2280. Upmarket tour company offering villas and hotels in the less touristy parts of Portugal, Greece, Turkey, Italy and Spain. In some destinations, can provide qualified, English-speaking nannies to come to your villa and look after the children.

In the USA

Travel With Your Children, 40 Fifth Ave, New York, NY 10011 ☏ 212/477 5524 or 1-888/822-4388. Publish a regular newsletter, Family Travel Times (ⓦ www.familytraveltimes.com), as well as a series of books on travel with children including *Great Adventure Vacations With Your Kids*.

Directory

ADDRESSES are written as: c/Picasso 2, 4° izda. – which means Picasso street (*calle*) no. 2, fourth floor, left- (*izquierda*) hand flat or office; dcha. (*derecha*) is right; cto. (*centro*) centre. Other confusions in Spanish addresses result from the different spellings, and sometimes words, used in Catalan, Basque and Galician – all of which are to some extent replacing their Castilian counterparts – and from the gradual removal of Franco and other fascist heroes from the main *avenidas* and plazas. Note that a lot of maps – including the official ones – haven't yet caught up. In some towns dual numbering systems are also in effect, and looking at the plates it's difficult to tell which is the old and which the new scheme.

AIRPORT TAX You can happily spend your last euro – there's no departure tax.

ELECTRICITY Current in most of Spain is 220 or 225 volts AC (just occasionally it's still 110 or 125V); most European appliances should work as long as you have an adaptor for European-style two-pin plugs. North Americans will need this plus a transformer.

FEMINISM The Spanish women's movement, despite having to deal with incredibly basic issues (such as trying to get contraception available on social security), is radical, vibrant and growing fast. Few groups, however, have permanent offices, and if you want to make contact it's best to do so through the network of feminist bookshops in the major cities. Some of the more established are: Madrid – Librería de Mujeres, c/San Cristóbal 17, near Plaza Mayor (☎915 217 043); Valencia – Ideas, c/Gravador Esteve 33 (☎963 348 318); Sevilla – Librería Fulmen, c/Zaragoza 36. In Barcelona, the most useful contact address is Ca la Dona, c/Caspe 38 (☎934 127 161), a women's centre used for meetings of over twenty feminist and lesbian organizations.

FILM Movie-going remains a remarkably cheap and popular entertainment, with crowded cinemas in every town. The majori-

ty of what's screened is the usual Hollywood fare poorly dubbed into Spanish, but in the cities you will find some films in their original language with subtitles. Look for *voz* or *versión original* (*subtitulada*), abbreviated "v.o.", in the listings; "v.e." means *versión español*. An account of Spanish cinema is to be found in the Contexts section of this book.

FISHING Fortnightly permits are easily and cheaply obtained from any ICONA office – there's one in every big town (addresses from the local Turismo).

LANGUAGE COURSES are offered at most Spanish universities, and in a growing number of special language schools for foreigners. For details overseas and a complete list write to a branch of the Instituto Cervantes: the London one is at 102 Eaton Square, London SW1W (☎020/7235 0353) or check other centres on their website ⓦwww.cervantes.es. Many American universities also have their own courses based in Spain.

LAUNDRIES You'll find a few self-service laundries (*lavanderías automáticas*) in the major cities, but they're rare – you normally have to leave your clothes for the full (and somewhat expensive) works at a *lavandería*. Note that you're not allowed by law to leave laundry hanging out of windows over a street. A dry cleaner is a *tintorería*.

LEFT LUGGAGE You'll find self-service *consignas* at most important Spanish train stations. Lockers are large enough to hold most backpacks, plus a smaller bag, which cost about €1.80–3.60 a day; put the coins in to free the key or key-card. These are not a viable alternative for long-term storage, however, as they're periodically emptied out by station staff. Bus terminals have staffed *consignas* where you present a claim stub to get your gear back; cost is about the same.

SKIING There are resorts in the Pyrenees, Sierra Nevada, and outside Madrid and Santander, all detailed in the relevant chap-

△ Beware of the bulls

ters. The SNTO's *Skiing in Spain* pamphlet is also useful. If you want to arrange a weekend or more while you're in Spain, Viajes Ecuador (the biggest travel firm in the country, with branches in most cities) is good for arranging cheap all-inclusive trips.

SWIMMING POOLS Even quite small Spanish towns and villages have a public swimming pool, or *piscina municipal* – a lifesaver in the summer and yet another reason not to keep exclusively to the coast.

TIME Spain is one hour ahead of the UK, six hours ahead of Eastern Standard Time, nine hours ahead of Pacific Standard Time, except for brief periods during the changeovers to and from daylight saving. In Spain the clocks go forward in the last week in March and back again in the last week in October.

TOILETS Public ones are generally reasonably clean but very rarely have any paper (best to carry your own). They can very occasionally be squat-style. They are most commonly referred to and labelled *Los Servicios*, though signs may point you to *baños*, *aseos*, *retretes* or *sanitarios*. *Damas* (Ladies) and *Caballeros* (Gentlemen) are the usual distinguishing signs for sex, though you may also see the confusing *Señoras* (Women) and *Señores* (Men).

guide

guide

Madrid

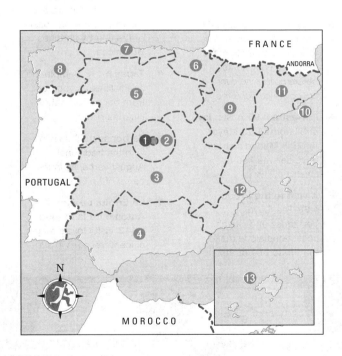

CHAPTER 1 # Highlights

✳ **Monasterio de las Descalzas Reales** p.91
A fascinating hoard of art treasures hidden away in the centre of Madrid.

✳ **El Palacio Real** p.92
Over-the-top royal opulence in this former royal residence.

✳ **A night on the tiles** p.126
Start late at a bar, then on to a club and try to make it into the early hours before collapsing over *chocolate con churros*.

✳ **El Rastro** p.95 A Sunday stroll from Plaza Mayor through Madrid's shambolic flea market, El Rastro.

✳ **A visit to the Prado** p.99 The Goya, Velázquez and Bosch collections alone make the trip to one of the world's greatest art museums worthwhile.

✳ **Guernica** p.106 See this icon of twentieth century art at the Reina Sofía museum.

✳ **Urban oases** p.107 & 109 Escape from the bustle of the city to the Retiro or the shady oasis of the nearby Jardines Botánicos.

✳ **Tapas** p.118 Sample the specialities as you hop from bar to bar in the Huertas district.

✳ **Verbenas** p.78 Join in with the traditional August *verbenas* in the *barrio* of La Latina.

✳ **La Ermita de San Antonio de la Florida** p.112 Visit Goya's magnificent frescoes *in situ*.

Madrid

M adrid became Spain's capital simply through its geographical position at the centre of Iberia. When Felipe II moved the seat of government here in 1561 his aim was to create a symbol of the unification and centralization of the country, and a capital from which he could receive the fastest post and communications from each corner of the nation. The site itself had few natural advantages – it is 300km from the sea on a 650-metre-high plateau, freezing in winter, burning in summer – and it was only the determination of successive rulers to promote a strong central capital that ensured Madrid's survival and development.

Nonetheless, it was a success, and today Madrid is a vast, predominantly modern city, with a population of some three million and growing. The journey in – through a stream of concrete-block suburbs – isn't pretty, but the streets at the heart of the city are a pleasant surprise, with pockets of medieval buildings and narrow, atmospheric alleys, dotted with the oddest of shops and bars, and interspersed with eighteenth-century Bourbon squares. By comparison with the historic cities of Spain – Toledo, Salamanca, Sevilla, Granada – there may be few sights of great architectural interest, but the monarchs did acquire outstanding picture collections, which formed the basis of the **Prado** museum. This has long ensured Madrid a place on the European art tour, and the more so since the 1990s arrival – literally down the street – of the **Reina Sofía** and **Thyssen–Bornemisza** galleries, state-of-the-art homes to fabulous arrays of modern Spanish painting (including Picasso's *Guernica*) and European and American masters.

Accommodation price codes

All the establishments listed in this book have been price-graded according to the following scale. The prices quoted are for the **cheapest available double room in high season**; effectively this means that anything in the ❶ and most places in the ❷ range will be without private bath, though there's usually a washbasin in the room. In the ❹ category and above you will probably be getting private facilities. Remember, though, that many of the budget places will also have more expensive rooms including en-suite facilities. Youth hostels are graded under ❶ as the price per person is less than half of the category's upper limit.

Note that in the more upmarket *hostales* and *pensiones*, and in anything calling itself a hotel, you'll pay a **tax** (IVA) of seven percent on top of the room price.

❶ Under €12	❹ €27–36	❼ €60–90
❷ €12–18	❺ €36–48	❽ €90–120
❸ €18–27	❻ €48–60	❾ Over €120

As you get to grips with the place you soon realize that it's the inhabitants – the **madrileños** – that are the capital's key attraction: hanging out in the traditional cafés or the summer terrazas, packing the lanes of the Sunday Rastro flea market, or playing hard and very, very late in a thousand **bars**, clubs, discos and *tascas*. Whatever Barcelona or San Sebastián might claim, the Madrid scene, immortalized in the movies of Pedro Almodóvar, remains the most vibrant and fun in the country. The city is also in better shape than for many years past, after a £500-million refurbishment for its role as 1992 European Capital of Culture and the ongoing impact of a series of urban rehabilitation schemes – funded jointly by the European Union and local government – in the older *barrios* (districts) of the city. Improvements are also being made to the transport network, with extensions to the metro, the construction of new ring roads and the excavation of a series of road tunnels designed to bring relief to the city's overcrowded streets. The authorities are even preparing a bid for the 2012 Olympics.

The city's development

Modern Madrid is enclosed by dreary suburbs: acres of high-rise concrete seemingly dumped without thought onto the dustiest parts of the plain. The great spread to suburbia was encouraged under Franco, who also extended the city northwards along the spinal route of the Paseo de la Castellana, to accommodate his ministers and minions during development extravaganzas of the 1950s and 1960s. Large, impressive, and unbelievably sterile, these constructions leave little to the imagination; but then, you're unlikely to spend much time in these parts of town.

In the centre, things are very different. The oldest streets at the very heart of Madrid are crowded with ancient buildings, spreading out in concentric circles which reveal the development of the city over the centuries. Only the cramped street plan gives much clue as to what was here before Madrid became the **Habsburg** capital (in 1561), but the narrow alleys around the Plaza Mayor are still among the city's liveliest and most atmospheric. Later growth owed much to the French tastes of the **Bourbon** dynasty in the eighteenth century, when for the first time Madrid began to develop a style and flavour of its own.

The early **nineteenth century** brought invasion and turmoil to Spain as Napoleon established his brother Joseph on the throne. Madrid, however, continued to flourish, gaining some very attractive buildings and squares. With the onset of the twentieth century, the capital became the hotbed of the political and intellectual discussions which divided the country; *tertulias* (political/philosophical discussion circles) sprang up in cafés across the city (some of them are still going) as the country entered the turbulent years of the end of the monarchy and the foundation of the Second Republic.

The **Civil War**, of course, caused untold damage, and led to forty years of isolation, which you can still sense in Madrid's idiosyncratic style. The Spanish capital has changed immeasurably, however, in the two and a half decades since Franco's death, guided by a poet-mayor, the late and much lamented Tierno Galván. His efforts – the creation of parks and renovation of public spaces and public life – have left an enduring legacy, and were a vital ingredient of the *movida madrileña*, the "happening Madrid", with which the city broke through in the 1980s. The present local authorities have adopted a more restrictive attitude towards bar and club licensing and unfortunately there has been a tendency towards homogenization with the rest of Europe as franchised fast-food joints and coffee bars spring up all over the place. Nevertheless, in making the transition from provincial backwater to major European capital, Madrid has still managed to preserve its own stylish and quirky identity.

Orientation, arrival and information

The city's layout is pretty straightforward. At the heart of Madrid – indeed at the very heart of Spain since all distances in the country are measured from here – is the **Puerta del Sol** (often referred to as just "Sol"). Around it lie the oldest parts of Madrid, neatly bordered to the west by the **Río Manzanares**, to the east by the park of **El Retiro**, and to the north by the city's great thoroughfare, the **Gran Vía**.

Within this very compact area, you're likely to spend most of your time. The city's three big museums – the **Prado, Thyssen–Bornemisza** and **Reina Sofía** – lie in a "golden triangle" just west of El Retiro and centred around Paseo del Prado, while over towards the river are the oldest, Habsburg parts of town, centred around the beautiful arcaded **Plaza Mayor**. After Gran Vía, the most important streets (*calles* – abbreviated as c/) are **c/Alcalá** and its continuation, **c/Mayor**, which cut right through the centre from the main post office at **Plaza de Cibeles** to the Bourbon **Palacio Real**.

Arrival

If Madrid is your first stop in Spain, by **air**, **train** or **bus**, you are likely to arrive a little way from the centre. Transport into the centre, however, is relatively cheap, easy and efficient.

By air

The **Aeropuerto de Barajas** (☎913 058 343) is 16km east of the city, at the end of Avenida de América (the NII road). It is in the process of being extended and modernized and now has three interconnecting terminals: T1 for nearly all international flights (*vuelos internacionales*); T2 for domestic flights (*nacionales*) plus some of Iberia's flights from continental Europe; T3 for the Puente Aéreo (the air shuttle with Barcelona).

From the airport, the new **metro** link takes you from T2 via Line 8 into the centre in about thirty minutes (daily 6am–1.30am, 2.30am on Fri & Sat; €0.90), with a change at Mar de Cristal (Line 4). A more direct route straight to Nuevos Minsterios, where check-in facilities are planned, is due to open in March 2003 and cut the journey time to about fifteen minutes. The route by road to central Madrid is more variable, depending on rush-hour traffic, and can take anything from twenty minutes to an hour. Outside the terminal, there is a **shuttle bus** every ten to fifteen minutes (5.17am–1.51am; €2.40) to an underground terminal in the central Plaza Colón, with pedestrian entrance from the c/Goya or Metro Serrano. If your plane arrives outside these times, there should be additional special connecting bus services. **Taxis** are always available outside, too, and cost around €12 to the centre, unless you get stuck in traffic.

Half a dozen or so **car rental** companies have stands at the airport and can generally supply clients with maps and directions (see p.143 for addresses and phone numbers of car rental offices in the city). Other airport facilities include 24-hour currency exchange, a post office, left luggage lockers in T1 and T2, a RENFE office for booking train tickets (daily 8am–9pm), a chemist, a tourist office and hotel reservations desk.

By train

Trains from France and north/northeast Spain arrive at the **Estación de Chamartín**, a modern terminal isolated in the north of the city; it has all the

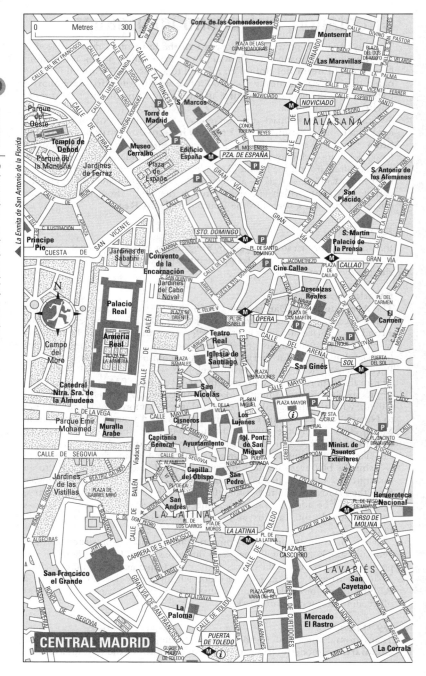

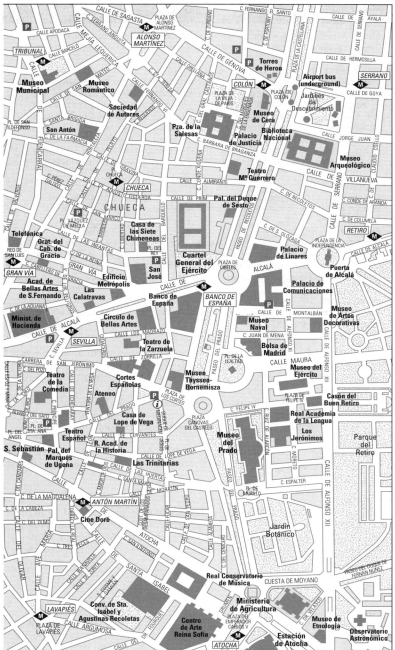

Estación Sur de Autobuses

Madrid's fiestas

Look out for **fiestas** whenever you're in Madrid: there are dozens, some of which involve the whole city, others just an individual *barrio*. The more important dates are listed below.

Also well worth checking out are cultural festivals organized by the city council, in particular the **Veranos de la Villa** (July–Sept) and **Festival de Otoño** (Sept–Nov) concerts (classical, rock, flamenco), theatre and cinema. Many events are free and, in the summer, often open air, taking place in the city's parks and squares. One of the nicest venues is the courtyard of the Antiguo Cuartel del Conde Duque (Ⓜ Ventura Rodríguez), where weekly flamenco recitals are held. Annual festivals for alternative theatre (Feb), flamenco (Feb), dance (mid-May to mid-June), photography (mid-June to mid-July) and jazz (Nov) are also firmly established on the cultural agenda. Full programmes are published in the monthly *En Madrid* tourist hand-out.

January
5 *Cabalgata de los Reyes* (Cavalcade of the Three Kings); an evening procession through the city centre in which children are showered with sweets.

February
Week before Lent *Carnaval* – is the excuse for a lot of partying and fancy-dress parades, especially in the gay zone around Chueca. The end of *Carnaval* is marked by the bizarre and entertaining parade, *El Entierro de la Sardina* (The Burial of the Sardine), on the Paseo de la Florida.

March/April
Easter Week *Semana Santa* is celebrated in Madrid, but with less spirit and processional activity than in Toledo.

---

usual big station facilities, including currency exchange. A metro line connects Chamartín with the centre, and there are also regular connections by the commuter *trenes de cercanías* with the much more central Estación de Atocha; just take any *cercanía* headed in that direction.

The **Estación de Atocha**, expanded and imaginatively remodelled back in the early 1990s, has two separate terminals: one for **Toledo** and other local services, the other for all points in **south and eastern Spain**, including the high speed AVE trains.

If you're coming from local towns around Madrid, you may arrive at **Príncipe Pío** (aka Estación del Norte), fairly close to the centre below the Palacio Real.

By bus
Bus terminals are scattered throughout the city, but the largest – used by all of the international bus services – is the Estación Sur de Autobuses on c/Méndez Alvaro on the corner of c/Retama, 1.5km south of the Atocha train station (Ⓜ Méndez Alvaro). For details of others, see the "Travel details" section at the end of this chapter (p.145).

By car
All the main roads into Madrid bring you right into the city centre, although eccentric signposting and even more eccentric driving can be very unnerving. The inner ring road, the M30, and the Paseo de la Castellana are all notorious bottlenecks, although virtually the whole city centre can be close to gridlock during the peak **rush-hour periods** (Mon–Fri 7.30–9.30am & 6–8.30pm).

May

2 *Fiesta del Dos de Mayo* in Malasaña and elsewhere in Madrid. Bands and party-ing around the Plaza Dos de Mayo – a bit low-key in recent years, having been the funkiest festival in the city during the 1980s.

15 *Fiestas de San Isidro* – Madrid's patron saint – spread for a week either side of this date, and are among the country's biggest festivals. A nonstop round of carni-val events: bands, parades and loads of free entertainment, usually centred around Plaza Mayor. There's a band each night in the Jardines de las Vistillas (south of the Palacio Real), and the evenings there start out with *chotis* (a dance typical of Madrid) music and dancing. The fiestas also herald the start of the bullfighting season.

June

13 *Fiesta de la Ermita de San Antonio de la Florida*; events around the church and in the adjacent Parque de la Bombilla.

17–24 *Fiestas de San Juan*; bonfires and fireworks in El Retiro.

July

9–16 *La Virgen del Carmen*; local fiesta in Chamberí *barrio*, north of the city centre.

August

6–15 *Castizo fiestas.* Traditional *fiestas* of *San Cayetano*, *San Lorenzo* and *La Virgen de la Paloma* in La Latina and Lavapiés *barrios*. Much of the activity takes place around the Plaza de la Paja and the Jardines de las Vistillas.

December

31 New Year's Eve (*nochevieja*) is celebrated at bars, restaurants and parties all over the city, and there are bands in some of the squares. Puerta del Sol is the custom-ary place to gather, waiting for the strokes of the clock – it is traditional to swallow a grape on each strike.

Be prepared for a long trawl around the streets to find **parking**, and even then you will need to buy the coupons available at *estancos* if you want to avoid the threat of a fine. A better, and safer, option is to put your car in one of the many signposted *parkings*. Your own transport is really only of use for out-of-town excursions, so it's advisable to find a hotel with or near a car park and keep your car there during your stay in the city. If you are staying more than a cou-ple of weeks, you can get long-term parking rates at neighbourhood garages.

Information and maps

There are year-round **turismo** offices at the following locations: Aeropuerto de Barajas (Mon–Fri 8am–8pm, Sat 9am–3pm; ☎913 058 656); Estación de Atocha (Mon–Fri 9am–9pm, Sat & Sun 9am–1pm; ☎902 100 007); Estación de Chamartín (Mon–Fri 8am–8pm, Sat 9am–1pm; ☎913 159 976); Plaza Mayor 3 (Mon–Fri 10am–8pm, Sat 10am–2pm; ☎915 881 636); Mercado Puerta de Toledo, Ronda de Toledo 1 (Mon–Fri 9am–7pm, Sat 9.30am–2.30pm; ☎913 641 876); c/Duque de Medinaceli 2 (Mon–Fri 9am–7pm, Sat 9am–3pm; ☎914 294 951; ⓜ Banco de España). The Madrid tourist board has a web page at ⓦwww.munimadrid.es and the regional authority has one at ⓦwww.comadrid.es. In the **summer**, turismo posts operate at popular tourist spots such as the Puerta del Sol and the Prado, and there are staff (in blue and yellow uniforms) on call outside the Palacio Real, *ayuntamiento* (town hall) and the Prado, and in the Plaza Mayor and Puerta del Sol. You can **phone for information** in English on ☎010 within the city and ☎915 404 040 from outside. There is also a tourist information line on ☎901 300 600.

Free **maps** of Madrid are available from any of the turismos detailed above. However, if you intend to do more than just a day's sightseeing, you would be well advised to invest in the Almax *Madrid Centro* map (€2), available from just about any kiosk in the city; this is very clear, 1:10,000 in scale, fully street-indexed, and has a colour plan of the metro on the reverse. The area covered on this represents just about everything of interest; if you want more, Almax also produces a rather less clear, 1:12,000-scale *Madrid Ciudad* (€4.70) that goes right out into the suburbs. Again, it's widely available.

Safety and crime

As far as safety goes, there's little cause for concern. Central Madrid is so populated – and so busy at just about every hour of the day and night – that it never seems to carry any "big city" threat. Which is not to say that **crime** is not a problem, nor that there aren't sleazy pockets to be avoided. Madrid has a big drug problem, all too evident around the Plaza de España and some of the streets just north of Gran Vía. Drugs, it is reckoned, account for ninety percent of crimes in Madrid, and if you are unlucky enough to be threatened for money, it's unwise to resist.

In recent years parts of the *barrio* of Lavapíes have also been a focus of night-time criminal activity so it is best to stick to the busier streets here. Be aware that the main routes through the Casa de Campo and the Parque del Oeste have been appropriated by prostitutes and their clients and are best steered clear of at night.

Tourists in Madrid, as everywhere, are prime targets for pickpockets, and petty thieves. The main shopping areas, parks, the metro and anywhere with crowds, are their favourite haunts; burger bars and the Rastro market seem especially popular. Be aware that they often work in groups, and associates will try to distract your attention while your pocket is being picked. Tourists are also obvious targets for muggers and in all areas it is advisable to keep jewellery, watches and cameras hidden, and to stay away from dark, empty streets at night.

Unless they have rented expensive garage space, drivers may well find their cars broken into and the radio stolen. The **police** are generally fairly sympathetic and will give you a report form for insurance claims. In an emergency, dial ☎112; English is usually spoken on this number.

City transport and tours

Madrid is a pretty easy city to get around. The central areas are walkable, the metro is modern and efficient, buses serve out-of-the-way districts, and taxis are always available.

If you're using public transport extensively and staying long-term, **passes** (*abonos*) covering the metro, train and bus, and available for each calendar month, are worthwhile. If you have an InterRail or Eurail pass, you can use the RENFE urban and suburban trains (*cercanías*) free of charge – they're an alternative to the metro for some longer city journeys.

The metro

The clean and highly efficient **metro** is by far the quickest way of getting around Madrid, serving most places you're likely to want to get to. It runs from

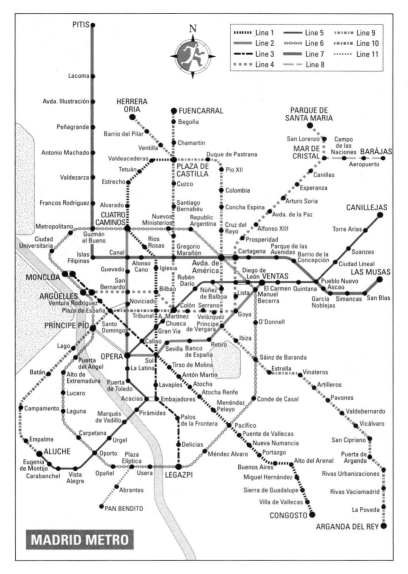

MADRID METRO

6am until 1.30am (Fri & Sat until 2.30am); the flat fare is €0.90 for nearly all journeys, or €4.60 for a ten-trip ticket (*bono de diez viajes*), which can be used on buses too. Lines are colour-coded, and the direction of travel is indicated by the name of the terminus station. Note that some stations or sections may be subject to periodic closures as a result of the modernization and extension programme which is due to be finished in 2003. You can get a free colour map of the system (*plano del metro*) at any station.

Buses

The urban **bus network** is comprehensive but fairly complicated: in the text, where there's no metro stop, we've indicated which bus to take. There are information booths in the Plaza de Cibeles and Puerta del Sol, which dispense a huge route map (*plano de los transportes de Madrid*), and – along with other outlets – sell bus passes. Fares are the same as for the metro, at €0.90 a journey, or €4.60 for a ten-trip ticket (*bono de diez viajes*) which can be used on both forms of transport. When you get on a bus, you punch your ticket in a machine by the driver.

Buses run from 6am to midnight. In addition, there are around twenty **all-night** (*búho*) lines around the central area: departures are half-hourly 12.30am–2am, hourly 2–6am, from Plaza de Cibeles and Puerta del Sol.

Taxis

One of the best things about Madrid is that there are thousands of **taxis** – white cars with a diagonal red stripe on the side – which are reasonably cheap; €4.80 will get you most places within the centre and, although it's common to round up the fare, you're not expected to tip. They charge supplements on the metered fair for baggage, for going to the train and bus stations or outside the city limits (which includes going to the airport) and for night trips (11pm–7am). In any area in the centre, day and night, you should be able to wave down a taxi (available ones have a green light on top of the cab) in a couple of minutes. To phone for a taxi, call ☎915 478 200, 915 478 500, 914 051 213 or 914 459 008.

Local trains

The **local train** network, or *Cercanías*, is the most efficient way of connecting between the main railway stations and provides the best route out to many of the suburbs and to nearby towns such as Alcalá de Henares. Most trains are air-conditioned, fares are cheap and there are good connections with the metro. Trains generally run every fifteen to thirty minutes from 6am to midnight/1am. For more information go to the RENFE web page at ⓦwww.renfe.es and click on the *Cercanías* section for Madrid.

City tours

The turismo in Plaza Mayor (see above) can supply details of guided English-language **walking tours** around the city. A tour of *Madrid de los Austrias* departs at 10am on Saturdays from the Plaza Mayor tourist office and costs €3 (for more information ⓦwww.descubremadrid.munimadrid.es; reservations ☎902 488 488 or 915 882 906). For a **bus tour** of all the major city sites try Madrid Vision, c/San Bernardo 23 (☎917 671 743, ⓦwww.trapsa.com/madridvision; Ⓜ Noviciado); a 75-minute tour costs between €10.25 and €10.80, allowing you to jump off at various sites throughout the city. Pick-up points include Puerta del Sol and the Prado.

Accommodation

Madrid has lots of accommodation, and – business hotels apart – most of it is pretty central. It is, on the whole, pretty functional, too. Few places, at any price range, have great character, and you're basically paying for location and facilities. At the lower end of the range, there are bargains to be had, with double rooms as low as €20 a night – and less if you are looking for an extended stay.

Move up a few notches and you can find plenty of places at around €38–50 a night, offering a comfortable room with a private bath or (more often) shower. Few places, however, justify paying prices much higher than that and, assuming money is limited and Madrid is not your only destination in Spain, you'd be better off splashing out for luxury elsewhere.

If you prefer to have others find you a room, there are accommodation services at the airport, the Estación Sur de Autobuses, and Chamartín train station. Brújula is particularly helpful, with offices at Atocha station (open daily 8am–10pm; ☎915 391 173) and Charmartín (daily 7.30am–11pm; ☎913 257 894). The service covers the whole of Spain and there is a €2.40 booking fee.

Pensiones, hostales and hotels

The main factor to consider in choosing a hotel is location. If you want to be at the heart of the old town, you'll probably choose the areas around **Plaza de Santa Ana** or **Plaza Mayor**; if you're into nightlife, **Malasaña** or **Chueca** may appeal; if you want a bit of class, there are the **Paseo del Prado**, **Recoletos** or **Salamanca** areas. You'll notice that buildings in the more popular hotel/*hostal* areas often house two or three separate establishments, each on separate **floors**; these are generally independent of each other. Floors (*pisos*) are written as 1° (first floor in British parlance, second in American), 2° and so on, and often specify *izquierda* (*izq* or *izda*) or *derecha* (*dcha*), meaning to the left or to the right of the staircase. A problem with some of the *hostales* in larger buildings – on Gran Vía, for example – is that they are often inaccessible at night, unless you've been given a front-door key, as there's not always an entryphone or doorbell at street level. If you book a room and intend to arrive after, say, 9pm, check that you will be able to get in.

Around Estación de Atocha

Much of the cheapest accommodation in Madrid is to be found in the area immediately around the Estación de Atocha. However, the *pensiones* closest to the station are often grim, catering for migrants looking for work, and the area can be a little threatening after dark. The five places below, however, are good, safe choices.

Hostal Barrera, c/Atocha 96, 2ª ☎915 275 381, ☎915 273 950, ✉snowy@accesocero.es; Ⓜ Antón Martín. Friendly, good-value sixteen-room *hostal* with an English-speaking owner. Rooms have bath or shower, but most have no toilet. Internet access available. ❺

Hotel Mediodía, Plaza del Emperador Carlos V 8 ☎915 273 060, ☎915 307 008; Ⓜ Atocha. Huge 165-roomed hotel right next to the Reina Sofía and the Estación de Atocha. The simple but comfortable rooms, all with bathroom and TV, are excellent value. ❺–❻

Hotel Mercator, c/Atocha 123 ☎914 290 500, ☎913 691 252, ✉hotel.mercator@infonegocio.com; Ⓜ Atocha. Slightly fading hotel popular with tour groups. Good value and near the station; also handy if you are coming by car as it has its own car park. ❼

Pensión Mollo, c/Atocha 104, 4° ☎915 287 176; Ⓜ Atocha/Antón Martín. Closest reasonable *hostal* to the station, although it is up a steep hill and has no lift, so inconvenient if you're heavily laden. Doubles have en-suite showers. ❸

Hotel NH Sur, Paseo de la Infanta Isabel 9, ☎915 399 499, Ⓦ www.nh-hoteles.es; Ⓜ Atocha. Part of the NH chain, this smart 68-room hotel is right alongside the station and close to the Retiro. Special promotion rates can bring the price down to as low as €51 a night. ❾

Around Plaza de Santa Ana

Plaza de Santa Ana is at the heart of Madrid nightlife, with cafés open until very late at night. The recommendations following are all within a block or two of the square. The metro stations Antón Martín, Sevilla and Sol are all close by.

MADRID ACCOMMODATION

Hostal Alonso, c/Espoz y Mina 17, 3º ☏ 915 315 679; Ⓜ Sol. Basic but very good-value and friendly *hostal* popular for its location. Book ahead if you can. ③

Hostal Carreras, c/Príncipe 18, 3º ☏ & Ⓕ 915 220 036; Ⓜ Sevilla. Large light rooms in this very pleasant *hostal*. Cheaper rooms have handbasins only, others have showers or baths. ④

Gran Hotel Reina Victoria, Plaza de Santa Ana 14 ☏ 915 314 500, Ⓕ 915 220 307, Ⓦ www.solmelia.com; Ⓜ Sol. Lovely old hotel in a historic building, where the bullfighters stay when they're in town. Rooms are a hefty €180 a night, but this is the pick of Madrid's class hotels in this price range. ⑨

Hotel Persal, Plaza del Ángel 12 ☏ 913 694 643, Ⓕ 913 691 952, Ⓔ hostalpersal@mad.servicom.es; Ⓜ Sol. Friendly and excellent-value 100-room hotel. All rooms have air conditioning, bathroom

and TV. Breakfast is included. ⑥

Hostal Plaza D'Ort, Plaza del Ángel 13 ☏ 914 299 041, Ⓕ 914 201 297, Ⓦ www.plazadort.com; Ⓜ Sol. Next door to the *Hotel Persal*, all rooms in this very clean *hostal* have a shower or bath, TV and telephone. There are also several self-catering apartments, making it a good family or group option. ⑤

Hostal Regional, c/Príncipe 18, 4º ☏ 915 223 373; Ⓜ Sol. Small, basic rooms in an elegant old building off Plaza de Santa Ana. ③

Hotel Santander, c/Echegaray 1 ☏ 914 296 644, Ⓕ 913 691 078; Ⓜ Sevilla. Spacious, spotless rooms – many have a small seating area – in this pleasant, friendly 35-room two-star hotel. ⑥

Hostal Valencia, c/Espoz y Mina 7, 4º ☏ 915 211 845, Ⓕ 915 235 381; Ⓜ Sol. The very friendly multilingual owner of this six-room *hostal* will do everything he can to make your stay as comfortable as

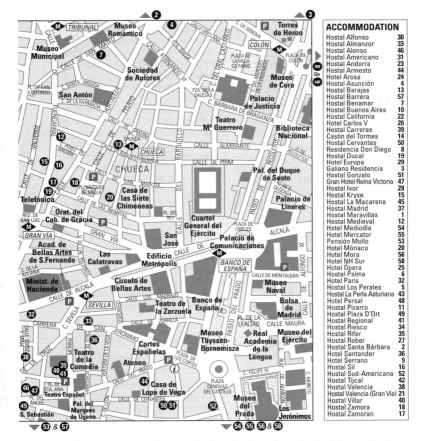

MADRID | Accommodation

ACCOMMODATION

Hostal Alfonso	30
Hostal Almanzor	33
Hostal Alonso	46
Hostal Americano	31
Hostal Andorra	23
Hostal Armesto	44
Hotel Arosa	24
Hostal Asunción	4
Hostal Barajas	13
Hostal Barrera	57
Hostal Benamar	7
Hostal Buenos Aires	10
Hotel California	22
Hotel Carlos V	26
Hostal Carreras	39
Casón del Tormes	14
Hostal Cervantes	50
Residencia Don Diego	8
Hostal Ducal	19
Hotel Europa	29
Galiano Residencia	3
Hostal Gonzalo	51
Gran Hotel Reina Victoria	47
Hostal Ivor	28
Hostal Kryse	15
Hostal La Macarena	45
Hostal Madrid	37
Hostal Maravillas	1
Hostal Medieval	12
Hotel Mediodia	54
Hotel Mercator	55
Pensión Mollo	53
Hotel Mónaco	20
Hotel Mora	56
Hotel NH Sur	58
Hotel Ópera	25
Hostal Palma	6
Hotel Paris	32
Hostal Los Perales	5
Hostal La Perla Asturiana	43
Hotel Persal	48
Hostal Pizarro	11
Hostal Plaza D'Ort	49
Hostal Regional	41
Hostal Riesco	34
Hostal Rifer	35
Hostal Rober	27
Hostal Santa Bárbara	2
Hotel Santander	36
Hotel Serrano	9
Hostal Sil	16
Hostal Sud-Americana	52
Hostal Tijcal	42
Hostal Valencia	38
Hostal Valencia (Gran Vía)	21
Hostal Villar	40
Hostal Zamora	18
Hostal Zamoran	17

possible. Large rooms, all with bathroom and TV. ❹
Hostal Villar, c/Príncipe 18, 1º ☎ 915 316 600 or 915 316 609, ☏ 915 215 073, ⓦ www.arrakis.es/~h~villar; ⓜ Sevilla. Large *hostal* in the same building as the *Regional* and *Carreras*. The standard rooms have small bathrooms, and all have TV and telephone. Air conditioning is available for a supplement of €6 per night. ❹

Sol, Ópera and Plaza Mayor

This really is the heart of Madrid and prices, not surprisingly, are a bit higher, though you can still find bargains in the slightly battered streets towards the Plaza Mayor.

Hostal Alfonso, Pza Celenque 1, 2º ☎ 915 319 840, ☏ 915 329 225; ⓜ Sol/Ópera. Nicely located just off c/Arenal this clean, friendly *hostal* has fourteen doubles, two triples and a handful of singles at a very competitive price, all with bathrooms and TV. ❹
Hostal Americano, Puerta del Sol 11, 3º and 4º ☎ 915 222 822, ☏ 915 221 192; ⓜ Sol. Nicely furnished hostal, with recently improved bathrooms and a pleasant communal living room, but you're paying extra for the location. ❺
Hotel Carlos V, c/Maestro Vitoria 5 ☎ 915 314 100, ☏ 915 313 761, ⓦ www.hotelcarlosv.com; ⓜ Sol. Large, plush rooms at this century-old hotel, in a pedestrianized part of town, just off c/Preciados behind the Descalzas Reales monastery. Some rooms have large balconies. Price includes breakfast. ❽

1

Hotel Europa, c/Carmen 4 ☎ 915 212 900, Ⓕ 915 214 696, ⓌⓌ www.hoteleuropa.net; ⓂSol. Well-established, family-run hotel with recently refurbished rooms and a new restaurant. **❻**

Hostal Ivor, c/Arenal 24, 2º ☎ 915 471 054, Ⓕ 915 471 054; ⓂÓpera. Good standard *hostal* with comfortable en-suite rooms, all with TV. **❺**

Hostal La Macarena, Cava de San Miguel 8, 2º ☎ 913 659 221, Ⓕ 913 642 757; ⓂSol. Fine, refurbished, family-run *hostal* in a characterful alley just off the Plaza Mayor. The rooms are on the small side, but do have air-conditioning. **❻**

Hostal Madrid, c/Esparteros 6, 2º ☎ 915 220 60, Ⓕ 915 323 510; ⓂSol. The owners of this slightly expensive but very convenient hostal are anxious to please. Well-kept rooms all have bathrooms and TVs. Four good-value apartments also available for €60–90. **❻**

Hotel Ópera, c/Cuesta de Santo Domingo 2 ☎ 915 412 800, Ⓕ 915 416 923, Ⓔhotelopera@ sinix.net; ⓂÓpera. With a very pleasant location near the Plaza de Oriente, this modern hotel has comfortable, large rooms at a pretty reasonable price. The café downstairs, appropriately enough, offers dinner served by singing waiters. **❽**

Hotel Paris, c/Alcalá 2 ☎ 915 216 496, Ⓕ 915 310 188; ⓂSol. Smart, old-fashioned hotel right on the Puerta del Sol. Half the rooms have air-conditioning. Very good value for so central a position. Price includes breakfast. **❼**

Hostal La Perla Asturiana, Plaza de Santa Cruz 3 ☎ 913 664 600, Ⓕ 913 664 608 Ⓔperlaasturi-ana@mundivia.es; ⓂSol. Small rooms in this nicely located hostal, overlooking a pleasant square. **❹**

Hostal Riesco, c/Correo 2–3 ☎ 915 222 692, Ⓕ 915 329 088; ⓂSol. Old-style, characterful place in a street just off Sol. All rooms are en suite and have air-conditioning. **❹**

Hostal Rifer, c/Mayor 5, 4º ☎ 915 323 197, Ⓕ 915 323 197; ⓂSol. Clean, bright rooms in the highest – and therefore quietest – of three options in this block, with a friendly owner. **❹**

Hostal Rober, c/Arenal 26, 5º ☎ 915 419 175; ⓂÓpera. One of several reasonable *hostales* at the Ópera end of c/Arenal. The thirteen rooms all have a bathroom and TV. **❹**

Hostal Tijcal, c/Zaragoza 6 ☎ 913 655 910, Ⓕ 913 645 260, ⓌⓌ www.hostaltijcal.com; ⓂSol. Situated between Plaza Santa Cruz and Plaza Mayor, this recently remodelled *hostal* offers rooms with air-conditioning, bathroom and TV (some also have good views). **❺**

Around Paseo del Prado

This is a quieter area, though still very central, which hosts some of the city's most expensive hotels – as well as some more modest options.

Hostal Almanzor, c/San Jerónimo 11, 2º ☎ 914 293 801; ⓂSol. Clean and welcoming, with a French-speaking *dueño*. **❹**

Hostal Armesto, c/San Agustín 6, 1º ☎ 914 299 031; ⓂAntón Martín. Another clean and friendly option, in a quiet street near the tourist office. The best rooms overlook the pleasant little garden in the Casa de Lope de Vega next door. **❺**

Hostal Cervantes, c/Cervantes 34, 2º ☎ 914 298 365 or 914 292 745, Ⓕ 914 298 365; ⓂAntón Martín. If you can't get in to the *Gonzalo* on the floor above, this is an equally friendly *hostal*, although slightly more expensive. All rooms have their own bathroom, TV and ventilator and are pleasantly furnished. **❺**

Hostal Gonzalo, c/Cervantes 34, 3º ☎ 914 292 714, Ⓕ 914 202 007; ⓂAntón Martín. Don't let the ancient lift put you off – this recently refurbished hotel has bright, en-suite rooms and a charming owner. Highly recommended. **❺**

Hotel Mora, Paseo del Prado 32 ☎ 914 201 569, Ⓕ 914 200 564; ⓂAtocha. Friendly, recently refurbished, 62-room hotel. All rooms have air-conditioning and some have pleasant views along the Paseo del Prado. Perfectly positioned for all the galleries on the Paseo del Arte. **❻**

Hostal Sud-Americana, Paseo del Prado 12, 6º ☎ 914 292 564; ⓂAntón Martín. Large, simple, but clean rooms with leafy views in this good-value *hostal* (though facilities are shared). Closed Aug. **❹**

Plaza de España and Gran Vía

The huge old buildings along the Gran Vía – which stretches all the way from Plaza de España to c/Alcalá – hide a vast array of hotels and *hostales* at every price, often with a delightfully decayed elegance, though also noisy from outside traffic. After dark, the area can feel somewhat seedy.

Hostal Andorra, Gran Vía 33, 7º ☎ 915 323 116, Ⓕ 915 217 931, Ⓔandorra@arrakis.es; ⓂCallao.

Smart, clean and quiet, with bathrooms in all the rooms. **❺**

Hotel Arosa, c/Salud 21 ℡ 915 321 600, Ⓕ 915 313 127, ✉arosa@hotelarosa.com; Ⓜ Gran Vía/Sol. Friendly, well-equipped and very good-value hotel right in the heart of town between Sol and Gran Vía. Spacious, air-conditioned rooms. Some of the surrounding streets are a bit down at heel but don't let this put you off. ❼

Hostal Buenos Aires, Gran Vía 61, 2º ℡ 915 420 102, Ⓕ 915 422 869; Ⓜ Plaza de España. Well-appointed *hostal*, at the Plaza de España end of this street. Rooms have air-conditioning, TV and en-suite bathroom. ❺

Hostal California, Gran Vía 38 ℡ 915 224 703, Ⓕ 915 316 101; Ⓜ Callao. Well-placed, but some-what pricey *hostal* with its own bar and café. Bright, new and relatively quiet rooms. ❼

Casón del Tormes, c/Río 7 ℡ 915 419 746, Ⓕ 915 411 852; Ⓜ Plaza de España. Plush 63-room hotel in a surprisingly quiet street off Plaza de España. Rooms are comfortable, en suite and air-conditioned, and the English-speaking staff are helpful. A very good option in this price range. ❽

Hostal Valencia, Gran Vía 44, 5º & 6º ℡ 915 221 115, ✉hostalvalencia@terra.es; Ⓜ Callao). Best of a whole block of *hostales*, though rooms at the front can be noisy. ❺

North of Gran Vía

North of Gran Vía, there are further wedges of *hostales* on and around c/Fuencarral and c/Hortaleza, near Metro Gran Vía, and c/Luna, behind Metro Callao. Fuencarral itself can be almost as noisy as Gran Vía, however, so ask for a room facing away from the street; the streets around its southern end form a red-light district, so take care after dark. The higher the street numbers, the fur-ther these streets are from Gran Vía – and the nearer to Malasaña (see below).

Hostal Ducal, c/Hortaleza 3, 3º ℡ 915 211 045, Ⓕ 915 215 064; Ⓜ Gran Vía. Pleasant *hostal* with flower-laden verandas overlooking the city. All rooms are en suite. ❹

Hostal Kryse, c/Fuencarral 25, 1º ℡ 915 311 512, Ⓕ 915 228 153; Ⓜ Gran Vía. One of a trio of clean, friendly places run by the same manage-ment. Small bathroom, TV and ceiling fans in all rooms. ❹

Hostal Medieval, c/Fuencarral 46, 2º ℡ 915 222 549; Ⓜ Chueca. Well-run, friendly place with a range of rooms, in an old building overlooking a square. All of the airy rooms have showers, but toilets are shared. Triples available for €40. ❹

Hotel Mónaco, c/Barbieri 5 ℡ 915 224 630, Ⓕ 915 211 601; Ⓜ Gran Vía/Chueca. A former bor-dello, and once a wonderfully characterful hotel, but now rather shabby and certainly not as friendly as it once was. The fittings aren't always up to scratch, but there are a couple of delightfully quirky Art Deco double rooms for the adventurous. Can be noisy at night with nearby *discobares*. ❼

Hostal Pizarro, c/Pizarro 14, 1º ℡ 915 319 158; Ⓜ Plaza de España. Comfortable, fairly upmarket *hostal* on a street just off c/Luna. ❹

Hostal Sil, c/Fuencarral 95, 3º ℡ 914 488 972, Ⓕ 914 474 829; Ⓜ Tribunal. Quiet and friendly *hostal* with air-conditioning. All rooms have bath-rooms and TV. Very handy for Malasaña. ❻

Hostal Zamora, Plaza Vázquez de Mella 1, 4º Izda. ℡ 915 217 031; Ⓜ Gran Vía. Seventeen rooms in this pleasant hostal, most of which overlook the recently spruced up plaza. All of the simple rooms have bathrooms, TV and air-conditioning. There are good-value family rooms for €59. ❺

Hostal Zamoran, c/Fuencarral 18, 2º ℡ 915 322 060; Ⓜ Gran Vía. Good-value *hostal*, with large, clean, en-suite rooms (all with TV). ❹

Malasaña

Malasaña, west of c/Fuencarral and centred around Plaza Dos de Mayo, is an old working-class district, and one of the main nightlife areas of Madrid. The *hostales* here tend towards the basic, but if you stay you'll get a feel for what the city is really like – and you'll still be in walking distance of the sights.

Hostal Barajas, c/Augusto Figueroa 17 ℡ 915 324 078, Ⓕ 915 310 209; Ⓜ Tribunal/Chueca. Unusually fancy *hostal* for this area, offering en-suite rooms, all with TV. ❺

Hostal Maravillas, c/Manuela Malasaña 23, 1º ℡ 914 484 000; Ⓜ Noviciado. Lively location for this bland but low-priced *hostal*. Shared facilities. ❸

Hostal Palma, c/Palma 17, 1º ℡ 914 475 488; Ⓜ Tribunal. Basic but clean rooms (some with bal-cony), behind the metro station. ❸

Hostal Los Perales, c/Palma 61, 1º ℡ 915 227 191; Ⓜ Noviciado. Best budget option in a building with several *hostales*. ❶–❷

Chueca and Santa Bárbara

Chueca, east of c/Fuencarral, is another nightlife centre and the city's *zona gay*. After some years of neglect, the barrio has been given a new lease of life with the opening of numerous new bars, clubs and restaurants. The northern reaches of Chueca, around Plaza Santa Bárbara (Ⓜ Alonso Martínez), are rather more spacious and still full of nightlife.

Hostal Asunción, Plaza Santa Bárbara 8, 2° Ⓣ 913 082 348, Ⓕ 913 100 478, Ⓔhostalasuncion@hotmail.com; Ⓜ Alonso Martínez. Small but well-furnished rooms with bath, TV and minibar. Pretty position overlooking the square. ❺

Hostal Benamar, c/San Mateo 20, 2° Ⓣ 913 080 092, Ⓔbenamar@nexo.es; Ⓜ Tribunal. A good budget option. Some of the 22 clean rooms have air-conditioning and all have washbasins. Four shared bathrooms. ❸

Hostal Santa Bárbara, Plaza Santa Bárbara 4, 3° Ⓣ 914 457 334 or 914 469 308, Ⓕ 914 462 345; Ⓜ Alonso Martínez. Nice, air-conditioned *hostal* in a good location, with English-speaking Italian *dueño*. ❻

Recoletos and Salamanca

This is Madrid at its most chic: the Bond Street/Rue de Rivoli region of smart shops and equally well-heeled apartment blocks. It's a safe, pleasant area, just north of the Parque del Retiro, but the pavements are notorious for dog shit – poodles being almost as ubiquitous here as fur coats.

Residencia Don Diego, c/Velázquez 45, 5° Ⓣ 914 350 760, Ⓕ 914 314 263; Ⓜ Velázquez. This is a comfortable little hotel – rooms are air-conditioned and have satellite TV. Quite reasonably priced for the area. ❼

Galiano Residencia, c/Alcalá Galiano 6 Ⓣ 913 192 000, Ⓕ 913 199 914; Ⓜ Colón. Hidden away in a quiet street off the Paseo de la Castellana, this small hotel has a sophisticated feel and friendly service. Car parking facilities. ❽

Hotel Serrano, c/Marqués de Villamejor 8 Ⓣ 914 355 200, Ⓕ 914 354 849; Ⓜ Rubén Darío. Small, modern hotel, handily sited between c/Velázquez and Paseo de la Castellana. Rooms look out onto a back courtyard so are fairly quiet. ❼

Youth hostels and campsites

Madrid has two youth hostels and, following the closure of *Camping Madrid* (still listed in some camping guides), just one "local" campsite.

Camping Osuna, Avda. de Logroño s/n, out near the airport, just north of the NII road to Barcelona Ⓣ 917 410 510, Ⓕ 913 206 365; Ⓜ Canillejas, then bus #105. Friendly, with good facilities, reasonable prices and plenty of shade, but the ground is rock hard and, with planes landing and taking off overhead, it's extremely noisy. ❶

Hostel Richard Schirmann, in the Casa de Campo Ⓣ 914 635 699, Ⓕ 914 644 685; Ⓜ Lago or bus #33. Not very convenient (about 45min walk from Sol) but friendly, comfortable and clean with disabled access, plenty of fresh air and an enjoyably noisy bar. You can call and they'll pick you up at Lago metro station, roughly 1km away; you shouldn't walk there alone after dark as the area is frequented by prostitutes and their clients. YH card needed, but can be bought at hostel. ❶

Hostel Santa Cruz de Marcenado, c/Santa Cruz de Marcenado 28 Ⓣ 915 474 532, Ⓕ 915 481 196; Ⓜ Argüelles. This is a 20-min walk (or an easy metro ride) northwest of the centre, east of c/Princesa. It's a modern, reasonably pleasant building, with good local bars. Reception is open 9am–1pm, and doors stay open to 1.30am. Try to book ahead if possible. YH card needed, but can be bought at hostel. ❶

The City

Madrid's main sights occupy a compact area between the **Palacio Real** (Royal Palace) and the gardens of **El Retiro**. The great trio of museums – the **Prado**, **Thyssen-Bornemisza** and **Reina Sofía** – are ranged along the Paseo del Prado, over towards the Retiro. The oldest part of the city, an area known as

Summer in Madrid

Madrid virtually shuts down **in the summer**; from around July 20 you'll sudden-ly find that many of the bars, restaurants and offices are closed, and their inhabitants gone to the coast and countryside. Only in September does the city open proper-ly for business again.

Luckily for visitors, and those *madrileños* who choose to remain, most sights and museums stay open, and a summer nightlife takes on a momentum of its own in out-door terrace bars, or terrazas. In addition, the city council has in recent years initi-ated a major programme of summer entertainment, *Los Veranos de la Villa*. It's not a bad time to be in town at all, so long as you're not trying to get anything done.

Note that, throughout the year, most museums (and many bars and restaurants) **close on Monday**. Major attractions that stay open on Mondays include the Reina Sofía and the Palacio Real.

Madrid de los Austrias after the Habsburg monarchs who built it, is centred on the gorgeous, arcaded **Plaza Mayor**, just to the east of the Palacio Real.

If you have very limited time, you might well do no more sightseeing than this. However, monuments are not really what Madrid is about, and to get a feel for the city you need to branch out a little, and experience the contrast-ing character and life of the various *barrios*. The most central and rewarding of these are the areas **around Plaza de Santa Ana and c/Huertas**, east of Puerta del Sol; **La Latina and Lavapiés**, south of Plaza Mayor, where the Sunday market, **El Rastro**, takes place; and **Malasaña and Chueca**, north of Gran Vía. By happy circumstance, these *barrios* have some of Madrid's finest concentrations of tapas bars and restaurants (see p.115).

Sol, Plaza Mayor and Ópera:
Madrid of the Austrias

Madrid de los Austrias – Habsburg Madrid – was a mix of formal planning, at its most impressive in the expansive and theatrical Plaza Mayor, and areas of shanty-town development, knocked up as the new capital gained an urban pop-ulation. The central area of old Madrid still reflects both characteristics, with its twisting grid of streets, alleyways and steps, and its Flemish-inspired architecture of red brick and grey stone, slate-tiled towers, and Renaissance doorways.

Puerta del Sol

The obvious starting point for exploring Habsburg Madrid (and most other areas of the centre) is the **Puerta del Sol** (Ⓜ Sol). This square marks the epi-centre of the city – and, indeed, of Spain. It is from this point that all distances are measured, and here that six of Spain's *Rutas Nacionales* (the roads known as the NI, to Burgos, the NII, to Zaragoza, and so on) officially begin. On the pavement outside the clock-tower building on the south side of the square, a stone slab shows Kilometre Zero.

The square is a popular meeting place, especially by the fountain, or at the corner of c/Carmen, with its statue of a bear pawing a *madroño* (strawberry tree) – the city's emblem. These apart, there's little of note, though the square fulfils something of a public role when there's a demonstration or celebration. At New Year, for example, it is packed with people waiting for the clock to chime midnight. The square's main business, however, is shopping, with giant branches of the **department stores** El Corte Inglés and the French chain FNAC in c/Preciados, at the top end of the square.

Plaza Mayor

Follow c/Mayor (the "Main Street" of the medieval city) west from the Puerta del Sol and you could easily walk right past Madrid's most important landmark: **Plaza Mayor**. This is set back from the street and, entered by stepped passageways, appears all the more grand in its continuous sweep of arcaded buildings. It was planned by Felipe II – the monarch who made Madrid the capital – as the public meeting place of the city, and was finished thirty years later in 1619 during the reign of Felipe III, who sits astride the stallion in the central statue. The architect was Juan Gómez de Mora, who was responsible for many of the civic and royal buildings in this quarter.

The square, with its hundreds of balconies, was designed as a theatre for public events, and it has served this function throughout its history. It was the scene of the Inquisition's *autos-de-fé* (trials of faith) and the executions which followed; kings were crowned here; festivals and demonstrations passed through; plays by Lope de Vega and others received their first performances; bulls were fought; and gossip was spread. The more important of the events would be watched by royalty from their apartments in the central **Casa Panadería**, a palace named after the bakery which it replaced. It was rebuilt after a fire in 1692 and subsequently decorated with frescoes. However, the present delightful, and highly kitsch, array of allegorical figures that adorn the facade were only added in 1992. Today the palace houses municipal offices and an exhibition centre displaying temporary exhibits on the history of Madrid (Mon–Fri 11am–2pm & 5–8pm, Sat, Sun & holidays 11am–2pm; free).

Nowadays, Plaza Mayor is primarily a tourist haunt, full of expensive outdoor cafés and restaurants (best stick to a drink). However, an air of grandeur clings to the plaza, which still performs public functions. In the summer months and during the major *madrileño* fiestas (see box p.78–79) it becomes an outdoor **theatre** and **music stage**; in the autumn there's a **book fair**; and in the winter, just before Christmas, it becomes a **bazaar** for festive decorations and religious regalia. Every Sunday, too, stamp and coin sellers set up their stalls.

In the alleys just below the square, such as c/Cuchilleros and c/Cava de San Miguel, are some of the city's oldest *mesones*, or taverns. Have a drink in these in the early evening and you are likely to be serenaded by passing *tunas* – musicians and singers dressed in traditional costume of knickerbockers and waistcoats who wander around town playing and passing the hat. These men-only troupes are attached to various faculties of the university and are used by students to supplement their grants.

Plaza de la Villa, San Miguel and San Ginés

West along c/Mayor, towards the Royal Palace, is **Plaza de la Villa**, an example of three centuries of Spanish architectural development. Its oldest surviving building is the recently renovated fifteenth-century **Torre de los Lujanes**, a fine Mudéjar (Moors working under Christian rule) tower, where Francis I of France is said to have been imprisoned in 1525 after his capture at the Battle of Pavia in Italy. Opposite is the old town hall, the **ayuntamiento**, begun in the seventeenth century, but remodelled in a Baroque mode (tours in Spanish only at 5pm every Monday; free). Finally, fronting the square is the **Casa de Cisneros**, built by a nephew of Cardinal Cisneros in the sixteenth-century Plateresque ("silversmith") style. Baroque is also seen round the corner in c/San Justo, where the parish church of **San Miguel** (Mon–Sat 11am–12.15pm & 5.30–7pm) shows the imagination of the eighteenth-century Italian architects who designed it.

Another fine – but much more ancient – church is **San Ginés**, north of Plaza Mayor on c/Arenal. This is of Mozarabic origin (built by Christians under

Madrid's freebies

Free entrance can be gained to many of Madrid's premier attractions. Sites classed as *Patrimonio Nacional* such as the Palacio Real, the Convento de la Encarnación, El Pardo (see p.115) and the Monasterio de las Descalzas are free to EU citizens on Wednesdays (bring your passport). Most museums are free for under 18s and the retired, and give substantial discounts to students (bring ID in all cases). In addition many museums and sights that normally charge entry set aside certain times when entrance is free. These include the following:

Centro de Arte Reina Sofía: Sat after 2.30pm & Sun 10am–2.30pm.
Ermita de San Antonio de la Florida: Wed 10am–2pm & 4–8pm & Sun 10am–2pm.
Museo de América: Sat 2–3pm & Sun 10am–2.30pm.
Museo Arqueológico: Sat 2.30–8.30pm & Sun 9.30am–2.30pm.
Museo de Artes Decorativas: Sun 10am–2pm.
Museo Cerralbo: Sun 10am–2pm & Wed 9.30am–2.30pm.
Museo del Ejército: Sat 10am–2pm.
Museo Lázaro Galdiano: Sat 10am–2pm.
Museo Municipal: Sun 10am–2pm & Wed 9.30am–8pm.
Museo del Prado: Sat after 2.30pm & Sun 9am–2pm.
Museo Romántico: Sun 10am–2pm.
Real Academia de Bellas Artes: Sat & Sun 9am–2.30pm.

Moorish rule) and has an El Greco canvas of the moneychangers being chased from the temple on show in the Capilla del Cristo (daily 9am–1pm & 6–9pm; entrance on c/Bordadores). The church itself is open only during services. Alongside the church, in somewhat uneasy juxtaposition, stands a cult temple of the twentieth century, the *Joy Madrid* disco, and, behind it, the **Chocolatería San Ginés**, a Madrid institution, which at one time catered for the early-rising worker but now churns out *churros* and hot chocolate for the late nightclub crowd (see p.134).

Descalzas Reales and Encarnación convents

A couple of blocks north of San Ginés is one of the hidden treasures of Madrid, the **Monasterio de las Descalzas Reales** at Plaza de las Descalzas Reales 3 (ⓂSol/Callao). This was founded by Juana de Austria, daughter of the Emperor Carlos V, sister of Felipe II, and, at age nineteen, already the widow of Prince Don Juan of Portugal. In her wake came a succession of titled ladies (*Descalzas Reales* means "Barefoot Royals"), who brought fame and, above all, fortune. The place is unbelievably rich, though beautiful and tranquil, too, and still in use as a convent, with shoeless nuns tending patches of vegetable garden.

Whistle-stop guided tours (Tues–Thurs & Sat 10.30am–12.45pm & 4–5.45pm, Fri 10.30am–12.45pm, Sun & holidays 11am–1.45pm; €4.80, free on Wed for EU citizens, joint ticket with Convento de la Encarnación €5) conduct visitors (usually in Spanish only) through the cloisters and up an incredibly fancy stairway to a series of chambers packed with art and treasures of every kind. The dormitories are perhaps the most outstanding feature, decorated with a series of Flemish tapestries based on designs by Rubens and a striking portrait of St Francis by Zurbarán. These were the sleeping quarters for all the nuns – who included, for a time, St Teresa of Ávila – except for the empress María of Germany, who endowed the convent with her own luxurious private chambers. The other highlight of the tour is the Joyería (Treasury), piled high with jewels and relics of uncertain provenance. The nuns kept no records of their gifts, so no one is quite sure what many of the things are – there is a bizarre cross-sectional model of Christ – nor which bones came from which saint. Whatever the case, it's an exceptional hoard.

Over towards the Palacio Real in Plaza de la Encarnación is the **Convento de la Encarnación** (Tues–Thurs & Sat 10.30am–12.45pm & 4–5.45pm, Fri 10.30am–12.45pm, Sun & holidays 11am–1.45pm; €3.50, free on Wed for EU citizens, joint ticket with Monasterio de las Descalzas Reales €6; Ópera). This was founded a few years after Juana's convent, by Margarita, wife of Felipe III, though it was substantially rebuilt towards the end of the eighteenth century. It houses an extensive but disappointing collection of seventeenth-century Spanish art, and a library-like reliquary which is reputed to be one of the most important in the Catholic world.

Ópera: Plaza de Oriente and the cathedral

West of Sol, c/Arenal leads to the **Teatro Real** or Ópera (tours Tues–Fri 1pm, Sat, Sun & holidays 10.30am–1.30pm; €3; tickets on sale from 10am; Ópera), which gives this area its name. Built in the mid-nineteenth century, it almost sank a few decades later as a result of subsidence caused by underground canals; it reopened in 1998 after a ten-year refurbishment that should have lasted just four and which ended up costing a mind-boggling 25 billion pesetas.

Around the back, the opera house is separated from the Palacio Real by the **Plaza de Oriente**, a pleasant square that is surprisingly under used, perhaps a hangover from the bad old days when Franco used to address crowds here; neo-Fascists still gather here on the anniversary of his death on November 21. However, the completion of a major pedestrianization project, diverting the busy c/Bailén beneath the square, has turned the plaza into one of the most agreeable open spaces in Madrid. One of the square's main attractions – and the focus of its life – is the elegant *Café del Oriente*, whose summer terraza is one of the stations of Madrid nightlife. The café (which is also a prestigious restaurant) looks as traditional as any in the city but was in fact opened in the 1980s by a priest, Padre Lezama, who ploughs his profits into various charitable schemes.

The café apart, the dominant features of Plaza de Oriente are statues: 44 of them, depicting Spanish kings and queens, which were designed originally to go on the palace facade but found to be too heavy (some say too ugly) for the roof to support. The **statue of Felipe IV** on horseback, in the centre of the square, clearly belongs on a different plane; it was based on designs by Velázquez, and Galileo is said to have helped with the calculations to make it balance.

Facing the Palacio Real to the south, across the shadeless Plaza de la Armería, is Madrid's cathedral, **Nuestra Señora de la Almudena** (Mon–Sat 10am–1.30pm & 6–8.30pm, Sun 10am–2.30pm & 6–8.30pm; Ópera), its Neoclassical bulk as undistinguished inside as out. The cathedral was planned centuries ago, bombed out in the Civil War, worked upon at intervals since, plagued by lack of funds and eventually opened for business in 1993 by Pope John Paul II.

South again from here, c/Bailén crosses c/Segovia on a high **viaduct** (now lined with panes of reinforced glass to prevent once-common suicide attempts) which was constructed as a royal route from the palace to the church of San Francisco el Grande, avoiding the rabble and river which both flowed below. Close by is a patch of **Moorish wall** from the medieval fortress here, which the original royal palace replaced. Across the aqueduct, the **gardens** of Las Vistillas ("the views") beckon, with their summer terrazas looking out across the river.

El Palacio Real

The **Palacio Real** or Royal Palace (April–Sept Mon–Sat 9am–6pm, Sun & holidays 9am–2.30pm; Oct–March Mon–Sat 9.30am–5pm, Sun & holidays 9am–2pm; closed occasionally for state visits; free on Wed for EU citizens) scores high on statistics. It claims more rooms than any other European palace; a library with one of the biggest collections of books, manuscripts, maps and musical scores in the world; and an armoury with an unrivalled collection of weapons dating back to the fifteenth century. If you are around on the first Wednesday of the month (except July & Aug) at noon–1pm, look out for the changing of the guard outside the palace, a tradition which has recently been revived.

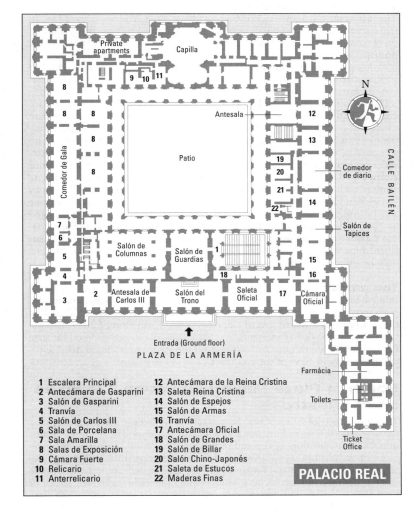

PALACIO REAL

1 Escalera Principal
2 Antecámara de Gasparini
3 Salón de Gasparini
4 Tranvía
5 Salón de Carlos III
6 Sala de Porcelana
7 Sala Amarilla
8 Salas de Exposición
9 Cámara Fuerte
10 Relicario
11 Anterrelicario
12 Antecámara de la Reina Cristina
13 Saleta Reina Cristina
14 Salón de Espejos
15 Salón de Armas
16 Tranvía
17 Antecámara Oficial
18 Salón de Grandes
19 Salón de Billar
20 Salón Chino-Japonés
21 Saleta de Estucos
22 Maderas Finas

Optional **guided tours** in various languages (€6.90; usually with a wait for a group to form) have been abbreviated in recent years, now taking in around 25 (rather than 90) rooms and apartments, including the Royal Armoury Museum and Royal Pharmacy. Nevertheless, they're still a pretty hard slog, rarely allowing much time to contemplate the extraordinary opulence: acres of Flemish and Spanish tapestries, endless Rococo decoration, bejewelled clocks and pompous portraits of the monarchs, as well as a permanent display of Goya's cartoons and tapestries. You're probably better off going **without a guide** (€6), as each room is clearly signed and described in English anyway, the main disadvantage being trying to fight your way past the guided groups.

The palace and outhouses

The Habsburgs' original palace burned down on Christmas Day 1734. Its replacement, the current building, was based on drawings made by Bernini for the Louvre. It was constructed in the mid-eighteenth century and was the principal royal residence from then until Alfonso XIII went into exile in 1931; both Joseph Bonaparte and the Duke of Wellington also lived here briefly. The present royal family inhabits a considerably more modest residence in the western outskirts of the city, using the Palacio Real on state occasions only.

The **Salón del Trono** (Throne Room) is the highlight for most visitors, containing the new thrones installed for Juan Carlos and Sofia, the current monarchs, as well as the splendid ceiling by Tiepolo, a giant fresco representing the glory of Spain – an extraordinary achievement for an artist by then in his seventies.

The palace outbuildings and annexes include the recently refurbished **Armería Real** (Royal Armoury), a huge room full of guns, swords and armour, with such curiosities as El Cid's sword and the suit of armour worn by Carlos V in his equestrian portrait by Titian in the Prado. Especially fascinating are the complete sets of armour, with all the original spare parts and gadgets for making adjustments. There is also an eighteenth-century **Farmacia**, a curious mixture of alchemist's den and laboratory, whose walls are lined with jars labelled for various remedies. The **Biblioteca Real** (Royal Library) can now only be visited by prior arrangement for research purposes.

The gardens

Immediately north of the palace, the disappointing **Jardines Sabatini**, are also open to the public, while to the rear the larger, and far more beautiful, park of the **Campo del Moro** (April–Sept Mon–Sat 10am–8pm, Sun 9am–8pm, Oct–March Mon-Sat 10am–6pm, Sun 9am–6pm; occasionally closed for state visits; access only from the far west side off the Paseo de la Virgen del Puerto) affords a splendid view of the western facade of the palace.

South of Plaza Mayor: La Latina, Lavapiés and El Rastro

The areas south of Plaza Mayor have traditionally been tough, working-class districts, with tenement buildings thrown up to accommodate the huge expansion of the population in the eighteenth and nineteenth centuries. In many places these old houses survive, huddled together in narrow streets, but the character of **La Latina** and **Lavapiés** has changed as their inhabitants, and the districts themselves, have become younger and more fashionable. The streets of Cava Baja and Cava Alta, for example, in La Latina, include some of the city's most fashionable bars and restaurants. These are attractive *barrios* to explore,

Madrid's flea market, **El Rastro**, is as much part of the city's weekend ritual as a Mass or a *paseo*. This gargantuan, thriving, thieving shambles of a street market sprawls south from Metro Latina to the Ronda de Toledo, especially along Ribera de Curtidores. Through it, crowds flood between 10am and 3pm every Sunday and increasingly on Fridays, Saturdays and public holidays too. On offer are second-hand clothes, military surplus items, budgies and canaries, sunshades, razor blades, fine antiques and Taiwanese transistors, cutlery and coke spoons – in fact just about anything you might (or more likely, might not) need.

Some of the goods – broken telephone dials, plastic shampoo bottles half-full of something which may or may not be the original contents – are so far gone that you can't imagine any of them ever selling. Other items may be quite valuable, but on the whole it's the stuff of markets around the world you'll find here: pseudo-designer clothes, bags and T-shirts. Don't expect to find fabulous bargains, or the hidden Old Masters of popular myth; the serious antique trade has mostly moved off the streets and into the shops along the street, while the real junk is now found only on the fringes. Nonetheless, the atmosphere of the Rastro is always enjoyable and the bars around these streets are as good as any in the city.

One warning: keep a close eye on your bags, pockets, cameras (best left at the hotel), and jewellery. The Rastro rings up a fair percentage of Madrid's tourist thefts.

particularly during the Sunday morning flea market, **El Rastro**, which takes place along and around the Ribera de Curtidores (Ⓜ La Latina or Tirso de Molina).

Around La Latina

La Latina is a short walk from Plaza de la Villa (see p.90) and, if you're exploring Madrid de los Austrias, it's a natural continuation, as some of the squares, streets and churches here date back to the early Habsburg period. One of the most attractive pockets is around the recently renovated **Plaza de la Paja**, an acacia-shaded square, behind the large church of San Andrés. In summer, there are usually a couple of terrazas here, tucked well away from the traffic. If it is open, you might look into the Gothic **Capilla del Obispo** (Tues–Sun 11am–2pm & 4–9pm), which backs on to San Andrés; long under restoration, this has an elaborate Renaissance interior, endowed by one of Fernando and Isabel's counsellors. Another of the adjoining chapels, the Baroque **Capilla de San Isidro** (Mon–Sat 8.30am–11.30pm & 6–8pm, Sun 9am–2pm), is also worth a look for its richly decorated interior with a beautifully sculpted dome.

Over to the west of here is one of Madrid's grandest, richest and most elaborate churches, **San Francisco el Grande** (Ⓜ Puerta de Toledo/La Latina). Built towards the end of the eighteenth century as part of Carlos III's renovations of the city, it has a dome even larger than that of St Paul's in London. Inside (Tues–Sat: June–Sept 11am–1pm & 5–8pm; Oct–May 11am–1pm & 4–7pm; €0.30 with guided tour) are paintings by, among others, Goya and Zurbarán, and frescoes by Bayeu. They're not all that easy to see, however, as scaffolding is in place for a painfully slow restoration. Work is scheduled to be completed in 2012.

A short walk up the Carrera de San Francisco opposite the entrance to the church brings you to the lively series of plazas close to the Mercado de la Cebada. The Plaza de San Andrés is now home to the city's newest museum, the **Museo de San Isidro** (Tues–Fri 9.30am–8pm, Sat & Sun 10am–2pm; August Tues–Sat 9.30am-2.30pm, Sat & Sun 10am–2pm; free) housed in a sixteenth century mansion owned by the counts of Paredes and supposedly once the home to the city's patron saint. The archeological collection, which consists of relics from the earliest settlements along the Manzanares river, has been transferred here to the basement, while the rest of the museum has been given over to the patron saint and his miraculous activities. The museum is still in the process of building up its collections, but there are plans afoot to extend its exhibits on the early history of Madrid.

The Ribera de Curtidores, heart of the Rastro, begins just behind another vast church, **San Isidro** (Mon–Sat 8am–12.30pm & 6–8.30pm; Sun & holidays 9am–2pm & 6–8.30pm). Isidro is the patron saint of Madrid – his remains are entombed within – and his church acted as the city's cathedral prior to the completion of the Almudena by the Palacio Real. Relics apart, its chief attribute is size – it's as bleak as it is big. Next door is the **Instituto Real**, a school which has been in existence considerably longer than the church and counts among its former pupils such literary notables as Calderón de la Barca, Lope de Vega, Quevedo and Jacinto Benavente.

If you continue to the end of Ribera de Curtidores, whose antique shops (some, these days, extremely upmarket) stay open all week, you'll see a large arch, the **Puerta de Toledo**, at one end of the Ronda de Toledo. The only surviving relation to the Puerta de Alcalá in the Plaza de la Independencia, this was built originally as a triumphal arch to honour the conquering Napoleon. After his defeat in the Peninsular Wars, it became a symbol of the city's freedom. Just in front of the arch, the **Mercado Puerta de Toledo**, once the city's fish market, has pretensions to be a stylish arts and crafts centre, but in reality stands practically empty, apart from the under-used tourist office that lies within.

Lavapiés and the Cine Doré

A good point to start exploring Lavapiés is the Plaza Tirso de Molina (⑩ Tirso de Molina). From here, you can follow c/Mesón de Paredes, stopping for a drink at *Taberna Antonio Sánchez* at no. 13, down past rows of wholesale shops to **La Corrala**, on the corner of c/Sombrerete. This is one of many traditional *corrales* – tenement blocks – in the quarter, built with balconied apartments opening onto a central patio. Plays – especially farces and *zarzuelas* (a kind of operetta) – used to be performed regularly in Spanish *corrales*, and the open space here usually hosts a few performances in the summer. It has been well renovated and declared a national monument.

From Lavapiés, you can take c/Argumosa towards the Centro de Arte Reina Sofía (see p.106). Don't miss out the opportunity to sample some of the excellent local bars on this pleasant tree-lined street while you are here. To the north of the quarter, near Metro Antón Martín, is the **Cine Doré**, the oldest cinema in Madrid, dating from 1922, with a late *modernista*/Art Nouveau facade. It has been converted to house the Filmoteca Nacional, an art-film centre (see p.138) and it has a pleasant and inexpensive café/restaurant (Tues–Sun 1.30pm–12.30am).

East of Sol: Plaza de Santa Ana and Huertas

The **Plaza de Santa Ana/Huertas** area forms a triangle, bordered to the east by the Paseo del Prado, to the north by c/Alcalá, and along the south by c/Atocha, with the Puerta del Sol at the western tip. The city reached this district after extending beyond the Royal Palace and the Plaza Mayor, so the buildings date predominantly from the nineteenth century. Many of them have literary associations: there are streets named after Cervantes and Lope de Vega

△ Bullfight ticket office, Madrid

(where one lived and the other died), and the *barrio* is host to the Atheneum club, Círculo de Bellas Artes (Fine Arts Institute), Teatro Español, and the Congreso de los Diputados (parliament). Just to the north, there is also an important museum, the **Real Academia de Bellas Artes de San Fernando**.

For most visitors, though, the major attraction is that in this district are some of the best and most beautiful bars and *tascas* in the city. They are concentrated particularly around Plaza de Santa Ana, which – following a rather seedy period – has been smartened up by the council.

Santa Ana and around

The bars around **Plaza de Santa Ana** (⊗Sol/Sevilla) really are sights in themselves. On the square itself, the dark-panelled **Cervecería Alemana** was a firm favourite of Hemingway and has hardly changed since the turn of the twentieth century. It's a place to drink beer, and go easy on tapas (the *empanadillas* are good) if you don't want to run up a significant bill. Another notable place is the *Bar Torero* of the **Gran Hotel Reina Victoria**, the smart hotel flanking Plaza de Santa Ana; this is where bullfighters stay when in town, and the bar is packed with taurine memorabilia.

Viva Madrid, on the northeast corner at c/Manuel Fernández y González 7, should be another port of call, if only to admire the fabulous tilework, original zinc bar and a ceiling supported by wooden caryatids. One block east from here is **c/Echegaray**, where one of the highlights is **Los Gabrieles** at no. 17. This is a bar with museum-piece *azulejos* (tiles), endowed by sherry companies in the late nineteenth century and fabulously inventive: there are skeletons climbing over barrels, Goya-esque idylls with sherry and bulls, and a superb co-opting of Velázquez's *Los Borrachos*.

Huertas, the Cortes and the Círculo de Bellas Artes

The area around c/Huertas itself is workaday enough – and again packed with bars. North of the street, and parallel, are two streets named after the greatest figures of Spain's seventeenth-century literary golden age, Cervantes and Lope de Vega. Bitter rivals in life, both are probably spinning in their graves now, since Cervantes is interred in the Convento de las Trinitarias on the street named after Lope de Vega, while the latter's house, the **Casa de Lope de Vega** (Tues–Fri 9.30am–2pm, Sat 10am–1.30pm, closed mid-July to mid-Aug; €1.20; ⊗Antón Martín), finds itself at c/Cervantes 11. The latter is well worth visiting for its reconstruction of life in seventeenth-century Madrid; ring the bell and someone will take you on a short tour (usually English is spoken).

A block to the north is **El Congreso de Los Diputados** (⊗Sevilla), an unprepossessing nineteenth-century building where the congress (the lower house) meets. Sessions can be visited by appointment only, though anyone can turn up (with a passport) for a tour on Saturday mornings (tours every 30 mins, 10.30am–12.30pm; closed Aug). You're shown, amongst other things, the bullet holes left by Colonel Tejero and his Guardia Civil associates in the abortive coup attempt of 1981.

Cut across to c/Alcalá from the Plaza de las Cortes and you will emerge close to the **Círculo de Bellas Artes** at Marqués de Casa Riera 2 (⊗Sevilla), a strange-looking 1920s building crowned by a statue of Pallas Athene. This is Madrid's best arts centre, and includes a theatre, music hall, cinema, exhibition galleries (Tues–Fri 5–9pm, Sat 11am–2pm & 5–9pm, Sun 11am–2pm) and a very pleasant bar (daily 8am–2am) – all marble and leather decor, with a nude statue reclining in the middle of the floor. It attracts Madrid's arts and media crowd but is not in the least exclusive, nor expensive, and there's an adjoining terraza, too. The Círculo is theoretically a members-only club, but it issues €0.60 day membership on the door, for which you get access to all areas.

Calle Alcalá to Cibeles

At the Círculo, you are on the corner of Gran Vía (see p.110), and, only a hundred metres to the east, c/Alcalá meets the Paseo del Prado at the **Plaza de la Cibeles**. The wedding-cake building on the far side of this square is Madrid's main post office, the aptly entitled **Palacio de Comunicaciones**. Constructed from 1904 to 1917, it is vastly more imposing than the parliament and runs the Palacio Real pretty close. It's a fabulous place, flanked by polished brass postboxes for each province and preserving a totally Byzantine system within, where scores of counters each offer just one specific service, from telegrams to string, and, until quite recently, scribes.

Awash in a sea of traffic in the centre of the square is a **fountain** and statue of the goddess Cibeles, which survived the bombardments of the Civil War by being swaddled from helmet to hoof in sandbags. It was designed, as were the two other fountains gushing magnificently along the Paseo del Prado, by Ventura Rodríguez, who is honoured in modern Madrid by having a metro station and a street named after him. The fountain is the scene of celebrations for victorious Real Madrid fans (Atlético fans bathe in the fountain of Neptune just down the road).

Madrid's three principal art museums, the Prado (see below), Thyssen-Bornemisza (see p.104) and Centro de Arte Reina Sofía (see p.106), all lie to the south of here, along the Paseo del Prado. To the north, on Paseo de Recoletos, are a couple of the city's most lavish **traditional cafés**, the *Café Gijón* at no. 21 and *Café del Espejo* at no. 31 (see box on p.123).

Real Academia de Bellas Artes de San Fernando

Art buffs who have some appetite left after the Prado, Thyssen-Bornemisza and Reina Sofía, will find the **Real Academia de Bellas Artes de San Fernando**, at c/Alcalá 13 (Tues–Fri 9am–7pm, Mon, Sat, Sun & holidays 9am–2.30pm; €2.40, free Sat & Sun; ⓜSevilla), next on their list. Admittedly, you have to plough through a fair number of dull academic canvases, but there are hidden gems, particularly in the second and third rooms. These include a group of small panels by **Goya**, in particular *The Burial of the Sardine*; portraits of the monks of the Merced order by Zurbarán and others; and a curious *Family of El Greco*, which may be by the great man or his son. Two other rooms are devoted to foreign artists, especially Rubens. Upstairs, there is a series of engravings by Picasso, and scattered throughout the museum is a dismembered *Massacre of the Innocents* by sculptor José Ginés. The gallery is also home to the national chalcography (copper or brass engraving) collection (Mon–Fri 10am–2pm, Sat 10am-1.30pm; free) which includes a number of Goya etchings.

Museo del Prado

The **Museo del Prado** (Tues–Sat 9am–7pm, Sun & holidays usually 9am–2pm but closed New Year's Day, Good Friday, May 1 & Christmas Day, in July and Aug the museum has experimented with opening until 7.30pm on Sundays so it might be worth checking if this is still in operation; €3, free on Sat after 2.30pm & Sun; ⓦwww.museoprado.mcu.es; ⓜBanco de España/Atocha) is Madrid's premier tourist attraction, and one of the oldest and greatest collections of art in the world. Built as a natural science museum in 1775, the Prado opened to the public in 1819, and houses the finest works collected by Spanish royalty – for the most part avid, discerning, and wealthy

MUSEO DEL PRADO

N

- Spanish painting
- Flemish painting
- French painting
- British painting
- Italian painting
- Classical and
- Renaissance sculpture
- Dutch painting
- German painting

Second Floor

Drawing collection

80
81
82
83
79
76
77
78

First Floor

Goya's Cartoons

90
85
91
92
93
94
86
87
88
89

Goya

Goya drawing collection

Velázquez

Rubens

15a
16a
17a 18a
16
17
18
15
14
12
11
10a
10
9a
9
8a
8
7a
7
10b
9b
8b
7b

16b
29
28
27
26
25
24

32

19 20 21 22 23
39
34 35 36 37 38

Goya

El Greco

Bosch

Giftshop

5 6
4
3
2
1

Puerta alta de Goya

Cloakroom

Ground Floor

Titian

Goya's Black Paintings

67
65 66
64
74
71
72
73

62a 64a
61a 63
60a 62 63b
61 62b
60 61b
59
75

Salón de actos

Bookshop

47

Giftshop

Puerta de Velázquez

54
55a
55
55b
56a
56
56b
57a
57
57b
58a
58
49

51c
50
51b
51
51a

Cloakroom

Puerta baja de Goya

Puerta de Murillo

To Basement, the Dauphin's Treasure & Cafeteria

buyers – as well as Spanish paintings gathered from other sources over the past two centuries. There are 7000 paintings in all, of which around 1500 (still a pretty daunting tally) are on permanent display. A controversial plan to modernize and extend the museum (adding three nearby buildings) will enable the Prado to double the number of works currently on show. Local residents are opposing the proposed plan, designed by Spain's leading architect Rafael Moneo, to construct a new glass-fronted building to house the museum's offices in the cloisters of the church of San Jerónimo el Real.

The museum's highlights are its Flemish collection – including almost all of **Bosch**'s best work – and of course its incomparable display of Spanish art, in particular that of **Velázquez** (including *Las Meninas*), **Goya** (including the *Majas* and the *Black Paintings*), and **El Greco**. There's also a huge section of Italian painters (**Titian**, notably) collected by Carlos V and Felipe II, both great patrons of the Renaissance, and an excellent collection of seventeenth-century Flemish and Dutch pictures gathered by Felipe IV. The museum has also hosted an increasing number of temporary displays in recent years. Even in a full day you couldn't hope to do justice to everything here, and it's perhaps best to make a couple of more focused visits. If you are tempted to take advantage of the long opening hours, however, there's a decent cafeteria and restaurant in the basement.

Organization, catalogues and entrances

After recent major work at the museum, including the installation of air conditioning and the remodelling of the roof to let in more light, most of the national schools now look to have found a permanent home although it is worth bearing in mind that paintings are sometimes moved around; any changes will be shown on the **free maps** available on your way into the museum.

> If you plan to visit all three art museums on the Paseo del Prado during your stay, it's well worth buying the under-advertised **Paseo del Arte ticket** (€7.70) which is valid for a year and allows one visit to each museum at a substantial saving.

What follows is, by necessity, only a brief guide to the museum contents. Illustrated **guides and catalogues** (€15–22.90) describing and explaining the paintings are on sale in the museum shop and there are useful **colour booklets** (€0.60) on Velázquez, Goya, El Greco, Titian and Bosch available in their respective galleries.

There are two main **entrances** to the museum: the **Puerta de Goya**, which has an upper and a lower entrance opposite the Hotel Ritz on c/Felipe IV, and the **Puerta de Murillo** on Plaza de Murillo, opposite the botanical gardens. The Puerta de Goya upper entrance takes you up to the first floor (US second floor), with the seventeenth-century Flemish and Dutch art giving way to the main Spanish collections; its ground-floor entrance is the one to take if you want to embark on a chronological tour and for some inexplicable reason often seems to have less of a queue to get in. The Puerta de Murillo steers you past the impressive classical sculpture and on to the Italian Renaissance galleries.

Spanish painting

The Prado's collections of Spanish painting begin with the cycles of twelfth-century **Romanesque frescoes** (Room 51c; being restored at the time of writing, but due to be returned to their original location in this room), reconstructed from a pair of churches from the Mozarabic (Muslim rule) era in Soria and Segovia. **Early panel paintings** – exclusively religious fourteenth- and fifteenth-century works – include a huge *retablo* (altarpiece) by Nicolás Francés; the anonymous *Virgin of the Catholic Monarchs*; Bermejo's *Santo Domingo de Silos*; and Pedro Berruguete's *Auto-de-Fé*.

The Golden Age: Velázquez and El Greco

Collections from Spain's Golden Age – the late sixteenth and seventeenth centuries under Habsburg rule – are prefigured by a collection of paintings (rooms 60a, 61a and 62a) by **El Greco** (1540–1614), the Cretan-born artist who worked in Toledo from the 1570s. You really have to have taken in the works in Toledo to appreciate fully his extraordinary genius, but the portraits and religious works here, ranging from the Italianate *Trinity* to the visionary late *Adoration of the Shepherds*, are a good introduction.

Upstairs, in rooms 12, 14, 15, 15ª, 16 and 27 you confront the greatest painter of Habsburg Spain, **Diego Velázquez** (1599–1660). Born in Portugal, Velázquez became court painter to Felipe IV, whose family is represented in many of the works: "I have found my Titian," Felipe is said to have remarked on his appointment. Velázquez's masterpiece, *Las Meninas*, is displayed alongside studies for the painting: Manet remarked of it, "After this I don't know why the rest of us paint," and the French poet Théophile Gautier asked "But where is the picture?" when he saw it, because it seemed to him a continuation of the room. *Las Hilanderas*, showing the royal tapestry factory at work, *Christ Crucified*, *Los Borrachos* (The Drunkards) and *The Surrender of Breda* (note the compositional device of the lances) are further magnificent works. In fact, almost all of the fifty works on display (around half of the artist's surviving output) warrant close attention. Don't overlook the two small panels of the *Villa Medici*, painted in Rome in 1650, in virtually Impressionist style.

In the adjacent rooms are examples of just about every significant Spanish painter of the seventeenth century, including many of the best works of **Francisco Zurbarán** (1598–1664), **Bartolomé Esteban Murillo** (1618–82), **Alonso Cano** (1601–67), **Juan de Valdes Leal** (1622–60), and **Juan Carreño** (1614–85). Note, in particular, Carreño's portrait of the last Habsburg monarch, the drastically inbred and mentally retarded Carlos II, rendered with terrible realism. There's also a fine selection of works by **José Ribera** (1591–1625), who worked mainly in Naples, and was influenced there by Caravaggio. His masterpieces are considered *The Martyrdom of St Bartholomew* and the dark, realist portrait of *Archimedes*.

Goya

The final suite of Spanish rooms (rooms 32–39 and 85–94) provides an awesome and fabulously complete overview of the works of **Francisco de Goya** (1746–1828), the largest and most valuable collection of his works in the world with some 140 paintings and 500 drawings and engravings. Goya was the greatest painter of Bourbon Spain, a chronicler of Spain in his time and an artist whom many see as the inspiration and forerunner of Impressionism and modern art. He was an enormously versatile artist: contrast the voluptuous *Maja Vestida* and *Maja Desnuda* (The Clothed and Naked Belles) with the horrors depicted in *Dos de Mayo* and *Tres de Mayo* (on-the-spot portrayals of the rebellion against Napoleon in the streets of Madrid and the subsequent reprisals). Then there are the series of pastoral cartoons – designs for tapestries – and the extraordinary *Black Paintings*, a series of murals painted on the walls of his home by the deaf and embittered painter in his old age. His many portraits of his patron, Carlos IV, are remarkable for their lack of any attempt at flattery while those of Queen María Luisa, whom he despised, are downright ugly.

Italian painting

The Prado's early Italian galleries (49, 56b, 60–63b and 75) are distinguished principally by **Fra Angelico**'s *Annunciation* (c. 1445) and by a trio of panels by **Botticelli** (1445–1510). The latter illustrate a deeply unpleasant story from the *Decameron* about a woman hunted by hounds; the fourth panel (in a private collection in the US) gives a happier conclusion.

With the sixteenth-century Renaissance, and especially its Venetian exponents, the collection really comes into its own. The Prado is said to have the most complete collection of Titian and painters from the Venice school in any single museum. There are major works by **Raphael** (1483–1520), including a fabulous *Portrait of a Cardinal*, and epic masterpieces from the Venetians, **Tintoretto** (1518–94), including *The Lavatorio*, bought by Felipe IV when Charles I of England was beheaded and his art collection was auctioned off, and **Veronese** (1528–88), as well as **Caravaggio** (1573–1610). The most important group of works, however, are by **Titian** (1487–1576). These include portraits of the Spanish emperors, *Carlos V* and *Felipe II* (Charles's suit of armour is preserved in the Palacio Real), and a famous, much-reproduced piece of erotica, *Venus, Cupid and the Organist* (two versions are displayed here), a painting originally owned by a bishop.

Flemish, Dutch and German painting

The biggest name in the **early Flemish collection** (rooms 55–58a) is **Hieronymus Bosch** (1450–1516), known in Spain as "El Bosco". The Prado has several of his greatest triptychs: the early-period *Hay Wain*, the middle-period *Garden of Earthly Delights* and the late *Adoration of the Magi* – all familiar from countless reproductions but infinitely more chilling in the original. Bosch's hallucinatory genius for the macabre is at its most extreme in these triptychs, but is reflected here in many more of his works, including three versions of *The Temptations of Saint Anthony* (though only the smallest of these is definitely an original). Don't miss, either, the amazing table top of *The Seven Deadly Sins*.

Bosch's visions find an echo in the works of **Pieter Brueghel the Elder** (1525–69), whose *Triumph of Death* must be one of the most frightening canvases ever painted. Another elusive painter, **Joachim Patinir**, is represented by four of his finest works. From an earlier generation, **Rogier van der Weyden**'s *Deposition* is outstanding; its monumental forms make a fascinating contrast with his miniature-like *Pietà*. There are also important works by Memling, Bouts, Gerard David and Massys.

The collection of over 160 works of **later Flemish and Dutch** art has been imaginatively rehoused in a new suite of twelve rooms on the first floor (rooms 7–11). Grouped by themes, such as religion, daily life, mythology, and landscape, the rooms have been tastefully decorated, while many of the paintings have been given a new lease of life by their restoration to their startling original colours. There are enough works to make an excellent comparison between the flamboyant Counter-Reformation propaganda of Flanders and the more austere bourgeois tastes of Holland.

Rubens (1577–1640) is extensively represented with the beautifully restored *Three Graces*, *The Judgement of Paris* and by a series of eighteen mythological subjects designed for Felipe IV's hunting lodge in El Pardo (though he supervised rather than executed these). There are, too, a fine collection of works by his contemporaries, including **Van Dyck**'s dramatic *Piedad* and his magnificent portrait of himself and Sir Endymion Porter. **Jan Brueghel**'s representations of the five senses and **David Teniers**' scenes of peasant lowlife also merit a closer look. For political reasons, Spanish monarchs collected few works painted from seventeenth-century Protestant Holland; an early **Rembrandt**, *Artemesia*, in which the artist's pregnant wife served as the model is, however, an important exception.

The **German room** (54) on the ground floor is dominated by **Dürer** (1471–1528) and **Lucas Cranach the Elder** (1472–1553). Dürer's magnificent *Adam and Eve* was saved from destruction at the hands of the prudish Carlos III only by the intervention of his court painter, Mengs. The most interesting of Cranach's works are a pair of paintings depicting Carlos V hunting with Ferdinand I of Austria.

The Tesoro del Dauphin and the Casón del Buen Retiro

The museum's basement houses the **Tesoro del Dauphin** (Treasure of the Dauphin), a display of part of the collection of jewels that belonged to the Grand Dauphin Louis, son of Louis XIV and father of Felipe V, Spain's first Bourbon king. The collection includes goblets, cups, trays, glasses and other pieces richly decorated with rubies, emeralds, diamonds, lapis lazuli and other precious stones.

Just east of the Prado is the **Casón del Buen Retiro** (currently undergoing restoration) which used to be a dance hall for the palace of Felipe IV, but is now devoted to nineteenth-century Spanish art. It is included in the entrance ticket to the main museum but, considering the riches which have gone before, is not of compelling interest.

Museo Thyssen-Bornemisza

The **Museo Thyssen-Bornemisza** (Tues–Sun 10am–7pm; the museum has also experimented with opening on Mondays during July & Aug, but this may not be a permanent arrangement, so check beforehand; €4.80; Ⓦ www.museothyssen.org; Ⓜ Banco de España) occupies the old Palacio de Villahermosa, diagonally opposite the Prado, at the end of the Carrera de San Jerónimo. This prestigious site played a large part in Spain's acquisition – for a knock-down $350 million in June 1993 – of what many argue was the world's greatest private art trove after that of the British royals: 700-odd paintings accumulated by father-and-son German-Hungarian industrial magnates. Another trump card was Baron Thyssen's current (fifth) wife, "Tita" Cervera, a former Miss Spain, who steered the works to Spain against the efforts of Britain's Prince Charles, the Swiss and German governments, the Getty foundation, and other suitors.

A terribly kitsch portrait of Tita with a lapdog hangs in the great hall of the museum, alongside those of her husband and King Juan Carlos and Queen Sofía. Pass beyond, however, and you are into seriously premier-league art: **medieval to eighteenth-century** on the top floor, **seventeenth-century Dutch** and **Rococo and Neoclassicism to Fauves and Expressionists** on the first floor, and **Surrealists**, **Pop Art** and the **avant-garde** on ground level. Highlights are legion in a collection that displays an almost stamp-collecting mentality in its examples of nearly every major artist and movement: how the Thyssens got hold of classic works by everyone from Duccio and Holbein, through El Greco and Caravaggio, to Schiele and Rothko, takes your breath away.

The museum had no expense spared on its design – again in the hands of the ubiquitous Rafael Moneo, responsible for the remodelling of Atocha and the current works at the Prado – with stucco walls (Tita insisted on salmon pink) and marble floors. There's a handy cafeteria and restaurant in the basement which allows re-entry, so long as you get your hand stamped at the exit desk. The basement is also home to a temporary exhibition space, which has staged a number of interesting and highly successful shows (separate entry fee of €3.60 and often with extended opening hours). There's also a shop, where you can buy the first instalments of the fifteen-volume catalogue of the baron's collection as well as the more modest, but informative, illustrated **guide** to the museum (€10.80). Around half of the collection is now on show, either here, or at the Monestir de Pedralbes in Barcelona, which houses around eighty works of sacred art (see p.720). Plans are afoot to extend the museum into some of the nearby buildings to accommodate some of Tita's own collection.

European old masters: the second floor

Take a lift to the second floor and you will find yourself at the chronological start of the museum's collections: European painting (and some sculpture) from the fourteenth to eighteenth century. The core of these collections was accumulated in the 1920s and 1930s by the present baron's father, Heinrich, who was a friend of the art critics Bernard Berenson and Max Friedländer.

He was clearly well advised. The early paintings include incredibly good (and rare) devotional panels by the Sienese painter **Duccio di Buoninsegna**, and the Flemish artists, **Jan van Eyck** and **Rogier van der Weyden**. You then move into a fabulous array of Renaissance portraits (Room 5), which include three of the very greatest of the period: **Ghirlandaio**'s *Portrait of Giovanna Tornabuoni*, **Hans Holbein**'s *Portrait of Henry VIII* (the only one of many variants in existence which is definitely genuine), and **Raphael**'s *Portrait of a Young Man*. *A Spanish Infanta* by **Juan de Flandes** may represent the first of Henry VIII's wives, Catherine of Aragón, while the *Young Knight* by **Carpaccio** is one of the earliest known full-length portraits. Beyond these is a collection of **Dürers** and **Cranachs** to rival that in the Prado, and as you progress through this extraordinary panoply, display cases along the corridor contain scarcely less spectacular works of sculpture, ceramics and gold- and silverwork.

Next in line, in Room 11, are **Titian** and **Tintoretto**, and three paintings by **El Greco**, one early, two late, which make an interesting comparison with each other and with those in the Prado. **Caravaggio**'s monumental *St Catherine of Alexandria* is the centrepiece of an important display of works by followers of this innovator of chiaroscuro. And finally, as you reach the eighteenth century, there is a room containing three flawless **Canaletto** views of Venice.

Americans, Impressionists and Expressionists: the first floor

The present baron, Hans Heinrich Thyssen, began collecting, according to his own account, to fill the gaps in his late father's collection, after it was split among his siblings. He, too, started with old masters – his father thought nineteenth- and twentieth-century art was worthless – but in the 1960s started on German Expressionists, closely followed by Cubists, Futurists, Vorticists and De Stijl, and also American art of the nineteenth century. The first floor, then, is largely down to him.

After a comprehensive round of seventeenth-century Dutch painting of various genres, Rococo and Neoclassicism, you reach the **American painting** in rooms 29 and 30. The collection, one of the best outside the US, concentrates on landscapes and includes James Goodwyn Clonney's wonderful *Fishing Party on Long Island Sound*, and works by James Whistler, Winslow Homer and John Singer Sargent. It is followed by a group of European **Romantics** and **Realists**, including Constable's *The Lock*, bought not so long ago for £10.8 million, forming one of a group of British representatives at the museum, along with a Henry Moore (Room 45) and a Sisley (Room 32).

Impressionism and **post-Impressionism** are another strong point of the collection – with works by Manet, Monet and Renoir from the former and Gauguin, Degas, Lautrec and Cézanne from the latter (Room 33) – and it is especially strong in the choice of paintings by Vincent van Gogh, which include one of his last and most gorgeous works, *Les Vessenots*. **Expressionist** representatives, meanwhile, include an unusually pastoral Edvard Munch, *Evening* (Room 35), Egon Schiele's Mondrian-like *Houses on the River*, and some stunning work by Ernst Ludwig Kirchner, Wassily Kandinsky and Max Beckmann.

Avant-gardes: the ground floor

Works on the ground floor run from the beginning of the twentieth century through to around 1970. The good baron doesn't, apparently, like contemporary art: "If they can throw colours, I can be free to duck," he explained, following the gallery's opening.

The most interesting work in his "experimental avant-garde" sections is from the **Cubists**. There is an inspired, side-by-side hanging of parallel studies by Picasso (*Man with a Clarinet*), Braque and Mondrian (Room 41). Later choices – a scattering of Joan Miró, Jackson Pollock, Magritte and Dalí, Rauschenberg and Liechtenstein – do less justice to their artists and movements, though there is a great work by Edward Hopper, *Hotel Room*, and a fascinating **Lucian Freud**, *Portrait of Baron Thyssen*, posed in front of the Watteau *Pierrot* hanging upstairs.

Centro de Arte Reina Sofía

It is fortunate that the **Centro de Arte Reina Sofía** (Mon & Wed–Sat 10am–9pm, Sun 10am–2.30pm; €3, free on Sat after 2.30pm and Sun; ⓦmuseoreinasofia.mcu.es; ⓜAtocha), facing Atocha station at the end of Paseo del Prado, keeps slightly different opening hours and days to its neighbours. For this leading exhibition space and permanent gallery of modern Spanish art – its centrepiece is Picasso's greatest picture, *Guernica* – is another essential stop on the Madrid art circuit, and one that really mustn't be seen after a Prado-Thyssen overdose.

The museum, a vast former hospital, is a kind of Madrid response to the Pompidou centre in Paris. Transparent lifts shuttle visitors up the outside of the building, whose levels feature a cinema, excellent art book and design shops, a print, music and photographic library, a restaurant, bar and café in the basement and a peaceful inner courtyard garden, as well as the exhibition halls and the permanent collection of twentieth-century art (second and fourth floors). Like the other two great art museums it too has plans to extend – here the French architect Jean Nouvel is supervising a scheme which will add a state-of-the-art extension behind the main building and will increase the floor space by 55 percent.

The permanent collection

It is for **Picasso's Guernica** that most visitors come to the Reina Sofía, and rightly so. Superbly displayed, this icon of twentieth-century Spanish art and politics carries a shock that defies all familiarity. Picasso painted it in response to the bombing of the Basque town of Gernika by the German Luftwaffe, acting in concert with Franco, in the Spanish Civil War. In the preliminary studies, displayed around the room, you can see how he developed its symbols – the dying horse, the woman mourning her dead, the bull, the sun, the flower, the light bulb – and then return to the painting to marvel at how he made it all work.

The work was first exhibited in Paris in 1937, as part of a Spanish Republican Pavilion in the Expo there, and was then loaned to the Museum of Modern Art in New York, until, as Picasso put it, Spain had rid itself of fascist rule. The artist never lived to see that time but in 1981, following the restoration of democracy, the painting was, amid much controversy, moved to Madrid to hang (as Picasso had stipulated) in the Prado. Its recent transfer to the Reina Sofía in 1992, again prompted much soul-searching and protest, though for anyone who saw it in the old Prado annexe, it looks truly liberated in its present setting.

Guernica hangs midway around the permanent collection on the second floor, although Picasso himself is actually a starting point: symbolically, no painter represented here was born before Picasso (in 1881). It is preceded by strong sections on **Cubism** and the **Paris School**, in the first of which Picasso is again well represented, alongside an intriguing straight Cubist work by Salvador Dalí. There are also good collections of other avant-garde Spaniards of the 1920s and 1930s, including Juan Gris.

In the post-*Guernica* halls, **Dalí**'s more familiar Surrealism seems trite and **Miró** less engaging than usual. The final rooms are stimulating: entitled **"Proposals"**, they comprise an evolving display of contemporary art, both Spanish and foreign.

The Spanish realists, such as **Antonio López**, are on the fourth floor, where you will find a **Francis Bacon** and a **Henry Moore**, along with interesting works by **Tapiès** and **Chillida**.

Parque del Retiro and around

When you get tired of sightseeing, Madrid's many parks are great places to escape for a few hours. The most central and most popular of them is **El Retiro**, a delightful mix of formal gardens and wider open spaces. Nearby, in addition to the Prado, Thyssen-Bornemisza and Reina Sofía galleries, are a number of the city's **smaller museums**, plus the startlingly peaceful **Jardines Botánicos**.

Parque del Retiro

Originally the grounds of a royal retreat (*retiro*) and designed in the French style, the **Parque del Retiro** (Ⓜ Retiro) has been public property for more than a hundred years. In its 330 acres you can jog (there is a council-sponsored track), row in the lake (you can rent boats by the Monumento a Alfonso XII), picnic (though officially not on the grass), have your fortune told, and – above all – promenade. The busiest day is Sunday, when half of Madrid, spouses, in-laws and kids, turn out for the *paseo*. Dressed for show, the families stroll around among the various activities, nodding at neighbours and building up an appetite for a long Sunday lunch.

Strolling aside, there's almost always something going on in the park, including a good programme of **concerts** and **ferias** organized by the city council. Concerts tend to be held in the Quiosco de Música in the north of the park. The most popular of the fairs is the *Feria del Libro* (Book Fair), held in early June, when every publisher and half the country's bookshops set up stalls and

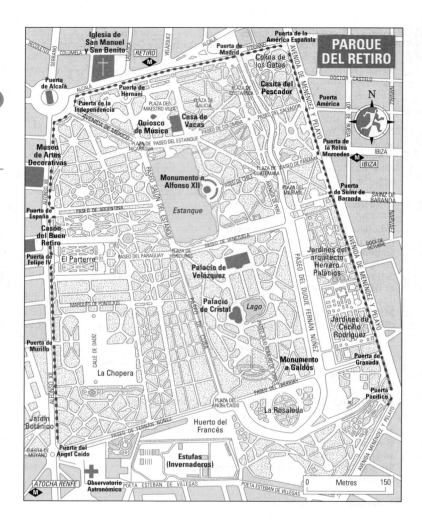

offer a 25-percent discount on their wares. At weekends there are **puppet shows** by the Puerta de Alcalá entrance (1pm, 7pm & 8pm) and on Sundays, you can often watch groups of Peruvian musicians or Catalans performing their counting dance, the **sardana**.

Travelling art exhibitions are frequently housed in the beautiful **Palacio de Velázquez** (June–Sept Mon & Wed–Sat 11am–8pm, Sun 11am–4pm; Oct–May Mon & Wed–Sat 10am–6pm, Sun 10am–4pm; free) and the nearby **Palacio de Cristal** (during exhibitions same hours; ☎915 746 614 for information) and **Casa de Vacas** (daily 10.30am–2.30pm & 4–8pm, closed Aug; free). Look out, too, for **El Ángel Caído** (Fallen Angel), the world's only public statue to Lucifer, in the south of the park. A number of **stalls and cafés** along the Salón del Estanque sell drinks, *bocadillos* and *pipas* (sunflower seeds), and there are terrazas, too, for *horchata* and *granizados*. The park has a safe reputation, at least by day; in the late evening it's best not to wander alone and there are plans to close the park completely at night because of an increase in petty vandalism. Note also that the area east of La Chopera is known as a cruising ground for gay prostitutes.

Puerta de Alcalá to San Jerónimo: some minor museums

Leaving the park at the northwest corner takes you to the Plaza de la Independencia, in the centre of which is one of the two remaining gates from the old city walls. Built in the late eighteenth century, the **Puerta de Alcalá** was the biggest in Europe at that time and, like the bear and bush, has become one of the city's monumental emblems.

South from here, you pass the **Museo de Artes Decorativas** (Tues–Fri 9.30am–3pm, Sat & Sun 10am–2pm; €2.40, free on Sun; ⓜBanco de España/Retiro), which has its entrance on c/Montalbán 12. The furniture and decorations here are not very thrilling but there are some superb *azulejos* and other decorative ceramics.

A couple of blocks west, in a corner of the Naval Ministry at c/Montalbán 2, is a **Museo Naval** (Tues–Sun 10.30am–1.30pm, closed mid-July to end of Aug; free; ⓜBanco de España), strong, as you might expect, on models, charts and navigational aids from or relating to the Spanish voyages of discovery. The army has its museum, the **Museo del Ejército**, just to the south of here at c/Méndez Núñez 1 (Tues–Sun 10am–2pm; €0.60, free on Sat; ⓜRetiro). The museum is likely to be moved to the Alcázar at Toledo (see p.161) in the future as the building features as part of the Prado extension plans. It is a traditional display, packed with arms and armour (including a sword of El Cid and *conquistador* breastplates), and models and memorabilia of various battles, from earliest times to the Civil War – in which Franco, here, remains the good guy.

South again, past the Prado's Casón del Buen Retiro annexe (part of the original Retiro palace, see p.104), is **San Jerónimo el Real** (Mon–Fri 8am–1.30pm & 6–8pm, Sat & Sun 9am–1.30pm & 6.30–8pm, Oct–July opens one hour earlier in the afternoon), Madrid's society church, where in 1975 Juan Carlos (like his predecessors) was crowned. Opposite is the **Real Academía Española de la Lengua** (Royal Language Academy), whose job it is to make sure that the Spanish language is not corrupted by foreign or otherwise unsuitable words; the results are entrusted to their official dictionary – a work that bears virtually no relation to the Spanish you'll hear spoken on the streets.

The botanical gardens and Atocha

Immediately south of the Prado are the delightful, shaded **Jardines Botánicos** (daily 10am–dusk; €1.50). Opened in 1781 by Carlos III (known as *El Alcalde* – "the mayor" – for his urban improvement programmes), they once contained over 30,000 plants. The numbers are down these days, though the gardens were well renovated in the 1980s, after years of neglect, and the worldwide collection of flora is fascinating for any amateur botanist; don't miss the hothouse with its tropical collection and amazing cacti. Under an edict issued when the gardens were opened, *madrileños* are still theoretically entitled to help themselves to cuttings of any plant or medicinal herb.

On the other side of the botanical gardens is the sloping Cuesta de Moyano, lined with **bookstalls**; though it's at its busiest on Sundays, some of the stalls are open every day. Across the way, the **Estación de Atocha** is worth a look even if you're not travelling out of Madrid. It's actually two stations, old and new: the former, a glorious 1880s glasshouse, was revamped in the early 1990s as a kind of tropical garden. It's a wonderful sight from the walkways above, and train buffs and architects will want to take a look at the high-speed AVE trains (Sevilla in two and a half hours) and the station beyond.

Also in this area, at c/Alfonso XII, is the **Museo Nacional de Antropología/Etnología** (Tues–Sat 10am–7.30pm, Sun 10am–2pm; €3, free Sat after 2.30pm & Sun), designed to give an overview of different cultures of the world, in particular those intertwined with Spanish history. The most unusual exhibits are to be found in a side room on the ground floor – a macabre collection of deformed skulls, a Guanche (the original inhabitants of the Canary Islands) mummy and the skeleton of a circus giant (2.35m tall). A little further to the east, the **Real Fábrica de Tapices** at c/Fuenterrabia 2 (Mon–Fri 9am–12.30pm, closed Aug; €1.50; Ⓜ Menéndez Pelayo) still turns out handmade tapestries, many of them based on the Goya cartoons in the Prado. They are fabulously expensive, but the entrance fee is a bargain if you ask for a tour of the fascinating manufacturing process. Lastly, to the south of this area is Parque Enrique Tierno Galván (Ⓜ Méndez Alvaro), which houses the **Planetarium** (shows: Tues–Fri 5.30pm & 6.45pm, Sat & Sun 11.30am, 12.45pm, 5.30pm & 6.45pm; €3) and the futuristic Imax cinema (see p.138).

The Gran Vía, Chueca and Malasaña

The **Gran Vía**, Madrid's great thoroughfare, runs from Plaza de Cibeles to Plaza de España, effectively dividing the old city to the south from the newer parts northwards. Permanently jammed with traffic and crowded with shoppers and sightseers, it's the commercial heart of the city, and – if you spare the time to look up – quite a monument in its own right, with its turn-of-the-twentieth century, palace-like banks and offices, and the huge hand-painted posters of the cinemas. Look out, too, for the towering **Telefónica** building, which was the chief observation post for the Republican artillery during the Civil War, when the Nationalist front line stretched across the Casa de Campo to the west.

North of the Telefónica, c/Fuencarral heads north to the Glorieta de Bilbao. To either side of this street are two of Madrid's most characterful *barrios*: **Chueca**, to the east, and **Malasaña**, to the west. Their chief appeal lies in an amazing concentration of bars, restaurants and, especially, nightlife. However, there are a few reasons – bars included – to wander around here by day.

Chueca

Plaza de Chueca (Ⓜ Chueca) once teetered on the verge of infamy, owing to its popularity with drug dealers and prostitutes. However, most of the addicts have been moved on and there is now a strong neighbourhood feel, with kids and grannies giving a semblance of innocence by day, and a lively gay scene springing into action at night. It is also fronted by one of the best old-style *vermut* bars in the city, *Bodega Ángel Sierra*, on c/Gravina at the northwest corner. The whole area has become somewhat gentrified in recent years with the rise of a host of stylish bars, cafés and restaurants many of which have been established by the local gay community.

From Plaza de Chueca east to **Paseo Recoletos** (the beginning of the long Paseo de la Castellana) are some of the city's most enticing streets. Offbeat restaurants, small private art galleries, and odd corner shops are to be found here in abundance and the **c/Almirante** has some of the city's most fashionable clothes shops too. On the parallel c/Prim, **ONCE**, the national association for the blind, has its headquarters. ONCE is financed by a lottery, for which the blind work as ticket sellers, and many come here to collect their allocation of tickets. The lottery has become such a major money-spinner that the organization is now one of the wealthiest businesses in Spain; oddly, perhaps, it is also the sponsor of one of the world's top cycling teams.

To the south, the Ministry of Culture fronts the **Plaza del Rey**, which is also worth a look for the other odd buildings surrounding it, especially the **Casa de las Siete Chimeneas** (House of Seven Chimneys), which is supposedly haunted by a mistress of Felipe II who disappeared in mysterious circumstances.

To the north, on the edge of the Santa Bárbara *barrio*, on c/Fernando VI, is the **Sociedad de Autores** (Society of Authors), housed in the only significant *modernista* building in Madrid, designed by José Grasés Riera, part of the Gaudí school. Nearby, the **Museo Romántico**, at c/San Mateo 13 (Tues–Sat 9am–2.45pm, Sun 10am–1.15pm, closed Aug; €2.40, free on Sun; ⓜTribunal), has its admirers for its late-Romantic-era furnishings, though casual visitors are unlikely to be impressed. The **Museo Municipal** at c/Fuencarral 78 (Tues–Fri 9.30am–8pm, July & Aug 9.30am-2.30pm, Sat & Sun 10am–2pm; €1.80, free on Wed & Sun; ⓜTribunal) is more interesting for its models and maps of old Madrid, which show the incredible expansion of the city in the last century. The building itself has a superb Churrigueresque facade by Pedro de Ribera.

Malasaña

The heart, in all senses, of Malasaña is the **Plaza Dos de Mayo**, named after the insurrection against Napoleonic forces on May 2, 1808; the rebellion and its aftermath are depicted in a series of Goyas at the Prado (see p.102). The surrounding district bears the name of one of the martyrs of the uprising, fifteen-year-old Manuela Malasaña, who is also commemorated in a street (as are several other heroes of the time). On the night of May 1 all of Madrid shuts down to honour its heroes, and the plaza is the scene of festivities lasting well into the night.

More recently, the quarter was the focus of the *movida madrileña*, the "happening scene" of the late 1970s and early 1980s. As the country relaxed after the death of Franco and the city developed into a thoroughly modern capital under the leadership of the late mayor, Galván, Malasaña became the mecca of the young. Bars appeared behind every doorway, drugs were sold openly in the streets, and there was an extraordinary atmosphere of new-found freedom. Times have changed – and *chocolate* (dope) sellers are less tolerated by residents and police alike. A good deal of renovation has been going on in recent years, but the *barrio* retains a somewhat alternative – nowadays rather grungey – feel, with its bar custom spilling onto the streets, and an ever-lively scene in the Plaza Dos de Mayo terrazas.

The corner of c/Barceló and c/Fuencarral has become the centre of the *litrona* scene and a bit of an eyesore to boot. On Friday and Saturday nights hundreds of under-age drinkers come here with their *litronas* – litre bottles of coke or soft drinks to mix with spirits - and *calimochos* – a mixture of cheap red wine and Coca-Cola – and create an impromptu open-air terraza in the plaza only to leave the whole area strewn with bottles and rubbish the next morning.

There are no regular sights in this quarter but the streets have an interest of their own and some fine traditional bars – *Casa Camacho* at c/San Andrés 2 is a great place for *vermut*. There are also some wonderful old shop signs and architectural details, best of all the **old pharmacy** on the corner of c/San Andrés and c/San Vicente Ferrer, with its irresistible 1920s *azulejo* scenes depicting cures for diarrhoea, headaches and suchlike.

Plaza de España, Parque del Oeste and Casa de Campo

The **Plaza de España** (ⓜ Plaza de España), at the west end of Gran Vía, was home, until the flurry of corporate building in the north of Madrid, to two of the city's tallest buildings – the **Torre de Madrid**, which has a top-storey bar, and the **Edificio de España**. These rather stylish 1950s buildings look over an elaborate monument to Cervantes in the middle of the square, which in turn overlooks the bewildered-looking bronze figures of Don Quixote and Sancho Panza.

The plaza itself is a little on the seedy side especially at night. However, to its north, **c/Martín de los Heros** is a lively place, day and night, with three of the city's best cinemas, and behind them the **Centro Princesa**, with shops, clubs, bars and a 24-hour branch of the ubiquitous VIPS – just the place to have your film developed at 4am, or a bite to eat before heading on to a small-hours club. Up the steps opposite the Centro Princesa is c/Conde Duque, dominated by the massive former barracks of the royal guard, constructed in the early eighteenth century by Pedro de Ribera. The barracks have been turned into a dynamic cultural centre, **El Centro Cultural de Conde Duque** (Tues–Sat 10am–2pm & 5.30–9pm, Sun & holidays 10.30am–2.30pm; free), which is home to the city's collection of contemporary art; it also hosts a variety of temporary exhibitions, and stages concerts, plays and dance as part of the *Veranos de la Villa* season. Just to the east of this, the **Plaza de las Comendadoras** – named after the convent that occupies one side of the square – is a tranquil space bordered by a variety of interesting craft shops, bars and cafés.

A block to the west is the **Museo Cerralbo**, c/Ventura Rodríguez 17 (Tues–Sat 9.30am–2.30pm, July closes 2pm; Sun 10am–2pm; closed Aug; €2.40, free on Wed & Sun; ⓜ Ventura Rodríguez), an elegant mansion endowed with its collections by the Marqués de Cerralbo. The rooms, stuffed with paintings, furniture, armour and artefacts, provide insights into the lifestyle of the nineteenth-century aristocracy, though there is little of individual note.

Parque del Oeste – and Goya's Ermita frescoes

The **Parque del Oeste** stretches northwest from the Plaza de España, following the railway tracks of Príncipe Pío up to the suburbs of Moncloa and Ciudad Universitaria (see below). On its south side, five minutes' walk from the square, is the **Templo de Debod** (April–Sept Tues–Fri 10am–2pm & 6–8pm, Sat & Sun 10am–2pm; Oct–March Tues–Fri 9.45am–1.45pm & 4.15–6.15pm, Sat & Sun 10am–2pm; €1.80, free on Wed & Sun), a fourth-century BC Egyptian temple given to Spain in recognition of the work done by Spanish engineers on the Aswan High Dam (which inundated its original site). Reconstructed here stone by stone, it seems comically incongruous but provides a good concert venue nonetheless. In summer, there are numerous terrazas in the park, while, year-round, a **teleférico** (April–Sept daily 11am–2.30pm & 4.30pm–dusk; Oct–March Sat, Sun & holidays noon–2.30pm & 4.30pm–dusk; €2.60 single, €3.60 return; ⓜ Argüelles/Ventura Rodríguez) shuttles its passengers high over the river from Paseo del Pintor Rosales to the middle of the Casa de Campo (see opposite), where there's a bar/restaurant with pleasant views back towards the city.

Rail lines from commuter towns to the north of Madrid terminate at the **Príncipe Pío** (Estación del Norte), a quietly spectacular construction of white enamel, steel and glass which enjoyed a starring role in Warren Beatty's film *Reds*. About 300m from the station along the Paseo de la Florida is the *Casa Mingo* (see "Restaurants"), an institution for chicken and cider take-outs for the Casa de Campo, and, almost alongside it, at Glorieta de la Florida 5, the **Ermita de San Antonio de la Florida** (Tues–Fri 10am–2pm & 4–8pm, closed afternoons July 13–23; Sat & Sun 10am–2pm; €1.80, free on Wed & Sun; ⓜPríncipe Pío). If you can, go on Saturdays, when there are guided tours in English three times a day. This little church on a Greek cross plan was built by an Italian, Felipe Fontana, between 1792 and 1798, and decorated by **Goya**, whose frescoes are the only reason to visit. In the dome is a depiction of a miracle performed by St Anthony of Padua. Around it, heavenly bodies of angels and cherubs hold back curtains to reveal the main scene: the saint resurrecting a dead man to give evidence in favour of a prisoner falsely accused of murder (the saint's father). Beyond this central group, Goya created a gallery of highly realist characters – their models were court and society figures – while for a lesser fresco of the angels adoring the Trinity in the apse, he took prostitutes as his models. The *ermita* also houses the artist's mausoleum.

Moncloa

The wealthy suburb of **Moncloa** contains the Spanish prime ministerial home and is worth a visit even if you are not using the bus terminal for El Pardo and El Escorial (see p.99). The metro will bring you out opposite the imposing Ministry of Defence building and the impressive Arco de la Victoria, marking Napoleon's exit from the capital. Beyond this lies the leafy expanses of the Parque del Oeste and the campuses of the **Ciudad Universitaria**. During term time, the end of each day sees the area become one big student party, with huddles of picnickers and singing groups under the trees. Take the Plaza de Moncloa metro exit and the path on your right through the trees will lead you to the **Mirador del Faro** (Tues–Sun: June–Aug 11am–1.45pm & 5.30–8.45pm; Sept–May 10.30am–2pm & 5.30–8pm; €1.25), a futuristic 92-metre-high tower with stunning views over the city and to the mountains beyond. Just past this, with its main entrance on Avda. Reyes Católicos 6, the **Museo de América** (Tues–Sat 10am–3pm, Sun 10am–2.30pm; €3, free on Sat after 2pm and Sun) contains a fine collection of artefacts, ceramics and silverware from Spain's former colonies in Latin America. The highlight is the fabulous Quimbayas treasure – a breathtaking collection of gold objects and figures from the Quimbaya culture of Colombia.

Casa de Campo

If you want to jog, play tennis, swim, picnic, go to the fairground or see pandas, then the **Casa de Campo** is the place to head. This enormous expanse of heath and scrub is in parts surprisingly wild for a place so easily accessible from the city; other sections have been tamed for more conventional pastimes. Far larger and more natural than the city parks, the Casa de Campo can be reached by metro (ⓜBatán/Lago), various buses (#33 from Príncipe Pío is the easiest), or the cable car mentioned above. The walk from the Príncipe Pío station via the Puente del Rey isn't too strenuous either.

Throughout the park there are picnic tables and café-bars, a **jogging track** with exercise posts, a municipal open-air **swimming pool** (daily June–Sept 10.30am–8pm; €3) close to Metro Lago, tennis courts, and rowing boats to hire on the **lake** (again near Metro Lago).

Sightseeing attractions include a **Zoo** (daily 10.30am–dusk; €11.20; ⓦwww.zoomadrid.com), which is perennially popular and has an impressive aquarium. Adjoining it is a large and recently modernized amusement park, the **Parque de Atracciones** (July & Aug daily noon–midnight, Fri & Sat till 2am; Sept–June daily noon–11pm, Sat till 1am; access only €4.20, €18.60 for a day ticket, which includes most rides, children €11.10; ⓦwww.parqueatracciones.es), with its assorted restaurants and cafés; during the summer, a variety of **concerts** are held in the auditorium within. Both are easiest reached by bus (#33 and #65 from Príncipe Pío), which will take you right to the gates; the Batán metro station is a ten-minute walk through scrubland. Be warned that many of the **main access roads** through the park have been taken over by prostitutes (banished from the city streets by the council), and can become crowded with kerb-crawlers, both day and night.

Salamanca and the Paseo de la Castellana

Salamanca, the area north of the Parque del Retiro, is a smart address for apartments and, even more so, for shops. The *barrio* is the haunt of *pijos* – universally denigrated rich kids – and the grid of streets between c/Goya and c/José Ortega y Gasset contains most of the city's designer emporiums. The buildings are largely modern and undistinguished, though there is a scattering of museums and galleries that might tempt you up here, in particular the Lázaro Galdiano, the pick of Madrid's smaller museums.

Taking the area from south to north, the first point of interest is **Plaza de Colón** (ⓜColón), endowed at street level with a statue of Columbus (Cristóbal Colón) and some huge stone blocks arranged as a megalithic monument to the discovery of the Americas. Below it is the 1970s **Centro Cultural Villa de Madrid**, which is still a good place for film and theatre and occasional exhibitions (Tues–Sat 10am–9pm Sat & Sun 10am–2pm). Across the square, if your taste runs to tableaux of *matadores* being gored, or vain attempts to recognize Juan Carlos, there is diversion at Paseo de Recoletos 41 in the **Museo de Cera** (Mon–Fri 10.30am–2.30pm & 4.30–8.30pm, Sat & Sun 10.30am–8.30pm; €9; ⓜColón), a pretty lamentable wax museum.

Off the square, too, with its entrance at c/Serrano 13, is the **Museo Arqueológico Nacional** (Tues–Sat 9.30am–8.30pm, closes 6.30pm in July & Aug; Sun 9.30am–2.30pm; €3, free Sat 2.30–8.30pm & Sun; ⓜSerrano). As the national collection, this has some impressive pieces, among them the celebrated Celto-Iberian busts known as *La Dama de Elche* and *La Dama de Baza*, and a wonderfully rich hoard of Visigothic treasures found at Toledo. The exhibition, however, is very old-fashioned and rooms are often closed for somnolent rearrangement, sometimes at very short notice. In the gardens, downstairs to the left of the main entrance, is a reconstruction of the Altamira Caves, with their prehistoric wall paintings.

The **Museo Lázaro Galdiano** (Tues–Sun 10am–2pm, July & Sept guided tours in the evenings 7-11pm, closed Aug; €3, free Sat; ⓦwww.flg.es; ⓜGregorio Marañon/Rubén Darío; closed until the end of 2002 for extension and refurbishment) is some way north at c/Serrano 122. This former private collection was given to the state by José Galdiano in 1948 and spreads over the four floors and 37 rooms of his former home. It is a vast jumble of art works, with some very dodgy attributions, but includes some really exquisite and valuable pieces. Among painters represented are El Greco, Bosch, Gerard David, Dürer and Rembrandt, as well as a host of Spanish artists, including Berruguete, Murillo, Zurbarán, Velázquez and Goya. Other exhibits include a collection of clocks and watches, many of them once owned by Carlos V.

Not far to the west of here, across the Paseo de la Castellana, is another enjoyable gallery, the **Museo Sorolla**, c/General Martínez Campos 37 (Tues–Sat 10am–3pm, July & Aug closes 2.30pm; Sun 10am–2pm; €2.40, free Sun; Ⓜ Gregorio Marañon/Iglesia). This is a large collection of work by the painter Joaquín Sorolla (1863–1923), displayed in his old home and studio; the best paintings are striking, impressionistic plays on light and texture. The house itself, with its cool and shady Andalucian-style courtyard and gardens, is worth the visit alone.

A little to the north just off the Paseo de la Castellana on c/José Gutiérrez Abascal is the **Museo de Ciencias Naturales**, or Natural History Museum (Tues–Fri 10am–6pm, Sat 10am–8pm, Sun 10am–2.30pm; €2.40; Ⓜ Nuevos Ministerios), one of the most interactive of the traditional museums in the city centre, with audiovisual displays on the evolution of life on earth and plenty of dinosaur exhibits. Further north along the Paseo de la Castellana, you reach the **Zona Azca** (Ⓜ Nuevos Ministerios/Santiago Bernabéu), one of Madrid's newest business quarters, with its tallest skyscraper – the 43-storey Torre Picasso (designed by Minori Yamasaki) – and corporate headquarters. Just beyond it, and easily the most famous sight up here, is the magnificent **Santiago Bernabéu** football stadium, home of Real Madrid.

El Pardo

Franco had his principal residence at **EL PARDO**, a former royal hunting ground, 9km northwest of central Madrid. A garrison still remains at the town – where most of the Generalísmo's staff were based – but the stigma of the place has lessened over the years, and it is now a popular excursion for *madrileños*, who come here for long lunches in the terraza restaurants, or to play tennis or swim at one of the nearby sports centres.

The tourist focus is the **Palacio del Pardo** (April–Sept Mon–Sat 10.30am–6pm, Sun 9.30am–1.30pm; Oct–March Mon–Sat 10.30am–5pm, Sun 10am–1.30pm; closed occasionally for official visits; guided tours €4.80, free Wed for EU citizens), rebuilt by the Bourbons on the site of a hunting lodge of Carlos V. The interior is pleasant enough, with its chapel and theatre, a portrait of Isabel la Católica by her court painter Juan de Flandes, and an excellent collection of tapestries, many after the Goya cartoons in the Prado. Guides detail the uses Franco made of the *palacio*, but pass over some of his stranger habits. He kept by his bed, for instance, the mummified hand of Santa Teresa of Ávila. Tickets to the palace are also valid for the **Casita del Príncipe** (closed for refurbishment), though this cannot be entered from the gardens and you will need to return to the main road. Like the *casitas* (pavilions) at El Escorial, this was built by Juan de Villanueva, and is highly ornate.

You can reach El Pardo by local **bus** (every fifteen minutes until midnight from the bus terminal at Metro Moncloa), or by any city **taxi**.

Restaurants and tapas bars

The sections below review Madrid's best places for **eating and drinking** and include bars, cafés, cervecerías (beer halls), *marisquerías* (seafood bars) and *restaurantes*. They have been divided simply between "**tapas bars**" and "**restaurants**", depending on whether they concentrate more on bar food or sit-down meals. Sometimes this division is arbitrary, as many places have a bar area, where you can get tapas, together with a more formal *comedor* (canteen) or restaurant

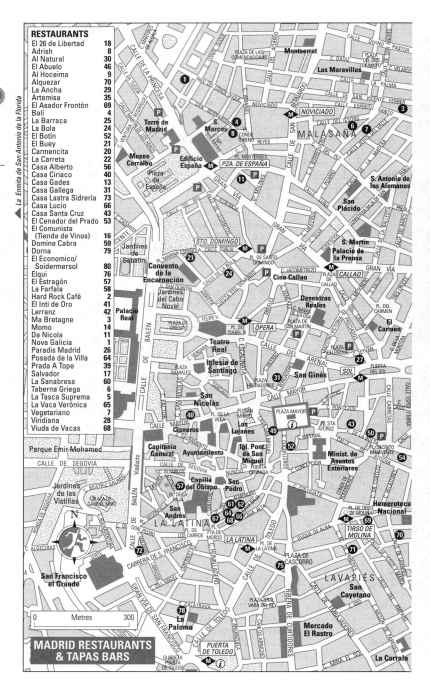

◄ La Ermita de San Antonio de la Florida

RESTAURANTS

El 26 de Libertad	18
Adrish	8
Al Natural	30
El Abuelo	46
Al Hoceima	9
Alquezar	70
La Ancha	29
Artemisa	35
El Asador Frontón	69
Bali	4
La Barraca	25
La Bola	24
El Botín	52
El Buey	21
Carmencita	20
La Carreta	22
Casa Alberto	56
Casa Ciriaco	40
Casa Gades	13
Casa Gallega	31
Casa Lastra Sidrería	73
Casa Lucio	66
Casa Santa Cruz	43
El Cenador del Prado	53
El Comunista	
(Tienda de Vinos)	16
Domine Cabra	59
Dorna	79
El Economico/	
Soidermersol	80
Elqui	76
El Estragón	57
La Farfala	58
Hard Rock Café	2
El Inti de Oro	41
Lerranz	42
Ma Bretagne	3
Momo	14
Da Nicola	11
Nova Galicia	1
Paradis Madrid	26
Posada de la Villa	64
Prada A Tope	39
Salvador	17
La Sanabresa	60
Taberna Griega	6
La Tasca Suprema	5
La Vaca Verónica	65
Vegetariano	7
Viridiana	28
Viuda de Vacas	68

MADRID RESTAURANTS & TAPAS BARS

0   Metres   300

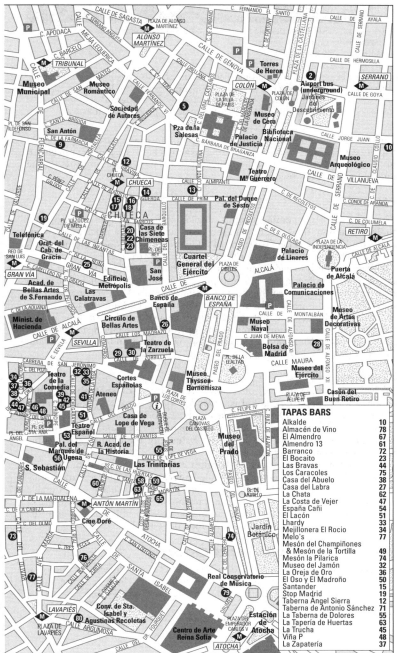

TAPAS BARS

Alkalde	10
Almacén de Vino	78
El Almendro	67
Almendro 13	61
Barranco	72
El Bocaito	23
Las Bravas	44
Los Caracoles	75
Casa del Abuelo	38
Casa del Labra	27
La Chata	62
La Costa de Vejer	47
España Cañí	54
El Lacón	51
Lhardy	33
Mejillonera El Rocio	34
Melo's	77
Mesón del Champiñones & Mesón de la Tortilla	49
Mesón la Pilarica	74
Museo del Jamón	32
La Oreja de Oro	36
El Oso y El Madroño	50
Santander	15
Stop Madrid	19
Taberna Angel Sierra	12
Taberna de Antonio Sánchez	71
La Taberna de Dolores	55
La Tapería de Huertas	63
La Trucha	45
Viña P	48
La Zapatería	37

Estación Sur de Autobuses

out the back or upstairs. At almost any of our recommendations you could happily eat your fill – money permitting – though at bars *madrileños* usually eat just a tapa or share a *ración* of the house speciality, then move on to repeat the procedure down the road.

Hours

The hours for having **cañas y tapas** (drinks and tapas) are from around noon to 2pm, and 8pm to 10pm, though most bars will do you a snack at any hour of the day, and they generally stay open till midnight or beyond. Summer hours are generally later than winter, and Sundays are early to bed.

Restaurant meals (*comidas*) are taken very late: few *madrileños* will start lunch before 2pm or dinner much before 10pm, and if you turn up much earlier you may find yourself alone, or the restaurant (in the evening) not yet open. On the other hand, most people do arrive for dinner by 10.30pm; Madrid being Madrid, though, there are quite a number of late-night options and the listings magazines all have sections for restaurants open past midnight (*después de media noche/de madrugada*). Many restaurants close on Sundays and/or Mondays and for all or part of July and August.

Cuisines

Madrid's restaurants and bars offer every regional style of **Spanish cooking**: Castilian for roasts (*horno de asar* is a wood-burning oven) and stews (such as the meat and chickpea *cocido*), *gallego* for seafood, *andaluz* for fried fish, Levantine (Valencia/Alicante) for paella and other rice (*arroz*)-based dishes, Asturian for winter stews like *fabada* and Basque for the ultimate gastronomy (and correspondingly high prices).

Over the last few years, dozens of **foreign cuisines** have appeared. There are some good Peruvian, Argentinian, Middle Eastern and Italian places and a scattering of enjoyable Indonesian and Japanese restaurants. With a few honourable exceptions, though, Indian and Chinese restaurants are fairly dire, as too, alas, are most of the Mexican and Brazilian ones. There has also been an unfortunate rise of franchised restaurant chains and coffee bars.

Sol, Plaza Mayor and Ópera

The central area is the most varied in Madrid in terms of price and choice of food. Indeed, there can be few places in the world which rival the streets around Puerta del **Sol** for sheer number of places to eat and drink. Around the smarter **Ópera** district, you need to be more selective, while on **Plaza Mayor** itself, stick to drinks. Unless we indicate otherwise, all these places are easily reached from **Metro Sol**.

Tapas bars

Las Bravas, c/Alvarez Gato 3. As the name suggests, *patatas bravas* (spicy potatoes) are the tapa to try at this bar, just south of Puerta del Sol; the *tortilla* is tasty, too. On the outside of the bar are novelty mirrors, a hangover from the days when this was a barber's and the subject of a story by Valle Inclán. Standing room only, but if it's too crowded you'll find other branches nearby at c/Espoz y Mina 13 and Pasaje Mathéu 5.

Casa del Abuelo, c/Victoria 12. Tiny, highly atmospheric bar serving just their sweet, rich red house wine and cooked prawns – try them *al ajilo* (in garlic) or *a la plancha* (fried). You'll be given a voucher for a free glass of wine at the sister bar round the corner in c/Nuñez de Arce (see also "Restaurants", below).

Casa del Labra, c/Tetuán 12 – opposite El Corte Inglés. Order a drink at the bar and a *ración* of cod fried in batter (*bacalao*) or some of the best *croquetas* in town at the counter to the right of the door (see also "Restaurants", below).

Lhardy, Carrera de San Jerónimo 8 ☎ 915 213 385. *Lhardy* is one of Madrid's most famous and expensive restaurants. Once the haunt of royalty, it's a beautiful place but greatly overpriced. Downstairs, however, there's a wonderful bar, where you can snack on canapés, *fino* (dry sherry) and *consommé*, without breaking the bank.

Mejillonera El Rocio, Pasaje Matheu. Mussels (*mejillones*) served in every way conceivable at one of many bars on this pedestrian-only alleyway between c/Espoz y Mina and c/Victoria, south of Puerta del Sol.

Mesón del Champiñones and Mesón de la Tortilla, Cava de San Miguel 17 & 15. These are two of the oldest *tabernas* in Madrid, just down the steps at the southwest corner of Plaza Mayor. They specialize, as you'd imagine, in mushrooms and *tortilla*, respectively. At weekends, both places come alive as people gather to sample the excellent wines and *sangría*.

Museo del Jamón, Carrera de San Jerónimo 6. The largest branch of this Madrid chain, from whose ceilings are suspended hundreds of *jamones* (hams). The best – and they are not cheap – are the *jabugos* from the Sierra Morena, though a ham croissant will set you back under €1.75.

La Oreja de Oro, c/Victoria 9. Standing room only in this bar just opposite *La Casa del Abuelo*. Try the excellent *pulpo a la Gallega* (sliced octopus served on a bed of potatoes fried in olive oil and seasoned with cayenne pepper) washed down with Ribeiro wine served in terracotta bowls. Plenty of other seafood tapas on offer too. Closed Aug.

El Oso y El Madroño, c/Bolsa 4. A tiny *castizo*

(traditional *madrileño*) bar where you can have a drink to the accompaniment of the *madrileño chotis* and chat to the barmen who seem to have been there forever. Specialities are *cocido*, snails, *sangría* and *jerez* (sherry).

La Zapatería, c/Victoria 8. A relative newcomer on the scene which has carved out a niche of its own with its excellent *patatas a lo pobre* (pan-fried potatoes) mixed with either *chorizo* or *morcilla* (blood sausage). Does a nice line in *caracoles* (snails) too.

Restaurants

El Abuelo, c/Núñez de Arce 3. There's a *comedor* at the back of this spit-and-sawdust bar, where you can order a selection of delicious *raciones* – the *croquetas* are especially good – and a jug of house wine. Inexpensive.

El Botín, c/Cuchilleros 17 ☎ 913 664 217; Ⓜ Sol/Tirso de Molina. One of the city's oldest restaurants, established in 1725, highly picturesque and favoured by Hemingway. Inevitably, it's a tourist haunt but not such a bad one, with creditable if not tremendously inspired roasts – especially suckling pig (*cochinillo*) and lamb (*lechal*). The *menú* is €27 but you could eat for less. Expensive.

Casa Ciriaco, c/Mayor 84 ☎ 915 595 066; Ⓜ Ópera. Attractive, old-style *taberna*, long reputed for traditional Castilian dishes – trout, chicken and so on, served up in old-style portions. The *menú* is €16.25; main *carta* dishes a bit less. Closed Wed & Aug. Moderate.

Casa Gallega, c/Bordadores 11 ☎ 915 419 055; Ⓜ Ópera/Sol. An airy and welcoming *marisquería* that has been importing seafood on overnight trains from Galicia since it opened in 1915. Costs vary greatly according to the rarity of the fish or shellfish that you order. *Gallego* staples such as *pulpo* (octopus) and *pimientos de Padrón* (tiny, randomly piquant peppers) are brilliantly done and inexpensive but the more exotic seasonal delights will raise a bill for two to around the €60 mark. Another branch at Plaza San Miguel ☎ 915 473 055. Expensive.

Casa del Labra, c/Tetuán 12 ☎ 915 310 081; Ⓜ Sol. A great, traditional place where the Spanish Socialist Party was founded, which retains much of its original 1869 interior. The restaurant is through the bar on the right: an old panelled room, with classic *madrileño* food on offer. Moderate to expensive.

Casa Santa Cruz, c/Bolsa 12 ☎ 915 218 623; Ⓜ Sol. Formerly a hermitage and later the Stock Exchange, this beautiful place is not remotely cheap but the food – a mixture of *nueva cocina* and Castilian staples – has the same top quality as the decor. A rather restrained atmosphere compared to some of its more lively neighbours. Expensive.

Around Santa Ana and Huertas

You should spend at least an evening eating and drinking at the historic, tiled bars in this central area. Restaurants are good, too, and frequented as much by locals as tourists.

Tapas bars

La Costa de Vejer, corner of c/Núñez de Arce and c/Alvarez del Gato; Ⓜ Sol. The speciality here is prawns (*gambas*), grilled with garlic, which are an absolute must, but you can't go wrong with the rest of the tapas either.

España Cañi, Plaza del Ángel 14; Ⓜ Sol. An attractive tiled exterior fronts this attractive bar with a fine selection of *tapas*; a great place to soak up flamenco sounds and the house *sangría*.

El Lacón, c/Manuel Fernández y González 8; Ⓜ Sol. Large Galician bar-restaurant with plenty of seats upstairs. Great *pulpo*, *caldo gallego* (meat and vegetable broth) and *empanadas* (pastry slices filled with tuna and vegetables). Closed Aug.

La Taberna de Dolores, Plaza de Jesús 4; Ⓜ Antón Martín. Splendid canapés at this popular and friendly tiled bar at the bottom of Huertas. The beer is really good, and the food specialities include Roquefort and anchovy, and smoked-salmon canapés. Get here early if you want a space at the bar.

La Tapería de Huertas, c/Santa María 28; Ⓜ Antón Martín. An ideal place to go if you want to try a wide variety of tapas without having to eat a *ración* of each dish: the neat little *cazuelitas* are just the right size for two. A good selection of wines and plenty of tapas that will suit vegetarians.

La Trucha, c/Manuel Fernández y González 3; Ⓜ Antón Martín. If you're not going to end up at the restaurant here (see below), at least call in for a tapa at the bar. Smoked fish and *pimientos de Padrón* are specialities. Usually very crowded. Closed Sun.

Viña P, Plaza de Santa Ana 3; Ⓜ Sol. Very friendly staff serving a great range of tapas in a bar decked out with bullfighting mementos and posters. Try the asparagus, stuffed mussels and the mouthwatering *almejas a la marinera* (clams in a garlic and white wine sauce).

Restaurants

Casa Alberto, c/Huertas 18 ☎ 914 299 356; Ⓜ Antón Martín. Traditional *taberna* with a zinc bar and a small dining room at the back. Specialities include *albondigas* (meatballs) and *rabo de toro* (oxtail). Closed Sun night & Mon. Moderate to expensive.

El Cenador del Prado, c/Prado 4 ☎ 914 291 561; Ⓜ Sevilla. Relaxing and stylish decor serve as the backdrop to imaginative cuisine combining Spanish, Mediterranean and Far Eastern influences. There's a *menú de degustación* at €21 and some spectacular desserts. Closed Sat lunch & Sun.

Domine Cabra, c/Huertas 54 ☎ 914 294 365; Ⓜ Antón Martín. Interesting mix of traditional and modern, with *madrileña* standards given the *nueva cocina* treatment. Very good-value *menús* at €13.25 & €18. Closed Sun night. Moderate.

La Farfala, c/Santa María 17 ☎ 913 694 691; Ⓜ Antón Martín. The place to go for late-night food and a lively party atmosphere in the Huertas area. Good range of tasty pizzas and Argentinian-style meat. Open till 4am at weekends. Inexpensive.

El Inti de Oro, c/Ventura de la Vega 12 ☎ 914 296 703; Ⓜ Sevilla. An ideal introduction to Peruvian cuisine. Try the *cebiche de merluza* (a refreshing raw fish salad) and the *aji de gallina* (chicken in walnut sauce); the local liqueurs are worth sampling too. Moderate.

Lerranz, c/Echegaray 26 ☎ 914 291 206; Ⓜ Sevilla. Designerish touches to the decor and the food in this small bar-restaurant; the set menu is around €6. Moderate.

Prada A Tope, c/Príncipe 11 ☎ 914 295 221; Ⓜ Sevilla. Excellent quality produce from El Bierzo in León; the *pimientos asados*, *morcilla* and *tortilla* are extremely tasty. Closed Mon. Moderate.

La Sanabresa, c/Amor de Diós 12 ☎ 914 290 338; Ⓜ Antón Martín. A real local with a TV in one corner and an endless supply of customers who come for its excellent and reasonably priced dishes. Don't miss the grilled aubergines. Closed Sun. Inexpensive.

La Trucha, c/Manuel Fernández y González 3 – off c/Echegaray ☎ 914 295 833; Ⓜ Antón Martín. This is a treat: call in to reserve a table while you have drinks at nearby *Los Gabrieles* and *La Venencia*, then fight your way through the bar to a half-dozen tables at the back (or in the basement). Highlights include the *plato de verbena* (salmon and caviar canapés) and *fritura variada* (a huge platter of fried fish); decline the house wine and order a bottle instead. Moderate.

La Vaca Verónica, c/Moratín 38 ☎ 914 297 827; Ⓜ Antón Martín. Excellent Argentinian-style meat, really good fresh pasta in imaginative sauces, quality fish dishes and tasty vegetables. Try the *Filet Verónica* and the *carabinero con pasta*. The *menù del día* is a good deal at €11.50, and the service is friendly. Closed Sat lunch & Sun. Moderate.

Gran Vía and Plaza de España

On the **Gran Vía**, burger bars fill most of the gaps between shops and cinemas. However, head a few blocks in and there's plenty on offer, including a good cluster of ethnic restaurants on c/San Bernardino (north of the Plaza de España).

Tapas bars

Stop Madrid, c/Hortaleza 11; Ⓜ Gran Vía. An old-time spit-and-sawdust bar specializing in products from Extremadura, revitalized with Belgian, Mexican and German beers as well as *vermut* on tap. Tapas are largely *jamón* and *chorizo*, with the *Canapé Stop* of ham and tomato doused in olive oil well worth a try.

Restaurants

Adrish, c/San Bernardino 1 ☏ 915 429 498; Ⓜ Plaza de España. One of the city's better Indian restaurants, nicely decorated and with a vast selection of dishes. The cooking is mild, so if you like your curries hot, let the waiter know. Closed Sun. Moderate.

Bali, c/San Bernardino 6 ☏ 915 419 122; Ⓜ Plaza de España. Indonesian food; the speciality is the all-encompassing *rijsttafel*. Closed Sun night & Mon lunch. Moderate.

La Barraca, c/Reina 29 ☏ 915 327 154; Ⓜ Gran Vía/Banco de España. Step off the dingy street into this little slice of Valencia for some of the best *paellas* in town. Service is attentive but not over-fussy, the starters are excellent and a great lemon sorbet for dessert. A three-course meal with wine

will set you back somewhere around €30 a head. Expensive.

La Bola, c/Bola 5 ☏ 915 476 930; Ⓜ Santo Domingo. Established back in 1870, this is the place to go for *cocido madrileño* (soup followed by chickpeas and other vegetables and then a selection of meats), which is only served at lunchtime. Don't plan on doing anything energetic afterwards as it is incredibly filling. No cards. Closed Sun night. Moderate.

El Buey, Plaza de la Marina Española 1 ☏ 915 413 041; Ⓜ Santo Domingo. A meat-eaters' paradise specializing in steak which you fry up yourself on a hotplate. Very good side dishes, including a great leek and seafood pie and excellent home-made desserts. Moderate.

Da Nicola, Plaza Los Mostenses ☏ 915 422 574; Ⓜ Santo Domingo. Extremely popular (so book ahead) Italian restaurant just to the north of Gran Vía.

Nova Galicia, c/Conde Duque 3 ☏ 915 594 260; Ⓜ Plaza de España. Excellent-value Galician restaurant specializing in seafood tapas and *arroz con bogavante* (rice with lobster). Pass through the ordinary-looking front bar and into the dining room hidden behind. Closed second half of Aug. Moderate.

La Latina and Lavapiés: the Rastro area

South from Sol and Huertas are the quarters of La Latina and Lavapiés whose tiny streets retain an appealing neighbourhood feel, and have a great selection of bars and restaurants.

Tapas bars

Almacén de Vinos, c/Calatrava 21; Ⓜ La Latina. A neighbourhood tapas bar in the best tradition. Well worth a call.

El Almendro, c/Almendro 27; Ⓜ La Latina. On the corner of the Plaza de San Andrés, this is just the place for highly original seated tapas. Imaginatively presented and very tasty.

Almendro 13, c/Almendro 13; Ⓜ La Latina. Fashionable wooden-panelled bar that serves great *fino* from chilled black bottles. Tuck into the original tapas of *huevos rotos* (fried eggs on a bed of crisps) and *roscas rellenas* (rings of bread stuffed with various meats).

Barranco, San Isidro Labrador 14; Ⓜ La Latina. Come here for *gambas* after a trek around the Rastro. Very popular.

Los Caracoles, Plaza Cascorro 18; Ⓜ La Latina. A favourite since the 1940s, this does a good range of tapas as well as its namesake *caracoles* (snails).

La Chata, c/Cava Baja 24; Ⓜ La Latina. One of the most traditional, and popular, tiled tapas bars in Madrid, with hams hanging from the ceiling, taurine and football mementos on the walls, and a good selection of *raciones*, including *cebolla rellena* and *pimientos del piquillo rellenos* (stuffed onions and peppers). Closed Sun night.

Melo's, c/Avemaría 44; Ⓜ Lavapiés. Standing room only at this very popular Galician bar serving huge *zapatillas (*hunks of Galician country bread filled with *lacón* and *queso*) and great *pimientos de Padrón*.

Madrid's vegetarian restaurants

Madrid can be an intimidating city for veggies, given the mass of ham, fish and seafood on display in bar and restaurant windows and on counters. However, you can order vegetables separately at just about any restaurant in the city – Argentine steakhouses, perhaps, excepted – and there is good pizza and pasta to be had at a number of Italian places. You can even find the odd vegetarian paella.

More crucially, the capital now has half a dozen decent and inexpensive **vegetarian restaurants**, scattered about the centre. These include:

Al Natural, c/Zorilla 11 ⓣ913 694 709; ⓜBanco de España. Veggie and non-veggie food, including a very good mushroom and spinach pie. Excellent wines and a good-value *menú del día* at €7.50. Closed Sun night. Inexpensive to moderate.

Artemisa, c/Ventura de la Vega 4 ⓣ914 295 092; ⓜSevilla; c/Tres Cruces 4 ⓣ915 218 721; ⓜGran Vía. A popular place (you may have to wait for a table), best for its veggie pizzas and an imaginative range of salads. No smoking – even more of a novelty than veggie food in Madrid. Closed Sun night. Moderate.

Elqui, c/Buenavista 18 ⓣ914 680 462; ⓜLavapíes/Antón Martín. Excellent vegetarian venue in the heart of Lavapíes. Light and very tasty main courses, imaginative soups and some great fruit-based drinks. There's a self-service lunch-time *menú* for €6.60. No smoking. Open Tues-Fri for lunch and Fri and Sat evenings.

El Estragón, Plaza de La Paja 10 ⓣ913 658 982; ⓜLa Latina. Good vegetarian tapas, leek pie and chocolate cake. Economical *menú del día* at €7.20 (dinner *menú* is over double the price) and a fine setting on the edge of this ancient plaza. Inexpensive to moderate.

La Granja, c/San Andrés 11 ⓣ915 328 793; ⓜBilbao/Tribunal. Good-value set menu that changes every day, offering a choice of soup, salad, a main dish of vegetables, rice and fruits topped with sauce, dessert and drinks. Open Mon–Wed 1.30–4.30pm & 9pm–midnight, Thurs–Sun 1.30–4.30pm. Inexpensive.

Vegetariano, c/Marqués de Santa Ana 34 ⓣ915 320 927; ⓜTribunal. Excellent salads and Mediterranean vegetables. No smoking. Closed Sun night & Mon. Inexpensive.

Taberna de Antonio Sánchez, c/Mesón de Paredes 13 ⓣ915 397 826; ⓜTirso de Molina. Seventeenth-century bar – said to be the oldest *taberna* in Madrid – decorated with a wooden interior and a stuffed bull's head (one of which killed Antonio Sánchez, the son of the founder). Lots of *finos* on offer, plus *jamón* and *queso* tapas or *tortilla de San Isidro* (with salted cod). Closed Sun night.

Restaurants

Alquezar, c/Lavapíes 53 ⓣ915 277 261; ⓜTirso de Molina. Authentic and good-value Middle Eastern food in the heart of the cosmopolitan Lavapíes *barrio*. Moderate.

El Asador Frontón, Plaza Tirso de Molina 7, 1º – entrance just off the square ⓣ 913 691 617; ⓜTirso de Molina. Old, charming neighbourhood restaurant, where publishers and the like settle down for a long afternoon's lunch. Wide range of classic Castilian dishes – all delicious. Moderate.

El Economico/Soidermersol, c/Argumosa; ⓜLavapíes. Traditional workmen's *comedor* with an unbeatable €4.75 lunchtime *menú*. Inexpensive.

Casa Lastra Sidrería, c/Olivar 3 ⓣ913 690 837; ⓜAntón Martín/Tirso de Molina. Very popular restaurant serving classic Asturian fare: *chorizo a la sidra* (chorizo in cider), *entrecot al cabrales* (steak in a strong blue-cheese sauce), *fabada* (a warming winter stew of beans, *chorizo* and *morcilla*) and, of course, *sidra natural* (cider). Closed July. Moderate.

Casa Lucio, c/Cava Baja 35 ⓣ913 653 252; ⓜLa Latina. *Madrileños* come here for the expected: classic Castilian dishes such as *cocido*, *callos* (tripe) and roasts, cooked to perfection. It is where Queen Sofía took George Bush's wife when the US president visited recently. Booking is essential. Closed Sat lunch & Aug. Expensive.

Café life

Madrid has a number of cafés that are institutions. They serve food but are much more places to drink coffee, have a *copa* or *caña*, or read the papers. They're also a meeting place for the semi-formal *tertulia* – a kind of discussion/drinking group, popular among Madrid intellectuals of the past and revived in the 1980s. Many cafés also have summer – or all-year – terrazas (outside terraces), though be aware that sitting outside puts up the prices. Other cafés and *pastelerias* are simpler affairs, good places to grab a breakfast croissant or a teatime snack. Good choices include:

Café los Austrias, Plaza de Ramales Ⓜ Opera. Relaxing café with marble table-tops and dark-wood interior; a good stop after a visit to the Palacio Real.

Café Barbieri, c/Ave María 45 Ⓜ Lavapiés. Well-known café with a vaguely intellectual reputation. It's a relaxed place with unobtrusive music, lots of wooden tables, old-style decor, newspapers, and a wide selection of coffees.

Café El Botánico, c/Espalter/Plaza Murillo Ⓜ Atocha. A quiet place to sit with a drink, opposite the south entrance of the Prado.

Café Central, Plaza del Ángel 10 Ⓜ Sol. A jazz club by night but a regular café by day, again with newspapers supplied.

Café Comercial, Glorieta de Bilbao Ⓜ Bilbao. One of the city's most popular meeting points – a lovely traditional café, well poised for the Chueca/Santa Bárbara area.

Café del Espejo, Paseo de Recoletos 31 Ⓜ Colón. Opened in 1991 but you wouldn't guess it – mirrors, gilt, and a wonderful glass pavilion, plus a leafy outside terraza.

Café Gijón, Paseo de Recoletos 21 Ⓜ Banco de España. Famous literary café – and a centre of the intellectual/arty *movida* in the 1980s – decked out in Cuban mahogany and mirrors. Has a summer terraza.

Café Manuela Malasaña, c/San Vicente Ferrer 29 Ⓜ Tribunal. Wonderful mirrors and fittings and a very civilized atmosphere, with live piano music and *tertulias*, in different languages, most nights.

Café de Oriente, Plaza de Oriente 2 Ⓜ Ópera. Elegant, traditional-style café founded a decade or so ago by a priest, as part of a charity rehab programme for ex-convicts. Has a popular terraza.

Círculo de Bellas Artes, c/Alcalá 42 Ⓜ Banco de España. Day membership to the Círculo is €0.60, which gives you access to exhibitions, and to a most luxurious bar, where you can loll on sofas and have drinks at normal prices. Outside, in summer, there's a comfortable terraza.

Croissantería, c/Corredera Alta de San Pablo – just off Plaza San Ildefonso Ⓜ Tribunal. Some of the best stuffed croissants in the city, plus ice cream and coffee.

La Mallorquina, Puerta del Sol 2 Ⓜ Sol. Good for breakfast or snacks – try one of their *napolitanas* (cream slices) in the sunny upstairs salon.

Yenes, c/Mayor 1 Ⓜ Sol. Wedge yourself on to a bar stool and enjoy a fine array of cakes and croissants; less bustling than *La Mallorquina* opposite.

Posada de la Villa, c/Cava Baja 9 ☎ 913 661 860; Ⓜ La Latina. The most attractive-looking restaurant in Latina, spread over three floors of a seventeenth-century mansion. Cooking is typically *madrileña*, including superb roast lamb. Reckon on a good €42 per person for the works – though you could get away with less. Closed Sun night & Aug. Expensive.

Viuda de Vacas, c/Cava Alta 23 ☎ 913 665 847; Ⓜ La Latina. Highly traditional, family-run restaurant. The place looks rather down-at-heel, but the good-quality Castilian fare certainly isn't. Closed Thurs and Sun nights. Inexpensive to moderate.

Chueca and Santa Bárbara

Chueca – and **Santa Bárbara** to its north – have some superb traditional old bars and bright new restaurants, and a vast amount of nightlife. The southern part of Chueca, however, around the metro station, and south to Gran Vía, is also quite a big drug area, which can leave you feeling a little uneasy after dark.

Tapas bars

El Bocaíto, c/Libertad 4–6 Ⓜ Chueca. Munch away on a variety of delicious canapés and tapas, washed down by a cold beer, at this busy bar; watch out for the *Luisito*, the hottest canapé your taste buds are ever likely to encounter. Closed Sat lunch, Sun & two weeks in Aug.

Cervecería Santa Bárbara, Plaza Santa Bárbara 8 Ⓜ Alonso Martínez. Popular, but pricey, meeting place in this part of town, with *cañas* and prawns to keep you going.

Santander, c/Augusto Figueroa 25 Ⓜ Chueca. It's worth a visit to this bar in the heart of Chueca for the good range of tapas, including *empanadas*, *tortillas* and quiche lorraine, as well as a huge variety of fresh home-made canapés at reasonable prices. Closed Aug.

Taberna Ángel Sierra, c/Gravina 11, on Plaza Chueca Ⓜ Chueca. One of the great bars of Madrid, with a traditional zinc counter, constantly washed down. Everyone drinks *vermut*, which is on tap and delicious, and free tapas of the most exquisite *boquerones en vinagre* are despatched (*raciones*, too, for the greedy – though they are expensive).

Restaurants

El 26 de Libertad, c/de la Libertad 26 ☎ 915 222 522; Ⓜ Chueca. Imaginative cuisine served up in an attentive, but unfussy manner in this brightly decorated restaurant popular with the Chueca locals. Closed Sun night in July & Aug. Moderate.

Al Hoceima, c/Farmacia 8 ☎ 915 319 411; Ⓜ Tribunal. Elegant little Moroccan restaurant, with decent couscous and *tajines*. Closed Mon & Tues lunch. Moderate.

Annapurna, c/Zurbano 5 ☎ 913 198 716; Ⓜ Colón. To say this is the best Indian restaurant in Madrid is faint praise – however, *Annapurna* could hold its own in London, especially if you go for the tandoori dishes or thali. Closed Sat lunch & Sun. Moderate to expensive.

Carmencita, c/Libertad 16 ☎ 915 316 612; Ⓜ Chueca. Beautiful old restaurant, dating back to 1830, with panelling, brass, marble tables – and a new Basque-influenced chef. Lunch *menú* is a

bargain €7.25, but eating à la carte is expensive. *Gallina en pepitoria* (chicken in almond sauce) is the speciality. Closed Sat night, Sun & holidays. Moderate to Expensive.

La Carreta, c/Barbieri 10 ☎ 915 327 042; Ⓜ Chueca/Banco de España. Argentinian restaurant, heavy on steaks and red meat. From Wed to Sun there's a trio playing tango; on Tues you can learn to dance. A good late-night option in this area, as it's open daily to 5am. Moderate to expensive.

Casa Gades, c/Conde de Xiquena 4 ☎ 915 312 637; Ⓜ Chueca/Banco de España. Very attractive restaurant in a fashionable area on the edge of Chueca, owned by the flamenco dancer Antonio Gades. Food is a mix of Spanish and Italian. Closed Mon. Moderate.

El Comunista (Tienda de Vinos), c/Augusto Figueroa 35 – between Libertad and Barbieri Ⓜ Chueca. Long-established *comedor*, its unofficial (but always used) name dates back to its time as a student haunt under Franco. The garlic soup is recommended. Inexpensive.

Hard Rock Café, Paseo de la Castellana 2 ☎ 914 350 200; Ⓜ Colón. Predictable American fast-food and loud music, but with a pleasant terrace which overlooks Plaza de Colón. Open daily until 1.30am. Inexpensive.

Momo, c/Augusto Figueroa 41 ☎ 915 327 162; Ⓜ Chueca. Kitsch decor and creative cuisine at very reasonable prices – €7 for the *menú del día* – in this very popular restaurant in the heart of Chueca. Inexpensive.

Salvador, c/Barbieri 12 ☎ 915 214 524; Ⓜ Chueca. Bullfighting decor and traditional specialities such as *rabo de toro* (bull's tail), *gallina en pepitoria* (chicken fricassee), fried *merluza* (hake) and *arroz con leche* (rice pudding) – all excellent. Closed Sun night and Aug. Moderate to expensive.

La Tasca Suprema, c/Argensola 7 ☎ 913 080 347; Ⓜ Alonso Martínez. Very popular neighbourhood local, worth booking ahead. Castilian home cooking to perfection, including *cocido* on Mon & Thurs and excellent *pimientos de piquillo* (piquant red peppers). Open for lunch only; closed Sun & Aug. Inexpensive.

Malasaña and north to Bilbao

Malasaña is another characterful area, with a big nightlife scene and dozens of bars. Further north, the area around Plaza de Olavide – a real neighbourhood square – offers some good-value places, well off any tourist trails.

Tapas bars

Albur, c/Manuela Malasaña 15 Ⓜ Bilbao. Wooden tables, rustic decor and excellent food, although the service can be a little slow. The *champiñones en salsa verde* and the *patatas albur* are both worth sampling; the well-kept wines are the ideal accompaniment.

La Camocha, c/Fuencarral 95 Ⓜ Bilbao. Asturian cider bar serving splendid *pulpo* and *almejas a la sidra*. You can use the special cider-pouring instruments stuck to the wall to make sure it is properly aerated.

Casa Camacho, c/San Andrés 2 – just off Plaza Dos de Mayo Ⓜ Tribunal. Irresistible old *bodega*, with a traditional bar counter, *vermut* on tap, and basic tapas. An ideal place to start the evening. Packed out at weekends.

Restaurants

Balear, c/Sagunto 18 ☎ 914 479 115; Ⓜ Iglesia. This Levantine restaurant serves only rice-based dishes, but they're superb. There's an inexpensive house *cava*, and you can turn up any time before midnight. Closed Sun & Mon night. Moderate.

Castilla, c/Manuel Malasaña 37 ☎ 914 484 016; Ⓜ Bilbao. Modern Spanish cooking – imaginative and tasty. The *endivias con nueces y roquefort* (chinese leaf with walnut and blue-cheese sauce) and the duck are very good options. Closed Sun & half of Aug. Moderate.

La Despensa, c/Cardinal Cisneros 6 ☎ 914 461 794; Ⓜ Bilbao. Good standard, no-nonsense lunchtime fare with an inexpensive *menú del día*. Inexpensive.

La Gata Flora, Plaza Dos de Mayo 1 ☎ 915 212 020; Ⓜ Tribunal. Argentine-Italian cooking of a pretty high quality, considering the low prices. Open till midnight on weekdays, 1am on Fri & Sat. Inexpensive.

La Giralda, c/Hartzenbush 12 ☎ 914 457 779; Ⓜ Bilbao. An *andaluz* fish and seafood restaurant of very high quality: perfectly cooked *chipirones*, *calamares*, and all the standards, plus wonderful *mero* (grouper). A second branch, across the road at no. 15, does a similarly accomplished job on *pescados fritos*. Closed Sun & holidays. Moderate to expensive.

Ma Bretagne, c/San Vicente Ferrer 9 ☎ 915 817 774; Ⓜ Tribunal. Tiny place with good crepes, open until after midnight. Closed Mon. Inexpensive.

Mesón Do Anxó, c/Cardenal Cisneros 6 Ⓜ Bilbao. A *gallego* café-restaurant with formica tables – as unpretentious as they come – but serving superb *pulpo*, *pimientos de Padrón*, and other staples of the region. Closed Sun. Moderate.

Taberna Griega, c/Tesoro 6 ☎ 915 321 892; Ⓜ Tribunal. Enjoyable Greek restaurant, with live bouzouki music most weekends. Open until well after midnight. Inexpensive.

La Zamorana, c/Galileo 21 ☎ 914 471 169; Ⓜ San Bernardo. Attractive, tiled restaurant, with good-value Basque cooking – including lots of dishes based on *bacalao* (dried cod). Closed Sat lunch & Sun. Moderate (just).

Paseo del Prado, Recoletos and Retiro

This is a fancier area with few bars of note but some extremely good, if expensive, restaurants, well worth considering, even if you're not staying at the *Ritz*.

Tapas bars

Mesón la Pilarica, Paseo del Prado 39 Ⓜ Atocha. One of the nearest decent places to the Prado on this road, this is a good place to sample *serrano* ham.

Restaurants

La Ancha, c/de Zorrilla 7 ☎ 914 298 186; Ⓜ Sevilla/Banco de España. Highly regarded restaurant in a rather gloomy street behind the Cortes – hence popular with politicians. Mahogany-panelled decor, and imaginative variations on traditional Castilian dishes. Good-value lunchtime *menú*. Closed Sun & holidays. Expensive.

Dorna, c/Atocha 118 ☎ 915 275 299; Ⓜ Atocha. Bustling place with somewhat brusque waiters, but a decent stop before (or after) a visit to the Reina Sofía. Inexpensive to moderate.

Paradis Madrid, c/Marqués de Cubas 14 ☎ 914 297 303; Ⓜ Banco de España. There are Paradises in Barcelona and New York – the chain is run by a Catalan duo – and the American influence is apparent in designerish details like a *carta* for olive oils. Nonetheless, the cooking is light, Mediterranean and tasty; try the wonderful *arroz*

negro with seafood. Stays open till 1.30am if it's busy. Closed Sat lunch, Sun & Aug. Expensive.
Viridiana, c/Juan de Mena 14 ☎ 915 315 222; Ⓜ Retiro. Bizarre temple of Madrid *nueva cocina*, offering mouthwatering creations like *solomillo*

(sirloin) with black truffles, and herrings with avocado and mango. Dishes often arrive with sparklers or other pyrotechnic devices attached. Main courses are around €20; no cards accepted. Closed Sun & Aug. Expensive.

Salamanca

Salamanca is Madrid's equivalent of Bond Street or Fifth Avenue, full of designer shops and expensive-looking natives. Recommendations below are correspondingly pricey but high quality.

Tapas bars

Alkalde, Jorge Juan 10 ☎ 915 673 359; Ⓜ Serrano. This serves up pricey Basque tapas, a treat which you could turn into a tasty meal.
Hevia, c/Serrano 118 Ⓜ Núñez de Balboa. Plush venue and clientele for pricey, but excellent tapas and canapés – the hot Camembert is a must.
José Luís, c/Serrano 89 ☎ 915 630 958; Ⓜ Serrano. Upmarket tapas bar with dainty and delicious sandwiches laid out along the bar. You take what you fancy, in the safe knowledge that

the barman will have notched up another few hundred pesetas to expand his chain of bars in the Americas.
Pil, Pil Madrid, c/Alberto Alcocer 33 Ⓜ Columbia. A takeaway, shop and bar all rolled into one. The speciality is *bacalao* (salted cod) served in a myriad of fashions. Closed Sun night.

Restaurants

El Amparo, Callejón Puigcerdá 8 ☎ 914 316 456; Ⓜ Serrano. Most critics rate this designer

Terrazas and chiringuitos

Madrid is a different city during summer, as temperatures soar, and life moves outside, becoming even more late-night. In July and August, those *madrileños* who haven't headed for the coast meet up with each other, from 10pm onwards, at one or other of the city's immensely popular **terrazas**. These can range from a few tables set up outside a café or alongside a **chiringuito** – a makeshift bar – in one of the squares, to extremely trendy (and very expensive) designer bars, which form the summer annexe of one or other of the major clubs or *discotecas*. Most places offer cocktails, in addition to regular drinks, and the better or more traditional ones also serve *horchata* (an almond-ish milk shake) and *granizado* (crushed-ice lemon). A few of the terrazas operate year-round.

Terrazas run by the **clubs** vary their sites year by year, often locating way out from the centre, necessitating long and expensive taxi rides.

Paseo de Recoletos and Paseo de la Castellana

The biggest concentration of terrazas is to be found up and down the grass strip in the middle of the Paseo de Recoletos and its continuation, Paseo de la Castellana. On the nearer reaches of Paseo de Recoletos are terrazas of the **old-style cafés** *Gran* (no. 8), *Gijón* (no. 21) and *Espejo* (no. 31), which are popular meeting points for *madrileños* of all kinds.

Past Plaza de Colón, the **trendier terrazas** begin, most pumping out music, and some offering entertainment – especially midweek, when they need to attract custom. They are extremely posey places, with clubbers dressing up for a night's cruise along the length – an expensive operation, with cocktails at €7 a shot, and even a *caña* costing €3.50. If you want to take in a good selection, walk up from Plaza de Colón for around 500m. Alternatively, take a taxi or the metro up to Plaza de Lima, where you'll find *Castellana 99* – a fashionable terraza and bar that's open year-round. For some reason, most of the Castellana terrazas are known only by their (approximate) street number.

restaurant among the top five in Madrid – and you'll need to book a couple of weeks ahead to get a table. If you strike lucky, the rewards are faultless Basque cooking from a woman chef, Carmen Guasp – "Guaspi" to the Spanish media. Main dishes are around the €20 mark so expect a bill of at least €40 a head. Closed Sat lunch & Sun. Expensive.

Casa Portal, c/Dr Castelo 26 ⓣ 915 742 026; ⓜ Retiro. Superlative Asturian cooking – go for the *fabada* (beans and sausage stew) or *besugo* (bream). Closed Sun & Mon night, holidays & Aug. Moderate.

El Pescador, c/José Ortega y Gasset 75 ⓣ 914 021 290; ⓜ Lista. One of the city's top seafood restaurants, run by *gallegos* and with specials flown in from the Atlantic each morning. The clientele can be a bit intimidating – it is reputedly one of Felipe González's favourites – but you'll rarely experience better seafood cooking. Closed Sun &

Aug. Expensive.

Ribeira do Minho, c/Doctor Fleming 52 ⓣ 913 597 917; ⓜ Cuzco. A good place to sample top-quality traditional Galician food and wine. Expensive.

Suntory, Paseo de la Castellana 36 ⓣ 915 773 733; ⓜ Rubén Darío. Authentic and upmarket Japanese restaurant, where a mixed sushi will set you back around €25. The best bet is to go for the lunchtime set menu. Closed Sun & holidays. Expensive.

Teatriz, c/Hermosilla 15 ⓣ 915 775 379; ⓜ Serrano. As the name suggests, this was once a theatre, and the layout has been maintained by designers Philippe Starck and Mariscal – as trendy a European combination as could be conceived. Although primarily a nightspot (see p.133), there's a fine restaurant in the old "circle", with light, *nouvelle cuisine*-influenced dishes. (Surprisingly) moderate.

Elsewhere in Madrid

Antiguo Cuartel del Conde Duque ⓜ Ventura Rodríguez. This is a beautiful patio, inside an old military barracks. The council puts on weekly flamenco recitals and concerts in July & Aug., with a small admission charge, but most nights there's free entry.

Jardines de Conde Duque, at the corner of c/Conde Duque 11 and c/Santa Cruz del Marcenado ⓜ Ventura Rodríguez. The summer base of *Zanzibar* in recent years.

Jardines Las Vistillas, c/Bailén – on the south side of the viaduct (ⓜ La Latina – though it's not very close). This area, due south of the royal palace, has a number of terrazas and *chiringuitos*. It's named after the "little vistas" to be enjoyed in the direction of the Guadarrama mountains to the northwest.

Paseo del Pintor Rosales ⓜ Argüelles. There is a clutch of late-night terrazas around the base of the *teleférico*, with views across the river to the Casa de Campo.

Plaza de Comendadoras ⓜ Ventura Rodríguez. One of the city's nicest squares, this has a couple of terrazas –

attached to the *Café Moderno* and to a not very good Mexican restaurant.

Plaza Dos de Mayo ⓜ Tribunal. The *chiringuito* on Malasaña's main square is always diverting, though the square has something of a reputation for drug addicts.

Plaza de Olavide ⓜ Quevedo. An attractive neighbourhood square, with more or less year-round terrazas belonging to four or five cafés and tapas bars.

Plaza de Oriente ⓜ Ópera. The *Café de Oriente* terraza is a station of Madrid nightlife.

Plaza de Santa Ana ⓜ Sol. Several of the *cervecerías* here have seats outside and there's a *chiringuito* in the middle of the square from June to September.

La Vieja Estación, Glorieta de Carlos V ⓜ Atocha. Above the main entrance to Atocha station, this attracts a glamorous clientele ranging from football stars to TV personalities. If you don't fancy people-watching, there are concerts, talent contests and exhibitions laid on for good measure.

The west

Picnicking in the Casa de Campo aside, the west doesn't hold much in the way of culinary interest. However, two excellent restaurants deserve a mention.

Casa Mingo, Paseo de la Florida 2 – next to the chapel of San Antonio de la Florida ☎915 477 918; Ⓜ Príncipe Pío. Famous Asturian café-restaurant where you eat roast chicken – which is basically all they serve – washed down with *sidra* (cider), and followed up by *yemas* (candied egg yolk) or aged Roquefort-like cheese (*cabrales*). Good value and great fun. You can also buy a takeout (chicken and cider) for a picnic in the Casa de Campo, if you prefer. Moderate.

La Vaca Argentina, Paseo del Pintor Rosales 52 ☎915 596 605; Ⓜ Argüelles. Good views and great grilled steaks (*churrasco*) at this Argentinian restaurant overlooking the Parque del Oeste. Its terrace is a very pleasant place to eat in summer. Other branches at c/Bailén 20 ☎913 656 654; Ⓜ La Latina, c/Caños del Peral ☎915 413 318; Ⓜ Ópera, and Ribera del Manzanares 123 ☎915 593 780; Ⓜ Príncipe Pío with a fine riverside terrace. Moderate.

Nightlife

Madrid **nightlife** is a pretty serious phenomenon. This is one of the few cities in Europe where you can get caught in traffic jams at 4am, when the clubbers are either going home or moving on to the dance-past-dawn discos.

As with everything *madrileño*, there is a bewildering variety of nightlife venues – all of which are covered, to some degree, in the area reviews following. Most common are the **discobares** – bars of all musical and sexual persuasion, whose unifying feature is background (occasionally live) rock, dance or salsa music. These get going from around 11pm and will stay open routinely to 2am or 3am, as will the few quieter **cocktail bars** and **pubs**.

Discotecas – which we've separated in the listings – are rarely worth investigating until around 1am (the *madrugada* – early morning). Most of them pick their clientele through a dress code exclusivity and you may at times need to ingratiate yourself with the doorman. Being foreign, oddly enough, seems to make it easier to get in. Entry charges are quite common and quite hefty (€3.50–18) at *discotecas* (and some of the more disco-like *discobares*) but tend to cover you for a first drink. Free entries can sometimes be picked up from touts in the streets, in tourist offices or bars. Be aware that many *discotecas* in Spain are fairly ephemeral institutions and frequently only last a season before opening up somewhere else under a different name, so it's a good idea to consult *La Guía del Ocio* or *Metrópoli* (see p.135) for the very latest information.

Bars

Madrid's bar scene has something to offer every conceivable taste in terms of drinks, music and atmosphere. In recent years the notoriously late opening hours have been somewhat curtailed by the local authorities who are attempting to close bars by 3am, but there are still plenty of opportunities to dance the night away if you head for a disco afterwards. In *discobares* and *discotecas*, *bakalao*, a Spanish (originally Ibizan) version of house music, is still horribly popular. Perhaps in reaction to it, the more traditional bar scene has revived and expanded, and in the listings below you'll find a fair number of *bares de copas* (drinking bars) where the music is restrained – and even a couple with chamber orchestras.

△ Tiled bar, Madrid

Gay and lesbian Madrid

Much of Madrid's nightlife has a big gay input and gay men especially will feel at home in most of the listings in our clubs/*discotecas* section. However, around Plaza Chueca, graffiti-plastered walls proclaim the existence of a *zona gay*, and the surrounding streets, especially c/Pelayo, harbour at least a dozen exclusively gay bars and clubs, as well as a café that's traditionally gay – the *Café Figueroa* at c/Augusto Figueroa 17. Wandering about, be aware that Chueca is also something of a drug centre, so taxis are best late at night. The lesbian scene, which is rather less developed, has a current focus in Lavapiés.

The main gay organization in Madrid is Coordinadora Gay de Madrid, c/Fuencarral 37 (Mon–Fri 5–9pm, Aug from 7pm; ☎ 915 224 517; Ⓜ Chueca), which can give information on health, leisure and gay rights. The Chueca website Ⓦ www.chueca.com is full of information about everything going on in the area.

Gay Bars and Discotecas

Café Acuarela, c/Gravina 10 Ⓜ Chueca. Very comfortable café, stylish decor and the perfect place for a quiet drink. Popular with a mixed crowd.

Cruising, c/Pérez Galdós 5 Ⓜ Chueca. This *discobar* is strictly for leather boys, with a dark room and bar upstairs and a small, intimate disco below. It has a slightly tense atmosphere and you have to order your drinks at the door before you come in.

Liquid, c/Barquillo 8 Ⓜ Chueca. Smart and stylish new arrival on the gay scene. The two bars are lined with video screens playing a selection of modish music.

La Lupe, c/Torrecilla del Leal 12 Ⓜ Antón Martín. Mixed gay, lesbian and alternative bar that has received a recent make-over. Good music, cheap drinks and occasional cabaret.

Medea, c/Cabeza 33 Ⓜ Tirso de Molina. Women-only disco which has a huge dance floor and wide-ranging selection of danceable music. Gets going from about 1am.

New Leather Bar, c/Pelayo 42 Ⓜ Chueca. The name implies a leather scene but this bar has a mixed gay crowd.

Ricks, c/de las Infantas 26 Ⓜ Banco de España. Mixed straight/gay *discobar* which gets wild at weekends when every available space is used for dancing. Open and light, with a friendly atmosphere – plus table football at the back. Pricey drinks.

La Sastrería, c/Hortaleza 74 Ⓜ Chueca. This popular two-floored café-bar is a great place for an afternoon coffee, tea or fruit juice as well as an evening drink.

Shangay Tea Dance, at the *Flamingo Club*, c/Mesonero Romanos 13 Ⓜ Callao. A compulsory Sunday night stop, featuring live shows and 70s disco hits. €6 entry including first drink. Open Sun 9pm–2am.

Stars Dance Café, c/Marqués de Valdeiglesias 5 Ⓜ Gran Vía. Quiet and low-key during the day and gradually livens up as the night goes on. Popular meeting point for the gay community but clientele is mixed.

Sol, Plaza de Santa Ana and Huertas

Cervecería Alemana, Plaza de Santa Ana Ⓜ Sol. Recently refurbished but still stylish old beer house, frequented by Hemingway and, these days, seemingly every other American tourist. Order a *caña* and go easy on the tapas, as the bill can mount up fast.

Cervecería Santa Ana, Plaza de Santa Ana Ⓜ Sol. Cheaper than the *Alemana*, with tables outside,

friendly service, and a good selection of tapas.

La Comedia, c/Príncipe 16 Ⓜ Sevilla. Modern, relaxing bar for a quiet drink by day, which gets livelier as the night progresses; from Thursday to Saturday it's open until 5am and is a favourite haunt for staff from earlier-closing bars.

La Fidula, c/Huertas 57 Ⓜ Antón Martín. A fine bar where you can sip *fino* to the accompaniment of classical tunes, performed from the tiny stage.

Los Gabrieles, c/Echegaray 17 Ⓜ Sol. This tiled

bar is a Madrid monument and it's worth going earlier than is cool to appreciate the fabulous tableaux, created by sherry companies in the 1880s. Drinks are reasonable, considering the venue; tapas don't go much beyond olives and crisps. Very crowded after 10pm, especially at weekends.

Naturbier, Plaza de Santa Ana 9 Ⓜ Sol. Next door to the *cervecerías Alemana* and *Santa Ana*, the *Naturbier* brews its own tasty, cloudy beer and serves a variety of German sausages to accompany it.

No se lo digas a nadie, c/Ventura de la Vega 7 Ⓜ Sol. This was founded (and is still run) by a women's co-op, though it has mellowed a bit in recent years (the toilets no longer proclaim *nosotras* and *ellos* – "us" and "them"). Nonetheless, it retains a political edge, hosting benefit events from time to time, and has a different atmosphere from other bars in this area. There is no door policy or dress code and the drinks are reasonably priced. Upstairs there's a pool table and plenty of places to sit; downstairs is a disco playing mainly dance music.

Reporter, c/Fucar 6. The cool terrace garden in this neat bar just off Huertas makes a great place for a relaxing cocktail. Also does tapas and a *menú del día* during the day.

Salón del Prado, c/Prado 4 Ⓜ Sol. Elegant café-bar which hosts classical concerts on Thursday nights at 11pm. Turn up early if you want a table.

La Taberna de Dolores, Plaza de Jesús 4 Ⓜ Antón Martín. Splendid canapés at this popular and friendly tiled bar at the bottom of Huertas. Decorated with beer bottles from around the world, the beer is really good, and the food specialities include Roquefort and anchovy, and smoked-salmon canapés. Get here early if you want a space at the bar.

La Venencia, c/Echegaray Ⓜ Sol. For a real taste of old Madrid, this is a must: a long, narrow bar, serving just sherry – try the extra dry *fino* – cheese, and delicious cured tuna (*mojama*) and olives. Decoration is unchanged for decades, with ancient barrels and posters.

Viva Madrid, c/Manuel Fernández y González 7 Ⓜ Antón Martín. Another fabulous tiled bar – both outside and in – with wines and sherry, plus basic tapas. Open to 2.30am and always crowded.

Gran Vía

Carpe Diem, Plaza Conde de Toreno 2 Ⓜ Plaza de España/Noviciado. Part of the takings of this single-roomed bar goes towards overseas projects and it often stages markets in aid of developing countries. Happy hour goes on until midnight, with

a variety of Spanish pop and salsa played.

El Cock, c/Reina 16 – just behind *Museo Chicote* Ⓜ Gran Vía. A smart wooden-panelled bar, styled like a gentlemen's club, and very *de moda*. The music is good, although there's no dancing. *Cañas* or wine cost around €4.

Del Diego, c/Reina 12 Ⓜ Gran Vía. Stylish Art Deco cocktail bar set up by a former *Museu Chicote* waiter who personally mixes all the excellent cocktails. Friendly, unhurried atmosphere and open until the early hours. The house special, vodka-based *Del Diego,* is the one to go for. Closed Sun & Aug.

Museo Chicote, Gran Vía 12 Ⓜ Gran Vía. *Chicote* is a piece of design history, virtually unaltered since it opened in 1931, full of Art Deco lines and booths and once a haunt of Buñuel and Hemingway. They will mix you any (expensive) cocktail, alcoholic or not. Busiest after midnight. Open Mon–Sat 5pm–1.30am.

La Latina and Lavapiés

Aloque, c/Torrecilla del Real 20 Ⓜ Antón Martín. Relaxed wine bar where you can try top-quality wine by the glass; the innovative tapas are excellent too.

Avapiés, c/Lavapiés 5 Ⓜ Lavapiés/Tirso de Molina. Excellent music and nightly cabaret at around 10pm. Closes at 3.30am.

Montes, c/Lavapiés 40 Ⓜ Lavapiés/ Tirso de Molina. A Lavapiés favourite for those in search of a decent glass of wine. Ask owner César for advice and he'll help you find one to suit. A great place to start the evening.

El Tempranillo, Cava Baja 38 Ⓜ La Latina. Excellent little bar serving tasty tapas and a vast range of Spanish wines by the glass – a great place to discover your favourite variety.

El Viajero, Plaza de la Cebada. Ⓜ La Latina. Bar, disco, restaurant and summer terraza on different floors of this fashionable La Latina nightspot. Great views of San Francisco El Grande from the terraza at the top. The food (meat, pizzas and pastas) is good too. Tues–Sun 2pm–2.30am, Fri & Sat till 3am.

Chueca and Santa Bárbara

Big Bamboo, c/Barquillo 42 Ⓜ Alonso Martínez. Reggae music and great cocktails, including an upside-down margarita poured directly down the throat – mixing takes place by vigorous shaking of the head before you swallow. Plenty of room for dancing. Open daily 10.30pm–5am, Fri & Sat till 6am.

Café de Belén, c/Belén 5 Ⓜ Chueca/Alonso Martínez. A café by day, in the evenings there's a

Irish pubs

Although a pint of the "black stuff" has long been available in Madrid, specialist **Irish pubs** have sprung up all over the city in the last ten years. Theme pubs based on village shops, Dublin streets, country cottages and breweries have all appeared, while the Celtic music scene has taken off in a big way with a number of bands now firmly established on the pub circuit. Drinks aren't cheap, but if you want to be assured of a great St Patrick's night or just feel a little homesick you could try some of the following:

Finnegans, Plaza de las Salesas 9 Ⓜ Colón. Large bar with several rooms, complete with bar fittings and wooden floors brought over from Ireland. English-speaking staff and TV sports.

La Fontana de Oro, c/Victoria 1 Ⓜ Sol. Although it's a heresy to have turned this ancient bar (dating back over two hundred years and featuring in Benito Pérez Galdós's book of the same name) into an Irish pub, it's an attractive and lively venue with some swinging Celtic sounds.

The Harp, c/Jesús del Valle Ⓜ Tribunal. Riotous bar which is packed at weekends. Occasional live music.

The Irish Rover, Avda. Brasil 7 Ⓜ Lima. Just behind the concrete jungle of the Azca centre, off the Paseo de la Castellana. Inside it is modelled on an Irish street, but the clientele is more Spanish than most of the Irish pubs. Particularly popular with young *madrileños* and packed at weekends.

The Quiet Man, c/Valverde 44 Ⓜ Tribunal. One of the first on the scene, designed in the style of a turn-of-the-twentieth-century Dublin pub and full of authentic fittings.

Taberna del León de Oro, c/del León 10 Ⓜ Antón Martín. Popular bar, serving both Guinness and Newcastle Brown Ale to homesick foreign residents.

The Triskel Tavern, c/San Vicente Ferrer 3 Ⓜ Tribunal. Jazz nights on Tuesday and the open mic session on Thursday are often worth a visit: there's also a Monday quiz and, to complete a typical pub night out, they even do curries.

radical change to cocktails, hip-hop, acid jazz and trip-hop. Open daily 3.30pm–3am.

Cliché, c/Barquillo Ⓜ Chueca. Best of many bars along this street – a relaxed yet funky place, with clientele as eclectic as the decor, and all ages from fifteen to fifty. Open till 3am.

La Fábrica de Pan, c/Regueros Ⓜ Chueca. Deep in the heart of Chueca, this has a relaxed atmosphere and good music. On any day of the week you'll find people drinking till 4am, or playing board games in the room at the back. Perhaps best enjoyed during the week, as it's a small place and gets packed at weekends. *Cañas* are a modest €2.

Impacto, c/Campoamor 3 Ⓜ Alonso Martínez. Inside is a mini-labyrinth of little rooms and bars around every corner. A fairly trendy, slightly older crowd. Reasonably priced drinks and a good variety of music, despite the lack of dance floor. Door policy of sorts.

Kingston's, c/Barquillo 29 Ⓜ Chueca. Relaxed multicultural *discobar*. Music ranges from soul and funk to reggae and rap. At the weekend professional dancers get things going. Open Mon–Thurs 11pm–5am, Fri, Sat & Sun 11pm–6am.

Malasaña and north

Al Lab'Oratorio, c/Colón 14 Ⓜ Tribunal. Famous 1980s bar with very loud rock music on the sound system, and often live on a little stage downstairs. No entry charge but the drinks are expensive. Open 9pm–3am.

Bar Plaza Dos de Mayo, Plaza Dos de Mayo Ⓜ Tribunal. Old-style wood and tiles bar, which gets packed at weekends. Good music, regular prices, and it opens up in the summer so you can watch the goings-on in the square.

Café del Foro, c/San Andrés 38 Ⓜ Tribunal. Expensive but enjoyable bar with live music or some form of entertainment most nights. Attracts a slightly older, fairly smart crowd. The decor is designed by Costus, who was Almodóvar's sidekick. Open daily 7pm till 3am or 4am.

Café Libertad 8, c/Libertad 8 Ⓜ Chueca. The place to go to listen to budding *cantautores* (singer-songwriters). Some big names – including Rosana and Pedro Guerra – started off in this café, which has been going for more than 25 years. Open Mon–Thurs 5pm–2am, Fri 5pm–3am, Sat 7pm–3am & Sun 6pm–1am.

Casa Quemeda, c/Cardenal Cisneros 56 ⓜ Quevedo. Unusual for this bar-packed area in that it's old, with an all-wood decor, and very peaceful. There's a car stuck in the window – one of the first assembly-line models produced in the country. *Sangría* is a modest €5.25 a jug.

Pepe Botella, c/San Andrés 12 – on Plaza Dos de Mayo ⓜ Tribunal. Formerly a restaurant, now a relaxed wine bar, with friendly staff, decent music and no fruit machine.

Tupperware, c/Corredera Alta de San Pablo 26 ⓜ Tribunal. *The* place to go for the latest on the indie scene, with a mixture of grunge, Brit pop and old classics from the punk era.

La Vaca Austera, c/Palma 20 ⓜ Tribunal. American-style rock bar playing punk/indie classics, with pool tables, mixed clientele and friendly atmosphere.

Vía Lactea, c/Velarde 18 ⓜ Tribunal. Call in here to see where the *movida* began. *Vía Lactea* was a key meeting place for Spain's designers, directors, pop stars and painters in the 1980s, and it retains its original decor from the time, billiard tables included. Stage downstairs. Young studenty clientele.

Warhol's Club, c/Luchana 20 ⓜ Bilbao. Very popular *discobar* open until 10am – and until noon on Sundays. It is spread over two floors, with lots of chrome, glass, video screens, and ultraviolet lighting. Attracts an early-twenties crowd. No door policy.

Salamanca

Avión Club, c/Hermosilla 99 ⓜ Goya. This was one of the most popular clubs in the gloomy post-Civil War years, when it was adopted by the remains of the left. It hasn't changed an iota in the last sixty years and even the pianist, at ninety-odd, is virtually original. Daily 7pm–3am.

El Cabaret de Madrid, c/Jorge Juan 20 ⓜ Colón. Relaxing and characterful bar with downstairs cabaret acts that get going after 1am.

Teatriz, c/Hermosilla 15 ⓜ Serrano. This former theatre, redesigned by the Catalan, Mariscal, together with Philippe Starck, is as elegant a club/bar as any in Europe. There are bars on the main theatre levels, watched over by a restaurant in the circle. Down in the basement there's a library-like area and small disco. Drinks are fairly pricey (€9 for spirits) but there's no entrance charge. Bar 9pm–3am; restaurant 1.30–4.30pm & 9pm–1am; closed Sat lunch, Sun & Aug.

Discotecas

Discotecas – or clubs – aren't always that different from *discobares*, though they tend to be bigger and flashier, with a lot of attention to the lights, sound system and decor, and stay open very late – most until 4am, some till 6am, and a couple till noon. In summer, many of the trendier clubs suspend operations and set up outdoor *terrazas* (see pp.126–127).

Sol, Ópera and Plaza de Santa Ana

Joy Madrid, c/Arenal 11 ⓜ Sol. This big-name disco is frequented by musicians, models and media folk, for whom the €15 entry and rigorous door policy hold no fear. If you can't get in – and 3–5am is the hippest time here – console yourself with the *Chocolatería San Ginés* (see next page), on the street behind. Open 11.30pm–5.30am, Fri & Sat till 6am.

Kapital, c/Atocha 125 ⓜ Atocha. Seven floors to cater for most tastes in this macro-disco, with two dance floors, a cinema and a top-floor terrace. Open Thurs–Sat midnight–6am.

Palacio de Gaviria, c/Arenal 9 ⓜ Ópera/Sol. Aristocratic, nineteenth-century palace where you can wander through a sequence of extravagant salons, listen to a chamber concert in the ballroom, watch a live show or simply dance the night away. Entrance is €15 which includes a first drink. After this, expect to pay €9 a drink.

Gran Vía

Arena, c/Princesa 1 ⓜ Plaza de España. Big, modern and very popular former cinema. Reggae and funk progresses to house music during the night. Occasional live concerts too – Paul Weller and the Asian Dub Foundation are among the artists that have performed here recently. Open Fri & Sat from midnight.

Bash Line, Plaza de Callao 4 ⓜ Callao. There's funk on Wed, disco on Thurs and the OHM club on Fri & Sat, which is popular with a gay crowd. For those with real stamina there's also a Sun night session called "Weekend". Entry around €9.

Davai, c/Flor Baja 1, esq. Gran Vía 59 ⓜ Santo Domingo/Plaza de España. A two-floor multi-club operating under several different names during the week and catering for a wide range of musical tastes with everything from house to 1970s disco. Open daily 11pm–5am.

El Morocco, c/Marqués de Leganes 7 ⓜ Santo Domingo. Venture by rock singer Alaska, long-time mover of the *movida*, and mate of Pedro Almodóvar. The crowds here could well be from an Almodóvar movie (it's likely that some, at least, have acted in one), and they get a club in their own image, including a cabaret show at 2am, the odd (and odd is the word) band, and a dance floor open till 9am. There's an occasional entrance charge and you'll need to look the part to get past the doorman.

El Sol, c/Jardines 3 Ⓜ Gran Vía. Hosts around twenty live concerts a month, but continues afterwards (usually from about 1.30am) as a disco playing house, soul and acid jazz. Entry €6–12. Open daily 11.30pm–5am, Fri & Sat till 5.30am.

Chocolate before bed

If you stay up through a Madrid night, then you must try one of the city's great institutions – the **Chocolatería San Ginés** (Tues–Sun 6pm–7.30am) on Pasadizo de San Ginés, off c/del Arenal between the Puerta del Sol and Teatro Real. Established in 1894, this serves *chocolate con churros* to perfection – just the thing after a night's excess. There's an almost mythical *madrileño* custom of winding up at San Ginés after the clubs close (not that they do any longer), before heading home for a shower and then off to work. And why not?

La Latina

Amnesia/Deep Dance Club, Puerta de Toledo 1 Ⓜ Puerta de Toledo. Pick your night in this mega club with a big dance floor and all the special effects you could wish for. Wed for funk, Thurs for retro 70s and 80s, soul and ragga, Fri & Sat for house. Entry from €9 with drink. Open midnight–6.30am.

Chueca and Santa Bárbara

Boccaccio, c/Marqués de la Ensenada 16 Ⓜ Colón. This is an all-nighter, kicking off about midnight with a business-type crowd, with a younger, trendier crew taking over from 2am till noon. Plush interior with a bar upstairs and a disco down, playing mainly *bakalao*. Entrance is €6 for men, free for women.

Pachá, c/Barceló 11 Ⓜ Tribunal. An eternal survivor on the Madrid disco scene. Once a theatre and still very theatrical, it is exceptionally cool during the week, less so at the weekend when the out-of-towners take over. Good if you like techno. Entry €12 with drink.

Speakeasy, c/Fernando VI 6 Ⓜ Alonso Martínez. Good-value, friendly disco that holds "International Parties" for foreigners new to the city. Good resident DJ.

Out of the centre

Cats, c/Julia Romeo 4 Ⓜ Guzmán El Bueno.

Moncloa is a popular student area, towards the end of c/ Princesa, and it has a good range of bars and discos. *Cats* is one of the best: a large bar surrounded by various dance floors, podiums and chill-out areas. Young crowd and an emphasis firmly on dancing to house and *bakalao*. Recently in trouble for overcrowding. Open daily 9pm–5.30am.

Cocoon, c/Abdón Terradas 5 Ⓜ Moncloa. Keeping track of the latest dance vibes with a string of top notch DJs, this club has now moved to bigger premises in Moncloa. Chill-out upstairs or brave the hard-techno below. Entry €9–10.80. Open Fri & Sat 1am–6am.

Divino Aqualung, Paseo del Ermita Santo 48 Ⓜ Puerta del Angel. New disco which promises to "bring the spirit of Ibiza back to Madrid". Six bars, light shows, go-go dancers and a capacity for 2500 people. Entry €9 with drink. Open Fri & Sat midnight–6am.

Galileo Galilei, c/Galileo 100 Ⓜ Canal. Bar, concert venue and disco all rolled into one. Check the *Guía del Ocio* to find out whether it's the night for cabaret, salsa or a singer-songwriter.

Space of Sound/Macumba Club, Estación de Chamartín s/n Metro Chamartín. If you've still got energy left, this after-hours club on top of the Chamartín train station will allow you to strut your stuff all morning; if you can take the constant bombardment of *bakalao*, that is. Open Sat, Sun & holidays 6.30am–noon.

Performance: music, film and theatre

Most nights in Madrid, you can take in performances of **flamenco**, **salsa**, **rock** (local and imported), **jazz**, **classical music** and **opera** at one or other of the city's venues. Often, it's the smaller, offbeat clubs that are the more enjoyable, though there are plenty of big auditoria – including the football stadiums and bullring – for big-name concerts. In summer, events are supplemented by the council's **Veranos de la Villa** cultural programme and in autumn by the **Festival de Otoño**. These also encompass **theatre** and **film**, both of which have fairly healthy year-round scenes.

Flamenco

Flamenco underwent something of a revival in Madrid in the 1990s, in large part due to the "new flamenco" artists, like Ketama and Joaquín Cortes, who are unafraid to mix it with a bit of blues, jazz, even rock. The city has its own flamenco festival each February, when you can stand a chance of catching some of the bigger names. The club listings below span the range between purist flamenco and crossover experiments and most artists – even major stars – appear in them. Although the following clubs and cafés may open earlier, be aware that in many cases performances won't really get going until around midnight.

Café de Chinitas, c/Torija 7 ☎ 915 595 135; Ⓜ Santo Domingo. One of the oldest flamenco clubs in Madrid, with a dinner-dance spectacular. It's expensive but the music is authentic and the audience is predominantly Spanish. Reservations are essential, though you may get in late when people start to leave (at this time you don't have to eat and the steep entrance fee of around €25.25 does at least include your first drink). Open Mon–Sat 9pm–2am.

Candela, c/Olmo 2 ☎ 914 673 382; Ⓜ Antón Martín. A legendary bar frequented by musicians – the late, great Camarón de la Isla is reputed to have sung here until 11am on one occasion.

Caracol, c/Bernardino Obregón 18 ☎ 915 308 055; Ⓜ Embajadores. The top names tend to

---

Madrid listings and the madrugada

Listings information is in plentiful supply in Madrid. The newspapers *El País* and *El Mundo* have excellent daily listings, and on Fridays both publish sections devoted to events, bars and restaurants in the capital. Of the two, *El Mundo*'s **Metrópoli** is the better – a separate colour magazine, full of previews and details of the week's exhibitions, films, theatre and concerts, and with extensive listings of clubs, bars and restaurants (including opening hours and average prices – usually on the high side of what you'll spend).

If your time in Madrid doesn't coincide with the Friday *Metrópoli* supplement, or you want maximum info, pick up the weekly listings magazine **Guía del Ocio** (Ⓦ www.guiadelocio.com; €0.90) at any kiosk. It's not quite as clear or discriminating as *Metrópoli*, but it's functional enough. The *ayuntamiento* also publishes a monthly "What's On" pamphlet, **En Madrid**, which is free from any of the tourist offices and lists forthcoming events in the city. Alternatively, try calling the English-language telephone listings service on ☎ 914 811 248. *In Madrid,* meanwhile, is a free monthly magazine – available in many bars – which bills itself as "Madrid's English monthly for the Hip, Cool and Transient" and features useful reviews of clubs and bars.

One word that might perplex first-timers in Madrid – and which crops up in all the listings magazines – is **madrugada**. This refers to the hours between midnight and dawn and, in this supremely late-night/early-morning city, is a necessary adjunct to announcements of important events. *Tres de la madrugada* means an event is due to start at 3am.

appear at this venue which is popular with the young crowd, so it's worth getting here early. Flamenco is often mixed with jazz and blues; for pure flamenco, come on Thursday night (call first to check, as the programme can change). Entry €9 with drink.

Corral de la Morería, c/Morería 17 ☎ 913 658 446; Ⓜ La Latina. This is a good venue for some serious acts off the tourist circuit, but again expensive at about €24 for the show plus a drink. Open daily 9pm–2am, Sat opens 10.45pm.

Casa Patas, c/Cañizares 10 ☎ 913 690 496; Ⓜ Antón Martín. Small, but very popular flamenco *tablao* that gets its share of big names. The best

nights are Thurs and Fri. Entry €12. Open Mon–Sat 8pm–2am.

Peña Chaquetón, c/Canarias 39 ☎ 916 712 777; Ⓜ Palos de la Frontera. Fri nights only, but worth the effort; turn up early if there's a big name or you won't get in. Don't worry about the "members only" sign on the outside.

La Soleá, c/Cava Baja 34 ☎ 913 653 308; Ⓜ La Latina. This brilliant, long-established flamenco bar is the genuine article. People sit around in the salon, pick up a guitar or start to sing and gradually the atmosphere builds up until everyone else is clapping or dancing. Has to be seen to be believed. Open Mon–Sat 8.30pm–3am. Closed Aug.

Rock and blues

Madrid is very much on the international rock tour circuit and you can catch big (and small) American and British acts in front of enthusiastic audiences. One of the more endearing Spanish habits is to translate foreign names – including rock bands: thus, just as Prince Charles is always known as Príncipe Carlos, U2 are, of course, U–Dos. **Tickets** for most big rock concerts are sold by Madrid Rock, Gran Vía 25 (Ⓜ Callao), FNAC, c/Preciados 28 (Ⓜ Callao) and El Corte Inglés, c/ Preciados 1–4 (Ⓜ Sol). For telephone bookings, see ticket agencies in the "Listings" section (p.144).

In the smaller clubs, you have a chance of seeing a very wide range of local bands. Madrid has long been the heart of the Spanish rock scene (see "Music" in Contexts).

Clubs

Chesterfield Café, c/Serrano Jover 5 ☎ 915 422 817; Ⓜ Argüelles. As well as offering Tex-Mex-style food, this club is a live rock venue (Wed–Sun). Sets begin at midnight (1am on Fri and Sat).

La Coquette, c/Arenal 22, entrance at c/Hileras 14; Ⓜ Ópera. Small, smoky blues bar, where people sit around in the near dark watching the band perform on a tiny stage. Live music most nights. Open daily 8pm–2.30am.

Maravillas, c/San Vicente Ferrer 33 ☎ 915 233 071; Ⓜ Tribunal. Small but usually uncrowded indie venue where bands play anything from jazz to funk to reggae, often till around 4am.

Siroco, c/San Dimás 3 ☎ 915 933 070; Ⓜ San Bernardo. Live bands most nights at this popular little soul club, not far north of Gran Vía. Closed Sun.

El Sol, c/Jardines 3 ☎ 913 611 184; Ⓜ Sol/Gran Vía. Hosts around twenty live concerts a month; afterwards it continues as a disco. Very good acoustics. Open daily 11.30pm–5am.

Ya'sta La Trup, c/Valverde 10 Ⓜ Gran Vía. A weird and wonderful place for terminal insomniacs. Most nights there's a jam session from local rock musicians, then a disco plays rock and funk until about 8am. The door policy gets strict from 4am, so best turn up early.

Major concert venues

The city's main indoor arena, the **Palacio de Deportes**, was burned down recently so the following venues are likely to feature more frequently when bigger groups complete the Spanish leg of their European tours.

Auditorio Parque de Atracciones, Casa de Campo Ⓜ El Lago. Open-air summer venue within the precincts of the Parque de Atracciones, which hosts a number of the more popular family-oriented Spanish groups.

Caracol, c/Bernardino Obregón 18 ☎ 915 273 594; Ⓜ Embajadores. Originally a leading flamenco

night spot, but now one of the most popular venues for touring groups including, of late, Eagle Eye Cherry and the Manic Street Preachers. Good acoustics and visibility.

La Cubierta, Plaza de Toros de Leganés ☎ 917 651 890. Bullring in the southern industrial suburb of Leganés, often used as a venue for heavy rock artists of the Iron Maiden and Megadeth variety, although for a complete contrast a re-formed Soft Cell also made a recent appearance.

La Katedral, c/Fundadores 7 Ⓜ Manuel Becerra/O'Donnell. Relatively new venue which has hosted some big names, though most of these seem to be heading for *La Riviera* now.

Plaza de Toros de las Ventas, Las Ventas ☎ 913 562 200 or 917 264 800, Ⓦ www.las-ventas.com;

Ⓜ Ventas. The bullring is a pretty good concert venue, put to use in the summer festival. Tickets are usually one price, though you can pay more for a (good) reserved seat (*asiento reservado*).

La Riviera, Paseo Bajo Virgen del Puerto s/n, Puente de Segovia ☎ 913 652 415; Ⓜ Puerta del Ángel. Fun disco and concert venue right next to the river that has hosted Coldplay and David Byrne amongst other recent visitors.

Latin music

Madrid attracts big-name Latin artists and if you happen to coincide with the summer festival you'll stand a good chance of catching someone of the stature of Juan Luís Guerra from the Dominican Republic – a huge star in Spain. Gigs by top artists tend to take place at the venues listed above. The local scene is a good deal more low-key but there's enjoyable salsa, nonetheless, in a handful of clubs.

Café del Mercado, Ronda de Toledo 1, in the Centro Artesano Puerta de Toledo ☎ 913 653 786; Ⓜ Puerta de Toledo. Live music every day in a spacious, comfortable club and a *Gran Baile de Salsa* every Friday and Saturday at 2am.

Oba-Oba, c/Jacometrezo 4 Ⓜ Callao. Samba and lambada with lethal *caiprinhas* from the bar.

Pasadena, c/Fuencarral 29 Ⓜ Gran Vía. Large, popular venue with salsa a speciality.

Salsipuedes, c/Puebla 6 ☎ 915 228 417; Ⓜ Callao/Gran Vía. Serious salsa dancing to a live orchestra most weekdays in a "tropical" setting.

Strict door policy. Open daily 11pm–6am.

El Son, c/ Victoria 6 Ⓜ Sol. Live Cuban music Mon-Thurs at this small Latin club which has picked up where its predecessor Massai left off. There's no space to stand and watch so make sure you bring your dancing shoes. Open daily 7pm onwards.

Suristan, c/Cruz 7 ☎ 915 323 909; Ⓜ Sol. A wide range of ethnic music at this venue, including Cuban rock and other Latin sounds. Wednesday night is usually flamenco night. Closed Sun.

Jazz

Madrid doesn't rank with London, Paris or New York on the jazz front but the clubs are friendly, unpretentious places. Look out for the annual jazz festival staged at a variety of venues in November.

Bar Clamores, c/Albuquerque 14 ☎ 914 457 938, Ⓦ www.salaclamores.com; Ⓜ Bilbao. Large, low-key and enjoyable jazz bar with accomplished (if not very famous) artists, not too exorbitant drinks and a nice range of snacks. Last set finishes around 1.30am, though the bar stays open to 4am. €3–6 for gigs, otherwise free.

Café Central, Plaza del Ángel 10 ☎ 913 694 143; Ⓜ Sol. Once voted no. 6 in a "Best Jazz Clubs of the World" poll in *Wire* magazine, this is an attractive venue – small and relaxed – and it gets the odd big name, plus strong local talent. The Art Deco café is worth a visit in its own right. €8.50–10.25 for gigs, otherwise free.

Café Jazz Populart, c/Huertas 22 ☎ 914 298 407; Ⓜ Antón Martín. Nightly sets from jazz and blues bands. It's open from 6pm, gets cooking around 11pm and stays open till 2am or so. €6 for gigs, otherwise free.

Segundo Jazz, c/Comandante Zorita 8 ☎ 915 549 437; Ⓜ Nuevos Ministerios. Typical atmospheric basement club with live music during the week only. Last set at 2.15am.

Triskel Tavern, c/San Vicente Ferrer 3 ☎ 915 232 783; Ⓜ Tribunal. This Irish bar has a jazz night on Tuesday and it's worth popping in to see what's on.

Classical music and opera

The **Teatro Real** is the city's prestigious opera house and, along with the **Auditorio Nacional de Musica**, is home to the Orquesta Nacional de España. Equally enjoyable are the salons and small auditoria for chamber orchestras and groups.

Auditorio Nacional de Música, c/Príncipe de Vergara 146 ☎913 370 100, Ⓦauditorionacional. mcu.es; Ⓜ Cruz del Rayo. This is the home of the Spanish National Orchestra and host to most international visiting orchestras.

Centro de Arte Reina Sofía, c/Santa Isabel ☎914 675 062, Ⓦmuseoreinasofia.mcu.es; Ⓜ Atocha. This arts centre often has programmes of contemporary music.

La Corrala, c/Mesón de Paredes ☎915 309 600; Ⓜ Lavapiés. A surviving tenement block, once typical of working-class Madrid, which stages zarzuelas during the *Veranos de la Villa* summer season.

La Fídula, c/Huertas Ⓜ Antón Martín. A chamber orchestra plays most nights at 11.30pm in this café.

Fundación Juan March, c/Castelló 77 ☎914 354 240; Ⓜ Núñez de Balboa. Small auditorium used for recitals two or three times a week.

Salón del Prado, c/Prado 4 Ⓜ Sol. Another café venue which hosts classical musicians on Thursday nights at 11pm.

Teatro Calderón, c/Atocha 18 ☎916 320 114; Ⓜ Sol. Venue for a very popular annual opera season – a lot easier to get tickets here than at the Teatro Real.

Teatro Monumental, c/Atocha 65 ☎914 298 119; Ⓜ Atocha. A large theatre, offering orchestral concerts, opera, *zarzuela* and flamenco recitals. Tickets are sold for stalls (*butaca de patio*) or a series of dizzying circles (*entresuelo*).

Teatro Real, Plaza Isabel II info ☎915 160 660, tickets ☎902 244 824 or 915 588 787 from abroad, Ⓦ www.teatro-real.com; Ⓜ Ópera. Madrid's opera house.

La Zarzuela, c/Jovellanos 4 ☎915 245 400, Ⓦ teatrozarzuela.mcu.es; Ⓜ Sevilla. The main venue for Spanish operetta.

Film

Cines – cinemas or movie houses – can be found all over the central area. Major releases (which often make it here well before London) are dubbed into Spanish, though a number of cinemas have regular **original language** screenings, with subtitles; these are listed in a separate *versión original/subtitulada (v.o.)* section in the newspapers. **Tickets** for films cost around €5.40 but most cinemas have a *día del espectador* (usually Mon or Wed) with €3.90 admission. Be warned that on Sunday night half of Madrid goes to a movie and queues can be long.

Alphaville, **Renoir** and **Lumière**, c/Martín de los Heros – just north of the Plaza de España Ⓜ Plaza de España. This trio of multiscreen cinemas, within 200m of each other, show regular *v.o.* films.

California, c/Andrés Mellado 53 Ⓜ Moncloa. Giant single-screen cinema in the midst of studenty Moncloa. After a brief experiment showing dubbed foreign films it has reverted once again to *v.o.* only.

Ideal Yelmo Complex, c/Doctor Cortezo 6 Ⓜ Sol/Tirso de Molina. Nine-screen complex which shows a good selection of *v.o.* films.

Filmoteca/Cine Doré, c/Santa Isabel 3 Ⓜ Antón Martín. Beautiful old cinema, now home to an art-film centre, with imaginative programmes of classic and contemporary films, all shown in *v.o.* at an

admission price of just €1.25. In summer, there are open-air screenings on a little terraza – they're very popular, so buy tickets in advance.

Imax Madrid, Parque Tierno Galván, Meneses Ⓜ Méndez Alvaro. Three different types of screen at this futuristic cinema – a giant flat one, a dome-shaped one for all-round viewing and one for 3D projections. Continuous shows: Mon–Fri 11.20am–1pm & 3.45pm–1am, Sat & Sun 11.20am–2.15pm & 3.45pm–1am; €5.40–6.60.

Luna, c/Luna 2 Ⓜ Callao. Four-screen cinema showing some of the latest releases (often in *v.o*) located in a grim-looking square just north of the Gran Vía.

Theatre and cabaret

Madrid is enjoying a renaissance in theatre; you can catch anything from Lope de Vega to contemporary and experimental productions, and there's also a new wave of cabaret and comedy acts. Look out too for the annual *Festival de Otoño* running from September to November, and the alternative theatre festival in February.

Berlin Cabaret, Costanilla de San Pedro 11 ☎913 662 034; ⓜLa Latina. Varied cabaret and comedy in a traditional, slightly seedy club setting. Admission is normally free, but drinks are expensive. Open Mon–Sat 11pm–5am, Fri & Sat till 6am.
Centro Cultural de la Villa, Plaza de Colón ☎915 756 080; ⓜColón. Arts centre where you're likely to see some of the more experimental companies on tour as well as popular works and *zarzuela* performances.
Círculo de Bellas Artes, c/Marqués de Riera 2 ☎915 324 437 or 915 324 438; ⓜBanco de España. The Círculo includes a beautiful old theatre which puts on adventurous productions.
Teatro de la Abadía, c/Fernández de los Ríos 42 ☎914 481 627; ⓜQuevedo/Argüelles. Beautifully decorated theatre set in pleasant grounds just off the main street. It has staged some very successful productions and is especially popular in the *Festival de Otoño*.

Teatro Alfil, c/Pez 10 ☎915 215 827; ⓜNoviciado. Alternative theatre and comedy.
Teatro Español, c/Príncipe 25 ☎914 296 297; ⓜSol/Sevilla. Classic Spanish theatre.
Teatro de Madrid, Avda. de la Ilustración s/n ☎917 301 750; ⓜBarrio del Pilar. Large, modern theatre next to the large La Vaguada shopping centre in the north of the city, presenting some excellent ballet, drama and touring cultural shows.
Teatro María Guerrero, c/Tamayo y Baus 4 ☎913 194 769; ⓜColón. This is the headquarters of the Centro Dramático Nacional which stages high-quality Spanish and international productions in a beautiful neo-Mudéjar interior.
Teatro Muñoz Seca, Plaza del Carmen 1 ☎915 232 128; ⓜSol. This theatre hosts regular performances of *Sainetes,* traditional Spanish plays.
Teatro Nuevo Apolo, Plaza Tirso de Molina 1 ☎913 690 637; ⓜTirso de Molina. Madrid's principal venue for major musicals.

Shopping

Shopping districts in Madrid are pretty defined. The biggest range of stores are along Gran Vía and around Puerta del Sol, which is where the **department stores** – such as El Corte Inglés – have their main branches. For **fashion** (*moda*), the smartest addresses are c/Serrano, c/Goya and c/Velázquez, north of the Retiro, while more alternative designers are to be found in Malasaña and Chueca (c/Almirante, especially). The **antiques** trade is centred down towards the Rastro, on and around c/Ribera de Curtidores, or in the Puerta de Toledo shopping centre (ⓜPuerta de Toledo), while for **general weirdness**, it's hard to beat the shops just off Plaza Mayor, where luminous saints rub shoulders with surgical supports and fascist memorabilia. The cheapest, trashiest **souvenirs** can be collected at the Todo a Cien ("Everything at 100ptas") shops scattered all over the city. If you want international or speciality shops, head for Madrid 2, a huge hypermarket next to ⓜBarrio de Pilar or the upmarket ABC Serrano at c/Serrano 61 and Paseo de la Castellana 34 (ⓜNuñez de Balboa).

Most areas of the city have their own *mercados del barrio* – indoor **markets**, devoted mainly to food. Among the best and most central are those in Plaza San Miguel (just west of Plaza Mayor); La Cebada in Plaza de la Cebada (ⓜLa Latina); Antón Martín in c/Santa Isabel (ⓜAntón Martín); behind the Gran Vía in Plaza de Mostenses (ⓜPlaza de España); on c/Gravina in Chueca (ⓜChueca); on c/Barceló in Malasaña (ⓜTribunal); and Maravillas in c/Bravo Murillo 122 (ⓜCuatro Caminos). The city's biggest market is, of course, **El Rastro** – the flea market – which takes place on Sundays in La Latina, south

Opening hours and late-night shopping

Usual **opening hours** are Monday–Friday 9.30am–2pm & 5–8pm, Saturday 10am–2pm. Most shops are closed on Sunday, but the larger stores do open on the first Sunday of each month (not in Aug.) and those selling "cultural" goods such as books, CDs and videos can open every day. There are however, two chains of late-night shops – Vip's and 7 Eleven – that stay open into the small hours and on Sundays. Each branch sells newspapers, cigarettes, groceries, books, CDs – all the things you need to pop in for at 3am. Larger branches also have café-restaurants, one-hour photo developing and other services.

Central branches include:

Vip's (daily 9am–3am): Glorieta de Quevedo Ⓜ Quevedo; Gran Vía 43 Ⓜ Gran Vía; c/Fuencarral 101 Ⓜ Bilbao; c/Miguel Ángel 11 Ⓜ Rubén Darío; c/Serrano 41 Ⓜ Serrano; c/Velázquez 84 & 136 Ⓜ Velázquez.

7 Eleven (daily 24hr): c/Arenal 28 Ⓜ Sol/Opera; c/Toledo 80 Ⓜ La Latina; Agustín de Foxá 25 Ⓜ Plaza de Castilla; Avda. de América 18 Ⓜ Avda. de América; Capitán Haya 17–19 Ⓜ Lima; San Bernardo 33 Ⓜ Noviciados.

of Plaza Mayor. For details of this great Madrid institution, see the box on p.95. Other specialized markets include a second-hand **book market** on the Cuesta de Moyano, at the southwest corner of El Retiro (see p.107).

Crafts and miscellaneous

Alvarez Gómez, c/Serrano 14 Ⓜ Serrano. Gómez has been making the same perfumes in the same bottles for the past century. The scents – carnations, roses, violets – are as simple and straight as they come. Mon–Sat 9.30am–2pm & 4.45–8.15pm.

El Arco de los Cuchilleros, Plaza Mayor 9 – by the steps Ⓜ Sol. The location of this shop may be at the heart of tourist Madrid but the goods are a far cry from the swords, lace and castanets that fill most shops in the region. El Arco handles thirty or so workshops and artisans, who reflect Spanish *artesanía* at its most innovative and contemporary. They encompass ceramics (six of Madrid's top potters), leather (from Oviedo), wood (including some fine games), jewellery and textiles. Mon–Sat 11am–8pm, Sun 11am–2.30pm.

Conde Hermanos, c/Felipe II 2 Ⓜ Ópera (Mon–Fri 9.30am–1.30pm & 4.30–8pm) & **José Ramírez**, c/Concepción Jerónima Ⓜ Sol/Tirso de Molina (Mon–Fri 9.30am–2pm & 5–8pm, Sat 10am–2pm). Two of the most renowned guitar workshops in Spain; the latter even has a museum of antique instruments. Prices start at around €108 and head skywards for the quality models and fancy woods.

El Flamenco Vive, c/Unión 4 Ⓜ Ópera. Specializes in all things Andalucian; flamenco music, guitars, percussion, dance accessories, books etc. Mon–Sat 10.30am–2pm & 5–9pm.

Fútbol Total, c/Eloy Gonzalo 7 Ⓜ Quevedo & Estación de Trenes Charmartín Ⓜ Chamartín. Just the place to get your Real, Atlético or even Rayo shirt. In fact the strip of practically every Spanish team is available, for around €43. Mon–Sat: July–Sept 10.30am–2pm & 5.30–8.30pm; Oct–June 10.30am–2pm & 5–9pm.

Intermon, c/Alberto Aguilera 15 Ⓜ Argüelles. Arts and crafts from Asia, Africa and South America. Some of the profits are invested in development programmes. Mon–Sat 10am–2pm & 5–8pm.

Casa Jiménez, c/Preciados 42 Ⓜ Callao. If you want to buy a fan that's a work of art, this is the place to come. Mon–Sat 10am–1.30pm & 5–8pm, closed Sat pm in July and all day Sat in Aug.

Palomeque, c/Hileras 12 Ⓜ Ópera. A religious department store stocking everything from rosary beads and habits to your very own plastic baby Jesus. If you want to complete your postcard collection of Spanish saints and virgins, this is the place for you. Mon–Fri 10am–2pm & 5–8pm, Sat 10am–2pm.

Puck, c/Duque de Sesto 30 Ⓜ Goya. This is the best – indeed, about the only really decent – toy shop in central Madrid. Mon–Sat 10am–1.30pm & 4.30–8pm.

Puerta de Toledo shopping centre Ⓜ Puerta de Toledo. This centre has several shops specializing in antiques, jewellery and crafts. Closed Mon.

Seseña, c/Cruz 23 Ⓜ Sol. Tailor specializing in traditional *madrileño* capes for royalty and celebrities.

Clients have included Luis Buñuel and Gary Cooper. Mon–Sat 10am–1.30pm & 4.30–8pm.

Casa Yustas, Plaza Mayor 30 Ⓜ Sol. Madrid's oldest hat shop, established in 1894. Pick from traditional designs for men's and women's hats (*sombreros*), caps (*gorras*) and berets (*boinas*). No cards. Mon–Sat 9.30am–9.30pm, Sun & holidays 11am–1.30pm.

Books, comics and maps

Casa del Libro, Gran Vía 29 & Maestro Victoria 3 Ⓜ Callao. The city's biggest bookstore, with three floors covering just about everything, including a wide range of fiction in English. Mon–Sat 9.30am–9.30pm.

Desnivel, Plaza Matute 6 Ⓦ www.libreriadesnivel. com; Ⓜ Antón Martín. More centrally located than La Tienda Verde (see below), this bookshop stocks

a good range of guides and maps covering all parts of Spain.

FNAC, c/Preciados 28 Ⓜ Callao. The book department of this huge store is a good place to sit and peruse books and magazines in all languages.

Librería Antonio Machado, c/Fernando VI 17 Ⓜ Alonso Martínez. The city's best literary bookshop. All cards. Mon–Sat 10am–2pm & 5–8pm.

Pasajes, c/Genova 3 Ⓔ pasajes@infornet.es; Ⓜ Alonso Martínez/Colón. Specializes in English and foreign-language books. Also has a useful noticeboard service for flat-sharing and Spanish classes. Mon–Fri 10am–2pm & 5–8pm, Sat 10am–2pm.

La Tienda Verde, c/Maudes 23 & 38 Ⓜ Cuatro Caminos. Trekking and mountain books, guides and survey (*topográfico*) maps. Mon–Sat 9.30am–2pm & 4.30–8pm.

Fashion: clothes and shoes

Branches of chain stores such as Mango, Zara, Cortefiel and Springfield are scattered all over the city and at sale times in January and July there are often some great bargains to be picked up. If your tastes run to the more select in the fashion stakes try some of the shops listed below.

Adolfo Domínguez, c/José Ortega y Gasset 4 & c/Serrano 96 Ⓜ Serrano. The classic modern Spanish look – subdued colours, free lines. Domínguez's designs are quite pricey but he has a cheaper *Basico* range. Both branches have men's clothes; women's are only available at the Ortega y Gasset branch. Mon–Sat 10am–2pm & 5–8.30pm (Serrano branch open at lunchtime).

Agatha Ruiz de la Prada, c/Marqués de Riscal 8 Ⓜ Rubén Darío. Outlet for the striking clothes and accessories of this *movida* designer. Mon–Fri 10am–2pm & 5–8pm, Sat 10am–2pm.

Ararat, c/Conde Xiquena 13 Ⓜ Chueca & c/Almirante 10 & 11 Ⓜ Cheuca. A trio of shops with clubby Spanish and foreign designs at reasonably modest prices. Men's clothes in c/Conde Xiquena, women's in c/Almirante. Mon–Sat 11am–2pm & 5–8.30pm.

Berlín, c/Almirante 10 Ⓜ Chueca. Women's clothes from vanguard European designers. Mon–Sat 11am–2pm & 5–8.30pm.

Blackmarket, c/Colón 3 Ⓜ Chueca. Adventurous clothes for women. Mon–Sat 10.30am–2pm & 5–8.30pm.

Camper, c/Gran Vía 54 Ⓜ Callao. Spain's best shoe-shop chain, with covetable designs at modest prices. There are lots of other branches around the city. Men and women. Mon–Sat 10am–2pm & 5–8.30pm.

Caracol Cuadrado, c/Justiniano 6 Ⓜ Serrano. Bargain store selling last season's designs from

big names, including Sybilla – Spain's trendiest designer. Men and women. Mon–Sat 10.30am–2.30pm & 5–8.30pm.

Ekseptión, c/Velázquez 28 Ⓜ Velázquez. A dramatic walkway gives onto some of the most *moderno* clothes in Madrid, from Sybilla and Antoni Miró, among others. Expensive. Men and women. Mon–Sat 10.30am–2.30pm & 5–8.30pm.

Excrupulus Net, c/Almirante 7 Ⓜ Chueca. Groovy shoes from Spanish designers, Muxart and Looky. Men and women. Mon–Sat 11am–2pm & 5–8.30pm.

Glam, c/de Fuencarral 35 Ⓜ Gran Vía/Chueca & c/Hortaleza 62 Ⓜ Chueca. The clientele and the clothes wouldn't look out of place in an Almodóvar film. Mon–Sat 10am–2pm & 5–9pm.

Hernanz, c/Toledo 30 Ⓜ Tirso de Molina. This shoe shop stocks *alpargatas* – espadrilles – in just about every imaginable colour. No cards. Mon–Fri 9.30am–1.30pm & 5–8.30pm, Sat 9.30am–1.30pm.

Josep Font-Luz D'az, c/Serrano 58 – patio Ⓜ Serrano. Beautiful, minimalist shop, selling original and expensive women's designs by this young and *muy de moda* Catalan duo. Women only. Mon–Sat 10am–2pm & 5–8.30pm.

Manuel Herrero, c/Preciados 7 Ⓜ Sol. Traditional shop specializing in leather; particularly good for coats and jackets.

Sybilla, c/Jorge Juan 12 Ⓜ Retiro. Sybilla was Spain's top designer of the 1980s – a Vivienne

Westwood of Madrid, if you will. She remains at the forefront of the scene, and her prices show it. Women only. All cards. Mon–Sat 10am–2pm & 4.30–8.30pm.

Food and drink

Baco – La Boutique del Vino, c/San Bernardo 117 ⓜ Quevedo. Good-value range of quality Spanish wines, *cavas*, brandies and even Asturian cider. No cards. Mon–Fri 11am–2pm & 5–8pm, Sat 10am–2pm.

Casa Mira, Carrera de San Jerónimo 30 ⓜ Sol. Old, established *pasteleria*, selling delicious *turrón*, *mazapán*, *frutas glaseadas*, and the like. Daily 10am–2pm & 5–9pm.

Lafuente, c/Luchana 28 ⓜ Bilbao. Wines from Spain and abroad, including lots from Rioja, Ribera del Duero and Galicia, plus *cavas*. Mon–Sat 10am–2pm & 5–8.30pm.

Lhardy, Carrera de San Jerónimo 8 ⓜ Sol. This bar and deli is attached to one of Madrid's top restaurants – and is a lot more affordable. You can put together wonderful and elaborate picnics (the *croquetas* and *empanadillas* are legendary), assuming you can resist consuming them on the spot. Mon–Sat 9.30am–3pm & 5–9pm, Sun 9am–2pm.

Mallorca, c/Serrano 6 ⓜ Serrano. The main branch of Madrid's best deli chain – like *Lhardy*, a pricey but fabulous treasure trove for picnics, or cakes or chocs for presents. All branches have small bars for drinks and canapés. Daily 9.30am–9pm.

La Mallorquina, Puerta del Sol 2 ⓜ Sol. Wonderful-smelling pastry shop and café selling everything you've always been told not to eat. Mon–Sat 9am–9.45pm.

Mariano Aguado, c/Echegaray 19 ⓜ Sevilla. Fine selection of Spanish wines and, especially, sherries (*vinos de Jerez*). Mon–Sat 9.30am–2pm & 5.30–8.30pm.

Mariano Madrueño, c/Postigo San Martín 3 ⓜ Callao. The place to get wines and liqueurs such as *Pacharán* sloe gin. Mon–Fri 9.30am–2pm & 5–8pm, Sat 9.30am–2pm.

Tienda Olivarero, c/Mejia Lequerica 1 ⓜ Alonso Martinez. Outlet for olive growers' co-operative, with information sheets to guide you towards purchasing the best olive oils. Mon–Sat 9.30am–2pm & 5.30–7.30pm.

Records and CDs

FNAC, c/Preciados 28 ⓜ Callao. Large French store with a huge collection of cassettes and CDs.

Madrid Rock, Gran Vía 25 ⓜ Gran Vía. A big, slightly chaotic store, good for rock CDs and concert tickets. Daily 10am–10pm.

Toni Martín, c/Martín de los Heros 18 ⓜ Plaza de España. Rock CDs and discs, new and second-hand. Mon–Sat 10.30am–2pm & 5.30–8.15pm.

Children

Mothercare, Madrid 2, La Vaguada, Avda. Monforte de Lemos ⓜ Barrio del Pilar. As you would expect you'll find a wide range of clothes and every accessory you might conceivably require for a young child.

Prénatal, c/ Goya 99 ⓜ Goya, San Bernardo 97–99 ⓜ San Bernardo & Madrid 2, La Vaguada, Avda. Monforte de Lemos ⓜ Barrio del Pilar. Spanish equivalent of Mothercare with more branches around the city and often a little cheaper.

Listings

Airlines Many airlines have their offices along the Gran Vía or on c/Princesa, its continuation beyond the Plaza de España. Addresses include: British Airways, c/Serrano 60 5° ☎ 913 054 212 or 912 054 317, ⓜ Serrano; Iberia, c/Velázquez 130 ☎ 915 878 156 or 902 400 500, ⓜ Serrano; KLM, Gran Vía 59 ☎ 912 478 100, ⓜ Santo Domingo; and TWA, Plaza de Colón 2 ☎ 913 103 094, ⓜ Colón. Phone numbers for other airlines: Air Europa ☎ 913 936 732; Air France ☎ 913 300 440; Aer Lingus ☎ 915 414 216; and Sabena ☎ 913 300 460. The Iberojet counter at the airport sells discounted seats on all scheduled flights, if you're prepared to queue up and take the risk of not getting on. Tickets for the Puente Aéreo to Barcelona are available in terminal two.

Banks and exchange The main Spanish banks are concentrated on c/Alcalá and Gran Vía. Opening hours are normally Mon–Fri 9am–2pm, but they're also often open on Sat 9am–1pm from Oct to May. International banks include: Bank of America, c/Capitán Haya 1 ☎ 915 555 000, ⓜ Santiago Bernabéu; Barclays, Plaza de Colón 1 ☎ 914 102 800, ⓜ Colón; Citibank, c/José Ortega y Gasset 29 ☎ 914 355 190, ⓜ Núñez de Balboa; and Lloyds, c/Serrano 90 ☎ 915 767 000,

Núñez de Balboa. In addition to the banks, branches of El Corte Inglés department store all have exchange offices with long hours and highly competitive rates; the most central is on Puerta del Sol. Aeropuerto de Barajas has a 24-hr currency exchange office.

Bicycles Try Bicicletas Chapinal, c/Alcalá 242 ☎914 041 853 (Mon–Fri 10am–1.30pm & 4.30–8pm, Sat 10am–2pm; Ⓜ El Carmen); Calmera, c/Atocha 98 ☎915 277 574 (Mon–Sat 9.30am–1.30pm & 4.30–8pm; Ⓜ Antón Martín); and Karacol, c/Montera 32 ☎915 329 073 (Mon–Fri 10.30am–2pm & 5.30–8pm, Sat 10.30am–2pm; Ⓜ Gran Vía/Sol) and at c/Tortosa 8, nr Atocha ☎915 399 633; Ⓜ Atocha.

Bullfights Madrid's main Plaza de Toros, the monumental Las Ventas (c/Alcalá 237; Ⓜ Ventas), hosts some of the year's most prestigious events, especially during the May *San Isidro* festivities, though the main season runs from March to October. Tickets are available at the box office at Ventas (☎917 264 800 or 913 562 200, Ⓦ www.las-ventas.com; March–Oct Thurs–Sun 10am–2pm & 5–8pm) or at Localidades de Galicia (see "Ticket agencies" below); at the latter you pay around fifty percent more than the printed prices, which are for season tickets sold en bloc. There is a second bullring in the suburb of Carabanchel (Avda. Matilde Hernández; ☎914 220 780; Ⓜ Vista Alegre), about 4km to the southwest of the centre.

Car rental Major operators have branches at the airport and train stations. Central offices include: Atesa, c/Infanta Mercedes 90 ☎915 711 931, Ⓜ Estrecho; Avis, Gran Vía 60 ☎915 472 048, reservations ☎902 135 531, Ⓜ Plaza de España; Europcar, c/San Leonardo 8 ☎917 211 222, Ⓜ Plaza de España – also an office in Atocha station; and Hertz, Atocha station ☎914 681 318, Ⓜ Atocha. Easy-Rent-a-Car, c/Agustín de Foxa 27, Parking Centro Norte ☎0906 586 0586 (telephone bookings available from Britain only), Ⓜ Chamartín; Rent Me, Plaza de Herradores 6, just off Plaza Mayor ☎915 590 822, Ⓜ Sol, is a good-value local company.

Disabled access Madrid is not particularly well geared up for the disabled (*minusválidos*), although the situation is gradually improving. The Organizacíon Nacional de Ciegos de España (ONCE) at c/de Prado 24 (☎915 894 600 or 915 773 756) provides the best specialist advice. Wheelchair-adapted taxis can be ordered from Radio Taxi (☎915 478 200).

Embassies Australia, Plaza Descubridor Diego Ordás 3 ☎914 416 025, Ⓜ Ríos Rosas; Britain, c/Fernando el Santo 16 ☎913 192 630, Ⓜ Alonso Martínez; British Consulate c/Marqués Ensenada

16 ☎913 085 300; Canada, c/Núñez de Balboa 35 ☎914 314 300 or 914 233 250, Ⓜ Núñez de Balboa; Ireland, Paseo de la Castellana 46 ☎913 190 200, Ⓜ Rubén Darío; New Zealand, Plaza Lealtad 2 ☎915 230 226, Ⓜ Sevilla; USA, c/Serrano 75 ☎915 774 000, Ⓜ Rubén Darío.

Emergencies For an ambulance dial ☎112, 915 884 500 or 915 222 222 – or get a taxi, which will be quicker if no paramedics are necessary; ☎112 is also the number for the police.

Football The big teams are Real Madrid and their rivals, Atlético Madrid and Rayo Vallecano. Tickets can be bought in advance (and usually on the day) at the stadium for most matches, though derbies between Real and Atlético, or visits to either by Barcelona, are always sell-outs. **Real Madrid**: Estadio Santiago Bernabéu, c/Concha Espina s/n (info ☎902 271 707, ticket line ☎902 324 324; Ⓜ Santiago Bernabéu). Ticket office Mon–Fri 6–9pm; match days 11am–1.30pm. Tickets from €15 go on sale three days before each match. **Atlético Madrid**: Estadio Vicente Calderón, Paseo de la Virgen del Puerto 67 ☎913 664 707; Ⓜ Pirámides. Ticket office Mon–Fri 5–8pm; two days before each match also open 11am–2pm. Tickets from €18. **Rayo Vallecano**: Estadio de María Teresa Rivero, Avda. Payaso Fofó s/n ☎914 782 253; Ⓜ Portazgo. Ticket office Mon–Sat 5.30–8.30pm, and two hours before each match. Tickets from €12. If you fancy a Sunday afternoon game, the English **Five-a-side League** (EFL) sometimes need players if teams are short, with games usually at the Colegio del Niño Jesús near the Retiro (☎918 444 525).

Hospitals The most central hospitals are: El Clínico, Plaza de Cristo Rey ☎913 303 747, Ⓜ Moncloa; Hospital Gregorio Marañon, c/Dr Esquerdo 46 ☎915 868 000, Ⓜ O'Donnell; and Ciudad Sanitaria La Paz, Paseo de la Castellana 261 ☎913 582 831, Ⓜ Diego de León. First aid stations are scattered throughout the city and open 24hr a day: one of the most central is at c/Navas de Tolosa 10 ☎915 210 025, Ⓜ Callao. English-speaking doctors are available at the Anglo-American Medical Unit, c/Conde de Aranda 1 ☎914 351 823, Ⓜ Retiro; Mon–Fri 9am–8pm, Sat 10am–3pm.

Internet access Amiweb, c/Mayor 4, 4º, Oficina 8 (Ⓜ Sol) & Gran Vía 80 Piso 6 (Ⓜ Plaza de España); *Aroba 25*, Gran Vía 86 (Ⓜ Gran Vía); *Café Comercial*, Glorieta de Bilbao 7 (Ⓦ www.intervia.com/comercial; Ⓜ Bilbao); *Cybercafé*, c/Atocha 117 (Ⓔ cybermad@mail.com; Ⓜ Atocha);Cybermad, c/Laurel 6 (Ⓜ Embajadores/Acacias); *Easy Everything*, c/Montera 10-12

(Ⓦ www.easyeverything.com/spain; Ⓜ Sol; open 24 hrs); *Vortex*, c/Ave María 20, (Ⓜ Lavapiés/Antón Martín); *Xnet Café*, c/San Bernardo 81 (Ⓜ San Bernardo). Prices range from €1.75–3.50 per hour, often with a drink included.

Language schools Madrid has numerous language schools, offering intensive courses in Spanish language (and culture). One of the most established is International House, c/Zurbano 8 ☎ 913 101 314, Ⓔ ih-madrid@mad.servicom.es; Ⓜ Alonso Martínez.

Laundry Central *lavanderías* include: c/del Barco 26 (Ⓜ Gran Vía); c/de Cervantes 1–3 (Ⓜ Sol); c/Donoso Cortés 17 (Ⓜ Quevedo); c/de Hermosilla 121 (Ⓜ Goya); and c/de la Palma 2 (Ⓜ Tribunal).

Left luggage If you want to leave your bags there are *consignas* at the Barajas airport, the Estación Sur, Auto-Res and Continental Auto bus stations; and lockers at Atocha and Chamartín train stations.

Pharmacies *Farmácias* are distinguished by a green cross; each district has a rota with one staying open through the night – for details ☎ 098 or check the notice on the door of your nearest pharmacy or the listings magazines. Madrid also has quite a number of traditional herbalists, best known of which is Maurice Mességue, c/Goya 64 (Ⓜ Goya; Mon–Fri 10am–2pm & 5–8pm, Sat 10am–2pm).

Police If you've had something stolen call ☎ 900 100 333 (English spoken).

Post office The main one is the Palacio de Comunicaciones in the Plaza de las Cibeles (Mon–Sat 8am–midnight, Sun 8am–10pm for stamps and telegrams; Mon–Fri 9am–8pm, Sat 9am–2pm for *Lista de Correos* – poste restante). Branch offices, for example on c/Cruz Verde on the edge of Malasaña, are open Mon–Sat 9am–2pm, but the easiest places to buy stamps are the *estancos*, recognizable by their brown and yellow signs bearing the word *Tabacos*.

Scooter hire If you want to chance the traffic, scooters are delivered to and collected from your hotel by Alquiler de Scooter (☎ 902 102 020) at a charge of around €14 a day. Also worth trying is Motoalquiler at c/Conde Duque 13 (☎ 915 420 657; Ⓜ Noviciado).

Swimming pools and aquaparks The Piscina Canal Isabel II, Avda. de Filipinas 54 (daily 10am–8.30pm; Ⓜ Ríos Rosas), is a large and well-maintained outdoor swimming pool, and the best

central option. Alternatively, try the open-air *piscina* in the Casa de Campo (daily 10am–8.30pm; Ⓜ El Lago). Both these pools have café-bars attached. Also worth trying are the pools at Barrio del Pilar, Avda. Monforte de Lemos (Ⓜ Barrio del Pilar/Begoña), and La Elipa, Parque de la Elipa, c/O'Donnell s/n (Ⓜ Estrella). There are also a number of aquaparks around Madrid. The closest is Aquamadrid 16km out on the N2 Barcelona road (Bus Continental Auto #281, #282, #282, or #385 from Avda. de América). Note that the "swimming season" is from May to September, so outside these months, most outdoor pools are closed.

Telephones International calls can be made from any phone box or from any *locutorio*. The main *telefónica* office at Gran Vía 30 (Ⓜ Gran Vía) has ranks of phones and is open until midnight. Phone cards cost €6 or €12 and can be bought at post offices or *estancos*.

Ticket agencies For theatre and concert tickets try: Tele-Entradas, a telephone booking service run by BBVA ☎ 902 150 025, Ⓦ www.bbvaticket.com; Caja de Cataluña ☎ 915 383 333; Caja de Madrid ☎ 902 488 488; Caixa Catalunya/Tele Entrada ☎ 902 101 212; El Corte Inglés ☎ 902 400 222, Ⓦ www.elcorteingles.es; FNAC, c/Preciados 28 ☎ 915 956 100; Ⓜ Callao; Madrid Rock, Gran Vía 25 ☎ 915 210 239; Ⓜ Gran Vía; and Servi-Caixa ☎ 902 332 211. Localidades Galicia, Plaza del Carmen 1 ☎ 915 312 732 or 915 319131, Ⓦ www.eol.es/lgalicia.es; Ⓜ Sol, sells tickets for football games, bullfights, theatres and concerts.

Travel agencies Víajes Zeppelin, Plaza Santo Domingo 2 (☎ 915 477 904; Ⓜ Santo Domingo), are English-speaking, very efficient and offer some excellent deals on flights and holidays. Nuevas Fronteras, c/Luisa Fernanda 2 (☎ 915 423 990; Ⓜ Ventura Rodríguez), and in the Torre de Madrid, Plaza de España (☎ 912 474 200) can be good for flights, or try Top Tours, c/Capitán Haja 20 (☎ 915 550 604; Ⓜ Cuzco). For student and youth travel try TIVE, c/Fernando el Católico 88 (☎ 915 430 208; Ⓜ Moncloa). Many other travel agents are concentrated on and around the Gran Vía and c/Princesa.

Women's groups The best places to make contact are at the Centro de La Mujer, c/del Barquillo 44, 1º (☎ 913 193 689; Ⓜ Chueca), and at Madrid's feminist bookshop, the Librería de Mujeres, c/San Cristóbal 17, just east of Plaza Mayor (☎ 915 217 043; Ⓜ Sol).

Travel Details

Trains

For train **information and reservations** call ☎ 902 240 202 or 913 289 020. Tickets can be bought at the individual stations, at Aeropuerto de Barajas arrivals and at the city centre RENFE office, c/Alcalá 44 (☎ 915 623 333; Ⓜ Banco de España; Mon–Fri 8am–8pm). All Madrid trains run through one or more of the two stations below. **Chamartín**, in the north, has the most services and includes through trains to **Atocha**. If you arrive at (or are leaving from) Chamartín, you can use a *cercanía* train to/from Atocha, or catch the metro. Some through trains also stop at the Recoletos and Nuevos Ministerios stations. Note that the high-speed AVE trains to Córdoba and Sevilla run from Atocha. These must be booked in advance, either in person at Atocha, at the RENFE office at c/Alcalá 44, or by phone ☎ 913 289 020.

Atocha Station (Ⓜ Atocha): Alcalá de Henares (every 20 mins; 30min); Algeciras (2 daily; 6–10hr); Almería (1–2 daily; 6hr 45min); Aranjuez (every 15/30min; 40min); Badajoz (4 daily; 5hr 40min–7hr); Cáceres (6 daily; 3hr 20min–5hr); Cádiz (2 daily; 5hr); Ciudad Real (20 daily; 50min–1hr); Córdoba (23–29 daily; 2hr 20min; 1hr 40min AVE); Cuenca (4 daily; 2hr 30min); Granada (2 daily; 6hr–8hr 45min); Huelva (1 daily; 4hr 30min); Huesca (1 daily; 5hr); Jaén (3 daily; 4hr 15min); Jerez (2 daily; 4hr 10min); Málaga (8 daily; 4hr 10min–6hr 50min); Mérida (5 daily; 4hr 20min–6hr); Sevilla (19 daily; 3hr 15min; 2hr 30min AVE); Toledo (9 daily, 1hr 15min); Valencia (12 daily; 3hr 30min). Plus most destinations in the south and west.

Chamartín (Ⓜ Chamartín): A Coruña (2 daily; 8hr 30min–10hr); Albacete (22 daily; 2hr–2hr 20min);

Alicante (7 daily; 4hr); Ávila (24 daily; 1hr 20min–2hr 10min); Barcelona (7 daily; 6hr 30min–9hr); Bilbao (2–3 daily; 5hr 45min–8hr 45min); Burgos (7–8 daily; 3–4hr); Cartagena (4 daily; 5hr); Ferrol (1 daily; 11hr 30min); Gijón (3 daily, 6hr 30min–10hr); Guadalajara (every 30min; 1hr); León (7 daily; 4hr–4hr 30min); Lisbon (1 daily; 10hr); Lugo (1 daily; 9hr 30min); Oviedo (3 daily; 6–9hr); Pamplona (2 daily; 5hr); Paris (1 daily; 13hr 30min); Pontevedra (2 daily; 8hr 30min–10hr); Salamanca (3 daily; 2hr 40min); San Sebastián (3 daily; 6hr); Santander (3 daily; 5hr 30min); Santiago (2 daily; 7hr 15min–9hr 30min); Segovia (9 daily; 1hr 50min–2hr); Valladolid (17 daily, 2hr 30min); Vigo (2 daily; 7hr 50min–10hr); Vitoria (7 daily, 4hr 30 min–6hr 45min); Zamora (2 daily; 3hr–3hr 30min); Zaragoza (12 daily; 3hr–3hr 40min). Plus most other destinations in the north-east and northwest.

Buses

A bewildering number of companies operate buses from Madrid, each from their own garage or terminus. Many of the services, however, run through the **Estación Sur de Autobuses** (☎ 914 684 200), to the south of Atocha on the circular #6 metro line. Note that companies and services change with great frequency and it's always worth checking schedules with the turismo or the **Information line** (☎ 914 352 266).

Estación Sur de Autobuses, c/Méndez Álvaro s/n Ⓜ Méndez Álvaro: Albacete (11 daily; 3hr); Alicante (8 daily; 5hr); Almería (3 daily; 6hr 30min); Aranda (4 daily; 2hr); Ávila (8 daily, 1hr 30min); Barcelona (15 daily; 7hr 30min–8hr); Ciudad Real (2–4 daily; 3hr); Córdoba (7 daily; 4hr 30min); Gijón (15 daily; 5hr); Granada (12 daily; 5hr); Jaén (2–6 daily; 5hr); León (11 daily; 4hr 15min); Málaga (10 daily; 6hr); Marbella (10 daily; 6hr); Oviedo (15 daily; 5hr); Palencia (5 daily; 3hr); Pontevedra (3 daily; 7hr); Santiago (4 daily; 9hr); Sevilla (11 daily; 6hr); Toledo (every 15min; 1hr

15min); Valencia (12 daily; 4hr); Vallodolid (18 daily; 2hr 15min); Zaragoza (17 daily; 4hr); and international services to France and Portugal. **Auto-Res**, Fernández Shaw 1 ☎ 915 517 200, www.auto-res.es; Ⓜ Conde Casal: Badajoz (9 daily; 4hr 30min–5hr); Cáceres (7–10 daily; 3hr 50min–4hr 30min); Ciudad Rodrigo (1-2 daily; 3hr 40 min-4hr); Cuenca (10 daily; 2hr–2hr 30min); Mérida (10 daily; 4–5hr); Salamanca (24 daily; 2hr 15min–2hr 30min); Trujillo (10 daily; 4–5hr); Zamora (9 daily; 2hr 45min–3hr 15min). **Continental Auto**, Avda. de América 9 ☎ 917 456

300; Ⓜ Avda. de América: Alcalá (every 15 min; 40min); Bilbao (10 daily; 4hr 30min); Burgos (9 daily; 2hr 45min); El Burgo de Osma (2 daily; 4hr); Guadalajara (15 daily; 1hr); Logroño (5 daily; 4hr 30min–5hr 30min); Pamplona (4 daily; 5–6hr); San Sebastián (9 daily; 6–8hr); Santander (7 daily; 5hr 45min); Soria (5 daily; 2hr 30min–3hr); Vitoria (8 daily, 5hr).

Herranz, Intercambiador de Autobuses de Moncloa ☎ 918 904 100, an underground terminal just above Metro Moncloa: El Escorial (approx. every 30min). Onward connections to El Valle de los Caídos.

La Sepulvedana, Paseo de la Florida 11 ☎ 915 304 800, Ⓦ www.lasepulvedana; Ⓜ Pío: Ávila (8 daily; 1hr 30min); Segovia (31 daily; 1hr 15min).

MADRID | Travel Details

1

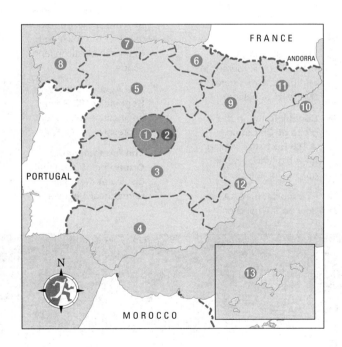

Around Madrid

FRANCE

ANDORRA

PORTUGAL

MOROCCO

N

CHAPTER 2 Highlights

* **A view of El Greco's Toledo** p.150 The terrace bar of the *parador* provides the perfect viewing point of the ancient city.

* **The Cathedral in Toledo** p.157 A splendid mixture of decorations and styles befitting a former capital.

* **Strawberries and cream at Aranjuez** p.165 Indulge yourself in one of the street cafés by the royal palace.

* **Sunday lunch in the plaza at Chinchon** p.166 No better setting for a big lunch and a drop of local anís.

* **El Escorial** p.167 A window on the mind of

Philip II, perched spectacularly in the foothills of the Sierra Guadarrama.

* **A hike in the sierra** p.171&178 Head out to Gredos or Guadarrama for a break from the city heat.

* **A walk along the walls at Ávila** p.172 Superb views of the town and the harsh Castilian landscape.

* **The Aqueduct at Segovia** p.185 Roman engineering at its most impressive.

* **The fountains at La Granja** p.188 A beautiful display at the royal retreat near Segovia.

2

Around Madrid

The lack of historic monuments in Madrid is more than compensated for by the region around the capital. Within a radius of 100km – and within an hour's travel by bus or train – are some of the greatest cities of Spain. Above all, there is **Toledo**, which preceded Madrid as the Spanish

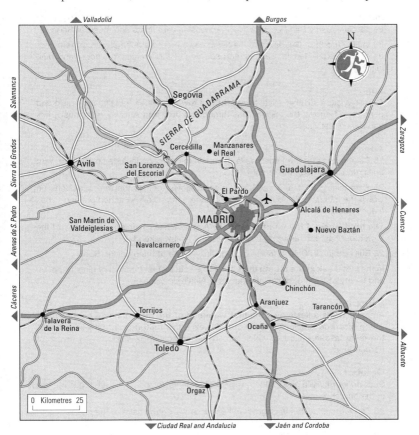

Fiestas

February
First Sunday in the month *Santa Agueda* women's festival in Segovia, when married women take over city administration and parade and celebrate in traditional costume. Occurs to an extent throughout the province, especially in Zamarramala just outside the city.

Week before Lent *Carnaval* is the excuse for lively fiestas all over the place.

March/April
Holy Week *Semana Santa* is celebrated everywhere, but with great formality and processions in Toledo and an impressive Passion play on Saturday in the Plaza Mayor at Chinchón.

Mid-April *Fiesta del Anís y del Vino* in Chinchón.

May
Corpus Christi (variable – the Thursday after Trinity, which sometimes falls in June) sees a very solemn, costumed religious procession in Toledo.

June
24–29 *San Juan y San Pedro*. A lively procession with floats and music in Segovia.

30 In Hita (north of Guadalajara) the fiesta has a medieval theme, with performances of old theatre, feasts, dances, and sporting events including falconry and bull-lancing.

July
There's a big festival in Ávila in **mid-July**; a rowdy affair with bullfights, music and dances. In Segovia the festival runs throughout **July and August**, with music, folk and dance festivities.

August
15 Celebrations for the *Virgen de la Asunción* in Chinchón include an *encierro*, with bulls running through the street.

25 Entertaining fiestas in La Granja (near Segovia; one of the rare occasions on which the monumental fountains in the palace gardens are switched on) and Orgaz (near Toledo).

The **third week of the month** marks the August fiestas in Toledo, in honour of the *Virgen del Sagrario*; amazing fireworks on the final weekend.

28 Bull running in Cuéllar (north of Segovia) – some of the oldest in Spain.

In the **last week in the month** there are some spectacular parades of giant puppets, and plenty of theatre, music and dance in Alcalá de Henares.

September
Aranjuez holds a fiesta over the **first weekend of the month**, and a re-enactment of the *Motín de Aranjuez* (Mutiny of Aranjuez) – the 1808 popular rebellion against the royal favourite Godoy, which forced the abdication of Carlos IV in favour of Fernando VII.

October
Second week Ávila goes wild for the *Feria de Santa Teresa*. There are organ recitals in the churches too.

25 *San Frutos*. Fiestas in Segovia in honour of the patron saint of the city.

Accommodation price codes

All the establishments listed in this book have been price-graded according to the following scale. The prices quoted are for the **cheapest available double room in high season**; effectively this means that anything in the ❶ and most places in the ❷ range will be without private bath, though there's usually a washbasin in the room. In the ❹ category and above you will probably be getting private facilities. Remember, though, that many of the budget places will also have more expensive rooms including en-suite facilities. Youth hostels are graded under ❶ as the price per person is less than half of the category's upper limit.

Note that in the more upmarket *hostales* and *pensiones*, and in anything calling itself a hotel, you'll pay a **tax** (IVA) of seven percent on top of the room price.

❶ Under €12	❹ €27–36	❼ €60–90
❷ €12–18	❺ €36–48	❽ €90–120
❸ €18–27	❻ €48–60	❾ Over €120

capital. Immortalized by El Greco, who lived and worked there for most of his later career, the city is a living museum to the many cultures – Visigothic, Moorish, Jewish and Christian – which have shaped the destiny of Spain. If you have time for just one trip from Madrid, there is really no other choice.

That said, **Segovia**, with its stunning Roman aqueduct and irresistible, Disney-prototype castle, puts up strong competition, while Felipe II's vast palace-mausoleum of **El Escorial** is a monument to out-monument all others. And there are smaller places, too, less known to foreign tourists: **Aranjuez**, an oasis in the parched Castilian plain, famed for its asparagus, strawberries and lavish Baroque palace; the beautiful walled city of **Ávila**, birthplace of St Teresa; and Cervantes's home town, **Alcalá de Henares**, with its sixteenth-century university. For walkers, too, trails amid the sierras of **Gredos** and **Guadarrama** provide enticing escapes from the midsummer heat.

All of the towns in this chapter can be visited as an easy day-trip from Madrid, but they also offer interesting jumping-off points into Castile and beyond; details of onward travel follow each main entry. Wherever you're going, it's a good idea to pick up leaflets in advance from one of the tourist offices in Madrid.

Toledo

Despite its reputation as one of Spain's greatest cities, **TOLEDO** can, in some ways, be a bit of a disappointment. Certainly, it's a city redolent of past glories, and is packed with sights – hence the whole city's status as a National Monument and UNESCO Patrimony of Mankind – but the extraordinary number of day-trippers has taken the edge off what was once the most extravagant of Spanish experiences. Still, the setting is breathtaking, and if you're an **El Greco** fan, you'd be mad to miss this city.

In a landscape of abrasive desolation, Toledo sits on a rocky mound isolated on three sides by a looping gorge of the Río Tajo. Every available inch of this outcrop has been built upon: churches, synagogues, mosques and houses are heaped upon one another in a haphazard spiral which the cobbled lanes infiltrate as best they can. To see Toledo at its best, you'll need to stay at least a night: a day-trip will leave you hard pressed to see everything. More importantly, in the evening with the crowds gone and the city lit up by floodlights – resembling one of El Greco's moonlit paintings – Toledo is a different place entirely.

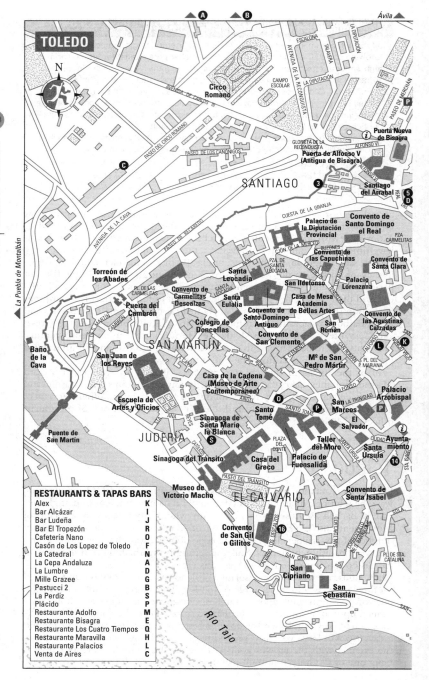

TOLEDO

N

Ávila

A   B

La Puebla de Montalbán

La Diputación

Circo Romano

Campo Escolar

Puerta Nueva de Bisagra

Puerta de Alfonso V (Antigua de Bisagra)

SANTIAGO

Santiago del Arrabal

Palacio de la Diputación Provincial

Convento de Santo Domingo el Real

Convento de las Capuchinas

Convento de Santa Clara

Torreón de los Abades

Convento de Carmelitas Descalzas

Santa Leocadia

San Ildefonso

Palacio Lorenzana

Convento de Santa Clara

Puerta del Cambrón

Santa Eulalia

Casa de Mesa Academia de Bellas Artes

Baño de la Cava

Colegio de Doncellas

Convento de Santo Domingo Antiguo

San Román

Convento de las Agustinas Calzadas

San Juan de los Reyes

SAN MARTÍN

Convento de San Clemente

Mª de San Pedro Mártir

Casa de la Cadena (Museo de Arte Contemporáneo)

Palacio Arzobispal

Escuela de Artes y Oficios

Sinagoga de Santa María la Blanca

Santo Tomé

San Marcos

El Salvador

Puente de San Martín

JUDERÍA

Taller del Moro

Santa Úrsula

Ayuntamiento

Sinagoga del Tránsito

Casa del Greco

Palacio de Fuensalida

Museo de Victorio Macho

EL CALVARIO

Convento de Santa Isabel

Convento de San Gil o Gilitos

San Cipriano

San Sebastián

Río Tajo

RESTAURANTS & TAPAS BARS

Alex	K
Bar Alcázar	I
Bar Ludeña	J
Bar El Tropezón	R
Cafetería Nano	O
Casón de Los Lopez de Toledo	F
La Catedral	N
La Cepa Andaluza	A
La Lumbre	D
Mille Grazee	G
Pastucci 2	B
La Perdiz	S
Plácido	P
Restaurante Adolfo	M
Restaurante Bisagra	E
Restaurante Los Cuatro Tiempos	Q
Restaurante Maravilla	H
Restaurante Palacios	L
Venta de Aires	C

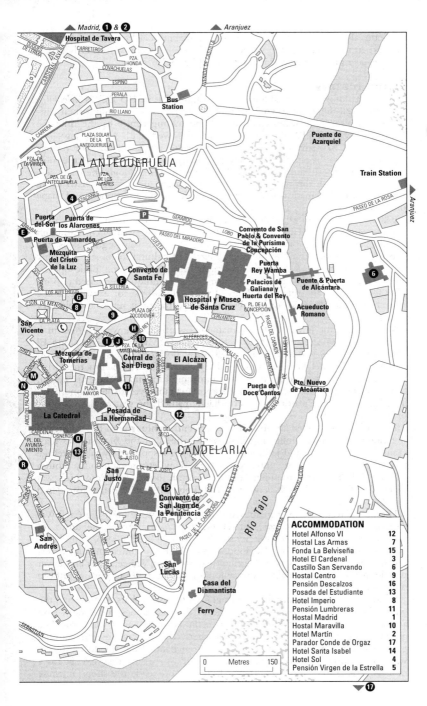

Hospital de Tavera

PZA. HONDA

CARRETEROS

COVACHUELAS

ESPINO

PERALA

Bus Station

RÍO LLANO

PLAZA SOLAR DE LA ANTEQUERUELA

Puente de Azarquiel

LA ANTEQUERUELA

PZA. DE LA VIRGEN

PZA. DE LA ANTEQUERUELA

PZA. DE LOS ALFARES

Train Station

PASEO DE LA ROSA

▲ *Aranjuez*

4

AZACANES

P

GERARDO

Puerta del Sol **Puerta de los Alarcones**

E

CARRETAS

PASEO DEL MIRADERO

LOBO

Convento de San Pablo & Convento de la Purísima Concepción

Puerta de Valmardón

Mezquita del Cristo de la Luz

Convento de Santa Fe

G

8

CJON. DE MENORES

9

San Vicente

Mezquita de Tornerías

Corral de San Diego

Puerta Rey Wamba

Palacios de Galiana y Huerta del Rey

Puente & Puerta de Alcántara

6

Hospital y Museo de Santa Cruz

PL. DE LA CONCEPCIÓN

Acueducto Romano

CERVANTES

ALFÉRECES PROVISIONALES

H

I **J**

PZA. DE LA MAGDALENA

El Alcázar

10

M

N

PLAZA MAYOR

11

Puerta de Doce Cantos

Pte. Nuevo de Alcántara

La Catedral

Posada de la Hermandad

12

CARDENAL CISNEROS

PL. DEL AYUNTA-MIENTO

Q

13

PL. DEL SECO

R

PL. DE S.JUSTO

LA CANDELARIA

San Justo

CTA. DE S.JUSTO

15

Convento de San Juan de la Penitencia

Río Tajo

San Andrés

PASEO DE LA CANDELARIA

San Lucas

Casa del Diamantista

Ferry

SEBASTIÁN

ACCOMMODATION	
Hotel Alfonso VI	12
Hostal Las Armas	7
Fonda La Belviseña	15
Hotel El Cardenal	3
Castillo San Servando	6
Hostal Centro	9
Pensión Descalzos	16
Posada del Estudiante	13
Hotel Imperio	8
Pensión Lumbreras	11
Hostal Madrid	1
Hostal Maravilla	10
Hotel Martín	2
Parador Conde de Orgaz	17
Hotel Santa Isabel	14
Hotel Sol	4
Pensión Virgen de la Estrella	5

0	Metres	150

17

Toledo also hosts one of the most extravagant celebrations of **Corpus Christi** in the country, with street processions and all the works. Other local festivals take place on May 25 and August 15 and 20.

Some history

Toledo was known to the Romans, who captured it in 193 BC, as *Toletum*, a small but well-defended town. Taken by the Visigoths, who made it their capital, it was already an important cultural and trading centre by the time the **Moors** arrived in 712. The period which followed, with Moors, Jews and Mozárabes (Christians subject to Moorish rule) living together in relative equality, was one of rapid growth and prosperity and Toledo became the most important northern outpost of the Muslim emirates. Though there are few physical remains of this period, except the miniature mosque of **Cristo de la Luz**, the long domination has left a clear mark on the atmosphere and shape of the whole city.

When the Christian king Alfonso VI "reconquered" the town in 1085, with the assistance of El Cid, Moorish influence scarcely weakened. Although Toledo became the capital of Castile and the base for campaigns against the Moors in the south, the city itself was a haven of cultural tolerance. Not only was there a school of translators revealing the scientific and philosophical achievements of the East, but Arab craftsmen and techniques remained responsible for many of the finest buildings of the period: look, for example, at the churches of **San Román** or **Santiago del Arrabal** or at any of the old **city gates**.

At the same time Jewish culture remained powerful. There were, at one time, at least seven **synagogues** – of which two, **Santa María la Blanca** and **El Tránsito**, survive – and Jews occupied many positions of power. The most famous was Samuel Levi, treasurer and right-hand man of Pedro the Cruel until the king lived up to his name by murdering him and stealing his wealth. From this period, too, dates the most important purely Christian monument, Toledo's awesome **Catedral** (the city has remained the seat of the Catholic primate to this day).

This golden age ended abruptly in the sixteenth century with the transfer of the capital to Madrid, following hard on the heels of the Inquisition's mass expulsion of Muslims and Jews; some of the latter responded by taking refuge in Catholicism, becoming known as *Conversos*. Few Jews remain today, though Samuel Toledano, late president of the Spanish Israelite Community, was descended from a fifteenth-century grand rabbi, his family name considered proof of his descent from *Conversos*.

The city played little part in subsequent Spanish history until the Civil War (see the box on the **Alcázar**, p.161) and it remains, despite the droves of tourists, essentially the medieval city so often painted by El Greco. Sadly, however, the Tajo, the city's old lifeblood, is now highly polluted, and its waters greatly depleted by industry and agriculture. And, as in Venice, fewer and fewer people live in the city centre; most who work there prefer to commute from the expanding suburbs.

Toledo has been a byword for fine **steel** for a thousand years or more and the glint of knives in souvenir shops is one of the first things you'll notice on arrival. Some have traced the craft back to the Romans and it was certainly a growth industry when the Moors were here. By the seventeenth century, Samuel Butler was complaining that "the trenchant blade, Toledo trusty, for want of fighting was growing rusty". Today it's surprising that, except for a modern display in the Alcázar, there's little to see outside the shops; in these you can still admire attractive damascene steel swords and knives, with handles inlaid with decorative gold and silver filigree.

Arrival and information

General orientation is pretty straightforward in Toledo, with the compact old city looped by the Tajo, and the new quarters across the bridges. **Getting to the city**, too, is easy, with nine trains per day (fewer on Sat & Sun) from Madrid Atocha (6.30am–8.30pm; 1hr 15min), plus buses every thirty minutes from the Estación Sur (6.30am–10pm; 1hr 15min).

Toledo's **train station**, a marvellous 1919 mock-Mudéjar creation, is some way out on the Paseo de la Rosa, a beautiful twenty-minute walk – take the left-hand fork off the dual carriageway and cross the Puente de Alcántara – or a bus ride (#5 or #6) to the heart of town. The **bus station** is on Avenida de Castilla la Mancha in the modern, lower part of the city; buses run frequently to Plaza de Zocódover, though if you take short cuts through the *barrio* at the bottom of the hill just inside the walls, it's a mere ten minutes to the Puerta Nueva de Bisagra.

If you're **driving** – and from Madrid there's little point if you're not going on elsewhere – be aware that parking in Toledo is a problem: the only 24-hour car park is on Paseo del Miradero, below the Plaza de Zocódover, and it's expensive (€11 per day). If your hotel hasn't got its own parking facilities (and with creeping pedestrianization, this is increasingly likely), leave your car outside the city walls at, say, Paseo de Merchán; remember that the city tow-truck is very active.

Information

Toledo's main **turismo** (Mon–Sat 9am–7pm, winter closes 6pm, Sun 9am–3pm; ☎925 220 843, ⓦwww.jccm.es/turismo and ⓦwww.diputoledo.es) is outside the city walls opposite the Puerta Nueva de Bisagra and next to a convenient taxi rank; it has full lists of places to stay, maps showing the monuments, admission times and charges. There's also a smaller but more central turismo run by the local *ayuntamiento* in the plaza opposite the cathedral (Mon–Fri 9am–2pm & 4–6pm; ☎925 254 030, ⓔturitoledo@line-pro.es).

Accommodation

Booking a **room** in advance is important, especially at weekends, or during the summer. If you're on a limited budget, hotel choice is complemented by private rooms, but you'll need to arrive early in the day. At slow times of the year "agents" hover in the Plaza de Zocódover, pouncing on those arriving by bus and offering to find a room for a small fee. Since places are scattered all over town, and the guides will know which have space, this can save time and trouble.

Budget options

Hostal Las Armas, c/Armas 7 ☎925 221 668. Nineteen small rooms with shared bathroom in a pleasant old house, conveniently located next to Plaza de Zocódover; can be noisy at night. Open April–Oct. ❸

Fonda La Belviseña, Cuesta del Can 5 ☎925 220 067. South of the Alcázar; cheap, good-value *fonda* with shared bathrooms; popular, so the dozen rooms fill up quickly. ❷–❸

Castillo San Servando, across the Puente de Alcántara and just off Paseo de la Rosa ☎925 224 554, ⓕ925 267 760. Toledo's youth hostel and student residence is on the outskirts of town in a wing of the fourteenth-century Castillo San Servando; a fifteen-minute walk (signposted) from the train station. It's a good option, with a fine view of the city, and booking is advised. YH card required. Closed mid-Aug to mid-Sept. ❶

Pensión Lumbreras, c/Juan Labrador 9 ☎925 221 571. Simple rooms around a courtyard; those on top floor have fine rooftop views. Rooms with bath available. **④**

Pensión Segovia, c/Recoletos 2 ☎925 211 124. On a narrow street off c/Armas. Well maintained and cheap; the rooms have washbasins – you pay extra for showers. **❸**

Pensión Virgen de la Estrella, c/Real del Arrabal 18, 1º ☎925 253 134. Small, with shared facilities, but decent enough, on the main road up to the old town, near Puerta de Bisagra – ask at the bar of the same name across the road. **❸**

Moderate and expensive options

Hotel Alfonso VI, c/General Moscardó 2 ☎925 222 600, ⓕ925 214 458. Pleasant hotel facing the Alcázar; some of the 83 rooms with balconies have views of the Río Tajo. **❽**

Hotel El Cardenal, Paseo de Recaredo 24 ☎925 224 900, ⓕ925 222 991, ⓔcardenal@macom.es. Splendid old palace with famous restaurant, located outside the city wall, near Puerta Nueva de Bisagra. **❼**

Hostal Centro, c/Nueva 13 ☎925 257 091, ⓕ925 257 848, ⓔjavirodriguez@worldonline.es. New and very pleasant 23-room *hostal* situated close to Plaza de Zocódover. A reasonable price too. **❺**

Pensión Descalzos, c/Descalzos 30 ☎ & ⓕ925 222 888, ⓔh-descalzos@jet.es. Centrally located *pensión*, handy for the main sights. Modern en-suite rooms. **❺**

Posada del Estudiante, Callejón de San Pedro 2 ☎925 210 069, ⓕ 925 226 527. Hidden down a side street near the cathedral, this former student residence offers good-value accommodation. **④**

Hotel Imperio, c/Cadenas 5–7 ☎925 227 650 ⓕ925 253 183, ⓔhimperio@teleline.es. Modern and decently furnished with an in-house coffee shop and reasonable restaurant next door. Handy for Plaza de Zocódover. **❺**

Hostal Madrid, c/Marqués de Mendigorría 7 ☎925 221 114, ⓕ925 228 113. Comfortable

hostal now with air-conditioning, but a bit of a way from the old town. **④–❺**

Hostal Maravilla, Plaza Barrio Rey 5 & 7 ☎925 228 317, ⓕ925 228 155. A prime location just off Plaza de Zocódover. All rooms are en suite and air-conditioned. **❺**

Hotel Martín, c/Covachuelas 12 ☎ & ⓕ925 221 733, ⓔhotel-martin@pymex.es. Relatively new and good value for money, in a residential area close to the bus station. **❻**

Parador Conde de Orgaz, Cerro del Emperador s/n ☎925 221 850, ⓕ925 225 166, ⓔtoledo@parador.es. Superb views of the city from the terrace of Toledo's top hotel, but a good walk from the centre. **❽**

Hotel Santa Isabel, c/Santa Isabel 24 ☎925 253120, ⓕ925 253136. Best of the mid-range hotels, right in the centre, with safe parking. **❺**

Hotel Sol, c/Azacanes 15 ☎925 213650, ⓕ925 216159, ⓔhotel.sol@to.adade.es. Good value, on a quiet side street just off the main road up to the Plaza de Zocódover before the Puerta del Sol. The owners also run the cheaper *hostal* across the street – ask at reception. **❺**

Camping

Camping El Greco, Ctra. De Toledo-Puebla de Montalbán s/n ☎ & ⓕ 925 220 090 ⓔelgreco@retemail.es. Much the best campsite in the area and a thirty-minute walk from the Puerta de Bisagra: cross the Puente de la Cava towards Puebla de Montalbán, then follow the signs. There are great views of the city from here – and a bar to enjoy them from – plus a swimming pool to cool off in after a hard day's sightseeing. Open all year.

Camping Circo Romano, Avda. Carlos III 19 ☎925 220 442. Nearer town, but a rundown site and not particularly friendly; worth considering only if the *El Greco* is full. Open all year.

Camping Toledo, Autovia Madrid–Toledo, km 63 ☎ & ⓕ925 353 013. 9km northeast of Toledo, off the Madrid road by the village of Olias del Rey. This is a handy site if you have your own vehicle. Open April–Sept.

The City

The street layout and labelling in Toledo can be confusing, but the old core is so small that you'll soon find your way around; part of the city's charm is that it's a place to wander and absorb, so don't overdose on "sights" if you can avoid it. You shouldn't leave without seeing at least the El Grecos, the cathedral, the synagogues and Alcázar, but give it all time and you may stumble upon things not listed in this or any other guidebook. Enter any inviting doorway and you may find stunning patios, rooms and ceilings, often of Mudéjar workmanship.

The cathedral

In a country so overflowing with massive religious institutions, the metropolitan **Catedral** has to be something special – and it is. A robust Gothic construction which took over 250 years (1227–1493) to complete, it has a richness of internal decoration in almost every conceivable style, with masterpieces of the Gothic, Renaissance and Baroque periods. The exterior is best appreciated from outside the city, where the 100-metre spire and the weighty buttressing can be seen to greatest advantage. From the street it's less impressive, so hemmed in by surrounding houses that you can't really sense the scale or grandeur of the whole.

There are eight doorways, but the main entrance is at present through the **Puerta Llana** on the southern side of the main body of the cathedral. Tickets (€3, free Wed pm) for the various chapels, chapter houses and treasuries that require them are sold in the cathedral shop opposite. The main body of the cathedral is closed from noon to 3.30pm; the parts which need tickets can be visited daily from Monday to Saturday 10.30am to 6pm and Sunday 2 to 6pm (in September through to April, open to 7pm). The *coro* is closed on Sunday morning, and the New Museums on Monday.

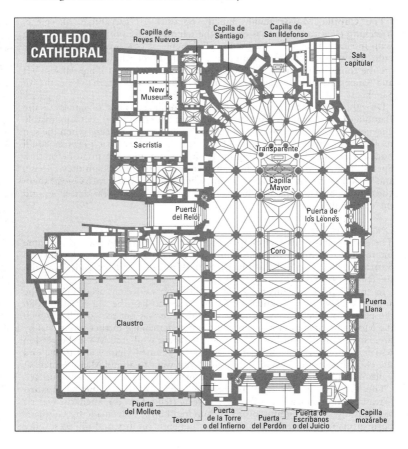

TOLEDO CATHEDRAL

Capilla de Reyes Nuevos — Capilla de Santiago — Capilla de San Ildefonso — Sala capitular — New Museums — Sacristía — Transparente — Capilla Mayor — Puerta del Reloj — Puerta de los Leones — Coro — Puerta Llana — Claustro — Puerta del Mollete — Tesoro — Puerta de la Torre o del Infierno — Puerta del Perdón — Puerta de Escribanos o del Juicio — Capilla mozárabe

The Coro and Capilla Mayor

Inside the cathedral, the central nave is divided from four aisles by a series of clustered pillars supporting the vaults, 88 in all, the aisles continuing around behind the main altar to form an apse. There is magnificent **stained glass** throughout, mostly dating from the fifteenth and sixteenth centuries, particularly beautiful in two rose windows above the north and south doors. Beside the south door (Puerto de los Leones) is a huge, ancient **fresco of St Christopher**.

At the physical heart of the church, blocking the nave, is the **Coro** (Choir), itself a panoply of sculpture. The carved wooden stalls are in two tiers. The lower level, by Rodrigo Alemán, depicts the conquest of Granada, with each seat showing a different village being taken by the Christians. The portraits of Old Testament characters on the stalls above were executed in the following century, on the north side by Philippe Vigarni and on the south by Alonso Berruguete, whose superior technique is evident. He also carved the large **Transfiguration** here from a single block of alabaster. The *reja* (grille) which encloses the *coro* is said to be plated with gold, but it was covered in iron to disguise its value from Napoleon's troops and has since proved impossible to renovate.

The **Capilla Mayor** stands directly opposite. Its gargantuan altarpiece, stretching clear to the roof, is one of the triumphs of Gothic art, overflowing with intricate detail and fanciful embellishments. It contains a synopsis of the entire New Testament, culminating in a Calvary at the summit. On either side are the tombs of the mighty, including (on the left) those of kings Alfonso VII and Sancho III and the powerful Cardinal Mendoza and (on the right) that of Sancho II.

Directly behind the main altar is an extraordinary piece of fantasy – the Baroque **Transparente**. Wonderfully and wildly extravagant, with its marble cherubs sitting on fluffy marble clouds, it's especially magnificent when the sun reaches through the hole punched in the roof for just that purpose. You'll notice a red cardinal's hat hanging from the vaulting just in front of this. Spanish primates are buried where they choose, with the epitaph they choose, and with their hat hanging above them, where it stays until it rots. One of them chose to be buried here, and there are other pieces of headgear dotted around the cathedral.

Chapels and treasures

There are well over twenty **chapels** around the walls, all of which are of some interest. Many of them house fine tombs, particularly the **Capilla de Santiago**, the octagonal **Capilla de San Ildelfonso** and the gilded **Capilla de Reyes Nuevos**.

In the **Capilla Mozárabe**, Mass is still celebrated daily according to the ancient Visigothic rites. When the Church tried to ban the old ritual in 1086 the people of Toledo were outraged. The dispute was put to a combat, which the Mozárabe champion won, but the Church demanded further proof: trial by fire. The Roman prayer book was blown to safety, while the Mozárabe version remained, unburned, in the flames. Both sides claimed victory, and in the end the two rituals were allowed to coexist. If you want to attend Mass, be there at 9.30am and look out for the priest – you may well be the only celebrant.

The Capilla de San Juan houses the riches of the cathedral **Tesoro** (Treasury), most notably a solid silver *custodia* (repository for Eucharist wafers) ten-foot high and weighing over two hundred kilos. It was made by German-born silversmith Enrique de Arfe in the sixteenth century, and gilded seventy years later. An even more impressive accumulation of wealth is displayed in the **Sacristía** (Sacristy), where paintings include a *Disrobing of Christ* and portraits of the Apostles by El Greco, Velázquez's portrait of Cardinal Borja and Goya's *Christ Taken by the Soldiers*.

In the adjoining rooms, the so-called **New Museums** house works of art that were previously locked away or poorly displayed. Among them are paintings by Caravaggio, Gerard David and Morales, and El Greco's most important piece of sculpture (only a few pieces survive), a polychromed wooden group of San Ildefonso and the Virgin. The **Sala Capitular** (Chapter House) has a magnificent sixteenth-century *artesonado* ceiling and portraits of all Spain's archbishops to the present day.

Santo Tomé and the Casa del Greco

The outstanding attraction of Toledo is El Greco's masterpiece, *The Burial of the Count of Orgaz*. It's housed, alone, in a small annexe to the church of **Santo Tomé** (daily 10am–6.45pm, winter closes 5.45pm; €1.25, free Wed pm) and depicts the count's funeral, at which St Stephen and St Augustine appeared in order to lower him into the tomb. It combines El Greco's genius for the mystic, exemplified in the upper half of the picture where the count's soul is being received into heaven, with his great powers as a portrait painter and master of colour. The identity of the sombre-faced figures watching the burial has been a source of endless speculation. On two identities, however, there is universal agreement; El Greco painted himself sixth from the left and his son in the foreground. Less certain are the identities of the rest of the mourners; Cervantes and Lope de Vega are unlikely to have been included as neither had achieved fame by 1586, but the odds are on for Felipe II's presence among the heavenly onlookers, even though he was still alive when it was painted. A search for the count's bones came to an end in early 2001 when they were unearthed from a tomb located, appropriately enough, directly below the painting.

El Greco – and a view of Toledo

Even if you've never seen Toledo – and even if you've no idea what to expect – there's an uncanny familiarity about your first view of it, with the Alcázar and the cathedral spire towering above the tawny mass of the town. This is due to **El Greco**, whose constant depiction of the city (as background, even, for the Crucifixion) seems to have stuck, albeit unwittingly, somewhere in everyone's consciousness. Domenico Theotocopoulos, "the Greek", was born in Crete in 1541 and settled in Toledo in about 1577 after failing to get work on the decoration of the Escorial. His paintings – the most individual, most intensely spiritual visions of all Spanish art – are extraordinary; however often he repeats the same subject, they always offer some surprise or insight.

For thrilling, uncluttered **views** of Toledo, walk along the Carretera de Circunvalación which runs along the south bank of the Tajo – the opposite bank from the city – from one of the medieval fortified bridges to the other. This takes about an hour, and will show to advantage the skyline so familiar from various El Grecos (though several bridges have disappeared in the intervening centuries). For the panorama most resembling *Storm Over Toledo* (now in New York's Metropolitan Museum of Art), you have to climb the hill above the westerly bridge of San Martín.

Midway between the bridges, there is access to a little landing stage, by an old chain ferry, where for most of the year a **boatman** shuttles passengers across the river. This is an informal service and the boatman responds to waves or shouts from one or other bank; you tip whatever you feel is appropriate.

From Santo Tomé the c/de los Amarillos leads down to the old **Judería** (Jewish quarter) and to the **Casa del Greco** (Tues–Sat 10am–2pm & 4–6pm, Sun 10am–2pm; €2.50, free Sat 4–6pm & Sun; currently closed for refurbishment), which despite its name wasn't the artist's actual home – the building in fact dates from the beginning of this century – although the evidence suggests that he lived nearby. The living quarters, furnished in sixteenth-century style, are closed for restoration, but the museum part of the house displays many classic El Grecos, among them his famous *View and Map of Toledo* and another complete series of the Twelve Apostles, completed later than the set in the cathedral and subtly different.

The Taller del Moro, two synagogues and San Juan de los Reyes

Between Santo Tomé and the Casa del Greco you pass the entrance to the **Palacio de Fuensalida** (Palace of the Counts of Fuensalida), a beautiful fifteenth-century mansion where Carlos V's Portuguese wife Isabel died. You used to be able to visit her treasures but the palace is now closed to the public. A garden separates it from the **Taller del Moro** (Tues–Sat 10am–2pm & 4–6.30pm, Sun 10am–2pm; €0.50, combined ticket with Museo de Arte Contemporaneo & Museo de Arte Visigótico €1, free Sat pm & Sun), three fourteenth-century rooms of a Mudéjar palace which were later used by masons working on the cathedral, with magnificent Mudéjar decoration and doorways intact. It is approached through its own entrance in the c/Taller del Moro.

Almost next door to the Casa del Greco, on c/Reyes Católicos, is the **Synagoga del Tránsito**, built along Moorish lines by Samuel Levi in 1366. It became a church after the expulsion of the Jews, but is currently being restored to its original form. The interior is a simple galleried hall, brilliantly decorated with polychromed stuccowork and superb filigree windows. Hebrew inscriptions praising God, King Pedro and Samuel Levi adorn the walls. Nowadays it houses a small **Sephardic Museum** (Tues–Sat 10am–2pm & 4–6pm, Sun 10am–2pm; €2.50, free Sat pm & Sun), tracing the distinct traditions and development of Jewish culture in Spain. During restoration, however, the museum may be closed temporarily.

The only other surviving synagogue, **Santa María la Blanca** (daily 10am–2pm & 3.30–7pm, winter closes 6pm; €1.25), is a short way down the same street. Like El Tránsito, which it predates by over a century, it has been both church and synagogue, though it looks more like a mosque. Four rows of octagonal pillars each support seven horseshoe arches, all of them elaborate and individual designs moulded in plaster, while a fine sixteenth-century *retablo* has been preserved from its time as a church. The whole effect is quite stunning, accentuated by a deep red floor tiled with decorative *azulejos*.

Continuing down c/Reyes Católicos, you come to the superb church of **San Juan de los Reyes** (daily 10am–1.45pm & 3.30–6.45pm, winter closes 5.45pm; €1.25, free Wed pm), its exterior bizarrely festooned with the chains worn by the Christian prisoners from Granada released on the reconquest of their city. It was originally a Franciscan convent founded by the "Catholic Kings", Fernando and Isabel, to celebrate their victory at the Battle of Toro, and in which, until the fall of Granada, they had planned to be buried. Designed by Juan Guas in the decorative late-Gothic style known as Isabelline (after the queen), its double-storeyed cloister is quite outstanding: the upper floor has an elaborate Mudéjar ceiling, and the crests of Castile and Aragón – seven arrows and a yoke – are carved everywhere in assertion of the new unity brought by the royal marriage. This theme is continued in the airy church where imperious eagles support the royal shields.

From the Puerta del Cambrón to Santo Cristo de la Luz

If you leave the city by the **Puerta del Cambrón** you can follow the Paseo de Recaredo, which runs alongside a stretch of Moorish walls, to the **Hospital de Tavera** (daily 10.30am–1.30pm & 3.30–6pm; €3). This, a Renaissance palace with beautiful twin patios, houses the private collection of the Duke of Lerma. The gloomy interior is a reconstruction of a sixteenth-century mansion scattered with fine paintings, including a *Day of Judgement* by Bassano; the portrait of Carlos V by Titian is a copy of the original in the Prado. The hospital's archives are kept here, too: thousands of densely handwritten pages chronicling the illnesses treated. The museum contains several works by El Greco and Ribera's gruesome portrait of a freak "bearded woman". Also here is the death mask of Cardinal Tavera, the hospital's founder, and in the church of the hospital is his ornate marble tomb – the last work of Alonso Berruguete.

Toledo's main gate, the sixteenth-century **Puerta Nueva de Bisagra**, is marooned in a constant swirl of traffic, but it still seems a formidable obstacle for any would-be invader to overcome. Its patterned-tile roofs bear the coat of arms of Carlos V. Alongside is the gateway that it replaced, the ninth-century Moorish portal through which Alfonso VI and El Cid led their triumphant armies in 1085. The main road bears to the left, but on foot you can climb towards the centre of town – after a glance at the intriguing exterior of the Mudéjar church of **Santiago del Arrabal** – by a series of stepped alleyways.

The Cuesta del Cristo de la Luz leads up here past the tiny mosque of **Mezquita del Cristo de la Luz** (currently undergoing restoration). Although this is one of the oldest Moorish monuments in Spain (it was built by Musa Ibn Ali in the tenth century on the foundations of a Visigothic church), only the nave, with its nine different cupolas, is the original Arab construction. The apse was added when the building was converted into a church, and is claimed to be the first product of the Mudéjar style. The head of a Visigoth peering out from one of the capitals is proof, if any were needed, of Moorish tolerance. According to legend, as King Alfonso rode into the town in triumph, his horse stopped and knelt before the mosque. Excavations revealed a figure of Christ, still illuminated by a lamp which had burned throughout three and a half centuries of Muslim rule – hence the name *Cristo de la Luz*.

The mosque itself, set in a small park and open on all sides to the elements, is so small that it seems more like a miniature summer pavilion, but it has an elegant simplicity of design that few of the great monuments can match. It is fenced in and cannot normally be visited, but the caretaker lives across the street at c/Cristo de la Luz 11, and will sometimes let visitors in; he might also show you through the garden where you can climb to the battlements of the **Puerta del Sol**, a great fourteenth-century Mudéjar gateway. Occasionally you'll see the mosque used for prayer by visiting Muslims.

The Alcázar

At the heart of modern Toledo is the **Plaza de Zocódover** (its name derives from the Arabic word *souk*), where everyone converges for an afternoon *copa*. Dominating this square, indeed all Toledo, is the bluff, imposing **Alcázar** (Tues–Sun 9.30am–2pm; €1.25, free Wed for EU citizens), entrance off Cuesta del Alcázar. There has probably always been a fortress at this commanding

The siege of the Alcázar

At the outset of the Spanish Civil War, on July 20, 1936, Colonel José Moscardó – a leading Nationalist rebel – and the cadets of the military academy under his command were driven into the Alcázar. They barricaded themselves in with a large group that included six hundred women and children, and up to a hundred left-wing hostages (who were never seen again).

After many phone calls from Madrid to persuade them to surrender, a Toledo attorney phoned Moscardó with an ultimatum: within ten minutes the Republicans would shoot his son, captured that morning. Moscardó declared that he would never surrender and told his son, "If it be true, commend your soul to God, shout *Viva España*, and die like a hero." (His son was actually shot with others a month later in reprisal for an air raid.) Inside, though not short of ammunition, the defenders had so little food they had to eat their horses.

The number of Republican attackers varied from 1000 to 5000, with people coming from Madrid to take pot shots from below. Two of the three mines they planted under the towers exploded but nothing could disturb the solid rock foundations. The besiegers tried spraying petrol all over the walls and setting fire to it, but with no effect. Finally, General Franco decided to relieve Moscardó and diverted an army that was heading for Madrid. On September 27, General José Varela commanded the successful attack on the town, which was followed by the usual bloodbath – not one prisoner being taken.

As the historian Raymond Carr put it "in civil war, symbols count". The day after Franco entered Toledo to consolidate his victory, he was declared head of state and spoke to the nation – according to Radio Castillo, he was "the authentic voice of Spain in the plenitude of its power".

location, but the present building was originated by Carlos V, though it has been burned and bombarded so often that almost nothing remaining is original. The most recent destruction was in 1936 during one of the most symbolic and extraordinary episodes of the Civil War, involving a two-month siege of the Nationalist-occupied Alcázar by the Republican town (see box, above).

After the war, Franco's regime completely rebuilt the fortress as a monument to the glorification of its defenders – the fascist newspaper *El Alcázar* also commemorates the siege – and their propaganda models and photos are still displayed. Objectionable exercise though this is, it's a fascinating story, and the Alcázar also offers the best views of the town, its upper windows level with the top of the cathedral spire (though in recent years access has been restricted – part of the building is still occupied by the military). Across the river, next to a modern military academy, stands the ancient **Castillo de San Servando**, Arabic in origin and remodelled in Mudéjar style in the fourteenth century; one wing of the castle now serves as a youth hostel.

Other museums

The **Hospital y Museo de Santa Cruz** (Mon 10am–2pm & 4–6.30pm, Tues–Sat 10am–6.30pm, Sun 10am–2pm; €1.25, free Sat pm & Sun), a superlative Renaissance building with a fine Plateresque facade, houses some of the greatest El Grecos in Toledo, including *The Assumption*, a daringly unorthodox work of feverish spiritual intensity, and a *Crucifixion* with the town as a backdrop. As well as outstanding works by Goya and Ribera, the museum also contains a huge collection of ancient carpets and faded tapestries (including a magnificent fifteenth-century Flemish tapestry called *The Astrolabe*), a military display (note the flags borne by Don Juan of Austria at the Battle of Lepanto), sculpture and a small archeological collection. Don't miss the patio with its ornate staircase – the entrance is beside the ticket office.

The **Museo de Arte Visigótico** (Tues–Sat 10am–2pm & 4–6.30pm, Sun 10am–2pm; €0.50, combined ticket with Taller del Moro & Museo de Arte Contemporaneo €1, free Sat pm & Sun) can be found in a very different, though equally impressive building, the church of **San Román**. Moorish and Christian elements – horseshoe arches, early murals and a splendid Renaissance dome – combine to make it the most interesting church in Toledo. Its twelfth-century Mudéjar tower originally stood apart from the main body of the church, in the manner of Muslim minarets. Visigothic jewellery, documents and archeological fragments make up the bulk of the collection.

A few new museums have opened in Toledo in recent years. Not far from the Visigothic museum, in the **Convento de Santo Domingo Antiguo**, the nuns display their art treasures in the old choir (Mon–Sat 11am–1pm & 4–7pm, Sun 4–7pm; winter open Sat, Sun & holidays only; €1.20, free Tues). More interesting is the high altarpiece of the church, El Greco's first major commission in Toledo. Unfortunately, most of the canvases have gone to museums and are here replaced by copies, leaving only two *St Johns* and a *Resurrection in situ*. The **Posada de la Hermandad**, near the market square at the back of the cathedral, is a recently restored Gothic building, now used for temporary exhibitions. Other exhibitions are staged at the **Museo de Arte Contemporáneo** (Tues–Sat 10am–2pm & 4–6.30pm, Sun 10am–2pm; €0.50, combined ticket with Taller del Moro & Museo de Arte Visigótico €1, free Sat pm & Sun) in the Casa de la Cadena, a refurbished sixteenth-century house near Santo Tomé. A few hundred metres south of here, splendidly situated on a spur overlooking the Tajo, is the **Museo de Victorio Macho**, Plaza de Victorio Macho 2 (Mon–Sat 10am–7pm, Sun 10am–3pm; €3), which contains the sculptures, painting and sketches of the famous Spanish sculptor after whom the museum is named. The auditorium on the ground floor shows a documentary film about the city and its history. In the Mezquita de las Tornerías on c/Tornerías, the **Centro de Promoción de la Artesanía** (Tues–Sat 10am–2pm & 5–8pm, Sun 10am–2pm; free), houses good displays of beautiful local crafts, mainly pottery. The renovated eleventh-century mosque, deconsecrated by the Reyes Católicos around 1500, is worth a visit in itself.

Eating, drinking and nightlife

Toledo is a major tourist centre and inevitably many of its cafés, bars and restaurants are geared to passing trade. However, the city is as popular with Spanish as with foreign visitors, so decent, authentic places do exist – and there's a bit of nightlife, too, for the local population.

Most **restaurants** in town do a good-value lunchtime *menú*, with game such as partridge (*perdiz*), pheasant (*faisán*) or quail (*cordoniz*) appearing in the more upmarket places, and everyone offering a tasty local speciality, *carcamusa* – a meat stew in a spicy tomato sauce. In the evenings, on a budget, you need to be selective: this can be an expensive town. As a rule, the nearer you get to the centre, the more you'll pay.

Inexpensive restaurants

Alex, Plaza de Amador de los Ríos 10, at the top end of c/Nuncio Viejo. Reasonable-value restaurant with a much cheaper café at the side. *Conejo* and *perdiz* are the specialities here. Nice location and a shady summer terrace.

Bar Alcázar aka *Champi*, c/Sierpe 5. A fairly standard bar, but it serves a good range of tapas and *raciones*.

Bar Ludeña, Plaza Magdalena 13. One of many places around this square, offering a cheap *menú* and the best *carcamusa* in town.

Bar El Tropezón, Travesía de Santa Isabel 2. A stone's throw from the cathedral, this outdoor bar offers generous meals for around €6. The fish is particularly good.

Cafetería Nano, c/Santo Tomé 10. Good-value chain where you can eat well for €9. You'll find it under the trees, near the church entrance.

La Catedral, c/Nuncio Viejo 1. Wide range of tapas and wines at this modern bar in the heart of the city.

La Cepa Andaluza, Avda. Méjico 11. Bar with dependable Andalucian cooking – fried fish and the like.

Pastucci 2, c/Columbia 8. Very reasonable pizzeria with a pleasant atmosphere.

Posada del Estudiante, Callejón de San Pedro 2. Secluded workers' café near the cathedral open only for very cheap lunchtime *menú* – well worth hunting out.

Restaurante Bisagra, c/Real del Arrabal 14. Reasonably priced *menú* in elegantly refurbished surroundings.

Restaurante Palacios, c/Alfonso X El Sabio 3. Friendly and popular local restaurant, with two *menús* – the cheaper one costing €6.

Moderate and expensive restaurants

Casón de Los Lopez de Toledo, c/Silleria 3. Upmarket restaurant in a quiet street close to Plaza Zocódover with a tasty *menú* at €18.

La Lumbre, c/Real de Arrabal 3. Well-regarded restaurant, just above the Puerta de Bisagra, specializing in meat dishes and local cuisine.

Mille Grazee, c/de las Cadenas 2. Popular restaurant with a wide variety of Italian dishes. The tortellini with nut and cream sauce is particularly good. Closed Mon & Sun evening.

La Perdiz, c/Reyes Católicos 7. Quality restaurant which does a very good *menú de degustación* for €21. A good selection of local wines.

Plácido, c/Santo Tomé 2. Good standard Toledan cuisine with a cool terrace and patio for the summer.

Restaurante Adolfo, c/Granada 6. One of the best restaurants in town, tucked behind a marzipan café, in an old Jewish town house (ask to see the painted ceiling downstairs), and serving very imaginative food. Allow €33 a head. Closed Sun evening.

Restaurante Los Cuatro Tiempos, c/Sixto Ramón Parro 5 at southeast corner of the cathedral. Excellent mid-price restaurant with local specialities and good tapas, including very good *caracoles*.

Restaurante Maravilla, c/Barrio Rey 7. In the *hostal* of the same name, and offering an excellent *menú*, which includes traditionally prepared *perdiz*.

Venta de Aires, c/Circo Romano 35. Popular restaurant housed in a famous old inn, a little way out of the centre, with outdoor eating in the summer. Allow €24 a head.

Late bars and entertainment

By Spanish standards, Toledo's **nightlife** is rather tame. You'll find most late-night bars running along c/de la Sillería and its extension c/de los Alfileritos, west of Plaza de Zocódover. *Picaro* on c/de las Cadenas is one of the liveliest *discobares* in town, while *La Abadía*, c/Nuñez de Arce 3, is a fashionable but civilized bar which serves a large range of foreign beer and attracts an older crowd than most along here.

Two alternative places are *Broadway Jazz Club*, on Plaza Marrón near the Taller del Moro, and *La Boîte de Garcilaso*, a similar place nearby at the corner of c/Alfonso XII and c/Rojas; both have occasional live jazz.

Out of the tourist season (Sept–March), **classical concerts** are held in the cathedral and other churches; details can be obtained from the turismo.

On from Toledo

The train line comes to a halt at Toledo but there are **bus** connections south to **Ciudad Real** (see p.208), west to **La Puebla de Montalbán** (see p.212) and **Talavera de la Reina** (see p.212) on the way to Extremadura, and east to **Cuenca** (see p.201). If you have transport of your own, or fancy slow progress by bus and on foot, the **Montes de Toledo** (see p.211), southwest of the city, are an interesting rural backwater.

More local excursions, by bus, to the south of Toledo, could include **Guadamur** (14km from Toledo), whose outstanding castle stands on a nearby hilltop, and **Orgaz**, once home to the count of El Greco's masterpiece *The Burial of the Count of Orgaz*, now a quiet village with a beautiful plaza, a magnificent Baroque church and a small fifteenth-century castle overlooking the main road to Ciudad Real.

Aranjuez and Chinchón

The frequent Madrid–Toledo trains run via **Aranjuez**, a little oasis in the beginnings of New Castile, where the eighteenth-century Bourbon rulers set up a spring and autumn retreat. Their palaces and luxuriant gardens, which inspired the composer Joaquín Rodrigo to write the famous *Concierto de Aranjuez*, and the summer strawberries (served with cream – *fresas con nata* – at roadside stalls), combine to make it an enjoyable stop. In summer (Sat & Sun end of April to July & Sept to mid-Oct), an old wooden **steam train**, the Tren de la Fresa, makes runs between Madrid and Aranjuez; it leaves Atocha station at 10.05am and returns from Aranjuez at 6.13pm, arriving back at Atocha at 7pm. Train enthusiasts won't begrudge the extra cost (€20.40), which includes a guided bus tour in Aranjuez, entry to the monuments and *fresas con nata* on the train. The less romantic, but highly efficient, standard trains leave every 15–30 minutes from Atocha, with the last train returning from Aranjuez at about 11.30pm.

Nearby, too, connected by sporadic buses from Aranjuez at c/Almíbar 138 (Mon–Fri 4 daily, Sat 2 daily) and hourly services from Madrid, is **Chinchón**, a picturesque village that is home to Spain's best-known *anís* – a mainstay of breakfast drinkers across Spain.

Aranjuez

The beauty of **ARANJUEZ** is its greenery – it's easy to forget just how dry and dusty most of central Spain is until you come upon this town, with its lavish palaces and luxuriant gardens. In summer, Aranjuez functions principally as a weekend escape from Madrid and most people come out for the day, or stop en route to or from Toledo. If you wanted to break your journey, you'd need to camp or reserve a room in advance, as there's very little accommodation available.

The eighteenth-century **Palacio Real** (Tues–Sun: April–Sept 10am–6.15pm; Oct–March 10am–5.15pm; €4.81, Wed free for EU citizens) and its **gardens** (daily: April–Sept 8am–8.30pm; Oct–March 8am–6.30pm; free) were an attempt by the Spanish Bourbon monarchs to create a Versailles in Spain; Aranjuez clearly isn't in the same league but it's a pleasant enough place to while away a few hours.

The palace is more remarkable for the ornamental fantasies inside than for any virtues of architecture. There seem to be hundreds of rooms, all exotically furnished, most amazingly so the **Porcelain Room**, entirely covered in decorative ware from the factory which used to stand in Madrid's Retiro park. The **Smoking Room** is a copy of one of the finest halls of the Alhambra in Granada, though executed with less subtlety. Most of the palace dates from the reign of the "nymphomaniac" Queen Isabel II, and many of the scandals and intrigues which led to her eventual abdication were played out here.

Outside, on a small island, are the fountains of the **Jardín de la Isla**. The **Jardín del Príncipe**, on the other side of the main road, is more attractive, with shaded walks along the river and plenty of spots for a siesta. At its far end is the **Casa del Labrador** (June-Sept: Tues-Sun 10am-6.15pm; Oct-March: Tues-Sun 10am-5.15pm; visits by appointment only – ☎918 910 305; €4.81, Wed free for EU citizens), which is anything but what its name (Peasant's House) implies. In a hotchpotch of styles, ranging from Neoclassical to Rococo, it was described by Richard Ford well over a century ago as "another plaything of that silly Charles IV, a foolish toy for the spoiled children of fortune, in which great expense and little taste are combined to produce a thing which is perfectly useless". Great expense is right, for the house contains more silk, marble, crystal and gold than would seem possible in so small a place, as well as a huge collection of fancy clocks. The guided tour goes into great detail about the weight and value of every item.

Also in the gardens, by the river, is the small **Casa de los Marinos** or **Museo de Faluas** (Tues–Sun: April–Sept 10am–6.15pm; Oct–March 10am–5.15pm; €3, Wed free for EU citizens), a museum containing the brightly coloured launches in which royalty would take to the river.

A bus service occasionally connects the various sites, but all are within easy walking distance of each other, and the town's a very pleasant place to stroll around. Look out for the suitably regal eighteenth-century **Plaza de Toros** and the newly inaugurated exhibition space entitled *Aranjuez – una gran fiesta* (summer Tues–Sun 10am–6.30pm; winter Tues–Sun 10am–5.30pm; €3, Wed free for EU citizens), part of which is a **museo taurino** with its *trajes de luces*, swords and associated taurine memorabilia, and part of which traces the town's history and royal heritage. Nearby in c/Naranja and c/Rosa are a number of **corralas**, traditional-style wooden-balconied tenement blocks.

Practicalities

The best **hostal** choices are the *Rusiñol*, c/San Antonio 76 (☎918 910 155, ℱ918 925 345; ❹), in the centre of town, and the *Castilla*, Carrera de Andalucia 98 (☎918 912 627, ℱ918 916 133; ❺). The **campsite**, *Soto del Castillo*, Soto del Rebollo (☎918 911 395, ℱ918 914 197), is on a far bend of the Río Tajo; it's equipped with a swimming pool, and hires out bicycles and rowing boats. You'll find a helpful **turismo** in the Casa de Infantes, facing the Plaza de San Antonio (summer Tues–Sun 10am–2pm & 4–6pm; winter Tues–Sat 10am–1pm & 3–5pm, Sun 10am–2pm; ☎918 910 427, ⓦwww.aranjuez.net).

With plenty of fresh produce around (including the famous strawberries and asparagus in season), the splendid nineteenth-century **Mercado de Abastos** on c/Stuart is a good place to buy your own food for a picnic. If you're after a memorable **restaurant** meal, *Casa José*, c/Abastos 32 (closed Sun eve & Mon), offers good, but expensive *nouvelle cuisine*, while *Casa Pablo*, c/Almíbar 42 (closed Aug), is more traditional, with walls covered with pictures of local dignitaries and bullfighters; its nearby offshoot, *Casa Pablete*, c/Stuart 108 (closed Tues & Aug), is good for tapas. Probably the best-known restaurant is the pleasant riverside *La Rana Verde*, c/Reina 1, which dates back to the late nineteenth century and serves a wide-ranging *menú* at €10.80.

Chinchón

CHINCHÓN, 45km southeast of Madrid, is an elegant little town, with a fifteenth-century castle and a fine Plaza Mayor, next to which stands the **Iglesia de la Asunción**, with a panel by Goya of *The Assumption of the Virgin*. It is as the home of *anís*, however, that the town is best known; your best bet for a sample of the local spirit is one of the local bars or the Alcoholera de Chinchón, a shop on the Plaza Mayor. Most visitors come for a tasting and then eat out at one of the town's traditional *mesones*: try the *Mesón del Comendador*, one of a cluster of good restaurants serving classic Castilian fare on the Plaza Mayor, or the *Mesón del Duende* – both are modestly priced. More expensive is the *Mesón Cuevas del Vino*, an old olive oil mill which today has its own *bodega* (wine cellar). If you fancy an overnight **stay** you could splash out on the *Parador de Chinchón* (☎918 940 836, ℱ918 940 908, ⓔchinchon@

parador.es; ⑧) which has been established in the former Augustinian monastery just off the Plaza Mayor. A more modest option is the pleasant *Hostal Chinchón* (☎918 935 398, ⓕ918 940 108; ⑤), also close to the Plaza Mayor in c/José Antonio.

If you're visiting over Easter, you'll be treated to the townsfolk's own enactment of the *Passion of Christ*, though be aware that the small town becomes packed with visitors at this time. In April 1995 the town launched its *Fiesta del Anís y del Vino*, an orgy of *anís* and wine tasting; understandably it was an immediate success and is now held every mid-April. An older annual tradition takes place on July 25, when the feast of St James (*Santiago* in Spanish) is celebrated with a bullfight in the Plaza Mayor.

El Escorial, El Valle de los Caídos and the Sierra de Guadarrama

Northwest of Madrid, in the foothills of the Sierra de Guadarrama, is one of Spain's best-known and most visited sights – Felipe II's vast monastery-palace of **El Escorial**. Travel writers tend to go into frenzies about the symbolism of this building – "a stone image of the mind of its founder" was how the nineteenth-century writer Augustus Hare described it – and it is indeed a key historic sight. The town around the monastery, **San Lorenzo del Escorial**, is an easy day-trip from Madrid, or if you plan to travel on, rail and road routes continue to Ávila (see p.172) and Segovia (see p.180). The heart of the **Sierra de Guadarrama**, too, lies just to the north, offering Madrid's easiest mountain escape.

Tours from Madrid to El Escorial often take in **El Valle de los Caídos** (The Valley of the Fallen), 9km north. This is an equally megalomaniac yet far more chilling monument: an underground basilica hewn under Franco's orders, allegedly as a monument to the Civil War dead of both sides, though in reality as a memorial to the Generalísmo and his regime.

El Escorial

The monastery of **EL ESCORIAL** was the largest Spanish building of the Renaissance: rectangular, overbearing and severe, from the outside it more resembles a prison than a palace. Built between 1563 and 1584, it was originally the creation of Juan Bautista de Toledo, though his one-time assistant, **Juan de Herrera**, took over and is normally given credit for the design. **Felipe II** planned the complex as both monastery and mausoleum, where he would live the life of a monk and "rule the world with two inches of paper". Later monarchs had less ascetic lifestyles, enlarging and richly decorating the palace quarters, but Felipe's simple rooms, with the chair that supported his gouty leg and the deathbed from which he could look across into the church where Mass was constantly celebrated, remain the most fascinating.

There's more to see than you can fit into a single day without total exhaustion, and you're liable to end up agreeing with Augustus Hare that while the Escorial "is so profoundly curious that it must of necessity be visited, it is so utterly dreary and so hopelessly fatiguing a sight that it requires the utmost patience to endure it".

Arrival, information and accommodation

From **Madrid** there are up to 31 **trains** a day (5.45am–11.30pm from Atocha, calling at Chamartín, and up to twelve every weekday going on to Ávila), with **buses** (from the *intercambiador* at Moncloa) running every thirty minutes on weekdays and hourly at weekends. If you arrive by train get straight on the local bus which shuttles you up to the centre of town – they leave promptly and it's a long uphill walk. If you're travelling by bus, stay on it and it will take you right up to the monastery. The **turismo** (Mon–Thurs 11am–6pm, Fri–Sun 10am–7pm; ☎918 905 313, ✉oflocaalt@worldonline.es) is at c/Grimaldi 2, the small street to the north of the visitors' entrance to the monastery and running into c/Floridablanca.

If you want to stay in the town, San Lorenzo del Escorial, there's a range of **accommodation**, but none of it is particularly cheap and in summer it's essential to book in advance. At the lower end of the scale is the recently refurbished *Hotel Tres Arcos*, c/Juan de Toledo 42 (☎918 906 897, ☏ 918 907 997; ❹–❺). A little more expensive are *Hostal Cristina*, c/Juan de Toledo 6 (☎918 901 961, ☏918 901 204, ✉hcristina@jazzviajeros.com; ❺), and *Hotel Parilla Príncipe*, c/Floridablanca 6, near the turismo (☎918 901 611, ☏918 907 601; ❻). If you've got the cash to splash out, head for the *Hotel Florida* next to the turismo (☎918 901 721, ☏918 901 715, ⓦwww.hflorida.com; ❼), or the plush *Hotel Botánico*, c/Timoteo Padrós 16 (☎918 907 879, ☏918 908 158;❽), set in the verdant grounds of a former palace.

You'll also find a well-equipped **campsite** with several swimming pools 6km out on the road to Ávila, *Caravaning El Escorial* (☎918 902 412, ☏918 961 062, ✉planeta.azul@retemail.es), and two **youth hostels**: *El Escorial*, c/Residencia 14 (☎918 905 924, ☏918 900 620; ❷), and *Santa María del Buen Aire*, Finca la Herrería (☎918 903 640, ☏918 903 792; ❷), which has a pool and camping space, but is usually packed with school groups; both are open to YHA members only. You're best off arriving in El Escorial early, spending the day here, and then continuing in the evening to Ávila or heading back to Madrid. Moving on to Segovia by train is a bit trickier as it involves backtracking to Villalba (15min) and hooking up with a Madrid–Segovia train from there.

The monastery

Visits to the **Real Monasterio del Escorial** (Tues–Sun: April–Sept 10am–7pm; Oct–March 10am–6pm; €6 non-guided, €6.90 guided, combined ticket for monastery & El Valle de los Caídos €8.40, Wed free for EU citizens) used to be deeply regulated, with compulsory guided tours to each section. Recently, they've become more relaxed and you can use your ticket (purchased in the **visitors' entrance**) to enter, in whatever sequence you like, the basilica, sacristy, chapter houses, library and royal apartments. The outlying **Casita del Príncipe** (aka **de Abajo**) and **Casita del Infante** (aka **de Arriba**) have separate opening hours and admission fees. To escape the worst of the crowds avoid Wednesdays and try visiting just before lunch, or pick that time for the royal apartments, which are the focus of all the bus tours. At present the Sala de Batallas – a long gallery lined with paintings of important imperial battles – and the Casita del Príncipe are closed as part of the programme of ongoing restoration.

For sustenance, you'll find a **cafetería** near the ticket office; drinks are OK but meals a bit of a rip-off.

The Biblioteca, Patio de los Reyes, Basilica and courtyards

A good starting point is to head for the west gateway, facing the mountains, and go through the traditional **main entrance**. Above it is a gargantuan stat-

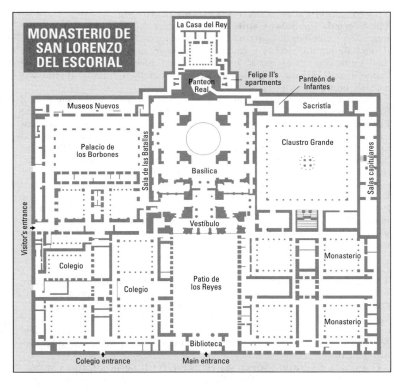

ue of San Lorenzo holding a gridiron, the emblem of his martyrdom. Within is the **Biblioteca**, a splendid hall, with shelves designed by Herrera to harmonize with the architecture, and frescoes by Tibaldi and his assistants, showing the seven Liberal Arts. Its collections include the tenth-century *Codex Albeldensis*, St Teresa's personal diary, some gorgeously executed Arabic manuscripts, and a Florentine planetarium of 1572 demonstrating the movement of the planets according to the Ptolemaic and Copernican systems. Beyond is the **Patio de los Reyes**, named after the six statues of the kings of Israel on the facade of the basilica straight ahead. Off to the left is a school, to the right the monastery, both of them still in use.

In the **Basilica**, notice the flat vault of the *coro* above your head as you enter, which is apparently entirely without support, and the white marble Christ carved by Benvenuto Cellini, and carried here from Barcelona on workmen's shoulders. This is one of the few things permanently illuminated in the cold, dark interior, but put some money in the slot to light up the main altarpiece and the whole aspect of the church is brightened. The east end is decorated by Italian artists: the sculptures are by the father-and-son team of Leone and Pompeo Leoni, who also carved the two facing groups of Carlos V with his family and Felipe II with three of his wives; Mary Tudor is excluded.

You can also wander at will in some of the Escorial's courtyards; most notable is the **Claustro Grande**, with frescoes of the life of the Virgin by Tibaldi, and the **Jardín de los Frailes** on the south side.

The treasuries, Mausoleum and royal apartments

The **Sacristía** and **Salas Capitulares** (Chapter Houses) contain many of the monastery's religious treasures, including paintings by Titian, Velázquez and José Ribera. Beside the sacristy a staircase leads down to the **Panteón Real**, the final resting place of all Spanish monarchs since Carlos V, with the exception of Felipe V and Fernando VI. Alfonso XIII, who died in exile in Rome, was recently brought to join his ancestors.

The deceased monarchs lie in exquisite gilded marble tombs: kings (and Isabel II) on one side, their spouses on the other. Just above the entry is the Pudridero Real, a separate room in which the bodies rot for twenty years or so before the cleaned-up skeletons are moved here. The royal children are laid in the **Panteón de los Infantes**; the tomb of Don Juan, Felipe II's bastard half-brother, is grander than any of the kings', while the wedding-cake babies' tomb with room for sixty infants is more than half full.

What remains of the Escorial's art collection — works by Bosch, Gerard David, Dürer, Titian, Zurbarán and many others, which escaped transfer to the Prado — is kept in the elegant suite of rooms known as the **New Museums**. Finally, there are the treasure-crammed **Royal Apartments**. On no account miss the spartan **quarters of Felipe II** and the adjacent **Maderas Finas** rooms with their magnificent inlaid wood.

Outlying lodges

The **Casita del Príncipe** (June–Sept Sat & Sun 10am–1pm & 3.30–6.30pm; €3.50; compulsory tours every 30min for a maximum of 10 people) and the **Casita del Infante** (Easter & mid-July to mid-Sept Tues–Sun 10am–6pm; €3, Wed free for EU citizens) are two eighteenth-century royal lodges, both full of decorative riches, and built by Juan de Villanueva, Spain's most accomplished Neoclassical architect — so worth seeing in themselves as well as for their formal gardens.

The Casita del Infante, which served as present King Juan Carlos's student digs, is a short way up into the hills and affords a good view of the Escorial complex; follow the road to the left from the main entrance and then stick to the contours of the mountain around to the right — it's well signposted. The Casita del Príncipe, in the Jardines del Príncipe below the monastery, is larger and more worthwhile, with an important collection of Giordano paintings and four pictures made from rice paste.

The Silla de Felipe

Around 7km out of town, is the **Silla de Felipe** — "Felipe's Seat" — a chair carved into a rocky outcrop with a view out towards the palace. His majesty is supposed to have sat here to watch the construction going on. If you have a car, it still offers a great view; take the Ávila road and turn off after 3km.

Eating and entertainment

You'll need to head away from the monastery for something **to eat**, up c/Reina Victoria into town. The *Hotel Parilla Príncipe* has a good restaurant, while *La Cueva*, c/San Antón 4, is elegant but expensive. Also at the top end of the scale, *El Charolés*, c/Floridablanca 24, is renowned for its fish and stews. More reasonable is *La Fonda Genara*, Plaza de Las Animas 2, near the *coliseo*, which is filled with theatrical mementoes. The *Cervecería Los Pescaítos*, c/Joaquín Costa 8, is a friendly bar serving fish dishes. Alternatively, grab a *bocadillo* from a drinks stand on c/Floridablanca and save your appetite for later.

For purely liquid refreshment *Bar Erriuga*, on c/Ventura Rodríguez 7, is one of the best bets.

If by design or default you end up staying the night in El Escorial, there are no fewer than eight **cinemas**, along with the eighteenth-century **Coliseo** where you'll find jazz and classical **concerts** and theatrical productions year-round. Details of shows can be picked up from the turismo, or check out the free weekly *La Semana del Escorial*.

El Valle de los Caídos

The entrance to the **Valle de los Caídos** (Valley of the Fallen) lies 9km north of El Escorial: from here a road (along which you are not allowed to stop) runs 6km into the underground basilica. Above it is a vast cross, reputedly the largest in the world, and visible for miles along the road to Segovia. To visit El Valle de los Caídos from El Escorial, there is a local bus run by Herranz, which starts from the office on c/Juan de Toledo, just north of the visitors' entrance to the monastery. The bus runs from El Escorial at 3.15pm, returning at 5.30pm (Tues–Sun).

The **basilica complex** (Tues–Sun: April–Sept 9.30am–7pm; Oct–Mar 10am–6pm; €4.80, combined ticket with El Escorial €8.40, Wed free for EU citizens) denies its claims of memorial "to the Civil War dead of both sides" almost at a glance. The debased and grandiose architectural forms employed, the grim martial statuary, the constant inscriptions "Fallen for God and for Spain", and the proximity to El Escorial clue you in to its true function: the glorification of General Franco and his regime. The dictator himself lies buried behind the high altar, while the only other named tomb, marked simply "José Antonio", is that of his guru, the Falangist leader José Antonio Primo de Rivera, who was shot dead by Republicans at the beginning of the war. The "other side" is present only in the fact that the complex was built by the Republican army's survivors – political prisoners on quarrying duty.

From the entrance, a shaky funicular (Tues–Sun: April–Sept 11am–1.30pm & 4–6.30pm; Oct–Mar 11am–1.30pm & 3–5.30pm; €3) ascends to the base of the **cross**, offering, as you can imagine, a superlative view over the Sierra de Guadarrama and a closer look at the giant figures propping up the base of the cross.

The Sierra de Guadarrama

The routes from Madrid and El Escorial to Segovia strike through the heart of the **Sierra de Guadarrama** – a beautiful journey, worth taking for its own sake. The road is occasionally marred by suburban development, especially around **Navacerrada**, Madrid's main ski station, but from the train it's almost entirely unspoiled. There are plenty of opportunities for walking, but make sure you buy the appropriate maps in Madrid.

If you want to base yourself in the mountains for a while you'd do best to head for **Cercedilla**, 75 minutes by train on the Madrid–Segovia line – and a little way off the main road. Alternatively, over to the east, there is **Manzanares el Real**, with an odd medieval castle and a reservoir-side setting.

Cercedilla and the Puerto de Navacerrada

CERCEDILLA is an alpine-looking village and an excellent base for summer walking; it is much frequented by *madrileños* at weekends. **Accommodation** is limited to the *Hostal El Aribel*, near the station (☎918 521 511, ✆918 521

561; ⑤), and two **youth hostels** up on the Dehesas road: *Villa Castora* (☎918 520 334, ⓕ918 522 411; ②) and, 2km up the road, *Las Dehesas* (☎918 520 135, ⓕ918 521 836; ②). Further up still, you'll find a helpful **information booth** (daily 10am–6pm; ☎918 522 213). There are several **eating** places in town: *Los Frutales* on the Carretera de las Dehesas does good *croquetas* and *judias con perdiz* (partridge and beans), the train station has a restaurant on the first floor or you could try the restaurant at *Hostal El Aribel*.

From Cercedilla, you can embark on a wonderful little train ride to the **Puerto de Navacerrada**, the most important pass in the mountains and the heart of the ski area, or a little further on to **Cotos** where a number of well-maintained walks around the **Parque Natural de Peñalara** begin. The train runs hourly over weekends and holidays and passes through the *parque natural*, an extension of the upper Manzanares basin: watch out for roe deer and wild boar. For the more energetic there is a very pleasant five-hour round-trip **walk** along the pine-fringed Calzada Romana (old Roman road) up to the Puerto de la Fuenfría (1796m) with its striking views down into Segovia province.

From **Madrid** to Cercedilla, there are over twenty **trains** a day (6am–11pm from Atocha, calling at Chamartín, and nine daily going on to Segovia) and **buses** leaving every half-hour from the Intercambiador de Autobuses de Moncloa.

Manzanares el Real

Some 50km north of Madrid, on the shores of the Santillana *embalse* (reservoir), lies **MANZANARES EL REAL**, a town which in former times was disputed between the capital and Segovia. Nowadays it's a somewhat tatty resort, geared to Madrid weekenders, whose villas dot the landscape for miles around. Nearby however, the ruggedly beautiful **La Pedriza**, a spur of the Sierra de Guadarrama, has been declared a regional park (access limited to 500 cars a day at weekends; free), and has some enjoyable walks, as well as some much-revered technical climbs, notably the ascent to the jagged Peña del Diezmo. It is also home to a very large colony of griffon vultures.

In Manzanares itself, the one attraction is the **castle** (daily 10am–1pm & 3–5.30pm; free), which despite its eccentric appearance is a perfectly genuine fifteenth-century construction, built around an earlier chapel. It was soon modified into a palace by the architect Juan Guas, who built an elegant gallery on the south side, false machicolations on the other, and studded the tower with stones resembling cannonballs. The interior has been heavily restored.

As befits Manzanares, **accommodation** is expensive and limited to *Hostal Tranco* (☎918 530 423; ④), and *Hotel Parque Real* (☎918 539 912, ⓕ918 539 960; ⑥). However, there is usually space at one of the two **campsites**, *El Ortigal* (☎918 530 120) at the foot of La Pedriza or the well-equipped *La Fresneda* (☎ & ⓕ918 476 523) on the Carretera M608 towards Soto del Real. **Food** is not cheap either, but good meals can be had at *Los Arcos* in c/Real and the *Restaurante Parra* in c/Panaderos. **Buses** from Madrid run hourly (7.30am–9.30pm) from c/Mateo Inurria 11 (Metro Plaza de Castilla).

Ávila

Two things distinguish **ÁVILA**: its eleventh-century **walls**, two perfectly preserved kilometres of which surround the old town, and the mystic writer **Santa Teresa**, who was born here and whose shrines are a major focus of religious pilgrimage. Set on a high plain, with the peaks of the Sierra de Gredos

ÁVILA

Segovia (N110) ▲ Train ▲ Station ▲ **3** ▲ Madrid (C505)

12 & Monasterio de Santo Tomás ▶

◀ Convento de la Encarnación

◀ Cáceres

B, Los Cuatro Postes & Salamanca (N 501)

▼ Toledo (N403)

Metres 0 — 100

ACCOMMODATION

Hostal Bellas	9
Hostería de Bracamonte	4
Hostal Casa Felipe	7
Hostal Continental	8
Duprier	12
Hostal Elena	2
Hostal Jardín	5
Palacio de Valderrábanos	10
Palacio de los Velada	6
Parador Raimundo	1
Hostal El Rastro	11
Pensión Santa Ana	3

RESTAURANTS & TAPAS BARS

Bar El Rincón	A
Los Cancelas	C
Casa Patas	F
La Casona	E
El Molino de la Losa	B
La Posada de la Fruta	D

behind, the town is quite a sight, especially if you time it right and approach with the evening sun highlighting the golden tone of the walls and the details of the 88 towers.

The walls were ordered by Alfonso VI, after his capture of the city from the Moors in 1090; they took his Muslim prisoners nine years to construct. At closer quarters, they prove a bit of a facade, as the old city within is sparsely populated and a little dishevelled, most of modern life having moved into the new developments outside the fortifications. However, the fine **Romanesque churches** dotted in and about the old city, plus good walks around the walls, make the town an excellent night's stopover, either combined with El Escorial, or en route to Salamanca.

Arrival and information

From **Madrid** (Chamartín station) there are up to 24 **trains** a day to Ávila; **buses** are less frequent (eight on weekdays, three at weekends). The train station is a fifteen-minute walk to the east of the old town, or a local bus into Plaza de la Victoria. On foot, follow the broad Avenida José Antonio to its end, by the large church of Santa Ana, and bear left up c/Duque de Alba to reach Plaza Santa Teresa. Buses use a terminal on the Avenida de Madrid, a little closer in: walking from here, cross the small park opposite, then turn right up c/Duque de Alba, or take a local bus to Plaza de la Victoria near the cathedral. **Driving**, follow signs for the walls (*murallas*) or the *parador* and you should be able to park just outside the old town.

Ávila's walls make orientation straightforward, with the **cathedral** and most other sights contained within. Just outside the southeast corner of the walls is the city's main square, **Plaza Santa Teresa**, and the most imposing of the old gates, the **Puerta del Alcázar**. Within the walls, the old market square, **Plaza de la Victoria**, fronts the *ayuntamiento* at the heart of the old city.

The main **turismo** (Mon-Fri 9am-2pm & 5-7pm, Sat & Sun 10am-2pm & 5-8pm; ☎920 211 387, ✉turismo@ayuntavila.com) is in the Plaza de la Catedral, and there's another, smaller office next to the Basílica de San Vicente (open July–Sept only; same hours).

Accommodation

There are numerous cheap *hostales* around the train station and along Avenida José Antonio, but you should be able to find something nearer the walled centre of town. You'll find a well-maintained **campsite**, *Camping Sonsoles* (☎920 256 336; open June–Sept) 2km out on the Toledo road, near a football stadium.

Budget options

Hostal Continental, Plaza de la Catedral 4 ☎920 211 502 or 920 211 563, ☎920 251 691. An attractive old hotel, opposite the cathedral; its charms are fading fast, but the rooms are large and en suite and some have great views onto the square. ❹

Duperier, Avda. de Juventud s/n ☎ & ☎920 221 716. Small youth hostel (with 11pm curfew) out past the monastery, near the local swimming pool. Rooms with bath and meals available. Open July to mid-Aug. ❷

Hostal Elena, c/Marqués de Canales y Chozas 1 ☎920 252 496. Small *hostal* near the *parador*, with some en-suite rooms. ❹

Pensión Santa Ana, c/Alfonso de Montalvo 2 ☎920 220 063. Fail-safe option between the train station and city centre. Eight rooms with shared facilities. ❸

Moderate and expensive options

Hostal Bellas, c/Caballeros 19 ☎920 212 910, ☎920 256 011. Friendly and fairly central, most rooms have showers and there are discounts out of season. ❺

Hostería de Bracamonte, c/Bracamonte 6 ☎920 251 280, ☎920 253 838. Atmospheric and elegant hotel, between the city walls and the Plaza de la

Victoria, created from a number of converted Renaissance mansions. **❼**

Hostal Casa Felipe, Plaza de la Victoria 12 ☎920 213 924. Reasonable and centrally located; some rooms have showers and overlook the square. **❹**

Hostal Jardín, c/San Segundo 38 ☎920 211 074. Large *hostal* near Puerta de los Leales, which often has rooms when others are full. **❹–❺**

Palacio de Valderrábanos, Plaza de la Catedral 9 ☎920 211 023, ☎920 251 691, ⓦwww.palaciovalderrabanos.com. This former bishop's palace beats the *parador* for ambience. **❽**

Palacio de los Velada, Plaza de la Catedral 10 ☎920 255 100, ☎920 254 900. Beautifully con-

verted sixteenth-century palace and the priciest hotel in town; it's part of the Melia chain and bears their usual stamp of gracious living. **❽**

Parador Raimundo de Borgoña, c/Marqués de Canales y Chozas 2 ☎920 211 340, ☎920 226 166, ⓔavila@paradores.es. A converted fifteenth-century mansion – not the most exciting *parador* in Spain, but pleasant enough, with the usual comforts. It's the cheapest of Ávila's top hotels. **❽**

Hostal El Rastro, Plaza del Rastro 1 ☎920 211 218, ☎920 251 626. A good mid-range option, this characterful old inn is set right against the walls, with a pleasant garden and popular restaurant. **❺**

The Town

The focus of Ávila's sights is, inevitably, **Santa Teresa**, with whom most of the numerous convents and churches claim some connection. On the secular front, a circuit outside the **walls** makes a fine walk, and from the Puerta del Alcázar you can climb up and stroll around a section.

Santa Teresa in Ávila

The obvious place to start a tour of Teresa's Ávila is the **Convento de Santa Teresa** (daily 8.30am–2pm & 3.30–8pm; free), built over the saint's birthplace just inside the south gate of the old town – entered off the Paseo del Rastro. Most of the convent remains *de clausura* but you can see the very spot where she was born, now an elaborate chapel in the Baroque church, which is decorated with scenes of the saint demonstrating her powers of levitation to various august bodies. In a small reliquary (daily: 9am–1.30pm & 3.30–7.30pm; summer 10am–1pm & 4–7.30pm; free), beside the gift shop, is a **museum** (daily 10am–1pm & 4–7pm; €1.80) containing memorials of Teresa's life, including not only her rosary beads, but also one of the fingers she used to count them with.

Santa Teresa de Ávila

Santa Teresa (1515–82) was born to a noble family in Ávila and from childhood began to experience visions and religious raptures. At the age of seven she attempted to run away with her brother to be martyred by the Moors: the spot where they were recaptured and brought back, **Los Cuatro Postes**, is a fine vantage point from which to admire the walls of the town.

Teresa's religious career began at the Carmelite convent of La Encarnación, where she was a nun for 27 years. From this base, she went on to reform the movement and found convents throughout Spain. She was an ascetic, but her appeal – and her importance to the Counter-Reformation – lay in the mystic sensuality of her experience of Christ, as revealed in her autobiography, for centuries a bestseller in Spain. As joint patron saint of Spain (together with Santiago – or St James), she remains a central pillar in Spanish Catholicism and schoolgirls are brought into Ávila by the busload to experience first-hand the life of the woman they are supposed to emulate.

On a more bizarre note, one of Santa Teresa's mummified hands has now been returned to Ávila after spending the Franco years by the bedside of the great dictator.

Heading through the old town, and leaving by the Puerta del Carmen, you can follow a lane, c/Encarnación, to the **Convento de la Encarnación** (daily: summer 9.30am–1pm & 4–7pm; winter 9.30am–1pm & 4–6pm; €1.20). Each of the rooms here is labelled with the act Teresa performed, while everything she might have touched or looked at is on display. A small museum section also provides a reasonable introduction to the saint's life, with maps showing the convents, and a selection of her sayings – the pithiest, perhaps, "Life is a night in a bad hotel."

A third Teresan sight lies a couple of blocks east of the Plaza de Santa Teresa. This is the **Convento de San José** (daily: summer 10am–1.30pm & 4–7pm; winter 10am–1.30pm & 3–6pm; €0.60), also known as San José, the first monastery that the saint founded, in 1562. Its museum contains relics and memorabilia, including the coffin in which Teresa once slept, and assorted personal possessions. The tomb of her brother Lorenzo is in the larger of the two churches.

Lastly, you might want to make your way up to **Los Cuatro Postes**, a little four-posted shrine, 1500m along the Salamanca road west of town. It was here, aged seven, that the infant Teresa was recaptured by her uncle, running away with her brother to seek Christian martyrdom from the Moors.

The cathedral and other sights

The three most beautiful churches in Ávila – the cathedral, San Vicente, and the Monasterio de Santo Tomás – are less directly associated with its most famous resident. Around the cathedral and Santo Tomé el Viejo (just outside the northeast corner of the walls), there is also a scattering of impressive **Renaissance mansions** – none of them are open to visitors but they give a glimpse of old Castilian wealth in their coats of arms and decorative facades.

Ávila's **Catedral** (Mon–Fri 9.30am–6.30pm, Sat 9.30am–7pm, Sun noon–7pm; closed Jan 1 & 6, Oct 15 & Dec 25; €1.80) was started in the twelfth century but has never been finished, as evidenced by the missing tower above the main entrance. The earliest Romanesque parts were as much fortress as church, and the apse actually forms an integral part of the city walls. Their defensive function was real, with the twelfth-century Bishop Sancho providing sanctuary here for the young Alfonso IX, prior to his accession.

Inside, the succeeding changes of style are immediately apparent; the **Romanesque** parts are made of a strange red-and-white mottled stone, then there's an abrupt break and the rest of the main structure is pure white stone and **Gothic** forms. Although the proportions are exactly the same, this newer half of the cathedral seems infinitely more spacious. The *coro*, whose elaborate carved back you see as you come in, and two chapels in the left aisle, are **Renaissance** additions. Here you can admire the carved stalls in the *coro* (the work of a Dutch sculptor, Cornelius) and the elaborate marble tomb of a fifteenth-century bishop known as El Tostado (the "toasted" or "swarthy"). The thirteenth-century *sacristia* with its star-shaped cupola and gold inlay decor, and the treasury-museum with its monstrous silver *custodia* and ancient religious images are also worth a visit.

The basilica of **San Vicente** (daily 10am–1.30pm & 4–6.30pm; €1.20), like the cathedral, is a mixture of architectural styles. Its twelfth-century doorways and the portico which protects them are magnificent examples of Romanesque art, while the church itself shows the influence of later trends. San Vicente was martyred on this site, and his tomb depicts a series of particularly gruesome deaths; in the crypt you can see the slab on which he and his sisters were executed by the Romans. This church shares with **San Pedro**, on

Plaza de Santa Teresa, a warm pink glow from the sandstone of its construction – a characteristic aspect of Ávila but seen most clearly here.

The **Monasterio de Santo Tomás** (daily 10am–1pm & 4–8pm, closed Jan 1 & 6, Feb 1-6, Oct 15 & Dec 25; *coro* and cloisters €0.50, museum €1.20) is a Dominican monastery founded in 1482, but greatly expanded over the following decade by Fernando and Isabel, whose summer palace it became. Inside are three exceptional cloisters, the largest of which contains an **oriental collection**, a strangely incongruous display built up by the monks over centuries of missionary work in the Orient. On every available surface is carved the yoke-and-arrows motif of the Reyes Católicos, surrounded by pomegranates, symbol of the newly conquered kingdom of Granada (*granada* means "pomegranate" in Spanish). In the **church** is the elaborate tomb of Prince Juan, Fernando and Isabel's only son, whose early death opened the way for Carlos V's succession and caused his parents so much grief that they abandoned their newly completed home here. It was subsequently damaged by Napoleon's troops, who stabled their horses in the church. Notice also the tomb of the prince's tutors, almost as elaborate as his own, and the thrones occupied by the king and queen during services. The notorious inquisitor Torquemada is buried in the sacristy. Santo Tomás is quite a walk downhill from the south part of town – you can get back up by the #1 bus, which takes in much of the old city on its circular route.

The small **Museo Provincial** is housed in the sixteenth-century Palacio de los Deanes (Tues–Sat 10am–2pm & 4.30–7.30pm, Sun 10.30am–2pm; €1.20, free Sat & Sun) which once housed the cathedral's deans. Today, its eclectic exhibits include collections of archeological remains, ceramics, agricultural implements, traditional costumes and furnishings from around the Ávila province, as well as some fine Romanesque statues and a wonderful fifteenth-century triptych depicting the life of Christ. The ticket also allows you entry to the museum storeroom in the church of Santo Tomé El Viejo just opposite.

It's possible to walk along the **city walls** from Puerta del Alcázar to Puerta del Rastro (Tues–Sun 11am–8pm; €1.80); the view of the town is stunning. Tickets are available from the green kiosk by the Puerta del Alcázar.

Eating and drinking

Ávila has a decent if unexceptional array of **bars** and **restaurants**, some of them sited just outside the walls. Within the walls, a stroll from Plaza de la Victoria along c/Vallespin will allow you to compare *menús* and prices. **Local specialities** include the Castilian standby *cordero asado* (roast lamb), *judias del barco con chorizo* (haricot beans with sausage), *mollejas* (cow's stomach) and *yemas de Santa Teresa* (candied egg-yolk) – the last of these sold in confectioners all over town. For **nightlife** head outside the city walls to c/Capitán Peña where the strip of four *discobares* next to each other keeps the walking to a minimum.

Bar El Rincón, Plaza Zurraquín 6. To the north of Plaza de la Victoria, this bar serves a generous three-course *menú* for €9.00.

Los Cancelas, c/Cruz Vieja 6. Next to the cathedral and in the hotel of the same name, this friendly restaurant is popular with locals; the *menú* is €10.80.

Casa Patas, c/San Millán 4. Pleasant bar, with good tapas, and a little *comedor* (evenings only), near the church of San Pedro. Closed Wed & Sept.

La Casona, Plaza de Pedro Dávila 6. Popular restaurant specializing in lamb, with *menús* starting at €9.60.

Hostería de Bracamonte, c/Bracamonte 6. Comfy, rustic atmosphere in this restaurant housed within the walls of a converted Renaissance mansion. Speciality is *codero asado* for €13.20. Closed Tues.

Mesón del Rastro, Plaza del Rastro 1. Excellent bar, attached to the *hostal* of the same name, with a range of tapas. Behind it is a modest-priced restaurant, an old-fashioned place with solid, traditional food.

El Molino de la Losa, c/Bajada de la Losa 12 ☎920 211 101. Converted fifteenth-century mill out by Los Cuatro Postes, with a deserved reputation and handy if you're with kids (there's a play area in the garden). The *menú* is €18. Closed Mon & mid-Oct to mid-March.

La Posada de la Fruta, Plaza de Pedro Dávila 8. With an attractive, sunny, covered courtyard, this is a nice place for a drink, and also serves some good standard Castilian fare.

On from Ávila

Ávila is quite a nexus with road and rail routes to Salamanca and Valladolid, from where you can get to just about anywhere in northern Spain, while to the east Segovia (see p.180) is less than two hours away by bus. Within striking distance, too, to the south, is the beautiful Sierra de Gredos (see below).

On the **Salamanca route**, both road and rail routes pass through **Peñaranda de Bracamonte**, a crumbling old town with a couple of large plazas and ancient churches. From here, if you have your own vehicle, you can continue to Salamanca on a slightly longer route through **Alba de Tormes**. Santa Teresa died here, and the Carmelite convent which contains the remains of her body (not much of it to judge by the number of relics scattered around Spain) is another major target of pilgrimage. There are the remains of a castle here too, and several other interesting churches.

Heading north **towards Valladolid**, road and rail both pass through **Medina del Campo** with its beautiful castle (see p.414).

The Sierra de Gredos

The **Sierra de Gredos** continues the line of the Sierra de Guadarrama, enclosing Madrid to the north and west. A major mountain range, with peaks in excess of 2500m, Gredos offers the best trekking in central Spain, including high-level routes across the passes as well as more casual walks among the villages.

By bus, the easiest access is from Madrid to **Arenas de San Pedro**, from where you can explore the range, and then move on west into the valley of La Vera in Extremadura (see p.214). If you have your own transport, you could head into the range south from Ávila along the C502, and you might prefer to base yourself in one of the villages on the north side of the range, along the **Tormes valley**, and do circular walks from there. The *casas rurales* that are scattered throughout the villages often make a good base, especially if you are travelling in a group (☎902 4224 141, ⓦwww.casasgredos.com).

Arenas de San Pedro and Mombeltrán

ARENAS DE SAN PEDRO is a sizeable town with a somewhat prettified fifteenth-century **castle** and a good range of **accommodation**: pleasant options include the *Hostería Los Galayos* (☎ & ⓕ920 371 379, ⓦlosgalayos.com; ⑤), which also has a reliable restaurant, the roomy *Posada de la Triste Condesa* (☎920 372 567; ⑤), and *Hostal Castillo* (☎920 370 091; ③). If you haven't already obtained **maps** of Gredos, you can pick up a functional pamphlet from the **turismo** (Mon–Fri 9.30am–1.30pm & 4.30–7.30pm, Sat 9.30am–1.30pm; ☎920 372 368) on c/Triste Condesa, or buy more detailed sheets from the bookshop Librería Nava on the same road.

MOMBELTRÁN, 12km north (an enjoyable, mainly downhill, walk from Arenas), is an attractive alternative stop, with its fifteenth-century **castle** of the Dukes of Albuquerque set against a stunning mountain backdrop. The village has two **hostales**, the *Albuquerque* (☎920 386 032; ④) and *Marji* (☎920 386

031; **⑥**), and a summer-only **campsite**, *Prados Abiertos* (☎920 386 061), 4km south of the centre towards Arenas de San Pedro.

El Arenal and El Hornillo

The main reason to stop in Arenas de San Pedro is to make your way up to the villages of El Hornillo and El Arenal, respectively 6km and 9km to the north, the trailheads for some excellent **mountain walks**. There are no buses but it's a pleasant walk up from Arenas to El Arenal on a track running between the road and the river – start out past the sports centre and swimming pool in Arenas.

EL ARENAL has the accommodation, including the *Hostal Isabel* (☎920 375 148; **❸**), whose owner is knowledgeable about routes through the range. You can walk over the top of Gredos from El Arenal – the path via the pass at Puerto de la Cabrilla has been somewhat improved recently – and strike out along the ridge in either direction, to the main road at Puerto del Pico or back to El Arenal. **EL HORNILLO**, however, is the more common trailhead, and the beginning of the Circo de Gredos, one of the main recognized trekking routes over the Gredos watershed.

An alternative trek is to head due south from El Arenal, along a well-defined path over a broad pass to Candeleda (see below); this is a long day's walk but it's more or less all downhill.

The Circo de Gredos

The walk from El Hornillo over the **Gredos watershed** takes most of a day to accomplish, exchanging the pine and granite of the steep south slopes for the *matorral* (scrub thickets), cow pastures and wide horizons on the northern side. Over the top, you'll emerge on a twelve-kilometre stretch of paved road linking Hoyos del Espino, a village in the Tormes valley, and the so-called **Plataforma**, jumping-off point to the highest peaks of the Gredos. It's best to call it a day just above the Plataforma, where there's lots of camping space in the high Pozas meadows. From here, you can proceed up to the Circo de Laguna Grande, two hours' walk beyond Pozas on a well-defined path.

Circo de Laguna Grande
and Circo de las Cinco Lagunas

The **Circo de Laguna Grande** is the centrepiece of the Gredos range, with its highest peak, **Almanzor** (2593m), looming above, surrounded by pinnacles sculpted into utterly improbable shapes. The valley with its huge lake is popular with day-trippers and weekenders, as you can drive up here from Hoyos del Espino, and its **refugio** (mountain hut) is often full, especially at weekends; camping out by the refugio is, however, an accepted alternative.

The valley path, actually Alfonso XIII's old hunting route, continues west for a couple of hours before ending abruptly at the edge of a sharp, scree-laden descent into the **Circo de las Cinco Lagunas**. The drop is amply rewarded by virtual solitude, even in midsummer, and sightings of *Capra pyrenaica gloriae*, the graceful (and almost tame) Gredos mountain goat. Protected by law since the 1920s, they now number several thousand and frequent the north slopes of Gredos in the warmer months.

The Tormes valley: Navarredonda

On the north side of Gredos is the Tormes valley, trailed by the C500 to the main N110 at El Barco de Ávila. There is accommodation at **NAVARREDONDA**, including a **youth hostel** (☎920 348 005; **❷**), a campsite, *Camping Navagredos* (☎920 207 476; May–Sept) and Spain's first ever **parador** (☎920 348 048, ☏920 348 205, ✉gredos@parador.es; ⑦) at km 43 on the C500.

Candeleda and Madrigal de la Vera

The village of **CANDELEDA**, on the Arenas–Jarandilla road, is nothing special but it's amazingly popular with Spanish summer holiday-makers, who book its *hostales* weeks in advance. The **turismo** is in the Casa Cultura, close to the Plaza Mayor (daily 10am–1.30pm & 5–8pm; ☎920 380 396), and can provide helpful information on walking and hiking in the area. If you're planning ahead, the best-value **place to stay** is *Hostal La Pastora* (☎920 382 127; ④) and the fanciest the *Hostal Pedrós* (☎920 380 951; ④). Campers sometimes set up their tents alongside the river, west of town.

At **MADRIGAL DE LA VERA**, a more attractive village 12km to the west of Candeleda, there's an official campsite, *Alardos* (☎927 565 066; March–Sept), and yet another route across the Gredos, this time leading to **Bohoyo**, a hamlet 4km southwest of El Barco de Ávila.

Segovia and around

After Toledo, **SEGOVIA** is the outstanding trip from Madrid. A relatively small city, strategically sited on a rocky ridge, it is deeply and haughtily Castilian, with a panoply of squares and mansions from its days of Golden Age grandeur, when it was a royal resort and a base for the Cortes (parliament). It was in Segovia – in the unremarkable church of San Miguel, off the Plaza Mayor – that Isabel la Católica was proclaimed queen.

For a city of its size, there are a stunning number of outstanding architectural monuments. Most celebrated are the **Roman aqueduct**, the **cathedral** and the fairy-tale **Alcázar**, but the less obvious attractions – the cluster of ancient churches and the many mansions found in the lanes of the old town, all in a warm, honey-coloured stone – are what really make it worth a visit. Just a few kilometres outside the city and reasonably accessible from Segovia are two Bourbon palaces, **La Granja** and **Riofrío**.

Arrival and information

Well connected by road and rail, Segovia is an easy trip from Madrid with nine trains daily from Charmartín and Atocha, as well as up to 31 buses (operated by La Sepulvedana, Paseo de la Florida 11; Metro Príncipe Pío). The city's own **train station** is some distance out of town – take bus #3 to the central Plaza Mayor; the **bus station** is on the same route.

The **turismo** (Mon–Fri 9am–2pm & 5–7pm, Sat & Sun 10am–2pm; ☎921 460 334, ⊛www.ctv.es/aytosego), in the **Plaza Mayor**, offers a list of local accommodation plus a *Guía Semanal* with transport timetables and current events; most significant facts are displayed in the window if it's closed. You'll find a second tourist office in the busy **Plaza de Azoguejo** (daily 10am–8pm, ☎921 462 914).

Accommodation

Most of the **accommodation** is to be found in the streets around the Plaza Mayor and Plaza de Azoguejo, but rooms can be hard to come by even out of season, so it's worth booking ahead if you're considering more than a day-trip. Be warned that in winter, at over 1000m, the nights can be very cold and sometimes snowy, and the more basic rooms aren't generally heated.

Budget options

Pensión Aragón, Plaza Mayor 4 ☎921 460 914. Rotten rooms and communal bathrooms but an ideal position and as cheap as they come. Triples are a bargain at €21.75. ❷

Emperador Teodosio, Paseo Conde de Sepúlveda 4 ☎921 441 111. Pleasant, spacious student residence which becomes a youth hostel just for July and August. Located between the train and bus stations. ❷

Pensión Ferri, c/Escuderos 10 ☎921 460 957. On a street off Plaza Mayor, quiet, clean and with a small garden. ❷–❸

Moderate and expensive options

Hotel Acueducto, Avda. Padre Claret 10 ☎921 424 800, ⓕ921 428 446, ⓔ hacueducto@ interbook.net. Pleasant hotel outside the city walls, near the aqueduct. The restaurant gets busy with bus parties during the day, but is quiet most evenings. ❼

Hostal Don Jaime, c/Ochoa Ondategui 8 ☎921 444 787, ⓕ921 444 790. Excellent *hostal* near Plaza de Azoguejo. All doubles have their own bathroom. ❺

Hostal Hidalgo, c/José Canalejas 3 & 5 ☎921 463 529, ⓕ921 463 531. Small, beautiful old building overlooking the church of San Martín, with a good restaurant. *El Hidalgo 2*, the sister *hostal* nearby at c/Juan Bravo 21 (☎921 463 529), is also worth a try. Both ❹–❺

Hotel Infanta Isabel, c/Isabel la Católica 1 ☎921 461 300, ⓕ921 462 217. Comfortable new hotel – better value than the *parador* – ideally positioned on Plaza Mayor. ❼

Hostal Juan Bravo, c/Juan Bravo 12 ☎921 463 413. Lots of big, comfortable rooms and plant-festooned bathrooms. ❹

Hotel Los Linajes, c/Dr Velasco 9 ☎921 460 475, ⓕ921 460 479. Good-value cosy hotel set in part of an old palace in a quiet corner of the walled city. It has a fine garden overlooking the river valley, and all rooms are air-conditioned. ❼

Parador de Segovia, Carretera de Valladolid s/n ☎921 443 737, ⓕ921 437 362, ⓔ segovia@paradores.es. Not very convenient for visiting the sights (you'll need a car), but for facilities and fantastic views of the city – especially beautiful when illuminated at night – it can't be beaten. ❽.

Hostal Plaza, c/Cronista Lecea 11 ☎921 460 303, ⓕ921 460 305. Clean *hostal*, centrally located just off the Plaza Mayor. Also has a garage. ❺

Camping

Camping Acueducto, Avda. Don Juan de Borbón 49 ☎ & ⓕ 921 425 000, ⓔ acueducto@ mmteam.interbook.net; open Easter–Sept. The nearest campsite, a couple of kilometres out on the road to La Granja; take a #6 "Nueva Segovia" bus from the Plaza Mayor.

The City

Segovia has more than a full day's worth of sights. If you're on a flying visit from Madrid, obvious priorities are the **cathedral** and **Alcázar** in the old town, and the church of **Vera Cruz** and **aqueduct**, just outside the walls to west and east respectively. Given more time, take a walk out of the city for the **views**, or just wander at will through the **old quarters** of the city, away from the centre: each has a village atmosphere of its own.

The cathedral to the Alcázar

Construction on Segovia's **Catedral** (daily: April–Oct 9am–6.30pm; Nov–March 9.30am–5.30pm) began in 1525, on the orders of Carlos V to make amends for the damage done to the city during the *comuneros* revolt. However, it was not completed for another 200 years, making it the last major Gothic building in Spain, and arguably the last in Europe. Accordingly it takes the style to its logical – or perhaps illogical – extreme, with pinnacles and flying buttresses tacked on at every conceivable point. Though impressive for its size alone, the interior is surprisingly bare for so florid a construction and its space cramped by a great green marble *coro* at its very centre. The treasures are

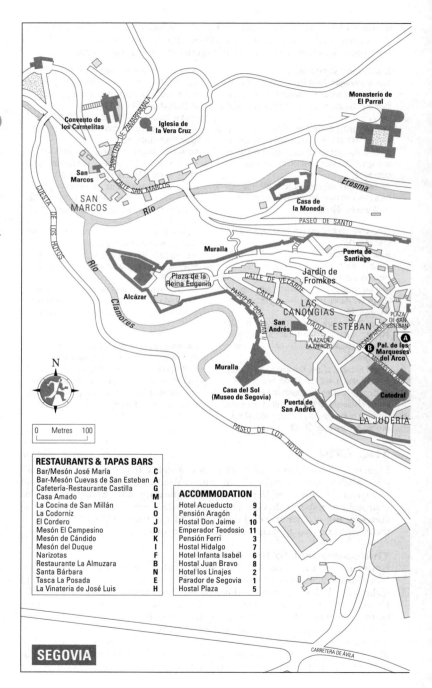

N

| 0 | Metres | 100 |

RESTAURANTS & TAPAS BARS

Bar/Mesón José María	**C**
Bar-Mesón Cuevas de San Esteban	**A**
Cafetería-Restaurante Castilla	**G**
Casa Amado	**M**
La Cocina de San Millán	**L**
La Codorniz	**O**
El Cordero	**J**
Mesón El Campesino	**D**
Mesón de Cándido	**K**
Mesón del Duque	**I**
Narizotas	**F**
Restaurante La Almuzara	**B**
Santa Bárbara	**N**
Tasca La Posada	**E**
La Vinateria de José Luis	**H**

ACCOMMODATION

Hotel Acueducto	**9**
Pensión Aragón	**4**
Hostal Don Jaime	**10**
Emperador Teodosio	**11**
Pensión Ferri	**3**
Hostal Hidalgo	**7**
Hotel Infanta Isabel	**6**
Hostal Juan Bravo	**8**
Hotel los Linajes	**2**
Parador de Segovia	**1**
Hostal Plaza	**5**

SEGOVIA

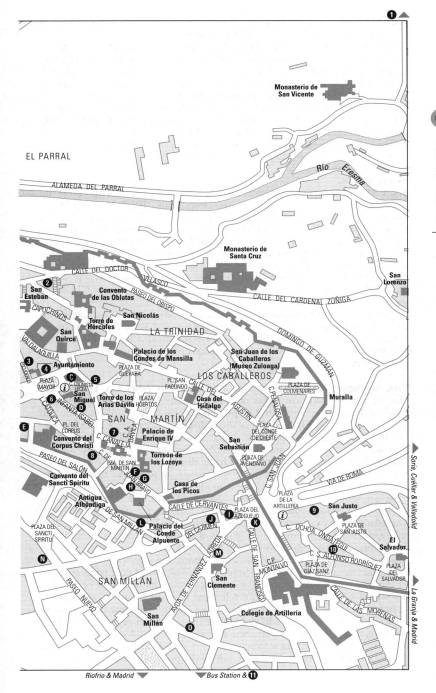

EL PARRAL

Río Eresma

ALAMEDA DEL PARRAL

Monasterio de
San Vicente

Monasterio de
Santa Cruz

San
Lorenzo

CALLE DEL DOCTOR

VELASCO

CALLE DEL CARDENAL ZÚÑIGA

② San
Esteban

Convento
de las Oblatas

PASEO DEL OBISPO

CAPUCHINOS

San Nicolás

LA TRINIDAD

DOMINGO DE GUZMÁN

Torre de
Hércules

San
Quirce

Palacio de los
Condes de Mansilla

San Juan de los
Caballeros
(Museo Zuloaga)

Muralla

VALDELAGUILLA

③

④ Ayuntamiento

PLAZA DE
GUEVARA

PL. SAN
FACUNDO

LOS CABALLEROS

PLAZA DE
COLMENARES

ESCUDEROS

C. PEÑALOSA

PLAZA
MAYOR

ⓒ C. CRONISTA
LECEA

⑤

Casa del
Hidalgo

CALLE DEL

San
Miguel

ⓓ

Torre de los
Arias Dávila

PLAZA
HUERTOS

AGUSTÍN

CATÓLICA

⑥ INFANTA ISABEL

SAN

MARTÍN

PLAZA
DEL CONDE
DE CHESTE

PL. DEL
CORPUS

⑦ C.A.
DÁVILA

Palacio de
Enrique IV

San
Sebastián

Ⓔ

Convento del
Corpus Christi

C. CANALEJA

PLAZA DE
AVENDAÑO

VÍA DE ROMA

PASEO DEL SALÓN

⑧

L. DE

PZA. DE SAN
MARTÍN

Torreón de
los Lozoya

C. SAN JUAN

Convento del
Sancti Spíritu

Ⓕ

Ⓖ

Ⓗ JUAN BRAVO

Casa de
los Picos

PLAZA
DE LA
ARTILLERÍA

ⓘ

Antigua
Alhóndiga

DE SAN MILLÁN

CALLE DE CERVANTES

Ⓘ

PLAZA DEL
AZOGUEJO

⑨ San Justo

C. OCHOA ONDATEGUI

PLAZA DE
SAN JUSTO

Ⓛ

Palacio del
Conde
Alpuente

DEL CARMEN

Ⓙ

Ⓚ

⑩ El
Salvador

PLAZA DEL
SANCTI
SPÍRITU

CALLE DE SAN FRANCISCO

C. S. ALFONSO RODRÍGUEZ

PLAZA
DEL
SALVADOR

Ⓝ

Ⓜ

C.P.
MONTALVO

PLAZA DE
DÍAZ SANZ

PASEO NUEVO

SAN MILLÁN

San
Clemente

CALLE DE LAS MORENAS

San
Millán

Ⓞ

Colegio de Artillería

Soria, Cuéllar & Valladolid

La Granja & Madrid

Riofrío & Madrid ▼   ▼ Bus Station & ⑪

almost all confined to the museum (same hours as cathedral, except Sun opens at 2.30pm; €1.80) which opens off the cloisters.

Down beside the cathedral, c/Daoiz leads past a line of souvenir shops to the twelfth-century Romanesque church of San Andrés and on to a small park in front of the **Alcázar** (daily: May–Sept 10am–7pm; Oct–April 10am–6pm; €3, Tues free for EU citizens). An extraordinary fantasy of a castle, with its narrow towers and flurry of turrets, it will seem eerily familiar to just about every visitor, having served as the model for the original Disneyland castle in California. It is itself a bit of a sham. Although it dates from the fourteenth and fifteenth centuries, it was almost completely destroyed by a fire in 1862 and rebuilt as a deliberately hyperbolic version of the original. Still, it should be visited, if only for the magnificent panoramas from the tower.

Vera Cruz

The best of Segovia's ancient churches is undoubtedly **Vera Cruz** (Tues–Sun 10.30am–1.30pm & 3.30–7pm, winter closes 6pm; closed Nov; €1.20), a remarkable twelve-sided building outside town in the valley facing the Alcázar. It was built by the Knights Templar in the early thirteenth century on the pattern of the church of the Holy Sepulchre in Jerusalem, and once housed part of the True Cross (hence its name; the sliver of wood itself is now in the nearby village church at Zamarramala). Inside, the nave is circular, and its heart is occupied by a strange two-storeyed chamber – again twelve-sided – in which the knights, as part of their initiation, stood vigil over the cross. Climb the tower for a highly photogenic vista of the city.

While you're over here you could take in the prodigiously walled **Convento de las Carmelitas** (daily summer: 10am–1.30pm & 4.30–8pm, winter: 10am–1.30pm & 4.30-7pm, closed Mon 10am–1.30pm; free), which is also referred to as the monastery of San Juan de la Cruz, and contains the gaudy mausoleum of its founder-saint.

The synagogue, Plaza de San Martín and La Trinidad

One of the lesser-known sights of Segovia is the **Synagogue**, which now serves as the convent church of **Corpus Cristi**, in a little courtyard at the end of c/Juan Bravo near the east end of the cathedral. You can see part of its exterior from the Paseo del Salón, near which are the streets of the old *Judería*. It's very similar in style to Santa María la Blanca in Toledo, though less refined. During the nineteenth century it was badly damaged by fire, so what you see now is a reconstruction, but historic synagogues are so rare in Spain that this is still of interest. Opening times are unpredictable.

Just east of the synagogue is the **Plaza de San Martín**, one of the city's grandest squares, whose ensemble of buildings include the fourteenth-century **Torreón de Lozoya** (open for exhibitions Mon–Sat 7–9pm & Sun noon–2pm & 7–9pm), and the twelfth-century church of **San Martín**, which demonstrates all the local stylistic peculiarities, though the best of none of them. It has the characteristic covered portico, a fine arched tower, and a typically Romanesque aspect; also, like most of Segovia's churches, it can be visited only when it's open for business, during early morning or evening services. In the middle of the plaza is a **statue of Juan Bravo**, a local folk hero who led the *comuneros* rebellion against Carlos V in protest against tax increases, the undermining of local power and the influence of foreign advisers. Around the square, notice the facades of the buildings, many of which display the local taste for plaster decoration (*esgrafiado*) which is as common on new structures as it is on old. A good example is the **Teatro Juan Bravo** on the northern side of the plaza, opened in 1918.

North of here, the church of **La Trinidad** (daily 10am–2pm & 4.30–7.30pm) preserves the purest Romanesque style in Segovia: each span of its double-arched apse has intricately carved capitals, every one of them unique. Nearby – and making a good loop to or from the Alcázar – is the **Plaza San Esteban**, recently restored and worth seeing for its superb, five-storeyed, twelfth-century tower.

The aqueduct, San Millán and San Justo

The granite **aqueduct**, over 800m long, supported by 166 arches and 120 pillars and at its highest point towering some 30m above the Plaza de Azoguejo, stands up without a drop of mortar or cement. No one knows exactly when it was built, but probably around the end of the first century BC under either Emperor Domitian or Trajan. It no longer carries water from the Río Frío to the city and in recent years traffic vibration and pollution have been threatening to undermine the entire structure. If you climb the stairs beside the aqueduct you can get a view looking down over it from a surviving fragment of the city walls.

Another fine Romanesque church in the typical Segovian style, with *mozárabe* tower and open porticoes, is **San Millán** (daily 10am–2pm & 4.30–7.30pm), which lies between the aqueduct and the bus station. Its interior has been restored to its original form. Also, beyond the aqueduct, you'll find **San Justo** (Tues–Sat: summer noon–2pm & 5–7pm; winter 11am–1.45pm & 4–7pm) which has a wonderful Romanesque wall painting in the apse.

Museums

The **Museo de Segovia** (Tues–Sat 10am–2pm & 5–7pm, Sun 10am–2pm; €0.60, free Sat & Sun), which was recently reopened in the Casa del Sol, the former town abattoir perched on the walls between the Puerta de San Andrés and the Alcázar, has closed once more for further refurbishment and looks like remaining so for some time to come. When it does reopen, it promises to display an enlarged collection of fine arts, sculpture and ceramics, and ethnological and archeological exhibits. The **Casa-Museo de Antonio Machado**, c/Desamparados 5 (Tues–Sun: summer 11am–2pm & 4.30–7.30pm; winter 11am–2pm & 4–6pm; €1.20, free Wed), displays the spartan accommodation and furnishings of one of Spain's greatest poets of the early twentieth century; he is generally more associated with Soria but spent the last years of his life teaching here.

Walks around Segovia and the Monasterio del Paral

Segovia is an excellent city for **walks**. Follow the signposted bypass road outside the city on the south side, and you'll get ever-changing views of the cathedral and the Alcázar from across the valley. The road then doubles back along the other side of the Alcázar, passing near the Convento de los Carmelitas and Vera Cruz.

From there you could continue to the **Monasterio de El Parral** (Mon–Sat 10am–12.30pm & 4.30–6.30pm, Sun 10–11.30am & 4.30–6.30pm; free); or better still, follow the track which circles behind Vera Cruz to the monastery. El Parral is a sizeable and partly ruined complex occupied by Hieronymites, an order found only in Spain. Ring the bell for admission and you will be shown the cloister and church; the latter is a late-Gothic building with rich sculpture at the east end. Gregorian Masses can be heard during the week at 1pm and on Sundays at noon.

For the **best view** of all of Segovia, however, take the main road north for 2km or so towards Cuéllar. A panorama of the whole city, including the aqueduct, gradually unfolds.

△ View of Toledo

Eating and drinking

Segovia takes its cooking seriously, with restaurants of Madrid quality – and prices. **Culinary specialities** include roast suckling pig (*cochinillo asado*), displayed in the raw in the windows of many restaurants, and the rather healthier *judiones*, large white beans from La Granja. There is a concentration of cheaper **bar-restaurants** on c/de la Infanta Isabella, off the Plaza Mayor, and late-night bars on c/Escuderos and c/Judería Vieja, and along Avenida Fernández Ladreda. *La Escuela*, at c/San Millán 5, is a youthful bar with occasional **live bands**.

Inexpensive restaurants and bars

Bar José María, c/Cronista Lecea 11, just off Plaza Mayor. Bar-annexe to one of Segovia's best restaurants (see below), serving delicious and modest-priced tapas.

Bar-Mesón Cuevas de San Esteban, c/Valdelaguila 15, off the top end of Plaza San Esteban. A cavern-restaurant and bar (serving draught beer), popular with locals and excellent value.

Cafetería-Restaurante Castilla, c/Juan Bravo 58. Generous helpings and friendly service – and you can eat out on a terrace.

La Codorniz, c/Ancieto Marinas 1, opposite San Millán church. Inexpensive *menús* and lots of *combinados* featuring *cordoniz* (quail).

El Cordero, c/Carmen 4 & 6. Plenty of variety here, with no less than seven different *menús* to choose from, ranging in price from €7.50–15.

Mesón El Campesino, c/Infanta Isabella 12. One of the best budget restaurants in town, serving decent-value *menús* and *combinados* to a young crowd. Closed Aug.

Restaurante La Almuzara, c/Marqués del Arco 3. Just behind the cathedral, this is a good-value, genuine vegetarian restaurant, with some non-veggie dishes on offer too. Closed Aug.

Tasca La Posada, c/Judería Vieja 19. A fine *bar-mesón* for tapas, *raciones*, or a *menú*.

La Vinatería de José Luis, c/Herreria 3. Imaginative tapas and good selection of wines in this friendly bar off c/Juan Bravo.

Moderate and expensive restaurants

Casa Amado, Avda. Fernández Ladreda 9 ☎921 432 077. Popular local restaurant serving traditional dishes, near the Plaza Azoguejo. Allow €24 per head. Closed Wed & Nov.

La Cocina de San Millán, c/San Millán 3 ☎921 460 233. Nestling below the steps which lead up to the old town, this cosy restaurant serves up imaginative cooking at reasonable prices. Closed Sun night & Jan 7–31.

Mesón de Cándido, Plaza Azoguejo 5 ☎921 428 103. The city's most famous restaurant, reopened in 1992 by the founder's son and still the place for *cochinillo* and other roasts. The *menú* is €18, although with the *cochinillo* you are more likely to top €24.

Mesón del Duque, c/Cervantes 12 ☎921 462 487. Rival to the nearby *Cándido*, and also specializing in Castilian roasts.

Mesón José María, c/Cronista Lecea 11, just off Plaza Mayor ☎921 461 111. Currently reckoned to be the city's best and most imaginative restaurant, with modern variations on Castilian classics. The *menú* is a hefty €24 but there are combinations costing around €12.

Narizotas, Plaza Medina Campo 1 ☎921 462 679. Bar-restaurant with a bright, relaxed atmosphere, good service and innovative *menús*.

Santa Bárbara, c/Ezequiel González 32 ☎921 434 806. Extensive menu and excellent seafood.

Out of town

La Posada de Javier, in the village of Torrecaballeros, 8km northeast on the N110 ☎921 401 136. Serious *madrileño* – and *segoviano* – gourmands eat out in the neighbouring villages, and this lovely old farmhouse is one of the most popular choices. It is, however, pricey with a *menú* costing at least €24. Booking is essential at weekends. Closed Sun night, Mon & July.

La Granja and Riofrío

Segovia has a major outlying attraction in the Bourbon summer palace and gardens of **La Granja**, 10km southeast of the town on the N601 Madrid road, and connected by regular bus services. True Bourbon aficionados, with time and transport, might also want to visit a second palace and hunting museum 12km west of La Granja at **Riofrío**.

La Granja

LA GRANJA (or San Ildefonso de la Granja, to give it its full title) was built by the reluctant first Bourbon king of Spain, Felipe V, no doubt homesick for the luxuries of Versailles. Its glories are the mountain setting and the extravagant wooded grounds and gardens, but it's also worth casting an eye over the **palace** (June–Sept Tues–Sun 10am–6pm; Oct–May Tues–Sat 10am–1.30pm & 3–5pm, Sun 10am–2pm; compulsory guided tour €4.80, Wed free for EU citizens). Though destroyed in parts and damaged throughout by a fire in 1918, much has been well restored. Everything is furnished in plush French imperial style but it's almost all of Spanish origin; the majority of the huge chandeliers, for example, were made in the **crystal factory** still operating in the village of San Ildefonso (June–Sept Tues–Fri 10am–8pm, Sat, Sun & holidays 10am–7pm; Oct–May Tues–Sat 10am–6pm, Sun 10am–3pm; €3). The palace is also home to a superlative collection of sixteenth-century tapestries, one of the most valuable in the world.

The highlight of the **gardens** (daily summer: 10am–9pm, winter 10am–6pm; €3, Wed free for EU citizens) is its series of fountains, which culminate in the fifty-foot-high jet of La Fama. They're really fantastic and on no account to be missed, which means timing your visit from 5.30pm on Wednesdays or weekends, when some are switched on. Only on three saints' days in the year – normally May 30 (San Fernando), July 25 (Santiago) & August 25 (San Luis) – are all of the fountains set to work, with accompanying crowds to watch.

The **village** of San Ildefonso de la Granja is a pleasant place to while away any spare time, with several decent **bars** and **restaurants**: try the *Bar La Villa* off the main square for tapas, *Casa Zaca*, also off the square, for lunch, or *Bar Madrid*, near the palace. There's a range of **accommodation**, too, if you prefer to stay here rather than Segovia: try the friendly *Hotel Roma* at c/Guardas 2 (☎921 470 752, ℱ921 470 278; ❻), right outside the palace gates, or the cheaper *Pensión Pozo de la Nieve*, c/Baños 4 (☎921 470 598; ❸).

Riofrío

The palace at **RIOFRÍO** (June–Sept Tues–Sun 10am–6pm; Oct–May Tues–Sat 10am–1.30pm & 3–5pm, Sun 10am–2pm; €4.80) was built by Isabel, the widow of Felipe V, who feared she would be banished from La Granja itself by her stepson Fernando VI. He died however, leaving the throne for Isabel's own son, Carlos III, and Riofrío was not occupied until the nineteenth century when Alfonso XII moved in to mourn the death of his young queen Mercedes. He, too, died pretty soon after, which is perhaps why the palace has a spartan and slightly tatty feel.

The complex, painted in dusty pink with green shutters, is surrounded not by manicured gardens but by a **deer park**, which you can drive through but not wander into. Inside the palace, you have to join a guided tour, which winds through an endless sequence of rooms, none stunningly furnished. About half the tour is devoted to a **museum of hunting**; the most interesting items here are reconstructions of cave paintings, including the famous Altamira drawings.

North from Segovia

Heading **north from Segovia**, you're faced with quite a variety of routes. The train line heads northwest towards Valladolid and León, past the castles of **Coca** and **Medina del Campo** – two of the very finest in Spain. If you have transport of your own, or time for convoluted local bus routes, you can take in further impressive castles in Segovia province at **Pedraza**, **Turégano** and **Cuéllar**, and still more by striking north again to **Peñafiel** and the chain of castles along the River Duero. If you are looking for a night's stop in a small town, Pedraza and Turégano, around 40km from Segovia, would fit the bill nicely.

For details on this area, see the "Old Castile and Léon" chapter.

East of Madrid: Alcalá de Henares, Nuevo Baztán, Guadalajara and the Alcarria

East of the capital there's considerably less to detain you. The only tempting day-trips are to the old university town of **Alcalá de Henares**, Cervantes's birthplace and, for Baroque enthusiasts, to **Nuevo Baztán**, an eighteenth-century new town planned by José de Churriguera. Further afield, the largely modern city of **Guadalajara** has little to recommend it, although the region southwest of here, the **Alcarria**, has its charms, especially if you want to follow the footsteps of Spain's Nobel prizewinner, Camilo José Cela, who described his wanderings here in the 1940s in his book, *Viaje a la Alcarria*.

Alcalá de Henares

ALCALÁ DE HENARES, a little over 30km from Madrid, is one of Europe's most ancient university towns, and renowned as the birthplace of Miguel de **Cervantes**. In the sixteenth century the university was a rival to Salamanca's, but in 1836 the faculties moved to Madrid and the town went into decline. Almost all the artistic heritage was lost in the Civil War and nowadays it's virtually a suburb of Madrid. It is not somewhere you'd want to stay longer than it takes to see the sights, but that's no problem with regular trains (Chamartín or Atocha; every 15–30min from 5.30am-11.45pm) and buses (every 15min, operated by Continental Auto) from Madrid throughout the day. If you like everything organized for you, the **Tren de Cervantes** leaves Atocha at 11am on Saturday and Sunday (May, June & Oct–Dec; €13.20; ☎915 066 356 or 915 067 103) complete with staff wearing period costume and includes a guided tour of the main sites, before returning to Madrid at 7pm.

The **Universidad Antigua** (45-minute guided tours Mon–Fri 11.30am, 12.30pm, 1.30pm, 4.30pm & 5.30pm, Sat, Sun & holidays 11am–2pm & 5–8pm; €2.10) stands at the heart of the old town in Plaza de San Diego. It was endowed by Cardinal Cisneros (also known as Cardinal Jiménez) at the beginning of the sixteenth century and features a fabulous Plateresque facade and a Great Hall, the **Paraninfo** (entered through the *Hostería del Estudiante*, an expensive restaurant at the back), with a gloriously decorated Mudéjar *artesonado* ceiling. Next door, the **Capilla de San Ildefonso** has another superb ceiling, intricately stuccoed walls, and the Italian marble tomb of Cardinal Cisneros.

The **Museo Casa Natal de Cervantes** at c/Imagen 2 (Tues–Sun 10.15am–1.30pm & 4–6.15pm; free) claims to be the birthplace of Cervantes in 1547: though the house itself is hardly thirty years old, it's authentic in style, furnished with genuine sixteenth-century objects, and contains a small museum with a few early editions of *Don Quixote* and other curiosities related to the author.

To the west of the university, the **Monasterio de San Bernardo**, Via Complutense (guided tours Mon–Fri 1.45pm & 6.30pm, Sat & Sun 12.30pm, 1.30pm, 5pm, 5.45pm, 6.30pm, 7.15pm & 8pm; €2.10), was founded by the Cistercians in 1617 and has recently opened its doors as a museum of religious art, re-creating the atmosphere of a monastery of that era, complete with cells and kitchen.

Just off the central Plaza Cervantes is the oldest surviving public theatre in Europe, the **Cervantes Theatre**, whose twenty-year restoration is nearing completion, although dispute continues over the theatre's future use. Discovered beneath a crumbling old cinema by two drama students in 1980, the theatre, like Shakespeare's Globe, was a hub of rowdy heckling and lively dramatics throughout the first half of the seventeenth century.

The local **turismo** (daily: summer 10am–2pm & 5–7.30pm, closed Mon in July & Sept; winter 10am–2pm & 5–6.30pm; ☎918 892 694, ⓦalcalaturismo. com), just off the central Plaza de Cervantes, can arrange guided tours for €4.50–5, has maps and other handy information, and from here nothing of interest is more than a short walk away. There is another office in Plaza de los Santos Niños (same hours, but closed Tues in July & Aug; ☎918 810 634). You'll find no shortage of places to eat centrally and, if you want to **stay**, there are several *pensiones* on the Plaza de Cervantes itself as well as the *Hostal Jacinto* (☎ & Ⓕ918 891 432; ❺), conveniently located by the train station.

Nuevo Baztán

Twenty kilometres southeast of Alcalá, or 45km from Madrid, **NUEVO BAZTÁN** should appeal to anyone interested in architecture, planning or merely the unusual. It was designed and built in 1709–13 by José de Churriguera in response to a commission from the royal treasurer, who aimed to develop a local decorative arts industry. Today it's semi-deserted, though brash modern villas are being built nearby for well-heeled commuters to the capital. As a focus, Churriguera built a **palace** and **church** as a single architectural unit; the latter has a massive twin-towered facade and a central dome and *retablos* by the architect within. Behind the palace, now fenced off, is the **Plaza de Fiestas**, complete with balconies for watching celebrations. The houses of the workers comprise the rest of the settlement.

The best day to visit Nuevo Baztán is Sunday. Empresa Izquierdo, c/Goya 80 (Metro Goya), runs two buses daily from Madrid but only on Sunday do these allow you any time here, and this is also the only day the church is sure to be open.

Guadalajara

GUADALAJARA, north from Alcalá de Henares, is not terribly exciting despite its famous name. Severely battered during the Civil War, it's now a small industrial city, provincial and scruffy. There are, however, a few worthwhile buildings which survived bombardment, notably the **Palacio del Infantado** (Tues–Sat 10.30am–2pm & 4.15–7pm, Sun 10.15am–2pm; €1.20) and an assortment of medieval churches. The *palacio*, the former home of the Duke of Mendoza, boasts a wonderful decorative facade and cloister-like **patio** (Mon–Fri 9am–9pm, Sat & Sun 10am–2pm & 4–8pm; free), and now houses a fairly average local art museum. It is to be found a few blocks to the northwest of the town's large, park-like central square, Plaza Capitán Beixareu Rivera.

There's a friendly **turismo** opposite the palace (Mon–Sat 10am–2pm & 4–7pm, Sun 10am–2pm; ☎949 211 626). If you needed, or wanted, **to stay**, the recently refurbished *Hotel España*, c/Teniente Figueroa 3 (☎949 211 303, ⓕ949 211 305; ❺) is a decent option; even cheaper is *Pensión Galicia*, c/San Roque 16 (☎949 220 059, ⓕ949 214 807; ❹). **Bars** and **restaurants** are plentiful, too. *Can Vic* on Plaza Fernando Beládiez is a good, low-priced place, or for a seafood and fish blow-out there's *Casa Victor* at c/Bardales 6. Late-night and music bars are mostly to be found along c/Sigüenza. There is a regular train service from Madrid running every 15–30 minutes from Atocha from 5.30am–11.45 pm with a journey time of about 50 minutes.

Moving on

The main road and rail lines from Madrid to Zaragoza and Barcelona both pass through Alcalá and Guadalajara, and continue more or less parallel throughout their journeys. Sigüenza (see p.199) and Medinaceli (see p.425) each make excellent resting points on your way. From Guadalajara you can also cut down to Cuenca, and from there continue towards Valencia and the coast. This is a very beautiful drive, past the great dams of the Embalse de Entrepeñas and Embalse de Buendía, and takes you through the heart of the Alcarria region.

The Alcarria

The **Alcarria** has few particular monuments but the wild scenery and sporadic settlements are eerily impressive, especially coming upon them so close to Madrid. Many of the high sierra villages, north of the N320, were deserted during the Nationalist advance on Madrid in the Civil War and today have only a handful of permanent inhabitants, plus a few *madrileño* weekenders who are restoring the old cottages.

The largest town of the region, **PASTRANA**, 15km south of the N320, merits a diversion. The museum of its vast **Colegiata** church (daily 10.30am–1.30pm & 4.30–6.30pm; €1.75) contains some wonderful fifteenth-century tapestries depicting the conquest of Tangier and Asilah by Alfonso V of Portugal, as well as richly decorated ebony and bronze altarpieces from the Philippines. These were brought to Pastrana by the princess of Eboli, duchess of the town, who after a court scandal was imprisoned in the palace overlooking the central square and allowed to sit out on the balcony overlooking the square (now known as Plaza de la Hora), for one hour a day. Also of interest is the **Convento del Carmen**, a ten-minute walk out of town. This Carmelite convent was founded by St Teresa and within you'll find a small museum of assorted religious art and yet more relics of the saint (daily 9.30am–1pm & 3.30–7pm; 300ptas/€1.80). Part of this convent has recently become a **hotel**, the *Hospedería Real de Pastrana* (☎949 371 060, ⓕ949 371 058; ❻). The only other place to stay is back in town at *Hostal Moratín*, c/Moratín 3 (☎949 370 628, ⓕ949 370 116; ❹), a clean and comfortable place on the main road. Meanwhile, Pastrana's twisting streets, including its former **Jewish and Arab quarters**, offer endless rambling, and there's a modest **turismo** (Fri 4–8pm, Sat 10am–2pm & 4–8pm, Sun 10am–2pm; ☎949 370 672) on the edge of town, but there's little diversion to be had in the evening.

Travel Details

Trains

From Madrid Atocha station (Metro Atocha) to: Alcalá (every 15–30min; 30min); Aranjuez (every 15–30min; 45min); Cuenca (4 daily; 2 hr 45 min); El Escorial via Chamartín (31 daily; 1hr); Guadalajara via Chamartín (47 daily; 50min); Segovia via Chamartín (9 daily; 1hr 50min–2hr); Toledo via Aranjuez (9 daily; 1hr 15min).

Chamartín (Metro Chamartín) to: Ávila (24 daily; 1hr 20min–2hr 10min); Cercedilla (23 daily; 1hr 15min).

Aranjuez to: Cuenca (5 daily; 1hr 50min–2hr); Madrid (every 15–30min; 45min); Toledo (10 daily; 30min).

Ávila to: Madrid (35 daily; 1hr 30min–1hr 50min); El Escorial (10 daily; 1hr); Medina del Campo (15 daily; 20min); Salamanca (5 daily; 1hr 45min); Valladolid (14 daily; 1hr–1hr 20min).

Cercedilla to: Madrid (23 daily; 1hr 25min); Puerto de Navacerrada (13 daily; 30–45min); Segovia (9 daily; 1hr).

El Escorial to: Ávila (7 daily; 1hr 10min); Madrid (27 daily; 1 hr).

Segovia to: Cercedilla (9 daily; 45min); Madrid (9 daily; 1hr 40min).

Toledo to: Aranjuez (8–9 daily; 30min); Madrid (9 daily; 1hr 15min).

Buses

From Madrid: Estación Sur de Autobuses, c/Méndez Álvaro s/n ☎914 684 200 (Metro Méndez Álvaro) to: Aranjuez (9–43 daily; 1hr); Ávila 4-8 daily; 2hr); Toledo (every 30min; 1hr 15min); Arenas de San Pedro (5 daily; 2hr 15min).

Auto-Res, Plaza Conde de Casal ☎902 020 999 (Metro Conde de Casal) to: Cuenca (6-8 daily; 2hr-2hr 30min); Salamanca (8-13 daily; 2hr 30 min–3hr)

La Veloz, Avda. del Mediterráneo 49 ☎914 097 602 (Metro Conde de Casal) to: Chinchón (10–15 daily; 1hr).

Argabus, Intercambiador de Autobuses, Avda. de América ☎914 339 149 (Metro Avda. de América) to: Nuevo Baztan (3–9 daily; 1hr 15min).

Herranz, Intercambiador de Autobuses, Moncloa (Metro Moncloa) to: El Escorial (every 30min; 1hr).

La Sepulvedana, Intercambiador de Autobuses, Moncloa ⓦwww.sepulvedana.es (Metro Moncloa) to: Cercedilla (every 30min; 45min).

La Sepulvedana, Paseo de la Florida 11 ☎915 304 800, ⓦwww.sepulvedana.es (Metro Príncipe Pío) to: Ávila (8 daily; 1hr 30min); Segovia (31 daily; 1hr 15min).

Continental Auto, Avda. de América 9 ☎917 456 300 (Metro Avda. de América) to: Alcalá (every 15min; 40min); Guadalajara (every 30min; 45min).

Intercambiador de Autobuses, Plaza de Castilla (Metro Plaza de Castilla) to: Manzanares del Real (hourly; 40min).

Ávila to: Arenas de San Pedro (1 daily Mon–Fri; 1hr 30min); Madrid (8 daily; 1hr 30min); Salamanca (2–3 daily; 1hr 30min); Segovia (2–7 daily; 1hr).

El Escorial to: Guadarrama (every 30min–1hr; 15min); Madrid (every 15–30min; 1hr); Valle de los Caídos (1 daily; 15min).

Segovia to: Ávila (2–3 daily; 1hr); La Granja (12 daily; 20min); Madrid (every 30min; 1hr 30min); Salamanca (1–3 daily; 2–3hr); Valladolid (5–9 daily; 2hr 30min).

Toledo to: Ciudad Real, for the south (1 daily; 2hr); Cuenca (1 daily Mon–Fri, 2hr 30min); Guadamur (7 daily; 20min); Madrid (every 30min; 1hr 15min); Orgaz (3–10 daily; 30min); La Puebla de Montelban (5 daily Mon–Fri, 1 daily Sat; 40min); Talavera de la Reina, for Extremadura (10 daily; 1hr).

New Castile and Extremadura

Highlights

New Castile and Extremadura

The vast area covered by this chapter is some of the most travelled, yet least visited, country in Spain. Once south of Toledo (covered in the previous chapter, "Around Madrid"), most tourists thunder non-stop across the plains of New Castile to Valencia and Andalucía, or follow the great rivers through Extremadura into Portugal. At first sight this is understandable. **New Castile** in particular is Spain at its least welcoming: a vast, bare plain, burning hot in summer, chillingly exposed in winter. But the first impression is not an entirely fair one – away from the main highways the villages of the plain are as welcoming as any in the country, and in the northeast, where the mountains start, are the extraordinary cliff-hanging city of **Cuenca** and the historic cathedral town of **Sigüenza**. New Castile is also the agricultural and wine-growing heartland of Spain and the country through which Don Quixote cut his despairing swathe.

It is in **Extremadura**, though, that there is most to be missed. This harsh environment was the cradle of the *conquistadores*, men who opened up a new

Accommodation price codes

All the establishments listed in this book have been price-graded according to the following scale. The prices quoted are for the **cheapest available double room in high season**; effectively this means that anything in the ❶ and most places in the ❷ range will be without private bath, though there's usually a washbasin in the room. In the ❹ category and above you will probably be getting private facilities. Remember, though, that many of the budget places will also have more expensive rooms including en-suite facilities. Youth hostels are graded under ❶ as the price per person is less than half of the category's upper limit.

Note that in the more upmarket *hostales* and *pensiones*, and in anything calling itself a hotel, you'll pay a **tax** (IVA) of seven percent on top of the room price.

❶ Under €12	❹ €27–36	❼ €60–90
❷ €12–18	❺ €36–48	❽ €90–120
❸ €18–27	❻ €48–60	❾ Over €120

world for the Spanish empire. Remote before and forgotten since, Extremadura enjoyed a brief golden age when its heroes returned with their gold to live in a flourish of splendour. **Trujillo**, the birthplace of Pizarro, and **Cáceres** both preserve entire towns built with *conquistador* wealth, the streets crowded with the ornate mansions of returning empire builders. Then there is **Mérida**, the most

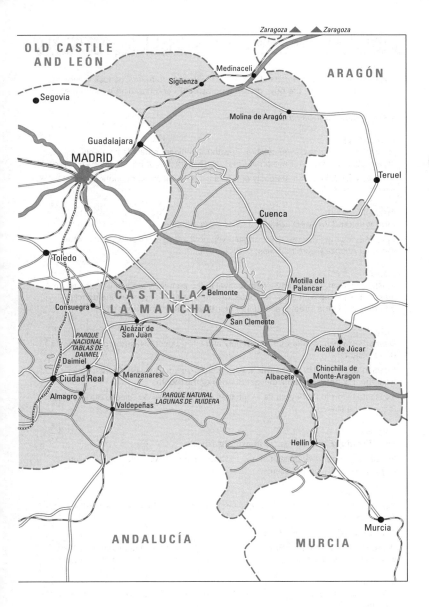

completely preserved Roman city in Spain, and the monasteries of **Guadalupe** and **Yuste**, the one fabulously wealthy, the other rich in imperial memories. Finally, for little-visited wild scenery and superb fauna, northern Extremadura has the **Parque Natural de Monfragüe**, where even the most casual bird-watcher can look up to see eagles and vultures circling the cliffs.

February

First weekend *La Endiablada* at Almonacid Marquesado (near Cuenca), a very old festival which sees all the boys dressing up as devils and parading through the streets.

Week before Lent *Carnaval* everywhere.

March/April

Holy Week (*Semana Santa*) celebrated with magnificent ritual (floats, penitents, etc) in Cuenca. *Pascua* (Passion of the Resurrection). Major Easter fiesta in Trujillo.

April 23 *San Jorge*. Tremendously enthusiastic celebrations that continue for several days in Cáceres.

May

First weekend WOMAD Festival at Cáceres (see p.228).

Late May Fair at Cáceres. Also – again with no fixed date – *Cabalata*, muleteer races, at Atienza (30km northeast of Sigüenza).

June

23–27 *San Juan*. Particularly manic festival in the picturesque town of Coria (50km west of Plasencia) with a bull let loose for a few hours a day, everyone dancing and drinking in the streets, and running for their lives when it appears.

July

Drama Festival in Mérida throughout July and into August, when the plays move on to Alcántara.

Spanish Classical Drama Festival at Almagro (25km southwest of Ciudad Real) – from the first Thursday until the last Sunday of the month.

14 Fiestas start in La Puebla de Montalbán, in the Montes de Toledo. Bulls are let loose in the streets.

August

First Tuesday *Fiesta de Martes Mayor*, Plasencia.

24–25 *San Bartolomé*. Fiestas at any town or church named after the saint, particularly at Jerez de los Caballeros.

September

First week *Vendimia* – grape harvest – celebrations at Valdepeñas. Major fair at Trujillo also early in the month.

7–17 *Virgin of Los Llanos*, Plasencia.

Week leading up to third Sunday Festivals in Jarandilla and Madrigal de la Vera with bulls running in front of cows – which are served up on the final day's feast.

October

1 *San Miguel*. Fiestas at any town or church named after the saint, particularly at Badajoz.

New Castile

The region that was for so long called **New Castile** – and that until the 1980s held Madrid in its domain – is now officially known as **Castilla-La Mancha**. Although the heavily cultivated plains that cover much of the terrain are less bleak than they once were – the name La Mancha comes from the Arab *manxa*, meaning steppe – the main points of interest are widely spaced on an arc drawn from Madrid, with little between that rewards exploration. If you are travelling east on **trains and buses** towards Aragón, there's little to justify a stop other than Sigüenza (en route to Zaragoza) or Cuenca (en route to Teruel). To the south, Toledo has bus links within its own province but heading for Andalucía or Extremadura you'd do better returning to Madrid and starting out again; the Toledo rail line stops at the town.

If you do have a **car**, and are **heading south**, the Toledo–Ciudad Real road, the Montes de Toledo and the marshy Parque Nacional de las Tablas de Daimiel all provide good alternatives to the sweltering NIV *autovía*. **Heading east**, through Cuenca to Teruel, the best route is to follow the Río Júcar out of the province, by way of the weird rock formations in the Ciudad Encantada and the source of the Río Tajo. **Heading west**, into Extremadura, the NV is one of the dullest and hottest roads in Spain and can be avoided by following the C501 through the Sierra de Gredos (see previous chapter, "Around Madrid") or by cutting onto it from Talavera de la Reina; this would bring you to the Monastery of Yuste by way of the lush valley of La Vera.

The sections following cover the main sights and routes of New Castile in a clockwise direction, from northeast to southwest of Madrid.

Sigüenza

SIGÜENZA, 120km northeast of Madrid, is a sleepy little town with a beautiful cathedral. At first sight it seems quite untouched by the twentieth century, though appearances are deceptive: taken by Franco's troops in 1936, the town was on the Nationalist front line for most of the Civil War, and its people and buildings paid a heavy toll. However, the postwar years have seen the cathedral restored, the Plaza Mayor recobbled and the bishop's castle rebuilt, so that the only evidence of its troubled history is in the facades of a few buildings, including the pencil-thin cathedral bell tower, pock-marked by bullets and shrapnel.

Sigüenza's main streets lead you towards the hilltop **Catedral** (Tues–Sun 9.30am–1.30pm & 4.30–7.30pm, Sun noon–1pm & 4.30–5.30pm; guided tours of chapels Tues–Sat 11am, noon, 4.30pm, & 5.30pm, Sun noon & 5.30pm; €1.80), built in the pinkish stone which characterizes the town. Begun in 1150 by the town's first bishop, Bernardo de Toledo, it is essentially Gothic, with three rose windows, though it has been much altered over the years. Facing the main entrance is a huge marble *coro* with an altar to a thirteenth-century figure of the Virgin. To the right of the *coro* is the cathedral's principal treasure, the alabaster tomb of Martín Vásquez de Arce, known as *El Doncel* (the page boy); a favourite of Isabel la Católica, he was killed fighting the Moors in Granada. On the other side of the building is an extraordinary

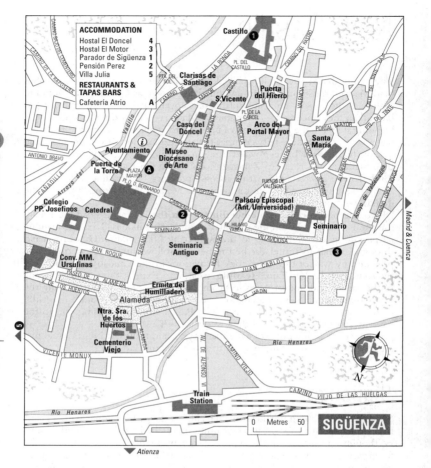

ACCOMMODATION
Hostal El Doncel	4
Hostal El Motor	3
Parador de Sigüenza	1
Pensión Perez	2
Villa Julia	5

RESTAURANTS & TAPAS BARS
Cafetería Atrio	A

SIGÜENZA

Atienza

doorway: Plateresque at the bottom, Mudéjar in the middle and Gothic at the top – an amazing amalgam, built by a confused sixteenth-century architect. Take a look, too, at the sacristy, whose superb Renaissance ceiling has 304 heads carved by Covarrubias. In a chapel opening off this (with an unusual cupola, best seen in the mirror provided) is an El Greco *Annunciation*.

More treasures are displayed in the **cloister**, while further art works from local churches and convents, including a saccharine Zurbarán of *Mary as a Child*, are displayed in the nearby **Museo Diocesano del Arte** (Tues–Sun 11am–2pm & 4–7pm; €1.80).

The cathedral looks out over the **Plaza Mayor** – which was used for bull-fighting until 1985 – from where c/Mayor leads up to the castle, passing close by the church of **San Vicente**. This is much the same age as the cathedral and is interesting mainly as a chance to see just how many layers of remodelling had to be peeled off by the restorers; an ancient figure of Christ above the altar is the only thing to detain you inside.

The **castle** started life as a Roman fortress, was adapted by the Visigoths and further improved by the Moors as their Alcazaba. Reconquered in 1124, it became the official residence of the warlike Bishop Bernardo and his successors. The Civil War virtually reduced the castle to rubble, but it was almost completely rebuilt in the 1960s and converted into a *parador*.

Practicalities

There's a rather lacklustre **turismo** in the town hall, at the top end of the Plaza Mayor (Tues–Fri 9am–2pm, Sat 9am–3pm & 4–7pm, Sun 9am–3pm; ☎949 347 007). **Accommodation** is not usually a problem. Central places include the *Pensión Perez*, c/García Atance 9 (☎949 391 269; ❸), *Hostal El Doncel*, Paseo de la Alameda 1 (☎ & ℱ949 391 090, ✆hostaldoncel@futurnet. es; ❺), and the slightly more upmarket *El Motor*, Avda. Juan Carlos I 2 (☎949 390 827, ℱ949 390 007; ❺). The *Villa Julia*, Paseo de las Cruces 27 (☎949 393 339; ❻), is a pricey but extremely comfortable *casa rural* (private house) with just five double en-suite rooms, while the *Parador de Sigüenza* (☎949 390 100, ℱ949 391 364, ✉siguenza@parador.es; ❽) is a bit soulless but has fine views from the upper floors. For **meals**, try the hotel restaurants at *El Motor* and *El Doncel*, or settle for excellent tapas at the *Cafetería Atrio* on the Plaza Mayor.

Heading north from Sigüenza, **Medinaceli** is just over the border in Old Castile, a couple of stops on the Zaragoza line (only slow trains call at Sigüenza and Medinaceli). Heading south, a good route for drivers leads **towards Cuenca**, past great reservoirs watered by the Tajo and Guadiela rivers, and skirting around the **Alcarria** region.

Cuenca and around

The mountainous, craggy countryside around **CUENCA** is as dramatic as any in Spain, and all the more so in the context of New Castile. The city itself, too, the capital of a sparsely populated province, is an extraordinary-looking place, enclosed on three sides by the deep gorges of the Huécar and Júcar rivers, with balconied houses hanging over the cliff top – the finest of them converted to a museum of abstract art. No surprise, then, that this is a popular weekend outing from Madrid; to get the most from a visit, try to come on a weekday, and take the time to stay a night and absorb the atmosphere.

Arrival and information

The old town of Cuenca – the **Ciudad Antigua** – stands on a high ridge, looped to the south by the Río Huécar and the **modern town** and its suburbs. If you're driving in, follow signs for the Catedral and try one of the car parks up in the old town. The **train and bus stations** are next to each other at the southern edge of the modern part of town. To get to the old town from here, head to the Puerta de Valencia, from where it's a steep climb; bus #1 or #2 will save you the walk.

Cuenca's helpful **turismo** is at Plaza Hispanidad (Mon–Thurs 10am–2pm & 5–8pm, Fri & Sat 10am–8pm, Sun 10am–2pm; summer Fri & Sat till 10pm; ☎902 100 131, ℱ969 235 356, ✆www.citelan.es/cuenca & www.citelan.es/quixote), a ten-minute walk from the stations along c/Fermin Caballero, and provides information and maps on the town and the whole province. **Internet access** is available in the *locutorio* at c/Colón 52 (Mon–Fri 9am–2pm & 5–11pm, Sat 5–8.30pm; €3.05 per hour).

CUENCA

Teruel, Valencia & Albacete (N320)

Alcázar de San Juan

Madrid & Guadalajara (N320)

Madrid & Guadalajara (N320)

La Ciudad Encantada & Nacimiento del río Cuervo

RESTAURANTS & TAPAS BARS

Figón de Pedro	F
Mesón Casas Colgadas	A
La Ponderosa	E
Posada San Julián	C
Restaurante Plaza Mayor	B
Taverna Tintes	D
Togar	G

ACCOMMODATION

Hotel Alfonso VIII	9
Hotel Arévalo	6
Hostal Avenida	11
Pensión Central	10
Pensión Cuenca	12
Hotel Figón de Pedro	8
Hotel Leonor de Aquitania	7
Pensión Marín	4
Parador de Cuenca	3
Hostal Posada de San José	5
Pensión Real	2
Pensión Tabanqueta	1

Parque de San Fernando

Bus Station

Train Station

Parque de Santa Ana

Parque de los Moralejos

Diputación Provincial

Parque de San Julián

Parador Nacional (Cvto. de S. Pablo)

Casas Colgadas (Museo de Arte Abstracto)

Museo Arqueológico

Catedral & Museo Diocesano

Ayuntamiento

Torre de Mangana

San Felipe

El Salvador

Palacio de Justicia

Castillo

San Pedro

San Miguel

Ntra. Sra. de las Angustias

Ntra. Sra. de la Luz

BARRIO DE LOS TIRADORES

BARRIO DE SAN ANTÓN

Río Júcar

Paseo del Júcar

Hoz del Júcar

Jardín de los Poetas

Metres   0   100

Accommodation

You'll find most **places to stay** in the new town, with a concentration of *hostales* along c/Ramón y Cajal, but there are several reasonably priced options in the old town.

Budget options

Pensión Central, c/Alonso Chirino 9 ☎969 211 511. Good-value *pensión* offering large rooms with separate bath. ❷

Pensión Cuenca, Avda. República Argentina 8 ☎969 212 574. Modern *pensión* located near the train and bus stations offering some rooms with showers. ❸

Pensión Marín, c/Ramón y Cajal 53 ☎969 221 978. Basic, but clean and central. ❷

Pensión Real, c/Larga 39 ☎969 229 977. The last building in the old town, with commanding views of Cuenca. Four rooms, with shared bathroom/shower. ❸

Pensión Tabanqueta, c/Trabuco 13 ☎969 211 290. The best *pensión* in town with wonderful views and a lively bar which serves good food at affordable prices. Shared bathrooms. ❸

Moderate and expensive options

Hotel Alfonso VIII, Parque de San Julián 3 ☎969 214 325, ℻969 214 325, ✆www.hotel-alfonsoviii. com. Nicely located – but pricey – hotel in the new town, facing the park. ❼

Hotel Arévalo, c/Ramón y Cajal 29 ☎969 223 979. Centrally located hotel with secure parking. ❺

Hostal Avenida, Avda. Carretería 39 ☎969 214 343, ℻969 212 335. Near the park, and well located for the old town, this *hostal* is functional but comfortable. All rooms have TV and bath. ❹

Hotel Figón de Pedro, c/Cervantes 17 ☎969 224 511. Well-run hotel at the heart of the modern town, with an excellent restaurant. ❺

Hotel Leonor de Aquitania, c/San Pedro 58–60 ☎969 231 000. Cuenca's prime hotel, beautifully situated in the old town, with superb views and prices to match. ❼

Parador de Cuenca, Convento de San Pablo ☎969 232 320, ℻969 232 534, ✉cuenca@parador.es. Expensive, but nothing special; head for *Leonor de Aquitania* for better value and views. ❽

Hostal Posada de San José, c/Julián Romero 4 ☎969 211 300, ℻969 230 365. Lovely old building in the old town near the cathedral, with only 30 rooms (21 with bath), so be sure to book ahead. ❻

Camping

Camping Cuenca, 6km north of the city on the CU921 ☎969 231 656. Surrounded by shady pines and open from mid-March to December. No bus.

The Ciudad Antigua

Cross one of the many bridges over the River Huécar and you start to climb steeply (most of the streets are stepped) towards the **Ciudad Antigua**, a narrow wedge of lanes, petering out in superb views to west and east.

More or less at the centre of the quarter is the Plaza Mayor, a fine space, entered through the arches of the Baroque *ayuntamiento* and ringed by cafés. Occupying most of its east side is the **Catedral** (daily 10am–2pm & 4–6pm; free), whose ugly, unfinished facade betrays a misguided attempt to beautify a simple Gothic building. The interior is much more attractive, especially the carved Plateresque arch at the end of the north aisle, and the chapel next to it, with distinctly un-Christian carvings round its entrance. The east chapel, directly behind the high altar, has a superb *artesonado* ceiling, which can just about be glimpsed through the locked door.

Alongside is a small **Museo Catedralicio** (daily 10am–2pm & 4–6pm; €1.20) which contains some beautiful gold and silver work as well as doors by Alonso Berruguete. The ceiling here, now a sea of Baroque icing-sugar shades, was originally a beautiful Mudéjar work like the one in the east chapel. Further religious treasures are to be found down c/Obispo Valero in the **Museo Diocesano** (Tues–Fri 11am–2pm & 4–6pm, Sat 11am–2pm & 4.30–6.30pm,

Sun 11am–2pm; €1.20), including two canvases by El Greco, a magnificent *Crucifixion* by Gerard David, and a Byzantine diptych unique in Spain. Right opposite is an excellent **Museo Arqueológico** (Tues–Fri 11am–2pm & 4–6pm, Sat 11am–2pm & 4.30–6.30pm, Sun 11am–2pm; €1.20), showcasing local Roman finds.

The artistic highlight of Cuenca, however, has to be the **Museo de Arte Abstracto** (Tues–Fri 11am–2pm & 4–6pm, Sat 11am–2pm & 4–8pm, Sun 11am–2.30pm; €3), a gallery established in the 1960s by Fernando Zóbel, one of the leading artists in Spain's "abstract generation". It is now run by the prestigious Fundación Juan March, which displays works from a core collection of abstract painting and sculpture by, among many others, Eduardo Chillida, José Guerrero, Lucio Muñoz, Antonio Saura and Fernando Zóbel, and hosts some of the best exhibitions to be found in provincial Spain. The museum itself is a stunning conversion from the extraordinary *Casas Colgadas* ("hanging houses"), a pair of fifteenth-century houses, with cantilevered balconies, literally hanging from the cliff face.

There are other monuments signposted in Cuenca, but the greatest attraction is the place itself. Have a drink in one of the bars opposite the cathedral in the Plaza Mayor, or walk along the gorge of the Huécar and look up at the *Casas Colgadas* and the other less secure-looking buildings high above the river. At night the effect is even more dramatic.

Eating, drinking and nightlife

There are plenty of **places to eat** around the Plaza Mayor, though you will eat better down at the bars and restaurants of the modern town. Some of the best places are reviewed below – note that almost all shut at around 11pm.

The Plaza Mayor is the place to head for evening *copas*, however, with its vibrant and diverse range of **bars**. The liveliest places are along c/Seuro Catalina, where you'll find *La Repos*, a good stand-up drinking bar, and the *Taberna-Artistica Los Elefantes*, a long-time artists' hangout playing an excellent range of alternative music – the nearby **club**, *Metro*, on c/Comillo, has a similar sound and stays open past dawn. Another popular area is on and around c/Parque del Huécar, where the crowds start off around midnight, moving on later to c/Alferez Rubianes, where the *Millennium* **disco** is popular with aficionados of *makina* (techno). If this isn't to your taste, there are a host of bars around the stations which play salsa.

Figón de Pedro, c/Cervantes 15 ☎969 226 821. Renowned restaurant, serving classic Castilian roasts and superb fish dishes. Closed Sun evening. Expensive – even the *menú* is over €18.

Mesón Casas Colgada, c/Canónigos 3 ☎969 223 509. A good restaurant up in the old town, housed in a fine hanging house. Features suckling pig and other Castilian specialities. Closed Mon evening. Expensive.

La Ponderosa, c/San Francisco 20. The best tapas selection in a street full of worthwhile *mesónes*. Closed Sun & July.

Posada San Julián, c/de las Torres 1. Housed in a sixteenth-century town house, with a decent, inexpensive *menú* (not served Sun).

Restaurante Plaza Mayor. Local specialities and liquor (*resoli*) served in this restaurant on the main plaza. Allow €12–18 per head, though you could get away with less.

Taverna Tintes, c/Tintes 7. This popular and atmospheric local serves up a wide range of moderately priced dishes. Closed Mon.

Togar, Avda. República Argentina 3. Popular restaurant – newly renovated – with cellar serving local dishes and regional specialities. €18 per head or go for the €9.60 *menú*. Closed Tues.

La Ciudad Encantada – and on towards Albarracín

The classic excursion from Cuenca is to the **Ciudad Encantada**, a twenty-square-kilometre "park" of limestone outcrops, sculpted by erosion into a bizarre series of abstract, natural and animal-like forms. A few of the names – "fight between an elephant and a crocodile", for example – stretch the imagination a little, but the rocks are certainly amazing, and many of the creations really do look knocked into shape by human hands.

The most interesting area of sculptures is enclosed (admission daily 9am–dusk; €1.80), and the extensive car park and restaurants outside testify to its popularity with weekending *madrileños*. However, off season, or during the week, you can have the place almost to yourself. You will need transport to get to the park, which is around 20km northeast of Cuenca, on signed backroads towards Albarracín. If you get stuck, there is a **hostal**, the *Ciudad Encantada* (☎969 288 194; ❺), opposite the entrance gate.

To the source of the Tajo

If you have transport, the route west from the Ciudad Encantada towards Albarracín (see the "Aragón" chapter) is a delight, edging through the verdant **Júcar Gorge** and across the wild, scarcely populated Serranía de Cuenca. En route, still in Cuenca Province, you might stop at **UÑA**, a village sited between a lagoon and a barrage, where the *Hotel Agua Riscas* (☎969 281 332; ❺) has decent rooms, a panoramic restaurant and a garden bar.

Just over the provincial border, in Teruel Province, the road between Uña and Frías de Albarracín runs past a point known as García, where a signpost directs you to the **source of the Río Tajo**. Below a hideous 1960s sculpture a trickle of muddy water seeps out, setting the course of one of Iberia's great rivers on its way to the Atlantic Ocean at Lisbon.

Belmonte, El Toboso and Alarcón

Travelling south from Cuenca – or west from Toledo – Cuenca Province has a couple more places where you might consider breaking your journey if you have your own transport: the castle villages of **Belmonte** (on the N420) and **Alarcón** (just off the NIII to Valencia).

Belmonte and El Toboso

The village of Belmonte is partly encircled by a vast curtain wall, at the corner of which is a magnificent fourteenth-century castle (daily 10am–2pm & 4–7pm; €1.80). Partially rebuilt in the last century, it is really little more than a shell, although belated restoration is revealing what must once have been stunning Mudéjar *artesonado* ceilings. The village, too, has seen better days, though it has a fine collegiate church, and a pleasant little hotel, *La Muralla* (☎967 171 045; ❷), on c/Isabel I de Castilla.

Continuing west from Belmonte, Cervantes enthusiasts might consider a detour to the attractive village of **EL TOBOSO** (ⓦwww.eltoboso.org), on a minor road south of the N301. This was the home of Don Quixote's mistress, Dulcinea, whose "house" has of course been identified and turned into a **small museum** (Tues–Sat 10am–2pm & 4–6.30pm, Sun 10am–2pm; €0.60, free Sat pm and Sun), with an adjoining restaurant. West again from here, you could cut across country – and past the NIV – to **Consuegra** (see p.207), with its dozen windmills.

Alarcón

ALARCÓN occupies an impressive defensive site sculpted by the burrowing of the Río Júcar. Almost completely encircled and walled, the village is accessible by a spit of land just wide enough to take a road which passes through a succession of **fortified gateways**. Unlike Belmonte, Alarcón has a bit of life about it, at least at weekends, as many of the old escutcheoned houses have been restored as retreats by *madrileños*.

At the top of the village is an exquisite **castle**, eighth-century in origin and captured from the Moors in 1184 after a nine-month siege. This has been converted to house an expensive **parador**, the *Parador Marqués de Villena* (⊕969 330 315, ⊕969 330 303; ❽), one of the country's smallest and most characterful. More affordable accommodation is provided by the *Pensión El Infante*, c/Dr Tortosa 6 (⊕969 330 323; ❹). Either option should be booked ahead in summer or at weekends.

Albacete Province

Travelling between Madrid or Cuenca and Alicante or Murcia, you'll pass through **Albacete Province**, one of Spain's more forgettable corners. Hot, arid plains for the most part, this is very much the Spain of Castilla–La Mancha, with a dull provincial capital, **Albacete**, to match. Scenically, the only relief is in the hyperactive **Río Júcar**, which, in the north of the province, sinks almost without warning into the plain.

The Río Júcar: Alcalá del Júcar

If you are driving, it is worth a detour off the main roads east to cross the Río Júcar, cutting between **Casas-Ibáñez** (on the N322) and **Ayora** (on the N330) by way of the village of **ALCALÁ DEL JÚCAR**. Almost encircled by the river, the village is an amazing sight, with its houses built one on top of the other and burrowed into the white cliff face. Several of these **cuevas** (caves) have been converted into bars and restaurants and they are well worth a stop, with rooms carved up to 170m through the cliff and windows overlooking the river on each side of the loop. They're open daily in summer but otherwise only at weekends. Alcalá also boasts a **castle** – adapted at intervals over the past 1500 years, though today just a shell – with great views. If you want to stay, there are two **hostales** on the main road at the bottom of the village.

Albacete

ALBACETE was named *Al-Basit* – the plain – by the Moors, but save for a few old backstreets, it is basically a modern city. The underworked **turismo**, c/del Finte 2 (Mon–Fri: summer 10am–2pm & 6–8pm; winter 10am–2pm & 4.30–6.30pm, Sat 10am–6pm, Sun 10am–3pm; ⊕967 580 522), lists only two places of interest on its map. You could dispense with one of these, the **Catedral**, which is noted only for the presence of Ionic columns instead of normal pillars astride its nave. The **Museo de Albacete** (Tues–Fri 10am–2pm & 4.30–7pm, Sat 9am–7pm, Sun 9am–2pm; €0.60, free Sat & Sun), however, has a more than respectable archeological and ethnographical collection, whose prize exhibits are five small Roman dolls, perfectly sculpted and jointed, and an array of local Roman mosaics. For Spaniards, Albacete is synonymous with high-quality knives, a speciality which, as with Toledo, can be traced back to the Moors: if you're after some top cutlery, now's your chance.

Albacete has plenty of **accommodation**, but there's no real reason to stay. Don't be tempted, either, by signs to Albacete's *parador*, a modern creation southeast of the town, right on the flight path of a military airfield.

Chinchilla de Monte Aragón

Thirteen kilometres southeast of Albacete, **CHINCHILLA DE MONTE ARAGÓN** is a breezy hilltop village worth a look if you're passing by, though most of its grand mansions and churches are either decayed or locked up for restoration. The hill-top **fortress**, so impressive from the road below, is a windy ruin not really worth the climb, but the **Convento de Santo Domingo**, in the lower part of the village, has interesting fourteenth-century Mudéjar work. There is also a small but nationally represented **Museo de Cerámica** at c/de la Penuela, open on Saturday afternoons and Sundays.

Ciudad Real and the heartland of La Mancha

There is a huge gap in the middle of the tourist map of Spain between Toledo and the borders of Andalucía, and from Extremadura almost to the east coast. This, the province of **Ciudad Real**, comprises the heartland of **La Mancha**. The tourist authorities try hard to push their *Ruta de Don Quixote* across the plains, highlighting the windmills and other Quixotic sights: the signposted route, which starts at Belmonte and finishes at Consuegra, can be done in a day, but much of it is fanciful and, unless you're enamoured of the book, it's of only passing interest.

Nonetheless, there are a few places which merit a visit if you've got time to spare, most notably **Consuegra**, for the best windmills, **Almagro**, for its arcaded square and medieval theatre, and **Calatrava**, for the castle ruins of its order of knights.

Consuegra

CONSUEGRA lies just to the west of the NIV *autovía*, roughly midway from Madrid to Andalucía, and has the most picturesque and typical of Manchegan settings, below a ridge of twelve restored (and highly photogenic) windmills. The first of these is occupied by the town's **turismo**, with uncertain opening hours (indeed, truly Quixotic), but good for information on the *Ruta de Don Quixote*, while others house shops and workshops. They share their plateau with a ruined **castle**, once the headquarters of the order of St John in the twelfth century, which offers splendid views of the plain from its windswept ridge. The town below, in spite of having perhaps the most potholed roads in Spain, is also attractive, with a lively Plaza Mayor and many Mudéjar churches.

Places to stay are limited to the friendly *Hostal-Restaurant San Poul* (☎925 481 315 or 925 482 304; ❻) in the centre and the busy and comfortable *Hotel Las Provincias* (☎925 480 300, ☏925 482 000; ❹), within walking distance on the main road north of town.

Don Quixote

The romantic adventures of **Don Quixote**, set against the backdrop of La Mancha, with its castles, windmills, cornfields and vineyards, have captivated readers ever since *Don Quixote de La Mancha* was first published in 1604.

Not a novel in the modern sense, **Miguel Cervantes'** book is a sequence of episodes following the adventures of a country gentleman in his fifties, whose mind has been addled by romantic tales of chivalry. In a noble gesture, he changes his name to Don Quixote de la Mancha, and sets out on horseback, in rusty armour, to right the wrongs of the world. At his side throughout is **Sancho Panza**, a shrewd, pot-bellied rustic given to quoting proverbs at every opportunity. During the course of the book, Quixote, an instantly sympathetic hero, charges at windmills and sheep (mistaking them for giants and armies), makes ill-judged attempts to help others, and is mocked by all for his efforts. Broken-hearted but wiser, he returns home and, on his deathbed, pronounces: "Let everyone learn from my example... look at the world with common sense and learn to see what is really there."

Cervantes' life was almost as colourful as his hero's. The son of a poor doctor, he fought as a soldier in the sea battle of **Lepanto**, where he permanently maimed his left hand and was captured by pirates and put to work as a slave in Algiers. Ransomed and sent back to Spain, he spent the rest of his days writing novels and plays in relative poverty, dying ten years after the publication of *Don Quixote*, "old, a soldier, a gentleman and poor".

Spanish academics have spent as much time dissecting the work of Cervantes as their English counterparts have Shakespeare's. Most see the story as a satire on the popular romances of the day, with the central characters representing two forces in Spain; Quixote the dreaming, impractical nobility, and Sancho the wise and down-to-earth peasantry. There are also those who read in it an ironic tale of a visionary or martyr frustrated in a materialistic world, while yet others see it as an attack on the church and establishment. Debates aside, this highly entertaining adventure story, rich in characters, and with an eminently lovable hero, is said to have been reprinted so often that, worldwide, it is second only to the Bible in the printing stakes.

Out of the wealth of artistic interpretations inspired by Cervantes's holy fool (including a bizarre and original short story by Jorge Luís Borges), perhaps the most enduring are **Jules Massenet's** folksy opera and **Strauss's** symphonic poem, in which the hero is portrayed by a lofty cello.

Ciudad Real

CIUDAD REAL, capital of the province at the heart of this flat country, makes a good base for excursions and has connections by bus with most villages in the area. It has a few sights of its own, too, including a Mudéjar gateway, the **Puerta de Toledo**, which fronts the only surviving fragment of its medieval walls, at the northern edge of the city on the Toledo road. Further in, take a look at fourteenth-century **San Pedro**, an airy, Gothic edifice, housing the alabaster tomb of its founder and a good Baroque *retablo*, and the **Museo Provincial** (Tues–Sat 10am–2pm & 5–8pm, Sun 10am–2pm; free), a modern building opposite the cathedral, with two floors of local archeology (the second also has some stuffed local wildlife) and a third devoted to artists of the region.

The local **turismo** (Mon–Sat 10am–2pm & 4–7pm, Sun 10am–2pm; ☏&℻926 200 037, ☜www.elquiujote.com or www.dipurcr.es) is at c/Alarcos 21 in the centre of town, a ten-minute walk from the **bus station** on the Ronda de Ciruela. Ciudad Real's new **train station**, with high-speed AVE connections to Madrid, lies out of town at the end of Avenida de Europa; bus #5 connects with the central Plaza de Pilar.

Accommodation is not always easy to find, particularly at the lower end of the scale, so it's worth booking ahead. Decent options include *Pensión Esteban*, c/Reyes 15 (☎926 224 578; ❸), *Pensión Santa Cruz*, Avda. Pio XII 6 (☎926 214 156; ❸), *Pensión Escudero*, c/Galicia 48 (☎926 252 309; ❸), and *Hotel Santa Cecilia*, c/Tinte 3 (☎926 228 545, ℗926 228 618; ❽). An impressive range of **tapas bars** includes *Casa Lucio*, off c/Montesa at Pasaje Dulcinea del Toboso, and *Gran Mesón*, Ronda Ciruela 34, which also has a swankier restaurant, *Miami Park*, down the road at no. 48. The town's **nightlife** at the weekend generally starts off with tapas on c/Palma, carrying on to the bars along Avenida Torreón del Alcázar and around. For those with the energy, it then moves off under the train tracks to the *Playa Park* complex, where there's *makina* at *Isla Tòrtuga* and salsa at *La Ribera*.

Almagro

Twenty kilometres east of Ciudad Real is **ALMAGRO**, an elegant little town, which for a period in the fifteenth and sixteenth centuries was quite a metropolis in southern Castile. Today, its main claim to fame is the **Corral de las Comedias**, in the Plaza Mayor, a perfectly preserved sixteenth-century open-air theatre, unique in Spain. Plays from its sixteenth- and seventeenth-century heyday – the golden age of Spanish theatre – are performed regularly in the tiny auditorium and in July it hosts a fully fledged theatre festival. By day the theatre is open to visitors (April–June & Sept Tues–Fri 10am–2pm & 5–8pm, Sat 10am–2pm & 5–8pm, Sun 11am–2pm; July & Aug Tues–Fri 10am–2pm & 6–9pm, Sat 11am–2pm & 6–8pm, Sun 11am–2pm; Oct–March Tues–Sat 10am–2pm & 4–7pm, Sat 10am–2pm & 4–6pm, Sun 11am–2pm; €2.40). Across the square on Callejon de Villar the **Museo del Teatro** (same hours as theatre except July & Aug open on Saturday until 9pm), houses photos, posters, model theatres and other paraphernalia, but is probably only of passing interest to anyone other than theatre buffs.

The **Plaza Mayor** itself is magnificent: more of a wide street than a square, it is arcaded along its length, and lined with rows of green-framed windows – a north European influence brought by the Fugger family, Carlos V's bankers, who settled here. Also resident in Almagro for a while were the Knights of Calatrava (see opposite), though their power was on the wane by the time the **Convento de la Asunción de Calatrava** was built in the early sixteenth century. Further traces of Almagro's former importance are dotted throughout the town in the grandeur of numerous **Renaissance mansions**.

Back in the Plaza Mayor, you can have an open-air snack or browse among the shops in the arcades, where **lacemakers** at work with bobbins and needles are the main attraction. On Wednesday mornings there's a lively **market** in c/Ejido de San Juan.

Practicalities

There's a small **turismo** just south of Plaza Mayor on c/Bernadas 2 (April–June & Sept Tues–Fri 10am–2pm & 5–8pm, Sat 11am–2pm & 5–8pm, Sun 11am–2pm; July & Aug Tues–Fri 10am–2pm & 6–9pm, Sat 11am–2pm & 6–9pm, Sun 11am–2pm; Oct–March Tues–Fri 10am–2pm & 4–7pm, Sat 10am–2pm & 4–6pm, Sun 11am–2pm; ☎926 860 717, ⓦwww.ciudad-almagro.com). Almagro invites a stay more than anywhere in this region, although **accommodation** can be fairly limited during the theatre festival and at holiday weekends. Cheapest options are the *Hostal Los Escudos*, c/Bolaños 55 (☎926 861 574; ❺), and, next to the convent, the *Hospedería Almagro*, Ejido de

Calatrava (☎926 882 087, ⓕ926 882 122; ⑤). The *Hotel Don Diego*, on the Ronda de Calatrava (☎926 861 287, ⓕ926 860 574; ⑦), due east of the plaza, is a good mid-range hotel, and there is also a very good *parador* (☎926 860 100, ⓕ926 860 150, ⓔalmagro@parador.es; ⑧) in a former Franciscan convent on c/Gran Maestre.

A number of **bars**, good for tapas, are to be found around the Plaza Mayor, and the *bodega* at the *parador* is worth a stop for a drink, too. The best **restaurant** in town is the *Mesón El Corregidor* at Jerónimo Ceballos 2 (closed Mon & first week in Aug); it's moderately expensive at €21–24 per head. A cheaper option is *La Cuerda*, in front of the train station at Plaza del General Jorreto 6, which has a good *menú* specializing in fish and *arroz* for €7.20 (closed Mon evening and first fortnight in Sept).

Moving on, Almagro has two direct **trains** a day to Madrid, and five trains and **buses** daily to Ciudad Real; buses stop near the *Hotel Don Diego* on the Ronda de Calatrava.

Calatrava La Nueva

The area known as the **Campo de Calatrava**, south of Almagro and Ciudad Real, was the domain of the **Knights of Calatrava**, a Cistercian order of soldier-monks at the forefront of the reconquest of Spain from the Moors. So influential were they in these parts that Alfonso X created Ciudad Real as a royal check on their power. Even today, dozens of villages for miles around are suffixed with their name.

In the opening decades of the thirteenth century, the knights pushed their headquarters south, as land was won back, from Calatrava La Vieja, near Daimiel, to a commanding hilltop 25km south of Almagro, protecting an important pass – the Puerto de Calatrava – into Andalucía. Here, in 1216, they founded **Calatrava La Nueva**, a settlement that was part monastery and part

---

Wet la Mancha and two parks

A respite from the arid monotony of the Castilian landscape, and a treat for bird-watchers, is provided by the oasis of **La Mancha Húmeda** ("Wet La Mancha"). This is an area of lagoons and marshes, both brackish and fresh, along the high-level basin of the **Río Cigüela** and **Río Guadiana**. Although drainage for agriculture has severely reduced the amount of water, so that lakes almost dry up in the summer, there is still a good variety of interesting plant and bird life to be found here. You're best off visiting from April to July when the water birds are breeding, or from September to midwinter when birds are passing through on migration.

Major parks between Ciudad Real and Albacete include the **Parque Nacional de las Tablas de Daimiel**, 11km north of Daimiel itself, which is renowned for its bird life. There's an **information centre** (daily winter: 8am–6.30pm, summer: 8.30am–8pm; ☎926 693 118) alongside the marshes, but the park is accessible only by car or taxi, and Daimiel has little **accommodation** on offer outside the upmarket *Hotel Las Tablas* (☎926 852 107, ⓕ926 852 189; ⑤).

More traveller-friendly is the **Parque Natural de las Lagunas de Ruidera**, which lies northeast of Valdepeñas (with frequent buses from Albacete). You'll find an **information centre** (July & Aug daily 10am–9pm, Sept–June Wed–Sun 10am–2pm & 4–6pm; ☎926 528 116) on the roadside, and several nature trails inside the park, as well as swimming and boating opportunites. You can also stay overnight; **accommodation** ranges from a campsite, *Los Molinos* (☎926 528 089; July to mid-Sept), to *Hostal Las Norias* (☎926 528 032; ③) and the comfortable *Hotel Entrelagos* (☎ & ⓕ926 528 022; ⑤).

castle, and whose main glory was a great Cistercian church. The site (Tues–Sun: summer 10am–2pm & 5–8pm; winter 10am–2pm & 4–7pm; free) is reached by turning west off the main road (C410) and following the signposts uphill. Once there, you will get a good idea of what must have been an enormously rich and well-protected fortress. The church itself is now completely bare but preserves the outline of a striking rose window and has an amazing stone-vaulted entrance hall.

On the hill opposite is a further castle ruin, known as **Salvatierra**, which the knights took over from the Moors.

Valdepeñas and beyond

The road from Ciudad Real through Almagro continues to **VALDEPEÑAS**, centre of the most prolific wine region in Spain and handily situated just off the main Madrid–Andalucía motorway. You pass many of the largest **bodegas** on the slip road into town coming from the north and Madrid; most of them offer free tastings – ask at the **turismo** on the Plaza Mayor (Tues–Sat 10am–2pm & 5–7pm; ☎926 312 552, ⊛www.ayto-valdepenaas.org). Another option is the recently inaugurated and appropriately hi-tech **museo del vino** at c/Princesa 39 close to Plaza de España (Tues–Sat 10am–2pm & 5–7pm, Sun noon–2pm; free). Wine aside, the only "sight" is a **windmill**, again on the Madrid road, which is supposedly the biggest in Spain; it houses a museum of the works of local artist Gregorio Prieto. Behind it is the public swimming pool.

South from Valdepeñas

Heading south beyond Valdepeñas you enter Andalucía through the **Gorge of Despeñaperros** (literally, "throwing over of the dogs"), a narrow mountain gorge once notorious for bandits and still a dramatic natural gateway which signals a change in both climate and vegetation, or as Richard Ford put it (travelling south to north), "exchanges an Eden for a desert".

The first towns of interest across the regional border, and more tempting places to break your journey than anywhere in this part of La Mancha, are **Úbeda** and **Baeza** (see p.345). Both towns are connected by bus with the train station of **Linares-Baeza**, which is also where you'll change trains if you're heading for Córdoba. The provincial capital of **Jaén** (see p.343), the first city on the main bus and train routes, is comparatively dull.

The Montes de Toledo and west into Extremadura

The **Montes de Toledo** cut a swathe through the upper reaches of La Mancha, between Toledo, Ciudad Real and Guadalupe. If you're heading into Extremadura, and have time and transport, the deserted little roads across these hills (they rise to just over 1400m) provide an interesting alternative to the main routes. This is an amazingly remote region to find so close to the centre of Spain: its people are so unused to visitors that in the smaller villages you'll certainly get a few odd looks. Covered below, too, is the **main route west** from Toledo into Extremadura, which runs just north of the hills.

Toledo to Navalmoral

The C502, west of Toledo, provides a direct approach into **Extremadura**, linking with the NV from Madrid to Trujillo, and with roads north into the valley of **La Vera** (see sections following). It follows the course of the Río Tajo virtually all the way to **Talavera de la Reina**, beyond which an attractive minor road, from **Oropesa**, with its castle *parador*, runs to **El Puente del Arzobispo** and south of the river to the Roman site of **Los Vascos**.

La Puebla de Montalbán – and Montalbán Castle

LA PUEBLA DE MONTALBÁN, the first town west of Toledo, offers one of the best approaches into the Montes de Toledo. In itself, it is an unexceptional little place but it has a claim to fame as the birthplace of **Fernando de Rojas**, a precursor of the golden age dramatists, whose play *La Celestina* was first published in 1500 and is still performed in Spain. He is remembered by a plaque in the Plaza Mayor on the *ayuntamiento*, a building, like those surrounding it, endowed with an attractive facade of pillars and balconies. Across the square, the sixteenth-century **Palacio de los Condes de Montalbán** is an impressive, rambling affair, brooding behind small, barred windows.

There's a **hostal** on the Toledo side of town, the *Legázpiz* (☎925 750 032; ❷), though there's little reason to stay unless you happen to coincide with the July fiestas, which include bull-running through the streets.

South of La Puebla de Montalbán, the C403 leads into the foothills of the Montes de Toledo. At kilometre stone 31 (15km south of La Puebla), a track leads 2km west to the **Castillo de Montalbán**. This is clearly visible from the road – a low, golden-brown edifice with central turrets – though close up you discover that only the walls actually survive. The interior is open for visits on Saturday mornings.

Talavera de la Reina, Oropesa and Navalmoral de la Mata

Continuing west from La Puebla de Montalbán you reach **TALAVERA DE LA REINA**, an unremarkable town at the junction of major road and rail routes. The town has long been one of the most important centres of ceramic manufacture in Spain, and there are thirty functioning porcelain factories still here. If you decide to stop, take a look round the many shops down the main street displaying the local products: much is the usual mass-produced tourist trash, but there are still a few genuine craftsmen working here. The most attractive part of town is the park on the banks of the Río Tajo, where you'll find a friendly **turismo**, a *hostal* and a few places to eat.

Far more promising for a night's stop is **OROPESA**, which lies 33km further west, overlooking the busy NV. The *Parador Virrey de Toledo* (☎925 430 000, ℉925 430 777, ©oropesa@parador.es; ❽) is installed in part of the village **castle**, a warm, stone building on a Roman site, rebuilt from Moorish foundations in the fifteenth century by Don García Álvarez de Toledo. Below it, stretches of the old town walls survive, along with a few noble mansions and a pair of Renaissance churches.

West again, **NAVALMORAL DE LA MATA** has nothing to offer other than its road, rail and bus connections to more engrossing places such as the **Monastery of Yuste** across the rich tobacco-growing area to the north, **Plasencia** to the west, and **Trujillo** and **Guadalupe** to the south.

El Puente del Arzobispo and Los Vascos

EL PUENTE DEL ARZOBISPO, astride the Río Tajo 14km south of Oropesa, is, like Talavera, famed for the production of pottery and decorated tiles. Approaching from the south, you drive in across the ancient **bridge** over the river which gives the place its name. According to legend this was built after the villagers appealed to a fourteenth-century archbishop to build them a bridge across the river. At first he refused, and when pressed pulled a ring from his finger and flung it into the Tajo, saying that he would build the bridge when the ring came back to him. Three days later he cut open his dinner of fish from the river, only to find the ring inside.

Today the ceramics industry dominates, with small factories and shops selling their products everywhere. The wares are not terribly exciting but the tiles do brighten up the Plaza Mayor, with its tile-covered benches, and the exuberantly ornate archbishop's house.

The other local attraction is the ruined **Roman city of Los Vascos**, in beautiful country some 10km southeast of town, near the village of Navalmoralejo. There's little to see beyond a few walls, but it's an enjoyable excursion.

Into the hills

The most accessible route into the Montes de Toledo is the C403 south of La Puebla de Montalbán, which runs through the backwater village of **Las Ventas Con Peña Aguilera**, overlooked by rock-studded hills, including a curious outcrop shaped like three fat fingers – the name Peña Aguilera means "Crag of Eagles". Southwest of Las Ventas, a tiny road leads to **San Pablo de los Montes**, a delightful village of fine stone houses nestling against the mountains. Beyond here, you can walk over the hills to the spa of **Baños del Robledillo**, a spectacular five- to six-hour trek (get directions locally).

If you keep to the C403 south of Las Ventas, you will come to the main pass over the Montes de Toledo, the **Puerto del Milagro**, with great views of the hills dipping down on either side to meet the plain. Past the Puerto del Milagro, you can drive through lovely scenery towards Ciudad Real, or turn right at the El Molinillo junction to follow a road through the hills via Retuerta del Bullaque to **Navas de Estena**. Here the road curves round to the north, passing a large crag with caves 5km beyond Navas, allowing you to loop round to Navahermosa and on to the C401 to Guadalupe.

The western villages

If isolated villages and obscure roads appeal, you could strike south from the C401, or west from the C403 (just south of the Puerto del Milagro), into the most remote part of the Montes de Toledo. The latter approach would take you some 54km, without a village, before you reached **Valdeazores**, itself scarcely inhabited with a population of just 35. You could bypass this, if you wanted, following a road past the Cijara reservoir, and on to the N502 at Puerto Rey, passing nothing save the odd *finca* (farmhouse).

Coming from the C401, the first place you reach is **Roblado del Buey**, where there's a single bar. From here, a pine forest extends south to Los Alares. To the west, and the only place in these parts that gets any visitors, is **Piedraescrita**, a well-kept village with an incredibly spruce bar, and a miraculous image of the Virgin that pulls in the odd Spanish pilgrim. West again is the area's main administrative centre, **Robledo del Mazo**, with a doctor, pharmacy and bar.

Extremadura

Extremadura is slowly getting on the tourist trail – and deservedly so. The grand old *conquistador* towns of **Trujillo** and **Cáceres** are excellent staging posts en route south from Madrid or from Salamanca to Andalucía; **Mérida** has numerous Roman remains and an exemplary museum of local finds; and there is superb bird life in the **Parque Natural de Monfragüe**. Almost inaccessible by public transport, but well worth visiting, is the great **Monastery of Guadalupe**, whose revered icon of the Virgin has attracted pilgrims for the past five hundred years.

This section of the chapter is arranged north to south, starting with the lush hills and valley of **La Vera**, the first real patch of green you'll come to if you've driven along the NV west from Madrid.

La Vera and the Monasterio de Yuste

La Vera lies just south of the Sierra de Gredos (see p.178), a range of hills tucked above the **Río Tiétar** valley. It is characterized by the streams or *gargantas* which descend from the mountains and in spring and summer attract increasing bands of weekenders from Madrid. At the heart of the region is the **Monasterio de Yuste**, the retreat chosen by Carlos V to cast off the cares of empire.

Jarandilla and around

La Vera really comes into its element between Candeleda and Jarandilla de la Vera, along the C501, as the *gargantas* flow down from the hills. They are flanked in summer by some superb seasonal **campsites**: *Minchones* (☎927 565 403; Easter & June to mid-Sept) is just outside **Villanueva de la Vera**, a village which gained British media notoriety in the 1980s with its *Pero Palo* fiesta, in which donkeys are horribly mistreated. It seems strange to imagine any cruelty, given the rural idyll hereabouts and the incredibly house-proud appearance of the villages, especially **Losar**, which has an almost surreal display of topiary.

The main village in these parts is **JARANDILLA DE LA VERA**, a good target if you want a roof over your head, with a choice of three **hostales**, the *Marbella* (☎927 560 218; ❺), *Jaranda* (☎927 560 206; ❻) and *Posada de Pizarro* (☎927 560 727; ❺), plus a fifteenth-century **castle-parador**, the *Parador Carlos V* (☎927 560 117, ☎927 560 088, ✉jarandilla@parador.es; ❽), in the castle where the emperor stayed during the construction of Yuste. If you've got a tent to pitch, head for the attractive *Camping Jaranda* (☎927 560 454; mid-March to Sept). In the village there is a scattering of bars and a Roman bridge. Buses run through here, en route between Madrid and Plasencia; the stop is outside *Bar Charly* on the main road.

There is good walking around Jarandilla. A track into the hills leads to the village of **El Guijo de Santa Barbara** (4.5km) and then ends, leaving the ascent of the rocky valley beyond to walkers. An hour's trek away is a pool known as *El Trabuquete* and a high meadow with shepherds' huts known as *Pimesaíllo*. On the other side of the valley – a serious trek needing a night's camping and good area maps – is the *Garganta de Infierno* (Stream of Hell) and natural swimming pools known as *Los Pilones*.

The Monasterio de Yuste

There is nothing especially dramatic about the **Monasterio de Yuste** (Mon–Sat 9.30am–12.30pm & 3–6pm, summer till 6.30pm, Sun 9.30–11.30am & 3.30–6.30pm; compulsory guided tour in Spanish €0.60; closed for restoration at the time of writing), the retreat created by Carlos V after renouncing his empire: just a simple beauty and the rather gloomy accoutrements of the emperor's last years. The monastery had existed here for over a century before Carlos's retirement and he had earmarked the site for some years, planning his modest additions – which included a pleasure garden – while still ruling his empire from Flanders. He retired here with a retinue that included an Italian clockmaker, Juanuelo Turriano, whose inventions were his last passion.

The imperial apartments are draped throughout in black, and exhibits include the little sedan chair in which he was brought here, and another designed to support the old man's gouty legs. If you believe the guide, the bed and even the sheets are the very ones in which Carlos died, though since the place was sacked during the Peninsular War and deserted for years after the suppression of the monasteries, this seems unlikely. A door by the emperor's bed opens out over the church and altar so that even in his final illness he never missed a service.

Outside, there's a snack bar and picnic spots, and you'll find a track signposted through the woods to Garganta La Olla (see below).

Cuacos de Yuste

The monastery is 2km into the wooded hills from **CUACOS DE YUSTE**, an attractive village with a couple of squares, including the tiny Plaza de Don Juan de Austria, named after the house (its upper floor reconstructed) where Carlos's illegitimate son Don Juan lived when visiting his father. The surrounding houses, their overhanging upper floors supported on gnarled wooden pillars, are sixteenth-century originals, and from the beams underneath the overhang tobacco is hung out to dry after the harvest. There are several **bars**, a good family-run **hotel**, *La Vera* (☎927 172 178, ⊕ 927 172 026; ⑤), an inexpensive **pensión**, *Sol* (☎927 172 241; ②) and a shady **campsite**, *Carlos I* (☎927 172 092; late-March to mid-Sept).

Jaraíz de la Vera and Garganta La Olla

West towards Plasencia, one last place you might be tempted to stop is **JARAÍZ DE LA VERA**. This has pleasant walking and a couple of reasonable **places to stay**: *Hostal Dacosta* (☎927 460 219, ⊕ 927 460 900; ⑤) and the comfortable *Hotel Jefi* (☎927 461 363, ⊕927 170 564; ⑤), which has a good restaurant.

Just outside Jaraíz, a left turning leads to **GARGANTA LA OLLA**, a beautiful, ramshackle mountain village set among cherry orchards. There are several things to look out for: the **Casa de Putas** (a brothel for the soldiers of Carlos V's army, now a butcher's but still painted the traditional blue) and the **Casa de la Piedra** (House of Stone), a house whose balcony is secured by a three-pronged wooden support resting on a rock. The latter is hard to find; begin by taking the left-hand street up from the square and then ask. If you want to spend the night here, it's Hobson's choice of the tiny *Hostal Yuste* (☎927 179 604; ⑤).

From Garganta, there is a short-cut track to the Monasterio de Yuste (see above).

El Valle de Jerte

Immediately north of La Vera, the main Plasencia–Avila road follows the valley of the **Río Jerte** (from the Greek *Xerte*, meaning "joyful") to the pass of Puerto de Tornavacas, the boundary with Ávila Province. The villages here are more developed than those of La Vera but the valley itself is renowned for its cherry trees, which for a ten-day period in spring cover the slopes with white blossom. If you're anywhere in the area at this time, it's a beautiful spectacle.

If you have transport, you can follow a minor road across the sierra to the north of the valley from **Cabezuela del Valle** to **Hervás**, where there's a fascinating former Jewish quarter. This is the highest road in Extremadura, rising to 1430m.

On the **southern side** of the valley, the main point of interest is the **Puerto del Piornal** pass, just behind the village of the same name. The best approach is via the villages of **Casas del Castañar** and **Cabrero**. Once at the pass you can continue over to Garganta La Olla in La Vera.

Plasencia

Set in the shadow of the Sierra de Gredos, and surrounded on three sides by the Río Jerte, **PLASENCIA** looks more impressive from afar than it actually is. Once you get up into the old city the walls are hard to find – for the most part they're propping up the backs of houses – and the cathedral is barely half-built, but it still merits a visit. Plasencia has some lively bars, delightful cafés and a fine, arcaded **Plaza Mayor**, the scene of a farmers' **market** every Tuesday morning, held here since the twelfth century.

Arrival and information

Plasencia's **turismo** is on Plaza de la Catedral (daily 11am–2pm & 5–7pm; ☎927 423 843, ⓦwww.plasencia.com), and there's a **provincial office** on c/del Rey 8, off the Plaza Mayor (summer Tues–Fri 9am–2pm & 5–7pm, Sat & Sun 9.30am–2pm; winter Tues–Fri 9am–2pm & 4–7pm, Sat & Sun 9.30am–2pm; ☎927 422 159, ⓦwww.turismodeextremadura.com). If you arrive by **bus**, you'll be about fifteen minutes' walk from the centre, along the gently inclining Avenida del Valle to the west; the **train station** is much further out – take a taxi (around €3) unless you fancy the hike. There are up to five trains a day to and from Madrid and many more buses. If you're driving, be warned that navigation in and around town is notoriously difficult.

Accommodation

Good **places to stay** include two reasonably priced options near the Plaza Mayor: the *Hostal La Muralla*, c/Berrozana 6 (☎927 413 874; ❸), and *Hotel Rincón Extremeño*, c/Vidrieras 6 (☎927 411 150, ☏927 420 627, ✉rincon@ cempresarial.com; ❺), which has twelve en-suite rooms with TV and air-conditioning, as well as cheaper rooms without. For more comfort, there's *Hotel Los Álamos* on the Cáceres road facing the tobacco factory (☎ & ☏927 411 550; ❺), and *Hotel Alfonso VIII*, c/Alfonso VIII 32 (☎927 410 250, ☏927 418 042, ✉hotelalfonsoviii@cajaextremadura.es; ❽), on the main road near the post office. Both of these have good, but pricey restaurants, as does the new *parador* (☎927 425 870, ✉plasencia@parador.es; ❻), housed in a beautiful restored fifteenth-century Gothic convent and centrally located on Plaza de

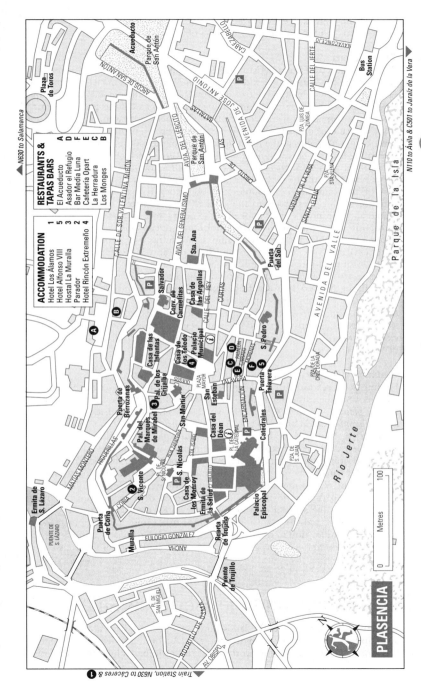

PLASENCIA

ACCOMMODATION
Hotel Los Alamos 1
Hotel Alfonso VIII 5
Hostal La Muralla 3
Parador 2
Hotel Rincón Extremeño 4

RESTAURANTS & TAPAS BARS
El Acueducto A
Asador el Refugio D
Bar Media Luna F
Cafetería Opart E
La Herradura C
Los Monges B

▲ N630 to Salamanca

▼ N110 to Ávila & C501 to Jaraíz de la Vera

◀ Train Station, N630 to Cáceres & ①

Metres 0   100

San Vincente Ferrer. There's also a **campsite** with a swimming pool 2.5km out on the Ávila road, *La Chopera* (☎927 416 660; March–Sept).

The Town

Plasencia's **Catedral** (summer Mon–Sat 9am–12.30pm & 5–7pm, Sun 9am–1pm; winter Mon–Sat 9am–12.30pm & 4–6pm, Sun 9am–1pm) is in fact two churches – old and new – built back-to-back. Work began on the second at the beginning of the sixteenth century and continued under two architects for almost forty years, but when neither managed to finish it, the open end was simply bricked up. The fact that the completed building would have been a particularly lofty Gothic construction only adds to the foreshortened feel of the interior. It does have some redeeming features, however, most notably the Renaissance choir stalls intricately carved by Rodrigo Alemán and described with some justice by the National Tourist Board as "the most Rabelaisian in Christendom". The older, Romanesque part of the cathedral now houses the obligatory **museum**, and the €0.90 entrance fee includes access to the similarly aged **cloisters**. Free tours of the cathedral (in Spanish) can be booked at the nearby tourist office.

Opposite the cathedral is the **Casa del Deán** (Dean's House), with an interesting balcony like the prow of a ship. Continuing away from the cathedral along c/Blanca you come out at the **Plaza de San Nicolás**, where, according to local tradition, the church was built to prevent two local families from shooting arrows at each other from adjacent houses. On c/Trujillo, near the hospital, the **Museo Etnográfico Textil Provincial** (July & Aug Mon–Sat 9.30am–2.30pm & 5–8pm, Sun 11am–2pm; rest of year Wed–Sat 11am–2pm & 5–8pm, Sun 11am–2pm; free) is worth a look for its colourful costumes and local crafts, excellently displayed in a fourteenth-century hospital. Many of the exhibits are still much in evidence in the more remote villages in the north of Plasencia province.

Eating and drinking

Finding good **restaurants** is not as easy as finding bars in Plasencia, but try the area between the cathedral and the Plaza Mayor. Easily the best budget options are the *platos* at *Cafeteria Opart*, c/Bravo 7, off c/Talavera, and the €5.40 *menú* at *Restaurante Los Monges,* c/Sor Valentina Mirón 24, just up from Puerta Berronzana. Another good, and rather fancier, place is *El Acueducto*, also on c/Sol Valentina Mirón, near the monument from which it takes its name.

Bars are much thicker on the ground, with over fifty in the old town alone. This is the land of the *pincho*, a little sample of food provided free with your beer or wine – among which is the local *pitarra* wine. A high tally of promising bars is to be found in c/Patalón (go down c/Talavera from the main square and it's the second turning on the left); *La Herradura* is good for *pinchos* and *pitarra*, and the *Asador el Refugio* for fish, squid and octopus *pinchos*. In the next street down, the atmospheric *Bar Media Luna* is famous for its ham (*jamón Iberico*) – it's expensive, but if you're lucky you'll get a taste as a *pincho*.

Las Hurdes and the Sierra de Gata

Las Hurdes, the abrupt rocky lands north of Plasencia, have always been set apart and are a rich source of mysterious tales. According to legend, the region was unknown to the outside world until the time of Columbus, when two lovers fleeing from the Court of the Duke of Alba chanced upon it. The people who welcomed them were supposedly unaware of the existence of other people or other lands. Shields and other remnants belonging to the Goth Rodrigo and his court of seven centuries earlier were discovered by the couple, giving rise to the saying that the *Hurdanos* are descendants of kings.

Fifty years ago, the inhabitants of the remoter areas were still so unused to outsiders that they hid in their houses if anyone appeared. **Luis Buñuel** filmed an unflatteringly grotesque documentary, *Las Hurdes: Tierra Sin Pan* ("Land Without Bread"), here in 1932, in which it was hard to discern any royal descent in his subjects. Modernity has crept up on the villages these days, though they can still feel very remote, and the soil is so barren that tiny terraces have been constructed on the riverbeds as the only way of getting the stubborn land to produce anything. To explore the region, you really need transport of some kind and certainly a detailed local **map** – regular Spanish road maps tend to be pretty sketchy.

Las Hurdes villages

You could approach Las Hurdes from Plasencia, Salamanca or Ciudad Rodrigo (the region borders the Sierra Peña de Francia – see p.418). From Plasencia or Salamanca, the approach is along the C512. Turn off along this road at Vegas de Coria and you will reach **NUÑOMORAL**, a good base for excursions, with an excellent and inexpensive **hostal**, *El Hurdano* (☎927 433 012; ❷); this does big dinners, and there is a bank alongside – not a common sight in these parts. For hire of mules, donkeys and horses at reasonable prices, ask for Amable in *Bar Emiliano* at the top of the town opposite the medical centre. Nuñomoral is also the village best connected to the outside world, with early-morning buses to both Ciudad Rodrigo and Plasencia.

To the north of Nuñomoral, the tiny village of **LA HUETRE** is worth a visit; take a left fork just before the village of Casares de las Hurdes. The typical slate-roofed houses are in better-than-usual condition and have an impressive setting, surrounded by steep rocky hills. Walkers might also head for the remote and disarmingly primitive settlement of **EL GASCO**, at the top of Valle de Malvellido, the next valley to the south, where there is a huge waterfall beneath the Miacera Gorge.

The Sierra de Gata

The **Sierra de Gata** creates a westerly border to Las Hurdes, in a series of wooded hills and odd outcrops of higher ground. It is almost equally isolated – in some of the villages the old people still speak *maniego*, a mix of Castilian Spanish and Portuguese – and its wooded valleys are in parts stunningly beautiful. Unfortunately, much has been damaged in recent summers by forest fires, which, like similar fires in Las Hurdes, are said to have been deliberately started to claim insurance money.

For a trip into the heart of the region, take the C512 south from Las Hurdes to **Villanueva de la Sierra** and follow the C513 west. A couple of kilometres past the Río Arrago, a very minor road veers north towards **Robledillo de Gata**, a village of old houses packed tightly together. A shorter, easier detour, south of the C513, around 5km on, is provided by the hill-top village of **Santibáñez el Alto**, whose oldest houses are built entirely of stone, without windows. At the top of town, look out for a tiny bullring, castle remains and the old cemetery – there's a wonderful view over the Borbollón reservoir from here. Another 3km along the C513, a turn-off to the north takes you on a winding road up to **GATA**, a pretty village with rooms at the *Pensión Avenida* (☎927 642 271; ❸).

On to the west, keeping to the C513, is **HOYOS**, the largest village of the region, with some impressive mansions. There's only one *hostal* in the village, *Pensión El Redoble*, c/La Paz 14 (☎927 514 018; ❷), but there's pleasant **camping** 3km below the village by a natural swimming pool, created by the damming of the river. Lastly, further along the C513, another turning leads north to **SAN MARTÍN DE TREVEJO**, one of the nicest of the many lonely villages around; if you're here at mealtime there's good, cheap village fare in great abundance at the *Bar Avenida del 82* (aka *Casa de Julia*). If you need to stay, there are comfortable rooms at *Hostal O'Soitu* (☎927 144 201; ❹).

South to Cáceres:
Coria and the Convento del Palancar

Heading south from the Sierra de Gata towards Cáceres along the C526, **CORIA** makes an interesting stop. It looks nothing much from the main road, but a visit reveals a cool and quiet old town with lots of stately whitewashed houses, enclosed within third- and fourth-century **Roman walls**. For the most part the walls are built into and around the houses, but a good stretch is visible between the deserted tower of the fifteenth-century castle, built by the Dukes of Alba, and the cathedral.

The **Catedral** (daily: summer 9.30am–1.30pm & 4–8pm; winter 9.30am–1pm & 4–7pm) has beautifully carved west and north portals in the Plateresque style of Salamanca and, inside, the choir stalls and *retablo* are worth seeing. The building overlooks a striking medieval bridge across fields, the river having changed course three hundred years ago.

Coria has a small **turismo** (☎927 501 351) of uncertain hours inside the *ayuntamiento* on Avenida de Extremadura, as well as plenty of **accommodation**. The *Pensión Casa Piro*, Plaza del Rollo 6 (☎927 500 027; ❷), is cheap and well placed, facing a gate in the walls; *Hotel Los Kekes*, Avda. Sierra de Gata 49 (☎927 504 400, ☎927 504 080; ❻), has more comforts and a decent restaurant; and *Pensión Bravatas* (☎927 500 401; ❸) is a budget place on the other side of the Avenida Sierra de Gata at no. 32.

Convento del Palancar

A detour off the C526, south of Coria, will take you to the **Convento del Palancar**, a monastery founded by San Pedro de Alcántara in the sixteenth century and said to be the smallest in the world at only seventy square metres. It's hard to imagine how a community of ten monks could have lived in these cubbyholes, though San Pedro himself set the example, sleeping upright in his cubicle. A small monastic community today occupies a more modern monastery alongside; ring the bell (daily except Wed 10am–1pm & 4–6.45pm; closed Wed; voluntary contribution) and a monk will come and show you around.

To reach Palancar, turn left off the C526 just after Torrejoncillo and follow the road to **Pedroso de Acim**; a left turn just before the village leads to the monastery.

The Parque Natural de Monfragüe

South of Plasencia a pair of dams, built in the 1960s, have turned the **Río Tajo** into a sequence of vast reservoirs. It's an impressive sight, driving across one of the half-dozen bridges, and it's a tremendous area for wildlife. Almost at random here, you can look up to see storks, vultures and even eagles circling the skies.

The best area for concerted wildlife viewing – and some very enjoyable walks – is the **PARQUE NATURAL DE MONFRAGÜE**, Extremadura's only protected area, which extends to either side of the Plasencia–Trujillo road, with its headquarters at **Villareal de San Carlos**. The landscape is a wonderful diversity of rivers, woods, scrubland and pasture, and attracts an incredible range of flora and fauna. It has been spared the blights of much of the region hereabouts, which, after the completion of the dams, saw the widescale destruction of wildlife habitats and the indiscriminate planting of inflammable eucalyptus by the rapidly expanding paper industry, despite the fire risk involved.

There are over two hundred **species of animals** in the park, including the ultra-rare Spanish lynx (which you are most unlikely to see). Most important is the **bird population**, especially the black stork – this is the only breeding population in western Europe – and birds of prey such as the black vulture (not averse to eating tortoises), the griffon vulture (partial to carrion intestine), the Egyptian vulture (not above eating human excrement), the rare Spanish imperial eagle (identifiable by its very obvious white shoulder patches), the golden eagle and the eagle owl (the largest owl in Europe).

Ornithologists should visit Monfragüe in May and June, botanists in March and April, and everybody should avoid July to September, when the heat is stifling.

Park practicalities

The easiest **approach to the park** is along the C524 from Plasencia to Trujillo, which runs past the park headquarters at Villareal de San Carlos. Transport of your own is an advantage unless you are prepared to do some walking. There is just one **bus** along the road, which runs daily between Plasencia and Torrejón El Rubio, 16km south of Villareal de San Carlos, and on Mondays and Fridays covers the whole distance to Trujillo. It's not a promising hitching route, though at weekends you should get a lift with Spanish birdwatchers.

VILLAREAL DE SAN CARLOS has a couple of bars and a restaurant, plus an **information centre** (daily: summer 9am–2.30pm & 5–7pm; winter 9am–2.30pm & 4–6pm; ☎927 199 134), where you can pick up a colourful leaflet with a map detailing three colour-coded walks from the village. There is also a seasonal shop, selling wildlife T-shirts and the like, and a useful guide to the park (in Spanish) by José Luís Rodríguez.

There's no **accommodation** in Villareal, and camping is prohibited in the park, but there are two friendly *pensións* in **TORREJÓN EL RUBIO**: the *Monfragüe* (☎927 455 026; ❸) and the *Avenida* (☎927 455 050; ❷). More expensive, but good value for money, is the *Hotel Carvajal*, Plaza de Pizarro 54 (☎927 455 254, ⓦbme.es/ctrmonfrague/hotel; ❹). The nearest **campsite** is *Camping Monfragüe* (☎927 459 233, ⓦwww.telexion.com/camping), a well-equipped, year-round site with a swimming pool and restaurant, 12km north of Villareal on the Plasencia road. It is near the turning to the train station of Palazuelo–Empalme (a stop for slow trains on the Madrid–Cáceres line) and it also has **bikes for rent** (for €9 a day) to get to Monfragüe.

Into the park

Walking in Monfragüe, it is best to stick to the colour-coded paths leading from Villareal de San Carlos. Each of them is well paint-blobbed and leads to rewarding bird-watching locations. Elsewhere, it is not easy to tell where you are permitted to wander, and all too easy to find yourself out of the park area in a private hunting reserve.

The **Green Route**, to the Cerro Gimio, is especially good, looping through woods and across streams, in a landscape unimaginable from Villareal, to a dramatic cliff-top viewing station. The longer **Purple Route** heads south of Villareal, over a bridge across the Río Tajo, and past a fountain known as the *Fuente del Francés* after a young Frenchman who died there trying to save an eagle. Two kilometres further is a great crag known as the *Peñafalcón*, which houses a large colony of griffon vultures, and the Castillo de Monfragüe, a castle ruin high up on a rock, with a chapel next to it; there is an observation post nearby. All these places are accessible from the C524 and if you're coming in on the bus, you could ask to get off here.

On the south side of the park, towards Trujillo, you pass through the **dehesas**, strange Africa-like plains which are among the oldest woodlands in Europe. The economy of the *dehesas* is based on grazing, and the casualties among these domestic animals provide the vultures of Monfragüe with their daily bread.

Trujillo

TRUJILLO is the most attractive town in Extremadura: a classic *conquistador* stage-set of escutcheoned mansions, stork-topped towers and castle walls. Much of it looks virtually untouched since the sixteenth century, and is redolent above all of the exploits of the conquerors of the Americas; Francisco Pizarro, the conqueror of Peru, was born here, as were many of the tiny band who with such extraordinary cruelty aided him in defeating the Incas.

Arrival and information

Trujillo could be visited easily enough as a day-trip from Cáceres, but if you can book, it is worth staying the night. There is no train station, but the town is well served by **buses**, with up to eight a day to and from Madrid. Coming in by bus, you'll arrive in the lower town, just five minutes' walk from the Plaza Mayor, where there is a **turismo** (daily 10am–2pm & 4–7/8pm; ☎927 322 677, ⓦwww.ayto-trujillo.com). If you're driving, follow the signs to the Plaza Mayor, where, with luck, you'll be able to park.

Accommodation

Places to stay are in high demand – so book ahead if you can. The turismo can provide accommodation lists. The nicest rooms are around the Plaza Mayor, or, if money is no object, at the *parador*.

Budget options

Pensión Boni, c/Domingo de Ramos 11 ☎927 321 604. Cheap and meticulously run, just off the northeast corner of the Plaza Mayor. ❸

Pensión Casa Roque, c/Domingo de Ramos 30 ☎927 322 313. Excellent and well-located *pen-*

sión. The owner runs the Margarita gift shop on the Plaza Mayor. ❸

Pensión Emilia, c/General Mola 28 ☎927 320 083. Clean and comfortable *pensión* with an economical restaurant and bar downstairs. ❸

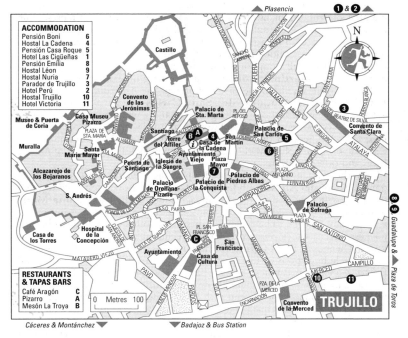

ACCOMMODATION

Pensión Boni	6
Hostal La Cadena	4
Pensión Casa Roque	5
Hotel Las Cigüeñas	1
Pensión Emilia	8
Hostal Léon	9
Hostal Nuria	7
Parador de Trujillo	3
Hotel Perú	2
Hostal Trujillo	10
Hotel Victoria	11

Castillo

Museo & Puerta de Coria

Casa Museo Pizarro

Convento de las Jerónimas

Palacio de Sta. Marta

Santiago

Muralla

Torre del Alfiler

Casa de la Cadena

San Martín

Palacio de San Carlos

Convento de Santa Clara

Santa María Mayor

Puerta de Santiago

Ayuntamiento Viejo

Plaza Mayor

Iglesia de la Sangre

Alcazarejo de los Bejaranos

S. Andrés

Palacio de Orellana-Pizarro

Palacio de Piedras Albas

Palacio de la Conquista

Palacio de Sofraga

Casa de los Torres

Hospital de la Concepción

Pl. San Francisco

San Francisco

Ayuntamiento

Casa de Cultura

RESTAURANTS & TAPAS BARS

Café Aragón	C
Pizarro	A
Mesón La Troya	B

0 Metres 100

Convento de la Merced

TRUJILLO

Cáceres & Montánchez ▼   ▼ Badajoz & Bus Station

Moderate and expensive options

Hostal La Cadena, Plaza Mayor 8 ☎927 321 463, ℻927 323 116. Attractive hotel, with rooms overlooking all the action and a decent restaurant. ④

Hotel Las Cigüeñas, Avda. Madrid ☎927 321 250, ℻927 321 300. Pleasant, modern accommodation down on the main road, but a bit inconvenient for the major sites. ⑦

Hostal Léon, General Mola 23–25 ☎927 321 792, ℻927 322 981. Decent *pensión* with the advantage of secure parking. ⑥

Hostal Nuria, Plaza Mayor 27 ☎927 320 907. Comfortable *hostal* with good views over the Plaza Mayor. ④

Parador de Trujillo, Plaza Santa Beatriz de Silva ☎927 321 350, ℻927 321 366 ✉trujillo@ parador.es. Luxurious accommodation in a sixteenth-century former *convento* north of the Plaza Mayor. ⑧

Hotel Perú, Avda. Madrid ☎927 320 745, ℻927 320 799. A large, drab hotel above a bar, whose one virtue is that it may have rooms long after everywhere else is full. ④

Hostal Trujillo, c/Francisco Pizarro 4 ☎927 322 274, ℻927 322 274 ✉www.arrakis.es/-hstruji/ hostal or ✉hstruji@arrakis.es. A pleasant *pensión* between the Plaza Mayor and the bus station. ④

Hotel Victoria, Plaza de Campillo 22 ☎927 321 819, ℻927 323 084. Modern and friendly hotel, with a pool, good restaurant and comfortable en-suite rooms with TV. ⑥

The Town

Trujillo is a very small place, still little larger than its extent in *conquistador* times. At the centre of a dense web of streets is the **Plaza Mayor**, a grand square overlooked by a trio of palaces and churches, and ringed by a half-dozen cafés and restaurants, around which life for most visitors revolves. In the centre is a bronze statue of Pizarro – oddly, the gift of an American sculptor, one Carlos Rumsey, in 1929. In the square's southwest corner is the **Palacio de la Conquista** (closed for restoration at the time of writing), the grandest of Trujillo's mansions with its roof adorned by statues representing the twelve months. Just one of many built by the Pizarro clan, it was originally inhabited by Pizarro's half-brother and son-in-law Hernando, who returned from the conquests to live here with his half-Inca bride (Pizarro's daughter). Diagonally opposite, and with a skyline of storks, is the bulky church of **San Martín**. Its tombs include, among others, that of the family of Francisco de Orellana, the first explorer of the Amazon. Adjacent is the **Palacio de los Duques de San Carlos** (daily 9.30am–1pm & 4.30–6.30pm; €1.20), home to a group of nuns who moved out of their dilapidated convent up the hill and restored this palace in return for the lodgings. The chimneys on the roof boast aggressively of cultures conquered by Catholicism in the New World – they are shaped like the pyramids of Aztecs, Incas and others subjected to Spanish rule.

From the plaza, c/de Ballesteros leads up to the walled upper town, past the domed **Torre del Alfiler** with its coats of arms and storks' nests, and through the gateway known as the Arco de Santiago. Here, to the left, is **Santa María Mayor** (daily 10am–2pm & 4.30–8pm; €1.20), the most interesting of the town's many churches. The building is basically Gothic but contains a beautiful raised Renaissance *coro* noted for the technical mastery of its almost flat vaults. There is a fine Hispano-Flemish reredos by Fernando Gallego, and tombs including those of the Pizarros – Francisco was baptized here – and Diego García de Paredes, a man known as the "Sansón Extremeño" (Extremaduran Samson). Among other exploits, this giant of a man, armed only with his gargantuan sword, is said to have defended a bridge against an entire French army and to have picked up the font, now underneath the *coro*, to carry holy water to his mother.

Further up the hill, in the Pizarros' former residence, the **Casa Museo Pizarro** (daily 10am–2pm & 4–7/8pm; €1.20) is a small, dull and overpriced affair, with little beyond period furniture and a few panels on the conquest of Peru. More detailed exhibits on the conquest are to be found in the nearby **Museo de la Coria** (Sat, Sun & public holidays 11.30am–2pm; free), which is housed in an old Franciscan convent.

The **castle** (daily 10am–2pm & 4–7pm; €1.20) is now virtually in open countryside; for the last hundred metres of the climb you see nothing but the occasional broken-down remnant of a wall clambered over by sheep and dogs. The **fortress** itself, Moorish in origin but much reinforced by later defenders, has recently been restored, and its main attraction is the panoramic view of the town and its environs from the battlements. Looking out over the barren heath which rings Trujillo, the extent to which the old quarter has fallen into disrepair is abundantly evident, as is the castle's superb defensive position.

Of the many other town mansions, or *solares*, the most interesting is the **Palacio de Orellana-Pizarro**, just west of the main square Mon–Sat 10am–1pm & 4–6pm, Sat & Sun 11am–2pm & 4.30–7pm; voluntary contribution). Go in through the superb Renaissance arched doorway to admire the courtyard, an elegant patio decorated with the alternating coats of arms of the Pizarros – two bears with a pine tree – and the Orellanas.

Eating, drinking and nightlife

There are plenty of **bar-restaurants** right in the Plaza Mayor, the best known of which is probably *Mesón La Troya*, which offers a huge *menú* for €12 – you'll find a giant salad and omelette on your plate before they've even asked what you want to order – although it is a case of quantity over quality. The *Pizarro*, next door, has much better food, costing €10.25 for the *menú* or around €18 a head à la carte. There are excellent *raciones* and tapas at the *Bar Las Cigüeñas* (in the hotel of the same name) and – more cheaply – in the old town at *Café Aragón*, c/Plazuela de Aragón 5. Otherwise, for budget eating, all the *pensiones* along c/General Mola have reasonably priced *menús* on offer – the cheapest being the *Emilia*. If you're driving, you could try out *La Majada*, 4km south of town on the road to Mérida for good fish, local sausages and partridge. At the weekend Trujillo's **nightlife** revolves around c/Ballesteros, north of Plaza Mayor, where you'll find most of its youth at the new *Bar Sotana*.

Guadalupe

The small town of **GUADALUPE** is dominated in every way by the great **Monasterio de Nuestra Señora de Guadalupe**, which for five centuries has brought fame and pilgrims to the area. It was established in 1340, on the spot where an ancient image of the Virgin, said to have been carved by St Luke, was discovered by a shepherd fifty or so years earlier. The delay was simply a question of waiting for the Reconquest to arrive in this remote sierra, with its lush countryside of forests and streams.

Arrival and information

Guadalupe's generally helpful **turismo** is in the arcaded Plaza Mayor (summer Tues–Fri 10am–2.30pm & 5–7pm, Sat & Sun 10am–2.30pm; winter: Tues–Fri 10am–2.30pm & 4–6pm, Sat & Sun 10am–2.30pm ☎927 154 128). **Banks** and a **post office** are to be found close by this central square, near the steps of the monastery church. **Buses** leave from either side of Avenida de Barcelona uphill from the *ayuntamiento*, 200m from the Plaza Mayor: Mirat operates services to Trujillo and Cáceres, Doalde runs buses to Madrid (though you might have to change at Talvera de Reina).

Accommodation

There are plenty of **places to stay** in Guadalupe and the only times you're likely to have difficulty finding a room are during Easter Week or around September 8, the Virgin's festival day. The **campsite**, *Las Villuercas* (☎927 367 139; open all year), is 2km out of town towards Trujillo, close to the main road.

Hospedaría del Real Monasterio, Plaza Juan Carlos 1 ☎927 367 000, ℗927 367 177. Housed in a wing of the monastery and popular with Spanish pilgrims, it's better value than the *parador*. ❻

Hostal Alfonso XI, c/Alfonso Onceno 21 ☎ & ℗927 154 184, ℮juanplaza@mixmail.es. Comfortable, nicely furnished *hostal*. ❻

Hostal Isabel, Plaza Santa María 13 ☎927 367 126. Modern *hostal* offering rooms with bath, and a bar downstairs. ❹

Hostal Lujuan, c/Gregorio López 19 ☎927 367 170. Decent, mid-priced rooms, reasonably central

and with a reliable restaurant (the *menú* costs €7.20). ❸

Parador de Guadalupe, c/Marqués de la Romana 12 ☎927 367 075, ℗927 367 076, ℮guadalupe@parador.es. Beautiful *parador*, housed in a fifteenth-century hospital, with a swimming pool and immaculate patio gardens. ❽

Hostal Taruta, c/Alfonso Onceno 16 ☎927 154 144. This *hostal* can arrange rooms in private houses if its own are fully booked, and offers discounts for full board, with meals in a *comedor* downstairs – which also serves an inexpensive range of *platos*. ❹

△ Storks' nests, Extremadura

The Town

In the fifteenth and sixteenth centuries, Guadalupe was among the most important pilgrimage centres in Spain: Columbus named the Caribbean island in honour of the Virgin here, and a local version was adopted as the patron saint of Mexico. Much of the monastic wealth, in fact, came from returning *conquistadores*, whose successive endowments led to a fascinating mix of styles. The **monastery** was abandoned in the nineteenth-century dissolution, but early this century was reoccupied by Franciscans, who continue to maintain it.

The town itself is a fitting complement to the monastery and countryside: a net of narrow cobbled streets and overhanging houses constructed around the Plaza Mayor, the whole overshadowed by the monastery's bluff ramparts. There's a timeless feel, only slightly diminished by modern development on the outskirts, and a brisk trade in plastic copies of religious treasures.

The church and monastery

The **monastery church** (daily 9am–8.30pm; free) opens onto the Plaza Mayor (aka Plaza de Santa María). Its gloomy Gothic interior is, like the rest of the monastery, packed with treasures from generations of wealthy patrons. Note especially the incredibly ornate *rejas* (grilles).

The entrance to the **monastery** proper (daily 9.30am–1pm & 3.30–6.30pm; €1.80) is to the left of the church. The (compulsory) guided tour begins with a Mudéjar **cloister** – two brick storeys of horseshoe arches with a strange pavilion or tabernacle in the middle – and moves on to the **museum**, with an apparently endless collection of rich vestments, early illuminated manuscripts and religious paraphernalia, along with some fine art works including a triptych by Isenbrandt and a small Goya. The **Sacristía**, beyond, is the finest room in the monastery. Unaltered since it was built in the seventeenth century, it contains eight paintings by Zurbarán, which, uniquely, can be seen in their original context – the frames match the window frames and the pictures themselves are a planned part of the decoration of the room.

Climbing higher into the heart of the monastery, you pass through various rooms filled with jewels and relics before the final ascent to the Holy of Holies. From a tiny room high above the main altar you can look down over the church while a panel is spun away to reveal the climax of the tour – the bejewelled and richly dressed **image of the Virgin.** The Virgin is one of the few black icons ever made - originally carved out of dark cedarwood, its colour has further deepened over the centuries under innumerable coats of varnish (replicas of this image are sold in the town's many souvenir shops).

On the way out, drop in at the **Hospedaría del Real Monasterio**, around to the right. The bar in its Gothic cloister, with lovely gardens outside, is one of the world's more unusual places to enjoy a *Cuba libre*.

Eating and drinking

You can **eat** at most *hostales* and *pensiones,* with just about everywhere – including the restaurants on Plaza Mayor – serving €7.20 *menús*. The one at *Hostal Lujuan* is particularly good value, while the *Hospedaria del Real Monasterio* has a courtyard setting. Perhaps the best restaurant in town is the *Mesón del Cordero* at c/Alfonso Onceno 27, a more expensive place with home cooking and grand views from the dining room. What there is of Guadalupe's **nightlife** takes place at the bottom of c/Alfonso Onceno, where *Casamalia*, at no. 14, is a young and lively bar.

The Sierra de Guadalupe: routes to Trujillo

A truly superb view of Guadalupe set in its sierra can also be enjoyed from the road (C713) north to Navalmoral. Five kilometres out of town, the **Ermita del Humilladero** marks the spot where pilgrims to the shrine traditionally caught their first glimpse of the monastery.

The surrounding **Sierra de Guadalupe** is a wild and beautiful region, with steep, rocky crags abutting the valley sides. If you have your own transport, a good route is to strike northwest of the C401 at Cañamero, up to the village of **Cabañas del Castillo**, a handful of houses, most of them empty as only twelve inhabitants remain, nestling against a massive crag and ruined castle. Beyond here, you can reach the main **Navalmoral–Trujillo road** close to the **Puerto de Miravete**, a fabulous viewpoint, with vistas of Trujillo in the far distance. Another great drivers' route, again leaving the C401 at Cañamero, is to follow the narrow road **through Berzocana** to Trujillo.

Cáceres

CÁCERES is in many ways remarkably like Trujillo. It features an almost perfectly preserved walled town, the Ciudad Monumental, packed with *solares* built on the proceeds of American exploration, while even more than in Trujillo every available tower and spire is crowned by a clutch of storks' nests. As a provincial capital, however, Cáceres is a much larger and livelier place, especially in term-time, when the students of the University of Extremadura are in residence. With its Roman, Moorish and *conquistador* sights, and a lively bar and restaurant scene, it is an absorbing and highly enjoyable city. It also provides a dramatic backdrop for an annual **WOMAD** festival, held over the second weekend in May and attracting up to 70,000 spectators.

The walled **old town** stands at the heart of Cáceres, with a picturesque **Plaza Mayor** just outside its walls. Almost everything of interest is contained within – or a short walk from – this area, and you would do well to base yourself as close to it as possible.

Arrival and information

If you arrive by **train or bus**, you'll find yourself around 3km out from the old town, at the far end of the Avenida de Alemania. It's not an enjoyable walk, so take bus #1, which runs down the *avenida* to Plaza de San Juan, a square adjoining the Plaza Mayor; an irregular shuttle bus from the train station (free if you show a rail ticket) also runs into town, to the Plaza de América, a major traffic junction west of the old town. If you're driving, be warned that increasing pedestrianization is making access to some streets impossible by car; your best bet is to try and park in the Plaza Mayor, or if that's full the car park on Avenida de España.

Cáceres has a helpful regional **turismo** (Mon–Fri 9.30am–2pm & 4–7.30pm, winter closes 6.30pm; Sat & Sun 9.30am–2pm; ☎927 246 347, ⊛www.turismoextremadura.com) in the Plaza Mayor, with a smaller municipal office (daily 10am–1pm & 4–6pm) nearby that organizes hourly guided tours of the main sites (1hr 30min; €3 including entry fees). The main **post office** is at c/Miguel Primo Rivera 2, near the Plaza de América, and **Internet access** is available on Plaza de Bruselas at *Cibercity* (daily 10am–10pm; €2.40 per hour).

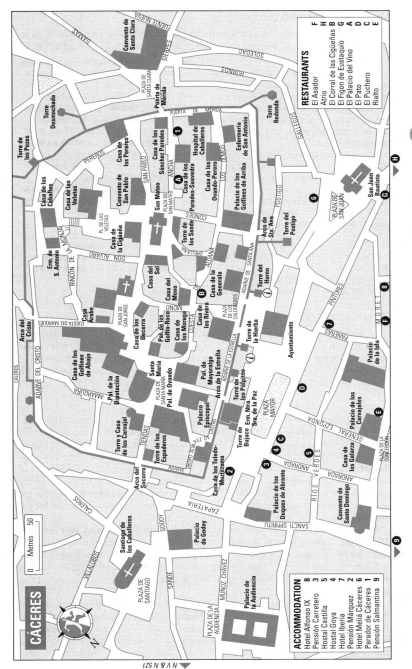

CÁCERES

▲ N V & N 521

RESTAURANTS

El Asador F
Atrio H
El Corral de las Cigüeñas B
El Fígon de Eustaquio G
El Palacio del Vino A
El Pato D
El Puchero C
Rialto E

ACCOMMODATION

Hotel Alfonso IX 8
Pensión Carretero 3
Hostal Castilla 5
Hostal Goya 4
Hotel Iberia 7
Pensión Márquez 2
Hotel Meliá Cáceres 6
Parador de Cáceres 1
Pensión Salmantina 9

0 Metres 50

Accommodation

There is usually plenty of **accommodation** to go round (much of it over-priced), but it's a good idea to book ahead if you're visiting during Easter.

Budget options

Pensión Carretero, Plaza Mayor 22–23 ☎927 247 882. Best value in town – very basic, large rooms, spotless bathrooms and a TV lounge – though some rooms can be noisy at the weekend. ❸

Pensión Castilla, c/Ríos Verdes 3 ☎927 244 404. Just off the Plaza Mayor, with small, clean rooms, and separate bath. ❸

Pensión Márquez, c/Gabriel y Galán 2 ☎927 244 960. Just off the Plaza Mayor, the cheapest place in town and fairly decent; it's popular, so check in early. ❸

Pensión Salmantina, c/General Margallo 36a ☎927 244 218. Centrally located *pensión* with shared bathroom and small, extremely basic rooms. ❸

Moderate and expensive options

Hotel Alfonso IX, c/Moret 20 ☎927 246 400, ☎927 247 811. Nicely located on a pedestrianized street off c/Pintores, this slightly aged hotel offers en-suite rooms with air-conditioning and satellite TV. ❻

Hostal Goya, Plaza Mayor 11 ☎927 249 950, ☎927 213 758. Upmarket (and good-value) *hostal* on the Plaza Mayor, with en-suite rooms. ❻

Hotel Iberia, c/Pintores 2 ☎927 247 634, ☎927 248 200. Tastefully restored building in a corner of the Plaza Mayor. ❺

Hotel Meliá Cáceres, Plaza de San Juan 11 ☎927 215 800, ☎927 214 070, ✉melia.caceres@solmelia.es. Part of the growing Meliá chain, this hotel is in a sixteenth-century palace, just outside the walls of the old town, and is in many ways a nicer place than the *parador*. ❾

Parador de Cáceres, c/Ancha 6 ☎927 211 759, ☎927 211 729, ✉caceres@parador.es. The *parador* occupies a *conquistador* mansion in the Ciudad Monumental – the only hotel within the walls. ❽

The Town

The **walls** of the Ciudad Monumental are basically Moorish in construction, though parts date back to the Romans – notably the **Arco del Cristo** – and they have been added to, refortified and built against pretty much throughout the centuries. The most intact section, with several original adobe Moorish towers, runs in a clockwise direction, facing the walls from the Plaza Mayor.

Around the old town

Entering the old town – the **Parte Vieja**, as it's also known – from the Plaza Mayor, you pass through the low **Arco de la Estrella**, an entrance built by Manuel Churriguera in the eighteenth century. To your left, at the corner of the walls, is one of the most imposing *conquistador solares*, the **Casa de Toledo-Montezuma** with its domed tower. It was to this house that a follower of Cortés brought back one of the New World's more exotic prizes, a daughter of the Aztec emperor, as his bride. The building has recently been restored – it was in imminent danger of collapse – to house the provincial historical archives, and it also stages occasional exhibitions.

Walking straight ahead through the Arco de la Estrella, brings you into the **Plaza de Santa María**, flanked by another major *solar*, the Casa de los Golfines de Abajo, the Palacio Episcopal, and the Gothic church of Santa María – Cáceres's finest. Inside, you can illuminate a fine sixteenth-century carved wooden *retablo*, while in the surrounding gloom are the tombs of many of the town's great families.

A couple of blocks away, at the town's highest point, is the Plaza de San Mateo, flanked by the church of **San Mateo**, another Gothic structure with fine chapels, and the **Casa de la Cigüeña** (House of the Stork), whose narrow tower was the only one allowed to preserve its original battlements when the rest were shorn by royal decree. It is now a military installation and, although the tower features on half the postcards in Cáceres, soldiers discourage the taking of further snapshots.

In the Plaza de las Veletas is the **Casa de las Veletas**, which houses the archeology and ethnology sections of the **Museo Provincial** (Tues–Sat 9am–2.30pm, Sun 10.15am–2.30pm; €1.80, free to EU citizens). The collections here take second place to the building itself. Typical of the local style, its beautifully proportioned rooms are arrayed around a small patio and preserve the *aljibe* (cistern) of the original Moorish Alcázar with its horseshoe arches. It also has an extraordinary balustrade, created from Talavera ceramic jugs.

From here, a footbridge leads to the museum's contemporary art section in the **Casa de los Caballos** (House of Horses). Two floors of modern art and sculpture include works by Miró, Picasso and Eduardo Arroyo, alongside up-and-coming contemporary artists.

Something could be said about almost every other building within the old walls, but notice above all the **family crests** – in particular on the **Casa del Sol** – and the magnificent facade of the **Casa de los Golfines de Abajo**. It was in this latter *conquistador* mansion that Franco had himself proclaimed *Generalísimo* and head of state in October 1936. Near the Casa del Sol is another *solar*, the **Casa del Mono** (House of the Monkey), which is now a public library; the facade is adorned with grotesque gargoyles and a stone monkey is chained to the staircase in the courtyard.

Outside the walls

Outside the walls, it's worth wandering up to the sixteenth-century church of **Santiago de los Caballeros**, which fronts the plaza of the same name, opposite a more or less contemporary mansion, **Palacio de Godoy**, with its corner balcony. The church, open only for Masses, has a fine *retablo* by Alonso Berruguete.

You might take time, too, for a visit to the **Casa Árabe** (daily 10.30am–1.30pm & 4.30–7.30pm; €1.50), off Plaza San Jorge at Cuesta del Marqués 4. The owner of this Moorish house has had the bright idea of decorating it more or less as it would have been when occupied by its original owner. The Alhambra it's not, and the red lights in the "harem" are a dubious touch, but it at least provides a context for all the horseshoe arches and curving brick ceilings.

If you want to enjoy a good view of the old town, go through the Arco del Cristo down to the main road and turn right onto c/de Fuente Concejo, following the signs for about five minutes or so, and you will have the whole town set out below you.

Eating, drinking and nightlife

There is a good range of **bars, restaurants and bodegas** in and around the Plaza Mayor, while the old town offers a bit more style at not too inflated a price.

Cáceres has the best **nightlife** in the region – especially during term-time – with the night starting off in the bars along c/Pizarro, south of Plaza de San Juan, moving on to c/Dr Fleming and the discos in the nearby Plaza de Albatros. These are all pretty similar – the usual mix of salsa and Spanish pop – though the *Rita* plays an interesting mix of alternative tunes. There are also several late-night bars around Plaza Mayor, and live music can be heard in many places along the nearby c/General Ezpondaz.

Restaurants

El Asador, c/Moret 34. Reasonably priced restaurant, off c/Pintores, serving local dishes and fronted by a popular tapas bar.

Atrio, Avda. de España 30, block B. Good, upmarket restaurant, southwest of Plaza Mayor, with extensive menu. Closed Sun evening. Allow €27–33 per head.

El Corral de las Cigüeñas, Cuesta de Aldana 6. A beautiful spot to enjoy a meal in the old town, with tables in a large, palm-shaded courtyard; reasonably priced *platos combinados*.

El Figón de Eustaquio, Plaza de San Juan 12. This features an extensive list of regional dishes, cooked with care and flair. It's not cheap; allow €18–30 a head, or try the €11.40 *menú*.

El Palacio del Vino, c/Ancha 4. Pleasant, traditional *mesón* near the *parador* in the old town; allow around €15 a head.

El Pato, Plaza Mayor 24. Popular restaurant fronting the square – slightly more expensive than its neighbours but probably worth the extra.

El Puchero, Plaza Mayor 10. The cheapest restaurant on the plaza, with an ever-popular *terraza*.

Rialto, Plaza de la Concepción 29. No frills but good-value restaurant popular with young locals.

Bars

Bar del Jamón, Plaza de San Juan 10. Small place to enjoy *pitarra* and a *pincho*.

El Extremeño, Plaza del Duque 10 – off the Plaza Mayor. A student favourite with Guinness on tap and beer sold by the metre.

Lancelot, Rincon de la Monja 2. Opposite the Casa Arabé, a relaxed English-run bar.

La Machacona, c/Andrada 8 – down an alley under the arcades off the Plaza Mayor. Good place to hear Latin sounds and occasional live music.

El Torre de Babel, c/Pizarro 8. Laid-back café with occasional live music, plus clothes and jewellery stalls downstairs.

Northwest of Cáceres: Arroyo and Alcántara

Northwest of Cáceres is the vast **Embalse de Alcántara**, one of a series of reservoirs harnessing the power of the Río Tajo in the last few kilometres before it enters Portugal. The scheme swallowed up large tracts of land and you can see the old road and railway to Palencia disappearing into the depths of the reservoir (their replacements cross the many inlets on double-decker bridges), along with the tower of a castle.

The C523 loops away to the south of the reservoir, through **Arroyo de la Luz** and **Brozas**, each with fine churches, before reaching **Alcántara**, with its superb Roman bridge across the Tajo. The Portuguese border – and the road to Costelo Branco and Coimbra – is just a dozen kilometres beyond.

Arroyo de la Luz and Brozas

ARROYO DE LA LUZ (Stream of Light), despite its romantic name, is one of the least memorable Extremaduran towns. However, it does have one sight of note: the gaunt, late-Gothic church of **La Asunción**, which houses a huge *retablo* of twenty panels by Luís Morales. This Extremaduran artist (1509–86) is known to the Spanish as "El Divino", though his heart-on-sleeve style has never found much favour with art historians. His work is certainly a lot more impressive seen here, *in situ*, than in a museum. To view it, ask for the keys from the local police at the side door of the *ayuntamiento*, which faces the south side of the church, and bring some coins for the meter.

Arroyo has a single **hostal**, inevitably called the *Divino Morales* (☎927 270 257; ❺), at the edge of town where the buses stop, and a couple of basic restaurants. A more pleasant place to eat, drink, or stay, however, is the old *Hostal La Posada* (☎927 395 019; ❹–❺) at **BROZAS**, 35km on towards Alcántara. Brozas itself is an old *conquistador* town, centred on a seventeenth-century castle. Its Gothic church of Santa María La Mayor has a spectacular Baroque *retablo*. More impressive still are the fantastic views over the plain and the low hills to the south.

Alcántara

The name **ALCÁNTARA** comes from the Arabic for "bridge" – in this case a beautiful six-arched **Puente Romano** spanning a gorge of the Río Tajo. Completed in 105 AD, and held together without mortar, it was reputed to be the loftiest bridge ever built in the Roman empire, although it's far from certain which bits, if any, remain genuinely Roman.

The bridge is quite a distance from the town itself, which is built high above the river; if you're on foot, don't follow the signs via the road – instead, head to the far side of the town and down a steep cobbled path.

Further Roman remains include a **triumphal arch** dedicated to Trajan and a tiny **classical temple**. The dominating landmark, however, is the recently restored **Convento San Benito**, erstwhile headquarters of the Knights of Alcántara, one of the great orders of the Reconquest. For all its enormous bulk, the convent and its church are only a fragment; the nave of the church was never built. Outside, the main feature is the double-arcaded Renaissance gallery at the back; it serves as the backdrop for a season of classical plays which moves here from Mérida in August. Entry to the convent (summer: Mon–Fri 10am–2pm & 4–6.30pm, Sat 11am–2pm & 4–6.30pm, Sun 11am–2pm; winter: Mon–Fri 10am–2pm & 4.30–5pm, Sat 11am–2pm & 4.30–5pm, Sun 11am–2pm; free) is through the adjacent *Fundación de San Benito*, who have been making attempts to restore the cloister and the Plateresque east end with its elaborate wall tombs.

Alcántara also contains the scanty remains of a **castle**, numerous **mansions** and street after street of humbler whitewashed houses. The place is marvellous for scenic walks, whether in the town, along the banks of the Tajo, or – best of all – in the hills on the opposite bank.

Practicalities

The **turismo**, Avda. de Merida 21 (May–Sept Tues–Fri 10am–2pm & 5–7pm, Sat & Sun 10.30am–12.30pm; Oct–April Tues–Fri 10am–2pm & 4.30–6.30pm, Sat & Sun 10.30am–12.30pm; ☎927 390 863, Ⓔoficiturismo@inicia.es), is very helpful and can provide a town map.

The town has one **hostal**, the *Kantara Al Saif*, just out of town on the Avenida de Mérida (☎927 390 246, Ⓕ927 390 833, Ⓔal-saif@teleline.es; ❹), with an

---

Jamón serrano: a gastronomic note

Extremadura, to many Spaniards, means ham. Together with the Sierra Morena in Andalucía, the Extremaduran sierra is the only place in the country which supports the pure-bred Iberian pig, source of the best *jamón serrano*. For its ham to be as highly flavoured as possible, the pig, a subspecies of the European wild boar exclusive to the Iberian peninsula, is allowed to roam wild and eat acorns for several months of the year. The undisputed kings of hams in this area, praised at length by Richard Ford in his *Handbook for Travellers*, are those that come from Montánchez, in the south of the region. The village is midway between Cáceres and Mérida, so if you're in the area try some in a bar, washed down with local red wine – but be warned that the authentic product is extremely expensive, a few thinly cut slices often costing as much as an entire meal. The local wine *pitarra* is an ideal accompaniment.

adjoining restaurant and café. **Buses**, which run twice a day to and from Cáceres, stop at a little square ringed by cafés at the entrance to the historic part of the town. Here you can **eat** cheaply at *Restaurante El Gorrón* and at *Restaurante Antonio*, near the turismo building.

Mérida

The former capital of the Roman province of Lusitania, **MÉRIDA** (the name is a corruption of *Augusta Emerita*) contains more **Roman remains** than any other city in Spain. Even for the most casually interested, the extent and variety of the remains here are compelling, with everything from engineering works to domestic villas, by way of cemeteries and places of worship, entertainment and culture. With a little imagination, and a trip to the wonderful modern museum, the Roman city is not difficult to evoke – which is just as well, for the modern city, in which the sites are scattered, is no great shakes.

Each July and August, the Roman theatre in Mérida hosts a **theatre festival**, including performances of classical Greek plays and Shakespeare's Roman tragedies.

Arrival and information

Mérida sees a lot of visitors and has plenty of facilities to cater for them. If you want maps, guidebooks or information on the region, look in at the helpful **turismo** (summer Mon–Fri 9am–1.45pm & 5–7.15pm, Sat & Sun 9.30am–2pm; winter Mon–Fri 9am–1.45pm & 4–6.30pm, Sat & Sun 9am–1.45pm; ☏924 315 353, ⓦwww.turismoextremadura.com), just outside the gates to the theatre and amphitheatre site.

The **train station** is pretty central, with the theatre site and Plaza de España no more than ten minutes' walk away. The **bus station** is on the other side of the river and is a grittier twenty minutes' walk from the town centre, along Avenida de Libertad, which extends from the new single-arch bridge. For inexpensive time online, *Ware Nostrum*, c/Baños 24, is a friendly **Internet café** (daily 4pm–1am; €1.80 per hour).

Accommodation

There is no shortage of **places to stay**, but prices tend to be high; if you're on a tight budget, be prepared to do some searching.

Budget options

Pensión El Arco, c/Cervantes 16 ☏924 318 321. Cheap and friendly *pensión*. ❸

Hostal Bueno, c/Calvario 9 ☏924 302 977. Basic but clean *hostal* – all the rooms have (tiny) bathrooms. ❸–❹

Moderate and expensive options

Hotel Cervantes, c/Camilo José Cela 8 ☏924 314 961, ☏924 311 342, ⓦwww.hotelcervantes.com. Comfortable hotel, off c/Cervantes, with secure parking. Ask to see the rooms, as some are on the small side. ❻

Hotel Emperatriz, Plaza de España 19 ☏924 313 111, ☏924 313 305. Attractive old hotel in a former palace, bang on the main square, and with a patio garden. ❼

Hotel Lusitania, c/Oviedo 12 ☏924 316 112, ☏924 316 109. Reliable but unremarkable hotel, best kept in reserve if everywhere else is full. ❺.

Hotel Nova Roma, c/Suavez Somontes 42 ☏924 311 261, ☏924 300 160. Large, modern hotel in central location. Book ahead if you're coming during the theatre festival. ❼

Hostal Nueva España, Avda. de Extremadura 6 ☏924 313 356. Good-value *hostal* with large rooms, out towards the train station. ❹

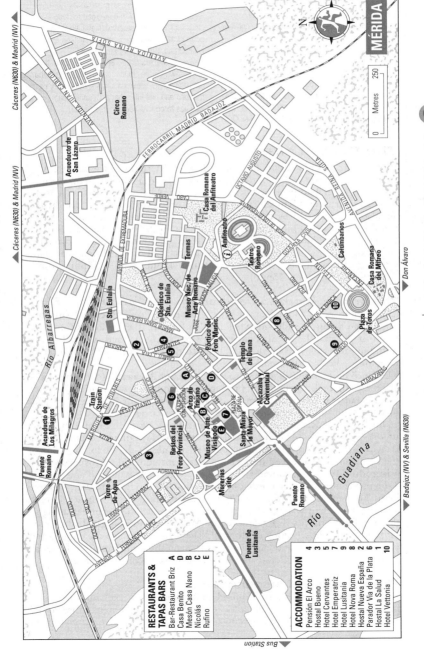

MÉRIDA

N

Cáceres (N630) & Madrid (NV) ▲

Cáceres (N630) & Madrid (NV) ▲

0   Metres   250

▼ Don Álvaro

▼ Badajoz (NV) & Sevilla (N630)

▼ Bus Station

Circo Romano

Acueducto de San Lázaro

FERROCARRIL MADRID BADAJOZ

AVENIDA REINA SOFIA

AVENIDA JUAN CARLOS

Casa Romana del Anfiteatro

ⓘ Anfiteatro

Termas

Teatro Romano

Columbarios

Sta. Eulalia

Obelisco de Sta. Eulalia

Museo Nac. de Arte Romano

Pórtico del Foro Munin.

Templo de Diana

Casa Romana del Mitreo

Plaza de Toros

⑩

⑧

⑨

Río Albarregas

Acueducto de Los Milagros

Puente Romano

Train Station

❷

❹
⑤

Ⓐ

❻

Restos del Foro Provincial

Ⓒ
Ⓓ

Arco de Trajano

❼

Museo de Arte Visigodo

Ⓔ

Santa María la Mayor

Alcazaba y Conventual

❶

❸

Torre de Agua

Murerías site

Puente de Lusitania

Puente Romano

Río Guadiana

AVENIDA DE EXTREMADURA

RESTAURANTS & TAPAS BARS

Bar-Restaurant Briz	A
Casa Benito	D
Mesón Casa Nano	B
Nicolás	C
Rufino	E

ACCOMMODATION

Pensión El Arco	4
Hostal Bueno	3
Hotel Cervantes	5
Hotel Emperatriz	7
Hotel Lusitania	9
Hotel Nova Roma	8
Hostal Nueva España	2
Parador Via de la Plata	6
Hostal La Salud	1
Hotel Vettonia	10

Parador Vía de la Plata, Plaza Constitución 3
☎924 313 800, ⓕ924 319 208,
ⓔmerida@parador.es. Well-run and friendly
parador in an eighteenth-century Baroque convent,
near the Arco de Trajano. ❽
Hostal La Salud, c/Vespasiano 41 ☎ & ⓕ924
312 259, ⓔhsalud@bluenet.com. Small, simple
rooms in this good-value *hostal* near the
Acueducto de los Milagros. ❹
Hotel Vettonia, c/Calderón de la Barca 26 ☎924
311 462/3. Comfortable, small hotel with easy
parking right outside and wheelchair access. ❹

Camping
Camping Lago de Proserpina ☎924 123 055.
Signposted off the NV and the road to Caceres, a
pleasant site by the reservoir (see below) 5km
north of town, offering swimming, fishing and
windsurfing. Open April to mid-Sept.
Camping Mérida ☎924 303 453. Located 4km
out of town on the Trujillo road (N430), this is the
closer of Mérida's two campsites, but is very near
the road and has little shade. Open all year and
also has three two-bed bungalows (❹).

The Roman sites

Built on the site of a Celto–Iberian settlement, Mérida was the tenth city of
the Roman empire and the final stop on the *Vía de la Plata*, the Roman road
which began in Astorga in northern Castile. The old city stretched as far as the
modern bullring and Roman circus, covering only marginally less than the triangular area occupied by the modern town. Visiting the sites, a single €4.80
combined ticket, which can be bought at any of the sites covers the Roman
theatre and amphitheatre, Casa Romana del Anfiteatro, Roman villas, the
archeological site at Morerías and the Alcazaba – all of which have the same
opening hours (daily: summer 9.30am–1.45pm & 5–6.15pm; winter
9.30am–1.45pm & 4–6.15pm).

The bridge, Alcazaba and around the centre
The obvious point to begin your tour is the magnificent **Puente Romano**,
the bridge across the islet-strewn Río Guadiana. It is sixty arches long (the
seven in the middle are fifteenth-century replacements) and was still in use
until the early 1990s, when the new **Puente de Lusitania** – itself a structure
to admire – was constructed.

Defence of the old bridge was provided by a vast **Alcazaba** (combined ticket or €2.40), built by the Moors to replace a Roman construction. The interior is a rather barren archeological site, although in the middle there's an *aljibe*
to which you can descend by either of a pair of staircases.

North of the Alcazaba, past the sixteenth-century Plaza de España, the heart
of the modern town, is the so-called **Templo de Diana**, adapted into a
Renaissance mansion, and further along are remains of the **Foro**, the heart of
the Roman city. To the west of the plaza, a convent houses the **Museo de Arte
Visigodo** (Tues–Sun: summer 10am–2pm & 5–7pm; winter 10am–2pm &
4–6pm; €2.40), with an unexciting collection of about a hundred lapidary
items. Just behind here is the great **Arco Trajano**, once wrongly believed to be
a triumphal arch; it was, in fact, a monumental gate to the forum. Heading to
the river from here you'll also discover the **Morerías archeological site** (combined ticket or €2.40) along c/Morerías, where you can watch the digging and
preservation of houses and factories from Roman through Visigoth to Moorish
times – particularly of interest are the well-preserved Roman mosaics.

The theatre and amphitheatre
A ten-minute walk northeast of the Plaza de España will take you to Mérida's
main archeological site (combined ticket or €3.60), containing the theatre and
amphitheatre. Immediately adjacent are a Roman villa and the museum of
Roman art.

The elaborate and beautiful **Teatro Romano** is one of the best preserved anywhere in the Roman empire. Constructed around 15 BC, it was a present to the city from Agrippa, as indicated by the large inscription above the passageway to the left of the stage. The stage itself, a two-tier colonnaded affair, is in a particularly good state of repair, while many of the seats have been entirely rebuilt to offer more comfort to the audiences of the annual July and August season of classical plays.

Adjoining the theatre is the **Anfiteatro**, a slightly later and very much plainer construction. As many as 15,000 people – almost half the current population of Mérida – could be seated to watch gladiatorial combats and fights with wild animals.

The **Casa Romana del Anfiteatro** (combined ticket or €2.40) lies immediately below the museum, and offers an approach to it from the site. It has wonderful mosaics, including a vigorous depiction of grape-treading.

The Museo Nacional de Arte Romano

The **Museo Nacional de Arte Romano** (May–Sept Tues–Sun 10am–2pm & 5–7pm, Oct–April Tues–Sun 10am–2pm & 4–6pm; €2.40, free Sat afternoons & Sun mornings), constructed in 1986 above the Roman walls, is a wonderfully light, accessible building, using a free interpretation of classical forms to present the mosaics and sculpture as if emerging from the ruins. Spain's leading architect, Rafael Moneo, achieved perfectly his aim here to allow visitors "to see the entire collection almost in a glance".

The exhibits, displayed on three levels of the basilica-like hall, live up to their showcase. They include statues from the theatre, the Roman villa of **Mithraeus** (Mitreo; see below) and the vanished forum, and a number of mosaics – the largest being hung on the walls so that they can be examined at each level. There are frescoes, too, including a complete room, reconstructed. Individually, the finest exhibits are probably the three statues, displayed together, depicting Augustus, the first Roman emperor; his son Tiberius, the second emperor; and Drusus, Augustus's heir apparent until (it is alleged) he was murdered by Livia, Tiberius's mother.

Further out: the hippodrome, aqueducts and Mitreo villa

The remaining monuments are further out from the centre, on the other side of the railway tracks. From the museum, it's a ten-minute walk out along the Avenida de Extremadura to the **Circo Romano**, essentially an outline, where horses and chariots once raced. Across the road from here, a stretch of the **Acueducto de San Lázaro** leads off towards the Río Albarregas.

The more impressive aqueduct, however, is the **Acueducto de los Milagros**, of which a satisfying portion survives in the midst of vegetable gardens, west of the train station. Its tall arches of granite, with brick courses, brought water to the city in its earliest days from the reservoir at Proserpina, 5km away (see below). The best view of the aqueduct is from a low and inconspicuous **Puente Romano** across the Río Albarregas; it was over this span that the *Vía de la Plata* entered the city.

Two further sights are the church of **Santa Eulalia**, by the train station, which has a porch made from fragments of a former Temple of Mars, and a second Roman villa, the **Mitreo**, in the shadow of the Plaza de Toros, south of the museum and theatres. The villa has a magnificent but damaged mosaic depicting river gods. A short walk away is a Roman burial ground with two family sepulchres.

Proserpina and Cornalvo reservoirs

You can swim in the **Embalse de Proserpina,** a Roman-constructed reservoir 5km north of town, and a popular summer escape, with a line of holiday homes. Alternatively, if you have transport, head to the **Embalse de Cornalvo**, 18km east of Mérida (turn left after the village of Trujillanos). There's a Roman dyke here, and a small national park has recently been created in the area.

Eating and drinking

The whole area between the train station and the Plaza de España is full of **bars and cheap restaurants** – fliers for many of which will be stuffed into your hands outside the theatre site entrance. Alternatively, search out one of the following:

Bar-Restaurante Briz, c/Félix Valverde Lillo 5, just off Plaza de España. Reliable restaurant offering local speciality *raciones* and an €8.50 *menú*. Closed Sun evening.

Casa Benito, c/San Francisco 3. Bullfighters' ephemera line the walls of this bar, which serves the local speciality tapas and *pitarra* wine. Closed Sun.

Mesón Restaurante Casa Nano, c/Casterlar 3. Nice restaurant with a *menú* at around €18.

Restaurante Nicolás, c/Félix Valverde Lillo 13. Good range of Extremaduran dishes and *menú* at €12, otherwise allow €18–21 a head. Closed Sun evenings.

Restaurante Rufino, Plaza de Santa Clara 2 ☏924 312 001. Traditional dishes in pleasant surroundings at this centrally located restaurant, opposite the Museo Visigodo. Allow €12–18 a head or try the enormous €16.20 *menú*.

Badajoz

The valley of the Río Guadiana, followed by road and rail, waters rich farmland between Mérida and **BADAJOZ**. The main reason for visiting this provincial capital, traditional gateway to Portugal and the scene of innumerable sieges, is still to get across the border – it's not somewhere you'd want to stay long. Crude modern development has largely overrun what must once have been an attractive old centre, and few of the monuments have survived. The troubled history of Badajoz, springing from its strategically important position on the Río Guadiana, is in many ways more interesting than its present day. Founded by the Moors in 1009, the city was taken by the Christian armies of Alfonso IX in 1230, used as a base by Felipe II against the Portuguese in 1580, stormed by British forces under the Duke of Wellington in 1812, and taken by Franco's Nationalist troops in 1936.

Arrival and information

If you're arriving by **bus**, you'll have a fifteen-minute-plus walk to the centre, as the station is awkwardly located in wasteland beyond the ring road at the southern edge of the city. Your best bet is to hop on city bus #3 or #4 to Avenida de Europa or #6 to the Plaza de la Libertad. The **train station** is still further from the action, on the far side of the river, up the road which crosses the Puente de Palmas. Buses #1 and #2 go to the Plaza de la Libertad, or it's around €1.50 in a taxi. If you're looking for **parking**, follow the signs to Plaza de Minayo where you'll find an attended underground car park.

The town has two tourist offices. The efficient municipal **turismo** (June–Sept Mon–Fri 9.30am–2pm & 5–7.30pm, Sat 10am–2pm; Oct–May Mon–Fri 9.30am–2pm & 4–6.30pm, Sat 10am–2pm; ☏924 224 981, ⓦwww.turismoextremadura.com) is in c/de San Juan, just off Plaza de España,

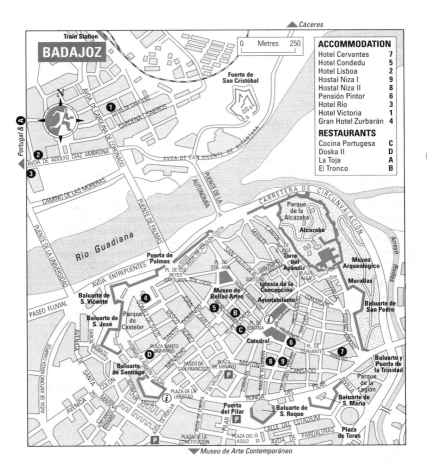

▲ *Cáceres*

BADAJOZ

Train Station

0   Metres   250

Fuerte de San Cristóbal

AVDA DE CAROLINA DE CORONADO

LUIS DE CAMÕES

CARDENA CISNEROS

AVDA. DE ADOLFO DIAZ AMBRONA

AVDA DE SAN VICENTE DE ALCÁNTARA

◀ Portugal & A

CAMINO DE LAS MORERAS

PUENTE DE PALMAS

AUTONOMIA

PUENTE DE LA

CARRETERA DE CIRCUNVALACIÓN

Río Guadiana

PUENTE DE LA UNIVERSIDAD

PASEO FLUVIAL

Parque de la Alcazaba

Alcazaba

Puerta de Palmas

Torre del Apéndiz

Museo Arqueológico

Murallas

Baluarte de S. Vicente

Baluarte de S. José

Parque de Castelar

Museo de Bellas Artes

Iglesia de la Concepción

Ayuntamiento

Baluarte de San Pedro

Catedral

Baluarte de Santiago

Baluarte y Puerta de la Trinidad

Parque de la Legión

Baluarte de S. María

Puerta del Pilar

Baluarte de S. Roque

CALLE DEL ESTADIUM

AVDA DE PARDALERAS

Plaza de Toros

PLAZA DE LA CONSTITUCIÓN

PLAZA DEL ASILO

▼ *Museo de Arte Contemporáneo*

while the **Junta de Extremadura** office (Mon–Fri 10am–2pm & 5–7pm, Sat & Sun 10am–2pm; ☎924 222 763), good for information on the whole region, is down the hill on Plaza de la Libertad – follow the signs from any approach to the town. For **Internet access**, go to Locutorio Público Extrameño, opposite the *Burger King* at Avda. Fernando Calzadilla 2 (7am–11pm; €3 per hour).

The Portuguese frontier is 4km west of Badajoz. You can get to the border by local bus, from where you can catch local Portuguese buses to Elvas, the first sizeable town on the Portuguese side of the border. There are two long-distance buses and one train to Lisbon daily, all via Elvas – the bus is by far the cheaper, faster and more hassle-free option.

Accommodation

There's plenty of **accommodation** available in Badajoz, much of it inexpensive, if not terribly desirable. The best location is around the Plaza de España, particularly on c/Arco Agüero.

Budget options

Hostal Niza I, c/Arco Agüero 34 ☎924 223 881. Cheap but decent *hostal*, with shared facilities. Can get noisy at weekends. ❸

Pensión Pintor, c/Arco Agüero 10 ☎924 224 228. Cheap but charming *pensión* on the first floor of this building, offering good value for money. ❸

Moderate and expensive options

Hotel Cervantes, c/Trinidad 2 ☎924 223 710, ℗924 222 935. On the Plaza Cervantes, by the cathedral, this hotel has impressive common areas but rather ordinary rooms. ❹

Hotel Condedu, c/Muñoz Torrero 27 ☎ 924 207 247, ℗924 207 248, ⓦwww.infonegocio.com/hotelcondedu. Comfortable and well-located hotel (aka Hotel Conde Duque), handy for the museum and cathedral. ❺ .

Gran Hotel Zurbarán, Paseo Castelar ☎924 223 741, ℗924 220 142, ⓔzurbaran@barcelo.com. Priciest hotel in town, with swimming pool and renowned restaurant. ❽

Hotel Lisboa, Avda. Díaz Ambrona 13 ☎924 272 900, ℗924 272 250. Large, comfortable hotel with en-suite rooms and a very reasonably priced restaurant. ❻

Hostal Niza II, c/Arco Agüero 45 ☎924 223 173, ⓦwww.coeba.es/hostalniza. Comfortable, en-suite rooms in this small *hostal* (check in early as it fills up quickly). ❺

Hotel Río, Avda. Adolfo Díaz Ambrona 13 ☎924 272 600, ℗924 273 874, ⓔhotelrio@htelrio.net. At the far end of Puente de la Universidad, with swimming pool, parking and a good restaurant (which is closed at weekends and Aug). ❽

Hotel Victoria, c/Luís de Camões 3 ☎924 271 662, ℗924 267 551. Good-value hotel near the train station, but a fair distance from the centre. Double rooms have bath and TV. ❹

The Town

At the heart of old Badajoz is the **Plaza de España** and the squat thirteenth-century **Catedral** (Tues–Sat 11am–1pm; free), a fortress-like building, prettified a little during the Renaissance by the addition of a portal and embellishment of the tower.

Northeast of the square, c/de San Juan leads to **Plaza Alta**, once an elegant arcaded concourse, now seedy, and what remains of the town's fortress, the **Alcazaba**. This is largely in ruins but preserves Moorish entrance gates and fragments of a Renaissance palace inside. Part of it houses a **Museo Arqueológico** (Tues–Sun 10am–3pm; €1.20), with local Roman and Visigothic finds. Defending the townward side is the octagonal Moorish **Torre del Aprendiz**, or *Torre Espantaperros* ("dog-scarer" – the dogs in question being Christians).

The Río Guadiana is the city's only other distinguished feature, and in particular the graceful **Puente de Palmas**, or Puente Viejo, spanning its course. The bridge was designed by Herrera (architect of El Escorial) as a fitting first impression of Spain, and leads into the city through the **Puerta de Palmas**, once a gate in the walls, now standing alone as a sort of triumphal arch.

From the plaza behind this arch, c/Santa Lucía leads to c/Duque de San Germán where you'll find the **Museo de Bellas Artes** (Tues–Fri 10am–2pm & 4–6pm, summer till 8pm, Sat & Sun 10am–2pm; free), which includes works by local boy Luís Morales, and a couple of good panels by Zurbarán. Near Plaza de la Constitución and off Avenida Calzadillas Maestre, is the **Museo de Arte Contemporáneo** (summer Tues–Sat 10.30am–1.30pm & 6–9pm, Sun 10.30am–1.30pm; winter Tues–Sat 10.30am–1.30pm & 5–8pm, Sun 10.30am–1.30pm; free). This striking building houses a wealth of modern paintings, installations and sculpture, by artists from Spain, Portugal and Latin America.

Eating, drinking and nightlife

The area around c/Muñoz Torrero, a couple of blocks below the Plaza de España, is the most promising site for reasonably priced food and tapas bars. For **nightlife**, *Mercantil* (daily 4.30pm–2/5am), off Plaza España at c/Zurbarán 10, is a stylish bar which also has live guitar-based music at the weekend.

Cocina Portugesa, c/Muñoz Torrero 1. Best budget bet in Badajoz with tasty, reasonably priced Portuguese cooking and a €5.10 *menú*.

Doska II, Avda. de Colom 3. Just off Plaza Santo Domingo, this well-priced place is very popular with locals, serving a wide range of generous, well-cooked specialities in the nautically themed restaurant. Under €12 a head, or there's a €7.80 *menú*.

Los Monjes, in the *Gran Hotel Zurbarán* ☎924 223 741. Probably the best food in town, with a pricey range of Spanish dishes, but a slightly char-

acterless place. À la carte will probably set you back around €30, though there's also a €11.40 lunchtime buffet. Reservation recommended.

La Toja, Avda. Elvas 22 – the Portugal road. An excellent restaurant, run by a *gallego*, so serving food from Extremadura and Galicia. A bit of a trek from the centre, though if you drive it has its own parking. Moderately pricey. Closed Sun pm.

El Tronco, c/Muñoz Torrero 16. Perhaps the best reason to stay in town – this has a vast range of superb-value bar snacks and excellent regional food and wine in the restaurant.

Southern Extremadura

The routes **south from Mérida or Badajoz** cross territory that is mostly harsh and unrewarding, fit only for sheep and the odd cork or olive tree, until you come upon the foothills of the Sierra Morena, on the borders of Andalucía. En route, **Olivenza**, a town that has spent more time in Portugal than Spain, is perhaps the most attractive stop, and offers a road approach to Évora, the most interesting city of southern Portugal.

Olivenza

Twenty-five kilometres southwest of Badajoz, whitewashed **OLIVENZA** seems to have landed in the wrong country; long disputed between Spain and Portugal, it has been Spanish since 1801. Yet not only are the buildings and the town's character clearly Portuguese, the oldest inhabitants still cling to this language – you may overhear them chatting as they relax in the main square, the Plaza de España, where the buses stop. There's a local saying here: "the women from Olivenza are not like the rest, for they are the daughters of Spain and the granddaughters of Portugal."

The town has long been strongly fortified, and traces of the **walls and gates** can still be seen, even though houses have been built up against them. They extend up to the **castle**, which has three surviving towers, and an ethnographic **museum** (Tues–Sun 11am–2pm & 5–8pm) within. Right beside the castle is the seventeenth-century church of **Santa María del Castillo** (daily 9am–1pm & 5–8pm), and around the corner, **Santa María Magdalena** (daily 9am–2pm), built a century later. The latter is in the distinctive Portuguese Manueline style, with arcades of twisted columns; the former is a more sober Renaissance affair with three aisles of equal height and a notable work of art in the huge "Tree of Jesse" *retablo*. Both have sturdy bell towers and light, airy interiors adorned with *azulejo* and ornate Baroque altars. Just across the street from Santa María Magdalena is a former **palace**, now the public library, with a spectacular Manueline doorway. Continuing down this street, then taking the first turning on the left onto c/Coridad, you come to the early sixteenth-century **Hospital**, which still serves its original purpose. Its chapel (staff will open it up for you on request) is covered with early-eighteenth-century *azulejos*.

There's a **turismo** kiosk on the Plaza de España (summer: Tues–Fri 10am–2.30pm & 5–7pm, Sat & Sun 10am–2pm; winter: Tues–Fri 10am–2.30pm & 4–6pm, Sat & Sun 10am–2pm; closed alternate weekends when the castle museum will provide information; ☎924 490 151, ⓔotolivenca@bme.es/). Should you want to stay in Olivenza, there's a **hotel** on the fringes of town, at the exit to Badajoz, the *Heredero* (☎924 490 835, ℗924 491 261; ⑤), which has a restaurant. Those on a budget should head for *Los Amigos* (☎924 490 725; ③), back in town on Avenida del Perú. You'll find a public **swimming pool** by the football ground, on Avenida Portugal, near the Badajoz exit.

Towards Portugal

Twelve kilometres northwest of Olivenza, a road heading towards Portugal stops abruptly at the ruined bridge of **Puente Ayuda**, where the Río Guadiana forms the border between the two countries. There's no way on other than to swim but it's a picturesque picnic spot; the river runs across many exposed rock beds giving good fishing, and it's also an ideal spot for some discreet camping. To **enter Portugal**, you need to follow the C436 south from Olivenza for 39km to the Spanish border at **Villanueva del Fresno**. From here it's 16km to **Mourao**, the first Portuguese town on this approach, which is on the main road (and bus route) to Évora.

South to Jerez de los Caballeros

The road from Badajoz to Jerez de los Caballeros is typical of southern Extremadura, striking across a parched landscape whose hamlets – low huts and a whitewashed church strung out along the road – look as if they have been dumped from some low-budget Western set of a Mexican frontier town. It's a cruel country which bred cruel people, if we are to believe the names of places like Valle de Matamoros (Valley of the Moorslayers), and one can easily understand the attraction which the New World and the promise of the lush Indies must have held for its inhabitants.

It is hardly surprising, then, that **JEREZ DE LOS CABALLEROS** produced a whole crop of *conquistadores*. The two most celebrated are Vasco Núñez de Balboa, discoverer of the Pacific, and Hernando de Soto (also known as the Conqueror of Florida), who in exploring the Mississippi became one of the first Europeans to set foot in North America. You're not allowed to forget it either – the bus station is in the Plaza de Vasco Núñez de Balboa, complete with a statue of Vasco in the very act of discovery, and from it the Calle Hernando de Soto leads up into the middle of town.

It's a quiet, friendly place, through which many tourists pass but few stay. Grass grows up through many of the cobbled streets and life goes on unhurriedly. From a distance it is the church towers that dominate the walled old town: a passion for building spires gripped the place in the eighteenth century, when three churches had new ones erected. The silhouette of each is clearly based on that of the Giralda at Sevilla, but they are all distinctively decorated: the first is **San Miguel**, in the central Plaza de España, made of carved brick; the second is the unmistakeable red-, blue- and ochre-glazed tower of **San Bartolomé**, on the hill above it, with a striking tiled facade; and the third, rather dilapidated, belongs to **Santa Catalina**, outside the walls.

Above the Plaza de España the streets climb up to the restored remains of a **castle** of the Knights Templar (this was once an embattled frontier town), mostly late thirteenth century but with obvious Moorish influences. Adjoining the castle, and predating it by over a century (as do the town walls), is the church of **Santa María**. Built on a Visigothic site, it's more interesting seen from the battlements above than from the inside. In the small park below the castle walls, a café commands fine views of the surrounding countryside and the magnificent sunsets.

There's a small **turismo** in the *ayuntamiento* on Plaza de San Agustín (daily

9.30am–2.30pm & 4.30–6.30pm; ☎924 730 372). **Places to stay** are few. By far the cheapest is the *Pensión El Gordito*, Avda. de Portugal 104 (☎924 731 452; ❶), which is good for the price. The more upmarket alternatives are the *Hotel Oasis*, c/El Campo 18 (☎924 731 836, ☏924 731 453, ✉doasis@interbook.net; ❺), and *Hostal Las Torres*, on the road out to Oliva de la Frontera (☎924 730 368; ❸). The *Oasis* has the only real **restaurant** in town; for tapas and *pitarra* wine, try *La Ermita*, an old chapel on c/Dr Benitez.

Zafra

If you plan to stick to the main routes or are heading south from Mérida, **ZAFRA** is rather less of a detour, though it's also much more frequented by tourists. It's famed mainly for its **castle** – now converted into a *parador* – which is remarkable for the white marble Renaissance patio designed by Juan de Herrera.

Two beautiful arcaded plazas, the Plaza Grande and the Plaza Chica, adjoin each other in the town centre. The most attractive of several interesting churches is **Nuestra Señora de la Candelaria** (summer: Mon–Sat 10.30am–1.30pm & 6.30–8.30pm, Sun 11am–1pm & 7–7.30pm; winter 10.30am–1pm & 5.30–7.30pm, Sun 11am–1pm), with nine panels by Zurbarán in the *retablo* and a chapel by Churriguera; the entrance is on c/José through a small gateway, around the side of the church. Also worth a look are the tombs of the Figueroa family (the original inhabitants of the castle) in the **Convento de Santa Clara** (daily: summer 6–8pm; winter 5–7pm), just off the main shopping street, c/Sevilla; ring the bell to get in.

This region is famous for its wines, and you can visit the **Bodega Medina**, c/Cestria (Mon–Fri 2–8pm); call in at the **turismo** in the Plaza de España (Mon–Fri 9.30am–4.30pm, Sat & Sun 10.30am–2.30pm; ☎924 551 036, ✉oitzafra@teleline.es) to make an appointment.

Accommodation options include the *parador* (☎924 554 540, ☏924 551 018; ❽), *Hotel El Ancla*, Plaza de España 8 (☎924 554 382; ❻), *Hotel Las Palmeras*, Plaza Grande 14 (☎924 552 208; ❻), and *Hostal Carmen*, Avda. Estación 9 (☎924 551 439; ❺), which also boasts an excellent medium-priced restaurant. The cheapest and best-value place, however, is the friendly *Hostal Arias* (☎924 554 855, ☏924 554 888; ❺), 200m out of town on the Carretera Badajoz–Granada, which has en-suite rooms and a good restaurant with a €7.25 *menú*.

South of Zafra: the Sierra Morena

Beyond Zafra the main road and the railway head straight down through the **Sierra Morena** towards **Sevilla**. By **road** it's more interesting – though bus services are less frequent – to go through **Fregenal de La Sierra** (where the road from Jerez de los Caballeros joins up) into the heart of the sierra around Aracena. On the **train** you can reach another interesting region by getting off at the station of Cazalla-Constantina, while if you're heading for **Córdoba** and eastern Andalucía, you should change at Los Rosales before reaching Sevilla.

Travel details

Trains

Albacete to: Alicante (7–9 daily; 1hr 35min); Madrid (23 daily; 2–3hr); Valencia (13 daily; 1hr 30min–2hr 20min).

Badajoz to: Cáceres (2 daily; 2hr); Lisbon via Elvas (1 daily; 5hr); Madrid (4 daily; 5–7hr); Mérida (7 daily; 50min); Plasencia (1 daily; 3hr).

Cáceres to: Badajoz (2 daily; 2hr); Lisbon (1 daily; 5hr 20min); Madrid (5 daily; 4–5hr); Mérida (5 daily; 1hr); Plasencia (4 daily; 1hr 10min); Sevilla (1 daily; 5hr 40min); Zafra (2 daily; 2hr 10min).

Ciudad Real to: Almagro (5 daily; 15min); Madrid (8 daily; 50min).

Cuenca to: Madrid (6 daily; 2hr 30min); Valencia (4 daily; 3hr 10min).

Madrid to: Albacete (15 daily; 2hr 10min); Almagro (1 daily; 2hr 30min); Badajoz (3 daily; 5hr 30min–7hr 30min); Cáceres (5 daily; 3hr 30min–4hr 30min); Ciudad Real (2 daily; 3hr; 8 daily AVE; 55min); Cuenca (6 daily; 2hr 30min); Mérida (6 daily; 6hr); Navalmoral (9 daily; 1hr 50min–2hr 25min); Plasencia (5 daily; 3hr 30min); Sigüenza (10 daily; 1hr 30min–2hr); Talavera de la Reina (8–9 daily; 2hr–2hr 25min).

Mérida to: Badajoz (7 daily; 50min); Cáceres (5 daily; 1hr); Madrid (6 daily; 6hr); Plasencia (6 daily; 2hr–2hr 25min); Sevilla (1 daily; 4hr 35min).

Plasencia to: Badajoz (1 daily; 3hr); Cáceres (4 daily; 1hr 10min); Madrid (5 daily; 3hr 30min); Mérida (3 daily; 2hr–2hr 25min).

Sigüenza to: Barcelona (1 daily; at least 6hr 30min), via Zaragoza (3–4hr); Madrid (9 daily; 1 hr 30min–2hr 15min); Medinaceli (1 daily; 15min).

Buses

Albacete to: Alicante (6 daily; 2hr 30min); Cuenca (2–3 daily; 2hr 45min); Madrid (6 daily; 3hr); Murcia (2–6 daily; 2hr 15min); Parque Natural de las Lagunes de Ruidera (Mon–Sat 1 daily; 2hr); Valencia (8 daily; 3hr).

Badajoz to: Cáceres (7 daily; 2hr); Caia (Portuguese frontier; 4 daily; 30min); Córdoba (3 daily; 5hr); Lisbon (2 daily; 7hr); Madrid (7 daily; 4hr 30min–5hr); Mérida (8 daily; 45min); Murcia (1 daily; 9hr 20min); Olivenza (12 daily; 30min); Sevilla (2–5 daily; 4hr 30min); Zafra (8 daily; 1hr 30min).

Cáceres to: Alcántara (2 daily; 1hr 30min); Arroyo de la Luz (8–15 daily; 30min); Badajoz (4 daily; 1hr 15min–1hr 45min); Coria (4 daily; 1hr 15min); Guadalupe (2 daily; 2hr 30min); Madrid (8 daily; 4hr); Mérida (4 daily; 1hr); Plasencia (4–5 daily; 1hr 20min); Salamanca (4 daily; 3hr 30min); Sevilla (8 daily; 4hr); Trujillo (8 daily; 45min).

Ciudad Real to: Almagro (6 daily; 1hr); Córdoba (1 daily; 4hr 30min); Jaén (2 daily; 4hr); Madrid (4 daily; 4hr); Toledo (1 daily; 3hr), Valdepeñas (3 daily; 2hr).

Cuenca to: Albacete (2–3 daily; 2hr 45min); Barcelona (1 daily; 9hr); Madrid (9 daily; 2hr–2hr 30min); Teruel (1 daily; 2hr 30min); Valencia (2–3 daily; 2hr 30min–3hr 30min).

Guadalupe to: Cáceres (2 daily; 2hr 30min); Madrid (2 daily; 4hr); Trujillo (2 daily; 2hr–2hr 30min).

Madrid to Albacete (7 daily; 3hr 45min); Badajoz (7 daily; 4hr 30min–5hr); Cáceres (8 daily; 4hr); Cuenca (9 daily; 2hr–2hr 30min); Jarandilla (1 daily; 3hr 30min); Mérida (8–9 daily; 4hr 20min); Plasencia (2 daily; 4hr); Talavera de la Reina (15 daily; 1hr 30min); Trujillo (11 daily; 3hr–3hr 30min).

Mérida to: Badajoz (8 daily; 45min); Cáceres (7 daily; 1hr); Guadalupe (4 daily; 2hr); Jerez de los Caballeros (1–3 daily; 2hr); Madrid (8–9 daily; 4hr 20min); Murcia (1 daily; 9hr); Salamanca (5 daily; 4hr); Sevilla (6–8 daily; 3hr 15min, some stopping in Zafra); Trujillo (4 daily; 2hr); Zafra (1–3 daily; 1hr 10min).

Navalmoral to: Jarandilla (2 daily; 3hr); Plasencia (2 daily; 2–4hr); Trujillo (6 daily; 1hr).

Plasencia to: Cáceres (4–5 daily; 1hr 20min); Jarandilla (2 daily; 2hr); Madrid (2 daily; 4hr); Salamanca (4 daily; 2hr).

Talavera de la Reina to: Guadalupe (2 daily; 2hr 30min); Madrid (15 daily; 1hr 30min); Toledo (10 daily; 1hr 30min).

Trujillo to: Cáceres (8 daily; 45min); Guadalupe (2 daily; 2hr); Madrid (13–16 daily; 3hr–3hr 30min); Mérida (4 daily; 2hr).

Andalucía

Highlights

4

Andalucía

bove all else – and there is plenty – it's the great **Moorish monuments** that compete for your attention in **Andalucía**. The Moors, a mixed race of Berbers and Arabs who crossed into Spain from Morocco and North Africa, occupied *al-Andalus* for over seven centuries. Their first forces landed at Tarifa in 710 AD and within four years they had conquered virtually the entire country; their last kingdom, Granada, fell to the Christian Reconquest in 1492. Between these dates they developed the most sophisticated civilization of the Middle Ages, centred in turn on the three major cities of **Córdoba**, **Sevilla** and **Granada**. Each one preserves extraordinarily brilliant and beautiful monuments, of which the most perfect is Granada's **Alhambra palace**, arguably the most sensual building in all of Europe. **Sevilla**, not to be outdone, has a fabulously ornamented Alcázar and the greatest of all Gothic cathedrals. Today, Andalucía's capital and seat of the region's autonomous parliament is a vibrant contemporary metropolis that's impossible to resist. Córdoba's exquisite **Mezquita**, the grandest and most beautiful mosque constructed by the Moors, is a landmark building in world architecture and also not to be missed.

These three cities have, of course, become major tourist destinations, but the smaller **inland towns** of Andalucía are often totally unspoiled. These offer amazing potential; Renaissance towns such as **Úbeda**, **Baeza** and **Osuna**, **Guadix** with its cave suburb, Moorish **Carmona** and the stark white hill towns around **Ronda**, are all easily accessible by local buses. Travelling for some time here you'll also get a feel for the landscape of Andalucía: occasionally

---

Accommodation price codes

All the establishments listed in this book have been price-graded according to the following scale. The prices quoted are for the **cheapest available double room in high season**; effectively this means that anything in the ❶ and most places in the ❷ range will be without private bath, though there's usually a washbasin in the room. In the ❹ category and above you will probably be getting private facilities. Remember, though, that many of the budget places will also have more expensive rooms including en-suite facilities. Youth hostels are graded under ❶ as the price per person is less than half of the category's upper limit.

Note that in the more upmarket *hostales* and *pensiones*, and in anything calling itself a hotel, you'll pay a **tax** (IVA) of seven percent on top of the room price.

❶ Under €12	❹ €27–36	❼ €60–90
❷ €12–18	❺ €36–48	❽ €90–120
❸ €18–27	❻ €48–60	❾ Over €120

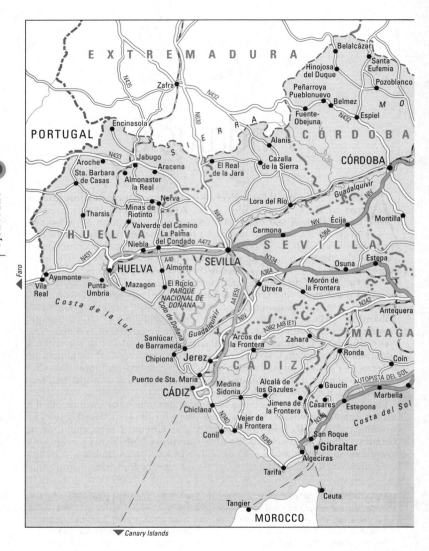

Canary Islands

spectacularly beautiful but more often impressive on a huge, unyielding scale, distinguished by a patchwork of colours and the interaction of land and buildings, or the gradual appearance of villages grouped beneath a castle and church.

The province also takes in mountains – including the **Sierra Nevada**, Spain's highest range. You can ski here in February, and then drive down to the coast to swim the same day. Perhaps more compelling, though, are the opportunities for walking in the lower slopes, **Las Alpujarras**. Alternatively, there's good trekking amongst the gentler (and much less-known) hills of the **Sierra Morena**, north of Sevilla.

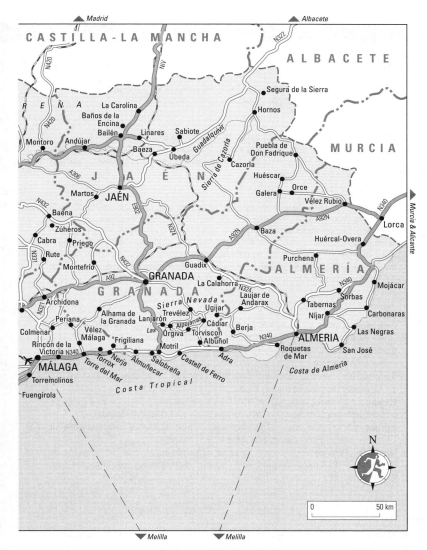

On the **coast** it's easy to despair. Extending to either side of **Málaga** is the **Costa del Sol**, Europe's most heavily developed resort area, with its beaches hidden behind a remorseless density of concrete hotels and apartment complexes. However, the province takes in two alternatives, much less developed and with some of the best beaches in all Spain. These are the villages **between Tarifa and Cádiz** on the Atlantic, and those **around Almería** on the southeast corner of the Mediterranean. The Almerian beaches allow warm swimming through all but the winter months; those near Cádiz, more easily accessible, are fine from about June to September. Near Cádiz, too, is the **Coto de**

Fiestas

January

1–2 *La Toma* celebration of the entry of the Reyes Católicos into the city – at Granada.

6 *Romería de la Virgen del Mar* pilgrimage procession from Almería.

17 *Romería del Ermita del Santo.* Similar event at Guadix.

February

1 *San Cecilio* fiesta in Granada's traditionally gypsy quarter of Sacromonte.

Week before Lent *Carnaval* is an extravagant week-long event in all the Andalucian cities. Cádiz, above all, celebrates, with uproarious street parades, fancy dress and satirical music competitions.

March/April

Holy Week (*Semana Santa*) has its most elaborate and dramatic celebrations in Andalucía. You'll find memorable processions of floats and penitents at Sevilla, Málaga, Granada and Córdoba and to a lesser extent in smaller towns such as Jerez, Arcos, Baeza and Úbeda. All culminate with dramatic candlelight processions at dawn on Good Friday, with Easter Day itself more of a family occasion.

Last week of April (approximately 2 weeks after Easter) Week-long *Feria de Abril* at Sevilla: the largest fair in Spain. A small April fair – featuring bull running – is held in Vejer.

May

First week *Cruces de Mayo* in Córdoba celebrates the Holy Cross and includes a "prettiest patio" competition in a town full of prize examples.

Early May (usually the week after Sevilla's fair). Somewhat aristocratic *Horse Fair* at Jerez de la Frontera.

3 *Moros y Cristianos* ("Moors and Christians") carnival at Pampaneira (Alpujarras).

17 *San Isidro Romería* at Setenil (Cádiz).

Pentecost (7 weeks after Easter) *Romería del Rocío*, when horse-drawn carriages and processions converge from all over the south on El Rocío (Huelva).

Corpus Christi (variable – Thursday after Trinity) Bullfights and festivities at Granada, Sevilla, Ronda, Vejer and Zahara de la Sierra.

Last week *Feria de la Manzanilla*, Sanlúcar de Barrameda. Prolonged binge to celebrate the town's major product, with flamenco and sporting events on the river beach.

Doñana national park, Spain's largest and most important nature reserve, which is home to a spectacular range of flora and fauna.

The realities of life in **contemporary Andalucía** can be stark. **Unemployment** in the region is the highest in Spain – over twenty percent in many areas – and an even larger proportion of the population is still engaged in agriculture. Rural life is bleak; you soon begin to notice the appalling economic structure, at its most extreme in this part of Spain, of vast absentee-landlord estates and landless peasants. The *andaluz* villages, bastions of anarchist and socialist groups before and during the Civil War, saw little economic aid or change during the Franco years – or indeed since. For the last twenty years, the province has been an **autonomous region** with its own parliament and a substantial degree of self-government.

June

Second week *Feria de San Bernabé* at Marbella, often spectacular since this is the richest town in Andalucía.

13 *San Antonio* fiesta at Trevélez (Alpujarras) with mock battles between Moors and Christians.

Third week The Algeciras fair and fiesta, another major event of the south.

23–24 *Candelas de San Juan* – bonfires and effigies at Vejer and elsewhere.

30 Conil *feria*.

End June/early July *International Festival of Music and Dance* – major dance/flamenco groups and chamber orchestras perform in Granada's Alhambra palace, Generalife and Carlos V palace.

July

Early July The *International Guitar Festival* at Córdoba brings together top international acts from classical, flamenco and Latin American music.

End of month *Virgen del Mar* – Almería's major annual shindig, with parades, horse-riding events, concerts and lots of drinking.

August

5 Trevélez observes a midnight *romería* to Mulhacén.

13–21 *Feria de Málaga* – one of Andalucía's most enjoyable fiestas for visitors, who are heartily welcomed by the ebullient *malagueños*.

15 *Ascension of the Virgin Fair* with *casetas* (dance tents) at Vejer and elsewhere. Riotous *Noche del Vino* wine festival at Competa (Málaga).

Third week The first cycle of horse races along Sanlúcar de Barrameda's beach, with heavy official and unofficial betting; the second tournament takes place a week later.

23–25 *Guadalquivir festival* at Sanlúcar de Barrameda with bullfights and an important flamenco competition.

September

First two weeks Ronda's annual *feria* with flamenco contests and *Corrida Goyesca* – bullfights in eighteenth-century dress.

1–3 Celebration of the *Virgen de la Luz* in Tarifa: processions and horseback riding.

First/second week *Vendimia* (celebration of the vintage) at Jerez.

29–Oct 2 *Feria* in Órgiva (Alpujarras).

October

1 *San Miguel* fiesta in Granada's Albaicín quarter and elsewhere, even at Torremolinos.

15–23 *Feria de San Lucas* – Jaén's major fiesta, dating back to the fifteenth century.

The day labourers, *jornaleros*, earn a precarious living from seasonal work, and as recently as 1986 the regional government instituted land reform in an effort to head off a peasants' revolt. Numerous instances of land occupation have resulted in violent clashes between labourers and the Civil Guard. Throughout the 1990s, tourism, and ventures such as Expo '92 in Sevilla, have brought some changes – above all radical improvements in infrastructure, with new road and rail projects aimed at providing faster connections within the region and with Madrid and Barcelona – but much still remains to be done.

For all its poverty however, Andalucía is also Spain at its most exuberant: the home of flamenco and the bullfight, and those wild and extravagant clichés of the Great Spanish Dream. These really do exist and can be absorbed at one of the hundreds of annual **fiestas**, **ferias** and **romerías**. The best of them include

Finding accommodation at Easter

Andalucía's major festival is the Easter processions, and you should be aware that during the whole of Easter week it is almost impossible to find accommodation in the cities of Málaga, Sevilla, Córdoba and Granada plus the other provincial capitals without booking well ahead. However, the smaller towns and villages surrounding them remain largely unaffected, should still have vacancies and are easy enough to reach with your own transport or by bus. However, it would still be wise to ring ahead first. Following Easter Sunday things revert to normal.

the giant **April Feria** in Sevilla, the ageless pilgrimage to **El Rocío** near Huelva in late May, and the dramatically moving **Semana Santa** (Easter) celebrations at Málaga, Granada, Sevilla, Córdoba and Jerez, as well as in countless small villages.

The Costa del Sol

The outstanding feature of the **Costa del Sol** is its ease of access. Hundreds of charter flights arrive here every week, and it's often possible to get an absurdly cheap ticket from other cities in Europe, particularly London. **Málaga**

The carretera nacional N340

A special note of warning has to be made about the **Costa del Sol's main highway**, which is one of the most dangerous roads in Europe. Nominally a national highway, it's really a 100-kilometre-long city street, passing through the middle of towns and *urbanizaciones*. Drivers treat it like a motorway, yet pedestrians have to get across, and cars are constantly turning off or into the road – hence the terrifying number of accidents, with, on average, over a hundred fatalities a year. A large number of casualties are inebriated British package tourists unfamiliar with left-hand-drive vehicles and traffic patterns. The first few kilometres, between the airport, with its various car rental offices, and Torremolinos, are among the most treacherous, but worse still is the stretch heading west from Marbella: around thirty accidents a year occur on each kilometre between Marbella and San Pedro.

A new four-lane toll motorway to replace it – the **Autopista del Sol** – linking Málaga with Estepona in the west and Nerja in the east has recently been completed but there has been a great protest from locals about the high charges to use it. High-season or summer tolls cost between €2.70 and €4.50 for relatively short stretches of road and around €8 for the whole Málaga–Estepona journey – low-season (Oct–May) rates are roughly half this – and due to misleading road signs it is easy to end up paying the toll without intending to. Unwilling to pay the charges, many locals have given the new road the thumbs down, leaving the N340 as bad as ever and the new *autopista* often devoid of traffic.

If you do use the N340 don't make dangerous (and illegal) left turns from the fast lane – use the "Cambio de Sentido" junctions which allow you to reverse direction. Also be particularly careful after heavy rain, when the hot, oily road surface sends you easily into a skid. **Pedestrians** should cross at traffic lights, a bridge or an underpass if possible.

airport is positioned midway between Málaga, the main city on the coast, and **Torremolinos**, its most grotesque resort. You can easily reach either town by taking the electric train which runs every thirty minutes (daily 7am–11.45pm) along the coast between Málaga and **Fuengirola**. Granada, Córdoba and Sevilla are all within easy reach of Málaga; so too, and covered in this section, are **Ronda** and the "White Towns" to the west, and a handful of relatively restrained coastal resorts to the east. **Beaches** along this stretch are generally grit-grey rather than golden, but the sea is reliably clean, after a lot of work on the sewerage system.

Economically, the coastal hinterland is undergoing a gradual resurgence, in contrast to the general decline in the rest of Andalucía. In recent years the cultivation of subtropical fruits such as mangos, papayas, guavas, lychees and avocados has replaced the traditional orange, lemon and almond trees. Most farm labourers, however, can't afford coastal land; those who buy are often former migrants to France and Germany who have been forced to return because of the unemployment situation there.

Málaga

MÁLAGA seems at first an uninviting place. It's the second city of the south (after Sevilla), with a population of half a million, and is also one of the poorest: official unemployment figures for the area estimate the jobless at one in four of the workforce. Yet though many people get no further than the train or bus stations, and though the clusters of high-rises look pretty grim as you approach, it has its attractions. The elegant central zone has a number of interesting churches and museums, not to mention the **birthplace of Picasso** and the new **Picasso Museum**, housing an important collection of works by Málaga's most famous son. Around the old fishing villages of **El Palo** and **Pedregalejo**, now absorbed into the suburbs, are a series of small beaches and a *paseo* lined with some of the best **fish and seafood cafés** in the province. And overlooking the town and port are the formidable Moorish citadels of the **Alcazaba** and **Gibralfaro** – excellent introductions to the architecture before pressing on to the main sites at Córdoba and Granada.

Arrival and information

From the **airport**, the **electric train** provides the easiest approach to Málaga (every 30min, 7am–11.45pm; €1). From the Arrivals hall, **go up one floor** to the *Salidas* or Departures hall, take any exit and then turn right to reach a pedestrian overpass at the end of the airport building. Follow the *Ferrocarril* signs and cross the overpass (trolleys allowed) to the unmanned station; you can buy tickets from the sweet kiosk, if open, from a ticket machine just next to it or on the train. Make sure that you're on the Málaga platform (the furthest away from you) and stay on the train right to the end of the line, the **Centro–Alameda** stop (about a 12min ride). The stop before this is RENFE, the main **train station**, a slightly longer walk into the heart of town (bus #3 runs from here to the centre every 10min or so). Alternatively, city **bus** #19 leaves from a stop outside the Arrivals hall (every 30min until midnight; €0.85) stopping at the train and bus stations en route to the centre and the Paseo del Parque near the port, from where you can also take it in the opposite direction to the airport.

The **bus station** is just behind the RENFE station, a bit to the right as you face the RENFE logo from the esplanade. All buses (run by a number of dif-

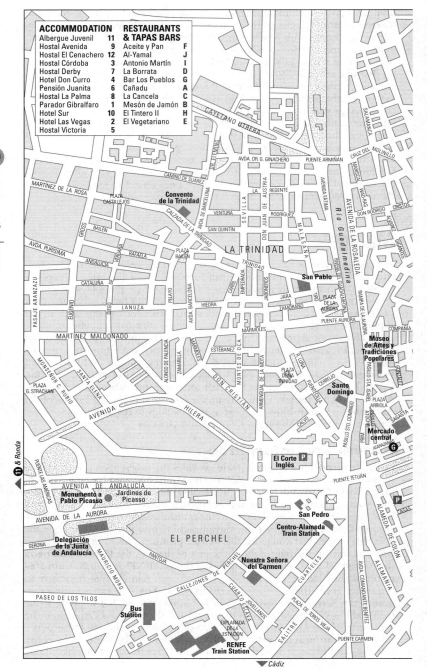

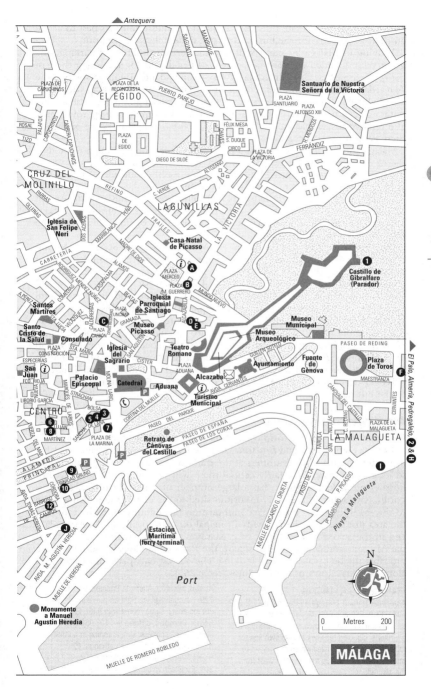

Antequera

PLAZA DE
CAPUCHINOS

PLAZA DE LA
RECONQUISTA

EL EGIDO

PUERTO PAREJO

Santuario de Nuestra
Señora de la Victoria

PLAZA
SANTUARIO

PLAZA
ALFONSO XIII

ROSAL

TIZO

ROSAL
PALAFOX
CASTICHINOS
CARRERA CAPUCHINOS

PLAZA
DE
EGIDO

FÉLIX MESA
S. DUQUE

PLAZA DE
LA VICTORIA

CIRCO

FERRANDIZ

OLLERAS

PARRAS

REFINO

DIEGO DE SILOÉ
ALTOZANO

CRUZ DEL
MOLINILLO

C. VERDE

LAGUNILLAS

LA VICTORIA

Iglesia de
San Felipe
Neri

DOS ACERAS
PEÑA
FRAILES

MARIBLANCA

Casa Natal
de Picasso

CARRETERÍA

MADRE DE DIOS

ÁLAMOS

RODRÍGUEZ
MÉNDEZ NÚÑEZ
COMETAS

ÁLAMOS

PLAZA
MERCED

Castillo de
Gibralfaro
(Parador)

SANTA LUCÍA
VELÁZQUEZ

CASAPALMA

PLAZA
M. GUERRERO

Iglesia
Parroquial
de Santiago

MUNDO NUEVO

Santos
Mártires

CARBONEROS

BEATAS

PLAZA
UNCIBAY
GRANADA

ALCAZABILLA

Santo
Cristo de
la Salud

Consulado

PLAZA
CAÑON

PARRAS

Museo
Picasso

Museo
Municipal

ESPECERÍAS

PLAZA
CONSTITUCIÓN
STA. MARÍA

Iglesia
del Sagrario

SAN AGUSTÍN

CISTER

Teatro
Romano

Museo
Arqueológico

PASEO DE REDING

San
Juan

FCO. RIOJA

MARQUÉS DE LARIOS

MOLINA LARIO

Palacio
Episcopal

Catedral

Aduana

PLAZA
ADUANA

Alcazaba

Ayuntamiento

GUILLÉN SOTELO

Fuente
(de)
Génova

Plaza
de Toros

LIBORIO GARCÍA

STRACHAN

Turismo
Municipal

AVDA. CERVANTES

MAESTRANZA

CÁNOVAS DEL CASTILLO

CERVANTES

CENTRO

PUERTA DEL MAR

SANCHA DE LARA

BOLSA

PLAZA
DE LA MARINA

CORTINA DEL MUELLE

PASEO DEL MUELLE

PASEO DEL PARQUE

C. REDING

SAN NICOLÁS

PLAZA DE LA
MALAGUETA

LA MALAGUETA

MARTÍNEZ

Retrato de
Cánovas
del Castillo

PASEO DE ESPAÑA

PASEO DE LOS CURAS

FAROLA

ALAMEDA PRINCIPAL

TRINIDAD GRUND

CÓRDOBA

BARROSO

ATARAZANAS HEREDIA

CAMPOS

Estación
Marítima
(ferry terminal)

MUELLE DE RICARDO G. DIBUELA

PASEO DE LA

PASEO MARÍTIMO
P. PICASSO

Playa La Malagueta

ANDA. M. AGUSTÍN HEREDIA

MUELLE DE HEREDIA

Monumento
a Manuel
Agustín Heredia

Port

N

0   Metres   200

MUELLE DE ROMERO ROBLEDO

MÁLAGA

El Palo, Almería, Pedregalejo,

255

ferent companies) operate from this terminal. In midsummer it's best to arrive an hour or so early for the bus to Granada, since tickets can sell out.

Arriving in Málaga by **car** you'll face the serious problem of parking; one good-value guarded car park (about €1.20 per day) is located along the east bank of the Río Guadalmedina (Avda. Comandante Benitez), below the Alameda. As **theft from cars** is rampant in Málaga you should strip your vehicle of all valuables before leaving it on the street overnight, or else use a hotel with a garage or one of the pay car parks marked on the city map. You should also remove any visible stickers bearing a car rental company's name or logo as these are a magnet for thieves.

Málaga also has the remnants of a **passenger ferry port**, though these days there's a service only to the Spanish enclave of Melilla in Morocco. If you're heading for Fes and eastern Morocco, this is a useful connection – particularly so for taking a car over – though most people go for the quicker services at Algeciras (see p.276) and Tarifa (see p.314) to the west. Sailings are daily except Sunday, generally leaving around 1pm; the crossing takes seven hours. Tickets are available from Transmediterranea (℡952 061 218 or 952 224 391) at the Estación Maritima south of Plaza de la Marina.

The **turismo**, Pasaje de Chinitas 4 (Mon–Fri 8.30am–8pm, Sat & Sun 10am–2pm; ℡952 213 445), can provide full accommodation lists and a detailed map of the city. There's also a useful turismo municipal, Avda. de Cervantes 1 (Mon–Fri 8.15am–2pm & 4.30–7pm, Sat 8.15am–2pm; ℡952 604 410), at the western end of the Paseo del Parque, and another helpful branch at the bus station. There are a couple of **Internet cafés** on the south side of Avenida de Andalucía, near the El Corte Inglés department store: *Cyber@lameda* (℡ & ℱ952 344 558) at no. 13 charges €5 per hour, whilst *Ciber Málaga* (℡952 040 303) at no. 11 will let you check your email at €1.50 for 15 minutes. *Pasatiempos* on Plaza Merced, near Picasso's birthplace, charges similar rates. Reliable and inexpensive **car rental** is available from Turarche, c/Roger de Flor 1 (℡952 318 069, ℱ952 316 342, ⓦwww.turarche.es) next to the bus station.

Accommodation

Málaga boasts dozens of **fondas** and **hostales**, so budget rooms are only really hard to come by around *feria* time, and there are some real bargains available in winter. You may well get offers at the train (or possibly the bus) station, and so long as the rooms are fairly central these will probably be as good as any. Further upmarket, the town has a large number of central **hotels** of all categories, with some of the more luxurious sited to the east of the bullring, close to the sea. Numerous budget accommodation possibilities are to be found in the area just south of the Alameda Principal (known locally as "La Alameda") and in the streets east and west of c/Marques de Larios which cuts between the Alameda and Málaga's main square, the Plaza de la Constitución; these are probably the best places to start looking. The nearest **campsite** lies 10km west along the coast towards Torremolinos (see p.266).

Budget options

Albergue Juvenil Málaga, Plaza de Pio XII ℡952 308 500, ℱ952 308 500. Modern youth hostel on the western outskirts of town, with double and single rooms, disabled facilities and its own sun terrace. Tends to fill up in season so ring ahead to make a reservation. Bus #18 heading west from the Alameda will drop you nearby. ❶

Hostal Avenida, Alameda Principal 5 ℡952 217 729. Functional place right on the Alameda, and not too noisy; some rooms with bath. ❸

Hostal Córdoba, c/Bolsa 9–11 ℡952 214 469. Inexpensive, spotless, simple rooms in a family-run establishment near the cathedral. ❸

Hostal Derby, c/San Juan de Dios 1 ℡952 221 301. Excellent-value fourth-floor *hostal*, just off the

Plaza de la Marina, with some en-suite rooms overlooking the harbour. ❸

Pensión Juanita, c/Alarcón Luján 8 ☏952 213 586. Basic, but clean and central *pensión* on the fourth floor (with a lift). ❸

Hostal La Palma, c/Martínez 7 ☏952 226 772. One of the best of the budget places with new air-conditioned en-suite doubles in addition to their simpler rooms; sometimes willing to give discounts. ❷

Moderate and expensive options

Hotel Don Curro, c/ Sancha de Lara 7 ☏952 227 200, ☏952 215 946. Central and comfortable, if rather featureless, hotel with air-conditioned rooms and car park. ❼

Hostal El Cenachero, c/Barroso 5 ☏952 224 088. Clean, quiet and reasonably priced *hostal*; left

off the seafront end of c/Córdoba. Some rooms en suite. ❹

Parador Gibralfaro, Monte de Gibralfaro ☏952 221 902, ☏952 221 904. You won't get a better panoramic view of the coast than from this eagle's nest on top of the Gibralfaro hill; it's quite small as *paradores* go, but has recently been refurbished and has a pool. Own garage. ❽

Hotel Sur, c/Trinidad Grund 13 ☏952 224 803, ☏952 212 416. Quiet, efficient and central hotel with secure garage; all rooms have bath and TV. ❻

Hotel Las Vegas, Paseo de Sancha 22 ☏952 217 712, ☏952 224 889. Smart hotel, reasonably close to the beach, with its own swimming pool and car park. ❻

Hostal Victoria, c/Sancha de Lara 3 ☏952 224 223. Pleasant, upmarket *hostal* with good-value double and single rooms, just north of the Alameda. ❺

The City

The city's position well east of the airport, and inside the ring road that carries traffic around it, means that most visitors to the Costa del Sol rarely visit the heart of Málaga itself. All this may be about to change as the city has embarked on a costly face-lift, with plans to create hotel-lined promenades along the beaches to the east and west of the centre already well advanced. Away from the seafront glitz, however, it's to be hoped that the city's unique and vibrant character will survive the development unscathed.

The Alcazaba and Gibralfaro

The impressive **Alcazaba** (Tue–Sun 9.30am–8pm; free) is the place to make for if you're killing time between connections. It lies just fifteen minutes' walk from the train or bus stations, and can be clearly seen from most central points. At its entrance stands a lost-looking **Roman theatre**, accidentally unearthed in 1951 and now a venue for various outdoor entertainments. The citadel, too, is Roman in origin, and, interspersed among the Moorish brick of the double- and triple-arched gateways, are blocks and columns of marble. The main structures, recently reopened following a costly three-year restoration, were begun by the Moors in the eighth century, probably soon after their conquest since Málaga was an important port, but the palace higher up the hill dates from the early decades of the eleventh century. It was the residence of the Arab emirs of Málaga, who carved out an independent kingdom for themselves upon the break-up of the western caliphate. Their independence lasted a mere thirty years, but for a while the kingdom grew to include Granada, Carmona and Jaén. The complex's palace, restored as an **archeological museum**, has some fine stuccowork and ceilings and good collections of pottery, for which Málaga was renowned during the thirteenth and fourteenth centuries.

Above the Alcazaba, and connected to it by a long double wall, is the **Gibralfaro castle** (daily 9.30am–8pm; free), reached either by climbing a path uphill from the rear of the museum or by taking the road to the right of the Alcazaba, then following a path up through gardens, a ramble of towers, bougainvillea-draped ramparts and sentry-box-shaped Moorish wells. You can also approach from the town side, as the tourist coaches do, but this is a very unattractive walk and not one to be done alone after sundown. If you want to

△ Casares, Andalucía

avoid the climb altogether, bus #35 goes east from the Paseo del Parque to drop you off just outside the entrance to the Gibralfaro. Last used in 1936 during the Civil War, the castle has, like the Alcazaba, been wonderfully restored and now houses an interesting **museum** dealing with the history of the Gibralfaro – a wonderful scale model lets you see how the city would have looked in Moorish times. A walk around the battlements affords terrific **views** over the city, while the nearby *parador* has a pleasant terrace café and restaurant.

The cathedral, Museo Picasso and other museums

Most conspicuous from the heights is Málaga's peculiar, unfinished **Catedral** (April–Sept 10am–6.45pm; Oct–March 10am–12.45pm & 4–6.45pm; closed Sun except for services; €1.80). Constructed between the sixteenth and eighteenth centuries, it is still lacking a tower on the west front because a radical *malagueño* bishop donated the earmarked money to the American War of Independence against the British. Unfortunately – and despite its huge scale – it also lacks any real inspiration and is distinguished only by an intricately carved and ultrarealistic seventeenth-century *sillería* (choir stall) by noted sculptor Pedro de Mena.

The former Museo de Bellas Artes, just around the corner from the cathedral on c/San Agustín, is to be reborn as the new **Museo Picasso**, housing 182 major works purchased (at a bargain price) from Picasso's daughter-in-law Christine Ruíz-Picasso, who felt that her inheritance should go to the artist's birthplace. Planned to open in the spring of 2002, this date may be put back due to archeological discoveries made during the renovation of the old Bellas Artes building, the former palace of the Counts of Buenavista. For the latest information check with the turismo. The **Bellas Artes collection** – including works by Murillo and Zurbarán – will eventually be housed in the old Aduana building on the Paseo del Parque which it will share with a new archeological museum. A selection of works from the Bellas Artes collection is currently being displayed in the Aduana (Tues 3–8pm, Wed–Fri 9am–8pm, Sat–Sun 9am–3pm; free), but when refurbishment of the building begins in 2002 it is likely to be closed for some time. Again consult the turismo or ⓦwww.andalucia.org for the latest news.

Picasso was born a couple of hundred metres away from his new museum in the Plaza de la Merced, where the **Casa Natal de Picasso** (Mon–Sat 11am–2pm & 5–8pm, Sun 11am–2pm; free) is home to the Fundación Picasso, a centre for scholars researching the painter's life and work. There's a photo display of Picasso's life here, as well as occasional exhibitions, but despite welcoming staff there's not an awful lot more to see. It was in the bars surrounding the square that the infant Pablo saw the first solid shape that he wanted to commit to paper: *churros*, those oil-steeped fritters that *malagueños* love to dip into their breakfast chocolate.

A recent addition to the city's museums is the **Museo Municipal**, Paseo de Reding 1 (Mon–Sat 10am–8pm; free) which is used to house visiting exhibitions from abroad. It's always worth checking out what's on here as recent offerings have included major exhibitions of Flemish and Italian art.

The Jardínes Botánicos La Concepción and El Retiro

There are a couple of pleasant trips out of town if you want to escape the fumes and concrete. The recently opened **Jardín Botánico La Concepción** (guided visits Tues–Sun: June–Sept 10am–7.30pm; Oct–May 10am–4.30pm; €2.75) is a spectacular tropical garden, with many of its botanical specimens planted in the nineteenth century. To get there, bus #2 from the north side of the Alameda will drop you at the gates on Saturday and Sunday, and on week-days at its terminus 700m short, leaving a ten-minute walk to the entrance; alternatively, you can take a taxi from town for about €4.50 one-way. The garden has no restaurant or bar but makes an ideal location for a discreet picnic.

The **El Retiro Jardín Botánico** (daily: April–Sept 9am–8pm; Oct–March 9am–6pm; €7.50, children and senior citizens half-price) lies just west of the airport in Churriana and makes an excellent place to kill a couple of hours while waiting for a flight. Founded by an eighteenth-century bishop of Málaga, the tranquil gardens are studded with fountains, lakes and sculptures and contain more than eight hundred species of plants and trees. The gardens also hold Andalucía's largest **aviary**, where more than a thousand exotic birds from all over the world can be viewed in depressingly cramped cages. El Retiro has a **restaurant** and **bar** but is not well served by public transport; the closest you can get is a bus to Churriana, and then ask for directions. To get there with your own vehicle, take the N340 out of Málaga towards the airport, leaving the road at the Coín–Churriana exit, just beyond the airport turnoff. The garden is sign-posted on the right, a little beyond Churriana village some 4km from the *autovía*. At the time of writing the ownership of El Retiro has changed hands, so check for possible new opening hours with the turismo in Málaga.

Eating and drinking

Málaga has no shortage of **places to eat and drink**, and, though it's hardly a gourmet paradise, the city has a justified reputation for its seafood.

Málaga's greatest claim to fame is undoubtedly its **fried fish**, acknowledged as the best in Spain. You'll find many fish restaurants grouped around the Alameda, although for some of the very best you need to head out to the suburbs of Pedregalejo and El Palo, served by bus #11 (from the Paseo del Parque). On the seafront *paseo* at **Pedregalejo**, almost any of the cafés and restaurants will serve you up terrific fish. Further on, after the *paseo* disappears, you find yourself amid fishing shacks and smaller, sometimes quite ramshackle, cafés. This is **El Palo**, an earthier sort of area for the most part, with a beach and fishing huts, and in summer or at weekends an even better place to eat.

Inexpensive restaurants

Aceite y Pan, c/Cervantes 5. Facing the eastern wall of the Plaza de Toros, this place serves up a wide variety of seafood. When you've chosen your fish from the chilled display you can eat inside or, more atmospherically, at tables on the pavement. Closed Mon.

Bar Los Pueblos, c/Ataranzas, almost opposite the market. Serves satisfying, inexpensive food all day – bean soups and *estofados* are its specialities; *gazpacho* is served in half-pint glasses.

La Borrata, c/Alcazabilla, just north of the Roman Theatre. Good dining place serving up the cheapest three-course *menú* in town for a remarkable €5 (including wine).

Cañadu, Plaza de la Merced 21. A rare vegetarian option serving a good selection of salad- and pasta-based dishes accompanied by organic wines and beers.

La Cancela, c/Denis Belgrano 3, off c/Granada. A *malagueño* institution – *ajo blanco* (chilled almond soup) is a must here – with an economical *ménu* and outdoor tables in a pleasant, pedestrianized street.

Mesón de Jamón, Plaza María Guerrero 5, just off the Plaza Merced. Good-value *menú* and a selection of *jamón* and cheese tapas.

Restaurante Arcos, Alameda 31. Efficient central place serving all-day *platos combinados* and late-night meals – for breakfast they also serve *pan tostada* with wholemeal bread, *pan integral*.

El Tintero II, El Palo. Right at the far east end of the seafront, just before the *Club Náutico* (bus #11; ask for "Tintero Dos"), this is a huge beach restaurant where the waiters charge round with plates of fish (all costing the same for a plate) and you shout for, or grab, anything you like. The fish to go for are, above all, *mero* (a kind of gastro-nomically evolved cod) and *rosada* (equally inde-finable), along with Andalucian regulars such as *boquerones* (fresh anchovies), *gambas* (prawns), *calamares*, *chopos*, *jibia* (different kinds of squid) and *sepia* (cuttlefish). It certainly isn't *haute cuisine* but for sheer entertainment it's a must.

El Vegetariano, Pozo del Rey 5, Just north of the Roman Theatre. Atmospheric – maybe too much so for some as smoking is permitted – little veggie place offering a variety of imaginative pasta-, cheese- and salad-based dishes. They have a twin restaurant, *El Vegetariano de San Bernardo*, at the junction of c/Niño de Guevara and c/Cañuelos de San Bernardo, a couple of blocks west of Plaza de la Merced.

Moderate to expensive restaurants

Al-Yamal, c/Blasco de Garay 3, near *Hostal El Cenachero*. Good North African restaurant serving up meat in spicy sauces, couscous and other typical Arab food.

Antonio Martín, Paseo Maritimo. One of Málaga's renowned fish restaurants and the traditional (and expensive) haunt of *matadores* celebrating their successes in the nearby bullring.

Parador Gilbralfaro, Monte Gilbralfaro. Superior dining on the terrace with spectacular views over the coast and town. The *menú* is excellent value at around €21. If you can't face the climb, bus #35 heading east along the Paseo del Parque will take you there.

Bars and cafés

A number of **traditional bars** serve the sweet **Málaga wine** (Falstaff's "sack"), made from muscatel grapes and dispensed from huge barrels; try it with shellfish at *Antigua Casa Guardia*, a great old nineteenth-century bar at the corner of c/Pastora, on the Alameda's north side. The new season wine, Pedriot, is incredibly sweet; much more palatable is Seco Añejo, which has matured for a year.

Málaga has plenty of good **tapas bars**: *Gorki*, in c/Strachan near the turismo is a popular place at *aperitivo* time, whilst the diminutive size of the bustling *Orellana* at c/Moreno Monroy 5, slightly north, is in inverse proportion to its reputation as one of the best tapas bars in town. Cheaper and earthier options include *La Manchega*, c/Marín García 4, off the west side of c/Larios, and the *Antigua Reja* on Plaza de Uncibay off c/de Méndez Núñez.

Nightlife

You'll find most of Málaga's **nightlife** northeast of the cathedral along and around calles Granada and Beatas and the streets circling **Plaza de Uncibay**, as well as in **Malagueta**, south of the bullring. At weekends and holidays dozens of youthful disco-bars fill the crowded streets in these areas with a cacophony of sound, and over the summer – it's dead out of season – the scene spreads out along the seafront to the suburb of **Pedregalejo**. Here, the streets just behind the beach host most of the action, and dozens of **discos** and smaller **bars** lie along and off the main street, Juan Sebastián Elcano. Málaga's daily paper, *El Sur*, is good for local entertainment listings – there's a weekly English edition.

Anden, Plaza de Uncibay. Disco-bar with a wild crowd and open till very late.

La Botellita, Pasaje Mitjana, slightly west of Plaza Uncibay, adjacent to *Luna Rubia*. Spanish music and a wide range of drinks at non-club prices; open till late.

La Chancla, on the beach in Pedregalejo. One of a recent rash of bars on the beach, this one bursts forth at midnight and continues until 3am or later.

Luna Rubia, Pasaje Mitjana 4, slightly west of Plaza Uncibay. Wide range of international sounds and open till dawn.

El Pimpi, c/Granada 62. Cavernous nightspot with flashing TV screens and a wide selection of sounds.

Salsa, at the top of c/Denis Belgrano, off c/Granada. Salsa and karaoke at weekends, samba and mambo on weekday nights. Dance tuition is also on offer for those who want to polish their moves.

Siempre Así, c/Convalecientes, north of Plaza Uncibay. Another late bar opening 11pm–3.30am and specializing in Spanish rock and techno.

Vankuver, Pasaje Mitjana, just off Plaza Uncibay. Wide range of international sounds and open until dawn.

El Chorro Gorge and Antequera

North of Málaga are two impressive sights: the magnificent limestone **gorge** near **El Chorro** and the prehistoric **dolmen caves** at **Antequera**. They lie close to the junction of roads inland to Sevilla, Córdoba and Granada and on direct train lines, and both are possible as day-trips from Málaga. Approaching Antequera along the old road from Málaga (MA423) via Almogía and Villenueva de la Concepción, you also pass the entrance to the popular national park, **El Torcal**.

El Chorro Gorge

Fifty kilometres north of Málaga, Garganta del Chorro is an amazing place – an immense five-kilometre-long cleft in a vast limestone massif – but its most stunning feature is a concrete catwalk, *El Camino del Rey*, which threads the length of the gorge, hanging precipitously halfway up its side. Built in the 1920s as part of a burgeoning hydroelectric scheme, it used to figure in all the guidebooks as one of the wonders of Spain; today it's largely fallen into disrepair, though a deal has recently been struck between the Madrid and Málaga governments to fund renovation works, due to begin at the end of 2001. At present, despite a few wobbly – and decidedly dangerous – sections (one tourist fell to her death in 1998), with random holes in the concrete through which you can see the gorge hundreds of feet below, it's still possible to walk much of its length. You will, however, need a very good head for heights, and at least a full day starting from Málaga. If you've neither, it's possible to get a glimpse of both gorge and *Camino* from any of the trains going north from Málaga – the line, slipping in and out of tunnels, follows the river for a considerable distance along the gorge, before plunging into a last long tunnel just before its head. If you're determined to walk the *Camino*, the safer way is to do it with an expert climbing guide (see below).

To explore the gorge, and walk the *Camino*, head for **EL CHORRO**, served by direct trains from Málaga. In the village there's an excellent **campsite** (☎952 112 696) with pool, reached by heading downhill to your right for 400m after getting off the train. Near the station, *Bar-Restaurante Garganta del Chorro* (☎952 497 219; ❹) has pleasant **rooms** inside a converted mill and overlooking a pool. Signs from the station will also direct you 2km to the *Finca La Campana* (☎ & ☎952 112 019, ✆*www.malaganet.com/lacampana*), with an economical bunkhouse (❶) and a couple of pleasant cottages (❸). Run by Swiss climber Jean Hofer and his wife Christine, the place also offers courses in rock climbing and caving, rents out mountain bikes, and can arrange horse-riding and hiking excursions, as well as **guided trips** along the *Camino* using ropes.

Into the gorge

From El Chorro it's a beautiful 12km to the start of the path and the gorge. From the train station, take the road signposted *Pantano de Guadalhorce*, which crosses over the dam, turns to the right and leads towards the hydroelectric plant. After 10km you'll come upon the bar-restaurant *El Mirador*, poised above the various lakes and reservoirs of the Guadalhorce scheme. From here a dirt track on the right covers the 2km to an abandoned power plant at the mouth of the gorge. The footpath to the left of this will take you into the chasm and to the beginning of **El Camino**.

Although it is marked "No Entry", you'll probably come upon a number of young Spaniards exploring the catwalk. The first section, at least, seems reasonably safe – despite places where it is only a metre wide and where parts of the handrail are missing – and this is in fact the most dramatic part of the canyon. Towards the end, where the passageway gets really dangerous, the gorge widens and it's possible to climb down and follow the riverbank or have a swim.

Antequera and around

ANTEQUERA, on the main rail line to Granada, is an ordinary, modern town, but it does have peripheral attractions in a Baroque church, **El Carmen** (Mon 11.30am–2pm, Tues–Sun 10am–2pm, Sat also 4–7pm; €1.20), which houses one of the finest *retablos* in Andalucía, and a group of three prehistoric **dolmen caves**. The most impressive and famous of these is the **Cueva de Menga** (Sun & Tues 9am–3.30pm, Wed–Sat 9am–6pm; free), its roof formed by an immense 180-tonne monolith. To reach this, and the nearby **Cueva de Viera** (same hours), take the Granada road out of town – the turning, rather insignificantly signposted, is after about 1km on the left. A third cave, **El Romeral** (same hours), is rather different (and later) in its structure, with a domed ceiling of flat stones; it also lies to the left of the Granada road, 2km further on, behind a sugar factory with a chimney.

If you want to **stay** in Antequera there's a good *pensión, Madrona,* c/Calzada 25 (☎952 840 014; ❸), near the market, which serves excellent food. Antequera also has a rather unattractive modern *parador* and several *hostales* on the roads in and out of town. Details of these, plus town maps and information on El Torcal (see below) are available from a helpful **tourist office** (Mon–Sat 10am–2pm & 5–8pm, Sun 10am–2pm; ☎952 843 573) on Plaza San Sebastián, alongside the church of the same name.

El Torcal, 13km south of Antequera, is the most geologically arresting of Spain's national parks. A massive high plateau of glaciated limestone tempered by a lush growth of hawthorn, ivy and wild rose, it can be painlessly explored using the **walking routes** that radiate from the centre of the park – trails are outlined in a leaflet available from the **Centro de Recepción** (Tues–Sun 10am–2pm & 4–6pm; ☎952 225 800). The only **waymarked route** (in green) is also the shortest (1.5km) and most popular, and in summer you may find yourself competing with gangs of schoolkids who arrive en masse for vaguely educational trips. A longer five-kilometre trail is more peaceful, great for strolling and taking in the looming limestone formations, eroded into vast, surreal sculptures. Camping is no longer allowed inside the park but there is a **campsite**, *Camping Torcal* (April–Sept), just off the A3310 6km south of Antequera. Five daily buses run from Málaga Monday to Friday and one runs on Sunday.

East from Málaga: the coast to Almería

The eastern stretch of the **Costa del Sol**, from Málaga to Almería, is uninspiring. Though far less developed than the wall-to-wall concrete from Torremolinos to Marbella in the west, it's not exactly unspoiled. If you're looking for a village and a beach and not much else, then you'll probably want to keep going at least to Almería.

Nerja and around

There's certainly little to tempt anyone before **NERJA**. This was a village before it was a resort, so it has some character, and development (more villas, fewer tower blocks) has been shaped around it. The beaches are also reasonably attractive, with a series of coves within walking distance if you want to escape the main mass of crowds. There are plenty of other great **walks** around Nerja, too, well documented in a locally available guide, *Twelve Walks Around Nerja, Frigiliana and Maro* by Elma and Denis Thompson, available from Librería Idiomas, almost opposite the turismo. For a little more freedom of movement Club Nautico de Nerja, Avda. Castilla Pérez 2 (☎952 524 654), west of the centre, rents out **mopeds** and **bikes**, as well as offering horse-riding and diving tuition.

Nerja's chief tourist attraction, the **Cuevas de Nerja** (daily 10am–2pm & 4–8pm; €4.50, kids €2.40), 3km from the town, are a heavily commercialized series of caverns, impressive in size – and home to the world's longest known **stalactite** at 63m – though otherwise not tremendously interesting. They also contain a number of prehistoric paintings, but these are not presently on public view.

Practicalities

The main **bus station** (actually a stand) is on c/San Miguel at the north end of the town close to Plaza Cantarero; from here hourly buses leave for the *cuevas*. It's a five-minute walk south from the station to the beach and centre, or old town, where you'll find the helpful **turismo** at c/Puerta del Mar 2 (April–Sept daily 10am–2pm & 5.30–8.30pm; ☎952 521 531), just to the east of the Balcón de Europa, an attractive palm–lined belvedere.

Nerja's main drawback, and a thorny problem through most of the summer, is scarce **accommodation**. There are a dozen or so *hostales*, most reserved well in advance, although some have arrangements with *casas particulares* who mop up the overflow; the turismo can provide a full accommodation list. Budget choices include the friendly *Hostal Montesol*, c/Pintada 130, just off Plaza Cantarero near the bus station (☎952 520 014; ❹), or, west of the turismo, the tidy *Hostal Atenbeni*, c/Diputación 12 (☎952 521 341; ❹), and the very pleasant *Hostal Mena*, c/El Barrio 15 (☎952 520 541; ❹), with a garden. Overlooking one of Nerja's most popular beaches, Playa de Burriana, are the *Parador Nacional*, c/Almuñécar 8 (☎952 520 050, ☎952 521 997, ✉nerja@parador.es; ❽), with a lift down the cliff, and the *Hotel Paraiso del Mar*, c/Carabeo 22 (☎952 521 621, ☎952 522 309; ❼). The **campsite**, *Nerja Camping* (☎952 529 714; open all year), with pool, bar and restaurant, is 4km east of town along the N340.

Almuñécar

Beyond Nerja the road climbs inland, running high above the coast until it surfaces at **LA HERRADURA**, a fishing village-resort suburb of Almuñécar, which is a good place to stop off and swim, and which also has three seafront summer **campsites**, the best of which is *La Herradura* (☎958 640 056), the westernmost of the three.

ALMUÑÉCAR itself is marred by a number of towering holiday apartments, though if you've been unable to find a room in Nerja you might want to stay here for a night. The rocky beaches are rather cramped and have grey sand, but the esplanade behind them, with palm-roofed bars (many offering free tapas) and restaurants, is fun, and the old town attractive.

Half a dozen good-value **fondas** and **hostales** ring the central Plaza de la Rosa in the old part of town; the cosy *Hostal Plaza Damasco*, c/Cerrajos 8 (☎958 630 165; ❹), and *Hostal Victoria*, Plaza de la Victoria (☎958 630 022; ❸), are two of the best. If you want to be right by the beach, try *Hotel Epsylon*, Paseo de la China 5 (☎ & ☎958 634 202; ❹), at the extreme western end of the seafront, a giant place with good value sea-view rooms with en-suite facilities. For a **campsite** you're much better off at La Herradura (see above) as Almuñécar's site, *El Paraíso* (☎958 632 370; open all year) at the eastern end of the seafront, can become an overcrowded hellhole in summer.

The **bus station**, which has frequent connections to Málaga and Granada, is located at the junction of Avenida Juan Carlos I and Avenida Fenicia, northeast of the centre, while the **turismo** (Mon–Sat 10am–2pm & 6–9pm; ☎958 631 125) can be found in an imposing neo-Moorish mansion on Avenida de Europa, behind the Playa San Cristóbal beach at the west end of the town. A couple of places worth seeking out for **eating and drinking** are *Bar-Restaurante Cuchi*, c/Alta del Mar 10, near Plaza de la Rosa, a small and friendly restaurant with a €5.25 *menú*, or, more upmarket, *Horno de Candida*, c/Orovia 3, close to the *ayuntamiento*, with a delightful roof terrace. For tapas, *Bodega Francisco*, c/Real 15, north of Plaza de la Rosa, is a wonderful old bar with barrels stacked up to the ceiling behind the counter and walls covered with ageing *corrida* posters and mounted boars' heads.

Salobreña and beyond

SALOBREÑA, 10km further east on the coast road, is infinitely preferable to Almuñécar. A white hilltop town gathered beneath the shell of a Moorish castle and surrounded by sugar-cane fields, it's set back 2km from the sea and is thus comparatively little developed. Its beach – a black sandy strip, only partially flanked by hotels and seafront *chiringuitos* – is a far more relaxed affair than that at Almuñécar.

Buses arrive and leave from Plaza de Goya, close to the **turismo** (Tues–Sun 10am–1.30pm & 5–8pm; ☎958 610 314). Along and off c/de Hortensia, the main avenue that winds down from the town to the beach, are a few **pensiones** and **hostales**: *Pensión Arnedo*, c/Nueva 15 (☎958 610 227; ❷), has the least expensive rooms, while *Pensión Mari Carmen* (☎958 610 906; ❷), over the road, is equally good, with fans in the rooms. The most atmospheric **places to eat** are the *chiringuitos* lining the seafront, among which *El Peñon*, on the promontory from which it takes its name, is good value and serves up great paella.

Just before **Motril**, the N323 heads north to Granada, a great route, skirting the Sierra Nevada. The coast road continues towards Almería through an unremarkable sprawl of resorts of which the most worthwhile is **CASTELL DE FERRO**. It's quite sheltered, still preserving remnants of its former existence as a small fishing village, with good, wide beaches to the east and west. Avoid the small town beach which is dirty and uninspiring. If you want to stay, head for the seafront where there are numerous possibilities: the friendly *Hostal Bahía*, Plaza de España 12 (☎958 656 060; ❸), is worth trying. The closest **campsite** to town is *El Sotillo* (☎958 656 078; June–Sept), near the beach. For the coast further east, see p.385.

The Costa del Sol resorts

West of Málaga – or more correctly, west of Málaga airport – the real **Costa del Sol** gets going, and if you've never seen this level of touristic development it's quite a shock. These are certainly not the kind of resorts you could envisage in Greece or even Portugal, with their 1960s and 1970s hotel and apartment tower blocks. In recent years, there has been a second wave of property development, this time villa homes and leisure complexes, funded by massive international investment. It's estimated that 300,000 foreigners now live on the Costa del Sol, the majority of them British and other northern Europeans, though custom marina developments such as Puerto Banús have also attracted Arab and Russian money.

Approached in the right kind of spirit it is possible to have fun in **Torremolinos** and, at a price, in **Marbella**. But if you've come to Spain to be in Spain, or even just to forget what inner-city housing looks like, put on the shades and keep going at least until you reach Estepona.

Torremolinos

The approach to Torremolinos – easily done via a 30min ride on the electric train from Málaga – is a rather depressing business. There are half-a-dozen beaches and stops, but it's a drab, soulless landscape of kitchenette apartments and half-finished developments. In recent years the local council have been trying to give the resort a facelift, the main feature of which has been the construction of a new seafront promenade and the renovation of the old town, the narrow alleyways of which are not without charm.

TORREMOLINOS, to its enduring credit, is certainly different: a vast, grotesque parody of a seaside resort, which in its own kitschy way is fascinating. This bizarre place, lined with sweeping (but crowded) beaches and infinite shopping arcades, crammed with (genuine) Irish pubs and (probably less genuine) real-estate agents, has a large permanent expatriate population of British, Germans and Scandinavians. It's a weird mix, which, in addition to thousands of retired people, has attracted – due to a previous lack of extradition arrangements between Britain and Spain – an extraordinary concentration of British crooks and more recently Russian mafia bosses. Torremolinos's social scene is strange, too, including, among the middle-of-the-road family discos, a thriving, pram-pushing, gay transvestite scene. All in all it's an intriguing blend of the smart and the squalid, bargains and rip-offs.

Practicalities

If any of these possibilities attracts you – or you're simply curious about the awfulness of the place – it's easy enough to **stay**. There are plenty of cheap *hostales* sandwiched between the high-rise horrors: *Pensión Beatriz*, c/Peligro 4 (☎952 385 110; ❸), and *Hostal Micaela*, c/Bajondillo 4 (☎952 383 310; ❹), are both near the beach and fairly cheap. The resort's **campsite** (☎952 382 602) lies 3km east of the centre on the main Málaga–Cádiz highway, 500m from the sea; get there by taking the *cercanía* train to the Los Alamos stop or bus "Línea B" from the central Plaza Costa del Sol. The **turismo** in Plaza Pablo Picasso (Mon–Fri 9.30am–1.30pm; ☎952 379 512) and a branch in Plaza del Lido on the seafront (daily 10am–2pm & 5–8pm) can provide more information on what accommodation is available.

The sheer competition between Torremolinos's **restaurants**, **clubs** and **bars** is so intense that if you're prepared to walk round and check a few prices you can have a pretty good night out on remarkably little. The more elegant part of the resort lies to the east at **La Carihuela**, where there's a decent beach, good seafood restaurants along the seafront and, if you're staying, the pleasant *Hostal Flor Blanco*, Paseo de la Carihuela 41 (☎952 382 071; ➎).

Fuengirola

FUENGIROLA, fifteen minutes along the train line from Torremolinos, is very slightly less developed and infinitely more staid. It's not so conspicuously ugly, but it is distinctly middle-aged and family-oriented. The huge, long beach has been divided up into restaurant-beach strips, each renting out lounge chairs and pedal-boats. At the far end is a windsurfing school.

Rooms are difficult to find in August, but you could try *Hostal Italia* (☎952 474 193; ➎), off the east side of the focal Plaza de la Constitución, which has rooms with bath, balcony and room-safe, or the slightly cheaper *Hostal Marbella*, c/Marbella 34, off the west side of the same square (☎952 475 802; ➎). Fuengirola's nearest **campsite** (☎952 474 108; open all year) lies 2km to the east of the centre and is reached by a turn-off near the junction of the N340 and the road to Mijas; bus "Línea Roja" from Avenida Ramón y Cajal on the main Marbella road will take you there. For excellent **seafood**, try the mid-priced *Bar La Paz Garrido* on Avenida de Mijas just north of the Plaza de la Constitución; alternatively, there are two seafront "as much as you can eat for €4.50" places, *Versalles*, Paseo Maritimo 3, and *Las Palmeras* nearby.

Marbella and around

MARBELLA stands in considerable contrast, after another sequence of apart-ment-villa *urbanizaciones*, to most of what's come before. It is undisputedly the "quality resort" of the Costa del Sol, where restaurants and bars are more styl-ish and everything costs considerably more. It has the highest per capita income in Europe and more Rolls Royces than any European city apart from London (although many of the classy cars here are rumoured to have been stolen else-where and re-registered in Spain). Recently the Spanish government and local police have been exercised by the arrival in Marbella of Russian and Italian mafia bosses who have been buying up property and using Marbella as a base to control their criminal empires, while in an ironic twist of history, there's been a massive return of Arabs to the area, especially since King Fahd of Saudi Arabia built a White House lookalike, complete with adjacent mosque, on the town's outskirts.

To be fair, the town has been spared the worst excesses of concrete architec-ture inflicted upon Torremolinos. Marbella also retains the greater part of its **old town** – set back a little from the sea and the new development. Centred on the Plaza de los Naranjos and still partially walled, the old town is hidden from the main road and easy to miss. Slowly, this original quarter is being bought up and turned into "quaint" clothes boutiques and restaurants, but this process isn't that far advanced. You can still sit in an ordinary bar in a small old square and look up beyond the whitewashed alleyways to the mountains of Ronda.

The truly rich don't stay in Marbella itself. They secrete themselves away in villas in the surrounding hills or lie around on phenomenally large and luxu-rious yachts at the marina and casino complex of **Puerto Banús**, 6km out of town towards San Pedro. If you're impoverished, this fact is worth noting as it's sometimes possible to find work scrubbing and repairing said yachts – and the pay can be very reasonable. As you'd expect, Puerto Banús has more than its complement of cocktail bars and seafood restaurants, most of them very pricey.

Practicalities

From the new **bus station** (☎952 764 400) in the north of the town, buses #2 or #7 will drop you close by the old town; otherwise it's a twenty-minute walk south along c/Trapiche. Rooms fill up fast here in July and August when you'll really need to ring ahead to be sure of getting a bed for the night. Marbella's only budget **pensiones** are on the eastern flank of the old town. The lowest priced are the friendly *Hostal Juan*, c/Luna 18 (☎952 779 475; ❹), with some en-suite rooms, and *Hostal Guerra*, Llanos de San Ramón 2 (☎952 774 220; ❹), on opposite sides of the main road as you come into town from the east. At c/Trapiche 2 to the north of the old town, the *Albergue Juvenil-Campamento* (☎952 771 491; ❶) has even cheaper beds in smart double and four-person en-suite rooms; there's a **campsite** with a pool too. There are plenty of more expensive places, too: *Hostal Enriqueta*, c/los Caballeros 18 (☎952 827 552; ❺), is comfortable and quiet, as is the charming *Hostal La Pilarica*, c/San Cristóbal 31 (☎952 774 252; ❹), in a street lined with potted plants – the work of the enthusiastic residents. The best seaside **campsite** for the town is *Marbella Playa* (☎952 833 998), located, confusingly, 12km east of the centre with a good beach.

If you need help in finding a room it is probably worth calling in at the **turismo** in Plaza de los Naranjos (Mon–Fri 9am–9pm, Sat & Sun 10am–2pm; ☎952 823 550), which will provide a street-indexed town map and list of addresses.

Food is available everywhere although it's worth avoiding the overpriced restaurants on the Plaza de los Naranjos, which turn the whole square into their dining terrace after dark. You're better off seeking out some of Marbella's excellent **tapas bars** such as *Bar Altamarino*, Plaza de Altamarino 4, just west of Plaza de los Naranjos or *Bar Guerra*, Avda. Ramón y Cajal 5, just south of the old quarter.

Estepona and beyond

The coast continues to be upmarket (or "money-raddled" as Laurie Lee put it) until you reach **ESTEPONA**, about 30km west, which is a more or less Spanish resort – in as much as that's possible round here. It lacks the enclosed hills that give Marbella character, but the hotel and apartment blocks which sprawl along the front are restrained in size, and there's space to breathe. The fine sand beach has been enlivened a little by a promenade studded with flowers and palms, and, away from the seafront, the old town is very pretty, with cobbled alleyways and two delightful plazas.

The **fish market** is definitely worth seeing: Estepona has the biggest fishing fleet west of Málaga, and the daily dawn ritual in the port, where the returning fleets auction off the fish they've just caught, is worth getting up early for – be there at 6am, since by 7am it's all over.

From May onward, Estepona's **bullfighting** season gets under way in a modern bullring reminiscent of a Henry Moore sculpture. At the beginning of July, the *Fiesta y Feria* week transforms the place, bringing out whole families in flamenco-style garb.

Beyond Estepona, 8km along the coast, there's a minor road leading into the hills to **CASARES**, one of the classic *andaluz* White Towns (see p.278). In keeping with the genre, it clings tenaciously to a steep hillside below a castle, and has attracted its fair share of arty types and expatriates. But it remains comparatively little known; bus connections are just about feasible for a day-trip (details from the turismo).

Further west, 3km inland from the village of Manilva, are some remarkably well-preserved **Roman sulphur baths**. If you want to partake of these health-giving waters you'll have to be prepared to dive into a subterranean cavern, and to put up with the overpowering stench of sulphur, which clings to your swimwear for weeks.

The beaches beyond Estepona have greyish sands (a trademark of the Costa del Sol that always seems surprising – you have to round the corner to the Atlantic coast at Tarifa before you meet yellow sand), and there are more greyish developments before the road turns inland towards San Roque and Gibraltar.

Practicalities

Estepona's **bus station** is on Avenida de España, to the west of the centre behind the seafront. The efficient and centrally located **turismo** (Mon–Fri 9.30am–9pm, Sat & Sun 9.30am–1.30pm; ☎952 800 913) is at Avda. San Lorenzo 1, east of the centre near the seafront. For **rooms**, *Hostal El Pilar* (☎952 800 018; ❹), on the pretty Plaza Las Flores, and the friendly *Pensión San Miguel*, c/Terraza 16 (☎952 802 616; ❸), a little to the west, with its own bar, are both good bets. Estepona's nearest **campsite** is *La Chullera III* (☎952 890 320; open all year), 8km south of town, just beyond the village of San Luís de Sabanillas. The town is well provided with **places to eat**, among them a bunch of excellent *freidurías* and *marisquerías* along c/Terraza, the main street which cuts through the centre – try *El Chanquete* or *La Gamba*. There's an excellent *churrería* towards the southern end of c/Mayor (one block back from, and parallel to, the promenade) – get there before 11am as they sell out early. Another good place for buying food is the covered **market** on c/Castillo, in the mornings. Estepona's **nightlife** centres on the recently pedestrianized c/Real, running behind and parallel to the seafront, whose **clubs** and **music bars** – with plenty of terrace tables on hot summer nights – compete for the custom of a mainly local clientele.

San Roque and La Línea de la Concepción

Situated 35km beyond Estepona in Cádiz province, **SAN ROQUE** was founded by the people of Gibraltar fleeing the British, who had captured the Rock and looted their homes and churches in 1704. They expected to return within months, since the troops that had taken the garrison in the name of the Archduke Carlos of Austria, whose rights Britain had been promoting in the War of the Spanish Succession. But it was the British flag that was raised on the conquered territory – and so it has remained.

The **"Spanish–British frontier"** is 8km away at **LA LÍNEA DE LA CONCEPCIÓN**, obscured by San Roque's huge oil refinery. In February 1985 the gates were reopened after a sixteen-year period of Spanish-imposed isolation, and since then crossing has become a routine affair of passport stamping, except for the odd diplomatic flare-up when the Spanish authorities have decided to operate a go-slow to annoy the Rock's inhabitants. If you're planning a stay in Gibraltar, be warned that accommodation there is very expensive and in summer the few budget places available are in tremendous demand; La Línea is more realistic, although even here prices have risen and it's now more expensive than neighbouring towns. There are no sights as such; it's just a fishing village which has exploded in size due to the jobs in Gibraltar and Algeciras.

Practicalities

At the heart of La Línea is the large, modern and undistinguished Plaza de la Constitución, where you'll find the *Correos*. The **turismo** (Mon–Fri 8am–3pm, Sat 9am–1pm; ☎956 769 950), which provides a useful town map labelling *hostales*, and **bus station** are both on Avenida 20 Abril, to the south of the square. Most of the budget **hostales** are also around Plaza de la Constitucíon. The friendly *La Campana*, c/Carboneras 3, just off the square (☎956 173 059; ❹), is clean, and has rooms with bath and TV; if this is full, *Hotel-Restaurante Carlos* (☎956 762 135; ❹) is almost opposite with the same facilities. Slightly further north, *Hostal Florida*, c/Sol 37 (☎956 171 300; ❸), is another possibility, with a good-value restaurant downstairs, and cheaper rooms are on offer at the basic but clean *Pensión La Perla*, c/Clavel 10 (☎956 769 513; ❷), off the north side of the square.

Off the east side of Plaza de la Constitución an archway leads to the smaller, pedestrianized Plaza Cruz de Herrera, with lots of reasonably priced **bars** and **restaurants**, among which *La Nueva Mesón Jerezana* does good *fino* and *jamón*. Slightly north lies c/Real, the main pedestrianized shopping street and another area with plenty of bars and cafés: just off the north side is *La Venta*, c/Dr Villar 19, which does a good-value *menú* and an excellent paella, while to the south at Avda. de España 22 is an excellent *marisquería*, *Bar Aquarium*. C/Clavel, signposted from the main plaza to the Plaza de Toros, has more options: *Bar Alhambra* halfway down is basic and excellent value.

Local **buses** from La Línea to Algeciras take thirty minutes, with departures every hour. The closest main-line **train station** is San Roque-La Línea, 12km away, from where you can pick up a train to Ronda and beyond. Buses link La Línea with Sevilla (daily; 4hr), Málaga (daily; 2hr 30min), Cádiz (daily; 2hr 30min) via Tarifa, and as far as Ayamonte on the Portuguese border (daily; 7hr).

Gibraltar

GIBRALTAR's interest is essentially its novelty: the genuine appeal of the strange, looming physical presence of its rock, and the dubious one of its preservation as one of Britain's last remaining colonies. For most of its history it has existed in a limbo between two worlds without being fully part of either, which makes it a curious place to visit, not least to witness the bizarre process of its opening to mass tourism from the Costa del Sol. Ironically, this threatens both to destroy Gibraltar's highly individual hybrid society and at the same time to make it much more British, after the fashion of the expatriate communities and huge resorts of the Costa. In recent years the economic boom Gibraltar enjoyed throughout the 1980s, following the reopening of the border with Spain, has started to wane, and the likely future of the colony – whether its population agrees to it or not – is almost certain to involve closer ties with Spain.

Arrival, information and orientation

If you have a **car**, don't attempt to bring it to Gibraltar – the queues at the border are always atrocious and parking is a nightmare due to lack of space. Use the underground car parks in La Línea – there's one beneath the central Plaza de la Constitución – instead, and either catch the **bus** (10min past or 20min to the hour) from the border, or take an easy ten-minute **walk** across part of the airport runway to the town centre.

The town and rock have a necessarily simple layout. **Main Street** (La Calle Real) runs for most of the town's length, a couple of blocks back from the port. In and around Main Street are most of the shops, together with many of the British-style pubs and hotels. For information, the main **tourist office** (Mon–Fri 10am–6pm, Sat 10am–2pm; ☎74805) is in Duke of Kent House on Cathedral Square, and there are also sub-offices in the Piazza on Main Street, at the airport, and in the customs and immigration building at the border. The John Mackintosh Hall at the south end of Main Street is a useful resource – it's the cultural centre, with exhibitions and a library. The local paper is the *Gibraltar Chronicle*, a stultifyingly parochial daily with little of interest to visitors. Much of Gibraltar – with the exception of the cut-price booze shops – closes down on Saturday afternoon, but the tourist sights remain open, and this can be a quiet time to visit.

The **currency** used here is the **Gibraltar pound** (the same value as the British pound, but different notes and coins); if you pay in euro while in Gibraltar, you generally fork out about five percent more. It's best to change your money once you arrive in Gibraltar, since the exchange rate is slightly higher than in Spain and there's no commission charged. Gibraltar pounds can be hard to change in Spain.

Accommodation

Shortage of space on the rock means that **places to stay** are at a premium, and you're much better off visiting on day-trips from Algeciras (buses on the hour and half-hour; 30min) or La Línea. The only remotely budget beds are at the friendly *Toc H Hostel* on Line Wall Rd (☎73431; about £6 a person) – and these are none too comfortable and almost always occupied by long-term residents – or the tiny, eccentric *Seruya's Guest House* at 92 Irish Town (☎73220; about £15 a double), which is also invariably full. There are also dorm beds at the basic *Emile Youth Hostel* at the Montagu Bastion, Line Wall Rd (☎51106; about £12 for a dorm bed including breakfast). Otherwise, you're going to have to pay normal British hotel prices: the next step up includes the *Queen's Hotel* on Boyd St (☎74000, ☎40030), the *Bristol* in Cathedral Square (☎76800, ☎77613), or the *Cannon Hotel*, 9 Cannon Lane, near the cathedral (☎ & ☎51711), all charging £35–65 for a double room.

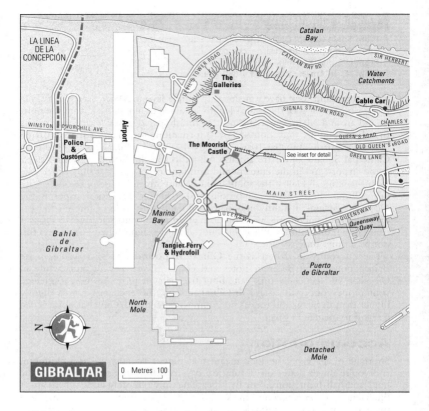

If this tempts you to find a bit of sand to bed down on, forget it: no camping is allowed and if you're caught sleeping rough or inhabiting abandoned bunkers, you are more than likely to be arrested and fined. This law is enforced by Gibraltar and Ministry of Defence police, and raids of the beaches are frequent.

Around the Rock

From near the end of Main Street you can hop on a **cable car** (Mon–Sat 9.30am–6pm, last trip down 5.45pm; £4.90 return, children under 10 half price) which will carry you up to the summit – **The Top of the Rock** as it's logically known – via **Apes' Den** halfway up, a fairly reliable viewing point to see the tailless monkeys and hear the guides explain their legend. From The Top you can look over the Strait of Gibraltar to the Atlas Mountains and down to the town, its elaborate water catchment system cut into the side of the rock, and ponder whether it's worth heading for one of the beaches. From the Apes' Den it's an easy walk south along St Michael's Road through the so-called "Nature Reserve" to **Saint Michael's Cave** (free entry with cable-car ticket), an immense natural cavern which led ancient people to believe the rock was hollow and gave rise to its old name of *Mons Calpe* (Hollow Mountain).

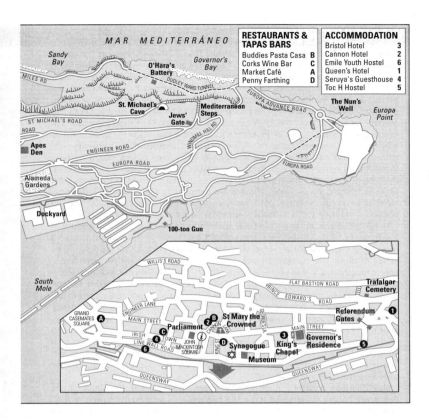

The cave was used during the last war as a bomb-proof military hospital and nowadays hosts occasional concerts. If you're adventurous you can arrange at the tourist office for a guided visit to Lower Saint Michael's Cave, a series of chambers going deeper down and ending in an underground lake.

Although you can take the cable car both ways, it's an interesting walk up via Willis's Road to visit the **Tower of Homage**. Dating from the fourteenth century, this is the most visible surviving remnant of the old **Moorish Castle**. Further up you'll find the **Upper Galleries** (aka the Great Siege Tunnels), blasted out of the rock during the Great Siege of 1779–82, in order to point guns down at the Spanish lines. To walk down, take the **Mediterranean Steps** – they're not very well signposted and you have to climb over O'Hara's Battery, a very steep descent most of the way down the east side, turning the southern corner of the Rock. You'll pass through the Jews' Gate and into Engineer Road. From here, return to town through the Alameda Gardens and the **Trafalgar Cemetery**, overgrown and evocative, with a good line in imperial epitaphs. The grand tour of the Rock takes a half to a full day, and all sites on it are open from 9.30am to 7pm in summer, 10am to 5.30pm in winter; if you visit all the attractions, buy a reduced-price ticket which includes the cave as well.

Back **in town**, incorporated into the **Gibraltar Museum** (Mon–Fri 10am–6pm, Sat 10am–2pm; £2), are two well-preserved and beautiful

British sovereignty in Gibraltar

Sovereignty of the Rock (a land area smaller than the city of Algeciras across the water) will doubtless eventually return to Spain, but at present neither side is in much of a hurry. For Britain it's a question of precedent – Gibraltar is in too similar a situation to the Falklands/Malvinas, the conflict over which pushed the Spanish into postponing an initial frontier-opening date in 1982. For Spain, too, there are unsettling parallels with the *presidios* (Spanish enclaves) on the Moroccan coast at Ceuta and Melilla – both at present part of Andalucía. Nonetheless, the British presence is in practice waning and the British Foreign Office clearly wants to steer Gibraltar towards a new, harmonious relationship with Spain. To this end they are running down the significance of the military base, and now only a token force of less than a hundred British troops remain – most of these working in a top-secret hi-tech bunker buried deep inside the Rock from where the Royal Navy monitors the sea traffic through the Strait (accounting for a quarter of the world movement of all shipping). In financial terms this has cut the British government's contribution to Gibraltar's GDP from 65 percent in the early 1980s to five percent today, and the figure is still falling.

The Gibraltarians, however, are firmly opposed to a return to **Spanish control** of the Rock. In 1967, just before Franco closed the border in the hope of forcing a quick agreement, the colony voted on the issue – rejecting it by 12,138 votes to 44 (a poll which was not recognized, incidentally, by the UN). Most people would probably sympathize with that vote – against a Spain that was then still a dictatorship – but more than thirty years have gone by, Spanish democracy is now secure, and the arguments are becoming increasingly tenuous. Despite its impressive claims to law and order, Gibraltar is no model society either; its dirty jobs, for instance, are nearly all done by Moroccans, who were recruited en masse to replace Spanish workers after the border between Gibraltar and Spain was closed by Franco in 1969, and who have always been treated as second-class citizens. This was underlined in the late 1990s by tough new immigration laws stripping them of residence, pension and health care rights, which were upheld by the colony's supreme court, despite appeals against "ethnic cleansing".

May 1996 saw a change in the trend of internal **politics**, with the defeat of Joe Bossano's Labour government (following two previous landslide victories). Voters, concerned that Bossano's pugnacious anti-Spanish stance jeopardized a viable economic future in which Spain must realistically play a role, elected a new Social Democratic administration led by Peter Caruana. However, whilst Caruana talked of opening up a more **constructive dialogue with Spain** during the election campaign, once in control he soon began to voice the traditional Gibraltarian paranoia. His stance has caused some dismay in Madrid and London, who were both behind Spain's offer in 1997 to give the colony the status of a Spanish autonomous region

fourteenth-century **Moorish Baths**. The museum, along with **Nelson's Anchorage** on Rosia Road – where the body of the naval commander was brought ashore following the Battle of Trafalgar – the **casino** and the **miniature golf**, is about the extent of the sightseeing, though you may also be interested in dolphin-spotting **boat trips**, run by two companies from the Queensway Quay (daily; ☎74958; £12–15 depending on company; reductions for kids); you should ring first to book places or ask the tourist office to do it for you.

Gibraltar has plans to reclaim an area equivalent to that of the present town from the sea, and is currently doing feasibility surveys on pumping up sand from the seabed. But at present there is just the one tiny fishing village at **Catalan Bay**, which is where you'll find the **beach** with most character. The inhabitants of the village like to think of themselves as very distinct from the townies on the other side of the Rock. About 48km of recent tunnels, or **galleries**, have been bored through the Rock for military purposes – these are

(similar to that of the Basques and Catalans) inside the Spanish state. The proposal was rejected out of hand by Caruana. After calling a snap election in February 2000, the Caruana government was returned for another four-year term with an increased majority. Caruana has also been urged by Britain (under pressure from Spain) to crack down on the smuggling of contraband cigarettes over the Spanish border and to curb the activities of the Rock's 75,000 "offshore" financial institutions – many of which Spain claims are guilty of involvement with money laundering by criminals from all parts of Europe and beyond. These claims were given some credibility by the EU's decision to start legal proceedings against a number of them in 1999.

What most outsiders don't realize about the political situation is that the Gibraltarians feel very vulnerable, caught between the interests of two big states; they are well aware that both governments' concerns are primarily strategic and political rather than with the wishes of the people of Gibraltar. Until very recently people were sent over from Britain to fill all the top civil service and Ministry of Defence jobs, a practice which, to a lesser degree, still continues – the present governor is David Durie, a senior Whitehall civil servant. Large parts of the Rock are no-go areas for "natives"; the South District in particular being taken up by military facilities. Local people also protest about the Royal Navy nuclear-powered submarines which dock regularly at the naval base, and secrecy surrounds the issue of whether nuclear warheads and/or chemical and biological weapons are stored in the arsenal, probably deep inside the Rock itself. This whole issue came to a head in the late summer of 2000 when the Royal Navy submarine *Tireless* limped into Gibraltar with a problem in its nuclear reactor. Tension mounted over the following months as the populations of the towns surrounding the Bay of Algeciras staged angry demonstrations sparked by the British Government's refusal to give any information about the potential dangers or when the sub would be leaving. It finally departed in May 2001 but the affair was a public relations disaster for Britain and Gibraltar and caused serious diplomatic strains between Madrid and London.

Yet Gibraltarians still cling to British status – perhaps simply because they have known nothing other than British rule since the former population was displaced – and all their institutions are modelled on British lines. Contrary to popular belief, they are of neither mainly Spanish nor British blood, but an ethnic mix descended from Genoese, Portuguese, Spanish, Minorcan, Jewish, Maltese and British ancestors. English is the **official language**, but more commonly spoken is what sounds to an outsider like perfect Andalucian Spanish. It is in fact **llanito**, an Andalucían dialect with borrowed words that reflect its diverse origins; ironically – in view of most of the colony's antipathy to their Iberian neighbour – only a Spaniard from the south can tell a Gibraltarian from an Andalucian.

now being adapted to help solve the territory's traffic-flow crisis brought on by the extraordinary surplus of cars.

Eating and drinking

Restaurants are far more plentiful than places to stay, though by Spanish standards they are still relatively expensive: pub snacks or fish and chips are reliable standbys. Main Street is crowded with touristy places, among which *Smiths Fish and Chip Shop*, at no. 295 near the Convent, is worth a try. Other good choices are the *Penny Farthing* on King Street, always busy for home-cooked food at reasonable prices, and *Buddies Pasta Casa* on Cannon Lane, serving up decent pasta in all its varieties. *Corks Wine Bar*, 79 Irish Town, is a pleasant place for light meals and the *Market Café* in the public market (off Casemates Square) serves up traditional English breakfasts all day long.

Pubs all tend to mimic traditional English styles (and prices), the difference being that they are open all day and often into the wee hours. For pub food, the *Royal Calpe*, 176 Main Street, *Calpe Hounds*, Cornwall's Lane, and *Clipper*, 78 Irish Town, are among the best. Of the obvious pubs grouped together on Main Street, the *Royal Calpe* has a beer garden, and *The Horseshoe* and the *Gibraltar Arms* have tables outside; places on Main Street, however, tend to be rowdy – often full of squaddies and visiting sailors at night. For a quieter alternative, try the *Cannon Bar* in Cannon Lane beside the cathedral, or the *Piccadilly Gardens Bar*, 3 Rosia Rd, just beyond the Referendum Gates. The *Star Bar*, 12 Parliament Lane, off the west side of Main Street near the Post Office, is reputedly Gibraltar's oldest and was a favourite hang-out of Lord Nelson when it traded under its original name, *La Estrella*.

Onward travel

One decidedly functional attraction of Gibraltar is its role as a **port for Morocco**, though the timetable is subject to weather conditions even at the best of times (the trip across the Strait is invariably very rough). The only ferry service currently operating is the *Estrella* to Tangier on Monday and Wednesday at 8.15am and Friday at 6.30pm, with the return on Sunday and Tuesday at 3pm and Friday at 9pm; the trip takes about two hours. Tickets cost around £18 one-way or £30 return for foot passengers and £40 single or £80 return for a four-seater car and passengers; however, things tend to change frequently and you should confirm timetables and ticket prices with the operator, Tourafrica, in the International Commercial Centre, 2a Main St (℡77666, ℻76754). A new **catamaran** service to Tangier, the *Mons Calpe*, leaves at 9.30am daily with additional sailings on Monday and Friday at 7pm; the crossing takes 1hr 15min and tickets cost £30 for a period return (valid three months) and £25 for a day-trip. Bookings and confirmation of timetables should be made through Bland Travel, Cloister Building, Irish Town (℡79200, ℻76189). There are also daily **flights** to London with GB Airways and Monarch Airlines as well as expensive daily flights to Casablanca and Marrakesh; details of these and travel connections with Spain are also available from Bland Travel.

Algeciras

ALGECIRAS occupies the far side of the bay from Gibraltar, spewing out smoke and pollution in the direction of the Rock. The last town of the Spanish Mediterranean, it must once have been an elegant resort; today it's unabashedly a port and industrial centre, its suburbs extending on all sides, and almost all construction is of modern vintage. When Franco closed the border with Gibraltar at La Línea it was Algeciras that he decided to develop to absorb the Spanish workers formerly employed in the British naval dockyards, thus breaking the area's dependence on the Rock.

Most travellers are scathing about the city's ugliness, and unless you're waiting for a bus or train, or heading for Morocco, there's admittedly little reason to stop. Yet some touch of colour is added by the groups of Moroccans in transit, dressed in flowing *jallabahs* and yellow slippers, and lugging unbelievable amounts of possessions (see box). Algeciras has a real port atmosphere, and even passing through it's hard to resist the urge to get on a boat south, if only for a couple of days in Tangier. Once you start to explore, you'll also discover that

Moroccans in Algeciras

It's easy to take a romantic view of the exotic hustle and bustle in the port area, but there's a miserable story behind some of it. Algeciras is the main port for **Moroccan migrant workers**, who drive home every year during their holidays from the factories, farms and mines of France, Germany and the Low Countries. Half a million cross Spain in the six weeks from the end of June to the beginning of August in often perilously overloaded vehicles, frequently becoming victims of all levels of racial discrimination (they are still referred to as *los Moros*), from being ripped off to being violently attacked and robbed.

the old town has some very attractive corners which seem barely to have changed in fifty years, especially around the Plaza Alta. The number of people passing through also guarantees endless possibilities for food and drink.

Practicalities

If you're waiting for a morning ferry, or want to stay awhile, Algeciras has plenty of budget **hostales** and **pensiones** in the grid of streets to the north of the railway line between the port and the train station. There are several in c/Duque de Almodóvar, c/José Santacana and c/Rafael de Muro. Try the basic but clean *Levante*, c/Duque de Almodóvar 21 (☎956 651 505; ❷), or the more comfortable *González*, c/José Santacana 7 (☎956 652 843; ❸), which has some rooms with bath. On Plaza Palma, the market square slightly in from the port, the surprisingly spruce *Hostal Nuestra Señora de la Palma* (☎956 632 481; ❸) is another good option with en-suite rooms. Algeciras's luxurious new **youth hostel**, Ctra. Nacional 340 (☎956 679 060; ❶), has a pool, tennis courts and double rooms with bath, but lies 8km west of town on the Tarifa road; buses heading for Tarifa will drop you there if you ask. Should you have trouble finding a place to stay, pick up a town plan and check out the full accommodation list in the **turismo**, c/Juan de la Cierva (official hours Mon–Fri 9am–2pm, but frequently fails to open; ☎956 572 636; English spoken), on the south side of the train track near the port. Prices tend to go up dramatically in midseason, but lots of simple *casas de huéspedes* are clustered round the market.

The port area also has plenty of **places to eat**. Across the train line from the turismo and invariably crowded is the good-value *Casa Gil* at c/Sigismundo Moret 2. Fifty metres further along the same street, *Casa Sánchez*, at the corner of c/Río, is another good place with a *menú*, and they also have a few **rooms** (❷). The bustling and colourful daily **market** in the nearby Plaza Palma is a useful place to buy food for travelling or picnics. Good **tapas** are on offer at *Bar Castro*, c/Castillo 14, just north of the market and en route uphill to the elegant main square, **Plaza Alta**, where there are more bars, cafés and *heladerías*.

Onward travel

If you are tempted to pop over to Morocco, it's easily enough done: in summer there are at least eighteen daily **crossings to Tangier** and half as many at other times of the year (2hr, or 1hr 30min with a fast ferry or *rapido*), and the same number to the Spanish *presidio* of **Ceuta** (1hr 30min), little more than a Spanish Gibraltar with a brisk business in duty-free goods, but a relatively painless way to enter Morocco. A hydrofoil service also goes to Tangier (1 daily; 30min). **Tickets** cost around €21.50 one-way to Tangier or Ceuta, with an additional €5.50 for hydrofoils, and are sold at scores of travel agents along the waterfront and on most approach roads; they all cost the same, though some places may give you a better rate of exchange than others if you want to pay in foreign currency. Viájes Transafric, Avda. Marina 4 (☎956 654 311), on the harbourfront, the nearby Transmediterranea (☎956 663 850) and the turismo (see above) are reliable and can provide up-to-date information on timetable changes.

Wait till Tangier – or if you're going via Ceuta, Tetouan – before buying any **Moroccan currency**; rates in the embarkation building kiosks are very poor. Make sure that your ticket is for the next ferry, and beware the ticket sellers who congregate near the dock entrance wearing official Ceuta/Tangier badges: they add a whopping "commission" to the normal price of a ticket. **InterRail/Eurail card holders** are entitled to a thirty percent discount on the standard ferry price; if you have trouble getting this, go to the official sales desk in the embarkation building.

At Algeciras the **train line** begins again, heading north to Ronda, Córdoba and Madrid. The route to Ronda – one of the best journeys in Andalucía – is detailed below; there are four departures a day. For Madrid (and Paris) there's a night express, currently leaving at 11pm, and also Linebus/Iberbus coaches to Paris and London. For Málaga, hourly **buses** leave from the *Empresa Portillo*, Avenida Virgen del Carmen on the waterfront (☎956 651 055); from here, too, there are less frequent, direct connections to Granada and Almería. Buses to Barcelona via Alicante and Valencia are operated by Bacoma (☎956 666 589) and leave from outside the harbour offices, but the journey is appallingly slow at 21 hours, with a change in Málaga. For Tarifa, Cádiz, Sevilla, Madrid and most other destinations you'll need the **main bus station** (☎956 653 456), in c/San Bernardo, behind the port, next to *Hotel Octavio* and just short of the **train station**: to get there follow the train tracks. The bus to La Línea also goes every half-hour from here.

Ronda and the White Towns

Andalucía is dotted with small, brilliantly whitewashed settlements – the **Pueblos Blancos** or "White Towns" – most often straggling up hillsides towards a castle or towered church. Places like **Mijas**, up behind Fuengirola, are solidly on the tourist trail, but even here the natural beauty is undeniable. All of them look great from a distance, though many are rather less interesting on arrival. Perhaps the best lie in a roughly triangular area between Málaga, Algeciras and Sevilla; at its centre, in a region of wild mountainous beauty, is the spectacular town of **Ronda**.

To Ronda from the coast

Of several possible approaches to Ronda from the coast, the stunningly scenic route up from Algeciras is the most rewarding – and worth going out of your way to experience. From Málaga, most of the buses to Ronda follow the coastal highway to San Pedro before turning into the mountains via the modern A376 *autovía*: dramatic enough, but rather a bleak route, with no villages and only limited views of the sombre rock face of the Serranía – an alternative route, via Álora and Ardales, is far more attractive. The train ride up from Málaga is better, with three connecting services daily, including a convenient 6.05pm departure after the last bus leaves.

The **Algeciras route** – via Gaucín – is possible by either bus or train, or, if you've time and energy, can be walked in four or five days. En route, you're always within reach of a river and there's a series of hill towns, each one visible from the next, to provide targets for the day. Casares is almost on the route, but more easily reached from Estepona (see p.268).

Castellar de la Frontera

The first White Town on the route proper is **CASTELLAR DE LA FRONTERA**, 27km north from Algeciras, a bizarre village within a thirteenth-century castle, whose population, in accord with some grandiose scheme, was moved downriver in 1971 to the "new" town of Nuevo Castellar, whose modern square frames an image of their former castle home on the hill behind. The relocation was subsequently dropped and a few villagers moved back to their old houses, but most of them were taken over by retired hippies (mainly German, mainly affluent). The result didn't entirely work, with suspicion from the locals and hostile exclusivity from some of the new arrivals fuelling tensions which remain today. Recent plans to rebuild the castle as a tourist centre – complete with *parador* – appear to have ground to a halt. The only **places to stay** inside the castle walls are *Casas Rurales Castillo* (T956 236 620, Wwww.cadiz.org/tugasa; ❻) which consists of a number of restored village houses, or the *Posada Antigua* (T956 236 101; ❸), with two en-suite rooms; *Hostal El Pilar* c/León Esquivel 4 (T956 693 022; ❸), lies below in the dull new town. There's a **bar** near the entrance to the castle and within the walls *El Aljibe* is a decent traditional **restaurant** attached to the *Casas Rurales* accommodation (above); an average *venta* at the start of the climb to the village on the main A369 is the only other food option, otherwise there's not a lot more to detain you.

Jimena de la Frontera and Gaucín

JIMENA DE LA FRONTERA, 20km further north along the A369, is a far larger and more open hill town, rising to a grand Moorish castle with a triple-gateway entrance. There are several **bars**, a beautiful old **fonda** (which has no sign – ask for the *Casa María*, c/Sevilla 36; ❶), the more expensive *Hostal El Anon* (T956 640 113, Eelanon@mx3redistb.es; ❺) with restaurant and rooftop pool at c/Consuelo 32, and another *hostal* at the train station, *Los Arcos* (T956 640 328; ❹), a little way out of town. The best place for **food** is *Restaurante-Bar Cuenca*, Avenida de los Deportes, on the way into town, which does wonderful tapas and meals and has a pretty terrace patio at the rear.

Beyond Jimena, it's 23km further along the A369 – or on foot a 16km climb – through woods of cork oak and olive groves to reach **GAUCÍN**; along the way there are bars at San Pablo, a hamlet about 7km out. Gaucín, almost a mountain village, commands tremendous views (to Gibraltar and the Moroccan coast on a very clear day), and makes a great place to stop over. **Rooms** and food are to be had at *Hostal Moncada*, c/Luís Armiñian (T952 151 324; ❸), next to the *gasolinera* as you enter the village from Jimena (get a room at the back for a view). Gaucín's charming *fonda*, the *Nacional*, c/San Juan de Dios 8, closed its doors a few years back after 125 years in business, but is steeped in history and still serves **meals**.

You can reach the village by bus, but far more rewarding is the 13km, mostly uphill, walk from its **train station**. Though it's now known as Gaucín, this station is actually at El Colmenar, on the fringes of the Cortés nature reserve: if you need to rest up before the hike (getting on for 3hr) there's a **hostal**, *Bar-Restaurante Flores* (T952 153 026; ❷) and several bars here. Should you chicken out, the *hostal* can arrange a taxi ride (about €12 one-way).

The train line between Gaucín and Ronda passes through a handful of tiny villages. En route, you can stop off at the station of Benaoján-Montejaque: from here it's an hour's trek to the prehistoric **Cueva de la Pileta** (see p.283). From Benaoján, Ronda is just three stops (and thirty minutes) down the line.

Ronda

Rising amid a ring of dark, angular mountains, the full natural drama of **RONDA** is best appreciated as you enter the town. Built on an isolated ridge of the sierra, it's split in half by a gaping river gorge, **El Tajo**, which drops sheer for 130m on three sides. Still more spectacular, the gorge is spanned by a stupendous eighteenth-century arched bridge, the **Puente Nuevo**, while tall whitewashed houses lean from its precipitous edges.

Much of the attraction of Ronda lies in this extraordinary view, or in walking down by the Río Guadalévin, following one of the donkey tracks through the rich green valley. Bird-watchers should look out for the lesser kestrels nesting in and launching themselves from the cliffs beneath the Alameda park. Lower down you can spot crag martins. The town itself is also of interest and, surprisingly, has sacrificed little of its character to the flow of day-trippers from the Costa del Sol.

Arrival, information and accommodation

Ronda's **train** and **bus stations** are both in the Mercadillo quarter to the northeast of the bullring. Trains arrive on Avenida Andalucía, a ten-minute walk or easy bus ride from the centre, and all the bus companies use the terminal close by on Plaza Redondo. The **turismo** (Mon–Fri 9am–7pm, Sat & Sun 10am–2pm; ☎952 871 272) is at the northern end of the focal Plaza de España, and can help with accommodation and provide a map. A new **municipal tourist office** (Mon–Fri 9.30am–8pm, Sat & Sun 10am–2pm & 3–7pm; ☎952 187 119) has opened nearby, opposite the south side of the bullring.

Most of the **places to stay** are also in the Mercadillo quarter, within easy walking distance of the central Plaza de España. Ronda's **campsite**, *Camping El Sur* (☎952 875 939) with pool, bar and restaurant lies 2km out of town along the road to Algeciras.

Alavera de los Baños, c/San Miguel s/n, next door to the Baños Arabes ☎ & ☎952 879 143, ⓦwww.andalucia.com/alavera. Enchanting small hotel with stylish rooms, garden, pool, restaurant and views from rear rooms to grazing sheep on the hill across the river. ⑥

Hostal Andalucía, c/Martínez Astein 19 ☎952 875 450. Pleasant en-suite rooms in leafy surroundings opposite the train station. ③

Hotel Colón, c/Pozo 1, on the Plaza de la Merced. Charming small hotel with sparkling en-suite facilities and – in rooms 301 & 302 – your own spacious roof terrace. ⑤

En Frente Arte, c/Real 40 ☎952 879 088, ⓦwww.enfrentearte.com. Stylish new hotel inside a restored mansion with distinctive and elegant rooms. Breakfast is included in the price as are soft drinks and draught beer. Additional luxuries include a delightful garden pool, games room, free sauna and internet access. ⑦ with reductions for longer stays.

Hotel La Española, c/José Aparicio 3 ☎952 871 052, ☎952 878 001. Cosy rooms with bath in the alley behind the turismo, some with amazing views, plus a terrace restaurant. ⑥

Parador de Ronda, Plaza de España ☎952 877 500, ☎952 878 188. Ronda's imposing *parador* has spectacular views overlooking El Tajo, plus a pool, terrace bar, restaurant, and all the facilities you'd expect from a hotel in this category. ⑧

Los Pastores, 3km outside town along the Algeciras road (A369), on the right with a red sign ☎952 114 464, ⓔnelske73@hotmail.com. Very pleasant rural option in a Dutch-owned former farmhouse surrounded by fine walking country. Three en-suite doubles; breakfast available. ④.

Hostal San Francisco, c/Cabrera-Prim 18 ☎952 873 299. At the end of c/Sevilla and just off Plaza Carmen Abela, this friendly *hostal* is excellent value, and all rooms come with bath. ③

The Town

Ronda divides into three parts: on the near (northwest) side of the gorge, where you'll arrive, is the largely modern **Mercadillo** quarter. Across the bridge is the old Moorish town, the **Ciudad**, and further south still, its **San Francisco** suburb.

The **Ciudad** retains intact its Moorish plan and a great many of its houses, interspersed with a number of fine Renaissance mansions. It is so intricate a maze that you can do little else but wander at random. However, at some stage, make your way across the bridge and along c/Santo Domingo, also known as c/Marqués de Parada, which winds round to the left. At no. 17 is the somewhat arbitrarily named **Casa del Rey Moro**, an early eighteenth-century mansion built on Moorish foundations. The gardens (but not the house itself) have recently been opened to the public (daily 10am–8pm; €3.60), and from here a remarkable underground stairway, the *Mina*, descends to the river; these 365 steps (which can be slippery after rain), guaranteeing a water supply in times of siege, were cut by Christian slaves in the fourteenth century. There's a viewing balcony at the bottom where you can admire the Tajo's towering walls of rock and its bird life.

Further down the same street is the **Palacio del Marqués de Salvatierra**, a splendid Renaissance mansion with an oddly primitive, half-grotesque frieze of Adam and Eve on its portal. The house is still used by the family and was closed to visitors in 2000, though visits may resume in the future (details from the turismo). Just down the hill you reach the two old town bridges – the **Puente Viejo** of 1616 and the single-span Moorish **Puente de San Miguel**; nearby, on the southeast bank of the river, are the distinctive hump-shaped cupolas and bizarre glass roof-windows of the old **Baños Árabes** (Tues 9.30am–1.30pm & 4–6pm, Wed–Sat 9.30am–3.30pm; free). Dating from the thirteenth century and recently restored, the complex is based on the Roman system of cold, tepid and hot baths and is wonderfully preserved; note the barrel-vaulted ceiling and brickwork octagonal pillars supporting horseshoe arches, all underlining the sophistication of the period.

At the centre of the Ciudad quarter on Ronda's most picturesque square, the Plaza Duquesa de Parcent, stands the cathedral church of **Santa María La Mayor** (daily 10am–7pm; €1.20), originally the Arab town's Friday mosque. Externally it's a graceful combination of Moorish, Gothic and Renaissance styles with the belfry built on top of the old minaret. The interior is decidedly less interesting, but you can see an arch covered with Arabic calligraphy, and just in front of the current street door, a part of the old Arab *mihrab*, or prayer niche, has been exposed. Slightly west of the square on c/Montero lies the **Casa de Mondragón**, probably the real palace of the Moorish kings (Mon–Fri 10am–7pm, Sat & Sun 10am–3pm; €1.50). Inside, three of the patios preserve original stuccowork and there's a magnificent carved ceiling, as well as a museum covering local archeology and aspects of Moorish Ronda.

To the northeast of the Plaza Duquesa de Parcent on c/Armiñan, which bisects La Ciudad, at no. 29 you'll find the new **Museo Lara** (daily 10am–8pm; €3.60), containing the collection of *rondeño* Juan Antonio Lara, a member of the family who own and run the local bus company of the same name. An avid collector since childhood, Señor Lara has filled the museum with a fascinating collection of antique clocks, pistols and armaments, musical instruments and archeological finds, as well as early cameras and cinematographic equipment.

Near the end of the Ciudad are the ruins of the **Alcázar**, destroyed by the French in 1809 ("from sheer love of destruction", according to Richard Ford), and now partially occupied by a school. Once it was virtually impregnable – as indeed was this whole fortress capital, which ruled an independent and isolated Moorish kingdom until 1485, just seven years before the fall of Granada.

The principal gates of the town, the magnificent Moorish **Puerto de Almocabar**, through which passed the Christian conquerors (led personally by Fernando), and the triumphal **Puerta de Carlos V**, erected later during the reign of the Hapsburg emperor, stand side by side to the southeast of the Alcázar at the entrance to the suburb of San Francisco.

The **Mercadillo** quarter, which grew up in the wake of the Christian conquest, is of comparatively little interest, with just a couple of buildings worth a quick look. The first is a remarkably preserved inn where Miguel Cervantes once slept, the sixteenth-century **Posada de las Ánimas** (also known as the Hogar del Pensionista) in c/Cecilia, the oldest building in the quarter. The other is the eighteenth-century **Plaza de Toros** (daily 10am–8pm; €3), close by the Plaza de España and the beautiful cliff-top *paseo* from which you get good views of the old and new bridges. Ronda played a leading part in the development of bullfighting and was the birthplace of the modern *corrida* (bullfight). The ring, built in 1781, is one of the earliest in Spain and the fight season here is one of the country's most important. At its September *feria* the *corrida goyesca*, honouring Spain's great artist Goya, who made a number of paintings of the fights at Ronda, takes place in eighteenth-century costume. You can visit the bullring to wander around the arena, and there's a museum inside.

The Puente Nuevo bridge's bar (now closed) was originally the town prison and last saw use during the Civil War, when Ronda was the site of some of the south's most vicious massacres. Hemingway, in *For Whom the Bell Tolls*, recorded how prisoners were thrown alive into the gorge. These days, Ronda remains a major military garrison post and houses much of the Spanish Africa Legion, Franco's old crack regiment, who can be seen wandering around town in their tropical green coats and tasselled fezzes. They have a mean reputation.

Eating and drinking

Most of the bargain **restaurants** are grouped round the far end of the Plaza del Socorro, though there are also some to be found near the Plaza de España.

Bar-Galeria Enfrente Arte, c/Espiritu Santo 9, close to the Puerta de Almocabar in La Ciudad. The bar of the hotel of the same name (see above) stages art exhibitions plus frequent musical and literary events. The views towards the Serranía de Ronda through panoramic windows are wonderful. Open till late.

Bar Luciano, c/Armiñan 42, La Ciudad. Pleasant bar-restaurant with a good-value *menú* for around €7.50.

Bar Valencia, c/Naranja 6, a couple of blocks east of Plaza del Socorro. Good *platos combinados* served up in an earthy atmosphere with an unbelievably cheap *menú* for around €3.50.

Bodega La Giralda, c/Nueva 19. Traditional and excellent tapas in a great setting.

Café Alba, c/Espinel 44. Piping hot *churros* and delicious breakfast coffee.

Don Miguel, Plaza de España. High-quality restaurant offering *rondeño* specialities such as

perdiz estofado (partridge stew) along with a *menú* and a terrace with a marvellous view of the Tajo.

Doña Pepa, Plaza del Socorro. Family-run and reliable restaurant with some vegetarian possibilities and a separate cafeteria-bar serving *bocadillos* and freshly squeezed orange juice.

La Farola, Plaza Carmen Abela 9. Friendly and economical *raciones* and *platos combinados* place; open till late.

Parador de Ronda, Plaza de España. The *parador*'s elegant restaurant has a menu offering an excellent choice of local and regional dishes, many of them appearing on a bargain *menú gastronomico* for around €25.

Hotel Polo, c/Mariano Soubirón 8. Pricey but excellent restaurant.

Restaurante La Merced, Plaza de la Merced s/n. Good place for well-prepared *platos combinados* and has a *menú* for around €6.

Around Ronda

Ronda makes an excellent base for exploring the superb countryside in the immediate vicinity or for visiting more of the White Towns. Fifteen kilometres away, **Setenil**, dug into the cliffs and with cave dwellings, is one of the most unusual – nearby **Olvera** and **Teba** are worth a visit, too. Other possible excursions are to the remarkable **Cueva de la Pileta**, with prehistoric cave paintings, and the Roman ruins of **Ronda la Vieja**.

Walks around Ronda

Good walking routes from Ronda are pretty limitless. One of the best, and a good way to get a sense of the town as a rural market centre set among farmland, is to take the path down to the gorge from the Mondragón palace terrace. In the fields below there's a network of paths and some stupendous views. A couple of hours' walk will bring you to the main road to the northwest where you can hitch or walk back the 4–5km into the Mercadillo. Another excursion is to an old, unused **aqueduct** set in rocky pasture – from the market square just outside the Ciudad in the San Francisco area, take the straight residential street which leads up and out of town. After about an hour this ends in olive groves, by a stream and a large water trough. A path through the groves leads to the aqueduct.

Further afield, if you're mobile or energetic, are the ruins of a town and **Roman theatre** at a site known as **Ronda la Vieja**, 12km from Ronda and reached by turning right 6km down the main A376 road to Arcos/Sevilla. At the site (Tues–Sun 10am–5pm; free) a friendly farmer, who is also the guardian, will present you with a plan (in Spanish) and record your nationality for statistical purposes.

Based on Neolithic foundations – note the recently discovered prehistoric stone huts beside the entrance – it was as a Roman town in the first century AD that Acinipo (the town's Roman name), reached its zenith. Immediately west of the theatre, the ground falls away in a startlingly steep escarpment, and from here there are fine views all around, taking in the hill village of Olvera to the north. From here a track leads off towards the strange "cave village" of Setenil (see below).

The Cueva de la Pileta

West from Ronda is the prehistoric **Cueva de la Pileta** (daily guided visits on the hour 10am–1pm & 4–6pm; €5.50, students €3; hourly visits on the hour with a strict limit of 25 persons per tour), a fabulous series of caverns with some remarkable paintings of animals (mainly bison), fish and what are apparently magic symbols. These etchings and the occupation of the cave date from about 25,000 BC – hence predating the more famous caves at Altamira in northern Spain – to the end of the Bronze Age. The tour lasts one hour on average, but can be longer, and is in Spanish – though the guide does speak a little English. There are hundreds of bats in the cave, and no artificial lighting, so visitors carry lanterns with them; you may also want to take a jumper, as the caves can be extremely chilly. Be aware if you leave a car in the car park that thieves are active here. To avoid disappointment in high summer (when there are often far more visitors than the stipulated maximum per visit) it's a good idea to **book** ahead on ☎952 167 343.

To reach the caves take either an Algeciras-bound local train (4 daily; 35min) to the Estación Benaoján-Montejaque, or a bus, which drops you a little closer in Benaoján. There's a bar at the train station if you want to stock up on drink before the hour-long walk (6km) to the caves. Follow the farm track from the right bank of the river until you reach the farmhouse (approximately 30min). From here, a track goes straight uphill to the main road just before the signposted turning for the caves. If you're driving, follow the road to Benaoján and take the turn-off, from where it is about 4km.

Setenil, Olvera and Teba

North of Ronda, and feasible as a day-trip from the town, are Setenil and Olvera. **SETENIL**, on a very minor road to Olvera, is the strangest of all the White Towns, its cave-like streets formed from the overhanging ledge of a gorge. Many of the houses – sometimes two or three storeys high – have natural roofs in the rock. There are a couple of bars, and a reasonably priced **hotel** with a good restaurant, *El Almendral* (☎956 134 029, ⓕ956 134 444; ❺), on the road just outside town. Four buses a day run from Ronda, or it's a possible walk from Ronda la Vieja. The train station is a good 8km from the village itself.

   OLVERA, 15km beyond, tumbles down a hill topped by its church and a fine Moorish castle. There's just one bus a day from Ronda, but there are a couple of **pensiones** if you want to stay and explore the region: the excellent-value *Maqueda*, c/Calvario 35 (☎956 130 733; ❷), and the nearby *Medina*, c/Sepulveda 6 (☎956 130 173; ❷), with plenty of neo-Moorish embellishments added by the proprietor. For **food**, superb *fino*, tapas and a budget *menú* are to be had at the friendly *Bar Manolo* in Plaza Andalucía, at the foot of the main street.

   TEBA is a small community with a calm and prosperous air situated in the mountains five or six kilometres south of the A382 between Campillos and Olvera, or straight up on the A367 from Ronda. It's easily seen from the A382 and is approached by way of a single, clearly marked road which winds its way up to the town. The lower square, Plaza de la Constitución, has all the **accommodation**: three clean, friendly and relatively inexpensive places, of which the best is *Hostal Sevillano*, c/San Francisco 26 (☎952 748 011; ❸), just off the plaza; it also serves food in its bar/restaurant below and has a good value *menú*. Sights around the village include the enormous Baroque church of **Santa Cruz** (daily 5–6pm; if closed at this time knock at the adjoining house of the *cura*), which is stuffed full of treasures, and the Plaza de España where there's a **monument** in Scottish granite to Robert Bruce. Bruce's recently rediscovered heart played a part in the battle against the Moors here in 1331; one of his knights carried the organ as a talisman and threw it into the Moorish ranks to encourage his timid soldiers to charge. On the hill above the town are the remains of a **Moorish castle**, constructed on Roman ruins, which has a superb keep. The views from here over the surrounding countryside are spectacular.

Towards Cádiz and Sevilla

Ronda has good transport connections in most directions (see "Travel details" at the end of this chapter). Almost any route to the north or west is rewarding, taking you past a whole series of White Towns, many of them fortified since the days of the Reconquest from the Moors – hence the mass of "de la Frontera" suffixes.

Grazalema, Ubrique and Medina Sidonia

Perhaps the best of all the routes, though a roundabout one, and tricky without your own transport, is to **Cádiz** via Grazalema, Ubrique, and Medina

Sidonia. This passes through the **Sierra de Grazalema Natural Park** before skirting the nature reserve of **Cortes de la Frontera** (which you can drive through by following the road beyond Benaoján) and, towards Alcalá de los Gazules, running through the northern fringe of the **Parque Natural de los Alcornocales**, which derives its name from the forests of cork oaks, one of its main attractions.

Twenty-three kilometres from Ronda, **GRAZALEMA** is a striking place at the centre of the Sierra de Grazalema Natural Park, with the **Puerto de las Palomas** (Pass of the Doves – at 1350m the second highest pass in Andalucía) rearing up behind. Cross this, and you descend to Zahara and the main road west (see below).

UBRIQUE, 20km southwest, is a natural mountain fortress which was a Republican stronghold in the Civil War. According to Nicholas Luard's book, *Andalucía*: "It proved so difficult for the besieging nationalists to take, they eventually called up a plane from Sevilla to fly over the town and drop leaflets carrying the message: "Ubrique, if in five minutes from now all your arms are not piled in front of the Guardia Civil post and the roofs and terraces of your houses are not covered in white sheets, the town will be devastated by the bombs in this plane." The threat was effective, although not quite in the way the nationalists had intended. Without spreading a single white sheet or leaving a gun behind them Ubrique's citizens promptly abandoned the town and took to the hills behind."

This is a Civil War story typical of these parts. More unusual, however, is that the town today is relatively prosperous, surviving very largely on its medieval guild craft of leather-making.

MEDINA SIDONIA, further west on the minor roads, is the old ducal seat of the Guzmáns, one of Spain's most famous families. Depopulated and now somewhat ramshackle, it nevertheless offers glimpses of sixteenth-century grandeur.

Zahara de la Sierra

Heading directly to Jerez or Sevilla from Ronda, a beautiful rural drive, you pass below **ZAHARA DE LA SIERRA** (or *de los Membrillos* – "of the Quinces"), perhaps the most perfect example of these fortified hill towns. Set in beautiful country, a landmark for miles around, its red-tiled houses huddle round a church and castle on a stark outcrop of rock. Once an important Moorish town, its capture by the Christians in 1483 opened the way for the conquest of Ronda – and ultimately Granada. There's a clutch of **places to stay**: the homely and simple *Pensión Gonzalo*, c/San Juan 9, with no sign, opposite the church (❷), *Los Estribos*, c/Fuerte 3 (☎956 137 445; ❸), near the swimming pool, and the excellent *Hotel Marqués de Zahara*, c/San Juan 3 (☎956 123 061; ❹), with a good **restaurant**. Zahara's pleasant **campsite** lies 3km outside the village along the old Ronda road (open April–Sept; a taxi costs about €3); here you can rent a tent complete with camp beds.

Arcos de la Frontera

Of more substantial interest, and a better place to break the journey, is **ARCOS DE LA FRONTERA**. This was taken from the Moors in 1264, over two centuries before Zahara fell – an impressive feat, for it stands high above the Río Guadalete on a double crag and must have been a wretchedly impregnable fortress. This dramatic location, enhanced by low, white houses and fine sandstone churches, gives the town a similar feel and appearance to Ronda – only Arcos is poorer and, quite unjustifiably, far less visited. The streets of the town, despite particularly manic packs of local bikers, are if anything more interesting, with their mix of Moorish and Renaissance buildings. At the heart is the Plaza del Cabildo, easily reached by following the signs for the *parador*, which occupies one side of it. Flanking another two sides are the castle walls and the large Gothic-Mudéjar church of **Santa María de la Asunción**; the last side is left open, offering plunging views to the river valley.

Practicalities

A **turismo** on the west side of Plaza del Cabildo (Mon–Fri 10am–2pm & 5.30–7.30pm, Sat 10am–2pm, Sun 10.30am–12.30pm; ☎956 702 264) can provide a town map and also does daily guided tours of the old town (except Sun). Budget **accommodation** in the **old town** is confined to the *Pensión de Callejón de las Monjas* (☎956 702 302; ❸), immediately behind the church of Santa María, and the very friendly *Bar San Marcos*, c/Marquéz de Torresoto 6 (☎956 700 721; ❸), the better option, with its own restaurant. More upmarket options are the elegant *parador* (☎956 700 500, ☎956 701 116; ❻), perched on a rock pedestal, the *Hotel Marqués de Torresoto*, c/Marqués de Torresoto 4 (☎956 700 717, ☎956 704 205; ❻), housed in a converted seventeenth-century mansion with colonnaded patio and Baroque chapel, and a new hotel, *La Casa Grande*, c/Maldonado 10 (☎ & ☎956 703 930, ⓦwww.lacasagrande.net; ❼), with beautiful rooms inside an eighteenth-century mansion and a stunning terrace view across the river valley. In the **new town** you'll find a couple of places on either side of the main street, c/Corredera, including the excellent *Hotel Fonda Comercio* (☎956 700 057; ❹), Arcos's oldest inn, welcoming visitors for well over a century, and recently refurbished.

Eating and drinking tends to be expensive in the old quarter, where most of the hotels have their own restaurants. A more modest good-value option is *La Terraza* in the gardens of the Paseo de Andalucía to the southwest of the Plaza del Cabildo, which serves a wide variety of *platos combinados* at outdoor tables, while *Alcaraván*, c/Nueva 1, close to the castle walls, is an interesting cave restaurant which does tapas and *platos asados* (roasts). In the new town *Los Faraones*, c/Debajo del Corral 14, is a well-established North-African restaurant with a €9 *menú*.

Just out of town, towards Ronda, a road leads down to a couple of sandy **beaches** on the riverbank (hourly buses from the bus station), where there's a pleasant two-star waterfront *hostal*, *La Molinera* (☎956 708 002; ❺), and a **campsite**, *Arcos de la Frontera* (☎956 708 333), close to the Bornos reservoir (aka Lago de Argos); bring mosquito protection if you stay at either, and if you swim here, or further along towards the namesake village, take care – there are said to be whirlpools in some parts.

Sevilla, the west and Córdoba

With the major exception of **Sevilla** – and to a slightly lesser extent **Córdoba** – the west and centre of Andalucía are not greatly visited. The coast here, certainly the Atlantic **Costa de la Luz**, is a world apart from the Mediterranean resorts, with the entire stretch between Algeciras and Tarifa designated a "potential military zone". This probably sounds grim – and in parts, marked off by *Paso Prohibido* signs, it is – but the ruling has also had happier effects, preventing foreigners from buying up land and placing strict controls even on Spanish developments. So, for a hundred or more kilometres, there are scarcely any villa developments and only a modest number of hotels and campsites – small, easy-going and low-key even at the one growing resort of **Conil**. On the coast, too, there is the attraction of **Cádiz**, one of the oldest and, though it's now in decline, most elegant ports in Europe.

Inland rewards include the smaller towns between Sevilla and Córdoba, Moorish **Carmona** particularly. But the most beautiful, and neglected, parts of this region are the dark, ilex-covered hills and poor rural villages of the **Sierra Morena** to the north and northwest of Sevilla. Perfect walking country with its network of streams and reservoirs between modest peaks, this is also a botanist's dream, brilliant with a mass of spring flowers.

On a more organized level, though equally compelling if you're into bird-watching or wildlife, is the huge nature reserve of the **Coto de Doñana**, spreading back from Huelva in vast expanses of *marismas* – sand dunes, salt flats and marshes. The most important of the Spanish reserves, Doñana is vital to scores of migratory birds and to endangered mammals such as the Iberian lynx.

Sevilla

"Seville," wrote Byron, "is a pleasant city, famous for oranges and women." And for its heat, he might perhaps have added, since **SEVILLA**'s summers are intense and start early, in May. But the spirit, for all its nineteenth-century chauvinism, is about right. Sevilla has three important monuments and an illustrious history, but what it's essentially famous for is its own living self – the greatest city of the Spanish south, of Carmen, Don Juan and Figaro, and the archetype of Andalucian promise. This reputation for gaiety and brilliance, for theatricality and intensity of life, does seem deserved. It's expressed on a phenomenally grand scale at the city's two great festivals – **Semana Santa** (in the week before Easter) and the **Feria de Abril** (which starts two weeks after Easter Sunday and lasts a week). Either is worth considerable effort to get to. Sevilla is also Spain's second most important centre for **bullfighting**, after Madrid.

Despite its elegance and charm, and its wealth, based on food processing, shipbuilding, construction and a thriving tourist industry, Sevilla lies at the centre of a depressed agricultural area and has an unemployment rate of nearly

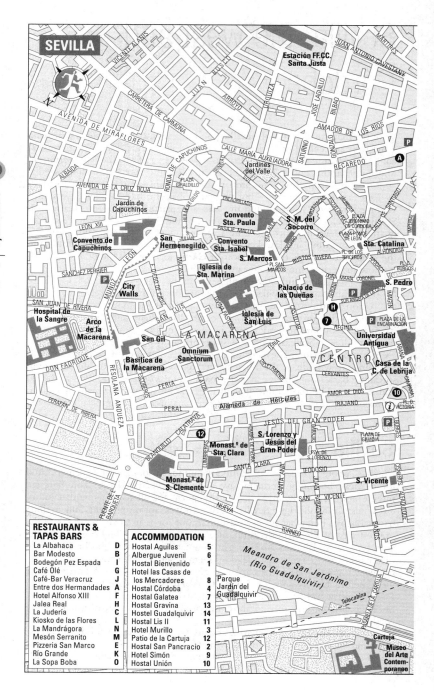

SEVILLA

Estación FF.CC. Santa Justa

Jardines del Valle

Convento Sta. Paula
S. M. del Socorro
Sta. Catalina
Convento de Capuchinos
San Hermenegildo
Convento Sta. Isabel
S. Marcos
S. Pedro
Jardin de Capuchinos
Iglesia de Sta. Marina
Palacio de las Dueñas
City Walls
Hospital de la Sangre
Iglesia de San Luis
Arco de la Macarena
San Gil
LA MACARENA
Universidad Antigua
Basílica de la Macarena
Omnium Sanctorum
CENTRO
Casa de la C. de Lebrija
Alameda de Hércules
JESÚS DEL GRAN PODER
S. Lorenzo y Jesús del Gran Poder
Monast.ᵉ de Sta. Clara
S. Vicente
Monast.ᵉ de S. Clemente

Meandro de San Jerónimo (Río Guadalquivir)

Parque Jardin del Guadalquivir

Telecabina

Cartuja

Museo del Arte Contemporaneo

RESTAURANTS & TAPAS BARS	
La Albahaca	D
Bar Modesto	B
Bodegón Pez Espada	I
Café Olé	G
Café-Bar Veracruz	J
Entre dos Hermandades	A
Hotel Alfonso XIII	F
Jalea Real	H
La Judería	C
Kiosko de las Flores	L
La Mandrágora	N
Mesón Serranito	M
Pizzeria San Marco	E
Río Grande	K
La Sopa Boba	O

ACCOMMODATION	
Hostal Aguilas	5
Albergue Juvenil	6
Hostal Bienvenido	1
Hotel las Casas de los Mercadores	8
Hostal Córdoba	4
Hostal Galatea	7
Hostal Gravina	13
Hostel Guadalquivir	14
Hostal Lis II	11
Hotel Murillo	3
Patio de la Cartuja	12
Hostal San Pancracio	2
Hotel Simón	9
Hostal Unión	10

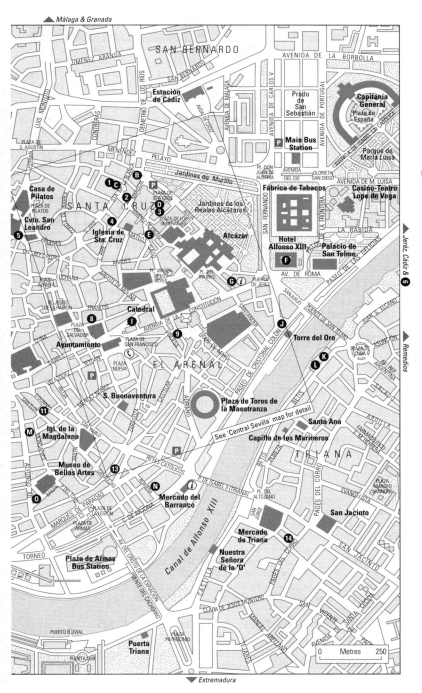

Málaga & Granada

SAN BERNARDO

AVENIDA DE LA BORBOLLA

Estación
de Cádiz

Prado
de
San
Sebastián

Capitanía
General
Plaza de
España

Main Bus
Station

Parque de
María Luisa

PLAZA DE
S. AGUSTÍN

Jardines de Murillo

Fábrica de Tabacos

Casino-Teatro
Lope de Vega

Casa de
Pilatos

SANTA CRUZ

Jardines de los
Reales Alcázares

LA RÁBIDA

Cvto. San
Leandro

Iglesia de
Sta. Cruz

Alcázar

Hotel
Alfonso XIII

Palacio de
San Telmo

PL. DEL
TRIUNFO

PUERTA
DE JEREZ

AV. DE ROMA

Catedral

PASEO DE LAS DELICIAS

Torre del Oro

Ayuntamiento

PLAZA DE
SAN FRANCISCO

EL ARENAL

S. Buenaventura

Plaza de Toros de
la Maestranza

Igl. de la
Magdalena

Santa Ana

See 'Central Sevilla' map for detail

Capilla de los Marineros

TRIANA

Museo de
Bellas Artes

Mercado del
Barranco

San Jacinto

Plaza de Armas
Bus Station

Mercado
de Triana

Canal de Alfonso XIII

Nuestra
Señora
de la 'O'

Puerta
Triana

PUERTO FLUVIAL

PUERTA SUR

0   Metres   250

Extremadura

Jerez, Cádiz & 6

Remedios

Moorish Sevilla

Sevilla was one of the earliest **Moorish conquests** (in 712) and, as part of the caliphate of Córdoba, became the second city of *al-Andalus*. When the caliphate broke up in the early eleventh century it was by far the most powerful of the independent states (or *taifas*) to emerge, extending its power over the Algarve and eventually over Jaén, Murcia and Córdoba itself. This period, under a series of three Arabic rulers from the Abbadid dynasty (1023–91), was something of a golden age. The city's court was unrivalled in wealth and luxury and was sophisticated too, developing a strong chivalric element and a flair for poetry – one of the most skilled exponents being the last ruler, al-Mu'tamid, the "poet-king". But with sophistication came decadence and in 1091 Abbadid rule was usurped by a new force, the **Almoravids**, a tribe of fanatical Berber Muslims from North Africa, to whom the Andalucians had appealed for help against the rising threat from the northern Christian kingdoms.

Despite initial military successes, the Almoravids failed to consolidate their gains in *al-Andalus* and attempted to rule through military governors from Marrakesh. In the middle of the twelfth century they were in turn supplanted by a new Berber incursion, the **Almohads**, who by about 1170 had recaptured virtually all the former territories. Sevilla had accepted Almohad rule in 1147 and became the capital of this last real empire of the Moors in Spain. Almohad power was sustained until their disastrous defeat in 1212 by the combined Christian armies of the north, at Las Navas de Tolosa. In this brief and precarious period Sevilla underwent a renaissance of public building, characterized by a new vigour and fluidity of style. The Almohads rebuilt the **Alcázar**, enlarged the principal **mosque** – later demolished to make room for the Christian cathedral – and erected a new and brilliant minaret, a tower over 100m tall, topped with four copper spheres that could be seen for miles round: the **Giralda**.

forty percent – one of the highest in Spain. The total refurbishment of the infrastructure boosted by the 1992 Expo – including impressive new roads, seven bridges, a high-speed rail link and a revamped airport – was intended to regenerate the city's (and the region's) economic fortunes but has hardly turned out to be the catalyst for growth and prosperity promised at the time. Indeed, some of the colossal debts are still unpaid a decade later.

Meantime, **petty crime** is a big problem, and the motive for stealing is usually cash to feed drug addiction. Bag-snatching is common (often Italian-style, from passing *motos*), as is breaking into cars. There's even a special breed called *semaforazos* who break the windows of cars stopped at traffic lights and grab what they can. Be careful, but don't be put off. Despite a worrying rise in the number of muggings in recent years, when compared with cities of similar size in northern Europe, violent crime is still relatively rare.

Sevilla's most famous present-day native son is the former prime minister, **Felipe González**, who led the Socialist administration that governed Spain for fourteen years until his defeat in 1996. Another, more bizarre Sevillano is one **Gregorio XVII**, who calls himself the true pope; in defiance of his excommunication by the Vatican, "Pope Greg" is leader of a large ultra-reactionary order which has made the dead Franco a saint and has built an extensive new "Vatican" in the countryside to the south of the city.

Arrival, orientation and information

Bisected by the Río Guadalquivir, Sevilla is fairly easy to find your way about (though hell if you're driving). The **old city** – where you'll want to spend most of your time – takes up the east bank. At its heart, side by side, stand the three great monuments: the **Giralda tower**, the **Cathedral** and the **Alcázar**, with the cramped alleyways of the **Barrio Santa Cruz**, the medieval Jewish quarter and now the heart of tourist life, extending east of them. North of here is the main shopping and commercial district, its most obvious landmarks the **Plaza Nueva** and **La Campana**, and the smart pedestrianized **c/Sierpes** which runs between them. From La Campana, c/Alfonso XII runs down towards the river by way of the **Museo de Bellas Artes**, second in importance in Spain only to the Prado in Madrid. Across the river is the earthier, traditionally working-class district of **Triana**, flanked to the south by the **Los Remedios** *barrio*, the city's wealthier residential zone where the great April *feria* takes place.

Points of arrival, too, are straightforward, though the **train station**, Santa Justa, is a fair way out on Avenida Kansas City, the airport road. Buses #27 and #32 will take you from outside here to the Plaza de la Encarnación (roughly dead centre of our city map), from where all sights are within easy walking distance; alternatively buses #70, #C1 and #C2 will take you to the main bus station. The **airport** bus, operated by Amarillos (hourly; €2.10), terminates in the centre at the Puerta de Jerez, at the top of Avenida Roma between the turismo and the Fábrica de Tabacos. To take the same trip by taxi costs around €15.

The **main bus station** is at the Prado de San Sebastián. Most companies and destinations go from here: exceptions include buses for Badajoz, Extremadura (the provinces of Cáceres and Badajoz), Huelva, Madrid and international destinations which arrive and depart from the station at Plaza de Armas by the Puente del Cachorro on the river.

The main **turismo** is at Avda. de la Constitución 21 (Mon–Sat 9am–7pm, Sun 10am–2pm; ☎954 221 404); they have good city maps, accommodation lists and you can get a copy of the very useful free listings magazine *Giraldillo*, here too. There's also a less chaotic **municipal tourist office** at c/Arjona 28 just north of the bullring (Mon–Fri 8am–8pm, Sat & Sun 8.30am–2.30pm) by the Puente de Triana, with a sub-office at the Santa Justa train station.

One way to get to grips with the city is to take an **open-top bus tour** – especially good if you're pressed for time. This hop-on hop-off service is operated by Sevirama (☎954 560 693) and the buses leave half-hourly from the riverside Torre del Oro, stopping at or near the main sites (all-day tickets cost around €9).

Accommodation

The most attractive **area to stay** is undoubtedly the **Barrio Santa Cruz**, though this is reflected in the prices. In mid-season or during the big festivals you can find yourself paying ridiculous amounts for what is little more than a cell; rooms are relatively expensive everywhere, in fact. Nonetheless there are reasonable places to be found in the *barrio* and on its periphery (especially immediately north, and south towards the bus station) and they're at least worth a try before heading elsewhere. Slightly further out, another promising area is to the north of the Plaza Nueva, and especially over towards the river and the Plaza de Armas bus station. It's always worth trying to bargain the price down a little, though you may not always succeed.

At peak times you may face quite a walk and if you're planning to arrive during any of the major festivals you'd be advised to book ahead. The list overleaf is no more than a start, and it's worth checking at the places you'll pass between all these. If you're still unable to find anything (which can happen at busy periods) the turismo has complete lists and should be able to help.

Semana Santa and the Feria de Abril

Sevilla boasts two of the largest festival celebrations in Spain. The first, **Semana Santa** (Holy Week), always spectacular in Andalucía, is here at its peak with extraordinary processions of masked penitents and carnival-style floats. The second, the **Feria de Abril**, is unique to the city: a one-time market festival, long converted to a week-long party of drink, food and flamenco. The *feria* follows close on the heels of *Semana Santa*. If you have the energy and time, experience both.

Semana Santa

Semana Santa may be a religious festival, but for most of the week solemnity isn't the keynote – there's lots of carousing and frivolity, and bars are full day and night. In essence, it involves the marching in procession of fifty-odd brotherhoods (many now including women) of the church (*cofradías*) and penitents, followed by *pasos*, elaborate platforms or floats on which sit seventeenth-century images of the Virgin or Christ in tableaux from the Passion. For weeks beforehand the *cofradías* painstakingly adorn the hundred or so *pasos*, spending vast amounts on costumes and precious stones. The bearers (*costaleros*) walk in time to stirring, traditional dirges and drumbeats from the bands, which are often punctuated by impromptu and moving street-corner *saetas* from the citizenry – short, fervent, flamenco hymns about the Passion and the Virgin's sorrows.

The last lap of the official **route** for every *paso* goes from La Campana south along c/Sierpes, through the cathedral, and around the Giralda and the Bishop's Palace. Throughout the week *pasos* leave churches all over town from early afternoon onward, snaking through the city and back to their resting place many hours later. **Good Friday** morning is the climax, when the *pasos* leave the churches at midnight and move through the town for much of the night, watched by large crowds. The highlight is the arrival at the cathedral of the *paso* bearing *La Macarena*, an image of the patroness of bullfighters and, by extension, of Sevilla itself.

The pattern of events changes every day; banks, hotels and businesses produce free skeleton **timetables**, and route maps are also issued with local papers, which are essential if you want to know which events are where – the ultra-Catholic *ABC*

Budget options

Hostal Águilas, c/Águilas 15 ☎954 213 177. Small comfortable and quiet *hostal* with some en-suite rooms, near the Casa de Pilatos. ❹

Albergue Juvenil Sevilla, c/Isaac Peral 2 ☎954 613 150 (they tend not to answer). Leafy if often crowded youth hostel some way out in the university district; take bus #34 from the Puerta de Jerez by the turismo or Plaza Nueva. ❶

Hostal Bienvenido, c/Archeros 14 ☎954 413 655. East of c/Santa María la Blanca, this *hostal* offers simple small rooms but has a nice roof terrace. ❸

Hostal Gravina, c/Gravina 46 ☎954 216 414. Pleasant, family-run *hostal* close to the Museo de Bellas Artes. ❷

Hostal Lis II, c/Olavide 5, a couple of blocks east of the Museo de las Bellas Artes ☎954 560 228, ⊚www.sol.com/hostalisii. A clean and simple place offering rooms with and without bath and offering internet access (extra charge) to guests. ❸.

Hostal San Pancracio, c/Cruces 9 (☎954 413

104). Decent range of room options here, some with bath – so check what's available. ❸

Moderate and expensive options

Hotel Las Casas de los Mercaderes, c/Álvarez Quintero 12 (☎954 225 858, ☎954 229 884, ⊚www.lascasas.zoom.es). Near the cathedral, this converted former *bodega* has been transformed into a very comfortable hotel with a delightful seventeenth-century patio, a roof terrace and great views from some rooms (especially nos. 201–206). ❼

Hostal Córdoba, c/Farnesio 12 ☎954 227 498. Good standard (if slightly overpriced) *hostal*, offering some rooms with bath, close to the church of Santa Cruz. ❺

Hostal Galatea, Plaza San Juan de la Palma 4, northwest of the church of San Pedro ☎954 563 564, ☎954 563 517. Friendly *hostal* in a restored town house in the heart of the atmospheric Macarena quarter; some rooms with bath. ❹

paper has the best listings with piles of background and historical info on each brotherhood. On Maundy Thursday women dress in black and it's considered respectful for tourists not to dress in shorts or T-shirts. Triana is a good location on this day, and there's always a crush of spectators outside the cathedral and on c/Sierpes, the most awe-inspiring venue. Plaza de la Virgen de los Reyes under the Giralda is a good viewing point but even here it gets chaotic. The best way of all to see the processions is to pick them up near their starting and finishing points in their respective *barrios*; here you'll see the true *teatro de la calle* – theatre of the streets.

Feria de Abril

The **Feria de Abril** is staged a fortnight after Semana Santa ends and lasts nonstop for a week. For its duration a vast area on the far bank of the river in the *barrio* of Los Remedios, the *Real de la Feria*, is totally covered in rows of *casetas*, canvas pavilions or tents of varying sizes. Some of these belong to eminent *sevillano* families, some to groups of friends, others to clubs, trade associations or political parties. In each one – from around nine at night until perhaps six or seven the following morning – there is flamenco singing and dancing. Many of the men and virtually all the women wear traditional costume, the latter in an astonishing array of brilliantly coloured, flounced gypsy dresses.

The sheer size of this spectacle is extraordinary, and the dancing, with its intense and knowing sexuality, a revelation. But most infectious of all is the universal spontaneity of enjoyment; after wandering around staring with the crowds you wind up a part of it, drinking and dancing in one of the "open" *casetas* which have commercial bars. Among these you'll usually find lively *casetas* erected by the anarchist trade union CNT and various leftist groups.

Earlier in the day, from 1pm until 5pm, Sevillana society **parades** around the fairground in carriages or on horseback. An incredible extravaganza of display and voyeurism, this has subtle but distinct gradations of dress and style; catch it at least once. Each day, too, there are **bullfights** (at around 5.30pm; very expensive tickets in advance from the ring), generally reckoned to be the best of the season.

Hostal Guadalquivir, c/Pagés del Corro 53 ☎954 332 100, ℱ954 332 104. The *barrio* Triana's only *hostal* is atmospheric and friendly; some rooms en suite. ❹

Hotel Murillo, c/Lope de Rueda 7 ☎954 216 095, ℱ954 219 616, ⊛www.sol.com/hotel.murillo. Traditional hotel in restored mansion with all facilities plus amusingly kitsch features such as suits of armour and paint-palette key rings. Close to the Plaza Santa Cruz. ❻

Patio de la Cartuja, c/Lumbreras 8, off west side of Alameda's northern end ☎954 900 200, ℱ954 902 056, ⊛www.patiosdesevilla.com. Stylish and excellent-value apart-hotel created from an old *sevillano corral*; en-suite apartments with balconies, kitchen and lounge are set around a tiled patio. Own garage. ❼

Hotel Simón, c/García de Vinuesa 19 ☎954 226 660, ℱ954 562 241. Well-restored mansion in an excellent position across from the cathedral. All rooms are en suite and air-conditioned and this can be a bargain out of high season. ❻

Hostal Unión, c/Tarifa 4 ☎954 229 294. Slightly east of the Plaza Duque de la Victoria and one of the best-value places in this area. Clean, economical rooms with bath. ❹

Camping

Camping Sevilla ☎954 514 379. Right by the airport, so some noise but otherwise not a bad site; has a pool. The airport bus will get you there or take bus #70 from outside the main Prado de San Sebastián bus station and ask to be dropped at "Parque Alcosa". The site has its own thrice-daily minibus service ferrying clients to and from central Sevilla.

Club de Campo ☎954 720 250. About 12km south of the centre in Dos Hermanas, with a pool. Half-hourly Amarillos buses from the main bus station or c/Palos de la Frontera, south of the cathedral.

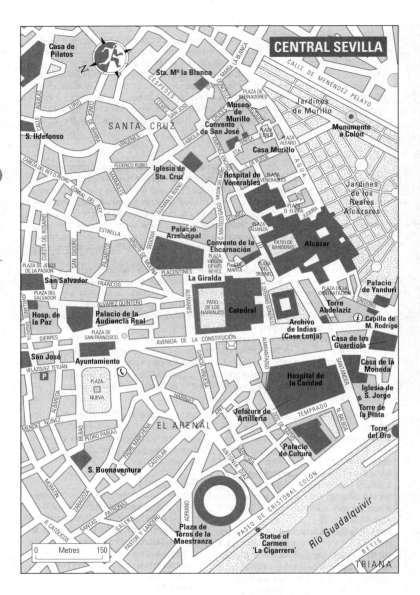

The Cathedral

Sevilla's **Catedral** (Mon–Sat 11am–5pm, Sun 2–6pm; €4.80 including admission to the Giralda, free Sun; students & senior citizens €1.20) was conceived in 1402 as an unrivalled monument to Christian glory: "a building on so magnificent a scale that posterity will believe we were mad". To make way for this new monument, the Almohad mosque (see box on p.290) that stood on the proposed site was almost entirely demolished. Meanwhile the canons, inspired by their vision of future repute, renounced all but a subsistence level of their incomes to further the building.

The cathedral was completed in just over a century (1402–1506), an extraordinary achievement as it's the largest Gothic church in the world. As Norman Lewis says, "It expresses conquest and domination in architectural terms of sheer mass." Though it is built upon the huge, rectangular base-plan of the old mosque, the Christian architects (probably under the direction of the French master architect of Rouen Cathedral) added the extra dimension of height. Its central nave rises to 42 metres, and even the side chapels seem tall enough to contain an ordinary church. The total area covers 11,520 square metres, and new calculations, based on cubic measurement, have now pushed it in front of St Paul's in London and St Peter's in Rome as the largest church in the world.

From the old mosque, the magnificent **Giralda** and the Moorish entrance court, the **Patio de los Naranjos**, were spared, though the patio is somewhat marred by Renaissance embellishments. The patio was originally entered from c/Alemanes, through the **Puerta del Perdón**, the original main gateway and now the **visitor** exit – the **main visitor entrance** is on the cathedral's south side, through the Puerta de San Cristóbal.

The interior

Entering the cathedral by the Puerta de San Cristóbal, you are guided through a reception area which brings you into the church to the west of the portal itself. Turn right once inside to head east, where you will soon be confronted by the **Monument to Christopher Columbus** (*Cristóbal Colón* in Spanish), actually the explorer's tomb, and aptly located before the doorway dedicated to the saint he was named after. Columbus's remains were originally interred in the cathedral of Havana, on the island that he had discovered on his first voyage in 1492. But during the upheavals surrounding the declaration of Cuban independence in 1902, Spain transferred the remains to Sevilla and the monumental tomb – in the late Romantic style by Arturo Mélida – was created to house them. The mariner's coffin is held aloft by four huge allegorical figures, representing the kingdoms of León, Castile, Aragón and Navarra; the lance of León should be piercing a pomegranate (which recently went missing), symbol of Granada (and the word for the fruit in Spanish), the last Moorish kingdom to be reconquered.

Moving into the **nave**, sheer size and grandeur are, inevitably, the chief characteristics of the cathedral. But as you grow accustomed to the gloom, two other qualities stand out with equal force: the rhythmic balance and interplay between the parts, and an impressive overall simplicity and restraint in decoration. All successive ages have left monuments of their own wealth and style, but these have been limited to the two rows of side chapels. In the main body of the cathedral only the great box-like structure of the **coro** stands out, filling the central portion of the nave.

The *coro* extends and opens onto the **Capilla Mayor**, dominated by a **vast Gothic retablo** composed of 45 carved scenes from the life of Christ. The lifetime's work of a single craftsman, Fleming Pieter Dancart, this is the supreme masterpiece of the cathedral – the largest and richest altarpiece in the world and one of the finest examples of Gothic woodcarving. The guides provide staggering statistics on the amount of gold involved.

Before proceeding around the edge of the nave in a clockwise direction it's best to backtrack to the church's southeast corner to take in the **Sacristía de los Cálices** where many of the cathedral's main art treasures are displayed, including a masterly image of *Santas Justa y Rufina* by Goya, depicting Sevilla's patron saints, who were executed by the Romans in 287. Should you be interested in studying the many canvases here or the abundance of major artworks placed in the various chapels, it's worth calling at the bookshop near the entrance to purchase a copy of the official *Guide to the Cathedral of Seville* which deals with them in detail. Alongside this room is the grandiose **Sacristía Mayor** which houses the treasury. Embellished in the Plateresque style, it was designed in 1528 by Diego de Riaño, one of the foremost exponents of this predominantly decorative architecture of the late Spanish Renaissance. Amid a confused collection of silver reliquaries and monstrances – dull and prodigious wealth – are displayed the **keys** presented to Fernando by the Jewish and Moorish communities on the surrender of the city; sculpted into the metal in stylized Arabic script are the words "May Allah render eternal the dominion of Islam in this city." Through a small antechamber here you enter the oval-shaped **Sala Capitular** (chapter house) with paintings by Murillo and an outstanding **marble floor** with geometric design.

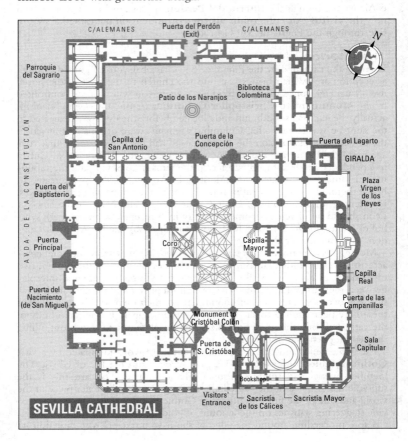

The route continues by proceeding to the southwest corner and the Puerta del Nacimiento and then turning right (or north) along the west wall, passing the Puerta Principal. In the northwest corner the **Capilla de San Antonio** has Murillo's *Vision of St Anthony* depicting the saint in ecstatic pose before an infant Christ. The nave's north side leads to the Puerta de la Concepción, through which you will exit – but before doing so, continue to the northeast corner to view the domed Renaissance **Capilla Real** (which is not always open), built on the site of the original royal burial chapel and containing the body of Fernando III (*El Santo*) in a suitably rich, silver shrine before the altar. The large tombs on either side of the chapel are those of Fernando's wife, Beatrice of Swabia, and his son, Alfonso the Wise.

The Giralda

The **entrance to the Giralda** (same ticket as cathedral) lies to the left of the Capilla Real in the cathedral's northeast corner. Unquestionably the most beautiful building in Sevilla, the **Giralda**, named after the sixteenth-century *giraldillo* or weather vane on its summit, dominates the city skyline. From the entrance you can ascend to the **bell chamber** for a remarkable **view** of the city – and, equally remarkable, a glimpse of the Gothic details of the cathedral's buttresses and statuary. But most impressive of all is the tower's inner construction, a series of 35 gently inclined ramps wide enough to allow two mounted guards to pass.

The **minaret** was the culmination of Almohad architecture, and served as a model for those at their imperial capitals of Rabat and Marrakesh. It was used by the Moors both for calling the faithful to prayer (the traditional function of a minaret) and as an observatory, and was so venerated that they wanted to destroy it before the Christian conquest of the city. This they were prevented from doing by the threat of Alfonso (later King Alfonso X) that "if they removed a single stone, they would all be put to the sword". Instead it became the bell tower of the Christian cathedral.

The Moorish structure took twelve years to build (1184–96) and derives its firm, simple beauty from the shadows formed by blocks of brick trelliswork, different on each side, and relieved by a succession of arched niches and windows. The original harmony has been somewhat spoiled by the Renaissance-era addition of balconies and, to a still greater extent, by the four diminishing storeys of the belfry – added, along with the Italian-sculpted bronze figure of "Faith" which surmounts them, in 1560–68, following the demolition by an earthquake of the original copper spheres. Even so, it remains in its perfect synthesis of form and decoration one of the most important and beautiful monuments of the Islamic world.

To reach the cathedral's **exit**, retrace your steps to the Puerta de la Concepción (see above) and beyond this cross the **Patio de los Naranjos** to the Puerta del Perdón, the former main entrance. In the centre of the patio remains a **Moorish fountain** used for the ritual ablutions before entering the mosque. Interestingly, it incorporates a sixth-century font from an earlier Visigothic cathedral, which was in its turn levelled to make way for the mosque.

Archive of the Indies and Ayuntamiento

If the Columbus monument has inspired you, or you have a fervent interest in the navigator's travels, visit **La Casa Lonja**, an austerely impressive sixteenth-century edifice and the city's old stock exchange (*lonja*), opposite the cathedral. This now houses the remarkable **Archivo de las Indias** (Mon–Fri 10am–

Sevilla's parish churches

Sevilla's parish **churches** display a fascinating variety of architectural styles. Several are converted mosques with belfries built over their minarets, others range through Mudéjar and Gothic (sometimes in combination), Renaissance and Baroque. Most are kept locked except early in the morning, or in the evenings from about 7 until 10pm – a promising time for a church crawl, especially as they're regularly interspersed with bars.

For a good circuit make first towards Gothic **San Pedro**, where a marble tablet records Velázquez's baptism, and **San Marcos**, with a fine minaret tower. Nearby, in this old cobbled part of town, is the fifteenth-century **Convento de Santa Paula** (Tues–Sun 10.30am–12.30pm & 4.30–6.30pm; free, but donations welcome), its church decorated with a vivid ceramic facade and superb *azulejos*, with an excellent museum containing fine artworks by Zurbarán and Ribera among others. Further on you meet the last remaining stretch of Moorish **city walls** – remains of the Almoravid fortifications which once spanned 12 gates and 166 towers. Now there's only one gate, the **Puerta Macarena**; beside it a basilica houses the city's cult image and patroness of matadors, *La Esperanza Macarena*, a tearful Virgin seated in the midst of gaudy magnificence.

Looping down towards the river, you reach the **Monasterio de Santa Clara** (entered from c/Santa Clara no. 40) – once part of the palace of Don Fadrique, brother of Alfonso X, and with a Romanesque-Gothic **tower** dating from 1252 (tower currently visitable only by appointment ℡ 954 224 808). A couple of blocks away are the distinctive columns (two at the far end are Roman) of the **Alameda de Hércules**. This leads back towards the town centre, with two more churches worth a look on the way: the Renaissance chapel of the **Universidad Antigua** and Baroque **San Salvador**, the latter built on the site of Sevilla's first Friday mosque (part of whose minaret is incorporated in its tower).

1pm; free), a monumental storehouse of the archives of the Spanish empire. Among the selection of documents on display are Columbus's log and a changing exhibition of ancient maps and curiosities. At the time of writing the building is undergoing an extensive **refurbishment** with no reopening date scheduled; consult the turismo for the current situation. Another building worth a look and sited slightly to the north of the cathedral is the sixteenth-century **Ayuntamiento** on Plaza de San Francisco, with a richly ornamented Plateresque facade by Diego de Riaño. The interior is open for infrequent guided visits (Tue & Wed 5.30–6.30pm; free).

The Alcázar

Rulers of Sevilla have occupied the site of the **Alcázar** (Apr–Sept Tues–Sat 9.30am–7pm, Sun 9.30am–6pm; Oct–Mar Tues–Sat 9.30am–6pm, Sun 9.30am–1.30pm; €4.20, children under 12, students & senior citizens, free) from the time of the Romans. Here was built the great court of the Abbadids, which reached a peak of sophistication and exaggerated sensuality under the cruel and ruthless al-Mu'tadid – a ruler who enlarged the palace in order to house a harem of eight hundred women, and who decorated the terraces with flowers planted in the skulls of his decapitated enemies. Later, under the **Almohads**, the complex was turned into a citadel, forming the heart of the town's fortifications. Its extent was enormous, stretching to the Torre del Oro on the bank of the Guadalquivir.

Parts of the Almohad walls survive, but the present structure of the palace dates almost entirely from the Christian period. Sevilla was a favoured residence of the Spanish kings for some four centuries after the Reconquest – most particularly of **Pedro the Cruel** (1350–69) who, with his mistress María de Padilla, lived in and ruled from the Alcázar. Pedro embarked upon a complete rebuilding of the palace, employing workmen from Granada and utilizing fragments of earlier Moorish buildings in Sevilla, Córdoba and Valencia. Pedro's works form the nucleus of the Alcázar as it is today and, despite numerous restorations necessitated by fires and earth tremors, it offers some of the best surviving examples of **Mudéjar architecture** – the style developed by Moors working under Christian rule. Later monarchs, however, have left all too many traces and additions. Isabel built a new wing in which to organize expeditions to the Americas and control the new territories; Carlos V married a Portuguese princess in the palace, adding huge apartments for the occasion; and under Felipe IV (c. 1624) extensive renovations were carried out to the existing rooms. On a more mundane level, kitchens were installed to provide for General Franco, who stayed in the royal apartments whenever he visited Sevilla.

Entry – the Salón del Almirante

The Alcázar is entered from the Plaza del Triunfo, adjacent to the cathedral. The gateway, flanked by original Almohad walls, opens onto a courtyard where Pedro (who was known as "the Just" as well as "the Cruel", depending on one's fortunes) used to give judgement; to the left is his **Sala de Justicia** and beyond this the **Patio del Yeso**, the only surviving remnant of the Almohads' Alcázar. The main facade of the palace stands at the end of an inner court, the **Patio de la Montería**; on either side are galleried buildings erected by Isabel. This principal facade is pure fourteenth-century Mudéjar and, with its delicate, marble-columned windows, stalactite frieze and overhanging roof, is one of the finest things in the whole Alcázar. But it's probably better to look round the **Salón del Almirante** (or *Casa de Contración de Indias*), the sixteenth-century building on the right, before entering the main palace. Founded by Isabel in

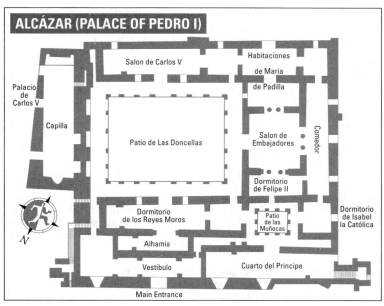

ALCÁZAR (PALACE OF PEDRO I)

Salon de Carlos V

Habitaciones de Maria de Padilla

Palacio de Carlos V

Capilla

Patio de Las Doncellas

Salon de Embajadores

Comedor

Dormitorio de Felipe II

Dormitorio de los Reyes Moros

Patio de las Muñecas

Dormitorio de Isabel la Católica

N

Alhamia

Vestibulo

Cuarto del Principe

Main Entrance

1503, this gives you a standard against which to assess the Moorish forms. Here most of the rooms seem too heavy, their decoration ceasing to be an integral part of the design. The only notable exception is the **Sala de Audiencias** (Chapel of the Navigators) with its magnificent *artesonado* ceiling inlaid with golden rosettes; within is a fine sixteenth-century **retablo** by Alejo Fernández depicting Columbus (in gold) and Carlos V (in a red cloak) sheltering beneath the Virgin. In the rear, to the left, are portrayed the kneeling figures of the Indians to whom the dubious blessings of Christianity had been brought by the Spanish conquest.

The palace

As you enter the **Main Palace** the "domestic" nature of Moorish and Mudéjar architecture is immediately striking. This involves no loss of grandeur but simply a shift in scale: the apartments are remarkably small, shaped to human needs, and take their beauty from the exuberance of the decoration and the imaginative use of space and light. There is, too, a deliberate disorientation in the layout of the rooms which makes the palace seem infinitely larger and more open than it really is. From the entrance court a narrow passage leads straight into the central courtyard, the **Patio de las Doncellas** (Patio of the Maidens), its name recalling the Christians' tribute of one hundred virgins presented annually to the Moorish kings. The court's stuccowork, *azulejos* and doors are all of the finest Granada craftsmanship. Interestingly, it's also the only part of the palace where Renaissance restorations are successfully fused – the double columns and upper storey were built by Carlos V, whose *Plus Ultra* ("yet still further") motto recurs in the decorations here and elsewhere.

Past the **Salón de Carlos V**, distinguished by a superb ceiling, are three rooms from the original fourteenth-century design built for María de Padilla (who was popularly thought to use magic in order to maintain her hold over Pedro – and perhaps over other gallants at court, too, who used to drink her bath water). These open onto the **Salón de Embajadores** (Salon of the Ambassadors), the most brilliant room of the Alcázar, with a stupendous *media naranja* (half-orange) wooden dome of red, green and gold cells, and horseshoe arcades inspired by the great palace of Medina Azahara outside Córdoba. Although restored, for the worse, by Carlos V – who added balconies and an incongruous frieze of royal portraits to commemorate his marriage to Isabel of Portugal here – the salon stands comparison with the great rooms of Granada's Alhambra. Adjoining are a long dining hall (*comedor*) and a small apartment installed in the late sixteenth century for Felipe II.

Beyond is the last great room of the palace – the **Patio de las Muñecas** (Patio of the Dolls), which takes its curious name from two tiny faces decorating the inner side of one of the smaller arches. It's thought to be the site of the harem in the original palace. In this room Pedro is reputed to have murdered his brother Don Fadrique in 1358; another of his royal guests, Abu Said of Granada, was murdered here for his jewels (one of which, an immense ruby which King Pedro later gave to Edward, the "Black Prince", now figures in the British crown jewels). The upper storey of the court is a much later, nineteenth-century restoration. On the other sides of the patio are the **bedrooms** of Isabel and of her son Don Juan, and the arbitrarily named Dormitorio del los Reyes Moros (Bedroom of the Moorish Kings).

Palacio de Carlos V and the gardens

To the left of the main palace loom the large and soulless apartments of the **Palacio de Carlos V** – something of an endurance test, with endless tapestries and pink–orange or yellow paintwork. Their classical style asserts a different and inferior mood. Best to hurry through to the beautiful and rambling **Alcázar gardens**, the confused but enticing product of several eras, where you can take a well-earned rest from your exertions. Here you'll find the vaulted baths in which María de Padilla is supposed to have bathed (in reality, an auxiliary water supply for the palace) and the **Estanque de Mercurio** with a bronze figure of the messenger of the gods at its centre. This pool was specially constructed for Felipe V in 1733, who whiled away two solitary years at the Alcázar fishing here and preparing himself for death through religious flagellation. Just to the left of the pool a path beyond the Puerta de Marchena leads to a pleasant **cafetería** with a terrace overlooking the gardens. South of here towards the centre of the gardens there's an unusual and entertaining **maze** of myrtle bushes and, nearby, the **pavilion of Carlos V**, the only survivor of several he built for relaxation.

The Plaza de España and María Luisa Park

Laid out in 1929 for an ill-fated "Fair of the Americas", the Plaza de España and adjoining María Luisa Park are among the most pleasant – and impressive – public spaces in Spain. They are an ideal place to spend the middle part of the day, just ten minutes' walk to the east of the cathedral.

En route you pass by the **Fábrica de Tabacos**, the city's old tobacco factory and the setting for Bizet's *Carmen*. Now part of the university, this massive structure was built in the 1750s and for a time was the largest building in Spain after El Escorial. At its peak in the following century it was also the country's largest single employer, with a workforce of some 4000 women *cigarreras* – "a class in themselves," according to Richard Ford, who were forced to undergo "an ingeniously minute search on leaving their work, for they sometimes carry off the filthy weed in a manner her most Catholic majesty never dreamt of".

The **Plaza de España**, beyond, was designed as the centrepiece of the Spanish Americas Fair, which was somewhat scuppered by the Wall Street crash. A vast semicircular complex, with its fountains, monumental stairways and mass of tile work, it would seem strange in most Spanish cities but here it looks entirely natural, carrying on the tradition of civic display. At the fair, the Plaza de España was used for the Spanish exhibit of industry and crafts, and around the crescent are *azulejo* scenes representing each of the provinces – an interesting record of the country at the tail end of a moneyed era.

Spaniards and tourists alike come out to the plaza – recently restored to its former glory in a grand refurbishment – to potter about in the little boats hired out on its tiny strip of canal, or to hide from the sun and crowds amid the ornamental pools and walkways of the **Parque de María Luisa**. The park is designed like the plaza in a mix of 1920s Art Deco and mock-Mudéjar. Scattered about, and round its edge, are more buildings from the fair, some of them amazingly opulent.

Towards the end of the park, the grandest mansions from the fair have been adapted as **museums**. The furthest now houses the city's **Museo Arqueológico** (Tues 3–8pm, Wed–Sat 9am–8pm, Sun 9am–2pm; €1.50, free to EU citizens), the most important archeology collection in Andalucía. The main exhibits include a hoard of prehistoric treasure found in the Sevilla suburb of Camas in 1958, as well as Roman mosaics and artefacts from nearby Italica and a unique Phoenician statuette of Astarte-Tanit, the virgin goddess once worshipped throughout the Mediterranean. Opposite, the fabulous-look-

△ Semana Santa outfitters, Sevilla

ing **Popular Arts Museum** (Tues 3–8pm, Wed–Sat 9am–8pm, Sun 9am–2pm; €1.50, free to EU citizens) is often besieged by schoolkids but has interesting displays relating to traditional arts and crafts and the April *feria*.

Barrio Santa Cruz, the river and Triana

Santa Cruz is very much in character with the city's romantic image, its streets narrow and tortuous to keep out the sun, the houses brilliantly whitewashed and barricaded with *rejas* (iron grilles), behind which girls once kept chaste evening rendezvous with their *novios*. Of numerous mansions, by far the finest is the so-called **Casa de Pilatos** (daily 9am–8pm, closes 6pm Oct–June; €6; free on Tues 1–5pm), built by the Marqués de Tarifa on his return from a pilgrimage to Jerusalem in 1519 and popularly thought to have been in imitation of the house of Pontius Pilate. In fact it's an interesting and harmonious mixture of Mudéjar, Gothic and Renaissance styles, featuring brilliant *azulejos*, a tremendous sixteenth-century stairway and the most elegant domestic patios in the city.

Patios are a feature of almost all the houses in Santa Cruz: they are often surprisingly large and in summer they become the principal family living room. One of the most beautiful is within the Baroque **Hospicio de los Venerables Sacerdotes** (daily 10am–2pm & 4–8pm; guided visits every 30min; €3.60), near the centre in a plaza of the same name – one of the few buildings in the *barrio* worth actively seeking out. A couple of blocks east of the Hospicio is the **Museo de Murillo**, c/Santa Teresa 8 (closed at the time of writing, enquire at turismo for latest information), the seventeenth-century *sevillano* artist's former home; it's furnished with contemporaneous artworks, craftsmanship and furniture – though no original artworks of his own.

Down by the **Guadalquivir** are pedal-boats for idling away the afternoons, and at night a surprising density of local couples. The main riverside landmark here is the twelve-sided **Torre del Oro**, built by the Almohads in 1220 as part of the Alcázar fortifications. It was connected to another small fort across the river by a chain which had to be broken by the Castilian fleet before their conquest of the city in 1248. The tower was later used as a repository for the gold brought back to Sevilla from the Americas – hence its name. It now houses a small **naval museum** (Tues–Fri 10am–2pm, Sat & Sun 11am–2pm; closed Aug; €0.60).

One block away, with its entry on c/Temprado, is the **Hospital de la Caridad** (Mon–Sat 9am–1.30pm & 3.30–6.30pm, Sun 9am–1pm; €2.40), founded in 1676 by Don Miguel de Mañara, the inspiration for Byron's Don Juan. According to the testimony of one of Don Miguel's friends, "there was no folly which he did not commit, no youthful indulgence into which he did not plunge . . . (until) what occurred to him in the street of the coffin." What occurred was that Don Miguel, returning from a reckless orgy, had a vision in which he was confronted by a funeral procession carrying his own corpse. He repented his past life, joined the Brotherhood of Charity (whose task was to bury the bodies of tramps and criminals), and later set up this hospital for the relief of the dying and destitute, for which purpose it is still used. Don Miguel commissioned a series of eleven paintings by Murillo for the chapel, six of which remain. Alongside them hang two *Triumph of Death* pictures by Valdés Leal. One, depicting a decomposing bishop being eaten by worms (beneath the scales of justice labelled *Ni más, Ni menos* – No More, No Less), is so powerfully repulsive that Murillo declared that "you have to hold your nose to look at it".

Museo de Bellas Artes

North of the hospital, near the Plaza de Armas bus station, lies one of Spain's most impressive art galleries, the **Museo de Bellas Artes** (Tues 3–8pm, Wed–Sat 9am–8pm, Sun 9am–2pm; €1.50, free to EU citizens), housed in recently modernized premises in a beautiful former convent. You should be aware that the museum has a policy of rotating its collection and not all the works mentioned here may be exhibited.

Among the highlights of an outstanding collection is a wonderful late-fifteenth-century sculpture in painted terracotta in Room 1, *Lamentation over the Dead Christ*, by the Andalucian Pedro **Millán**, the founding father of the Sevilla school of sculpture. A marriage of Gothic and expressive naturalism, this style was the starting point for the outstanding seventeenth-century period of religious iconography in Sevilla. Room 3 has a *retablo* of the Redemption, c.1562, with fine woodcarving by Juan Giralte, while a monumental *Last Supper* by Alonso Vázquez covers an end wall of Room 4.

Beyond a serene patio and cloister, Room 5 is located in the monastery's former church, where the recently restored paintings on the vault and dome by the eighteenth-century *sevillano*, Domingo Martínez, are spectacular. Here also is the nucleus of the collection: **Zurbarán**'s *Apotheosis of St Thomas Aquinas*, as well as a clutch of works by **Murillo** in the apse, crowned by the great *Immaculate Conception* – known as "*la colosal*" to distinguish it from the other work here with the same name. In an alcove nearby you'll see the same artist's *Virgin and Child*: popularly known as *La Servilleta* because it was said to have been painted on a dinner napkin, the work is one of Murillo's greatest.

Upstairs, Room 6 (quadrated around the patio) displays works from the Baroque period, among which a moving *Santa Teresa* by **Ribera** – Spain's master of *tenebrismo* (darkness penetrated by light) – and a stark *Crucifixion* by Zurbarán stand out. Room 10 contains more imposing canvases by Zurbarán, including *St Hugo visiting the Carthusian monks at supper* and another almost sculptural *Crucifixion* to compare with the one in Room 6.

The collection ends with works from the Romantic and Modern eras, where an austere late work by **Goya**, in Room 11, of the octogenarian *Don José Duaso* compensates for some not terribly inspiring works accompanying it. Room 14 contains *Juan Centeno y su cuadrilla* by Huelvan artist (and friend of Picasso) Daniel Vázquez Díaz: this monumental image of the *torero* and his team provides an appropriately *andaluz* conclusion to a memorable museum.

Triana and La Cartuja

Over the river is the **Triana** *barrio*, scruffy, lively and well away from the tourist trails. This was once the heart of the city's *gitano* community and, more specifically, home of the great flamenco dynasties of Sevilla who were kicked out by developers earlier this century and are now scattered throughout the city. The *gitanos* lived in extended families in tiny, immaculate communal houses called *corrales* around courtyards glutted with flowers; today only a handful remain intact. Triana is still, however, the starting point for the annual pilgrimage to El Rocío (at the end of May), when a myriad of painted wagons leave town, drawn by oxen. It houses, too, the city's oldest working ceramics factory, Santa Ana, where the tiles, many still in the traditional, geometric Arabic designs, are painted by hand.

At Triana's northern edge lies **La Cartuja** (Tues–Fri 10am–8pm, Sat 11am–8pm, Sun 10am–3pm; €1.80, free Tues for EU citizens), a fourteenth-century former Carthusian monastery expensively restored as part of the Expo '92 world fair. Part of the complex is now given over to the **Centro Andaluz de Arte Contemporáneo** (same hours and ticket as La Cartuja), which, in addition to work by *andaluz* artists, frequently stages important exhibitions by international painters and sculptors.

The remnants of much of the **Expo '92 site** itself have been incorporated into the **Isla Mágica** (open April–Sept Tue–Thur 11am–7pm, Fri–Sun 11am–10pm; €20.50, half-day €13.80), an amusement park based on the theme of sixteenth-century Spain, with water and rollercoaster rides, shows and period street animations.

Outside the city: Roman Italica

The Roman ruins and remarkable mosaics of **ITALICA** (Apr–Sept Tues–Sat 9am–8.30pm, Sun 9am–3pm; Oct–Mar Tues–Sat 9am–5.30pm, Sun 10am–4pm; €1.50, free to EU citizens) lie some 9km to the north of Sevilla, just outside the village of Santiponce. There's also a well-preserved **Roman theatre** in Santiponce itself, signposted from the main road.

Italica was the birthplace of two emperors (Trajan and Hadrian) and one of the earliest Roman settlements in Spain, founded in 206 BC by Scipio Africanus as a home for his veterans. It rose to considerable military importance in the second and third centuries AD, was richly endowed during the reign of Hadrian (117–138), and declined as an urban centre only under the Visigoths, who preferred Sevilla, then known as *Hispalis*. Eventually the city was deserted by the Moors after the river changed its course, disrupting the surrounding terrain.

Throughout the Middle Ages the ruins were used as a source of stone for Sevilla, but somehow the shell of its enormous **amphitheatre** – the third largest in the Roman world – has survived. Today it's crumbling perilously, but you can clearly detect the rows of seats, the corridors and the dens for wild beasts. Beyond, within a rambling and unkempt grid of **streets** and **villas**, about twenty **mosaics** have been uncovered. Most are complete, including excellent coloured floors depicting birds, Neptune and the seasons, and several fine black-and-white geometric patterns.

Getting to Italica, buses depart every half-hour from the Plaza de Armas station for the twenty-minute journey; you need the Empresa Casal service to Santiponce, which departs from Bay 33. Santiponce is not well endowed with facilities but the *Ventarillo Canario* **restaurant** almost opposite the Italica site entrance does good *platos combinados* and is famous for its grilled steaks served on wooden slabs with *papas arrugadas* – small baked potatoes in *mojo* spicy sauce.

Eating and drinking

Sevilla is packed with lively and enjoyable bars and restaurants, and you'll find somewhere to eat and drink at just about any hour. With few exceptions, anywhere around the sights and the **Barrio Santa Cruz** will be expensive. The two most promising central areas are down **towards the bullring** and north of here towards the Plaza de Armas bus station. The **Plaza de Armas** area is slightly seedier but has the cheapest *comidas* this side of the river. Wander down c/Marqués de Paradas, and up c/Canalejas and c/San Eloy, and find out what's available. Across the river in **Triana**, c/Betis and c/Pureza are also good hunting grounds.

Restaurants and cafés

La Albahaca, Plaza Santa Cruz 29. Charming, traditional and expensive restaurant with outdoor tables in one of the Barrio Santa Cruz's prettiest squares. Closed Sun.

Bar Modesto, c/Cano y Cueto. At the north end of Santa Cruz, this mid-priced bar-restaurant offers a tempting *menú* (€12) and great tapas.
Bodegón Pez Espada, c/Hernando Colón 8. Near

the cathedral, and one of the few inexpensive places to eat in the Barrio Santa Cruz. Excellent seafood and *paella* with a buffet where you can refill your plate as many times as you like.

Café-Bar Veracruz, opposite the Torre del Oro near the river. Simple no-frills roadside place offering a bargain €6 *menú*; makes a good lunch stop.

Café Olé, c/Miguel de Mañara 9. Pleasant lunchtime venue serving *raciones* and salads at outdoor tables in a pedestrianized street behind the turismo.

Entre dos Hermandades, c/Recaredo 13, near the Casa de Pilatos. Friendly restaurant and bar with perhaps the best value *menú* in town; €4.50 gets you three courses with wine and bread.

Hotel Alfonso XIII, c/San Fernando 2 ☎954 222 850. Swankiest place in town constructed to house guests visiting the 1929 exhibition; worth a look at this beautiful building and its stunning patio even if you don't sit down in the pricey restaurant.

Jalea Real, c/Sor Ángela de la Cruz 37, near the church of San Pedro. Excellent vegetarian restaurant run by a friendly and enthusiastic *sevillana*. Closed Mon.

La Judería, c/Cano y Cueto 13, near the Iglesia de Santa María la Blanca. Solid mid-priced restaurant with a tempting *menú* for around €12. *Revueltos* are a speciality here.

Kiosko de las Flores, c/Betis next door to the Río Grande (below). One of Sevilla's best-loved fried fish emporia has been evicted (to make way for a subterranean car park) from its ancient location tucked into the side of the Puente de Triana (Isabel II bridge) to a new riverside site with delightful terrace; tapas served in the bar and *raciones* on the terrace – just the place on a summer night. Closed Mon.

La Mandrágora, c/Albuera 11, just north of the Maestranza bullring, across c/Reyes Católicos. Sevilla's second vegetarian restaurant, with a wide range of dishes and a *menú*.

Mesón Serranito, Alfonso XII 9, behind the El Corte Inglés department store. Cosy little restaurant beyond the tapas bar out front with excellent fish and meat dishes and a €7.20 *menú*.

Pizzeria San Marco, c/Meson del Moro 4, Santa Cruz. Delicious Italian food and pizzas served inside a remarkable twelfth-century Moorish bathhouse.

Río Grande, c/Betis 70. This Triana restaurant has the best view in town from its terrace on the river's west bank, and a medium-priced *menú*. It's tapas bar is also worth a visit.

La Sopa Boba, c/Bailén 34, just off the Plaza del Museo on the Museo de Bellas Artes' doorstep. Tasty experimental home cooking, with a good-value *menú*.

Bars

For straight drinking and occasional tapas you can be much less selective. There are **bars** all over town – a high concentration of them with barrelled sherries from nearby Jerez and Sanlúcar (the locals drink the cold, dry *fino* with their tapas, especially shrimp); a *tinto de verano* is the local version of *sangría* – wine with lemonade, a great summer drink. Outside the centre, you'll find lively bars in the **Plaza Alfafa** area, and across the river in **Triana** – particularly in c/Castilla, c/Betis, and in and around c/Salado. A new zone that has emerged as a focus for artistic, student and gay barhoppers is the **Alameda** (de Hércules).

In summer much of the action emigrates to the bars along the **river's east bank** to the north of the Triana bridge as far as the spectacular Puente de la Barqueta, built for Expo '92. Many of these open for a season only, springing up the following year under a new name and ownership.

The **gay scene** has a cluster of bars on the city side of the Puente de Triana, where *Isbiliyya*, *Tócame* and other bars get lively around midnight.

Anima, c/Miguel Cid 80, north of the Museo de Bellas Artes. Lovely old tiled bar which mounts periodic art and photo exhibitions.

Bar Eslava, c/Eslava 3–5, near the church of San Lorenzo. Very good and extremely popular – which often means you can't get through the door – tapas bar with restaurant attached.

Bar Giralda, c/Mateus Gagos 1. Excellent and popular bar in converted ancient Moorish bath-

house, with a wide selection of tapas.

Bar Modesto, c/Cano y Cueto 5, at the north end of Santa Cruz (ask for it by name, it's well known). Perhaps the best tapas bar in the city, with just about every imaginable snack.

La Barqueta, just south of the bridge of the same name. Stylish open-air bar which puts on music, concerts, theatre and shows throughout the summer.

Capote, c/Radio Sevilla off c/Arjona, close to the Puente de Triana. Popular summer terrace bar with a varied clientele which gets younger as the night wears on.

Casa Morales, c/García de Vinuesa 11. Atmospheric traditional bar (founded 1850) with barrelled wine.

La Gitanilla, c/Ximénez de Enciso s/n. One of the liveliest places in Santa Cruz, with inexpensive drinks, but pricey tapas.

La Otra Orilla, Paseo de Nuestra Señora de la "O" s/n, near the Puente de Triana. Riverside open-air bar owned by the proprietors of *La Barqueta* (above) with a similar ambience.

El Refugio, c/Huelva 5. Slightly west of Plaza del Salvador, this serves a wide variety of snacks, including vegetarian tapas.

El Rinconcillo, c/Gerona 32, by the church of Santa Catalina. Sevilla's oldest bar (founded in 1670) does a fair tapas selection as well as providing a hangout for the city's literati.

Las Teresas, c/Santa Teresa 2, to the north of Plaza Santa Cruz. Good beer and sherry served in this atmospheric bar with hanging cured hams and tiled walls lined with faded *corrida* photos. It's also worth stopping here for breakfast the morning after.

Nightlife

Sevilla is a wonderfully late-night city, and in summer and during fiestas, the streets around the central areas are often packed out until the small hours.

Flamenco

Flamenco music and dance is on offer at dozens of places in the city, some of them extremely tacky and expensive. Unless you've heard otherwise, avoid the fixed "shows" or *tablaos* (many of which are a travesty, even using recorded music). The spontaneous nature of flamenco makes it almost impossible to timetable into the two-shows-a-night cabaret demanded by impresarios. The nearest you'll get to the real thing is at *Los Gallos*, in the Plaza Santa Cruz, which has a professional cast. However, it is pricey (€21 including one drink), and you'd probably do just as well at *El Tamboril*, a renowned flamenco bar in the opposite corner of the same square. Singers and dancers aren't guaranteed to drop in (around midnight is best), but when they do, you're in for an unforgettable night.

Another excellent bar which often has spontaneous flamenco (try Mon or Thurs after 10pm) is *La Carbonería*, c/Levies 18, just to the northeast of the church of Santa Cruz. It used to be the coal merchant's building (hence the name) and is a large, simple and welcoming place. *Quita Pesares*, in the Plaza Jerónimo de Córdoba near the church of Santa Catalina, is run by a flamenco singer, and is a chaotic place where there's often impromptu music (especially at weekends) when things get lively around midnight. A couple more places to try are *Café Lisboa*, c/Alhondiga 43, near the church of Santa Catalina, which stages flamenco nights on Thursdays with free entry, and *Salamandra*, c/Torneo 49, near the east bank of the river, which puts on flamenco on Saturday nights after 10pm for €7.20 (including one drink).

Live music and clubs

For **rock music** the bars around Plaza Alfalfa and the Alameda de Hércules have most of the best action. Recommended music bars on the Alameda include *Bulebar* and *La Habanilla* at the northern end, *El Baron Rampante* in c/Arias Montano about halfway along and *Fun Club* – which stages frequent live gigs – on the Alameda proper. At c/Adriano 10, on the north side of the bullring, *Arena* is another popular music bar specializing in rock, jazz and funk. Over in Triana, *Druida*, c/Rodrigo de Triana, often has live music. **Live jazz** can be found at *Bluemoon*, c/J.A. Cavestany s/n, near the Santa Justa train station, or the popular *Naima*, just off the Alameda at c/Trajano 47 (both closed

Aug). The vibrant café-bar *La Imperdible*, Plaza San Antonio de Padua, between the Alameda de Hércules and the river, puts on live jazz on Tuesdays, with various other entertainments throughout the week. Major **concerts**, whether touring British and American bands or big Spanish acts like Paco de Lucía, Alejandro Sanz or Ketama, often take place in the old Expo site across the river in Cartuja or in one or other of the football stadiums. Check *El Giraldillo* (the turismo's free listings magazine), the local paper *El Correo* or street posters for possibilities. La Teatral, c/Velázquez 12 near the Plaza del Duque de la Victoria (☎954 228 229) are the official ticket agents for many concerts, and tickets are also sold by the El Corte Inglés department store.

A strong night-time **club and disco** scene in Triana livens up c/Betis and its northern extension c/Castilla where the disco-club *Boss*, c/Betis 67, is a popular venue as is *La Otra Orilla* (on the river behind the church of Nuestra Señora de la O) with a great terrace overlooking the river. Another popular hot-spot for late night clubbing is *Luna Park*, Avda. de María Luisa s/n near the Plaza de España (top right-hand corner of our city map) with dance spaces offering salsa, *bacalao* (Iberian techno) and more – weekends are best, and not before midnight.

Listings

Airport For flight information, call ☎954 449 000. For internal flights run by Iberia contact their office at c/Almirante Lobo 2 ☎954 228 901; ☎954 516 111 for flight information.

Banks and currency exchange ATMs are located throughout the centre of town, for example around the Avda. de la Constitución and around Plaza Duque de la Victoria. *Bureaux de change* can be found on Plaza Nueva but banks – which no longer charge commission – are a cheaper option. American Express, Plaza Nueva 7 ☎954 211 617 (Mon–Fri 9.30am–1.30pm & 4.30–8pm, Sat 9.30am–1pm), and the El Corte Inglés department store on Plaza Duque de la Victoria (Mon–Sat 10am–9.30pm) offer good exchange rates, and most large hotels change notes (although rates tend to be poor).

Bike and scooter rental Sevilla Mágica, c/Miguel Mañara 11 ☎ & ☎954 563 838, through the arch behind the turismo, rents out cycles by the day or half-day (€12 per day). Motorcycles and scooters can be rented from Alkimoto, c/Fernando Tirado 5 ☎954 584 927, slightly south of the Santa Justa train station; prices start at €18 per day for a scooter.

Books and newspapers A wide range of books in English is stocked by Vértice, c/San Fernando 33 near the Alcázar. The Beta chain is good for guides and maps; central branches include Avda. de la Constitución 9 and 27 and Plaza de la Gavidia 7. El Corte Inglés on Plaza Duque de la Victoria stocks English titles and international press. A more comprehensive range of international newspapers is stocked by Esteban, c/Alemanes 15, next to the cathedral.

Bullfights Details and tickets from the Plaza de Toros on fight days from 4.30pm or in advance (with commission) from a kiosk at c/Adriano 36.

Car rental Avis ☎954 537 861 and Europcar ☎954 533 914 are located at the Santa Justa train station. Good local deals are to be had from Atlantic, c/Almirante Lobo 2 ☎954 227 893, just off the Puerta de Jerez, and Alquila un Coche, Avda. Constitución 15 ☎954 216 549.

Cinema Most movies showing are listed in *El Giraldillo*, the listings mag available from the turismo; "*V.O.*" indicates a screening in the original-language. A "*V.O.*" venue, Cine Avenida, c/Marqués de Paradas 15, specializes in original language films (mainly English). Open-air "*cines de verano*" (July & Aug) are great places for a beer and a *tapa* while watching a movie – you should consult the turismo for the latest locations as they tend to change yearly.

Consulates Australia, c/Federico Rubio 14 ☎954 220 971; Canada, nearest in Madrid: ☎914 233 250; Ireland, Plaza Santa Cruz 6, Bajo A ☎954 216 361; UK, nearest in Málaga: ☎952 217 571; USA, Paseo de las Delicias 7 ☎954 231 885.

Flea market A *rastro* takes place on Thursday mornings along the c/Feria past the Plaza Encarnación, and a bigger one on Sunday at the Alameda de Hércules.

Football Sevilla has two major teams: Sevilla CF play at the Sánchez Pizjuan stadium ☎954 489 400 and Real Betis use the Estadio Benito Villamarín ☎954 610 340. Match schedules are in the local or national press.

Hiking maps 1:50,000, 1:100,000 and 1:200,000 maps can be purchased from Cartolap, Edificio

Sevilla, c/San Francisco Javier 9 ☏ 954 656 612, south of the Santa Justa train station. A "made-to-measure" map service will make up maps in the above scales for a defined area; ring Francisco Marquez, c/Las Cruzadas 7, immediately behind the Plaza de España ☏ 954 423 063.

Hospital English-speaking doctors available at the Hospital Universitario Virgen Macarena, c/Dr Marañon s/n ☏ 955 614 140) behind the Andalucía parliament building to the north of the centre. For emergencies, dial ☏ 061.

Internet access New internet cafés are opening all across the city. *Alfalfa 10*, Plaza de Alfalfa 10 near the dead centre of our main city map (daily noon–1am; ☏ 954 213 841; €3.60 per hr) is probably the city's most attractive internet café. *Sevilla Internet Centre*, Calle Almirantazgo 2 (daily 9am–10pm; ☏ 954 500 275; €2.50 per hr) close to the cathedral's western entrance is the most central. *Ciber-Café Undernet* (☏ 954 991 419; €1.80 per hr) has branches at c/O'Donnell 19 (10am–10pm), near Plaza Duque de la Victoria,

and Pages del Corro 182 (11am–3am), in Triana.

Police Bag-snatching is big business. If you lose something, get the theft documented at the Plaza de la Gavidia station ☏ 954 289 300, near Plaza de la Victoria. Dial ☏ 092 (local police) or ☏ 091 (national) in an emergency.

Post office Avda. de la Constitución 32, by the cathedral; *Lista de Correos* (poste restante) open Mon–Fri 8.30am–8.30pm, Sat 9.30am–2pm.

Taxis The main central taxi ranks are in Plaza Nueva, the Alameda de Hércules and the Plaza de Armas and Prado de San Sebastián bus stations. A reliable taxi service, Radio Taxi, will come and collect you if you ring them on ☏ 954 580 000.

Telephones c/Sierpes 11, down a passageway (Mon–Fri 10am–2pm & 5–8.30pm, Sat 10am–2pm).

Train information For tickets/info go to the RENFE office, off the Plaza Nueva at c/Zaragoza 29 ☏ 954 222 693; Mon–Fri 9.15am–1.15pm & 4–7pm for information and reservations. The Santa Justa train station number is ☏ 902 240 202.

The Sierra Morena

The longest of Spain's mountain ranges, the **Sierra Morena** extends almost the whole way across Andalucía – from Rosal on the Portuguese frontier to the dramatic pass of Despeñaperros, north of Linares. Its hill towns marked the northern boundary of the old Moorish caliphate of Córdoba and in many ways the region still signals a break, with a shift from the climate and mentality of the south to the bleak plains and villages of Extremadura and New Castile. The range is not widely known – with its highest point a mere 1110m, it's not a dramatic sierra – and even Andalucians can have trouble placing it.

Climate, flora and fauna

The Morena's climate is mild – sunny in spring, hot but fresh in summer – but it can be very cold in the evenings and mornings. Tracks are still more common than roads, and tourism, which the government of Andalucía is keen to encourage, has so far meant little more than a handful of new signs indicating areas of special interest.

A good **time to visit** is between March and June, when the flowers, perhaps the most varied in the country, are at their best. You may get caught in the odd thunderstorm but it's usually bright and hot enough to swim in the reservoirs or splash about in the clear springs and streams, all of which are good to drink. If your way takes you along a river, you'll be entertained by armies of frogs and turtles plopping into the water as you approach, by lizards, dragonflies, bees, hares and foxes peering discreetly from their holes – and, usually, no humans present for miles round.

The locals maintain that, while the last bears disappeared only a short time ago, there are still a few wolves in remoter parts. Of more concern to anyone trekking in the Sierra Morena, however, are the **toros bravos** (fighting bulls), since you are quite likely to come across them. They should always be in fenced-off pastures with explicit signs warning you to keep out (*toros peligros* are the words to look out for), but these often disappear or are not put up in the first place. Apparently a group of bulls is less to be feared than a single one, and a single one only if he directly bars your way and looks mean. The thing to do, according to expert advice, is to stay calm, and without attracting the bull's attention, go round. If you even get a whiff of a fighting bull, though, it might well be best to adopt the time-honoured technique – drop everything and run.

Getting around the sierra

East–west **transport** in the sierra is very limited. Most of the bus services are radial and north–south, with Sevilla as the hub, and this leads to ridiculous situations where, for instance, to travel from Santa Olalla to Cazalla, a distance of some 53km, you must take a bus to Sevilla, 70km away, and then another up to Cazalla – a full day's journey of nearly 150km just to get from one town to the next. The best solution if you want to spend any amount of time in Morena is to organize your routes round **treks**. A bicycle, too, could be useful, but your own car much less so – this is not Michelin car-window-view territory. If you have a **bike**, you'll need plenty of gears, especially for the road between El Real de la Jara and El Pintado (Santa Olalla–Cazalla), while the roads round Almonaster, and between Cazalla and Constantina, are very bad for cycling.

    Buses from Sevilla to the sierra leave from the Plaza de Armas station. If you just want to make a quick foray into the hills, **Aracena** is probably the best target (and the most regularly served town). If you're planning on some walking it's also a good starting point: before you leave Sevilla, however, be sure to get yourself a decent **map** (see Sevilla "Listings") which, though it will probably be crammed with misleading information, should point you in the right direction to get lost somewhere interesting.

Aracena – and its sierra

The highest town in the Sierra Morena – guarded to its south by a small off-shoot of the range – **ARACENA** has sharp, clear air, all the more noticeable after Sevilla. Capital of the western end of the sierra with 10,000 inhabitants, it's a substantial but pretty town, rambling up the side of a hill topped by the **Iglesia del Castillo**, a Gothic-Mudéjar church built by the Knights Templar around the remains of a Moorish castle.

    Although the church is certainly worth the climb, Aracena's principal attraction is the **Gruta de las Maravillas** (daily 10.30am–1.30pm & 3–6pm; guided hourly visits, half-hourly at weekends; €5.40), the largest and arguably the most impressive cave in Spain. Supposedly discovered by a local boy in search of a lost pig, the cave is now illuminated and there are guided tours as soon as a dozen or so people have assembled. On Sunday there is a constant procession, but usually plenty of time to gaze and wonder. The cave is astonishingly beautiful, and funny too – the last chamber of the tour is known as the Sala de los Culos (Room of the Buttocks), its walls and ceiling an outrageous, naturally sculpted exhibition, tinged in a pinkish orange light. Close by the cave's entrance are a couple of excellent restaurants, open lunchtime only. Aracena is at the heart of a prestigious *jamón*-producing area, so try to sample some, and, when they're available, the delicious wild asparagus and local snails – rooted out from the roadside and in the fields in spring and summer respectively.

Practicalities

Aracena has a **turismo**, located at the Gruta (Mon–Sat 9am–2pm & 4–7pm; ℡959 128 206). There are limited **places to stay**, the best of which, at the bot-

tom end of the scale, is *Casa Manolo*, below the main square at c/Barberos 6
(☎959 128 014; ❸). Alternatively, the *Hotel Sierra de Aracena*, Gran Vía 21 (☎955
126 175; ❺), offers relative luxury. There's also a **campsite** with pool (☎959
501 005; April–Sept) about 3km out along the Sevilla road, then left for 500m
on the road towards Corteconcepción. For **meals**, the medium-priced
Restaurante José Vicente, Avda. Andalucía 51, opposite the park, specializes in
jamón and pork dishes, including a mouthwatering *solomillo* (pork loin); a recent
addition here is an outstanding tapas bar. Good tapas and *platos combinados* are
on offer at the more basic *Café-Bar Manzano*, at the southern end of the main
square, Plaza Marqués de Aracena. If you intend to do some **walking in the
sierra**, ask the turismo for a pamphlet entitled *Senderismo* (paths) which details
waymarked trails between the local villages.

Villages around Aracena

Surrounding Aracena you'll find a scattering of attractive but economically
depressed villages, most of them dependent on the **jamón industry** and its
curing factory at Jabugo. *Jamón serrano* (mountain ham) is a *bocadillo* standard
throughout Spain and some of the best, *jamón de bellotas* (acorn-fed ham),
comes from the Morena, where herds of sleek grey pigs grazing beneath the
trees are a constant feature. In October the acorns drop and the pigs, waiting
patiently below, gorge themselves, become fat and are promptly whisked off to
be slaughtered and then cured in the dry mountain air.

The **sierra villages** – Jabugo, Aguafría, Almonaster La Real – all make
rewarding bases for walks, though all are equally ill-served by public transport
(details from the Aracena turismo). The most interesting is **ALMONASTER
LA REAL**, whose castle encloses a tiny ninth-century mosque, **La Mezquita**
(daily 10am–sunset), with what is said to be the oldest **mihrab** in Spain. Tacked
onto the mosque is the village bullring which sees action once a year in August
during the annual fiesta. The village also has a couple of **places to eat and
stay**: the very hospitable *Pensión La Cruz*, Plaza El Llano 8 (☎959 143 135; ❸),
in the centre with a good restaurant, and *Hostal Casa García* (☎955 143 109;
❸), at the entrance to the village, which also has a fine restaurant, with great
jamón and *ensaladilla*. There are some superb paint-splashed waymarked walks
northwest of the village, off the Cortegana road; a leaflet detailing these and
other walks in the area can be found at the *ayuntamiento* on Plaza de la
Constitución.

Zufre and east to Cazalla and Constantina

From Aracena a single daily **bus** (except Sun) – currently at 5.30pm, connecting with the bus from Sevilla – covers the 25km southeast to Zufre. Timetables
and frequency of service change so check with the turismo in Aracena for the
latest information. Ten kilometres out of Aracena you come upon the **Embalse
de Aracena**, one of the huge reservoirs that supply Sevilla, and from here a
lovely but circuitous route will take you down towards Zufre along the **Rivera
de Huelva**. From Zufre east there are no buses directly linking the villages en
route to Cazalla.

Zufre

ZUFRE must rank as one of the most spectacular villages in Spain, hanging
like a miniature Ronda on a high palisade at the edge of a ridge. Below the
crumbling Moorish walls, the cliff falls away hundreds of feet, terraced into
deep green gardens of orange trees and vegetables. Within the town the **ayun-**

tamiento and **church** are both interesting examples of Mudéjar style, the latter built in the sixteenth century on the foundations of a mosque. In the basement of the *ayuntamiento*, too, are a gloomy line of stone seats, said to have been used by the Inquisition. The focus of town, however, is the **Paseo**, a little park with rose gardens, a balcony, a bar at one end and a *Casino* (bar-club) at the other. Here the villagers gather for much of the day: there is little work either in Zufre or its surrounding countryside. For **accommodation** Zufre has a new *hostal*, *La Posa*, C/Cibarranco 5 (☎959 198 110; ❸), with en-suite rooms, while for **food and drink** a couple of bars – *Aleman* and *Benito* on the Plaza La Quebrada in the warren of Moorish streets above the park – serve tapas.

Santa Olalla

SANTA OLALLA DEL CALA, the next village to the east, is a walkable 16km from Zufre, which – without transport of your own – may be your only option as there is no bus link, although locals are often willing to give lifts. It's a flattish route through open country with pigs and fields of wheat and barley, and then a sudden view of the Moorish **castillo** above the town. There have been several half-hearted attempts to reconstruct the castle but they haven't been helped by its adaptation in the last century as the local cemetery – the holes for coffins in the walls rather spoil the effect. Below its walls is the fifteenth-century parish **church**, with a fine Renaissance interior.

Coming from Zufre it's a surprise to find several **hostales** in Santa Olalla, but the town is actually on the main Sevilla–Badajoz road and sees a fair amount of traffic – and regular buses to both cities, which stop outside the friendly *Bar Primitivo*, c/Marina 3. Nearby, rooms are to be had at the comfortable *Casa Carmelo*, c/Marina 23 (☎959 190 169; ❸), some with bath. For **food** both places serve economical *menús*, with the latter specializing in the excellent *jamones* and *salchichas* from the pig farms hereabouts.

Real de la Jara

After 4km of winding through stone-walled olive groves, the road flattens out into a grassy little valley above the **Río Cala** – a spot where the villages of Real and Olalla hold their joint *romería* at the end of April. These country *romerías* are always good to stumble upon, and if you happen on one in the Sierra Morena you should be well looked after. Proceedings start with a formal parade to the local *ermita* but they're very soon given over to feasting and dancing, the young men wobbling about on donkeys and mules in a wonderful parody of the grand *hidalgo* doings of Jerez and Sevilla, children shrieking and splashing in the river, and everyone dancing *sevillanas* to scratchy cassettes.

REAL DE LA JARA, 8km east of Santa Olalla, is in much the same mould with two impressive, ruined Moorish *castillos*. For **rooms** there's a friendly *casa de huéspedes* at c/Real 70 (❷); also there are a few bars serving food and a very welcome public swimming pool. Cazalla de la Sierra, the next village, is some 45km along a mountainous route which sees few cars.

Cazalla and the central sierra

Another regional sierra "capital", **CAZALLA DE LA SIERRA** seems quite a metropolis with its comparative abundance of facilities, and in fact the town dates back to the times of the Romans – its original name of *Callentum* was later changed to *Kazalla* ("fortified city") by the Moors.

The main sight is the church of **Nuestra Señora de la Consolación** at the southern end of town, an outstanding example of *andaluz* "mix and match" architecture – begun in the fourteenth century, continued with some nice Renaissance touches and finally completed in the eighteenth century.

There are also some fine spots within easy wandering distance of the town: a walk of just 5km will take you east to the **Ermita del Monte**, a little eighteenth-century church on a wooded hill above the Rivera de Huesna.

A rather sleepy **tourist office** at Paseo del Moro 2 (Mon–Fri 9.30am–2pm & 5–7pm; ☎954 883 562) has information on the region but not a town map; this is available from the *ayuntamiento* (same hours) a five-minute walk away at Plaza Dr. Narcea 1. Among a number of **hostales** in Cazalla the best is perhaps *La Milagrosa*, c/Llana 29, on the main street (☎954 884 260; ❸). There are also several upmarket hotels, including the charming *Posada del Moro*, c/Paseo del Moro s/n (☎954 884 326, ⑥954 884 858; ❺), with its own good restaurant and delightful rooms overlooking a garden and pool. There are numerous bars around the centre of town and plenty of **places to eat** – *Bar Gonzalo*, c/Caridad 3, in the centre, serves a good-value *menú*, and the *casino* on the central La Plazuela serves simple and hearty meals. The *casino* is essentially a place to drink and relax – quieter and more comfortable than most of the bars – and serves as a kind of club, with locals paying a nominal monthly membership charge. Most towns of Cazalla's size have one, and tourists and visitors are always welcome to use the facilities free of charge – worth doing since the membership rule means everybody drinks at reduced prices.

Cazalla is well served by public transport, with daily **buses** connecting it with Sevilla. Buses also run at 7am and 11.45am to the Estación de Cazalla y Constantina, twenty minutes to the east, from where there are three or four **trains** a day northwest to Zafra and Extremadura, and a similar number that follow the river down towards El Pedroso and ultimately Sevilla. If you're making for El Pedroso, though, you might consider walking from the station – a lovely route, with great river swimming and a fabulous variety of valley flora and fauna; it takes about five hours. A kilometre south of the station there's also an excellent place to stay, the *Molino del Corcho* with rooms and food (☎955 954 249; ❸).

El Pedroso and Constantina

EL PEDROSO is a pretty little town with a notable Mudéjar church. **Accommodation** is limited, though the town now boasts a sparkling new hotel, the *Casa Montehuéznar*, Avda. de la Estación 15 (☎954 889 000; ❺), up the street opposite the station in a restored mansion with its own good restaurant. For more simple rooms enquire at the train station *cantina* (bar) or *Bar Serranía*, an excellent **tapas bar**, across the road from the station, which serves up local specialities such as venison, hare, pheasant and partridge.

Eighteen kilometres further to the east – and perhaps as good a place as any to cut back to Sevilla if you're not counting on trekking the whole length of the range – lies **CONSTANTINA**, a lively and beautiful mountain town with a population of almost 15,000, founded in the fourth century by the Romans during the reign of the Emperor Constantine, and named after his son. High above the town is the impressive **Castillo de la Armada**, surrounded by shady gardens descending in terraces to the old quarters. At the base is the sixteenth-century parish church of **La Encarnación**, once again with a Mudéjar tower, Moorish influence having died hard in these parts.

Constantina has a **tourist office** inside the *ayuntamiento*, c/Eduardo Dato 7 (Mon–Fri 8am–3pm; ☎954 880 000), which can provide a useful town map. The cheapest of the **places to stay** is the modern youth hostel, c/Cuesta Blanca s/n (☎955 881 589; ❶), uphill behind a pump station at the south end of the town with single and twin rooms. Everything else is priced above the budget category, including the delightful *Casa Mari Pepa*, c/José de la Bastida 25 (☎955 880 158; ❺), with distinctively decorated en-suite rooms in a refurbished mansion. There are plenty of places for **eating and drinking** along and around c/Mesones, the main street, and there's even a bit of **nightlife** here with a clutch of discos – *Bonny Dog* is the most central – drawing the younger set in from miles around at weekends. Travelling on to Sevilla, there are two buses a day currently running at 6.45am and 3pm but check with the tourist office or the operator Linesur (☎954 902 368) for the latest information.

The Costa de la Luz

Stumbling on the villages along the **Costa de la Luz**, between Algeciras and Cádiz, is like entering a new land after the dreadfulness of the Costa del Sol. The journey west from Algeciras seems in itself a relief, the road climbing almost immediately into rolling green hills, offering fantastic views down to Gibraltar and across the Strait to the just-discernible white houses and tapering mosques of Moroccan villages. Beyond, the Rif Mountains hover mysteriously in the background and on a clear day, as you approach Tarifa, you can distinguish Tangier on the edge of its crescent-shaped bay.

Tarifa and around

TARIFA, spreading out beyond its Moorish walls, was until the mid-1980s a quiet village, known in Spain, if at all, for its abnormally high suicide rate – a result of the unremitting winds that blow across the town and its environs. Today it's a prosperous, popular and at times very crowded resort, following its discovery as Europe's prime **windsurfing** spot. There are equipment rental shops along the length of the main street, and regular competitions held year-round. Development is moving ahead fast as a result of this new-found popularity, but for the time being it remains a fairly attractive place.

If windsurfing is not your motive, there can still be an appeal in wandering the crumbling ramparts, gazing out to sea or down into the network of lanes that surround the fifteenth-century, Baroque-fronted church of **San Mateo** (daily 9am–1pm & 6–8.30pm), which has a beautiful late Gothic interior. Also worth a look is the **Castillo de Guzman** (Tues–Sun 10am–2pm & 4–8pm; €1.20), the site of many a struggle for this strategic foothold into Spain. It is named after Guzmán el Bueno (the Good), Tarifa's infamous commander during the Moorish siege of 1292, who earned his tag for a superlative piece of tragic drama. Guzmán's nine-year-old son had been taken hostage by a Spanish traitor and surrender of the garrison was demanded as the price of the boy's life. Choosing "honour without a son, to a son with dishonour", Guzmán threw down his own dagger for the execution. The story – a famous piece of heroic resistance in Spain – had echoes in the Civil War siege of the Alcázar at Toledo, when the Nationalist commander refused similar threats, an echo much exploited for propaganda purposes.

A new attraction in Tarifa is popular **whale and dolphin spotting** excursions to the Strait of Gibraltar which leave daily from the harbour. The trip is a fairly steep €27 (reductions for under 14s), but this includes another trip free of charge if there are no sightings. Places must be booked in advance from either of two non-profit-making organizations: Whale Watch, *Café Continental*, Paseo de la Alameda (☎956 684 776), or FIRMM (Foundation for

Information and Research on Marine Mammals; ☎ & ☎956 627 008, or mobile ☎919 459 441) at c/Pedro Cortés 3, slightly west of the church of San Mateo, off c/El Bravo.

Practicalities

The **turismo** (Mon–Fri 10am–2pm & 6–8pm; ☎956 680 993) on the central Paseo la Alameda can help with maps and accommodation. Tarifa has plenty of **places to stay**, though finding a bed in summer can be a struggle, with crowds of windsurfers packing out every available *hostal*. The *Hostal-Restaurante Villanueva*, Avda. Andalucía 11 (☎956 684 149; ❸), is very clean and has a good restaurant, while the excellent *Hostal La Calzada*, c/Justina Pertiñez 7 (☎956 680 366; ❹), near San Mateo church, and the charming *Pensión Correo*, c/Coronel Móscardo 8 (☎956 680 206; ❹), located in the old post office, just south of the church entrance, are also recommended.

On the main Algeciras–Cádiz road (c/Batalla del Salado) you'll find the **bus station**, a supermarket, many of the larger hotels and, further out of town, plenty of **campsites** (see opposite). The same street also has the enterprising Aky Oaky at no. 37 (☎956 680 993) who hire out **mountain bikes**, organize horse treks and run visits to local *ganaderías* (breeding ranches) to see *toros bravos* (fighting bulls).

For **meals**, the restaurant of the *Hostal Villanueva* (see above) specializing in *urta* (Cádiz sea bream) is a good bet, as is the pricier *Restaurante Alameda*, Paseo Alameda 4, near the turismo, which does a variety of *platos combinados* and has a pleasant terrace. Of the dozen or so **bars** dotted around the centre, the German-run *Bistro Point* is a windsurfers' hang-out and a good place for finding long-term accommodation as well as secondhand windsurfing gear. *Bar Morilla*, facing San Mateo's main entrance, is a favourite meeting place with locals and a good tapas stop. *Bar El Trato*, c/Sancho El Bravo IV 28, doubles as Tarifa's **internet centre** where you can pick up your emails over a beer (€0.60 for 10min).

Tarifa Beach

Heading northwest from Tarifa, you find the most spectacular **beaches** of the whole Costa de la Luz – wide stretches of yellow or silvery-white sand, washed by some magical rollers. The same winds that have created such perfect conditions for windsurfing can, however, sometimes be a problem for more casual enjoyment, sandblasting those attempting to relax on towels or mats and whipping the water into whitecaps.

The beaches lie immediately west of the town. They get better as you move past the tidal flats and the mosquito-ridden estuary – until the dunes start and the first camper vans lurk among the bushes. At **TARIFA BEACH**, a little bay 9km from town, there are restaurants, a windsurfing school, campsites and a pricey *hostal*, *Millon* (☎956 685 246; ❼) at the base of a tree-tufted bluff. For more seclusion head for one of the numerous **beach campsites** on either side, signposted from the main road or accessible by walking along the coast. All of these – the main ones are *Río Jara* (☎956 680 570), *Tarifa* (☎956 684 778), *Torre de la Peña* (☎956 684 903) and *Paloma* (☎956 684 203) – are well equipped, inexpensive and open all year.

On to Morocco

Tarifa offers the tempting opportunity of a quick approach **to Morocco**, with Tangier feasible as a day-trip by boat on the once-daily seasonal ferry (May–Sept). Tickets are available from the Tourafrica office (☎956 684 751) on

Tuna fishing

The catch of the **bluefin tuna** is a ritual which has gone on along the Costa de la Luz for a thousand years and, today, still employs many of the age-old methods. The bluefin is the largest of the tuna family, weighing in at around 200 kilos each, and the season lasts from April to June as the fish migrate south towards the Mediterranean, and from early July to mid-August when they return, to be herded and caught by huge nets. The biggest market is Japan, where tuna is eaten raw as sushi. Tuna numbers, however, are declining and the season shortening – probably the result of overfishing – much to the concern of the people of Conil de la Frontera and Zahara de los Atunes, for whom the catch represents an important source of income.

the quayside, or from travel agents along c/Batalla del Salado. The boat normally leaves at 9.30am, returning from Tangier at 4.30pm or 6pm (Spanish time – which is 1hr ahead of Moroccan); check current times with Tourafrica or the turismo. The crossing takes an hour, leaving you just enough time for a brief look around. An overnight stay probably makes more sense, especially as a return ticket costs around €36. It's wise to book a few days ahead, as tour companies often take over the whole boat. This crossing is a lot more expensive than going from Algeciras, but might be a better bet if the latter is chock-a-block in summer or when Moroccans are returning home for the two major Islamic festivals (which rotate between January, February and March).

The coast west of Tarifa

Around the coast from *Paloma* campsite are extensive ruins of the Roman town of **BOLONIA**, or *Baelo Claudia* as the Romans knew it, where you can make out the remains of three temples and a theatre, as well as a forum and numerous houses (July–Aug 10am–1.30pm & 4.30–8pm; rest of year 10am–2.30pm & 4–5.30pm; closed Mon; €1.50, free to EU citizens). The site can be reached down a small side road which turns off the main Cádiz road 15km after Tarifa. There's also a fine **beach** here with bars and eating places and a pleasant **place to stay**, *Hostal Baelo*, c/El Lentiscal 15 (☎956 688 562; ❺). Alternatively it's a good walk along the coast from either *Paloma* or, from the west, Zahara de los Atunes (3–4hr).

ZAHARA DE LOS ATUNES, a small fishing village beginning to show signs of development, has a fabulous 8km-long strand, soon to be backed by the almost obligatory *paseo marítimo* (promenade), currently under construction. Best of a number of **places to stay** is the friendly *Hostal Monte Mar*, c/Peñon 12 (☎956 439 047; ❹), bang on the beach, with sea-view balcony rooms. **Camping** is also feasible at *Bahía de la Plata* (☎956 439 040) at the south end of the beach, but don't forget the insect repellent.

Vejer de la Frontera

While you're on the Costa de la Luz, be sure to take time to visit **VEJER DE LA FRONTERA**, a classically white, Moorish-looking hill town set in a cleft between great protective hills that rear high above the road from Tarifa to Cádiz. If you arrive by bus, it's likely to drop you well below the town at two *hostal-restaurantes* – one of them, *La Barca de Vejer* (☎956 450 083, ⓕ956 451 083; ❹), does superb *bocadillos de lomo*. The road winds up for another 4km, but just by one of the bus-stop cafés there's a donkey path that takes only about twenty minutes to reach the town. This is a perfect approach – for the drama of Vejer is in its isolation and its position, which gradually unfold before you. If you don't fancy the walk, though, taxis are usually available.

Until the last decade, the women of Vejer wore long, dark cloaks that veiled their faces like nuns' habits; despite being adopted as the town's tourist icon, this custom seems now to be virtually extinct, but the place has a remoteness and Moorish feel as explicit as anywhere in Spain. There's a castle and a church of curiously mixed styles (mainly Gothic and Mudéjar) but the main fascination lies in exploring the brilliant white and labyrinthine alleyways, wandering past iron-grilled windows, balconies and patios, and slipping into a succession of **bars**. Try the *Bar Chirino* on La Plazuela, which contains a photographic history of the town.

There's a **turismo** at c/Marqués de Tamarón 10, uphill from the central La Plazuela (Mon–Fri 8am–2pm & 6–9pm, Sat 9am–2pm; ☎956 450 191), which can provide a good town map, accommodation list and information on the budget *casas particulares* nearby. Outside August, finding **accommodation** shouldn't be a problem. A good place to start looking is at the excellent *Hostal la Janda*, c/Cerro Clarisas s/n (☎956 450 142; ❸), or the delightful, upmarket *Hotel Convento San Francisco* (☎956 643 570; ❻) on La Plazuela, which also stocks town maps if the turismo is closed. Both are rather hidden away, so ask for directions. A welcome addition to Vejer's hotel range is *La Casa del Califa*, Plaza de España 16 (☎956 447 730, ⓦwww.vejer.com; ❻) in a refurbished ancient town house, where stylish rooms come internet-equipped and guests have use of two patios and a library and the price includes buffet breakfast. More economical options are available at nos. 7 or 16 c/Filmo, around the corner from the turismo, where families let out rooms during the summer. Vejer's **campsite** (☎956 450 098; June–Sept) lies below the town on the main N340 Málaga to Cádiz road.

Conil

Back on the coast, a dozen or so kilometres on, **CONIL** is an increasingly popular resort. Outside July and August, though, it's still a good place to relax, and in mid-season the only real drawback is trying to find a room. Conil town, once a poor fishing village, now seems entirely modern as you look back from the beach, though when you're actually in the streets you find many older buildings too. The majority of the tourists are Spanish (with a lesser number of Germans), so there's an enjoyable atmosphere, and if you are here in mid-season, a very lively nightlife.

The **beach**, Conil's *raison d'être*, is a wide bay of brilliant yellow stretching for miles to either side of town and lapped by an amazingly, not to say disarmingly, gentle Atlantic – you have to walk halfway to Panama before it reaches waist height. The area immediately in front of town is the family beach; up to the northwest you can walk to some more sheltered coves, while across the river to the southeast is a topless and nudist area. Walking along the coast in this direction the beach is virtually unbroken until it reaches the cape, the familiar-sounding **Cabo de Trafalgar**, off which Lord Nelson achieved victory and met his death on October 21, 1805. If the winds are blowing, this is one of the most sheltered beaches in the area. It can be reached by road, save for the last 400 metres across the sands to the rock.

Practicalities

Most **buses** use the Transportes Comes station on c/Carretera; walk towards the sea and you'll find yourself in the centre of town. There's a helpful **turismo** (Mon–Sat 9.30am–1.30pm & 6–9pm, Sun 9.30am–1.30pm; ☎956 440 501) along the way at the junction of c/Carretera and c/Menéndez Pidal – it's worth picking up a copy of their useful free booklet *Conil en su Bolsillo*, which details all the town's tapas bars, restaurants, and much more. **Accommodation** needs are served by numerous hotels and *hostales*. The central *Hostal La Villa*, Plaza de España 6 (☎956 441 053; ❹), is one of the most reasonable, and nearby is the even cheaper and more atmospheric *Pensión Los Hermanos*, c/Virgen 2 (☎956 440 196; ❷), Conil's oldest *fonda*. Conil also has private rooms for rent; the easiest way to find one of these is to go to the first "supermarket" on the right-hand side of the road to Playa Fontanilla (the road opposite the *Rinkon Way* open-air disco), where they have a complete list – there are good ones at c/Velásquez 1. **Campsites** include *Fuente del Gallo* in the nearby *urbanización*, Fuente del Gallo (☎956 440 137; March–Oct), a 3km walk despite all signs to the contrary.

Seafood is king here and Conil has lots of good **restaurants** along the front; try the *ortiguillas* – deep-fried sea anemones – which you see only in the Cádiz area. Two of the best restaurants, *Francisco* and *La Fontanilla*, are to be found side by side on the Playa de la Fontanilla, the town's northernmost beach. During the summer, Conil's great **nightlife** attraction is *Las Carpas* ("the tents"), a huge triple entertainment complex on the beach which caters for all ages and features techno, salsa, dance bands and flamenco shows, often all in action at the same time in the separate venues. It's all provided by the town council and, best of all, it's absolutely free.

Cádiz

CÁDIZ is among the oldest settlements in Spain, founded about 1100 BC by the Phoenicians and one of the country's principal ports ever since. Its greatest period, however, and the era from which the central part of town takes most of its present appearance, was the eighteenth century. Then, with the silting up of the river to Sevilla, the port enjoyed a virtual monopoly on the Spanish-American trade in gold and silver, and on its proceeds were built the cathedral – itself golden-domed (in colour at least) and almost Oriental when seen from the sea – the public halls and offices, and the smaller churches.

Inner Cádiz, built on a peninsula-island, remains much as it must have looked in those days, with its grand open squares, sailors' alleyways and high, turreted houses. Literally crumbling from the effect of the sea air on its soft limestone, it has a tremendous atmosphere – slightly seedy, definitely in decline, but still full of mystique.

Arrival, information and accommodation

Arriving by **train** you'll find yourself on the periphery of the old town, close to the Plaza de San Juan de Dios, busiest of the city's many squares. By **bus** you'll be a few blocks further north, along the water – either at the Los Amarillos terminal (serving Rota, Chipiona and the resorts west of Cádiz) or a few blocks north at the Estación de Comes station in Plaza Independencia, near Plaza de España (used by buses from Sevilla, Tarifa and most other destinations toward Algeciras). Los Amarillos also runs a twice-daily service through Arcos to Ubrique, with a connection there to Ronda – by far the best route. There's a **turismo** on Avda. Ramón de Carranza s/n (Mon–Fri 9am–2pm & 5–8pm; ☎956 258 646) near to Plaza de San Juan de Dios and a municipal tourist information **kiosk** on the plaza itself (Mon–Fri 9am–2pm ☎956 241 001). **Internet access** is available at *La Sal*, c/Dr Marañon 14 (☎956 211 539; €1.20 per 30min), a stone's throw from the *Hotel Atlántico parador* (see opposite).

Accommodation

Radiating around the Plaza de San Juan de Dios is a dense network of alleyways crammed with **hostales** and **fondas** and a few less inviting options. More salubrious places to stay are to be found a couple of blocks away, towards the cathedral or Plaza de Candelaria.

Pensión La Argentina, c/Conde O'Reilly 1 ☏ 956 223 310. Simple, cheap and spotless rooms close to the Plaza de España. ❷

Hotel Atlántico, Parque Genovés 9 ☏ 956 226 905, ☏ 956 214 582. Functional, modern *parador* with Atlantic views and an outdoor pool. ❼

Hostal Bahía, c/Plocia 5 ☏ 956 259 061. Excellent, friendly *hostal*, offering pleasant rooms with bath. ❺

Las Cuatro Naciones, c/Plocia 3 ☏ 956 255 539. Clean, unpretentious place with low-priced rooms, close to Plaza San Juan de Dios. ❷

Hostal España, Marqués de Cádiz 9 ☏ 956 285 500. Pleasant *hostal* with reasonable rooms (some en suite) ranged around a patio. ❹

Hostal Fantoni, c/Flamenco 5 ☏ 956 282 704. Good-value *hostal* in renovated town house with lots of *azulejos*, cool marble and en-suite rooms. ❹

Hostal Manolita, c/Benjumeda 2 ☏ 956 211 577. Simple rooms in a friendly, family-run place. ❸

Quo Qádis Youth Hostel, c/Diego Arias 1, close to Plaza Manuel de Falla ☏ & ☏ 956 221 939. Somewhat eccentrically run and privately owned hostel in a restored mansion with dormitory, single and double rooms. Hires out bicycles to residents, as well as offering courses in flamenco and trips around the city and to surrounding beauty spots. Prices include breakfast and there's a restaurant with vegetarian options. ❶–❸

The Town

Unlike most other ports of its size, Cádiz seems immediately relaxed, easygoing, and not at all threatening, even at night. Perhaps this is due to its reassuring shape and compactness, the presence of the sea and the striking **sea fortifications** and waterside **alamedas** making it impossible to get lost for more than a few blocks. But it probably owes this tone as much to the town's tradition of liberalism and tolerance – one maintained all through the years of Franco's dictatorship even though this was one of the first towns to fall to his forces, and was the port through which the Nationalist armies launched their invasion. In particular, Cádiz has always accepted its substantial gay community, who are much in evidence at the city's brilliant *carnaval* celebrations.

Cádiz is more interesting in its general ambience – its blind alleys, cafés and backstreets – than for any particular buildings. As you wander, you'll find the **Museo de Bellas Artes**, at Plaza de Mina 5 (Tues 2.30–8pm, Wed–Sat 9am–8pm, Sun 9.30am–2.30pm; Oct–Mar Tue–Sat closes 6pm; €1.50, free to EU citizens), just across the square from the turismo. This contains an impressive local archeological display and a quite exceptional series of saints painted by **Francisco Zurbarán**, brought here from the Carthusian monastery at Jerez and one of only three such sets in the country (the others are at Sevilla and Guadalupe) preserved intact, or nearly so. With their sharply defined shadows and intense, introspective air, Zurbarán's saints are at once powerful and very Spanish – even the English figures such as Hugh of Lincoln, or the Carthusian John Houghton, martyred by Henry VIII when he refused to accept him as head of the English Church. Perhaps this is not surprising, for the artist spent much of his life travelling round the Carthusian monasteries of Spain and many of his saints are in fact portraits of the monks whom he met.

Even if you don't normally go for High Baroque it's hard to resist the attraction of the huge and seriously crumbling eighteenth-century **Catedral Nueva** (visits, including museum: Tues–Sun 10am–1pm, plus Tue–Fri 4–7pm; €3), now undergoing a belated (and astronomically expensive) restoration. The cathedral is decorated entirely in stone, with no gold or white in sight, and in absolutely perfect proportions. In the crypt you can see the tomb of Manuel

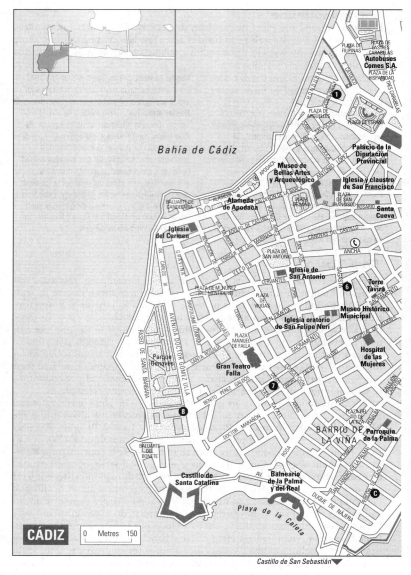

Bahía de Cádiz

PLAZA DE
FILIPINAS

PLAZA DE
BASTRES
CARABELAS

**Autobuses
Comes S.A.**

PLAZA DE LA
HISPANIDAD

TRES CARABELAS

❶

PLAZA DE
ARGÜELLES

PLAZA DE ESPAÑA

**Palacio de la
Diputación
Provincial**

**Museo de
Bellas Artes
y Arqueológico**

**Iglesia y claustro
de San Francisco**

PLAZA
DE SAN
FRANCISCO

ROSARIO

**Santa
Cueva**

BALUARTE DE
CANDELARIA

**Alameda
de Apodaca**

PLAZA
DE MINA

CÁNOVAS DEL CASTILLO

**Iglesia
del Carmen**

ANCHA

ⓒ

PLAZA DE
SAN ANTONIO

**Iglesia de
San Antonio**

❻

**Torre
Tavira**

PLAZA DE M. NUÑEZ
DEL MONTERO

PLAZA
DE
VIUDAS

**Museo Histórico
Municipal**

**Iglesia oratorio
de San Felipe Neri**

PLAZA
MANUEL
DE FALLA

SACRAMENTO

HOSPITAL DE MUJERES

**Hospital
de las
Mujeres**

AVENIDA DOCTOR GÓMEZ ULLA

PASEO DE SANTA BÁRBARA

**Parque
Genovés**

SANTA ROSALÍA

**Gran Teatro
Falla**

❼

BENITO PÉREZ GALDÓS

❽

DOCTOR MARAÑÓN

ROSA

PLAZA DEL
TÍO DE
LA TIZA

**BARRIO DE
LA VIÑA**

**Parroquia
de la Palma**

BALUARTE
DEL
BONETE

**Castillo de
Santa Catalina**

AV

**Balneario
de la Palma
y del Real**

DUQUE DE NÁJERA

ⓒ

Playa de la Caleta

CÁDIZ

0   Metres   150

Castillo de San Sebastián ▼

de Falla, the great *gaditano* composer of such Andalucía-inspired works as *Nights in the Gardens of Spain* and *El Amor Brujo*.

Over on the seaward side of the mammoth complex, the "old" cathedral, **Santa Cruz**, is also worth a look, its interior liberally studded with coin-in-the-slot votive candles. A **Roman theatre** (Tues–Sun 11am–1.30pm; free) has recently been excavated behind. To the north of the cathedral along

4

ANDALUCÍA | Cádiz

320

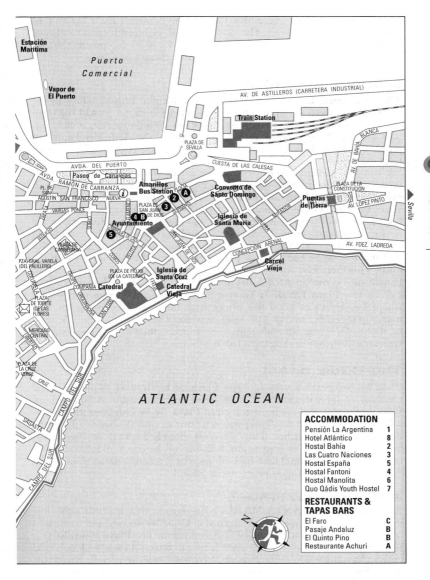

ACCOMMODATION	
Pensión La Argentina	1
Hotel Atlántico	8
Hostal Bahía	2
Las Cuatro Naciones	3
Hostal España	5
Hostal Fantoni	4
Hostal Manolita	6
Quo Qádis Youth Hostel	7

RESTAURANTS & TAPAS BARS	
El Faro	C
Pasaje Andaluz	B
El Quinto Pino	B
Restaurante Achuri	A

c/Sacramento, the **Torre Tavira** (daily: June–Sept 10am–8pm; Oct–May 10am–6pm; €3), c/Marqués del Real Tesoro 10, is an eighteenth-century mansion with the tallest tower in the city, from where there are great **views** over the rooftops to the sea beyond; it also houses an entertaining **camera obscura**. Lastly, there are two churches of note for the paintings they contain. Foremost of these is the chapel of the **Hospital de las Mujeres** (Mon–Fri

10am–1pm; €0.60; ask the porter for admission), which has a brilliant **El Greco**, *St Francis in Ecstasy*. The other, an oval, eighteenth-century chapel, **Santa Cueva** (Mon–Sat 10am–1pm, plus Tue–Fri 4.30–7.30pm; €0.30), on c/Rosario, has three fine frescoes on Eucharistic themes by **Goya**.

Eating and drinking

Take-away **fried fish** was invented in Cádiz (despite English claims to the contrary) and there are numerous *freidurías* (fried-fish shops) around the town as well as stands along the beach in season; few eating experiences here can beat strolling the city streets while dipping into a *cartucho* (paper funnel) of *pescado frito*. In the bars, *tortilla de camarones* (shrimp omelette) is another superb local speciality.

A couple of *freidurías* worth seeking out are the *Freiduría Las Flores* on the square of the same name and the equally good *Freiduría Sopranis*, c/Sopranis 2, just off **Plaza San Juan de Dios**. The Plaza de San Juan de Dios, protruding across the neck of the peninsula from the port and the first long stretch of Cádiz's naval dockyards, has several cafés and inexpensive **restaurants**. In the square's southwest corner, *Pasaje Andaluz*, with a terrace, and the nearby and diminutive *El Quinto Pino*, c/San Fernando 2, are good places to try. Superior quality fare is to be had at the popular *Restaurante Achuri*, c/Plocia 15 off the square's northern end (closed Sun–Wed evenings), serving up some excellent Basque and *andaluz*-inspired dishes in a pleasant setting. For fish you must also visit the tiny **Plaza Tío de la Tiza**, in the old fishing quarter near the beach, which has dozens of good fish places, with outdoor tables filling the surrounding streets in summer. The more upmarket *El Faro*, c/San Félix 15, nearby, is one of the best fish restaurants in Andalucía – their *menú* is good value – with an equally outstanding tapas bar attached.

The Cádiz coast

Cádiz has two beaches – the excellent **Playa de la Victoria**, to the left of the promontory approaching the town (reached from the centre on bus #1 from Plaza de España), and the none-too-clean **Playa de la Caleta** on the peninsula's western tip – but for clearer waters it's best to cross the bay to **El Puerto de Santa María**. Further along the coast towards Sanlúcar de Barrameda, beaches are more or less continuous, with two of the best flanking the resorts of **Rota** and **Chipiona**. These are both popular weekend retreats from Cádiz, and during July and August pretty much packed.

El Puerto de Santa María

EL PUERTO DE SANTA MARÍA is the obvious choice, a traditional family resort for both *gaditanos* (as inhabitants of Cádiz are known) and *sevillanos* – many of whom have built villas and chalets along the fine **Playa Puntillo**. This strand is a little way out from the town (a ten- to fifteen-minute walk or a local bus), a pleasant place to while away an afternoon; there are friendly beach bars where for ridiculously little you can nurse a litre of *sangría* (bring your own food). In the town itself the principal attraction is a series of **sherry bodegas** – long, whitewashed warehouses flanking the streets and the banks of the river. Until the train was extended to Cádiz, all shipments of sherry from Jerez came through Santa María, and its port is still used to some extent. Many of the firms offer free tours and tastings to visitors (Mon–Fri from around 10am till noon), though this is not a regular process and you need to phone in advance or organize a visit through the turismo, either in Cádiz or Puerto de Santa María itself. The most worthwhile tours are offered by two of the town's major producers, Osborne y Cía, c/Fernán Caballero 3 (Mon–Fri: visits at 10.30am in English, 11am & noon in Spanish; ☎956 855 211; €1.80), and Fernando de Terry, c/Santísima Trinidad 2 (Mon–Fri: visits at 9.30am, 11am & 12.30pm; ☎956 857 700; €2.10), situated in a beautiful, converted, seventeenth-century convent.

The **ferry** (known locally as *El Vapor*, alluding to the earlier steamboats) from Cádiz is quicker and cheaper than the bus at €1.70 one-way; the forty-minute trip across the bay departs from the Estación Marítima at 10am, noon, 2pm, 6.30pm and 8.30pm (summer only), returning to Cádiz at 9am, 11am, 1pm, 3.30pm and 7.30pm with extra sailings in season according to demand (especially in the evening). A new **catamaran** service operated by the MareSur 2000 company (mobile: ☎670 697 905) leaves from the same quay 7 times daily between 7.25am and 5.30pm, and does the trip in half the time of the *vapor* (20 minutes); tickets cost €2.25 one-way or €4.20 return. El Puerto's **turismo** is situated at c/Luna 22 (daily 10am–2pm & 6–8pm; ☎956 542 413), near the Plaza de las Galeras Reales where the ferry drops you. Close by you'll also find some excellent seafood **restaurants**, including the justly famous and great fun *Romerijo*, c/Ribera del Marisco, one of the most popular *marisquerías* in town, where you can buy your choice of shellfish in a *cartucho* (paper funnel) and eat on their terrace with a beer. Bus #2 from the Plaza de las Galeras Reales goes to the **campsite** at Playa Las Dunas (☎956 872 210; open all year), near the beach with plenty of shade.

Rota and Chipiona

ROTA, 16km along the coast, is marred by its proximity to one of the three major **US bases** in Spain – installed in the 1950s as part of a deal in which Franco exchanged strips of Spanish sovereign territory for economic aid and international "respectability". As a resort, it's no great shakes, but does boast two splendid beaches, and enough discos, bars and fish restaurants to satisfy your needs should you decide to stay.

CHIPIONA, at the edge of the next point, is simpler: a small, straightforward seaside resort crammed with family *pensiones*. Older tourists come here for the **spa waters**, channelled into a fountain at the church of Nuestra Señora de Regla, but for most it's the **beaches** that are the lure. South of the town and lighthouse is the long **Playa de Regla**, where, outside July and August, it's easy enough to leave the crowds behind; northeast, towards Sanlúcar, are sand bars and rocks. If you're planning on staying in the town, the **hostales** along the beach are the most attractive; in mid-season you'll need help getting a room from the women who meet new arrivals at the bus station; failing this, a **turismo** inside the Casa de Cultura on the central Plaza de Andalucía (Mon–Fri 10am–1.30pm & 7–9pm; ☎956 372 828) should be able to advise. The combined **campsite and youth hostel**, *Pinar de Chipiona* (☎956 371 480; open all year), is 3km out of town towards Rota – any Rota-bound bus will drop you off.

Sanlúcar de Barrameda

Like Puerto Santa María, **SANLÚCAR DE BARRAMEDA** also has its sherry connections. Set at the mouth of the Guadalquivir, it's the main depot for **Manzanilla** wine, a pale, dry variety much in evidence in the bars, which you can also sample during visits (booked in advance by phone) to the town's **bodegas**: *Bodega Antonio Barbadillo*, c/Eguilaz 11 (☎956 360 894; Wed & Thurs only, 12.30pm; €1.80), the town's major producer, has the most interesting visits and makes the famous *La Gitana* brand. Sanlúcar is also the setting for some exciting horse races along the beach in the last two weeks of August, the best time to be here.

There's not a great deal to see, although the attractive old quarter in the upper town, or Barrio Alto, is worth taking time to explore. The town's port was the scene of a number of important maritime exploits: Magellan set out from here to circumnavigate the globe, Pizarro embarked to conquer Peru, and 4km upriver, from the fishing harbour of Bonanza, Columbus sailed on his third voyage to the Americas. The few buildings of interest – the ducal palace of **Medina Sidonia**, the **Palacio de Orleáns y Borbón** (guided visits 10am–2pm; closed Wed; €0.60) built by the dukes of Montpensier and decorated in a wild neo-Mudéjar style, the thirteenth-century church of **Nuestro Señora de la O** with its fine Gothic-Mudéjar portal, and the substantial remains of the Moorish **Castillo de Santiago** – are all perched above the main part of town on the Cuesta de Belén in the Barrio Alto.

One of the best things about Sanlúcar is its shell-encrusted **river beach** and warm waters, a couple of kilometres' walk from the town centre and usually quite deserted. This is flanked, on the opposite shore, by the beginnings of the **Coto Doñana National Park** (see p.326), whose vast marshy expanses (strictly regulated access) signal the end of the coast road to the west. Visits to the park from Sanlúcar are now possible with a new boat cruise which, while it doesn't allow for serious exploration, is nevertheless a wonderful introduction to this remarkable area. The trip lasts approximately four hours and allows two short guided walks inside the park. The *Real Fernando* leaves daily from the Bajo de Guia quay (April–Sept 9.30am & 5pm; Oct–March 10am only; ☎956 363 813; €13.20 under-12s half price; advance booking essential). Tickets should be collected from the Fábrica de Hielo, Bajo de Guía s/n, the national park's **exhibition centre** (daily 9am–8pm).

Accommodation is limited especially in summer. For a central position try the *Pensión Blanca Paloma*, Plaza San Roque 9 (☎956 363 644; ❸), or seek assistance from the **turismo**, Calzada del Ejército (Mon–Fri 9am–2pm & 6–9pm, Sat & Sun 10am–1pm; ☎956 366 110), on the avenue leading to the sea, which can also provide a good town map.

Jerez de la Frontera

JEREZ DE LA FRONTERA, inland towards Sevilla, is the home and heartland of sherry (itself an English corruption of the town's Moorish name – *Xerez*) and also, less known but equally important, of Spanish brandy. An elegant and prosperous town, it's a tempting place to stop, arrayed as it is round the scores of wine *bodegas* with plenty of sights to visit in between. Life is lived at a fairly sedate pace for most of the year here, although things liven up considerably when Jerez launches into one or other of its two big **festivals** – the May Horse Fair (perhaps the most snooty of the Andalucian *ferias*), or the celebration of the vintage towards the end of September. Jerez is also famous throughout Spain for a long and distinguished **flamenco** tradition and if you're interested in finding out more about Andalucía's great folk art then a visit to the **Centro Andaluz de Flamenco**, Plaza de San Juan (Mon 9am–2pm, Tues–Fri 9am–2pm & 5–7pm; free), in the atmospheric *gitano* quarter, the Barrio de Santiago, is a must; here you can see videos of past greats and get information on flamenco venues in the town.

The **tours of the sherry and brandy processes** can be interesting – almost as much as the sampling that follows – and, provided you don't arrive in August when much of the industry closes down, there are a great many firms and *bodegas* to choose from. The visits are conducted either in English (very much the second language of the sherry world) or a combination of English and Spanish and last for about an hour. Jerez's "big two" are **González Byass**, c/Manuel González s/n (tours: March–Sept Mon–Sat 9.30am–1pm & 5–7pm, Sun 9.30am–1pm; rest of year ring the bodega for hours; book in advance on ☎956 357 016, English spoken, or ⓦwww.gonzalezbyass.es/; €6) makers of the famous *Tio Pepe* brand and the more central, and **Pedro Domecq**, c/San Ildefonso 3 (tours: Mon–Fri 9am–1.30pm & 5–7pm; advance booking on ☎956 151 500 or ⓦwww.domecq.es/; €3 morning visits, €4.50 afternoon) producers of *La Ina*; besides manufacturing sherry both *bodegas* are major brandy producers, too. Many of these firms were founded by British Catholic refugees, barred from careers at home by the sixteenth-century Supremacy Act, and even now they form a kind of Anglo-Andalucian tweed-wearing and polo-playing aristocracy (on display, most conspicuously, at the Horse Fair). The González cellars – the *soleras* – are perhaps the oldest in Jerez and, though it's no longer used, preserve an old circular chamber designed by Eiffel (of the tower fame). If you feel you need comparisons, you can pick up a list of locations and opening times of the other *bodegas* from the turismo (see below) or from any travel agent in the centre when this is closed.

The most attractive of the town's buildings – including the imposing Gothic-Renaissance **Catedral de San Salvador** (daily 5.30–8pm and morning service, or ring ☎956 348 482) and the impressive eleventh-century Moorish **Alcázar** (daily: May–Sept 10am–8pm; Oct–April 10am–6pm; €1.50) next to the González *bodega* – are within a couple of minutes' walk of the central Plaza del Arenal. An excellent **Archeological Museum** (June–Aug 10am–2.30pm, closed Mon; Sept–May Tues–Fri 10am–2pm & 4–7pm, Sat & Sun 10am–2.30pm; €1.50) lies five minutes north of the centre in the Plaza del Mercado on the edge of the Barrio de Santiago; star exhibits include a seventh-century BC Greek military helmet, a Visigothic sarcophagus and a fine Caliphal bottle vase. Evidence of Jerez's great enthusiasm for horses can be seen at the **Royal Andalucian School of Equestrian Art**, Avda. Duque de Abrantes s/n, which offers the chance to watch them performing to music (Thurs noon; March–Oct also Tues noon; ☎956 319 635; €12–18). Training, rehearsals (without music) and visits to the stables take place on other weekdays between 11am and 1pm, when admission is a more affordable €6.

Practicalities

The **turismo**, c/Larga 39 (Mon–Fri 8am–2pm & 5–8pm, Sat 10am–2pm; ☎956 331 150), is located halfway along the town's pedestrianized main street, to the north of the focal Plaza del Arenal. For **accommodation**, the best budget rooms are at *Pensión Los Amarillos*, c/Melina 39 (☎956 342 296; ❷), which you reach by turning left from the bus station and walking three blocks. The nearby *Hostal Las Palomas*, c/Higueras 17 (☎956 343 773; ❷), also has clean and simple rooms, while a bit further out in the suburbs is the good-value *Albergue Juvenil*, Avda. Carrero Blanco 30 (☎956 143 901; ❶), with a pool; bus #9 from outside the bus station will take you there. Moving upmarket, there's the excellent *Hostal San Andrés*, c/Morenos 12 (☎956 340 983, ☉956 343 196; ❸), which has rooms with bath, and the friendly *Hotel Torres*, c/Arcos 29 (☎956 323 400, ☉956 321 816; ❺), both northeast of the bus station, with similar facilities and charming patios. For **food** there are tapas bars and eating places all over the central zone; one of the best tapas venues is *Juanito*, c/Pescadería Vieja 4 (off the east side of the central Plaza del Arenal) and, right opposite in the same alleyway, is a decent modest-priced restaurant, *Almenas*, with a budget menú.

The **train** and **bus** stations are more or less next door to each other, eight blocks east of the González *bodega* and Plaza del Arenal.

Huelva Province

The **province of Huelva** stretches between Sevilla and Portugal, but aside from its scenic section of the Sierra Morena (see p.309) to the north and a chain of fine **beaches** to the west of the provincial capital it's a pretty dull part of Andalucía, laced with large areas of swamp – the *marismas* – and notorious for mosquitoes. This distinctive habitat is, however, particularly suited to a great variety of wildlife, especially birds, and over 60,000 acres of the delta of the Río Guadalquivir (the largest roadless area in western Europe) have been fenced off to form the **Coto de Doñana National Park**. Here, amid sand dunes, pine woods, marshes and freshwater lagoons, live scores of flamingos, along with rare birds of prey, 25 pairs of lynx, mongooses and a startling variety of migratory birds.

Coto de Doñana National Park

The seasonal pattern of its delta waters, which flood in winter and then drop in the spring, leaving rich deposits of silt, raised sandbanks and islands, give **Coto Doñana** its special interest. Conditions are perfect in winter for ducks and geese, but spring is more exciting: the exposed mud draws hundreds of flocks of breeding birds. In the marshes and amid the cork-oak forests behind you've a good chance of seeing squacco herons, black-winged stilt, whiskered tern, pratincole and sand grouse, as well as flamingos, egrets and vultures. There are, too, occasional sightings of the Spanish imperial eagle, now reduced to fourteen breeding pairs. Conditions are not so good in late summer and early autumn, when the *marismas* dry out and support far less bird life.

The park, however, is under threat from development. Even at current levels the drain on the water supply is severe, and made worse by **pollution** of the Guadalquivir by farming pesticides, Sevilla's industry and Huelva's mines. The seemingly inevitable disaster finally occurred in 1998 when an upriver mining dam used for storing toxic waste burst, unleashing millions of litres of pollutants into the Guadiamar river which flows through the park. The noxious tide was stopped just 2km from the park's boundary, but catastrophic damage was done to surrounding farmland, with nesting birds decimated and fish poisoned.

Equally disturbing are the proposals for a huge new tourist centre to be known as the **Costa Doñana**, on the very fringes of the park. Campaigning by national and international environmental bodies resulted in this project being shelved, but the threat remains, much of the pressure stemming from local people who see much-needed jobs in the venture. Large demonstrations have been organized by both sides, and an uneasy truce endures with persistent and mysterious outbreaks of vandalism against park property.

Visiting the park
Visiting the Doñana involves (perhaps understandably) a certain amount of frustration. At present it's open only to a boat cruise from Sanlúcar (see p.323) and to brief, organized **tours** (spring & summer daily 8.30am & 5pm; €16.50 a seat) by all-terrain 24-seater buses – four hours at a time along one of five

charted, 80km routes. The starting point for these, and the place to book them (essential and as far ahead as possible in high season), is at the Centro de Recepción de Acebuche (☎959 448 711, English spoken; ✉donana@mma.es), 4km north of Matalascañas towards El Rocío and Almonte, or at the Cooperativa Marismas del Rocío, Plaza del Acebuchal 16, El Rocío (☎959 430 432, ☎959 430 451). The tours are quite tourist-oriented (binoculars are pretty essential), and point out only spectacular species like flamingos, imperial eagles, deer and wild boar. If you're a serious ornithologist, the tour isn't for you; instead, enquire at the Centro about organizing a private group tour. There are excellent bird-watching **hides** (daily 8am–8pm) at the El Acebuche, La Rocina and El Acebron reception centres, as well as a 1500m footpath from El Acebuche, which creates a mini-trek through typical *cotos* or terrains to be found in the reserve. Although binoculars are on hire, they sometimes run out, and you'd be advised to bring your own. The natural history exhibition at the Centro is in itself worthy of a visit.

Matalascañas

Birds and other wildlife apart, the resort settlement of **MATALASCAÑAS** on the park's coastal edge is unlikely to excite; with its large hotel complexes and a concrete shopping centre, it would be difficult to imagine a more complete lack of character. In summer, too, the few **hostal rooms** are generally booked solid and, unless you plan in advance, you'll probably end up camping – either unofficially at the resort itself, or at the vast *Camping Rocío Playa* (☎959 430 238; open all year), 1.5km down the road towards Huelva. This site is a little inconvenient without your own transport if you're planning to take regular trips into the Doñana, but if you just want a **beach**, it's not a bad option. Playa Doñana and its continuation Playa Mazagón (with another campsite, *Doñana Playa*; ☎959 536 281; open all year) are fine strands stretching the whole distance to Huelva, and with hardly another foreign tourist in sight. This route is covered by three daily buses in both directions.

El Rocío

Set on the northwestern tip of the *marismas*, **EL ROCÍO** is a tiny village of white cottages and a church stockade where perhaps the most famous pilgrimage-fair of the south takes place annually at Pentecost. This, the **Romería del Rocío**, is an extraordinary spectacle, with whole village communities and local "brotherhoods" from Huelva, Sevilla and even Málaga converging on horseback and in lavishly decorated ox carts. Throughout the procession, which climaxes on the Saturday evening, there is dancing and partying, while by the time the carts arrive at El Rocío they've been joined by busloads of pilgrims. The fair commemorates the miracle of Nuestra Señora del Rocío (Our Lady of the Dew), a statue found, so it is said, on this spot and resistant to all attempts to move it elsewhere. The image, credited with all kinds of magic and fertility powers, is paraded before the faithful early on the Sunday morning.

El Rocío is a nice place to stay, with wide, sandy streets, cowboy-hatted horse-riding farmers and a frontier-like feeling. **Accommodation** prices, however, tend to be on the high side; do not even think about a getting a room during the *romería* as they not only cost over ten times normal prices, but are booked up years ahead. Worth a try in quieter times are the *Hostal Isidro*, Avda. los Ansares 59 (☎959 442 242; ❺), and *Hostal Cristina*, c/Real 32 (☎959 406 513; ❹). Moving upmarket, there's a choice between the inviting *Hotel Toruño*, Plaza Acebuchal 22 (☎959 442 323, ☎959 442 338; ❻), with *marismas* views, and the even plusher *Puente del Rey*, Avda. Canaliega 1 (☎959 442 575, ☎959

442 070; ❼). In the spring, as far as **bird-watching** goes, the town is probably the best base in the area. The *marismas* and pine woods adjacent to the town are teeming with birds, and following tracks east and southeast of El Rocío, along the edge of the reserve itself, you'll see many species (up to a hundred if you're lucky).

Huelva and the coast down to Portugal

Large, sprawling and industrialized, **HUELVA** is the least attractive and least interesting of Andalucía's provincial capitals. It has claims as a "flamenco capital", but unless you're really devoted it's unlikely you'll want to stop long enough to verify this. By day – and in the evening as well – the most enticing thing to do is to take the hourly ferry (summer only) across the bay to **Punta Umbría**, the local resort, also linked by a new road bridge spanning the marshlands of the Río Odiel estuary. This is hardly an inspiring place either, but it does at least have some life, a fair beach, numerous *hostales* and a campsite.

The Columbus Trail

Across the Río Tinto estuary from Huelva, the monastery of La Rábida and the villages of Palos and Moguer are all places connected with the voyages of Columbus to the New World.

La Rábida (hourly tours Tues–Sun 10am–1pm & 4–6.15pm; donations), 8km from Huelva and easily reached by bus, is a charming and tranquil fourteenth-century Franciscan monastery whose abbot was instrumental in securing funds for the voyage from the monarchs Fernando and Isabel. Nearby, on the estuary, the **Harbour of the Caravels** (April–Sept Tues–Fri 10am–2pm & 5–9pm, Sat & Sun 11am–8pm; Oct–March Tues–Fri 10am–2pm, Sat & Sun 11am–8pm; €2.60) has impressive full-size replicas of the three caravels which made the epic voyage to the New World and an adjoining museum, which features among its displays a geography book annotated in Columbus's own hand. At **PALOS**, 4km to the north, is the church of **San Jorge** where Columbus and his crew heard Mass before setting sail from the now silted-up harbour. A further 8km north, at the whitewashed town of **MOGUER**, is the fourteenth-century **Convent of Santa Clara** in whose church Columbus spent a whole night in prayer as thanksgiving for his safe return. The small town is a beautiful place, the birthplace of the Nobel prize-winning poet Juan Ramón Jiménez, and boasts a scaled-down, whiter version of Sevilla's Giralda attached to the church of **Nuestra Señora de la Granada**. If you want to stay overnight, *Hostal Pedro Alonso Niño*, c/Pedro Alonso Niño 13 (☎959 372 392; ❷), is delightful and has excellent-value en-suite rooms. One **bar** worth seeking out is *Mesón El Lobito* at c/La Rabida 31, which is in a bizarre league of its own when it comes to decor; it also sells wine at crazy prices (€0.15 per glass) and does decent fish and meat dishes *a la brasa*.

West to Portugal

From Huelva it's best either to press on inland to the Sierra Morena or straight **along the coast to Portugal**. There are a number of good beaches and some low-key resorts noted for their seafood, such as **Isla Cristina**, along the stretch of coastline between Huelva and the frontier town of **Ayamonte**, but not much more to detain you. A good bus service along this route and a new road suspension bridge across the Rio Guadiana estuary and border, linking Ayamonte and **Villa Real de Santo Antonio**, make for a relatively painless crossing into Portugal. From this approach, a good first night's target in Portugal is Tavira, on the Algarve train line.

Sevilla to Córdoba

The direct route from **Sevilla to Córdoba**, 135km along the valley of Guadalquivir, followed by the train and some of the buses, is a flat and rather unexciting journey. There's far more to see following the route just to the south of this, via **Carmona** and **Écija**, both interesting towns, and more still if you detour further south to take in **Osuna** as well. There are plenty of buses along these roads so there's no real need to stay – **Carmona** in particular is an easy day-trip from Sevilla.

Carmona

Set on a low hill overlooking a fertile plain, **CARMONA** is a small, picturesque town made recognizable by the fifteenth-century tower of the Iglesia de San Pedro, built in imitation of the Giralda. The tower is the first thing you catch sight of and it sets a tone for the place – an appropriate one, since the town shares a similar history to Sevilla, less than 30km distant. It was an important Roman city (from which era it preserves a fascinating subterranean necropolis) and under the Moors was often governed by a brother of the Sevillan ruler. Later, Pedro the Cruel built a palace within its castle, which he used as a "provincial" royal residence.

The **Iglesia de San Pedro** (Tues–Sat 9.30am–2.30pm; €1.20) is a good place to start exploring the town; it dominates Carmona's main thoroughfare, c/San Pedro and has a splendid Baroque *sagrario* (sacristy) within. Buses stop just short of the church in the Paseo del Estatuto, from where, looking east, you get a view of the magnificent Moorish **Puerta de Sevilla**, a grand and fortified Roman gateway to the old town which now houses the turismo (see "Practicalities" below). The **old town** is circled by 4km of ancient walls, inside which narrow streets wind up past Mudéjar churches and Renaissance mansions. Follow c/Prim uphill to the **Plaza San Fernando** (or Plaza Mayor), modest in size but dominated by splendid Moorish-style buildings. Behind it there's a bustling fruit and vegetable market most mornings.

Close by to the east is **Santa María la Mayor** (Tues–Sat 9.30am–2.30pm, Sun & Mon service times; €1.20), a fine Gothic church built over the former main mosque, whose elegant patio it retains; like many of Carmona's churches it is capped by a Mudéjar tower, possibly utilizing part of the old minaret. Dominating the ridge of the town are the massive ruins of **Pedro's Alcázar**, destroyed by an earthquake in 1504 and now taken over by a remarkably tasteful but very expensive *parador* (see below). To the left, beyond and below, the town comes to an abrupt and romantic halt at the Roman **Puerta de Córdoba**, from where the ancient Córdoba road (once the mighty Via Augusta heading north to Zaragoza and Gaul, now a dirt track) drops down to a vast plain.

The extraordinary **Roman necropolis** (guided tours: June–Sept Tues–Sat 9am–2pm; Oct–May Tues–Fri 9am–5pm, Sat & Sun 10am–2pm; €1.50, free to EU citizens) lies on a low hill at the opposite end of Carmona; walking out of town from San Pedro take c/Enmedio, the middle street (parallel to the main Sevilla road) of three that leave the western end of the Paseo del Estatuto; follow this for about 450m. Here, amid the cypress trees, more than nine hundred family tombs dating from the second century BC to the fourth century AD can be found. Enclosed in subterranean chambers hewn from the rock, the tombs are often frescoed and contain a series of niches in which many of the funeral urns remain intact. Some of the larger tombs have vestibules with stone benches for funeral banquets, and several retain carved family emblems (one is of an elephant, perhaps symbolic of long life). Most spectacular is the **Tumba de Servilia** – a huge colonnaded temple with vaulted side chambers. Opposite is a partly excavated **amphitheatre**, though as yet it isn't included in the tour.

Practicalities

The **turismo** (Mon–Sat 10am–6pm, Sun 10am–3pm; ☎954 190 955), in the arch of the Puerta de Sevilla, is well stocked with information and can provide a town map and guide to Carmona's tapas bars. Budget **accommodation** is limited: the best bets are *Pensión El Comercio* (☎954 140 018; ❹), built into the town's gateway, or the nearby *Hostal San Pedro*, c/San Pedro 17 (☎954 140 572; ❸), close to the church of the same name. If you're on a tight budget you could try the seedy, but clean, *El Potro*, c/Sevilla 78 (☎954 141 465; ❷), some 100m back along the Sevilla road. The *Parador Alcázar del Rey Don Pedro* (☎954 141 010, ☎954 141 712, ✉carmona@parador.es; ❽), in the ruins of the palace, is Carmona's most atmospheric upmarket hotel, and even if you don't stay it's worth calling at the bar for a drink to enjoy the fabulous views from its terrace.

The old town is an expensive place for **food**; cheapest places are the tapas bars on c/Prim, off the west side of Plaza de San Fernando – *Bar Goya* and *El Tapeo* are two worth seeking out – while *El Potro* (see above) has a decent and economical, if rather soulless, restaurant. For more elaborate fare, *Molino de la Romera*, c/Pedro s/n, near the *parador*, has a great terrace view across the plain and serves a good value *menú*.

Écija

Lying midway between Sevilla and Córdoba in a basin of low sandy hills, **ÉCIJA** is known, with no hint of exaggeration, as *la sartenilla de Andalucía* ("the frying pan of Andalucía"). In mid-August it's so hot that the only possible strategy is to slink from one tiny shaded plaza to another, or with a burst of energy to make for the riverbank.

The heat is worth enduring, since this is one of the most distinctive and individual towns of the south, with eleven superb, decaying church towers, each glistening with brilliantly coloured tiles. It has a unique domestic architecture, too – a flamboyant style of twisted and florid forms, best displayed on c/Castellar where the magnificent painted and curved frontage of the huge **Palacio de Peñaflor** (Mon–Fri 10am–1pm, Sat 11am–1pm; free) runs along the length of the street. Other sights not to be missed are the beautiful polychromatic tower of the church of **Santa María**, overshadowing the main Plaza de España, and the **Palacio de Benamejí**, a stunning eighteenth-century palace on c/Castillo, south of Plaza de España, with a beautiful interior patio, now declared a national monument. This building houses the town **museum** (daily 9am–2pm; free) displaying archeological finds from all periods, with a particularly interesting section on *Astigi's* (the town's Roman name) role in the olive-oil trade.

The Palacio de Benamejí also has the **turismo** (daily 9am–2pm; ☎955 900 240) with maps to help you find the thirty-plus other notable buildings throughout the town, and a good **restaurant**, *Las Ninfas*, with a pleasant terrace. Other places to eat are to be found along the streets surrounding the Plaza de España. On the square itself the *Cafetería Herrera* does tapas and *platos combinados* or there's more choice at *La Reja*, c/Garcilopez 1, close to the *Hotel Platería* (below). **Places to stay** are limited; the only budget option is the friendly *Pensión Santa Cruz*, c/Romero Gordillo 8 (☎954 830 222; ❸), off the eastern end of Plaza de España. The *Hotel Platería*, c/Garcilópez 1 (☎955 902 752, ✉hotel@plateria.com; ❺) just around the corner, is a step upmarket with decent modern rooms, while the *Hotel Sol Pirula* (☎954 830 300, ☎954 835 879; ❺), south of the centre at c/Cervantes 50, has comfortable air-conditioned rooms and a restaurant.

Osuna

OSUNA (like Carmona and Écija) is one of those small Andalucian towns which are great to explore in the early evening: slow in pace and quietly enjoyable, with elegant streets of tiled, whitewashed houses interspersed by fine **Renaissance mansions**. The best of these are off the main street, c/Carrera, which runs down from the central Plaza Mayor, and in particular on c/San Pedro which intersects it; at no. 16 the **Cilla del Cabildo** has a superb geometric relief round a carving of the Giralda, and further along the eighteenth-century **Palacio de los Marqueses de Gomera** – now a restaurant – is a stunning Baroque extravaganza. There's also a marvellous **casino** – with 1920s Mudéjar-style decor and a grandly bizarre ceiling – on Plaza Mayor which is open to all visitors and makes an ideal place for a cool drink.

Two huge stone buildings stand on the hilltop: the old university (suppressed by reactionary Fernando VII in 1820) and the lavish sixteenth-century **Colegiata** (guided tours: Mon–Sat 10am–1.30pm & 4–7pm, Sun 10am–1.30pm; €1.80), which contains the gloomy but impressive **pantheon and chapel** of the dukes of Osuna, descendants of the kings of León and once "the lords of Andalucía", as well as a **museum** displaying some fine artworks, including canvases by Ribera. Opposite the entrance to the Colegiata is the Baroque convent of **La Encarnación** (same hours as Colegiata; €1.50), which has a fine plinth of ninth-century Sevillan *azulejos* round its cloister and gallery.

Osuna has plenty of **accommodation** but not a lot of budget options. Lowest priced is *Hostal Cinco Puertas*, c/Carrera 79 (☎ & ☎954 811 243; ❸), with some en-suite rooms, while the *Hostal Caballo Blanco*, in a restored coaching inn opposite (☎954 810 184; ❹), is friendly, has a decent restaurant and is worth the extra. The **turismo** on the Plaza Mayor (Mon–Sat 9.30am–2.30pm & 4–7pm, Sun 10am–2.30pm; ☎955 821 400) can also help with finding accommodation. There are plenty of **food and drink** possibilities along c/Carrera and around the Plaza Mayor – one restaurant worth seeking out is the *Mesón del Duque*, Plaza de la Duquesa 2, uphill behind the casino, where you can eat out on a jasmine-fringed terrace.

Córdoba

CÓRDOBA lies upstream from Sevilla beside a loop of the Guadalquivir, which was once navigable as far as here. It is today a minor provincial capital, prosperous in a modest sort of way. Once, however, it was the largest city of Roman Spain, and for three centuries it formed the heart of the western Islamic empire, the great medieval caliphate of the Moors.

It is from this era that the city's major monument dates: the **Mezquita**, the grandest and most beautiful mosque ever constructed by the Moors in Spain. It stands right in the centre of the city, surrounded by the old Jewish and Moorish quarters, and is a building of extraordinary mystical and aesthetic

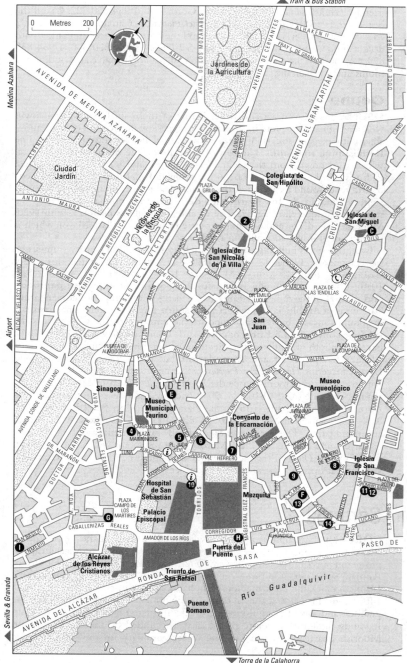

0 Metres 200

N

ANDALUCÍA | Córdoba

4

◀ Medina Azahara

AVENIDA DE MEDINA AZAHARA

Ciudad Jardín

ANTONIO MAURA

ALBEÑIZ

CAMINO DE LOS SASTRES

◀ Airport

ALCALDE VELASCO NAVARRO

AVENIDA CONDE DE VALLELLANO

DOCTOR BARRAQUER

DR. MARAÑON

DOCTOR FLEMING

M. RUA

◀ Sevilla & Granada

332

AVENIDA DE LA REPÚBLICA ARGENTINA

PASEO DE LA VICTORIA

Jardines de la Victoria

AVDA. DE LOS MOZÁRABES

Jardines de la Agricultura

ARTE

AVENIDA DE CERVANTES

ALHAKEN II

FRAY L. DE GRANADA

AVENIDA DEL GRAN CAPITÁN

DOCE DE OCTUBRE

CABRERA

Colegiata de San Hipólito

PLAZA A. GRILO

B

2

Iglesia de San Nicolás de la Villa

GÓNGORA

E. LUCENA

MORERA

Iglesia de San Miguel

C

S. ZOILO

S. ÁLVARO

CRUZ CONDE

ALFONSO XIII

PLAZA R. Y CAJAL

PLAZA DR. EMILIO LUQUE

S. MÁLAGA

PLAZA DE LAS TENDILLAS

CLAUDIO

San Juan

JUAN DE MENA

PLAZA DE LA COMPAÑÍA

PUERTA DE ALMODÓBAR

FERNÁNDEZ RUANO

TEIVA AGUILAR

LA JUDERÍA

Sinagoga

Museo Municipal Taurino

E

4 CARDENAL SALAZAR

PLAZA MAIMÓNIDES

5

6

ALBUCASIS

Museo Arqueológico

PLAZA DE JERÓNIMO PÁEZ

Convento de la Encarnación

7

CARDENAL HERRERO

Iglesia de San Francisco

8

9

11 12

Hospital de San Sebastián

i 10

TORRIJOS

Mezquita

F

13

14

Palacio Episcopal

PLAZA CAMPO DE LOS MÁRTIRES

G

CABALLERIZAS REALES

CORREGIDOR

PLAZA ALHÓNDIGA

PASEO DE

AMADOR DE LOS RÍOS

Puerta del Puente

H

I

SAN BASILIO

ENMEDIO

Alcázar de los Reyes Cristianos

Triunfo de San Rafael

RONDA DE ISASA

Río Guadalquivir

AVENIDA DEL ALCÁZAR

Puente Romano

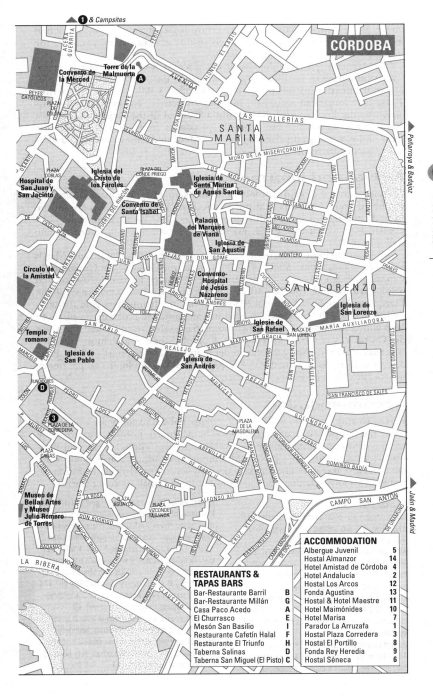

CÓRDOBA

Convento de la Merced
Torre de la Malmuerta
Santa Marina
Las Ollerías
Peñarroya & Badajoz

Hospital de San Juan y San Jacinto
Iglesia del Cristo de los Faroles
Plaza del Conde Priego
Iglesia de Santa Marina de Aguas Santas
Convento de Santa Isabel
Palacio del Marqués de Viana
Iglesia de San Agustín
Círculo de la Amistad
Convento-Hospital de Jesús Nazareno
San Lorenzo
Iglesia de San Lorenzo
Templo romano
Iglesia de San Pablo
Iglesia de San Rafael
Iglesia de San Andrés
Plaza de San Lorenzo
María Auxiliadora
San Francisco de Sales
Plaza de la Magdalena
Jaén & Madrid
Museo de Bellas Artes y Museo Julio Romero de Torres
Plaza de la Corredera
Campo San Antón
La Ribera

RESTAURANTS & TAPAS BARS

Bar-Restaurante Barril	**B**
Bar-Restaurante Millán	**G**
Casa Paco Acedo	**A**
El Churrasco	**E**
Mesón San Basilio	**I**
Restaurante Cafetín Halal	**F**
Restaurante El Triunfo	**H**
Taberna Salinas	**D**
Taberna San Miguel (El Pisto)	**C**

ACCOMMODATION

Albergue Juvenil	5
Hostal Almanzor	14
Hotel Amistad de Córdoba	4
Hotel Andalucía	2
Hostal Los Arcos	12
Fonda Agustina	13
Hostal & Hotel Maestre	11
Hotel Maimónides	10
Hotel Marisa	7
Parador La Arruzafa	1
Hostal Plaza Corredera	3
Hostal El Portillo	8
Fonda Rey Heredia	9
Hostal Séneca	6

power. Make for it on arrival and keep returning as long as you stay; you'll find its beauty and power increase with each visit, as of course is proper, since the mosque was intended for daily attendance.

The Mezquita apart, Córdoba itself is a place of considerable charm. It has few grand squares or mansions, tending instead to introverted architecture, calling your attention to the tremendous and often wildly extravagant **patios**. These have long been acclaimed, and they are actively encouraged and maintained by the local council, which runs a "Festival of the Patios" in May. Just 7km outside the town more Moorish splendours are to be seen among the ruins of the extravagant palace complex of **Medina Azahara** which is undergoing fascinating reconstruction.

Arrival and information

Finding your way around Córdoba is no problem. From the magnificent new combined **train and bus station** on the Plaza de las Tres Culturas, off the Avenida de America at the northern end of town, the broad Avenida del Gran Capitán leads down to the old quarters and the Mezquita (a fifteen-minute walk or bus #3).

The main **turismo** (Mon–Sat 9.30am–8pm, Sun 10am–2pm; Nov–March Mon–Sat closes 6pm; ☎957 471 235) is at the Palacio de Congresos y Exposiciones at c/Torrijos 10, alongside the Mezquita. There's also a small and helpful **municipal tourist office** nearby in Plaza Judá Leví, west of the Mezquita (April–Sept Mon–Sat 9.30am–8pm, Sun 10am–2pm; ring for winter hours; ☎957 200 522), which gives out an illustrated brochure on places to visit, with a town plan. For information on fringe theatre and music, the **Casa de Cultura** is at Plaza del Potro 10. Córdoba's best – and most central – **Internet café** is *El Navegante*, Llano del Pretorio 1, on the north side of Plaza de Colón (daily 9am–1am; ☎957 497 536; €1.50 for 15min, €3.60 per hour); the tourist offices have details of others.

Accommodation

Places to stay can be found all over Córdoba, but the majority are concentrated in the narrow maze of streets above the Mezquita. Less obvious are some recently refurbished *fondas* in the Plaza de la Corredera. This is a wonderful, ramshackle square (although a prolonged refurbishment means that building work often disrupts the atmosphere), like a decayed version of Madrid's Plaza Mayor, and worth a look whether you stay or not; it hosts a small morning market.

Budget options

Fonda Agustina, c/Zapatería Vieja 5 ☎957 470 872. Charming and spotlessly clean little *fonda*, with basic rooms in a tranquil location. ❷

Albergue Juvenil, Plaza Judá Leví ☎957 290 166, ☎957 290 500. Excellent modern youth hostel (with twin, triple and four-person en-suite rooms), which also serves meals. ❶

Hostal Almanzor, Corregidor Luís de la Cerda 10 ☎957 485 400. East of the Mezquita, this small, but very charming *hostal* has rooms with or without bath. ❷–❸

Hostal Los Arcos, c/Romero Barros 14 ☎957 485 643, ☎957 486 011. Excellent *hostal* with simple rooms around a delightful patio. ❸

Hostal Plaza Corredera, c/Rodríguez Marín 15 at the corner of Plaza Corredera ☎957 484 570. Clean, friendly and recently refurbished place with simple rooms and great views over the plaza from some. ❸

Hostal El Portillo, c/Cabezas 2 ☎ & ☎957 472 091. Beautiful old *hostal* with elegant patio, offering both singles and doubles with shared bath. ❷

Fonda Rey Heredia, c/Rey Heredia 26 ☎957 474 182. Clean and airy simple rooms in one of three very reasonable *fondas* on this street. ❷

Hostal Séneca, c/Conde y Luque 7 ☎ & ☎957 473 234, just north of the Mezquita. Wonderful place to stay with simple rooms around a stunning patio where you can take breakfast. Very popular, so booking ahead advised. ❸

Moderate and expensive options

Hotel Amistad Córdoba, Plaza de Maimónides 3
☎957 420 335, ⓕ957 420 365. Stylish hotel
incorporating two eighteenth-century mansions,
near the old wall in the Judería. They also put a
number of rooms on weekend discount which
reduces prices by a third. ⑨

Hotel Andalucía, c/José Zorilla 3, near the church
of San Hipolito ☎957 476 000, ⓕ957 478 143.
Handy hotel for drivers who want to avoid the
Mezquita maze, offering pleasant rooms with bath,
and relatively easy parking. ⑤

Hostal & Hotel Maestre, c/Romero Barros 4 & 16
☎ & ⓕ957 475 395. Excellent *hostal* between
c/San Fernando and the Plaza del Potro; their
neighbouring hotel has air-conditioned rooms with
TV. If you're carrying a *Rough Guide,* they'll offer
you free parking in their garage. ④–⑤

Hotel Maimónides, c/Torrijos 4 ☎957 471 500,
ⓕ957 483 803. This upmarket hotel has a particularly central and attractive location, near to the turismo – it also has a garage. ⑧

Hotel Marisa, c/Cardenal Herrero 6 ☎957 473
142, ⓕ957 474 144. Two-star hotel with a superb
position immediately outside the Mezquita. Own
garage. ⑥

Parador La Arruzafa, Avda. de la Arruzafa s/n, off
the Avda. El Brillante ☎957 275 900, ⓕ957 280
409, ⓔcordoba@parador.es. Córdoba's modern
parador is located on the outskirts of the city 5km
to the north of the Mezquita, but compensates
with pleasant gardens, pool and every other
amenity to justify the price. ⑧

Camping

Campamento Municipal, Avda. El Brillante 50
☎957 278 481. Córdoba's local campsite (with
restaurant and pool) is 2km north of the centre in
the *barrio* El Brillante, and served by bus #10 from
the bus station. They also rent out tents and equipment. Open all year.

Camping Los Villares ☎957 330 145. If you
have your own transport, this site (7km north of
the city along a minor road to Santo Domingo; the
campsite lies just beyond this) is a better option,
set in woodland with nature trails and a restaurant. Open all year.

Moorish Córdoba and the Mezquita

Córdoba's **domination of Moorish Spain** began thirty years after its conquest – in 756, when the city was placed under the control of **Abd ar-
Rahman I**, the sole survivor of the Umayyad dynasty which had been blood-
ily expelled from the eastern caliphate of Damascus. He proved a firm but
moderate ruler, and a remarkable military campaigner, establishing control over
all but the north of Spain and proclaiming himself emir, a title meaning both
"king" and "son of the caliph". It was Abd ar-Rahman who commenced the
building of the Great Mosque (*La Mezquita*, in Spanish), purchasing from the
Christians the site of the cathedral of St Vincent (which, divided by a partition
wall, had previously served both communities). This original mosque was completed by his son **Hisham** in 796 and comprises about one-fifth of the present building, the first dozen aisles adjacent to the Patio de los Naranjos.

The **Cordoban emirate**, maintaining independence from the eastern
caliphate, soon began to rival Damascus both in power and in the brilliance of
its civilization. **Abd ar-Rahman II** (822–52) initiated sophisticated irrigation
programmes, minted his own coinage and received embassies from Byzantium.
He in turn substantially enlarged the mosque. A focal point within the culture
of *al-Andalus*, this was by now being consciously directed and enriched as an
alternative to Mecca; it possessed an original script of the Koran and a bone
from the arm of Muhammad and, for the Spanish Muslim who could not go
to Mecca, it became the most sacred place of **pilgrimage**. In the broader
Islamic world it ranked third in sanctity after the Kaaba of Mecca and the Al
Aksa mosque of Jerusalem.

In the tenth century, Córdoba reached its zenith under a new emir, **Abd ar-
Rahman III** (912–61), one of the great rulers of Islamic history. He assumed
power after a period of internal strife and, according to a contemporary historian, "subdued rebels, built palaces, gave impetus to agriculture, immortalized
ancient deeds and monuments, and inflicted great damage on infidels to a point

where no opponent or contender remained in *al-Andalus*. People obeyed en masse and wished to live with him in peace." In 929, with Muslim Spain and part of North Africa firmly under his control, Abd ar-Rahman III adopted the title of "caliph". It was a supremely confident move and was reflected in the growing splendour of Córdoba, which had become the largest, most prosperous city of Europe, outshining Byzantium and Baghdad (the new capital of the eastern caliphate) in science, culture and scholarship. At the turn of the tenth century, Moorish sources boast of the city's 27 schools, 50 hospitals (with the first separate clinics for the leprous and insane), 900 public baths, 60,300 noble mansions, 213,077 houses and 80,455 shops.

The **development of the Great Mosque** paralleled these new heights of confidence and splendour. Abd ar-Rahman III provided it with a new minaret (which has not survived and provided the core for the later belfry), 80m high, topped by three pomegranate-shaped spheres, two of silver and one of gold and each weighing a ton. But it was his son **al-Hakam II** (961–76), to whom he passed on a peaceful and stable empire, who was responsible for the most brilliant expansion. He virtually doubled its extent, demolishing the south wall to add fourteen extra rows of columns, and employed Byzantine craftsmen to construct a new *mihrab* or prayer niche; this remains complete and is perhaps the most beautiful example of all Moorish religious architecture.

Al-Hakam had extended the mosque as far to the south as was possible. The final enlargement of the building, under the chamberlain-usurper **al-Mansur** (977–1002), involved adding seven rows of columns to the whole east side. This spoiled the symmetry of the mosque, depriving the *mihrab* of its central position, but Arab historians observed that it meant there were now "as many bays as there are days of the year". They also delighted in describing the rich interior, with its 1293 marble columns, 280 chandeliers and 1445 lamps. Hanging inverted among the lamps were the bells of the pilgrimage cathedral of Santiago de Compostela. Al-Mansur made his Christian captives carry them on their shoulders from Galicia – a process which was to be observed in reverse after Córdoba was captured by Fernando el Santo (the Saint) in 1236.

Entering the Mezquita

As in Moorish times the **Mezquita** (April–Sept Mon–Sat 10am–7pm; Oct–March 10am–5pm; €6.10; free entrance at side doors 8.30am–10am for services but without lighting) is approached through the **Patio de los Naranjos**, a classic Islamic ablutions court which preserves its orange trees, although the fountains for ritual purification before prayer are now purely decorative. Originally, when in use for the Friday prayers, all nineteen naves of the mosque were open to this court, allowing the rows of interior columns to appear an extension of the tree with brilliant shafts of sunlight filtering through. Today, all but one of the entrance gates is locked and sealed and the mood of the building has been distorted from the open and vigorous simplicity of the mosque, to the mysterious half-light of a cathedral.

Nonetheless, a first glimpse inside the Mezquita is immensely exciting. "So near the desert in its tentlike forest of supporting pillars," Jan Morris found it, "so faithful to Mahomet's tenets of cleanliness, abstinence and regularity." The mass of supporting pillars was, in fact, an early and sophisticated innovation to gain height. The original architect had at his disposal columns from the old Visigothic cathedral and from numerous Roman buildings; they could bear great weight but were not tall enough, even when arched, to reach the intended height of the ceiling. His solution (which may have been inspired by

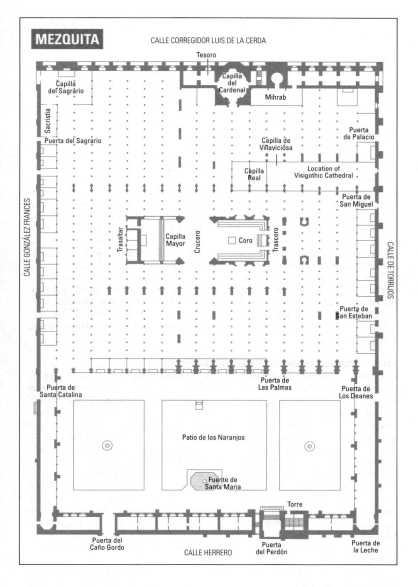

Roman aqueduct designs) was to place a second row of square columns on the apex of the lower ones, serving as a base for the semicircular arches that support the roof. For extra strength and stability (and perhaps also deliberately to echo the shape of a date palm, much revered by the early Spanish Arabs) the architect introduced another, horseshoe-shaped arch above the lower pillars. A second and purely aesthetic innovation was to alternate brick and stone in the arches, creating the red-and-white striped pattern which gives a unity and distinctive character to the whole design.

The Mihrab

This uniformity was broken only at the culminating point of the mosque – the domed cluster of pillars surrounding the sacred **Mihrab**, erected under al-Hakam II. The *mihrab* had two functions in Islamic worship: it indicated the direction of Mecca (and hence of prayer) and it amplified the words of the *imam*, or prayer leader. At Córdoba it was also of supreme beauty. As Titus Burckhardt wrote, in *Moorish Art in Spain*:

"The design of the prayer niche in Córdoba was used as a model for countless prayer niches in Spain and North Africa. The niche is crowned by a horseshoe-shaped arch, enclosed by a rectangular frame. The arch derives a peculiar strength from the fact that its central point shifts up from below. The wedge-shaped arch stones or *voussoirs* fan outwards from a point at the foot of the arch and centres of the inner and outer circumferences of the arch lie one above the other. The entire arch seems to radiate, like the sun or the moon gradually rising over the edge of the horizon. It is not rigid; it breathes as if expanding with a surfeit of inner beatitude, while the rectangular frame enclosing it acts as a counterbalance. The radiating energy and the perfect stillness form an unsurpassable equilibrium. Herein lies the basic formula of Moorish architecture."

The inner vestibule of the niche (which is roped off – forcing you to risk the wrath of the attendants in getting a glimpse) is quite simple in comparison, with a shell-shaped ceiling carved from a single block of marble. The chambers to either side – decorated with exquisite Byzantine mosaics of gold, rust-red, turquoise and green – constitute the *maksura*, where the caliph and his retinue would pray.

The cathedral and other additions

Originally the whole design of the mosque would have directed worshippers naturally towards the *mihrab*. Today, though, you almost stumble upon it, for in the centre of the mosque squats a Renaissance **cathedral coro**. This was built in 1523 – nearly three centuries of enlightened restraint after the Christian conquest – and in spite of fierce opposition from the town council. The erection of a *coro* and *capilla mayor*, however, had long been the "Christianizing" dream of the cathedral chapter and at last they had found a monarch – predictably Carlos V – who was willing to sanction the work. Carlos, to his credit, realized the mistake (though it did not stop him from destroying parts of the Alhambra and Sevilla's Alcázar); on seeing the work completed he told the chapter, "You have built what you or others might have built anywhere, but you have destroyed something that was unique in the world." To the left of the *coro* stands an earlier and happier Christian addition – the Mudéjar **Capilla de Villaviciosa**, built by Moorish craftsmen in 1371 (and now partly sealed up). Beside it are the dome and pillars of the **earlier mihrab**, constructed under Abd ar-Rahman II.

The **belfry**, at the corner of the Patio de los Naranjos, is contemporary with the cathedral addition. If it's open after restoration, the climb is a dizzying experience and the views over the Mezquita and town are tremendous. Close by, the **Puerta del Perdón**, the main entrance to the patio, was rebuilt in Moorish style in 1377. Original "caliphal" decoration (in particular some superb latticework), however, can still be made out in the gates along the east and west sides of the mosque.

The rest of town

After the Mezquita, Córdoba's other remnants of Moorish – and indeed Christian – rule are not individually very striking. The river, though, with its great **Arab waterwheels** and **Roman bridge** (the Puente Romano), is an attractive area in which to wander. At the bridge's eastern end the medieval **Torre de la Calahorra** (daily 10am–2pm & 4.30–8.30pm; €3.60) houses a gimmicky, hi-tech museum containing models of the pre-cathedral Mezquita, weird talking tableaux and a rather incongruous multimedia presentation on the history of man; there's a great panoramic view though, from the top of the tower towards the city. On the western riverbank the wheels, and the ruined mills, were in use for several centuries after the fall of the Muslim city, grinding flour and pumping water up to the fountains of the Alcázar, or Palace Fortress. This originally stood beside the Mezquita – on the site now occupied by the **Episcopal Palace** (aka Museo Diocesano de Bellas Artes; Mon–Fri 9.30am–1.30pm & 3.30–5.30pm, Sat 9.30am–1.30pm; last entry 30min before closing; €0.90, or free with Mezquita ticket), now a museum of religious art with some fine examples of medieval wood sculpture. After the Christian conquest the Alcázar was rebuilt a little to the west by Fernando and Isabel, hence its name, **Alcázar de los Reyes Cristianos**. The buildings (Tues–Sat 10am–2pm & 5.30–7.30pm, Sun 9.30am–3pm; last entry 30min before closing; €1.80, free Fri) are a bit dreary, having served as the residence of the Inquisition from 1428 to 1821. However, they display some fine mosaics from Roman Córdoba, among which is one of the largest complete Roman mosaics in existence, and the **gardens** are very attractive.

Judería

Between the Mezquita and the beginning of the Avenida del Gran Capitán lies the **Judería**, Córdoba's old Jewish quarter, and a fascinating network of lanes – more atmospheric and less commercialized than Sevilla's Barrio Santa Cruz, though souvenir shops are beginning to gain ground. Near the heart of the quarter, at c/Maimónides 18, is a **synagogue** (Tues–Sat 10am–1.30pm & 3.30–5.30pm, Sun 10am–1.30pm; last entry 30min before closing; €0.30, free to EU citizens), one of only three in Spain – the other two are in Toledo – that survived the Jewish expulsion of 1492. This one, built in 1316, is minute, particularly in comparison with the great Santa María in Toledo, but it has some fine stuccowork elaborating on a Solomon's-seal motif and retains its women's gallery. Outside is a statue of Maimónides, the Jewish philosopher, physician and Talmudic jurist, born in Córdoba in 1135.

Nearby is a rather bogus **Zoco** – an Arab *souk* turned into a crafts arcade – and, adjoining this, a small **Museo Taurino** (Tues–Sat 10am–2pm & 5.30–7.30pm, Sun 9.30am–2.30pm; €2.70, free Fri). The latter warrants a look, if only for the kitschy nature of its exhibits: row upon row of bulls' heads, two of them given this "honour" for having killed matadors. Beside a copy of the tomb of Manolete – most famous of the city's fighters – is exhibited the hide of his taurine nemesis, Islero.

Other museums and mansions

More interesting, perhaps, and more rewarding, is the **Museo Arqueológico** (Tues 3–8pm, Wed–Sat 9am–8pm, Sun 9am–3pm; last entry 30min before closing; €1.50, free to EU citizens). During its original conversion, this small Renaissance mansion was revealed as the unlikely site of a genuine Roman patio. As a result it is one of the most imaginative and enjoyable small museums in the country, with good local collections from the Iberian, Roman and

Moorish periods. Outstanding is an inlaid tenth-century bronze stag found at the Moorish palace of Medina Azahara (see below) where it was used as the spout of a fountain.

A couple of blocks below the Archeological Museum, back towards the river, you'll come upon the **Plaza del Potro**, a fine old square named after the colt (*potro*) which adorns its fountain. This, as local guides proudly point out, is mentioned in *Don Quixote*, and indeed Cervantes himself is reputed to have stayed at the inn opposite, the **Mesón del Potro**, which now houses the Casa de Cultura and is used for *artesanía* displays and art exhibitions. On the other side of the square is the **Museo de Bellas Artes** (Tues 3–8pm, Wed–Sat 9am–8pm, Sun 9am–3pm; last entry 30min before closing; €1.50, free to EU citizens), with paintings by Ribera, Valdés Leal and Zurbarán, and across its courtyard is the small **Museo Julio Romero de Torres** (Tues–Sat 10am–2pm & 5.30–7.30pm, Sun 9.30am–2.30pm; last entry 30min before closing; €2.70, free Fri) devoted to the Cordoban artist **Romero de Torres** (1885–1930), a painter of some sublimely dreadful canvases, many of which depict reclining female nudes with furtive male guitar players.

In the north of town, towards the train station, are numerous Renaissance churches – some converted from mosques, others showing obvious influence in their minarets – and a handful of convents and palaces. The best of these, still privately owned, is the **Palacio del Marqués de Viana** (guided tours: Mon–Fri 10am–1pm & 4–6pm, Sat 10am–1pm; patios €3, house additional €3) whose main attraction for many visitors are its twelve flower-filled patios.

Eating, drinking and nightlife

Bars and **restaurants** are on the whole reasonably priced – you need only to avoid the touristy places round the Mezquita. There are lots of good places to eat not too far away in the Judería and in the old quarters off to the east, above the Paseo de la Ribera.

Restaurants

Bar-Restaurante Barril, c/Concepción 16. Super-efficient tapas and breakfast bar with a small terrace and serving all day *platos combinados*.

Bar-Restaurante Millán, Avda. Dr. Fleming 14, just northwest of the Alcázar. Tranquil, economical restaurant with a charming *azulejo*-lined room. The *rabo de toro* (Córdoba's traditional dish – a very superior oxtail stew) and *salmorejo* are excellent here.

Casa Paco Acedo, beneath the ancient Torre de Malmuerta at the northern end of town. The house speciality at this celebrated *cordobés* institution is a memorable *rabo de toro*.

El Churrasco, c/Romero 16 (not c/Romero Barros); ☎957 290 819. Expensive and renowned restaurant, famous for its *churrasco* (a grilled pork dish, served with pepper sauces) and *salmorejo* (a thick Cordoban version of *gazpacho* with hunks of ham and egg).

Mesón San Basilio, c/San Basilio 19, west of the Alcázar. Good and unpretentious local restaurant offering well-prepared fish and meat *raciones* and *platos combinados* plus a *menú* for around €6.

Restaurante Cafetín Halal, c/Rey Heredia 28. Islamic cultural centre serving excellent, inexpensive food with vegetarian options. No alcohol.

Restaurante El Triunfo, c/Corregidor Luís de la Cerda 79, facing the Mezquita. One of the few worthwhile places near the Mezquita, with plenty of cool marble and offering a wide range of mid-priced meat and fish dishes.

Taberna Salinas, c/Tundidores 3, just off the Plaza Corredera. Century-old taberna with dining rooms around a charming patio. Good *raciones* place – try their *naranjas con bacalao* (cod with oranges) – and serves a great *salmorejo*.

Taberna San Miguel (El Pisto), Plaza San Miguel 1, behind the church. Known to all as *El Pisto* (the barrel) this is one of the city's legendary bars – over a century old – and not to be missed. Wonderful *montilla* and tapas; *rabo de toro* and *callos en salsa picante* (tripe in a spicy sauce) are house specials.

Bars and flamenco

The local barrelled **wine** is predominantly Montilla-Moriles – brewed in the towns of the same name just to the south – which vaguely resembles mellow, dry sherry and is magnificent here on its own turf. The *Bar Plateros* opposite the *Hostal Maestre* specializes in *montilla* and also turns out great tapas; the same chain has another branch at c/Deanes 5, near the top left-hand corner of the Mezquita; in summer both are good places to try their *fiti-fiti* ("fifty-fifty") comprising a half-and-half combo of white and sweet white wine. One bar not to be missed is the century-old *Taberna San Miguel* (aka *El Pisto*), behind the church of the same name to the north of Plaza Tendillas, which is hung with guitars and faded *corrida* posters and has excellent tapas, especially *callos* (tripe) and *manitas* (trotters) in sauce. A new beer bar serving beers from all over the world is *El Borracho de Oro*, c/San Felipe 15, off the south end of Avenida del Gran Capitán.

Córdoba takes it's tranquillity seriously, especially after dark, so the in-town **nightlife** scene is confined to a few music bars and clubs to the north of Plaza de las Tendillas and – moving east from here – in and around c/Alfaros and c/Alfonso XIII near the Roman temple (roughly dead centre of our city map). In the first group, *Seven* at c/Cruz Conde 32 (down a passage) is a popular club full of smoke, the occasional drag queen and techno sounds which closes at 7am, whilst the nearby *Golden*, c/H. Diaz del Moral 3, and *Qu*, c/Gongora 10 are equally frenzied at weekends. Near the Roman temple, at c/Alfonso XIII 3, *Soul* is a popular bar with students and often stages live gigs, while *Velvet Café* and *Millenium* (sic) are similar places along c/Alfaros, slightly north. To really let their hair down well away from any restraints, Córdoba's younger set migrates in summer to the **El Brillante** suburb, to the north of the central zone. Here at the junction of c/Poeta Emilio Prados and Avenida del Brillante (bus #10 from the bus station or a taxi for around €3.60), the focal *Bar Terra* gives access to a whole square behind filled with drinking and music bars where carousing goes on until dawn.

You'll find the best, and most authentic, **flamenco** in town at *Tablao Cardenal*, c/Torrijos 10 (next to the turismo), though it doesn't come cheap at around €18 a ticket (includes one drink). Performances begin at 10.30pm and you can book a good table by phone (☎957 483 320; closed Sun).

Medina Azahara

Seven kilometres to the northwest of Córdoba lie the vast and rambling ruins of **Medina Azahara**, a palace complex built on a dream scale by **Caliph Abd ar-Rahman III**. Naming it after a favourite, az-Zahra (the Radiant), he spent one-third of the annual state budget on its construction each year from 936 until his death in 961. Ten thousand workers and 1500 mules and camels were employed on the project and the site, almost 2000m long by 900m wide, stretched over three descending terraces. In addition to the palace buildings, it contained a zoo, an aviary, four fish ponds, 300 baths, 400 houses, weapons factories and two barracks for the royal guard. Visitors, so the chronicles record, were stunned by its wealth and brilliance: one conference room was provided with pure crystals, creating a rainbow when lit by the sun; another was built round a huge pool of mercury.

Medina Azahara was a perfect symbol of the western caliphate's extent and greatness, but it was to last for less than a century. **Al-Hakam II**, who succeeded Abd ar-Rahman, lived in the palace, continued to endow it, and enjoyed a stable reign. However, distanced from the city, he delegated more and more authority, particularly to his vizier Ibn Abi Amir, later known as **al-Mansur** (the Victor). In 976 al-Hakam was succeeded by his eleven-year-old son Hisham II and, after a series of sharp moves, al-Mansur assumed the full powers of government, keeping Hisham virtually imprisoned at Medina Azahara, to the extent of blocking up connecting passageways between the palace buildings.

Al-Mansur was equally skilful and manipulative in his wider dealings as a dictator, retaking large tracts of central Spain and raiding as far afield as Galicia and Catalunya; consequently Córdoba rose to new heights of prosperity. But with his death in 1002 came swift decline as his role and function were assumed in turn by his two sons. The first died in 1008; the second, Sanchol, showed open disrespect for the caliphate by forcing Hisham to appoint him as his successor. At this a popular revolt broke out and the caliphate disintegrated into civil war and a series of feudal kingdoms. Medina Azahara was looted by a mob at the outset and in 1010 was plundered and burned by retreating Berber mercenaries.

The site

For centuries **the site** (May–Oct daily 10am–8pm; phone for Nov–April hours on ☎957 329 130; €1.50, free to EU citizens) continued to be looted for building materials; parts, for instance, were used in the Sevilla Alcázar. But in 1944 excavations unearthed the remains of a crucial part of the palace – the **Royal House**, where guests were received and meetings of ministers held. This has been meticulously reconstructed and, though still fragmentary, its main hall must rank among the greatest of all Moorish rooms. It has a different kind of stuccowork from that at Granada or Sevilla – closer to natural and animal forms in its intricate Syrian *Hom* (Tree of Life) motifs. Unlike the later Spanish Arab dynasties, the Berber Almoravids and the Almohads of Sevilla, the caliphal Andalucians were little worried by Islamic strictures on the portrayal of nature, animals or even men – the beautiful hind in the Córdoba museum is a good example – and it may well have been this aspect of the palace that led to such zealous destruction during the civil war.

The reconstruction of the palace gives a scale and focus to the site. Elsewhere you have little more than foundations to fuel your imaginings, amid an awesome area of ruins, hidden beneath bougainvillea and rustling with cicadas. Perhaps the most obvious of the outbuildings yet excavated is the **mosque**, just beyond the Royal House, which sits at an angle to the rest of the buildings in order to face Mecca.

To reach Medina Azahara, follow the Avenida de Medina Azahara out of town, onto the road to Villarubia and Posadas. About 4km down this road, make a right turn, after which it's another two or three kilometres. City **bus** #1 from a stop on the Paseo de la Victoria (almost opposite the *Melia* hotel) will drop you off at the intersection for the final 3km walk to the site – ask the driver for the "Cruz de Medina Azahara". A **taxi** will cost you about €15 one-way for up to five people or there's a special round-trip deal ("Taxi-Tour Córdoba") for around €25 which includes a one-hour wait at the site while you visit – the turismo can help in arranging this. Alternatively Córdoba Vision runs **guided trips** to the site (10.30am, also 4pm Oct–April; not Mon; ☎957 231 734; €15); buses leave from the Triunfo de San Rafael monument close to the turismo, which can also help with booking.

Eastern Andalucía

There is no more convincing proof of the diversity of Andalucía than its eastern provinces: **Jaén**, with its rolling, olive-covered hills; **Granada**, dominated by Spain's highest peaks, the Sierra Nevada; and **Almería**, waterless and in part semi-desert.

Jaén is slightly isolated from the main routes around Andalucía, but if you're coming down to Granada from Madrid you might want to consider stopping over in the small towns of **Úbeda** or **Baeza**, both crammed with Renaissance architectural jewels and served on the main train line by their shared station of Linares-Baeza. Úbeda also serves as the gateway to **Cazorla** and its neighbouring natural park.

Granada, a prime target of any Spanish travels, is easily reached from Sevilla, Córdoba, Ronda, Málaga or Madrid. When you've exhausted the city, there are dozens of nearby possibilities, perhaps the most enticing being the walks in the newly created **national park of the Sierra Nevada** and its lower southern slopes, **Las Alpujarras**. The **Almería beaches**, least developed of the Spanish Mediterranean, are also within striking distance.

Jaén Province

There are said to be over 150 million olive trees in the **province of Jaén**. They dominate the landscape as infinite rows of green against the orange-red earth, occasionally interspersed with stark white farm buildings. It's beautiful on a grand, sweeping scale, though concealing a bitter and entrenched economic reality. The majority of the olive groves are owned by a mere handful of families, and for most residents this is a very poor area.

Jaén

JAÉN, the provincial capital and by far the largest town, is an uneventful sort of place with traces of its Moorish past in its ruined castle and in the largest surviving Moorish baths in Spain. The town is centred around the Plaza de la Constitución and its two arterial streets, Paseo de la Estación and Avenida de Madrid.

West of the main plaza is the imposing seventeenth-century Renaissance **Catedral** (daily 8.30am–1pm & 5–8pm; free), while to the north, between the churches of San Andrés and Santo Domingo, you'll find the painstakingly restored Moorish *hammam* in the **Baños Arabes** (Tues–Fri 9am–8pm, Sat & Sun 9.30am–2.30pm; free). Among the finest of their kind in Spain, the baths were originally part of an eleventh-century Moorish palace, and are now located inside the Palacio de Villardompardo, which was constructed over the Moorish palace. Jaén's **Museo Provincial**, Paseo de la Estación 29 (Tues 3–8pm, Wed–Sat 9am–8pm, Sun 9am–3pm; €1.50, free to EU citizens), has a large archeological collection including some remarkable fifth-century BC Iberian sculptures, now set to become the centrepiece of a major new museum of Iberian art.

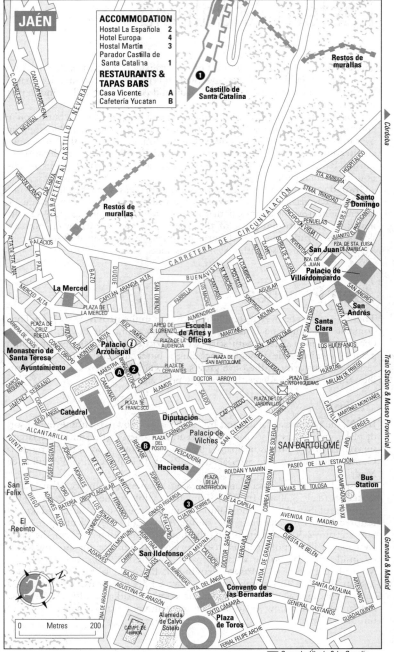

JAÉN

ACCOMMODATION

Hostal La Española	2
Hotel Europa	4
Hostal Martín	3
Parador Castilla de Santa Catalina	1

RESTAURANTS & TAPAS BARS

| Casa Vicente | A |
| Cafetería Yucatan | B |

Restos de murallas

Castillo de Santa Catalina

Restos de murallas

▶ Córdoba

▶ Train Station & Museo Provincial

▶ Granada & Madrid

▼ Granada, Úbeda & La Guardia

Practicalities

Jaén's **turismo**, c/Maestra 13 (Mon–Fri 10am–8pm, Sat & Sun 10am–1pm; ☎953 242 624), with good town maps, is located slightly to the north of the cathedral, and the **train station** is further north along the same street (bus #10 from the centre). The **bus station** (☎953 250 106) is on Plaza Coca de la Pinera, also off the Paseo de la Estación. If you want to **stay**, budget options include the basic *Hostal Martín*, c/Cuatro Torres 5 (☎953 220 633; ❷), near the Plaza de la Constitución, and *Hostal La Española*, c/Bernardo López 9 (☎953 230 254; ❸), by the cathedral. There are more expensive options on the Paseo de la Estación and Avenida de Madrid, including *Hotel Europa*, Plaza de Belén 1, just off Avda. de Madrid (☎953 222 700, ☎953 222 692; ❺). Overlooking the town and built in the shell of a Moorish castle with stunning views, is the *Parador Castillo de Santa Catalina* (☎953 230 000, ☎953 230 930; ❽), one of the most spectacularly sited hotels in Spain; even if you're not staying, it's worth calling in for a drink at the bar.

Calle Nueva, immediately east of Plaza de la Constitución, has a whole crowd of **bars** and **places to eat**. Alternatively *Casa Vicente*, c/Maestre 8, just north of the cathedral is one of the best restaurants in town with prices to match, while *Cafetería Yucatan*, up a flight of steps off the Plaza del Posito, is a good breakfast bar and serves *platos combinados* until late. For **late-night drinking** and music bars head for the streets in the Barrio de San Ildefonso to the east of the cathedral, focusing on c/Hurtado, where the friendly *Bar Azulejo* at no. 8 gives a complimentary *tapa* with every drink.

Baeza and Úbeda

Less than an hour from Jaén are the rarely visited, elegant towns of **Baeza** and **Úbeda**. Each has an extraordinary density of exuberant Renaissance palaces and richly endowed churches, plus fine public squares. Both towns were captured from the Moors by Fernando el Santo and, repopulated with his knights, stood for two centuries at the frontiers of the reconquered lands facing the Moorish kingdom of Granada.

Baeza

BAEZA is tiny, compact and provincial, with a perpetual Sunday air about it. At its heart are the Plaza Mayor – in fact comprised of two linked plazas, the Plaza de la Constitucíon at the southern end with a garden, and the smaller Plaza de España to the north – and *paseo*, flanked by cafés and very much the hub of the town's limited animation.

The **Plaza de Leones**, an appealing cobbled square enclosed by Renaissance buildings, stands slightly back at the far end. Here, on a rounded balcony, the first Mass of the Reconquest is reputed to have been celebrated; the mansion beneath it houses the **turismo** (Mon–Fri 9am–2.30pm, Sat 10am–1pm; ☎953 740 444), where you can pick up a map (which conveniently incorporates an Úbeda town map as well) and English-language walking-tour brochure of the town. There are no charges to enter any of Baeza's monuments but you may offer the guardian a small *propina* (tip).

Finest of Baeza's mansions is the **Palacio de Jabalquinto** (patio open Tues–Sun 10am–1pm & 4–6pm), now a seminary, with an elaborate "Isabelline" front (showing marked Moorish influence in its stalactite decoration). Close by, the sixteenth-century **Catedral** (daily 10am–1pm & 5.15–7pm), like many of Baeza and Úbeda's churches, has brilliant painted *rejas* (iron screens) created in the sixteenth century by Maestro Bartolomé, the

Spanish master of this craft. In the cloister, part of the old mosque has been uncovered, but the cathedral's real novelty is a huge silver *custodia* – cunningly hidden behind a painting of St Peter which whirls aside for a 100ptas coin (which they may eventually get around to converting to take euros).

There are some good walks around town: wandering up through the Puerta de Jaén on the Plaza de los Leones and along the Paseo Murallas/Paseo de Don Antonio Machado takes you round the edge of Baeza with good views over the surrounding plains. You can cut back to the Plaza Mayor via the network of narrow stone-walled alleys – with the occasional arch – that lie behind the cathedral.

Accommodation is adequate but mostly upmarket: for budget options try the *Hostal El Patio*, c/Conde Ramones 13, near the Plaza de Leones (☎953 740 200; ❷–❸), an old Renaissance mansion set around an enclosed courtyard with a wood-beamed dining hall; or the *Hostal Comercio* (☎953 740 100; ❸) on c/San Pablo, a main road at the end of the central square, at no. 21 – both have some rooms with bath. Best of the central pricier places is *Hotel Baeza*, c/Concepción 3, near the Plaza de España (☎953 748130, ℉953 742519; ❼), partly set inside a former Renaissance palace. Good bets for **food** and **drink** include the ancient *Cafetería Mercantil*, on the Plaza de España, which besides being the best place for a lazy terrace breakfast offers decent tapas and *raciones* later in the day. Nearby, *Casa Lucas*, Plaza España 13, is a local favourite for more tapas and economical *platos combinados*. For a bit more style try the pleasant terrace of the mid-priced *Restaurante Sali* around the corner at c/Benavides 9 with a view of Baeza's magnificent sixteenth-century *ayuntamiento*. *Casa Pedro* at no. 3 on the same street is another possibility, with a *menú* for around €12.

The nearest **train station** is Linares-Baeza 14km from Baeza and served by frequent trains from Sevilla, Córdoba and Granada (there is a connecting bus for most trains, except on Sun; €12 taxi ride). Most bus connections are via Úbeda.

Úbeda

ÚBEDA, 9km east of Baeza, is a larger town with modern suburbs. Follow the signs to the *Zona Monumental* and you'll eventually reach the **Plaza de Vázquez de Molina**, a tremendous Renaissance square which is one of the most impressive of its kind in Spain.

Most of the buildings round the square were the late sixteenth-century work of Andrés de Vandelvira, the architect of Baeza's cathedral and numerous churches in both towns. One of these buildings, the **Palacio de las Cadenas**, originally a palace for Felipe II's secretary, houses Úbeda's *ayuntamiento* and features a magnificent facade fronted by monumental lions. In another part of the same building the **Museo de Alfarería** (Tues–Sat 10.30am–2.30pm & 5.30–8pm, Sun 10.30am–2pm; €2.40) displays pottery of varying ages and types from all over Spain as well as Úbeda itself, still an important centre of ceramic craftsmanship. At the opposite end of the square, the **Capilla del Salvador** (daily 10am–2pm & 5–7.30pm; €2.10, free Mon–Thurs 6.30–7.30pm), erected by Vandelvira, though actually designed by Diego de Siloé, architect of the Málaga and Granada cathedrals, is the finest church in Úbeda. It's a masterpiece of Spanish Renaissance architecture with a dazzling Plateresque facade, its highlight a carving of the Transfiguration of Christ flanked by statues of St Peter and St Paul. Inside, the Transfiguration theme is repeated in a brilliantly animated *retablo* by Alonso de Berruguete, who studied under Michelangelo.

Following c/Horno Contado out of the Plaza de Vázquez de Molina leads to yet another delightful square, the Plaza del Primero de Mayo, and the idiosyncratic church of **San Pablo**, with a thirteenth-century balcony (a popular feature in Úbeda) and various Renaissance additions.

The **turismo** (Mon–Sat 8am–3pm; ☎953 750 897) is housed in its own Renaissance mansion, the Palacio del Marqués de Contadero, c/Baja Marqués 4, just to west of the Plaza de Vázquez de Molina, and can provide a town map. Most of the budget **accommodation** options are grouped around the main **bus station** on Avenida de Ramón y Cajal, in the modern part of town – the *Hostal Castillo* at no. 16 (☎953 750 430; ❸) and *Hostal Sevilla* at no. 9 (☎953 750 612; ❸) are both reasonable, and have better rooms with bath. For some of the least expensive rooms in town, try *Hostal San Miguel*, Avda. Libertad 69 (☎953 752 049; ❸), a fifteen-minute walk from the bus station. In the monumental quarter, the only option is the *Parador Condestable Dávalos*, Plaza de Vázquez de Molina 1 (☎953 750 345, ☎953 751 259; ❽), housed in yet another fabulous sixteenth-century Renaissance mansion.

There are plenty of **places to eat** around Avenida Ramón y Cajal: *El Gallo Rojo*, c/Torrenueva 3, has outdoor tables in the evening; *El Olivo*, Avda. Ramón y Cajal 6, serves good *platos combinados*; and *Hostal Castillo* has its own excellent-value restaurant with an economical *menú*. For a treat, the elegant restaurant of the *parador* offers a great-value lunch *menú* – with regional specialities – for about €21.

Cazorla and the Parque Natural

During the reconquest of Andalucía, **CAZORLA** acted as an outpost for Christian troops, and the two castles which still dominate the town testify to its turbulent past – both were originally Moorish but later altered and restored by their Christian conquerors. Today it's the main base for visits to the **Parque Natural de las Sierras de Segura y Cazorla**, a vast protected area of magnificent river gorges and forests. Cazorla also hosts the **fiesta de Cristo del Consuelo**, with fairgrounds, fireworks and religious processions on September 16–21.

Cazorla itself is constructed around three main squares. Buses arrive in the busy, commercial **Plaza de la Constitución**, where there's a privately run **tourist office**, Quercus (Mon–Fri 9am–2pm, Sat & Sun 9am–2pm & 6–9pm; ☎953 720 115), offering Land Rover and horse-riding day trips into the park. The main c/de Muñoz connects with the second square, the **Plaza de la Corredera** (or *del Huevo*, "of the Egg", because of its shape). The seat of the administration, the *ayuntamiento*, is here, a fine Moorish-style palace at the far end of the plaza. Beyond, a labyrinth of narrow, twisting streets leads to Cazorla's liveliest square, the **Plaza Santa María**. This takes its name from the old cathedral which, damaged by floods in the seventeenth century, was later torched by Napoleonic troops. Its ruins, now preserved, and the fine open square form a natural amphitheatre for concerts and local events as well as being a popular meeting place. The square is dominated by **La Yedra**, an austere, reconstructed castle tower, which houses the **Museo de Artes y Costumbres** (Mon–Sat 9.30am–2.30pm; free), an interesting folklore museum displaying domestic utensils and furniture.

Cazorla practicalities

Cazorla's official **turismo** (April–Sept Mon–Fri 10am–2pm; ☎953 710 102) is at Paseo del Santo Cristo 17, 100m north of Plaza de la Constitución, and can provide a useful town map. There is a surprising range of **accommodation** in Cazorla. *Pensión Taxi*, Travesía de San Antón 7 (☎953 720 525; ②), off Plaza de la Constitución, is at the bottom end; as a resident, you can also eat for very little in their *comedor*. Better facilities are available at the very friendly *Hotel Guadalquivir*, c/Nueva 6 (☎953 720 268; ③), off Plaza de la Corredera, while in the square itself, the equally friendly *Hostal Betis* (☎953 720 540; ②) has some rooms overlooking the plaza. There is also a clutch of more upmarket places, of which the *Villa Turística de Cazorla*, Ladera de San Isidro s/n (☎953 710 100, ⓕ953 710 152; ⑦), is the best; it's a five-minute walk from Plaza de Santa Maria along c/Fuente de la Peña. If you have a car there are some very attractive alternatives out in the sierra, including the *Hotel Sierra de Cazorla* (☎953 720 015, ⓕ953 720 017; ⑤), 2km outside the town, with a pool, and the *Parador El Adelantado* (☎953 727 075, ⓕ953 727 077; ⑦), a well-designed modern building with pool in a wonderful setting 25km away in the park. Cazorla also has an efficient **youth hostel**, at Mauricio Martínez 2 (☎953 710 329; ①; open April–Oct, Christmas and Easter), reached by following c/Juan Domingo from Plaza de la Constitución. Ask at the *Mesón la Cueva* (see below) if you want to **rent an apartment** for a longer stay.

For **eating** and **drinking** there are several spit-and-sawdust **bars** with good tapas clustered round the Plaza Santa María, along with the rustic *Mesón la Cueva*, which offers authentic local food cooked on a wood-fired range – the *conejo* (rabbit) is recommended – though when they are overrun in high season things can tend to deteriorate. Other places where you can **eat** well are *Mesón Don Chema*, down some steps off c/Muñoz, serving *platos combinados* and an economical *menú*, or the more expensive *La Sarga*, Plaza del Mercado, at the bottom of the same steps, where regional dishes are prepared with flair.

The Parque Natural

Even casual visitors to the park are likely to see a good variety of wildlife, including *Capra hispanica* (Spanish mountain goat), deer, wild pig, birds and butterflies. Ironically, though, much of the best viewing will be at the periphery, or even outside the park, since the wildlife is most successfully stalked on foot and walking opportunities within the park itself are surprisingly limited.

Information

The official **information office** for the park is located in Cazorla at c/Martínez Falero 11, just off Plaza de la Constitución. The main information centre inside the park is the Torre del Vinagre Centro de Interpretación (daily 11am–2pm & 5–8pm; ☎953 713 040; see box opposite). It's worth getting a good **map** from one of these: the 1:100,000 map, *Parque Natural de las Sierras de Cazorla y Segura*, and the 1:50,000 version, *Cazorla*, are recommended, but best of all are the new 1:40,000 set of map and guide packs to the Sierras de Cazorla and Segura (divided into three zones) published by Editorial Alpina, which have the most accurate maps available, detailing *senderos* (footpaths), mountain-bike routes, refuges, campsites and hotels.

Transport and accommodation

Public transport into the park is sparse. Two daily **buses** (except Sun) link Cazorla with **Coto Ríos** (a 1hr 15min journey) in the middle of the park: one at 6.45am, the other at 2.30pm; there's also a 6.30pm bus on Saturday. Return buses from Coto (not Sun) leave at 8am and 4.15pm. Distances between points are enormous, so to explore the park well you'll need a car or be prepared for long treks. Such problems are complicated by the fact that most of the *camping*

The Río Borosa walk

The classic **walk along the Río Borosa** can currently be done as a day-trek even if you are relying on public transport – though you should check the bus timetables before setting out. The early-morning bus to Coto Ríos can drop you at the visitors' centre at Torre del Vinagre where the route begins. Cross the road and take the path to the side of the Jardín Botanico. When you reach an electricity pylon turn left onto a downhill track. After passing a campsite and sports field to the left cross a foot-bridge over the river and turn right, aiming for a white building peeping above the trees. Soon you'll pass a small campsite (with an open-air bar in summer) and about a kilometre from the footbridge you'll come to a car park at a trout hatchery (*pisci-factoría*).

From here follow the rough track along the northwest (right) bank of the Borosa, swift and cold even in summer. Within a few minutes a signposted footpath diverges to the right; this also marks the beginning of the **gorge**. Two or three wooden bridges now take the path back and forth across the river, which is increasingly confined by sheer rock walls. At the narrowest points the path is routed along planked catwalks secured to the limestone cliff. The walk from Torre de Vinagre to the end of the narrows takes about two hours.

There the footpath rejoins the track; after another half-hour's walk you'll see a turbine and a long metal pipe bringing water from **two lakes** – one natural, one a small dam – up the mountain. The road crosses one last bridge over the Borosa and stops at the turbine house. When you get to a gate, beyond which there's a steeply rising gully, count on another full hour up to the lakes. Cross a footbridge and start the steep climb up a narrow track over the rocks below the cliff (at one point the path passes close to the base of the palisade – beware falling stones). At the top of the path is a cavernous amphitheatre, with a waterfall in winter. The path ends about halfway up the cliff, where an artificial tunnel has been bored through rock; walk through it to get to the lake.

Allow three and a half hours' walking time from Torre del Vinagre, slightly less going down. It's a full day's excursion but you should have plenty of time to catch the afternoon bus back – it currently passes the visitors' centre at 4.30pm, but it would be a good idea to confirm this before starting out. This walk is clearly detailed on the relevant Editorial Alpina map (see information opposite).

libre (free camping) areas shown on the 1:100,000 map have been closed recently; one still functioning is to be found beyond El Tranco on the dam. There is more accommodation at Coto Ríos, with three privately run **camp-sites** and a succession of *hostales*. Before setting out you should get the latest update on transport and accommodation from the turismo in Cazorla.

Walks

There are only three signposted **tracks** in the park, all pitifully short. One leads from the Empalme de Vadillo to the Puente de la Herrera via the Fuente del Oso (2km each way); another of about 1700m curls round the Cerrada (narrows) de Utrero near Vadillo-Castril village; and the best marked segment, through the lower Borosa gorge (see below), is also a mere 1700m long.

Granada

If you see only one town in Spain it should be **GRANADA**. For here, extraordinarily well preserved and in a tremendous natural setting, stands the **Alhambra** – the most exciting, sensual and romantic of all European monu-

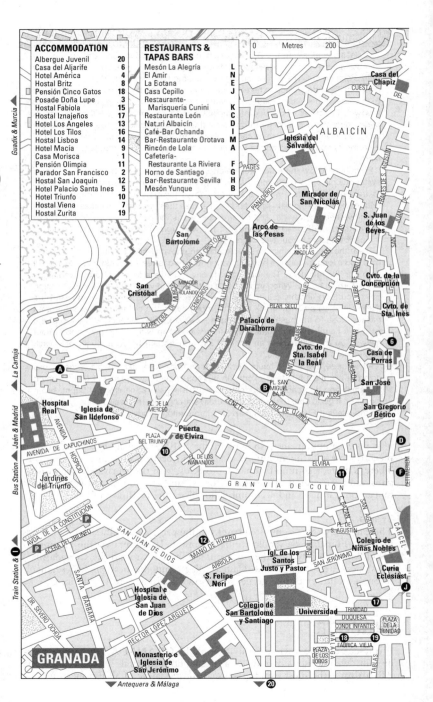

ACCOMMODATION

Albergue Juvenil	20
Casa del Aljarife	6
Hotel América	4
Hostal Britz	8
Pensión Cinco Gatos	18
Posade Doña Lupe	3
Hostal Fabiola	15
Hostal Iznajeños	17
Hotel Los Angeles	13
Hotel Los Tilos	16
Hostal Lisboa	14
Hotel Macía	9
Casa Morisca	1
Pensión Olimpia	11
Parador San Francisco	2
Hostal San Joaquin	12
Hotel Palacio Santa Ines	5
Hotel Triunfo	10
Hostal Viena	7
Hostal Zurita	19

RESTAURANTS & TAPAS BARS

Mesón La Alegría	L
El Amir	N
La Botana	E
Casa Cepillo	J
Restaurante-Marisquería Cunini	K
Restaurante León	C
Naturi Albaicín	D
Cafe-Bar Ochanda	I
Bar-Restaurante Orotava	M
Rincón de Lola	A
Cafetería-Restaurante La Riviera	F
Horno de Santiago	G
Bar-Restaurante Sevilla	H
Mesón Yunque	B

0 Metres 200

Guadix & Murcia

Casa del Chapiz

CUESTA DEL

ALBAICÍN

Iglesia del Salvador

PAGES

PANADEROS

S. Juan de los Reyes

Mirador de San Nicolás

Arco de las Pesas

PL. DE S. NICOLAS

San Bartolomé

LARGA SAN CRISTÓBAL

Cvto. de la Concepción

Cvto. de Sta. Inés

San Cristóbal

MIRADOR DE ROLANDO

CARRETERA DE MURCIA

CENICEROS

PILAR SECO

Palacio de Daralhorra

Cvto. de Sta. Isabel la Real

Casa de Porras

La Cartuja

Jaén & Madrid

Bus Station

Train Station

Hospital Real

Iglesia de San Ildefonso

PL. DE LA MERCED

ZENETE

PL. SAN MIGUEL BAJO

CRUZ DE QUIROS

SAN JOSÉ

San José

San Gregorio Bético

AVENIDA DE CAPUCHINOS

HOSPICIO

PLAZA DEL TRIUNFO

Puerta de Elvira

PL. DE LOS NARANJOS

ELVIRA

GRAN VÍA DE COLÓN

Jardines del Triunfo

AVDA. DE LA CONSTITUCIÓN

ACERA DEL TRIUNFO

SAN JUAN DE DIOS

MANO DE HIERRO

PL. DE S. AGUSTÍN

SAN AGUSTÍN

SAN JERÓNIMO

Colegio de Niñas Nobles

Curia Eclesiást.

SANTA BÁRBARA

DR. SEVERO OCHOA

RECTOR LÓPEZ ARGÜETA

ARRIOLA

Igl. de los Santos Justo y Pastor

S. Felipe Neri

TENDILLAS

Hospital e Iglesia de San Juan de Dios

Colegio de San Bartolomé y Santiago

Universidad

TRINIDAD

DUQUESA

CONDE INFANTES

PLAZA DE LA TRINIDAD

FÁBRICA VIEJA

PLAZA DE LOS LOBOS

Monasterio e Iglesia de San Jerónimo

MÁLAGA

TABLAS

GRANADA

Antequera & Málaga

▲ Sacromonte

Palacio
de los
Córdoba

CHAPIZ

DE LA VICTORIA
1

SACROMONTE

PASEO DE LAS ADELFAS

CIPRESES

Teatro

P
Entrance

Río Darro

CUESTA DEL REY CHICO

La Alhambra
2

CARMEN
DE LOS
MÁRTIRES

N

LOS REYES

Paseo de
los Tristes
Palacio de
los Leones
Palacio de
Comares
Baños de
Comares
Cuarto
Dorado
Palacio del
Mexuar
Palacios
Nazaries

Chirimías

Casa de
Castril

San Pedro
y San Pablo

Cvto. de Sta.
Catalina

Baños
Árabes
5

Puente
del Cadí

Carrera
del Darro
Casa de los
Ágreda

Sta. Ana

PLAZA
NUEVA

Real
Chancillería

7
8

9

C

CALDERERIA

Patio
de los
Leones

Jardines
del Partal

3

4 Sta. María de
la Alhambra

Palacio de
Carlos V

La Alcazaba

PASEO CENTRAL

PEÑA PARTIDA

ANTEQUERUELA ALTA CAMPO DE LOS MÁRTIRES

ANTEQUERUELA BAJA CUESTA DEL CAIDERO

San Cecilio

VARGAS

BELÉN

MOLINOS

10

CUESTA DE GOMÉREZ

LOS ALAMILLOS

Campo del
Príncipe

CUESTA DE REALEJO

MOLINOS

SANTIAGO

SANTIAGO

Casa de
los Tiros

PAVANERAS

E

Santo
Domingo

PL. SANTO
DOMINGO

P

P.S DE LUCENA

SOLARES

DEL PESCADO

Mon. a las
Capitulaciones

Cvto. de
S. Francisco

Capilla
Real

L

Madraza o
Univ. Árabe

Catedral

H

PL.
PASIEGOS

PL. BIB.
RAMBLA.

Palacio de
Abrantes

Alcaicería

PLAZA DEL
CARMEN

PL. Isabella Católica
Corral de
Carbón

i

PLAZA
GAMBOA

14

Ayuntamiento

15

L

GAMBOA

16

PESCADERIA

PL.A
CANO

K

Palacio
Arzobispal

MESONES

ALHÓNDIGA

ANGEL GANIVET

San Matías

SAN MATÍAS

LAS NAVAS

PLAZA DE
LOS CAMPOS

PLAZA DE
MARIANA PINEDA

G

CUARTO REAL

ANCHA DE LA VIRGEN

i

Palacio de
Bibataubín
(Dip. Prov.)

P

P

CARRERA DEL GENIL

Virgen de
las Angustias

HUMILLADERO

PASEO DEL SALÓN

ACERA DEL CASINO

PUERTA
REAL

A C E R A   D E L   D A R R O

PLAZA DE
LAS ARENAS

RECOGIDAS

SAN ANTÓN

P

CIPARRAGA

PUENTEZUELAS

REJAS DE LA VIRGEN

SAN ISIDRO

▼ **M** ▼ Purchil, Motril & **N**

► Sierra Nevada & Alhambra & **13**

ments. It was the palace-fortress of the Nasrid sultans, rulers of the last Spanish Moorish kingdom, and in its construction Moorish art reached a spectacular and serene climax. But the building seems to go further than this, revealing something of the whole brilliance and spirit of Moorish life and culture. There's a haunting passage in Jan Morris's book, *Spain*, which the palace embodies: "Life itself, which was seen elsewhere in Europe as a kind of probationary preparation for death, was interpreted [by the Moors] as something glorious in itself, to be ennobled by learning and enlivened by every kind of pleasure."

Arrival and information

Virtually everything of interest in Granada – including the hills of the **Alhambra** (to the east) and **Sacromonte** (to the north) – is within easy walking distance of the centre.

The **train station** (☎958 271 272) is a kilometre or so out on Avenida de Andaluces, off Avenida de la Constitución; to get into town, buses #3, #4, #6 and #9 run direct to Gran Vía de Colón and the centre of town, and bus #11 takes a circular route – inbound on the Gran Vía and back out via the Puerta Real and Camino de Ronda. The most central stop is by the cathedral on the Gran Vía.

The city's main **bus station**, Carretera de Jaén s/n, is some way out of the centre in the northern suburbs, and handles all services except those to the Sierra Nevada, Valencia and Barcelona. Bus #3 leaves from outside and will

---

Moorish Granada

Granada's glory was always precarious. It was established as an **independent kingdom** in 1238 by **Ibn Ahmar**, a prince of the Arab Nasrid tribe which had been driven south from Zaragoza. He proved a just and capable ruler but all over Spain the Christian kingdoms were in the ascendant. The Moors of Granada survived only through paying tribute and allegiance to Fernando III of Castile – whom they were forced to assist in the conquest of Muslim Sevilla – and by the time of Ibn Ahmar's death in 1275 theirs was the only surviving Spanish Muslim kingdom. It had, however, consolidated its territory (stretching from just north of the city down to a coastal strip between Tarifa and Almería) and, stimulated by refugees, developed a flourishing commerce, industry and culture.

By a series of shrewd manoeuvres Granada maintained its autonomy for two and a half centuries, its rulers turning for protection, in turn as it suited them, to the Christian kingdoms of Aragón and Castile and to the Merinid Muslims of Morocco. The city-state enjoyed a particularly confident and prosperous period under **Yusuf I** (1334–54) and **Mohammed V** (1354–91), the sultans responsible for much of the existing Alhambra palace. But by the mid-fifteenth century a pattern of coups and internal strife became established and a rapid succession of rulers did little to stem Christian inroads. In 1479 the kingdoms of Aragón and Castile were united by the marriage of Fernando and Isabel and within ten years had conquered Ronda, Málaga and Almería. The city of Granada now stood completely alone, tragically preoccupied in a **civil war** between supporters of the sultan's two favourite wives. The Reyes Católicos made escalating and finally untenable demands upon it, and in 1490 war broke out. **Boabdil**, the last Moorish king, appealed in vain for help from his fellow Muslims in Morocco, Egypt and Ottoman Turkey, and in the following year **Fernando and Isabel** marched on Granada with an army said to total 150,000 troops. For seven months, through the winter of 1491, they laid siege to the city, and on January 2, 1492, Boabdil formally surrendered its keys. The Christian Reconquest of Spain was complete.

drop you near the cathedral (a fifteen-minute journey). For information on bus departures check with the individual companies: Alsina Graells (☎958 185 480) at the main bus station runs services to and from Madrid, Jaén, Úbeda, Córdoba, Sevilla, Málaga, Alpujarras, Motril, Guadix, Almería and the coast; Empresa Bonal (☎958 273 100), Avda. Constitución 34, has buses to the north side of the Sierra Nevada; Empresa Autedía (☎958 153 636), c/Rector Martín 10, off Avda. Constitución, runs more services to Guadix; and Empresa Bacoma (☎958 284 251), Avda. Andalucía 12, near the train station, has buses to Valencia/Alicante and Barcelona. All terminals are on bus routes #3, #4 and #11.

Arriving **by air**, there's a bus (7 daily; 30min; €4.40 one way) connecting the airport, 17km west of the city on the A92 *autovía*, with Plaza Isabel La Católica; alternatively, a taxi should cost about €15.

Full details and bus timetables – and much else besides – should be posted on the walls of the **turismo** (Mon–Sat 9am–7pm, Sun 10am–2pm; ☎958 225 990), c/Mariana Pineda, in the Corral del Carbón near the cathedral, just off the eastern side of c/Reyes Católicos. There's also a very helpful (and less frenetic) **municipal tourist office** (Mon–Fri 9.30am–7pm, Sat 10am–2pm; ☎958 226 688) at Plaza Mariana Pineda 10. For listings, the monthly *Guía del Ocio* (available from newspaper *kioscos*) details most of what's happening on the cultural and entertainment front, though it tends to be less up-to-date than the city's daily paper, *Ideal*, which is particularly good in its weekend editions.

Accommodation

Finding a **place to stay** in the centre of town, along the Gran Vía, c/Reyes Católicos or in the Plaza Nueva and Puerta Real is usually easy enough except at the very height of season (Semana Santa is impossible), although ringing ahead to book could save you legwork or tedious phoning around when you arrive. Otherwise, try the streets to either side of the Gran Vía, at the back of the Plaza Nueva, round the Puerta Real and Plaza de Carmen (particularly c/Las Navas), the Plaza de la Trinidad in the university area (and east of there), or along the Cuesta de Gomérez, which leads up from the Plaza Nueva towards the Alhambra. **Hostales** and **pensiones** are so plentiful round here – and turnaround of guests so regular – that individual places are hard to recommend; those below are no more than an indication of some that have proved good. The main problem, almost anywhere, is **noise**, though the new road to the Alhambra, diverting traffic away from the centre, has transformed the Cuesta de Gomérez, which is now a semi-pedestrianized street (taxis and buses only). Don't waste shoe leather trying to find "interesting" accommodation in the Albaicín area – there are only a handful of upmarket options, the best of which are listed below.

Budget options

Albergue Juvenil, Camino de Ronda 171, at the junction with Avda. Ramón y Cajal ☎958 002 900, ☎958 285 285. If you arrive late in the day, Granada's youth hostel is conveniently close to the train station: turn left onto Avda. de la Constitución and left again onto Camino de Ronda. From the bus station, take bus #3 to the cathedral and then the circular #11, which will drop you outside. Recently renovated with lots of facilities, all rooms are en-suite doubles, staff are friendly but the food is institutional; it can also be booked up for days ahead in summer. ❶

Hostal Britz, Cuesta de Gomérez 1 ☎958 223 652. Very comfortable and well-placed *hostal*, en route to the Alhambra. Some rooms with bath. ❸

Pensión Cinco Gatos, c/Fabrica Vieja 4 ☎958 203 680. Homely *pensión* with clean, inexpensive rooms – some with bath – and an ebullient *dueña*. ❸

Posada Doña Lupe, Avda. del Generalife s/n ☎958 221 473, ☎958 221 474. A stone's throw from the new entrance to the Alhambra, with economically priced rooms (some en suite) and a rooftop pool, but blighted by a rule-ridden student hostel ambience. ❸

Hostal Fabiola, c/Ángel Gavinet 5 ☎958 223
572. Close to the Puerta Real; on the third floor
and relatively quiet. All rooms with bath and many
with sun balcony. ❸

Hostal Iznajeños, c/Lucena 1, a tiny street just
off Plaza de la Trinidad ☎958 278 255. Very
friendly family pensión with spotless, economical
rooms. ❷

Pensión Olimpia, c/Alvaro de Bazán 6, off Gran
Vía de Colón opposite Banco de Jeréz building
☎958 278 238. Friendly, central *pensión* offering
good-value basic accommodation. ❷

Hostal San Joaquin, c/Mano de Hierro 14, close
to the church of San Juan ☎958 282 879. Great,
rambling old *hostal*, with simple rooms and
charming patios. ❸

Hostal Viena, c/Hospital de Santa Ana 2 ☎958
221 859. In a quiet street (first left off the Cuesta
de Gomérez), this is a friendly, efficient Austrian-
run *hostal* offering some rooms with bath. If full,
they have other places nearby. ❸

Hostal Zurita, Plaza de la Trinidad 7, west of the
cathedral ☎958 275 020. Friendly place where
immaculate rooms come with and without bath,
and all have TV and air-conditioning. Has own
garage. ❸

Moderate and expensive options

Casa del Aljarife, Placeta de la Cruz Verde 2 ☎
& ℱ958 222 425, ℮most@mx3.redestb.es. The
Albaicín's solitary upmarket *hostal* occupies a
restored sixteenth-century mansion near the heart
of the *barrio*, has charming en-suite air-conditioned rooms and allows use of email and fax. ❻

Hotel América, Real de la Alhambra 53 ☎958
227 471, ℱ958 227 470. Simple, one-star hotel,
in the Alhambra grounds; you're paying for the
location, but repeated price hikes call into question
whether it's worth it. Booking essential. ❼

Hotel Macía, Plaza Nueva 4 ☎958 227 536,
ℱ958 227 535. Centrally located hotel, with comfortable rooms overlooking the atmospheric
square. ❻

Hostal Lisboa, Plaza del Carmen 27 ☎958 221
413. Clean and comfortable central *hostal*, offering
rooms with and without bath. ❹

Hotel Los Angeles, Cuesta Escoriaza 17 ☎958
221 423, ℱ958 222 125. Pleasant modern hotel
on leafy, quiet avenue within easy walking distance of the Alhambra. All rooms come with terrace balcony and there's a garden, pool and car
park. ❼

Casa Morisca, Cuesta de la Victoria 9 ☎958 215
796, ℱ958 215 796. Romantic small new hotel
inside an immaculately renovated fifteenth-century Moorish mansion with exquisite patio below the
walls of the Alhambra in the Albaicín; there are re-
created Moorish furnishings throughout, and
Room 15 (with Alhambra views) is the one to go
for. ❽

Hotel Palacio Santa Inés, Cuesta de Santa Inés
9 ☎958 222 362, ℱ958 222 465. Sumptuous six-
room hotel in a restored sixteenth-century mansion on the edge of the Albaicín, with views of the
Alhambra. ❼

Parador San Francisco, Real de la Alhambra
☎958 221 440, ℱ958 222 264. Without question
the best – and most expensive – place to stay in
Granada; a converted monastery in the Alhambra
grounds. Advance booking essential. ❾

Hotel Los Tilos, Plaza de Bib-Rambla 4 ☎958
266 712, ℱ958 266 801. Plain, two-star hotel well
located near the cathedral on a pleasant square;
make sure to request an exterior room if you don't
want to overlook a gloomy light well. ❺

Hotel Triunfo, Plaza del Triunfo 19 ☎958 207
444, ℱ958 207 673. Well-appointed upmarket
hotel on the edge of the Albaicín, flanked by an
imposing Moorish arch, the Puerta de Elvira. Own
garage. ❽

Camping

Camping Sierra Nevada, Avda. de Madrid 107
☎958 150 062 (March–Oct). Closest site to the
centre (bus #3 from the centre or a 3min walk
south from the bus station), and – with a welcome
pool – probably the best too.

Camping Reina Isabel, 4km along the Zubia road
to the southwest of the city ☎958 590 041. With a
pool, this is a less noisy and shadier site than the
one above, making a pleasant rural alternative;
with your own transport the city is still in easy
reach.

The Alhambra

There are three distinct groups of buildings on the Alhambra hill: the **Palacios
Nazaríes** (Royal Palace, or Nasrid Palaces), the palace gardens of the
Generalife, and the **Alcazaba**. This last, the fortress of the eleventh-century
Ziridian rulers, was all that existed when the Nasrid ruler Ibn al-Ahmar made
Granada his capital, but from its reddish walls the hilltop had already taken its
name: *Al Qal'a al-Hamra* in Arabic means literally "the red fort". Ibn al-Ahmar

rebuilt the Alcazaba and added to it the huge circuit of walls and towers which forms your first view of the castle. Within the walls he began a palace, which he supplied with running water by diverting the River Darro nearly 8km to the foot of the hill; water is an integral part of the Alhambra and this engineering feat was Ibn al-Ahmar's greatest contribution. The Palacios Nazaríes was essentially the product of his fourteenth-century successors, particularly Yusuf I and Mohammed V, who built and redecorated many of its rooms in celebration of his accession to the throne (in 1354) and the taking of Algeciras (in 1369).

After their conquest of the city, **Fernando and Isabel** lived for a while in the Alhambra. They restored some rooms and converted the mosque but left the palace structure unaltered. As at Córdoba and Sevilla, it was **Emperor Carlos V**, their grandson, who wreaked the most insensitive destruction, demolishing a whole wing of rooms in order to build a Renaissance palace. This and the Alhambra itself were simply ignored by his successors and by the eighteenth century the Palacios Nazaríes was in use as a prison. In 1812 it was taken and occupied by **Napoleon's forces**, who looted and damaged whole sections of the palace, and on their retreat from the city tried to blow up the entire complex. Their attempt was thwarted only by the action of a crippled soldier who remained behind and removed the fuses.

Two decades later the Alhambra's "rediscovery" began, given impetus by the American writer **Washington Irving**, who set up his study in the empty palace rooms and began to write his marvellously romantic *Tales of the Alhambra* (on sale all over Granada – and good reading amid the gardens and courts). Shortly after its publication, the Spaniards made the Alhambra a **national monument** and set aside funds for its restoration. This continues to the present day and is now a highly sophisticated project, scientifically removing the accretions of later ages in order to expose and meticulously restore the Moorish creations.

Approaches and orientation

The standard **approach** to the Alhambra is along the Cuesta de Gomérez, the semi-pedestrianized road which climbs uphill from Granada's central Plaza Nueva. The only vehicles allowed to use this road in daytime are taxis and the **Alhambrabus** (line #30), a dedicated minibus service (daily 7am–10pm, every 10min; €0.75) linking Plaza Nueva with the Alhambra palace. To get there **by car** you will need to use the route which is signed from the Puerta Real, to the south of the cathedral; this guides you along the Paseo del Salón and the Paseo de la Bomba eventually bringing you to the Alhambra's car park, close to the new entrance on the eastern edge of the complex.

Should you decide to **walk** up the hill along the Cuesta de Gomérez (a pleasant twenty-minute stroll from the Plaza Nueva), after a few hundred metres you reach the **Puerta de las Granadas**, a massive Renaissance gateway erected by Carlos V. Here two paths diverge to either side of the road: the one on the right climbs up towards a group of fortified towers, the **Torres Bermejas**, which may date from as early as the eighth century. The left-hand path leads through the woods past a huge terrace-fountain (again courtesy of Carlos V) to the main gateway – and former entrance – of the Alhambra. This is the **Puerta de la Justicia**, a magnificent tower which forced three changes of direction, making intruders hopelessly vulnerable. It was built by Yusuf I in 1340 and preserves above its outer arch the Koranic symbol of a key (for Allah the Opener) and an outstretched hand, whose five fingers represent the five Islamic precepts: prayer, fasting, alms-giving, pilgrimage to Mecca and the oneness of God. The **new entrance** to the Alhambra – at the eastern end, near to

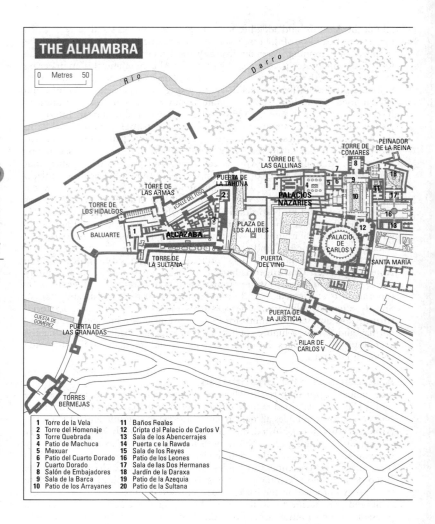

THE ALHAMBRA

0 Metres 50

1 Torre de la Vela	11 Baños Reales
2 Torre del Homenaje	12 Cripta del Palacio de Carlos V
3 Torre Quebrada	13 Sala de los Abencerrajes
4 Patio de Machuca	14 Puerta de la Rawda
5 Mexuar	15 Sala de los Reyes
6 Patio del Cuarto Dorado	16 Patio de los Leones
7 Cuarto Dorado	17 Sala de las Dos Hermanas
8 Salón de Embajadores	18 Jardín de la Daraxa
9 Sala de la Barca	19 Patio de la Azequia
10 Patio de los Arrayanes	20 Patio de la Sultana

the Generalife gardens – lies a further five-minute walk uphill, reached by following the wall to your left.

Within the citadel stood a complete "government city" of mansions, smaller houses, baths, schools, mosques, barracks and gardens. Of this only the **Alcazaba fortress** and the **Palacios Nazaríes** remain; they face each other across a broad terrace (constructed in the sixteenth century over a dividing gully), flanked by the majestic though incongruous **Palace of Carlos V**.

Within the walls of the citadel, too, are the beautiful *Parador San Francisco* (a converted monastery, where Isabel was originally buried – terrace bar open to non-guests), and the *Hotel América*. There are a handful of **drinks stalls** around as well, including one, very welcome, in the Portal gardens (towards the Carlos V Palace after you leave the Palacios Nazaríes).

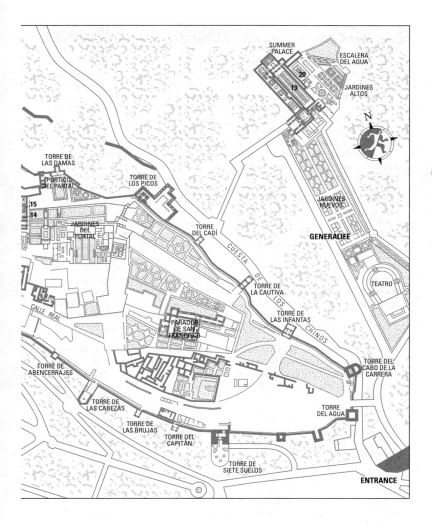

The Alcazaba

The new entrance to the Alhambra now brings you into the complex at the eastern end, near to the Generalife gardens. However, as you will have a time slot for entering the Palacios Nazaríes (usually up to an hour ahead), it makes sense chronologically and practically to start your visit with the **Alcazaba** at the Alhambra's opposite, or western, end. To get there from the entrance, walk up the short avenue lined with cypresses to a three-way fork, taking the signed path to the Alhambra. Cross the bridge over the "moat" following signs to the Alcazaba and Palacios Nazaríes, and you will eventually pass the gates of the *Parador de San Francisco* (on your right) and the *Hotel America* to enter the Calle Real. Continue alongside the Palace of Carlos V to pass through the **Puerto**

Admission to the Alhambra

To protect the Alhambra only 7700 daily admissions are allowed (March–Oct 8.30am–8pm; Nov–Feb 8.30am–6pm; €6). If you are buying your **tickets** in person you have two options: they can be purchased at the entrance (ticket office opens at 8am and shuts one hour before the closing time above) but the overwhelming number of visitors to the monument has made it imperative to turn up as early in the day as possible to be sure of getting in, and you should be prepared for queues of one to two hours in high season. Alternatively, they can be bought on the day from the main Granada branch of the Banco de Bilbao Vizcaya Argentaria (BBVA; Mon–Fri 9am–2pm; €0.75 commission per ticket), Plaza Isabel la Católica 1, in the centre.

However, the best way to **avoid the queues** is to use a new reservation system (English spoken), also operated by the BBVA, which enables you to **book your tickets in advance** from anywhere in Spain or abroad (inside Spain ☏902 224 460; outside Spain ☏+34 913 465 936; ⓦhttp://decompras.bbv.es) a minimum of one day, or a maximum of one year, ahead. This scheme accounts for 75 percent of tickets sold and you are strongly advised to use it to avoid tedious queuing or disappointment if your time in Granada is restricted. You can usually choose your time slot for the Palacios Nazaríes (see below) but at peak periods a time will be allocated to you. You are required to pay for the tickets with a **credit card** (Visa or Mastercard only) and a commission of €0.75 is levied for each ticket. Once your booking is confirmed you are given a code number which allows you to collect your tickets from any of the 2800 BBVA branches in Spain (at least one day before the visit takes place) or the Alhambra ticket office (at least two hours before your allotted visit time). For both points of collection you will need to provide the code number and your passport. Tickets can also be reserved on the Alhambra's Spanish website ⓦwww.alhambratickets.com which is easy to get the gist of and can be accessed from abroad; the same collection conditions apply.

The tickets have **sections** for each part of the complex – Alcazaba, Palacios Nazaríes, Generalife – which must be used on the same day. Note that you will not be allowed to enter the complex (even with pre-booked tickets) less than an hour before closing time. To alleviate the severe overcrowding of recent years, tickets are stamped with a half-hour time slot during which you *must* enter the Palacios Nazaríes. You will not be allowed to enter before or after this time, but once inside you can stay as long as you like.

The Alhambra is also open for **floodlit visits** (limited to the Palacios Nazaríes; €6) on Tuesday to Saturday nights from March to October (10–11.30pm; ticket office open 9.45–10.15pm only) and on Friday and Saturday nights from November to February (8–9.30pm; ticket office open 7.45–8.15pm only), and occasional concerts are held in its courts (details from the turismo). The two **museums** in the Palace of Carlos V have separate admission fees and hours (see p.361).

To check any changes to opening times, admission charges or booking procedures visit the Alhambra's **website** ⓦwww.alhambra-patronato.es where the latest information is posted.

del Vino – named from its use in the sixteenth century as a wine cellar – into the Alcazaba.

The Alcazaba is the earliest and most ruined part of the fortress. At its summit is the **Torre de la Vela**, named after a huge bell on its turret which until recent years was rung to mark the irrigation hours for workers in the *vega*, Granada's vast and fertile plain. It was here, at 3pm on January 2, 1492, that the Cross was first displayed above the city, alongside the royal standards of Aragón and Castile and the banner of St James. Boabdil, leaving Granada for exile in the Alpujarras, turned and wept at the sight, earning from his mother Aisha the famous rebuke: "Do not weep like a woman for what you could not defend like a man." The **Aljibe**, a cistern beneath the area between the Alcazaba and Palacios Nazaríes, is open for viewing on Monday, Wednesday and Friday from 9.30am to 1.30pm.

The Palacios Nazaríes

It is amazing that the **Palacios Nazaríes** has survived, for it stands in utter contrast to the strength of the Alcazaba and the encircling walls and towers. It was built lightly and often crudely from wood, brick and adobe, and was designed not to last but to be renewed and redecorated by succeeding rulers. Its buildings show a brilliant use of light and space but they are principally a vehicle for ornamental stucco decoration. This, as Titus Burckhardt explains in *Moorish Culture in Spain*, was both an intricate science and a philosophy of abstract art in direct contrast to pictorial representation:

4

With its rhythmic repetition, [it] does not seek to capture the eye to lead it into an imagined world, but, on the contrary, liberates it from all pre-occupations of the mind. It does not transmit any specific ideas, but a state of being, which is at once repose and inner rhythm.

Burckhardt adds that the way in which patterns are woven from a single band, or radiate from many identical centres, served as a pure simile for Islamic belief in the oneness of God, manifested at the centre of every form and being. **Arabic inscriptions** feature prominently in the ornamentation. Some are poetic eulogies to the buildings and builders, others to various sultans (notably Mohammed V). Most, however, are taken from the Koran, and among them the phrase *Wa-la ghaliba illa-Llah* (There is no Conqueror but God) is tirelessly repeated. This became the battle cry (and family motto) of the Nasrids upon Ibn al-Ahmar's return in 1248 from aiding the Castilian war of Fernando III against Muslim Sevilla; it was his reply to the customary, though bitterly ironic, greetings of *Mansur* (Victor), ridiculing his role as a feudal puppet of the Christian enemy.

Wa-la-ghaliba illa-Llah stylized inscription from the Alhambra

The palace is structured in three parts, each arrayed round an interior court and with a specific function. The sultans used the **Mexuar**, the first series of rooms, for business and judicial purposes. In the **Serallo**, beyond, they received embassies and distinguished guests. The last section, the **Harem**, formed their private living quarters and would have been entered by no one but their family or servants.

The Mexuar

The council chamber, the main **reception hall** of the Mexuar, is the first room you enter. It was completed in 1365 and hailed (perhaps formulaically) by the court poet and vizier Ibn Zamrak as a "haven of counsel, mercy, and favour". Here the sultan heard the pleas and petitions of the people and held meetings with his ministers. At the room's far end is a small oratory, one of a number of prayer niches scattered round the palace and immediately identifiable by their distinctive alignment (to face Mecca). This "public" section of the palace, beyond which few would have penetrated, is completed by the Mudéjar **Cuarto Dorado** (Golden Room), decorated under Carlos V, whose *Plus Ultra* motif appears throughout the palace, and the **Patio del Cuarto Dorado**. This has perhaps the grandest facade of the whole palace, for it admits you to the formal splendour of the Serallo.

The Serallo

The Serallo was built largely to the design of Yusuf I, a romantic and enlightened sultan who was stabbed to death by a madman while worshipping in the Alhambra mosque. Its rooms open out from delicate marble-columned arcades at each end of the long **Patio de los Arrayanes** (Patio of the Myrtles).

At the court's north end, occupying two floors of a fortified tower, is the royal throne room, known as the **Salón de Embajadores** (Hall of the Ambassadors). As the sultan could be approached only indirectly, it stands at an angle to the entrance from the Mexuar. It is the largest room of the palace, perfectly square and completely covered in tile and stucco decoration. Among the web of inscriptions is one that states simply "I am the Heart of the Palace." Here Boabdil signed the terms of his city's surrender to the Catholic kings, whose motifs (the arms of Aragón and Castile) were later worked into the room's stunning wooden dome, a superb example of *lacería*, the rigidly geometric "carpentry of knots". Here too, so it is said, Fernando met Columbus to discuss his plans for finding a new sea route to India – which led to the discovery of the Americas. The dome itself, in line with the mystical-mathematical pursuit of medieval Moorish architecture, has a complex symbolism representing the seven heavens. Carlos V tore down the rooms at the southern end of the court; from the arcade there is access to the gloomy **Chapel Crypt** of his palace which has a curious "whispering gallery" effect.

The Harem

The **Patio de los Leones** (Court of the Lions), which has become the archetypal image of Granada, constitutes the heart of the harem section of the palace. The stylized and archaic-looking lions beneath its fountain probably date, like the patio itself, from the reign of Mohammed V, Yusuf's successor; a poem inscribed on the bowl tells how much fiercer they would look if they weren't so restrained by respect for the sultan. The court was designed as an interior garden and planted with shrubs and aromatic herbs; it opens onto three of the palace's finest rooms, each of which looks onto the fountain.

The most sophisticated rooms in this part of the complex, apparently designed to give a sense of the rotary movement of the stars, are the two facing each other across the court. The largest of these, the **Sala de los Abencerrajes**, has the most startlingly beautiful ceiling in the Alhambra: sixteen-sided, supported by niches of stalactite vaulting, lit by windows in the dome and reflected in a fountain on the floor. This light and airy quality stands at odds with its name and history, for here Abu'l-Hasan (Boabdil's father) murdered sixteen princes of the Abencerraje family, whose chief had fallen in love with his favourite, Zoraya; the rust stains in the fountain are popularly supposed to be the indelible traces of their blood.

At the far end is the **Sala de los Reyes** (Hall of the Kings), whose dormitory alcoves preserve a series of unique paintings on leather. These, in defiance of Koranic law, represent human scenes; it's believed that they were painted by a Christian artist in the last decades of Moorish rule. The second of the two facing chambers on the court's north side, the **Sala de las Dos Hermanas** (Hall of the Two Sisters), is more mundanely named – from two huge slabs of marble in its floor – but just as spectacularly decorated, with a dome of over five thousand "honeycomb cells". It was the principal room of the sultan's favourite, opening onto an inner apartment and balcony, the **Mirador de Daraxa** (known in English as the "Eyes of the Sultana"); the romantic garden patio below was added after the Reconquest.

Beyond, you are directed along a circuitous route through **apartments** redecorated by Carlos V (as at Sevilla, the northern-reared emperor installed fireplaces) and later used by Washington Irving. Eventually you emerge at the **Peinador**, or Queen's Tower, a pavilion that served as an oratory for the sultanas and as a dressing room for the wife of Carlos V; perfumes were burned beneath its floor and wafted up through a marble slab in one corner.

From there, passing the **Patio de la Reja** (Patio of the Grille) added in the seventeenth century, you reach the **Baños Reales** (Royal Baths). These are tremendous, decorated in rich tile mosaics and lit by pierced stars and rosettes once covered by coloured glass. The central chamber was used for reclining and retains the balconies where singers and musicians – reputedly blind to keep the royal women from being seen – would entertain the bathers.

Towers and the Palacio de Carlos V

Before leaving the palace compound, there are a number of the **towers** worth a look. Most are richly decorated – particularly the first, the **Torre de las Damas** (Ladies' Tower) – which stands in front of its own patio (restored to the original design).

The usual exit from the Palacios Nazaríes leads through the courtyard of the **Palacio de Carlos V**, where bullfights were once held. The palace itself (begun in 1526 but never finished) seems totally out of place here, but is in fact a distinguished piece of Renaissance design in its own right – the only surviving work of Pedro Machuca, a former pupil of Michelangelo. On its upper floors is a mildly interesting **Museo de Bellas Artes** (Tues 2.30–6pm, Wed–Sat 9am–6pm, Sun 9am–2.30pm; €1.50, free for EU citizens) with some notable examples of *andaluz* wood sculpture. The lower floor holds the **Museo de la Alhambra** (aka Museo Hispano-Musulman; Tues–Sat 9am–2pm; free), a small but fascinating collection of Hispano-Moorish art, displaying many items discovered during the Alhambra restoration; the star exhibit is a beautiful fifteenth-century metre-and-a-half-high **Alhambra vase** (Jarrón de las Gacelas), made from local red clay enamelled in blue and gold and decorated with leaping gazelles. Note, however, that both museums frequently fail to open on their advertised days and are liable to close early in slack periods.

The Generalife

Paradise is described in the Koran as a shaded, leafy garden refreshed by running water where the "fortunate ones" may take their rest. It is an image which perfectly describes the **Generalife**, the gardens and summer palace of the sultans. Its name means literally "garden of the architect" and the grounds consist of a luxuriantly imaginative series of patios, enclosed gardens and walkways.

By chance, an account of the gardens during Moorish times, written rather poetically by the fourteenth-century court vizier and historian Ibn Zamrak,

△ Mudejar arch, Grenada

survives. The descriptions that he gives aren't all entirely believable, but they are a wonderful basis for musing as you lie around by the patios and fountains. There were, he wrote, celebrations with horses darting about in the dusk at speeds that made the spectators rub their eyes (a form of festival still indulged in at Moroccan *fantasías*); rockets shot into the air to be attacked by the stars for their audacity; tightrope walkers flying through the air like birds; and men bowled along in a great wooden hoop, shaped like an astronomical sphere.

Today, devoid of such amusements, the gardens are still evocative – above all, perhaps, the **Patio de los Cipreses** (aka Patio de la Sultana), a dark and secretive walled garden of sculpted junipers where the Sultana Zoraya was suspected of meeting her lover Hamet, chief of the unfortunate Abencerrajes. Nearby, too, is the inspired flight of fantasy of the **Camino de las Cascadas**, a staircase with water flowing down its stone balustrades. This is just above the wonderful little **Summer Palace**, with its various decorated belvederes. From just below the entrance to the Generalife the **Cuesta del Rey Chino** – an alternative route back to the city – winds down towards the River Darro and the old Arab quarter of the Albaicín (see below).

The Albaicín and around the town

If you're spending just a couple of days in Granada it's hard to resist spending both of them in the Alhambra. There are, however, a handful of minor Moorish sites and, climbing up from the Darro, the run-down medieval streets of the **Albaicín**, the largest and most characteristic Moorish quarter that survives in Spain. In addition, it's worth the distinct readjustment and effort of will to appreciate the city's later Christian monuments.

The Albaicín and other Moorish remains

The Albaicín stretches across a fist-shaped area bordered by the river, the Sacromonte hill, the old town walls and the winding Calle de Elvira (parallel to the Gran Vía de Colón, the main avenue which bisects central Granada). The best approach is along the Carrera del Darro, beside the river. At no. 31 on this street are the remains of the **Baños Árabes** (Tues–Sat 10am–2pm; free), marvellous and very little-visited Moorish public baths. At no. 43 is the **Casa de Castril** (Tues 3–8pm, Wed–Sat 9am–8pm, Sun 9am–2.30pm; €1.50, free to EU citizens), a Renaissance mansion which houses the town's **Archeological Museum**. Of particular note here are some remarkable finds from the Neolithic Cueva de los Murciélagos (Cave of the Bats) in the Alpujarras; there are also exhibits from Granada's Phoenician, Roman, Visigothic and Moorish periods. Beside the museum a road ascends to the church of San Juan (with an

---

Security in the Albaicín

Although you certainly shouldn't let it put you off visiting the atmospheric **Albaicín quarter**, it's worth bearing in mind that the area has recently seen an escalating number of **thefts** from tourists, typically carried out by drug addicts to fund their addiction. To ensure your visit is a happy one, take all the usual precautions: avoid carrying around large amounts of money or valuables (including airline tickets and passports), and keep what you have in safe pockets instead of shoulder bags. If you do get something snatched, don't offer resistance; crime in these streets rarely involves attacks to the person, but thieves will be firm in getting what they want. Finally, try not to look like an obvious tourist (map/guidebook in hand is a dead giveaway) and keep to the streets where there are other people about, particularly at night.

intact thirteenth-century minaret) and to **San Nicolás**, whose square offers a **view of the Alhambra** considered to be the best in town.

Outside the Albaicín are two of the most interesting Moorish mansions: the **Corral del Carbón**, a fourteenth-century *caravanserai* (an inn where merchants would lodge and, on the upper floors, store their goods), now home of the turismo; and the nearby **Casa de los Tiros**, actually built just after the Reconquest, which has a curious facade adorned with Greek deities and a number of stone muskets projecting from the upper windows. Perhaps the most interesting Moorish building in the lower town, though, and oddly one of the least well known, is the so-called **Palacio Madraza** (Mon–Fri 8am–10pm; closed Aug; free), a strangely painted building opposite the Capilla Real. Built in the early fourteenth century, this is a former Islamic college (*medressa* in Arabic) and retains part of its old prayer hall, including a magnificently decorated *mihrab*.

Just to the east of Plaza Nueva behind the church of Santa Ana, the Baños Arabes Al Andalus, c/Santa Ana 16 (reservation required ☏958 229 978; bath €10.50) gives you some idea of what a **Moorish bathhouse** would have been like when functioning. Here you can wallow in the graded temperatures of the re-created traditional baths – decorated with mosaics and plaster arabesques – or take tea in the peaceful *tetería* (tea room) upstairs.

The Capilla Real, cathedral and churches

The **Capilla Real** (April–Sept Mon–Sat 10.30am–1pm & 4–7pm, Sun 11am–1pm & 4–7pm; Oct–March Mon–Fri 10.30am–1pm, Sat & Sun 11am–1pm; €2.10), in the centre of town at the southern end of Gran Vía de Colón, is an impressive building, flamboyant late Gothic in style and built ad hoc in the first decades of Christian rule as a mausoleum for Los Reyes Católicos, the city's "liberators". The actual **tombs** are as simple as could be imagined: Fernando (marked with an "F") and Isabel, flanked by their daughter Joana ("the Mad") and her husband Felipe ("the Handsome"), resting in lead coffins placed in a plain crypt. But above them – the response of their grandson Carlos V to what he found "too small a room for so great a glory" – is a fabulously elaborate **monument** carved in Carrara marble by Florentine Domenico Fancelli in 1517, with sculpted Renaissance effigies of the two monarchs; the tomb of Joana and Felipe alongside is a much inferior work by Ordóñez. In front of the monument is an equally magnificent **reja**, the work of Maestro Bartolomé of Baeza, and a splendid **retablo** behind depicts Boabdil surrendering the keys of Granada.

Isabel, in accordance with her will, was originally buried on the Alhambra hill (in the church of San Francisco, now part of the *parador*) but her wealth and power proved no safeguard of her wishes. The queen's final indignity occurred during the 1980s when the candle that she asked should perpetually illuminate her tomb was replaced by an electric bulb – it was restored in 1999 following numerous protests. In the Capilla's **Sacristy** is displayed the sword of Fernando, the crown of Isabel and her outstanding personal collection of **medieval Flemish paintings** – including important works by Memling, Bouts and van der Weyden – and various Italian paintings, including panels by Botticelli and Pedro Berruguete.

For all its stark Renaissance bulk, Granada's **Catedral**, adjoining the Capilla Real and entered from the door beside it (April–Sept Mon–Sat 10.45am–1.30pm & 4–7pm, Sun 4–7pm; Oct–March Mon–Sat 10.30am–1.30pm, Sun 4–7pm; €2.10), is a disappointment. It was begun in 1521, just as the chapel was finished, but was then left incomplete well into the eighteenth century. At least it's light and airy inside, though, and it's fun to go round putting coins in the slots to light up the chapels, where an El Greco *St Francis* and sculptures by Pedro de Mena and Montañes will be revealed.

Other churches have more to offer, and with sufficient interest you could easily fill a day of visits. North of the cathedral, ten minutes' walk along c/San Jerónimo, the Baroque **San Juan de Dios**, with a spectacular *retablo*, is attached to a majestically portalled hospital (still in use; porter will allow a brief look). Close by is the elegant Renaissance **Convento de San Jerónimo** (April–Sept Mon–Sat 10am–1.30pm & 4–7.30pm, Sun 11am–1.30pm; Oct–March Mon–Sat 10am–1.30pm; €2.10), founded by the Catholic kings, though built after their death, with two imposing patios and a wonderful frescoed church. Lastly, on the northern outskirts of town, is **La Cartuja** (April–Sept Mon–Sat 10am–1pm & 4–8pm, Sun 10am–noon & 4–8pm; Oct–March Mon–Sat 10am–1.30pm, Sun 10am–noon; €2.10), perhaps the grandest and most outrageously decorated of all the country's lavish Carthusian monasteries. It was constructed at the height of Baroque extravagance – some say to rival the Alhambra – and has a chapel of staggering wealth, surmounted by an altar of twisted and coloured marble. It's a further ten- to fifteen-minute walk beyond San Juan de Dios (or take bus #8 or #C from the centre going north along Gran Vía).

Fuente Vaqueros Lorca museum

To the west of the city, in the pleasant *vega* village of Fuente Vaqueros, the birthplace of Federico García Lorca, Andalucía's greatest poet and dramatist, has been transformed into a **museum** (guided visits on the hour Tues–Sun 10am–1pm & 5–7pm; €1.80), and contains a highly evocative collection of Lorca memorabilia. Buses operated by Ureña (hourly from 8am; 20min) leave from Granada's Avenida de Andaluces, fronting the train station.

Eating and drinking

When it comes to **restaurants** Granada certainly isn't one of the gastronomic centres of Spain, possibly due in part to the *granadino* **tapas bars** which tempt away potential diners by giving out some of the most generous tapas in Andalucía – one comes free with every drink. We have recommended a few of the best of these below, and the municipal tourist office gives out a handy tapas bar leaflet to help you locate more (see p.353). A flavour of North Africa is to be found along c/Calderería Nueva and its surrounds in "Little Morocco", where you'll find health-food stores as well as numerous Moroccan tearooms and eating places. This street is useful for assembling **picnics** for Alhambra visits, as is the revamped ultramodern Mercado Municipal in Plaza San Agustín just north of the cathedral (Mon–Fri early until 1.30pm). Inexpensive restaurants – most serving an economical *menú del día* – can be found among the inevitable tourist traps all over Granada. The warren of streets between **Plaza Nueva** and **Gran Vía** has plenty of good-value places, particularly tapas bars, as does the area around **Plaza del Carmen** (near the *ayuntamiento*) and along c/Navas leading away from it. Another good location is the **Campo del Principe**, a pleasant square below the south side of the Alhambra hill, with a line of open-air restaurant terraces, highly popular on summer nights.

City centre

Bar-Restaurante Sevilla, c/Oficios, opposite the entrance to the Capilla Real. One of the few surviving prewar restaurants, and a haunt of Lorca, with

a good-value *menú* and an outdoor terrace in the evenings.

Cafetería-Restaurante La Riviera, c/Cettimeriem 5. Popular café with a good *menú* *económico*, including a vegetarian option.

Casa Cepillo, c/Pescadería, off c/Príncipe behind the Alcaicería. Cheap *comedor* very popular with locals for its great-value *menús* – fish and squid are the specialities.

Horno de Santiago, Plaza de Los Campos 2. Probably the city's best restaurant, offering classic *granadino* meat, fish and game dishes in a pleasant setting. There's a *menú de degustación* for about €20. Closed Aug.

Mesón La Alegría, c/Moras 4, east of Puerta Real. This *mesón* is a favourite of *granadinos* working nearby and specializes in *carnes asados* (roasted meats).

Mesón Yunque, Plaza San Miguel Bajo in the Albaicín. Great atmosphere, with tasty meat and fish dishes served at indoor and outdoor tables on this delightful square.

Naturi Albaicín, c/Calderería Nueva 10. Imaginative vegetarian cooking, serving up fine salads, stuffed mushrooms, and the like.

Restaurante León, c/Pan 3. Long-established *cordobés* restaurant serving many *carne de monte* (game) dishes with a cheap *menú del día*, plus a good tapas bar on the other side of the street.

Restaurante-Marisquería Cunini, c/Pescadería 9. One of Granada's established upmarket restaurants, serving mainly fish, with an outstanding (and cheaper) tapas bar attached.

Around town

El Amir, General Narváez 3, in the south of the city near the Plaza de Gracia. Superb, and expensive, Arab restaurant with delicious hummus and falafel, wonderful dishes of rice and ground meat with pine nuts and cinnamon, and meatballs in a spicy sauce.

Bar-Restaurante Orotava, junction of c/Pedro Antonio de Alarcón and c/Sol. This no-frills diner serves up what has to be Granada's cheapest *menú del día* at €3.60 for three courses including bread and wine.

La Botana, Santa Escolástica s/n, near the Casa de los Tiros. Stylish restaurant and bar with raucous musical background and an eclectic cuisine, including some vegetarian options.

Café-bar Ochando, Avda. de los Andaluces. Situated right by the train station and open 24 hours, this café is handy for late or early travellers, and serves a good breakfast.

Rincón de Lola, Plazita Rosales near the Hospital Real. Good little vegetarian restaurant with well-prepared dishes and tasty home-made desserts.

Bars and nightlife

Enjoyable central **bars** include *Bodegas Castañeda* on the corner of c/Elvira and c/Almireceros, near the top of the Gran Vía, a traditional, though modernized, *bodega,* the lively *Bodegas La Mancha*, c/Joaquín Costa 10 around the corner, and the earthy *Bar Sabanilla*, c/San Sebastián 14, up an alley off the southeast corner of Plaza Bib Rambla, which claims to be the oldest bar in Granada, and serves a free *tapa* with every drink. The bar of the *Hotel Reina Cristina*, c/Tablas 4 off the Plaza de la Trinidad – the building in which Lorca spent his last days before being seized by the fascists – is also an excellent place for a *tapa* and a glass of *fino*. All these stay open until around midnight.

If you want to go on **drinking through the early hours**, head out to the student areas round the university. Calle San Juan de Dios (and its continuations c/Gran Capitán and Plaza Gran Capitán), Carril del Picón and c/Pedro Antonio de Alarcón are all extremely lively. The streets to the east of the latter – c/Casillas de Prats, c/Trajano and Plaza Menorca – have most of the **pubs** and **disco-bars**; current vogue places include *Biblioteca*, *Gente Guapa*, *Black is Beautiful*, *Pub M*, *Babel* and *Chueka* (a popular **gay bar** in nearby c/Goya), though new places open almost weekly in summer. Other places to try are *Granada 10*, near the cathedral at c/Carcel Baja 10, a beautifully restored retro cinema that reopens as a disco when the films finish; *Dar Ziryab*, nearby at c/Calderería Nueva 11, an Arabic cultural centre that often stages live traditional music; and, just south of Plaza de la Trinidad, *Salsero Mayor*, c/La Paz 20, which specializes in salsa, *merengue* and Latin jazz. The Campo del Príncipe, a square on the eastern slopes of the Alhambra, is another popular drinking haunt, as are the areas around Plaza Nueva, where on weekend evenings throngs of drinkers jam the streets solid, and the Carrera del Darro (running alongside the Río Darro below the Alhambra) – *La Sal*, c/Marqués de Falces, *Pie de la Vela*, a gay and lesbian (but not exclusively so) bar just off Plaza Nueva on Paseo de los Tristes, and *Rincon de San Pedro*, Carrera del Darro, a mixed-music gay bar, are all worth seeking out.

For **flamenco**, one of the most touristy and heavily promoted of shows is *Los Jardines Neptuno*, c/Arabial (near the Parque García Lorca in the south of the city; ☎958 522 533; tickets about €24), best avoided in summer when they bus in the tour groups but better in winter, with an intimate atmosphere and a log fire in the bar. Alternatively *Eshavira*, c/Postigo Cuna (off Gran Vía), is a jazz/flamenco bar with a great atmosphere and live performances.

Sacromonte

Like many cities of Andalucía, Granada has an ancient and still considerable *gitano* population, from whose clans many of Spain's best flamenco guitarists, dancers and singers have emerged. Traditionally the gypsies inhabit cave homes on the **Sacromonte hill**, and many still do, giving displays of *zambras* to the tourists. These can occasionally be good, though more often they're straight-faced and fabulously shameless rip-offs: you're hauled into a cave, leered at if you're female, and systematically extorted of all the money you've brought along (for the dance, the music, the castanets, the watered-down sherry . . .). The simple solution is to take only as much money as you want to part with. Turn up mid-evening; the lines of caves begin off the Camino de Sacramonte, just above the Casa del Chapiz. When the university is in session, several of the cave dwellings are turned into **discos**, packed with students at weekends.

Listings

Airport Granada airport (☎958 245 223) handles domestic flights to Madrid and Barcelona; details from Air Aviaco (☎958 227 592), Air Europa (☎902 240 042) or Iberia (☎958 229 971).

Books, newspapers and maps Metro, c/Gracia 31, off c/Alhóndiga, to the southwest of Plaza de la Trinidad, is the best international bookshop with a wide selection of books on Granada, Lorca etc, plus walking maps. For maps, try also the Librería Dauro at c/Zacatín 3 (a pedestrian street between the cathedral and c/Reyes Católicos) or for a more specialist selection Cartografica del Sur, c/Valle Inclán 2, southwest of the train station. Foreign press is sold by the *kioscos* in Plaza Nueva and Puerta Real.

Bullfights are held in season at the Plaza de Toros, Avda. del Doctor Olóriz 25. The bullring's ticket office (☎958 271 950) or any of the tourist offices has details of upcoming *corridas*.

Car rental Autos Fortuna, c/Infanta Beatriz 2 ☎958 260 254, are a reliable local outfit who undercut the big boys (prices from €36–42 per day). Atesa, c/Rector Marín Ocete 8 ☎958 288 755, has reasonable deals with national back-up.

Football C.F. Granada play in Spain's lower league, Segunda División "B", and tickets are easy to come by in season. The stadium, Nuevo los Cármenes ☎958 253 300, lies northwest of the Hospital Real.

Hospital Cruz Roja (Red Cross), c/Escoriaza 8 ☎958 222 222, or Hospital Clinico San Cecilio, Avda. Dr Olóriz, near the Plaza de Toros ☎958 270 200.

Internet access *Internet*, Plaza de los Girones 3, near the Casa de Los Tiros (Mon–Sat 9am–11pm, Sun 4–11pm; ☎958 289 269; €2.40 per hr, 25-percent discount for *Rough Guide* readers), is Granada's most efficient online operation; they have another branch at c/Buen Suceso 22 ☎958 226 919 (same hours) just off Plaza de la Trinidad.

Laundry Lavandería La Paz, c/La Paz 19, just west of Plaza Trinidad, is Granada's last remaining launderette and will wash, dry and fold 6kg of washing the same day for €7.20.

Police The Policía Nacional are located at c/Duquesa 15 off Plaza Trinidad ☎958 278 300. The Policía Local station is in the *ayuntamiento* building on Plaza del Carmen ☎958 209 461.

Post office Puerta Real; Mon–Fri 9am–8.30pm, Sat 9am–2pm.

Shopping Artesanía El Suspiro, Plaza Santa Ana 1 at the northeast end of Plaza Nueva, has a selection of ceramics from surrounding *granadino* villages, as well as Moroccan pottery and jewellery; its charming Scottish *dueña* is a fund of local information. Castellano, c/Almireceros 6, between c/Elvira and Gran Vía, is the best place to buy jamón serrano and also stocks regional wines and brandies. Traditional perfumes are made by Aromas de Al-Andalus, c/Almireceros 5 (near Castellano above), using ancient Moorish formulas. La Alcena, c/San Jerónimo 3, on the cathedral's north side, is a great place to find the special products of Andalucía, including olive oil, wines, cheeses, *embutidos* and lots more; the friendly proprietor speaks good English. Handmade (on the premises) guitars can be tried out and purchased at a number of shops along the Cuesta de Gomérez, leading to the Alhambra.

Swimming pool Piscina Miami ☎958 250 031, junction c/Arabial and c/Virgen Blanca (west of the centre), has an Olympic-size pool, kids' pool, sunbeds and a good restaurant.

The Sierra Nevada

The mountains of the **Sierra Nevada**, designated Andalucía's second **national park** in 1999, rise to the south of Granada, a startling backdrop to the city, snowcapped for much of the year and offering good trekking and also skiing from late November until late May. The ski slopes are at **Solynieve** ("Sun and Snow", aka Pradollano), an unimaginative, developed resort just 28km away from the city centre. From here, you can make the two- to three-hour trek up to **Veleta** (3470m), the second highest peak of the range (and of the Iberian peninsula); this is a perfectly feasible day-trip from Granada by bus. For more serious enthusiasts, the renowned trek across the sierra is the **Ruta de los Tres Mil**.

The best **map** of the Sierra Nevada including the lower slopes of the Alpujarras (see p.370) is the one co-produced by the Instituto Geográfico Nacional and the Federación Española de Montañismo (1:50,000), which is generally available in Granada. A new 1:40,000 **map and guide set**, *Sierra Nevada and La Alpujarra*, published in English by Editorial Alpina (see "Books", p.1061) is also good. The turismo in Granada can advise on **snow conditions** in the mountains, as can the Sierra Nevada Club (☎958 249 119).

Flora and fauna

The Sierra Nevada is particularly rich in **wild flowers**, with fifty varieties unique to these mountains. **Wildlife** abounds away from the roads; one of the most exciting sights is the *Cabra hispanica*, a wild horned goat which (with luck) you'll see standing on pinnacles, silhouetted against the sky. Bird-watching is also superb, with the colourful hoopoe – a bird with a stark, haunting cry – a common sight.

The Veleta/Mulhacén ascent

The Sierra Nevada is easily accessible from Granada. Throughout the year, Autocares Bonal (☎958 273 100) runs a single daily bus to the Solynieve resort, southeast of the city and, just above this, to the *Parador de Sierra Nevada* (see below). The bus leaves from *Bar Ventorillo*, Paseo Violón, next to the Palacio de Congresos, southeast of the centre (bus #1 going east along Gran Vía, will drop you off very near), from April to September daily at 9am, returning from the *parador* at 5pm and passing the Solynieve ski resort ten minutes later. If there are passengers, the bus will continue the short distance beyond the *parador* to the *Albergue Universitario* (see below). For the winter service (Oct–March) ring the bus company.

With your own transport, take the Acera del Darro east from the Puerta Real and follow the signs for the Sierra Nevada. At the 22km mark and signposted just off the road is the **Sierra Nevada National Park Information Centre** (daily 10.30am–2.30pm & 4.30–7pm; ☎958 340 625), which sells guidebooks, maps and hats (sun protection is vital at this altitude), and has a permanent exhibition on the park's flora and fauna. There's also a pleasant **cafetería** with a stunning terrace view.

From the *parador*, the Capileira road (closed to vehicles) continues to climb and actually runs past the **peak of Veleta**; now asphalted, it is perfectly – and tediously – walkable, but most hikers follow the well-worn shortcuts between the snakes the road is forced to make. With your own transport it's possible to shave a couple of kilometres off the walk to the summit by ignoring the no-entry signs at the car park near to the *Albergue Universitario* and continuing on to a second car park further up the mountain from which point the road is then barred. Although the peak of the mountain looks deceptively close from here, you should allow two to three hours up to the summit and two hours down. As there is no water to be had on the way up you'd be advised to take some along, and the summit makes a great place for a picnic (don't leave rubbish behind). Weather permitting, the **views** beyond the depressing trappings of the ski resort are fabulous: the Sierra Subbética of Córdoba and the Sierra de Guadix to the north, the Mediterranean and Rif Mountains of Morocco to the south, and nearby to the southeast, the towering mass of **Mulhacén** (3479m), the Spanish mainland's highest peak.

With a great deal of energy you could conceivably walk the mountain route all the way to Capileira, though it's a good 30km, there's nothing along the way and temperatures drop pretty low by late afternoon. An hour beyond Veleta you pass just under Mulhacén, two hours of exposed and windy ridge-crawling from the road.

Solynieve

SOLYNIEVE, which lies outside the boundaries of the new national park, is a hideous-looking ski resort regarded by serious Alpine skiers as something of a joke, but with snow lingering so late in the year, it does have obvious attractions. For budget **accommodation** try the modern and comfortable *Albergue Juvenil*, c/Peñones 22 (☎958 480 305, ⓕ958 481 377; ❷; open all year), on the edge of the ski resort, where you can get great-value double and four-bed rooms, all en suite. They also rent out skis and equipment in season. Other places here are incredibly **expensive** in season (and often closed outside it), with even the cheapest doubles priced at around €60. Should you wish to stay in summer, the Granada tourist offices have accommodation lists.

Three kilometres away in isolated Peñones de San Francisco are a couple more options: the *Albergue Universitario* (☎958 481 003, ⓕ958 480 122; ❸, half board; open all year), with bunk rooms, doubles and a restaurant, and the bleakly modern *Parador Sierra Nevada* (☎958 480 661, ⓕ958 480 212; ❺), no longer part of the state *parador* chain, and open only in the ski season. The only **campsite** in this area is at the Ruta del Purche (☎958 340 407; open all year), 15km out of Granada and halfway to Solynieve, with a supermarket and restaurant. The bus will drop you at the road leading to the site (a good kilometre walk).

Ruta Integral de los Tres Mil (High Peaks Traverse)

The classic **Ruta Integral de los Tres Mil**, a complete traverse of all the sierra's peaks over 3000m high, starts in Jerez del Marquesado on the north side of the Sierra Nevada (due south of Guadix) and finishes in Lanjarón, in the Alpujarras; an exhausting three- to four-day itinerary. Taking four days entails overnight stays near Puntal de Vacares, in the Siete Lagunas valley, at the *Refugio de la Caldera*, and at the Cerro Caballo hut. Slightly shorter, and more practicable, variations involve a start from the Vadillo refuge in the Estrella valley (northwest of Vacares), or from Trevélez in the Alpujarras, and a first overnight at Siete Lagunas.

Whichever way you choose, be aware that the section between Veleta and Elorrieta calls for rope, an ice axe (and crampons before June) and good scrambling skills. There is another difficult section between Peñón Colorado and Cerro de Caballo. If you're not up to this, it is possible to **detour** round the Veleta–Elorrieta section, but you will end up on the ridge flanking the Lanjarón river valley on the east rather than on the west; here there is a single cement hut (the *Refugio Forestal*), well placed for the final day's walk to Lanjarón.

For any major **exploration of the Sierra Nevada**, it is essential to take a tent, proper gear and ample food. It's a serious mountain and you should be prepared for the eventuality of not being able to reach or find the huts (which are marked correctly on the 1:50,000 map) or the weather turning nasty.

An easier alternative

The full *Ruta* is probably more than most people – even hardy trekkers – would want to attempt. A modified version, starting in **Trevélez** and ending in **Lanjarón** (with the detour noted above), is more realistic, though still strenuous.

Ascending Mulhacén from Trevélez is a full six hours up, four hours down – assuming that you do not get lost or rest (both unlikely) and that there is no snowpack on Mulhacén's east face (equally unlikely until July). If you decide to try, be prepared for an overnight stop. Heading out of Trevélez, make sure that you begin on the higher track over the Crestón de Posteros, to link up with *acequias* (irrigation channels) coming down from the top of the Río Culo Perro (Dog's Arse River) valley; if you take the main, tempting trail which goes toward Jerez del Marquesado, and then turn into the mouth of the Río Culo Perro, you face unbelievable quagmires and thorn patches. The standard place to **camp** is in the Siete Lagunas valley below the peak, allowing an early-morning ascent to the summit before the mists come up.

Continuing the traverse, you can drop down the west side of Mulhacén (take care on this awkward descent) to the dirt road coming from Veleta. Follow this towards Veleta, and you can turn off the road to spend a second night at the *Refugio de la Caldera* or, 3km further on, at the very basic *Refugio Villa Vientos*. Moving on, to the west, plan on a third night spent at either the *Refugio Elorrieta*, *Refugio Cerro del Caballo*, *Refugio Ventura* or the *Refugio Casa Forestal*, depending on your capabilities.

Las Alpujarras

Beyond the mountains, further south from Granada, lie the great **valleys of the Alpujarras**, first settled in the twelfth century by Berber refugees from Sevilla, and later the Moors' last stronghold in Spain.

The valleys are bounded to the north by the Sierra Nevada, and to the south by the lesser sierras of Lujar, La Contraviesa and Gador. The eternal snows of the high sierras keep the valleys and their seventy or so villages well watered all summer long. Rivers have cut deep gorges in the soft mica and shale of the

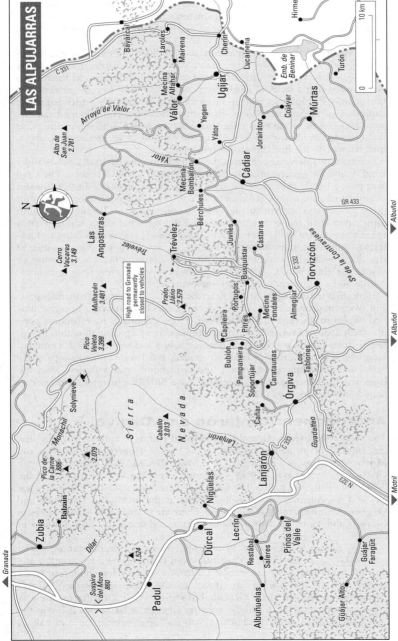

LAS ALPUJARRAS

High road to Granada permanently closed to vehicles

upper mountains, and over the centuries have deposited silt and fertile soil on the lower hills and in the valleys; here the villages have grown, for the soil is rich and easily worked. The intricate terracing that today preserves these deposits was begun as long as 2000 years ago by Visigoths or Ibero-Celts, whose remains have been found at Capileira.

The **Moors** carried on the tradition, and modified the terracing and irrigation in their inimitable way. They transformed the Alpujarras into an earthly paradise, and here they retired to bewail the loss of their beloved lands in *al-Andalus*, resisting a series of royal edicts demanding their forced conversion to Christianity. In 1568 they rose up in a final, short-lived revolt, which led to the expulsion of all Spanish Moors. Even then, however, two Moorish families were required to stay in each village to show the new Christian peasants, who had been marched down from Galicia and Asturias to repopulate the valleys, how to operate the intricate irrigation systems.

Through the following centuries, the land fell into the hands of a few wealthy families, and the general population became impoverished labourers. The Civil War passed lightly over the Alpujarras: the occasional truckload of Nationalist youth trundled in from Granada, rounded up a few bewildered locals, and shot them for "crimes" of which they were wholly ignorant; Republican youths came up in their trucks from Almería and did the same thing. Under Franco the stranglehold of the landlords increased and there was real hardship and suffering. Today, the population has one of the lowest per capita incomes in Andalucía, with – as a recent report put it – "a level of literacy bordering on that of the Third World, alarming problems of desertification, poor communications and a high degree of underemployment".

Ironically, the land itself is still very fertile – oranges, chestnuts, bananas, apples and avocados grow here – while the recent influx of **tourism** is bringing limited wealth to the region. The so-called "High" Alpujarras have become popular with Spanish tourists; Pampaneira, Bubión and Capileira, all within half an hour's drive from Lanjarón, have been scrubbed and whitewashed. Though a little over-prettified, they're far from spoiled, and have acquired shops, lively bars, good unpretentious restaurants and small, family-run *pensiones*. Other villages, less picturesque, or less accessible, have little employment, and are sustained only by farming.

Approaches: Lanjarón and Órgiva

The road **south from Granada to Motril** climbs steeply after leaving the city, until at 860m above sea level it reaches the **Puerto del Suspiro del Moro** – the Pass of the Sigh of the Moor. Boabdil, last Moorish king of Granada, came this way, having just handed over the keys of his city to the Reyes Católicos (see p.352). From the pass you catch your last glimpse of the city and the Alhambra. Just beyond Béznar, is the turning to **Lanjarón** and **Órgiva**, the market town of the region. There are several buses a day from both Granada and Motril to Lanjarón and Órgiva, and one a day from Almería in the east.

There's also a bus (currently 8.30am & 6pm from the main bus station) which goes to Ugíjar, in the "Low" Alpujarras, from Granada, via a less scenic route through Lanjarón, Órgiva, Torvizcón, Cadiar, Yegen and Valor; about four hours to the end of the line. A bus direct to the more spectacular **"High" Alpujarras** leaves the main Granada bus station at 10.30am (terminating at Pitres), noon and 5.15pm daily. It goes via Trevélez as far as Bérchules; in the other direction it leaves Bérchules at 5am and 5pm, passing Trevélez half an hour later, arriving in Granada at 8.45am and 8.45pm respectively (with a service from Pitres to Granada at 3.30pm). Further information on these services is available from the bus operator Alsina Graells (☎958 185 480).

Lanjarón

LANJARÓN has been subject to tourism and the influence of the outside world for longer than anywhere else in the Alpujarras due to the curative powers of its **spa waters**, sold in bottled form throughout Spain. Between March and December the spa baths are open, and the town fills with the aged and infirm. The place itself is little more than a ribbon of buildings, mostly modern, flanking the road through the village, the Avenida Alpujarra, and its continuation, the Avenida Andalucía. Below, marking Lanjarón's medieval status as the gateway to the Alpujarras, is a Moorish castle, now dilapidated and barely visible. A ten-minute stroll reveals its dramatic setting – follow the signs down the hill from the main street and out onto the terraces and meadows below the town.

The countryside and mountains within a day's walk of Lanjarón, however, are beyond compare. Walk up through the backstreets behind the town and you'll come across a track that takes you steeply up to the vast spaces of the **Reserva Nacional de la Sierra Nevada**. For a somewhat easier day's walk out of Lanjarón, go to the bridge over the river just east of town and take the sharply climbing, cobbled track which parallels the **river**. After two to two-and-a-half hours through small farms, with magnificent views and scenery, a downturn to a small stone bridge permits return to Lanjarón on the opposite bank. Allow a minimum of six hours.

Should you wish to try a cure at the **Balneario** on Avenida Alpujarra (open March–Dec), a basic soak will cost about €9, with add-ons for massage, mud baths and all kinds of other alarming-sounding *tracciónes* and *inyecciónes*. Opposite is Lanjarón's semi-official **information kiosk** (open office hours; ☎958 770 282), and midway along the same street is the Alsina Graells **bus terminal**.

Largely to cater for the Balneario's clients, there's no shortage of **hotels** and **pensiones** in the town. The grand-looking *Hotel España*, Avda. Alpujarra 42 (☎ & ⓕ958 770 187; ❹), next door to the *balneario*, is very friendly and has a pool. Further along the road, a signed turnoff leads downhill to the delightful *Apartamentos Castillo Alcadima*, c/General Rodrigo 3 (☎ & ⓕ958 770 809, ⓦwww.castillo-alcadima.es; ❺), which has excellent studio apartments with kitchenette and stunning balcony views over the castle below the town, as well as a pool and pleasant terrace restaurant. The proprietor also hires out mountain bikes and offers horse-riding treks and rock-climbing courses. Towards the east end of town and before the church, *Bar Galvez*, c/Real 95 (☎958 770 087; ❷), offers the cheapest rooms in town and has excellent meals, while 1km east of town, there are peaceful inexpensive en-suite rooms with great views, plus tasty tapas and a €6 *menú*, at the *Venta El Buñuelo* (☎958 770 350; ❷).

Lanjarón has plenty of **restaurants** and tapas bars too, many attached to the hotels. The *Manolete*, c/San Sebastián 3, is much esteemed by the locals for its tapas, while the more expensive *El Club* at Avda. de Andalucía 18 specializes in Alpujarran dishes and is reckoned to serve the best food in town. For seafood (also offering some meat and vegetarian dishes) try *Los Mariscos*, Avda. de La Alpujarra 6, in a small square off the east end of the main street. There's even a **nightclub**, *Noche Azul*, on the corner of the main square, while a new disco-bar, *El Barco*, has opened down a flight of steps opposite.

Órgiva

Eleven kilometres east of Lanjarón is **ÓRGIVA** (also spelled Órjiva), the "capital" of the western Alpujarras. It is closer to the heart of the valley but is still really a starting point; if the bus goes on to Capileira, you may want to stay on it. If you're **driving** it's worth noting that petrol stations become scarcer from this point on.

Órgiva is a lively enough town, though, with a local produce market on Thursdays, and a number of good bars and hotels. On the main street is a sixteenth-century Moorish palace which today houses various shops. A yoga centre, Cortijo Romero, just 1km east of town, is a sign of the times hereabouts; Órgiva, and surrounding farms and villages, are attracting a growing band of expatriate "New Age" Europeans. The **mercado** building in town has wholefood stalls and the occasional juggler, and there's a **tepee village**, "El Beneficio" on the edge of town, where assorted Europeans and their offspring endure freezing winters under canvas.

For budget **accommodation**, one of the nicest places is the pretty *Alma Alpujarreña* (☎958 784 085; ❸), a little beyond the traffic lights at the town's main (and solitary) intersection, with a leafy terrace restaurant. Cheaper rooms are to be had at *Bar El Semáforo* (❷), set a little back from the traffic lights along Avenida Gonzalez Robles, and on the way in there's another decent *hostal*, the recently refurbished *Hostal Mirasol* (☎958 785 159; ❸), which has rooms with and without bath. Órgiva's **campsite** (☎958 784 307; open all year), with a pool, bar and restaurant, lies 2km south of town, reached by continuing along the road where the bus drops you. For **food** both the *Alma Alpujarreña* and the *Hostal Mírasol* do good tapas and reasonable *menús*. The best tapas, though, are at the *Bar El Semáforo*, particularly the *calamares*. For good meals at reasonable prices try the quiet, family-run *Mirasierra* at the bottom of town.

The mountains behind Órgiva form the **Sierra de Lujar**, running into the **Sierra la Contraviesa**. The whole range of hills on the south side of the valley was once densely forested, indeed many years ago the whole of the Alpujarras was well covered with trees. But in 1980 a great forest fire swept for miles along the hillsides, scorching the life from the trees but leaving the wood undamaged; tens of thousands of acres of forest were ruined overnight. It's alleged that a pulp paper company paid hoodlums to start the fire – the next day they were buying up the dead trees at a fraction of the real price.

Houses in the Alpujarras

Houses in the valleys are built of grey stone, flat-roofed and low; whitewashing them is a recent innovation. The coarse walls are about 750cm thick, for summer coolness and protection from winter storms. Stout beams of chestnut, or ash in the lower valleys, are laid from wall to wall; on top of these is a mat of canes or split chestnut; upon this flat stones are piled, and on the stones is spread a layer of *launa*, the crumbly grey mica found on the tops of the Sierra Nevada. It must, and this maxim is still observed today, be laid during the waning of the moon for the *launa* to settle properly and thus keep rain out. Gerald Brenan wrote in *South from Granada* of a particularly ferocious storm: "As I peered through the darkness of the stormy night, I could make out a dark figure on every roof in the village, dimly lit by an esparto torch, stamping clay into the holes in the roof."

The High (Western) Alpujarras

The best way to experience the **High Alpujarras** is to walk, and there are a number of paths between Órgiva and Cadiar, at the furthest reaches of the western valleys (see box, below). Equip yourself with a compass and the Instituto Geográfico Nacional/Federación Española de Montañismo 1:50,000 map or the Editorial Alpina map (see p.26), which cover all the territory from Órgiva up to Bérchules (Alpina) and Berja (IGN/FEM) respectively. Alternatively, a bus leaves daily from Lanjarón at 1pm and winds through all the upper Alpujarran villages; hitching, too, is generally good in these rural areas, though cars are few and far between.

Cañar, Soportújar and Carataunas

Heading on from Órgiva, the first settlements you reach, almost directly above the town, are **CAÑAR** and **SOPORTÚJAR**, the latter a maze of sinuous white-walled alleys. Like many of the High Alpujarran villages, they congregate on the neatly terraced mountainside, planted with poplars and laced with irrigation channels. Both have bars where you can get a **meal** and Soportújar can provide excellent-value en-suite **rooms** for the night; ask at *Bar Correillo* (☎958 787 578; ❷) on c/Real (behind the church). Both villages are perched precariously on the steep hillside with a rather sombre view of Órgiva in the valley below, and the mountains of Africa over the ranges to the south. Just below the two villages, the tiny hamlet of **CARATAUNAS** is particularly pretty, and offers a comfortable place to stay, *El Montañero* (☎958 787 528; ❺), which has a pool and offers a variety of activities, such as mountain-biking, horse-riding and mountain walks. Two kilometres out of Carataunas a turn-off on the left (signed "*Camino Forestal*") beyond the *Los Llanos* restaurant ascends 6km (the last three a rugged unpaved track) to the Buddhist monastery of Osel Ling (see below).

The Poqueira Gorge and up to Capileira

Shortly after Carataunas the road swings to the north, and you have your first view of the **Poqueira Gorge**, a huge sheer gash into the heights of the Sierra

---

Trekking in the Alpujarras

Half a century ago the **Camino Real** (Royal Way), a mule track that threaded through all the high villages, was the only access into the Alpujarras. Today the little that's left is quiet, used only by the occasional local mule or foreign walker. At their best, Alpujarran paths follow mountain streams, penetrate thick woods of oak, chestnut and poplar, or cross flower-spangled meadows; in their bad moments they deteriorate to incredibly dusty firebreaks, forestry roads or tractor tracks, or (worse) dead-end in impenetrable thickets of bramble and nettle. Progress is slow, grades are sharp and the heat (from mid-June to Sept) is taxing. A reasonable knowledge of Spanish is a big help.

For the determined, the most rewarding **sections of treks** include:

Pitres to Mecina Fondales: Twenty minutes' trek, and then a good hour-plus from neighbouring Ferreirola to Busquistar.

Busquistar towards Trevélez: One hour's trek, and then two-plus hours of road walking.

Pórtugos towards Trevélez: Two hours' trek, meeting the tarmac a little beyond the end of the Busquistar route.

Trevélez to Berchules: Four hours' trek, but the middle two hours is dirt track.

Trevélez to Juviles: Three hours' trek, including some sections of firebreak.

Nevada. Trickling deep in the bed of the cleft is the Río Poqueira, which has its source near the peak of Mulhacén. The steep walls of the gorge are terraced and wooded from top to bottom, and dotted with little stone farmhouses. Much of the surrounding country looks barren from a distance, but close up you'll find that it's rich with flowers, woods, springs and streams.

A trio of villages – three of the most spectacular and popular in the Alpujarras – teeters on the steep edge of the gorge among their terraces. The first is **PAMPANEIRA**, neat, prosperous and pretty. On its leafy main square is Nevadensis, an **information centre** (Mon & Tues 10am–3pm, Wed–Sat 10am–2pm & 4–6pm, Sun 10am–3pm; ☎958 763 127, ⒲www.nevadensis.com) for the Natural and National Parks of the Sierra Nevada; they also offer horse-riding tours and **guided treks** including an ascent of Mulhacén. The same square also has a number of bars, restaurants and **pensiones**; try *Casa Diego* by the fountain (☎958 763 015; ❷), or the plusher *Hostal Ruta del Mulhacen* (☎958 763 010, Ⓕ958 763 010; ❸) at the entry to the village for rooms with bath. A weaving workshop just down the hill specializes in traditional *alpujarreño* designs.

Above Pampaneira, on the very peak of the western flank of the Poqueira Gorge, is the **Tibetan Buddhist Monastery of Osel Ling** ("Place of Clear Light"), founded in 1982 by a Tibetan monk on land donated by the communities of Pampaneira and Bubión. Three years later, in 1985, a baby born to Spanish parents in Granada was recognised by the Dalai Lama as the reincarnation of the former head lama – one Yeshé – and the youth is currently undergoing training under the Dalai Lama in the Himalayas. The simple stone-built monastery complete with stupas and stunning **views** across the Alpujarras welcomes visitors between 3 and 6pm daily; lectures on Buddhism are held regularly and facilities exist for those who want to visit for periods of retreat in cabins dotted around the site (☎958 343 134 for details).

BUBIÓN is the next of the three villages up the hill, backed for much of the year by snowcapped peaks. The village now has a private **museum**, the Casa Alpujarreña, just off Plaza de la Iglesia, the main square (daily except Tues 11am–2pm, Sat & Sun also 5–7pm; €1.80), displaying aspects of the folklore, daily life and architecture of the Alpujarras in a traditional house. For **places to stay**, there's a fancy hotel, *Villa Turística del Poqueira* (☎958 763 111, Ⓕ958 763 136; ❼) with its own restaurant, and a comfortable *pensión*, *Las Terrazas* (☎958 763 034, Ⓕ958 763 252; ❸), which also has some excellent apartments (☎958 763 217; ❹) downhill at c/Parras that come with terrace, kitchen and satellite TV; the proprietors also rent out **mountain bikes**. A decent **restaurant**, *La Artesa*, at c/Carretera 2, turns out *alpujarreño* specialities and has an economical *menú*. There is also a ranch, *Dallas*, 2km above the village, which will arrange **horse-riding trips** of from one to five days for groups with a guide (☎958 763 038). The private **tourist office**, Rustic Blue (☎958 763 381, ⒲www.rusticblue.com; English spoken), on the main road to the right as you enter the village, can also book horse-riding and walking tours and help with accommodation in fully equipped houses across the Alpujarras (minimum two nights' stay; from around €310 per week).

Capileira

CAPILEIRA is the highest of the three villages and the terminus of the road – Europe's highest, but now closed to traffic – across the heart of the Sierra Nevada from Granada (see p.368). In addition to the direct daily afternoon **bus** from Granada, continuing to Murtas and Bérchules, anything going to Ugíjar and Berja will come very close to Capileira; the bus out to Granada currently passes by at 6.20am, 3.50pm and 6.20pm.

The **kiosco** at the centre of the village near where the bus drops you hands out a **village map**, sells newspapers and large-scale walking maps, and acts as an information office. Just downhill from here lies the village's **museum**, containing displays of regional dress and handicrafts, as well as various bits and pieces belonging to, or produced by, Pedro Alarcón, the nineteenth-century Spanish writer who made a trip through the Alpujarras and wrote a (not very good) book about it. There are numerous **places to stay and eat**. One of the quietest places in town, well away from the main road, is the *Fonda Restaurante El Tilo*, Plaza Calvario (☎958 763 181; ❷), which also does a *menú*. Further uphill the pleasant *Finca Los Llanos* (☎958 763 071, ☞958 763 206; ❺) has apartment-style rooms with kitchenette and terrace together with its own pool and a good restaurant, while the *Mesón-Hostal Poqueira* (☎ & ☞958 763 048; ❸) near the bus stop has en-suite heated rooms, and also offers a substantial *menú* for around €6 in its terrace restaurant at the rear. Near the church, the *Casa Ibero* (aka the *Mesón Alpujarreón*) serves excellent food and has vegetarian options.

Capileira is a handy base for easy **day walks** in the Poqueira Gorge. For a not-too-strenuous example, take the northernmost of three paths below the village, each with bridges across the river. This sets off from alongside the *Pueblo Alpujarreño* villa complex. The path winds through the huts and terraced fields of the river valley above Capileira, ending after about an hour and a half at a dirt track within sight of a power plant at the head of the valley. You can either retrace your steps or cross the stream over a bridge to follow a dirt track back to the village. In May and June, the fields are tended – laboriously and by hand – as the steep slopes dictate. Reasonably clear paths or tracks also lead to **Pampaneira** (2–3hr, follow lower path to the bridge below Capileira), continuing to Carataunas (1hr, mostly road) and Órgiva (45min, easy path) from where you can get a bus back. In the other direction, taking the Sierra Nevada road and then the first major path to the right, by a ruined stone house, you can reach **Pitres** (2hr), Pórtugos (30min more) and Busquístar (45min). Going in the same direction but taking the second decent-sized path (by a sign encouraging you to "conserve and respect nature"), **Trevélez** is some five hours away – you can also get to Pórtugos this way. More fine walking routes in this zone are detailed in *Landscapes of Andalucía* by John and Christine Oldfield and the *Discovery Walking Guide* (see "Books", p.1061).

Along the High Route to Trevélez

PITRES and **PÓRTUGOS**, the next two villages on the High Route, are perhaps more "authentic" and less polished. You're more likely to find rooms here during the summer months, while all around spreads some of the best Alpujarran walking country. For **accommodation** in Pitres try the *Fonda Sierra Nevada* (☎958 766 017; ❷), on the main square; they also rent out apartments nearby with *salón*, kitchen and bath (❸). On the village's eastern edge the *Refugio de los Albergues* (☎958 766 004; ❶) is an old Civil War hostel with very cheap dormitory beds and cooking facilities. Close by, and on the main road, *El Jardín* is a British-run restaurant with garden terrace, great views and an eclectic vegetarian menu. Pitres's **campsite**, *Balcón de Pitres* (☎958 766 111; March–Oct), with restaurant and pool, is located in a stunning position 1km west of the village. Pórtugos has the *Hostal Mirador* (☎958 766 014; ❸), on the main square, and a *fonda* (❷) at Los Castaños, 1km east.

Down below the main road (GR421) linking Pitres and Pórtugos are the three villages of Mecina Fondales (and its offshoot Mecinilla), Ferreirola and Busquístar; along with Pitres, these formed a league of villages known as the

Taha under the Moors. **FERREIROLA** and **BUSQUISTAR** are especially attractive, as is the path between the two, clinging to the north side of the valley of the Río Trevélez. You're out of tourist country here and the villages display their genuine characteristics to better effect. In Busquistar there's an **inn**, the *Hostal Mirador de la Alpujarra* (① & ⑤958 857 470; ④), just uphill from the church, with great views and a restaurant. **MECINILLA** also has a charming *hostal*, *L'Atelier*, c/Alberca s/n (① & ⑤958 857 501, ⑥mecinilla@yahoo.com; ④), in traditional dwellings; it's run by a friendly French chef who prepares outstanding dishes in the adjoining vegetarian **restaurant**.

TREVÉLEZ, at the end of an austere ravine carved by the Río Trevélez, is purportedly Spain's highest permanent settlement, with cooler temperatures year-round than its neighbours. In traditional Alpujarran style it has lower, middle and upper quarters (*barrios bajo, medio* and *alto*) overlooking a grassy, poplar-lined valley where the river starts its long descent. The village is well provided with **hostales**; if you are susceptible to low temperatures, outside July and August you may want a place with efficient heating. In the *barrio medio*, *Hostal Fernando* (①958 858 565; ③) is friendly and has heated rooms, as does the comfortable *Hotel La Fragua*, c/Antonio 4 (①958 858 626, ⑤958 858 614; ④), in the *barrio alto*, which has an excellent restaurant. Another **place to eat** is the *Río Grande*, down near the bridge, which serves good, solid mountain food and is often the only place open in the evening. Trevélez's *jamón serrano* is a prized speciality and an obsession throughout Andalucía, and good places to try it here include *Mesón del Jamón* above the Plaza de la Iglesia or *Mesón Joaquín* in the lower *barrio*.

Although Capileira is probably the more pleasant base, Trevélez is traditionally the jump-off point for the **high sierra peaks** (to which there is a bona fide path) and for treks across the range (on a lower, more conspicuous track). The latter begins down by the bridge on the eastern side of the village. After skirting the bleak Horcajo de Trevélez (3182m), and negotiating the Puerto de Trevélez (2800m), the path drops gradually down along the north flank of the Sierra Nevada to Jerez del Marquesado (see the "Ruta de los Tres Mil", p.369).

East from Trevélez

Heading east from Trevélez, you come to **JUVILES**, an attractive town straddling the road. At its centre is an unwhitewashed, peanut-brittle-finish church with a clock that's usually running slow (like most things round here). A single all-in-one *fonda-restaurante-store*, *Bar Fernandez* (①958 769 168; ②; meals on demand), is simple and very friendly, with great views from the second floor east over the valley to Cadiar. *Pensión Tino* (①958 769 174; ③), a little back along the main street, has rooms with bath and serves *raciones*.

BÉRCHULES, a high village of grassy streams and chestnut woods, lies only 4km beyond Juviles, but a greater contrast can hardly be imagined. It is a large, abruptly demarcated settlement, three streets wide, on a sharp slope overlooking yet another canyon. For **accommodation** the *Fonda-Restaurante Carayol*, c/Iglesia 18 below the church (aka *Pensión Resu*; ①958 769 092; ②), has rooms with bath; *La Posada* (①958 852 541; ③), on the central Plaza Victoria (aka Plaza Abastos), is another possibility; and on the main road the more expensive *Hotel Bérchules* (① & ⑤958 852 530; ⑤) has comfortable rooms above its own restaurant. For **food**, *Bar Vaqueras*, also on Plaza Victoria, does decent tapas, and there's an excellent grocery in the village – a godsend if you're planning on doing any walking out of here, since most village shops in the Alpujarras are rather primitive.

Just below Bérchules, **CADIAR**, the central town of the Alpujarras, is more attractive than it seems from a distance, and there are a handful of **hostales** and *camas* if you want to stay. The friendly *Hostal Montoro*, c/San Isidro 20 (☎958 768 068; ❷), near the central plaza, has excellent-value en-suite heated rooms, while for **food**, the very good *Bar-Restaurante La Pará de La Suerte*, near the petrol station as you come in from Bérchules, is owned by the same people. There's a colourful **produce market** on the 3rd and 18th of every month, sometimes including livestock, and from October 5 to 9 the **Fuente del Vino** wine and cattle fair takes place, turning the waters of the fountain literally to wine.

Cadiar and Bérchules mark the end of the western Alpujarras, and a striking change in the landscape; the dramatic, severe, but relatively green terrain of the Guadalfeo and Cadiar valleys gives way to open rolling land that's much more arid, a prelude to the deserts of Almería that lie ahead.

Eastern Alpujarras

The villages of the eastern Alpujarras display many of the characteristics of those to the west but as a rule they are poorer and much less visited by tourists. There are vineyards on the hills in the south of this region and the good dry red wine available in most of the Alpujarran villages, west or east, is always worth asking for.

Yegen and Ugíjar

In **YEGEN**, some 7km northeast of Cadiar, there's a plaque on the house (just along from the central fountain) where **Gerald Brenan** lived during his ten or so years of Alpujarran residence. His autobiography of these times, *South from Granada*, is the best account of rural life in Spain between the wars, and describes the visits made here by Virginia Woolf, Bertrand Russell and the arch-complainer Lytton Strachey. Disillusioned with the strictures of middle-class life in England after World War I, Brenan rented a house in Yegen and shipped out a library of 2000 books, from which he was to spend the next eight years educating himself. He later moved to the hills behind Torremolinos, where he died in 1987, a writer better known and respected in Spain (he made an important study of St John of the Cross) than in his native England.

Brenan connections aside, Yegen is still one of the most characteristic Alpujarran villages, with its two distinct quarters, cobbled paths and cold-water springs. It has a **fonda**, *Bar La Fuente* (☎958 851 067; ❷), opposite the fountain in the square, or there are rooms with bath at *El Tinao* (☎958 851 212; ❸), on the main road. Heading east out of the village, more upmarket accommodation is available at *El Rincón de Yegen* (☎958 851 270; ❹), where heated rooms come with TV and where there are apartments (❻) for longer stays, as well as a pool and good restaurant with an economical *menú*.

UGÍJAR, 12km on from Yegen, is the largest community of this eastern zone, and an unassuming, quiet market town. There are easy and enjoyable walks to the nearest villages (up the valley to Mecina-al-Fahar, for example), and plenty of **places to stay**: try the relatively luxurious *Pensión Pedro*, c/Fabrica, near the church (☎958 767 149; ❸), which has en-suite rooms and a restaurant, or *Hostal Vidaña* (☎958 767 010, 🖷958 854 004; ❸), nearby on the Almería road, with a terrace restaurant. There is a **bus** service on to Almería (3hr).

The southern ranges

The tiny hamlets of the southern Alpujarras have an unrivalled view of the Mediterranean, the convexity of the hills obscuring the awful development that mars the coast. There are few villages of any size, but the hills host the principal **wine-growing district** of the Alpujarras. For a taste of the best of its wine, try the *venta* (wine shop) at Haza del Lino (Plain of Linen); the house brew is a full-bodied rosé.

Inland towards Almería: Guadix

An alternative **route from Granada to Almería** runs via **GUADIX**, a crumbling old Moorish town with a vast and extraordinary cave district. This, the **Barrio Santiago**, still houses some 10,000 people and it's well worth a stop.

The quarter extends over a square mile or so in area, just beyond the ruined **Alcazaba** (Mon–Fri 9am–2pm & 4–7pm, Sat 9am–2pm; €0.60), which is signposted as you come into the old walled part of town and is entered from the adjoining theological school. The entrance to the Barrio is behind the whitewashed church of Santiago. The lower caves, on the outskirts, are really proper cottages with upper storeys, electricity, television and running water. But as you walk deeper into the suburb, the design quickly becomes simpler – just a whitewashed front, a door, a tiny window and a chimney. Penetrating right to the back you'll come upon a few caves which are no longer used: too squalid, too unhealthy, their long-unrepainted whitewash a dull brown. Yet right next door there may be a similar, occupied hovel, with a family sitting outside and other figures following dirt tracks still deeper into the hills. A **Cueva Museo** opposite the church of San Miguel, in Plaza Padre (Mon–Sat 10am–2pm & 5–7pm, Sun 10am–2pm; €1.20), provides insight into cave culture, with intriguing reconstructions of troglodytic life.

Guadix itself is a pleasant, modest old place with an impressive sixteenth-century red-sandstone **cathedral** (Mon–Sat 10am–1pm & 4–6pm; €1.20) a grand Plaza Mayor and some good-looking mansions. A map from the **turismo**, Ctra. de Granada just west of the cathedral (Mon–Fri 8am–3pm; ☎958 662 665) will help you find your way around. There's little in the way of budget **accommodation**, but you could try the *Hotel Mulhacen* on c/Buenos Aires, the main road into town from the north (☎958 660 750, ℱ958 660 661; ●). If you can afford the extra, however, you should stay at the *Hotel Comercio*, c/Mira de Amezcua 3, east of the imposing cathedral (☎958 660 500, ℱ958 665 072; ●), an elegant and refurbished turn-of-the-twentieth-century hotel. For **food**, the *Hotel Comercio* has an excellent restaurant with a good-value *menú*. Otherwise try the Plaza de Naranjos, a stone's throw east of the cathedral, where there are plenty of popular eating places, such as *Cafetería Hawaii*, serving up tapas and *raciones* as well as hamburgers and an economical *menú*.

Buses run direct from Granada to Guadix (Empresa Autodia from c/Rector Marín). The bus station in Guadix is a five-minute walk outside the walls. Guadix's **train station**, 2km north-east of the centre along the Murcia road, is served by four daily trains (in each direction) from Granada and Almería.

On from Guadix

En route towards Almería you pass through more of the strange, tufa-pocked landscape from which the Guadix caves are hewn. The main landmark, 16km beyond Guadix, is a magnificent sixteenth-century castle on a hill above the village of **La Calahorra**. One of the finest in Spain with a remarkable Renaissance patio within, it's open Wednesdays only (10am–4pm & 4–6pm; free); outside these times visit the guardian's house – avoiding siesta time – at c/de los Claveles 2, and he will open it up for a consideration. Guadix–Almería buses normally follow the train line, along the minor N324 over the last section. If you're driving, you might want to keep going straight on the main road, meeting the Almería–Sorbas road at what has become known as **Mini Hollywood** (see p.384), the preserved film set of *A Fistful of Dollars*.

Almería Province

The **province of Almería** is a strange corner of Spain. Inland it has an almost **lunar landscape** of desert, sandstone cones and dried-up riverbeds. On the coast it's still largely unspoiled; lack of water and roads frustrated development in the 1960s and 1970s and it is only now beginning to take off. A number of **good beaches** are accessible by bus, and in this hottest province of Spain they're worth considering during what would be the "off season" elsewhere, since Almería's summers start well before Easter and last into November. In midsummer it's incredibly hot (frequently touching 100°F/38°C in the shade), while all year round there's an intense, almost luminous, sunlight. This and the weird scenery have made Almería one of the most popular film locations in Europe – much of *Lawrence of Arabia* was shot here, along with scores of spaghetti westerns.

Almería

ALMERÍA is a pleasant, modern city, spread at the foot of a stark grey mountain. At the summit is a tremendous **Alcazaba** (daily 9am–8.30pm; Oct–Mar closes 6pm; €1.50, free for EU citizens), probably the best surviving example of Moorish military fortification, with three huge walled enclosures, in the second of which are the remains of a mosque, converted to a chapel by the Reyes Católicos. In the eleventh century, when Almería was an independent kingdom and the wealthiest, most commercially active city of Spain, this citadel contained immense gardens and palaces and some 20,000 people. Its grandeur was reputed to rival the court of Granada but comparisons are impossible since little beyond the walls and towers remains, the last remnants of stuccowork having been sold off by the locals in the eighteenth century.

From the Alcazaba, however, you do get a good view of the coast, of Almería's **cave quarter** – the Barrio de la Chanca on a low hill to the left – and of the city's strange fortified **Cathedral** (Mon–Fri 10am–4.30pm, Sat 10am–1pm, Sun service hours; €1.80), built in the sixteenth century at a time when the southern Mediterranean was terrorized by the raids of Barbarossa and other Turkish and North African pirate forces; its corner towers once held cannons. There's little else to do in town, and your time is probably best devoted to sampling the cafés, tapas bars and *terrazas* in the streets circling the Puerta de Purchena, the focal junction of the modern town, and strolling along the main Paseo de Almería down towards the harbour, and taking day-trips out to the beaches along the coast. The city's own **beach**, southeast of the centre beyond the train lines, is long but dismal.

Practicalities

The **turismo** (Mon–Fri 9am–7pm, Sat 10am–2pm; ☎950 274 355) is on c/Parque de Nicolás Salmerón facing the commercial harbour. They have a list of most buses out of Almería in all directions, as well as train and boat schedules. Almería's gleaming new international **airport** is 8km out of town with a

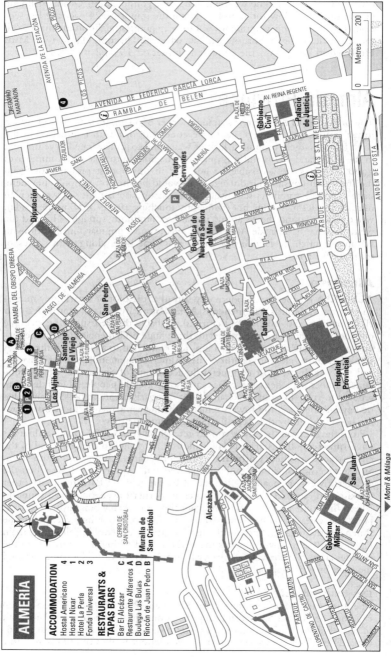

▲ Bus & Train Stations

ALMERÍA

ACCOMMODATION
Hostal Americano 4
Hostal Nixar 1
Hotel La Perla 2
Fonda Universal 3

RESTAURANTS & TAPAS BARS
Bar El Alcázar C
Restaurante Alfareros A
Bodega Las Bolas D
Rincón de Juan Pedro B

Motril & Málaga ▼

The landscape of Almería

The **landscape of Almería**, like much of southern Spain, is dominated by mountain chains composed of hard, ancient rocks, separated by lower-lying basins filled with younger, softer rocks. The highest mountains – the Sierra Nevada, Sierra de Gádor, Sierra de Baza and the Sierra de los Filabres, which reach altitudes of over 2000 metres – were created by the collision of the African and Eurasian tectonic plates which took place at around the same time as the Alps were being formed, ending some ten million years ago. The basins between the mountain ranges were once below sea level and rivers cut into them, leading to the creation of the stunning landscapes that we see today.

Almería is also one of the driest parts of Europe, with an average rainfall of only 250–300mm per year. When rainfall does occur, however, it can be of very high intensity: the storms which swept the region in the winter of 1993 deposited 247mm of rain in just four days, causing flash flooding and severe erosion of hill slopes – something the region is prone to with its semi-arid climate and relatively sparse vegetation cover.

The landscape which most vividly illustrates the interaction between tectonic uplift and erosion is the area of "badlands" to the west of **Tabernas**, which can be best viewed from the road behind Mini Hollywood leading up to the radio mast on the summit of the Sierra Alhamilla. The badlands have been caused by tributaries of the Tabernas and Gérgal rivers cutting into soft limestone and sandstone deposits between the Sierra Alhamilla and Sierra de los Filabres. As the basin was uplifted, so the rivers cut deeper into the landscape, creating the stunning setting used by numerous Almería-made Westerns.

There are also a number of excellent raised beaches near **Mojácar** and **La Garrucha**, which were once at sea level but have been uplifted by tectonic movements to heights of several metres above the present beach. You'll have to be quick to see them, however, as many of the better sites are being progressively bulldozed to make way for villa developments.

connecting bus service (#14, labelled "El Alquián") every half-hour from the junction of the Avenida Federico García Lorca and c/Gregorio Marañon (just above the top right corner of our city map). There is also a **daily boat to Melilla** on the Moroccan coast throughout the summer (less often out of season), a six-hour journey which can pay dividends in both time and money over Algeciras if you're driving – information from Transmediterránea, Parque Nicolás Salmerón 19, near the port (℡950 263 714).

Rooms are not normally difficult to come by at any time of the year, and a good place to start looking is around the Puerta de Purchena, the hub of the modern town. Just off this intersection, the recently refurbished *Hotel La Perla*, Plaza del Carmen 7 (℡950 238 877, ℻950 275 816; ❻), is Almería's oldest hotel. Just behind is a cheaper option, *Hostal Nixar*, c/Antonio Vico 24 (℡ & ℻950 237 255; ❹); ask for a high, airy room. On the square itself, the atmospheric *Fonda Universal*, Puerta de Purchena 3 (℡950 235 557; ❷), with a fabulous foyer staircase from its previous incarnation as a minor *casa señorial*, is very basic but clean, while close to the bus station, *Hostal Americano*, Avda. de la Estación 6 (℡950 258 011; ❹), is handily placed if you're arriving on a late bus. The *Albergue Juvenil Almería*, c/Isla de Fuerteventura s/n (℡950 269 788; ❷), is a swish new 150-double-roomed affair on the east side of town next to the Estadio Juventud sports arena; take bus #1 from the junction of Avenida Federico García Lorca and c/Gregorio Marañon. The nearest **campsite**, *La Garrofa* (℡950 235 770; open all year), is on the coast at La Garrofa, some 5km west, easily reached by the buses to Aguadulce and Roquetas de Mar (℡950 343 809; open all year).

When it comes to **eating** and **drinking**, the Puerta de Purchena is a great place to head for, particularly at night. On the north side, in a small street, *Restaurante Alfareros*, c/Marcos 6, has an excellent-value *menú* for around €6. On the opposite side of the junction, there's a popular *marisquería*, *Bar El Alcázar*, Paseo de Almería 4, with plenty of tapas possibilities. Just in from here, you'll find an alley, c/Tenor Iribarne, filled with tables from many other tapas establishments and, close by, *Bodegas Las Botas*, c/Fructuoso Perez 3, is well worth seeking out. Alternatively, the *Rincón de Juan Pedro*, Plaza del Carmen, is one of the town's better restaurants, serving top-quality Almerian specialities. For **bars**, try the streets around Plaza Masnou off the southern end of the Alameda.

Inland: Mini Hollywood

Rather livelier than the eastern resorts is the strip of coast between Carboneras and La Garrucha, centred on the town of Mojácar. This is some way up the coast and to get there you'll have to travel through some of Almería's distinctive desert scenery (see box, p.383). There are two possible routes: via Níjar to Carboneras, or via Tabernas and Sorbas to Mojácar.

NÍJAR is a neat, white and typically Almerían town, with narrow streets designed to give maximum shade, and it makes a good base from which to explore the coast. There are two or three small **hostales**; try *Montes*, Avda. García Lorca 26 (☎951 360 157; ➋), with en-suite rooms, a *comedor* on the main road into town. For **food**, further up the same street *Casa Pedro* is a very good bar-restaurant and there are more tapas and *raciones* bars in the upper square beyond the church.

The most dramatic landscapes, however, lie further north, between **TABER-NAS** and **SORBAS**. Both towns look extraordinary, especially Sorbas, whose houses overhang an ashen gorge, but neither is really a place to linger – this is the middle of a desert. Just outside Tabernas, in a particularly gulch-riven landscape, is **Mini Hollywood** (daily: July–Sept 10am–9pm; Oct–June 10am–7pm; €9 or €14.50 including zoo; reductions for kids), the set of the spaghetti western *A Fistful of Dollars* and various other movies. This has been preserved and opened up as a tourist attraction: you can wander into the saloon for a drink, and three times a day in season (noon, 5pm & 8pm) the fantasy is carried a step further with an acted-out "show" including a mock bank raid. The complex has now also added a somewhat incongruous **zoo**, featuring birds and reptiles as well as lions and other big cats prowling depressingly small cages.

The beaches

Almería's best **beaches** lie on its eastern coast; those to the west of the city, particularly Aguadulce and Roquetas de Mar, have already been exploited and although they're not quite as bad as many on the Costa del Sol, they're not a lot better either. Either place is an easy day-trip, however, with hourly buses along the coast. The eastern stretch of the Almerian coastline offers some of the most relaxing beaches left in Spain: half-abandoned fishing communities which have only recently begun to be promoted for tourists. Outside the centres of Mojácar and San José development is low-key and with a short walk along the coast you should be able to find plenty of relatively secluded spots to lay your towel.

El Cabo de Gata and San José

Heading east, the closest resort with any appeal is the modest **EL CABO DE GATA**, where there is a lovely expanse of coarse sand. Five buses a day run between here and Almería, making an intermediate stop at Retamar, a retirement/holiday development. Arriving at El Cabo, you pass a lake, the **Laguna de Rosa**, protected by a conservation society and home to flamingos and other waders throughout the summer. Around the resort are plentiful bars, cafés and shops, plus a fish market. **Accommodation** is limited and in high season often impossible to find; the two *hostales* (③) above the bars *Playa* and *Mediterráneo* (☎950 371 137) on the beach are both quite expensive for basic accommodation. The new *Hostal Las Dunas*, c/Barrionnuevo 58 (☎950 370 072; ⑤), set back from the beach, is an even pricier option for en-suite rooms. Nearby there's a campsite, *Cabo de Gata* (☎950 160 443; open all year) with its own pool and restaurant. The beach gets windy in the afternoons, and it's a deceptively long walk eastwards to **Las Salinas** (The Salt Pans – exactly that) for a bar and café.

Beyond lies **SAN JOSÉ**, also reached by bus from Almería. This is an established and popular resort, set back from a sandy beach in a small cove, with shallow water, and fine beaches within walking distance. **Accommodation**, however, can be hard to come by in summer. *Casa de Huéspedes Costa Rica* (☎950 380 103; ③), on the main road a little way out, is one of the most inexpensive and also serves a reasonable *menú. Hostal Bahia*, c/Correos 5 (☎950 380 114; ⑤), is a comfortable modern *hostal* in the centre, and the more upmarket *Hotel Las Gaviotas* on the way into the village (☎950 380 010; ⑥) has decent en-suite rooms. You'll also find a good **campsite**, *Camping Tau* (☎950 380 166; April–Oct), close to the beach. There are again numerous excellent bars, restaurants and cafés, and a well-stocked supermarket.

Next along the coast is **LOS ESCULLOS**, with a reasonable beach and a pleasant, if slightly overpriced, beachfront hotel-restaurant, *Casa Emilio* (☎950 389 761; ⑤). Two kilometres further east, **LA ISLETA** is another fishing town, with a sleepy atmosphere, a sandy beach and a **hostal** overlooking the harbour, *Hostal Isleta de Moro* (☎951 389 713; ④); this reasonably priced place has a popular **bar-restaurant** for tapas and meals. At **LAS NEGRAS**, 5km further on, there's a cove with a pebbly beach and a few bars and restaurants; there's a brand-new **hostal**, *Arrecife* (☎950 388 140; ④), close to the village *estanco*; if it's full, you can enquire here about a room in a private house or renting an apartment nearby.

Mojácar

MOJÁCAR, Almería's main and growing resort, takes its name from the ancient hill village which lies a couple of kilometres back from the sea, a striking agglomeration of white cubist houses wrapped round a harsh outcrop of rock. In the 1960s, when the main Spanish *costas* were being developed, this was virtually a ghost town, its inhabitants having long since taken the only logical step and emigrated. The town's fortunes suddenly revived, however, when the local mayor, using the popularity of other equally barren spots in Spain as an example, offered free land to anyone willing to build within a year. The bid was a modest success, attracting one of the decade's multifarious "artist colonies", and now, twenty years later, they are quickly being joined by package-holiday firms and second-home professionals. A plush new 280-room hotel has opened, as well as a *parador* on the beach, and a burgeoning foreign jet set now lives here for half the year and migrates in summer.

If you want to stay in the **upper village** there are a handful of small

hostales; try *Casa Justa*, c/Morote 5 (☎950 478 372; ❹), or the cheaper *La Esquinica* on nearby c/Cano (☎950 475 009; ❸). For cheap **eats** up here, *Rincón de Embrujo*, on the plazuela fronting the church, does a good-value *menú*. Down at **the beach**, there's a good **campsite**, *El Cantal de Mojácar* (☎950 478 204; open all year), rooms to let and several *hostales*. Among the **hotels**, try either the good-value *Puntazo* (☎951 478 229, ℻951 478 285; ❺), to the south of the *centro comercial* on the seafront, or the nearby *Hostal Bahía* (☎951 478 010; ❹), with rooms around a pleasant patio. The modern and rather dull *Parador Reyes Católicos* (☎950 478 250, ℻950 478 183; ❽) is set in a palm-tree landscape right by the beach. For a decent no-frills **meal**, head for the *Cafetería Rosa*, facing the south side of the *centro comercial*. Other restaurants, mostly of indifferent quality, are to be found along the seafront, where you'll also find lots of fine beach **bars** (currently a little overwhelmed by Spanish techno). **Nightlife** happens all along the beach strip throughout the summer and it's fun just to cruise and see what's on offer. The sassiest of the discos is *Pascha*, easily tracked down at the foot of the strobe light it beams into the sky every night, and the beachfront *Goa* is similar. The **beach** itself is excellent and the waters (like all in Almería) are warm and brilliantly clear.

Carboneras, Agua Amarga and La Garrucha

South of Mojácar beach lie a succession of small, isolated coves, the most accessible of them reached down a rough coastal track that turns off towards the sea just under 4km down the road to Carboneras. The scenic Mojácar–Carboneras road itself winds perilously through the hills some way inland, and offers only occasional access to some tempting beaches. There's no bus on this stretch either, and you'd need to be very intent on escaping the crowds to want to drive this way.

CARBONERAS has an average beach and a few *hostales* but is scarred by the shadow of a massive cement factory, which dominates its bay. Beyond, a small road extends to the isolated fishing hamlet of **AGUA AMARGA**, an infinitely more attractive spot with a fine beach backed by a tasteful crop of villas. There are limited **places to stay**, of which the best is easily the French-run *Pensión Family* (☎950 138 014, ℻950 138 208; ❺), which has a good restaurant with a great value *menú*; you'll need to book well ahead in high season. Both Carboneras and Agua Amarga are served by bus from Almería.

North from Mojácar there's easier access, with occasional buses and reasonably easy hitching, to **LA GARRUCHA**, a lively, if unattractive, town and fishing harbour. This is in the process of development, with villas now thick on the ground and many more in the offing, but it does have a life of its own besides tourism. There are several expensive **hostales** and a summer-only **youth hostel**, but you're more likely to visit its reasonable beach as a good afternoon's break from Mojácar. There are also some fine fish **restaurants** around the fishing harbour; *El Almejero*, with its terrace actually fronting the quayside, is one of the best − if the fish landed don't meet their high standards, they don't open − and they have an equally excellent tapas bar, too.

Travel details

Trains

Algeciras to: Córdoba (2 daily; 4hr 30min); Granada (2 daily; 4hr–4hr 30min); Madrid (3 daily; 12hr 30min–15hr; 6hr 30min with AVE from Sevilla). All Algeciras trains via Ronda and Bobadilla.

Almería to: Granada (4 daily; 2hr 10min); Guadix

(4 daily; 1hr 15min); Madrid (2 daily; 6hr 40min–8hr 40min); Sevilla (3 daily; 5hr 30min).
Cádiz to: Córdoba (4 daily; 3hr); Madrid (AVE 2 daily; 5hr); Sevilla (12 daily; 2hr).
Córdoba to: Algeciras (2 daily; 4hr 30min); Cádiz (4 daily; 3hr); Granada (2 daily; 3hr 20min); Jáen (1 daily; 1hr 30min); Madrid (13 daily, 4–6hr; AVE 14 daily, 1hr 45min); Málaga (2 daily; 3hr); Sevilla (6 daily, 1–2hr; AVE 16 daily, 45min).
Granada to: Algeciras (2 daily; 4hr 30min); Almería (4 daily; 2hr 10min); Antequera (3 daily; 1hr 50min); Córdoba (2 daily; 3hr 20min); Guadix (4 daily; 1hr 10min); Linares-Baeza (1 daily; 2hr 30min); Madrid (2 daily; 6–8hr); Málaga (2 daily; 3hr 30min); Ronda (3 daily; 3hr); Valencia (3 daily; 8–10hr, 1 via Linares-Baeza).
Huelva to: Madrid (AVE 1 daily; 4hr 15min); Sevilla (3 daily; 1hr 30min); Zafra (2 daily; 4hr 30min).
Jaén to: Cádiz (1 daily; 4hr 30min); Córdoba (1 daily; 1hr 30min); Sevilla (1 daily; 2hr 50min).
Málaga to: Algeciras (3 daily; 3hr); Córdoba (2 daily, 3hr 10min; AVE 6 daily, 2hr 10min); Fuengirola (every 30min; 50min); Granada (1 daily; 3hr 30min); Madrid (5 daily; 6–8hr; AVE 5 daily; 4hr 10min); Ronda (3 daily; 1hr); Sevilla (6 daily; 2hr 15min–3hr 30min); Torremolinos (every 30min; 30min).
Sevilla to: Algeciras (2 daily; 5hr); Badajoz (4 daily; 5–7hr); Cádiz (12 daily; 1hr 30min–2hr); Córdoba (6 daily, 1–2hr; AVE 17 daily, 45min); Huelva (3 daily; 1hr 30min); Madrid (12 daily; AVE 2hr 15min or 6–9hr); Mérida (4 daily; 3hr 30min).

Buses

Algeciras to: Cádiz (9 daily; 2hr 30min); La Línea (for Gibraltar: hourly; 30min); Madrid (1 daily; 10hr); Sevilla (5 daily; 3hr 30min); Tarifa (11 daily; 30min).
Almería to: Agua Amarga (1 daily; 1hr 15min); Alicante (2 daily; 7hr); Cabo de Gata/San José (6 daily; 30min/45min); Carboneras (3 daily; 1hr 15min); Córdoba (2 daily; 5–6hr); Granada (5 daily; 2hr 15min); Guadix (9 daily; 2hr); Laujar de Andarax (5 daily; 1hr 15min); Málaga (8 daily; 4hr 30min); Mojácar (2 daily; 2hr); Níjar (1 daily; 45min); Sevilla (daily; 5–6hr); Tabernas (6 daily; 1hr); Ugíjar (2 daily; 1hr 30min).
Cádiz to: Algeciras (8 daily; 2hr 45min); Arcos de la Frontera (5 daily; 2hr); Chipiona (7 daily; 1hr 30min); Conil (13 daily; 1hr); Granada (2 daily; 8hr); Jerez de la Frontera (14 daily; 45min); Málaga (3 daily; 5hr); El Puerto de Santa María (15 daily; 40min); Sanlúcar de Barrameda (8 daily; 1hr 15min); Sevilla (12 daily; 1hr 30min); Tarifa (1 daily; 2hr); Vejer de la Frontera (10 daily; 1hr 15min).

Córdoba to: Badajoz (1 daily; 6hr 30min); Écija (5 daily; 1hr 15min); Granada (8 daily; 2hr 30min); Jaén (7 daily; 2hr); Málaga (7 daily; 3hr 30min); Madrid (6 daily; 4hr 30min); Sevilla (11 daily; 2hr 30min).
Granada to: Alicante (5 daily; 4hr 45min–6hr 45min); Almería (8 daily; 2hr 15min); Cádiz (2 daily; 5hr); Cazorla (2 daily; 2hr 45min); Córdoba (7 daily; 2hr 30min); Guadix (12 daily; 1hr 15min); Jaén (12 daily; 2hr); Madrid (9 daily; 5–6hr); Málaga (15 daily; 2hr); Mojácar (2 daily; 3hr 30min); Motril (9 daily; 1hr 30min); Ronda (3 daily; 3hr); Sevilla (9 daily; 3hr 30min–4hr 30min); Sierra Nevada/Alpujarras (5 daily to Lanjarón and Órgiva in 1hr; 2 daily to most of the other villages along most of the routes); Solynieve (2 daily; 45min); Valencia (5 daily; 7hr 30min); Úbeda/Baeza (7 daily; 2hr 30min–3hr 30min).
Huelva to: Aracena (2 daily; 1hr 30min); Ayamonte/Portuguese frontier (9 daily; 1hr); Granada (1 daily; 4hr); Isla Cristina (3 daily; 1hr); Matalascañas (6 daily; 1hr 15min); Moguer/Palos (12 daily; 45min); Punta Umbria (hourly; 30min); Sevilla (14 daily, 6 direct; 1hr 15min–1hr 45min).
Jaén to: Almería (2 daily; 4hr 30min); Baeza/Úbeda (14 daily; 1hr–1hr 30min); Cazorla (2 daily; 2hr); Córdoba (8 daily; 2hr); Granada (14 daily; 2hr); Madrid (6 daily; 6hr); Málaga (4 daily; 4hr); Sevilla (3 daily; 5hr).
Jerez to: Algeciras (3 daily; 2hr); Arcos de la Frontera (17 daily; 30min); Cádiz (21 daily; 45min); Chipiona (8 daily; 40min); Córdoba (1 daily; 3hr 30min); El Puerto de Santa María (6 daily; 30min); Ronda (3 daily; 2hr 30min); Sanlúcar de Barrameda (16 daily; 30min); Sevilla (6 daily; 1hr); Vejer de la Frontera (2 daily; 1hr 30min).
Málaga to: Algeciras (12 daily; 2hr 30min); Almería (8 daily; 4hr 30min); Almunecar (11 daily; 1hr 15min); Cádiz (3 daily; 2hr 30min); Córdoba (5 daily; 3hr 30min); Fuengirola (every 40min; 45min); Gibraltar (1 daily; 4hr 30min); Granada (15 daily; 2hr 30min); Huelva (1 daily; 5hr 30min); Jaén (3 daily; 4hr 30min); Jerez (1 daily; 3hr); Madrid (6 daily; 6hr); Marbella (every 30min; 30min); Motril (10 daily; 1hr 30min); Nerja (11 daily; 1hr 30min); Ronda (6 daily; 2hr 30min); Salobrena (11 daily; 45min); Sevilla (9 daily; 2hr); Torremolinos (every 15min; 30min); Úbeda-Baeza (1 daily; 4hr).
Ronda to: Arcos de la Frontera (5 daily; 1hr 30min); Cádiz (3 daily; 3hr 30min); Jerez (5 daily; 2hr 30min); Málaga (6 daily; 2hr) Olvera (2 daily; 30min); San Pedro de Alcántara (4 daily; 1hr 30min, continuing to Málaga); Setenil (2 daily; 20min); Sevilla (5 daily; 2hr 45min); Ubrique (2 daily; 45min).

Sevilla to: Albufeira, Portuguese Algarve (via Ayamonte and Faro; 2 daily; 2hr 30min); Algeciras (5 daily; 3hr 30min); Almería (3 daily; 6hr); Aracena (2 daily; 2hr); Badajoz (2 daily via Zafra, 2 daily via Jerez de los Caballeros; 3hr 30min); Cádiz (8 daily; 1hr 30min–2hr 30min); Carmona (34 daily; 45min); Córdoba (11 daily; 1hr 45min–3hr 15min); Écija (11 daily; 2hr); El Rocío (5 daily; 2hr 30min); Granada (7 daily; 4–5hr); Huelva (11 daily; 1hr 30min); Jerez (6 daily; 1hr); Madrid (12 daily; 5–8hr); Málaga (6 daily; 2hr); Matalascañas (3 daily; 3hr); Mérida (6 daily; 3hr 30min); Ronda (5 daily; 3hr).

Ferries

Algeciras to: Ceuta (18 boats daily, 1hr 30min; seasonal hydrofoil, 1 daily, 30min); Tangier (18 boats daily; 2hr; seasonal hydrofoil, 1 daily; 1 hr).

Almería to: Melilla (April–Sept daily; 6hr); Nador (April–Sept daily; 6hr).

Cádiz to: El Puerto de Santa María (4–6 daily; 40min); Las Palmas (every 2 days in season, every 5 out; 48hr); Tangier (2 daily; 3hr); Tenerife (every 2 days in season, every 5 out; 36hr).

Gibraltar to: Tangier (Mon, Wed & Fri; 2hr; 1 daily catamaran, 2 daily on Mon & Fri; 1hr 15min).

Málaga to: Melilla (daily except Sun; 7hr).

Tarifa to: Tangier (seasonal boat, 1 daily; 1hr 30min).

Old Castile and León

Highlights

5

Old Castile and León

The foundations of modern Spain were laid in the kingdom of **Castile**. A land of frontier fortresses – the *castillos* from which it takes its name – it became the most powerful and centralizing force of the Reconquest, extending its domination through military gains and marriage alliances. By the eleventh century it had merged with and swallowed **León**; through Isabel's marriage to Fernando in 1469 it encompassed Aragón, Catalunya and eventually the entire peninsula. The monarchs of this triumphant and expansionist age were enthusiastic patrons of the arts, endowing their cities with superlative monuments, above which, quite literally, tower the great Gothic cathedrals of Salamanca, León and Burgos.

Salamanca and **León** are the two outstanding highlights, ranking in interest and beauty alongside the other great cities of Spain, such as Toledo, Sevilla and Santiago. Try to take in some of the lesser towns, too, such as **Ciudad Rodrigo** and **El Burgo de Osma**, or the village of **Covarrubias**. In all of them you'll be struck by a wealth of mansions and churches incongruous with present, or even imagined past, circumstances and status. In the people, too, you may notice something of the classic Castilian *hidalgo* archetype – a certain haughty solemnity of manner and a dignified assumption of past nobility, however straitened present circumstances.

Over the past decade, the historic cities have grown to dominate the region more than ever. Although the Castilian soil is fertile, the harsh extremes of land and climate don't encourage rural settlement, and the vast central plateau – the 700- to 1000-metre-high *meseta* – is given over almost entirely to grain. Huge areas stretch into the horizon without a single landmark, not even a tree.

Accommodation price codes

All the establishments listed in this book have been price-graded according to the following scale. The prices quoted are for the **cheapest available double room in high season**; effectively this means that anything in the ❶ and most places in the ❷ range will be without private bath, though there's usually a washbasin in the room. In the ❹ category and above you will probably be getting private facilities. Remember, though, that many of the budget places will also have more expensive rooms including en-suite facilities. Youth hostels are graded under ❶ as the price per person is less than half of the category's upper limit.

Note that in the more upmarket *hostales* and *pensiones*, and in anything calling itself a hotel, you'll pay a **tax** (IVA) of seven percent on top of the room price.

❶ Under €12	❹ €27–36	❼ €60–90
❷ €12–18	❺ €36–48	❽ €90–120
❸ €18–27	❻ €48–60	❾ Over €120

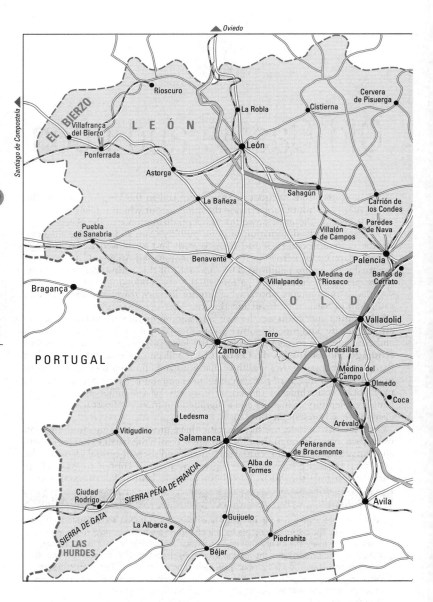

Oviedo

Santiago de Compostela

EL BIERZO

Rioscuro

Cervera
de Pisuerga

La Robla

Cistierna

LEÓN

Villafranca
del Bierzo

León

Ponferrada

Astorga

Sahagún

Carrión de
los Condes

La Bañeza

Paredes
de Nava

Puebla
de Sanabria

Villalón
de Campos

Palencia

Benavente

Bragança

Villalpando

Medina de
Rioseco

Baños de
Cerrato

O   L   D

Valladolid

Toro

PORTUGAL

Zamora

Tordesillas

Medina del
Campo

Olmedo

Coca

Ledesma

Arévalo

Vitigudino

Salamanca

Peñaranda
de Bracamonte

Alba de
Tormes

Ciudad
Rodrigo

SIERRA PEÑA DE FRANCIA

Avila

SIERRA DE GATA

La Alberca

Guijuelo

Piedrahita

LAS
HURDES

Béjar

Surprisingly, however, the Duero River, which has the most extensive basin in Spain, runs right across the province and into Portugal. And despite being characterized by *meseta* landscape, there are enclaves of varied scenery – in particular, the **valley of Las Batuecas** and the lakeland of the **Sierra de Urbión**, where the Duero begins its course.

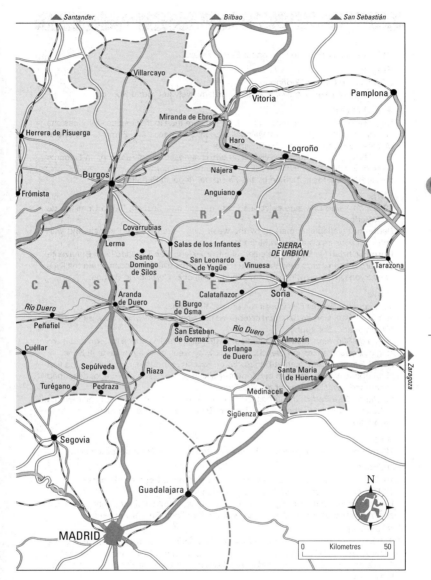

Villarcayo

Vitoria

Pamplona

Miranda de Ebro

Herrera de Pisuerga

Haro

Logroño

Burgos

Nájera

Frómista

Anguiano

R I O J A

Covarrubias

Lerma

Salas de los Infantes

SIERRA
DE URBIÓN

Santo
Domingo
de Silos

San Leonardo
de Yagüe

Vinuesa

Tarazona

C A S T I L E

Aranda
de Duero

Calatañazor

Soria

Río Duero

El Burgo
de Osma

Peñafiel

San Esteban
de Gormaz

Río Duero

Almazán

Cuéllar

Berlanga
de Duero

Sepúlveda

Riaza

Santa Maria
de Huerta

Turégano

Pedraza

Medinaceli

Sigüenza

Segovia

N

Guadalajara

MADRID

0   Kilometres   50

Zaragoza

The sporadic and depopulated villages, bitterly cold in winter, burning hot in summer, are rarely of interest – travel consists of getting as quickly as you can from one grand town to the next. The problem with many of the smaller places, and even some of the larger ones, is that they have little appeal beyond their monuments: **Burgos** and **Valladolid**, for example, are important historically

January
30 Processions in Burgos to honour *San Lesmes*.

February
3 *Romería* to Ciudad Rodrigo.
Week before Lent *Carnaval* is also particularly lively in Ciudad Rodrigo.

March/April
Holy Week is even more fanatically observed here than in most areas – processions in all the big cities, particularly Valladolid, León, Salamanca and Zamora. The one at Medina de Rioseco is also worth aiming for.
Good Friday in Bercanos de Aliste (Zamora) is almost chillingly solemn, participants dressed in white gowns which will later become their shrouds.
Week after Easter is marked by the *Fiesta del Ángel* in Peñafiel.

May
12 *Día de Santo Domingo* celebrated with a traditional fiesta in Santo Domingo de la Calzada.
Pentecost (variable) is marked by the week-long *Feria Chica* in Palencia and with more religious celebrations in Miranda de Ebro.
Corpus Christi (variable) sees celebrations in Palencia and Valladolid; in Benavente the *Toro Enmaromado* runs through the streets in the evening, endangering the lives of everyone. The following day sees the festival of *El Curpillos* in Burgos.

June
11 Logroño's *Fiestas Bernabeas* run around this date.
12 *Día de San Juan de Sahagún* celebrated in Salamanca (of which he is patron) and his birthplace, Sahagún.
24 *Día de San Juan* sees a secular fiesta with bullfights and dance in León and more religious observances in Palencia. The following week sees a big fiesta in Soria.
23–26 *Fiesta de San Juan* at San Pedro de Manrique (northeast of Soria) – the first night opens with the famous barefoot firewalking of the *Paseo del Fuego*, described in Norman Lewis's *Voices of the Old Sea*.
29 *Día de San Pedro*. In Burgos the start of a two-week-long feria; lesser events in León, and in Haro there's the drunken *Batalla del Vino* celebrating local wine production.

July
22 In Anguiano performance of the famous stilt dance – *danza de los zancos*.

August
15 Colourful festivals for the Assumption in La Alberca, Coca and Peñafiel.
16 *Día de San Roque* fiesta in El Burgo de Osma.
Last week *Fiesta de San Agustín* in Toro, with the "fountain of wine" and *encierros*, and in Medinaceli, musical evenings with medieval and Renaissance music.

September
8 A big day everywhere – the first day of Salamanca's major fiesta, beginning the evening before and lasting two weeks, as well as a famous bull running in Tordesillas.
21 *Día de San Mateo*. Major *ferias* in Valladolid and especially Logroño, where the Rioja harvest is celebrated.

October
First Sun *Fiesta de las Cantaderas* in León.
Valladolid's *International Film Week* also falls in Oct.

November
13 The *Toro Júbilo* runs through the streets of Medinaceli on the night of the nearest Saturday.

but their "sights" lack a stimulating setting. The most impressive of the castles are at **Coca**, **Gormaz** and **Berlanga de Duero**. The other architectural feature of the region is the host of Romanesque churches, monasteries and hermitages, a legacy of the **Camino de Santiago** (pilgrim route) which cut across the top of the province.

Technically, parts of the **Picos de Europa** lie in León province, and there are good approaches to the region from the south. However, this mountain range – with its superb villages, wildlife and treks – is covered in the chapter "Cantabria and Asturias", where its heartland lies.

Southern Old Castile: Salamanca to Soria

This first part of the chapter follows a route across **Southern Old Castile**, from west to east, starting at Salamanca and covering the provinces of Salamanca, Zamora, Valladolid, Palencia, the northern part of Segovia and Soria. From Zamora on, it follows the path of the **Río Duero** with its plethora of magnificent castles, to the crags and lakes of the wild Sierra de Urbión beyond Soria. Most of this region is well covered by **bus** and **train** routes, with Salamanca, in particular, a nexus of transport, with links to Ávila/Madrid, Zamora/León, Valladolid/Burgos and beyond.

Salamanca and around

SALAMANCA is the most graceful city in Spain. For four centuries it was the seat of one of the most prestigious universities in the world and, despite losing this reputation in the seventeenth century, it has kept the unmistakeable atmosphere of a seat of learning. It's still a small place, and is given a gorgeous harmony by the golden sandstone from which almost the entire city seems to be constructed.

Two great architectural styles were developed, and see their finest expression, in Salamanca. **Churrigueresque** takes its name from José Churriguera (1665–1723), the dominant member of a prodigiously creative family. Best known for their huge, flamboyant altarpieces, they were particularly active around Salamanca. The style is an especially ornate form of Baroque, long frowned upon by art historians from a north European, Protestant tradition. **Plateresque** came earlier, a decorative technique of shallow relief and intricate detail named for its resemblance to the art of the silversmith (*platero*); Salamanca's native sandstone, soft and easy to carve, played a significant role in its development. Plateresque art cuts across Gothic and Renaissance frontiers – the decorative motifs of the university, for example, are taken from the Italian Renaissance but the facade of the New Cathedral is Gothic in inspiration.

SALAMANCA

Metres
0   150

▲ Train Station & ❶

ACCOMMODATION

Hotel Amefa	3
Hotel Emperatriz	7
Pensión Estefanía	9
Pensión Lisboa	6
Pensión Los Angeles	4
Pensión Marina	5
Hostal Mindonao	10
Palacio de Castellanos	12
Hotel Paris	2
Parador de Salamanca	14
Hotel Rector	13
Hostal Tormes Confort	11
Pension Las Vegas	8
Pensión Virginia	1

RESTAURANTS & TAPAS BARS

El Bardo	H
El Candil	C
Cervecería del Comercio	A
Chez Victor	E
Freduria Marín	G
Mesón Cervantes	D
Restaurante Río de la Plata	F
Restaurante Roma	B

Santo Tomás Canturiense

Convento de Santa Clara

MARQUESA ALMARZA

LOS MARTIRES

PASEO DE CANALEJAS

IMPERIAL

GÓMEZ VILA

PASEO DE SAN ANTONIO

ALAMEDILLA

ALAMEDILLA

PLAZA DE ESPAÑA

Iglesia de Sancti Spiritus

SANCTI SPIRITUS

CUESTA

EL PINTO

ASADERIA

BODEGONES

SOLEDAD

EL GRILLO

PLAZA SAN CRISTÓBAL

BANZO

LA PARRA

COMEDIAS

GRAN VÍA

COSOS

SANTA CLARA

PLAZA DE LA CONSTITUCIÓN

Torre del Aire

PLAZA DE STA EULALIA

PLAZA DE LA REINA

CAMINAS

VARILLAS

PLAZA DE SAN JUSTO

SAN JUSTO

MININAGUSTIN

CONSUELOS

CALDEREROS

ROSA

AZUCENA

POZO AMARILLO

PLAZA DEL MERCADO

PLAZA DEL ÁNGEL

Iglesia de San Martín

PLAZA DEL CORRILLO

EL AZAFRANAL

PLAZA MAYOR

TORO

EL SOL

LOS

NOVIOS

CASAS

BROCENSE

PADRE LAS CASAS

PADILLEROS

EL CONCEJO

ESPOZ Y MINA

DEL CARMEN

Casa de las Muertes

PLAZA DE LOS BANDOS

PRIOR

AVENIDA DE MIRAT

JOSE JAUREGUI

EL ARCO

SOL ORIENTE

ZAMORA

S. MARCOS

PLAZA DEL EJERCITO

Iglesia de San Marcos

CONDES DE CRESPO RASCÓN

RONDA DEL CORPUS

PERDONES

San Juan de Barbalos

PLAZA DE LA FUENTE

CUESTA

Convento de Santa Úrsula

SORIAS

ARRIBA

ABAJO

DE LOS CARMELITAS

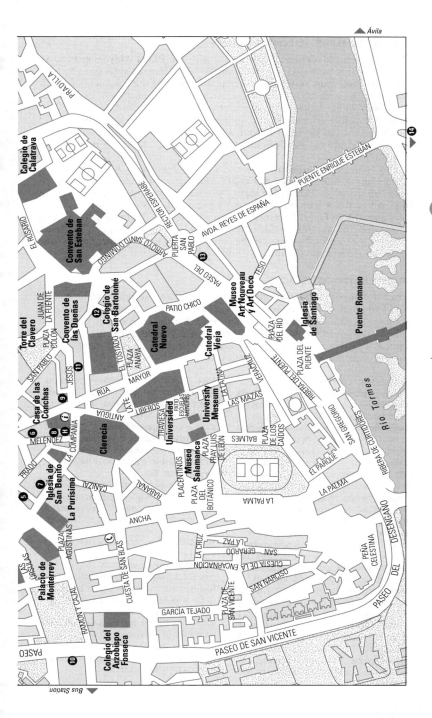

▲ *Ávila*

▼ *Bus Station*

Colegio de Calatrava

PRADILLA

EL ROSARIO

Convento de San Esteban

Torre del Clavero

JUAN DE LA FUENTE

PLAZA COLON

Convento de las Dueñas

SAN PABLO

RECTOR ESPERABÉ

ARROYO SANTO DOMINGO

PUERTA SAN PABLO

PUENTE ENRIQUE ESTEBAN

AVDA. REYES DE ESPAÑA

Museo Art Nouveau y Art Deco

PASEO DEL

TESO

PATIO CHICO

Colegio de San Bartolomé

Catedral Nuevo

Catedral Vieja

Iglesia de Santiago

PLAZA DEL RÍO

Puente Romano

JESÚS

EL TOSTADO

PLAZA ANAYA

RÚA

MAYOR

Casa de las Conchas

LATE

LIBEROS

Clerecía

ANTIGUA

COMPANIA

LA PATINA

VERACRUZ

Río Tormes

PLAZA DEL PUENTE

RIBERA DEL PUENTE

SAN GREGORIO

RIBERA DE CURTIDORES

MELENDEZ

PRADO

Iglesia de San Benito

La Purísima

Universidad

PATIO ESCUELAS MENORES

University Museum

LAS MAZAS

PLAZA DE LOS CAIDOS

EL PARQUE

TRAVIESA

Museo Salamanca

PLAZA FRAY LUIS DE LEÓN

BALMES

LA PALMA

CAÑIZAL

RABANAL

PLACENTINOS

PLAZA DEL BOTÁNICO

LA PALMA

PLAZA AGUSTINAS

ANCHA

CUESTA DE SAN BLAS

Palacio de Monterrey

LAS URSULAS

RAMON Y CAJAL

GARCÍA TEJADO

CUESTA DE LA ENCARNACIÓN

SAN NARCISO

PLAZA DE SAN VICENTE

LA CRUZ

SAN GERARDO

LA PAZ

PEÑA CELESTINA

DESENGAÑO

PASEO DEL

PASEO DE SAN VICENTE

PASEO

Colegio del Arzobispo Fonseca

▲ Ávila

Arrival and information

The compact **old centre** of Salamanca, with the **Plaza Mayor** at its heart, spreads back from the Río Tormes, bounded by a loop of avenues and *paseos*. The **bus and train stations** are on opposite sides of the city, each about fifteen minutes' walk from the centre. From the bus station at Avda. de Filiberto Villalobos 73–83 simply turn right and you'll eventually end up in the Plaza Mayor. If you've arrived by train, go left down the Paseo de la Estación and you'll reach Plaza de España, from where c/Toro leads to the Plaza Mayor; alternatively, take bus #1 from the station to Plaza del Mercado, right next to the Plaza Mayor.

The main city **turismo** (Mon–Sat 9am–2pm & 4.30–6.30pm, Sun 10am–2pm & 4.30–6.30pm; ☎923 218 342, ✉ayuntamiento@aytosalamanca.es) is on the Plaza Mayor, and there are summer-only information booths at the train and bus stations. There's also a regional tourist office for Salamanca province (Mon–Fri 9am–2pm & 5–7pm, Sat & Sun 10am–2pm & 4–7pm; ☎923 268 571) around the side of the Casa de las Conchas, facing Rúa Mayor. Information on local events can be found in a monthly guide, *Lugares*, free from bars, restaurants and the city tourist office.

Accommodation

Prices for **accommodation** in Salamanca are reasonable, but it can be hard to find a room in high season – especially at fiesta time in September. During the summer months you may well be approached at the train or bus station and offered *casas particulares* (private rooms). These are often the lowest-priced options available as many of the *pensiones* are more or less permanently occupied by students during the academic year.

Budget options

Pensión Estefanía, c/Jesús 3–5 ☎923 217 372. Brave one of Salamanca's dingiest staircases to reach this cheap and clean *pensión*, centrally located on a relatively quiet side street very close to the Casa de las Conchas. Rooms are a bit gloomy, though most have small balconies. ❸

Pensión Lisboa, c/Meléndez 1, 2º ☎923 214 333. Smart *pensión* on one of the liveliest squares in the city. Rooms – some en suite – are excellent value, though those facing the street can be a bit noisy, and you'll have to contend with the eccentric management too. ❸

Pensión Los Angeles, Plaza Mayor 10 ☎ & ☎923 218 166. Friendly, no-frills *pensión* with four basic en-suite rooms boasting stunning views over the Plaza Mayor, plus another five shared-bath doubles with good views over the old city. ❸–❹

Pensión Marina, c/Doctrinos 4 ☎923 216 569. Just five basic doubles sharing one huge bathroom in this very friendly establishment, tucked away in a peaceful side street close to the Plaza Mayor. ❸

Hostal Mindonao, Paseo de San Vicente 2 ☎923 263 080, ☎923 263 080. Large, modern *hostal* with comfortable en-suite rooms, situated just outside the old city, a ten-minute walk from the Plaza

Mayor. A decent budget alternative to the old-city *pensiones* if you don't mind the rather uninspiring setting next to a busy main road – try to get an inward-facing room. ❸

Pensión Las Vegas, c/Meléndez 13 ☎923 218 749, ✉lasvegas@iponet.es. Five large, light rooms (one single, one double and three triples) in this attractive, plant-filled flat on one of the old city's liveliest streets. ❸

Pensión Virginia, Paseo de la Estación 109–115, 2º☎923 241 016. A well-run *pensión*, right in front of the train station – convenient if you've a train to catch, though quite a way from the city centre. ❸

Moderate and expensive options

Hotel Amefa, c/Pozo Amarillo 18–20 ☎923 218 189, ☎923 260 200. Understated, good-quality hotel in an extremely central location, even if it's on one of old Salamanca's least scenic roads. ❻

Hotel Emperatriz, c/Compañía 44 ☎923 219 200, ☎ 923 219 201. Two-star hotel in a beautiful old mansion on a lovely pedestrianized Salamantine street. Rooms are comfortable enough, and good value, even if they don't quite live up to the historic setting. ❺

Palacio de Castellanos, c/San Pablo 58–64 ☏ 923 261 818, ⓕ 923 261 819. Opulent, marbled four-star hotel set in a fifteenth-century palace facing the Convento de San Esteban. The entrance area – a glassed-in Renaissance cloister converted into a drawing room – is stunning, as it should be for this price. ❾

Parador de Salamanca, Toso de Feria 2 ☏ 923 192 082, ⓕ 923 192 087, ✉ salamanca@parador.es. Modern building with swimming pool and great views, situated just across the Puente Romano. ❽

Hotel París, c/Padilla 1–5 ☏ 923 262 970 ⓕ 923 260 991. Thirteen plush rooms in the modern town on the way to the train station – good value, though it's a bit of a walk from the sights. ❻

Hotel Rector, Paseo del Rector Esperabé 10 ☏ 923 218 482, ⓕ 923 214 008, ✉ hotelrector@teleline.es. Setting by side of dusty main road does nothing to detract from this superb boutique hotel with just 14 gorgeously outfitted rooms. ❽

Hostal Tormes Confort, c/Jesus 22 ☏ 923 271 773, ⓕ 923 219 688. Brand-new mid-range *hostal* excellently located in a quiet but very central side street, with ten surgically clean en-suite rooms. ❺

Camping

Camping Regio ☏ 923 138 888, ⓕ 923 138 044. Salamanca's excellent campsite is open all year round, 4km along the Ávila road behind the *Hotel Regio*.

The City

The city's architectural sights seem endless: two **cathedrals**, one Gothic, the other Romanesque, vie for attention with Renaissance **palaces** and gems of Plateresque decoration. The **Plaza Mayor** is the finest in Spain; and the surviving university buildings are tremendous throughout – all of them distinguished by the same warm stone.

The Plaza Mayor and around

The grand **Plaza Mayor** is the hub of Salamantine life. You get the impression that everyone passes through its cafés and arcaded walks at least ten times a day. Its bare central expanse, in which bullfights were staged as late as 1863, is enclosed by a continuous four-storey building, broken only by the grand, three-storey *ayuntamiento* on its northern side. Decorated with iron balconies and medallion portraits, including a much-abused image of General Franco in the northeast corner, the building was the work of Andrea García Quiñones and Alberto Churriguera, younger brother of José, and nowhere is the Churrigueras' inspired variation of Baroque so refined as here.

Leave Plaza Mayor via the southwest corner, past the Romanesque Iglesia de San Martín, and walk straight down c/Meléndez to reach the vast Baroque church of **La Clerecía**. The church itself is opened only for Mass, though you can visit the patio to the right of the church (daily 8am–3pm; free), a grandiose Baroque courtyard that looks a little like a miniature version of the Plaza Mayor. Opposite stands the city's most distinctive (and photographed) building, the early sixteenth-century mansion, **Casa de las Conchas** (House of Shells), named after the rows of carved scallop shells, symbol of the pilgrimage to Santiago, which decorate its facade. It's worth popping into the recently restored courtyard (Mon–Fri 9am–9pm, Sat 9am–2pm & 4–7pm, Sun 10am–2pm & 4–7pm; free), a quaint mishmash of Gothic and Renaissence elements with a good view of La Clerecía from the upper storey.

The University and around

From the Casa de las Conchas, turn right onto Rua Antigua then left along c/de los Libreros to reach the **University** (Mon–Sat 9.30am–1.30pm & 4–7pm, Sun 10am–1pm; €1.80). The ultimate expression of Plateresque, the **facade** is covered with medallions, heraldic emblems and a profusion of floral decorations, amid which lurks a hidden frog said to bring good luck and

The university at Salamanca

Salamanca University was founded by Alfonso IX in the 1220s, and after the union of Castile and León swallowed up the University of Palencia to become the most important in Spain. Its rise to international stature was phenomenal and within thirty years Pope Alexander IV proclaimed it equal to the greatest universities of the day. As at Oxford, Paris and Bologna, theories formulated here were later accepted as fact throughout Europe. It made major contributions to the development of international law, and Columbus sought support for his voyages of discovery from the enlightened faculty of astronomy. The university continued to flourish under the Reyes Católicos, even employing a pioneering woman professor, Beatriz de Galindo, who tutored Queen Isabel in Latin. In the sixteenth century it was powerful enough to resist the orthodoxy of Felipe II's Inquisition but, eventually, freedom of thought was stifled by the extreme clericalism of the seventeenth and eighteenth centuries. Books were banned for being a threat to the Catholic faith, and mathematics and medicine disappeared from the curriculum. Decline was hastened during the Peninsular War when the French demolished 20 of the 25 colleges, and by the end of the nineteenth century there were no more than 300 students.

Today, although socially prestigious, Salamanca University ranks low academically, well behind Madrid, Barcelona and Sevilla. It does, however, run a highly successful language school – nowhere else in Spain will you see so many young Americans.

marriage within the year to anyone who spots it unaided. The centre is occupied by a portrait of Isabel and Fernando, surrounded by a Greek inscription commemorating their devotion to the university; above them is the coat of arms of Carlos V, grandson and successor of Isabel.

Inside, the old **lecture rooms**, surprisingly small for a seat of learning that once boasted over 7000 students, are arranged round a courtyard. The **Aula Fray Luís de León**, on the left side of the ground floor, preserves the rugged original benches and the pulpit where this celebrated professor lectured. In 1573, the Inquisition muscled its way into the room and arrested Fray Luís for alleged subversion of the faith; five years of torture and imprisonment followed, but upon his release he calmly resumed his lecture with the words "*Dicebamus hesterna die…*" ("As we were saying yesterday…").

The remainder of the heavily restored lower floor has surprisingly little to show for its illustrious past, though look out for the bizarre **Sala de las Tortugas** (Tortoise Room), a dusty collection of expired tortoises and polished shells in various states of decay – it's reckoned to be the second largest such collection in the world. An elegant Plateresque stairway leads to the upper floor, where you'll find a section of fanciful Moorish *techumbre* ceiling and, next to it, the old university **library**, stuffed with thousands of antiquated books on wooden shelves and huge globes of the world, whose faded magnificence gives some idea of Renaissance Salamanca's academic splendour.

Facing the university entrance is the **Patio de las Escuelas**, a tiny square surrounded by further university buildings. At the back of the square, an arch leads through to the Renaissance courtyard of the **Escuelas Menores**, which served as a kind of preparatory school for the university proper. On the far side of this courtyard, the **University Museum** (same hours as university & included in entry price) has a fine zodiacal ceiling, moved here from the chapel after two-thirds of it was destroyed by tremors from the 1755 Lisbon earthquake.

Just behind the Patio de las Escuelas Menores (walk left down Traviesa then left again to the Plaza del Fray Luís de León), the **Museo Salamanca**, also known as the Museo de Bellas Artes (Tues–Sat 10am–2pm & 4.30–7.30pm,

Sun 10am–2pm; €1.20) occupies an exquisite fifteenth-century mansion – originally the home of Isabel's personal physician – which is at least as interesting as the mildly diverting collection of Spanish religious paintings and sculpture contained within it.

The cathedrals

The **Catedral Nueva** (daily: April–Sept 9am–2pm & 4–8pm; Oct–March 10am–1pm & 4–6pm; free) was begun in 1512 as a declaration of Salamanca's prestige, and in a glorious last-minute assertion of Gothic architecture. It was built within a few yards of the university and acted as a buttress for the Old Cathedral, which was in danger of collapsing. The main Gothic-Plateresque entrance is contemporary with that of the university and equally dazzling in its wealth of ornamental detail, while the doorways on the north side facing Plaza de Anaya are scarcely less fine. For financial reasons, construction spanned two centuries and thus the building incorporates a range of styles, with some Renaissance and Baroque elements and a tower modelled on that of the cathedral at Toledo; stand under the dome to see the transition from Gothic at the bottom to late Baroque at the top. Alberto Churriguera and his brother José both worked here – the former on the choir stalls, the latter on the dome.

The Romanesque **Catedral Vieja** (daily: April–Sept 10am–1.30pm & 4–7.30pm; Oct–March 10am–12.30pm & 4–5.30pm; €1.80) is dwarfed by its neighbour, through which it's also entered. Its most striking feature is the massive fifteenth-century *retablo* by Nicolás Florentino: fifty-three paintings of the lives of the Virgin and Christ surmounted by a powerfully apocalyptic portrayal of the Last Judgement. A thirteenth-century fresco on the same theme is hidden away in the **Capilla de San Martín** at the back of the building.

The chapels opening off the cloisters were used as university lecture rooms until the sixteenth century. One, the **Capilla de Obispo Diego de Anaya**, contains the oldest organ in Europe (mid-fourteenth century); the instrument shows Moorish influence and, in the words of Sacheverell Sitwell, "is one of the most romantic, poetical objects imaginable". In the Chapter House there's a small **museum** with a fine collection of works by Fernando Gallego, Salamanca's most famous painter. Active in the late fifteenth century, he was a brilliant and conscious imitator of early northern Renaissance artists such as Roger van der Weyden.

Outside, the cathedral's most distinctive feature is its *media naranja* dome, known as the **Torre de Gallo** (Cock Tower) on account of its rooster-shaped weathervane. Shaped like the segments of an orange, the dome derives from Byzantine models and is similar to those at Zamora and Toro; there's a good view of it from Patio Chico around the back of the cathedrals.

The Art Nouveau Museum and Puente Romano

Right behind the Old Cathedral stands Salamanca's newest and quirkiest museum, the **Museo Art Nouveau y Art Deco** (April to mid-Oct Tues–Fri 11am–2pm & 5–9pm, Sat & Sun 11am–9pm; mid-Oct to March Tues–Fri 11am–2pm & 4–7pm, Sat & Sun 11am–8pm; €1.80). The development of these two, closely linked, movements – Art Nouveau and Art Deco – from the *belle époque* years at the turn of the twentieth century through to the 1930s, is illustrated here by a miscellany of objects including paintings, bronze statues, porcelain figures, lamps, vases, jewellery and furniture. Among the most notable exhibits are the glass vases and lamps created by Emile Gallé (Room 5), one of the most eminent Art Nouveau artists; the famous scent bottles René Lalique designed for Guerlain and Worth (Room 4); and Hagenauer's highly stylized and instantly recognizable carved figures (Room 13). The chief attraction, however, is the building itself, the Casa Lis, which was built for an Art Nouveau enthusiast at the turn of the twentieth century and appears to be half-constructed from amazing, vibrantly painted glass.

Just south of the Casa Lis, the Rio Tormes is straddled by the majestic **Puente Romano** (Roman Bridge; currently closed for restoration), some 400m long, from where there's a stunning panoramic view of the old city up on the hill above.

West of the Plaza Mayor

There's another swathe of impressive buildings west of the Plaza Mayor. Following Calle de la Compañía from the Casa de las Conchas takes you past the rather severe Iglesia de San Benito, with some fine Renaissance mansions on the tiny plaza behind, before reaching the Plaza Agustinas. In front is the large **Palacio de Monterrey**, a sixteenth-century construction with end towers, unfortunately not seen to best advantage in the narrow street. Across from it is the seventeenth-century Augustinian monastery usually called **La Purísima**, for which Ribera painted several fine altarpieces, including the main "Immaculate Conception".

Behind the Palacio de Monterrey there's another interesting convent, **Las Ursulas** (daily 11am–1pm & 4.30–6.30pm; €0.60), a tall, plain structure recognizable by its unusual open-topped tower; its church contains the superb marble tomb of Archbishop Alonso Fonseca by Diego de Siloé. Facing the east wall of this church is the impressive Plateresque facade of the **Casa de las Muertes** (House of the Dead), the mansion of leading Salamantine architect Juan de Álava, named after the four skulls at the base of the upper windows.

West from Las Ursulas across a small park, c/de Fonseca leads to the magnificent Plateresque **Colegio del Arzobispo Fonseca** (daily 10am–2pm & 4–6pm; €0.60, free Mon am), a corporate work by many of the leading figures of Spanish architecture in the early sixteenth century, including Diego de Siloé (who designed the facade, an unusually restrained affair for the period), and Juan de Álava. The two-storey Renaissance cloister is particularly fine, with beautifully carved portrait medallions, each distinctly characterized, while the chapel contains a fine *retablo* with paintings and sculptures by Alonso Berruguete.

San Esteban, Santa Clara and around

Just west of the New Cathedral, the facade of the **Convento de San Esteban** (daily 9am–1pm & 4–6pm; €1.20) is another faultless example of Plateresque art, covered in a tapestry of sculpture, the central panel of which depicts the stoning of its patron saint, St Stephen. The east end of the church is occupied by a huge Baroque *retablo* by José Churriguera, a lavish concoction of columns, statuary and floral decoration. The monastery's cloisters, through which you enter, are magnificent too.

The most beautiful cloisters in the city, however, stand across the road in the **Convento de las Dueñas** (daily 10.30am–1pm & 4.30–6pm; €1.20). Built on an irregular pentagonal plan in the Renaissance-Plateresque style of the early sixteenth century, the imaginative upper-storey capitals are wildly carved with human heads and skulls. On the opposite side of San Esteban stands the **Colegio de Calatrava**, a large and rather sober structure designed by José de Churriguera. It's occasionally open for temporary exhibitions.

Just north of here is the thirteenth-century **Convento de Santa Clara** (Mon–Fri 9.30am–1.40pm & 4–6.40pm, Sat & Sun 9am–2.40pm; €1.20), out-

△ Cloisters, Salamanca

wardly plain but with beautiful interior features which encompass virtually every important feature of Spanish architecture and design. In 1976 the walls of the chapel, whitewashed during a long-forgotten cholera epidemic, were found to be covered with an important series of frescoes from the thirteenth to the eighteenth century, while further probing of the ceiling revealed medallions similar to those in the Plaza Mayor. Romanesque and Gothic columns, and a stunning sixteenth-century polychrome ceiling, were also uncovered in the cloister. But the most incredible discovery was made in the church, where the Baroque ceiling constructed by Joaquín de Churriguera was found to be false; rising above this, you can see the original fourteenth-century beams, decorated with heraldic motifs of the kingdoms of Castile and León. The prize-winning restoration is fascinating, and the icing on the cake is perhaps the city's best view of the New Cathedral.

From Santa Clara, head east to reach the **Torre de Clavero**, a fifteenth-century octagonal tower with quaint Gothic pepperpot turrets. Its precise function remains obscure, though it was probably attached to a (now-vanished) mansion.

Eating, drinking and nightlife

Salamanca is a great place for hanging out in bars and cafés. Those in the Plaza Mayor are nearly twice the usual price but worth every peseta. Close at hand in the Plaza del Mercado (by the **market**, itself a good source of provisions), there's a row of lively **tapas bars**. Just south of Plaza Mayor, the adjacent c/Meléndez and Rua Mayor are packed with **bars** and **restaurants**, with tables set out in the pedestrianized streets; Plaza Corilla, where the two streets join, is particularly lively. There is another good, more budget-oriented, selection of places to eat and drink around the university area, particularly along the streets between the Casa de las Conchas and the Museo Salamanca.

El Bardo, c/Compañía 8. Good-value restaurant next to the Casa de las Conchas, with a lively bar attached. *Menús* go for around €6, and there's often a vegetarian option.

El Candil, c/Ruiz Aguilera 14–16. Secate old Salamantine restaurant with pricey but excellent Castilian dishes including regional specialities such as roast kid goat (*cabrito asado*).

Cervecería del Comercio, c/Pozo Amarillo 23. Gorgeous tiled bar decorated with bullfighting photos and Salamanca's largest collection of used beer cans conceals this relaxed restaurant serving moderately priced Castilian meat and fish dishes.

Chez Victor, c/Espoz y Mina 26. Upmarket French-influenced restaurant specializing in game. Reckoned to be Salamanca's finest. Closed Sun night, Mon & Aug.

Freduría Marín, c/del Prado 11. Cosy bar specializing in seafood *raciones* and, for its summer speciality, frogs' legs fried in batter.

Mesón Cervantes, Plaza Mayor 15. Pleasant upstairs bar-restaurant overlooking the Plaza Mayor – though you'll be lucky to get a window seat – with cheap, basic *platos combinados* from around €4.80 and more sophisticated *raciones*.

Restaurante Río de la Plata, Plaza Peso 1. Quality Castilian home cooking with a long menu of meat and fish dishes ranging from *lomo de cerdo* (€6) to *chateaubriand de ternera* (€15). A few vegetarian options too. Closed Mon & July.

Restaurante Roma, c/Ruíz Aguilera 8. Inexpensive place to try *chanfaina* – a rice-based dish with meats cooked in spicy juices and the nearest Spanish cuisine gets to a curry.

Nightlife

Nightlife happens everywhere in Salamanca: the presence of so many local and foreign students and tourists makes it easily the liveliest city in Old Castile. There's a whole host of student-oriented **bars and clubs** in the rectangle of streets on the southeast edge of the old town formed by Gran Vía, c/Calderos, c/Consuelo and c/Varillos. Those along Gran Vía, such as *El Gran Café Moderno* at no. 75 (with an excellent DJ and live sets), are better established, while those in the other streets tend to be impromptu student hang-outs with dodgy paint-jobs and raucous music. Just over Grand Vía at c/San Justo 27, the mainly gay *De Laval Genovés*, popularly known as "Submarino" due to its nautical decor (look for the ships' lanterns outside the discreet entrance), plays good music, has three bars and stays open until 5am. Back in the old town, *Camelot*, near the convent of Las Ursulas on c/Bordadores, is the place to watch American language students lose it completely.

There are also many laid-back **cafés** where you can hear live music: try *El Corrillo* in Plaza San Benito for jazz, or *El Callejón*, Gran Vía 68, for folk. Also good for folk is the excellent *Country Bar* at c/Juan de Almeida 5 (round the corner from *El Gran Café Moderno*). There's no sign anywhere, just an unpromising black door, but downstairs you'll find a small, atmospheric tavern covered wall-to-wall in beautiful, swirling mosaics (the owner is a Gaudí fanatic).

Listings

Bookshops Cervantes Humanidades, Plaza de Santa Eulalia 13 (not to be confused with the orginal Cervantes bookshop just round the corner on c/Azafranel), stocks a meagre range of English-language books; a similarly small selection is available at Librería Portonaris, Rúa Mayor 35.

Bus information ☎923 236 717.

Car rental Major operators include Avis, Paseo de Canalejas 49 ☎923 269 753; Europcar, Paseo de Canalejas 123 ☎923 269 041; Eurodollar-Atesa, Avda. de Comuneros 30 ☎923 249 901; Goyacar, Paseo Dr Torres Villarroel 49 ☎923 233 526; and Hertz, Avda. de Portugal 131 ☎923 243 134.

Internet access *Internet Bar*, c/Zamora 7 (Mon–Fri 9.30am–2am, Sat & Sun 11am–2am; €1.80 for 30min, €3 for 1hr), immediately north of Plaza Mayor.

Language courses Spanish language courses are big business in Salamanca, and the following is only a small selection: Colegio de España, c/Compañía 65 ☎923 214 788, ℱ923 218 791; Colegio de Estudios Hispanicos, c/Bordadores 1 ☎923 214 837, ℱ923 215 607; Cursos Internacionales de la Universidad de Salamanca, Patio de Escuelas Menores ☎923 294 408, ℱ923 294 504.

Laundry There are a couple of self-service *lavanderías* out by Plaza del Oeste (northwest of the ring road) but none in the centre.

Post office The main *Correos* is at Gran Vía 25.

Taxis There are two 24-hour companies: Radio Tele-Taxi ☎923 250 000 and Radio Taxi ☎923 271 111.

Train information ☎923 120 202.

Around Salamanca

The countryside around Salamanca is an attractive swathe of New Castile, particularly along the Río Tormes, which flows into the Duero to the northwest. The small hillside town of **ALBA DE TORMES**, 20km southeast of Salamanca and connected to it by regular bus (16 daily; 30min), makes an interesting day's excursion. The main attraction here is the **Convento de Carmelitas** (daily 9am–1.30pm & 4–6.30pm, Oct–April closes 7.30pm), founded by Santa Teresa in 1571, with an ornate Renaissance facade and a rather dubious reconstruction of the cell in which Teresa died. Alba is a centre for making traditional Castilian **pottery**, and you can watch its manufacture at Bernardo Pérez Correas on c/Matadero near the river. If you want to **stay the night**, the lowest-priced rooms – some en suite – are at the *Hostal América*, across the bridge on c/La Guía (☎923 300 071, ℱ923 300 346; ❹). For something more spacious try the *Hotel Alameda*, Avenida Juan Pablo II (☎923 300 031, ℱ923 370 281; ❹–❺), which also has a good restaurant.

In the opposite direction, heading northwest from Salamanca, a delightful minor road via Ledesma makes an excellent alternative route to **Zamora**. For most of the way this route trails the beautiful Río Tormes, where there's excellent fishing (for giant carp), herons and storks in the trees, enormous, delicious mushrooms (*setas*) in autumn and a variety of meadow flowers in spring. **LEDESMA** itself – little more than a large village these days – retains its ancient walls, the remains of a Roman bridge and baths, and a couple of attractive churches. If you're staying overnight, the *Fonda Mercado*, c/Mercado 12 (T 923 570 146; ❷), is good. The greenery round here seems atypical of Castile – it's created in large part by the **Embalse de Almendra**, a dam almost at the Portuguese border, whose reservoir stretches all the way back to Ledesma.

Ciudad Rodrigo and the Sierra Peña de Francia

In the far southwest corner of Salamanca province, the unspoiled frontier town of **Ciudad Rodrigo** – astride the road and rail line to Portugal – is worth a detour even if you don't plan to cross the border. East of the town lies the **Sierra Peña de Francia**, with good walking and a stunning village, **La Alberca**, the whole of which has been declared a national monument.

Ciudad Rodrigo

CIUDAD RODRIGO is an endearingly sleepy old place which, despite an orgy of destruction during the Peninsular War, preserves streets full of **Renaissance mansions**. The best way to get an overview of the town is by making a circuit of the impressive **walls** – originally twelfth century, with seventeenth-century additions. En route you'll pass an austere **castle** (now the *Parador Enrique II* – see below), which overlooks a Roman bridge on the Río Águeda and commands an enticing view across into Portugal. If you're around over the weekend, the **Centro de Interpretación de la Ruta de las Fortificaciones** (Sat & Sun 10.30am–2.30pm & 5–7pm; €1.50), on the northern edge of the old town, has entertaining displays on the history of the walls – ask nicely and they may even let you try on one of their suits of armour.

Inside the walls, Ciudad Rodrigo's empty streets are ideal for aimless wandering. All roads lead sooner or later to the picture-perfect **Plaza Mayor**, while north of here on Plaza Conde are three of the town's most imposing mansions: the **Palacio de los Castro**, the **Palacio Alba de Yeltes** and the

---

Ciudad Rodrigo in the Peninsular War

Along with Badajoz, Ciudad Rodrigo was a crucial border point in the Peninsular War. No army could cross safely between Spain and Portugal unless these two towns to its rear were secured. Ciudad Rodrigo fell to the French in 1810, despite valiant resistance from General Herrasti's Spanish garrison – in admiration for whose bravery, the French permitted them to march away from the devastated city.

Britain's Duke of Wellington retook Ciudad Rodrigo with a devastatingly rapid siege in 1812. Aware that French reinforcements were approaching, Wellington had announced "Ciudad Rodrigo must be stormed this evening" – his soldiers duly did so, embarking on a triumphant rampage of looting and vandalism. When order was restored, the troops paraded out dressed in a ragbag of stolen French finery. A bemused Wellington muttered to his staff, "Who the devil *are* those fellows?"

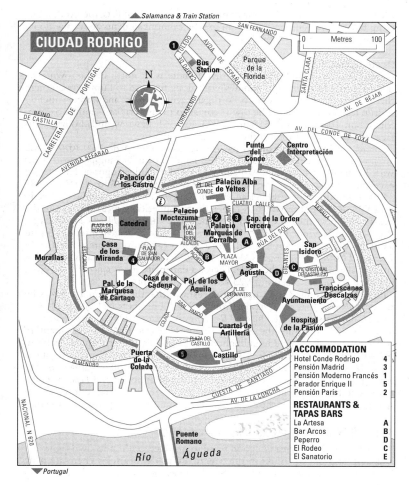

CIUDAD RODRIGO

Salamanca & Train Station

Metres

Bus Station

Parque de la Florida

Punta del Conde

Centro Interpretación

Palacio de los Castro

Palacio Alba de Yeltes

PL DEL CONDE

CUATRO CALLES

Palacio Moctezuma

Cap. de la Orden Tercera

Catedral

Palacio Marqués de Cerralbo

PLAZA DE HERRASTI

Casa de los Miranda

PLAZA DE SAN SALVADOR

PLAZA MAYOR

San Isidoro

Murallas

PLAZA DEL BUEN ALCALDE

San Agustín

Casa de la Cadena

Pal. de los Águila

PL DE CRISTOBAL DE CASTILLEJO

Pal. de la Marquesa de Cartago

PL DE CERVANTES

Franciscanas Descalzas

Ayuntamiento

Cuartel de Artillería

Hospital de la Pasión

PLAZA DEL CASTILLO

Puerta de la Colada

Castillo

Puente Romano

Río Águeda

Portugal

ACCOMMODATION

Hotel Conde Rodrigo	4
Pensión Madrid	3
Pensión Moderno Francés	1
Parador Enrique II	5
Pensión París	2

RESTAURANTS & TAPAS BARS

La Artesa	A
Bar Arcos	B
Peperro	D
El Rodeo	C
El Sanatorio	E

Palacio de Moctezuma (now the town's Casa Municipal de la Cultura). Just west of the Plaza Conde is the **Catedral** (daily 10am–1pm & 4–7pm), built in a mixture of styles but originally Transitional Gothic: take a look at the unusual eight-part vaults, dome-like in shape. You'll need to find the sexton to see the building's other interesting features: the *coro*, with wonderfully grotesque stalls carved by Rodrigo Alemán, who also created those at Toledo and Plasencia; the narthex, with statues of Apostles; and the cloisters (€1.20, free Wed pm), half of which are fourteenth century and half sixteenth century, with lurid carvings of biblical scenes.

A monument to **General Herrasti** and his men (see box opposite) stands in the little square beside the cathedral. A plaque in the corner of the walls near this marks the site of the Great Breach through which the British entered Ciudad Rodrigo; from outside the walls the position of the hole, later patched up with differently coloured stone, is clearly visible. The British guns were on the two ridges opposite (the lower one with the block of flats, the other higher up beyond the rail line) – you can see the cannonball dents above the doorway on this side of the cathedral.

Practicalities

Ciudad Rodrigo's **bus station** is a five-minute walk north of the town centre; the **train station** is ten minutes' walk along the road to Lumbreras, though there's only one train a day into Portugal leaving at 6am, and another nightly to Irún leaving at 1.15am. The town's **turismo** (Mon–Fri 9am–2pm & 5–7pm, Sat & Sun 10am–2pm & 5–8pm; ☎923 460 561, ⓦwww.ciudadrodrigo.net) faces the cathedral at the northern entrance to the town.

For reasonable budget **rooms** try *Pensión Madrid*, c/Madrid 20 (☎923 462 467), which has a couple of doubles (❷ –❸) and three fully equipped apartments with kitchen and bath for 2–5 people (❹). Other budget options include the excellent *Pensión París*, in the centre of the old town at c/Toro 10 (☎923 482 349;❸), and the impeccably clean *Pensión Moderno Francés*, c/Campo de Toledo 8 (☎923 461 968;❸), which is rather unatmospherically located opposite the bus station, above the bar of the same name (there's no sign). *Hotel Conde Rodrigo*, Plaza de San Salvador (☎ & ⓕ 923 461 408, ⓔh_c_rodrigo@ntserver.codeinf .com;❻), offers more comfort and is located in an attractive square, while *Parador Enrique II* (☎923 460 150, ⓕ923 460 404, ⓔciudadrodrigo@parador.es;❽) has an unrivalled location in the castle. There's a **campsite**, *La Pesquera*, by the river, just off the road to Cáceres (☎923 481 348; April–Sept).

Plaza Mayor is lined with **bars and restaurants**: the pleasant *La Artesa*, by the *ayuntamiento*, has good *menús* (from €9) and breakfasts (€1.70), while further along the square the cheaper *Bar Arcos* has reasonable-value *platos combinados*. Directly opposite the *Arcos* is the atmospheric little bar-restaurant *El Sanatorio*, its walls covered in bullfighting memorabilia, with cheap snacks (from €2.40) and meat dishes (€4–9). For even cheaper meals, head just north of the Plaza Mayor to c/Gigantes, where several restaurants offer bargain *menús*, among them the pleasantly old-fashioned *El Rodeo* at no. 10, and *Peperro*, which has less ambience but more choice, including a few vegetarian options. For a splurge, the restaurant at the *parador* is the best and most expensive in town.

The Sierra Peña de Francia

The village of La Alberca is a good place to head for, both in its own right, and as a starting point for walks in the **Sierra Peña de Francia**. There are daily buses from Salamanca, but only on Sunday does the timetable make a day-trip possible.

La Alberca

LA ALBERCA has an extraordinary collection of houses, constructed from diverse materials: wood, pebbles, stone and rubble built in amongst the rocks. Due to its national monument status, plenty of tidying-up is going on, and "local craft" shops have sprung up all over, but the character of a rural community remains: horses still take precedence over cars, the restorers use donkeys instead of vans, and goats, sheep and poultry often block the streets.

The most elegant houses are in the **Plaza Mayor**, which is dominated by a Calvary. Look into the church in the square behind for its elaborate polychromed pulpit, carved in a popular style. These days most of the houses in the Plaza Mayor seem to serve as cafés for the tourist trade, but there is an air of timelessness to the place. Many age-old traditions, including costume, have survived, and the local celebration of the Feast of the Assumption on August 15 is considered to be the best in Spain.

There's a shortage of budget **accommodation**, the only reliable place being *Pensión Hernandez* off the Plaza Mayor at c/Tablado 3 (☎923 415 039; ❸). If money's no problem, the four-star *Hotel Doña Teresa* (☎923 415 308, ℹ923 415 309; ❼), on the road to Mogarraz, is very chic and well equipped (with Jacuzzi, gym, sauna and sunbeds), while the long-established *Hotel Las Batuecas* (☎923 415 188, ℹ923 415 055; ❻), on the road to Las Batuecas, has a more rustic feel and an excellent restaurant. There is a campsite, the *Al-Bereka* (☎923 415 195; April–Sept), with a pool, on the Salamanca road.

La Peña de Francia

A very circuitous road behind La Alberca climbs to the summit of the **Peña de Francia**. The road emerges from the trees halfway up to give fine panoramas not only of the mountain itself (disfigured by a television tower serving the whole province and beyond) and the plains below, but also out over the wild hills of Las Hurdes to the south and the Sierra de Gredos to the east. At the top you can have lunch or refreshments at the *hospedería* of the **Monasterio Peña de Francia**, where it's also possible to stay overnight (☎923 164 000, ℹ923 164 001; ❻).

Valle de Las Batuecas

Another excellent trip from La Alberca is south to the **Valle de Las Batuecas**, a national reserve bordering Las Hurdes (see p.219). This makes an impressive day-long walk or a beautiful drive; you'll need to take a picnic, for although fresh water abounds, there isn't a bar, restaurant or even house in sight until you reach the village of Las Mestas, just over the Extremaduran border, some 19km away.

From La Alberca, take the minor road south out of the village. After 2km you'll come to the pass of **El Portillo**, surrounded by solemn, rugged hills. From here, the road dips and loops spectacularly, offering a different vista at every turn. You reach the valley floor at the 12km point, and a short road leads to the gate of the **Carmelite Monastery**, founded at the beginning of the seventeenth century for a reclusive community. One of the first tasks of the monastery was to exorcize the demons and evil spirits which supposedly inhabited the nearby valleys of Las Hurdes. In 1933, the great film-maker **Luis Buñuel** stayed in the monastery – then a hotel – while shooting his early masterpiece, *Land Without Bread,* about the extremely primitive lifestyle of the people of these valleys.

A footpath skirts the outside of the monastery's perimeter wall and follows the course of the river, which forms a gorge with splendid rock formations. There are **caves** with prehistoric rock paintings here, but unfortunately the most important ones have had to be closed in order to preserve them from deterioration and vandalism.

If you're walking back to La Alberca after exploring the valley, you're faced with a daunting climb; there is little traffic, although the chances of a lift from cars that do pass are good. By car, it makes a good round trip to keep going beyond **Las Mestas**, turning east at the T-junction and crossing back into Salamanca province via **Miranda del Castañar**, with its pretty views and romantic, crumbling castle.

Zamora to Valladolid

Zamora is the quietest of the great Castilian cities, with a population of just 75,000. Its province is pretty low-key, too, though with a cluster of historic names. The road east from Zamora follows the **Río Duero** into the heartland of Old Castile, taking in **Toro**, the site of the battle which established Fernando and Isabel on the Spanish throne in 1476, and **Tordesillas**, where the treaty which ratified the division of lands discovered in the New World was signed in 1494.

Zamora

In medieval romances, **ZAMORA** was known as *la bien cercada* (the enclosed one) on account of its strong fortifications; one siege here lasted seven months. Its old quarters, still walled and medieval in appearance, are spread out along the top of a ridge which slopes down to the banks of the Río Duero (known as the Douro once it crosses into Portugal). The minor road heading east to Toro along the south bank of the river offers good opportunities for bird-watching and fishing.

Arrival and information

Zamora is very spread out, and arrival can be confusing. The **train station** and the **bus terminal** are close to each other, twenty minutes' walk north from the Plaza Mayor. From the bus station, turn right out of the main entrance then right again around the side of the terminal to reach the main road, the Avenida de las Tres Cruces; turn left along this road to reach the old town. From the train station walk straight out over the roundabout in front to join the Avenida de las Tres Cruces, which veers round to the right. The **turismo** (Mon–Fri 9am–2pm & 5–7pm, Sat & Sun 10am–2pm & 5–8pm; ☎980 531 845, ⓦwww.ayto-zamora.com) is at c/Santa Clara 20. For **internet** access, head for *Ciberc@fé* on Plaza Viriato (daily 11am–3am).

Accommodation

Zamora has a reasonable spread of **accommodation**, most of it centred in the old quarter. Except during Easter week few places run out of space, but if you do get stuck the turismo can help you out.

Parador Condes de Alba de Aliste, Plaza de Viriato 1 ☎980 514 497, ⓕ980 530 063, ⒺSzamora@parador.es. One of Spain's most beautiful *paradores*, situated in a fifteenth-century ducal palace in the heart of town and with a superb restaurant attached. Go in for a look at the marvellous courtyard even if you're not staying. ❽
Hostería Real de Zamora, Cuesta Pizarro 7 ☎980 534 545, ⓕ980 534 522, Ⓔhostzamora@wanadoo.es. Gorgeous and surprisingly affordable hotel set in the 400-year-old Palacio de Inquisidores, complete with tiled staircases, cobbled Renaissance patio and goldfish pond. The larger downstairs rooms with river views are much better value than those upstairs. ❼
Hostal La Reina, c/La Reina 1, 1º ☎980 533 939. Best budget accommodation in town, with spacious and immaculate rooms (some en suite) overlooking the Plaza Mayor, and a very friendly *dueña*. ❸
Hostal Sol, c/Benavente 2, 3º ☎ & ⓕ 980 533 152; ❺. Modern rooms, a little on the small side, but smart and well equipped (all with bathroom, TV and phone). It's in the same block as two other, slightly cheaper, *hostales*: Hostal Luz ☎ 980 533 152 (❺), belonging to the same owners, and *Hostal Chiqui* ☎980 531 480 (❹).

The Town

In and around the old centre are a dozen **Romanesque churches** (most open March to mid-Oct Tues–Sun 10am–1pm & 5–8pm; mid-Oct to Dec Fri & Sat 10am–2pm & 4.30–6.30pm) which, with their unassumingly beautiful architecture and towers populated by colonies of storks, are the city's most distinctive feature. The majority date from the twelfth century and reflect Old Castile's sense of security following the victorious campaigns against the Moors by Alfonso VI and El Cid – notably the recapture of Toledo in 1085. **San Juan de Puerta Nueva**, in Plaza Mayor, and **Santiago del Burgo**, to

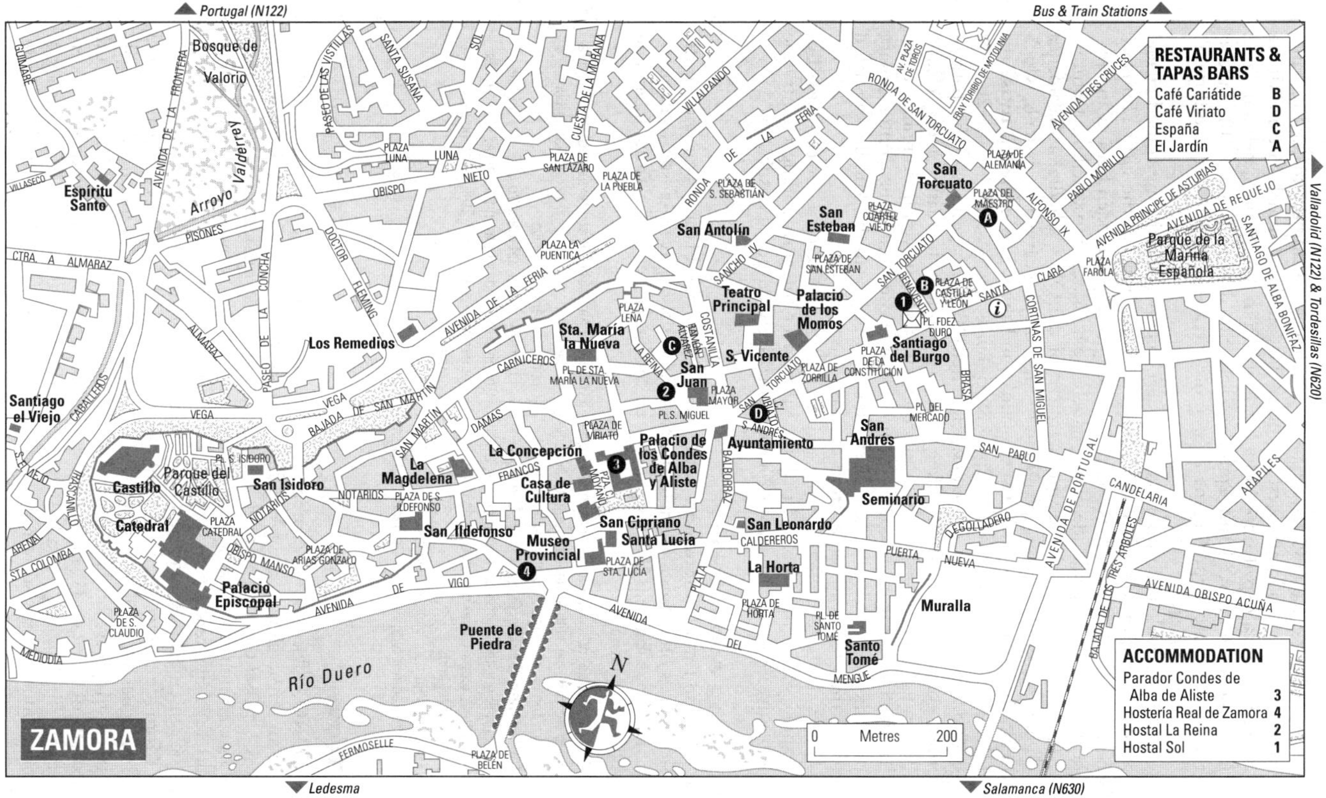

ZAMORA
RESTAURANTS & TAPAS BARS
Café Cariátide B
Café Viriato D
España C
El Jardín A
ACCOMMODATION
Parador Condes de Alba de Aliste 3
Hostería Real de Zamora 4
Hostal La Reina 2
Hostal Sol 1
0 Metres 200
N
Portugal (N122)
Bus & Train Stations
Valladolid (N122) & Tordesillas (N620)
Ledesma
Salamanca (N630)
Río Duero
Puente de Piedra
Bosque de Valorio
Arroyo Valderrey
Espíritu Santo
Santiago el Viejo
Castillo
Parque del Castillo
Catedral
Palacio Episcopal
San Isidoro
La Magdelena
San Ildefonso
Los Remedios
La Concepción
Casa de Cultura
Museo Provincial
San Cipriano
Santa Lucía
Palacio de los Condes de Alba y Aliste
Sta. María la Nueva
San Juan
S. Vicente
Teatro Principal
Palacio de los Momos
San Antolín
San Esteban
San Torcuato
Santiago del Burgo
Ayuntamiento
San Andrés
Seminario
San Leonardo
La Horta
Santo Tomé
Muralla
Parque de la Marina Española
AVENIDA PRINCIPE DE ASTURIAS
AVENIDA DE REQUEJO
SANTIAGO DE ALBA BONIFAZ
AVENIDA TRES CRUCES
PABLO MORILLO
ALFONSO IX
RONDA DE SAN TORCUATO
FRAY TORIBIO DE MOTOLINIA
AV. PLAZA DE TOROS
CORTINAS DE SAN MIGUEL
AVENIDA DE PORTUGAL
AVENIDA OBISPO ACUÑA
BAJADA DE LOS TRES ARBOLES
CANDELARIA
ARAPILES
SAN PABLO
DEGOLLADERO
PUERTA NUEVA
AVENIDA DEL MENGUE
AVENIDA DE VIGO
BALBORRAZ
CALDEREROS
COSTANILLA
SAN TORCUATO
RONDA DE LA FERIA
AVENIDA DE LA FERIA
VILLALPANDO
SANCHO IV
CUESTA DE LA MORANA
PASEO DE LAS VISTILLAS
SANTA SUSANA
SOL
OBISPO
NIETO
LUNA
DOCTOR FLEMING
PASEO DE LA CONCHA
PISONES
AVENIDA DE LA FRONTERA
CTRA. A ALMARAZ
ALMARAZ
GUIMARE
VILLASECO
CABALLEROS
VEGA
BAJADA DE SAN MARTIN
SAN MARTIN
DAMAS
FRANCOS
NOTARIOS
CARNICEROS
LA REINA
TRASCANILLO
ARENAL
STA. COLOMBA
MEDIODIA
OBISPO MANSO
FERMOSELLE
S. E. VIEJO
BRASA
CLARA
SANTA
BENAVENTE
C/ VIRIATO
S. ANDRÉS
PLAZA MAYOR
PL. S. MIGUEL
PLAZA DE VIRIATO
PZA. C. MOYANO
PLAZA DE STA. LUCÍA
PLAZA DE S. ILDEFONSO
PLAZA DE ARIAS GONZALO
PLAZA CATEDRAL
PL. S. ISIDORO
PLAZA DE S. CLAUDIO
PLAZA DE BELÉN
PL. DE STA. MARÍA LA NUEVA
PLAZA LENA
RAMÓN ALVAREZ
PLAZA DE ZORRILLA
PLAZA DE LA CONSTITUCIÓN
PL. DEL MERCADO
PL. FDEZ. DURO
PLAZA DE CASTILLA Y LEÓN
PLAZA DEL MAESTRO
PLAZA DE ALEMANIA
PLAZA CUARTEL VIEJO
PLAZA DE SAN ESTEBAN
PLAZA DE S. SEBASTIÁN
PLAZA DE LA PUEBLA
PLAZA DE SAN LÁZARO
PLAZA LA PUENTICA
PLAZA LUNA
PLAZA FAROLA
PLAZA DE HORTA
PL. DE SANTO TOMÉ

the east along c/Santa Clara, are two of the most rewarding. Attached to Santa María la Nueva, slightly west of Plaza Mayor, the unusual **Museo de la Semana Santa** (April–Sept Mon–Sat 10am–2pm & 5–8pm, Sun 10am–2pm; Oct–March Mon–Sat 10am–2pm & 4–7pm, Sun 10am–2pm; €1.80) contains the *pasos* – statues depicting the Passion of Christ – which are paraded through the streets at Easter.

The **Catedral** (same hours as churches), enclosed within the ruined citadel at the far end of town, has little of the discreet charm of the city's churches. Begun in 1151, its mainly Romanesque body is largely hidden behind an overbearing Renaissance facade, above which the building's most striking feature – a Byzantine-inspired dome similar to that of the Old Cathedral at Salamanca – perches in incongruous splendour. Inside, note the carved choir stalls, which depict lusty carryings-on between monks and nuns. The cathedral **museum** (Tues–Sat: April–Sept 11am–2pm & 5–8pm; Oct–March 11am–2pm & 4–6pm; €1.80) houses the city's celebrated "Black Tapestries". The patrons who commissioned these fifteenth-century Flemish masterpieces clearly demanded their money's worth, since every inch is woven in stunning detail. Traditional Greek and Roman themes were chosen but often contemporary dress and weaponry intruded, illustrating how nobles in the Middle Ages liked to see themselves as heroes from the past.

Next to the cathedral are the impressive moated remains of the **Castillo**; wander round the back for majestic views over the surrounding countryside and River Duero, along with Zamora's massively burgeoning suburbs.

Eating and drinking

You'll find most **restaurants and cafés** around the Plaza Mayor and on the side streets off c/Santa Clara to the east. There's also a lively cluster of no-nonsense **tapas bars** in the alleys between the eastern end of c/Santa Clara and Plaza de Alemania.

Café Cariátide, c/Benavente 5. Pleasant and spacious old café-bar with a modest range of *bocadillos* and tapas and a restaurant attached.

Café Viriato, c/Viriato. Elegant place to enjoy a quiet drink outside on the pavement by day; by night it attracts a young crowd, staying open until 5am at weekends.

España, c/Ramón Álvarez. Wonderfully old-fashioned restaurant with fusty 1950s decor and clientele to match. Choice of *menús* (€6) and cheap à la carte dishes, plus a few vegetarian options – none of them expensive.

El Jardín, Plaza del Maestro 5–8. One of the many lively tapas bars in this area; also serves gargantuan *menús* (€7.20) on the pleasant square outside.

Toro

TORO, 30km east of Zamora, looks dramatic: "an ancient, eroded, red-walled town spread along the top of a huge flat boulder", as Laurie Lee described it in *As I Walked Out One Midsummer Morning*. Its raw, red, hillside site is best contemplated from the rail line several hundred feet below the town in the Duero valley; at closer quarters it turns out to be a pleasant, rather ordinary provincial town, though embellished with one outstanding Romanesque reminder of past glory.

Toro did, however, play a role of vital significance in both Spanish and Portuguese history. The **Battle of Toro** in 1476 effectively ended Portugal's interest in Spanish affairs and laid the basis for the unification of Spain. On the death of Enrique IV in 1474, the Castilian throne was disputed: almost certainly his daughter Juana la Beltraneja was the rightful heiress, but rumours of illegitimacy were stirred up and Enrique's sister Isabel seized the throne.

Alfonso V of Portugal saw his opportunity and supported Juana. At Toro the armies clashed in 1476 and the Reyes Católicos – Isabel and her husband Fernando – defeated their rivals to embark upon one of the most glorious periods in Spanish history.

Toro had long been a major military stronghold, and the monument that hints most strongly at this former importance is the **Colegiata Santa María la Mayor** (Tues–Sun 10am–1pm & 5–8pm; €0.60). The West Portal (c. 1240) inside the church is one of the best-preserved and most beautiful examples of Romanesque art in the region, its seven recessed arches carved with royal and biblical themes, still retaining much of their colourful original paint. Outside, there are grand views over the *meseta*, with the River Duero far below.

The Dominican **Monasterio Sancti Spiritus** on the western edge of town (Tues–Sun 10.30am–12.30pm & 4.30–6.30pm, guided tours 10.30am, 11.15am, noon, 5.30pm, 6.15 pm & 7pm; €2.40) is worth a visit, too. It's a rambling fourteenth-century building containing some genuine treasures in amongst the mass of exhibits – chiefly a series of sixteenth-century Flemish tapestries depicting the betrayal and Crucifixion of Christ. In the church is the tomb of Beatriz of Portugal (wife of Juan I of Castile, died 1410), who lived here for various periods after she was widowed at the age of 18.

Practicalities

Trains to Toro are few and far between, and it's a steep 1.5km uphill walk from the station to the town. It's much easier to visit using one of the reasonably frequent Zamora–Valladolid **buses** (Mon–Sat 5–7 daily, Sun 3 daily); these drop passengers on the north side of town – walk through the big arch and straight on for about five minutes (passing directly under the church tower) to reach the *ayuntamiento*, where you'll find the **turismo** (Tues–Sun 10am–2pm & 4–8pm; Ⓦ www.toroayto.es). The Colegiata Santa María la Mayor is immediately behind here.

If you want **to stay**, there's a choice between the simple *Hostal Doña Elvira*, c/Antonio Miguélez 47 (Ⓣ 980 690 062; ❸), and the upmarket *Hotel Juan II* at Plaza del Espolón 1 (Ⓣ 980 690 300, Ⓕ 980 692 376; ❺), right by the Colegiata Santa María la Mayor. If you're coming by train, there's a *hostal*, *La Estación* (Ⓣ 980 692 936; ❸), next to the station. For **eating** and **drinking**, try the colourful line of bar-restaurants opposite the *ayuntamiento*.

Tordesillas

TORDESILLAS, like Toro, can boast an important place in Spain's history. It was here, under the eye of the Borgia Pope Alexander VI, that the **Treaty of Tordesillas** (1494) divided "All Lands Discovered, or Hereafter to be Discovered in the West, towards the Indies or the Ocean Seas" between Spain and Portugal, along a line 370 leagues west of the Cape Verde Islands. Brazil, allegedly discovered six years later, went to Portugal – though it was claimed that the Portuguese already knew of its existence but had kept silent to gain better terms. The rest of the New World, including Mexico and Peru, became Spanish.

Further fame was brought to Tordesillas by the unfortunate **Juana la Loca** (Joanna the Mad), who spent 46 years in a windowless cell here. She had ruled Castile jointly with her husband Felipe I from 1504–6 but was devastated by his early death and for three years toured the monasteries of Spain, keeping the coffin perpetually by her side, stopping from time to time to inspect the corpse. In 1509 she reached the Convent of Santa Clara in Tordesillas, where first Fernando (her father) and later Carlos V (her son) declared her insane, imprisoning her for half a century and assuming the throne of Castile for themselves.

Juana's place of confinement could have been worse. The **Real Monasterio de Santa Clara** (April–Sept Tues–Sat 10am–1pm & 3.30–6.30pm, Sun 10.30am–1.30pm & 3.30–5.30pm; Oct–March Tues–Sat 10.30am–1pm & 4–5.30pm, Sun 10.30am–1.30pm & 3.30–5.30pm; €3.50, free Wed, €2.25 for Arab baths by prior arrangement on ☎983 770 071) overlooks the Duero and is known as "The Alhambra of Castile" for its delightful Mudéjar architecture. Built as a royal palace by Alfonso el Sabio (the Wise) in 1340, its prettiest features are the tiny "Arab Patio" with horseshoe arches and Moorish decoration, and the superb *artesonado* ceiling of the main chapel, described by Sacheverell Sitwell as "a ceiling of indescribable splendour, as brilliant in effect as if it had panes or slats of mother-of-pearl in it".

Further places of interest in Tordesillas include the long medieval **bridge** over the Duero, the arcaded **Plaza Mayor** and the church of **San Antolín** (March–Nov Tues–Sun 10.30am–2pm & 4–7pm; rest of the year by prior arrangement on ☎983 770 980; €1.80), now a museum with an impressive collection of sculpture and excellent views from its tower.

Practicalities

The bus station is just outside the centre – you'll see the old town walls from the terminal. Inside the walls, all roads lead sooner or later to the Plaza Mayor. From here exit the square beneath the building sporting the clock and flags to reach a bluff overlooking the river. Turn left here to reach the Real Monasterio de Santa Clara or right to reach San Antolín, next door to which there's a small turismo (Tues–Sat 10am–1.30pm & 4–6.30pm, closes 7.30pm in summer, Sun 10am–2pm; ☎983 771 067).

There's nowhere **to stay** in the old town, and although there are plenty of options in the drab modern surrounding areas, they tend to be expensive. The lowest-priced is the *Lorenzo* (☎983 770 228; ❸), on the Salamanca road, and there's a cluster of uninspiring mid-range options around the bus station. Alternatively, *Los Toreros*, Avda. de Valladolid 26 (☎983 771 900, ℱ983 771 954; ❺), has immaculate rooms and a good restaurant. The modern *parador* (☎983 770 051; ℱ983 771 013; ❸) is on the Salamanca road, and there's a well-equipped **campsite** (☎983 770 953; April–Sept) opposite. Inexpensive **places to eat**, including the busy *Viky*, can be found on the Plaza Mayor and along c/San Anton. For a splurge, the restaurant at the *parador* is excellent.

Medina del Campo

MEDINA DEL CAMPO, 24km south of Tordesillas, and the major rail junction before Valladolid, stands below one of the region's great castles. The Moorish design of the brick-built **Castillo La Mota** (Mon–Sat 11am–2pm & 4–6pm, Sun 11am–2pm; €1.20) is similar to that at Coca further east, but less exotic and more robust. It was intended as another stronghold for the same family, the Fonsecas, but they were thrown out by the townsfolk in 1473. Queen Isabel lived here for several years (and died, in 1504, in a room overlooking the town's Plaza Mayor), after which the castle was reincarnated as a prison, then as a girls' boarding school, and more recently as a Casa de la Cultura. You can go inside the castle walls, but there are no rooms to see, and it is the exterior which is impressive.

In the fifteenth and sixteenth centuries, Medina del Campo (Market of the Field) was one of the most important market towns in the whole of Europe, with merchants converging from as far afield as Italy and Germany to attend its fairs. The largest sheep market in Spain is still held here and the beautifully ramshackle **Plaza Mayor** is evocative of the days when its bankers determined the value of European currencies.

Budget **rooms** are offered by *Pensión Medina* (✆983 802 603; ❷) and the smarter *Mesón la Plaza* (✆983 811 246; ❸), both on the Plaza Mayor (also known as Plaza de la Hispanidad). You could also try mid-range *Hostal-Residencia La Mota* (✆983 800 450; ❺) at c/Fernando el Católico 4, on the other side of the bridge from the centre. For **meals**, *Restaurante Monaco* on the Plaza Mayor is a splendid place with a bargain *menú*.

Valladolid

VALLADOLID, at the centre of the *meseta*, ought to be exciting. Many of the greatest figures of Spain's Golden Age – Fernando and Isabel, Columbus, Cervantes, Felipe II – lived in the city at some point and for many years it vied with Madrid as the royal capital. In reality its old quarter is today an oppressive labyrinth of dingy streets, and those of its palaces that survive do so in a woeful state of decline. Many of the finest have been swept away on a tide of speculation and official incompetence, to be replaced by a dull sprawl of high-rise concrete. Modern Valladolid may be an expanding industrial city of 400,000 inhabitants but it has lost much that was irreplaceable. The one time you might actively seek to be in Valladolid is **Semana Santa** – Easter week – when it is host to some of the most extravagant and solemn processions in Spain.

Arrival and information

Arrival points are centred around the Campo Grande, a large triangular park to the southwest of the city centre where Napoleon once reviewed his troops: the **train station** is on Paseo de Campo Grande, and the **bus station** is a ten-minute walk west at c/Puente Lodgante 2. The **turismo** is in the city centre at c/Santiago 19 (daily 9am–2pm & 5–7pm; ✆983 344 013, 🌐www.dip-valladolid.es), and there's an **internet** café, *Bocattanet*, at Maria de Molina 16, just north of Plaza de Zorilla.

Accommodation

Accommodation in Valladolid is plentiful and good value. The main concentration of rooms, in all price ranges, is in the pleasant area around the Plaza Mayor; there are also lots of cheaper options down the east side of Campo Grande on the way to the bus station.

Budget options

Pensión La Cueva, c/Correos 4 ✆983 330 072. Slightly frayed but perfectly comfortable en-suite rooms in an excellent location just off the Plaza Mayor. ❸

Pensión Dani, c/Perú 11, 1° ✆983 300 249. Atmospheric and beautifully maintained old *pensión* with creaky wooden floors and high ceilings, in a quiet side street five minutes south of the city centre. Excellent value. ❷

Pensión Dos Rosas, c/Perú 11, 2° ✆983 207 439. Upstairs from the *Pensión Dani* and equally good value – it's owned by the same family. ❷

Hostal Val II, Plaza del Val 6 ✆983 375 752. Twelve reasonable rooms with and without bath in the very central but slightly run-down market area just north of Plaza Mayor. ❸

Moderate and expensive options

Hotel La Enara, Plaza de España 5 ✆983 300 211, 🖷983 300 311. Reasonable hotel in a central location, with characterful wood-panelled and stained-glass entrance. Rooms are OK, though a little past their best. ❺

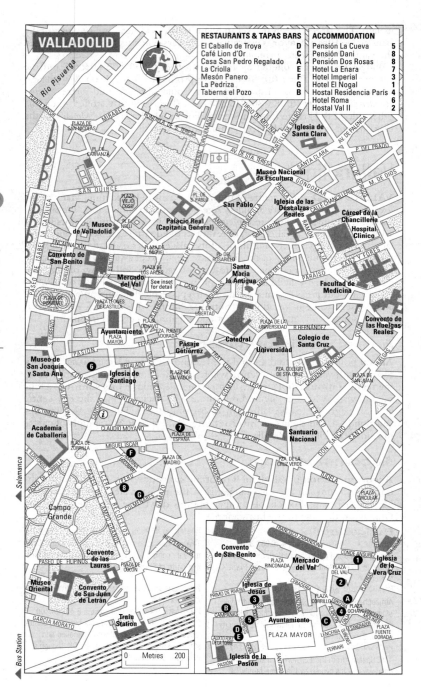

VALLADOLID

N

RESTAURANTS & TAPAS BARS

El Caballo de Troya	D
Café Lion d'Or	C
Casa San Pedro Regalado	A
La Criolla	E
Mesón Panero	F
La Pedriza	G
Taberna el Pozo	B

ACCOMMODATION

Pensión La Cueva	5
Pensión Dani	8
Pensión Dos Rosas	8
Hotel La Enara	7
Hotel Imperial	3
Hotel El Nogal	1
Hostal Residencia París	4
Hotel Roma	6
Hostal Val II	2

0   Metres   200

Hotel Imperial, c/del Paseo 4 ☎ 983 330 300, ⓕ 983 330 813, ⓦ www.vasertel.es/himpe. Swish hotel in a beautiful old-town mansion right by the Plaza Mayor. Worth visiting the bar for a drink among the Renaissance columns even if you're not staying. ❼

Hotel El Nogal, c/Conde Ansurez 10 ☎ 983 340 333, ⓕ 983 354 965. Pleasant and good-value little hotel with its own homely bar and restaurant, tucked away in a backstreet near the Plaza Mayor. ❻

Hostal Residencia París, c/Especería 2 ☎ 983 370 625, ⓕ 983 358 301. Comfortable and central hotel with its own car park and good-quality rooms grouped around a superb *modernista*-style staircase. ❻

Hotel Roma, c/Héroes del Alcázar de Toledo 6 ☎ 983 351 833, ⓕ 983 355 461. Plush, excellent-value rooms in a great location, with a good restaurant attached and its own parking. ❼

The City

Despite the despoliation of many of the city's finest monuments, there are a couple of terrific examples of late-Gothic architecture, an excellent Oriental museum and – above all – the finest collection of sculpture assembled anywhere in Spain. Aside from the national museum, almost all of the city's historic churches contain further examples of Valladolid's passionate religious sculpture.

The Plaza Mayor and around

The heart of Valladolid is the spacious **Plaza Mayor**, a broad, pedestrianized expanse surrounded by arcaded buildings painted a striking, uniform red. Originally laid out in the sixteenth century after a fire had devastated the city, it was the first plaza of its kind in the country, becoming the model for count-less similar civic centrepieces both in Spain and her South American colonies. Though much rebuilt since, it's still one of the grandest urban spaces in Spain and a pleasant place to watch the world go by, while many of Valladolid's best restaurants can be found in the narrow streets just off its western edge.

A few minutes' walk to the west of the plaza, the **Museo de San Joaquín y Santa Ana** (Mon 5–8pm, Tues–Sat 10am–1pm & 5–8pm, Sun 10am–1pm; €2) is filled mostly with religious dust-collectors but has a few good statues, plus three Goya paintings in the chapel. North of the plaza, beyond the down-at-heel area around the **Mercado del Val**, is the imposing **Convento de San Benito**, now used for temporary exhibitions. Continuing north up c/San Ignacio brings you to the **Museo de Valladolid** (Tues–Fri 9.45am–2pm & 4–7.15pm, Sat & Sun 9.45am–2.15pm; €1.80, free Sat & Sun), an archeologi-cal museum and art gallery set in a Renaissance mansion.

The cathedral and university

Ten minutes' walk east of the Plaza Mayor, the **Catedral** (Tues–Sat 10am–1.30pm & 4.30–7pm, Sun 10am–2pm) was designed but not completed by Juan de Herrera (architect of El Escorial) and later worked on by Alberto Churriguera; only half of it was ever built, but the model in its museum (same hours as cathedral; €2.10) shows how classically grand the original design was. What stands is a disappointment: the vast dimensions and sweeping arches do have something of Herrera's grandeur, but the overall effect is one of plainness and severity. Inside, the highlight is the *retablo mayor* by Juan de Juni, which was actually made for the Gothic Santa María la Antigua in the large plaza behind.

Just beyond the cathedral, Valladolid's **Universidad** has a portal by Narciso Tomé, the man who built the *Transparente* in Toledo Cathedral – one of his very few surviving works. Further on, part of the university administration is housed in the **Colegio de Santa Cruz**, a late-fifteenth-century edifice which signals the introduction of Renaissance architecture to Spain. The beautiful three-storey patio is open to the public during office hours.

San Pablo and the sculpture museum

North of the cathedral, c/de las Angustias leads a short distance to Plaza de San Pablo and its unmistakeable church. The exuberant facade of **San Pablo** is a wild mixture of styles: the lower part is a product of the lavish form of late Gothic known as Isabelline, whereas the upper part is a Plateresque confection, similar to the New Cathedral and San Esteban at Salamanca. The facade of the adjacent **Colegio de San Gregorio**, a purer example of the Isabelline style, is adorned with coats of arms, sculpted twigs, naked children clambering in the branches of a tree and several comical, long-haired men carrying maces. It's a lot like icing on a cake – Jan Morris, for one, was convinced that the flamboyant facades must be edible.

Behind the gaudy front, there's serious business, for San Gregorio houses the dynamic **Museo Nacional de Escultura** (Tues–Sat 10am–2pm & 4–6pm, Sun 10am–2pm; €2.40, free Sat 4–6pm & Sun), where some of the most brilliant works of the Spanish Renaissance are on display. Much the most important figures in this movement were Alonso Berruguete, Diego de Siloé and Juan de Juni: all three were active in the sixteenth century and spent several years in Florence where they perfected the realistic depiction of anatomy, fell heavily under the influence of Michelangelo and immersed themselves in the Italian Renaissance. Their genius lies in the adaptation of the classical revival to the religious intensity of the Spanish temperament. The masterpiece of **Alonso Berruguete** (1486–1561) is a massive, dismantled *retablo* which occupies the first three rooms of the museum – a remarkable demonstration of his skills in painting, relief sculpture and freestanding statuary. **Diego de Siloé** (1495–1565) was even more versatile. He created a classical building from the Gothic cathedral at Granada and was an equally accomplished sculptor – see his *Sagrada Familia* in Room 12 and the carved choir stalls in Room 11. Works of the Frenchman **Juan de Juni** (1507–77) show an almost theatrical streak and foreshadowed the emotional and naturalistic sculpture of the seventeenth and eighteenth centuries. This later period is best exemplified by the agonizingly realistic work of **Gregorio Fernández** (rooms 4 and 5, near the ticket desk) and **Alonso de Villabrille** (especially his *Head of San Pablo*, Room 27).

While here, you should also take in the beautiful **patio** with lacelike tracery, and several Moorish-inspired ceilings taken from other buildings in the city. The chapel (entrance is immediately left of the main door, opposite the ticket booth) has many interesting exhibits, including another *retablo* by Alonso Berruguete, this time intact (hours are the same as for the museum).

The Museo Oriental

The delightful **Museo Oriental** (Mon–Sat 4–7pm, Sun 10am–2pm; €2.70) is on the southern side of the city centre, near the train station. This occupies a dozen rooms in the Colegio de Agustinos, which sent missionaries to China and the Philippines for four centuries until their expulsion in 1952. Among the countless exquisite gems of Chinese art on show are some beautiful nature paintings on rice paper (mainly Sung dynasty; Room 9), three gorgeous porcelain pieces entitled *The Three Happy Chinamen: Fu, Shou and Lou* (Qing epoch; Room 2) and some stunning ivory carvings from the Philippines (Room 14). On the way out you can admire the lavishly decorated interior of the church, a good example of the academic style of Ventura Rodríguez, fashionable in the late eighteenth century. Have a look too at the elaborate facade of the **Convento San Juan de Letran** next door.

Eating, drinking and nightlife

The central area is the best place for **eating and drinking**. The Plaza Mayor is a popular place to linger, while c/Correos, just to the west, is packed with smart restaurants. There's a cluster of raucous late-opening **bars** northeast of the cathedral around Santa María la Antigua and up c/Marqués de Duero and c/Paraíso, and there's also **live jazz** in the *Café España* at Plaza Fuente Dorada 8, just east of the Plaza Mayor. For something a little different try the anti-quated *El Penicilino* on Plaza de la Libertad, by the cathedral, with an atmosphere more like an apothecary than a bar; its speciality is a lurid (but alcohol-free) range of fluorescent fruit liquors made on the premises.

El Caballo de Troya, c/Correos. Upmarket but affordable Castilian cuisine: choose between the award-winning restaurant or the slightly cheaper *taverna*, both with *menús* (€16.20 in the restaurant; €12 in the *taverna*) and pricier à la carte dishes. Alternatively, have a drink and tapas in the tiny gem of a Renaissance courtyard.

Café Lion d'Or, Plaza Mayor. Attractive old café on the Plaza Mayor with black marble pillars, gilt mirrors and wrought-iron furniture – somewhere between a Viennese coffee house and a garden centre – plus outside seating on the square; a good place to watch the world go by.

Casa San Pedro Regalado, Plaza del Ochavo 1. Nice little garlic-strung bar-restaurant close to Plaza Mayor, with traditional Castilian fare and good-value *menús* (€7.20).

La Criolla, c/Correos. One of many restaurants in town serving the Valladolid speciality, *lechazo asado* (roast lamb). Closed Mon.

Mesón Panero, c/Marina Escobar 1 ☎983 301 673. The city's gastronomic temple – pricey, but not horribly so. Closed Sun evening.

La Pedriza, c/Colmenares 10. No menu – only roast lamb served here (and at its best); moderately priced. Closed Mon.

Taberna el Pozo, c/de Campañas 2 (off c/Correos). Moderately priced Castilian specialities, plus a long and varied list of tapas and *raciones*; very popular with locals.

Palencia

PALENCIA is Castile's least known and least impressive province and its capital city is no exception. Despite a rich past, it has no great sights. There are numerous plazas, usually dominated by Romanesque churches built in a rather gaunt white stone, but while all are pleasant, none is outstanding.

The **Catedral** (Mon–Sat 10.30am–1.30pm & 4.30–6.30pm, closed Sun pm), a fourteenth- to fifteenth-century Gothic building, is plain by Spanish standards, except for the two south portals. Inside, most of the decoration is contemporary with, or only slightly later than, the architecture, thanks to the patronage of Bishop Fonseca. Soon after it was completed, Palencia fell into decline, hence the almost complete absence of Baroque trappings. Buy a ticket in the sacristy to see the artistic treasures; one of the staff will take you to the crypt (part Visigothic, part Romanesque) and the museum in the cloisters, which includes a very early *San Sebastián* by El Greco and Flemish tapestries. In addition, lights are switched on so you can see the various altars, and the chapel doors opened. The highlight is probably the *retablo mayor*, which contains twelve beautiful little panels, ten of them painted by Juan de Flandes, court painter to Isabel la Católica – it's the best collection of his work anywhere.

Practicalities

Palencia's **bus and train stations** are both on the Plaza Calvo Sotelo. Calle Mayor is over on the far side of the square to your left as you leave either terminal; walk down it for ten minutes, passing the Plaza Mayor en route, to reach the **turismo** (Mon–Fri 9am–2pm & 5–7pm, Sat & Sun 10am–2pm & 5–8pm;

ⓣ979 740 068, ⓦ www.palencia.com/ayuntamiento or www.dip-palencia.es) at c/Mayor 105, just before the end of the pedestrianized section (there's another, irregularly open kiosk in the park opposite). A couple of minutes' further on is the friendly *El Salón*, Avda. República Argentina 10 (ⓣ979 726 442; ❸), with thirteen spotless rooms in a modern block; *Hostal Ávila*, at c/Conde Vallellano 5 (ⓣ979 711 910, ⓕ979 711 910; ❻), is more luxurious but still good value; it's tucked away in the backstreets between Plaza Mayor and the turismo – turn left down c/San Bernado. For good tapas and *raciones* try *La Taberna Plaza Mayor* in the southeast corner of the Plaza Mayor, or *Casero*, slightly further along c/Mayor, which has a good *menú* and a big selection of tapas. For a mini-splurge, *Lorenzo*, Avda. Casado del Alisal 10 (closed mid-Sept to mid-Oct), is the city's top restaurant and quite modestly priced.

Around Palencia

South of Palencia, at the ugly, modern town of **Venta de Baños**, is an important train junction. If you are changing trains here, it's well worth following the signs to the village of **BAÑOS DE CERRATO**, 2km out of town. This has the oldest church in the peninsula – *Monumento Nacional 1* in the catalogue: a seventh-century basilica (Tues–Sun 10.30am–1.30pm) dedicated to **San Juan** by the Ostrogoth King Recesvinto. It has tiny lattice windows, horseshoe arches and incorporates materials from Roman buildings. The caretaker lives opposite.

PAREDES DE NAVA, on the train line to León, has another church of interest, **Santa Eulalia** (Sat 11am–1pm, Sun 5–7pm; other times by arrangement on ⓣ979 830 469). The great sculptor Alonso Berruguete was born here, as were many of his lesser-known relatives, and the parish church (with a beautifully tiled Romanesque tower) has been turned into a small museum full of their work. The collection is arranged in every available space, and includes pieces by many of the best-known of Berruguete's contemporaries, gathered from all the churches of this little town. Paredes also has a couple of **pensiones**: the *Sofia*, c/Santa María 3 (ⓣ979 830 774; ❸), and *La Venta*, on c/General Cabanellas (ⓣ979 830 495; ❺).

Castles south of the Duero

It is said there were once ten thousand castles in Spain. Of those that are left, some five hundred are in a reasonable state of repair, and Castile has far more than its fair share of them. The area south of Valladolid, and towards Segovia, is especially rich – ringed with a series of fortresses, many of them built in the fifteenth century to protect the royal headquarters.

Coca

Sixty kilometres south of Valladolid and connected with regular buses (Mon–Sat 2 daily), the village of **COCA** is home to the prettiest **fortress** imaginable (Mon–Fri 10.30am–1pm & 4.30–6pm, Sat & Sun 11am–1pm & 4.30–6pm, July–Sept closes 7pm, closed first Tues of each month; €2.10). Less a piece of military architecture than a country house masquerading as one, it's constructed from narrow pinkish bricks, encircled by a deep moat and fantastically decorated with octagonal turrets, merlons and elaborate castellation – an extraordinary design strongly influenced by Moorish architecture. The building dates from about 1400, and was the base of the powerful **Fonseca family**.

The village itself is pretty lifeless, but there are a few bars and if you ask in these you should be able to find a room for the night. While here, try to see the inside of the parish church of **Santa María**, where there are four tombs of the Fonseca family carved in white marble in the Italian Renaissance style. The power of the dynasty is indicated by the fact that they were able to hire Bartolomé Ordóñez, the sculptor of the tombs of the Reyes Católicos in Granada.

Cuéllar, Turégano, Pedraza and Sepúlveda

The route south by road from Valladolid passes another impressive ancient castle at **CUÉLLAR** (Sat & Sun 11am–2pm & 4–7pm), served by regular buses from Valladolid (Mon–Fri 12 daily, Sat & Sun 7 daily). Even more stunning is the one at **TURÉGANO**, 28km north of Segovia; it's essentially a fifteenth-century structure enclosing an early-thirteenth-century church, though it's currently closed for restoration (call ☎921 500 667 for up-to-date information).

East of Turégano, just off the main Segovia–Soria road, there are rewarding diversions to be made to Pedraza and Sepúlveda, both extraordinarily pretty villages. **PEDRAZA** is almost perfectly preserved from the sixteenth century, a homogeneity enhanced by the uniformity of the rich brown stone in which it's constructed. The village is protected on three sides by a steep valley; the only entrance is the single original gateway (which used to be the town prison) from where the narrow lanes spiral gently up towards a large **Plaza Mayor**, still used for a **bullfighting festival** in the first week in September. Pedraza also has a **castle** (privately owned), where the eight-year-old dauphin of France and his younger brother were imprisoned in 1526, given up by their father François I who swapped his freedom for theirs after he was captured at the battle of Pavia.

SEPÚLVEDA is less of a harmonious whole, but has a more dramatic setting, strung out high on a narrow spit of land between the Castilla and Duratón river valleys. Its physical and architectural high point is the distinctive Romanesque church of **El Salvador** (open third Sun in month), below which is a ruined castle out of which the town hall protrudes.

Both villages can be reached by bus from Valladolid, but are best avoided at weekends, when every *madrileño* with a Mercedes seems to descend on them for the local speciality, roast lamb. Sepúlveda is the better bet for **accommodation**, with three *hostales*: *Hernanz*, c/Conde de Sepúlveda 4 (☎921 540 378, ⓕ921 540 520; ⑤); *Postigo*, a few doors along at no. 22 (☎921 540 172; ④); and *Villa de Sepúlveda* on Ctra Boceguillas (☎921 500 302; ⑤). Pedraza has two hotels, both expensive (and luxurious): *De la Villa*, c/Calzada (☎921 508 651, ⓕ921 508 652; ⑦), and *La Posada de Don Mariano*, c/Mayor 14 (☎ & ⓕ921 509 886; ⑦).

The Pantano de Burgomillodo and Riaza

In addition to its castles, this area of Old Castile is rich in **wildlife**. The **Pantano de Burgomillodo**, a reservoir just to the west of Sepúlveda, is a particularly exciting spot for bird-watchers, surrounded by heaths of wild lavender which are the haunt of griffon vultures and other exotic species. From here you can head towards El Burgo de Osma on the road through **RIAZA**, skirting the foothills of the Sierra de Guadarrama. It's a lovely route, and Riaza itself is a pleasant place to stop with several good bars (try *El Museo*) and restaurants, and a couple of places offering rooms. There's also a station here on the main line from Madrid to Burgos.

Along the Duero: Valladolid to Soria

The **Duero**, east from Valladolid to Soria, is trailed by a further panoply of castles and old market towns; the river long marked the frontier between Christian and Arab territory. Road (and bus) routes follow the river, allowing leisurely and rewarding small-town stops.

Peñafiel

The reason for stopping at **PEÑAFIEL**, 60km east of Valladolid, is to see its fabulous elongated **castle** (Tues–Sun: Easter–Sept 11.30am–2.30pm & 4.30–8.30pm; Oct–Easter noon–2pm & 4.30–7.30pm; €1.50), which bears an astonishing resemblance to a huge ship run aground: it is 210m long but only 23m across, with its central tower playing the role of the ship's bridge. Built in 1466 out of the region's distinctive white stone, the castle was designed around the narrow ridge upon which it stands, a location best appreciated from the top of the tower. There's not much to see inside the castle, part of which has now been turned into a **Museo Provincial del Vino** (combined ticket with castle €4), but it's well worth going up to the battlements for the glorious panoramas over the surrounding countryside, including a tremendous view of Peñafiel from the "prow" of the castle.

In the town itself, the main sight is the extraordinary **Plaza del Coso**. All the buildings on this square are wooden, with several tiers of loggias, and it makes the most spectacular bullring in Spain when bullfights are held here in August. The nearby **San Pablo**, now a college, has a superb brick Gothic-Mudéjar apse, to which a Plateresque chapel was later added.

Practicalities

There are six daily **buses** (3–4 on Sun) to and from Valladolid (1hr). These drop you on the edge of town – turn right down Travesia de Calvario, walk over the bridge, then turn right again to reach San Pablo and the Plaza del Coso, where you'll find the **turismo** (daily 11am–2pm & 5–7.30pm; ☎983 881 526). If you need a **place to stay**, the *Hostal Linares* at Mercado Viejo 11 (☎983 880 942; ❹), right next to where the buses stop, has comfortable rooms. *Hostal Chicopa*, conveniently located next to the *ayuntamiento* in the centre of town, has cheap and tidy rooms (☎983 880 782; ❸) and a reasonable tapas bar downstairs, or for something more luxurious, Peñafiel offers one of the region's best hotels, the *Hotel Ribera de Duero*, Avda. Escalona 17 (☎983 881 616, ℗983 881 444; ❼), set in an incongruously grand old building with very stylish rooms, almost all with views of the castle. For **dinner**, the *Molino de Palacios* serves traditional Castilian dishes in a converted sixteenth-century watermill over the Duratón River, while *Bar Plata*, at c/Franco 22, does good tapas and is a bit of a nightspot.

El Burgo de Osma and around

EL BURGO DE OSMA, the episcopal centre of Soria Province, is a wonderfully picturesque place, with crumbling town walls and ancient colonnaded streets overhung by houses supported on precarious wooden props. In the relaxed village atmosphere of the Plaza de la Catedral, the **Catedral** (daily 10.30am–1pm & 4.30–6.30pm), one of the richest in Spain, seems more than usually over the top. Basically Gothic in style, it has had many embellishments over the years, notably the superb Baroque tower decorated with pinnacles and gables which dominates the town. If you buy a visitor's ticket (€2.10), lights will be switched on for you to see the theatrical *retablo mayor* by Juan de Juni and his pupils, and a series of dark chapels, one of which contains a powerful Romanesque carving of the Crucifixion; you'll also be shown the cloisters and the museum. Most impressive of all is the thirteenth-century painted stone tomb of San Pedro de Osma – an unusually naturalist treatment for its age. Just beyond the cathedral there's a small but impressive surviving stretch of the fifteenth-century town **walls**.

A couple of minutes' walk up the quaintly arcaded c/Mayor is Osma's other main square, the **Plaza Mayor**, flanked on opposite sides by the old Hospital de San Augustín of 1699 and the *ayuntamiento* of 1771 with its over-the-top iron steeples – quaint monuments to provincial self-esteem. Further evidence of Osma's former importance can be found slightly beyond here, at the junction of c/Mayor and c/Universidad, where the Instituto Santa Catalina occupies a fine old sixteenth-century mansion which was once the seat of the town's **university**.

Practicalities

The town's new **bus station**, just northwest of the Plaza Mayor, is due to open in late 2000; there are four services daily to Soria (1 Sun). It's a couple of minutes from here to the **turismo** (Wed–Sun 10am–2pm & 4–8pm; ☎975 360 116, 🌐www.burgosma.es) at Plaza Mayor 9.

Accommodation is limited: the very basic *Hostal Casa Agapito*, c/Universidad 1 (☎975 340 212; ❷), and the *Pensión El Arco*, c/General Alvarez de Castro 3 (☎975 360 462; ❹), are the only real budget options in town. *Hostal La Perdiz*, c/Universidad 33 (☎975 360 476; ❻), is reasonable value, though rather unpromisingly located a ten-minute walk up c/Universidad behind a petrol station. Better located, but overpriced, is the *Hostal El Mirador* (☎975 360 408; ❻), behind the Plaza Mayor on c/Marques de Vadillo 10. If money is no object, the town's best hotel is *Il Virrey* (☎975 341 311, 📠975 340 855, 🌐www.logiccontrol.es/virreypalafox; ❼) on the Plaza Mayor, complete with baronial wooden fittings, and a staircase and chandelier which are virtually tourist attractions in their own right. There's also a **campsite**, *La Pedriza* (☎975 340 806; June–Sept). For **food**, *Cafeteria 2000*, on Plaza Mayor, has reasonable *menús* (€7.20), or try the tapas bar in the *Hostal Mirador*.

San Esteban de Gormaz and Gormaz

Thirteen kilometres to the west of El Burgo de Osma, **SAN ESTEBAN DE GORMAZ** has a ruined castle and a pair of Romanesque churches. There's also a pleasant **hostal**, *El Moreno,* Avda. del Generalísimo 1 (☎975 350 217; ❸), which could be useful if you find everything full in Osma.

GORMAZ, 15km south of El Burgo de Osma, is a particularly intriguing fortification since it was originally built in the caliphate style, and two Moorish doorways dating from the tenth century have survived. Later captured and modified by Christians, it was one of the largest fortified buildings in the West – there are 28 towers in all, ruined but impressive. The inside is a shell, but there are good panoramas from here, and the wonderful views as you approach make the long walk up less daunting. Gormaz itself is little more than a hamlet, without any accommodation.

Calatañazor

Just off the main El Burgo–Soria road lies **CALATAÑAZOR**, a severely depopulated medieval village with walls and the ruins of a castle, chiefly remarkable for its **houses**, with their distinctive conical chimneys, decorative coats of arms and wooden balconies. A village guide is based at the *mesón*, where good simple meals are served. The only available **accommodation** is the *Hostal Calatañazor*, c/Real 10 (☏975 183 642 or 975 371 334; ❹), an ancient house on the main village street, but the place makes a good half-day excursion from either El Burgo de Osma or Soria, 30km east.

Berlanga de Duero and around

BERLANGA DE DUERO, east again along the Duero, stands just off the main road between El Burgo de Osma and Almazán; it can also be reached from Soria by daily **bus**.

Once again, the main attraction is a **castle**, whose massive cylindrical towers and older double curtain wall, reminiscent of Ávila, loom above the town. The way up is through a doorway in a ruined Renaissance palace at the edge of town (watch out for the lethal uncovered hole dropping down to an underground cavern); entrance is free. The other dominant monument is the **Colegiata** (usually open), one of the last flowerings of the Gothic style. Its unusually uniform design is a consequence of rapid construction – it was built in just four years. Berlanga also has an old-world **Plaza Mayor** (where markets are held regularly), several fine mansions, arcaded streets, an impressive entrance gateway and the unique **La Picota**, a pillar of justice to which offenders were tied (it's on waste ground outside the old town, where the buses stop).

The only **place to stay** in Berlanga is at the fairly upmarket *Hotel Fray Tomás*, c/Real 16 (☏975 343 033, ℉975 343 169; ❺), which also has a very good restaurant.

Ermita de San Baudelio de Berlanga

Eight kilometres south of Berlanga, the tiny **Ermita de San Baudelio de Berlanga** (April–June & Sept–Oct Wed–Sat 10.30am–2pm & 4–7pm, Sun 10.30am–2pm; July & Aug Wed–Sat 10.30am–2pm & 5–9pm, Sun 10.30am–2pm; Nov–March Wed–Sat 10.30am–2pm & 4–6pm, Sun 10.30am–2pm; €0.60) is the best-preserved and (with San Miguel de Escalada, see p.445) most important example of Mozarabic style in Spain. It was even better before the 1920s: five years after being declared a national monument, its marvellous cycle of frescoes was acquired by an international art dealer and exported to the USA. After much fuss, the Spanish government got some of them back on indefinite loan, but they are now kept in the Prado.

In spite of this loss, the hermitage remains a beauty. Its eight-ribbed interior vault springs from a central pillar, while much of the space is taken up by the tribune gallery of horseshoe arches. Some original frescoes do remain, including two bulls from the great sequence of animals and hunting scenes of the nave. You can also see the entrance to the cave below, which the hermit, San Baudelio, made his home.

Almazán

Some 35km due south of Soria lies **ALMAZÁN**, which despite a lot of ugly modern development still possesses complete **medieval walls**, pierced by three gateways. On the Plaza Mayor stands the fine Renaissance **Palacio Hurtado de Mendoza**, with a Gothic loggia at the rear, visible from the road around the walls. The church of **San Miguel**, across from the palace, has a memorable interior, with Romanesque and early Gothic features, and a remarkable dome in the Cordoban style. To gain access, try the parish offices in the adjacent Plaza Santa María, opposite the church of the same name.

Places to stay include *Hostal El Arco*, c/San Andrés 7 (℡975 310 228; ❸), and *Hostal Mateos*, c/San Lázaro 2 (℡975 301 400; ❹), across the river. The latter is also one of the few places to eat in town, along with *Restaurante Toma*, c/Manuel Cartel 11. However, you are not likely to want to stay long, and there are regular **bus** and **train** connections to Soria.

Medinaceli

MEDINACELI, perched in an exhilarating, breezy position above the Río Jalón, is something of a ghost town – steeped in history and highly evocative of its former glory as a Roman and Moorish stronghold. It's 76km south of Almazán and positioned on the main Madrid–Barcelona rail line. If you arrive this way, it's a three-kilometre climb by road up from the station to the village, though you can take a short cut straight up the hill to a distinctive Roman arch. The **Roman arch** – a triple arch in fact – is worn but impressive, and unique in Spain. Its presence is something of a mystery as such monuments were usually built to commemorate military triumphs but the cause of celebration at Medinaceli is unknown. Nearby stands the dilapidated Moorish **castle**, now a mere facade sheltering a Christian cemetery.

The quiet streets are full of ancient mansions with proud coats of arms, the grandest of which is the **Palacio de los Duques de Medinaceli** on the dusty and desolate Plaza Mayor. The palace was the seat of the family regarded as rightful heirs to the Castilian throne until, in 1275, Fernando, eldest son of Alfonso el Sabio (the Wise), died before he could assume his inheritance. His two sons were dispossessed by Fernando's brother Sancho el Valiente (the Brave), and their descendants, the dukes of Medinaceli, long continued to lay claim to the throne. Today Medinaceli is a declining village with no more than 900 inhabitants, though its *duquesa* remains the most titled woman in Spain.

There are several **places to stay** by the train station: *Hostal Nicolás* (℡975 326 004; ❹) and *Hotel Duque de Medinaceli* (℡975 326 111, ℻975 326 472; ❺) are both very pleasant. If you prefer to stay up in the old village there's *El Mirador*, Campo de San Nicolás (℡975 326 264; ❹), or the *Hostal Medinaceli*, c/del Portillo 1 (℡975 326 102; ❹), next to the Roman arch. *Las Llaves* (closed Sun evening & Mon), on the Plaza Mayor, is an attractive **restaurant**, stuffed with antiques.

Southwest of Medinaceli, Sigüenza (see p.199) is just 20km away across the border in New Castile, a couple of stops on any Madrid-bound train.

Santa María de Huerta

On the Aragonese border, 25km and just half an hour by train or bus from Medinaceli, lies **SANTA MARÍA DE HUERTA**. This tiny community is dominated by a Cistercian **monastery** (9am–1pm & 3–6.30pm), whose story of royal and noble patronage was brought to a sudden end by the First Carlist War in 1835. The buildings were repopulated in 1930, and the main church has recently been restored. The highlight of the complex is the French-Gothic refectory (1215–23), whose superb sexpartite vaulting and narrow pointed windows are worthy of the best church, let alone a dining room. Adjacent stands the kitchen with a mammoth chimney protruding above Plateresque upper cloisters. There's just one **pensión** in the village, the *Santa María* (℡975 327 218; ❸), on c/Marqués de Cerralbo.

Soria and around

SORIA is a modest little provincial capital – an attractive place, despite encroaching suburbs. It stands between a ridgeback of hills on the banks of the Duero, with a castle ruin above, a medieval centre dotted with mansions and Romanesque churches, and one of the country's most unusual set of cloisters.

Arrival, information and accommodation

Soria's **train station** is at the extreme southwest of the city; the **bus station** is on Avenida de Valladolid on the western side of the city, a twenty-minute walk from the centre. There's a helpful **turismo** (Mon–Fri 9am–2pm & 5–7pm, Sat & Sun 10am–2pm & 4–8pm; ☏975 212 052, ⊛www.sorianitelaimaginas.com) in the Plaza Ramón y Cajal, opposite the entrance to the large Alameda de Cervantes, a spacious park which is one of Soria's most attractive features.

Accommodation

Soria's tourists are rarely in great numbers, so finding a **place to stay** shouldn't be a problem. There are plenty of centrally located budget options, and a reasonable choice of mid-range and upmarket hotels.

Hostal Alvi, c/Albera 2 ☏975 228 112, ℉975 228 240. Well-equipped en-suite rooms in a central modern block with private parking. ❺

Pensión Carlos, Plaza del Olivio 2 ☏975 211 555. Ten very cheap but perfectly adequate rooms in the corner of a central but relatively quiet square. ❷

Parador Antonio Machado, Parque del Castillo ☏975 240 800, ℉975 240 803. Modern and relatively cheap *parador* in a beautiful hilltop location with great views. ❽

Hostal La Posada, Plaza San Clemente 6 ☏975 223 603. Good – though slightly expensive – rooms in this nicely located *hostal*, set in the corner of one of the city's most pleasant squares. ❺

Hostal Viena, c/García Solier 1 ☏975 222 109. Spacious and comfortable rooms in this pleasant and central mid-range *hostal*, with own restaurant attached. ❹

The Town

Over on the eastern edge of the city centre, Soria's cathedral, the **Concatedral de San Pedro**, is a rather stolid Plateresque building whose interior (open only for church services) takes the Spanish penchant for darkness to a ridiculous extreme. To the side are three bays of a superb Romanesque cloister (daily: May 10am–2pm & 4.30–7pm, June–Aug 10am–2pm & 5–8pm; Sept–April 10.30am–2pm & 4–6.30pm; €0.90), which belonged to the cathedral's predecessor.

From the cathedral, follow the main road that skirts the old town to reach the convent church of **Santo Domingo**. A twelfth-century building, its beautiful rose-coloured facade is decorated symmetrically with sixteen blind arches and a wheel window with eight spokes. The recessed arches of the main portal are excellently preserved and magnificently sculpted, with scenes from the life of Christ and a wonderful gallery of heavily bearded musicians who look uncannily like the lost medieval ancestors of ZZ Top – look out in particular for the fetching three-in-a-bed scene.

Also worth a look in the centre of town is **San Juan de Rabanera** (daily 11am–1pm & 3–5pm), another fine Romanesque church, the massive sixteenth-century **Palacio de los Condes de Gomara** and the **Museo Numantino** (June–Sept Tues–Sat 9am–2pm & 5–9pm, Sun 10am–2pm; Oct–May Tues–Sat 10am–7.30pm, Sun 10am–2pm; €2.10, free Sat & Sun),

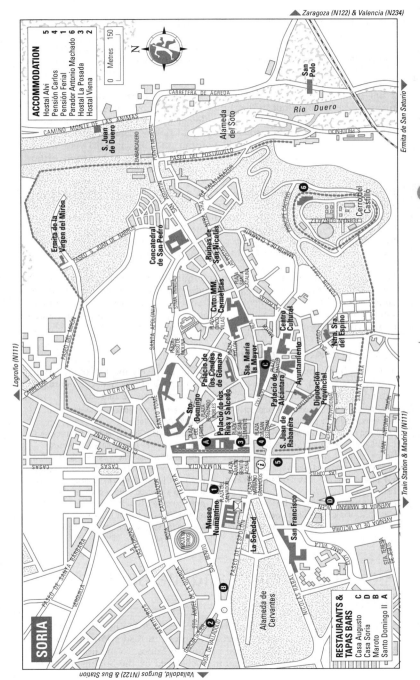

SORIA

ACCOMMODATION
Hostal Alvi	5
Pensión Carlos	4
Pensión Ferial	1
Parador Antonio Machado	6
Hostal La Posada	3
Hostal Viena	2

0 Metres 150

RESTAURANTS & TAPAS BARS
Casa Augusto	C
Casa Soria	D
Maroto	B
Santo Domingo II	A

Zaragoza (N122) & Valencia (N234)

Logroño (N111)

Valladolid, Burgos (N122) & Bus Station

Train Station & Madrid (N111)

Ermita de San Saturio

which features excellent displays of the finds from Numancia (see below) and Tiermes, another Celto-Iberic and Roman city, south of El Burgo de Osma.

Just across the Duero, some ten minutes' walk from the centre, stand the ruined cloisters of **San Juan de Duero** (April, May, Sept & Oct Tues–Sat 10am–2pm & 4–7pm, Sun 10am–2pm; June–Aug Tues–Sat 10am–2pm & 5–9pm, Sun 10am–2pm; Nov–March Tues–Sat 10am–2pm & 3.30–6pm, Sun 10am–2pm; €0.60, free Sat & Sun), one of the most bizarre medieval monuments in the region. Built in the thirteenth century by Mudéjar masons, each of the four sides of the cloister is in a different style: Romanesque, Transitional Gothic, Gothic, and finally a totally original section of vaguely Moorish-looking arches. If the cloisters are closed, you can get a partial aerial view from a low hill across the road. The church, converted into a museum, is more orthodox in style, but has two unusual little freestanding temples inside.

From here, there's a good walk south along the banks of the river, passing the former Templar church of **San Polo** (now a private home), and arriving, after 2km, at the **Ermita de San Saturio**, a two-tiered complex including an octagonal chapel with thirteenth-century frescoes (daily 10.30am–2pm & 4–6.30pm; free). The landscape here is typical of the province, with its parched, livid, orange earth and the solemn river lined by poplars.

The barren site of Roman **NUMANCIA** (same hours and admission as San Juan de Duero) stands on a hill above the village of **Garray**, 8km north of Soria. The Celto-Iberian town which originally occupied this site resisted Scipio and his legions for over a year and, when finally defeated, the inhabitants destroyed the town rather than surrender it. What survives – some excavated remains of the Roman city that replaced it, with the outline of the streets clearly visible – is really only of interest to archeologists.

Eating and drinking

The city's **bars and restaurants** are plentiful and lively, most of them serving excellent tapas. You'll find the best selection around Plaza San Clemente, just behind Citibank at the western end of the main drag, c/Zapatería.

Casa Augusto, Plaza Mayor 5. An excellent restaurant in a central location with a friendly owner and an affordable *menú*.
Casa Soria, Avda. Mariano Vicén 5. Slightly out of the way, but worth searching out this friendly local eaterie for its simple but good value *menú* (€6.60) and meat and fish dishes from €5.40. Open from 7am.
Maroto, Paseo del Espolón 20. Conservative and quite pricey, this is where Soria's well-heeled come to dine. Good Castilian food, beautifully presented – there's a *menú* for €13.80 plus à la

carte meat, fish and game (*caza*) dishes from €10.80. Closed Thurs.
La Posada, Plaza San Clemente 6. Downstairs from the *Hostal La Posada*, on Soria's liveliest square and serving some of the best tapas in town.
Santo Domingo II, c/Aduana Vieja 15. Upmarket restaurant, just south of Santo Domingo: €17.40 buys you a six-course *menú*, or choose from mouthwatering à la carte dishes such as oxtail in red wine (*rabo de buey al vino tinto*; €10.80) or kid goat fried with red peppers (*cabrito frito con ajillos*; €11.40).

Río Lobos Canyon and the Sierra de Urbión

Some of Castile's loveliest and least-visited countryside lies northwest of Soria, on either side of the N234 to Burgos. South of this road a **Parque Natural** has been created around the canyon of the Río Lobos. To the north rises the **Sierra de Urbión**, a lakeland region much loved by the Sorian-born poet,

Antonio Machado. The Cañón Río Lobos can also be approached on minor roads from El Burgo de Osma, to the south.

Río Lobos Canyon

The whole area of the **Parque Natural del Cañón del Río Lobos** is impressive, with fantastically shaped rocks on both sides of the canyon. The most interesting part lies 1km from the park's car park, southeast of San Leonardo de Yagüe. Here, as well as some of the prettiest rock formations, there's a **Romanesque chapel** founded by the Templars (kept locked) and, behind this, a beautiful natural **cave**. From here, the path continues through the Lobos gorge; at times the river is a mere trickle – its tributaries have dried up completely, providing ready-made walking tracks. For this, or more adventurous treks into the high ground, you really need proper walking boots, but any shoes will do on the main paths. The park will appeal to bird-watchers; eagles and vultures are often seen, even though they are not protected here.

SAN LEONARDO DE YAGÜE makes a convenient base, with a good hostal, the Torres, c/Magdalena 4 (☎975 376 156; ④). Alternatively, you can camp in the officially designated areas around the entrance to the park (☎975 363 565; mid-March to mid-Oct).

Vinuesa and the Sierra de Urbión

For the **Sierra de Urbión**, the most obvious base is **VINUESA**, situated just north of an enormous man-made reservoir, **Pantano de la Cuerda del Pozo**. On a slow country bus route between Soria and Burgos, it's a spaciously laid-out village with many fine old houses and plenty of **accommodation** to choose from down by the bridge: *Visontium* (☎975 378 354, ⓕ975 378 362; ④), and *Santa Inés* (☎975 378 126; ④), both on Carretera Laguna Negra, are two attractive *hostales* owned by brothers; the slightly more expensive *Hostal Urbión* on Avenida Constitución (☎975 378 494; ⑤) also has good rooms, and in the middle of the village there's an excellent *pensión*, *Mesón Tito*, c/Reina Sofía 30 (☎975 378 031; ③). All these places except the last have their own restaurant. There's also a **campsite** 2km along the Montenegro road (☎975 378 331; April to mid-Oct), which has bikes for hire.

Nineteen kilometres north of Vinuesa lies the most famous of the lakes, the beautiful **Laguna Negra**. There's no public transport to it, but a good road leads through thickly wooded country before climbing steeply up the green mountainside. For the last couple of kilometres, by the side of a ravine, the road is much rougher; finally, a path leads to the lagoon. Ice Age in origin, and set in an amphitheatre of mountains from which great boulders have fallen, it presents a primeval picture – Machado was inspired to write some of his most purple verse here. The area remains delightfully unspoiled, though, and the **bar** (June–Sept only) and **picnic area** are out of sight, 3km down the mountain.

Serious hikers can make a tortuous ascent from the Laguna Negra to the **Laguna de Urbión**, just over the border in Logroño Province – a route that takes in a couple of other tiny, glacially formed lakes. A less taxing version of the same excursion is to take the long way round, from the village of **Duruelo de La Sierra**, some 20km west of Vinuesa.

The Camino de Santiago: from Logroño to León

This part of the chapter is laid out in an east–west direction, following, more or less, the **Camino de Santiago**, the great pilgrim route to the shrine of St James at Compostela (see p.586). The route had many variants but its most popular point of entry to Spain was – and remains – the pass of Roncesvalles in the Pyrenees. From there, the old paths strike south through Navarra to Logroño and then west across Castile through the great cathedral cities of **Burgos** and **León**. These are major architectural sights but each of the smaller towns along the *camino* has some treasure or reminder – a bridge, a Romanesque church, or a statue of the saint. For uncommitted pilgrims, the highlights of the route can be taken in by car, bus, or sometimes train.

Old Castile, in this section, is used in a loose, historical sense, for this region actually takes in two other provinces. In the east is **La Rioja**, Spain's premier wine-producing region, with its capital in **Logroño** and wine trade centre in nearby **Haro**. Over to the west is the old kingdom of **León**, whose northern reaches merge with Asturias in the Picos de Europa mountains (see p.539).

Logroño

LOGROÑO is a modern, prosperous city, lacking in great monuments, but pleasant enough with its broad, elegant streets and open squares. It has a lively old section, too, stretching down towards the Río Ebro from the twin-towered cathedral. Whether you stay or not, you're likely to pass through Logroño at some point since it lies on the borders of Old Castile, the Basque provinces and Navarra, a position that has stimulated commerce and light industry. Most importantly, however, this is the very heart of the **Rioja wine region**.

The Town

Before the wine trade and industry brought prosperity to Logroño, it owed its importance for some six centuries to the **Camino de Santiago**. In almost every town on the route you can still find a church dedicated to the saint; in Logroño it stands close to the iron bridge over the Río Ebro – the lofty sixteenth-century Gothic structure of **Santiago el Real**. High on its south side, above the main entrance, is a magnificent eighteenth-century Baroque equestrian statue of the saint, mounted in full glory in his role of *Matamoros* (Moorslayer), on a stallion which Edwin Mullins, in his fascinating book *The Pilgrimage to Santiago*, describes as "equipped with the most heroic genitals in all Spain, a sight to make any surviving Moor feel inadequate and run for cover".

Other fine Logroño churches include **San Bartolomé**, which has an unrefined but richly carved Gothic portal, and the **Catedral de Santa María la Redonda** (Mon–Sat 7.45am–1pm & 6.30–9pm, Sun 8.15am–1.15pm). The latter was originally a late-Gothic hall church with a lovely sweeping elevation

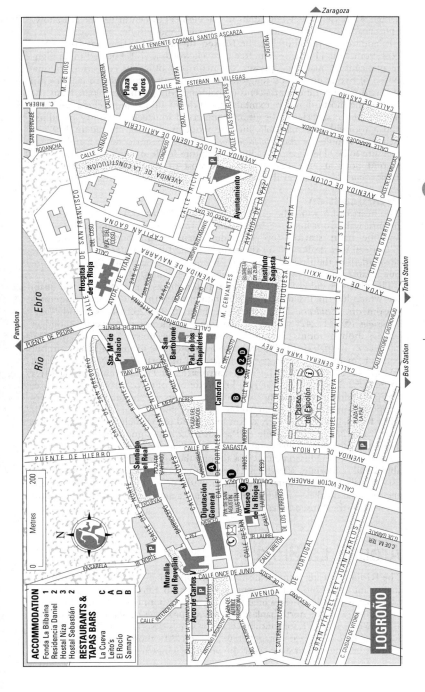

LOGROÑO

ACCOMMODATION
Fonda La Bilbaína   1
Residencia Daniel   2
Hostal Niza   3
Hostal Sebastián   2

RESTAURANTS &
TAPAS BARS
La Cueva   C
Leito's   A
El Rocío   D
Samary   B

▲ Zaragoza

CALLE TENIENTE CORONEL SANTOS ASCARZA

Plaza
de
Toros

CALLE ESTEBAN M. VILLEGAS

AVENIDA DE LA CONSTITUCIÓN

Ayuntamiento

Instituto
Sagasta

Ebro

◄ Pamplona

PUENTE DE PIEDRA

Río

Hospital
de la Rioja

Sta. Mª de
Palacio

San
Bartolomé

Pal. de los
Chapiteles

Catedral

PUENTE DE HIERRO

Santiago
el Real

Diputación
General

Museo
de la Rioja

Muralla
del Revellín

Arco de Carlos V

Paseo
del Espolón

► Train Station

► Bus Station

N

Metres
0   200

PASARELA

CALLE ONCE DE JUNIO

GRAN VÍA DEL REY JUAN CARLOS I

which was extended at both ends in the eighteenth century – the twin-towered facade is a fine example of the Churrigueresque style.

In addition to the churches, the **Museo de la Rioja** (Tues–Sat 10am–2pm & 4–9pm, Sun 11.30am–2pm; free), is well worth a visit. Located in an eighteenth-century mansion opposite the main post office, its collection is composed of two main groups: religious art taken from abandoned monasteries in the region, and nineteenth-century paintings on permanent loan from the Prado. The most impressive exhibits are on the first floor and include *Las Tablas de San Millán*, a series of beautifully preserved fourteenth-century paintings, and a roomful of remarkable, life-size wooden carvings created in 1597 by Pedro de Arbulo for the *retablo mayor* of the Monasterio de la Estrella. It's a pleasure to be able to see this kind of sculpture so close up and well lit. On the second floor are the Prado paintings, most of which won medals in the *Exposiciones Nacionales* in the late nineteenth century.

Practicalities

The heart of Logroño, the gardens of the wide **Paseo del Espolón**, is a five-minute walk from both the **bus station** (straight up c/General Vara de Rey) and the **train station** (up Avda. de España to the bus station, then up c/General Vara de Rey). The **turismo** is located in a modern building inside the gardens of the Paseo del Espolón (summer Mon–Sat 10am–2pm & 5–8pm, Sun 10am–2pm & 5–8pm; winter daily 10am–2pm; ☎941 291 260).

The northern side of the Paseo del Espolón marks the start of the old quarter, which has the liveliest bars and restaurants and the lowest-priced **accommodation**. *Residencia Daniel*, c/San Juan 21 (☎941 252 948; ❸), and *Hostal Sebastián* (☎941 242 800; ❸) in the same block are two excellent budget places, though rooms facing the street can be noisy. *Fonda La Bilbaína*, c/Gallarza 10 (☎941 254 226; ❸), also has reasonable rooms with and without bath, or for more comfort, try the functional modern *Hostal Niza*, c/Gallarza 13 (☎941 206 044; ❺). The local **campsite**, *La Playa*, Avenida de la Playa (☎941 252 253; open all year), is a kilometre out of town across the Río Ebro, and lies beside its own sandy river beach; campers get free entrance to a nearby sports complex with an enormous outdoor pool.

For **tapas**, head to the lively c/San Juan: good places include the *Samary* (no. 3) and *La Cueva* (no. 1), while *El Rocío* at no. 23 does good menús for €8.10. The best selection of **restaurants** is along c/San Agustín, c/Laurel and c/del Peso, around the Museo de la Rioja, though the top restaurant in town is probably *Leito's*, c/Portales 30, which has *menús* for €11.40 and €17.40, and a small list of elaborate *à la carte* dishes from €9. For snacks – including superb *empanadas* and cakes – make a detour to *El Paraíso*, a bakery at c/San Agustín 27, next to the Museo de la Rioja.

Around La Rioja

The **Rioja** area takes its name from the Río Oja, which flows into the Tirón and thence into the Ebro to the northwest of Logroño. Effectively, though, it is the Ebro that waters the vines, which are cultivated on both banks. Many of the best vineyards are on the north bank in the Basque province of Alava, an area known as the *Rioja Alavesa*. Look out above all for wines described as *Reserva* or *Gran Reserva*, and for the great vintages of '68, '69 and '70 – though many say that with controls getting stricter every year, the younger wines are the better ones.

La Rioja's wines

Wine is at the very heart of La Rioja's identity, and few people will pass through Haro without wanting to buy a few bottles. It's a good idea to equip yourself with some **vocabulary** so you know what you're buying: *cosecha* (which literally means harvest), when used on its own, refers to young wines in their first or second year, which tend to have a fresh and fruity flavour; *crianzas* are wines which are at least in their third year, having spent at least one year in an oak cask and several months in the bottle; *reservas* are vintages that have been aged for three years with at least one year in the oak; and *gran reservas* have spent at least two years in oak casks and three years in the bottle. **Good years** to look out for include '75,'78,'81,'82,'91,'94 and '95.

The most convenient **place to buy** your wine is at *Mi Bodega*, c/Santo Tomás 13 (just off the Plaza de la Paz), whose dark cellars stock a vast range of wines; a similar outlet is El Rincón de Quintín near the bus station. You can expect to buy decent *crianzas* from around €3 and *reservas* from around €5. The *bodegas* themselves, most of which are down by the train station, are reluctant to open their doors unless you're with a group; your best bet is to try to get on a tour organized by the turismo or ask at the campsite (see opposite) about getting one together. Failing this, try hanging around the gates looking interested but not too thirsty. Among the most famous *bodegas* are Bodegas Bilbaínas, CVNE (pronounced Cune), and Muga. If you want to find out more about how the wine's produced, the high-tech **Museo del Vino** (Tues–Sat 10am–2pm; €1.80, free Wed), in the Estación Erológica on c/Breton de los Herreros, behind the bus station, has detailed and highly complicated displays of the processes involved, but no tastings.

Haro

The main centre of Rioja production is **HARO**, an attractive, working town, 40km northwest of Logroño. In addition to **wine-tasting** possibilities, it has some lovely reminders of a grand past, notably the Renaissance church of **San Tomás** with its wedding-cake tower, an imposing sight on any approach to town. The old quarter around it is attractive in a low-key, faded kind of way, its lower margins marked by the **Plaza de la Paz**, a glass-balconied square whose mansions overlook an archaic bandstand.

The best time to be in Haro is in the last week of June, during the **fiestas** of San Juan, San Felices and San Pedro. All the *bodegas* bring their wares to the main square for tastings and bargain buys; there are free outdoor concerts, and you'll see parades through the streets of elaborately costumed characters on giant stilts. The climax of these fiestas is the riotous *batalla del vino* on June 29, when thousands of people climb the Riscos de Bilibio (a small mountain near the town) to be drenched from head to foot in wine; if this annual ritual does not take place, the Riscos will by law be passed to the jurisdiction of Miranda de Ebro.

Practicalities

Haro's **train station** is some distance out of town; to get to the centre, walk down the hill to the main road, turn right and when you reach the bridge (campsite off to the right), cross it and head straight uphill. **Buses** stop in Plaza Castañares, a ten-minute walk from the centre (follow signs for *centro* straight up c/la Ventilla). The **turismo** is on Plaza M. Florentino Rodríguez (Mon–Sat 10am–2pm & 4.30–7.30pm, Sun 10am–2pm; ☎941 303 366).

There's plenty of moderately priced **accommodation** in town: *Pensión la Peña*, Plaza de la Paz 17, 2° (☎941 310 022; ❹), has spotless rooms, some of them en suite and most with a balcony overlooking the plaza, and there are more modern (though smaller) rooms attached to *Bar-Restaurante Vega*, Plaza Juan García Gatio 1 (℡941 312 205; ❸). *El Maño*, Avda. de la Rioja 27 (℡941 310 229; ❸), is also very comfortable, but if it's luxury you're after, head for *Los Agostinos*, c/San Agustín 2 (℡941 311 308, ℱ941 303 148; ❼), a superb hotel in a converted Augustinian monastery. There's also an excellent **campsite** (℡941 312 737; open all year), down by the river below town with a bar and swimming (in the river or pool) nearby.

Even the humblest *menú del día* in town is transformed by a bottle of Rioja, and you'll get more wine – and very cheaply – in the many good **bars** that lie between the *ayuntamiento* and the church of San Tomás. Best of the **restaurants** are *Beethoven*, c/San Tomás 5 (closed Mon night, Thurs, July 1–15 & Dec), and *Terete*, c/General Franco 26 (closed Sun night & Mon); prices at both are moderate.

Nájera

Fifteen kilometres south of Haro, **NÁJERA** is dramatically situated below a pink rock formation, and has an interesting Gothic monastery, **Santa María la Real** (daily 9.30am–12.30pm & 4–7.30pm; €0.60). This contains a royal pantheon of ancient monarchs of Castile, León and Navarra – a host of sarcophagi and statues, some of which seem to have been made long after the death of the sitter. Best of all is the cloister of rose-coloured stone and elaborate tracery, closer to the Manueline style of Portugal than anything in Spain. There is nothing more to detain you, but if you want to stay there are several cheap restaurants, a **hostal**, *San Fernando* (℡941 363 700, ℱ941 363 399; ❺), and a *fonda*.

Burgos

BURGOS was for some five hundred years the capital of Old Castile and with its dark-stone old town and castle it remains redolent of these years of power and military strength. It has historic associations as the home of El Cid in the eleventh century, and as the base two centuries later of Fernando el Santo (Fernando III), the reconqueror of Murcia, Córdoba and Sevilla. It was Fernando who began the city's famous Gothic **cathedral**, one of the greatest in all Spain, though it, too, seems to share in the solemnity and severity of the city's history.

To Spaniards, the city has more modern military connotations. A large military garrison was stationed here for many years following the Civil War, when Franco temporarily installed his fascist government in the city. Burgos also owes much of its modern industry and expansion to Franco's "Industrial Development Plan", a strategy to shift the country's wealth away from Catalunya and the Basque country and into Castile. Even now, such connotations linger.

The most exciting times to be in Burgos are during **El Curpillos**, which takes place the day after the feast of Corpus Christi, and at the end of June for the two-week **Fiesta de San Pedro**, when *gigantillos* parade in the streets, and there are bullfights and all-night parties.

Arrival, orientation and information

Orientation in Burgos could not be simpler, since wherever you are the cathedral makes its presence felt. The Río Arlanzón bisects the city and neatly delimits the old quarters. The main pedestrian bridge is the **Puente de Santa María**, nearest the cathedral and facing the gateway of the same name. The **bus station** is on the "new" side of the river at c/Miranda 4; the **train station** is a short walk away at the bottom of Avenida Conde Guadalhorre. The **turismo** (Mon–Fri 9am–2pm & 5–7pm, Sat & Sun 10am–2pm & 5–8pm; ℡ 947 203 125, ⓦ www.patroturisbur.es) is at Plaza de Alonso Martínez 7, a five-minute walk northeast of the cathedral.

Accommodation

Rooms can often be difficult to come by; they're at a premium in late June and July, while during the university year many of the cheaper *pensiones* are brimful of students, so it's worth calling ahead to check. The best place to try for inexpensive accommodation is around the Plaza de Vega, and any road off towards the bus station as far as c/de San Pablo. There are plenty of smart, upmarket hotels in town, as well as one of the region's most luxurious and memorable places to stay just out of town on the road to Madrid.

The local **campsite**, *Camping Fuentes Blancas* (℡ 947 486 016; April–Sept) is out by the Cartuja de Miraflores (see p.440 for directions), 45 minutes' walk or a bus ride from the centre (buses hourly between 11am and 9pm, leaving from the Cid statue) – it's a very good site with excellent facilities, including a pool.

Budget options

Pensión Arribas, c/Defensores de Oviedo 6 ℡ 947 266 292. Cheap and reliable *pensión* in a convenient – though dreary – location right behind the bus station. ❸

Pensión Dallás, Plaza de Vega 6 ℡ 947 205 457. Reasonable rooms in this *pensión* on a busy roundabout right on the river front. ❸

Hostal Hidalgo, c/Almirante Bonifaz 14 ℡ 947 203 481. Large, moderate-value rooms in a rather gloomy block on a central but very quiet street. ❹

Pensión Paloma, c/Paloma 39, 3º ℡ 947 276 574. Warm, clean and bang next to the cathedral. ❷

Pensión Peña, c/Puebla 18 ℡ 947 206 323. Easily the top budget option in Burgos, this welcoming and immaculate *pensión* offers outstanding value in a quiet but central location. ❷

Moderate and expensive options

Del Cid, Plaza de Santa María 8 ℡ 947 208 715, Ⓕ 947 269 460. Facing the cathedral, this is the poshest hotel in the old town, in a handsome old building and a modern block opposite, with its own parking. ❽

Hotel Conde de Miranda, c/Miranda 4 ℡ 947 265 267, Ⓕ 947 207 770. Smart and comfortable rooms, if not particularly cheap, located (literally) on top of the bus station. ❻

Hotel Cordón, c/Puebla 6 ℡ 947 265 000, Ⓕ 947 200 269. Central Burgos's most characterful hotel, with very smart rooms in a beautiful, glass-balconied building. ❽

Landa Palace, Carretera Madrid–Irún ℡ 947 206 343, Ⓕ 947 264 676. A stunning and fabulously expensive hotel in a medieval tower, just out of town on the road to Madrid, complete with antique furnishings and a renowned restaurant. ❾

Hostal Lar, c/Cardenal Benlloch 1 ℡ 947 209 655, Ⓕ 947 209 655. Burgos's best mid-range option, despite its location on a busy main road, with big, comfy en-suite rooms and very friendly owners. ❺

Hostal Manjón, c/Conde Jornada 1 ℡ 947 208 689. Ten clean, comfortable and good-value modern rooms – some en suite – on the edge of the old town, a ten-minute walk from the cathedral. ❹–❺

The City

Heading in across the Puente de Santa María you are confronted with the great white bulk of the **Arco de Santa María**. Originally this gateway formed part of the town walls; its facade was castellated with towers and turrets and embellished with statues in 1534–36 in order to appease the wrath of Carlos V after Burgos's involvement in a revolt by Spanish noblemen against their new Belgian-born king. Carlos's statue is glorified here in the context of the great-

BURGOS

CAMINO DE LAS CORAZAS

CALLE DE FRANCISCO DE SALINAS

EL POLVORÍN

LAS MURALLAS

SAN JACINTO

CALLE DE SAN FRANCISCO

CONSULADO

SAN MIGUEL

CORAZAS

TRINIDAD

S. Gil

Puerta de
S. Esteban

ALV. YÁÑEZ

HOSPITAL DIEGOS

FERNÁN GONZÁLEZ

AVELLANOS

A

Castillo

SAN ESTEBAN

SALDAÑA

V. PALENCIA

C. HUERTO DEL REY

CALLE LAÍN CALVO

C. CARDENAL SEGURA

P

C

Arco de
S. Martín

EMPERADOR

Seminario Mayor
San Jerónimo

S. Esteban

LLANAS DE
AFUERA

CALLE DE LA PALOMA

SOMBRERERÍA

PLAZA
MAYOR

P

BENEDICTINAS DE SAN JOSÉ

DOÑA JIMENA

POZO SECO

Arco de Fernán
González

S. Nicolás

E

Solar
del Cid

CALLE DE SANTA ÁGUEDA

Santa
Águeda

7

Catedral

PL. REY

PLAZA DE
STA. MARÍA

SAN FERNANDO

F

6

G

Ayuntamiento

PASEO DEL ESPOLÓN

LAVADORES

PASEO DE LOS CUBOS

NTRA. SRA. DE LAS SOLANÍN

Arco de
Sta. María

PUENTE DE
STA. MARÍA

PASEO DE

EDUARDO

MARTÍNEZ DEL CAMPO

8

PASEO DE LA ISLA

Parque de
la Isla

BARRANTES

APARICIO Y RUIZ

Palacio
Arzobispal

CALLE DEL GENERALÍSIMO

CALLE DE LA MERCED

Casa de Angulo

PLAZA
DE
VEGA

La Merced

SAN COSME

AVENIDA DE PALENCIA

PRADOLUENGO

AV. M. DE LAS HUELGAS

DE LA BUREBA

ARANGO

PLAZA DE
CESTILLA

AVENIDA DEL ARLANZÓN

Río Arlanzón

CALLE DE

PLAZA DEL
DR. ALBINANA

CALLE CONCEPCIÓN

Instituto

SAN COSME

S. Cosme &
S. Damián

P. MEDIA LUNA

PASEO DE LASERNA

C. CONDE DE GUADALHORCE

PASEO DEL EMPECINADO

Iglesia del
Carmen

CALLE DEL CARMEN

CALLE BERRIO GIMENO

CALLE DE LUIS RODRÍGUEZ

Seminario
Menor
San José

CALLE DE LA ESTACIÓN

C. SANTA DOROTEA

PLAZA DE LA
ESTACIÓN

CALLE DE LA ESTACIÓN

Train
Station

◄ Monasterio de las Huelgas

RESTAURANTS & TAPAS BARS	
Bar La Cabaña Arandina	F
Casa Ojeda	D
Gaona	G
Marisquería Bringas	B
Mesón el Avellano	A
Mesón Burgos	E
Prego	C

est Burgalese heroes: Diego Porcelos, founder of the city in the late ninth century; Nuño Rasura and Laín Calvo, two early magistrates; Fernán González, founder of the Countship of Castile in 932; and **El Cid Campeador**, who was surpassed only by Santiago *Matamoros* in his exploits against the Moors. El Cid was born Rodrigo Díaz in the village of Vivar, just north of Burgos, though his most significant military exploits actually took place around Valencia; *Cid*, inci-

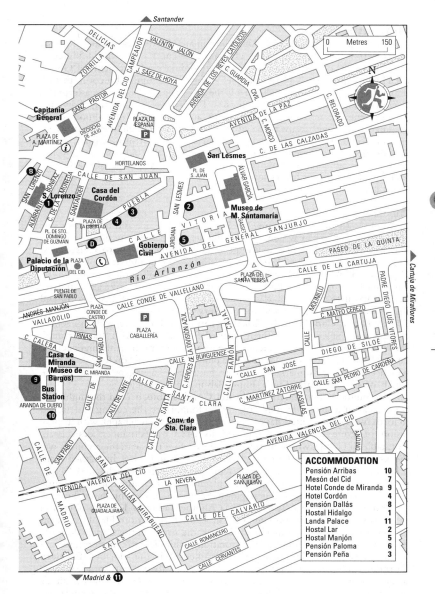

ACCOMMODATION

Pensión Arribas	10
Mesón del Cid	7
Hotel Conde de Miranda	9
Hotel Cordón	4
Pensión Dallás	8
Hostal Hidalgo	1
Landa Palace	11
Hostal Lar	2
Hostal Manjón	5
Pensión Paloma	6
Pensión Peña	3

dentally, derives from the Arabic *sidi* (lord), and *Campeador* means "supreme in valour". There's a splendid **equestrian statue** of him – with flying cloak, flowing beard and raised sword – lording over the **Puente de San Pablo**, the main road bridge to the old town. The statue, one of the city's principal landmarks, stands at the end of the **Paseo del Espolón**, a fashionable tree-lined promenade round which most of the evening life takes place.

The cathedral

The old quarters of Burgos are totally dominated by the **Catedral** (Mon–Sat 9.30am–1pm & 4–7pm, Sun 9.30–11.45am & 4–7pm), whose florid filigree of spires and pinnacles is among the most extraordinary achievements of Gothic art. The building is such a large complex of varied and opulent sections that it's difficult to appreciate it as a whole; it is the sheer accumulation of masterpieces – both inside and out – that impresses. Burgos has outstanding individual achievements in ironwork, woodcarving and sculpture, and almost every entrance and chapel seems to be of interest. Oddly enough, the most ornate entrance of all, the **Puerta de la Pellejería** at the northeast corner, is in a Renaissance-Plateresque style, quite different from the bulk of the exterior. Most of the cathedral has now emerged from a lengthy period of restoration, looking cleaner than it has for a number of centuries, though the central tower is still currently under wraps.

The Chapels

Inside the cathedral you're immediately struck by the size and number of side chapels, the greatest of which, the Capilla del Condestable, is almost a cathedral in itself. The most curious, though, is the **Capilla del Santo Cristo** (first right) which contains the bizarre *Cristo de Burgos*, a cloyingly realistic image of Christ (c. 1300), endowed with real human hair and nails and covered with the withered hide of a water buffalo, still popularly believed to be human skin. Legend has it that the icon was modelled directly from the Crucifixion and that it requires a shave and a manicure every eighth day.

The adjacent **Capilla de la Consolación** has a distinctive, early sixteenth-century star-shaped vault, a form adapted from the Moorish "honeycomb" vaults of Granada. Similar influences can also be seen in the cathedral's central dome (1568), highlighted with gold and blue and supported on four thick piers which fan out into remarkably delicate buttresses – a worthy setting for the **tomb of El Cid**, marked by a simple slab in the floor below.

The sumptuous, octagonal **Capilla del Condestable**, behind the high altar, contains a third superb example of star-vaulting. Here the ceiling is designed to form two eight-pointed stars, one within the other. The chapel, with its profusion of stone tracery, was founded in 1482 by Fernández de Velasco, Constable of Castile, whose marble tomb lies before the altar; the architect was the German Simón de Colonia. Between 1442 and 1458 his father Hans (Hispanicized as Juan) had built the twin openwork spires of the west facade, possibly modelling them on the spires planned for the cathedral in his home city of Cologne. In the third generation, Francisco de Colonia built the central dome and the Puerta de la Pellejería. Another father-and-son combination of artists was that of Gil and Diego de Siloé, the former from Flanders but his son born and raised in Spain. Gil worked on the *retablo* in the Capilla de Santa Ana (second left; currently under restoration), while Diego's masterpiece, one of the crowning achievements of the cathedral, is the glorious **Escalera Dorada**, a double stairway in the north transept. To get into some of these smaller chapels you'll have to buy a Treasury ticket (€3.60), which also admits you to the cloisters, the Diocesan Museum inside them, the Capilla del Condestable and the **Coro** at the heart of the cathedral, which affords the best view into the dome.

San Nicolás and San Esteban

Overlooking the plaza in front of the cathedral stands the fifteenth-century church of **San Nicolás** (July–Sept Mon–Sat 9am–2pm & 4–8pm; Oct–June

Tues–Fri 6.30–7.30pm, Sat 9.30am–2pm & 5–7pm, Sun 9am–2pm; €0.60). Unassuming from the outside, it has an altarpiece within by Francisco de Colonia which is as rich as anything in the city. At the side of San Nicolás, c/Pozo Seco ascends to the early Gothic church of **San Esteban**, which now houses the mildly interesting **Museo del Retablo** (*Retablo* Museum; July–Aug Mon–Sat 10.30am–2pm & 4.30–7pm, Sun 10.30am–2pm; Sept–June Tues–Sat 10.30am–2pm & 4.30–7pm, Sun 10.30am–2pm; €1.20).

Monasterio de las Huelgas

Inevitably the lesser churches of Burgos tend to be eclipsed by the cathedral, but on the outskirts are two monasteries which are by no means overshadowed. The closer, the Cistercian **Monasterio de las Huelgas** (April–Sept Tues–Sat 10.30am–1.15pm & 3.30–5.45pm, Sun 10.30am–2.15pm; Oct–March Tues–Fri 11am–1.15pm & 4–5.15pm, Sat 11am–1.15pm & 4–5.45pm, Sun 10.30am–2.15pm; €4.80, free Wed), is remarkable for its wealth of Mudéjar craftsmanship. It lies on the "new side" of the river, a twenty-minute walk from the city centre: cross Puente de Santa María, turn right and follow the signs along the riverbank. Founded in 1187 as the future mausoleum of Alfonso VIII and Eleanor of Aquitaine, wife of Henry II of England, it became one of the most highbrow and powerful convents in Spain. It was popularly observed that "if the pope were to marry, only the abbess of Las Huelgas would be eligible!" The main **church**, with its typically excessive Churrigueresque *retablo*, contains the tombs of no fewer than sixteen Castilian monarchs and nobles. Priceless embroidery, jewellery and weaponry of a suitably regal splendour were discovered inside the tombs and are exhibited in a small museum.

Among the highlights in the rest of the monastery are a set of delicate Romanesque cloisters, **Las Claustrillas**, and the ceiling of the main Gothic cloisters, which is adorned with patches of Mudéjar decoration, including the familiar eight-pointed stars and rare peacock designs – a bird holy to the Moors. The **Capilla de Santiago**, an obvious reminder that Las Huelgas stood on the pilgrim route, also has a fine Mudéjar ceiling and pointed horseshoe archway. Its cult statue of St James has an articulated right arm, which enabled him to dub knights of the Order of Santiago (motto: "The Sword is Red with the Blood of Islam") and on occasion even to crown kings. Note that the chapel is currently under restoration, during which time the statue may be temporarily moved to a different part of the monastery. The convent was also responsible for the nearby Hospital del Rey where food and shelter were provided free for two nights. It is presently in a very bad state of neglect, although the portals merit a visit.

The Cartuja de Miraflores

The second of the town's two notable monastaries, the **Cartuja de Miraflores** (Mon–Sat 10.15am–3pm & 4–6pm, Sun 11.20am–12.30pm, 1–3pm & 4–6pm; free), is famous for three dazzling masterpieces by Gil de Siloé. The buildings are still in use as a monastery and most are closed; you can, however, visit the **church**, built between 1454 and 1488 by Juan and Simón de Colonia. In accordance with Carthusian practice, it is divided into three sections for the public, the lay brothers and the monks. In front of the high altar lies the star-shaped joint tomb of Juan II and Isabel of Portugal, of such perfection in design and execution that it forced Felipe II and Juan de Herrera to admit "we did not achieve very much with our Escorial". Isabel la Católica, a great patron of the arts, commissioned it from Gil de Siloé in 1489 as a memorial to her parents. The same sculptor carved the magnificent altarpiece, which was plated with the first gold shipped back from America. His third masterpiece is the tomb of the Infante Alfonso, through whose untimely death in 1468 Isabel had succeeded to the throne of Castile.

Miraflores lies in a secluded spot about 4km from the centre: turn left from the Puente de Santa María along c/de Valladolid, from where the monastary is well signposted. There's a good restaurant in the nearby park. A bus runs on Sunday but returns right after the well-attended Mass; there's also a bus to the nearby campsite (see p.435).

Eating, drinking and nightlife

You'll find plenty of **restaurants** in Burgos serving the traditional dishes, *cordero asado* (roast lamb) and *morcilla* (a kind of black pudding with rice), but there's also a wide choice of other food and, due to the large student population, a lively **bar** scene.

Bar La Cabaña Arandina, c/Sombrerería. Looking oddly like a marooned American diner, this fun eaterie around the back of Plaza Mayor serves up cheap *platos combinados* and *bocadillos* around a big three-sided bar stuffed with tapas.

Casa Ojeda, c/Vitoria 5. Huge bar-cum-deli-cum-patisserie-cum-restaurant complex, with a smart Castilian restaurant upstairs, a less expensive *comedor* downstairs, or tapas at the bar. À la carte dishes in the restaurant start at €10.80; *platos combinados* at €9.

Gaona, c/de la Paloma 41. Formal and upmarket Spanish restaurant, very close to the cathedral, with a huge menu of meat and fish dishes from

around €11.40 and no less than eight *menús* (€10.20–21).

Marisquería Bringas, c/Laín Calvo 50. Very good fish restaurant when you're fed up with *asados* and Castilian cuisine.

Mesón el Avellano, c/Avellanos. One of several excellent tapas bars along this lively street.

Mesón Burgos, c/Sombrerería 8. Small, old-fashioned wooden bar, with cosy restaurant behind serving Castilian meat and fish standards from €6.

Prego, c/Huerto del Rey. Pleasant if not particularly cheap Italian restaurant with a big menu including pasta (from €6), meat dishes (€7.80) and pizza (from €10).

Nightlife

What **nightlife** there is in staid Burgos is mainly generated by the local students, who hang out in the noisy and (mainly) nasty bars down c/Huerto del Rey and around Llanas de Afuera, just behind the cathedral: *Warhol*, at c/Huerto del Rey 15, is as good a place as any to go deaf in quickly. Alternatively, try the lively bunch of **tapas bars** in c/Avellanos and on Plaza de San Martín by the turismo. After 3am, head for the **clubs** in the new district of Bernardos round c/Las Calzadas and Avenida de la Paz, just to the east of the old city. Most places play loud rock and dated heavy metal; for a more relaxed atmosphere and soothing jazz music try *Café La Cabala*, c/Puebla 7, or, back towards the cathedral, *Café de España*, at c/Laín Calvo 12.

Listings

Bus information ☎947 265 565.
Car rental Operators include Díaz Espartosa, Avda. General Vigón 52 ☎947 223 803; Europcar, c/Santa Clara 32 ☎947 273 745; and Hertz, c/General Mola 5 ☎947 201 675.
Internet access *Ciber-Café*, c/Puebla 21 (Mon–Thurs 4pm–2am, Fri 4pm–4am, Sat 5pm–4am & Sun 5pm–2am; €3 for 30min, €4.80 for 1hr).

Laundry Lavasec, Plaza Santiago 4, has self-service facilities.
Post office The main office is at Plaza de Conde de Castro, by the Puente San Pablo.
Taxis Abutaxi ☎947 277 777 and Radio Taxi ☎947 481 010; both offer a 24-hour service.
Train information ☎947 203 560.

Southeast of Burgos

Southeast of Burgos, off the road to Soria, are a trio of sights: the great monastery of **Santo Domingo de Silos**; the town of **Covarrubias**, a medieval treasure on the Río Arlanza; and, at **Quintanilla de las Viñas**, a tiny Visigothic church and hermitage. These are easy excursions if you have transport. If you don't, you'll need commitment and time to get the daily early evening bus from Burgos to Silos via Lerma, staying overnight (or two nights if you go on Saturday, since there's no bus back until Monday), and returning the following morning. Pilgrims, of course, used to (and still do) walk to Silos as a detour from the *camino*.

Santo Domingo de Silos and around

The Benedictine abbey of **SANTO DOMINGO DE SILOS** is one of Spain's greatest Christian monuments. Its main feature is a great double-storey eleventh-century **Romanesque cloister** (Mon & Sun 4.30–6pm, Tues–Sat 10am–1pm & 4.30–6pm; €1.50), whose beautiful sculptural decoration is in many ways unique. The most remarkable features of the cloister are eight almost life-sized **reliefs** on the corner pillars. They include *Christ on the Road to Emmaus*, dressed as a pilgrim to Santiago (complete with scallop shell), a detail that shows that pilgrims made a detour from the route to see the tomb of Santo Domingo, the eleventh-century abbot after whom the monastery is named.

The same sculptor was responsible for about half of the **capitals**. Besides a famous bestiary, these include many Moorish motifs, giving rise to speculation that he may even have been a Moor. Whatever the case, it is an early example of the effective mix of Arab and Christian cultures, which was continued in the fourteenth century with the painted Mudéjar vault showing scenes of everyday pastimes. A quite different sculptor carved many of the remaining capitals, including the two that ingeniously tell the stories of the Nativity and the Passion in a very restricted space. A third master was responsible for the pillar with the Annunciation and Tree of Jesse, which is almost Gothic in spirit.

Visits to the monastery also include entry to the eighteenth-century **pharmacy**, which has been reconstructed in a room off the cloister, and the **museum**, which houses the tympanum from the destroyed Romanesque church. The **church** itself is an anticlimax, a rather nondescript construction designed by the eighteenth-century academic architect Ventura Rodríguez. Its Romanesque predecessor was too dark for the taste of the times; fortunately, the cloister's size and spaciousness saved it from a similar fate. The monks are considered one of the two or three best choirs in the world, and it's particularly worth attending the morning Mass (Mon–Sat 9am, Sun noon) or even better, vespers, which currently start at 7pm.

Practicalities

Men can **stay** in the monastery itself if they contact the Guest Master (*Padre Hospedería*) in advance (☎947 380 768); he prefers people to stay a few days. This is a wonderful bargain, with comfortable single rooms and good food at a ridiculously low cost (€13.20 per night). There are also some excellent places to stay in the village: the *Hotel Arco de San Juan*, Pradera de San Juan 1 (☎ & ⓕ947 390 074; ❺), very near the cloister entrance, which has a lovely garden; the new, clean and well-furnished *Hostal Cruces* in the Plaza Mayor (☎947 390 064; ❹), which has an informative, English-speaking manager and serves good-value evening meals; and the *Hotel Tres Coronas de Silos*, Plaza Mayor 6 (☎947 390 125, Ⓕ947 390 124; ❺), an imposing stone house which dominates the square.

The Gorges of Yecla

The landscape around Silos is some of the most varied in Castile. A short walk up the hill gives a superb bird's-eye view of the village and the surrounding countryside and a couple of kilometres away are the impressive **gorges of Yecla**.

To reach these, take the road to Burgos, heading west of Silos, and turn left at the first road you come to, shortly after leaving the village. You cross two rivers in quick succession, the Mataviejas and the Yecla. A few hundred metres later, a path off to the left leads through an incredibly narrow rocky gorge – the **Desfiladero de la Yecla** – which was impassable until a series of wooden walkways and plank bridges was built in the 1930s. It makes a spectacular hike, with the birds of prey circling high in the thin strip of visible sky.

If you continue west from the gorge rather than heading straight back to Silos, you can climb to the picturesque hilltop village of **Hinojar de Cervera**, and descend on the far side, after a couple of kilometres, to the **Cueva de San García**. This is a small cave containing various faded and rudimentary specimens of prehistoric art.

Covarrubias

The superbly preserved small town of **COVARRUBIAS** is just under 20km north of Silos, on the C110 between Lerma and the Burgos–Soria road. The main sight is the town itself: many of its white houses are half-timbered, with shady arcades, and remnants of the fortifications are still standing, including a tenth-century tower. The **Colegiata** (Mon & Wed–Sun 10.30am–2pm & 4–7pm; €1.50) looks plain from the outside, but a visit to the interior is a must. Inside you'll find a late-Gothic hall church crammed with tombs, giving an idea of the grandeur of the town in earlier times. The organ is an amazing seventeenth-century instrument still in good working order; you'll probably have to be content with hearing a recording. There are several good paintings in the museum, but the chief attraction is a triptych whose central section, a polychromed carving of the *Adoration of the Magi*, is attributed to Gil de Siloé.

Public **transport** is limited: there's no bus service between Covarrubias and Silos, although it is just possible to see both towns in a day on foot; the alternative is to come direct on the single daily bus from Burgos. If you plan **to stay** in Covarrubias, bear in mind that apart from the expensive (but excellent) *Hotel Arlanza*, Plaza Mayor 11 (☎947 406 441, Ⓕ947 406 359; ❻), and the equally upmarket *Hotel Rey Chindasvinto*, Plaza del Rey Chindasvinto 5 (☎947 406 560; ❻), the only other place to stay is above the restaurant *Casa Galín* (☎947 406 552, Ⓕ947 406 552; ❸), which is also the best place to **eat** in the village.

Quintanilla

An equally important monument, this time a rare Visigothic survival, is to be found at **QUINTANILLA DE LAS VIÑAS**, which lies 4km north of Mazanriegos on the main Burgos–Soria road, about 40km southeast of Burgos. Signs labelled *Turismo* lead to a house where the caretaker of the **Ermita de Santa María** (April–Nov Wed–Sun 9.30am–2pm & 4–7pm, Oct–March Wed–Sun 10am–5pm, closed last weekend in each month) lives; if he isn't there, he'll probably be at the hermitage itself, 1km further north. It's a simple building, of which only the transept and the chancel survive. Dating from about 700, it's remarkable for its unique series of sculptures: the outside bears delicately carved friezes, and inside there's a triumphal arch with capitals representing the sun and moon, and a block which is believed to be the earliest representation of Christ in Spanish art.

Burgos to León

The pilgrim route west from Burgos to León is one of the most rewarding sections in terms of art and architecture. The N120 between the two cities passes through **Carrión de los Condes** and **Sahagún**, and the other stops on the *camino* are only a short detour off the main road.

Frómista

FRÓMISTA was the next important pilgrimage stop after Burgos. The present-day town is much decayed, with a fraction of the population it once had. There's only one sight of any note – the extremely beautiful church of **San Martín**, which was originally part of an abbey which no longer exists, and is now deconsecrated (daily: summer 10am–2pm & 4.30–8pm; winter 10am–2pm & 3–6.30pm; free). Carved representations of monsters, human figures and animals run right around the church, which was built in 1066 in a Romanesque style unusually pure for Spain, with no traces of later additions. In fact, what you can see now is a result of an early-twentieth-century restoration which was perhaps rather too thorough, although it is pleasing to the eye. Its beauty is enhanced by being completely devoid of furnishings; there's nothing to detract from the architecture, and the only colour is provided by twin wooden statues of San Martín and Santiago. The other church associated with the pilgrimage, **Santa María**, is near the train station, but it is also redundant and is kept locked.

If you want to **stay** there are three comfortable places: *Pensión Camino de Santiago*, Avda. Ejercito 11 (☎979 810 053; ❹), on the square on the road north to Santander, *Pensión Marisa* (☎979 810 023; ❸), behind San Martín, and the slightly more upmarket *Hotel San Martín*, Plaza San Martín 7 (☎ & ℱ979 810 000; ❹), which also does a very popular lunchtime *menú*. The *Hostería de Los Palmeros*, Plaza Mayor (☎988 810 067), is a former medieval pilgrims' *hostal* now converted into an excellent restaurant. The **turismo** (daily in summer 10am–2pm & 4.30–8pm; ☎979 810 113) is at the crossroads in the centre of town where the **buses** stop. Frómista is connected with Burgos by a daily bus, although it's reached more easily from Palencia since it lies on the Palencia–Santander rail line.

Villalcázar de Sirga

Thirteen kilometres from Frómista lies **VILLALCÁZAR DE SIRGA**, notable for a **church** built by the Knights Templar: from a distance it seems to crush the little village by its sheer mass, and originally its fortified aspect was even more marked. The Gothic style here begins to assert itself over the

Romanesque, as witnessed by the figure sculpture on the two portals and the elegant pointed arches inside. The **Capilla de Santiago** has three polychromed tombs, among the finest of their kind and contemporary with the building. If the church is closed, as it usually is, take the street to the left in front of it and turn left at the corner; the sexton's house is the first brick building on the right.

In the square itself are a few medieval houses, one of which has been converted into the excellent **restaurant**, *El Mesón de Villasirga*. There is no accommodation, however, and Villalcázar is probably best seen as a day's excursion from Carrión de los Condes, 5km away.

Carrión de los Condes

The dusty, quiet atmosphere of **CARRIÓN DE LOS CONDES** belies its sensational past. It's reputed to be the place where, before the Reconquest, Christians had to surrender one hundred virgins annually to the Moorish overlords – a scene depicted on the portal of **Santa María** (situated at the edge of town, where the buses stop). For finer sculpture, however, look at the doorway of **Santiago**'s own church in the centre of town, overlooking the Plaza Mayor. Time has not treated this kindly; burned out during the last century, the church was rebuilt but now stands disused and neglected. Look out for the extraordinarily delicate covings above the door, which depict the trades and professions of the Middle Ages. The town's third main monument is the Plateresque cloister of the **Monasterio de San Zoilo**, located over the sixteenth-century bridge; a side room off the cloister contains the tombs of the counts of Carrión, from whom the town's name comes. The nuns of **Santa Clara** have opened a small **museum** (April–Sept Tues–Sun 10.30am–12.30pm & 5–7pm; Oct–March Tues–Sun 10.30am–12.30pm & 4–6pm, closed mid-Oct to mid-Nov) with a moderately interesting collection, including one of Spain's oldest organs. Their main work of art, however, the theatrical *Pietà* by Gregorio Fernández, is kept in the church, which is open only for the early-morning Mass.

For **accommodation**, *Hostal La Corte* at c/Santa María 34 (℡ & ℻979 880 138; ❺) in Carrión is good value, and boasts an excellent cheap **restaurant**. Another restaurant, *El Resbalón*, c/Ferman Gomez 19, also offers rooms (℡979 880 433; ❸), though they have seen better days. By far the most atmospheric place to stay is at the splendid *Hotel Real Monasterio San Zoilo* (℡979 880 049, ℻979 881 090; ❺), recently converted from part of the monastery. There's plenty of room for unofficial **camping** down by the river, or in the shady and modern official campsite, *El Edén* (℡979 881 152), also by the river and back from the main road. Carrión is linked by **bus** to both Burgos and Palencia.

Sahagún and San Miguel de Escalada

From Carrión the route west continues to **Sahagún.** No other town so clearly illustrates the effect of the decline from the heyday of the pilgrimage. Once the seat of the most powerful monastery in all Spain, it's now a largely modern town, above which the towers of the remaining old buildings rear up like dinosaurs in a zoo. The nearby monastery at **San Miguel de Escalada** has similarly slipped into insignificance.

Sahagún

SAHAGÚN is generally thought to be the birthplace of the Mudéjar brick churches built by the Moorish craftsmen who stayed on to work for the Christians after the Reconquest. Unfortunately, its great Benedictine **monastery** is these days little more than a largely ruined shell whose main

surviving sections – the gateway and belfry – date from a period of reconstruction in the seventeenth century. Right beside these is the most delicate of
Sahagún's Mudéjar churches, the twelfth-century **San Tirso** (Tues–Sun
10am–2pm & 4.30–8pm, closed Sun pm), now beautifully restored and looking almost unnaturally pristine in comparison to the monastery remains scattered around it. Just to the other side of San Tirso is the plain building of the
Monasterio Santa Cruz, whose museum (daily 10.30am–12.30pm &
4–6.30pm) houses the great *custodia* made by Enrique de Arfe, founder of a
dynasty of silversmiths. Its big sister is the famous one at Toledo; like that one,
the only airing it gets is during the Corpus Christi celebrations. The nuns prefer only to open up to groups, but try anyway if you're on your own – many
pilgrims pass by here to get the official stamp for their *Camino de Santiago* card.

Walking across town you'll see the grand brick towers of further Mudéjar edifices rising incongruously above Sahagún's otherwise dull and modern skyline.
The most imposing is the church of **San Lorenzo**, just off the Plaza Mayor up
the unnamed road behind the Banco Herrero. The exterior is very grand, though
the inside has been heavily restored and is open only for Mass at the weekend
(Sat 9.30am, Sun noon & 2pm). It's also worth hunting out **La Peregrina**, on
the edge of town five minutes' walk beyond San Tirso, a thirteenth-century
monastery now crumbling into atmospheric rubble, though there's a beautiful
little restored chapel inside (ask at San Tirso about visiting) with fine stuccowork.

Practicalities

Buses leave from the Plaza Mayor but are very infrequent; it's much easier to
come by **train** from León or Palencia (13 daily in each direction). Turn right
out of the train station down Avenida Constitución to reach Plaza Mayor, a
ten-minute walk. En route you'll pass several of the town's **accommodation**
options: the good-value *Hostal-Restaurante Don Pacho* (☎987 780 775; ❸–❹),
with both en-suite and shared-bath rooms; the slightly pricier *La Cordoniz* (☎
& ⓕ 987 780 276; ❺); and, just off on a side street to the left, the *Alfonso VI*
(☎987 781 144, ⓕ987 781 258; ❺). There's a nice **restaurant** at the *Don Pacho*
with a *menú* for €6, while bar-restaurant *Luís* on Plaza Mayor and the *Cafetería
Caracas* just up the hill on Avenida Constitución are both good places for a
drink or snack.

San Miguel de Escalada

Although León is just a short distance further on from Sahagún, the medieval
pilgrim would probably first have made a slight detour to see the monastery of
SAN MIGUEL DE ESCALADA, a precious Mozarabic survival from the
tenth century. Founded by refugee monks from Córdoba, it's a touching little
building, with a simple interior of horseshoe arches, and a later portico, again
Moorish in style. You'll need your own transport to visit: although there are
two buses a day to and from León, one turns back thirty minutes after it arrives,
while the other requires spending the night – and there's nowhere to stay.

León

Even if they stood alone, the stained glass in the cathedral of **LEÓN** and the
Romanesque wall paintings in its Royal Pantheon would merit a very considerable journey, but there's much more to the city than this. For León is as attractive – and enjoyable – in its modern quarters as it is in those parts that remain
from its heyday: a prosperous provincial capital and lively university town.

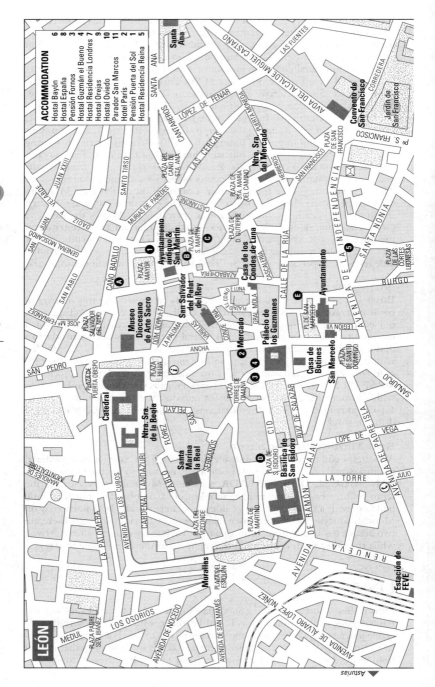

LEÓN

ACCOMMODATION

Hostal Bayón	6
Hostal España	8
Pensión Fornos	3
Hostal Guzmán el Bueno	4
Hostal Residencia Londres	7
Hostal Orejas	9
Hostal Oviedo	10
Parador San Marcos	11
Hotel París	2
Pensión Puerta del Sol	1
Hostal Residencia Reina	5

Asturias ▶

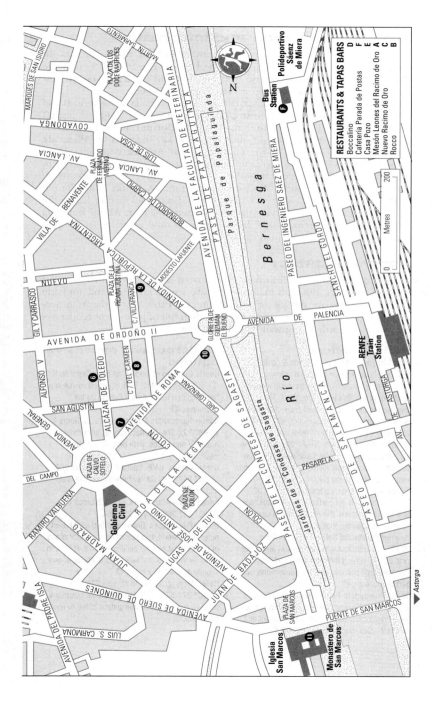

N

RESTAURANTS & TAPAS BARS

Boccalino	D
Cafetería Parada de Postas	F
Casa Pozo	E
Mesón Leones del Racimo de Oro	A
Nuevo Racimo de Oro	C
Rocco	B

0   Metres   200

Bus Station   **F**

Polideportivo Sáenz de Miera

MARQUÉS DE SAN ISIDRO

PLAZA DE LOS DOCE MÁRTIRES

MARTÍN SARMIENTO

COVADONGA

AV. LANCIA

LUIS DE SOSA

AV. LANCIA

PLAZA DE FERNANDO MERINO

AVENIDA DE LA FACULTAD DE VETERINARIA

PASEO DE PAPALAGUINDA

Parque de Papalaguinda

VILLA DE

BENAVENTE

BERNARDO DEL CARPIO

B e r n e s g a

PASEO DEL INGENIERO SÁEZ DE MIERA

NUEVO

GIL Y CARRASCO

PLAZA DE LA PIEDRA

SANTA JUSTINA

MODESTO LAFUENTE

AVENIDA DE LA REPÚBLICA ARGENTINA

C/ VILLAFRANCA   **9**

AVENIDA DE ORDOÑO II

ALFONSO V

SAN AGUSTÍN

ALCÁZAR DE TOLEDO   **6**

C/ DEL CARMEN   **8**

GLORIETA DE GUZMÁN EL BUENO

AVENIDA   DE   PALENCIA

RENFE Train Station

AVENIDA GENERAL

DEL CAMPO

PLAZA DE CALVO SOTELO

AVENIDA DE ROMA   **10**

CARD LORENZANA

PASEO DE LA CONDESA DE SAGASTA

R í o

PASEO DE SALAMANCA

SANCHO EL GORDO

ASTORGA

DE ASTORGA

AV.

RAMIRO VALBUENA

JUAN MADRAZO

Gobierno Civil

ROA DE LA VEGA   **7**

AVENIDA DE JOSÉ ANTONIO

PLAZA DE COLÓN

LUCAS DE TUY

COLÓN

JARDINES DE LA CONDESA DE SAGASTA

PASARELA

LUIS S. CARMONA

AVENIDA DEL PADRE ISLA

AVENIDA DE SUERO DE QUIÑONES

JUAN DE BADAJOZ

PLAZA DE SAN MARCOS

PUENTE DE SAN MARCOS

Iglesia San Marcos

Monasterio de San Marcos   **11**

▶ Astorga

Arrival, orientation and information

León's modern sectors have been imaginatively laid out with wide, straight streets radiating like spokes from three focal plazas. The first of these is the **Glorieta de Guzmán el Bueno** near the river and the **train station**. Just south of here is the **bus station** on Paseo Ingeniero Miera.

From the Glorieta one can see straight down the Avenida de Ordoño II and across the **Plaza de Santo Domingo** to the towers of the cathedral. Just off the Plaza de Santo Domingo stands the **Casa de Botines**, an uncharacteristically restrained work by Antoni Gaudí. The third key square is the **Plaza de Calvo Sotelo**, connected to the Glorieta by the Avenida de Roma. Head straight up from Plaza de Santo Domingo to the cathedral and you'll arrive in the Plaza Regia; here, directly opposite the cathedral's great west facade, stands the main **turismo** (Mon–Fri 9am–2pm & 5–7pm, Sat & Sun 10am–2pm & 5–8pm; ☎987 237 082, ⓦwww.aytoleon.com). León's old quarter lies to the south of the cathedral, occupying the streets around the Plaza Mayor and Plaza San Martin; it now seems a little shabby in the daytime, especially in comparison with the smart modern city centre.

Accommodation

Most budget **accommodation** is concentrated in the downtown area just north of the river, although many places have seen better days and are fairly poor value. There are also lots of rooms round the Plaza Mayor: they're generally less expensive, but dingy and noisy, and often full of permanent residents – certainly not worth a long walk with heavy bags.

Budget options

Hostal Bayón, c/Alcázar de Toledo 6 ☎987 231 446. Best budget accommodation in town: stripped-pine floors, high ceilings, large windows, quiet rooms and firm beds throughout. There are only five rooms though, so best book ahead. ❸

Hostal España, c/del Carmen 3 ☎987 236 014. Good-value, clean *hostal* in a quiet side street. ❸

Pensión Fornos, c/Cid 8 ☎987 236 921. Above a popular restaurant of the same name, this *pensión* offers comfortable rooms in a good location in a quiet side road in the centre of town. ❸

Hostal Oviedo, Avda. de Roma 26 ☎987 222 236. Slightly worn but perfectly comfortable rooms near the train station; the *Hostal Europa* downstairs is cheaper but shabbier. ❸

Pensión Puerta del Sol, c/Puerta del Sol 1 ☎987 211 966. Reasonable rooms in an excellent location overlooking the attractive Plaza Mayor; about the only *pensión* here not permanently occupied by students. ❸

Hostal Residencia Reina, Puerto de a Reina 2 ☎987 205 212. Neat, modern little eleven-room *hostal*, quite centrally located, with pleasant and excellent-value rooms, some en suite. ❹

Moderate and expensive options

Hostal Guzmán el Bueno, c/López Castrillón 6 ☎ & ⒻF987 236 412. Well-equipped rooms in a handy central location near Palacio de los Guzmanes. ❹

Hostal Residencia Londres, Avda. de Roma 1 ☎987 222 274. Spotless rooms, all with bathroom, TV and phone, with nice views; good value. ❺

Hostal Orejas, c/Villafranca 8 ☎987 252 909, ⒻF987 252 909). Comfortable rooms with bath and TV. ❺

Parador San Marcos, Plaza San Marcos 7 ☎987 237 300, ⒻF987 233 458, Ⓔleon@parador.es. Once described as the best hotel in the world, this sensational *parador* in one of León's most historic buildings (see p.450), with antiques in the rooms, seems quite cheap at only slightly over €120 a night. ❾

Hotel París, c/Ancha 18 ☎987 238 600, ⒻF987 271 572, Ⓔhparis@lesin.es. Luxurious modern rooms in a former palace close to the cathedral. ❼

The City

In 914, as the Reconquest edged its way south from Asturias, Ordoño II transferred the Christian capital from Oviedo to León. Despite being sacked by the dreaded al-Mansur in 996, the new capital rapidly eclipsed the old – a scenario that was to repeat itself as the Reconquest unfolded. As more and more territory came under the control of León, it was divided into new administrative groupings: in 1035 the county of Castile matured into a fully fledged kingdom with its capital at Burgos. For the next two centuries León and Castile jointly spearheaded the war against the Moors – as often as not under joint rule – until, by the thirteenth century, Castile had come finally to dominate her mother kingdom. These two centuries were nevertheless the period of León's greatest power, from which date most of her finest monuments.

The cathedral

León's Gothic **Catedral** (Mon–Fri 8.30am–1.30pm & 4.30–7.30pm, July & Aug afternoon hours are 4–8pm, Sun 8.30am–2.30pm & 5–7pm, July & Aug Sun closes at 8pm) dates from the final years of the city's period of greatness. Its stained-glass **windows** (thirteenth-century and onwards) are equal to any masterpiece in any European cathedral – a stunning kaleidoscope of light streaming in through walls of multicoloured glass. While such extensive use of glass is purely French in inspiration, the colours used here – reds, golds and yellows – are strictly Spanish. Other elements which take the cathedral further away from its French model are the cloister (admission €3, including entrance to the Diocesan Museum – see below) and the later addition of the *coro*, whose glass screen, added this century to give a clear view up to the altar, enhances the sensation of light with its bewildering refractions.

Outside, the magnificent **west facade**, dominated by a massive rose window, comprises two towers and a detached nave supported by flying buttresses – a pattern repeated at the south angle. The inscription *locus appelationis* on the main porch indicates that the Royal Court of Appeal was held here, and amid the statuary a king ponders his verdict, seated on a throne of lions. Above the **central doorway** a more sublime trial – the Last Judgement – is in full swing. The sculpture on this triple portal of the facade is some of the finest on the Pilgrim Route, although later in date than most. The doorways of the south transept and the polychromed door to the north transept (shielded from the elements by the cloister) are other attractions. The cloister houses the rather eclectic **Diocesan Museum** (July–Sept Mon–Fri 9.30am–2pm & 4–7.30pm, Sat 9.30am–2pm & 4–7pm, Oct–May Mon–Fri 9.30am–1.30pm & 4–7pm, Sat 9.30pm–1.30pm, €3).

The Pantéon

From the Plaza de Santo Domingo, Avenida de Ramón y Cajal leads to the church of San Isidoro (open all day) and the Royal Pantheon of the early kings of León and Castile. Fernando I, who united the two kingdoms in 1037, commissioned the complex as a shrine for the bones of San Isidoro and a mausoleum for himself and his successors. The church dates mainly from the mid-twelfth century and shows Moorish influence in the horseshoe arch at the west end of the nave and the fanciful arches in the transepts. The bones of the patron saint lie in a reliquary on the high altar.

The **Pantéon** (daily 10am–1.30pm & 4–6.30pm, closed Sun pm; €3), reached through the door to the left of the main entrance and comprising two surprisingly small crypt-like chambers, was constructed between 1054 and

1063 as a narthex or portico preceding the west facade of the church. It's one of the earliest Romanesque buildings in Spain, and the carvings on the portal which links the Panteón and church herald the introduction of figure sculpture into the peninsula. In contrast, the capitals of the side piers and the two squat columns in the middle of the Panteón are carved with thick foliage which is still rooted in Visigothic tradition. Towards the end of the twelfth century, the extraordinarily well-preserved vaults were vividly covered in some of the most significant, imaginative and impressive paintings of Romanesque art. The central dome is occupied by Christ Pantocrator surrounded by the four Evangelists depicted with animal heads – allegorical portraits which stem from the apocalyptic visions in the Bible's Book of Revelation. One of the arches bordering the dome is decorated with quaint rustic scenes which represent the months of the year. Eleven kings and twelve queens were laid to rest here but the chapel was desecrated during the Peninsular War and the remaining tombs command little attention in such a marvellous setting.

You can also visit the treasury and library; the former contains magnificent reliquaries, caskets and chalices from the early Middle Ages, but only reproductions of the manuscripts are on view.

San Marcos

If the Panteón is a perfect illustration of the way Romanesque art worked its way into Spain along the Pilgrim Route from France, the opulent **Monasterio de San Marcos** (reached from the Plaza de Calvo Sotelo via Avenida de José Antonio) stands as a more direct reminder that León was a station on this route. Here, on presentation of the relevant documents, pilgrims were allowed to regain their strength before the gruelling Bierzo mountains west of León. The original monastery was built in 1168 for the Knights of Santiago, one of several chivalric orders founded in the twelfth century to protect pilgrims and lead the Reconquest. Eventually these powerful, ambitious and semi-autonomous knights posed a political threat to the authority of the Spanish throne, until in 1493 Isabel la Católica subtly tackled the problem by "suggesting" that her husband Fernando be "elected" Grand Master. Thus the wealth and power of this order was assimilated to that of the throne.

In time, the order degenerated to little more than a men's club – Velázquez, for instance, depicts himself in its robes in *Las Meninas* – and in the sixteenth century the monastery was rebuilt as a kind of palatial headquarters. Its massive facade is lavishly embellished with Plateresque appliqué designs: over the main entrance Santiago is once again depicted in his battling role of *Matamoros*; more pertinently, the arms of Carlos V, who inherited the grand mastership from Fernando in 1516, protrude above the ornate balustrade of the roofline. The monastery is now a *parador* (see p.448), and is officially off-limits to nonresidents beyond its foyer and (modern) bar and restaurant, though you may be able to sneak in for a discreet look at the fine cloisters and the *coro alto* of the church (access only from the hotel), which has a fine set of stalls by Juan de Juni.

Adjacent to the main facade stands the **Iglesia San Marcos**, vigorously speckled with the scallop shell motif of the pilgrimage. Its sacristy houses a small **museum** (May–Sept 10am–2pm & 5–8.30pm, Oct–April Tues–Sat 10am–2pm & 4.30–8pm, Sun 10am–2pm), whose most beautiful and priceless exhibits include a thirteenth-century processional cross made of rock crystal and an eleventh-century ivory crucifix.

Eating, drinking and nightlife

Along with Salamanca, León is the best place to eat and drink in Old Castile. The liveliest **bars and restaurants** are those in and around the small square of San Martín – an area known as the **Barrio Húmedo** (the Wet Quarter) for the amount of liquid sloshing around. All the bars here will give you a *pincho* with every drink, so you can eat pretty well if you drink enough, especially hopping from bar to bar ordering *cortos* – small tumblers of beer for about €0.50. The garlic-smothered potatoes dished up in *El Rincón del Gaucho* are particularly delicious.

Things really take off during **Semana Santa**, and for the **fiestas** of San Juan and San Pedro in the last week of June. The celebrations, concentrated around the Plaza Mayor, get pretty riotous, with an enjoyable blend of medieval pageantry and buffoonery.

Boccalino, Plaza de San Isidoro 9. Beautifully located restaurant, with outdoor seating on the square facing San Isidoro and (given the setting) surprisingly cheap pizza and pasta (from €6), plus slightly more expensive Castilian fare.

Cafetería Parada de Postas. Vast restaurant in the unlikely setting of the bus terminal, serving one of the best lunchtime *menús* (€7.10) in northern Spain.

Casa Pozo, Plaza San Marcelo 15 ☎ 987 223 039. Excellent *bodega* for traditional Leónese dishes, behind the *ayuntamiento*, with *menús* from €9 and à la carte dishes from €12. Closed Sun in July & Aug.

Mesón Leones del Racimo de Oro, Caño Badillo 2. Authentic and modest-priced *mesón* in slightly olde-worlde surroundings just behind Plaza Mayor. There's a good *menú,* or try regional speciality

morcillo estofada (stewed black sausage; €9). Closed Sun night & Tues.

Nuevo Racimo de Oro, Plaza San Martín 8. Slightly formal restaurant offering an oasis of restraint on the corner of León's wackiest square. À la carte dishes (from €9) are expensive, but worth it. Closed Wed in winter.

Restaurante Fornos, c/Cid 8. Down-to-earth restaurant with good atmosphere serving cheap, basic fill-you-up dishes like roast chicken (€4.50) and more expensive concoctions like clams with French beans (*alubias con almejas*; €7.20). Closed Sun night & Mon.

Rocco, Plaza de San Martín 5. One of the few half-decent pizzerias between Madrid and Lisbon, and cheap too, with a big list of offerings from €4.20 dished up in cosy surroundings on the city's liveliest square.

Listings

Bus information ☎ 987 211 000.
Car rental Operators include Atesa, Plaza Condesa de Sagasta 46 ☎ 987 233 589; Avis, c/Condesa Sagasta 34 ☎ 987 270 075; and Europcar, c/Juan de Badajoz 7 ☎ 987 271 980.
Internet access Locutorio Telefónica, c/La Rua 8 (Mon–Fri 9.30am–2.30pm & 4.30–9pm, Sat 10am–2pm & 5–9.30pm; €2.40 per hour).

Post office The main branch is at the southern end of Avda. de Independencia, by the Plaza de San Francisco.
Taxis Radio Taxi León ☎ 987 261 415; Taxi Trabajo Villaquilambe ☎ 987 285 355.
Train information RENFE ☎ 987 270 202; FEVE ☎ 987 271 210.

Astorga and beyond

For the fittest of the pilgrims it was one day's walk 29 miles southwest of León to the next major stop at Astorga. On the way – at **Puente de Orbigo** – you pass the most ancient of the bridges along the route (probably the oldest in all Spain), now bypassed by the new road and offering a delightful and popular spot for a riverside stroll or picnic. As you get closer to Galicia, the terrain becomes mountainous and offers spectacular views. Beyond the valley town of **Ponferrada**, weary pilgrims confronted the mountains of **El Bierzo**, a region linked historically with León though distinct in more than just geography; in remoter villages you'll hear *gallego* spoken and see rather hopeful graffiti demanding independence for the area.

Astorga

ASTORGA resembles many of the smaller cities along the *camino*: originally settled by the Romans, it was sacked by the Moors in the eleventh century, then rebuilt and endowed with the usual hospices and monasteries, but as the pilgrimage lost popularity in the late Middle Ages the place fell into decline. It's now a small but lively provincial capital with a smattering of museums, an incongruously grand cathedral and the bizarre **Palacio Episcopal** – commissioned by a Catalan bishop from his countryman Antoni Gaudí. The palace's appearance will not surprise anyone who has seen Gaudí's work in Barcelona. Surrounded by a moat and built of light grey granite, it resembles some horror-movie Gothic castle from the mountains of Transylvania with an equally striking, remarkably spacious interior. For half a century it stood empty and was considered a scandalous and expensive white elephant, but nowadays it houses the unique and excellent **Museo de los Caminos** (Tues–Sat 10am–2pm & 4–8pm, Sun 10am–2pm; €2.40, €3 joint ticket with Museo Catedralicio). A host of knick-knacks throws interesting sidelights on the story of the pilgrimage: hanging on the wall are examples of the documents issued at Santiago to certify that pilgrims had "travelled, confessed and obtained absolution", and there are photographs of the myriad villages and buildings along the way, and charts to show the precise roads taken through the towns.

Opposite – though stylistically worlds apart – stands the florid **Catedral**. Built between 1471 and 1693, it combines numerous architectural styles, but still

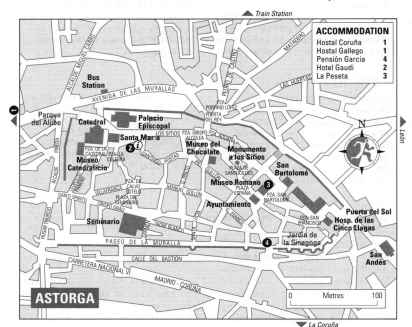

Astorga is the traditional market town of the **Maragatos**, a mysterious race of people, possibly descended from the Berbers of North Africa, who crossed into Spain with the first Moorish incursions of the early eighth century. Marrying only among themselves, they maintained their traditions and individuality well into recent decades. For several centuries almost the entire carrying trade of Spain was in their hands, but muleteers no longer have a role. Nowadays you're unlikely to come across them unless you're plodding through the fields along the Pilgrim Route, and their only obvious legacy to the town is a pair of colourful clockwork figures dressed in Maragato costume who jerk into action to strike the hour on the town hall clock in Plaza de España.

manages to be totally upstaged by the palace. The **Museo Catedralicio** (daily: summer 10am–2pm & 4–8pm; winter 11am–2pm & 3.30–6.30pm; €1.50, €3 joint ticket with Museo de los Caminos; entrance to the left of the main facade) is interesting, however, especially for its beautiful twelfth-century wooden tomb painted with scenes from the lives of Christ and the Apostles.

While you're here, you could also take in the **Museo del Chocolate**, c/José María Goy (Tues–Sun 10.30am–2pm & 4.30–8pm, closed Sun pm; €0.60), which charts the growth of Astorga's flourishing chocolate industry during the eighteenth and nineteenth centuries. There are also 75-minute guided walks departing from the turismo (around 12 daily; €1.20) along the **Ruta Romana**, which take you through Astorga's Roman remains, while the **Museo Romano** (Tues–Sun: Easter–Sept 11am–2pm & 5–8pm; Sept–Easter 11am–2pm & 4–6pm; closed Sun pm all year; €1.20; closed for restoration at the time of writing) displays various bits of Roman stonework recovered by archeologists from the area.

Practicalities

Astorga connects with León by train but the **train station** is a long way from the centre of town. It makes far more sense to arrive and depart by **bus** as the station is very conveniently placed opposite the Palacio Episcopal. The **turismo** (Tues–Sat 10.30am–2pm & 4–7pm, Sun 10am–2pm; ☏987 618 222, ⓦwww.ayuntamientodeastorga.com) is located opposite the Palacio Episcopal at c/Eduardo de Castro 5.

Several of Astorga's better **restaurants** are attached to accommodation: the homely little *comedor* in the *Pensión García* has a good *menú* for €9.60, or try the slightly more upmarket restaurant in the *Peseta*, where award-winning Castilian dishes start at a reasonable €7.20. For a splurge, the restaurant in the *Hotel Gaudí* is the best in town. **Accommodation** is limited, and what there is isn't particularly good value, so you might prefer to visit on a day-trip from León. If you do want to stay, it's worth booking ahead.

Hostal Coruña, Avda. Ponferrada 72 ☏ & ⓕ 987 615 009. Decent *hostal*, though unattractively located on a dreary road ten minutes' walk from the cathedral. ❺

Hostal Gallego, Avda. de Ponferrada 78 ☏ 987 615 013, ⓕ 987 615 450. Bigger and slightly more expensive than the almost adjacent *Coruña*, and in a similarly uninspiring setting, though the rooms themselves are perfectly OK. ❺

Pensión García, c/Bajada del Postigo 3 ☏ 987 616 046. Just inside the old town, with basic but clean rooms and a good *comedor*. ❸

Hotel Gaudí, c/Eduardo de Castro 6 ☏ 987 615 654, ⓕ 987 615 040. Astorga's top hotel, with classy rooms looking directly onto Gaudí's palace. The restaurant and wood-panelled bar are rather fine too. ❼

La Peseta, Plaza de San Bartolomé 3 ☏ 987 617 275, ⓕ 987 615 300. Smart but overpriced *hostal* above an excellent restaurant. ❺

Ponferrada

At first sight the heavily industrialized, bowl-shaped valley, centred on the large town of **PONFERRADA**, seems to have little to offer, but the mountainous terrain around has scenery as picturesque as any in Spain. The town of Ponferrada itself sums up this dichotomy, dominated by a huge slag heap and spreading suburbs, yet with a quiet, unspoiled old quarter. The two are separated by a river blackened by coal mining and spanned by the iron bridge that has given Ponferrada its name. Above the sharp valley the fancy twelfth-century turrets and battlements of the **Castillo de los Templarios** (Tues–Sat 10am–2pm & April–May 4.30–8pm, June–Sept 5–9pm, Oct–March 4–6pm, Sun 10am–2pm €1.50) may look like gingerbread, but they were built to protect pilgrims against the very real threat of the Moors, and the arcaded streets and overhanging houses of the old quarter grew up in their protective shadow. A quaint Puerta del Reloj (Clock Gateway) leads into the **Plaza Mayor**, with a late seventeenth-century *ayuntamiento*, similar in design to its contemporary counterpart at Astorga.

There are several churches in the town but the most important is a short walk away in the northeast outskirts: **Santo Tomás de las Ollas**, a small Mozarabic church dating from the tenth century with nine round Moorish horseshoe arches and Visigothic elements.

Practicalities

Bus and train stations, and most accommodation, are in the new part of town, which can be quite difficult to find your way around. From the **bus station**, head across the open space outside to the far left-hand corner to pick up c/General Gomez Nuñez (subsequently Avenida Perez Colino) and walk straight down it for 10–15 minutes to reach the river, from where you'll see the castle up on your left. The **train station** is more centrally located, right on the edge of the town centre. The **turismo** (summer Mon–Fri 10am–3pm & 4–9pm, Sat 10am–2pm & 4–8pm, Sun 11am–2pm; winter Mon–Sat 10am–2pm & 4–6pm, Sun 10am–2pm; ☎987 424 236) is next to the castle.

The best low-price **place to stay** is the nice *Hostal Santa Cruz*, c/Marcelo Macías 4 (☎ & ℱ987 428 351, ℮hsantacruz@usuarios.retecal.es; ❹). For something plusher, try the *Hotel Madrid*, Avda. de la Puebla 44 (☎987 411 550, ℱ987 411 861; ❻), while for real luxury, Ponferrada has its own four-star palace, the *Hotel del Temple*, on Avenida de Portugal (☎987 410 058, ℱ987 423 525, ℮comercial@hotelestemple.com; ❼). There's a good, if pricey, **restaurant** in the *Hotel Madrid*, while the *Rincon de los Templarios*, just off the Avda. del Castillo, by the main gate to the castle, serves lavish portions of home-cooked food at rock-bottom prices (closed Mon).

Las Médulas

Twenty kilometres southwest of Ponferrada lies **LAS MÉDULAS**, the jagged remains of Roman strip mining for gold. Nine hundred thousand tonnes of the precious metal were ripped from the hillsides using carefully constructed canals, leaving an eerie scene reminiscent of Arizona, peppered with caves and needles of red rock. From **Carucedo**, a road leads for 4km up to the village of Las Médulas; from here you can walk right through the zone. It's a good idea to make for the ridge overlooking the whole desolation; the quarry visible in the background from here is a reminder of how nature can turn man's devastation into beauty given a few thousand years. Another road leads from this viewpoint back down to Carucedo; the round trip takes about four or five hours.

Villafranca del Bierzo

The last halt before the climb into Galicia, **VILLAFRANCA DEL BIER-ZO**, was where pilgrims on their last legs could chicken out of the final trudge. Those who arrived at the Puerta del Perdón (Door of Forgiveness) at the church of **Santiago** could receive the same benefits as in Santiago de Compostela itself. The simple Romanesque church is of little interest, and the impressive castle opposite is in private hands and unvisitable, but the town itself is quietly enchanting, with slate-roofed houses, cool mountain air and the clear Burbia River providing a setting reminiscent of the English Lake District. Of the other churches the most rewarding is **San Francisco** just off the Plaza Mayor; it has a beautiful Mudéjar ceiling, a *retablo* so warped that it makes you dizzy to contemplate it, and an unusual well. If either church is locked, the bookshop on the plaza has the keys.

Regular half-hourly **buses** from Ponferrada stop near the *parador*. **Places to stay** include the modern *Parador de Villafranca del Bierzo*, Avenida Calvo Sotelo (✆987 540 175, ℻987 540 010, ✉villafranca@parador.es; ❼), and the *Hostal Comercio*, Puente Nuevo 2 (✆987 540 008; ❷–❸), a beautiful fifteenth-century house whose spacious rooms are a real bargain. *Don Nacho*, in a little alley off the Plaza Mayor, is a good place to **eat**, serving tapas, *menús* and fish specialities.

Travel details

Trains

Burgos to: Ávila (4–6 daily; 2hr 30min); Barcelona (4 daily; 8hr 30min); Bilbao (3–6 daily; 3hr 30min); Haro (3 daily; 1hr 40min); Irún (7–8 daily; 3hr 30min); León (4 daily; 2hr); Logroño (3 daily; 2hr); Lugo (2 daily; 6hr 30min); Madrid (7–8 daily; 3hr); Palencia (4 daily; 1hr); Valladolid (12–14 daily; 1hr 20min); Vitoria (12 daily; 1hr 30min–2hr); Zamora (1 daily except Sun; 3hr 45min); Zaragoza (4 daily; 4hr).

León to: Ávila (7 daily; 3hr); Barcelona (3 daily; 11hr); Bilbao (1 daily; 5hr); Burgos (4 daily; 2hr); A Coruña (3 daily; 7hr); Logroño (2 daily; 4hr); Lugo (2–3 daily; 5hr); Madrid (7 daily; 4hr–6hr 20min); Medina del Campo (7 daily; 2hr); Ourense (4 daily; 4hr); Oviedo (5 daily; 2hr); Ponferrada (9 daily; 2hr) Santiago de Compostela (1 daily; 5hr 40min); Valladolid (3–5 daily; 1hr 30min); Vigo (4 daily; 6hr); Vitoria (2 daily; 3hr); Zaragoza (3 daily; 5hr 30min).

Logroño to: Barcelona (3 daily; 6hr 30min); Bilbao (2–3 daily; 2hr 30min); Burgos (3–4 daily; 2hr); León (2 daily; 3hr 45min); Madrid (1 daily except Sat; 5hr 30min); Valladolid (2 daily; 3hr); Zamora (1 daily except Sun; 6hr); Zaragoza (5–8 daily; 1hr 50min).

Medina del Campo to: Barcelona (2 daily; 11hr); Bilbao (3 daily; 5hr); León (7 daily; 2hr); Lugo (1 daily except Sat; 7hr); Madrid (14–18 daily; 2hr 15min); Ourense (2–3 daily; 3hr 40min); Oviedo (2–3 daily; 4hr); Valladolid (hourly; 20min); Vigo (2 daily; 6hr); Zamora (3–4 daily; 1hr); Zaragoza (2–3 daily; 6hr–7hr 30min).

Salamanca to: Ávila (4 daily; 1hr 30min); Burgos (4 daily; 2hr 30min); Madrid (2–4 daily; 2hr 30min); Valladolid (7 daily; 1hr 30min).

Valladolid to: Ávila (15 daily; 1hr); Barcelona (1–2 daily; 10–12hr); Bilbao (2–3 daily; 4hr 30min); Burgos (12 daily; 1hr 20min); León (10 daily; 1hr 30min); Lisbon (1 daily; 7hr 40min); Logroño (2 daily; 3hr); Madrid (16 daily; 2hr 30min); Medina del Campo (hourly; 20min); Palencia (hourly; 30min); Salamanca (7 daily; 1hr 30min); San Sebastián (4 daily; 4–5hr); Zamora (1–2 daily; 1hr 30min); Zaragoza (2 daily; 5hr 30min–6hr 30min).

Zamora to: Ávila (2 daily; 1hr 30min); A Coruña (2 daily; 5hr 20min); Madrid (2 daily; 3hr); Medina del Campo (4 daily; 1hr); Santiago de Compostela (2 daily; 4hr 20min); Toro (1–2 daily; 30min); Valladolid (1–2 daily; 1hr 30min); Vigo (2 daily; 5hr).

Buses

Burgos to: Bilbao (8 daily; 2–3hr); Carrión de los Condes (1 daily; 1hr 30min); Ciudad Rodrigo (1 daily; 5hr); Covarrubias (1 daily; 1hr); Frómista (1 daily; 1hr); León (1 daily; 3 hours); Logroño (7 daily; 2hr); Madrid (10 daily; 3hr); Palencia (1 daily; 1hr); Pamplona (5 daily; 3hr 30min); Sahagún (1

daily; 2hr 30min); Salamanca 3 daily; 2hr 45min);
San Sebastián (5 daily; 3hr); Santander (4 daily;
2hr 30min); Santo Domingo de la Calzada (5 daily;
1hr 30min); Soria 2 daily; 3hr–3hr 30min);
Valladolid (3 daily; 1hr 45min); Vinuesa (2 daily;
2hr 45min); Zamora (1 daily; 2hr 45min); Zaragoza
(4 daily; 3hr 45min).

León to: Astorga (hourly; 45min); Bilbao (1 daily;
5hr 45min); Burgos (1 daily; 3hr 30min; Logroño
(2 daily; 4hr); Lugo (2 daily; 4hr); Madrid (10 daily;
4hr 30min); Oviedo (8 daily; 1hr 45min); Palencia
(1 daily; 2 hours); Ponferrada (11 daily; 2hr);
Salamanca (5 daily; 2hr 40min); Santander (2
daily; 3hr); Valladolid (7 daily; 1hr 30min);
Villafranca del Bierzo (3 daily; 3hr); Zamora (3
daily; 2hr 30min).

Logroño to: Barcelona (3 daily; 6hr); Bilbao (5
daily; 2hr 30min); Burgos (7 daily; 2hr); Haro (5
daily; 1hr); León (2 daily; 4hr); Pamplona (5 daily;
2hr); Santander (1 daily; 3hr 30min); Santo
Domingo de la Calzada (9 daily; 45min); Soria (5
daily; 1hr 30min); Vitoria (6 daily; 1hr); Zamora (3
daily; 4hr 30min); Zaragoza (6 daily; 2–3hr).

Palencia to: Burgos (3 daily; 1hr); Carrión de los
Condes (3 daily; 45min); A Coruña (3 daily; 6hr);
León (1 daily; 2 hours); Lugo (5 daily; 5hr 30min);
Madrid (6 daily; 3hr); Salamanca (3 daily; 2hr
30min); Valladolid (9 daily; 1hr); Zamora (2 daily;
2hr 30min); Zaragoza (2 daily; 5hr).

Salamanca to: Ávila (4 daily; 1hr 30min); Badajoz
(2 daily; 4hr 30min); Barcelona (2 daily; 11hr
30min); Burgos (1 daily; 2hr 45min); Cáceres (4
daily; 3hr 30min); Ciudad Rodrigo (12 daily; 1hr
30min); Madrid (13 daily; 2hr 30min); Palencia (3
daily; 2hr 30min); Santander (2 daily; 5hr 30min);
Sevilla (4 daily; 7hr); Soria (2 daily; 4hr 30min);
Valladolid (6 daily; 1hr 30min); Zamora (hourly;
50min).

Soria to: Almazán (2–3 daily; 45min); Barcelona (2
daily; 6hr); Berlanga de Duero (1 daily; 1hr 15min);
Burgos (4 daily; 3hr–3hr 30min); El Burgo de
Osma (2 daily; 1hr); Logroño (5 daily; 1hr 30min);
Madrid (7 daily; 2hr 30min); Medinaceli (2 daily;
1hr 15min); Pamplona (4 daily; 2–3hr); Peñafiel (4
daily; 2hr 30min); Salamanca (2 daily; 4hr 30min);
Valladolid (3 daily; 3hr); Vinuesa (2 daily; 45min);
Zaragoza (6 daily; 2hr 15min).

Valladolid to: Burgos (3 daily; 1hr 30min); León
(8 daily; 2hr); Madrid (16 daily; 2hr 40min);
Palencia (9 daily; 1hr); Peñafiel (5 daily; 1hr);
Salamanca (4 daily; 1hr 30min); Zamora (9 daily,
3 on Sun; 1hr 15min); Zaragoza (3 daily; 7hr
30min).

Zamora to: Burgos (1 daily; 2hr 45min); León (3
daily; 2hr 30min); Logroño (2 daily; 4hr 30min);
Madrid (7 daily; 3hr 15min); Palencia (2 daily; 2hr
30min); Salamanca (hourly; 50min); Valladolid (7
daily, 3 on Sun; 1hr 15min).

Euskal Herria

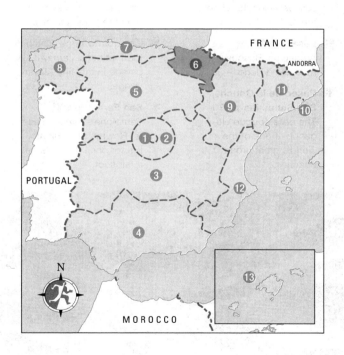

CHAPTER 6 # Highlights

* **Euskara – Bat, bi, hiru...** p.462 The Basque language has survived 3000 years of isolation. Impress locals by learning some.

* **Pintxos** p.463 Basque gourmet bar snacks are the way to dine in the *cascos viejos* throughout the region.

* **Lesaka** p.467 Archetypal Basque mountain village.

* **Paseo de la Concha, San Sebastián** p.473 The *belle époque* elegance of one of the world's great urban beaches.

* **Mundaka Estuary** p.483 Sublime scenery and world-class surfing, an enchanted forest and Gernika, the Basque spiritual capital.

* **Guggenheim Museum, Bilbao** p.489 The giant titanium sculpture that has become the symbol of the regenerated city.

* **Zalduondo** p.497 Catch the traditional *carnaval* parade in this tiny Alavan village.

* **San Fermin** p.500 Pamplona's famous fiesta. Rowdy, dirty, lunatic, but for once the bulls get a fair shot.

Euskal Herria: the País Vasco & Navarra

E uskal Herria is the name the Basque people give to their own land, an area that covers the three Basque provinces – **Gipuzkoa**, **Bizkaia**, and **Alava**, known collectively as the País Vasco – together with **Navarra**, and part of southwestern France. It's an immensely beautiful region – mountainous, green and thickly forested. It rains often, and much of the time the countryside is shrouded in a fine mist. But the summers, if you don't mind the occasional shower, are a glorious escape from the unrelenting heat of the south.

Despite some of the heaviest industrialization on the peninsula, Euskal Herria is remarkably unspoiled – neat and quiet inland, rugged and wild along the coast – and transport everywhere is easy and efficient. **San Sebastián** is the big draw on the coast, a major resort with superb but crowded beaches, but there are any number of lesser-known, equally attractive villages along the coast all the way to **Bilbao**, home to the magnificent **Guggenheim Museum**. Inland there's **Pamplona**, with its exuberant **Fiestas de San Fermín**, as well as many other destinations with charms of their own, from the drama of the **Pyrenees** to the laid-back elegance of **Vitoria**.

Accommodation price codes

All the establishments listed in this book have been price-graded according to the following scale. The prices quoted are for the **cheapest available double room in high season**; effectively this means that anything in the ❶ and most places in the ❷ range will be without private bath, though there's usually a washbasin in the room. In the ❹ category and above you will probably be getting private facilities. Remember, though, that many of the budget places will also have more expensive rooms including en-suite facilities. Youth hostels are graded under ❶ as the price per person is less than half of the category's upper limit.

Note that in the more upmarket *hostales* and *pensiones*, and in anything calling itself a hotel, you'll pay a **tax** (IVA) of seven percent on top of the room price.

❶ Under €12	❹ €27–36	❼ €60–90
❷ €12–18	❺ €36–48	❽ €90–120
❸ €18–27	❻ €48–60	❾ Over €120

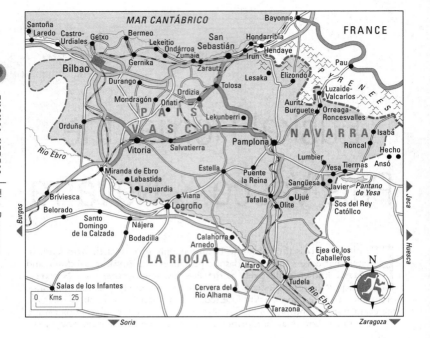

The Basques

The origin of **the Basques** is something of a mystery. They are a distinct people, generally with a different build from the French and Spanish and a different blood group distribution from the rest of Europe. Their language, the complex *Euskara*, is unrelated to any other, and was already spoken here when Indo-European languages such as Celtic and Latin began to arrive from the east some 3000 years ago. Written records were scarce until the first books in *Euskara* were published in the mid-sixteenth century; language and culture were maintained instead through oral traditions, including that of the *bertsolariak*, popular poets specializing in improvised verse, a tradition still alive today.

Archeological and genetic evidence suggests that the Basque people may be the last surviving representatives of Europe's aboriginal population. Skull fragments of late Cro-Magnon man believed to date from the Paleolithic era, around 9000 BC, have been shown to be identical to present-day Basque cranial formation. Much anthropological work, above all by the revered Joxe Miguel Barandiaran (who died in December 1991, aged 101), lends itself to the view that the Basques have continuously inhabited the western Pyrenees for thousands of years.

Some history

At the time of the **Roman invasion**, large areas of south-western Gaul and parts of northern Iberia were inhabited by an ethnic group called the *Aquitani*, who spoke an ancestral version of Basque. Most of the *Aquitani* were defeated and Romanized, but the invaders, for once, saw little to gain from subjugating the *Vascones*, wild tribes living in the infertile mountains of Euskal Herria. In exchange for allowing the Romans trading rights and free passage through their territory, the *Vascones* were allowed to retain their tribal customs, language, and independence.

After the fall of Rome, the new rulers were not so accommodating. Successive **Visigoth** kings attempted to eradicate the Basques, but the Basques gave as good as they got. The **Moors**, as they stormed through Spain, conquered the lowlands of Alava and Navarra as far north as Pamplona, but never really had a firm grip on the mountainous north. This new enemy, however, forced the Basques, hitherto a collection of more-or-less allied tribes, to unite, and in 818 one Basque leader, Iñigo Iñiguez, was proclaimed the first ruler of the **Kingdom of Navarre**. Inevitably, in the context of the holy wars sweeping Europe, the Basques at last embraced Christianity, while maintaining many of their ancestral beliefs and customs. Chief among these customs were the ancient laws by which the Basques governed themselves, maintained by oral tradition until the twelfth century, when they were first written down (in Spanish) and known as **fueros**.

Once the Reconquest was complete and Spain was being welded into a single kingdom, Navarre (by now ruled by French monarchs) was one of the missing pieces. The Reyes Católicos persuaded the Bizkaians, Gipuzkoans and Alavans to split away from Navarre and join Castile. In return, their ancient laws and privileges, the *fueros*, including exemption from customs duty, conscription and central taxation, would be respected. Under duress, the Navarrese agreed to the same deal, and by 1512 all four territories were subject to rule from Madrid.

Having given up their political independence in return for the right to self-government, the Basques would jealously defend this right for the next four centuries. It was not until 1876 and the final defeat of the **Carlists**, whom most Basques supported as upholding their traditional rights, that the victorious Liberals finally abolished the *fueros* altogether. However, this only served to inflame the Basque desire for self-government, and the late nineteenth and early twentieth centuries saw the beginnings of Basque nationalism as an ideology. The conservative **Basque Nationalist Party** (PNV) was founded in 1895 by Sabino Arana, the son of a Carlist shipbuilder.

At the start of the Civil War, the predominantly rural, conservative Navarrans and Alavans sided with the Nationalists. Bizkaia and Gipuzkoa, dominated by left-leaning industrial cities, supported the Republic. Irún was quickly captured by Navarrese troops (in September 1936), cutting off the northern Republican zone from France. San Sebastián was quickly surrendered to spare its avenues from bombardment. An autonomous Basque government, in practice limited to Bizkaia, was declared with José Antonio Aguirre as *lehendakari* (president); it was to last only nine months. After failing to capture Madrid, Franco turned on the Basques, who were finally conquered in June 1937, after a vicious campaign that included the infamous German bombing of **Gernika**.

After the war Franco's boot went in hard, and as many as 21,000 people died in his attempts to tame the Basques. Public use of the language was forbidden and central control was asserted with the gun. But state violence succeeded only in nurturing a new resistance, **ETA** (*Euskadi ta Askatasuna* – "Basque Homeland and Freedom"), whose most spectacular success was the assassination in Madrid of Franco's right-hand man and probable successor, Admiral

Basque names

Almost everywhere in the province, street and road signs are in both Basque and Castilian, but the latter is often painted over. Many town halls have officially chosen to use the Basque names and this is reflected on new tourist brochures and maps. We have, therefore, used the Basque name for towns, giving the Castilian in brackets. Some towns, however, including Pamplona and Bilbao, are still generally referred to by their Castilian names and in these cases we have supplied the Basque name in brackets.

It is worth noting a couple of key letter changes which may help to decipher initially confusing words on, for example, menus and signs: notably, the Castilian *ch* becomes *tx* (*txipirones* as opposed to *chipirones*), *v* becomes *b* and *y* becomes *i* (*Bizkaia* as opposed to *Vizcaya*). Above all, *Euskara* features a proliferation of *ks*, as this letter replaces the Castilian *c* (*Gipuzkoa* instead of *Guipúzcoa*) and *qu* (*Lekeitio* instead of *Lequeitio*) and is also used to form the plural and the possessive (e.g. *Bilboko* means "of Bilbao").

Castilian name	Basque name			
Fuenterrabía	Hondarribia		*Egun on*	Good morning
Motrico	Mutriku		*Ongi etorri*	Welcome
Oñate	Oñati		*Mesedez*	Please
Lequetio	Lekeitio		*Eskerrik asko*	Thank you very
Zarauz	Zarautz			much
Guernica	Gernika		*Bai*	Yes
Guetaria	Getaria		*Ez*	No
Mundaca	Mundaka		*Bat*	1
Pasajes	Pasaia Donibane		*Bi*	2
Marquina	Markina		*Hiru*	3
Zumaya	Zumaia		*Lau*	4
Pamplona	Iruña		*Bost*	5
Bilbao	Bilbo		*Zenbat da?*	How much is it?
San Sebastián	Donostia		*Aparkalekua*	Car park
Vitoria	Gasteiz		*Hondartza*	Beach
			Jatetxea	Restaurant
			Turismo Bulegoa	Tourist Office
Some common words			*Udaletxea*	Town hall
Kaixo	Hello		*Ertzantza*	Autonomous
Agur	Goodbye			police
Gabon	Goodnight		*Udaltzaingoa*	Municipal police

Carrero Blanco. In contrast to the PNV, ETA became increasingly identified with the radical left, in opposition to Franco.

Things changed following the **transition to democracy**. The new constitution granted the Basques limited autonomy, with their own parliament and tax collection. Today, there's a regional police force, the *ertzaintza* (distinguished by its red berets) much in evidence in the streets, and the Basque **language** is taught in schools and universities. The Basque flag (the *ikurriña*), banned under Franco, flies everywhere. Basque demands for independence have not ended, however, and nor has the **violence**. ETA's attacks have continued against a diversity of targets, from members of the Spanish police and armed forces to Basque businessmen and politicians, academics, journalists, the tourist industry and random civilians. The total number of deaths caused by ETA exceeds 800. Meanwhile, human rights organizations continue to denounce not only ETA's activities, but also widespread police brutality, torture, and the dispersal of ETA prisoners to jails around Spain.

The **ceasefire** declared in September 1998 was heralded as a major breakthrough. But talks between Basque nationalists and the governing PP (Popular Party) broke down over the perennial issue of constitutionality: the Spanish constitution, whose validity many Basque nationalists deny, is founded on the indivisible unity of the nation.

With the talks in ruins, ETA returned to violence. Since January 2000 more than thirty people, including journalists and PP representatives in the País Vasco, have been killed. Each death has been met with enormous popular demonstrations, and, in May 2001, a stinging rebuke from the electorate to ETA's political allies, EH (*Euskal Herritarok* – Basque People's Party), who lost half their seats in the regional parliament to the PNV. The terrorists, however, have not relented, and summer 2001 saw renewed bombing attacks on Spain's tourist industry. There remains a small but solid nucleus of support for EH and ETA, and although the overwhelming majority of both Basques and Spaniards believe in a peacefully negotiated solution, there seems to be no end in sight to the violence.

Fortunately, visitors to Euskal Herria aren't in any danger. Despite the presence of threatening graffiti, you're extremely unlikely to meet with any type of violence here.

Food

Basque cuisine is accepted as Spain's finest, and the people here are compulsive eaters: try *bacalao* (cod) *a la vizcaina* or *al pil-pil*, *merluza* (hake) *a la vasca*, *chipirones en su tinta* (squid cooked in its ink) or *txangurro* (spider crab), which you'll find in very reasonably priced roadside *caseríos* (*baserri* in Basque), on the outskirts of towns throughout the region. You'll also come across traditional Basque food in the form of tapas (known in the Basque country as *pintxos*) in virtually every bar, freshly cooked and usually excellent.

The tradition of **gastronomic societies**, unique to the Basque country, deserves special mention: first founded in the mid-nineteenth century, they came about originally as socializing places for different craftsmen. Controversy has surrounded them due to the traditional barring of women (although this is changing); all cooking is done by men who pay a token membership fee for the facilities. Members prepare elaborate dishes to perfection as a hobby and it could be said that true Basque cookery has largely retreated to these societies. The so-called *Nueva Cocina Vasca* (New Basque Cookery), heavily influenced by French cuisine, is becoming increasingly evident on menus throughout the country.

Sport

The **Basque sport** of *pelota* (otherwise known as *jai alai*, Basque for "happy party") is played all over Spain, but in Euskal Herria even the smallest village has a *pelota* court or *fronton*, and betting on the sport is rife. Rowing is another Basque obsession, and regattas are held every weekend in summer. Other unique Basque sports include *aizkolaritza* (log-chopping), *harri-jasotzea* (stone-lifting), *soka-tira* (tug-of-war) and *segalaritza* (grass-cutting). The finest exponents of the first two in particular are popular local heroes (the world champion stone-lifter Iñaki Perurena's visit to Japan resulted in the sport being introduced there – he remains the only lifter to surpass the legendary 315-kilo barrier). All Basque sports form an important part of the many local fiestas.

January
19–20 *Festividad de San Sebastián*, 24 hours of festivities, including *tamborrada* (a march with pipes and drums).

February
Weekend before Ash Wednesday *Carnaval* throughout, but especially Bilbao, San Sebastián and Tolosa; traditional parade in Zalduondo.

March
4–12 A series of pilgrimages to the castle at Javier, birthplace of San Francisco Javier.

April
Extensive **Easter** celebrations in Vitoria and Balmaseda.
28 *Fiesta de San Prudencio* is celebrated with *tamborradas*, and a re-enactment of the retreat is staged in Vitoria.

June
24 *Fiestas de San Juan* in Lekeitio, Laguardia-Biasteri and Tolosa.

July
First week sees the great fiesta at Zumaia with dancing, Basque sports and an *encierro* on the beach.
7–14 *Fiestas de San Fermín* in Pamplona, featuring running with the bulls.
16–20 International Jazz Festival in Vitoria.
22 *Fiesta de la Magdalena* in Bermeo, with torch-lit processions of fishing boats and the usual races and Basque sports.
25 *Santiago Apóstol*, International Paella Competition in Getxo.
Mid- to late July Jazz Festival in San Sebastián.
Last week in July Fiesta de San Pedro in Mundaka (2km south of Bermeo), with Basque dancing.
31 *Día de San Ignacio Loyola*, celebrated throughout, but above all in Loyola and Getxo where there are fireworks, jazz and a cycling competition.

August
First weekend Patron saint's celebration in Estella.
4–9 *Fiesta de la Virgen Blanca* in Vitoria with bullfights, fireworks and *gigantones*.
15 *Semana Grande* witnesses an explosion of celebration, notably in Bilbao, with Basque games and races; Zarautz with rowing regattas; Gernika and Tafalla with an *encierro* and San Sebastián where the highlight is an International Fireworks Competition.

September
First week *Euskal Jaiak* (Basque feasts) in San Sebastián.
4 *Fiesta de San Antolín* in Lekeitio, where the local youth attempt to knock the head off a goose.
9 *Euskal-Jaia* in Zarautz and *Día del Pescador* in Bermeo.
12 Sangüesa holds its own *encierros*.
14 Patron saint's day in Olite, with yet more bulls.
19–28 International Film Festival in San Sebastián.

December
Christmas Celebrations are particularly exuberant in Pamplona. At midnight on **Christmas Eve** there's an open-air Mass by firelight in Labastida (Alava).

Accommodation

The main drawback to travelling in the region is that prices (apart from for food) are higher than in much of Spain, particularly for **accommodation**, although it's cheaper inland (with the exception of Pamplona). Accommodation in smaller towns had a substantial boost with the introduction of the Basque government's **nekazalturismoa** (*agroturismo* or homestay) programme, which offers the opportunity to stay in traditional Basque farmhouses and private homes, usually in areas of outstanding beauty, at very reasonable cost. In Navarra, as in much of the country, these are known as **casas rurales**. Properties participating in the programme are identified by a red and green circular sign. Lists showing facilities and prices may be obtained from regional tourist offices (who also handle bookings); alternatively, you can reserve through the central booking offices for País Vasco (☎946 201 188) and Navarra (☎948 229 328). Except in very small villages, there is usually a *fonda* or *hostal*; alternatively, entering any bar and asking for a room will generally produce results.

Irún and around

The Basque province of Gipuzkoa adjoins the French frontier, and its border town, **Irún**, is one of the major road and rail entry points into Spain. There are fast, regular onward connections to San Sebastián, although if you're travelling more slowly, the fishing ports of **Hondarribia** and **Pasaia Donibane** (Pasajes San Juan) are worth a stop. The main route to the south crosses quickly into Navarra and leads initially via the beautiful Valle de Bidasoa to Pamplona (Iruña).

Irún

Like most border towns, **IRÚN**'s chief concern is how to make a quick buck from passing travellers, and the main point in its favour is the ease with which you can leave; there are trains to **Hendaia** (Hendaye) in France and to San Sebastián throughout the day, and regular long-distance and international connections. If arriving by train from Paris (or elsewhere in France) at Hendaia, note that it is far quicker to take the *topo* (mole train, so called because of all the tunnels it goes through) from the separate platform on the right outside Hendaia's main station; it runs every thirty minutes to Irún station, at Avda. de Colón 52, then on to San Sebastián. Of the town's few attractions, the **Ermita de Santa Elena**, a museum containing Roman remains discovered here in 1969, is worth a visit.

Practicalities

If you do need to spend the night, there are plenty of bars and places to eat, and prices are markedly lower than in France or San Sebastián (which is no place to arrive late at night with nowhere to stay). In the vicinity of Irún's main train station are several small, reasonably priced **hostales** and **restaurants** specializing in good local food. *Pensión Bidasoa*, c/Estación 14 (☎943 619 913; ❹) and *Bar Pensión los Fronterizos*, c/Estación 7 (☎943 619 205; ❺) have some of the least expensive rooms; for more comfort try the nearby *Hostal Matxinbenta*, Paseo Colón 21 (☎943 621 384; ❺). There are also two reasonable **casas rurales** nearby: the *Mendiola*, Barrio Ventas, Landexte (☎943 629 763; ❹), 2km west of town on the N1 road, and the *Artzu* (☎943 640 530, ℻943 844 118; ❺), officially in Hondarribia but actually just northwest of Irún's giant rail-shunting yards.

Hondarribia

The fishing port of **HONDARRIBIA** (Fuenterrabía), 6km north of Irún and looking over the Bidasoa river mouth to Hendaia, is a far more attractive prospect, though the waterfront itself is disappointingly modern, enlivened with just a few cafés. The town's real appeal lies in main streets running parallel to the front, and the backstreets further inland, where traditional, wood-beamed Basque houses are interspersed with bars offering some of the best seafood and *pintxos* around. During the summer, the fine **beaches** just beyond the town are an escape from ultra-crowded San Sebastián.

Hondarribia has a picturesque, walled old town entered through the fifteenth-century **Puerta de Santa María**. Calle Mayor, leading up to the Plaza de Armas, has further fine examples of wood-beamed houses with wrought-iron balconies and studded doors, some displaying the family coats of arms above doorways; the square itself is dominated by the **Palacio de Carlos Quinto**, started originally in the tenth century by Sancho the Strong of Navarra and subsequently extended by Carlos V in the sixteenth. It is now a luxurious *parador* (see below), and it's worth at least having a drink at the bar inside.

Practicalities

The helpful **Turismo** is on Javier Ugarte 6 (July–Aug Mon–Sat 9am–8pm, Sun 10am–2pm; Sept–June Mon–Fri 9am–1.30pm & 4–6.30pm, Sat 10am–2pm; ☎943 645 458). There's a fair amount of characterful if rather pricey **accommodation** in Hondarribia: try *Hostal Álvarez Quintero*, c/Beñat Etxepare 2 (☎943 642 299; ❺), in the Edificio Miramar near the turismo, or the *Hostal San Nikolas* on Plaza de Armas 6 (☎943 644 278; ❺). Pick of the plusher establishments is the two-star *Hotel Obispo*, an old stone manor on Plaza del Obispo (☎943 645 400, ℉943 642 386; ❼), or for a splurge, there's the *Parador Nacional El Emperador Carlos V*, Plaza de Armas 14 (☎943 645 500, ℉943 642 153, ✉pilardemiguel@parador.es; occasionally closed Nov–Feb; ❾), stunningly located in the town's fortified *palacio*.

If you've transport, you'll get better value for money from the three excellent **casas rurales** just outside town, though they're very popular and must usually be reserved well in advance. The closest, uphill from the airport in Barrio Arkoll-Santiago, is *Iketxe* (☎ & ℉943 644 391; ❻), with wood-ceilinged en-suite rooms. Nearby stands *Maidanea* (☎ & ℉943 640 855; ❻), a modernized 400-year-old farmhouse with views out to France, or alternatively, 3km from town in Jaizubia hamlet, there's *Arotzenea* (☎ & ℉943 642 319; ❻), a half-timbered farmhouse. For the impecunious, the **youth hostel**, *Juan Sebastián Elkano*, is on Carretera Faro (☎943 641 550; ❶), though it's often packed out in summer with school groups; fork left beyond c/San Pedro on the way to the beaches. The closest **campsite**, *Camping Jaiz Kibel* (☎ & ℉943 642 653; open all year), is 2km out of town along Carretera Guadalupe towards Pasaia Donibane (Pasajes); there's no public transport.

The **restaurants** and **bars** along parallel c/Santiago and c/San Pedro, three to four short blocks in from the water, are the best hunting ground for **food** and **drink**. For something special, try the *Hermandad de Pescadores* (reservations on ☎943 642 738) on c/Zuloaga 12, parallel to the waterfront. This was once strictly the fishermen's clubhouse but is now open to all; expect to pay €10.25 for the *menú*, or €30 *a la carta*. Otherwise, in the old town, tucked away in a narrow, cobbled alley two streets behind c/Mayor, the *Mamutzar* restaurant serves a good-value *menú*, and next door, tapas are available in the tiny but lively *Hamlet* bar.

Pasaia Donibane

The one place you might consider stopping for any length of time en route between Irún and San Sebastián (frequent buses as well as trains) is the port of Pasaia. While much of the town is highly industrialized – cranes steadily pick through heaps of scrap metal on the south side of the bay – the old town, **PASAIA DONIBANE** (Pasajes San Juan), has retained its charm. The narrow cobbled c/San Juan (Victor Hugo once lived at no. 65, the house built over the tunnel) leads to Plaza de Santiago with its colourful houses. Pasaia Donibane is famous for its waterside **fish restaurants**, which are considerably less expensive than those in San Sebastían's old quarter. Two to try are *Casa Camara*, c/San Juan 79, for shellfish (from €18), and *Ziaboga* at no. 91 for fish (from €27). A **launch** (*txalupa*) runs throughout the day and evening across the harbour to Pasaia San Pedro, from where frequent buses depart to San Sebastián's Alameda del Boulevard.

Towards Pamplona

If you're heading straight down to Pamplona, you'll pass through the **Bidasoa valley** with its succession of beautifully preserved towns just off the N121a, the best of which are Bera-Vera de Bidasoa, Lesaka and Etxalar – all just over the border in Navarra. At Oieregi, just under halfway to Pamplona, there's a junction left for the Valle de Baztán, where the Navarran Pyrenees really start (see p.512). Both valleys are on direct bus routes from San Sebastián/Irún and Pamplona respectively.

Bera (Vera) de Bidasoa

BERA (VERA) DE BIDASOA offers some of the finest examples of old wood-beamed and traditional stone houses in the region; the brightly painted buildings along c/Altzarte and the main square are particularly attractive. About a hundred metres off the square, just past the old customs house, is the former home (no. 24) of the Basque writer Pío Baroja; at the time of writing this is closed indefinitely, but you can check the latest situation with the turismo in Pamplona (see p.512).

If you want to **stay**, there's the comfortable *Hostal Euskalduna*, c/Bidasoa 5 (☎948 630 392; ❺), with a good restaurant, or, just outside town in the Barrio de Zalain, the *Hostal Zalain* (☎948 631 106; ❸) and a *casa rural*, *Casa Etxebertzea* (☎948 630 272; ❹), which also offers pricier en-suite rooms (❺).

Six kilometres northeast of Bera, straddling the French border, **Monte Larroun** (900m) is an easy climb: from the summit you'll get spectacular views across the Pyrenees and the French Basque coast. There's a bar-restaurant at the top which serves tourists taking the rack-railway up from the French side.

Lesaka

Some 4km south of Bera along the Bidasoa valley, a right turn leads to **LESAKA**. Despite the large, eyesore factory on the outskirts of town, it's a beautiful place dominated by the hilltop parish church in which the pews bear family names of the local farms and mansions. On the banks of the irrigation channel which flows through town is one of the best remaining examples of a *casa torre* (fortified private house) of a design peculiar to the Basque country, dating back to the days when north Navarra was in the hands of a few powerful and constantly feuding families.

Places to stay include the simple *Pensión Tolareta*, Plaza Berria 2 (☎948 637 106; ❸), above a clothes shop just off the main square, the *Hostal Ekaitza* at

Plaza Berria 13 (☎948 627 547; ❺), and the slightly more upmarket *Hotel Bereau* (☎948 627 509, ☎948 627 647; ❻), near the main road.

Etxalar

ETXALAR is a small, bucolic place, 4km off the main road on the way up to a minor border crossing at the Lizarrieta pass, but it is perhaps the best-preserved village of the valley, famous for the impressive array of Basque funerary steles in the churchyard. Among numerous **casas rurales** here, two good ones with rooms available for short stays are the central *Casa Domekenea* (☎948 635 031; ❸) and the *Casa Herri-Gain* (☎948 635 208; ❸), the latter perched on a steep hill with fantastic views of the surrounding area. There are also a couple of restaurants and bars near the giant church, so you won't starve or go thirsty.

San Sebastián

The undisputed queen of the Basque resorts, **SAN SEBASTIÁN** (increasingly known by its Basque name of Donostia) is a picturesque – and expensive – seaside town with good beaches. Along with Santander, it has always been the most fashionable place to escape the heat of the southern summers, and in July and August it's packed. Although it tries hard to be chic, San Sebastián is too much of a family resort to compete in those terms with the South of France, which is all to its benefit. Set around the deep, still bay of La Concha and enclosed by rolling low hills, the town is beautifully situated; the old quarter sits on the eastern promontory, its back to the wooded slopes of Monte Urgull, while newer development has spread along the banks of the Urumea, around the edge of the bay to the foot of Monte Igeldo and onto the hills overlooking the bay.

Arrival and information

Most **buses** arrive at Plaza Pío XII, fifteen minutes' walk along the river from the centre of town (the ticket office for these companies is around the corner next to the river on Paseo de Bizkaia), but from Pasaia and Astigarraga they arrive on the Alameda del Boulevard, and from Hondarribia on Plaza de Gipuzkoa. RENFE's main-line **Estación del Norte** is across the Río Urumea on Paseo de Francia, although local lines of the *Eusko Tren* from Hendaia, or Bilbao via Zarautz and Zumaia (neither line accepts InterRail passes), have their terminus on Plaza Easo at the **Estación de Amara**. The **airport** is 22km from the city centre, just outside Hondarribia; an airport bus runs every fifteen minutes into town throughout the day.

The municipal **turismo** (June–Sept Mon–Sat 8am–8pm, Sun 10am–1pm; Oct–May Mon–Sat 9am–2pm & 3.30–7pm, Sun 10am–1pm; ☎943 481 166, ⓦpaisvasco.com/donostia/ingles/indexi.htm) is on c/Reina Regente in the Teatro Victoria Eugenia. For a greater selection of pamphlets there is the very useful regional turismo (Mon–Fri 9.30am–1.30pm & 3.30–6.30pm, Sat 9am–1pm & 3.30–6.30pm; July & Aug also open Sun 10am–1.30pm; Oct–May closed Sat pm & Sun; ☎943 426 282) at Paseo de los Fueros 1, just off the main Avenida de la Libertad.

San Sebastián is something of a travel hub for the region. Viajes TIVE, c/Tomás Gros 3 (☎943 276 934), is a youth/student **travel agency** that sells tickets for international buses and discount plane tickets. Another good general travel agency is Viajes Aran, c/Elkano 1 (☎943 429 009). For travel **books and maps** (both local and elsewhere), and for books on all things related to the Basque country, head for Graphos on the corner of Alameda del Boulevard and c/Mayor. Also recommended are Bilintx, c/Esterlines 10; Dr Camino, c/Treinta y Uno de Agosto 32–36; and the library, Koldo Mitxelena, c/Urdaneta 9.

Accommodation

Places to stay, though plentiful, can be pricey and hard to come by in season – if you arrive between mid-July and the end of August, or during the film festival in September, you'll have to start looking early in the day, or book ahead if possible. There is no great difference in rates between the cheapest places in the *parte vieja* (old quarter) and elsewhere, although *hostales* along the Alameda del Boulevard do tend to be slightly pricier. There is often more chance of finding space in the *zona romántica* district around c/Easo, c/San Martín, c/Hondarribia and c/San Bartolomé, or on the other side of the river in **Gros**, behind the RENFE station in **Egia**, or in the new part of town, **Amara Nuevo**, on the way to the Anoeta sports complex.

Parte Vieja

Pensión Amaiur, c/Treinta y Uno de Agosto 44, 2° ☎943 429 654. Pleasant, friendly *pensión* with carpeted doubles and a few triples, all with shared bath. ❹

Pensión Anne, c/Esterlines 15, 2° ☎943 421 438, Ⓔ pensionanne@euskalnet.net. Recently opened *pensión* with English-speaking staff. ❸

Pensión Arsuaga, c/Narrika 3, 3° ☎943 420 681. Very friendly *pensión* with simple, spacious doubles. Has its own restaurant which does a good *menú* for €6 and also offers full-board deals. ❹

Hostal La Estrella, Plaza de Sarriegi 1 ☎943 420 997. Attractive old *hostal*, offering old-fashioned but clean rooms – some en suite – either overlooking the plaza or Alameda del Boulevard. ❺

Pensión Kaia, c/Puerto 12, 2° ☎943 431 342. Pleasant, modern rooms with bath. Prices fall by a third out of season. ❻

Pensión Larrea, c/Narrika 21, 1°, corner c/Pescaderia ☎943 422 694. Clean, modern rooms but on a busy street corner, and a bit cramped and noisy. ❸

Hotel Parma, c/General Jauregi Gudalburuaren 11 ☎943 428 893, Ⓕ943 424 082, Ⓦwww. hotelparma.com. Nicely located between the *parte vieja* and Paseo Nuevo, this rather characterless modern building offers comfortable rooms with all amenities, the best ones overlooking the sea. ❼

Pensión San Jerónimo, c/San Jerónimo 25, 2° ☎943 420 830. Adequate *pensión*, though the rooms are spartan and the hallway and stairs somewhat the worse for wear. ❺

Pensión San Lorenzo, c/San Lorenzo 2, 1° ☎943 425 516. Backpackers' cheapo haven with just six shared-bath rooms and a self-catering kitchen; generally full, and does not accept advance reservations, so contact them the evening or morning before your intended stay. ❸

Pensión Urgull, c/Esterlines 10, 3° ☎943 430 047. Just five airy, spotless and tastefully furnished rooms – the English-speaking owner won't take reservations far in advance, so arrive early or book the same day. The nearby bars can be a bit noisy. ❹

Alameda del Boulevard and around

Pensión Boulevard, Alameda del Boulevard 24, 1° ☎943 429 405. Comfortable, modern rooms mostly with washbasins only, plus one en suite. ❺

Hostal Eder II, Alameda del Boulevard 16, 2° ☎943 426 449. Elegant hallway with fine wood panelling leads to spacious rooms, some with bath. ❻

Pensión Fernando, Plaza de Gipuzkoa 2, 1° ☎943 425 575. Fair-sized, relatively quiet rooms with washbasin, and showers out in the hall, at this friendly *pensión* overlooking a leafy square. ❺

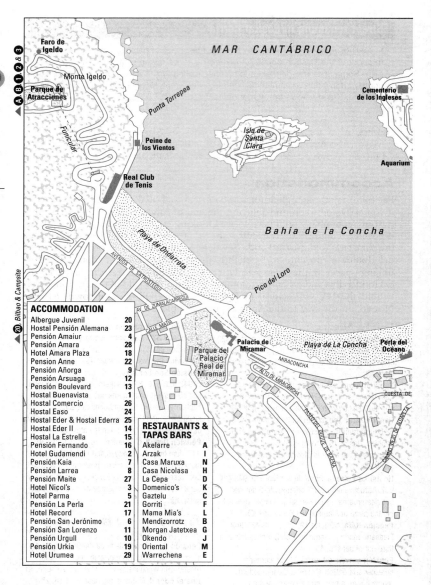

MAR CANTÁBRICO

Faro de Igeldo

Monte Igeldo

Parque de Atracciones

Funicular

Punta Torrepea

Peine de los Vientos

Real Club de Tenis

Playa de Ondarreta

AVENIDA DE SATRUSTEGUI

AV. DE ZUMALACARREGUI

CALLE MATIA

Isla de Santa Clara

Bahía de la Concha

Pico del Loro

Cementerio de los Ingleses

Aquarium

Parque del Palacio Real de Miramar

Palacio de Miramar

Playa de La Concha

MIRACONCHA

ALTO DE MIRACONCHA

CUESTA DE

Perla del Océano

PASEO DEL DUQUE DE BAENA

CONCHA DE AIDGETA

ACCOMMODATION

Albergue Juvenil	20
Hostal Pensión Alemana	23
Pensión Amaiur	4
Pensión Amara	28
Hotel Amara Plaza	18
Pension Anne	22
Pensión Añorga	9
Pensión Arsuaga	12
Pensión Boulevard	13
Hostal Buenavista	1
Hostal Comercio	26
Hostal Easo	24
Hostal Eder & Hostal Ederra	25
Hostal Eder II	14
Hostal La Estrella	15
Pensión Fernando	16
Hotel Gudamendi	2
Pensión Kaia	7
Pensión Larrea	8
Pensión Maite	27
Hotel Nicol's	3
Hotel Parma	5
Pensión La Perla	21
Hotel Record	17
Pensión San Jerónimo	6
Pensión San Lorenzo	11
Pensión Urgull	10
Pensión Urkia	19
Hotel Urumea	29

RESTAURANTS & TAPAS BARS

Akelarre	A
Arzak	I
Casa Maruxa	N
Casa Nicolasa	H
La Cepa	D
Domenico's	K
Gaztelu	C
Gorriti	F
Mama Mia's	L
Mendizorrotz	B
Morgan Jatetxea	G
Okendo	J
Oriental	M
Warrechena	E

Zona Romántica

Hostal Pensión Alemana, c/San Martín 53, 1° ☎943 462 544, ⊕943 461 771, ✉halemana@adegi.es. Perfectly located just behind La Concha, this fine *belle époque* two-star offers affordable splendour in its large en-suite rooms with all mod cons, and off-street parking.

Reservations required year-round. ❼

Pensión Añorga, c/Easo 12, 1° ☎943 467 945. Large, fairly plain *pensión* on two floors, but the rooms are clean and some have a bath. ❹

Hostal Comercio, c/Urdaneta 24 ☎943 464 414. Simply furnished *hostal*, offering reasonable rooms with washbasin and fan heaters. ❹

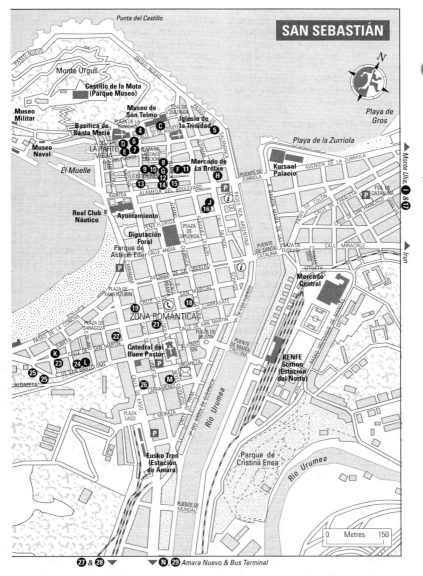

⑳ & ㉘ ▼   ▼ **Ⓝ, ㉙** Amara Nuevo & Bus Terminal

Hostal Easo, c/San Bartolomé 24 ☎943 453 912. Relatively low-priced rooms with washbasin or shower. ❺

Hostal Eder and **Hostal Ederra**, c/San Bartolomé 33 and 25 ☎943 464 969 or 943 426 449. Two *hostales* run by the same management as the *Eder II* in Alameda del Boulevard, with their location

close to La Concha the principal selling point. Open Easter & July–Sept only. ❺

Pensión La Perla, c/Inazio Loiola 10 ☎943 428 123. Excellent-value *pensión*, near Buen Pastor cathedral and the food market, offering spotless rooms with baths and TV. Half-board also available. ❹

Pensión Urkia, c/Urbieta 12, 3° ⊤ 943 424 436. Run by the sister of *La Perla*'s owner, this *pensión* has equally good en-suite rooms, though there is some street noise. If she's full up, you may be referred to yet another relative, *Casa Elisa* ⊤ 943 453 950. ➍

Hotel Urumea, c/Getaria 14, 1° ⊤ 943 424 605. Clean and pleasant, conveniently located for the bus and trian stations. ➎

Out of the centre

Pensión Amara, Isabel II 2, 1° ⊤ 943 468 472. Clean, comfortable accommodation in this highly recommended *pensión*. ➎

Hotel Amara Plaza, Plaza Pío XII 7 ⊤ 943 464 600, ⓕ 943 472 548, ⓦ www.paisvaswco.com /hotel/amara-plaza. Four-star hotel with all facilities in the Amara district. ➒

Hostal Buenavista, Barrio de Igeldo ⊤ 943 210 600. Stone-clad, mock-trad Basque chalet on the main road to Monte Igeldo, featuring sweeping sea views and a good restaurant. Good value for the area. ➏

Hotel Gudamendi, Paseo de Gudamendi, Monte Igeldo ⊤ 943 214 000, ⓕ 943 215 108. In a peaceful, park-like cul-de-sac near the top of the mountain, this rambling, slightly neglected, converted hunting lodge scores for its pleasant pool and common areas rather than the functional bedrooms. There are usually vacancies because it's somewhat overpriced, though rates fall significantly out of season. ➑

Pensión Maite, Avda. de Madrid 19, 1° B ⊤ 943 470 715, ⓕ 943 454 826. Good, clean rooms with shower and TV; handy for bus station, Astoria cinema and Anoeta football stadium. The owners also run the *Bar Maite* opposite. ➎

Hotel Nicol's, Paseo de Gudamendi, Monte Igeldo ⊤ 943 215 799, ⓕ 943 211 724. Just 200m shy of the *Hotel Gudamendi*, this one-star is not so grand as its neighbour, but is more reasonably priced and has a well-regarded restaurant. Prices fall out of season. ➐

Hotel Record, Calzada Vieja de Ategorrieta 35 ⊤ 943 271 255, ⓕ 943 278 521. At the far end of Gros and a pleasant alternative to the bustle of the *parte vieja* and *zona romántica*; well connected by bus, or a fifteen-minute walk from the centre, with plenty of parking. All rooms with shower or bath (though the cheapest lack toilet); the larger have terraces. ➏ –➐

Youth hostel and camping

Albergue Juvenil, Paseo de Igeldo ⊤ 943 310 268, ⓕ 943 214 090. San Sebastián's youth hostel, known as *La Sirena*, is just a few minutes' walk from the end of Ondarreta beach (or take bus #5 or #16). Open all year. ➊

Igeldo, Paseo Padre Orkolaga 69, Barrio de Igeldo ⊤ 943 214 502, ⓕ 943 280 411. San Sebastián's campsite is excellent if pricey, but it's 5km from the centre on the landward side of Monte Igeldo (up a steep hill), reached by bus #16 from the Alameda del Boulevard. Open all year.

The Town

The **parte vieja** (old quarter) is the town's highlight – cramped and lively streets where the crowds congregate in the evenings to wander among the many small bars and shops or sample the shellfish from the street traders down by the fishing harbour. Much of it was destroyed by a fire in 1813 and carefully restored, though the old medieval wall was swept away to allow expansion later the same century – the Alameda del Boulevard marks its former course.

The *parte vieja* contains San Sebastián's chief sights: the elaborate Baroque facade of the eighteenth-century church of **Santa María**, and the more elegantly restrained sixteenth-century Gothic church of **San Vicente**. The centre of the old quarter is **La Plaza de la Constitución** (known by the locals simply as *La Consti*) – the numbers on the balconies of the apartments around the square refer to the days when it was used as a bullring. Situated just off c/Treinta y Uno de Agosto (the only street to survive the great fire of August 31, 1813), behind San Vicente, is the excellent **Museo de San Telmo**. Its displays – around the cloisters of a former convent – include a fine Basque ethnographic exhibition and the largest collection of keyhole-shaped funerary steles in the País Vasco. The convent chapel is decorated with a series of frescoes by José Sert, depicting scenes from Basque life.

Behind the plaza rises **Monte Urgull**, crisscrossed by winding paths. From the mammoth figure of Christ on its summit, a 45-minute climb, there are great views out to sea and back across the bay to the town. On the way down you can stop at the **Aquarium** (mid-May to mid-Sept daily 10am–8pm; mid-Sept to mid-May Tues–Sun 10am–1.30pm & 4–7.30pm; €6.60) on the harbour; it contains the skeleton of a whale caught in the last century and an extensive history of Basque navigation. Although there are not a great deal of fish, you can walk through the middle of a giant aquarium in a Perspex tube. Close by, at Paseo de Muelle 24, is the **Museo Naval** (mid-June to mid-Sept Tues–Sat 10am–1.30pm & 5–8.30pm, Sun 11am–2pm; mid-Sept to mid-June Tues–Sat 10am–1.30pm & 4–7.30pm, Sun 11am–2pm), with video facilities and exhibits tracing the tradition and history of Basque fishing. On the quay outside the museum you can see the fishwives mending nets in the time-honoured and most picturesque fashion.

Still better views across the bay can be had from the top of **Monte Igeldo**: take the #16 bus marked *Igeldo* from the Boulevard or walk round the bay to its base near Real Club de Tennis, from where a **funicular** (daily: summer 10am–8pm, winter 11am–6pm; every 15min; €1 round trip) will carry you to the summit.

Continuing along the *paseo* past the tennis club you end up at Eduardo Chillida's striking iron **sculpture**, *El Peine de los Vientos* (The Comb of the Winds), looking as if it is trying to grasp the waves in its powerful rusting arms. More of Chillida's work is on display at the Chillida-leku museum in Hernani (see p.485).

Beaches

There are **four beaches** in San Sebastián: Playa de la Concha, Playa de Ondarreta, Playa de la Zurriola and Playa de Gros. **La Concha** is the most central and the most celebrated, a wide crescent of yellow sand stretching round the bay from the town. Despite the almost impenetrable mass of flesh here during much of the summer, this is the best (if most regimented) of the beaches, enlivened by sellers of peeled prawns and cold Cokes and with great swimming out to the diving platforms moored in the bay. Out in La Concha bay is a small island, **Isla de Santa Clara**, which makes a good spot for picnics; a boat leaves from the port every half-hour in the summer (daily 10am–8pm; €1.50 round trip).

La Concha and **Ondarreta** are the best beaches for swimming – the latter is a continuation of the same strand beyond the rocky outcrop which supports the **Palacio de Miramar**, once a summer home of Spain's royal family. Set back from Ondarreta beach are large villas, some of the most expensive properties in Spain, and mostly owned by wealthy families from Madrid who vacation here – the area used to be known as La Diplomática for this reason and has a reputation for being rather more staid than the central area, although the lively district of **El Antiguo** with its many bars is only a few minutes' walk beyond.

Far less crowded, and popular with surfers, **Playa de la Zurriola** and the adjacent **Playa de Gros** were regraded during the 1990s and breakwaters added to shield them from dangerous currents and river pollution. A recent addition to the elegant promenade is the giant beached glass cubes of Rafael Moneo's **Kursaal Palacio**. In addition to the auditorium and art gallery, the building houses a pleasant café-restaurant with an outside terrace in summer. One of the best views of the whole town and bay may be had by climbing up the steps to the cider house on the side of **Monte Ulia** from the far end of the beach. This walk can easily be extended for about 5km along the coast to the lighthouse overlooking the entrance to Pasaia harbour.

Eating, drinking and entertainment

If you're in the mood for a gastronomic treat, San Sebastián has some of the best **restaurants** in Spain, mostly in the *parte vieja* but a few in the *zona román-tica*, as well as plenty of lively **bars**. Note that most restaurants are closed Sunday evening and Monday. Prices tend to reflect the popularity of the old quarter, especially in the waterside restaurants, but lunchtime *menús del día* are generally good value, and the *pintxos* and *raciones* set out in all but the fanciest bars are a great way to eat cheaply in the evenings. For those on a budget, the **Mercado de la Bretxa** is conveniently situated in the centre of the *parte vieja* on c/San Juan.

Akelarre, Paseo de Padre Orkolaga 56 ☎943 212 052. In Barrio Igeldo well beyond the terminus for the #16 bus, this is reckoned one of the city's top restaurants with wonderful sea views. Put on your best rags and burn a hole in your pocket to the tune of €54 each.

Arzak, Alto de Miracruz 21, Monte Ulia ☎943 278 465. A shrine of Basque cuisine, with three Michelin rosettes and a superb *menú* for around €48.

Casa Maruxa, Paseo de Bizkaia 14, Amara. Specializes in food from Galicia and attracts the crowd on their way to the Astoria cinema complex just around the corner.

Casa Nicolasa, c/Aldamar 4, 1° ☎943 421 762. Classic – and expensive – Basque cookery; there's a €42 *menú*, while *a la carta* isn't much more.

La Cepa, c/Treinta y Uno de Agosto 7. Inexpensive *raciones* served amidst decor of bullfighting kitsch and dangling hams; also a pricier *comedor*. Closed Wed.

Domenico's, c/Zubieta 3 ☎943 471 537. Smart but affordable (€18–24) Italian restaurant with non-pizza-type food; very popular in season, so reservations mandatory.

Gaztelu, c/31 de Agosto 22. Fine choice in the *parte vieja* where you can choose from a selection of reasonably priced *raciones*; if you sit in the *comedor*, allow about €21.

Gorriti, c/San Juan, corner c/Fernando Calbetón.

One of the best counter-top collections of tapas and *pintxos* in a town not short of such.

Mama Mia's, c/San Bartolomé 18, corner c/Triunfo. Good, relatively inexpensive Italian restaurant serving vegetarian dishes and pizzas; allow about €18 for a meal.

Mendizorrotz, Barrio Igeldo, at the central plaza two stops from end of #16 bus line. Brief but superbly executed *carta*, with specialities like *pimientos de padrón* (grilled green peppers) and *puding de txangurro* (spider-crab mousse); reckon on €21–24 including local cider and dessert in the tiny *comedor* (reservations on ☎943 212 023) or have the cheap *menú* (Mon–Fri) at the bar tables.

Morgan Jatetxea, c/Narrika 7. Specializes in the French-influenced "new Basque" school of cook-ery, especially the lighter, tasty first courses. It's quite normal to order two of these instead of the heartier main courses.

Okendo, c/Okendo 8. A decor of cinema-festival posters, youngish crowd and an appetizing €8.10 *menú* make this an appealing target.

Oriental, c/Reyes Católicos 6. Best of several local Chinese restaurants in terms of quality of food, price and extremely friendly atmosphere; eat in or take away.

Warrechena, c/Nagusia (ex-Mayor), corner c/Puerto. Fairly busy place serving up basic fare in tarted-up London fish-and-chip-shop sur-roundings.

Nightlife

In the evenings, you'll find no shortage of action, with **clubs** and **bars** every-where. The two main areas are the **parte vieja**, especially lively c/Fermín Calbetón where virtually every address is a bar, and the area around the inter-section of c/Reyes Católicos and c/Larramendi, where a large number of the city's more expensive music pubs are located. For **jazz**, try *BeBop* on Paseo de Salamanca, *Etxekalte* or *Altxerri*, all on the edge of the *parte vieja*. Once the pubs close, usually by about 3.30am, the night continues at varous **clubs**, including the *Komplot*, a techno-disco on c/Pedro Egaña.

Sidrerías

If you're in San Sebastián between late January and early May, a visit to one of the many **sidrerías** (*sagardotegiak* in Basque, or cider houses) in the area around **Astigarraga**, about 6km from town, is a must – take the red Hernani-bound bus from the Alameda del Boulevard or a taxi for about €6.

Cider production is one of the oldest traditions in the Basque country – until the Civil War and the subsequent move towards industrialization, practically every farmhouse in Gipuzkoa and to a lesser extent the other provinces produced cider, which was a valuable commodity used for barter. Barter remained the main form of exchange in rural communities here until comparatively recently, and the farms were practically open houses where local people socialized – the *bertsolariak* tradition of oral poetry originated in these places – and drank cider.

Since the 1980s, cider houses are again flourishing, and for €9–18 you can feast on delicious food, drink unlimited quantities of cider and in general enjoy the raucous atmosphere. Of the fifty or so *sidrerías*, some of the most accessible include *Petritegi* and *Gartziategi*, just a few kilometres out of town, while many of the more rustic (ie authentic) ones, such as *Sarasola* and *Oiarbide*, are on the so-called *ruta de las sidrerías* (cider trail) beyond Astigarraga. Check in the turismo for a full list with phone numbers.

Festivals

Throughout the summer there are constant **fiestas**, many involving Basque sports including the annual rowing (*trainera*) races between the villages along the coast, which culminate in a final regatta on September 9. The **Jazz Festival** (Ⓦ www.jazzaldia.com), at different locations throughout the town for five days during the latter half of July, invariably attracts top performers as well as hordes of people on their way home from the fiesta in Pamplona. The week preceding August 15, known as **Semana Grande** (Ⓦ www.paisvasco.com/donostia/ingles/indexi.htm), sees numerous concerts, special events and fireworks laid on. There is also the **Film Festival** (Ⓦ www.sansebastianfestival.ya. com) in the second half of September and frequent theatrical and musical performances throughout the year at both the Teatro Victoria Eugenia and the Teatro Principal. The turismo produces a monthly guide to what's on.

Inland from San Sebastián: a circuit through Gipuzkoa

Gipuzkoa is the smallest province in Spain and public transport is good, meaning that most places of interest can be visited comfortably as a day-trip from San Sebastián. Alternatively, try the circuit set out below which can also act as a stepping stone to Vitoria and places further south.

Hernani

The reason for a visit to Hernani, 7km south of San Sebastián, is **Chillida-leku** (April–Oct 15, Mon, Wed–Sat 11am–6pm, Sun 11am–4pm; Oct 16–March, Mon, Wed–Sat 11am–4pm; €7.20; Ⓦ www.eduardo-chillida.com), the open-air museum dedicated to the life and work of Euskal Herria's most internationally renowned artist, sculptor Eduardo Chillida, whose massive works can be seen all over the Basque country and further afield, including San Sebastián (see p.483), Gernika (see p.492) and Gijón (see p.556). Buses leave every half hour from c/Okendo in San Sebastián, near the main tourist office.

The sculptures, housed in a beautifully refurbished 16th-century farmhouse and the surrounding field (which can be muddy), present an elemental solidity that almost seems to capture the essence of Basqueness. There's also an impressive video about Chillida's life.

Tolosa and Ordizia

Twenty-four kilometres south of San Sebastián is **TOLOSA**, famous for its **carnival** in February, celebrated here with fervour and considered by Basques to be superior to San Sebastián's (it was the only one whose tradition was maintained throughout the Franco era). In October, the town hosts an international choir festival. Although fairly industrialized, Tolosa has an extensive old quarter with an impressive old town square and is a lively place for a weekend night out. Make sure you sample a plate of *alubias* (kidney beans) in one of the many eating places – they're considered the best in Euskal Herria. If you want to **stay**, try *Hostal Oyarbide*, Plaza Gorriti 1 (T & F 943 670 017; ❺), or the more upmarket *Hotel Oria*, c/de Oria 2 (T 943 654 688, F 943 653 612; ❻), which has a new annexe at c/San Francisco 20.

A further 20km south, on the main railway line to Vitoria, is **ORDIZIA**, the fastest growing town in the Oria valley. If your visit coincides with a Wednesday, don't miss the weekly **market** of farm products when all the farmers in the region converge on the town to buy and sell livestock, cheese and the like. Ordizia is backed by the impressive peak of **Txindoki**, rising above the town like a mini-Matterhorn. You can climb it in about three hours from Larraitz, the highest village, and the whole thing can be done as a day-trip from San Sebastián or Tolosa.

The **Sierra de Aralar** stretching beyond Txindoki is a great place for a few days' walking – one possibility is to walk all the way from Larraitz to the **sanctuary of San Miguel de Aralar** in Navarra (see p. 504), 7–8 hours in all, largely on the flat over the plateau. In cold winters the range becomes a popular centre for cross-country skiing.

Segura and the monastery of Arantzazu

One of the most attractive inland villages in Gipuzkoa is **SEGURA**, about 5km southeast of Ordizia. An original seignorial village from where the powerful Guevara family once wielded power, there are various old mansions once belonging to the Guevaras and other families of note along its long, winding main street. Today, it's a sleepy backwater which comes alive during the **Easter processions** (not otherwise much celebrated in Euskal Herria) and which hosts one of the best village fiestas in Euskal Herria in mid-June.

Segura and Zegama, further south, were important stops on the ancient **Pilgrim Route** to Santiago, which joined up with the main route in Santo Domingo de la Calzada (La Rioja). The old Roman way the pilgrims once followed is still partly in evidence and you can walk a section of it as an easy daytrip, even without your own transport (although you should double-check all transport details before setting out). Take an early Vitoria-bound train from San Sebastián to **OTZAURTE**, a small halt south of Zegama. From here it's an hour's walk to the refuge of **San Adrián** (open weekends throughout the year and daily in summer; meals available). The best-preserved section of Roman road on the mountain is just beyond the natural tunnel of San Adrián above the refuge, from where it's downhill (2hr) to **Araia**, the first town in Araba just

△ Guggenheim Museum, Bilbao

off the Vitoria–Pamplona road; from here, a bus departs at 3.15pm for Vitoria and trains leave from the station 2km beyond town.

Alternatively, head west across the plateau or along the spectacular ridge of Aitzkorri to the refuge of **Urbia** (same hours as San Adrián) and the monastery of **Arantzazu** (3–4hr), where there are several *hostales* and hotels, best value of which is *Hospedería de Arantzazu* (☎943 781 313; ❸), or the slightly more expensive *Sindica* next door (☎943 781 303; ❹). This is the prime place of pilgrimage for Basques – **Our Lady of Arantzazu** is the patron saint of Gipuzkoa – and is located in a particularly spectacular setting, clinging to the mountainside above a gorge. Although a monastery on this site dates back to the fifteenth century, the present spiky, futuristic-looking building was built in 1950 and features contemporary work by the sculptors Chillida (the doors) and Sáenz de Oteiza (part of the facade). It's frankly hideous, but worth looking inside for the soaring stained-glass windows. It gets packed out on Sundays when worshippers come from all over the province and elsewhere.

Oñati

OÑATI, 8km below Arantzazu, is without doubt the most interesting inland town in Gipuzkoa, with some fine examples of Baroque architecture among its many historic buildings; indeed the Basque painter Zuloaga described it as the "Basque Toledo".

The old **university** dominates the town, built in 1548 and the only functioning university in Euskal Herria for hundreds of years. The facade with its four pilasters adorned with figures, and the serene courtyard, are particularly impressive. The Baroque town hall and parish church of **San Miguel** are at opposite ends of the arcaded Plaza de los Fueros. In the church crypt are buried all the Counts of Oñati from 988 to 1890; the cloister is unusual in that it is actually built over the river. Other fine buildings around the town include various *casas torres* of the type also found in northern Navarra, private family mansions and the Plateresque-style monastery of **Bidaurreta**.

Practicalities

You'll find a very helpful **turismo** at Foru Enparantza 11 (Mon–Fri 10.30am–1pm & 4–7.30pm, Sat 10am–1pm & 4–6.30pm, Sun 11am–2pm & 4.30–6.30pm; winter closed Sat & Sun pm; ☎943 783 453), which can arrange visits to the university and parish church, and provide a free map of the town, as well as plenty of leaflets detailing walking and motoring routes to places of interest nearby.

The *Bar-Restaurante Echeverria*, R.M. Zuazola 15 (☎943 780 460; ❸), is the only **hostal** in the town centre; the **restaurant** below also offers a reasonable *menú del día*. For an **agroturismo,** try *Arregi*, Garagaltza 19 (☎ & ☎943 780 824; ❹) – or enquire at the turismo about a private room.

There is a daily **bus** from Oñati to Bilbao, and another to Vitoria, changing at Mondragón – an otherwise unappealing town famous as the cradle of the Basque co-operative movement.

The Costa Vasca

Heading west from San Sebastián, both road and rail run inland, following the Río Oria, towards the coast at Zarautz. Along the way, the pretty fishing village of **Orio** on the estuary makes an enjoyable break in the journey. From

Zarautz onwards, the coastline of the **Costa Vasca** is glorious – rocky and wild, with long stretches of road hugging the edge of the cliffs – all the way to Bilbao. There are buses that take the motorway along this route, but even if you're not planning to stop (and there are plenty of picturesque villages to tempt you to do so) it's worth taking the old road for the scenery. The further you go, the less developed the resorts are.

Zarautz

ZARAUTZ itself is certainly not the most attractive spot along the coast. Developed as a fashionable overspill of San Sebastián, the old village has been swamped by a line of hotels and pricey cafés sandwiched between the busy road and the busier beach, a popular place for surfers. The town and surrounding area (and, to a lesser extent, towns further along the coast towards Bizkaia) are famous for the production of *txakoli*, a strong, dry white wine – the vineyards cling to hillsides along the coast from here to Getaria. The first week in September, Zarautz hosts "Basque Week", when you can watch traditional dances and hear *bertsolaris* performing improvised poetry in Basque.

The well-stocked **turismo** (Mon–Sat 9am–1pm & 3.30–7pm, Sun 10am–2pm; ☎943 830990, ⓦwww.zarautz.com) is on Avda. Navarra, the busy main road through town; staff here can advise on **accommodation**. There are several pricey hotels in town, including the *Zarautz* at Avda. Navarra 26 (☎943 830 200, Ⓕ943 830 193; ⑦), and some cheaper *pensiones*, such as *Lagunak* at c/San Francisco 10 (☎943 833 701, Ⓕ943 134 656; ⑤). One of the best places to stay, however, is a large and well-situated *agroturismo*, *Agerre-Goikoa* (☎943 833 248; ④), above the *Talai-Mendi* campsite (see below). The **youth hostel**, *Monte Albertia*, San Inazio 25 (☎943 132 910, Ⓕ943 130 006; ②), on the Meagas road out of town, is open all year. Zarautz has two **campsites**: *Gran Camping Zarauz* (☎943 831 238, Ⓕ943 132 486; open all year), on the cliff tops overlooking the beach, reached from town on the old San Sebastián road, with a marked turning on the left up the hill; and the cheaper *Talai-Mendi* (☎943 830 042), a short walk from the beach but open only from July to mid-September.

Getaria

Five kilometres on is **GETARIA**, a tiny fishing port sheltered by the hump-backed islet of **El Ratón** (The Mouse). It's a historic little place, one of the earliest towns on the coast, preserving the magnificent fourteenth-century church of San Salvador, whose altar is raised theatrically above the heads of the congregation. The first man to sail around the world, Juan Sebastián Elcano, was born here around 1487. His ship was the only one of Magellan's fleet to make it back home. Every four years on August 6, during the village's **fiestas**, Elcano's landing is re-enacted on the beach; the next will be in 2003. The *Mayflower* bar overlooking the harbour is worth a visit for the round-the-wall nautical map of the entire Basque coast, and there's a small but interesting **art gallery** of oil reliefs by local painter Elorza.

Getaria has a small, summer-only **turismo** at Aldamar Parkea 2 (mid-July to mid-Sept Mon 3–9pm, Wed 11.15am–1.15pm & 3–9pm, Thurs–Sun 10.15am–2.15pm & 3–9pm; ☎943 140 957); when it's closed, use the turismo in Zarautz. Check the prices at the tempting fish **restaurants** before you eat; many are expensive. **Accommodation** options include *Pensión Getariano*, c/Herrerieta 3 (☎943 140 567; ⑤), and three somewhat cheaper *agroturismos* a few kilometres up the hillside on the way to Meagas; check with the turismo for details.

Zumaia, Azpeitia and around

The coast becomes still more rugged on the way to **ZUMAIA** – an industrial-looking place at first sight, but with an attractive centre and pleasant waterfront along the estuary of the Río Urola. Zumaia's local **fiesta** in the first days of July is one of the region's most exuberant, with Basque sports, dancing and bullocks let loose on the beach to test the mettle of the local youth.

Zumaia has two very different **beaches** – one of these, over the hill behind the town, is a large splash of grey sand enclosed by extraordinary sheer cliffs of layered slate-like rock which channel the waves in to produce some of the best surfing on the coast. There are spectacular walks along the cliff tops to the west. The other beach, across the river from the port, is yellow and flat, sheltered by a little pine forest. On the road behind this you'll find the **Villa Zuloaga** (Wed–Sun 4–8pm; €3), former home of the Basque painter Ignacio Zuloaga, and now a small art museum displaying his work and that of other Basque artists, together with a rather bizarre exhibition of bull-fighting memorabilia.

There's a very helpful **turismo** on the main square (Easter & mid-June to mid-Sept Mon–Sat 10am–2pm & 4–8pm; ☎943 143 396, ⓦwww.paisvasco.com/zumaia), where you'll also find the cheapest **accommodation** in town, *Bar Tomás* (☎943 861 916; ❸). There are also a couple of hotels, the *Zumaia* at c/Alai 13 (☎943 143 441, ⓕ943 860 764; ❺), and the new *Ilzuren* on Playa de Ilzuren (☎943 865 100; ❺), the latter with a sea-water therapy centre.

Inland from Zumaia, 1km from the town of **AZPEITIA**, is the imposing eighteenth-century Baroque **Basilica of Loyola** (daily 8.30am–2pm & 3–9pm), built in honour of San Ignacio de Loyola, the founder of the Society of Jesus, with an impressive rotunda and marble decor – this is a major pilgrimage spot. Also nearby is the town of **ZESTOA**, which lies north of Azpeitia and has a rich supply of thermal and mineral waters. The luxurious (and pricey) *Gran Hotel Balneario Cestona* (☎943 147 064, ⓕ943 147 140; ❼) lies just off the main road (Carretera Provincial) and offers a wide range of spa treatments including thermal showers.

Mutriku

Beyond **Deva** (Deba), itself an unprepossessing place, the main road veers inland and the coastal route becomes still wilder as it enters the province of Bizkaia. The road is narrow and slow, but there are a fair number of buses from San Sebastián and hitching is surprisingly easy. There's a summer-only **turismo** near the port in Deva, at Puerto 1 (☎943 192 452, ⓦwww.deba.net).

MUTRIKU, despite some ugly recent construction above the town, has some attractive narrow streets leading down steeply to the fishing harbour. It's the centre of another *txakoli*-producing area. Admiral Churruca, the "Hero of Trafalgar" to locals, was born here; his imposing statue faces the incongruous church of Nuestra Señora de Asunción, built along the lines of a Greek temple. Mutriku has a **turismo** on Xemein Etorbidea 13 (mid–June to mid–Sept 10.30am–2pm & 4.30–8pm; ☎943 603 378) and no fewer than four **campsites** around several small beaches. There is also a choice of **agroturismos**: *Casa Matzuri* (☎943 603 001; ❸), just beyond town on the road to Ondarroa, and *Koostei* (☎943 583 008; ❸), perched high up in the hills several kilometres from the main road, which offers horse-riding. Beyond Mutriku, the road temporarily turns inland and reaches the coast once more at the beach of **Saturrarán**, very popular and crowded in summer, when there's a **campsite** (☎943 603 847; June–Sept).

Ondarroa

Around the headland from Saturrarán, **ONDARROA**, the first coastal town in Bizkaia, presents a very different aspect from the other small resorts further east. Here, the usual town beach and attractive tree-lined *rambla* end at a nononsense **fishing port** filled with an eclectic set of trawlers. In the early morning, an endless succession of trucks files in from the coastal road to fill up with fish – the traffic is so great that a large bridge has been built across the bay to channel the fishing trucks directly to the port. You're unlikely to want to stay more than one night, but Ondarroa is an interesting place to stop over, particularly in August when the town hosts its **fiestas**.

Ondarroa's **turismo** is at Konttoipe 3 (Easter & summer only; ☎946 833 090). If you want **to stay**, head for the *Hostal Vega*, c/Antiguako Ama 8 (☎946 830 002; ❹; April–Sept only), right by the fishing port and overlooking the water; the rooms are spacious and clean, some with massive picture windows, and the terrace **restaurant** serves a good €7.20 *menú*, incorporating whatever's been landed that day. The **bars** at the harbour stay open late (some 24hr) as deckhands come and go and, stuffed with a tempting array of seafood *pintxos*, they're accommodating enough to keep the promenading locals and occasional stray tourist happy.

Lekeitio

LEKEITIO is another good bet along this stretch. Still an active fishing port, it has two fine **beaches** – one beside the harbour, the other, much better, across the river to the east of town. It's worth stopping in at the **church** of Santa Maria, in the town centre, with a recently restored magnificent 16th-century Flemish Gothic altarpiece. There's a fair choice of **accommodation**: the best is the new *Hotel Emperatriz Zita*, c/Santa Elena s/n (☎946 842 655, ℻946 243 500; ❻), with excellent sea views from the better rooms. Otherwise, try the *Hotel Beitia*, Avda. Pascual Abaroa 25 (☎946 840 111, ℻946 842 165; ❺), or the *Hostal Piñupe*, Avda. Pascual Abaroa 10 (☎946 842 984, ℻946 840 772; ❺), both very popular in summer when the town becomes a prime destination for the masses from Bilbao. There are also self-catering apartments available along Avenida Pascual Abaroa; enquire at the tourist office, c/Gamarra 1 (☎946 243 365). Lekeitio is literally teeming with **bars**, many offering food, plus a couple of good (if pricey) seafood restaurants: *Kaia* at Txatxo Kaia 5, and *Txopi* on Foru Enparantza. A **campsite**, *Endai* (☎946 842 469; Easter & mid-June to mid-Sept only), can be found on the main road to Ondarroa; alternatively, head for *Leagi* (☎946 842 352), in the village of Mendexa, 3km inland between Ondarroa and Lekeitio, which is open all year. There is also a summer-only **agroturismo**, *Mendexakua* (☎946 243 108; ❹), near Mendexa. Horse-riding, mountain biking and kayaking are all available nearby.

Elantxobe

The road turns inland from Lekeitio, but the fishing village of **ELAN-TXOBE**, almost entirely in its original condition, is worth a detour back to the coast. Perched high above a small harbour, the village is connected to it by an incredibly steep cobbled street lined with attractive fishermen's houses. Calle Mayor continues up to the cemetery from where a signposted track leads to **Mount Ogoño** – at 280m the highest cliff on the Basque coast.

Elantxobe has a couple of small **restaurants** on c/Mayor, and one *pensión*, *Itsasmin Ostatua,* at c/Nagusia 32 (☎946 276 174, ℻946 276 293; ❹). Alternatively, you can stay at one of the two *agroturismos* located in Ibarrangelu, 1km from the crossroads in the direction of Gernika: *Caserio Arboliz*, at c/Arboliz 12 (⌾946 276 283; ❹), or *Etxetxu* (⌾946 276 337; ❸) next door.

Direct **buses** run between Elantxobe and Gernika (twice daily) or, from Lekeitio, take the Gernika bus to Ibarrangelu and walk 1km down to the village.

Gernika and around

Immortalized by Picasso's nightmare picture (finally brought home to Spain after the death of Franco, and now exhibited in the Centro de Arte Reina Sofía, Madrid (see p.106)), **GERNIKA**, inland and west of Lekeitio, is the traditional heart of Basque nationalism. It was here that the Basque parliament used to meet, and here, under the **Tree of Gernika** (the *Gernikako Arbola*), that their rights were reconfirmed by successive rulers. It was more for its symbolic importance than the presence of a small-arms factory that Gernika was chosen during the Civil War as the target for one of the first ever saturation bombing raids on a civilian centre. In just four hours on April 27, 1937, planes from the Condor Legion (lent to Franco by Hitler) destroyed the town centre and killed more than 1600 people. The nearby town of Durango had in fact been bombed a few days earlier, but because there were no foreign observers, the reports were simply not believed.

The parliament building, the **Casa de las Juntas** (Mon–Sat 10am–2pm & 4–6pm or 7pm in summer, Sun 10am–1.30pm; free), is well worth a visit for the stained-glass window depicting the tree and important scenes and monuments from the region. The adjacent church of Santa María la Antigua, adorned with portraits of the various nobles of Bizkaia who pledged allegiance to the *fueros*, traditionally served as a meeting-house (although in fine weather, assemblies were held under the tree). The parliament, church and tree remained miraculously unscathed by the bombing, but the rest of the town was rebuilt and is now nondescript, apart from the arcaded main street. Here you'll find the **Gernika Museum** (Sept to mid-June Mon–Sat 10am–2pm & 4–7pm, Sun 10am–2pm; mid-June to Aug Mon–Sat 10am–7pm, Sun 10am–2pm; €2.10), with a stirring display on the bombing, and a collection of Picasso's sketches for *Guernica*. For a Basque, at least, a visit to Gernika is more pilgrimage than tourist trip. A walk through Europa Park with its ornamental gardens, fast-flowing stream and peace sculptures by Henry Moore and Eduardo Chillida captures something of the elegiac atmosphere.

Housed in the Palacio Udetxea next to the park is the headquarters of the **Urdaibai Biosphere Reserve** (Mon–Fri 9am–1.30pm & 3–5pm; free), which often holds exhibitions on environmental and cultural themes. The reserve itself, which encompasses the watershed of the Mundaka estuary, was declared by UNESCO in 1984 as an area of world cultural and natural heritage; it includes the most diverse range of habitats in Euskal Herria and is the resting place for hosts of migrating birds.

Practicalities

There's a helpful **turismo** at c/Artekale 8 (Mon–Sat 10am–1pm & 4–7.30pm, Sun 10am–1pm; ⌾946 255 892, ⓦwww.gernika-lumo.net) in the arcaded main street, with one of the best selections of pamphlets in English on all areas of Euskal Herria and details of **places to stay**. Otherwise, head for *Hostal Iratxe*, Industri Kalea 4 (⌾946 256 463; ❸), or for more luxury, *Gernika*, Carlos Gangoiti 17 (⌾946 254 948, Ⓕ946 255 874; ❻). If you have your own transport, the turismo can make bookings at any one of four **agro-**

turismos within a ten-kilometre radius of town. There's a good, inexpensive **menú** at *Jatetxea Madariaga*, c/Juan Madariaga 10. Hourly **buses** run via Zornotza to Bilbao starting at 7.10am. There is also a regular service to Bermeo (12 daily).

The Cueva de Santimamiñe and Bosque Encantado de Oma

Five kilometres from Gernika, off the Lekeitio road, lies the **Cueva de Santimamiñe** (guided tours Mon–Fri at 10am, 11.15am, 12.30pm, 4.30pm & 6pm; free but tipping customary). Inside are extraordinary rock formations and some Paleolithic cave paintings of bison – which are now, unfortunately, off limits due to deterioration brought about by rising temperatures.

Without your own transport, it may be worth coming on an organized tour (details from tourist offices in Gernika or Bilbao), as there is no public transport to the cave. You can, however, get a taxi from Gernika for about €7, or the thrice-daily Gernika–Lekeitio bus can drop you at Kortezubi from where it's a two-kilometre signposted walk. It's a steep climb up to the entrance and you may have to wait as numbers are limited to fifteen at one time – a good **bar-restaurant** in the car park helps pass the time. If you do have to wait, or wish to spend longer, the area is very scenic and walking trails from the cave are well signposted. For accommodation, try *Morgota* (☎946 252 772; ❹), a peaceful *agroturismo*, in sleepy Kortezubi.

From the *Lezika* restaurant on the Santimarniñe road, a single-track road leads to the lovely village of **OMA**, 5km away, tucked in a lush green valley. Here, veteran Basque artist Augustin Ibarrola has transformed an ordinary pine plantation into the **Bosque Encantado de Oma** (Enchanted Wood of Oma), by painting treetrunks in such a way that from certain points in the wood, where the trees line up correctly, pictures are formed – of rainbows, strange beasts and the like. The effect is quite eerie and impressive, and although the wood was recently vandalized by ETA supporters, it's still well worth the trip. As well as the road, there is a dirt road to the wood (also starting from the *Lezika*) which allows access with a reasonably sturdy vehicle, and also allows you to see the wood as part of a 10km circular walk (allow 4hr in total, including time in the wood). If you want to stay in Oma, there's a highly recommended *agroturismo, Bizketxe* (☎946 254 906; ❹) – you can book at the Gernika turismo.

Mundaka and Bermeo

Continuing the route west, the Río Mundaka flows from Gernika into a broad estuary fringed by hilly pine woods and dotted with islets. There's a succession of sandy coves to swim in, but the best spots are at Sukarrieta (Pedernales) and especially **MUNDAKA**, where there's a **campsite**, *Portuondo* (☎946 877 701; open all year), high above the water with steps leading down to a rocky beach, with magnificent surfing and the longest left break in the world; championships often take place here, and any windy day you can watch from the plaza next to the church as the surfers battle the waves. A passenger ferry plies across the river (June–Sept 10am–8pm; every twenty minutes; €1.20) to the **Playa de Laída**, an enormous area of white sand which at low tide stretches across the mouth of the bay in an unbroken crescent. There is a group of holiday villas here and another campsite, *Camping Arketa* (☎946 278 118); it's a small site, so book beforehand. Places to **stay** in Mundaka itself include the friendly *Hotel el Puerto*, c/Portu 1 (☎946 876 625, ℱ946 177 064; ❺), right on the fishing port; it gets very crowded in summer so book ahead.

The local *EuskoTren* train line from Bilbao and Gernika gives good access to the estuary beaches and continues beyond Mundaka to **BERMEO**, whose fishing fleet is the largest remaining in these waters, a riot of red, green and blue boats in the harbour. Worth checking out while you're here is the **Museo del Pescador** near the harbour (Tues–Sat 10am–1.30pm & 4–7.30pm, Sun 10am–1.30pm; free), full of local interest and more general maritime displays. Apart from a stroll through the narrow, cobbled streets, there's not much else to see, and no beach worth the name – but you should try some of the fish in the restaurants around the port: the local standards, *merluza* (hake) and *bacalao* (cod), are particularly good. Bermeo's **turismo** (daily 10am–1pm & 5–8pm; ☎946 179 154), just opposite the train station at Askatasun Bidea 2, has a good pamphlet detailing a walk through the town and can arrange **accommodation**. In town there are two *hostales, Subigane* (☎946 186 944; ❹) and *Aldatxeta*, c/Erremedio 24 (☎946 187 703; ❺), in a renovated building with bath and TV in all rooms, as well as the more upmarket *Hotel Txaraka*, Almike Bidea (☎946 885 558; ❼). There are also several *agroturismos* in the area.

Westwards, on the way to the sleepy resort town of **BAKIO**, the hermitage of **San Juan de Gaztelugatxe** stands on a rocky peninsula, connected to the shore by a long and winding flight of 231 steps at one of the most rugged parts of the Bizkaian coast. If you're travelling by bus, ask the driver to let you off at the cliff-top crossroads and walk down.

Bakio itself has a good **beach** and walking and mountain-bike trails in the quiet surrounding hills. If you fancy a bit of luxury, try the colonial-style *Hotel Joshe Mari*, c/Bentalde 31 (☎946 194 005, Ⓕ946 195 706; ❼), with excellent views and its own restaurant with a €24 *menú*.

After Bakio, the coast road passes **Lemóniz**, infamous for the government's attempt to build a nuclear power station and the Basques' fierce resistance to it. The project was shelved after one of its engineers was kidnapped and assassinated by ETA. The abandoned, half-finished power station, enclosed in a narrow valley, is a striking, if rather sinister, sight.

Bilbao

Stretching for some 14km along the narrow valley of the heavily polluted Río Nervión, **BILBAO** (Bilbo) is a large city that rarely feels like one, its urban sprawl having gradually engulfed a series of once-separate communities. Even in the city centre you can always see the green slopes of the surrounding mountains beyond the high-rise buildings. A prosperous, modern city with a busy and attractive centre, surrounded by grim, graffiti-covered slums and smoke-belching factories, Bilbao is in the process of reinventing itself after the collapse of its traditional industrial base in the 1980s and 1990s. Steel mills and shipyards have been transformed into conference centres and luxury flats, and the famous Guggenheim Museum, which opened in 1997, has sparked a tourism boom. A new metro and airport have opened and celebrations of Bilbao's 700th anniversary, in 2000, brought new impetus to the redevelopment programme. The city also has some of the best places to eat and drink in the whole of Euskal Herria, and very open, friendly inhabitants with a great abundance of civic pride.

Arrival, information and orientation

Most long-distance and international **bus** companies, including Alsa, Ansa, Bilmanbús, Enatcar, Saia, La Unión and Pesa, use the **Termibús station**

(☎944 395 077; Ⓜ San Mamés), which fills an entire block between Luis Briñas and Gurtubay in the new part of town. Many provincial buses depart from the **Bizkaiabus station** on c/Sendeja, next to the main turismo in the Parque del Arenal; the turismo has information on timetables. The bus for Bilbao's spanking new **airport** (☎944 869 300) leaves from Plaza Moyua in the centre of the new town and takes 40 minutes (€0.75).

The main RENFE train station is the **Estación de Abando** on Plaza Circular, but local services to San Sebastián, Gernika, Bermeo and Durango use the **Estación Atxuri** (Achuri), on the other side of the river, to the south of the *casco viejo*. FEVE services, along the coast to Santander and beyond, stop at the highly decorative **Estación de Santander**, on the riverbank right below the Estación de Abando.

The **P&O ferry** from Portsmouth in the UK docks at **Santurtzi**, across the river from Getxo (Las Arenas), to the north of the city centre. Regular buses and trains run from the docks to the centre of town. An unusual way to cross the Río Nervión is by the hundred-year-old *puente colgante* (hanging bridge) in Portugalete, some 3km south of the ferry terminal; either take the gondola across at street-level (24hrs/day, €0.20) or else get the lift up to the 43m-high viewing platform (10am–7pm; €2.40) and walk across.

Information and orientation

The well-stocked main **turismo** (Mon–Fri 9am–2pm & 4–7.30pm, Sat 9am–2pm, Sun 10am–2pm; ☎944 795 760, Ⓦwww.bilbao.net) is in the Parque del Arenal, near the Puente del Ayuntamiento. There's another turismo outside the Guggenheim Museum (July–Aug Mon–Fri 11am–2pm & 4–6pm, Sat 11am–2pm & 5–7pm, Sun 11am–2pm; rest of year closed Mon), a booth at the airport, and a helpful turismo on Getxo's seafront at Muelle de Ereaga (daily 10am–8pm; ☎944 910 800).

The new town (or "Ensanche") is situated in a broad loop of the Río Nervión, with the main radial avenues affording direct views of the mountains from the bustling streets. On the opposite (right) bank of the river, there's the *casco viejo* to the south, and Deusto, famous for its university, to the north.

Most facilities are along the city's main thoroughfare, the **Gran Vía Don Diego López de Haro**, where you'll find all the major **banks**, public buildings, expensive shops and El Corte Inglés. The Gran Vía goes straight through the heart of the modern city, from the Plaza Circular by the RENFE station, to the Plaza Sagrado Corazón, situated between the new **Euskalduna Palace** and the huge stadium of **San Mames**, the "cathedral of football" as the Basques would have it.

Transport around the city has recently been revolutionized by the completion of a spanking new **metro** system, designed by Lord Norman Foster; the distinctive tubelike entrances are popularly known as *fosteritos*. An easy, efficient service runs every four minutes along the single line from Plentzia (to the northeast of Getxo) to Bouleta, south of the city centre; free metro maps are available from the tourist offices. The 27 stops are divided into three zones, but all journeys in the city centre (including the *casco viejo*) are within one zone. For parts the metro doesn't reach, there are municipal **buses** – painted in red and white stripes – with route maps at the green bus shelters, or for longer journeys (including to the airport) the blue and yellow *Bizkaibuses*. A **tram** line is under construction, due to open sometime in 2002. The Bilbao transport system has won a European award – despite which traffic is awful and parking a nightmare, especially in the city centre.

If you're staying a few days, it's a good idea to get a *CrediMovil* travelcard, available in kiosks, newsagents and metro stations in denominations of €3, €6

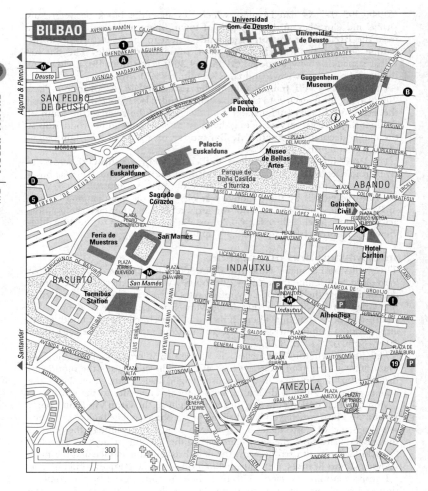

and €15. This smart card works for all Bilbao's various modes of transport – the metro, municipal and provincial buses, the Artxanda funicular and the *ascensors* at Puente la Salve and elsewhere – and cuts fares in half, to about €0.40 per trip.

Accommodation

Now that Bilbao is firmly on the tourist map, accommodation is frequently booked out, so it's well worth planning ahead to avoid a lot of phoning round. The best **places to stay** are mainly in the *casco viejo* – especially along **c/Bidebarrieta**, which leads from Plaza Arriaga to the cathedral, and in the streets around it: c/Lotería, c/Santa María and c/Barrencalle Barrena. Calle Barrencalle is best avoided if you value your sleep – the bars get very noisy at night. Rock-bottom options (rather grim *fondas* and *casas de huéspedes*) are on

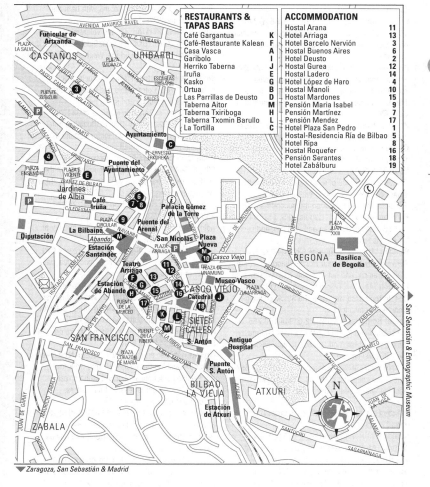

RESTAURANTS & TAPAS BARS

Café Gargantua	K
Café-Restaurante Kalean	F
Casa Vasca	A
Garibolo	I
Herriko Taberna	J
Iruña	E
Kasko	G
Ortua	B
Las Parrillas de Deusto	D
Taberna Aitor	M
Taberna Txiriboga	H
Taberna Txomin Barullo	L
La Tortilla	C

ACCOMMODATION

Hostal Arana	11
Hotel Arriaga	13
Hotel Barcelo Nervión	3
Hostal Buenos Aires	6
Hotel Deusto	2
Hostal Gurea	12
Hostal Ladero	14
Hotel López de Haro	4
Hostal Manoli	10
Hostal Mardones	15
Pensión Maria Isabel	9
Pensión Martínez	7
Pensión Mendez	17
Hotel Plaza San Pedro	1
Hostal-Residencia Ría de Bilbao	5
Hotel Ripa	8
Hostal Roquefer	16
Pensión Serantes	18
Hotel Zabálburu	19

▼ *Zaragoza, San Sebastián & Madrid*

the east bank around the Estación de Abando, particularly round the back on c/San Francisco. The parallel c/de las Cortes is the red-light district, and not for the nervous; avoid it if you can. Another decent area for rooms is in the streets leading down from Plaza Circular around c/Buenos Aires (Ⓜ Abando). Staying in **Deusto** is a good alternative, handy for the art galleries and main shopping districts and boasting its own crop of restaurants and bars. **Getxo** is another viable option, since with the metro it's easy to reach anywhere on the east bank in minutes; you can book accommodation in the Getxo turismo.

The nearest **campsites** are to the northeast, on the beaches at Sopelana, *Sopelana* (☏946 762 120; bus towards Plentzia or Metro Sopelana), and Gorliz, *Arrien* (☏946 771 911; just beyond Plentzia); both campsites are open all year.

Budget options

Hostal Gurea, Bidebarrieta 14, 3° ☎ & ⓕ944
163 299. In an old building that's falling apart, but
otherwise quite comfortable, cheap and convenient. ❹

Pensión Ladero, c/Lotería 1, 4° ☎944 150 932.
Friendly management and clean, good-value
rooms with modern furnishings. There is also a
fifth-floor annexe reached by a narrow spiral staircase. ❹

Pensión Manoli, c/Libertad-Askatasuna 2 ☎944
155 636. Spacious, clean rooms off Plaza Nueva.
❸ There's an annexe with similar prices just down
the street at c/Gordóniz 66.

Pensión Mardones, c/Jardines 4 ☎944 153 105.
Entrance at the side of a newspaper kiosk with
smart, clean rooms with or without bath.
Preferable to the annexe on the second floor. ❹

Pensión Maria Isabel, c/Amistad 5, 1° ☎944
248 566. Basic, but clean and well run, and useful
for the station. ❸

Pensión Martínez, c/Villarías 8 ☎944 239 178.
Conveniently located near *Hostal Buenos Aires*, but
a bit unfriendly, and not all rooms have windows. ❸

Pensión Mendez, c/Santa María 13 ☎944 160
364. In the *casco viejo* near the Stock Exchange;
clean and convenient. ❷

Hostal Roquefer, c/Lotería 2 ☎944 150 755. On
the second and fourth floors of a dark and musty
building. The best (and lightest) rooms overlook
the cathedral square. ❹

Pensión Serantes, c/Somera 14 ☎944 151 557.
This is the cheapest of the lot. Rather down-at-
heel but with friendly young staff. ❷

Moderate and expensive options

Hostal Arana, c/Bidebarrieta 2 ☎944 156 411,
ⓕ944 161 205. Friendly, very quiet and conveniently located *hostal* in the *casco viejo*. ❹

Hotel Arriaga, c/Ribera 3 ☎944 790 001. Best of
the medium-range hotels, near the Teatro, by the
river; modern, comfortable rooms with bath and
TV; garage available. ❻

Hotel Barcelo Nervión, Campo Volantín 11
☎944 454 700, ⓕ944 455 608. Plush new hotel
overlooking the Zubizuri bridge. Weekend reductions. ❼–❽

Hostal Buenos Aires, Plaza Venezuela 1, 3°
☎944 240 765. Comfortable and well-run *hostal*
with a pleasant lounge and small bar. ❺

Hotel Deusto, c/Francisco Macia 9 ☎944 760
006, ⓕ944 762 199, Ⓜ Deusto. Business hotel
near the University of Deusto, with substantial
weekend reductions. ❼–❽

Hotel Igeretxe, Playa Ereaga, Getxo ☎944 607
000, ⓕ944 608 599. Upmarket hotel right on the
seafront with a bar where you can watch the ships
coming in to port. ❽

Hotel López de Haro, Obispo Orueta 2 ☎944
235 500, ⓕ944 234 500, Ⓦwww.
hotellopezdeharo.com. Luxury, five-star hotel near
the Jardines de Albia. ❾

Hotel Neguri, Avda. Algorta 14, Getxo ☎944 910
509, ⓕ944 911 943. Decent and good value, with
plenty of facilities. ❼

Hostal Plaza San Pedro, c/Luzarra 7 ☎944 763
126, ⓕ944 763 895, Ⓜ Deusto. Across the river
in Deusto in a slightly grim-looking street, but with
very comfortable en-suite rooms with TV. ❺

Hostal-Residencia Ría de Bilbao, Ribera de
Deusto 32 ☎944 761 557,
Ⓦwww.riabilbao.arrakis.es, Ⓜ Deusto. Nice quiet
place overlooking the river, a 10-min walk from
the Palacio Euskalduna. Mainly a student residence, but with rooms reserved for visitors.
Garden and cooking facilities. ❺

Hotel Ripa, c/Ripa 3 ☎944 239 677, ⓕ944 231
816. Just over Puente del Arenal from the *casco
viejo*, on the street by the waterfront; good-value
rooms with bath and TV. ❺

Hotel Zabálburu, Pedro Martínez Artola 8 ☎944
437 100, ⓕ944 100 073. Good, clean doubles and
handy for train and bus terminals. ❻

The City

Bilbao's **casco viejo**, the old quarter on the east bank of the river, holds many
of the city's sights: the beautiful **Teatro Arriaga**, the elegantly arcaded **Plaza
Nueva** (or *de los Mártires*), the Gothic **Catedral de Santiago** and the **Museo
Arqueológico, Ethnográfico e Histórico Vasco** at c/Cruz 4 (Tues–Sat
10.30am–1.30pm & 4–7pm, Sun 10.30am–1.30pm; €1.80, free Thurs). The
museum is housed in the former School of San Andrés with its beautiful cloister and large selection of coats of arms of the former Bizkaian nobility – a lovely retreat from the city bustle. It has an intriguing and eclectic collection, from
an enormous, obsessively detailed three-dimensional map of Bizkaia on the top
floor, to an exhibition on Basque emigrants to the Americas. It's in the old
town too that the best bars and restaurants are situated, among the thronged

narrow streets and antiquated shops contained in the *siete calles* (seven streets) area bordered by c/de la Ronda and c/Pelota.

From the *casco viejo* it's a pleasant ramble along the river through the Parque del Arenal and past the *ayuntamiento* – a faviourite *paseo* for Bilbainos, although the smell of the River Nervión can be overpowering in hot weather. For some fresh air, leave the river at the Zubizuri bridge and head three blocks north to the Plaza Funicular, where the **Artxanda funicular** (€0.70) sweeps you up the mountain for a panoramic vista of the city; you can also see over into the next valley, with views of the new Calatrava-designed airport. The top station is a nice spot for a picnic, and you can stroll down the hill again (about 45min) through the lush suburbs of the *Ciudad Jardin* (Garden City).

The biggest attraction in Bilbao, however, is undoubtedly Frank O. Gehry's astounding **Guggenheim Museum** (Tues–Sun: July & Aug 9am–9pm; Sept–June 10am–8pm; €7.20), which dominates the quayside opposite the University of Deusto. You can cross the delicate arch of the Zubizuri footbridge to approach the museum from beneath along the west bank; or, for an aerial view, take the *ascensor* (or seven flights of steps) up to the Puente de la Salve. Described by architect Philip Johnson as "the greatest building of our time", the Guggenheim is the keystone of the Basque government's plans to revitalize the city; it has been developed in co-operation with the Solomon R. Guggenheim Foundation, and provides a European showcase for the Foundation's unmatched collection of twentieth-century art. The permanent collection, which rotates between Bilbao and the Foundation's other museums in New York and Venice, includes works by all the major modern and contemporary figures, including Kandinsky, Klee, Mondrian, Picasso, Cézanne, Chagall, Warhol and Rauschenberg, to name a few; the museum also hosts various top-flight temporary exhibitions. One painting, though, is conspicuous by its absence: Picasso's *Guernica* – in the Reina Sofia, Madrid – whose "return" the Basques have been demanding for years (indeed, some say they built the Guggenheim specially).

The art, however, takes a back seat to the **building** itself: a gargantuan sculpture whose sensual titanium curves glimmer like running water in the sun. The main entrance, on the city side, is home to *Puppy*, Jeff Koons' kitschy flower sculpture, which was originally installed as a temporary exhibit for the opening ceremony but became a permanent feature after Bilbainos clamoured for it to stay. It is now an inseparable part of the museum and has probably paid for itself many times over in *Puppy* key-rings and soft toys.

Inside the museum, galleries and walkways lead off a vast, light-filled atrium. Your ticket is valid for the whole day, so it's worth arriving early and taking a break for lunch – perhaps at the museum's classy **restaurant** (see "Restaurants and tapas bars"). Free guided tours (in English) start at 11am, 12.30pm, 4pm and 6.30pm. Major exhibitions are held in the 130m-long "Fish Gallery"; films, talks and other events are also organized regularly. To find out what's on, visit the museum's website ⓦwww.guggenheim-bilbao.es or call ☎944 359 080.

The area of former docks and rail depots to the west (downriver) of the Guggenheim, known as Abandoibarra, is under development, with plans for parks, luxury high-rise apartments and a giant shopping centre. Until this happens, you have to follow Alameda de Mazarredo – a conduit for heavy traffic from Puente la Salve – west from the Guggenheim's main entrance to get to the **Museo de Bellas Artes** (Tues–Sat 10am–8pm, Sun 10am–2pm; €3.60, free Wed), in the Parque de Doña Casilda de Iturriza. Although overshadowed by its world-famous neighbour, this houses a diverse, well-displayed collection, including works by El Greco, Goya and Van Dyck; Basque artists, of course, are also well represented. You can buy a combined ticket for both museums for €8.40.

Continuing through the park you come to the rusty iron bulk of the **Palacio Euskalduna**, another new piece in Bilbao's urban jigsaw, backed by the curved Euskalduna bridge. Built on the ruins of the city's last shipyard, which closed in the 1980s, the Palacio hosts conferences and classical performances (see "Bars and entertainment"). It's a beautiful building to look around – particularly the tiled floors inside – but staff are rather snooty to the casual visitor. However, there are one-hour guided tours (depart noon on Sat; €1.80), starting from door 4 on street level – just turn up fifteen minutes early to get your ticket.

Beaches

The city is well served with **beaches** along the mouth of the estuary and around both headlands. The metro means it's easier to reach the beaches on the east bank, such as those at **Sopelana** (Ⓜ Larrabasterra), including the nudist Playa de Barinatxe, and **Plentzia** – out to the north of the city – which is generally cleaner and not quite so crowded. **Getxo** (Ⓜ Algorta) has a pretty old quarter with white houses and green-painted doors, and an impressive waterfront promenade fringed with private mansions belonging to Bilbao's millionaire set.

Eating, drinking and nightlife

Bilbao is definitely one of those cities where the most enjoyable way to eat is to move from bar to bar, snacking on *pintxos*. The city can be very lively at night – and totally wild during the August **fiesta**, with scores of open-air bars, live music and impromptu dancing everywhere, and a truly festive atmosphere. The *casco viejo* has most of the interesting places to **eat and drink,** with almost wall-to-wall places on c/Santa María and c/Barrencalle Barrena.

If you want to get together something of your own, the attractive Art Nouveau **Mercado de la Ribera**, on c/de la Ribera towards the Estación Atxuri, offers a dazzling array of fresh produce, particularly seafood.

Café Gargantua, c/Barrencalle Barrena. Simple café serving sandwiches, and a selection of different priced *menús* and *platos combinados*.

Café-Restaurante Kalean, c/Santa María. Very popular, offering excellent economical *nueva cocina vasca*. After midnight, there's a resident pianist and great atmosphere.

Casa Vasca, Avda. Lehendakari Aguirre 13–15 Ⓜ Deusto. Traditional Basque restaurant in Deusto, across the bridge from the Museo de Bellas Artes; does great breakfasts (the hot chocolate is the best in town).

Garibolo, c/Fernandez del Campo 7 (in the centre just north of the Gran Vía). Good if unsurprising vegetarian restaurant does lunch Mon–Sat, dinner Fri & Sat.

Guggenheim Museum Restaurant, ☎944 239333. A surprisingly inexpensive lunch *menú* (€9.60) from the *nueva cocina vasca* school. Be sure to book by 1pm for lunch.

Herriko Taberna, c/de la Ronda 20. Excellent place for a straightforward, inexpensive meal; a strong Basque nationalist atmosphere and a great *menú*.

Iruña, Jardines de Albia. The spicy lamb *pintxos morunos* in this popular bar are indispensible to build your strength for a night out.

Kasko, c/Santa María. Trendy café offering *nueva cocina vasca* with a delightful evening *menú* for €15.

Ortua, Alameda Mazarredo 18. Vegetarian restaurant doing an excellent *menú* for €7.20 (lunch only). Convenient for a break from the Guggenheim.

Las Parrillas de Deusto, Travesía de los Espinos, 6 Ⓜ Deusto. You can't get more authentic than this locals' *cerveceria* 5 minutes' walk from the Euskalduna bridge. Good *menús* from €9 up – the *langostinos a la plancha* are great.

Taberna Aitor, c/Barrencalle Barrena. Excellent tapas bar and one for football fans, with the bonus

of a beautiful wooden interior.
Taberna Txiriboga, c/Santa María. Lively tapas bar in the heart of the *casco viejo*.
Taberna Txomin Barullo, c/Barrencalle. Great café-bar with nationalist murals, specializing in

more experimental *nueva cocina vasca* (lunch *menú* only Thurs–Sun) at reasonable prices.
La Tortilla, Plaza Ernesto Erkoreka. Opposite the *Ayuntamiento*, this bar offers *mejillones* of mythical quality.

Bars and entertainment

Bars can be found all through the **casco viejo**, with the traditional approach to drinking – *poteo* – consisting of a high-speed bar crawl, spending less than ten minutes in each place. If (as Bilbainos hold to be self-evident) Bilbao is the centre of the universe, then the *siete calles* on a Saturday night are the whirling hub of it all, with the heart of the madness centred on c/Barrenkale. For the more leisurely, *Lamiak* on c/Pelota is a café-bar full of students, with good music and a noticeboard worth checking for events, women's groups, work, flatshares and the like. *Txokolanda* is a **gay** bar, upstairs from *Solokuetxe*, reached via steps from c/de la Ronda, and, along with the *Lasaí* bar on c/de la Ronda itself, is one of the last places to close. For a relaxed drink in the early evening, head for the outdoor tables in the beautiful Plaza Nueva, not as pricey as you might expect. Bilbao's **historic cafés** include the gorgeous Art Nouveau *Boulevard* on c/Ribera near the Teatro Arriaga (which has free tango lessons upstairs at 9pm on the first Saturday of each month) and the *Granja* in Plaza Circular.

In the **new town**, lively areas with a slightly smarter atmosphere are near the Plaza Circular, between the Alameda de Mazarredo and c/de Buenos Aires, especially on c/Ledesma, a street teeming with bars and especially popular during early evening. *Bar Iruña*, on Colón de Larreategui, parallel to c/Ledesma, is marvellously atmospheric. Bilbao has a large number of **Irish** pubs; one of the best is *Dubliners,* in the heart of the new town on c/Elcano at Plaza Moyúa, with live sessions (musicians welcome) on Mondays at 10pm, and a free pub quiz (in English) on Wednesdays at 9.30pm.

Farther east, south of the Gran Vía, around the junction of c/de Licenciado Poza and Gregorio de Revilla, an area known as **Pozas (Ⓜ Indautxu)** is highly popular before lunch and in the early evening; *Ziripot* is a bar worth trying here. For action well into the night, one of the in-places is the cluster of bars known as the **Ripa** on the modern city side of the riverbank between Puentes del Arenal and the *ayuntamiento*, with a mixed crowd ranging from Basque yuppies to rockabillies.

Live music abounds in Bilbao; check the listings in the local newspaper *El Correo*. *Café Antxokia* on c/San Vicente is a theatre-turned-nightclub with an emphasis on folk- and punk-influenced groups, *La Merced-Bilborock*, across the Puente La Merced from the Casco Viejo, is the place for rock and alternative music, while *Palladium*, on c/Iparraguirre two blocks from the Guggenheim, has jazz on Fridays. Teatro Arriaga (☎944 163 333), in the *casco viejo*, hosts dance and music events as well as theatre, and the Palacio Euskalduna (☎944 035 000) offers opera and classical music, plus the odd wrinkly rocker, with ticket prices ranging from €6 to €60; you can pick up a bimonthly programme from the box office (downstairs on the river level; Mon–Fri 9am–2pm & 4–7pm.) *El Correo* also has **cinema** listings; few films are screened in English, but two venues that do show films in their original language are the Filmoteca at the Museo de Bellas Artes – films generally start around 5pm – and Multicines at José Maria Escuza 13.

Listings

Bookshops TinTas, c/General Concha 10 Ⓜ Indautxu, is a large travel bookshop with a wide range of maps and guides; Borda, c/Somera 45 Ⓜ Casco Viejo, also specializes in maps and guidebooks, including English-language publications, and sells hiking/travel gear; Mendiko Etxea, c/Autonomía 9 Ⓜ Indautxu, specializes in local trekking and cycling guides. The best place to buy English and other foreign newspapers (one day late) is Librería Cámara on c/Euskalduna 6, four streets up on the right from Plaza Circular along Hurtado de Amézaga, Ⓜ Abando.

Car rental Avis, Alameda Dr Areilza 34 ☎944 275 760; Europcar, Licenciado Poza 56 ☎944 422 849; Budget, Dr Nicolás Achúcarro 8 ☎944 150 870; all Ⓜ Indautxu. There are several booths at the airport as well, but watch out for the airport surcharge.

Consulates The British consulate is at Alameda Urquijo 2 ☎944 157 600, and the Irish at Amann 2, Getxo ☎944 912 575.

Hospital Hospital de Basurto, Avda. de Montevideo 18 ☎944 418 700, Ⓜ San Mames.

Call ambulances on ☎944 410 081 or 944 100 000 (24hr).

Internet access *Milenium*, Avda. Lehendakari Aguirre 36, Deusto (€3/hr); *Antxi*, Luis Briñas 13 (Ⓦ www.cybercafe-antxi.com; €2.40; Ⓜ Moyua); *El Señor de la Red*, Rodriguez Arras 69 Ⓜ Moyua or Avda. Lehendakari Aguirre, next to Deusto University (Ⓦ www.elsenordelared.com; €2.10/hr; Ⓜ Deusto; with free coffee).

Post office The main *Correos* is at Alameda Urquijo 19 (Mon–Fri 8am–9pm, Sat 9am–2pm; Ⓜ Abando or Moyua).

Taxi TeleTaxi (☎944 102 121) or Radio Taxi Bilbao (☎944 448 888).

Telephones There is a *telefónica* at c/Baroeta Aldamar 7, close to the Plaza Circular (Ⓜ Abando).

Travel agents Barcelo Viajes, Rodríguez Arias 8 ☎944 200 400; TIVE, Iparraguirre 3 ☎944 231 862, specializes in student/youth travel and international buses, as does USIT at Plaza Moyúa 6 ☎944 240 218. All Ⓜ Moyua.

Inland routes from Bilbao

Inland Bizkaia is well off the beaten track yet has much to offer, with spectacular walking and climbing country, particularly around Durango, and remarkable limestone caves, accessible as a day-trip from Bilbao.

Around Durango

The otherwise uninspiring factory town of **DURANGO** (easily accessible by train from Atxuri station) is the gateway to the impressive **Duranguesado Massif**. To explore this area of rocky peaks, the best access point is the Urkiola Pass (on the Durango–Vitoria road and bus route) from where it's about three hours to the highest peak, **Amboto**. This summit is a favourite with Basque walkers and climbers – the final scramble to the top can be a bit vertigo-inducing. Alternatively, head for the beautiful Atxondo valley off the Durango–Elorrio road. If you don't have your own transport, take the hourly buses as far as the signposted crossroads and then walk 2.5km to the village of **Axpe-Marzana**, nestling at the base of Amboto – a good base for a couple of days' walking. There is an **agroturismo**, *Imitte-Etxebarria* (☎946 231 659; ❹), 500m before the village, and another, *Olazabal Azpikoa* (☎946 813 872; ❹), in the village itself.

Markina and Bolibar

Some 40km east of Bilbao, on the bus route to Ondarroa, the attractive town of **MARKINA** is famous for producing many of the finest *pelota* players – the *frontón* here is known as *La Universidad de la Pelota*. If you want to stay, try *Hostal Vega* in the main square (☎946 866 015; ❹). From Markina you can visit the tiny village of **BOLIBAR**, ancestral home of the South American liberator, where there is a small museum depicting the great man's feats (Tues–Fri

10am–1pm, Sat & Sun noon–2pm; July & Aug also daily 5–7pm; free). From the village a short, restored stretch of a branch of the Camino de Santiago leads up to the **Colegiata de Zenarruza** (daily 10.30am–1.30pm & 4–7pm; Mass 12pm), a former pilgrims' *hostal* and hospital containing a beautiful sixteenth-century cloister and Romanesque church.

Orduña

Thirty-five kilometres south of Bilbao is **ORDUÑA**, a curious enclave of Bizkaia in Alava Province (served by several trains a day from Abando station). The Plaza de los Fueros boasts a collection of fine old buildings including the Neoclassical former customs house and a belfry where a pair of storks have taken up residence – apparently one of only three such nests in Euskal Herria. In the plaza is an old shop selling the local speciality, *Mantecadas de Badillo*, a kind of sweet spongecake, sold straight from the oven. You can walk up to **Fraileburu** (monk's head), a peculiarly shaped rock at the top of the escarpment immediately south of the town which is regarded as one of the prime hang-gliding and paragliding spots in Spain.

West to the limestone caves

The little-known area of **ENCARTACIONES**, west of Bilbao, makes another rewarding day-trip, with places to stay if you want to extend your visit. Head for the village of **Carranza** on the Bilbao–Ramales road (or one hour by train on the Santander line out of Abando station; no public transport onwards to the caves). On the way, you pass through the small village of **SOPUERTA**, where there's a new **museum** dedicated to the area (summer Tues–Sat 10am–2pm & 5–7pm, Sun 10am–2pm; winter Tues–Sat 10am–2pm & 4–6pm, Sun 10am–2pm; free). Four kilometres west of Carranza on the main road, just past a curious thermal spa resort run by German monks at **MOLINAR**, where you can stay and eat (☎946 806 002; ④), a road heads 3km up the mountain to the tiny village of **Ranero** and the **Cuevas de Pozalagua** (Sat & Sun 11am–2pm & 4–7pm; €3; groups must ring ahead – ☎946 806 012). The caves are remarkable for their eccentric coral-like stalactites, although some of the formations have unfortunately been damaged by previous dynamiting in local quarries. The area abounds with other caves, including the **Torca del Carlista**, one of the world's largest cave chambers; you can visit its entrance, a big hole in the ground hidden somewhere in the landscape behind Pozalagua – if you can find it.

A few kilometres north of Carranza, in the *barrio* of Biañez, the **Parque Ecologico Bizkaia** (Sat & Sun 11am–7pm; €1.80) is an unusual wildlife sanctuary which treats injured animals before, if possible, releasing them into the wild. It's a good place to see the native fauna, including brown bears from the Picos de Europa.

Vitoria and around

VITORIA (Gasteiz), the capital of Alava, crowns a slight rise in the heart of a fertile plain. Founded by Sancho el Sabio, King of Navarra, it was already a prosperous place by the time of its capture by the Castilian Alfonso VIII in 1200. Later, as the centre of a flourishing wool and iron trade, Vitoria became seriously rich, and the town still boasts an unusual concentration of Renaissance palaces and fine churches.

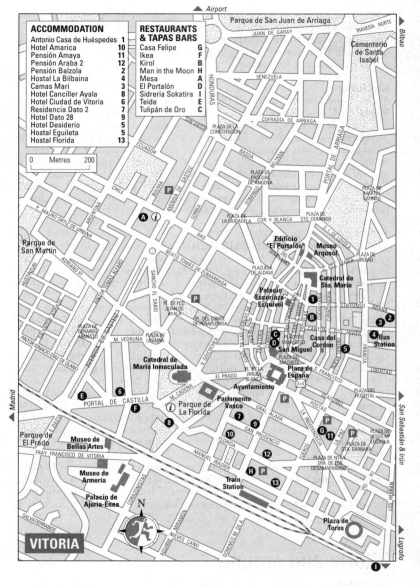

ACCOMMODATION
Antonio Casa de Huéspedes **1**
Hotel Amárica **10**
Pensión Amaya **11**
Pensión Araba 2 **12**
Pensión Balzola **2**
Hostal La Bilbaína **4**
Camas Mari **3**
Hotel Canciller Ayala **8**
Hotel Ciudad de Vitoria **6**
Residencia Dato 2 **7**
Hotel Dato 28 **9**
Hotel Desiderio **5**
Hostal Eguileta **5**
Hostal Florida **13**

RESTAURANTS & TAPAS BARS
Casa Felipe **G**
Ikea **F**
Kirol **B**
Man in the Moon **H**
Mesa **A**
El Portalón **D**
Sidreria Sokatira **I**
Teide **E**
Tulipán de Oro **C**

VITORIA

It's off the tourist circuit but by no means dull. There's a relaxed, easy-going attitude to life in comparison with the other Basque provinces, summed up in *Euskara* as *lasai* – perhaps best translated as "chill out". The old town is full of rowdy bars and *tabernas,* not to mention an abundance of excellent Basque restaurants, making it as pleasant a place as you'll find to pass a few days away from the crowds.

Arrival and information

The **bus station** is on c/los Herran, a two-minute walk (straight up the cobbled Cantón de San Francisco Javier) from the old town. The town's useful **turismo** (Mon–Sat 9am–1pm & 4–8pm, Sun 10am–2pm; ☎945 161 598 or 945 161 599, ⓕ945 161 105, ⓔturismo@vitoria-gasteiz.org) is at c/Dato, 11 (corner of c/General Alava), in the city centre straight up from the train station, with lots of colourful brochures and a good free map. The Alava regional turismo is at c/Ramón y Cajal (in the corner of Parque de la Florida; ☎943 131 321, ⓦwww.alava.net) a bit further away from the centre, is a second branch on the corner of Avenida de Gasteiz and c/de Chile (Mon–Sat 10am–7pm, Sun 11am–2pm).

The **post office**, c/de Postes, and most other services, including **banks**, are located in the central area around the Plaza de la Virgen Blanca.

Accommodation

The only time you might have trouble locating a room is during Vitoria's annual **jazz festival** in the third week of July, or during the town's summer **fiesta** (August 4–9). There are several budget **places to stay** near the train station, around the junction of c/de los Fueros and Ortiz de Zarate and near the bus station, but it's far nicer, if noisier, to stay in the old quarter near the action.

Budget options

Antonio Casa de Huéspedes, c/Cuchillería 66 ☎945 268 795. A rambling old building with friendly management, but a long hike to the bathrooms. ❷

Pensión Araba 2, c/Florida 25 ☎945 232 588. Centrally located *pensión*, offering four clean rooms with or without bath. ❸

Pensión Balzola, c/Prudencio María de Verástegui 6, 2° ☎945 256 279. Simple but clean, with doubles and singles; ring bell beside CH sign. ❷

Hostal La Bilbaina, c/Prudencio María de Verástegui 2 ☎945 254 400, ⓕ945 279 757. Comfortable rooms above a large *cafetería*, all with cable TV. ❸

Camas Mari, c/Prudencio María de Verástegui ☎945 277 303. Clean rooms with shared bath. ❸

Hostal Eguileta, c/Nueva Fuera 32 ☎945 251 700, ⓕ945 251 722. Cheaper annexe of the *Hotel Desiderio* opposite, offering reasonable doubles with washbasin. ❸

Moderate and expensive options

Hotel Amarica, c/Florida 11 ☎945 130 506. Popular modern hotel, offering two singles and eight doubles with bath and satellite TV. ❺

Pensión Amaya, c/La Paz 15 ☎945 255 497. No single rooms, but all have bath. ❹

Hotel Canciller Ayala, c/Ramón y Cajal 5 ☎945 130 000, ⓕ945 133 505. One of Vitoria's top hotels, situated on the edge of the Parque de la Florida. ❽

Hotel Ciudad de Vitoria, Portal de Castilla 8 ☎945 141 100, ⓕ945 143 616. Comfortable, upmarket accommodation. ❽

Residencia Dato 2, c/San Antoni 17 ☎945 130 400, ⓕ945 232 320. Bizarre decor – including a pair of plaster stags fighting in the lobby – but very comfortable and spacious. ❹

Hotel Dato 28, c/Dato 28 ☎945 147 230, ⓕ945 232 320. Excellent-value hotel on main pedestrian mall down from the station. There's a different colour scheme in every room, and colourful batik bedspreads. All rooms with bath and some have enclosed balcony. ❹

Hotel Desiderio, Colegio San Prudencio 2 ☎945 251 700, ⓕ945 521 722. Spacious rooms with bath and TV. ❺

Hostal Florida, c/Manuel Iradier 33 ☎945 260 675. Comfortable, well-furnished rooms on the first street down from the station towards the bullring. Has more expensive rooms with bath. ❹

The Town

The streets of the Gothic old town spread out like a spider's web down the sides of the hill, surrounded on level ground by a neater grid of later development. You'll get the feel of Vitoria simply by wandering through this old quarter. Although parts of it can be rather shabby, it is on the whole a harmonious

Fiesta de la Virgen Blanca

To experience Vitoria's annual festivities (4–9 August) is to see the good-natured Vitorians at their finest. On the first day of the festival you need to be in the Plaza de la Virgen Blanca with a blue and white festival scarf, a bottle of champagne, a cigar and wearing old clothes. At 6pm the umbrella-toting figure of Celedón appears from the church tower and flies through the air over the plaza. This is the signal to spray champagne everywhere (hence the old clothes), light the cigar and put on your scarf – which the real hard core don't take off until midnight on the 9th, when Celedón returns to his tower, signalling the end of the fiesta. In between the town is engulfed in a continuous party.

place, the graceful mansions and churches all built from the same greyish/gold stone. The porticoed **Plaza de España**, especially, is a gem, a popular location for early-evening strolling and drinking.

The heart of the old town is the old cathedral of **Santa María**, c/Correría 116, which is under serious reconstruction. Guided tours (Spanish only; €1.80; ☎945 255 135) take you through the different periods of construction, beginning in the thirteenth century when the cathedral was an integral part of the town's defences, and explain how Renaissance attempts to remodel the heavy Gothic structure resulted in serious structural defects – one look at the severely twisted arches that hold the whole thing up may send you running for the exit. The fourteenth century west doorway is superb, intricately and lovingly carved; seen from the level of the scaffolding, the faces of the saints appear distorted, since they were carved to be viewed from ground level.

Take time also to visit the church of **San Miguel** (Mon–Sat 11am–noon & 6.30–8pm, Sun 10.30am–2.30pm), just above the Plaza de España, which marks the southern end of the old town. Outside its door stands the fourteenth-century stone image of the Virgen Blanca, revered patron of the city. The streets below hold any number of interesting buildings, one of the finest being the **Escoriaza-Esquivel Palace** with its sixteenth-century Plateresque portal, on c/Fray Zacarías.

Behind the cathedral, down the hill on the left, the **Portalón** is the most impressive of the surviving trading houses of Renaissance Vitoria, its dusty red brick and wooden beams and balconies in marked contrast to the golden stone of the rest of the town. Today it is an extremely good, but expensive restaurant (see below). Over the road you'll find the province's **Museo Arqueológico** at c/Correria 116 (Tues–Fri 11am–2pm & 4–6pm, Sat 10am–2pm, Sun 11am–2pm; free). An annexe of this museum houses the unusual **Museo de Naipes** (same opening times; free), with over 6000 exhibits of playing cards from all corners of the globe. Southwest of the centre, on the attractive, pedestrianized, tree-lined Paseo de Fray Francisco, is the **Museo de Bellas Artes** (same opening times; free), which has a substantial collection of works by Spanish and Basque contemporary artists including Miró and Picasso. Nearby, the **Museo de Armería**, Paseo de Fray Francisco 3 (same opening times; free), features imaginative displays of medieval weapons and suits of armour.

Eating and drinking

The streets of the **old town** – particularly c/Cuchillería, c/Pintorería, c/Hurrería and c/Zapatería – are lined with lively **bars**, **tabernas** and **bodegas**, differentiated only by music and perhaps decor. Each, however, manages to spill onto the narrow pavements at night. For a good selection of restaurants and tapas bars head for the **casco histórico** to sample a selection of Basque dishes. Further down, on the pedestrianized section of c/Dato, you'll find a variety of bars and cafés with charming terraces which offer a quieter ambiance. Equally pleasant are the outdoor cafés of Plaza de España and those on the other pedestrian thoroughfares in the lower section of the new town.

Casa Felipe, c/Fueros 28 ☏945 134 554. Reasonably priced restaurant specializing in local dishes.

Ikea, Portal de Castilla 27 ☏945 144 747. Expensive, fashionable spot serving good Basque food. Closed Sun night & Mon.

Kirol, c/Cuchillería. This café-bar has an amazing selection of *raciones*, including – for the brave – deep-fried pig's ear.

Man in the Moon, c/Manuel Iradier. Desperately craving real ale in Vitoria? Very good English brew-pub with live jazz on Thursdays.

Mesa, c/Chile 1 ☏945 228 494. Basque specialities for around €21 a head and a good-value *menú* for €10.80. Closed Wed.

Restaurante Poliki, c/Manuel Iradier. Good-value *menu del día* for €7.80.

El Portalón, c/Correría 15 ☏945 142 755. Expensive restaurant specializing in traditional Basque cooking, set in beautiful 16th-century surroundings. Closed Sun.

Sidreria Sokatira, c/Las Trianas 15 ☏945 140 440. The most authentic *sidrería* in town. Often booked out with a party atmosphere at weekends.

Teide, Avda. de Gasteiz 61 ☏945 221 023. Solid Basque cuisine at moderate prices.

El Tulipan de Oro, c/Correría, two doors down from El Portalón. Serves *chorizo* flambéed at the bar over pig-shaped alcohol burners.

Around Vitoria

Attractive though the town is, a significant part of Vitoria's charm is the beauty of the surrounding **countryside**. Almost every hamlet of this once-rich farming territory has something of interest: an old stone mansion proudly displaying the family coat of arms, a lavishly decorated church, or a farmhouse raised Swiss-style on stilts.

A few kilometres to the west of Vitoria, a popular day-trip is to the village of **MENDOZA**, dominated by a fortified tower-house now established as the **Museo de Heraldica** (summer Tues–Fri 11am–2pm & 4–7.30pm, Sat & Sun 10am–2.30pm; winter Tues–Sun 11am–2.30pm; free), which contains a fascinating collection of coats of arms of the Basque nobility through the ages and an exhibition of the history of the principal clans and their often bloody feuds.

The **Embalse de Ulibarri** to the northeast of Vitoria is a large scenic reservoir very popular with the locals; the waterside villages of Gamboa-Ullibarri and Landa (both served by three buses daily) make a pleasant retreat on a hot summer's day.

To the east, on the **Llanada Alavesa** (Plain of Alava) are some of the best-preserved villages of inland Euskal Herria, all served by a twice-daily bus from Vitoria. With your own transport, take the A3012 off the main N1 *autovía* towards the village of Narvaja. From here, the road continues to **ZAL-DUONDO**, one of the highlights of the area, with a very good **museum** of local ethnography (Sat 5.30–7pm, Sun noon–2pm), which is housed in the sixteenth-century Palacio de los Lazárragas; look out for the heraldic crest over the main door, one of the most elaborate in the País Vasco. Zalduondo, although tiny, is famous for its traditional **carnaval** celebrations, where a Guy Fawkes-like figure, "Markitos", is ritually tried and then burned as a scapegoat for the misfortunes of the past year. From Zalduondo it's a pleasant 3km walk to **ARAÍA**, from where a branch of the Camino de Santiago leads to the San Adrián tunnel and its refuge (see p.476).

The main town on the plain, **SALVATIERRA**, situated on the Vitoria–Pamplona rail line, makes a good base for exploration. The old walled quarter rises above the countryside offering splendid views, and the Gothic church of Santa María is visible for miles around. At the other end of town, in the Plaza de San Juan, there's a **turismo** (T 945 312 535, W www.jet.es/touragurain), opposite which is a *fonda* attached to the *Bar Merino* (T 945 300 052; ❸); the town's other *fonda* is at c/Mayor 53 (❷). The town also has a convent whose nuns make and sell their own pastry.

South of Vitoria lies the wine-growing district of **Rioja Alavesa** and its town of **LAGUARDIA**, which is served by regular buses from Vitoria. If you're driving, don't miss stopping at the *Balcon de la Rioja*, a viewpoint 35km south of Vitoria, with magnificent views over the plain. Laguardia has a useful **turismo**, c/Sancho Abarca (Mon–Fri 10am–2pm & 4–6.30pm, Sat 10am–2pm, Sun 10.45am–2pm; T 941 600 845, W www.laguardia-alava.com), with a free map of the town as well as information on the many *bodegas* in the area – visits usually require a phone call beforehand. *Bodegas Palacio*, just out of town on the A3210 to Elciego, however, has scheduled tours (11.30am and 1.30pm Mon to Fri; just turn up).

Laguardia itself is an interesting old walled town of cobbled streets and historic buildings, entered through the Puerta de San Juan. The turismo has keys to the church of Santa María de los Reyes with its ornately carved Gothic doorway. One of the best places to **stay** is *Larretxori*, c/Portal de Páganos (T & F 941 600 763; ❹), a small *agroturismo* in the old town. You can also stay at one of the two *hostales* on the main road: *Pachico Martínez*, c/Sancho Abarca 20 (T 941 600 009, F 941 600 005; ❺), and *Marixa*, c/Sancho Abarca (T & F 941 600 165; ❺). If you're looking for a place to **eat**, *La Muralla*, Paganos 42, and *Los Rojillos*, c/Mayor 57, both serve a good *menú del día* for under €6.

The whole Rioja Alavesa area is great to explore (with your own transport): rolling countryside with sleepy villages like Elciego, Samaniego and Labastida, *bodegas* and farmhouses. Ask at the turismo in Laguardia (see above) for more information or check out the websites W www.laguardia-alva.com and W www.alvaturismo.com.

Pamplona and around

PAMPLONA (Iruña) has been the capital of Navarra since the ninth century, and long before that was a powerful fortress town defending the northern approaches to Spain at the foothills of the Pyrenees. Even now it has something of the appearance of a garrison city, with its hefty walls and elaborate pentagonal citadel. With a long history as capital of an often semi-autonomous state, Pamplona has plenty to offer around its old centre, the *casco antiguo* – enticing churches, a beautiful park, the massive citadel – and it's an enjoyable place to be throughout the year. But for anyone who has been here during the thrilling week of the **Fiestas de San Fermín**, a visit at any other time can only be an anticlimax.

San Fermín

From midday on July 6 until midnight on July 14 the city gives itself up entirely to riotous nonstop celebration. The centre of the festivities is the **encierro**, or the running of the bulls, which draws tourists from all over the world, but this has become just one aspect of a massive fair along with bands, parades and dancing in the streets 24 hours a day. You could have a great time here for a week without ever seeing a bull, but even if you are vehemently opposed to bullfighting, the *encierro* – in which the animals decisively have the upper hand – is a spectacle not to miss.

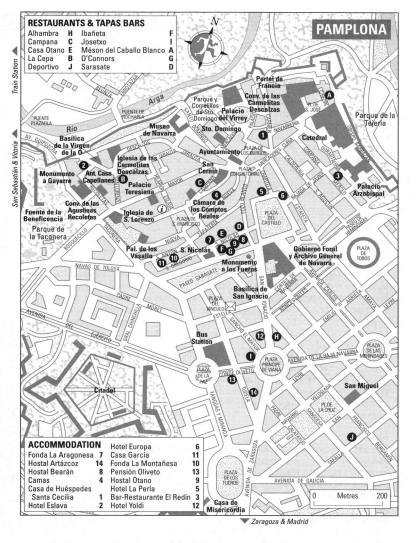

PAMPLONA

RESTAURANTS & TAPAS BARS

Alhambra	H	Ibañeta	F
Campana	C	Josetxo	I
Casa Otano	E	Méson del Caballo Blanco	A
La Cepa	B	O'Connors	G
Deportivo	J	Sarasate	D

ACCOMMODATION

Fonda La Aragonesa	7	Hotel Europa	6
Hostal Artázcoz	14	Casa García	11
Hostal Bearán	8	Fonda La Montañesa	10
Camas	4	Pensión Oliveto	13
Casa de Huéspedes		Hostal Otano	9
Santa Cecilia	1	Hotel La Perla	5
Hotel Eslava	2	Bar-Restaurante El Redín	3
		Hotel Yoldi	12

0   Metres   200

Zaragoza & Madrid

Six bulls are released each morning at eight (traditionally it was an hour earlier, so that the festival started on the seventh hour of the seventh day of the seventh month) to run from their corral near the Plaza Santo Domingo to the bullring. In front, around, and occasionally under them run the hundreds of locals and tourists who are foolish or drunk enough to test their daring against the horns. It was Hemingway's *The Sun Also Rises* that really put "Los San Fermines" on the map and the area in front of the Plaza de Toros has been renamed Plaza Hemingway by a grateful council. His description of it as "a damned fine show" still attracts Americans by the thousands. No amount of

San Fermín – the facts

Accommodation and security

Don't expect to find **accommodation** during the fiesta unless you have booked well in advance – the town is packed to the gills, and most rooms double in price. However, the turismo opposite the bullring fills with women willing to let **rooms** for the night at exorbitant prices. If you have no luck, accept that you're going to sleep on the ramparts, in the park or plaza (along with hundreds of others), and deposit your valuables and luggage at the bus station on c/Conde Oliveto – it's inexpensive, and you can have daily access (this fills early in the week, too – hang around and be insistent). There are also showers here.

Probably the **best plan**, though, is not to stay here at all: find a room somewhere else (Vitoria or Estella for instance), get plenty of sleep, leave your luggage there, and arrive in Pamplona by bus, staying as long as you can survive on naps in the park before escaping for some rest and a clean-up. You can always come back again. The first few days are best – by the end the place is getting pretty filthy.

Alternatively, there's a **campsite**, *Ezcaba* (T 948 330 315 or 948 331 665), 7km out of town on the road to France. You have to be there a couple of days before the fiesta to get a place. Facilities include good toilets and showers but they can't really handle the numbers during San Fermín – be prepared for long queues or for going "primitive", and bear in mind that the shop is only really well stocked in the drinks department. The main bonus is that security is tight – admission is by pass only and there's a guard who patrols all night. For the period of the fiesta there is a **free campsite**, by the river just below *Ezcaba*. Security is doubtful, however. The bus service, which goes to all the campsites, is poor (about five a day, first at 6am, last at 1am), but it's easy to hitch or, more expensively, get a lift on one of the tour buses that stay at the official campsite (they leave in time to see the *encierro*).

Wherever you sleep, keep an eye on everything you have with you – there's a very high rate of **petty crime** during the festival; cars and vans are broken into with alarming frequency and people are often robbed as they sleep, occasionally with violence. Several **banks** and a **post office** are open mornings during the festival, so changing travellers' cheques is no problem. Note that everything is closed over the weekend.

El Encierro

To watch the *encierro* it's essential to arrive early (about 6am) – crowds have already formed an hour before it starts. The best **vantage points** are near the starting point around the Plaza Santo Domingo or on the wall leading to the bullring. If possible, get a spot on the outer of the two barriers – don't worry when the one in front fills up and blocks your view, as all these people will be moved on by the police before the run. The event divides into two parts: firstly there's the actual running of the bulls, when the object is to run with the bull or whack it with a rolled-up newspaper. It can be difficult to see the bulls amid all the runners but you'll sense the sheer terror and excitement down on the ground; just occasionally this spreads to the watching crowd if a bull manages to breach the wooden safety barriers. Then there's a separate event after the bulls have been through the streets, when bullocks with padded horns are let loose on the crowd in the bullring. If you watch the actual running, you won't be able to get into the bullring (too many people), so go on two separate mornings to see both things. For the bullring you have to arrive at about 6am to get the free lower seats. If you want to pay for a seat higher up buy from the ticket office outside, not from the touts inside, who will rip you off. On Sunday you have to pay.

We advise against it, but if you do decide to **run**, remember that although it's probably less dangerous than it looks, at least one person gets seriously injured (sometimes killed) every year. Find someone who knows the ropes to guide you through the first time, and don't try any heroics; bulls are weighed in tonnes and have very sharp horns. Don't get trapped hiding in a doorway and don't get between a scared bull and the rest of the pack. Traditionally women don't take part, though more and more are doing so; if you do, it's probably best to avoid any officials, who may try to remove you. A glass of *pacharán*, the powerful local liqueur, is ideal for a dose of courage.

The only official way in is at the starting point, Plaza Santo Domingo, entered via Plaza San Saturnino; shortly before the start the rest of the course is cleared, and then at a few minutes before eight you're allowed to make your way along the course to your own preferred starting point (you should walk the course beforehand to get familiar with it). To mark the start, two rockets are fired, one when the bulls are released, a second when they are all out (it's best if these are close together, since the bulls are far safer if they're running as a herd rather than getting scared individually). As soon as the first goes you can start to run, though if you do this you'll probably arrive in the ring well before the bulls and be booed for your trouble; if you wait a while you're more likely to get close to the bulls. Although there are plenty of escape points, these are only for use in emergency – if you try to get out prematurely you'll be shoved back.

Other events

There are plenty of other hazardous things to do in Pamplona, especially once the atmosphere has got the better of a few people's judgement. Many people (especially tourists) have fun hurling themselves from the fountain in the centre of town and from surrounding buildings (notably *La Mesillonera* – the mussel bar), hoping their friends will catch them below. Needless to say, several people each year are not caught by their drunken pals.

Other events include **music** from local bands nightly from midnight in the bars and at Plaza del Castillo, continuing until about 4am in the fairground on the Avda. de Bayona, which is where local political groupings and other organizations have their stands. There are **fireworks** every evening in the citadel (about 11pm), and a **funfair** on the open ground beside it. Competing **bands** stagger through the streets all day playing to anyone who'll listen. If things calm down a bit you can sunbathe, take a shower, catch up on sleep and even swim at the public **swimming pool** outside the walls below the Portal de Zumalacárregui.

Bullfights take place daily at 6.30pm, with the bulls that ran that morning. Tickets are expensive (about €12–72), and if you have no choice but to buy from the touts, wait until the bullfight has begun, when you can insist on paying less (the price drops with each successive killing). You can also buy tickets the day before from the ticket office in Plaza de Toros (opens 8am), but be prepared to queue. At the end of the week (midnight, July 14) there's a mournful candlelit procession, the **Pobre De**, at which the festivities are officially wound up for another year.

If you're hooked on danger, many **other Basque towns** have fiestas which involve some form of *encierro*. Among the best are Tudela (July 24–28), Estella (first weekend in August, and one of the few that has no official ban on women participants), Tafalla (mid-Aug) and Ampuero in Cantabria (Sept 7–8).

outsiders, though, could outdo the locals in their determination to have a good time, and it's an indescribably exhilarating event in which to take part.

Arrival and information

Although Pamplona is a sizeable city, the old centre is remarkably compact – nothing you're likely to want to see is more than ten minutes from the main **Plaza del Castillo**. The **train station** is on Avenida San Jorge; bus #9 runs every ten minutes from here to the citadel end of the Paseo de Sarasate, a few minutes' walk from the Plaza del Castillo. There's a handy central RENFE ticket office at c/Estella 8 (Mon–Fri 9.30am–2pm & 4.30–7.30pm, Sat 9.30am–1pm; ☎948 227 282). The **bus station** is more central, on c/Conde Oliveto just in front of the citadel: schedules are confusing, given the number of companies operating from here – check the timetable posted at the station, or pick up one at the helpful **turismo** (summer daily 10am–7pm; winter Mon–Fri 10am–2pm & 4–7pm, Sat 10am–2pm; ☎948 206 540, ☎948 207 034) at c/Eslava 1, at the corner of Plaza San Francisco. The staff will also arrange accommodation, including advance bookings if you intend to strike out into the Pyrenees. During San Fermín, a municipal information bus also operates (10am–2pm & 5–8pm). Daily updates on the festivities are posted on ⓦwww.sanfermin.com.

Banks are scattered throughout the central area, with much-restricted, morning-only hours during the fiesta – one that also opens in the afternoons (4–6pm) is the Caja de Ahorros de Navarra in c/Roncesvalles. There's a central **post office** (Mon–Fri 8am–9pm, Sat 9am–7pm) on c/Estella, next to the RENFE office. A **laundry** (in case your clothes have borne the brunt of the festivities) can be found at c/de Descalzos, a couple of minutes' walk from the Plaza de San Francisco.

Accommodation

Most of the budget **fondas** and **hostales** are in c/San Nicolás and c/San Gregorio, off the Plaza del Castillo. Even outside San Fermín, when prices can double or triple, rooms fill up quickly in summer, and it might be easier to accept that you'll have to pay a little more to avoid the hassle of trudging around. If you want to continue looking, the streets around the cathedral, across the Plaza del Castillo, yield other possibilities. Further away from the Plaza del Castillo and the old town, there are several *hostales* in the more modern, yet not so interesting, central area.

Budget options

Fonda La Aragonesa, c/San Nicolás 32 ☎948 223 428. Reasonable *fonda* offering doubles with washbasin. ❷

Hostal Navarra, c/Tudela 9, 2°☎948 225 164, ☎948 223 426. Well-established *hostal* going back more than forty years; all rooms have en-suite facilities. ❺

Camas, c/Nueva 24, 1 ☎948 227 825. Next to the upmarket *Hotel Maisonnave*; well-furnished doubles and singles. ❸

Casa de Huéspedes Santa Cecilia, c/Navarrería 17, 1° ☎948 222 230. Spacious rooms in a former palace right by the fountain much splashed in during San Fermín. The place looks foreboding with a massive heavy door and grey facade, but the owner is extremely welcoming. ❸

Fonda La Montañesa, c/San Gregorio 2 ☎948 224 380. Doubles and singles; nothing very special. ❷

Moderate and expensive options

Hostal Bearán, c/San Nicolás 25 ☎ & ☎948 223 428. Comfortable, clean *hostal* offering rooms with TV. ❺

Hotel Eslava, Plaza Virgen de la O 7 ☎948 222 270, ☎948 225 157. Cosy, comfortable hotel run by the Eslava family in a quiet corner of the old city – views from balconies overlooking the plaza. Singles and doubles, with a bar in the basement. ❼

Hotel Europa, c/Espoz y Mina 11 ☎948 221 800, ☏948 229 235. Just off Plaza del Castillo; a good three-star hotel with a fine restaurant. ❼
Casa García, c/San Gregorio 12 ☎948 223 893. Double rooms without bath above a restaurant, with very reasonable full-board rate. ❹
Pensión Oliveto, Avda. de Conde Oliveto 3 ☎948 249 321, Just across the road from the bus station; nice rooms without bath but with satellite TV and plenty of hot water. ❹
Hostal Otano, c/San Nicolás 5 ☎948 227 036, ☏948 212 012. Well-run *hostal* above bar and restaurant which have been in the family since 1929. The restaurant serves a popular *menú del día* for €7.80. ❹

Hotel La Perla, Plaza del Castillo 1 ☎948 227 706. Great character; a few rooms have balcony overlooking the street (prices triple during San Fermín). Ernest Hemingway stayed in Room 217. ❼
Bar-Restaurante El Redín, c/Mercado 5 ☎948 222 182. Nicely located in the street by the market, within a stone's throw of the start of the *encierro*. Mostly double rooms with a bar-restaurant downstairs; full board available. ❹
Hotel Yoldi, Avda. de San Ignacio 11 ☎948 224 800, ☏948 212 045, ⓦwebs.navarra.net/hyoldi. This is where the bullfighters and VIPs from the *taurino* world stay during San Fermín. Garage parking. ❽

The Town

The **Plaza del Castillo**, a tree-lined square ringed with fashionable cafés, is the centre of the town and of much of its activity. The narrow streets of the former *Judería* fill the area to the south and west, towards the city walls by the cathedral; virtually the only trace of a large Jewish community that thrived here before the persecutions and expulsions of the Inquisition. From the opposite side of the square, c/San Nicolás runs down towards the citadel and the more modern area of the city to the east. It's in c/San Nicolás and its continuation, c/San Gregorio, that you'll find most of the *hostales* and *fondas,* a number of excellent small restaurants and loads of raucous little bars.

The **Catedral de Santa María** (Mon–Fri 10.30am–6pm, Sat 10.30am–1.30pm, mid-Sept to mid-July closed 1.30–4pm; €2.40) is basically Gothic, built over a period of 130 years from the late fourteenth to the early sixteenth century but with an unattractive facade added in the eighteenth. It doesn't look promising, but the interior, containing the tomb of Carlos III and Eleanor in the centre of the nave, and the ancient *Virgen de los Reyes* above the high altar, is fine, and the cloister is magnificent: don't miss the many sculpted doorways, particularly the *Puerta de la Preciosa*, and the chapel with a lovely star vault, built by a fourteenth-century bishop to house his own tomb. You enter the cathedral from c/Dormitalería, via the **Museo Diocesano**, a notable collection of Navarran sacred art housed in two superb buildings, the refectory and the kitchen – both worth seeing in their own right.

Behind the cathedral is one of the oldest parts of the city, an area known as **La Navarrería**. Here you'll find the best section of the remaining **city walls** with the Baluarte de Redín and Portal de Zumalacárregui (or de Francia) looking down over a loop of the Río Arga. If you head out through the gate, paths lead down to the river from where you get the full force of the impregnability of these defences. Follow the inside of the walls and you'll come to the **Museo de Navarra** (Tues–Sat 10am–2pm & 5–7pm, Sun & holidays 11am–2pm; €1.80) in the magnificent old hospital building on c/Santo Domingo. Inside is displayed material on the archeology and history of the old kingdom of Navarra, along with some good mosaics and an art collection that includes a portrait of the Marqués de San Adrián by Goya. Heading back to the plaza via c/Santo Domingo and the Plaza Consistorial you'll pass the **market** and the fine Baroque **ayuntamiento**.

There's much more to be seen within the old town, with ancient churches and elegant buildings on almost every street. In particular, though, take time to wander around the parks and gardens on Avenida Ejército that surround and include the ruinous **Citadel**, with its views over the new town, and a gallery (Tues–Sat 11.30am–1.30pm & 6–8pm, Sun 11am–2pm; free). From here you can follow the line of the old walls through the **Parque de la Taconera** and down to the river by an alternative route.

Eating and drinking

For good, inexpensive **menús**, and a wide range of **tapas** and *bocadillos*, head for the streets around c/Major, in particular c/San Lorenzo. The elegant *Café Iruña*, on Plaza del Castillo, is the place to sit over a leisurely coffee and take in the action, or try the more modern yet equally enjoyable *Café Niza* opposite the turismo on c/Duque de Ahumada. For **breakfast** in peaceful surroundings and a chance to read the paper, there's no better place than *Café Alt Wien*, known to the locals as *El Vienés*, in the Jardines de la Taconera – it can get crowded with families in the afternoon.

Alhambra, c/Bergamín 7. Good for local dishes, especially the stuffed lamb. Closed Sun.

Campana, c/Campana 12. Serves one of the best *menús* in town, near the church of San Saturino.

Casa Otano, c/San Nicolás. Popular *menú del día* at this restaurant which excels in *cocina Navarra*. Closed Sun night.

La Cepa, c/San Lorenzo 2. Fine selection of tapas and *bocadillos*.

Deportivo, c/Tafalla 34. Reasonably priced, tasty home cooking. Closed Thurs.

Ibañeta, c/San Nicolás 15. Basic, but good-value

dishes at this lively restaurant. Closed Sun night & Mon.

Josetxo, Plaza Príncipe de Viana ☏ 948 222 097. One of the best – and priciest – restaurants in town.

Méson del Caballo Blanco, c/Redín. Lots of character at this surprisingly inexpensive restaurant serving up *raciones* and traditional local cooking. Evenings only.

O'Connors, Paseo Sarasate 22. A pub serving a strange but excellent mixture of Irish and Spanish tapas. Very popular with locals.

Sarasate, c/San Nicolás 19. Very decent vegetarian restaurant.

Around Pamplona: the Sierra de Aralar

Some 30km to the northwest of Pamplona, the wooded **Sierra de Aralar** is a good hiking destination, with paths of all grades, mostly well marked, criss-crossing the sierra past prehistoric dolmens, waterfalls and caves. The sierra is also home to Navarra's oldest and most spectacularly situated church: the Sanctuario de San Miguel in Excelsis.

The village of **LEKUNBERRI**, 25km from Pamplona on the A5 Pamplona–San Sebastián motorway, is the best place to go for maps and information about the area. Its old railway station at c/Plazaola 21 has been converted into a helpful **turismo** (Mon–Sat 10am–2pm & 4–7pm, Sun 10am–2pm; ☏948 507 204, ✉oit.lekunberri@cfnavarra.es). From the doorstep you can set off along the former train tracks, now transformed into the picturesque Vía Verde de Plazaola ("**green way**") leading south to Pamplona and north into Gipuzkoa. The route is over 90km in all, mostly in poor condition, following the tracks all the way; the first 5km north from Lekunberri, however, are excellent, after which the track enters the 2.7km tunnel of Uitzi. Bring a torch (or follow the alternative path) to continue to the larger mountain village of Leitza, 8km further north, which has an impressive assortment of Basque *caserios* (houses).

Sanctuario de San Miguel in Excelsis

From Lekunberri, a road heads 17km up the mountainside through the beech and birch forest to the **Sanctuario de San Miguel in Excelsis**, passing on its way after 12km the *Casa Forestal (Guardetxea)*, a popular starting-point for hikers, which offers hearty home-cooked meals (lunch from €7.20). At the top (1237m), above a massive car park and a rather ugly bar, is the small, squat church of San Miguel (daily 9.30am–8pm), built mainly between 783 and 940, with some later additions. Although unimpressive from the outside, San Miguel's interior is beautifully simple and austere. The only ornamentation is in the shape of eight carved capitals, six of them in the tiny twelfth-century central chapel. The church houses two wonderful medieval enamel works: the shrine of the archangel in the central chapel, and the stunning twelfth-century gilt copper *retablo*, depicting a rosily smiling Madonna and Child flanked by Evangelists and Apostles. Not surprisingly, the sanctuary is an extremely popular pilgrimage destination – half the villages in Navarra have an annual *romería* to San Miguel, many centring around the saint's day of September 29.

Another route up to the church starts at the tiny village of **Arakil**, on the main train and bus routes between Vitoria and Pamplona. The single-track road is a tough but exhilarating climb whether on foot or by car, with breathtaking views across the valley and vultures circling overhead and below.

Practicalities

The Lekunberri area is not strong on **accommodation**: your best bet is the *Hostal Ayestarán*, c/Aralar 22 (☎ & ☎948 504 127; ❺), which also has a good-value restaurant. In nearby Aldatz, 2km away, there's an excellent *casa rural, Uhaldeko Borda* (☎948 396 013; ❹). Most of the other villages around have at least one *casa rural*, all of which can be booked from the turismo in Lekunberri. In Leitza, the new *Hostal Musunzar*, c/Elbarren 14 (☎948 510 607; ❹), has clean and spacious en-suite rooms with TV.

Buses to Lekunberri from Pamplona are operated by Roncalesa (☎948 222 079), Muguiroarra (☎948 227 172), and Leizaran-Mariaezcurrena (☎948 224 015); the last of these companies runs services via Lekunberri and Leitza to Santesteban on the Pamplona–Irún highway.

Southern Navarra

South of Pamplona, the country changes rapidly; the mountains are left behind and the monotonous plains so characteristic of central Spain begin to open out. The people are different, too – more akin to their southern neighbours than to the Basques of the north. There are regular bus and train services south to **Tudela**, the second city of Navarra, passing through **Tafalla** and **Olite**, once known as the "Flowers of Navarra", though little remains of their former glory. Many attractive smaller towns and villages dot the area, most looking as if not much has happened in them for the last five hundred years.

Tafalla

TAFALLA, 35km south of Pamplona, is a shabby provincial town apparently left behind by modern Spain. If you find yourself here, it's worth going to the parish church of **Santa María**, where there's a huge *retablo*, one of the finest in Spain. It was carved by Juan de Ancheta, among the most recognized of the Basque country's artists. The *retablo* was started in 1853 and completed after the artist's death in 1858 by his disciple Pedro Gonzalez de San Pedro.

There are a couple of overpriced places to **stay**: *Pensión Arotza*, Plaza de Navarra 3 (☎948 700 716; ❺; reception in *Bar Tubal*), and *Hostal Tafalla* (☎948

700 300, ⓕ948 703 052; ❼) on the main Pamplona–Zaragoza road, next to the service station.

Olite

OLITE is a more attractive proposition. Now hardly more than a village, it boasts a magnificent **castle** (April–June & Sept 10am–2pm & 4–7pm, July & Aug 10am–2pm & 4–8pm, Oct–March 10am–2pm & 4–6pm; €2.40) which was once the residence of the kings of Navarra. A ramble of turrets, keeps and dungeons straight out of Walt Disney, it is slowly being restored, and part of the building already houses a *parador*. There are also two gorgeous old churches, Romanesque **San Pedro** and Gothic **Santa María**, the latter with a superb carved *retablo*.

Olite's central square, Plaza Carlos III, sits atop a series of impressive **medieval galleries** (Mon–Fri 10am–2pm & 4–7pm, Sat & Sun 10am–2pm; free), whose existence was a local legend for centuries before they were unearthed in the 1980s. Their original purpose is still a mystery, although it is thought they could have been a market or crypt, or even part of a secret tunnel linking Olite with Tafalla. Today they house a somewhat random display on the town's history as well as Olite's **turismo** (same hours; ☎948 741 703, ⓦwww.animsa.es/navarra/olite), although there are plans to move the latter elsewhere because of the damp.

Olite has its own *encierro* during the exuberant Fiesta del Patronales, 13–19 September, and there's a medieval festival during the week leading up to the saint's day of Olite's patron, the "Virgin of the Cholera" on 26 August, which commemorates the town's salvation from the cholera epidemic of 1885.

Accommodation in Olite is generally expensive. Apart from the *Parador Príncipe de Viana*, Plaza de los Teobaldos 2 (☎948 740 000, ⓕ948 740 201; ❽), there are a couple of other pricey hotels: *Casa Zanito*, Rúa Mayor 16 (☎948 740 002, ⓕ948 712 087; ❻), among the old streets, is the more atmospheric, but frequently full during the summer, while *Hotel Carlos III el Noble*, Plaza Carlos III (☎948 740 644; ❺), has amazing stained-glass *miradores* and also offers a popular and good-value *menú* for €7.80. If you want to camp, head for *Camping Ciudad de Olite* two kilometres out of town on the Tafalla–Peralta Road (☎948 712 443; open all year).

Ujué

East of Tafalla and Olite in the direction of Sangüesa, a winding road branches off to the right at San Martín de Unx (a good place to stock up on wine from the local *bodega*), to the hilltop village of **UJUÉ** – one of the real jewels of Navarra. It's a perfect medieval defensive village perched up on the terraced hillside above the harsh, arid landscape and dominated by the thirteenth-century Romanesque church of **Santa María** (daily 10am–8pm), where the heart of King Carlos II of Navarra is supposedly preserved inside the altar. The church has Gothic additions dating from the fourteenth century and, from its balconied exterior, the view extends over the whole southern Navarra region of La Ribera. The main doorway contains some intricate sculptures depicting the Last Supper and the Three Kings. Ujué is the destination of one of Navarra's most notable *romerías* (pilgrimages), held on the first Sunday after St Mark's (April 25), when half the populace of Tafalla, among others, walk through the night to celebrate Mass here in commemoration of their town's reconquest from the Moors in 1043.

From the main square, a couple of pedestrianized cobbled streets plunge down to another beautiful little square and a *casa rural*, *Casa Isolina Jurio* (☎948 739 037; ❹); a second smaller one in the village, *Casa El Chófer* (☎948 739 011; ❹), also has a few rooms. There are at least ten *casa rurales* in the area, which can be booked through the turismo in Olite; ask here also about a guide and transport to the village from San Martín de Unx, as there is no public transport.

Tudela

The route south continues to **TUDELA** on the banks of the Ebro. On arrival, it seems as ugly a town as you could ever come across, but don't despair – a short walk down the main street takes you into the old town and an entirely different atmosphere. Around the richly decorated **Plaza de los Fueros** are a jumble of narrow lanes apparently little changed since the Moorish occupation of the city was ended by Alfonso I of Aragón in 1114. The twelfth-century **Colegiata de Santa Ana** is a fine, strong, Gothic construction. It has a rose window above the intricately carved alabaster west doorway which portrays a chilling vision of the Last Judgement. Inside there's an unusual *retablo* and some beautiful old tombs, while the Romanesque cloister has some deft primitive carvings, many badly damaged. The bizarre thirteenth-century **bridge** over the Ebro looks as if it could never have carried the weight of an ox cart, let alone seven centuries of traffic on the main road to Zaragoza.

There is a **turismo** on Plaza Vieja 1 (Mon–Sat 9am–3pm & 4–6pm, Sun 10am–2pm; ☎948 848 058), and a couple of pricey **hostales** on the main street through the new part of town: best value is *Hostal Remigio*, just off Plaza de los Fueros, at c/Gaztambide 4 (☎948 820 850, ⑤948 824 123; ④), which also has more expensive rooms with bath; *Delta*, Avda. Zaragoza 29 (☎948 821 400; ⑦), has rooms with TV and video; or try the *Casa de Huéspedes* at c/de Carniceras 13 (☎948 821 039; ②), above the *Restaurante La Estrella* in the old town. You'll find many other places to **eat and drink** around the Plaza de los Fueros; *Bar Arbella* is good for fresh *calamares fritos*.

The Pilgrim Route

The ancient **Pilgrim Route** to Santiago passed through Aragón (see p.623) and into Navarra just before Leyre, travelling through the province via **Sangüesa**, **Puente la Reina** (where it met an alternative route crossing the Pyrenees at Roncesvalles) and **Estella**, before crossing into Old Castile at Logroño.

The Camino de Santiago in Navarra

Following the European Parliament's decision to designate the **camino** Europe's first "cultural itinerary", Navarra has invested considerably in improving facilities along the route. There are around a dozen pilgrims' *hostales* within Navarra which bona fide pilgrims can use – to qualify you must show a letter of introduction from your parish church or town hall at the place where you plan to start the route (in Spain this is usually Roncesvalles or Somport, or the church of San Cernino or the archbishop's palace in Pamplona). You'll be given a "passport" as an accredited pilgrim which is then stamped at each *hostal* along the route. Most of the *hostales* have hot showers, some have kitchens and are either free or charge only a nominal €3 fee. A few of the *hostales* may be open only during the summer months, but regional turismos in Navarra can provide up-to-date details.

The route itself is clearly marked as long-distance footpath GR65. Long stretches do run alongside the main Pamplona–Estrella–Logroño road, but wherever possible the official walking route avoids major highways.

Yesa and the Monasterio de Leyre

The first stop for the pilgrims in Navarra is the **Monasterio de San Salvador de Leyre** (daily 10am–9pm), which stands amid mountainous country 4km from Yesa, on the main Pamplona–Jaca road, connected with both places by a daily **bus** in either direction. **YESA** has several **hostales**, the best being *El Jabalí* (☎948 884 042; ❸), on the main road, with a pool and restaurant.

From the village a good road leads up to Leyre, arriving at the east end of the monastery. Although the convent buildings are sixteenth to eighteenth century, the church is largely Romanesque; its tall, severe apses are particularly impressive. After languishing in ruins for over a century, it was restored and reoccupied by the Benedictines in the 1950s and now looks in immaculate condition. Inside, the crypt, with its sturdy little columns, can be illuminated by putting a coin in the slot. Try to catch a service if you can; the Benedictines here employ the Gregorian chant in their Masses and are well worth hearing.

The former pilgrims' guest house here is now run as a two-star **hotel**, the *Hospedería de Leyre* (☎948 884 100, ☎948 884 137; ❻), which, although far more expensive than staying in Yesa, is still a remarkable bargain. Men can stay at the monastery itself for a nominal fee, but anyone wanting to do this should phone ahead (☎948 884 011).

Javier

From Yesa it's only a few kilometres south to **JAVIER**, birthplace of San Francisco Xavier – one of the first Jesuits – and home to a fine **castle** (daily 10am–1pm & 4–7pm; free). Javier had nothing to do with the Pilgrim Route, but it is something of a place of pilgrimage in its own right, with a museum of the saint's life in the restored keep. Look out for the set of extraordinary demonic murals – recently discovered – depicting the Dance of Death.

It's a popular picnic spot and there's a **hotel** in the grounds, *Hotel Xavier* (☎948 884 006, ☎948 884 078; ❻), which has a good restaurant. Alternatively, try the cheaper *El Mesón*, Plaza de Javier (☎948 884 035, ☎948 884 226; ❺). Javier and Pamplona are connected by one daily **bus**.

Sangüesa

The Pilgrim Route proper next stops three kilometres away at **SANGÜESA,** a small, delightful town preserving many outstanding monuments, including several churches from the fourteenth century and earlier. See above all the south facade of the church of **Santa María Real** (at the far end of town beside the river), which has an incredibly richly carved doorway and sculpted buttresses: God, the Virgin and the Apostles are depicted amid a chaotic company of warriors, musicians, craftsmen, wrestlers and animals. Sangüesa is an enjoyable place simply to wander around. Many of its streets have changed little in centuries and aside from the churches – Romanesque Santiago is also lovely – there are some handsome mansions, the remains of a royal palace and a medieval hospital.

Sangüesa's helpful **turismo** is at Alfonte el Batallador 20 (Mon–Fri 10am–2pm & 4–7pm, weekends & holidays 10am–2pm; ☎948 860 329). Unfortunately, there's not much in the way of **accommodation**: the *Pensión Las Navas*, c/Alfonso el Batallador 7 (☎948 870 077; ❹), opposite the main bus stop, is the only convenient place to stay, though there's also a fairly fancy hotel, *Yamaguchi* (☎948 870 127, ☎948 870 700, ☎yamaguchi@interbook.net; ❻), on the road to Javier. If you want to camp, *Camping Cantolagua* (☎948 430 352, ☎camping.sanguesa@alva.net) is just outside town by the river, and has a great

△ San Fermín, Pamplona

swimming pool. Three **buses** daily run to and from Pamplona and one (leaving Sangüesa very early) goes to the Aragonese town of Sos del Rey Católico, 12km away.

Puente La Reina

Perhaps no town is more perfectly evocative of the days of the medieval pilgrimage than **PUENTE LA REINA**, 20km southwest of Pamplona. This is the meeting place of the two main Spanish routes: the Navarrese trail, via Roncesvalles and Pamplona, and the Aragonese one, via Jaca, Leyre and Sangüesa. From here onwards, all the pilgrims followed the same path to Santiago.

At the eastern edge of town, the **Iglesia del Crucifijo** (daily 9am–9pm) was originally a twelfth-century foundation of the Knights Templar, its porch decorated with scallop shells (the badge of the Santiago pilgrims). To one side is the former pilgrims' hospice, later in date, but still one of the oldest extant. In town, the tall buildings along c/Mayor display their original coats of arms, and there's another pilgrim church, Santiago (daily 9am–1pm & 5–8pm), whose Romanesque portal is sadly worn, but which has a notable statue of St James inside. The **bridge** at the end of the street gives the town its name. The finest medieval bridge in Spain, it was built at the end of the eleventh century by royal command and is still used by pedestrians and animals only – an ugly modern bridge has been constructed for vehicular traffic.

Accommodation in town is limited to *Hostal Puente*, Paseo de los Fueros (☎948 340 146; ❸), which is friendly, clean and serves good food, though it can be noisy. *Mesón del Peregrino* (☎948 340 075, ℉948 341 190; ❸), an ancient building with a modern pool, just out of town on the main road towards Pamplona, offers more luxury, or try next door at the *Hotel Jakue* (☎948 341 017, ℉948 341 120; ❼) for rooms of a good standard. There's a good **campsite**, *El Molino* (☎948 340604, ℉948 340 082; open all year) at **Mendigorría**, 5km south, with a large swimming pool. There are several places to **eat**, most near the main road which, thankfully, skirts the town. *La Conrada*, at Cerco Nuevo 77 (near *Hostal Puente*), has an excellent set menu for around €9, while *Sidrería Ilzarbe*, on c/Irundibea, offers delicious cider and tapas.

Estella

Twenty kilometres west lies **ESTELLA**, a town rich in monuments but surrounded by unattractive sprawl. During the nineteenth century this was the headquarters of the Carlists in the Civil Wars, and each May there is still a pilgrimage up a nearby mountain to honour the dead.

The centre of town, around **Plaza de los Fueros**, sits in a loop of the river Ega, but most of the interesting buildings are situated across the river in Barrio San Martín. Here on c/San Nicolás you'll find the twelfth-century **Palacio de los Reyes de Navarra**, Navarra's only large-scale Romanesque civil edifice, now open as an art gallery (Tues–Sat 11am–1pm & 5–7pm, Sun & holidays 11am–1pm; free) devoted to the Navarrese painter Gustave de Maeztu.

Estella has a wealth of churches, the interiors of which may only be visited just before or just after Mass (times vary, but normally Mon–Fri 7–8pm, Sun 11am–1pm), unless you're with a tour guide. Most are best seen from the outside, in any case. Particularly striking is the fortified pilgrimage church of **San Pedro de la Rúa**, just up the hill from the turismo, whose main doorway shows unmistakeable Moorish influence. From the former *ayuntamiento*, an elegant sixteenth-century building just opposite the Palacio, c/de la Rúa leads past many old merchants' mansions. Further along, past a stud farm, you reach the abandoned church of Santo Sepulcro with a carved fourteenth-century Gothic doorway. Cross the hump-backed bridge, take the first left, then right uphill, and you come to the church of **San Miguel**: not a terribly inspiring building in itself but with a north doorway that is one of the gems of the Pilgrim Route. Its delicate capitals are marvellous, as are the modelled reliefs of the *Three Marys at the Sepulchre* and *St Michael Fighting the Dragon*.

Practicalities

Estella's well-stocked **turismo** is next door to the Palacio de los Reyes de Navarra at c/San Nicolás 1 (April–Aug Mon–Sat 9am–8pm, Sun 10am–2pm; Sept Mon–Sat 10am–2pm & 4–7pm, Sun 10am–2pm; Oct–March Mon–Sat 10am–5pm, Sun 10am–2pm; ☏ & ℱ948 556 301, ℇoit.estella@cfnavarra.es); you can arrange to join a guided tour in English of the main monuments here (€3.60 per person, minimum 4 people) or else pick up a free street map and follow your own route.

If you want to **stay**, many of the budget places are located round the Plaza de los Fueros. *Pensión San Andrés*, c/Mayor 1 (☏948 554 158; ❹), is a good choice, while in the streets nearby several cheaper options include *El Volante*, c/Merkatondoa 2 (☏948 554 309; ❸), and *Fonda Izarra*, c/Calderería (☏948 550 678; ❸; closed Sept), which has a comfortable bar. For more comfort, head for *Hostal Cristina*, Baja Navarra 1 (☏948 550 450, ℱ948 550 772; ❺) or the clean and modern *Hotel Yerri*, Avda.Yerri, 35 (☏948 546 034, ℱ948 555 081; ❺). There's also a **casa rural**, *Casa Laguao* (☏948 520 203; ❸), 8km north in the village of Abarzuza, and a **campsite**, *Camping Lizarra* (☏948 551 733).

Estella has plenty of **bars**, many serving good-value *platos combinados*. If you're in the mood for local cuisine, try the *Casanova* at c/Fray Wenceslao de Oñate 7, which has a good weekday *menú* for €7.80, or the slightly pricier *Asador Astarriaga*, Plaza de los Fueros 12.

Buses operate to Pamplona (11 daily), Logroño (7 daily) and San Sebastián (4 daily).

Estella to Logroño

From Estella, the Pilgrim Route follows the main road to Logroño and there are a number of interesting stops. At **IRACHE**, near the village of Ayegui, there's a **Cistercian monastery** (Tues 9.30am–1.30pm, Wed–Fri 9.30am–1.30pm & 5–7pm, Sat & Sun 8.30am–1.30pm & 4–7pm), which boasts an ornate Plateresque cloister. Beside the adjacent **Museo de Vino** (Sat & Sun 10am–2pm & 4–8pm), principally a showroom for Bodega Irache, are two taps in the wall, ostensibly for use by pilgrims – out of one comes water and from the other, red wine. Seventeen kilometres further on is **LOS ARCOS**, whose handsome church of **Santa María** has a Gothic cloister which is open just before and just after Mass (Mon–Sat 8pm, Sun noon & 6pm). If you decide to **stay**, *Hostal Ezequiel* (☏948 640 296, ℱ948 640 278; ❹) is clean and comfortable, and has a special pilgrim rate; alternatively, *Hotel Monaco*, Plaza del Coso 22 (☏948 640 000; ❹) is a good bet, with en-suite rooms.

Of greater interest is **TORRES DEL RÍO**, 7km further still. This unpretentious village is built round the church of the **Holy Sepulchre**, a little octagonal building whose function is uncertain – it may have been a Knights Templar foundation or a funeral chapel. The names of the local women who look after the monument are posted on the wall of the church, and any one of them may be found to show visitors around (access at any reasonable time; €0.60). Inside it's a surprise to find that the dome is of Moorish inspiration.

VIANA, the last stop before the border and the place where Cesare Borgia died, is an attractive place with many beautiful Renaissance and Baroque palatial houses, in addition to the Gothic church of Santa María with its outstanding Renaissance carved porch. Logroño is only 10km away, but Viana's **pensión**, *La Granja*, c/Navarro Villoslada 19 (☎948 645 078; ❸), has comfortable rooms with bath. Viana also has a useful **turismo** on Plaza de los Fueros (Mon–Fri 10am–2pm & 4.45–8pm, Sat 10.15am–2pm; ☎948 446 302, Ⓦwww.animsa.es/navarra/viana).

The Pyrenees

The mountains of Navarra may not be as high as their neighbours to the east, but they're every bit as dramatic and far less developed. And there's not – as yet – a single ski lift in the province, though there's a busy nordic skiing centre at Belagoa. The historic **pass of Roncesvalles** is the major route northeast through the mountains from Pamplona, and always has been; it is celebrated in the *Song of Roland* and, more recently, by Jan Morris who called it "one of the classic passes of Europe and a properly sombre gateway into Spain". It was the route taken by countless pilgrims throughout the Middle Ages; Charlemagne's retreating army was decimated here by Basque guerrillas avenging the sacking of Pamplona; Napoleon's defeated armies fought a running battle along the pass as they fled Spain; and thousands of refugees from the Civil War made their escape into France along this narrow passage.

The beautiful Pyrenean valleys, particularly the **Valle de Baztán** due north of Pamplona, and the **Valle de Salazar** to the east, are a perfect place to relax, with the largest concentration of good-value **casas rurales** in the province. The Pyrenees really start to get serious at the top of the **Valle de Roncal**, where there's a large mountain refuge (the westernmost in the Spanish Pyrenees) and challenging hiking up to and along the karst ridges nearby.

Auritz-Burguete and Orreaga-Roncesvalles to France

Northeast of Pamplona, the N135 winds upwards and across two valleys until it reaches the neighbouring villages of **Auritz-Burguete** and **Orreaga-Roncesvalles**, about half an hour's walk apart. The surrounding rolling country is superb for gentle riverside strolls, or simply to sit back and admire. Beyond these villages, the road continues into France via the border settlement of **Luzaide-Valcarlos**.

Auritz-Burguete

AURITZ-BURGUETE, a typical Navarran Basque village straggling for a kilometre or so along its single street, has a pleasant atmosphere despite the through traffic, and if you've come on the daily bus from Pamplona you've little choice but to **stay** here, as it doesn't arrive until about 8pm. The best choice amongst the conventional lodgings is the *Hostal Burguete* at the north end of the main street (☎948 760 005; ❺), with its three echoing storeys of huge, spotless, squeaky-wood-floored rooms, most en suite. Hemingway stayed here in the early 1920s, and immortalized it in *Fiesta*; the room he occupied (no. 25, formerly no. 18), is still preserved much as he described it, save for discreetly placed photos of the great man. The four rooms of the *Hostal Juandeaburre* (☎948 760

078; ❸) at the south end of the high street are rather more basic, while directly opposite stands the charmless three-star *Hotel Loizu* (☎948 760 008, ☎948 790 444; ❻). Failing these, try one of the *casas rurales* for a more traditional feel: *Casa Loigorri* (☎948 760 016; ❸), *Casa Loperena* (☎948 760 068; ❸), above the **bank** (next-to-last one before the frontier), or *Casa Vergara* (☎948 760 044; ❹). There's also a **campsite**, *Urrobi* (☎948 760 200; April–Oct), 3km south of the village at Auritzberri-Espinal on the Pamplona road. **Eating** out, the *Loizu* has the best restaurant in town, with game- and meat-oriented meals for about €18; otherwise there's little to distinguish the cheaper, sustaining fare at the *Burguete*'s *comedor* from the *Txikipolit* across the way.

Orreaga-Roncesvalles

The few buildings at **ORREAGA-RONCESVALLES** are clustered around the Augustinian **Colegiata**, its echoing church and beautiful Gothic cloister somewhat spoiled by the abbey's glaring tin roofs and the swiveling tower-cranes overhead engaged in renovations. The *Sala Capitular* to one side of the cloister houses a prostrate statue of Sancho VII el Fuerte (the Strong) atop his tomb; measuring 2.25m long, it is supposedly life-size. Here also is a fragment of the chains that Sancho broke in 1212 at the battle of Navas de Tolosa against the Moors – a motif which found its way into the Navarrese coat of arms. Admission to the cloister (€1.80) includes entry to a small ecclesiastical **museum** next to the monastery (summer daily & weekends all year 10am–2pm & 4–8pm). A beautiful half-hour walk from the back of the monastery (on the marked GR65 path, the Camino de Santiago) will bring you up to the **Puerto de Ibañeta**, said to be the very pass used by Charlemagne.

Accommodation is fairly abundant: head for the small *Hostal Casa Sabina*, right next to the monastery (☎948 760 012; ❻), or the much larger *La Posada* (☎948 760 225; ❺), run by the monastery. Bona fide pilgrims following the Camino de Santiago can use the hostel at the monastery (token donation requested). There is a small, not particularly useful **turismo** housed in an eighteenth-century millhouse behind *Casa Sabina* (☎948 760 193).

Luzaide-Valcarlos

If you're continuing into France – a journey redolent with history – you'll come to the border village, **LUZAIDE–VALCARLOS**, 18km on. There's no bus service beyond Auritz-Burguete but hitching is easy or it's a pleasant walk. Luzaide-Valcarlos is a typical border town full of tatty souvenirs and booze – though the views are better than usual – with the *Hostal Maitena* (☎948 790 210; ❹–❺) conveniently situated on the main road with some en-suite rooms should you need to **stay**. On the Frenchward side of the village, the excellent *Casa Etxezuria* (☎948 790 011; ❸) has four beautifully furnished shared-bath rooms offering luxury at a bargain price – it's a big hit with pilgrims following the Camino de Santiago, so phone in advance if possible. There are four other **casas rurales**, including the remoter en-suite *Casa Navarlaz* (☎948 790 042; ❹), so – outside of August at least – you shouldn't be stuck.

Valle de Baztán

Due north of Pamplona, the heavily travelled N121a climbs over the Velate pass before descending to **ORONOZ-MUGAIRI** and the **Parque Señorio de Bértiz** (daily 10am–2pm & 4–7pm; €1.20), a combined botanical garden and managed recreational forest. Immediately beyond, at Oieregi, the N121a forks left to head up the scenic Valle de Bidasoa (see p.467) towards Irún and San

Sebastián. Continuing along the right fork and the N121, you enter the **Valle de Baztán** with its succession of villages, beautiful countryside and cave formations.

Elizondo

The "capital" of this most strongly Basque of Navarran valleys is **ELIZONDO**. What's visible from the through road leaves a poor impression, but once away from it the town is full of typical Basque Pyrenean architecture, especially alongside the river. Three **buses** run daily from both Pamplona and San Sebastián, but there is no public transport to the smaller villages beyond.

There are several places to **stay** in and around Elizondo, which make it a potential base for exploring the beautiful surrounding villages and countryside. One inexpensive option is *Casa Rural Jaén* (☎948 580 487; ❸), with six shared-bath rooms; the rooms above the *Restaurante Eskisaroi*, c/Jaime Urrutia 40 (☎948 580 013; ❸) make a good second choice. There are also two pricier places: the modern *Hotel Baztán* (☎948 580 050, ℱ948 452 323; ❼) on the Pamplona road south of town, complete with garden and pool, and in town itself, *Hostal Saskaitz*, 200m east of the through road at c/María Azpilikueta 10 (☎948 580 488, ℱ948 580 615; ❼).

Of the handful of **restaurants**, the *Txokoto*, c/Braulio Iriarte 25 (closed Wed), has been in the same family for three generations, and its cosy, water-view *comedor* has a good line in reasonable seafood and meat. Alternatively there's the nearby *Eskisaroi*, which is justly popular, with long waits for tables after 2.30pm, or the similarly priced *Galarza*, at the very northern town limits by the Río Baztan, which is strong on seafood (reckon on €18 minimum), though there's also a €9 *menú*.

Around Elizondo

In nearby **ARIZKUN**, beside the minor road to the Izepegui Pass and the French border, the seventeenth-century convent of Nuestra Señora de los Angeles flaunts its striking Baroque facade. Just beyond the village, there's a typical example of a fortified house (very common in the valley) where Pedro de Ursua, the leader of the Marañones expedition up the Amazon in 1560 in search of El Dorado, was born. You can **stay** in Arizkun at the friendly and well-run *Pensión Etxeberría*, near the west edge of town at c/Txuputo 43 (☎948 453 013; ❸), which does additional duty as a bar, general store and reasonable if basic restaurant.

Some 4km northeast and the last Spanish village before France, **ERRATZU** is another gem, with a few well-preserved **casas rurales**: *Casa Etxebeltzea* (☎948 453 157; ❺), a fourteenth-century seigneurial manor at the south edge of the medieval core; the more affordable *Casa Kordoa* (☎948 453 222; ❹); and, cheapest of all, *Casa Indatxipia* (☎948 453 121; ❸).

AMAIUR-MAIA, 6km north of Arizkun just off the N121, and scene of the last unsuccessful battle to preserve the independence of Navarra, is another unspoilt village worth a stop. The gateway to its single street displays the village shield depicting a red bell – most houses still proudly emblazon their door lintels with this coat-of-arms. There are several **casas rurales** here too, including the *Casa Goiz-Argi* (☎948 453 234; ❹) and the *Casa Miguelenea* (☎948 453 224; ❸).

Urdazubi-Urdax and Zugarramurdi

Northwest of Amaiur, the N121 climbs over the **Otxondo Pass** to the villages of Urdazubi-Urdax and Zugarramurdi, both potential stopovers between

Pamplona and the French Basque coastal towns of Biarritz and Bayonne. The only public transport on this stretch is the noon postbus from Elizondo – check in town to confirm departure.

URDAZUBI-URDAX, ringed by hills and guarded by a tiny castle, has three *hostales* and *pensiones*, the most upmarket and central of which is the *Hostal Irigoiena* (☎948 599 267, ℱ948 599 243, ✉hoirigoienea@jet.es; ❻), in a renovated farmhouse. If your budget won't stretch to that, try the more modest *Pensión Beotxea* on the Zugarramurdi road (☎948 599 114; ❹), or there's a **campsite**, *Josenea* (☎948 599 011; open all year), out on the main highway. For **eating**, the *Bar Restaurante Indianoa-Baita* opposite the church has reasonable *menús*.

ZUGARRAMURDI is famous for its caves, the **Cueva de las Brujas** (allow 45 minutes for a walking visit), whose highlight is the giant natural arch through which the *regata de infierno* (hell's stream) flows. The cavern was a major centre for witchcraft in the Middle Ages and consequently the area bore the brunt of persecution at the time of the Inquisition. Underneath the arch, *akelarres* or witches' sabbaths allegedly took place as recently as the seventeenth century, and have passed into Basque legend – and into the content of the local July "Witches' Festival". The appealing village itself makes a good base for excursions into the surrounding countryside; one possibility is to walk 3km along the track beyond the caves into France to another set of caves, the **Grottes de Sare**. Zugarramurdi has two **casas rurales** letting rooms short term, heavily subscribed at weekends: *Casa Sueldeguía* (☎948 599 088; ❸) and *Casa Teltxeguia* (☎948 599 167; ❸), both in the village centre.

Valle de Salazar

East of Pamplona, 13km before Yesa, the C127 road to Lumbier leads into the beautiful valley of the Río Salazar. One kilometre from **LUMBIER**, the first town en route, is the entrance to the **Foz de Lumbier**, a major nesting place for **eagles** which can usually be spotted high up in the walls of the gorge or circling overhead. But the most spectacular part of the lower valley is the **Foz de Arbaiun-Arbayún**, a deep, six-kilometre-long gorge which may be descended by the intrepid, but is also visible from a viewing platform by the road. Numerous **griffon vultures** scythe the skies above.

Some forty kilometres further on you reach the showcase Pyrenean village of **OTSAGI-OCHAGAVÍA**, served by one bus daily from Pamplona (except Sun). Cobbled lanes wander off from the tree-lined quays on each side of the river, crossed by a series of low stone bridges. On the east bank, the wood-and-antique-decor **rooms** – some en suite – of the *Hostal Urialde* (☎948 890 027; ❹) are better value than those of the *Hostal Auñamendi* on Plaza Gúrpide (☎948 890 189; ❻), though the latter has a decent **comedor**. There are also no fewer than thirteen **casas rurales** offering rooms in the traditional stone houses for which the town is famous; two worth singling out are *Casa Navarro* (☎948 890 355; ❸) and *Casa Osaba* (☎948 890 011; ❸) on the west bank.

The **forest of Irati** to the north is one of the most extensive pine and beech forests in Europe, and **Pico de Ori** (Orhy), the westernmost 2000m summit in the Pyrenees, offers some excellent walking and climbing options with views every bit as spectacular as the highest peaks. For those relying on public transport, the forest is inaccessible, but there are some excellent walks in the hills surrounding Ochagavía. Ask for details at Ochagavía's **turismo** (☎948 890 004), on the opposite side of the river to the bus stop, and/or lay hands on the Editorial Alpina 1:40,000 map-booklet *Roncesvalles Irati*.

Valle de Roncal – and the Parque Natural Pirenaico

If you're really serious about exploring alpine mountains, the **Valle de Roncal**, the next major valley to the east, is considerably more rewarding, although very popular in July and August. The bus route from Pamplona ventures briefly into Aragón by the huge Embalse de Yesa (whose recently approved enlargement is set to drown three villages and 20km of the Camino de Santiago), before heading north up the valley of the Esca and back into Navarra. It's a lovely route, crisscrossing the river all the way up through Burgui and Roncal to Isaba. There's a helpful regional **turismo** (summer Mon–Sat 10am–2pm & 4.30–7.30pm, Sun 10am–2pm; ☎948 475 136) in **ERRONKARI-RONCAL**, "capital" of the valley, as well as a *hostal*, the *Zaltua* (☎948 475 008; ❸–❹), on the through road, and several *casas rurales*, best of which is *Casa Villa Pepita* (☎948 475 133; ❸); this also provides *table d'hôte* meals at very reasonable cost, though you'll have more choice in Isaba.

Isaba and around

ISABA, with its network of streets looping around a giant fortified church, presents a more atmospheric prospect, with the small, sterile modern district at the south end of the village (home to a small **turismo** and a **bank** with an ATM) easily ignored. There are no fewer than eight **casas rurales** (all ❸) in the village, though expect to have to try several places at weekends since Isaba (along with Ochagavía) is a major touring centre for the western Pyrenees, as well as a nordic ski base in winter. The pick of conventional **accommodation**, east of the busy through road on narrow c/Mendigatxa, is the sleek and clean *Hostal Lola* (☎ & ℱ948 893 012, ✉hostallola@jet.es; ❺), with limited parking – a problem everywhere in Isaba – and the best restaurant in town (allow €21–24 *a la carta*). Alternatively, try *Pensión Txiki* (☎948 893 118; ❹), poised above the simple bar-restaurant of the same name at the junction of c/Mendigatxa and the high street, or the quiet *Pensión Txabalkua*, west of the through road at c/Izarjentea 16 (☎948 893 083; ❹). The *Albergue Oxanea* (☎948 893 153; ❶) on c/Bormapéa west of the main street is an unusually salubrious private **youth hostel**, which also offers meals, while Isaba's **campsite**, *Asolaze* (☎948 893 034; open all year), with bungalows for rent, is 6km upstream towards the border.

For the best walking and magnificent scenery, continue up the valley of the Río Belagoa to the *Refugio Angel Olorón de Belagoa* (☎ & ℱ948 394 002; ❶), almost at the border but just inside the **Parque Natural**. It stands in grand isolation, overlooking pastures and the high limestone peaks to the east, with the river gleaming between forested slopes below to the south. In summer the bus from Pamplona continues this far, or there's an 8am service up from Isaba. The refuge, run by the Club Deportivo Navarra, offers a complete programme of sports, both summer and winter (nordic skiing pistes begin at the door), as well as economical meals (though the most characterful local restaurant, the popular *Venta de Juan Pito*, is a couple of kilometres below, at the base of the road's hairpins). There are many **walks** you can undertake from here – the most obvious treks to peaks on the frontier ridge – but to do them in safety (the landscape abounds in deep sinkholes) you'll need a proper **map** (Editorial Alpina's 1:40,000 *Ansó-Hecho* covers the park), a compass and good conditions. Take advice from the refuge wardens.

Travel details

Trains

Bilbao Estación de Abando to: Alicante (5 daily; 16hr); Barcelona (2 daily; 10–12hr); Logroño (6 daily; 2hr 30min); Madrid (1 daily; 8hr); Orduña (hourly; 1hr); Salamanca (1 daily; 9hr).
Bilbao Estación Atxuri to: Durango (10–12 daily; 40min); Bermeo via Gernika (12–25 daily; 1hr 15min).
Bilbao Estación de Santander to: Karranza (3 daily; 1hr); Santander (3 daily; 2hr 25min); Balmaseda (15-30 daily; 50min).
Irún to: Hendaye, France (every 30min 7am–10pm; 5min); Paris (2 daily; 8hr); San Sebastián (every 30min 5am–11pm; 30min).

Pamplona to: Madrid (1 daily; 6hr); San Sebastián (1 daily; 2hr 30min); Tudela (1 daily; 1hr 15min); Vitoria (1 daily; 1hr); Zaragoza (7 daily; 2hr 30min).
San Sebastián to: Bilbao (9 daily; 2hr 30min–3hr); Burgos (12 daily; 4hr); Irún (every 30min; 30min); Madrid (4 daily; 6hr 30min–8hr 30min); Ordizia (every 30min; 50min); Pamplona (6 daily; 2–3hr); Salamanca (2 daily; 9hr); Valencia (1 daily; 12hr); Vitoria (7 daily; 1hr 50min); Zaragoza (4 daily; 4–5hr).
Vitoria to: Miranda del Ebro (1 daily; 1hr 25min); Pamplona (1 daily; 1hr); San Sebastián (7 daily; 2hr 30min).

Buses

Bilbao to: Barcelona (4 daily; 8hr); Bayonne (2 daily, 2hr 50min); Burgos (4 daily; 2hr); Durango (4 daily; 30min); Elantxobe (3 daily; 1hr 30min); Gernika (16 daily; 40min); Lekeitio (4 daily; 1hr 30min); León (daily; 7hr); Logroño (daily; 2hr 15min); Madrid (15 daily; 5hr 30min); Oñati (2 daily; 1hr 15min); Ondarroa via Markina (4 daily; 1hr 30min); Pamplona (3 daily; 4hr); San Sebastián (2 hourly; 1hr 10min); Santander (28 daily; 1hr 30min); Vitoria (12 daily; 1hr); Zaragoza (10 daily; 4hr).
Irún to: Pamplona (3 daily; 2hr); San Sebastián (constantly; 30min).
Pamplona to: Bilbao (3 daily; 4hr); Burguete (1 daily; 1hr 30min); Castro (2 daily, 2hr 40min); Elizondo (4 daily; 2hr); Estella (11 daily; 1hr); Irún (3 daily; 2hr); Isaba (1 daily; 2hr); Jaca (2 daily in summer, 1 in winter, except Sun; 2hr); Logroño (4 daily; 2hr); Madrid (2 daily; 6hr); Ochagavía (1 daily, except Sun; 2hr); Puenta la Reina (hourly;

30min); Roncal (1 daily; 1hr 45min); San Sebastián (6 daily; Autovista 1hr; others 3hr); Santander (2 daily, 3hr 45min); Tafalla (6 daily; 1hr); Tudela (6 daily; 1hr 30min); Vitoria (9 daily, fewer Sun; 1hr 30min); Yesa (1 daily; 1hr); Zaragoza (2–3 daily; 4hr).
San Sebastián to: Bilbao (13 daily; 1hr 10min); Elizondo (3 daily; 2hr); Hondarribia (every 20min; 30min); Irún (constantly; 30min); Lekeitio (3–5 daily; 2hr); Lesaka (2 daily; 1hr 15min); Pamplona (6 daily; Autovía 1hr; others 3hr); Bera-Vera de Bidasoa (2 daily; 1hr); Vitoria (7 daily; 2hr 30min); Zarautz (hourly; 30–40min); Zumaia (4 daily; 1hr).
Vitoria to: Araía (via villages of Llanada Alavesa; 2 daily; 1hr); Bilbao (8 daily; 1hr 30min); Durango (4 daily; 1hr); Estella (4 daily; 1hr 15min); Laguardia (4 daily; 1hr 45 min); Logroño (8 daily; 1hr); Pamplona (9 daily, fewer Sunday; 1hr 30min); Pantanos de Zadorra (3 daily; 30min); Santander via Castro Urdiales (7 daily; 2hr 15min).

Ferries

Bilbao to Portsmouth (departs Bilbao Thursday & Monday, departs Portsmouth Tuesday & Saturday; 36 hours).

Cantabria
and Asturias

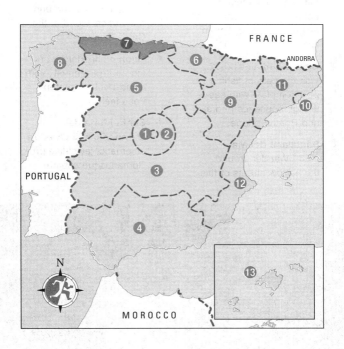

CHAPTER 7 # Highlights

* **Playas** From el Sardinero to el Tostadero, los Biquinis to los Locos – with 202 beaches to choose from, you needn't worry about finding space for your towel.

* **Sidra p.555** Asturia's national drink must be poured from a great height to attain optimum fizz.

* **Castro-Urdiales p.532** Visit the perfect fishing port complete with castle-lighthouse, cathedral and Roman bridge.

* **Santillana del Mar p.534** Wander around the narrow streets of this unbelievably chocolate-box village crammed with picturesque houses.

* **Naranjo de Bulnes p.546** This vast orange-tinted megalith is the icon of the Picos de Europa.

* **Ruta del Cares p.547** A horizontal walk through the vertical world of the Cares Gorge.

* **Gijon p.556** Hard-working and -playing city with a laid-back, unpretentious feel.

* **Santa Maria del Naranco p.563** Oviedo's enigmatic, jewel-like pre-Romanesque church.

Cantabria
and Asturias

he northern provinces of Cantabria and Asturias are popular holiday terrain for Spaniards and French, but hardly touched by the mass tourism of the Mediterranean coast, mostly because of the somewhat unreliable weather. But the sea is warm enough for swimming through the summer months, and the sun does shine, if not every day; it is the warm, moist climate too that gives rise to the wealth of forests and rich vegetation that give the region its name, *Costa Verde*, or the Green Coast. The provinces also boast old and elegant seaside towns, and a landscape that becomes more dramatic the further west you travel, with tiny, isolated coves along the coast and, inland, the fabulous Picos de Europa, with peaks, sheer gorges, flora and fauna enough to satisfy walkers and trekkers of all levels.

Cantabria, centred on the city of Santander, was formerly part of Old Castile, and was long a conservative bastion amid the separatist leanings of its coastal neighbours. **Santander**, the modern capital, is an elegant, if highly conventional, resort, with one of Spain's two ferry links with Britain – to Plymouth. More attractive, low-key resorts lie to either side, crowded and expensive in the Spanish and French holiday season – August especially – but

Accommodation price codes

All the establishments listed in this book have been price-graded according to the following scale. The prices quoted are for the **cheapest available double room in high season**; effectively this means that anything in the ❶ and most places in the ❷ range will be without private bath, though there's usually a washbasin in the room. In the ❹ category and above you will probably be getting private facilities. Remember, though, that many of the budget places will also have more expensive rooms including en-suite facilities. Youth hostels are graded under ❶ as the price per person is less than half of the category's upper limit.

Note that in the more upmarket *hostales* and *pensiones*, and in anything calling itself a hotel, you'll pay a **tax** (IVA) of seven percent on top of the room price.

❶ Under €12	❹ €27–36	❼ €60–90
❷ €12–18	❺ €36–48	❽ €90–120
❸ €18–27	❻ €48–60	❾ Over €120

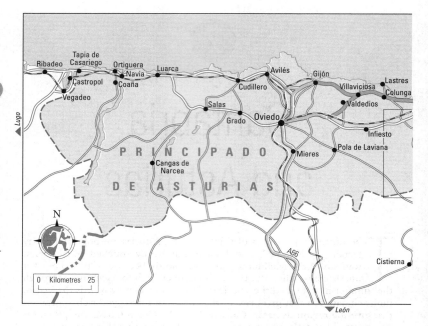

generally enjoyable; the best are **Castro Urdiales**, to the east, and **Comillas** and **San Vicente** to the west. Inland, there is a series of **prehistoric caves**, one of which can be seen at **Puente Viesgo**, near Santander, though the most famous, **Altamira**, can no longer be visited.

To the west are the harsh peaks and rugged coves of mountain-locked **Asturias**, a land with its own idiosyncratic traditions, which include status as a principality (the heir to the Spanish throne is known as the *Príncipe de Asturias*), and a distinctive culture that includes bagpipes and cider (*sidra* – served from above head height to add fizz). Asturias has a base of heavy industry, especially mining and steelworks, and a long-time radical and maverick workforce. Having conducted wildcat strikes during the early days of the Republic, Asturian miners were among the staunchest defenders of the Republic against Franco.

The coastline is a delight, with wide, rolling meadows leading down to the sea, so long as you steer clear of the steel mills of Avilés and the factories of Gijón. Tourism here is largely local, with a succession of old-fashioned and very enjoyable **seaside towns**: small places such as **Ribadesella**, **Llanes** and **Luarca**. Inland, everything is dominated by the **Picos de Europa**, though a quiet pleasure on the peripheries of the mountains, as in Cantabria, is the wealth of Romanesque, and even rare pre-Romanesque, churches found in odd corners of the hills. These reflect the history of the old Asturian kingdom – the embryonic kingdom of Christian Spain – which had its first stronghold in the mountain fortress of **Covadonga**, and was slowly to spread south with the Reconquest. The churches are often at their best when you come upon them by accident, rounding a corner in the countryside, though **Santa María del Naranco**, just outside Oviedo, is worth a special effort to see; **Oviedo**

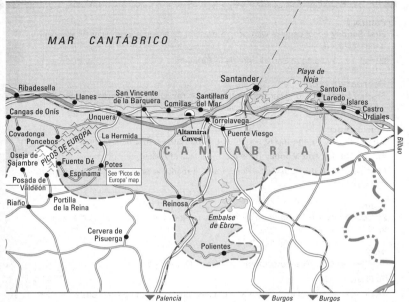

itself, a delightful regional capital, is perhaps the only big city in Asturias meriting a longer stay.

The Picos de Europa, in fact, take in parts of León, as well as Cantabria and Asturias, though for simplicity the whole National Park is covered in this chapter.

The FEVE railway

Communications in this region are generally slow, with the one main road following the coast through the foothills to the north of the Picos de Europa. If you're not in a hurry, you may want to make use of the **FEVE rail line**, which is unmarked on many maps and independent of the main RENFE system; note that rail passes are not valid on this service. The FEVE line begins at Bilbao in the Basque country and follows the length of the Cantabrian coast (with trains serving the triangle of Gijón, Avilés and Oviedo) to Ferrol in Galicia: a terrific route, skirting beaches, crossing *rías* and snaking through a succession of limestone gorges. An expensive "train hotel" runs at night, but it's not a practical way of getting about and it's certainly not the best way of seeing the scenery.

Santander

Long a favourite summer haunt of *madrileños*, **SANTANDER** is an elegant, refined resort – much in the same vein as Biarritz and San Sebastián – though away from the beaches, the modern city is rather unattractive. Some people

Fiestas

January

First Sunday Local carnival with people dressed as sheep and in other bizarre costumes, in Iguña.

22 Saint's day fiesta at San Vicente de la Barquera.

February/March

Start of Lent Week-long *carnaval* festivities in Avilés, Gijón, Oviedo, Mieres, Santoña – fireworks, fancy dress and live music.

March/April

Good Friday Over-the-top re-enactment of the Passion at Castro-Urdiales.

Easter Sunday and Monday *Bollo* (cake) festival at Avilés.

First weekend after Easter *La Folia*, torch-lit maritime procession at San Vicente de la Barquera.

June

29 Cudillero enacts *La Amuravela* – an ironic review of the year – and then proceeds to obliterate memories.

July

First Friday *Coso Blanco* nocturnal parade at Castro Urdiales.

10 Fiesta at Aliva.

15 Good solid festival at Comillas with greased-pole climbs, goose chases and other such events.

16, 17 & 18 Fiestas in Tapia de Casariego.

25 Festival of St James at Cangas de Onis.

Last Sunday *Fiesta de los Vaqueros* – cowboys – at La Brana de Aristebano near Luarca.

Through July Weekly fiestas in Llanes, with Asturian dancers balancing pine trees

---

find Santander a clean and restful base – indeed it's a popular centre for summer Spanish language courses – while others (especially younger Spaniards) will tell you it's dull and snobbish. On a brief visit, the balance is probably tipped in its favour by its variety of excellent beaches and the sheer style of its setting, despite the lack of sights in the town. The narrow Bahía de Santander is dramatic, with the city and port on one side in clear view of open countryside and high mountains on the other – a great first view of Spain if you're arriving on the ferry from Plymouth.

In the summer, the city holds an **international university**, augmented by a **music and cultural festival** throughout August. You'll need to book accommodation well ahead if you plan to stay at these times.

Information and orientation

The **centre** of Santander is a compact grid of streets, set between the city's two ports, the **Puerto Grande** (where the ferries arrive) and the **Puerto Chico** (which serves pleasure boats). The main square is **Plaza de Velarde**, where you'll find the **turismo** for the Cantabrian region (daily 9am–1pm & 4–7pm; ☎942 216 120, ℱ942 313 248, ⓦwww.cantabriaocio.com). Nearby, on Paseo

on their shoulders and swerving through the streets. Also, tightrope walking and live bands down at the harbour.

August

First or second weekend Mass canoe races from Arriondas to Ribadesella down the Río Sella, with fairs and festivities in both towns.

First Sunday Asturias Day, celebrated above all at Gijón.

12 Fiesta at Llanes.

15 *El Rosario* at Luarca – the fishermen's fiesta when the Virgin is taken to the sea.

31 Battle of the Flowers at Laredo.

Last week Fairly riotous festivities for San Timoteo at Luarca: best on the final weekend of the month, with fireworks over the sea, people being thrown into the river, and a Sunday *romería*.

Through August Music and cultural festival at Santander. This being one of the wealthiest cities of the north, you can usually depend on the festival featuring some prestigious acts.

September

7–8 Running of the bulls at Ampuero (Santander).

14 Bull running by the sea at Carreñón (Oviedo).

16 Llanes folklore festival, strong on dancing.

19 Americas Day in Asturias, celebrating the thousands of local emigrants in Latin America; at Oviedo there are floats, bands and groups representing every Latin American country. The exact date for this can vary.

21 *Fiesta de San Mateo* at Oviedo, usually a continuation of the above festival.

29 San Miguel *romería* at Puente Viesgo.

November

First or second weekend *Orujo* (local liquor) festival in Potes.

30 Small regatta for San Andrés day at Castro Urdiales.

Pereda, is the informative municipal **turismo** (summer daily 9am–2pm & 4–9pm; winter Mon–Fri 9.30am–1.30pm & 4–7pm, Sat 10am–1pm; ☎942 203 000, ⓦ www.santanderciudadviva.com). Around the waterfront to the east, **La Magdalena**, a wooded headland, shelters **Playa Magdalena**, on its near side and, beyond, the two-kilometre-long sands of **El Sardinero**, with its beachside suburb.

The **RENFE** and **FEVE** train stations are side by side on the Plaza Estaciones, just back from the waterside, under an escarpment which hides the main roads. A largely subterranean **bus station** faces them directly across the square. The **Aeropuerto de Santander** (☎942 202 100) is 4km out of town at Parayas on the Bilbao road – an inexpensive taxi ride.

City buses #1, #3, #4, #7, and #E shuttle daily between the centre and El Sardinero.

Accommodation

July and August aside, Santander usually has enough **accommodation** to go round. There is a choice of locations between the **centre** and **El Sardinero**, though many of the *pensiones* and *hostales* in the latter area don't open until July.

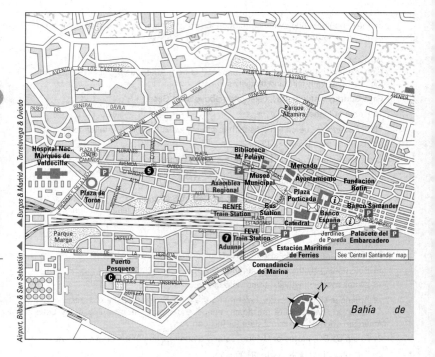

Bahía de

In the centre

Pensión Los Caracoles, Marina 1 ☎ 942 212
697. Centrally located and good-value *pensión*. ❸
Hostal Carlos III, Avda. Reina Victoria 135
☎&ⓕ 942 271 616. Well-run *hostal* in a wonderful
old mansion overlooking the Sardinero beach. ❻
Hostal Residencia La Corza, c/Hernán Cortés 25
☎ 942 212 950. Clean, friendly and very central. ❹
Pensión Gómez, c/Vargas 57A ☎ 942 376 622.
Small, friendly base not far from the station. ❺
Hostal Liébana, c/Nicolás Salmerón 9 ☎ 942 223
250, ⓕ 942 229 910. Pleasant, quiet *hostal* in the
centre of town. ❻
Hostal La Mexicana, Juan de Herrera 3 ☎ 942
222 350. Well-located and friendly *hostal*, offering
clean rooms with bath. ❺
Pensión La Porticada, c/Méndez Núñez 6 ☎ 942
227 817. Spotless, friendly and right next to the
bus and train stations. ❹
Hotel Real, Paseo Pérez Galdós 28 ☎ 942 272 550,
ⓕ 942 274 573. Elegant, upmarket hotel, near the
Playa de la Magdalena, with good sea views. ❾

El Sardinero

Pensión Coloma, Avda. Maura 23 ☎ 942 270 636.
Clean, airy and right next to the Sardinero beach. ❺

Hotel Hoyuela, Avda. de los Hoteles 7 ☎ 942 282
628, ⓕ 942 280 040. Traditional, upmarket and
expensive hotel, perfect for the beach. ❾
Hostal Paris, Avda. de los Hoteles 6 ☎ 942 272
350, ⓕ 942 271 744. Upmarket *hostal* well placed
just off Plaza Italia with some stylish balconied
rooms. ❻
Hotel Sardinero, Plaza de Italia 1 ☎ 942 271
100, ⓕ 942 271 698. Smart beachside hotel with
style and character. ❾
Hostal La Torre, Avda. de los Castros 53 ☎ 942
275 071. A good ten-minute walk from the beach,
but one of the few Sardinero *hostales* that stays
open all year round. ❺

Camping

Camping Bellavista ☎ 942 391 530, ⓕ 942 391
536; open all year and
Camping Cabo Mayor ☎ 942 391 542; June
15–Sept 30. Two well-equipped sites, 2km north
of the Casino on a bluff known as Cabo Mayor, not
far from the Sardinero beach and right next to a
smaller, less-frequented one, the Playa de
Mataleñas. Take bus #9 to Cueto from opposite the
ayuntamiento.

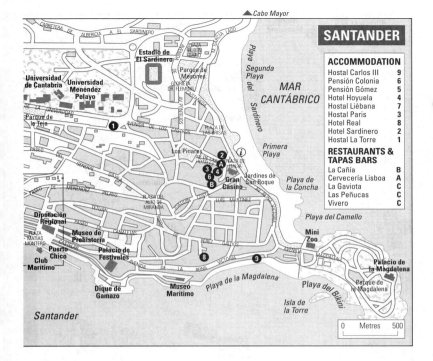

▲ *Cabo Mayor*

SANTANDER

ACCOMMODATION

Hostal Carlos III	9
Pensión Colonia	6
Pensión Gómez	5
Hotel Hoyuela	4
Hostal Liébana	7
Hostal Paris	3
Hotel Real	8
Hotel Sardinero	2
Hostal La Torre	1

RESTAURANTS & TAPAS BARS

La Cañía	B
Cervecería Lisboa	A
La Gaviota	C
Las Peñucas	C
Vivero	C

The Town

Santander was severely damaged by fire in 1941, when it lost most of its former pretensions, along with its medieval buildings. What was left of the old city was reconstructed on the grid around the cathedral but, while the avenues are pleasant enough, and some of the shops have their appeal, there is little of interest beyond a couple of museums. The appeal of the town lies firmly in its beaches.

Santander's **Catedral** (Mon–Fri 10am–1pm & 4–7.30pm, weekends & holidays 10am–1pm & 4.30–8.45pm) is a dull building, almost uniquely bereft of treasures, save for its Gothic-Romanesque **crypt** (separate entrance; daily 8am–1pm & 4–8pm). The **Museo Municipal** (June–Sept Mon–Fri 10.30am–1pm & 5.30–8pm, Sat 10.30am–1pm; Oct–May Mon–Fri 10am–1pm & 5–8pm, Sat 10.30am–1pm; free), nearby, is not much more promising, overburdened with nineteenth-century portraits. If you have time to fill, better to look in at the **Museo Marítimo** (Tues–Sat 11am–1pm & 4–7pm, Sun 11am–2pm; free), near the port, whose exhibits range from pickled two-headed sardines to entire whale skeletons, plus a real-life aquarium.

Kids might also enjoy the little seaside **zoo** (9am–10pm; free), on the Península de la Magdalena, with its lions and polar bears. This is housed in the gardens of the old **Palacio Real**, built at the end of the nineteenth century by Alfonso XIII, to whose residence Santander owed its initial fashionable success.

If you're planning to visit the caves at Puente Viesgo (see p.536), you might look in at the **Museo Provincial de Prehistoria**, c/Juan de la Costa 1

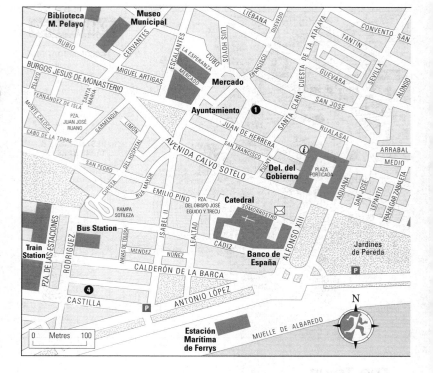

Central Santander

(Tues–Sat 10am–1pm & 4–7pm, Sun 11am–2pm; free). This is well arranged, displaying and reconstructing finds from the province's numerous prehistorically inhabited caves.

The beaches

The first of Santander's beaches, **Playa de la Magdalena**, begins on the near side of the headland. A beautiful yellow strand, sheltered by cliffs and flanked by a summer **windsurfing** school, it is deservedly popular. So, too, is **El Sardinero** itself: a further 2km of beach, beyond the headland, with its own flag announcing it as one of the eight cleanest beaches in the world. If you find both beaches too crowded, there are long stretches of dunes and excellent views across the bay at **Somo** (which has boards to rent and a summer **campsite**) and **Pedreña**; to get to them, jump on the taxi-ferry which leaves every fifteen minutes from the central Puerto Chico (€2.10 return).

Eating, drinking and nightlife

There is a huge choice of **cafés**, **bars** and **restaurants** in the centre, around the **Puerto Pesquero** (the fishing port), and at **El Sardinero**, while if you want to picnic or cook for yourself, there's a good food market behind the *ayuntamiento*.

Being a university town and a pretty flash resort, Santander also has plenty of **nightlife**, at its liveliest from Thursday to Saturday. **Calle Río de la Pila** is

CENTRAL SANTANDER

ACCOMMODATION

Pensión Los Caracoles	2
Hostal Residencia La Corza	3
Hostal La Mexicana	1
Pensión La Porticada	4

RESTAURANTS & TAPAS BARS

Bar Cantabria	A
Bar Cigaleña	E
Bar El Solórzano	F
Bodega Bringas & Bodega Mazon	G
Bodega del Riojano	B
La Conveniente	C
Restaurante/Bar Cañadio	D

the heart of the scene – a whole street of bars, with people spilling out into the small hours; a slightly older crowd is to be found 300m uphill (and left out of c/Río de la Pila) in **Plaza Cañadio** and out towards the **Puerto Chico**. Bright young Santanderians also leave town for **Renedo** on Saturday nights and **Solares** on Sundays, both nearby small towns, connected by RENFE and FEVE trains respectively.

Tapas bars and restaurants

Bar Cantabria, c/Río de la Pila 12. Tapas bar serving up wonderful *empanadas* and *pinchos*, with a little dining room at the back.

Bar Cigaleña, c/Daoiz y Velaverde. Atmospheric bar decorated with old bottles.

Bar El Solórzano, c/Peña Herbosa 17. Great neighbourhood bar with traditional music, *vermut* on tap, and the whole array of Cantabrian seafood.

Bodega Bringas and **Bodega Mazon**, c/Hernán Cortés 47 and 57. These *bodegas* serve tasty local food, wine and *sidra*, amidst vast wine vats. *Bringas* is open evenings only and reputed for its *anchoas* and *pimientos*; *Mazon* is good for *chipirones* and *tortilla*.

Bodega del Riojano, c/Río de la Pila, 5. Traditonal *bodega* with stacks of casks and good tapas. Popular with the thirty-something crowd.

La Caña, c/Joaquín Costa 45, Sardinero. Unpretentious restaurant with excellent seafood and a good *menú*.

Cervecería Lisboa, Plaza Italia, Sardinero. Ever-popular restaurant in front of the casino, with a summer *terraza*, and a good choice of *platos combinados*.

La Conveniente, c/Gómez Oreña 19. Nineteenth-century *bodega* with live music, fried fish and other delicious, but pricey, snacks.

La Gaviota, **Las Peñucas** and **Vivero**, c/Marqués de la Ensanada, Puerto Pesquero. Three popular and unpretentious seafood restaurants down by the fishing port. You can spend anything, from a few hundred pesetas for a *menú del día* or plate of sardines, to a small fortune for fishy exotica.

Restaurante Cañadio and **Bar Cañadio**, Plaza Cañadio ☎ 942 314 149. The *Cañadio* is the city's best restaurant, known far and wide for the sublime fish and regional cooking of its chef, Paco Quirós. If you can't spare €24 and up, don't despair – just join the foodies snacking on a fabulous spread of canapés at the much more modest bar. Closed Sun.

Bars and clubs

Agua de Valencia, c/Perines. Popular place to start the evening, with a killer house cocktail at €4.80 a jug.

Blues, Plaza Cañadio. Blues and jazz music bar, with an expensive connecting restaurant.

Castelar–5, c/Castelar 5. Pleasant music bar with a summer terraza.

The Celtic's Tavern, c/Gándara 3 (cnr General Mola). Live folk music, imported beers and English-speaking staff.

Cerveceria Cruz Blanca, c/Hernán Cortés 16. Another popular place to begin the evening, with a huge variety of international beers.

Escena, Plaza Rubén Darío, at the north end of Sardinero. Old-time dance club still frequented for *rumbas* and *sevillanas*.

El Grifo, Plaza Cañadio. Youthful bar with a choice of fifteen beers.

Maria's and **Indian's**, both on c/Casmiro Saiuz and open for dancing till dawn.

Pacha, c/General Mola 45. Biggest club in town with two floors (dance/latino) and a quieter bar area.

Rocambole, c/de Hernán Cortés 36. Late-night club attracting a young and trendy crowd from 3am; Motown music and expensive drinks.

Web-Site Story, c/Menéndez Pelayo 5. Funky café-pub with Internet access.

Listings

American Express c/o Viajes Altair, c/Calderón de la Barca 11 ☎ 942 311 700.

Car rental Atesa, c/Marcelino Sanz de Santuola, 2 ☎ 942 222 926; Budget, c/San Luis 8 ☎ 942 238 485; Europcar, c/Rodríguez 9 ☎ 942 214 706.

Consulates British Consulate, Paseo Pereda 27 ☎ 942 220 000.

Ferry tickets Tickets for the Brittany Ferries crossing to Plymouth are sold by Modesto Piñeiro at their office at the ferry dock (☎ 942 214 500, 🌐 www.brittany-ferries.com). Advance reservations are essential in summer, both for cars and passengers.

Hospital Santander's General Hospital is on Avda. Valdecilla (☎ 942 202 520).

Internet Santander's burgeoning crop of *ciber-cafés* include *The New*, c/ Perines, 35 (☎ 608 287 067, 🌐 www.cibercafethenew.com), with a bar downstairs; and *Batch-PC*, Camilo Alonso 26 (10am–1.30pm and 5pm–8.30 pm; ☎ 942 241670, 🌐 www.batch-pc.com), with 15 terminals.

Post office The city's main *Correos* is on Avda. Alfonso XIII (Mon–Fri 8am–9pm, Sat 9am–2pm).

Telephones The *Telefónica* is at c/de Hernán Cortés 37; in Sardinero there is a *locutorio* beside the casino.

Trekking Federación Cantabria de Montaña, c/Rubio 2 (☎ 942 373 378), provides information and organizes treks in the Picos de Europa.

East along the coast to Castro Urdiales

The coast east of Santander has been heavily developed, with villas and apartment complexes swamping most of the coves. **Noja**, until recently remarkable only for the strange-shaped rocks along its shore, now has seven campsites, while **Laredo** has become one of the north's major holiday resorts. Things improve as you move east, however, to the beach at **Islares**, or to the old town of **Castro Urdiales**.

Laredo and around

LAREDO pulls in a young, Spanish crowd with its summer profusion of pubs, clubs and discos. For a spell in the last century it was Cantabria's provincial capital, and the village-like core of the old town, the **Puebla Vieja**, rambles back from the harbour, with occasional traces of its former walls and gates, climbing up towards a splendid thirteenth-century parish church, **Santa María de la Ascunción** (daily 10am–1pm & 4–7.30pm). Beyond the church you can climb quickly out of town to the cliffs and to grand open countryside, while below lies the best **beach** this side of San Sebastián, a gently shelving crescent of sand, 5km long and well protected from the wind.

Practicalities

All **buses** stop outside the small ticket office adjoining the *Cafetería Orio*, on c/Jose Antonio 10. There isn't much in the way of budget **accommodation** in Laredo. The cheapest place you'll find is *Pensión Cantabria* on c/Menéndez Pelayo 7 (☎942 605 073; ❸); otherwise, *Hotel Montecristo*, c/Calvo Sotelo 2 (☎942 605 700; ❸), and *Hotel El Cortijo*, c/González Gallego 3 (☎942 605 600, ℉942 605 591; ❼; mid June–Sept), are both handy for the beach, and *Pensión Esmeralda*, c/Fuente Fresnedo 4 (☎942 605 219; ❹), is close to the nightlife in town. If money is no object, *Hotel El Risco*, Blvd. Arenosa (☎942 605 030, ℉942 605 055; ❸), perched on top of a hill with great views out to sea, is a fine bet; alternatively, head for the elegant *Hotel El Ancla*, c/Gonzáles Gallego 10 (☎942 605 500, ℉942 611 602; ❸). There are no less than four **campsites** close to the beach: *Laredo* (☎942 605 035; June–Sept), *Costa Esmeralda* (☎942 603 250; June–Sept), *Playa de Regatón* (☎942 606 995; April–Sept) and *Carlos V* (☎942 605 593; open all year).

You'll find bars and *cafeterías* on the beach, while in town Rúa de San Marcial has a good selection of **restaurants**. If you want the town's best, it is the *Mesón del Marinero* (☎942 606 008) on c/Zamanillo, a creative, though pricey, shell-fish specialist; *El Pescador*, on the seafront, is another good option – their catch of the day is always excellent.

Santoña

Just across the bay from the west end of Playa de Laredo lies the resort of **SANTOÑA**. Ferries run across the water to the small beach, or it's thirty minutes from Laredo by hourly bus. Santoña is, remarkably, still a working fishing port; you can watch the catch being unloaded and sample it in the tiny bars grouped around the streets leading up from the port, particularly c/General Salinas. There are grand views across the bay to Laredo from the hilltop castle of **Fuente de San Martín**.

Islares and Oriñon

If you're looking for somewhere more peaceful, the villages of **ISLARES** and **ORIÑON**, east from Laredo on opposite sides of the Rio Agüera, are pleasant and as yet little developed. Islares, on the east side of the river, has a small beach, but is somewhat overshadowed by the coast highway roaring past on the hillside above; Oriñon, down in the valley beside the main beach, sheltered by the mountains on either side, is a better bet. Another, much wilder beach is located 2km away around the headland below the village of Sonabia. From here you can see the strange rock formation known as the *ojos del diablo* (devil's eyes) on the mountainside above.

In Islares, *El Langostero* (☎942 871 212, ℉942 862 212; ❹), just off the main highway and virtually on the beach, is clean with nice views and its own restaurant. Closer to the main road, *Pensión Playamonte* (☎942 862 696; ❸) is a cheaper, but noisier, option. *Hostal Arenillas*, (☎942 860 766; ❹), Islares's original *hostal*, is still a good bet, though it can be very crowded in July and August. In Oriñon, El Conde (☎942 878 624; ❹; Easter & June–Sept), is a basic *pen-*

sión with shared bathrooms, and there is also a **campsite** (☏942 863 152). There are several bars which serve food in both villages although *El Langostero* is the best bet in the area.

Castro Urdiales

CASTRO URDIALES is a congenial and good-looking resort, less developed than Laredo, although experiencing a construction boom with apartment blocks, and hotel prices, shooting up everywhere. Rooms and space on the beaches are at a premium in high season and at weekends, when everyone descends from Santander and Bilbao. At such times, the main "town beach", **Playa del Brazomar**, a small strip of sand, hemmed in by a cement esplanade used for sunbathing, and bordered by two large hotels, can be very busy. However, the crowds can be left behind by heading further east to more secluded coves, or west to **Playa Ostende**, with its rough, dark sand. From this latter beach, there's an unusual walk back to town along the cliffs, most of which seem to be hollow – you can hear the sea pounding beneath you. Along the route is a tiny bay where the sea comes in under a spectacular overhang.

As well as its tourist functions, the town retains a considerable fishing fleet, gathered around a beautiful natural harbour. Above this looms a massively buttressed Gothic church, **Santa María**, and a lighthouse, built within the shell of a Knights Templar castle. These are linked to the remains of an old hermitage by a dramatic reconstructed **Roman bridge**, under which the sea roars at high tide. The old quarter, the **Mediavilla**, is relatively well preserved, with arcaded streets and tall, glass-balconied houses. The **turismo** (Mon–Sat 9am–2pm & 5–7pm; ☏942 871 512) is found on the main jetty, alongside an open-air fish grill serving fresh sardines and tuna in summer.

Accommodation

The town's best budget **accommodation** is scattered throughout the narrow, pedestrianized streets of the old town. For modern and expensive hotels, head towards the beach and the newer part of town. There is a **campsite** in Barrio Campijo near the beach *Castro*, Camino Allende Laguna (☏942 870 300, ⓕ942 870 306).

Pensión Alberto, Avda. República Argentina 2 ☏942 862 757. Comfortable rooms without bath. July–Sept only. ④

Pensión Catamaran, c/Victorina Gainza ☏942 860 496. Modern rooms in a noisy position opposite the bus station; try for a room that doesn't face the road, as noise starts early. ⑤

Pensión El Cordobes, c/Ardigales 15 ☏942 860 089. Attractive, old-fashioned *pensión* with good choice of clean, spacious rooms with or without bath. ⑤ –⑦

Pensión La Mar, c/La Mar 27 ☏942 870 524, ⓕ942 862 828. Smart, refurbished *pensión* in the old town, well located for bars and restaurants. ⑤

Hotel Miramar, Avda. de la Playa 1 ☏&ⓕ942 860 204. Modern hotel close to the beach with good panoramic views of the port. ⑦

Hotel Las Rocas, Avda. de la Playa ☏942 860 400, ⓕ942 861 382. Expensive hotel close to the beach in a residential area. ⑧

Pensión La Sota, c/La Correría 1 ☏942 871 188, ⓕ942 871 284. Just behind the *ayuntamiento*, this *pensión* makes an excellent base for exploring the harbour and castle. ⑥

Pensión El Viejo Baracaldo, c/Ardigales 4 ☏942 872 404. Small *pensión* in the old town. ⑥

Eating and drinking

Castro Urdiales has no shortage of places to **eat**. If you're on a budget, head for the less expensive places around the *ayuntamiento* at the castle end of the harbour, where there are some excellent fish/seafood bars around the square and on c/El Carrerias. The lively c/Ardigales is packed with *mesones* and *tabernas*,

△ Castro Urdiales, Cantabria

and is also the centre of the **nightlife** scene, with two discos, *Mambo* and *Safari*, and more fashionable disco-pubs and late-night bars continuing on down the same street into c/La Rua.

Bar Agora, c/Ardigales. Very reasonable Basque-run establishment with outdoor tables.

Bar Rincón, c/La Mar. Typical Basque setting with sawdust floors and men in berets; expect good *pinchos* and great atmosphere.

El Marichu, c/Ardigales. An excellent selection of *pinchos* – the mushrooms in oil and garlic are especially good.

Mesón Marinero, c/Correría 23 ☎ 942 860 005. Castro's renowned fish restaurant, in a huge building opposite the *ayuntamiento*, can be pricey, but if you sit at the bar and choose from the wide selection of *raciones* you can eat very well and relatively cheaply.

Restaurante Baracaldo, c/Matilde de la Torre 11 ☎ 942 862 012. Highly recommended restaurant with good seafood *menú*.

Moving on

The **bus stop**, shared by the companies Alsa-Turytrans and Encartaciones, is next to the *Cafetería Catamaran*, c/Victorina Gainza, four blocks from the seafront, where you'll also find a small ticket office. There are through services to towns between Irún and Gijón from here, while buses to **Bilbao** leave from the side road just next to the *Cafe-Bar Ronda* on the main N634.

Santillana and the prehistoric caves

If you see a postcard in Santander depicting gorgeous sandstone churches and mansions, it is **Santillana del Mar**, an outrageously picturesque village, 26km west of Santander, which has been prettified beyond belief for tourism. It remains beautiful, by the skin of its teeth, but in season it's a major tourist spot, and can be a nightmare to visit. The crowds would be even worse were the caves at **Altamira**, on the edge of the village, still open to visitors, for these contain Spain's most dramatic prehistoric drawings. A less impressive, but still very extensive, set of Altamira-epoch paintings is preserved in another set of caves at **Punte Viesgo**, 24km south of Santander on the N623 Burgos road.

Santillana

Jean-Paul Sartre (in *Nausea*) describes **SANTILLANA DEL MAR** as "*le plus joli village d'Espagne*" – an unlikely source, but none the less accurate for that. The village (once you reach it past the bus and car parks) is all ochre-coloured stone houses, mansions, and farms. It's known by locals as the "town of the three lies" – as it's neither very holy (*santi*) nor particularly flat (*llana*), and despite the *del Mar* actually stands some three or four kilometres back from the sea. While its fine houses flaunt their aristocratic origins, the village itself has long been completely rural. Its single pedestrianized street, with one loop and two plazas, saunters back from the access road towards a wonderful Romanesque collegiate church and then stops abruptly amidst farms and fields.

Santillana's fifteenth- to eighteenth-century **mansions**, vying with each other in the extravagance of their coats of arms, are as splendid as they are anomalous. One of the best is the **Casa de los Hombrones**, named after two moustachioed figures, flanking its grandly sculpted escutcheon. Another, the **Casa de Bustamentes**, established its credentials with a simple motto: "The Bustamentes marry their daughters to kings." Although many of the mansions still belong to the original families, their noble owners have rarely visited in the last couple of centuries; indeed, up until the 1970s, villagers kept their cattle in some of the less-used mansions.

Just down from the Casa de los Hombrones is the **Museo El Solar**, which actually houses two separate museums (daily 9.30am–10pm; €4.80 each): one displays an excellent, if disturbing collection of torture instruments, with historical notes in English, while the other is devoted to venomous animals. The village church, **La Colegiata** (daily 9am–1pm & 4–7pm) is dedicated to Santa Juliana, an early martyr whose tomb it contains; she is legendarily supposed to have captured the Devil and is depicted with him in tow in various scenes around the building. Its most outstanding feature, however, is the twelfth-century **Romanesque cloister** (€1.80), one of the best preserved in the whole country, with its squat, paired columns and lively capitals carved with animals and hunting scenes.

Also worth a look is the seventeenth-century **Convento de Regina Coeli** (same hours and tickets as the Colegiata cloisters), on the main road just across from the entrance to the village. This houses an exceptional museum of painted wooden figures and other religious art: pieces brilliantly restored by the nuns and displayed with great imagination to show the stylistic development of certain images, particularly of San Roque, a healing saint always depicted with his companion, a dog who licks the wound in his thigh. There is supposedly a resident ghost, too, on the first floor.

Practicalities

There are several direct **buses** daily to Santillana from Santander run by Autobuses Cantabria from the main station (July–Aug first bus 7.30am); you are dropped outside the convent with the town straight ahead across the main road. Buses on to Comillas and San Vicente de la Barquera leave from the same place at 8am, 11.10am, 1.40pm and 6.45pm although the service is reduced at weekends. You can also get to the village by regular buses from Torrelavega, which is on the FEVE railway line. You'll find a **turismo** (Mon–Sat 9.30am–1.30pm & 4–8pm, Sun 10am–1.30pm & 4–7.30pm; ☎942 818 251) in the Plaza de Ramón Pelayo – the square opposite the *parador*.

Santillana is an attractive **overnight stop** if you are travelling out of season, and it has rooms to suit most budgets, although these can be booked out in summer. Least expensive are the *casas de huéspedes* (guest houses), just off Plaza de Ramón Pelayo, and the *habitaciones* advertised by many of the bars in high season. *Casa Angelica*, c/Los Hornos 3 (☎942 818 238; ❸), is a decent, low-budget option, while *Casa Fernando*, (☎942 818 018; ❷), a little out towards Altamira, and more modern, is also good value. For more comfort, head for *Casa La Solana*, at the top of c/Los Hornos 12 (☎942 818 106; ❻), a beautifully restored country house, perched above the hustle and bustle of the village. *Posada del Organista*, on the same street (☎942 840 452; ✉organist@arrakis.es; ❺), is another beautiful eighteenth-century house and does great breakfasts. *Posada Gonzalez* (☎942 818 178; ❺), on the far side of Campo Revolgo at La Robleda, 13, is a very well-kept family house. The grand old *Hotel Altamira*, Cantón 1 (☎942 818 025, ℻942 840 136; ❼), is a good choice if you can afford to splash out, and also does a very good *menú* for €10.20; but Santillana's choicest accommodation is the *Parador Gil Blas*, housed in one of the town's finest mansions in the heart of the village (☎942 818 000, ℻942 818 391; ❽). There is also a **campsite**, *Camping Santillana* (☎942 818 250; June–Sept), 1km out along the Altamira road, which is large and soulless, but has a pool and good facilities.

Restaurants in Santillana are abundant but largely unexceptional. *Mesón de Los Villa*, c/Santo Domingo 5, is pleasant, serving meals outside in a little orchard in summer; *La Viga* has a lovely courtyard restaurant and is also one of the few bars staying open late.

The prehistoric caves

The prehistoric **Caves of Altamira** lie 2km west of Santillana. Dating from around 12,000 BC, they consist of an extraordinary series of caverns, covered in paintings of bulls, bison, boars and other animals etched in red and black with a few confident and impressionistic strokes. When discovered in the 1870s they were in near-perfect condition, with striking and vigorous colours, but in the 1950s and 1960s the state of the murals seriously deteriorated, and they are now **closed** to prevent the build-up of surplus moisture (from breathing) in the cavern's atmosphere. Visitors with a serious academic interest can apply in writing (at least three years in advance) to the Museo Altamira (39330 Santillana de Mar, Cantabria, ℱ942 840 157). Otherwise, there is a new **museum** (Tues–Sun 9am–1pm & 2–8pm; free) situated next to the caves, which contains a faithful replica of the drawings.

A more rewarding cave visit is to hand at **PUENTE VIESGO**, 24km out of Santander on the N623 road to Burgos (SA Continental bus from the main station in Santander). Around the village, set amid magnificent rolling green countryside, are four separate **prehistoric caves**, one of which, **Castillo**, is open to tours, conducted in Spanish only (April–Oct 10am–1pm & 3–7pm; Nov–March 10am–3pm; ☎942 598 425; €1.80, free for EU citizens); it's best to book at least twenty-four hours in advance. The cave is magnificent, with stalactites and stalagmites in the weirdest shapes, in addition to the remarkable paintings – clear precursors to the later developments at Altamira.

If you want **to stay**, the village has a luxurious four-star hotel on c/Manuel Pérez Mazo, the *Gran Hotel Balneario* (☎942 598 061, ℱ942 598 261; ➒), as well as a few budget places: *Hostal La Terraza* (☎942 598 102; ➌; open July–Sept), and *La Tropical* (☎942 598 117; ➋), set back a bit from the bus stop. Several other places also open up for the summer season.

South of Santander: Reinosa and the Ebro

South of Santander lies a large area of quiet Cantabrian countryside, dominated by the extensive **Pantano del Ebro**. The N611 to Palencia brushes the shores of this reservoir and passes through **Reinosa**, a transport hub for the region and a pleasant old town if you want to break your journey. To the west, the high Sierra de Peña Labra has **skiing** opportunities, with a small resort at **Alto Campoo**, 24km from Reinosa. To the east, the **Río Ebro** trails a lovely valley, past a succession of unspoilt villages, Romanesque architecture and cave churches.

Reinosa

REINOSA is a pretty, characteristically Cantabrian town with lots of glass-fronted balconies and *casonas* – seventeenth-century town houses – displaying the coat of arms of their original owners. The **turismo** (Mon–Fri 9am–2pm & Sat 10am–2pm; ☎942 755 215, ⓦwww.campoolosvalles.org) occupies one of these, midway down the main street, Avenida Puente Carlos III, near the distinctive Baroque church of **San Sebastián**.

Two inexpensive **places to stay** are *Hostal San Cristóbal*, c/Julióbriga 1 (☎942 751 768; ➌), and the nearby *Hostal Residencia Sema* (☎942 750 047; ➌), at c/Julióbriga 14, which is near the station and has a good restaurant. For a bit more comfort, head for *Hotel Rubén*, c/Abrego 12 (☎ & ℱ942 754 914; ➍), or, across the bridge, *Hostal Tajahierro*, c/Pellila 8 (☎942 753 524; ❹). For a small town, Reinosa has a surprising range of traditional **bodegas** and **mesones**. On the main street, *Pepe de los Vinos* is a good place for a glass of wine and a snack, while the restaurants *Avenida* and *Los Ángeles* offer more substantial meals; the latter is open late. While you're here, don't miss the tasty *pantortillas* (sweet pastries), which can be bought from most bakeries.

If you are pressing on deeper into the countryside, one local **bus** daily (Mon–Sat) goes south to Polientes, leaving at 10am, and another two travel east around the reservoir to **Cabañas** and **Arija**, departing at 11am (Mon–Sat) and 6pm (Mon–Fri).

Skiing: Alto Campoo

Twenty-four kilometres to the west of Reinosa lies the ski resort of **ALTO CAMPOO**, served by regular buses in season. It's a tiny resort, with a ski school, 20km of pistes and a three-star **hotel**, *La Corza Blanca* (☎ & ⓕ942 779 250; ❼).

Along the Ebro: Polientes

Southeast of Reinosa, a network of tiny, winding roads trail the Ebro river, passing through villages of no more than a few houses. The largest of these is **POLIENTES**, a lovely place, totally rural, though with a couple of places to stay: *Pensión Demetrio* (☎942 776 018; ❹) by the bus stop, and a *hostal* just down the road, *Sampatiel* (☎942 776 053, ⓕ942 776 136; ❸) – in season, be sure to ring before you arrive. The café-bar in the main square serves good **food** (it's run by the mayor) and the *hostal* does a good value *menú*, too.

East of Polientes, you'll need your own transport to continue along the valley and on to the Santander–Burgos road. Twelve kilometres from Polientes is the village of **San Martín de Elines**, with a twelfth-century Romanesque **Colegiata** containing medieval sarcophagi, and a church set into rock. At nearby **Cadalso**, you'll find another smaller rock church.

The coast: Comillas to Unquera

The coast west of Santillana, as far as **Unquera** at the border with Asturias, is dotted with a succession of small, low-key resorts. The main towns, **Comillas** and **San Vicente de la Barquera**, are attractive enough, having been spared the high-rise hotel and apartment treatment. The **FEVE line** runs inland along this stretch, but the towns are linked by regular bus services.

Comillas

COMILLAS, the first resort west of Santillana del Mar, is a curious rural town with pretty cobbled streets and squares, and an inland feel, despite it being only just set back from the sea. It has a pair of superb beaches: the **Playa de Comillas**, the closest, with a little anchorage for pleasure boats and a few beach cafés, and the longer and less developed **Playa de Oyambre**, 4km west out of town towards the cape.

Oddly out of place in the otherwise provincial town is a trio of mansions, including a Gaudí-designed villa, **El Capricho**, a short (and signposted) walk from the centre. This is now a restaurant but its gardens are open to visitors, and it's certainly worth a look even if you're not staying in Comillas, with its playful miniaturizations, futuristic use of colour and whimsical tower.

Next door to El Capricho is another nineteenth-century *modernista* flourish, the **Palácio de Marqués de Comillas**, designed by Gaudí's associate, Juan Martorell. It is closed to visitors but can be seen from the garden of El Capricho. The Marqués, an industrialist friend of Alfonso XII, also commissioned the huge **Seminario Pontífico**, on the hillside above, from Domenech y Montaner, another of the Barcelona *modernista* group.

Practicalities

Comillas is actually skirted by the FEVE line, though it has good **bus** connections with San Vicente de la Barquera to the west and Santillana and Santander to the east. Buses arrive at and leave from the Paseo de Solatorre, the main road at the bottom of the town overlooked by El Capricho. **Accommodation** is better priced than surrounding resorts, but in season you will need to book ahead, or arrange a private room through the **turismo** (summer Mon–Sat 10am–1pm & 5–9pm, Sun & holidays 11am–1pm & 5–8pm; winter Mon–Sat 11am–1pm & 4.30–7pm, Sun & holidays 11am–1pm; ☎942 720 768), centrally located at c/La Aldea 2.

You'll find good budget rooms at *Pensión Bolingas*, c/Gonzalo de la Torre (☎942 720 841; ❸), which is clean, friendly and just off the main square, and at *Pensión La Aldea*, c/La Aldea (☎942 721 046; ❹), which has a superb restaurant downstairs. *Pensión Villa*, Cuesta Carlos Diaz de la Campa 21 (☎942 720 217; ❸), has two buildings, one modern and comfortable above the main square and another more characterful house just off the Plaza de Ibañez. More upmarket choices include *Hotel Josein*, c/Manuel Noriega 27 (☎942 720 225, ☎942 720 949; ❼), with excellent coastal views, *Hostal Esmeralda*, c/Antonio López 7 (☎942 720 097, ☎942 722 558; ❺), a beautifully furnished place at the top of the town, and the *Fuente Real*, c/Sobrellano 19 (☎942 720 155; ❹), right beside El Capricho. There are **campsites** at both beaches, with the *Comillas* (☎942 720 074; July–Aug) on the east side of town significantly better than *El Rodero* at Oyambre (June–Oct).

Comillas has good **food** to offer. At the bottom end of the scale, *Picoteo*, just down from the *Esmeralda*, does generous meals at rock-bottom prices, while for good, cheap tapas, try the *Bar Filipinas* at the crossroads next to the bus stop. The main square is packed with outdoor tables and café-restaurants, most specializing in *barcas* (huge platters) of seafood. *Gurea* on c/Ignacio Fernandez de Castro (☎942 722 426) is an outstanding Basque restaurant offering a wide range of traditional dishes for around €21–24 for a three-course meal plus wine. If you want to really splash out, credit cards can pay for Gaudí decor and Spanish *nouvelle cuisine* at *El Capricho* (☎942 720 365).

Given its size, Comillas has a surprisingly lively nightlife, with a clutch of **disco-pubs** on c/Pérez de la Riva, above the sloping Plaza Generalísmo, including the excellent *Don Porfirio*, with gardens and a small dance floor.

San Vicente de la Barquera

The approach to **SAN VICENTE DE LA BARQUERA** is dramatic, with the town, marooned on both sides by the sea, entered across a long causeway, while inland, hills rise towards the Picos de Europa. Looking down from the hill which looms over the centre of town are an impressive Renaissance **ducal palace** and a Romanesque-Gothic church, **Santa María de los Ángeles**, the latter with restored, gilded altarpieces and a famous reclining statue of the Inquisitor Corro. The town itself, a thriving fishing port with a string of locally famed but expensive seafood restaurants, has had its old core encroached upon, and is split by the main coast road with its thundering lorries, but it still makes a good overnight stop. The seafront is more dedicated to work than tourism, but there's a good sweep of sand flanked by a small forest fifteen minutes across the causeway.

Practicalities

The local **turismo** (summer only daily 9.30am–2pm & 4.30–9pm; ☎942 710 797) is on the main road, at Avda. Generalísimo 20. **Accommodation** is easy enough to find. The central *Pensión Hostería La Paz*, c/Mercado 2 (☎942 710 180; ❹), is clean and spacious; *Pensión Liebana* (☎942 710 211; ❸) is at the top of the stairs leading from the back of the main square. More expensive options include *Hotel Boga Boga*, Plaza José Antonio 9 (☎942 710 135, ℗942 710 151; ❻), and on the main road, *Hotel Luzón*, Avenida Miramar (☎ & ℗942 710 050; ❺). There is a pleasant **campsite**, *El Rosal* (☎942 710 165), across the causeway from the town, situated in the woods beside the beach. For **food**, *Bar Colón*, on the right as you head westwards out of town, does good *raciones*, while a good place to try seafood or *sorropoton*, the local speciality tuna stew, is *El Pescador*, further down the same road and just beyond the turismo.

Using public transport, San Vicente is best left or approached by **bus** (Alsa serves the coast and Palomera or Cantabrica cover inland routes), as the FEVE station is about 4km south at **La Alcebasa**. Buses leave from the small bus station near the causeway, where there's a ticket office, but no left-luggage facilities.

Unquera

The last town in Cantabria is **UNQUERA**, 9km west of San Vicente. Here buses for the Picos de Europa turn south towards **Potes** (3 daily). Unquera itself is fairly dire, its only bright spots being the restaurants *Ríomar* and *Granja,* both on the main street; the latter also serves as the local bus stop and is just across from the FEVE station. The town is famous for its *anis*-flavoured *corbatas* (pastries), which are sold in many of the bars and bakeries along the main street. The small **turismo** (Mon–Fri 10am–1.30pm & 4–7.30pm, Sat 10am–12.30pm; ☎942 719 680) is open summer only.

The Picos de Europa

The **PICOS DE EUROPA**, although not the highest mountains in Spain, are the favourite of many walkers, trekkers and climbers. The range is a miniature masterpiece: a mere forty kilometres across in either direction, shoehorned in between three great **river gorges**, and straddling the provinces of Asturias, León and Cantabria. The whole area was made a National Park in 1995, although there remain problems in co-ordinating the activities of the three provinces. Asturians see the mountains as a symbol of their national identity, and celebrate a cave-shrine at **Covadonga**, in the west of the range, as the birthplace of Christian Spain.

Walks in the Picos de Europa are amazingly diverse, considering the size of the region, and they include trails for all levels of activity – from a casual morning's walk to two- and three-day treks. The most spectacular and popular walks are along the twelve-kilometre **Cares Gorge** – a route you can take in whole or part – and around the high peaks reached from a cable car (*teleférico*) at **Fuente Dé**. But there are dozens of other paths and trails, both along the river valleys and in woodlands, and up in the mountains. Take care if you go off the

PICOS DE EUROPA

Torrelavega & Santander

MAR CANTÁBRICO

San Vicente de la Barquera

Puentenansa

Pimiango
Bustio
Unquera
N 621
Colombres
Noriega
Villanueva
Alevia
Alles
Llonín
Mier
Ruenes
Trescares
Arangas
Carreña de Cabrales
Arenas de Cabrales
Poncebos
Tielve
Sotres

Panes
Sobrepeña
Piñeres
Linares
Santa María de Lebeña
La Hermida
Cabezón de Liébana
Tama
Ojedo
Potes
Turieno
Monasterio de Santo Toribio de Liébana
La Vega
Camaleño
Cosgaya
Espinama

Peña Tú
Vidiago
San Roque
Cué
Llanes
Parres
Caldueño
Meré
Benia (Onís)
Con
Labra
La Riera
Corao
Cangas de Onís
La Tornín
Arriondas

Destiladero de la Hermida

Deva

Tresviso

PICOS DE EUROPA

Terenosa
Bulnes
Naranjo de Bulnes 2519
Peña Vieja 2613
Refugio de Aliva
Teleférico
Fuente Dé

Vega de Ario
Camarmeña
Caín
Torre de Cerredo 2648
Cabaña Veronica
Mirador del Cable
Collado Jermoso

Vega de Urriello

Pto. de Pandetrave 1562

Portilla de la Reina, Riaño & León

Portilla de la Reina

Desfiladero del Cares

Cares

Soto de Valdeón
Santa Marina de Valdeón
Posada de Valdeón
Cordiñanes

Vega Huerta
Vegabaño

Lago Enol
Lago la Ercina
Vega Redonda

Cueva del Buxu
Covadonga
Cuera

Soto de Sajambre
Oseja de Sajambre

Amieva
Sames (Amieva)

Sella

Desfiladero de los Beyos

Viego

Beleño (Ponga)

Pto. de Panderruedas 1540

Puerto del Pontón

N 625

Riaño & León

Ribadesella

Oviedo

N

0   Kilometres   10

marked trails: the Picos are one of Europe's most challenging mountain ranges, with unstable weather and treacherous, unforgiving terrain, and what appears from a distance to be a slowly undulating plateau can too easily turn out to be a series of chasms and gorges. If you do leave the trails, be sure to have adequate equipment and preparation (see box above).

In addition to the walking, the Picos **wildlife** is a major attraction. In the Cares Gorge you're likely to see griffon vultures, kestrels, black redstarts, rock thrushes and, most exciting of all for the initiated, wallcreepers. Wild and domestic goats abound, with some unbelievably inaccessible high mountain pastures. Wolves are easy to imagine in the grey boulders of the passes, but bears, despite local gossip, and their picturesque appearances on the tourist board maps, are not a likely sight. An inbred population of about sixty specimens of *Ursus ibericus* remains in the southern Picos, most of them tagged with radio transmitters; another isolated group survives in western Asturias.

The Picos have long been on the map for trekkers and, over the last few years, as road access has opened up the gorges and peaks, have been brought increasingly into the mainstream of tourism. The most popular areas can get very crowded in July and August, as can the narrow roads, and the *teleférico* at Fuente Dé. If you have the choice, and are content with lower-level walks, spring is best, when the valleys are gorgeous and the peaks still snowcapped, although the changing colours of the beech forests in autumn give some competition.

You can **approach** – and leave – the Picos along half a dozen roads: from León, to the south; Santander and the coast, to the northeast; Oviedo and Cangas de Onis, to the northwest.

From the coast to Potes

The N621 heads inland from the coast at Unquera (see p.539), right on the Cantabria–Asturias border, between San Vicente de la Barquera and Llanes. From there, it follows the twisting course of the Río Deva, past **PANES**, where the C6312 forks west, along the upper reaches of the Río Cares to Arenas de Cabrales (see p.549) and Cangas de Onis. There is a very good **information office** (⊕985 414 008 or 985 414 297) in Panes, opposite the Caja de Asturias, where you can arrange walks and horse-riding.

Panes to Potes: the Deva Gorge

Continuing from Panes towards Potes, you enter the eerily impressive gorge of the Río Deva, the **Desfiladero de La Hermida**, whose sheer sides are so high that they deny the village of **LA HERMIDA** any sunlight from November to April. There are a few **places to stay** here if you want to break your journey, including the clean and modern *Pensión Marisa* (⊕ & Ⓕ942 733 545; ❸), on the road out towards Potes, the *Fonda de La Hermida* (⊕ & Ⓕ942 733 531; ❹), also on the main road, and a *posada rural*, *Campo* (⊕ & Ⓕ942 744 135; ❹). The popular **bar-restaurant** *Pagnín*, beneath *Hostal Marisa*, serves up fine traditional cooking. From nearby **Urdón**, a path leads west to Sotres (see p.546); it's a pleasant walk, with mountains looming up around you.

Around 10km beyond La Hermida, the village of **LEBEÑA** lies just east of the main road. It is worth a detour to see the church of **Santa María**, built in the early tenth century by "Arabized" Christian craftsmen and considered the supreme example of Mozarabic architecture. It makes an interesting visit with its thoroughly Islamic geometric motifs and repetition of abstract forms, and is set in beautiful countryside – the Hermida gorge having by now opened out into sheltered vineyards and orchards.

Picos practicalities

Accommodation *Albergues, pensiones* and *hostales* have proliferated in recent years in the more popular villages, but whenever you can it is worth phoning ahead to book a room – especially in summer or at weekends, when whole towns can be booked solid. Up in the mountains there are a number of alpine *refugios*, which range from organized hostels to free, unstaffed huts where you'll need to bring your own food and sleeping bag. Camping beside the *refugios* is accepted, and there are about half a dozen campsites, too, scattered around the villages. Camping outside these sites is officially prohibited below 1600m, and subject to on-the-spot fines, but unofficially you won't be disturbed once away from populated areas.

Banks are located on the periphery of the region: at Panes, Potes, Arenas de Cabrales, Riaño and Cangas de Onís.

Climate There are good days for walking in the valleys even in the depths of winter, but at high altitudes the walking season is from late June to September, varying according to the amount of snowfall the previous winter. All year round, the weather is unstable, with brilliant sunshine rapidly turning to clouds, cold rain or dense mist; in summer, cloud often descends on the valleys, while higher up it is bright and clear. Rain gear and a compass are therefore highly advisable.

Equipment Most trails in the Picos are stony, rugged and steep; walking boots are needed on all but the easiest routes. Safe, reliable water sources are sporadic and you'll need to carry a bottle. The routes given in this guide, unless mentioned otherwise, are straightforward and well marked; for walks at high altitude or off the marked trails, proper equipment and experience are essential, especially if you attempt any actual rock climbing.

Guided walks From June to September the National Park service runs free daily guided walks of easy to moderate standard, leaving from various points around the park's perimeter. They are an excellent way for novice walkers to get to know the

Potes and around

POTES is the main base on the east side of the Picos, still not all that high above sea level at 500m but beautifully situated in the shadow of tall white peaks. It is a small town and market centre (there's an open-air **flea market** on Monday mornings), with winding alleys and plenty of small shops and, although devoted largely to tourism, it retains some identity beyond it. Look out for the Torre del Infanto, which dates back to the thirteenth century and is now the site of the *ayuntamiento*.

This is a useful town to change money in, with the last banks before the mountains and, if you haven't already done so, to buy **trekking maps**. The latter are available from a number of shops, including Fotos Bustamente, in the main square, Plaza Jesús del Monasterio. You can rent **mountain bikes**, and arrange paragliding and canyoning at Picos Aventura next to the bridge.

Six kilometres south of Potes is the church of **Santa María Piasca**. This is pure Romanesque in style, beautifully proportioned, and with some terrific exterior sculpture. Like Santo Toribio de Liébana (see below) it was once a Cluniac monastery, and is flanked by the ruins of monastic and convent buildings.

Practicalities

You'll find a useful **turismo** (June–Sept Mon–Sat 9am–2pm & 4–7pm; ☎942 730 787), under the clock tower just behind the *ayuntamiento*, in Plaza

Picos, although guides won't necessarily speak any English. Call or visit the park offices for details. The National Park offices also have lists of guiding companies operating in each province.

Maps Best are the Adrados editions, in two 1:25,000 sheets, one covering the western massif, the other the central and eastern massifs. Adrados also publish good walking and climbing guides. The Topografico Nacional de España 1:25,000 series, in four sheets, is neither as accurate nor as useful. Maps are available in Cangas de Onis, Cain, Potes, Sotres, Bulnes and Arenas de Cabrales.

Mountain federations You can get further information on trekking and climbing in the Picos from these organizations: Federacíon Asturiana de Montaña, c/Melquiades Álvarez 16, Oviedo ☎ 985 252 362 (Mon–Thu 5–8pm) and Federacíon Cantabrica, c/Rubio 2, Santander ☎ 942 373 378.

National Park offices There are three offices, one in each province, providing information on routes, activities and wildlife within the park, although you may find each one short of information on the other two regions: Casa Dago, Cangas de Onis, Asturias (☎ 985 848 614); Camaleño, Cantabria (☎ 942 733 201, ⓦ www. concejodeonis.com/turismo/parque.htm); Posada de Valdeón, León (☎ 987 740 549, ⓦ www.liebanaypicosdeeuropa.com/visita/picos.htm).

Potholing federations For details on potholing in the area, contact Apt. de Correos 540, Oviedo ☎ 985 211 790 (Fri 7–9pm), Apt. de Correos 51, Santander, or c/Alfonso X el Sabio 1, Burgos (☎ 947 222 427). Permits are required from the National Park offices.

Transport There are no motorable roads which cross the Picos (except the 4WD track from Espinama to Sotres), and circuits by road are long and slow; if you plan to trek across the range, make sure you allow sufficient time to get back to your starting point. There are bus services along the main roads but they're limited to one or two a day and very sketchy out of season. Hitching is fairly easy, however, and can often be arranged at campsites and hostels; bike rental in Potes and other main towns is another option.

Jesús del Monasterio.

Potes has a good range of **accommodation**. If you want to be in town, *Casa Cayo*, c/Cántabra 6 (☎ 942 730 150, ☞ 942 730 119; ❹), is very friendly and welcoming, with a lively bar and excellent restaurant downstairs; at Plazuela del Llano, s/n, *Casa Cuba* (☎ 942 730 064; ❷) is much more basic. For a bit more comfort, head for the modern *Picos de Europa*, San Roque 6 (☎ 942 730 005, ☞ 942 732 060; ❹), the first hotel on the left coming into town from Panes, with a range of rooms with and without bath, or the *Rubio* (☎ 942 730 015, ☞ 942 730 405; ❺) next door, which has its own garage.

If you're unsure just how to tackle the Picos and don't speak much Spanish, the English-owned *Casa Gustavo Guesthouse* (☎ 942 732 010; ❸) is ideal, although 3km away in Aliezo. **Skiing** and **canoeing trips** for residents (and all-comers) are on offer here, and the guesthouse has an office in the UK (☎ 01629/813346), which takes bookings. Also good for activities is *Albergue El Portalón*, 6km south of Potes at Vega de Liébana (☎ & ☞ 942 736 048, ⓦ www.albergue-el-portalon.com; ❶). This is a private hostel, with dormitory rooms, and an "Escuela del aire libre" (Outdoor Activity Centre) offering **paragliding**, mountain-biking, climbing and trekking.

In summer there are three Palomera (☎ 942 880 611) **buses** daily from Potes to Fuente Dé (8.15am, 1pm and 8pm; returning at 9am, 5pm and 8.45pm). Services also run to Unquera and on to Santander three times a day (7am, 9.45am and 5.45pm).

Potes to Espinama and Fuente Dé

The road from **Potes** to **Espinama** and **Fuente Dé** runs below a grand sierra of peaks – the Macizo Oriental – and past a handful of villages, built on the slopes. In summer, and at weekends, there is near constant traffic towards the *teleférico* at Fuente Dé, which has spoilt the villages on the road. However, all have attractive walking, with woodland and streams, and from Espinama you can cut across the range to Sotres.

Turieno and Liébana

TURIENO, 3km west of Potes along the road to Espinama, is a quiet village, in sight of some tall peaks and well placed for acclimatizing to the mountains, with lots of short walks along narrow mule tracks to villages where the locals don't see many tourists and may well open up the bar just for you. The walk to the hamlets of **Lon** and **Brez** is especially worthwhile, through a profusion of wild flowers and butterflies. Turieno has two good rural hotels, *Posada Javier* (☎942 732 122; ❺) and *Posada Laura* (☎942 730 854, ℱ942 744 006; ❹), both about 2km out of town in idyllic settings, as well as a more centrally located *pensión*, the *Hospedería Floranes* (☎942 732 104; ❹). There's also an attractive **campsite**, *La Isla* (☎942 730 896; April–Oct), situated behind an orchard, with **pony-trekking** on offer and a swimming pool. If it's full, the *San Pelayo* campsite in Baró (☎942 733 087; Easter–Oct), a little further up the road towards Espinama, is just as good. Also in Baró is the excellent *Albergue Valdebaró* (☎ & ℱ942 733 092; ❷), located in an attractive nineteenth-century farmhouse.

Close by Turieno, but off the main road from Potes, is the eighth-century **Monasterio de Santo Toribio de Liébana** (daily 10am–2pm & 4–8pm; free), one of the earliest and most influential of medieval Spain. Although much reconstructed, it preserves fine Romanesque and Gothic details, the largest claimed piece of the True Cross, and some extraordinary Mozarabic paintings of the Visions of the Apocalypse (now replaced by reproductions). When the saint's day, April 16, falls on a Sunday (next due in 2006), the Puerto del Perdon (Door of Pardon) is opened, indicating the start of a Jubilee Year that lasts until the following April, during which the monastery is accorded the same pilgrimage status as Santiago de Compostela, Rome and Jerusalem – meaning a huge increase in the number of pilgrims and tourists.

Cosgaya

COSGAYA, midway between Potes and Espinama, can be an attractive base. If you feel like a little luxury before or after trekking, the Alpine-looking *Hotel del Oso* (☎942 733 018, ℱ942 733 036; ❻), on the main road, is the place, set in neat paddocks beside a tidy stream, and with a swimming pool in summer. The *Posada de la Casona* (☎942 733 077; ❹), a seventeenth-century farmhouse hidden away in the woods off the side of the road, is equally relaxing. Inexpensive rooms are provided by the *Mesón de Cosgaya* (☎942 733 047; ❹), which also does excellent meals.

Espinama

Twenty kilometres from Potes, **ESPINAMA** is really into the mountains. Like Cosgaya, its position and one-time isolation is marred by the road running through, but there are plenty of walks in the nearby woods and meadows for those seeking rural tranquillity.

You'll find comfortable accommodation at any of the four **hostales**: the excellent *Hospedaje Sobrevilla* (☎942 736 669; ❺) off the main road, the *Remoña* (☎ & ⓕ942 736 605; ❹), the *Puente Deva* (☎942 736 658, ⓕ942 736 659; ❹) and the *Nevandi* (☎942 736 613, ⓕ942 736 608; ❹). All of these serve **meals**; the *menú* at the *Remoña* is particularly good value at €6, but the *Vicente Campo* (*Puente Deva*'s restaurant) probably has the edge, if only for its feel of a wayfarers' inn, and a crackling fire in winter. The village also has a grocery store which provides for picnics and trekking snacks.

Fuente Dé and the *teleférico*

The road comes to a halt 4km past Espinama, in a steep-sided cul-de-sac of rock. This is the source of the Río Deva; debate as to whether its name should be Fuente de Deva or Fuente de Eva has left it called simply **FUENTE DÉ**. Here you can stay at the modern **parador**, *Río Deva*, next to the cable car (☎942 736 651, ⓕ942 736 654; ❼), or the attractive *Hotel Rebeco* (☎ & ⓕ942 736 600; ❻), nearby. There's also a **campsite**, *El Redondo* (☎942 736 699), with a basic dormitory (❶).

The **teleférico** (cable car) lurches alarmingly up 900m of sheer cliff. It's an extremely popular excursion throughout the year, and in summer a wait to ascend of between two and three hours is by no means uncommon, especially in the middle of the day. A system of numbered tickets (€7.80 return, €4.80 one-way) means that you can wait in the shelter of the **café-bar** at the bottom, as long as your Spanish is up to interpreting the garbled announcements of the PA. Remember that you may well have to queue again for an hour or two before coming down which, at 1900m above sea level, is not nearly so congenial in the mountain chill.

At the top is an extraordinary mountainscape, where on warm days Spanish day-trippers wander around in bathing suits. However, within a few minutes' walk there is hardly a soul. If you are on for a walk, you can follow a bulldozer track 4km to the **Refugio de Aliva** (☎942 563 736; ❺), which has hotel-like rooms and prices, a restaurant, and its own *fiesta* on July 2. From there, you can wind your way back down to Espinama on another rough track. It is also possible to arrange a lift in a **4WD** from the top of the *teleférico*, either to Aliva or to Sotres (see below).

Espinama to Sotres – and beyond

The **trek from Espinama to Sotres** is a superb route along a dirt track, practicable by 4WD, or around five hours on foot. If you are walking, set out north from the *Peña Vieja* bar in Espinama, under an arching balcony, and on to the twisting track behind. This, climbing stiffly, winds past hand-cut hay fields and through groups of barns, until tall cliffs on either side rise to form a natural gateway. Through this you enter a different landscape of rocky summer pasture and small streams. As you near the highest point the track divides at a small barn. Ignore the left-hand path which leads up to the Refugio de Aliva and the top of the cable car, and take the track ahead past a chapel (visible from the junction) up to the ridge forming the pass.

Over the divide the scenery changes again, into a mass of crumbling limestone. In spring or winter, the downhill stretch of track here is slippery and treacherous to all but goats – and perhaps 4WDs. The hamlet of **Vegas de Sotres**, at the bottom of the hill, has a seasonal bar selling drinks; from there you need to climb again slightly to reach Sotres, which, when it appears, has a grim, almost fortified feel, clinging to a cliff edge above a stark green valley.

Sotres

SOTRES is an established walkers' base – it is a trailhead for some superb treks – and has three fairly basic **places to stay**. The *Pensión Casa Cipriano* (☎985 945 024; ⑤) has good rooms but disappointing meals in a *comedor* with a €7.20–7.50 *menú*. It also has a basic *albergue* (①). The better *albergue*, however, is the *Peña Castil* (☎ & ℱ985 945 070; ①), and there is another *pensión*, *La Perdiz* (☎985 945 011; ③), a little further up the street. The bar at the north end of the village has good food and an excellent atmosphere.

The village **store** does good meals, and sells cured sheep's and cow's milk cheeses, as well as the five-month-fermented *cabrales*, a local speciality similar to Roquefort.

East to Tresviso

Until the late 1980s, only a mule path led east from Sotres to **TRESVISO**. This is now a paved road, though still a beautiful route. If you prefer your walking a bit rougher, you can cut down a footpath from this road, 5km out of Sotres, which leads through the **Valle de Sobra** down to **La Hermida**; the final stretch is a spectacular switchback.

In Tresviso, the local bar has clean, modern rooms (☎942 744 444; ③) and a restaurant.

West to Bulnes

Most walkers head west from **Sotres to Bulnes**, heading up to the broad, windy pass of **Pandébano** using the dirt road. This is officially closed to private traffic, although it is navigable by car, with care, and many do still drive up. At the top are high meadows still used for summer pasture by villagers from Bulnes, who live in simple stone dwellings there during the summer months. An old, steep cobbled path leads down to Bulnes.

BULNES is a delight, a remnant of the Picos before roads brought tourists and better living conditions. Previously the only access was by donkey track (see p.549); this changed with the opening in 2001 of a **funicular railway** from Poncebos. At the moment its use is limited to residents only, due to opposition by environmental groups who say that the thousands of predicted visitors will cause irreparable damage to the mountain ecosystem.

For now at least, Bulnes remains a sleepy village, in two parts, Castillos and La Villa. There are two *albergues,* both also offering breakfast and evening meal: the *Bar/Albergue Bulnes* (☎985 366 932; ①), and the *Albergue Peñamain* (☎985 945 939; ①). Camping is also tolerated.

The Naranjo de Bulnes – and across the massif

From the pass at Pandébano and from Bulnes village there are well-used paths up to the **Vega de Urriello**, the high pasture at the base of the **Naranjo de Bulnes**, the Picos' trademark peak – an immense slab of orange-tinted rock standing aloof from the jagged grey sierras around it. The approach from Pandébano is easier, a two- to three-hour hike along a track passing the small *refugio* of Terenosa. The direct path up from Bulnes is heavy-going, and can take up to six hours in bad conditions, with a slippery scree surface which can prove very difficult and dangerous when wet. Once up on the plateau you'll find another refugio, the Vega de Uriello (altitude 1953m), and a permanent spring, as well as large numbers of campers and rock-climbers, for whom the Naranjo is a popular target.

Experienced trekkers can stay the night in the Vega de Urriello *refugio* and then continue across the central massif, through a roller-coaster landscape unforgiving of mistakes, to the **Cabaña Veronica** *refugio*. Cabaña Veronica only has three bunks, so don't plan on sleeping; it's an easy descent from here to the top of the **Fuente Dé** cable car. Alternatively, you can continue west through further challenging terrain to another *refugio* at **Collado Jermoso** before a descent down the ravine of Asotín takes you finally to Cordiñanes at the top of the **Cares Gorge**. If you're planning this trek, make sure you go in a group with proper gear.

The Cares Gorge

The classic walk in the Picos – and deservedly so – is the **Cares Gorge**, which separates the central massif from the western one of Corñión. The most enclosed section **between Caín and Poncebos** – a massive cleft more than 1000m deep and some 12km long – bores through some awesome terrain along an amazing footpath hacked out of the cliff face. It's maintained in excellent condition by the water authorities (it was built to service a hydro-electric scheme) and is perfectly safe. With reasonable energy you can walk it both ways in well under a day – or you could, like many Spanish day-trippers, get a taste of it by walking just a section from Caín. Such is the popularity of this route that in August it can seem to be a stream of hikers – unless you're an early riser.

The usual **starting point** is from the southern trailheads, **Posada de Valdeón** and **Caín**, which can be reached from Potes via Portilla de la Reina, from Cangas de Onis via Oseja de Sajambre, or from León via Riaño. There is a single daily bus to Posada de Valdeón from León via **Portilla de la Reina**, an odd little hamlet at the bottom of a lichen-covered chasm of limestone; Portilla itself is on the León–Potes bus line. On foot, you can reach Posada de Valdeón from Fuente Dé in about four hours, over a mix of dirt tracks and footpaths; the occasional Land Rover makes the trip in summer.

Access from the north is, if anything, easier with a Land Rover bus connecting **Poncebos**, the northern trailhead, with Arenas de Cabrales – which has a regular bus service to Cangas de Onis, Llanes and Panes. Poncebos can also be reached on foot from Bulnes – see below.

Santa Marina and Posada de Valdeón, Cordiñanes and Caín

The bus from Portilla de la Reina gives out at **SANTA MARINA DE VALDEÓN**, transferring its passengers to a Land Rover for the final 3km ride on the narrow lane leading down to Posada. Santa Marina is a lovely village – still quite unspoilt – with a bar, *La Ardilla,* which rents out **rooms** (☎987 742 677; ➊), and a **campsite**, *El Cares* (☎987 742 676), which offers pony trekking.

POSADA DE VALDEÓN is very much on the tourist trail, though nothing can detract from the views of the huge mountains that hem in the valley to the south and shorten the days. The **National Park office** in the village (daily 9am–1pm & 4–7pm; ☎987 740 549) can provide information on the area. The most characterful **accommodation** is at the old *Pensión Begoña* (☎987 740 516; ➌ with bath); rooms are available at the *hostal* above the *Café-Bar Campo* (☎987 740 502; ➎), or you can get a dormitory bed at the *Albergue Cuesta-Valdeón* (☎987 740 560; ➊) on the northern edge of the village. For more comfort, head for *Cumbrés Valdeón* (☎987 742 701; ➎), which also has a smart restaurant. There is also a **campsite**, *El Valdeón* (☎987 742 605), 3km east of the village, at the hamlet of Soto de Valdeón. For **meals**, *Pensión Begoña* does a good set menu, or try the *Cafetería Campo* for more choice.

The **Río Cares** runs through Posada, and its gorge begins just north of the village. Over this first section – to Caín – it is relatively wide and is trailed by a road. However, it's still pretty delightful, with odd pockets of brilliant green meadows at the base of the cliffs. If you're pushed for time (or energy) there is a **Land Rover** service from Posada to the trailhead – €24 per carload – and hitching is easy enough. Most people will prefer to walk the distance, though, and some of the tarmac can be bypassed by taking a dirt track from the lower end of Posada to the **Mirador del Tombo**, just past the village of Cordiñanes. From there to Caín it's around 6km, along a downhill road.

CORDIÑANES makes for a pleasant night's stop – a quieter base than Posada or Caín – and has a couple of small **pensiones**: *El Tombo* (☎987 740 526; ④) and *El Rojo* (☎987 740 523; ④). In summer, **CAÍN** itself is quite a honeypot, full of cars, coaches, day-trippers and trekkers. It has a handful of bars and a supermarket, plying the trade. There is a single **hostal**, *La Ruta* (☎987 742 702; ⑤; March–Oct), right at the opening of the gorge path, although the *Casa Cuevas* (☎987 742 720; ②) also offers beds, and the nearby hotel, *La Posada del Montañero* (☎987 742 711; ④), is reasonable value, with a large restaurant and terrace. Alternatively, you can **camp** in the meadow nearby for the princely sum of €1.20 (no amenities whatsoever). For food supplies, *Casa Chevas* and *Bar La Senda* are reliable and convenient.

Into the gorge

Just beyond Caín the motorable road ends, the valley briefly opens out, then, following the river downstream, suddenly seems to disappear as a solid mountain wall blocks all but a thin vertical cleft. This is where the **gorge** really begins, the path along its course dramatically tunnelled within the rock in the early stages before emerging onto a broad, well-constructed and well-maintained footpath.

The path owes its existence to a long-established hydroelectric scheme, for which a canal was constructed (often buried inside the mountain) all the way from Caín to Poncebos, and into which the river can be diverted in varying quantities. The path is still used for maintenance and each morning a power-plant worker walks the entire length, checking water volume in the canal and waking up those who have elected to spend a night out in the mountains. If you feel like camping, but with more privacy, there is a side valley leading off to the east about 1km into the gorge.

The first stretch of the path is more of an engineering spectacle than anything else and in midsummer or at weekends is thronged with day-trippers strolling through the dripping tunnels and walkways. Once you get 4km or so from Caín, you're down to more committed walkers, and the mountains, freed of most waterworks paraphernalia, command your total attention. They rise pale and jagged on either side, with griffon vultures and other birds of prey circling the crags. The river drops steeply, some 150m below you at the first bridge but closer to 300m down by the end.

A little over halfway along, the canyon bends to the right and gradually widens along the **descent to Poncebos**. At about 7km and 9km into the gorge some enterprising individuals have cornered the summer market with makeshift refreshments stands, handy as there are no springs. For the final 3km of the gorge, the main route climbs a dry, exposed hillside; an alternative riverside path can be reached by a steep side trail that zigzags down the precipice. Just before Poncebos another side path leads up to the cliffside village of

CAMARMEÑA, where *La Fuentina* (☎985 846 625; ❶) has a bar, *camas* and tremendous perspectives on the Naranjo de Bulnes peak.

Poncebos – and a trail to Bulnes

At **PONCEBOS** you'll find **places to stay**, including the *Pensión El Garganta del Cares* (☎985 846 463; ❸) and, a bit further down past the bridge (coming from Caín), next to the power plant, the modern *Hostal Poncebos* (☎985 846 447; ❸), and the large *Mirador de Cabrales* (☎985 846 673, ℻985 846 685; ❹), which has a rather ugly self-service restaurant. Any of these might be welcome facilities at the end of a long day, but they're a bit institutional and somewhat gloomy due to blocked sunlight. They are, incidentally, the only buildings at Poncebos – in no sense is the place a village. If daylight permits, you might prefer to make the superb, but steep, hour-and-a-half trek up the gorge of the Tejo stream to **Bulnes** (see p.546) and stay overnight there. The path begins over the photogenic medieval bridge of Jaya, located just to the right (south) at the end of the marked Cares path – there's no need to descend to the hotels.

Arenas de Cabrales

The foothill area to the north of the Picos is known as **Cabrales**, as is the delicious and exceptionally strong fermented sheep's cheese made in a dozen-odd villages here. The C6312 runs through the valley; there are buses four times a day (Mon–Sat) between Cangas de Onis and Arenas de Cabrales, two of which run through to Panes and on to the coast. If you're driving, the minor roads to the coast are pleasant, allowing you to bypass traffic on the Cangas road.

ARENAS DE CABRALES (Las Arenas on some maps) is the main village of this region: a friendly place, and an excellent first or last stop in the Picos. There are three good **hotels**, the *Naranjo de Bulnes* (☎985 846 519; ❹), the luxurious *Picos de Europa*, (☎985 846 491, ℻985 846 545; ❻), and the elegant *Villa de Cabrales* (☎985 846 719, ℻985 846 733; ❺). Alternatively try the attractive self-catering *agroturismo*, *Apartments Montecaoru* in the village (☎639 001 691; ❹) with a booking office in the UK (☎07808/650 677, ✉fondon@mail.com). You'll also find a pair of *pensiones* just around the corner, *El Castañeu* (☎985 846 573; ❸) and *Covadonga* (❸), and there's a **campsite**, *Camping Naranjo de Bulnes* (☎985 846 578), 1km to the east. If all of the accommodation is full, there are three further *hostales* 3km down the road in Carreña de Cabrales, the best of which is *Hostal Cabrales* (☎985 845 006; ❸). Back in Arenas, the *Mesón Castañeu* has outstanding à la carte **food** at *menú* prices, while *Bar Palma*, past the BBVA bank, is a lively spot for an evening's drinking – they serve *queimadas* (hot Galician punch) if you're in a large enough group. *La Jueya* is a good new *sidrería* in the town centre.

Arenas also has a helpful **turismo** booth (summer only Tues–Sun 10am–2pm & 4–8pm; ☎985 846 484, ⓦhttp://turismo.cabrales.org/2/index.htm) to fill you in on mountain or transport details. Out of season, try the *ayuntamiento* (☎985 845 021). There are also two **banks** and various stores. On the last Sunday in August the village plays host to the **Asturian Cheese Festival**, an excuse for plenty of dancing and music but, oddly enough, not all that much cheese.

Over to the west: the Sella valley and Riaño

The road running along the western end of the Picos, the N625 between Cangas de Onis and Riaño, is arguably quite as spectacular as the Cares gorge.

Mountains rear to all sides and for much of the way the road traces the gorge of the **Río Sella**. The central section of this, the **Desfiladero de los Beyos**, is said to be the narrowest motorable gorge in Europe – a feat of engineering rivalling anything in the Alps and remarkable for the 1930s.

In summer there are daily EASA **buses** in each direction between Cangas and Posada de Valdeón via Oseja de Sajambre.

The Sajambre villages

Coming from Posada de Valdeón, you turn onto the N625 right by the 1290m **Puerto del Pontón**, a pass almost continually fogged in since the reservoir was built at Riaño to the south (see below). Heading north, the road passes through **OSEJA DE SAJAMBRE**, a very pretty village, high on the steep slope of a broad and twisting valley. Comfortable **rooms** and good **meals** are available at *Hostal de Pontón* (☎987 740 348; ❹).

Six kilometres above Oseja, to the east of the road, is **SOTO DE SAJAMBRE**, an excellent base for walkers, with a lovely **hostal**, the *Peña Santa* (☎987 740 395; ❸) which also has dormitory beds and a restaurant. This is a possible starting point for a south-to-north traverse of the western Picos massif to the Lakes of Covadonga, as well as for treks in the valley of the Río Dobra. There is a refuge, *Vegabaño*, one hour above the village.

Riaño and south towards León

South from the **Puerto del Pontón**, you descend to the spectacular **Pantano de Riaño** (see box below). The creation of this reservoir flooded half a dozen villages and a swathe of farmland – leaving just the odd tree top above water. The main village of the valley, **RIAÑO**, was relocated just above the reservoir, and has a hotel and a few bars. There are plans to turn it into a winter- and water-sports resort, though little has come of this so far.

Riaño: the making of a reservoir

Travelling in Asturias, you often see posters with the slogan "Don't let them destroy our Picos". The threat to the mountains is real: the Picos is a small range, and every year the despoliation of previously pristine areas seems to increase. The Asturians are doing what they can, but if you enter the Picos from the south, from León through Riaño, you'll see the worst that can (and has) happened – the loss of a whole valley.

In 1966 the Franco regime claimed right of eminent domain over the entire valley of **Riaño**, prior to turning it into a reservoir. Compensation of sorts was paid at that time, and then plans stalled until the 1980s, when the project was revived by the PSOE government. The inhabitants of Riaño, most of them children of those who had accepted the "settlement" in the 1960s, were forcibly evicted, with no further compensation offered. The newer generation erected a tent village overlooking their destroyed homes, but that too was bulldozed, after demonstrations broken up by riot police. On December 31, 1987, the dam was suddenly sealed, and flooding commenced. The authorities claimed that conditions were optimal – there was a storm in progress – but the reality was that the government had imposed a deadline and wanted no more protests.

The dam, clearly, has a value for the Spanish agricultural economy, irrigating the plains of León and Palencia to the south. But the investment came from outside corporations, and the local residents have seen none of the profits from the dam and few of the benefits.

Cangas de Onis, Covadonga and the lakes

The main routes between the Picos and central Asturias meet at **Cangas de Onis**, a busy market town, and a bit of a traffic bottleneck, especially so in summer and at weekends. If you're not intent on a visit to **Covadonga**, with its pilgrim shrine and **mountain lakes** beyond, or on making a canoe trip down the Río Sella, you may prefer to make a detour.

Cangas de Onis

The distant peaks around **CANGAS DE ONIS** provide a magnificent backdrop to its big sight – the so-called **Roman bridge**, festooned with ivy, which you'll see splashed across the front of many Asturian tourist brochures, although it has in fact been rebuilt many times, most recently in the twentieth century. The town's other attraction, less photogenic but perhaps more curious, is the **Capilla de Santa Cruz**, a fifteenth-century rebuilding of an eighth-century chapel founded over a Celtic dolmen stone. This, like the Liébana monastery at Potes, is among the earliest Christian sites in Spain, and Cangas, as an early residence of the fugitive Asturian-Visigothic kings, lays claim to the title of "First Capital of Christian Spain". Today, however, it belies such history: a functional town, muscled-in upon by new developments, though good for a comfortable night and a solid meal after a spell in the mountains, and a better base than Arriondas itself for the popular **canoe descents** of the Río Sella. These morning trips tend to last three hours or so, cost around €18 including transport, and are bookable through various tour operators in town.

Practicalities

Most facilities lie within a few hundred metres of the **bus station** (in front of the *ayuntamiento*). A **turismo** kiosk (July–Sept Mon–Fri 10am–10pm, Sat 10am–9pm, Sun 10am–3pm; ☎985 848 005) is on Avenida Covadonga, next to the park. More comprehensive information for trekkers and mountaineers is available from Casa Dago, a **National Park headquarters** (☎985 848 614), just up the road from the turismo.

There's a wide range of **accommodation**, although budget places tend to get booked out in summer. Good choices include the friendly *Hostal El Sella* (☎985 848 011; ❸), by the old bridge at Avda. de Castilla 4 and *Hotel Covadonga* at no. 38 in the same street (☎985 848 135, ⓕ985 947 054; ❸). More upmarket is the *Hotel Puente Romano*, at Puente Romano 8 (☎985 849 339, ⓕ985 947 284; ❹). If you want to camp, there is a **campsite** in Soto de Cangas: *Covadonga* (☎985 940 097; Easter & June–Sept). Two kilometres down the road to Arriondas there's the *Parador de Cangas de Onis* (☎985 849 402; ❽) in the sumptuously restored monastery of La Vega, and a youth hostel, *La Posada del Monasterio* (☎985 848 553, ⓕ985 947 502; ❶; March–Dec), a useful fallback when everywhere's full in town.

Freshwater fish and *sidra* are the specialities in the **bars and restaurants** here. The *Sidrería/Mesón Puente Romano* by the bridge has a grand outdoor setting under the plane trees, with good-value *menús*, while *Restaurante Los Arcos*, on Avenida Covadonga, has a less romantic setting but excellent, if slightly pricey, cooking.

Covadonga and the lakes

The **reconquista** is said to have begun at **COVADONGA**, 11km southeast of Cangas in a northerly sierra of the Picos. Here in 718 the Visigothic King Pelayo and a small group of followers repulsed the Moorish armies – at odds, according to Christian chronicles, of 31 to 400,000. In reality the Moors can hardly have been more than an isolated expeditionary force and their sights were already turned to the more lucrative lands beyond the Pyrenees, where in 732 they were defeated at Poitiers by Charles Martel. But the symbolism of the event is at the heart of Asturian, and Spanish, national history, and the defeat probably did allow the Visigoths to regroup, slowly expanding Christian influence over the northern mountains of Spain and Portugal.

Certainly, Covadonga is a serious religious shrine, with signs proclaiming it as a place of prayer, and daily Masses in the **cave** (8am–10pm; free), which is the focus of the pilgrimage. This shrine, said to have been used by Pelayo and containing his sarcophagus, is now a chapel, sited impressively on the side of a mountain above a waterfall and plunge pool. Across the road is a grandiose nineteenth-century pink basilica and, opposite this, the **Museo del Tesoro** (daily 10.30am–2pm & 4–7.30pm; €0.30) displaying various religious artefacts.

There is one inexpensive **fonda** on the road into town, the *Hospedería del Peregrino* (☎985 846 047, ℻985 846 051; ❹), which has an excellent restaurant, specializing in *fabada asturiana*. There is also a *casa rural*, *Casa Priena* (☎985 846 070; ❹), with bath, TV and telephone. For more upmarket accommodation, you'll find the *Auseva* nearby (☎985 846 023, ℻985 846 151; ❺), and *Hotel Pelayo* right next to the caves (☎985 846 061, ℻985 846 054; ❻).

Lakes Enol and Ercina

Beyond Covadonga the road begins to climb sharply, and after 12km you reach the **mountain lakes** of **Enol** and **Ercina**. These are connected to Covadonga by frequent buses (June 15 to September 15 only), but it's not difficult to hitch if you miss out. The **Mirador de la Reina**, a short way before the lakes, gives an inspiring view of the assembled peaks.

The **lakes** themselves are placid, but subject to quirky weather. Even if it's misty at Cangas or Covadonga, you may find that the cloud cover disperses abruptly just before the lakes. There is a basic **refugio** (☎985 848 043), with no eating or washing facilities, a **campsite** at the southwest corner of Lake Enol, and a bar-restaurant beside Ercina.

The Cornión Massif

From the higher Lake Ercina a good path leads east-southeast within three hours to the **Vega de Ario**, where there's a **refugio** (☎989 524 553), lots of campers on the meadow, and unsurpassed **views** across the Cares Gorge to the highest peaks in the central Picos. Unless you have serious hiking experience for the steep descent to the Cares, this is something of a dead end, since to cross the bulk of the western peaks you'll need to backtrack at least to Lake Ercina to resume progress south.

Most walkers, however, trek south from the lakes to the **Vega Redonda refugio** (☎985 848 516). This popular route initially follows a dirt track but later becomes an actual path through a curious landscape of stunted oaks and turf. Vega Redonda, about three hours' walk, overlooks the very last patches of green on the Asturias side of the Cornión massif. From here the path continues west for another hour up to the viewing point, the **Mirador de Ordiales**.

Beyond the Vega Redonda refugio, walks are in a different category of difficulty altogether. Nerve and skill are required to cross the barren land to **Llago Huerta**, the next feasible overnight spot – and like Redonda popular with potholers who disappear down various chasms in the area. From Llago Huerta it's possible to descend to Cordiñanes, Santa Marina de Valdeón or Oseja de Sajambre.

The coast: Llanes to Gijón

Once you get into Asturias, the coast becomes wilder and more rugged. You can never forget the presence of the **Picos de Europa** – just 20km inland from **Llanes**, the first major resort along the coast, and a good base for exploring the mountains. The **FEVE line** hugs the coast as far as **Ribadesella**, an attractive little fishing port, before turning inland in the direction of Oviedo. West of Ribadesella, the coast deteriorates towards Gijón, although there are some attractive spots such as the fishing villages of **Lastres** and **Villaviciosa**, and the small town of **Colunga**, famed for its cider.

Llanes

The delightful seaside town of **LLANES** is Asturias's easternmost resort – and one of its most attractive, crammed between the foothills of the Picos and a particularly dramatic stretch of the coast. To the east and west stretch sheer cliffs, little-known beaches and a series of beautiful coves, yours for the walking. The three town beaches are small, but pleasant, while the excellent **Playa Ballota** is only 3km to the east, with its own supply of springwater down on the sand (and a nudist stretch). A long *rambla*, the **Paseo de San Pedro**, runs along the top of the dramatic cliffs above the western town beach, the Playa del Sablón.

In the centre, a tidal stream lined with cafés and seafood restaurants runs down into a small harbour. On the west bank, tall medieval walls shelter a number of older buildings in various stages of restoration or decay, including a medieval tower, the semi-ruined Renaissance palaces of the **Duques de Estrada** and the **Casa del Cercau** (both closed for restoration), and the **Basilica**, built in the plain Gothic style imported from southern France, although the sculpted east door is preserved from an earlier Romanesque building. Around town you'll also see numerous larger houses built by *indianos*, nineteenth-century emigrants returning from the Americas eager to show off their newly acquired wealth.

Llanes makes an excellent base (or rest-cure) for the Picos, with good transport connections via nearby Unquera. Those with their own transport could also visit a curious Bronze Age monolith 10km east along the coast road at **Peña Tu**.

Practicalities

There's a useful **turismo**, open year-round, in the Torre Medieval (daily 10am–2pm & 4–6pm; ☎985 400 164), which can help with accommodation. Llanes's cheapest **rooms** are at the *Bar Colón* (☎985 400 883; ❷), overlooking the river, while another good budget option includes the old-fashioned and spacious *Hospedaje El Río*, Avda. de San Pedro 3 (☎985 401 191; ❸). *Pensión Iberia*, c/Las Barqueras (☎985 400 891; ❸), is a budget fallback near the bus station. For more comfort, *Sablon's Hotel* (☎985 400 787, ☎985 401 988; ❹) overlooks the Playa del Sablón, while *Pensión La Guía*, Plaza Parres Sobrino 1 (☎985 402 577; ❹), is smart and central. Slightly more pricey is *Don Paco* (☎985 400 150; ❼), which is run along *parador* lines in a converted seventeenth-century convent. A wide selection of *casas rurales* in this area includes *La Torre* (☎985 411 133; ❹), 5km away in Andrín. There is a large **campsite**, *Las Baracenas* (☎985 402 887; June–Sept), five minutes from town, although the slightly smaller *Entre Playas* (☎985 400 888; Easter & June–Oct), on the headland between the two town beaches to the east, has the better situation.

For good **seafood** – and Asturian *sidra* – head for *La Marina*, a restaurant shaped like a boat at the end of the harbour, where you can sit outside and tuck into swordfish steaks and sardines, or for one of the simple open-air **café-restaurants** by the river just inland from the bridge, which serve up above-average seafood *raciones*. At the *El Campanu*, and others here, you'll pay between €3.60 and €12 a dish; drink the *sidra* or the local white wine. *El Bodegón*, hidden in the tree-shaded Plaza de Siete Puertas, is good for *sidra* and Asturian *raciones*; for more formal meals and *menús*, try the restaurant behind *Bar Colón*, or one of the fairly similar places round the corner on c/Manuel Cué.

Villahormes and Nueva

Following the coast (and FEVE line), the next tempting stop to the west of Llanes is **VILLAHORMES**. This is an unprepossessing-looking place: no more than a train station, a handful of houses, a café-bar and a very shabby-looking *hostal*. Follow the rusty signpost to **Playa de la Huelga**, however, and, after 1500m of driveable track, you reach one of the best swimming coves imaginable, with a rock arch in the bay and an enclosed sea pool for kids to splash around in safety. It is flanked by a pleasant bar-restaurant. The **Playa de Gulpiyuri**, 1km to the north east, is an unusual beach set back from the shore line but fed by an underground channel of seawater.

A thirty-minute walk west of Villahormes, or five minutes more on the train, will get you to another hamlet, **NUEVA**, tucked into a fold of the hills, 3km inland from another gorgeous little cove. If you decide to **stay**, head for the *Ereba* (☎985 410 139; ❹), a pleasant *casa rural*; there is also a **campsite**, *Palacio de Garaña* (☎985 410 075).

Ribadesella

RIBADESELLA, 18km west of Llanes, is an unaffected old port, split into two by the Sella River, and bridged by a long causeway. On the east side is the old town, with the bus and FEVE stations and dozens of great little bars and *comedores* on the streets parallel to the **fishing harbour**. Freshly caught fish is still unloaded after midnight at the *lonja* and, although the catch is increasingly small, it's fun to hang out until then in the bars. In the seafood joints lining the harbour you can sample unusual delicacies such as limpets (*lapas*) in tomato sauce or boiled sea urchin (*erizos de mar*). On the west side, the new town contains the more upmarket accommodation, the excellent town **beach**, and the **Cueva Tito Bustillo** (April to mid-Sept Wed–Sun 10am–4.15pm; €1.80, free Wed; reservations on ☎985 861 118), an Altamira-style cave more impressive for its stalactites than its paintings, though it has a museum of prehistoric finds from the area. Only 375 visitors are allowed into the caves each day, so in summer you'll need to arrive first thing in the morning to get in.

Practicalities

Arriving by train, you'll emerge at the **FEVE station**, at the top end of town, on Carretera Santander; the **bus station** is on the main road at the entrance to the old town. There is a new **turismo** (summer only daily 10am–10pm; ☎985 860 038) in the old town just by the causeway at the entrance to the port.

Accommodation is a bit pricier than usual, although the impecunious may be able to find *camas*, and there's a **youth hostel** on c/Ricardo Cangas (☎985 400 205; ❶) in an old house on the east side of the estuary, although it is often booked out by groups. Among the *hostales*, try the *Sueve*, La Bolera 13 (☎985

860 369; ⑤), or the *Covadonga* (☎985 860 222; ❹), at the end of Gran Vía at c/Manuel Caso de la Villa 9. Ribadesella's top hotel, the old-fashioned *Gran Hotel del Sella* (☎985 860 150, ⓕ985 857 449; ❼), fronts the beach and the promenade. Also recommended is the *Hostal El Pilar* (☎985 860 446; ⑤), 2km south of the beach at Puente del Pilar, which has a restaurant serving traditional Asturian food. There is a *casa rural*, *La Llosona* (☎985 857 887; ⑤), 1km south of the new town in Granda-Ardines, with great views of the surrounding area, and there are also two **campsites**: *Los Sauces*, near the beach on Carretera San Pedro la Playa (☎985 861 312; Easter & June–Sept), and *Ribadesella* (☎985 858 293; April–Sept), just south of Puente del Pilar, at Sebreño.

For **meals**, the *Rompeolas* is a classic if slightly pricey *marisquería* in the old town, with piles of seafood lining its long wooden counter; alternatively, there's *Casa Basilio* on c/Manuel Caso de la Villa, which serves great tapas.

Lastres and Villaviciosa

Beyond Ribadesella the railway turns inland, as do most tourists, heading for Cangas de Onis and the western flanks of the Picos de Europa. The route into the mountains – the N634 and M625 – is a superb one, following the valley and gorge of the Río Sella. The coast itself deteriorates the closer you get to Gijón, Asturias's main industrial port, though there are a few last highlights, including the small resort of **La Isla** and the town of **Colunga**, both of which are noted for their seafood and cider, and the fishing villages of **Lastres** and **Villaviciosa**. Colunga has a useful **turismo**, located in an original *hórreo* in the town park (summer only Tues–Sat 10am–2pm & 5–8pm, Sun 10am–3pm; ☎985 852 200).

Lastres

LASTRES, a couple of kilometres north of Colunga off the Santander–Gijón highway, is a tiny fishing village built on a steep cliffside with a new harbour and a couple of good beaches on its outskirts. It has escaped much tourist attention so far and if you've just come from a few strenuous days' trekking in the Picos, this would be as good a spot as any to recuperate. **Buses** run from Ribadesella every two hours in summer.

Two neighbouring **restaurants** on the road down to the port, *Sidrería El Escanu* and *Bar Bitacora*, serve good seafood, with terrace views. There is only a handful of **hotels**, but *Casa Eutimio* (☎985 850 012; ❹), near the port in Plaza San Antonio and with its own seafood restaurant, is a good bet, and the nearby *Miramar*, Bajada al Puerto (☎985 850 120; ❼), has some rooms with great sea views. The *Hostal Mary Paz* (☎985 850 261; ❹), at the top of town, is a last resort, while if you've money to spare, there's also a luxury hotel, the *Palacio de los Vallados*, Pedro Villarta (☎985 850 444, ⓕ985 850 517; ❽). There are two *casas rurales*: *Pipo* in the tiny village of Sales, 4km away (☎985 856 590; ❹), and *Pernús* (☎985 928 819; ❹) in Pernús, the next village along. The excellent beach, Playa la Griega, 2km to the east, has a **campsite**, *Costa Verde* (☎985 856 373).

Villaviciosa and around

VILLAVICIOSA, 30km from Gijón, is set in beautiful Asturian countryside, on the shores of the Río Villaviciosa, and with green rolling hills behind. There's a market on Wednesday and an atmospheric old town where you'll find the thirteenth-century church of Santa María and the best restaurants. The town is famed as the "apple capital" of Spain, and visits to the **cider factory**,

El Gaitero, reveal how the country's most famous cider is manufactured (Mon–Fri 9am–12.30pm & 3–5.30pm, Sat 9am–12.30pm; free). There's a good **beach** for swimming nearby – Playa Rodiles, visible from the main road.

You'll find good-value **rooms** at the friendly *Pensión Sol*, c/Sol 27 (T985 891 130; ❷), and at the modern *Hostal El Congreso*, c/Generalísimo 25 (T985 891 180, F985 891 907; ❹), with its own restaurant. More upmarket places include *Hotel Carlos I*, Plaza Carlos I (T985 890 121, F985 890 051; ❹) and the new *Hotel Casa España*, opposite (T985 892 030, F985 892 682; ❺). The **turismo** (summer only Tues–Sat 10am–2pm & 5–8pm; T985 891 759) is in Parque Vallina.

Nine kilometres southwest of Villaviciosa, tucked away in the beautiful Puelles valley, lies the Cistercian monastery of **Valdedios** (daily: May–Oct 11am–1pm & 4.30–6.30pm; Nov–April 11am–1pm). Abandoned for many years, the buildings are now being restored and a small community of monks returned in 1992. It's worth a look around the grounds and impressive thirteenth-century monastery church, where you can attend one of the five offices sung daily, but the main sight is the wonderful **Iglesia de San Salvador**, built in the ninth century in the unique style known as Asturian, or pre-Romanesque; look out for the columns borrowed from a nearby Roman ruin and the beautiful geometric motifs in the stone windows. There are eight buses daily between Oviedo and Villaviciosa which stop at San Pedro de Ambas. From here, it's a one-kilometre walk downhill to the monastery, where it's sometimes possible to stay in the **hospedería** (T985 892 324).

Gijón and Avilés

Gijón and **Avilés** are Asturias's major industrial cities: daunting places, with their smoking factory chimneys, and best passed by if you are looking for a quiet seaside holiday. However, each of the cities has something going for it: Gijón in its big-city "feel", nightlife and summer **film festival** (late June/early July); Avilés in its well-preserved old centre. In addition, both cities know how to party, especially during **Carnaval** (see box, p.559) and during **Semana Santa**, when Avilés hosts some of the country's most spectacular parades.

Gijón

GIJÓN, the largest city in Asturias, was completely rebuilt after its destruction in the Civil War. It was the scene of one of the most intensive bombardments of the war, when, in August 1936, miners armed with sticks of dynamite stormed the barracks of the Nationalist-declared army. The beleaguered colonel asked ships from his own side, anchored offshore, to bomb his men rather than let them be captured.

Arrival, orientation and information

The city **centre** is a fairly small area, just south of the old town and headland. Its three main squares, separated by a couple of blocks each, are, from south to north, Plaza del Humedal, Plaza del Carmen and Plaza del Marqués (flanked by the Palacio de Revillagigedo). Two of the **train stations** (FEVE and RENFE local services) and the **bus station** (a wonderful piece of Art Deco) are just off Plaza del Humedal. Long-distance RENFE services use a third train station on Avenida de Juan Carlos I.

The **turismo** (☎985 346 046) is off the Plaza del Marqués. **Internet cafés** are beginning to spring up in Gijón, although most are rather pricey. Good value, and centrally located, is *Informatica Gijón* at c/Martínes Marina 3; also worth trying is *El Navegante de Internet* at c/Marqués de San Esteban 21, down by the port, and *Cafetería San Siro* at Avda. Rufo Rendueles 16, right next to the beach.

Accommodation

Finding a **place to stay** is rarely a problem, with a broad range of places to cater for all budgets. Most of the accommodation is concentrated at the lower end of town, beyond the Playa San Lorenzo; good streets to head for include c/San Bernardo, c/Santa Lucía and c/Pedro Duro. The pleasant municipal campsite is 1.5km east along the coast at Las Cascrias (☎985 365 755; Easter & June–Sept)

Hotel Asturias, Plaza Mayor 12 ☎985 350 600, ⓕ985 346 872. Friendly hotel on the atmospheric main square between the beach and port. ❻

Hostal Gijón, c/Tineo 5 ☎985 359 815. Cheap, basic bed for the night, not far from the bus station. ❹

Pensión Gonzalez, c/San Bernardo 30 ☎985 355 863 Highly recommended *pensión* with large, airy rooms in a well-furnished old mansion-house.

Pensión Argentina ☎985 344 481 upstairs is also a good bet. Both ❹

Hostal Manjón, Plaza del Marqués 1 ☎985 352 378. Nicely located *hostal*; ask for a room overlooking the harbour. ❹

Hostal Narcea, c/San Juan de la Cruz 5 ☎985 393 287. One of the cheapest places to stay, slightly outside the centre. ❸

Parador Molino Viejo, Parque de Isabel la Católica ☎985 370 511, ⓕ985 370 233. Luxury accommodation, set in an attractive park at the east end of the beach. ❽

Hotel Patho's, c/Santa Elena 6 ☎985 176 400. Upmarket business hotel offering internet access in the rooms, if that's what you want. ❻

The City

Although Gijón hosts a number of museums and other sights, the main attraction is its unpretentious feel, with great beaches and a serious party spirit. Once past the industrial outskirts, the city has quite a breezy, open feel about it, with a grid of streets backing onto the sands of the **Playa de San Lorenzo**, a surprisingly unpolluted beach. In winter, you'll find the occasional hardy surfer out here, while in the summer the whole city seems to descend for the afternoons and weekends.

The old part of town, **Cimadevilla**, occupies a headland northwest of the beach. Its chief monument is the eighteenth-century **Palacio de Revillagigedo** (summer Tues–Sat 11am–1.30pm & 4–9pm, Sun noon–2.30pm; winter Tues–Sat 10am–1pm & 4–8pm, Sun noon–2.30pm; free), built in a splendid mix of neo-Baroque and neo-Renaissance styles; it now houses a gallery of twentieth-century art, and hosts music, theatre and other cultural events. Facing the palace, in the centre of the square, is a statue of Pelayo, the seventh-century king who began the Reconquest. Nearby is the **Torre del Reloj**, c/Recoletas 5 (March–June & Sept Tues–Sat 10am–1pm & 5–8pm, Sun 11am–2pm; July & Aug Tues–Sat 11am–1.30pm & 5–9pm, Sun 11am–2pm; Oct–Feb Tues–Sat 10am–1pm & 5–7pm, Sun 11am–2pm; free), a modern tower built on the ruins of a sixteenth-century one, housing an interesting display about Gijón's history, but mainly worth climbing for the view across the city. At the end of the headland is the **Parque La Atalaya**, with great views of the Atlantic framed by Eduardo Chillida's sculpture *Elegy of the Horizon*.

West from Cimadevilla is the pretty **Puerto Deportivo**, the harbour area which is a focus for the city's evening and weekend *paseo*. There are a few scattered museums, the most interesting of which is the bagpipe museum, the **Museo de la Gaita**, Paseo Dr Fleming (summer Tues–Sat 11am–1.30pm & 5–9pm, Sun 11am–2pm; winter Tues–Sat 10am–1pm & 5–8pm, Sun 11am–2pm; free), an amazing array of instruments from all over the Celtic world and beyond. Gijón is also home to one of Spain's premier **football** clubs, Sporting Gijón; they play at a stadium just east of the beach.

Eating and drinking

The streets around the seafront and immediately behind contain a mass of little **café-restaurants**, all reasonably priced and most with a *menú*. **Fish** is a speciality here.

La Botica, c/San Bernardo 2. Typical *sidrería* (cider house) on the Plaza Mayor.

Heladería Islandia, c/San Antonio 4. Excellent ice-cream joint offering (among others) gazpacho, *fabada* and *cabrales* blue cheese flavours.

Casa Justo, Avda. del Hermanos Felgueroso 50. Superb *sidrería* with a good restaurant behind it.

Casa Zabala, c/Viz Compgrade ☎ 985 341 731. Good, traditional Asturian specialities, including

fabada – a rich sausage and bean stew. Closed Sun & Feb.

La Marina, c/Trinidad 9. Fine *sidra* and tapas.

La Pondala, Avda. Dionisio Cifuentes, Somio ☎ 985 361 160. Upmarket restaurant, famous for its seafood and rice. Closed Thurs & Nov.

El Retiro, c/Begoña 26, La Ruta. Asturian cooking with an excellent value €6 *menú*.

Torremar, c/Ezcurdía 120. Wonderful place for *sidra* and *parillas* (grills).

Nightlife

Gijón's **nightlife** scene centres around the area known as **La Ruta**, a grid enclosed by c/Santa Lucía, c/Buen Suceso and c/Santa Rosa, five minutes' walk from the harbour. There are scores of **disco-bars**, including the noisy and trendy *La Gruta de la Ruta*, and *El Viñedo*, which has a quieter, more old-fashioned feel. Later on, the **club and disco** scene is focused around **El Náutico** near the beach: *Amnesia*, c/Jacobo Olaneta, plays up-to-date dance; *Guantanamera*, further down the road, plays salsa and latino.

Avilés

AVILÉS, 20km from Gijón and inland, is the centre of the crumbling Asturian steel industry, and until not long ago had the unwelcome honour of being one of Europe's most polluted cities. As you approach, from any direction, it's not hard to see why: line upon line of grim factories ring the town, putting off even the hardiest of travellers. But press on to the tiny, arcaded old centre of town and you can forget they exist.

Arrival, information and accommodation

Avilés is a good transport junction and you may well find yourself here changing buses or trains. The **FEVE**, **RENFE** and **bus stations** are all sited in the same terminus on Avenida Telares just down from Parque Muelle and the old town. The **airport**, Aeropuerto de Asturias, is 13km away in Ranon, just off the N632 (☎ 985 127 500); Iberia flies direct to Stansted in the UK three times a week. The Viaca travel agency, at Plaza de la Merced, 5 (☎985 561 844), can be useful for last-minute flights and train tickets.

The city's **turismo** (Mon–Fri 9.30am–2pm; ☎985 544 325) is off Plaza de España, at c/Ruíz Gómez 21, and the main **post office** is on c/Doctor Graiño, in front of Parque Las Meanas.

Carnaval in Asturias

Carnaval, the *mardi gras* week of drinking, dancing and excess, takes place over late February and early March. In Spain, the celebrations are reckoned to be at their wildest in Tenerife, Cadiz and Asturias – and, in particular, **Avilés**.

Events begin in **Avilés** on the **Saturday** before Ash Wednesday, when virtually the entire city dons fancy dress and takes to the streets. Many costumes are bizarre works of art ranging from toothbrushes to mattresses and packets of sweets. By nightfall, anyone without a costume is likely to be drenched in some form of liquid, as gangs of nuns, Red Indians and pirates roam the streets. Calle Galiana is central to the action, and the local fire brigade traditionally hoses down the street, and any passing revellers, with foam. A parade of floats also makes its way down this street, amid the frenzy.

The festivities, which include live music, fireworks and fancy-dress competitions, last till dawn. It's virtually impossible to find accommodation but the celebrations continue throughout Asturias during the following week, so after a full night of revelling you can just head on to the next venue. The first buses leave town at 6.45am. Sunday is, in fact, a rest day before *Carnaval* continues in **Gijón** on the **Monday** night. Much the same ensues and fancy dress is again essential; La Ruta is the place to be for the start of the night, with people and events shifting between Plaza Mayor and the harbour area till dawn. On **Tuesday** night, the scene shifts to **Oviedo**: the crowds are smaller here and events are less frantic, but a fair part of the city again dons costume. There's a parade along Calle Uria, a midnight fireworks display in the Plaza Escandelera, and live bands in the Plaza Mayor.

Finally, on the Friday after Ash Wednesday, **Mieres**, a mining town, just southeast of Oviedo, plays host to *Carnaval*. Events take place in an area known as Calle del Vicio, which locals claim contains the highest concentration of bars in the province.

Staying in Avilés is surprisingly tricky as **accommodation** is scarce, and the few reasonably priced *hostales* are invariably full of business people. At the bottom end of the scale, head for *Pensión Puente Azud*, c/El Acero 5 (☏985 550 177; ④). More expensive is the *Hotel Luzana*, c/Fruta 9 (☏985 565 840, ℉985 564 912; ⑥), just off Plaza de España and with a good restaurant, while the upmarket *Hotel San Félix*, Avda. de Lugo 48 (☏985 565 146, ℉985 521 779; ⑤), is slightly out of town.

The City

The city's pleasant **old district**, strewn with fourteenth- and fifteenth-century churches and palaces, is about five minutes' walk from the bus and train terminus and not difficult to find. Most of the shops, bars and places to stay are here, too, and there's also a large and very pretty park, the Parque de Ferrera. Among several churches worth a closer look are the Romanesque church, **San Nicolás de Bari** on c/San Francisco, and the thirteenth-century **Santo Tomás**. La Iglesia de los Padres Franciscanos contains the tomb of the erstwhile governor of Florida, Don Pedro Menéndez de Avilés. There are also three superb palaces, namely the Baroque **Camposagrado**, built in 1663, in Plaza Camposagrado, the **Palacio de Llano Ponte**, which is now a cinema, and the seventeenth-century **Palacio de Marqués de Ferrera** both in Plaza de España. Nearby in c/San Francisco is the city's most distinctive monument, the seventeenth-century **Fuente de los Caños** with its six grotesque heads spouting water.

Eating, drinking and nightlife

The streets around Plaza de España are full of promising **bars and restaurants**, in particular c/del Ferrería, c/Rivero and c/Galiana. *Casa Lin*, Avda. Telares 3, is a fine *sidrería* with excellent seafood, while *Casa Tataguyo*, Plaza Carbayedo 6, a beautiful 1870s *mesón* (the oldest in town), serves Asturian specialities; both are moderately priced. If you're waiting for a bus or train, the bars along c/de la Estación diagonally across from the RENFE station offer excellent lunchtime *menús* for around €5.40. Late night, there are **music bars** on c/Galiana, an all-nighter at c/González Albarca 6, off Plaza de la Merced, and *Paradis*, a popular disco on c/Cátamara.

Oviedo

OVIEDO likes to set itself apart from the other cities of the region, and some would say sets itself above them too, its bourgeois culture in stark contrast with the working-class ethos of its neighbours. As the Asturian capital, it has long been fairly wealthy, a history which can be traced through its plethora of grand administrative and religious buildings, right down to the recent restoration and pedestrianization works which have transformed it into one of the most attractive cities in the north. The old quarter is a knot of squares and narrow streets built in warm yellow stone, while the newer part is redeemed by a huge public park right in the centre. Throughout the city are excellent bars and restaurants, many aimed at the lively student population. There are good transport links, too, with buses to just about everywhere in the province, and trains on both the FEVE and RENFE lines.

The principal reason for visiting the city, however, is to see three small **churches**. They are among the most remarkable in Spain, built in a style unique to Asturias which emerged in the wake of the Visigoths and before the Romanesque style had spread south from France. All of them date from the first half of the ninth century, a period of almost total isolation for the Asturian kingdom, which was then just 65km by 50km in area and the only part of Spain under Christian rule. Oviedo became the centre of this outpost in 810 with the residence of King Alfonso II, son of the victorious Pelayo (see p.551).

Arrival, information and orientation

Oviedo's transport connections are all conveniently located to the northeast of the city centre; the **RENFE** (☎985 250 202) and **FEVE** (☎985 284 096) **train stations** are both on Avenida de Santander, and the **bus terminal** (☎985 222 422) is nearby on Plaza Prime de Rivera.

Central Oviedo is bounded by a loop of roads. At its heart is the extensive **Campo de San Francisco**; the **Catedral** is a couple of blocks to the east of this, with the **Plaza de la Constitución** and *ayuntamiento* to its south. The city **turismo** (Mon–Fri 9.30am–1.30pm & 4.30–7.30pm, Sat 9am–2pm; ☎985 213 385, ℻985 228 459), which also covers the whole of Asturias, is in Plaza Alfonso II, the cathedral square; there's also a booth at Marqués de Santa Cruz 1 (Mon–Fri 10.30am–2pm & 4.30–7.30pm, Sat & Sun 11am–2pm; ☎985 227 586).

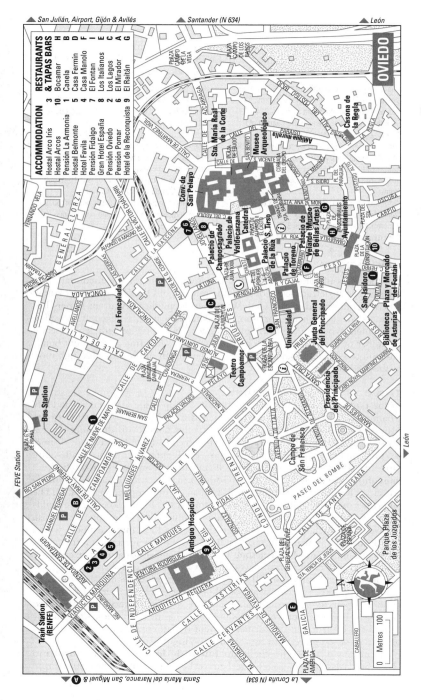

OVIEDO

ACCOMMODATION
Hostal Arco Iris	3
Hostal Arcos	10
Pensión La Armonía	1
Hotel Belmonte	5
Hotel Favila	4
Pensión Fidalgo	7
Gran Hotel España	8
Pensión Oviedo	2
Pensión Pomar	6
Hotel de la Reconquista	9

RESTAURANTS & TAPAS BARS
Bocamar	H
Canela	B
Casa Fermín	D
Casa Manolo	F
El Fontán	I
Los Italianos	E
Los Lagos	C
El Mirador	A
El Raitán	G

▲ San Julián, Airport, Gijón & Avilés   ▲ Santander (N 634)   ▲ León

▼ La Coruña (N 634)

▲ Santa María del Naranco, San Miguel & ⒶⒶ

Accommodation

Oviedo has a good supply of **accommodation**, with a concentration of *hostales* on c/de Uría, opposite the RENFE train station, along c/9 de Mayo and its continuation c/de Caveda, and along c/Jovellanos near the cathedral.

Hostal Arco Iris, c/de Uría 39 ☎ 985 245 908. Clean, friendly *hostal* offering large rooms. ❹
Hostal Arcos, c/Magdalena 3 ☎ 985 214 773. Friendly, good-value place, in the heart of old Oviedo, just off Plaza Mayor. ❸
Pensión La Armonia, c/Nueve de Mayo 14 ☎ 985 220 301. Small, family-run *pensión*. Good value. ❷
Hostal Belmonte, c/de Uría 31 ☎ 985 241 020, Ⓕ 985 242 578. Pleasant and newly refurbished rooms. ❹
Hotel Favila, c/de Uría 37 ☎ 985 253 877. Comfortable business hotel. ❺
Pensión Fidalgo, c/Jovellanos 5 ☎ 985 213 287. Cosy rooms with television, near the centre. ❺

Gran Hotel España, c/Jovellanos 2 ☎ 985 220 596, Ⓕ 985 222 140. Grand hotel, just as the name claims, close by the cathedral. Expensive, but reduced weekend rates. ❼
Pensión Oviedo, c/Uría 43 ☎ 985 241 000. Excellent, mid-priced *pensión*. ❺
Pensión Pomar, c/Jovellanos 7 ☎ 985 222 791. A little dingy, but central and very cheap. ❷
Hotel de la Reconquista, Gil de Jaz 16 ☎ 985 241 100, Ⓕ 985 241 166, Ⓦ www. hoteldelareconquista.com. Luxury accommodation in a seventeenth-century palace near Parque de San Francisco. ❾

The Town

Around the cathedral, enclosed by scattered sections of the medieval town walls, is a compact, attractive quarter, the remains of **Old Oviedo**. As at Gijón, much was destroyed in the Civil War when Republican Asturian miners laid siege to the Nationalist garrison; the defenders were relieved by a *gallego* detachment when on the brink of surrender. The centre nevertheless preserves a number of medieval churches and squares, and some fine government buildings and town houses built on the industrial wealth of the area, although most of these cannot be visited.

The cathedral and around

In the ninth century, King Alfonso II built a chapel, the Cámara Santa (Holy Chamber), to house the holy relics rescued from Toledo when it fell to the Moors. Remodelled in the twelfth century, this now forms the inner sanctuary of Oviedo's **Catedral** (Mon–Sat: March to mid-May & Oct 10am–1pm & 4–7pm; mid-May to June 10am–1pm & 4–8pm; July–Sept 10am–8pm; Nov–Feb 10am–1pm & 4–6pm; €2.40 including Cámara Santa & Diocesan museum), an unusually uncluttered Gothic structure at the heart of the modern city. The **Cámara Santa** is in fact a pair of interconnecting chapels. The innermost, with its primitive capitals, is thought to be Alfonso's original building. The antechapel, rebuilt in 1109, is a quiet little triumph of Spanish Romanesque; each of the six columns supporting the vault is sculpted with a pair of superbly humanized Apostles. Built around the attractive Gothic cloister, itself built on pre-Romanesque foundations, the **Diocesan museum** has a higher quality collection of devotional art and artefacts than is typical.

Around the cathedral, some of the city's ancient **palaces** – not least the archbishop's, opposite – are worth a look, though most are in government use and none is open to visitors. Of interest, too, is the **Museo Arqueológico** (Tues–Sat 10am–1.30pm & 4.30–6pm, Sun 11am–1pm; free), immediately behind the cathedral in the former convent of San Vicente. This displays various pieces of sculpture from the "Asturian-Visigoth" churches.

The nearest of these churches, **San Julián de los Prados**, or **Santullano** (Tues–Sun: May, June & Oct 11am–1pm & 4.30–6pm; July–Sept 9.30am–1pm

& 4.30–6pm; Nov–April noon–1pm & 4–5pm; free), is ten minutes' walk to the northeast along the c/de Gijón and by some unfortunate quirk of local city planning stands right next to a highway. However, it's well worth seeing. Built around 830, it is considerably larger and more spacious than the other Asturian churches, with an unusual "secret chamber" built into the outer wall. It is kept locked but the keys are available at the priest's house to the left; there are original frescoes inside, executed in similar style to those of Roman villas.

Santa María del Naranco

The greatest of the Asturian churches, indeed the architectural gem of the principality, is **Santa María del Naranco** (daily: May to mid-Oct 9.30am–1pm & 3–7pm; mid-Oct to April 10am–1pm & 3–5pm; closed Sun & Mon mornings; €1.20), majestically located on a wooded slope 3km above the city. It's an hour's walk from the centre, or 45 minutes from the station; the local tourist office has marked out a walking route, starting on one of the pedestrian streets in the town centre and leading on to a beautiful trail; by road, follow the signs for Monte Naranco.

Perhaps it's the walk, providing glimpses of the warm stone and simple bold outline of the church, that makes Santa María so special, almost mystical, a building. But when you've arrived and gazed upon it from all sides it still seems quite perfect in its harmony of form, decoration, and natural surroundings – "formidable beyond its scale", to use Jan Morris's phrase. Curiously, it was designed not as a church but as a palace or hunting lodge for Ramiro I (842–52), Alfonso's successor. The present structure was just the main hall of a complex that once included baths and stairways, features which the caretaker may point out. Architecturally, the open porticos at both ends are most interesting – an innovation developed much later in Byzantine churches – as well as the thirty or so decorative medallions which give the appearance of being suspended from the roof. The crypt bears a notable resemblance to the Cámara Santa back in town.

A couple of hundred metres beyond Santa María is King Ramiro's palace chapel, **San Miguel de Lillo** (same hours and ticket as Santa María), built with soft golden sandstone and red tiles. This is generally assumed to be by the same architect as Santa María, Tiodo (whom some scholars credit also with the Cámara Santa and San Julian de los Prados), though its design is quite different. In fact less than half of the original ninth-century church remains, the rest having collapsed and been rebuilt in the twelfth century. Much of its interior sculpture has been removed to the archeological museum, but look for the window grilles carved from single slabs of limestone, and the superb Byzantine-style carved doorframes depicting, incongruously enough, the investiture of a Roman consul, complete with circus-style festivities.

Further up from the two little churches is a Rio-style **figure of Christ** that looks out over the city and is spectacularly illuminated at night. It was built by Republican prisoners of war and although ugly close up (it's constructed from concrete blocks), there are wonderful views from the site.

Eating, drinking and nightlife

Head to the area around the cathedral for the best **eating and drinking**. You can't help but notice the *sidrerías*, spit-and-sawdust places with a lot of people pouring a lot of drink from a great height. This may baffle the newcomer, but just order a bottle (about €1.70), and you'll soon pick up the right drinking method. Most of the best are along c/Gascona, down from the cathedral. There are plenty of cafés and bars too, most with remarkable-value *menús* –

anything over €4.80 is expensive – as well as more pricey traditional *mesones* serving *fabada* and other Asturian fare. A pleasant place to while away some time is the café in the Corrada del Obispo, one of the most beautiful of Oviedo's squares.

Bocamar, Plaza Trascorrales 14. Terrific *sidrería-marisquería*: try the *fabas con almejas* (beans with clams) and the delicious rice dishes.

Canela, c/Campoamor 20 ☎ 985 220 045. Great little restaurant with quality cooking at a remarkable price; the *menú* is €12. Closed Sun, Feb 15–28 & Aug 1–15.

Casa Fermín, c/San Francisco 8 ☎ 985 216 497. A classic, much-written-about restaurant, serving imaginatively recreated Asturian dishes. The *menú* is a hefty €18 and you could easily spend a lot more. Closed Sun.

Casa Manolo, c/Altamirano 9 ☎ 985 212 561. Superior and pricey *sidrería* known for its game and tapas.

El Fontan, c/Fierro. Café-restaurant overlooking the market with good-value *menú*.

Los Italianos, Avda. de Galicia 15. Reliable pasta and pizza.

Los Lagos, Plaza del Carbayón 3. Excellent *sidrería* filled with the heady smell of strong Asturian foods, cider and sawdust. Another branch on c/Cervantes 7.

El Mirador, midway up the road to Naranco. Very decent restaurant with a terrace that looks out over the whole city and mountains beyond.

El Raitán, Plaza Trascorrales 6 ☎ 985 214 218. Superb restaurant in a delightful square off Plaza Mayor. The huge €24 *menú* offers a taste of several Asturian dishes, but you can eat for as little as half that.

Nightlife and entertainment

Oviedo can be quiet in summer when the local youth tends to flock to nearby resorts and the student population is away, but during the rest of the year there's a huge scene. Irish pubs have taken hold in a big way, particularly along c/Jovellanos, and you'll also find loud Irish music playing at the popular *Ca Beleño*, c/Martínez Vigil 4. Calle Mon is the place to go for the thriving **disco-pub** scene, with music to cater for most tastes. The *Diario Roma* is loud and crowded with a great atmosphere, while *Montañes* is a quieter refuge with cheaper drinks. *Monster* on the nearby Plaza de Sol plays indy/alternative rock and on the tiny c/Carta Puebla off c/Postigo Alto, *El Planeta Tierra* and *La Misión* host a more dance-oriented scene. *Salsipuedes*, c/Salsipuedes 3, is a relaxed place with a trio of bars and a great summer *terraza*.

Places on c/Altamirano stay open a bit later – *La Botica* has a good selection of dance music and *La Tamara* wonderful decor and a mixed crowd – but if you want to keep going into the small hours, a younger crowd moves out to the bars and **clubs** on c/Rosal and c/Gonzalez Besada ten minutes west of the old town; *Movie* on the latter is hugely popular. Two big popular clubs are *El Antiguo* on c/del Peso, off Plaza Mayor and *Stavaganza* on c/Santa Clara off Plaza del Carbayón. *La Real* on c/Cervantes is good for house and has a mixed gay/straight crowd.

For **classical music**, watch out for Oviedo's Orquestra de Asturias, who are based here and perform mainly in the Teatro Campoamor. There are usually a couple of concerts each week, and summer performances in the university and cathedral cloisters. For many years there has been an opera festival in September, but financing problems are leaving its immediate future in doubt.

Listings

Airport Aeropuerto de Asturias (☎ 985 547 733 or 985 561 709) is 13km away in Ranon, just off the N632.

American Express c/o Viajes Cafranga, c/Uría 26 ☎ 985 225 217.

Books Librería Cervantes, c/Dr Casal 3/9 has a good stock, including walking and wildlife guides to Asturias, and English-language novels.

Car rental Avis, c/Ventura Rodríguez 12 ☎ 985 241 383; Europcar, c/Uría, in RENFE station ☎ 985

245 712; National Atesa, c/Asturias 41 ☎ 985 243 576.

Internet access The funky *Café Bhet@* (daily 4pm–midnight) is in a restored railway carriage next to the RENFE station.

Post office The *Correos Principal* is at c/Alonso Quintanilla 1 (Mon–Fri 8.30am–8.30pm, Sat 9.30am–2pm).

Telephones The *Telefónica* is at c/Foncalada 6 (Mon–Sat 10am–2pm & 4–10.30pm).

Trekking The Federacíon Asturiana de Montaña, Avda. Julian Clavería (☎ 985 252 362), provides information and organizes treks in the Picos. The student agency, TIVE, c/Calvo Sotelo 5 (☎ 985 231 112), also offers good-value trekking trips.

Avilés and Oviedo to Galicia

The **coast west of Avilés**, as far as the Río Navia, is pretty rugged, with scarcely more than a handful of resorts carved out from the cliffs. The most attractive by far is the old port and resort of **Luarca**. West again from the Río Navia, the coast becomes marshy and, save for an honorary mention of the attractive fishing village of **Tapia de Casariego**, unexceptional. Again, the FEVE line trails the coast, with some spectacular sections, though some of the stations (including Cudillero and Luarca) are inconveniently sited some way out of town.

Inland from Oviedo, the N634 and C630 offer a winding approach over the hills to Lugo in Galicia. The old town of **Salas**, with its castle, is of passing interest, but the main appeal of the route is the mountainous wildness of this area, which hardly sees a tourist from one year to the next.

Cudillero

CUDILLERO is a small, active and picturesque fishing port, with brightly coloured arcaded houses rising one upon each other over a steep horseshoe of cliffs around the port. Despite rapidly encroaching tourism, the town nonetheless manages to retain its charm. As there's no beach as such here – the nearest is **Playa Aguilar**, 3km to the east – the most obvious attractions are the **fish tavernas** in its cobbled, seaside plaza; at weekends these are packed out, with prices geared to tourist rather than local trade. For *sidra* and *merluza*, *Méson El Pescador* is excellent.

Practicalities

Cudillero can be reached by **FEVE trains** from Avilés or Oviedo; the station is at the top of town, a fifteen-minute walk from the centre. The **bus station** is midway between here and the town centre, with twelve daily buses to Avilés and a sporadic service to Oviedo and Gijón, although you can walk 3km to **El Pito** on the main road to pick up the full coastal service. In summer, there's a **turismo** (Mon–Fri 10am–9pm, Sat & Sun 3–8pm; ☎ 985 590 020) on Plaza de San Pedro, just behind the port, and a booth next to the harbour which can help find accommodation.

The village is reasonably well supplied with **accommodation**, though it tends to be pricey. The hotels include *San Pablo*, c/Suarez Inclán 36–38 (☎ 985 591 155; ❻), and *Casona de Pio*, c/Rio Frio 3 (☎ 985 591 512; ❺). There are two *pensiones* on c/La Concha, the road out of town towards El Pito – *El Camarote* at no. 4 (☎ 985 591 202; ❺) and *Pensión Alver* at no. 8 (☎ 985 590 005; ❹) – while up on the main road itself is the very clean and modern *Pensión Álvaro* (☎ 985 590 204; ❹). The best of the town's **campsites** is *Camping Cudillero* (☎ 985 590 663; Easter & June–Sept), off the same road above Playa Aguilar.

Luarca

The coast west of Cudillero is rugged and the main highway, the N632, leaps over viaducts spanning deep, pine-wooded gorges. An enticing prospect if you've got time is to follow the **old N632**, which winds through the dark hills and across little bridges far beneath the roaring lorries. About 50km west of Cudillero is the port of **LUARCA**, accessed from the N632 by a road that dips down steeply to the coast. This is one of the most attractive towns along the whole northern coastline, a mellow place, built around an S-shaped cove surrounded by sheer cliffs. Down below, the town is bisected by a small, winding river, and knitted together by numerous narrow bridges.

Luarca is a seaside resort in a very modest sort of way, with a slim beach of slightly murky sand, a scattering of accommodation, and some excellent bars and restaurants. In contrast to Cudillero, Luarca has defiantly retained its traditional character, including a few *chigres* – old-fashioned Asturian taverns – where you can be initiated into the art of *sidra* drinking. The fishing harbour area is the best place for meals, too: cross the bridge from the plaza, follow the river, and pick from a line of good-value restaurants here. You can watch the small fishing boats returning at around midnight and see the catch auctioned off at the *lonja* at around 3pm the following afternoon.

Practicalities

The **turismo** (July & Aug only Tues–Sun 11am–2pm & 4–7pm; ☎985 640 083), at c/Olavarrieta 27, provides lists of private rooms and apartments; when it's closed, try the municipal library across the road for general information. On the way into town, there are some good **places to stay**, including *El Redondel* (☎985 640 733; ❺), on the main highway, 3km from the centre, in Almuña. In town, try *El Cocinero* (☎985 640 175; ❸), a fine, ramshackle eighteenth-century *fonda* in the main plaza; other budget places include *Pensión Cabas,* Plaza los Pachorros (☎985 640 070; ❹) and *Hostel Oria,* c/Crucero 7 (☎ 985 640 385; ❸). The upmarket choices include the *Hotel Gayoso,* Paseo Gómez 4 (☎985 640 054, ☎985 470 271; ❸–❼), a grand old hotel (reputedly Spain's oldest) with a cheaper annexe nearby in Plaza Alfonso; *Hotel Oviedo* (☎985 640 906; ❻) on c/del Crucero, a pedestrianized street behind the plaza; and the well-situated *Hotel Baltico* (☎985 640 991; ❺), overlooking the harbour.

The town **beach** is divided in two. The closer strip is narrower but more protected, the broader one beyond the jetty is subject to seaweed litter. On the cliff top on the other side of town is a hermitage chapel and a lighthouse, and facing these across a rocky cove is a **campsite**, *Los Cantiles* (☎985 640 938; open all year), with facilities to match its superb setting.

You'll find an excellent **restaurant**, *Casa Consuelo*, on the main road (Carreterra San Sebastián), which attracts people from miles around; try the *merluza con angulas* (hake with eels). In town, the gourmet choice is the excellent *Villablanca* on Avenida de Galicia, while in the port area, *El Barometro*, Plaza de Muelle 5, and *Sport*, c/Rivero 8, are both great for seafood. For cheaper but still high-quality cuisine try *La Montañesa*, Nicanor del Campo 2.

Luarca has good **bus** connections to Oviedo, Gijón, Avilés and into Galicia; you'll find the bus station just off c/del Crucero. The FEVE station is 2km out of town.

Luarca to Ribadeo

West from Luarca, you cross the wide Río Navia – a foretaste of Galicia's *rías* or estuaries – at **NAVIA**, a pleasant little port, though lacking the style and life of Luarca. If you have transport, the inland route from here to Lugo is fascinating. At **COAÑA**, 5km south of Navia and connected by local buses, there's a *castro*, or Celtic settlement (Tues–Sun 11–2.30pm & 4–7.30pm; free), and beyond that the road winds above the reservoirs of the Navia River before twisting into Galicia and the remote mountainous region around Fonsagrada. If you want **to stay** in Navia, the *Palacio Arias*, c/José Antonio 11 (☎985 473 675, ⓕ985 473 683; ❺–❼), is quite luxurious, especially in the less expensive modern annexe, while cheaper options include *La Barca*, c/Manuel Suárez 19 (☎985 473 477; ❺), and *Hostal La Marina*, c/Salazar 61 (☎985 630 602; ❸).

The best beach along this stretch is almost the last in Asturias, the **Playa de Los Campos**, which flanks the fishing village of **TAPIA DE CASARIEGO**. This is a lively place, with an entertaining "alternative" Teatro Popular, and a very helpful **turismo** (mid-June to mid-Sept Mon–Sat 10.30am–2pm & 5–8.30pm; ☎985 472 968) in a small kiosk in the plaza. There are three reasonably priced **hotels**, including *La Ruta* (☎985 628 138; ❹) and *Puente de los Santos* (☎985 628 155, ⓕ985 628 437; ❸), just opposite, which are both great value. Just outside town are two **campsites**, about 1km towards Ribadeo: *Playa de Tapia* (☎985 472 721; June–Sept) and *El Carbayín* (☎985 623 709; open all year). The port area is again the place to eat and drink, though many of the bars only open evenings and at weekends; head straight downhill from the main plaza. *La Marina* here does a very good *menú* for €7.80.

CASTROPOL, set back from the coast on the Río Eo – the border with Galicia – is a tiny, pretty place with a pair of *hostales*. However, you're better off staying across the border in Ribadeo (see p.575). There's a **turismo** (Tues–Sat 10am–2pm & 5–8pm, Sun 10am–3pm; ☎608 380 386) on the main highway, if you're entering from Galicia and want pamphlets and information on Asturias.

Salas

SALAS, 35km west of Oviedo, was the home of the Marqués de Valdés-Salas, founder of Oviedo University and one of the prime movers of the Inquisition. The town **castle** is actually the Marqués's old palace; you can climb an adjoining tower from the **turismo** (Mon–Sat: summer 11am–2pm & 4–8pm; winter 9am–2pm & 4–7pm; ☎985 830 988) for fine views of the town and surrounding countryside. Among the other monuments are a sixteenth-century **Colegiata** and, in the main square, the tenth-century church of **San Martín**.

If you want to **stay**, there are two options: the *Hotel Castillo de Valdés-Salas* (☎985 832 222, ⓕ985 832 299; ❺), in the castle, with an out-of-the-ordinary restaurant; and the *Casa Soto*, c/Arzobispo Valdés 9 (☎985 830 037; ❹), which has big, clean rooms. **Buses** to Oviedo leave on the hour from outside the *Café Berlin*.

Travel details

Trains

RENFE

Oviedo to: Alicante (1 daily; 11hr); Barcelona (2 daily; 12hr–13hr 30min); León (7 daily; 2hr 30min); Madrid (5 daily; 6hr); Vigo (2 daily; 9hr).
Santander to: Madrid (3 daily; 5hr 30min), change at Palencia for east–west routes including León.

FEVE

This delightful independent service runs along the north coast between **Bilbao, Santander, Oviedo** and **Ferrol**. The narrow-gauge railway has recently been modernized, and the line is punctual and scenic, though still slow for longer trips; the full journey from Ferrol to Bilbao can't be done in one day. Timetables can be picked up at any main station but these can be confusing. In practical terms it is best to think of the service divided between **through trains** that cover the longer distances between the big cities, and **local trains**, which run more frequently between the smaller towns. There are also a few *cercanías*, or local **branch lines**, most of which are centred around Gijón.

Through trains: Bilbao to Santander (3 daily; 2hr 25min); Santander to Oviedo (2 daily; 4hr 25min); Oviedo to Ferrol (2 daily; 6hr 40min).

Local trains: Bilbao to Orejo (3 daily; 2hr); Orejo to Santander (18 daily; 25min); Santander to Puente de San Miguel (42 daily; 30–40min); Puente de San Miguel to Cabezon de la Sal (20 daily; 20min); Cabezon to Llanes (2 daily; 1hr); Llanes to Ribadesella-Infiesto (3 daily in winter, 5 in summer; 35min); Ribadesella to Nava (7 daily; 1hr 8min); Nava to Oviedo (21 daily; 45min); Oviedo to Pravia (21 daily; 1hr); Pravia to Cudillero (18 daily; 20min); Cudillero to Navia (3 daily; 1hr 30min); Navia to Ribadeo (2 daily; 50min); Ribadeo to Ferrol (3 daily; 3hr).

Branch lines: Gijón to Avilés (30 daily; 40min); Gijón to Pravia (for main line to Ferrol; 15 daily; 30min).

Buses

The majority of buses along the coast, and all those covering longer distances, are run by the Alsa bus company. Some of these buses covering shorter distances are also labelled EASA or Turytrans, but the livery is the same distinctive blue-grey and all buses carry the Alsa logo. A number of smaller companies operate more local services between coastal resorts and inland destinations, but you should note that these buses often have reduced services outside July and August.

Castro Urdiales to: Bilbao (10 daily; 1hr); Santander (13 daily; 1hr); Vitoria (3 daily; 1hr 15min); Pamplona (2 daily; 2hr 40min).

Comillas to: San Vicente (3 daily; 30min); Santander (7 daily; 45min); Santillana (4 daily; 35min).

Gijón to: Bilbao via Oviedo (6 daily; 6hr); Irún via Oviedo (3 daily; 7hr 40min); León via Oviedo (8 daily; 2hr); Madrid via Oviedo (11 daily; 5hr 30min); Oviedo (every 15min; 30min); Ribadeo via Luarca, Navia, Castropol and Vegadeo (7 daily; 4hr); Salamanca (5 daily; 4hr 30min); Sevilla (2 daily; 12hr 30min); Villaviciosa (hourly; 45min).

Llanes to: Arenas (3 daily; 1hr); Madrid via Cangas and Oseja (daily; Mon, Wed & Fri only in winter); Oviedo via Ribadesella (10 daily; 1hr 30min); San Vicente (10 daily; 45min); Santander (12 daily; 1hr 30min); Unquera (11 daily; 30min).

Oviedo to: Avilés (every 30min; 30min); Cangas de Onis (10 daily; 1hr–1hr 30min); A Coruña via Betanzos (2 daily; 4hr 30min/5hr); Covadonga (5 daily; 1hr 45min); Cudillero (10 daily; 1hr); Gijón (every 15min; 30min); León (8 daily, 1hr 30min); Lugo (5 daily; 5hr 30min); Madrid (12 daily; 5hr 30min); Pontevedra (2 daily; 8hr); Ribadeo via Luarca (7 daily; 3hr 30min); Ribadesella (12 daily; 1hr 20min–2hr); Santander (8 daily; 3hr 30min); Santiago (3 daily; 5hr 30min); Sevilla (2 daily; 12hr); Valladolid (4 daily; 3hr 30min); Vigo (2 daily; 8hr 30min); Villaviciosa via San Pedro de Ambas (8 daily; 1hr 15min).

Picos buses Arenas de Cabrales–Cangas de Onis (4 daily; 45min); Bustio–Arenas via Panes (2 daily; 50min); Cangas de Onis–Covadonga (9 daily; 45min); Cangas de Onis–Posada de Valdeón via Sajambre (1 daily in summer; 2hr 15min); Llanes–Madrid via Cangas, Sajambre and Riaño (1 daily in summer; 3 weekly in winter; 6hr 15min); León–Posada de Valdeón via Riaño and Portilla de la Reina (1 daily; 3hr); Potes–Espinama–Fuente Dé (3 daily; 45min). Also Land Rover service between Valdeón and Caín.

Ribadesella to: Lastres (every 2hr in summer; 45min); Llanes (11 daily; 45min); Oviedo via Arriondas (change at Arriondas for Cangas; 12 daily; 1hr 20min–2hr); San Vincente (3 daily; 2hr); Villaviciosa (3 daily; 1hr).

San Vicente to: Comillas (3 daily; 30min); Llanes (12 daily; 45min); Potes via Unquera (2 daily; 1hr 30min); Ribadesella (3 daily; 2hr); Santander (12 daily; 1hr).

Santander to: Barcelona (2 daily; 9hr); Bilbao (28 daily, 10 of which continue to French border; 1hr 30min); Burgos (6 daily; 4hr); Castro Urdiales (11 daily; 1hr); Comillas (7 daily; 45min; more by changing in Torrelavega); Laredo (25 daily; 40min); León (3 daily, 1 via Potes; 5hr); Llanes (11 daily; 1hr 30min); Logroño (2 daily, 3hr 30min); Madrid (6 daily; 8hr); Oviedo (8 daily; 3hr 30min); Pamplona (3 daily, 3hr 45min); Potes via San Vicente and Unquera (3 daily; 3hr); Puente Viesgo (5 daily; 40min); Santiago, Vigo, and Portuguese border (2 daily; 10–12hr); Santillana (7 daily, 4 daily in winter; 45min); Santoña (7 daily; 1 hr); San Vicente la Barquera (7 daily; 1hr); Sevilla (1 in summer; 14hr); Vitoria via Castro Urdiales (7 daily; 2hr 15min); Zaragoza (8 daily, 4hr 30min).

Ferries

Car/passenger ferry from Santander to Plymouth (Tues & Thurs, 24hr; runs weekly only to Poole in February and early March, 28 hr).

8

Galicia

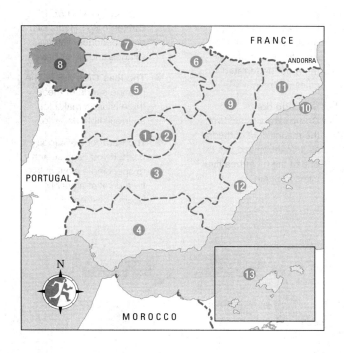

CHAPTER 8

Highlights

✳ **Pimientos de Padrón**
p.603 A delicious tapa of
randomly piquant green
peppers fried in hot oil
and sea salt.

✳ **A mariscada and some
Ribeiro wine** p.582
Galicia is renowned for
its delicious seafood and
white wine.

✳ **A Coruña** p.579
Perched on the rugged
northwestern coast this
Atlantic port is one of
the most underrated
cities in Spain.

✳ **Santiago de
Compostela** p.586 With
the magnificent cathedral
as its centrepiece this is
one of the most beautiful
cities in Spain.

✳ **Mass at the cathedral in
Santiago** p.592 A spec-
tacular experience if you
can time your visit to
coincide with the use of
the massive incense
burner, the "Botafumeiro".

✳ **Sunset at Finisterre**
p.599 For fantastic views
over the Atlantic.

✳ **Exploring the Rias
Baixas** p.601 Hosts of
great beaches, fishing
villages and great bars.

✳ **The Illas Cíes** p.614 The
pristine sands of these
three islands make for
an irresistible day-trip.

✳ **The Parador at Baiona**
p.615 If you can't stretch
to spending a night at least
try a drink at arguably
Spain's best hotel.

8

Galicia

Remote, rural, and battered by the Atlantic, Galicia is a far cry from the popular image of Spain. It not only looks like Ireland; there are further parallels in the climate, culture, and music, as well as the ever-visible traces of its Celtic past. Above all, despite its green and fertile appearance, Galicia has a similar history of famine and poverty, with a decline in population owing to forced emigration which is only now being reversed with government subsidies for returning emigrants of *gallego* ancestry.

Galicia is lush and heavily wooded in native oaks and pines, although subsidized plantations of imported eucalyptus are becoming dominant. The coastline is shaped by fjord-like inlets, source of some of the best seafood in Europe. In the north these *rías* shelter unspoiled old villages and fine beaches, while the sunnier southern coast is becoming increasingly built up with new resorts and roads. As you enter Galicia from the east, the rolling meadows of Asturias are replaced by a patchwork of tiny fields, with terraces of vines supported on granite props and allotments full of turnip-tops and cabbages growing on stalks. Archaic inheritance laws have meant a constant division and redivision of the land into little plots too small for machinery and worked with primitive agricultural methods; ox carts with solid wooden wheels are still seen on the backroads. Everywhere you see *hórreos*, granaries made here of granite rather than wood, with saints and sculpted air-vents, standing on pillars away from rodents and the damp.

While it is a poor part of the country, unlike the south it never seems oppressively so, and the wave of road improvements, motorways and new building in

Accommodation price codes

All the establishments listed in this book have been price-graded according to the following scale. The prices quoted are for the **cheapest available double room in high season**; effectively this means that anything in the ❶ and most places in the ❷ range will be without private bath, though there's usually a washbasin in the room. In the ❹ category and above you will probably be getting private facilities. Remember, though, that many of the budget places will also have more expensive rooms including en-suite facilities. Youth hostels are graded under ❶ as the price per person is less than half of the category's upper limit.

Note that in the more upmarket *hostales* and *pensiones*, and in anything calling itself a hotel, you'll pay a **tax** (IVA) of seven percent on top of the room price.

❶ Under €12	❹ €27–36	❼ €60–90
❷ €12–18	❺ €36–48	❽ €90–120
❸ €18–27	❻ €48–60	❾ Over €120

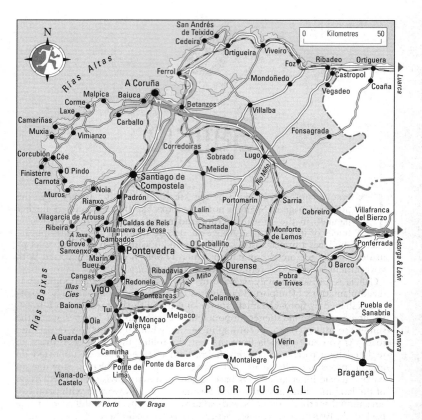

the last decade is rapidly changing the character of the region. Food is plentiful, most people being involved in its production, and there's a strength and solidity in the culture, run, uniquely for Spain, by the women. In the countryside, women and children traditionally work the land while the men work at sea, whether as merchant seamen or fishermen, catching octopus and lobster from rowing boats, and minding the *mejilloneiras* (the mussel rafts anchored in the *rías*). Others, undoubtedly, are engaged in the old standby of smuggling – which, these days, means drugs as well as more traditional contraband. For centuries men have also sought their fortunes abroad, traditionally in Argentina (there are said to be more *gallegos* in Buenos Aires than in Galicia), though more often these days as migrant labourers in northern Europe.

With so many men absent, and little heavy industry beyond the failing shipbuilding yards in Ferrol and Vigo, there is little of the radicalism of Asturias. Galicia has always been deeply conservative and since 1875 has provided Spain with a gallery of prominent right-wing leaders; it was the birthplace of General Franco, and is today dominated by the right-wing Partido Popular, whose founder, Manuel Fraga, is another local boy. Nonetheless, there is a strong and proud *gallego* nationalist movement, which may not approach the scale – or political intensity – of the Catalans and the Basques, but has formed links with Brittany and Ireland, and championed the revival of the long-banned local language.

The **gallego language** sounds like a fusion of Castilian and Portuguese, but has existed every bit as long as either, and is still spoken by an estimated 85 percent of the population. In the smaller communities few people speak anything else. It is definitely a living language, taught in schools and with its own literary heroes such as the poet Rosalia de Castro and the essayist and caricaturist Castelao. Road signs and maps these days tend to be in *gallego* (though the Castilian version is often given as well). We have therefore used the *gallego* name for towns, supplying the Castilian version in parentheses where it varies significantly, or is helpful. The most obvious characteristic of *gallego* is the large number of Xs, which in Castilian might be Gs, Js or Ss; these are pronounced as a soft *sh*. You will also find that the Castilian *plaza* becomes *praza* and *playa* becomes *praia,* while *la* is *a* (as in A Coruña), *el* is *o* (as in O Grove), *de la* is *da* and *del* is *do*.

The obvious highlight of the region is **Santiago de Compostela**, the greatest goal for pilgrims in medieval Europe and once again a flourishing centre for tourists. The cathedral, and the unified architecture of the whole city, with its granite colonnades and mossy facades, together make Santiago quite unforgettable. But there are smaller and equally charming old stone towns throughout Galicia, and those that have retained a vibrant sense of life and atmosphere, such as **Pontevedra** and **Betanzos**, are enjoyable bases for a touring holiday. The coastal countryside is always spectacular, but the best and safest swimming beaches are along the booming **Rías Baixas** towards Portugal, with **O Grove** and **Baiona** two of the most popular resorts. Far fewer visitors come here than to the Mediterranean, and while the sea is never as warm, the pine-fringed coves are delightful. Outside July and August accommodation prices drop considerably and you'll have the beaches virtually to yourself. Further north, the tiny, picturesque ports of the harsh **Costa da Morte** – the stretch of coast between **A Coruña** and **Noia** – still preserve the traditional *gallego* lifestyle of smallholdings and small-scale fishing.

Inland, Galicia can be bleak and empty; the most rewarding route is to follow the Minho river upstream from the Portuguese border to towns such as **Ribadavia** and **Celanova**, and then up to the Roman walls of **Lugo**.

The Rías Altas and Santiago

It's not nearly as difficult as it once was to move around the north coast of Galicia, where the **Rías Altas** (High Estuaries) include both the northernmost and westernmost points of Spain. Roads, which until relatively recently were poorly surfaced and barely frequented, are now reliable and safe, and the facilities for visitors have improved with the increasing importance of the revenues from tourism. The savagery of the ocean has created a wild and dramatic coastline that slows down travel, and even if you have a car it's advisable to choose

Fiestas

January
1 Livestock fair at Betanzos.
6 Horseback procession of *Los Reyes* (the Three Kings) in Baiona.
15 *San Mauro* – fireworks at Vilanova de Arousa.

March
1 Celanova's big festival, of *San Rosendo*, at the monastery above town.
Pre-Lenten *carnavales* throughout the region, along with the *Lazaro* festival, a gathering of both *gallego* and Portuguese folk groups, at Verín.

April
Palm Sunday Stations of the Cross at Monte San Tecla, near A Guarda.
Holy Week Celebrations include a symbolic *descendimiento* (descent from the Cross) at Viveiro on Good Friday and a Resurrection procession at Finisterre.
Second Monday after Easter *San Telmo* festival at Tui.
25 *San Marcos* observance at Noia.
Late April – Early May (dates vary from year to year) Festival at Ribadavia celebrating and promoting Ribeiro wines.

May
1 *Romería* at Pontevedra.
22 *Santa Rita* at Vilagarcía de Arousa.

June
Sundays Country fairs and roundups of wild horses, known as *curros*, are held on successive Sundays in the hills above Baiona and Oia; villages include La Valga, Torroña, Mougas and Pinzas.
Corpus Christi Flower festival, with flower "carpets" in the streets, in Ponteareas.
24–25 Two days of celebration for *San Juan* in many places, with processions of bigheads and *gigantones* on the 24th and spectacular parades with fireworks and bands through the following evening.

July
First weekend *Rapa das Bestas* – capture and breaking in of wild mountain horses – at Viveiro and San Lorenz (Pontevedra). At the latter the horses are raced before being let loose.
11 *San Benito* fiesta at Pontevedra, with river processions and competitions, and folk groups, and a smaller *romería* at Cambados.

just a couple of targets. **Viveiro**, to the east, and the **Costa da Morte**, the section of coastline to the west of A Coruña, are particularly good to explore. No words of praise could be too extravagant for **Santiago de Compostela**, and if you really want to appreciate this pilgrimage centre to the fullest it makes sense to approach it by the ancient Pilgrim Route from León. Its one drawback, often exaggerated, is the weather; Santiago must be one of the few cities in the world which actually boasts about its excessive rainfall. With the exception of Santiago and **A Coruña**, which preserves a beautiful medieval quarter amid the sprawl of the modern port, the cities of this area are best avoided; **Ferrol** in particular is deep in the throes of industrial decay.

16 *Virgen del Carmen*. Sea processions at Muros and Corcubión.
25 Galicia's major fiesta, in honour of St James, at Santiago de Compostela. It's worth attending Mass to see the National Offering to the Shrine (of the country and government) as well as the swinging of the *botafumeiro*. The evening before, there's a fireworks display and symbolic burning of a cardboard effigy of the mosque at Córdoba. The festival – also designated *Galicia Day* – has become a nationalist event with traditional separatist demonstrations and an extensive programme of political and cultural events for about a week on either side.
29 Octopus festival at Vilanova de Arousa.

August
First Sunday Wine festival at Cambados; bagpipe festival at Ribadeo; *Virgen de la Roca* observances outside Baiona; Viking *romería* in Catoira (Pontevedra).
9 *Percebe* (barnacle) festival in Finisterre.
Second Sunday *Fiesta del Pulpo* in O Carballiño (Ourense).
16 *San Roque* festivals at all churches that bear his name: at Betanzos there's a Battle of the Flowers on the river; at Sada (10km east of A Coruña) there are boat races and feasts.
24 Fiesta (and bullfights) at Noia.
25 *San Ginés* at Sanxenxo.
28 *Romería del Naseiro* outside Viveiro.
Last Sunday *Romería* sets out from Sanxenxo to the Praia de La Lanzada.

September
6–10 *Fiestas del Portal* at Ribadavia.
8 *San Andreu* at Cervo (20km east of Viveiro).
First Sunday after 8th *Romería* at Muxia.
14 Seafood festival at O Grove; *romería* with bigheads at Viveiro.

October
13 *Fiesta de la Exaltación del Marisco* at O Grove – literally "a celebration in praise of shellfish".

November
11 *Fiesta de San Martín* at Bueu.
Last Sunday Oyster festival at Arcade (10km south of Pontevedra).

December
Last week Crafts fair, *O Feitoman,* at Vigo.

The north coast

The closing stretch of the **FEVE railway** from Luarca to Ferrol, is perhaps the best, as long as you're in no hurry to arrive. It clings to every nuance of the coastline, looping around a succession of *rías* and rambling through the eucalyptus forests and wild-looking hills which buffer the villages from the harsh Atlantic. Settlements are concentrated at the sides of the estuaries, with the occasional beach tacked beside or below them. By **road**, too, it's a slow route, even though this stretch has recently been improved.

Along the FEVE

RIBADEO, the first *gallego* town and *ría*, makes a poor introduction to the region. It does have a certain crumbling charm, as well as a few places to stay –

such as the *Galicia*, Rúa Virgen del Camino 1 (☎982 128 777; ❹), and a *parador* on Rúa Amador Fernández (☎982 128 825, ❶928 100 346, ❷ribadeo@ parador.es; ❽) − but overall it's drab. The nearest **beach**, the Praia do Castro, is a few kilometres further west, with **campsites** at Benquerencia (☎982 124 450; June–Sept) and Reinante (☎982 134 005; June–Sept), but by now you're getting a bit too close to the industrial port of Foz. Beyond that, Cervo has little more to boast of than a huge, rust-red aluminium factory, although Mondoñedo, 20km up the valley of the Río Masma, is an attractive old riverside town.

Viveiro

Once a remote, elegant port, the area around **VIVEIRO** has seen an influx of summer visitors over the last decade, changing the character of the large *ría* with a rash of holiday homes spreading up the hillsides. The old town however, is protected by a circuit of Renaissance walls, and its narrow streets are largely closed to traffic and lined with glass-fronted houses in delicate white wooden frames.

The bay shelters several peaceful **beaches**, particularly the Praia de Faro up towards the open sea. The large town beach, the Praia de Covas, is a good ten minutes' walk from town across a causeway.

Practicalities

The **bus station** is on the waterfront Avenida de la Marina: turn right out of the station, and after 100m go left through a stone gateway to reach the Praza Maior. The **FEVE station** (3–4 trains daily in each direction to Ribadeo and Ferrol) is a ten-minute walk from the town centre: bear left out of the station to reach the main road, then turn left under the bridge and walk straight on to reach the bus station. The **turismo** (mid-June to mid-Sept daily 10am–2pm & 5.30–8.30pm) is in a wooden hut opposite the bus station.

Inside the walls there are a couple of good, inexpensive **places to stay**: *Hospedaje García*, Praza Maior 18 (☎982 560 675; ❸), has a few simple but immaculate balconied rooms overlooking the square (look for the blue "CH" sign as there's no other marker); nearby, *Nuevo Mundo*, Rúa María Teodoro de Quirós 14 (☎982 560 025; ❸), also has attractive balconied rooms, although those at the front are within ear-splitting distance of the bells of Santa María church opposite. More upmarket is the *Hostal Vila*, Rúa Nicolás Montenegro 57 (☎982 561 331, ❶982 563 112; ❺), in a rather drab street just outside the walls at the Porta del Vallado at the top end of town. For real luxury, head for *Hotel Orfeo*, Rúa García Navia Castrillón 2 (☎982 562 101, ❶982 560 453; ❼), with private parking and rooms overlooking the bay. There's a **campsite**, *Vivero* (☎982 560 004; June–Sept), behind the Praia de Covas.

Places **to eat** are fairly thin on the ground. The *Nuevo Mundo* has a good restaurant upstairs − €6 for a four-course feast − while *Laurel*, Rúa Melitón Cortiñas 26, three blocks south of the main square, has a range of (largely seafood-based) *menús* (€6.60) plus à la carte dishes. On the other side of the Praza Maior, just above San Francisco church at Rúa Antonio Bas 2, *Restaurante Serra* serves decent seafood and *menús* for around €9.

Porto do Barqueiro, Ortigueira and Porto de Vares

The next two *ría* villages (and FEVE stops) are **PORTO DO BARQUEIRO**, a tiny and very picturesque fishing port of slate-roofed houses near Spain's northernmost point, and the larger **ORTIGUEIRA**, set amid a dark mass of pines. The former has three places to stay dotted around its tiny harbour:

Estrellas del Mar (℡981 414 105; ❸), with great sea views; *La Marina* (℡981 414 098; ❸), a little smarter and pricier but with only two sea-facing rooms; and the stylish and very comfortable *Bodegón O Forno* (℡981 414 124; ❹), also looking onto the sea. Ortigueira, too, has a couple of decent *hostales*, including the *Monterrey*, at Avda. Franco 105 (℡981 400 135, Ⓕ981 400 417; ❸).

Drivers and cyclists, though, should take the opportunity to head the 7km north of Barqueiro up to the headland, through pine and eucalyptus forest, to straggly Vila de Vares. Two kilometres beyond, **PORTO DE VARES** is a highly attractive clump of fishermen's houses overlooking the bay, flanked to the south by a superb, wide, sandy beach, where you can camp. In the hamlet, there's a single *hostal*, the brand-new *Hostal Porto Mar* (℡981 562 803; ❸), with smart rooms and beautiful sea views. There's also a terrific seafood restaurant, *Marina*, with outdoor tables and window seats overlooking bay and beach. Fresh seafood meals – including great octopus and an *especial paella* – start from €9.60 a head, though the *paella* will set you back considerably more.

San Andrés de Teixido and around

The FEVE heads inland after Ortigueira, but drivers or the very determined could make a side-trip to the hermitage at **SAN ANDRÉS DE TEIXIDO**, which, like so many of Galicia's sanctuaries, is based on a pre-Christian religious site. The hermitage occupies an important place in the mythology of Galicia, where the saying goes: *a San Andrés de Teixido vai de morto o que non foi de vivo* ("those who don't go to San Andrés alive, will go once they're dead"). Those failing to make the pilgrimage in their lifetime become one of the dreaded Santa Compaña, their souls trapped in the skins of lizards and weasels living in the rocks around the hermitage. Even in recent times, some older Galicians have been known to buy bus tickets for recently deceased relatives in an attempt to avoid this fate. It is a dramatic spot, with the nearby cliffs at **Vixia de Herbeira** claiming the title of highest in Europe at over 600 metres. There are a couple of places to stay in **CEDEIRA**, a port with a long sweep of beach set in an attractive *ría* 12km away: try the comfortable *Avenida*, Rúa Cuatro Caminos 6 (℡981 480 998, Ⓕ981 492 112; ❻), or the basic *Hostal Chelsea*, Plaza Sagrado Corazón 15 (℡981 481 111; ❸).

Ferrol

The city of **FERROL**, historically one of Spain's principal naval bases and dockyards, is now struggling to survive the collapse of the shipbuilding industry. Unfortunately the navy and dockyards have usurped the best of the coastline, leaving a provincial centre dominated by a status-conscious, navy-oriented community and a large, paint-spattered statue of El Caudillo (the Chief), Francisco Franco, who was born here in 1892. Although frequently considered a bastion of conservatism, Ferrol was also the birthplace of Pablo Iglesias, founder of the Spanish Socialist Party, which until March 1996 ruled Spain for over a decade.

Getting out shouldn't be too difficult; the **FEVE** and **RENFE** stations are housed in the same building, and the **bus station** is just outside – exit and make two quick lefts, and you'll see it some 50m ahead of you. If you need **accommodation**, one of the more reasonable places is the spartan *Noray* on Rúa Venezuela 117 (℡981 310 079; ❷), and there are plenty of other choices along Rúa Pardo Bajo – the *Aloya* is at number 28 (℡981 351 231, Ⓕ981 351 231; ❹) – or Rúa del Sol and Rúa María, all within a few minutes' walk of the station and the central Praza de España. If you're driving, beware of outrageous traffic jams out of Ferrol on Friday and in again on Sunday nights, when the entire community heads out of the city for the weekend, blocking local roads solid.

The Ría de Betanzos

Ferrol stands more or less opposite A Coruña, only 20km away across the mouth of the **Ría de Betanzos**, but a seventy-kilometre trip by road or rail. The coast between the two cities is surprisingly rural, with the contours of the *ría* speckled with forests and secluded beaches.

Pontedeume, Perbes and Sada

Heading south from Ferrol, you cross the Río Eume either by the vast medieval bridge at **PONTEDEUME** (Puentedeume), or the vaster-still motorway flyover nearby. The stones on either side of the old bridge as you enter town are, in fact, boars from the arms of the once-powerful overlords, the counts of Andrade. Their tower overlooks the river at Pontedeume, and the Castelo de Andrade is perched on a hill over the town.

Just beyond, *Camping Perbes* (☎981 783 104; June–Sept) is sandwiched between woods and water on the popular **Praia Perbes** near Minho. At **SADA**, opposite, you'll find the *Marina Española* **youth hostel** (☎981 620 118; ❶), and there are also several **campsites** in the area.

Betanzos

The town of **BETANZOS** is an enjoyable place to stay, although as most visitors are day-trippers from A Coruña, accommodation is fairly limited. The site it's built on is so old, dating back from before the Romans, that what was once a steep seaside hill is now set well back from the coast, at the spot where the rivers Mendo and Mandeo meet. The base of the hill is surrounded by still-discernible fragments of the medieval walls, though these are now largely built over with houses, above which rise a mass of twisting and tunnelling narrow streets. Follow these, and you'll come to the twelfth-century church of **Santa María do Azougue**, reconstructed by the Andrade lords in the fourteenth century; Andrade influence probably explains the unlikely stone pig with a cross on its back over the adjacent and contemporary church of San Francisco.

The focus of Betanzos is the large, attractive main square, the **Praza dos Irmáns G. Naveira**, named after (and boasting a statue of) the two Betanzos-born brothers who left to make their fortunes in Argentina and then returned to endow the town with hospitals, schools and the remarkable O Pasatempo park (see below). Just behind the square, in Rúa Emilio Romay, the excellent **Museo das Mariñas** (summer Mon–Fri 10am–2pm & 4.30–6.30pm, Sat 10.30am–1pm; winter Mon–Fri 10am–2pm & 4–8pm, Sat 10.30am–1pm; €1.40) provides a fascinating insight into Betanzos and neighbouring *mariñas* (sea-facing villages) throughout their long history.

A ten-minute walk away on the edge of town is the remarkable "encyclopedia park", **O Pasatempo** (summer daily 4–8.30pm; winter Sat & Sun 4–6pm; free), recently rescued from almost total dereliction and restored to something resembling its original splendour. Founded by Juan García Naveira in 1893, the park's sculptures and murals were intended to give the folk of provincial Betanzos a picture in stone of all that was then newest or strangest in the world – a biplane, a deep-sea diver, the Great Wall of China, the Panama Canal – along with more purely whimsical elements like the strange grotto with Gaúdi-esque pillars and a bank of granite clocks showing times around the world (it's always midday in Betanzos), all of it looking as quaintly old-fashioned now as it might have seemed thrillingly modern then.

Practicalities

Half-hourly **buses** from A Coruña (a 45-minute journey) pull up right opposite the turismo, just behind the main square. Buses from Ferrol arrive at the Betanzos Ciudad RENFE **train station**, itself used only for the three daily trains to and from Ferrol; it's a ten-minute walk into town, across the park and over the bridge to the town walls. Other trains use the Betanzos Infesta station, 2.5km away at the top of a steep climb – you're better off coming by bus. The **turismo** (summer Mon–Fri 10am–2pm & 4.30–6.30pm, Sat 10.30am–1pm; winter 10am-1pm & 4–8pm, Sat 10.30am–1pm; ☎981 773 693, Ⓦwww.betanzos.net) is in the same building as the Museo das Mariñas in Rúa de Emilio Romay. If you need a **place to stay**, there are a few options just off the main square: at Rúa do Rollo 6, directly behind the statue of the Garciá brothers, *Hostal Barreiro* (☎981 772 259; ❷) fills up quickly in summer, but has pleasant, if basic rooms; just around the corner, the very basic *Fonda Universal*, Avda. Linares Rivas 18 (☎981 770 055; ❸), is a cheap fallback; and on the far side of the square, *Hotel Los Ángeles*, Rúa dos Ánxeles 11 (☎981 771 213, Ⓕ981 776 459, Ⓔhlosangeles@tpi.infomail.es; ❺), is professionally run, if a bit anonymous.

    Eating and drinking centre around the row of bars on the main square – with outdoor seating – and the two tiny alleys leading off it to the right of *Café La Galeta*. The popular *O Pote* on the first alley, the Travesía do Progreso, has a wide range of good tapas, though you may have to stand. The owner of the *Hostal Barreiros* also runs the rather classy, wood-panelled *Mesón dos Arcos* below the *hostal*, whose dining room serves an excellent-value *menú del día* and great grills.

A Coruña

Despite its long history, the port of **A CORUÑA** is surprisingly modern, focused more on the office blocks and apartments of its rising middle class than on its past. However, its situation is impressive, crammed onto a peninsular with one side looking across the *rías* to Ferrol, the other exposed to the Atlantic, and its medieval quarter remains fairly extensive. It's also a major transport nexus, with a cosmopolitan range of shops and services, a surprisingly good beach right in the centre, an excellent array of seafood restaurants and a vibrant nightlife that ends with 5am *chocolate con churros*, watching the fishing boats come in.

Arrival, information and accommodation

The **bus** and **train** stations are close to each other, a good twenty-minute walk from the city centre; take bus #1 or #1a to the Praza de María Pita. The **turismo** is at the Darsena de la Marina (Mon–Fri 10am–1.30pm & 4.30–6.30pm, Sat 10.30am–2pm & 4.30–7pm, Sun 10.30am–2pm; ☎981 221 822, Ⓦwww.turgalicia.es). Librería Colón, Rúa Riego de Agua 24, has possibly Galicia's best selection of English-language **books**, plus a wide range of foreign **newspapers**.

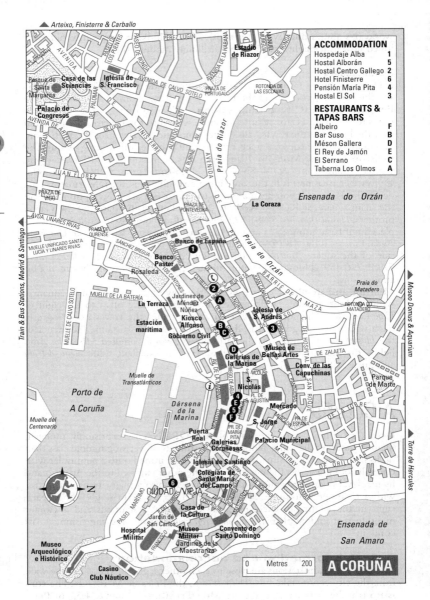

ACCOMMODATION

Hospedaje Alba	1
Hostal Alborán	5
Hostal Centro Gallego	2
Hotel Finisterre	6
Pensión María Pita	4
Hostal El Sol	3

RESTAURANTS & TAPAS BARS

Albeiro	F
Bar Suso	B
Méson Gallera	D
El Rey de Jamón	E
El Serrano	C
Taberna Los Olmos	A

A CORUÑA

Accommodation

Hospedaje Alba, Rúa San Andrés 145 ☎981 220 242. Cheap and spotless rooms, plus the use of a kitchen. ❸

Hostal Alboran, Rúa Riego de Agua 14 ☎981 226 579, ⓕ981 222 562,

ⓦwww.meiganet.com/hostalalboran. Excellent location on a pedestrianized street very close to Praza María Pita with thirty comfortable rooms, all with bath and TV, some with balconies overlooking the street. ❻

Hostal Centro Gallego, Rúa Estrella 2 ☎ 981 222 236. Pleasant and well-located *hostal* with comfortable modern rooms in a quiet side street. ❹

Hotel Finisterre, Paseo del Parrote ☎ 981 205 400, ℻ 981 208 462, Ⓦ www.hotelfinisterre.com. The top option in town, this vast orange waterfront palace comes complete with tennis courts, Olympic-size swimming pool and all mod-cons. ❾

Pensión María Pita, Rúa Riego de Agua 38 ☎ 981 221 187. Excellently located on a pedestri-

anized street in the heart of town, this is the best of the numerous budget options hereabouts, with a charming *dueña* and pleasant rooms; there are a couple of other *hospedajes* upstairs if you get stuck. ❸

Hostal El Sol, Rúa Sol 10 ☎ 981 210 019. Unprepossessing exterior, complete with bordello-style flashing sign, though inside rooms are surprisingly stylish and comfortable. ❻

The City

Departure point of the doomed 1588 Armada, and veteran of the Peninsular Wars, A Coruña has a lengthy history of naval combat. At the heart of the town is the huge, colonnaded **Praza de María Pita**, named after (and featuring a statue of) the spear-waving María Pita, a redoubtable local heroine who helped repel an English siege in 1589; local patriots like to have their photos taken in front of her. Some of the best of A Coruña's distinctive glassed-in balconies – a practical innovation against wind and showers – are on Rúa Riego de Agua, directly west of here, and on the nearby waterfront Dársena, from where the **Paseo Marítimo** walkway edges the city's extensive coastline, bending around the port and marina.

East of the plaza are the narrow and atmospheric streets of the medieval town, which wind around the Romanesque churches of **Santiago** and **Santa María del Campo** and are shielded from the sea by a high wall, much of which still remains, notably some fine sixteenth- and seventeenth-century gates. On the far side of the old town is the walled **Jardín de San Carlos** and, inside, the **tomb of Sir John Moore**, killed in 1809 during the British retreat from the French in the Peninsular Wars, and immortalized in the jingoistic rhythms of Reverend Charles Wolfe ("Not a drum was heard, not a funeral note . . .") which you will find here inscribed. Directly across the road, the **Museo Militar** (daily 10am–2pm & 4–7pm, closed Sun pm; free) has a huge collection of guns, ordnance, uniforms and toy soldiers from the Peninsular to Bosnian wars.

Beyond here, on a spit of land poking out into the sea, the restored Castelo San Antón was once a garrison and, until the 1960s, a military and political prison. Today it houses the **Museo Arqueolóxico e Histórico** (Tues–Sat 10am–7.30pm, July & Aug closes 9pm, Sun 10am–2.30pm; €1.80), worth the entrance fee if only for the view across the bay from the top and the medieval stone carvings at the back.

The city's much-trumpeted lighthouse, the **Torre de Hercules** (daily April–June & Sept 10am–7pm; July & Aug 10am–9pm, open till midnight on Fri and Sat; Oct–March 10am–6pm; €1.50), symbol of A Coruña, lies on a rocky outcrop north of the centre, reached by bus #3 or #3a from the gardens just behind the turismo. It has been warning ships off the treacherous Costa da Morte since Roman times, but was entirely recased in the eighteenth century and there's not a trace of ancient stone to be seen. The last victim of the coast was an oil tanker that went down in 1993; only a typically vicious storm saved the region from absolute ecological disaster, by breaking up the slick.

North of the city centre, on the opposite side of the headland from the Dársena, lies the huge **Praia del Orzán**, A Coruña's main beach. Follow this around northwards to reach the superbly designed **Museo Domus** (Museum of Mankind; daily: summer 11am–9pm; winter 10am–7pm; Ⓦ www.casaciencias .org; €1.80), whose interactive displays on how the human mind and body works are mostly aimed at children. The joint entry ticket also gets you in to the less-interesting **Casa de las Sciencias** (same hours), an interactive science museum in Parque de Santa Margarita, out towards the bus station.

A new state-of-the art **aquarium** (daily: July & Aug 10am–10pm, Sept–June 10am–7pm; €6) has been built on the headland just south of the Torre de Hercules. It has an impressive array of hands-on educational exhibitions and the 4.5-million-litre *nautilus* tank and viewing gallery - great for kids.

Eating, drinking and nightlife

The chain of small streets leading west from Praza de María Pita, from Rúa Franja, through to Rúa La Galera, Rúa Los Olmos and Rúa Estrella, are

---

Gallego food and drink

One of the most compelling attractions of Galicia is the local food. Gourmets claim the quality of the **seafood** here is to be equalled only in Newfoundland, and with a few exceptions it is not expensive, at least when eaten as tapas in bars. Local wonders to look out for include *vieiras* (the scallops whose shells became the symbol of St James), *mejillones* (the rich orange mussels from the *rías*), *cigallas* (a kind of crayfish usually and inadequately translated as shrimp), *anguilas* (little eels from the River Minho), *navajas* (razor-shells), *percebes* (barnacles) and *choquitos* and *chipirones* (different kinds of small squid best served in their own ink). *Pulpo* (octopus) is so much a part of *gallego* eating that there are special *pulperías* cooking it in the traditional copper pots, and it is a mainstay of local country fiestas. In the province of Pontevedra alone, Vilanova de Arousa has its own octopus festival, Arcade has one devoted to oysters, and O Grove goes all the way with a generalized seafood fiesta. One word of warning, however; although a wide variety of crab and lobster is always on display in the restaurants, make sure to have a price quoted in advance – the cost of these specialities is often exorbitant, and the demand so great that certain items such as *necoras* (spider crab) even have to be imported from England to keep up the supply.

Throughout Galicia there are superb **markets**; the coastal towns have their rows of seafront stalls with supremely fresh fish, while cities such as Santiago and Pontevedra have grand old arcaded market halls, piled high with farm produce from the surrounding countryside. Most enjoyable of all are the ports (such as Cambados and Marín), with *lonjas* open to the public, where you can wait for the fishing boats to come home (usually around midnight, but more like 6am in A Coruña) and watch the auctioning of their catch – much of which will have left Galicia well before dawn for the restaurants of Madrid, on the nightly special train.

Another speciality, imported from the second *gallego* homeland of Argentina, is the **churrasquería** (grill house). Often unmarked and needing local assistance to find, these serve up immense *churrascos* – what we inadequately call "spare ribs" (it's more like a steak with bones in it). The *gallegos* don't normally like their food highly spiced, but *churrascos* are traditionally served with a devastating garlic-based *salsa picante*. Other common dishes are *caldo gallego*, a thick stew of cabbage and potatoes in a meat-based broth, *caldeirada*, a filling fish soup, *lacon con grelos*, ham boiled with turnip greens, and the ubiquitous *empanada*, a light-crusted pasty, often filled with tuna and tomato.

The local **wines** can be great – both the whites (especially Albariño) and the thick port-like reds (some bars even serve a "black" wine) – and are still usually drunk from *tazas*, handleless ceramic cups; the best regions are Ribeiro and the Rias Baixas. The local beer is Estrella Galicia, good and strong. **Liqueurs** tend to be fiery, based on the clear *aguardiente* (which is elsewhere known as *eau de vie* or *aquavit*) nowadays often flavoured with herbs or coffee liquor; one much-loved *gallego* custom is the *queimada*, when a large bowl of *aguardiente* with fruit, sugar and coffee-grains is set alight and then drunk hot.

crowded with **bars** that, at their best, offer some of Spain's finest seafood, and excellent tapas. There's a cluster of *marisquerías* immediately west of Praza María Pita on Rúa Franja, including the popular *Albeiro* at no. 3. Beyond here there's a big selection of seafood tapas bars – try *Méson Gallera* at Rúa Galera 17, *Bar Suso* on the same street at no. 31 or *Taberna Los Olmos* at Rúa Olmas 22 – and several good *jamonerías*, such as *El Rey de Jamón*, Rúa Franja 45, and *El Serrano*, Rúa Galera 23. There's also a crowd of waterfront **restaurants** along the Dársena, though they're nothing special.

The **late-night** scene moves to the northern side of the isthmus around the two adjacent beaches of Praia do Riazor and Praia do Orzán; there's a cluster of bars on the Pasadizo Orzán (towards the Rotonda do Matadero at the northern end of the bay). At the other end of the bay you can dance the night away in the *discoteca, Praia Club*, on the seafront Avenida de Pedro Barrié da Maza. Inland, the more yuppified Rúa de Juan Florez has jazz, salsa and the perennial *Pirámide* nightclub.

Five kilometres out of town, the bars and clubs at **Praia Santa Cristina**, a lovely wooded spit of sand further up the *ría*, are lively throughout the summer. You can pick up a bus from the main station until 10pm, or a boat from the Dársena de la Marina until 8pm, but once there you'll either have to stay the course until the following morning or get a taxi back to town.

Inland to Santiago

The **Camino de Santiago**, the pilgrims' route, is the longest-established "tourist" route in Europe, and its final section through Galicia provides a fair representation of the medieval pilgrimage to the thousands who walk it every year, armed with the traditional staff and the shell emblem of St James. Hundreds more cycle the route, and it's possible to drive, too, although this is the least satisfying way of making the journey, offering tantalizing glimpses of ancient footpaths winding through woods as the road and footpath intertwine and then separate. Both routes are well signposted with yellow scallop shell symbols, and local buses cover much of the road route, a boon to the footsore. Basic hostels for pilgrims are set up along the way, with priority given to walkers. Walking or cycling, the *camino* is a tough but unforgettable experience. Local turismo offices have lists of the hostels and special pilgrim facilities (there are phone lines for medical emergencies); you'll also need a hat to guard against the hot sun, rainwear against *gallego* deluges, and a big stick to keep the dogs at bay.

The Pilgrim Route branches off the main Ponferrada–Lugo road at the **Pedrafita do Cebreiro** pass which marks the *gallego* frontier. This is a desolate spot, where hundreds of English soldiers froze or starved to death during Sir John Moore's retreat towards A Coruña in 1809. In such a forbidding landscape, you can only be impressed by the sheer scale of work that medieval builders put into providing spiritual and material amenities for the pilgrims. Crumbling castles, convents and humble inns line the road, and it's not hard to imagine what a welcome sight each must have been.

Cebreiro

The village of **CEBREIRO** itself is quite appallingly situated to catch the worst of the *gallego* wind and snow – not that you would realize that on one of the rare fine days of summer. It's highly picturesque, an undulating settlement of thatched stone huts (*pallozas*) surrounding a stark ninth-century church. No one actually lives in the *pallozas* any more, which are maintained as a national monument, with a guide on site to answer visitors' questions. In high season up to 1000 people per day pass this way; at other times it feels as remote as it ever did, and it's even possible to take refuge for the night in the former monastery next to the church. There are similar villages in the vicinity, where a few farmers still choose to live in the ancient dwellings; their children, however, seem to be unanimous in the desire to move away in pursuit of creature comforts, and the old way of life must surely be coming to an end.

Following the Pilgrim Route through Galicia

Many of the places along the Pilgrim Route that medieval travellers stopped at are now little more than ruins, but some survive. For example, the **Monasterio de Samos** (daily 10.30am–1pm & 4.30–7pm), 40km west of Cebreiro, famous for its library in the Middle Ages, and badly damaged by fire in 1951, has been restored, and its *hospedería* reopened for pilgrims. Its moss-covered exterior, pierced only by two small barred windows, leads to two sunny and peaceful cloisters.

The once-great monastery of **Sobrado dos Monxes** (daily 10.15am–1.30pm & 4.15–6.45pm), midway between Lugo, Santiago and Betanzos – was also allowed to decay for a long time, but the provincial government is beginning to repair and restore it, and with your own transport this remains a highly worthwhile detour. After the empty approach road, the huge cathedral church with its strong west towers comes as a dramatic shock. The range of the abbey buildings proclaims past royal patronage, their scale emphasized by the tiny village below. The church itself sprouts flowers and foliage from every niche and crevice, its honey-coloured stone blossoming with lichens and mosses. Within, all is immensely grand – long, uncluttered vistas, mannerist Baroque, and romantic gloom; there are superb, worm-endangered choir stalls (once in Santiago cathedral) and, through a small arch in the north transept, a small, ruined Romanesque chapel. These are the highlights, but take time to explore the outbuildings, too, including a magnificent thirteenth-century kitchen with a massive chimney flue. A small community of monks maintain the monastery and operate a small shop.

Equipped with a handful of *hostales* and cafés, **SARRÍA** makes a logical stopover on this part of the *camino*; try the *Londres*, Calvo Sotelo 13 (☎982 532 456, ⓕ982 533 006; ⑤). The lower part of town is unimpressive, but old Sarría straggles gloriously uphill, topped by a (privately owned) castle. Thirty kilometres along the route, the whole town of **PORTOMARÍN** was flooded by the damming of the Minho, but its Templar castle and church were carried stone by stone to a new site further up the hillside.

Lugo

The Camino de Santiago bypassed **LUGO**, although it was already an ancient city even a thousand years ago. Built on a Celtic site above the Minho (and named after the Celtic sun god Lug), it is the only Spanish town to remain

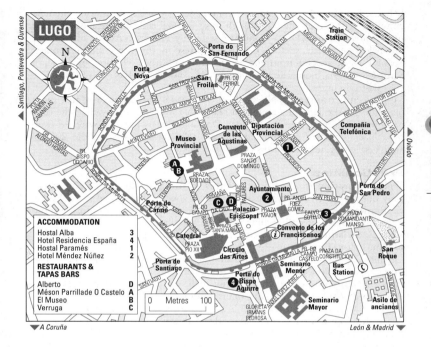

ACCOMMODATION

Hostal Alba	3
Hotel Residencia España	4
Hostal Paramés	1
Hotel Méndez Núñez	2

RESTAURANTS &
TAPAS BARS

Alberto	D
Méson Parrillade O Castelo	A
El Museo	B
Verruga	C

0   Metres   100

completely enclosed within superb **Roman walls**. These are ten to fifteen metres high, with 85 circular towers along a circuit of almost three kilometres, and are broad enough to provide a pleasant thoroughfare for walks around the city. Sadly, insensitive building has blocked out most of the views of the surrounding countryside, and a busy loop road makes it impossible to appreciate the walls from any distance outside. But the road does at least keep the traffic out of the centre, which itself maintains an enjoyable if neglected medley of medieval and eighteenth-century buildings.

The Town

Lugo may be short on great sights, but it's a fine place to wander around, savouring the many granite staircases, narrow arcades and relaxed open spaces. The largest and best of the city's gardens, the **Parque Rosalia de Castro**, has a fine little café and weekend performances by the local brass band. It's a popular destination for the evening *paseo*, positioned a little way out of the Porta de Santiago, with good views over the Minho valley.

The large mossy **Catedral** (daily 8am–8.30pm, museum Mon–Sat: July & Aug 11am–1pm; Sept–June 11am–noon; €1.20), flanked by three distinctive towers, was, like so many *gallego* churches, modelled after the one at Santiago de Compostela. Inside, choir stalls cramp the central space, forcing you around a ring of chapels, in one of which an imperial soldier in cherubic posture tramples a dying Moor. Walk down Rúa Nova and you'll come to Lugo's exceptionally good **Museo Provincial** (July & Aug Mon–Fri 11am–2pm & 5–8pm, Sat 10am–2pm; Sept–June Mon–Sat 10.30am–2pm & 4.30–8.30pm, Sat closes at 8pm; free, though you'll need to show a passport or driving licence), part-

585

ly housed in the old Convento de San Francisco – you'll see the stone kitchen, complete with a fireplace big enough to sit in. Well laid out, the museum features *gallego* art, including a wonderful statue by Francisco Asorey of a kneeling peasant woman, staff in one hand, priest in the other, contemporary Spanish work swiped from the Prado and an early collection of Galicia's Sargadelos china, alongside more predictable displays of Roman remains and ecclesiastical clutter.

Of the city's two squares, the graceful colonnades of the **Praza Maior** shelter some good cafés and a couple of reasonable restaurants (as well as the turismo in the *galerías*). The Praza Santo Domingo is less inviting, watched over by a black statue of a Roman imperial eagle, commemorating the 2000th anniversary of Caesar Augustus's entry to the city.

Practicalities

The **train station** (to the north) and **bus terminal** (to the east) are immediately outside the walls, a fair distance apart. If you enter the town at the **Porta de Santiago**, the best of its old gates, you can then climb up onto the most impressive stretch of wall, leading past the cathedral.

Lugo's **turismo** (July to mid-Sept Mon–Fri 10am–2pm & 4–8pm, mid-Sept to June Mon–Fri 9.30am–2pm & 4.30–6.30pm; ☎982 231 361, ⓦwww. turgalicia.es) is concealed in a small shopping arcade off the south side of the Praza España. Most of the budget **hostales** are outside the walls, around the train and bus stations, but it's more fun to be inside. *Hostal Paramés*, Rúa do Progreso 28 (☎982 226 251; ❹), offers comfortable, good-value rooms, while the *Alba*, Calvo Sotelo 31 (☎982 226 056; ❸), is very cheap but extremely basic. The only other place to stay within the town walls is at the upmarket *Hotel Méndez Núñez*, Rúa Raiña 1 (☎982 230 711, ⓕ982 229 738; ❻). Just outside the Porta do Bispo Aguirre you'll find the friendly and well-run *Hotel Residencia España*, Rúa Vilalba 2 (☎982 231 540; ❹).

The best selection of **restaurants** is on the long, straight Rúa Nova and the nearby Rúa da Cruz. *Méson Parrillade O Castelo*, Rúa Nova 23, has a good, cheap *menú* for €5.40, or try the *bodega*-cum-*pulpería El Museo* a couple of doors down at no. 21. In Rúa da Cruz, the swanky *Verruga* has top-notch seafood and a sensational window display of outlandish marine produce, as does the equally posh *Alberto* a few doors down. Rúa Nova is also the best place to look for **bars** and **tapas**.

Santiago de Compostela

Built in a warm golden granite, **SANTIAGO DE COMPOSTELA** is one of the most beautiful of all Spanish cities, rivalled in the north only by León and Salamanca. The medieval city has been declared in its entirety to be both a national monument and a UNESCO World Heritage site, and remains a remarkably integrated whole, all the better for being almost completely pedestrianized. The buildings and the squares, the long stone arcades and the statues, are hewn from the same granite blocks and blend imperceptibly one into the other, often making it impossible to distinguish ground level from raised terrace.

The **pilgrimage** to Santiago captured the imagination of Christian Europe on an unprecedented scale. At the height of its popularity, in the eleventh and twelfth centuries, the city was receiving over half a million pilgrims each year.

People of all classes came to visit the supposed shrine of St James the Apostle (Santiago to the Spanish, Saint Jacques to the French), making this the third holiest site in Christendom, after Jerusalem and Rome.

The atmosphere of the place is much as it must have been in the days of the pilgrims, with tourists now as likely to be attracted by Santiago's art and history as by religion. Not that the function of pilgrimage here is dead; it fell into decline with the Reformation – or as the local chronicler Molina reported, "the damned doctrines of the accursed Luther diminished the number of Germans and *wealthy* English" – but fortunes have revived of late. Each year at the **Festival of St James** (see p.575) on July 25, there is a ceremony dedicating the country and government to the saint at his shrine. Years in which the saint's day falls on a Sunday are designated "Holy Years", and the activity becomes even more intense; the next Holy Year is 2004 – after that you'll have to wait until 2015.

With its large population of students, most of whom live in the less appealing modern city slightly downhill, Santiago is always a lively place to visit, far more than a mere historical curiosity. Uniquely, it's also a city that's at its best in the rain; in fact it's situated in the wettest fold of the *gallego* hills, and suffers brief but constant showers. Water glistens on the facades, gushes from the innumerable gargoyles, and flows down the streets. As a result vegetation sprouts everywhere, with the cathedral coated in orange and yellow mosses, and grass poking up from the tiles and cobbles. It's also a manageable size – you can wander fifteen minutes out of town and reach wide-open countryside. You may well find yourself staying longer than you'd planned, particularly if you arrive when the great July 25 Festival is in full swing.

Arrival, orientation and information

Arriving at the **bus station** you are 1km or so northeast of the town centre; bus #10 will take you to Praza de Galicia. If you're walking, go straight ahead down the road in front of the terminal to the roundabout, then turn left and follow this road past the Convento de Santa Clara into town. The **train station** is slightly more centrally located: head straight out of the station up Rúa do Horreo to Praza de Galicia, a fifteen-minute walk. Labacolla **airport** (℡981 547 500) is some 13km east of town on the road to Lugo. Frequent buses run between the airport and bus station (1–2 hourly); there are also less frequent services from opposite the Iberia office at Rúa Xeneral Pardiñas 24. The **turismo**, at Rúa do Vilar 43 (Mon–Fri 10am–2pm & 4–7pm, Sat 11am–2pm & 5–7pm, Sun 11am–2pm; ℡981 584 081), can provide complete lists of accommodation. There is also a small office at the bus station (daily 10am–2pm & 4–8pm).

Accommodation

You should have no difficulty finding an inexpensive **room** in Santiago, though note that *pensiones* here are often called *hospedajes*, as elsewhere in Galicia. The biggest concentration of places is on the three parallel streets leading down from the cathedral: Rúa Nova, Rúa do Vilar, and Rúa do Franco (this last named after the French pilgrims, rather than the late dictator). Even during the July festival, there's rarely a problem, with half the bars in the city renting out beds, and landladies dragging you off on arrival; if anything, things can be more difficult out of season, when much of the cheaper accommodation is let long-term to students.

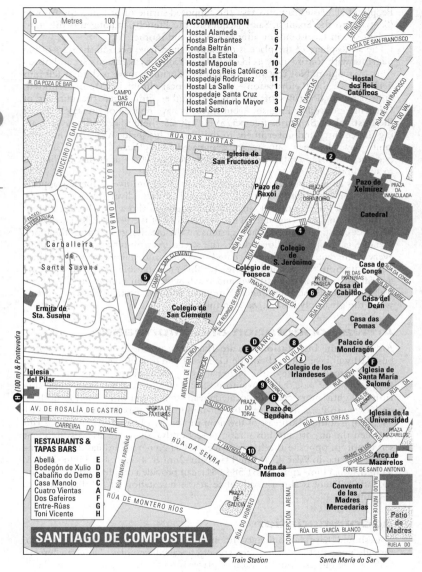

ACCOMMODATION

Hostal Alameda	5
Hostal Barbantes	6
Fonda Beltrán	7
Hostal La Estela	4
Hostal Mapoula	10
Hostal dos Reis Católicos	2
Hospedaje Rodríguez	11
Hostal La Salle	1
Hospedaje Santa Cruz	8
Hostal Seminario Mayor	3
Hostal Suso	9

RESTAURANTS & TAPAS BARS

Abellà	E
Bodegón de Xulio	D
Cabaliño do Demo	B
Casa Manolo	C
Cuatro Vientas	A
Dos Gafeiros	F
Entre-Rúas	G
Toni Vicente	H

SANTIAGO DE COMPOSTELA

▼ Train Station   Santa María do Sar ▼

Budget options

Fonda Beltrán, Rúa do Preguntoiro 36 ☎ 981 582 225. Attractive rooms in a beautiful, ancient house with friendly owners. The large living room has wonderful views of the cathedral. **❸**

Hostal La Estela, Avda. Rajoy 1 ☎ 981 582 796. Quiet, good-value *hostal* on a pretty street just off

the Praza do Obradoiro, with both en-suite and shared-bath rooms. **❸–❹**

Hostal La Salle, Rúa do San Roque 6 ☎ 981 584 611, ℻ 981 584 221. A modern students' residence, annexed to the Colexio la Salle, containing sixty or so small, functional rooms, all with private shower or bath. **❸**

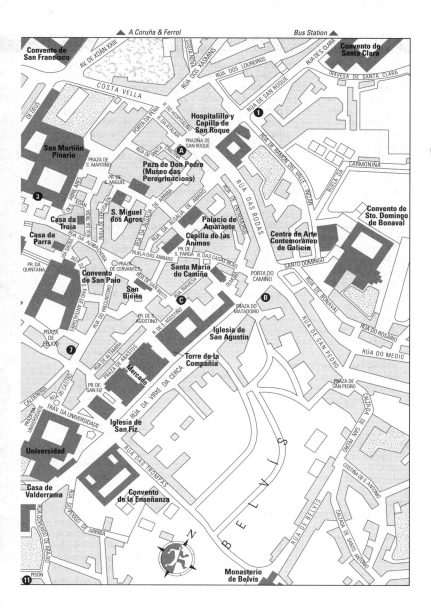

Within the map:

Convento de San Francisco

Convento de Santa Clara

AV. DE XOÁN XXIII
RÚA DOS XASMINS
RÚA DOS LOUREIROS
COSTA NOVA
RÚA DE S. CLARA
TRAVESA DE SANTA CLARA
COSTA VELLA
DE BEUS
R. DO HOSPITALIÑO
R. DA ATALAIA
PORTA DA PENA
RÚA DE SAN ROQUE
RÚA DE SANTA CRISTINA
CARMONINA
RÚA DE RAMÓN DEL VALLE-INCLÁN
RUELA DA

Hospitaliño y Capilla de San Roque

PRAZIÑA DE SAN ROQUE

San Martiño Pinario

PRAZA DE S. MARTIÑO

Pazo de Don Pedro (Museo das Peregrinacións)

PR. DE S. MIGUEL

RÚA DE ABRIL ARES
RÚA XOÁN
RÚA DA TROIA
RUELA XELMÍREZ
RÚA DA ALGALIA DE ARRIBA
RÚA DA ALGALIA DE ABAIXO
RÚA DAS RODAS
RÚA DE ENTREMUROS

S. Miguel dos Agros

Casa da Troia

Casa da Parra

Palacio de Amarante

Capilla de las Ánimas

Convento de Sto. Domingo de Bonaval

Centro de Arte Contemporáneo de Galicia

RÚA DA AZABACHERÍA
RÚA DA ACIBECHERÍA
RUELA DAS ÁNIMAS
PR. DE S. PARGA
RÚA DAS CASAS REAIS
SANTO DOMINGO

PR. DA QUINTANA

PRAZA DE CERVANTES

Santa María do Camiño

Convento de San Paio

San Bieito

PORTA DO CAMIÑO

RÚA DE BONAVAL

RÚA DE SAN BIEITO
RÚA TRAVESA
OMARÍA
PR. DE S. AGOSTIÑO
R. DE S. AGOSTIÑO

PRAZA DO MATADOIRO

RÚA DO ROSARIO

PRAZA DE FEIJOO

RÚA DO PREGUNTOIRO

Iglesia de San Agustín

RÚA DE SAN PEDRO

RÚA DO MEDIO

CALDERERÍA
RÚA DO CASTRO
PR. DE SAN FIZ
RÚA DE ALTAMIRA
PRAZA DE ABASTOS

Mercado

Torre de la Compañía

PRAZA DE SAN PEDRO

CALZADA DE SAN PEDRO

Iglesia de San Fiz

TRAV. DA UNIVERSIDADE

RÚA DA VIRXE DA CERCA

COSTIÑA DE S. ANTONIO

Universidad

PRAZA UNIVERSIDADE

RÚA DAS TROMPAS

Casa de Valderrama

Convento de la Enseñanza

RÚA DO PEXIGO DE ARRIBA
RÚA DOPEXIGO DE ABAIXO

RÚA DE BELVÍS

CALZADA DE SANTO ANTONIO

BELVÍS

PISÓN

Monasterio de Belvís

Hospedaje Santa Cruz, Rúa do Villar 42 ☎ 981 582 815. Large, basic rooms near the cathedral. ④

Moderate and expensive options

Hostal Alameda, Rúa do San Clemente 32 ☎ 981 588 100, ℱ 981 588 689. Smart, stylish rooms – some en suite – with polished floors, large windows and TV. Pleasantly located by a park. ④–⑤

Hostal Barbantes, Rúa do Franco 1 ☎ 981 581 077. Clean and light en-suite rooms, some with balconies overlooking a little square. There's a good bar and restaurant below. ④

The great **pilgrimage to Santiago** was the first exercise in mass tourism. Although the shrine was visited by the great – Fernando and Isabel, Carlos V, Francis of Assisi – you didn't have to be rich to come. The various roads through France and northern Spain which led here, collectively known as El Camino de Santiago (The Way of St James, or the Pilgrim Route), were lined with monasteries and charitable hospices for the benefit of the pilgrims. Villages sprang up along the route, and an order of knights was founded for the pilgrims' protection. There was even a guidebook – the world's first – written by a French monk called Aymery Picaud, which recorded, along with water sources and places to stay, such facts as the bizarre sexual habits of the Navarrese Basques (who exposed themselves when excited, and protected their mules from their neighbours with chastity belts). All in all it was an extraordinary phenomenon in an age when most people never ventured beyond their own town or village.

Why did they come? Some, like Chaucer's Wife of Bath, who had "been in Galicia at Seynt Jame", had their own private reasons: social fashion, adventure, the opportunities for marriage or even for crime. But for most pilgrims, it was simply a question of faith. They believed in the miraculous power of St James, and were told that the journey would guarantee them a remission of half their time in purgatory. Not for a moment did they doubt that the tomb beneath the high altar at Compostela Cathedral held the mortal remains of James, son of Zebedee and Salome and first cousin of Jesus Christ. It seems scarcely credible that the whole business was an immense ecclesiastical fraud.

Yet the legend, at each point of its development, bears this out. It begins with the claim, unsubstantiated by the Bible, that St James came to Spain, at some point after the Crucifixion, to spread the gospel. He is said, for example, to have had a vision of the Virgin in Zaragoza. He then returned to Jerusalem, where he was undoubtedly beheaded by Herod Agrippa. His body should, by all rights and reason, be buried somewhere in the Nile delta. But the legend records that two of James's disciples removed his corpse to Jaffa, where a boat appeared, without sails or crew, and carried them to Padrón, twenty kilometres downstream from

Hostal Mapoula, Rúa do Entremurallas 10 ☎ 981 580 124, ℱ 981 584 089. Good, friendly *hostal* with spacious, en-suite rooms, all with TV and phone. ❹

Hostal dos Reis Católicos, Praza do Obradoiro 1 ☎ 981 582 200, ℱ 981 563 094 ℰ santiago@parador.es. A modest €160 buys you a night in Spain's most famous *parador*, reputedly the oldest hotel in the world – see also p.593. ❾

Hospedaje Rodríguez, Ruela do Pison 4 ☎ 981 588 408. Pleasant en-suite rooms in a peaceful street off Patio de Madres, with a well-equipped kitchen for guests' use. ❹

Hostal Seminario Mayor, Praza da Inmaculada 5 ☎ 981 583 008, ℱ 981 572 867. Students' residence open as a hotel from July to September. Rooms are basic for the price, but the setting, in a

stunning former Benedictine monastery, is superb. ❹

Hostal Suso, Rúa do Vilar 65 ☎ 981 586 611. Neat, comfortable *hostal*, with a good bar-restaurant downstairs, located in a lively street, a few doors along from the turismo. ❹

Camping

As Cancelas ☎ 981 580 266. Open all year and within reasonable walking distance of the town (2.5km northeast of the cathedral). Reached via the road to A Coruña, branching off at the Avda. del Camino Francés; the route is also served by regular buses to the airport and the city bus #9.

Las Sirenas ☎ 981 698 722. Reasonable second choice 6km out on the Santa Comba road, with less frequent connecting buses.

The cathedral

All roads to Santiago lead to the **Catedral** (Mon–Sat 11am–1pm & 4–6pm, Sun 10am–1.30pm & 4–7pm), and this, as Jan Morris asserts, "is still, as it was

Santiago. The voyage took just seven days, at once proving the miracle "since", as Richard Ford wrote in 1845, "the Oriental Steam Company can do nothing like it".

At this stage the body was buried, lost and forgotten for the next 750 years. It was rediscovered at Compostela in 813, at a time of great significance for the Spanish Church. Over the preceding century, the Moors had swept across the Iberian peninsula, gaining control over all but the northern mountain kingdom of Asturias, and in their campaigns they had introduced a concept entirely new to the West: *jihad*, or holy war. They also drew great strength from the inspiration of their champion, the Prophet Muhammad, whose death (in 632) was still within popular memory and a bone from whose body was preserved in the Great Mosque of Córdoba. Thus the discovery of the bones of St James, under a buried altar on a site traditionally linked with his name, was singularly opportune. It occurred after a hermit was attracted to a particular spot on a hillside by visions of stars, and the hill was known thereafter as Compostela, from the Latin *campus stellae*, meaning "field of stars". Alfonso II, king of Asturias, came to pay his respects, built a chapel, and the saint was adopted as the champion of Christian Spain against the Infidel.

Within decades the saint had appeared on the battlefield. Ramiro I, Alfonso's successor, swore that he had fought alongside him at the Battle of Clavijo (844), and that the saint had personally slaughtered 60,000 Moors. Over the next six centuries *Santiago Matamoros* (Moor-killer) manifested himself at some forty battles, even assisting in the massacre of American Indians in the New World. It may seem an odd role for the fisherman-evangelist, but presented no problems to the Christian propagandists who portrayed him most frequently as a knight on horseback in the act of dispatching whole clutches of swarthy, bearded Arabs with a single thrust of his long sword. (With consummate irony, when Franco brought his expert Moroccan troops to Compostela to dedicate themselves to the overthrow of the Spanish Republic, all such statues were discreetly hidden under sheets.)

The cult of Santiago was strongest during the age of the First Crusade (1085) and the Reconquest; people wanted to believe, and so it gained a kind of truth. In any case, as Ford acidly observed, "If people can once believe that Santiago ever came to Spain at all, all the rest is plain sailing."

---

for those ancient pilgrims, one of the great moments of travel". Traditionally the first member of a party of pilgrims to catch sight of their goal would cry "Mon Joie!" and become "king" of the group; the hill on the eastern side of Santiago thus became known as "Mountjoy". But you first appreciate the sheer grandeur of the cathedral upon venturing into the vast expanse of the Praza do Obradoiro. Directly ahead stands a fantastic Baroque pyramid of granite, flanked by immense bell towers and everywhere adorned with statues of St James in his familiar pilgrim guise with staff, broad hat, and scallop-shell badge. This is the famous **Obradoiro facade**, built in the mid-eighteenth century by an obscure Santiago-born architect, Fernando Casas y Novoa. No other work of Spanish Baroque can compare with it, nor with what Edwin Mullins (in *The Road to Compostela*) sublimely calls its "hat-in-the-air exuberance".

The main body of the cathedral is Romanesque, rebuilt in the eleventh and twelfth centuries after a devastating raid by the Muslim vizier of Córdoba, al-Mansur, in 977. He failed to find the body of the saint (perhaps not surprisingly), but forced the citizens to carry the bells of the tower to the mosque at Córdoba – a coup which was later dramatically reversed (see p.336). The building's highlight – indeed one of the great triumphs of medieval art – is the **Pórtico de Gloria**, the original west front, which now stands inside the cathedral behind the Obradoiro. Completed in 1188 under the supervision of one Maestro Mateo, this was both the culmination of all Romanesque sculpture and a precursor of the new Gothic realism, each of its host of figures being strikingly relaxed and quietly humanized. They were originally painted, and still bear traces of a seventeenth-century renovation.

The real mastery, however, is in the assured marshalling of the ensemble. Above the side doors are representations of Purgatory and the Last Judgement, while over the main door Christ presides in glory, flanked by his Apostles (Matthew writing on his knees, Luke writing on a bull, John on an eagle and Mark on a lion), and surrounded by the 24 Elders of the Apocalypse playing celestial music. St James sits on the central column, beneath Christ and just above eye level in the classic symbolic position of intercessor, since it was through him that pilgrims could gain assurance of their destiny. To either side are the Prophets of the Old Testament, most famously Daniel, apparently smiling seraphically across at Esther on the other side of the portico. The pilgrims would give thanks at journey's end by praying with the fingers of one hand pressed into the roots of the Tree of Jesse below the saint. So many millions have performed this act of supplication that five deep and shiny holes have been worn into the solid marble. Finally, for wisdom, they would lower their heads to touch the brow of Maestro Mateo, the humble squatting figure on the other side.

The spiritual climax of the pilgrimage, however, was the approach to the **High Altar**. This remains a peculiar experience. You climb steps behind the altar, embrace the Most Sacred Image of Santiago, kiss his bejewelled cape, and are handed, by way of certification, a document in Latin called a *Compostela*. The altar is a riotous creation of eighteenth-century Churrigueresque, but the statue has stood there for seven centuries and the procedure is quite unchanged. (You also get a God's-eye view from up there, during services, of the priest and congregation.) The pilgrims would then make confession and attend a High Mass. You should try to do the latter at least, as a means of understanding Santiago's mystique.

You'll notice an elaborate pulley system in front of the altar. This is for moving the immense incense-burner, "**Botafumeiro**", which, operated by eight priests, is swung in a vast 30-metre ceiling-to-ceiling arc across the transept. It's stunning to watch, but takes place only at certain services and is unusual outside Holy Years. The saint's bones are kept in a **crypt** beneath the altar. They were lost for a second time in 1700, having been hidden before an English invasion, but were rediscovered during building work in 1879. In fact they found three skeletons, which were naturally held to be those of St James and his two disciples. The only problem was identifying which one was the Apostle. This was fortuitously resolved as a church in Tuscany possessed a piece of Santiago's skull which exactly fitted a gap in one of those here. Its identity was confirmed in 1884 by Pope Leo XIII, and John Paul II's visit in 1982 presumably reaffirmed official sanction.

The cathedral is full of collecting boxes; there are two on either side if you wish to kneel before the bones. But to visit the **Treasury**, **Cloisters**, **Buchería** (Archeological Museum), and Mateo's beautiful **Crypt of the Portico**, you need to buy a collective ticket for €3. The late Gothic cloisters in particular are well worth seeing; from the plain, mosque-like courtyard you get a wonderful view of the riotous mixture of the exterior, crawling with pagodas, pawns, domes, obelisks, battlements, scallop shells and cornucopias. Underneath the cloister in the Buchería, is Mateo's original stone choir and the remains of the thirteenth-century cloister. The crypt lies directly under the Portico de Gloria, accessed from beneath the main entry staircase; the museum and cloister entrance is just to the right on the cathedral square.

The rest of the city

The whole city, with its flagstone streets and arcades, is quietly enchanting, but if you want to add direction to your wanderings, perhaps the best plan is first to examine the buildings around the cathedral – the Pazo de Xelmírez and Hostal dos Reis Católicos – and then head for some of the other monasteries and convents. Finally, to get an overall impression of the whole architectural ensemble of Santiago, take a walk along the promenade of the **Paseo da Ferradura** (Paseo de la Herradura), in the spacious public gardens just southwest of the old part, at the end of Rúa do Franco.

Around the cathedral

The **Pazo de Xelmírez** (Palacio Arzobispal Gelmírez; April–Sept Tues–Sun 10am–1.30pm & 4–7.30pm; €1.20) occupies the building to the north side of the cathedral, balancing the cloister, with its entrance just to the left of the main stairs. Archbishop Xelmírez was one of the seminal figures in Santiago's development. He rebuilt the cathedral in the twelfth century, raised the see to an archbishopric, and "discovered" a ninth-century deed which gave annual dues to St James's shrine of one bushel of corn from each acre of Spain reconquered from the Moors – a decree which was repealed only in 1834. In his suitably luxuriant palace are a vaulted twelfth-century kitchen and some fine Romanesque chambers.

As late as the thirteenth century the cathedral was used to accommodate pilgrims (the Botafumeiro incense-burner was used at least in part as a fumigator), but slowly its place was taken by convents founded around the city. Fernando and Isabel, in gratitude for their conquest of Granada, added to these facilities by building a hostel for the poor and sick. This, the elegant Renaissance **Hostal dos Reis Católicos** (Hostal de los Reyes Católicos), fills the northern side of the Praza do Obradoiro in front of the cathedral. It is now a *parador*, which means that unless you're staying here, it's not all that easy to get in to see the four superb patios, the chapel with magnificent Gothic stone carving, and the vaulted crypt-bar (where the bodies of the dead were once stored). However, although do-it-yourself tours are frowned on, you can always stop in for a drink in the bar (which isn't that expensive, unlike the restaurant).

You could easily spend half an afternoon exploring the squares around the cathedral. The largest is the **Praza da Quintana**, where a flight of broad steps joins the back of the cathedral to the high walls of a convent. The "Porta Santa" doorway in this square is only opened during those Holy Years in which the Feast of Santiago falls on a Sunday. To the south is the **Praza das Praterías**, the silversmiths' square, centred on an ornate fountain of four horses with webbed feet, and to the north is the **Praza da Inmaculada**, dominated by the grand Baroque facade of San Martiño Pinario (see below).

Central churches and museums

From Praza da Inmaculada, walk round the side of the Benedictine monastery of **San Martiño Pinario** (Tues–Sun 10.30am–1.30pm & 4.30–6.30pm; €1.20), to reach the entrance to the monastery church on Praza de San Martiño; inside, the vast altarpiece ("a fricassee of gilt gingerbread", according to Ford) depicts its patron riding alongside St James. Nearby is the barn-like **San Francisco** (Tues–Sun 11am–1.30pm & 4–7pm; free), reputedly founded by the saint himself during his pilgrimage to Santiago.

East of San Martiño, the fascinating museum of pilgrimage, the **Museo das Peregrinacións** (Tues–Fri 10am–8pm, Sat 10.30am–1.30pm & 5–8pm, Sun 10.30am–1.30pm; free), lies just off Praza de San Miguel in a sixteenth-centu-

△ Detail of the cathedral, Santiago de Compostela

ry mansion, the Pazo de Don Pedro, also known as the Gothic House. It traces the history of the *camino*, the city and cathedral using excellent models and displays, and there is a comprehensive (and free) guide in English. The real jewel of the museum is the original copy of the twelfth-century *Codex Calixtinus*, a travel guide for pilgrims, which recommended routes and lodgings and pointed out the various dangers of the *camino*, such as the "malicious, swarthy, ugly, depraved, perverse, despicable, disloyal and corrupt" Navarrese.

Just outside to the east of the city, lies the old convent and church of **Santo Domingo**, featuring a magnificent seventeenth-century triple stairway, each spiral leading to different storeys of a single tower. Inside the convent buildings, the fascinating **Museo do Pobo Gallego** (Mon–Fri 10am–1pm & 4–7pm, Sat 4–7pm; Ⓦ www.museodeppobo.es), features *gallego* crafts and traditions. Many aspects of the way of life displayed haven't yet entirely disappeared, though you're today unlikely to see *corozas*, straw overcoats worn until recent decades by mountain shepherds. The convent gardens and orchards on the hillside behind are a wonderful spot for a little solace and a break from sightseeing. **The Centro de Arte Contemporáneo de Galicia** (Tues–Sat 11am–8pm, Sun 11am–2pm; free) opposite, a beautiful addition to Santiago's architectural heritage by the Portugeuse architect Álvaro Siza, houses interesting temporary exhibitions of contemporary art and sculpture.

Santa María do Sar

Outside the main circuit of the city, the one really worthwhile visit is the curious Romanesque church of **Santa María do Sar**. This lies about a kilometre down the Rúa de Sar, which begins at the Patio das Madres on the southern edge of the old city. Due to the subsidence of its foundations Santa María has developed an extraordinary slant of about fifteen degrees, though it remains utterly symmetrical. It also has a wonderfully sculpted cloister, reputedly the work of Maestro Mateo. The church is supposed to stay open all day, but you may have to ask around in the buildings at the back.

Eating, drinking and nightlife

The presence of so many students in Santiago guarantees that the city has a healthy animation to go with its past. In term-time the main **bar** scene is down in the new town, particularly on Rúa Nova de Abaixo. The slightly more expensive old town is lively throughout the year, particularly if you're lucky enough to witness (or foolhardy enough to attempt) the legendary **Paris–Dakar race**: participants must start at *Bar Paris* at the top of end of Rúa do Franco and have one drink at each of the 48 bars on the way down to *Bar Dakar* on Rúa da Raiña, finishing by midnight. It's on these two streets that you'll find the best **tapas bars**, although after midnight people tend to move on to the pubs scattered around the city.

Gallego food is also plentiful and excellent in Santiago, with a plethora of good, solid **places to eat**, particularly on Rúa do Franco, which is lined with seafood restaurants, most with your dinner displayed (live) in the window. If you're shopping for your own food, don't miss the large covered **market** held daily until 3pm in the old halls of the Praza de Abastos, on the southeast edge of the old city. Thursday is the main market day, when it is bustling. There are also a number of tiny delicatessens throughout the town which sell the traditional breast-shaped **cheese**, the rich *queso de tetilla*.

Santiago is also the best place in Galicia to hear the local Celtic **music**, played on *gaitas* (bagpipes), often by student groups known as *tunas* – they'll probably try and sell you a tape in Praza do Obradoiro.

Restaurants

Abellà, Rúa do Franco 30. One of this street's many seafood places, with generous portions and good service – try the *caldo gallego* (€2.10).

Bodegón de Xulio, Rúa do Franco 43. Good seafood place on this long restaurant-lined street.

Cabaliño do Demo, Porta do Camino 7. Reasonable vegetarian restaurant, with a €6 *menú* and an imaginative range of à la carte dishes, many of them with an Asian twist.

Casa Manolo, Rúa Traviesa 27. A superb and justly popular student haunt, with a vast €4.50 *menú* and wide choice. No smoking. Closed Sun pm.

Cuatro Vientas, Rúa Santa Cristina 19. Friendly and very cheap local diner – no main course costs more than €2.55 – offering simple, wholesome meals like cutlet and chips. Try the *tartas*, too.

Don Gaiferos, Rúa Nova. Superb – but expensive – seafood in attractive cellar-like surroundings, with fish dishes from €13.80.

Entre-Rúas, Callejon de Entre Rúas 2. Excellent seafood *raciones* at this small bar-restaurant, shoehorned into a tiny square up an even tinier alley between *rúas* Nova and Vilar.

Toñi Vicente, Avda. Rosalía de Castro 24. Very expensive *nouvelle cuisine* with *gallego* elements; winner of the 1998 prize for Spanish cuisine – main courses start at €17.40.

Bars

O Beiro, Rúa da Raíña 3. Pleasant *bodega* stocking a range of Spanish wines vast enough to suit even the most exacting vinophile.

Casa das Crechas, Via Sacra 3. Well-known folk bar, often with live *gallego*, Celtic or international folk music. *The* place to meet fellow bagpipe enthusiasts.

Fuco Lois, Rúa Gelmirez 25. Popular bar with eclectic live music, particularly midweek.

O Galo d'Ouro, Rúa Conga 14. Cosy cellar bar, and proud home of Santiago's only Wurlitzer.

O Gato Negro, Rúa da Raíña. Unprepossessing but unmissable old *tasca* that seems to be permanently packed solid with vociferous locals.

Klausura, Rúa San Pelayo 20. One of a cluster of brash, unatmospheric but strangely popular summer-night pubs on a tiny square.

Listings

Airlines Labacolla airport is served by a number of airlines, including: Iberia ☎981 597 550; Air Europa ☎981 594 950; and Spanair ☎902 567 022.

Bookshops Variable secondhand selection, including foreign-language titles and book-exchange, from Librería Vetusta, Rúa Nova 31. Huge choice of new titles at Librería Follas Novas, Rúa Montero Ríos 37, in the new town.

Bus information ☎981 587 700.

Car rental Operators include: Autos Brea, Rúa Gómez Ulla 8 ☎981 562 670; Avis, Rúa República de El Salvador 10 ☎981 573 718; Autotur-Budget, Rúa Xeneral Pardiñas 3 ☎981 586 493; and Atesa, Parador dos Reis Católicos ☎981 581 904.

Internet cafés Ciber...¿Qué?, Praza Cruceiro de San Pedro, halfway towards the bus station; *Ciber Dreams*, Rúa Diego de Muros 5, just south of Praza Roxa in the new town.

Laundry Lavandería la Económica is a self-service launderette at Rúa Ramón Cabanillas 1 (off Praza Roxa, a few blocks west of Praza de Galicia).

Post office The main office is on the corner of Travesía de Fonseca and Rúa do Franco.

Trains RENFE information ☎981 520 202 (long-distance reservations ☎981 153 338); information and booking also available from many of the travel agents in town.

The Costa da Morte

The wild, indented coastline to the west of A Coruña and Santiago is known as the **Costa da Morte** or Coast of Death; hundreds of shipwrecks litter the cliffs and rocks, and Celtic legends, as at the Breton Finisterre, tell of doomed cities drowned beneath the sea. The climate and landscape are harsher than that of the Rías Baixas further south, but beautiful nonetheless, with forests covering the mountain slopes and occasional fishing villages huddled up against the bleak headlands, battered by mighty Atlantic waves. For the medieval pilgrims this was the **end of the world**, and it remains relatively inaccessible and somewhat forbidding.

Regular Transportes Finisterre buses connect all the places mentioned below, but can be as infrequent as one a day, and often leave very early in the morning (for full details, see Travel Details on p.620 under "Costa da Morte"). Although some stretches have been improved, roads tend to be slow and winding, and there are no trains. If you have your own car, or you're prepared to hitch (it's one of the best places in Spain to try), it's well worth following the length of the coastal road from A Coruña down to **Finisterre** and around to **Muros** and **Noia**. Celtic dolmens and *castros* (forts) abound, but you'll need a good map and plenty of patience to find most of them.

You should also be warned that even where the isolated coves do shelter fine beaches, you will rarely find resort facilities. While the beaches may look splendid, braving the water is recommended only to the hardiest of swimmers, and the weather is significantly wetter and windier here than it is a mere 100km further south.

Malpica to Traba

There are few potential stopping points immediately west of A Coruña; your best bet is to get on a Transportes Finisterre bus and stay on it until you're well past Carballo (a busy inland road junction) after which the bus takes you to a succession of tiny seaside harbours. The first of these is **MALPICA**, crammed onto the neck of a narrow peninsula, with a harbour on one side and a marvellous – though exposed – beach hardly 100m away on the other. Out to sea are three desolate islands which make up a seabird sanctuary; access is possible only if you come to some informal arrangement with a fisherman. If you want a **place to stay**, *Hostal Panchito*, Praza Villar Amigo 6 (℡981 720 307; ❹), has smart rooms with private bath, while *Hostal JB* (℡981 721 906; ❹) is right on the beach. The best seafood **restaurants** here are *San Francisco*, Rúa Eduardo Pondal, where you can choose your dinner from a tankful of live sea creatures, and *O Burato*, overlooking the port off the square.

Unlike its neighbours, **CORME** lacks a developed seafront and so is hardly visited by tourists, which can be a relief in the high season. Across the headland from Malpica, it is set back above a deep, round bay, with three beaches just to the east: two in small rocky inlets and a larger one backed by sand dunes a walkable distance around the bay. The town itself has few bars or restaurants, only a few cramped streets leading to a minute *praza*. Even by the standards of local villages whose social structures are still clan-based, Corme is fiercely insular. In the 1940s and 1950s, it was the stamping-ground of *gallego* guerrillas, who swooped down from the hills to beat up the Civil Guard. In August 1993, 650 kilos of hashish appeared in the nets of a local fishing boat – to the amazement of no one. **Corme Aldea**, an agricultural settlement on the hill above the port, has perhaps more charm than its sea-based sister, but back in Corme the view across the harbour from the back of *O Biscoiteiro* bar, on Avenida Remedios, is lovely, and the food's good, too. There are **beds** available at *O'Cabazo*, Rúa Arnela 23 (℡981 738 077; ❸), if you want to stay. For **dinner**, try the *Café-bar Mendez* on the main road.

Midway between Malpica and Corme, Spanish people set up tents around small fires on the sheltered **Praia de Niñóns**. Follow the signposts from Corme and turn left at the granite cross – then follow the road between fields of maize to the sea. There's a *fuente* (fountain) beneath the granite church that overlooks the beach, and a solitary bar that closes at night; otherwise, you'll need to bring your own supplies. Another great, though illegal, campsite is at **Praia de Balarés**, below Corme and approaching Ponteceso – a lovely sheltered inlet with a couple of high-season bars, and relatively safe swimming.

An ancient bridge crosses the River Anllóns at **PONTECESO**, just beyond the stone mansion that was the home of the *gallego* poet, Eduardo Pondal (1835–1917) – you'll see roads named after him all over Galicia. A long sweep of fine, clean sand is backed by café-lined streets at **LAXE** (pronounced *lashay*), which offers the area's safest swimming, thanks to a formidable sea wall which also protects a small harbour. *Bar Mirador*, off the square, is owned by the descendant of a family of photographers who began work here in the 1870s – there's a pictorial history of the area up on the bar walls. The only **places to stay** here are the pleasant *Hostal Beiramar*, Rúa Rosalía de Castro 30 (☎ & ⓕ981 728 109; ❺), and the friendly *Hospedaje Pescador*, Rúa del Río (☎981 728 195; ❹), just off the plaza. Basic rooms are available at the *Restaurante Sardiñeira*, Rúa Rosalía de Castro 51 (☎981 728 029; ❷). Close by are two beaches, the deserted **Praia de Soesto**, which, though exposed, more than rivals the town beach, and a perfect cove, the **Praia de Arnado**. Nearby **TRABA** has its own massively long beach, the **Praia de Traba**, remote as anything, and backed by sand dunes and the jigsaw mini-fields of what is still basically strip farming, although newly collectivized.

Camariñas to Finisterre

The stretch of coast from Camariñas to Finisterre is the most exposed and westerly of all, and has long been known as the end of the world, or *finis terrae*, since a Roman expedition under Lucius Florus Brutus was brought short by what seemed to them an endless sea. The savagery of the currents and weather are notorious, and even scavenging for shellfish along the rocks can be lethal. This is prime territory for hunting *percebes* (barnacles), which have to be scooped up from the very waterline, and collectors have been known to be swept away by the dreaded "seventh wave", which can appear out of nowhere from a calm sea. *Percebes* are one of Galicia's most popular delicacies – you'll see them on sale in the markets at vastly inflated prices.

Camariñas

Picturesque **CAMARIÑAS** is back on the bus route: if you're planning a night's stay it has a definite edge over Finisterre. Curled around an attractive harbour containing a fishing fleet and the yachts of well-heeled visitors, Camariñas's buildings have white-painted, glassed-in balconies while the town sports a tradition in lacemaking – you'll see old women, with lacemaking pillows and extensive experience in markets, strategically placed to corner tourists.

For **accommodation**, *La Marina* (☎981 736 030; ⓕ981 736 030; ❸), Rúa Miguel Freijo 3, at the beginning of the harbour wall, has clean rooms, great views and a good restaurant. There's also *Hostal Plaza* in the old market square (☎981 736 103; ❸) and, about 1km out of town on Area de Vilá (by the sandy beach), *Triñanes II* (☎981 736 108; ❺).

You can trek out from Camariñas to **Cabo Vilán**, five kilometres away, where a lighthouse rising out of a huge mansion guards a rocky shore; climb the adjacent rocks for a stunning sea view. Winds whip viciously around the cape, which is why it was chosen for the site of the towering experimental wind-farm park next door to the lighthouse. Huge, sci-fi propellers spin in the wind – dramatic and, in the evening when lit by the searchlight beam of the lighthouse, rather eerie.

Muxía

On the tip of a rocky promontory across the *ría* from Camariñas, the small port of **MUXÍA** is nothing special, but from the Romanesque church on the hill above, there's a fabulous view to either side of the headland and a footpath down to the eighteenth-century **Santuario de la Virgen de la Barca**, once the second most important site of Galicia's pre-Christian animist cult after San Andrés de Teixido (see p.577). The cult was centred around the strangely shaped granite rocks at the furthest point of the headland, some of which are precariously balanced and said to make wonderful sounds when struck correctly; others are supposed to have healing power. In later times, the rocks were reinterpreted as being the remains of the stone ship which brought the Virgin to the aid of Santiago, an obvious echo of the saint's own landing at Padrón.

The best **place to stay** is the delightful *Casa Isolina* (℡981 742 367; ❸), a beautiful old house one block back from the seafront, with a vine-terraced garden behind. For great **seafood**, visit the tiny tumbledown *Casa Marujita*, up left from the far end of the seafront road.

On to Finisterre

The inland road (C552) from Carballo to Finisterre is surprisingly good, a result of the unprecedented burst of road-building over the past two decades that is changing Galicia forever. **VIMIANZO** has spent years restoring its picture-postcard thirteenth-century castle (Mon–Sat: summer 10.30am–2pm & 4–8.30pm; winter 9am–1pm & 3–6pm), which now makes a wonderful setting for a new cultural centre with paintings, photographs and costumes.

Heading west, 2km past the industrialized port of Cée, **CORCUBIÓN**, 14km northeast of Finisterre, retains some elegance, though ribbon-strip development has now joined it with its uglier neighbour. For a cheap room, try the small *La Sirena*, Rúa Antonio Porrua 15 (℡981 745 036; ❷), above the bar of the same name just off the square or, if you're after luxury, *El Hórreo* on the seafront (℡981 745 500, ℻981 745 563; ❼). Halfway between Corcubión and Finisterre, a fine white-sand beach nestles in a small cove at **ESTORDE**, 1km short of the larger village of **Sardiñeiro**. Overlooking the beach is a pleasant **hostal**, the *Praia de Estorde* (℡981 745 585; ❻), and just across the road, a small wooded **campsite**, *Ruta de Finisterre* (℡981 746 302; June–Sept).

Finisterre

The town of **FINISTERRE** (Fisterra) still feels as if it's ready to drop off the end of the world, but other than for its symbolic significance, there's no great reason to stay. It's no more than a grey clump of houses wedged into the rocks on the side of a headland away from the open ocean, but it does have a number of inexpensive **hostales**, the cheapest of which is the *Casa Velay* (℡981 740 127; ❷), overlooking the tiny bay just beyond the long harbour wall. *Hospedaje Lopez* (℡981 740 449; ❸) on the north side of the harbour has some rooms with balconies and views; the *Rivas*, Carreterra de Faro (℡981 740 027; ❸), is excellent value; and the *Cabo Finisterre*, Rúa Santa Catalina 1 (℡981 740 000, ℻981 740 054; ❸), is good too. For **food**, bypass the fancier restaurants with giant lobster tanks and head for the south side of the harbour where you'll find a cluster of places with *sardiñadas* (open-air sardine grills) and fresh *mariscos*.

The actual tip of the **headland** is a four-kilometre walk beyond, along a heathered mountainside, then through a newly planted pine forest. On the way out of town, stop at **Santa María das Areas**, a small, but atmospheric church with Romanesque and Gothic elements and a beautiful carved altar, which like the strange weathered tombs to the left of the main door, is considerably older than the rest of the building. At the cape, a lighthouse perches high above the waves and when, as so often, the whole place is shrouded in thick mist and the mournful foghorn wails across the sea, it's an eerie spot. When the sun shines, you're better steering clear of the ice-cream kiosks and shell-necklace sellers, and turning right up the zigzag road that climbs to the **Vista Monte do Facho**, high above the lighthouse, for stupendous views.

Ezaro, O Pindo and Carnota

Around **EZARO**, where the Río Xallas meets the sea, the scenery is marvellous. The rocks of the sheer escarpments above the road are so rich in minerals that they are multicoloured, and glisten beneath innumerable tiny waterfalls. Upstream there are warm natural lagoons and more cascades. In Ezaro itself, the *hostal* above the *Bar Stop* (℡981 7125 777; ❸) has inexpensive en-suite **rooms**, or you could continue another couple of kilometres to the little port of **O PINDO**. Beneath a stony but thickly wooded hill dotted with old houses, there's a small beach here and two **places to stay**, the *Hospedaje La Morada* (℡981 764 870; ❹) and *La Revolta* (℡981 764 927; ❹), with a recommended *marisquería*.

Towards **CARNOTA** the series of short beaches finally join together into a long unbroken line of dunes, swept by the Atlantic winds. The village of Carnota is 1km from the shore, but its palm trees and old church are still thoroughly caked in salt. Set in fields just outside town, *Casa Fandiño*, Rúa Calvo Sotelo 23 (℡981 857 020; ❷), is an excellent choice, with spotless, quiet rooms, while *Hostal Miramar*, Praza de Galicia (℡981 857 016; ❺), is nice but a little expensive.

Muros and Noia

Some of the best traditional *gallego* architecture outside Pontevedra can be found in the old town of **MUROS**, enhanced by a marvellous natural setting at the widest point of the Ría de Muros just before it meets the sea. The town rises in tiers of narrow streets from the curve of the seafront to the Romanesque Iglesia de San Pedro; almost everywhere you look are squat granite columns and arches, flights of wide steps, and benches and stone porches built into the house fronts. There's also a nice – though small – **beach** on the edge of town next to the road to Finisterre.

Any of the half-dozen **hostales** along the seafront Avenida Calvo Sotelo (later called Avenida de la Marina) would make for a pleasant stay, although you'll have to book ahead to get a sea-facing room: *Hostal Ría de Muros* (℡981 826 056; ❹), at Avda. de Calvo Sotelo 53, has spacious double rooms with balconies and views, while *A Muradana* (℡981 826 885; ❺), at Avda. de la Marina 107, is also recommended. There's a **campsite**, *A Bouga* (℡981 826 025; open all year), beside the beach 3km out at Louro. There's no shortage of **places to eat**. *Pulpería Pachanga*, at Avda. Calvo Sotelo 29, has a stone-vaulted interior, fresh seafood and grilled meats, while the *Dársena*, just down the road at no. 11, serves huge, cheap pizzas. One block back from the seafront immediately behind the *Hostal Ría de Muros*, the Praza da Pescadería has a couple of good café-restaurants under the arches. Castromil **bus** services stop by the *Ría de Muros*; Transportes Finisterre buses terminate 100m back down the seafront near the *A Muradana*.

The larger town of **NOIA** (Noya), near the head of the first of the Rías Baixas, is, according to a legend fanciful even by *gallego* standards, named after Noah, whose Ark is supposed to have struck land nearby. Scarcely less absurd is Noia's claim to be a "Little Florence", principally on the strength of a couple of nice churches and an arcaded street. If you do want **to stay**, the *Hostal Sol y Mar*, a dreary concrete box down by the small bridge on Avenida de San Lázaro (☎981 820 900; ❸), has lovely views over the river. Smarter and pricier – with some rooms en suite – is *Ceboleiro I*, Rúa Galicia 15 (☎ & ☎981 824 497; ❸–❺), opposite the grand *ayuntamiento*.

The southern side of the Ría da Noia, which is sometimes called the "Cockle Coast", is dauntingly exposed, although in good weather the dunes serve as excellent beaches. At **BAROÑA** (Basonas), a rocky outcrop juts from the sand into the sea, and built on top of it you can still see the ruins of an impregnable pre-Roman settlement, with round stone huts enclosed behind a fortified wall. From here you can follow the increasingly bleak coastal road around into the Ría de Arousa, or take a short cut through the deep lush gorges along the AC301 to Padrón.

The Rías Baixas and the Minho

In the three lowest of the **Rías Baixas** (Rías Bajas) – the *rías* of **Arousa**, **Pontevedra** and **Vigo** – Galicia is expanding its tourist industry at an enormous rate. The summer sun is fairly dependable and the climate mild, avoiding the worst of the Atlantic storms, which tend just to brush the northwest corner. Each of these inlets is sheltered by islands and sandbanks offshore. They are deep and calm beneath mountains of dark pines, busy with bright fishing boats and mussel rafts, and fringed with little towns of whitewashed houses and safe bathing beaches. Most visitors are Spanish or Portuguese and although there is none of the overexploitation of the Mediterranean resorts, the coastline is becoming increasingly built up along the new roads, particularly around Vigo and Vilagarcía.

To the south, the slow, wide, mist-filled Río Minho marks the border with Portugal, and can be followed inland in search of unspoiled towns and hilltop monasteries. The chief pleasures of the region however, are to be found by the sea, and the two most obvious places to base yourself are **Pontevedra** and **Vigo**, each dominating its own magnificent and spacious *ría*.

The region is also famous for its **wines**, although they are less well known outside Spain than the ubiquitous Rioja. The areas along the Minho and between Vilagarcía and Sanxenxo are particularly heavily cultivated, most famously with the pale Albariño grape which produces wonderful, flowery wine.

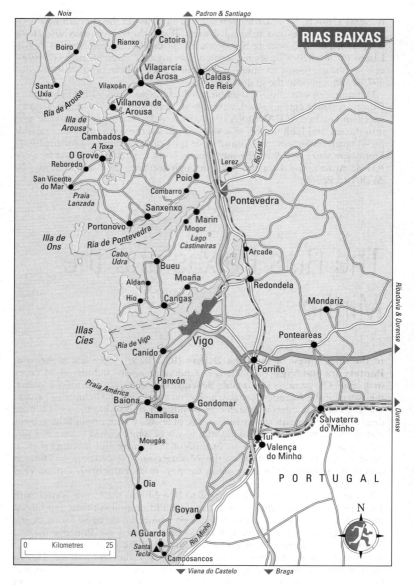

Ría de Arousa

Following the road and rail route south from Santiago, it will take you a while to realize that things are changing. **Padrón** and Catoira are not especially appealing, and in fact the train swings inland again at Vilagarcía without reaching the main resorts of this first *ría*, **Cambados** and **O Grove**. The northern shore is pretty inaccessible, and is still not sufficiently far south for travellers in search of beaches to feel confident of favourable weather.

Padrón and the north shore

According to legend, the corpse of St James arrived in Galicia by sailing up the Ría de Arousa as far as **PADRÓN**, where his miraculous voyage ended. The modern town along the highway has surprisingly little to show for the years of pilgrimage, except an imposing seventeenth-century church of Santiago in which, if you can find the boy in charge of the key, you can see the *padrón* (mooring post) to which the vessel was tied. Padrón is no longer on the sea – the silt of the Río Ulla has stranded it a dozen kilometres inland.

The poet **Rosalía de Castro** (1837–1885), still revered as one of the great champions of the *gallego* language, lived in Padrón, and a "*Circuit de Rosalía*" has been organized to take in the main sites of her life. Chief of these is her former house, which is now a **museum** (summer Tues–Sat 10am–2pm & 4–8pm, Sun 10am–1.30pm; winter Tues–Sat 10am–1.30pm & 4–7pm, Sun 10am–1.30pm; €1.20), furnished in period style. Rosalía's public image and cultural significance have made her a sort of *gallego* poet laureate, though unless you're already acquainted with her life and work the random jumble of texts, photographs and bric-a-brac on display here won't make a great deal of sense. The house is a ten-minute walk from the centre of Padrón, opposite the RENFE station – cross the railway line and turn left.

Padrón is also renowned in Galicia for its **peppers**, available in the summer months only. What you get in a tapas bar under the name of *pimientos de Padrón* might look like whole green peppers fried in a bit too much oil and sprinkled with sea salt, but perhaps through the intercession of Santiago they acquire a transcendent sweet flavour – though a few in each serving are memorably hot.

If you want **to stay** (though there's no very compelling reason to do so), the best-value place is the *Hostal Jardín*, Rúa Salgado Araújo 3 (☎981 810 950; ⑤), a beautiful eighteenth-century house overlooking a park. There's a small **turismo** kiosk (daily: June–Sept 10am–1.30pm & 4–8pm; Oct–May Mon–Fri 10am–1.30pm & 4–8pm; ☎627 210 777) on the main road close by, and a top-quality octopus **restaurant**, the *Pulpería Rial* on Plazuela de Traviesa.

The north side of the *ría* is quite underpopulated, with only Rianxo (Rianjo), Boiro and **RIBEIRA** large enough to support *hostales*. Ribeira (also known as Santa Eugenia, or Santa Uxía in *gallego*) is a thriving fishing port, which has good restaurants but also a lot of modern apartment buildings. On either side of the town there are long beaches; the small *Coroso* **campsite** (☎981 838 002; June–Sept) on the Praia de Coroso, next to the C550 road, provides an escape from staying centrally.

Vilagarcía to O Grove

The slow, cluttered road around the Ría de Arousa offers picture-postcard views across the water. Sprawling **VILAGARCÍA**, a major port and the drug-smuggling capital of Galicia, isn't short of a buck, and the main Avenida da Mariña – Vilagarcía's "waterfront", though it's actually separated from the sea by an ugly swathe of docks – is sprinkled with chic cafés. There's a seasonal **turismo** (June–Oct Mon–Fri 10am–2pm & 5–9pm, Sat & Sun 11am–2pm & 5–8pm; ☎600 370 275) at the south end of Avenida da Mariña, over the road from the fish market, and a couple of pleasant but pricey **hostales** on the other side of the market; better value is the attractive *Hostal Martis*, Praza Martín Gómez Abal 2 (☎986 505 410, ⓕ986 504 310; ③), in a small square just inland

> ## Smugglers
>
> **Smuggling** is a long-established tradition in Galicia. Not all the boats you see sailing into the picturesque fishing harbours are carrying fish; not all the lobster pots sunk offshore are used for holding crustaceans; not all those huts on the mussel rafts are occupied by shellfish-growers. All along the coast you'll find beaches known locally as the "Praia de *Winston*", notorious for the late-night arrivals of shipments of foreign cigarettes.
>
> Recently, however, it has become more difficult to laugh off the smugglers as latter-day Robin Hoods. Taking advantage of the infrastructure developed over the years by small-time tobacco smugglers, and of the endlessly corrugated coastline frequented by innumerable small boats, the big boys have moved in. At first, there were stories of large consignments of hashish brought in at night; now heroin abuse has become a major concern. At some point, the Medellín cartel of Colombia began to use Galicia as the European entrance point for large consignments of cocaine. Several major police crackdowns, particularly on the Isla de Arousa where certain segments of the population seemed all of a sudden to have become inexplicably rich, have yet to reverse the trend that has locals worrying that Galicia is heading towards becoming "another Sicily".

from the market. The best places **to eat** are all along the Avenida da Mariña: there's a nice bunch under the plane trees including the *Mesón da Mariña* at no. 58, and the *Café España* at no. 42.

The only real reason to venture into Vilagarcía is to visit the local **beaches**. There's a big and quite reasonable (if you don't mind the views of the dockside cranes) expanse of sand, the **Praia da Concha**, on the north side of the town, and buses leave from next to the fish market for the small beach at **Vilaxoán** (Villajuán). You'd do better, however, to go to the main bus station and head south to the wooded **Isla de Arousa** out in the *ría*. There are lots of pleasant beaches here, but the easiest to get to is the **Praia de Vao**, just to the right of the bridge as you cross over onto the island, where you'll also find a **campsite**, *Salinas* (☎986 527 444; June–Oct). There are a couple of *hostales* in the main village, including *Benalua*, Rúa Méndez Núñez (☎986 551 335; ❹).

On the road towards Vilaxoán, about 1km out of Vilagarcía (on the left), is what is popularly acknowledged to be the best **restaurant** in Galicia, *Chocolate's*. The walls are festooned with letters of praise from such sources as Juan Perón, La Oficina del Presidente, Buenos Aires, and Edward Heath, Westminster, London. The flamboyant owner personally serves clients with two-pound steaks impaled on pitchforks, and the fish is superb – though the prices are around €18–30 per head.

CAMBADOS, further south again, has a remarkable paved stone square, the **Praza de Fefiñanes**, with beautiful buildings on all sides, including a seventeenth-century church and a *bodega* where you can sample the excellent local white wines; otherwise, it's a fairly sleepy town with an unremarkable seafront. The helpful **turismo** (summer daily 10am–2pm & 4.30–8.30pm, Sun 11am–1.30pm & 5–9.30pm; winter daily 10am–2pm & 4.30–7.30pm) is housed in a small booth on the Praza do Concello at the junction of the main roads. If you can't afford to stay at the **parador** – the *Albariño*, on Paseo Cervantes (☎986 542 250, 📠986 542 068; ❽) – try *El Duende*, Rúa Ourense 10 (☎986 543 075, 📠986 542 900; ❹), just off the seafront and Praza do Concello, or the nearby *Pazos Feijoo*, Rúa Curros Enríquez 1 (☎986 542 810; ❹).

O Grove and A Toxa

The coast road curves back on itself to the resort of **O GROVE**, one of the few towns in Galicia whose principal raison d'être is the tourist trade. O Grove is specifically a "family" resort, full of inexpensive, small-scale bars, restaurants and places to stay, and not altogether without charm. There's also a fine aquarium, the **Acquariumgalicia** (daily June–Oct 10am–9pm, Nov–May 10am–7pm; €5.10), a 45-minute walk west across the headland towards the village of Reboredo – it's one of the largest in Spain, with a huge selection of Atlantic marine life. The aquarium also arranges ninety-minute trips on the *ría* in glass-bottomed boats (€9.60), a worthwhile excursion if you're interested in looking at Galicia's sea creatures rather than eating them.

Just across a bridge from O Grove is the pine-covered islet of **A TOXA** (La Toja), much-loved by Galicia's nouveaux riches, who stay in the couple of upmarket hotels and play the casino. Heavily coated with expensive holiday homes and manned by throngs of souvenir sellers, A Toxa is far from unspoilt, although the less developed half of the island, still largely covered in pine woods, is perfectly pleasant. Look out too for the little shell-covered **church**, most of whose cockles are now covered in amorous teenage graffiti. A Toxa actually owes much of its nationwide fame to the soap that's made from the salts of the spa here; Magno, the original brand, is pitch black and available from the shops on the island (and most Spanish supermarkets).

Practicalities

Regular **buses** from Pontevedra (1–2 hourly) and Santiago (8 daily) pull in to O Grove right by the port, where there's a small seasonal **turismo** (June–Nov daily 10am–9pm; ☎986 731 415) in a kiosk. There are dozens of **places to stay** along the waterfront Rúa Teniente Dominguez (facing the bridge leading over to A Toxa) and its continuation, Rúa Castelao, which heads inland through the middle of the town: try *Hostal Isolino* at Rúa Castelao 30 (☎986 730 236, ℗986 730 287; ❹), or *Casa Campaña*, on the same street at no. 60 (☎986 730 919, ℗986 732 277; ❺). There are also a number of **campsites** on the road west across the peninsula between Reboredo and San Vicente do Mar, served by a regular bus from the port at O Grove; these are packed throughout the summer, but there's room for everybody on the local beaches, especially on the vast La Lanzada (see p.608). For **eating**, the waterfront by the port is solid with the inevitable *marisquerías*; for something without tentacles, head for the *Amalfi*, also on the waterfront by the port, which has pizza and pasta from €4.80.

The inland route: Caldas de Reis

The motorway between Santiago and Pontevedra is expensive, though it does circumvent traffic jams around Padrón. If you take the inland road (the N550) you come, halfway between Padrón and Pontevedra, to the thermal spa town of **CALDAS DE REIS**, where there's a Roman fountain, the waters of which guarantee you will be married within a year should you be so foolhardy as to drink them. At the exact point where the road crosses the Río Umia, there's a gorgeous bar-restaurant, *O Muiño*, down under the bridge next to a weir; the barbecues and the octopus are unbeatable.

Ría de Pontevedra

Of all the Rías Baixas, the long narrow **Ría de Pontevedra** is the archetype, closely resembling a Scandinavian fjord with its steep and forested sides.

Pontevedra itself is a lovely old city, now set slightly back from the sea at the point where the Río Lérez begins to widen out into the bay. It's a good base for expeditions along either shore of its *ría* – such expeditions made necessary by the fact that the town itself doesn't have a beach. The **north coast** of the *ría* is the more popular with tourists, Sanxenxo (Sangenjo), the best-known resort with well over fifty hotels, often full of British and German visitors. If you want to avoid the crowds, head for the **south coast**, which stretches out past lovely beaches towards the rugged headland, ideal for camping in privacy.

Pontevedra

PONTEVEDRA is the definitive old *gallego* town, a maze of flagstoned alley-ways and colonnaded squares, with granite crosses and squat stone houses with floral balconies. There are some "sights" to see – the museum is good, and there are several interesting churches – but the real joy of visiting Pontevedra is to spend time in an ancient town so lively and lived-in. It's perfect for a night out, with the traditional local food and drink both at their best. The town is very compact, despite being the administrative capital of a district which includes the much larger city of Vigo. Pontevedra's growth was curtailed by the silting up of its medieval port (from which one of Columbus's ships supposedly sailed; there is even a long-standing claim that Columbus was born a *gallego* in Pontevedra). There are some slightly dismal industrial suburbs, but the old quarter, the *zona monumental*, remains distinct and unchanged, hard against the Río Lérez within the sweeping crescent of the main boulevards.

Arrival and orientation

Both the **bus** and **train** stations are about 1km southeast of the centre, side by side, and connected to the Praza de España in the centre by half-hourly buses. If you're coming in on foot, head out of the bus station and follow Rúa Calvo Sotelo as it bears round to the left; walk to the roundabout then straight over onto Avenida de Vigo and follow this all the way to the Praza da Peregrina on the edge of the old town. The **turismo** is nearby at Rúa Xeneral Guiterrez Mellado 3 (Mon–Fri 9.30am–2pm & 4.30–6.30pm, Sat 10am–12.30pm; ☎986 850 814).

Accommodation

Finding a **place to stay** in Pontevedra should be straightforward. The best-value places are in the winding streets of the *zona monumental*; the widest choice is among budget places, but there are also a couple of good upmarket options here. The new town offers a number of hotels on and around Avenida de Vigo, but these are mostly characterless and overpriced.

Casa Alicia, Avda. de Santa María 5 ☎986 857 079. Good-value, spotless rooms, all en suite, in a pleasant house on the edge of the old quarter. ❸

Fonda Chiquito, Rúa Charino 23 ☎986 862 192. The cheapest in town, but perfectly adequate. ❷

Casa O Fidel Pulpeiro, Rúa San Nicolás 7 ☎986 851 234. Pleasant, well-kept rooms above a friendly bar with great *pulpo*. ❸

Casa Maruja, Rúa Alta ☎986 854 901. Immaculate rooms – some en suite – in this comfortable modern *pensión* opposite *Casa Alicia*. ❸–❹

Parador Casa del Barón, Rúa del Barón 19 ☎986 855 800, ℱ986 852 195, 🖃pontevedra@parador.es. Housed in a historic stone mansion in the heart of the old quarter, this is the best – and most expensive – place to stay in Pontevedra. ❽

Hospedaje Penelas, Rúa Alta 17 ☎986 855 705. Atmospherically located *hospedaje* in the old quarter, with simple, but spotlessly clean, rooms with wafer-thin walls. ❸

Hotel Rúas, Rúa Padre Sarmiento 37 ☎986 846 416, ℱ986 846 411. Handsome old hotel in an excellent location, next to the Museo Provincial. ❻

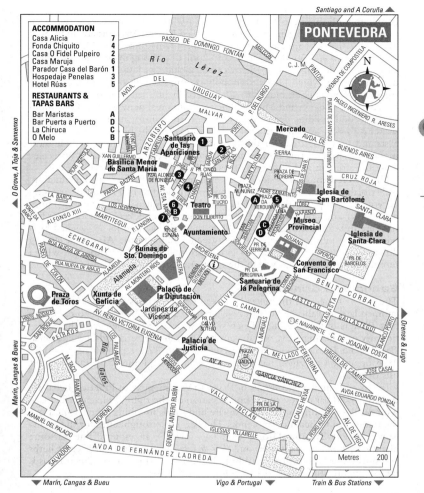

The Town

The boundary between Pontevedra's old and new quarters is marked by the **Praza da Peregrina** – site of a pilgrim chapel, the **Santuario de la Pelegrina**, a tall and eye-catching Baroque structure built in the shape of a scallop shell – and the **Praza da Ferrería** (known simply as the "Ferrería") a paved square lined by arcades on one side and rose trees on the other. To the east is the town's main church, **San Francisco**. Amid the surrounding fountains, gardens, and open-air cafés, are old women playing cards, teenagers courting and all the daily rituals of life in a town small enough for everyone to know everyone else.

A selection of narrow lanes leads north from the Ferrería into the **zona monumental**. Following Rúa Figueroa, you come to the small and shaded **Praza de Leña**, the postcard image of Pontevedra, a typical *gallego* square complete with granite columns and a Calvary. Two of its mansions have been joined to form the elegant and well-conceived **Museo Provincial** (June–Sept Tues–Sat 10am–2.15pm & 5–8.45pm, Sun 11am–2pm; Oct–May Tues–Sat 10am–1.30pm & 4.30–8pm, Sun 11am–2pm; free, though you'll need to show a passport or driving licence). Star exhibits include jet jewellery from Santiago de Compostela, which held a monopoly on the stone throughout the Middle Ages, pre-Roman gold, and a fair – though badly lit – selection of Spanish masters: Ribera, Zubarán and Murillo. The museum's real draw is a top-floor room in the second building devoted to the twentieth-century artist, caricaturist and writer Alfonso Castelao, author of *Sempre en Galizia*, the bible of *gallego* nationalists and now a set text for the region's schools. His drawings, at their most moving when depicting prewar poverty and the horror of the Civil War, celebrate the strength and resilience of the *gallego* people and their culture.

The covered **market** beside the river is an attractive old two-tier building, well worth taking a look at even if you don't intend to buy anything – as long as you can cope with the sight of disembowelled cows hanging from meathooks, and still-hairy muzzles poking out from buckets of blood. The fish stalls are full of glistening goodies, while the walls on all sides are stacked high with muddy piles of nameless edible greenery. Finally, the **Alameda** leading down from Praza de España is a grand promenade down to the sea, with a monument to Columbus where the river empties into the Atlantic.

Eating and drinking

The twisting streets of the *zona* are packed with tiny **bars** and **restaurants** and jammed late into the night with revellers. You'd probably do best to eat in the bars. Platters of fish and jugs of rich white wine are available everywhere, particularly on Rúa Figueroa, which runs between the Ferrería and Praza da Leña; *Bar Puerta a Puerto* at no. 1 and *La Chiruca* at no. 17 are particularly good. *O Melo*, opposite *Casa Alicia*, has a decent *menú* (€6) and one of the city's longest lists of tapas.

Try to end up at *Bar Maristas* in Praza da Vedura, next to Praza da Leña (it's the unmarked bar closest to the police station on the right), a characterful place with outdoor seating on a lovely square and locals imbibing white wine from the traditional Galician ceramic pots. The bar is also sought after for the astonishing liqueur **Tumba Dios** ("God falls down"), an esoteric but fearsome blend of *aguardiente* (firewater) and *licor de café*, laced with sundry secret herbs and spices. For **late-night drinking**, the area around Praza das Cinco Rúas is full of raucous student disco-bars – follow the noise.

The north shore of the Ría

To the north, 5km from Pontevedra, is the seventeenth-century Benedictine **Monasterio de Poyo**, with a *hospedería* (☎986 770 000) and further along the coast the village of **COMBARRO**, justly famed for its large collection of waterfront *hórreos*, resembling miniature chapels with their granite crosses. Beyond is the resort of **SANXENXO** (Sangenjo), the area's main venue for a serious summer night out. From 10pm onwards, the seafront bars and cafés are packed with revellers, the clubs playing Eurodance music to a lively crowd. You can judge the scale of things from the fact that there are over sixty hotels between here and the similar resort of **PORTONOVO**, but prices are high; you'd be lucky to find a room under €30.

A few kilometres beyond begins the vast **beach** of **La Lanzada**, a favourite with strong swimmers and windsurfers. In the summer there are temporary enclaves of cafés and restaurants, and **campsites** such as the recommended

Muiñeira (☎986 738 404), or *O Espiño* (☎986 738 048); during the rest of the year it's left to the wild ocean waves.

The south shore and the Península do Morrazo

The southern side of the Ría de Pontevedra is less developed and has fewer visitors, although once past Marín (see below) it's quite superb. The first stretch, however, is off-putting in the extreme. Just outside (and upwind from) Pontevedra sits a monstrous paper factory, **La Cellulosa**, where a titanic yellow metal spider spouts mountains of sawdust and emits a staggering stench; on a bad day you can smell it fifty kilometres away. Buses run roughly every twenty minutes from Pontevedra (departing from Praza de Galicia, not the main bus station), travelling right around the headland to Marín.

Marín

Nearby **MARÍN** is not on first impression all that appealing. It's a very busy port, with the seafront cut off from the town by forbidding walls for most of its length, and is populated largely by bored cadets from the local naval academy. Even the wooded island in the middle of the *ría* belongs to the navy, and is inaccessible.

However, Marín did boast the best **churrasquería** in Spain, the *Cantaclaro*, which was very cheap and almost impossible to find, housed in what looked like a deserted blue shed very near the harbour, about a mile back towards Pontevedra from the middle of town. The prawns and charcoal-grilled meat of all kinds were delicious. Unfortunately, as this edition went to press news reached us that the place had burnt down, but that there were plans to reopen: if you're in the area, it's definitely worth checking out.

Isla de Ons

Marín is also the most convenient starting point for an excursion to the beautiful **Isla de Ons**. Four ferries a day run from Marín to the island in high season (mid-July to mid-Sept; €9 return); there are also services from Sanxenxo via Portnovo during the same period (8 daily; same price) and from Bueu (June–Sept 2–6 daily; same price). Wilder and more windswept than the nearby Illas Cíes (see p.614), the island is still home to a community of local fishermen and some interesting birdlife, and has good walking tracks with terrific views of coast and sea – you can hike round the entire island in about three hours. There are some nice **beaches** too – in particular Praia Melide, a gorgeous stretch of white sand a couple of kilometres north of the jetty – and a handful of bars and restaurants. If you want to stay, you can **camp** for free in the specified "camping zone" (*zona de acampada*).

Mogor, Bueu and beyond

Once past Marín, the scenery rapidly improves, the bay broadening into a whole series of breathtaking sandy coves. A narrow side road drops away from the main coast road immediately beyond the naval academy outside Marín, leading to three beaches. The second of these, the **Praia de Mogor** (on the bus route from Pontevedra), is perfect, with fields of green corn as the backdrop to a crescent of fine, clean sand, one end of which is shielded by a thick headland of dark green pines. There are a couple of bars overgrown with vines, and the villagers' rowing boats are pulled up in the shade of the trees.

BUEU (pronounced *bwayo*) is a quiet market town and port about 12km beyond Marín, and offers pleasant strips of **beach** stretching away from its rambling waterfront; the quieter spots are round the headland to the west. **Accommodation** here is mostly expensive; you'll get little for less than €36 in the summer, although the unmarked *Hostal Fazanes*, Rúa Eduardo Vincenti 29 (☎986 320 046; ❸) has cheap, basic rooms in the town centre. Other options include the *Incamar*, Rúa Montero Ríos 147 (☎986 320 067, ⓕ986 320 784; ❺), or to the east, *A Centoleira*, Praia de Beluso (☎986 320 896; ❹).

A smaller road turns away from the sea at Bueu, towards Cangas, and is served by half-hourly buses in summer, but if you make your way along the coast, towards the village of **ALDÁN** and the cape of **Hio**, you'll find an unspoiled expanse of pine trees and empty beaches – an ideal place to go **camping** if you stock up in advance. Particularly worth following is the unpaved road to the huge boulders at **Cabo Udra**, where wild horses roam the hillsides and the waves come crashing down in deserted coves. For those without transport, it may be easier to access the more southerly areas via Cangas (see opposite).

Ría de Vigo

Following the main road south from Bueu, you cross the steep ridge of the Morrazo peninsula to astonishing views on the far side over the **Ría de Vigo**, one of the most sublime natural harbours in the world. This region was once a hotbed of witchcraft, although *gallegos* are careful to distinguish between *brujas* (malevolent witches) and *meigas* (wise women herbalists with healing powers). Tradition tells of a local woman who was accused of trafficking with the Devil by the Inquisition in the seventeenth century; she proved her claim to be a *meiga*, and was sentenced to stand outside Cangas church in her oldest clothes every Sunday for six months. Presumably she fell foul of the Holy Inquisition in one of its more lenient moods. Even today, you'll find charms against witches (in the shape of a clasped hand) on sale everywhere in Galicia, often next to crucifixes.

The *ría's* narrowest point is spanned by a vast suspension bridge which carries the Vigo–Pontevedra highway; you'll see its twin towers from all around the bay. On the inland side is what amounts to a saltwater lake, the inlet of **San Martín**. The road and railway from Pontevedra run beside it to **Redondela**, separated from the sea by just a thin strip of green fields, and pass close to the tiny San Martín islands, once a leper colony and used during the Civil War as an internment centre for Republicans. The calm waters here are deceptive; somewhere under them lies a fleet of galleons lost in 1702. Seeking shelter from a storm, the ships foundered on hidden sandbanks and went down with the largest single shipment of silver ever sent from the New World.

The city of **Vigo** looks very appealing, spread along the waterfront, but apart from its possibilities for sleeping and eating, it's not a particularly interesting place to stay. If Vigo is your point of arrival in this region, one obvious alternative is to head down to the waterfront and get a **ferry** across to the little resort of **Cangas**; another would be to take a bus (the train doesn't follow the coast any further) out to **Baiona**, at the edge of the ocean. Wherever you end up staying, be sure not to miss the boat trip out to the wonderful **Illas Cíes**.

Cangas and Moaña

CANGAS, where the road south from Bueu descends, is today a burgeoning resort, at its most lively during the Friday **market**, when the seafront gardens are filled with stalls. It's worth visiting just for the superb, twenty-minute **ferry** trip across the *ría* from Vigo (every 30min 6.30am–10pm, hourly at weekends; €1.35), and there's an excellent beach too, the **Praia de Rodeira**, a beautiful 500-metre stretch of sand with majestic views across the water – alight from the ferry, turn left and walk along the seafront for ten minutes to reach it.

The **bus** station is right next to where ferries dock, and there's a **turismo** booth here too (daily 10am–2pm & 5–8pm, Sat & Sun closes 9pm). Ferry services to the Illas Cíes (July to mid-Sept 4–6 daily) also depart from here when weather permits. The cheapest **rooms** in town are at *Hostal Belén*, tucked away in a hard-to-find backstreet on Rúa Antonio Nores (☎986 300 015; ❹), and the *Playa*, Avda. Ourense 78 (☎986 303 674; ☏986 301 363; ❺), at the beginning of the Praia de Rodeira; both fill up quickly in summer, though prices fall sharply outside high season.

The main cluster of **bars and restaurants** is around the port. The *Bar Celta*, looking out over the bay at Rúa Alfredo Saralegui 28, up some steps slightly to the left of the jetty as you face the town, is an excellent old-fashioned tapas bar whose *comedor* serves bargain budget meals; a few doors along at no. 11 is *O Balcón do Porto*, a wonderful little restaurant with excellent home cooking and great views out to sea. En route to the Praia de Rodeira, *Taberna O Arco*, on Praza do Arco, and *O Porrón* at Paseo de Castelao 15 (just beyond the fish market), are two very good bars specializing in seafood.

Hourly boats from Vigo (6.30am–9.30pm; €1.20) also leave for **MOAÑA**, 5km along the coast from Cangas, and similar to it in feel. Again, much of the appeal of a trip here is the ferry ride, which takes you right alongside the local *mejilloneiras* – ramshackle rafts, perched on the river like water-spiders and sometimes topped by little wooden huts, which are used for cultivating mussels. Moaña itself boasts a fine, long beach, but relatively few facilities for visitors. Places to stay include *Hostal Prado Viejo*, Rúa Ramón Cabanillas 16 (☎986 311 634; ❹), with en-suite rooms and private parking, and *Hostal Antonio*, Rúa Méndez Núñez 2 (☎986 313 684; ❹), which has rooms both with and without bath.

West of Cangas, the beaches and hills are stunning and all but deserted. In summer, hourly buses take you from Cangas to **Nerga**, from where it's a short walk to the huge sandy strip extending from the Praia de Nerga to the nudist Praia de Barra. There is also a 2pm bus (returning at 7.30pm) to **Donon**, from where it's a two-kilometre walk to the Praia de Melide on the tip of the peninsula, an isolated cove backed by woods and a lighthouse, with superb walks along the cape.

Vigo

VIGO is a large and superbly situated city, dominating the broad expanse of its *ría*. Seen from a ship entering the harbour, it is magnificent, though once ashore you may find the views back out to sea to be its most attractive feature. It is so well sheltered from the Atlantic that the wharves and quays which make it Spain's chief fishing port stretch along the shore for nearly 5km.

Arrival and information

Vigo's **turismo** is located at the port (July & Aug daily 9.30am–2pm & 4.30–6.30pm; Sept–June Mon–Fri 9.30am–2pm & 4.30–6.30pm, Sat 10am–noon; ☎986 430 577, ☯www.vigotour.net), and offers a free map with accommodation marked on it. The **RENFE station**, on the edge of the city centre, has direct services to Santiago, Barcelona and Madrid, and down into Portugal. The **bus station** is further out, around 1.5km from the centre; from

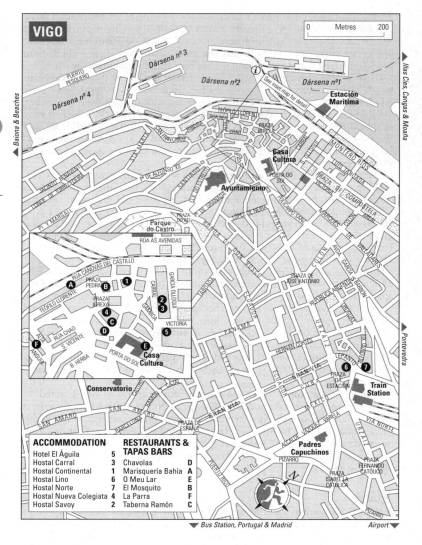

VIGO

| 0 | Metres | 200 |

Baiona & Beaches ◄

▲ Illas Cíes, Cangas & Moaña

► Pontevedra

Dársena nº 3

Dársena nº 2

Dársena nº 1

Dársena nº 4

PUERTO PESQUERO

Estación Marítima

Casa Cultura

Ayuntamiento

Parque do Castro

RÚA AS AVENIDAS

PRAZA DE JOSÉ ANTONIO

Train Station

Conservatorio

Casa Cultura

Padres Capuchinos

N

▼ Bus Station, Portugal & Madrid

Airport ▼

ACCOMMODATION		RESTAURANTS & TAPAS BARS	
Hotel El Águila	5		
Hostal Carral	3	Chavolas	D
Hostal Continental	1	Marisquería Bahía	A
Hostal Lino	6	O Meu Lar	E
Hostal Norte	7	El Mosquito	B
Hostal Nueva Colegiata	4	La Parra	F
Hostal Savoy	2	Taberna Ramón	C

the stop just outside the station entrance, bus #12 runs half-hourly and #7 hourly to the central Porta do Sol; bus #23 runs every ninety minutes to Rúa Areal, just east of the port.

Accommodation

Places to stay tend to be reasonably priced and are concentrated in two main areas: up by the train station, and down by the port. The latter is more atmospheric and is also where you'll find the best restaurants and bars.

Hotel El Águila, Rúa Victoria 6 ☎986 431 398, ℻986 437 007. Friendly, old-fashioned hotel in the old quarter, with lots of charm. All rooms are en suite, though some are a bit small. ❹

Hostal Carral, Rúa Carral 18 ☎986 224 927. Reasonable budget rooms (if the owner isn't in, ask in the amusement arcade a couple of doors down, which he also runs). ❸

Hostal Continental, Baixada a Fonte 3 ☎983 220 764, ℻986 223 887. Good en-suite rooms in a lovely location just back from the waterfront. ❺

Hostal Lino, Rúa Lepanto 26 ☎986 447 004, ℻986 449 663. Close to the train station, with a range of rooms (some smart and modern; some older and cheaper), all en suite and with TV; breakfast included. ❺–❻

Hostal Norte, Rúa Alfonso XIII 29 ☎986 223 805, ℻986 437 007. Conveniently located next to the train station; most rooms have bath, TV and phone, and there are some cheaper ones without. ❹

Hostal Nueva Colegiata, Praza da Igrexa 3 ☎986 220 952. Well-kept and good-value *hostal* on a lovely central square; all rooms en suite. ❸

Hostal Savoy 2, Rúa Carral 20 ☎986 432 541. Probably Vigo's best budget option, with simple but clean and comfortable rooms in a rather grand old hotel building. ❸

The City

Today Vigo's passenger port may be declining, but it has kept the prime spot in the middle of this stretch of shore. This was where Laurie Lee disembarked "with the whole of Spain to walk through", a journey marvellously recorded in *As I Walked Out One Midsummer Morning*. Here, too, generations of *gallego* emigrants have embarked for and returned from the Americas, and Caribbean immigrants have had their first glimpse of Europe. Although, these days, the only tourists who arrive at the **Estación Marítima de Ría** are those who have come on the ferry from Cangas and Moaña, the steep, winding streets of the old city remain crammed with tiny shops and bars catering for the still-plentiful sailors.

The cobbled streets around the **Rúa Real** (once the main street, and what Todman called "the best drinking street in Christendom", though things are a lot quieter now) remain a focal point for visitors. Along the seafront early in the morning, kiosks revive fishermen with strong coffee, while there and in the nearby **market** their catch is sold: from early morning to mid-afternoon women stand at granite tables rooted in **Rúa da Pescadería**, with plates of fresh oysters set out for passers-by. On **Rúa Carral** shops sell kitsch marine souvenirs, and in the evening the myriad bars on all the tiny streets come alive.

For the most part, the **beaches** adjacent to Vigo are crowded and not nearly as appealing as those further along, or across the *ría* – and certainly not a patch on the Illas Cíes (see below). Heading south, however, the beaches of **Samil** and **Vao** are better, and very popular for late Saturday night revels; take bus #L15 or #L27 from Rúa Colón and return on the #LN. A little further on, the beach at **Canido**, 10km from Vigo, is also quite reasonable, and equipped with campsites – try *Canido* (☎986 491 920; June–Sept) – and *hostales*, though it's spoilt by seaweed wrack.

Eating and drinking

Rúa da Pescadería is a lively place for **lunch** at an outdoor table amongst the oyster sellers; most of one side of the street is taken up by the *Marisquería Bahía*, allegedly the largest seafood restaurant in Spain, with seating for 1200 people. Among the budget **restaurants**, *O Meu Lar* on Rúa Fermín Penzol, off Rúa Carral, offers a decent set menu for €5.40. If you're prepared to pay €21 and up, *El Mosquito* on the Praza A Pedra is a classy option. Virtually all of the **bars** in the old streets serve great tapas, but *Chavolas* (for cuttlefish) and *Taberna Ramón*, both on Rúa dos Cesteiros, off the Praza Almeida, and *La Parra* on Rúa Alta (try the octopus) stand out. Look out too for the local delicacy, *anguilas*, the baby eels which come swimming up the Río Minho, ready to be eaten.

The Illas Cíes

The most irresistible sands of the Ría de Vigo must be those of the **Illas Cíes**. These three islands protect the entrance to the *ría*, and can be reached by boat from Vigo, and (less regularly) from Baiona and Cangas. The islands were once a refuge used by Sir Francis Drake when conducting pirate raids on Spanish shipping, and are now a nature reserve. One is an off-limits bird sanctuary; the other two are joined by a narrow causeway of sand, which forms a beach open on one side to the Atlantic and on the other to a placid lagoon. Most visitors stay on the beach, with its sprinkling of bars and a campsite in the trees, so it's easy to escape the crowds and find a deserted spot all your own – which can feel particularly remote on the Atlantic side of the islands. A long climb up a winding rocky path across desolate country leads to a lighthouse with a commanding ocean view.

The **campsite** (☎986 438 358; June–Sept) is the only legal accommodation on the islands, so if you want to stay in mid-season, book ahead to make sure there's room. There is a small shop, as well as a couple of restaurants which aren't at all bad, but these are free to charge more or less what they choose, so you might prefer to take your own food and drink. In the summer (roughly mid-June to mid-Sept) there are ten **ferries** per day **from Vigo**'s Estación Marítima (hourly 9am–7pm, though note that some services may not run in bad weather), the last one back leaving the islands at 8pm, with the return trip costing €12. In addition, there are boats **from Baiona** and **from Cangas** (July to mid-Sept 4–6 daily) – you can call Vigo's Estación Marítima on ☎986 225 272 to confirm all timetables. Only a certain number of visitors are allowed to go to the Cíes on any one day; aim for an early boat to make sure. The season lasts from mid-June to mid-September, and during the rest of the year you can't get out there at all.

Baiona and around

BAIONA (Bayona) is situated just before the open sea at the head of a miniature *ría*, the last and the smallest in Galicia. It is arguably the region's best resort, not yet over-exploited for all its popularity with the Spanish. This small and colourful port was the first place in Europe to hear of the discovery of the New World, when Columbus's *Pinta* appeared on March 1, 1493. Nowadays the harbour contains at least as many pleasure yachts as fishing boats.

The **medieval walls**, surrounding the wooded promontory which is Baiona's most prominent feature, enclose an idyllic *parador* (see below). It's definitely worth paying the €0.60 fee to walk around the parapet, with an unobstructed view in every direction, across the *ría* and along the chain of rocky islets which leads to the Illas Cíes. There's a footpath beneath the walls at sea level, barely used, which gives access to several diminutive beaches. These are not visible from the town proper, which has only a small patch of sand despite its fine esplanade.

Practicalities

Buses (every 30min from Vigo; 3 daily from A Guarda) stop by Praza Pedro de Castro on the esplanade right in the middle of town; the land-side stop is for buses to Vigo and the local beaches, the sea-side stop for buses to A Guarda. There's a seasonal **turismo** (March–Oct Mon–Fri 10.30am–1pm & 4–7pm, Sat & Sun 10am–1.30pm & 4–7.30pm; ☎986 687 067, ⓦwww.baiano.org) by the entrance to the *parador*. Most **accommodation** and restaurants are along either the seafront esplanade or Rúa Ventura Misa, the narrow pedestrianized street that runs just behind it. Cheapest is the cramped but well-located *Hospedaje Kin*, Rúa Ventura Misa 27 (☎986 355 695; ❸). For a step up in comfort take a short walk out to the *Mesón del Burgo* (☎986 355 309; ❹) by the Praia Santa Marta (next to the Campsa petrol station, a ten-minute walk from the centre back towards Vigo), which has sunny, spacious rooms looking out to sea. The *Hotel Tres Carabelas* (☎986 355 441, ☞986 355 921, ⓦ *www.hoteltrescarabelas.com*; ❻), Rúa Ventura Misa 61, is a smart mid-range option, while if you've got the money (and even if you haven't) it's hard to resist the gorgeous *Parador Conde de Gondomar* (☎986 355 000, ☞986 355 076, ⓔbaiona@parador.es; ❾), which boasts a reputation as Spain's best hotel. It has a couple of bars, including a nice one standing alone in the grounds.

There's a superabundance of **seafood restaurants** around Praza Pedro de Castro and along Rúa Ventura Misa and the esplanade, including *El Túnel*, at Ventura Misa 21, with tanks stuffed full of doomed marine creatures. The **bars** along the Rúa Ventura Misa are excellent, too.

Praia de América, Ramallosa and Sabaris

There are two good **beaches** next to the road in from Vigo a couple of kilometres before Baiona. The first is the **Praia de América** – take the Vigo–Baiona bus via Panxon (Panjón), not Nigrán – a superb, long curve of clean sand backed by rows of vacation villas. This has its own **campsite**, *Playa América* (☎986 365 404; March–Oct); however, the *Bayona Playa* (☎986 350 035; June–Sept) is nearer the town (and accessible on both bus routes) on the shorter and scruffier **Praia Ladeira**, about a kilometre east of the centre of Baiona. The inlet here is popular with **windsurfers**.

Look out for the wonderful Roman stone footbridge at **RAMALLOSA**, next to the road between the two beaches, and in Sabaris climb up the hill opposite the Praia Ladeira road for good food at the very welcoming and gregarious *Churrasquería Franky*. If you keep going up this road, you'll reach the bleak plateau at the very top. It's a great place for long walks in the woods, and there's a scattering of old villages up there where life seems to go on as it always did, oblivious to the developments below.

The coastal route towards Portugal

The road between Baiona and A Guarda, which once threaded through a deserted, windswept wilderness, has recently been improved and is now scattered with *hostales* and hotels. There are no beaches (although the sight of the ocean foaming through the rocks is mightily impressive), or even shops, and only three buses per day.

Just outside Baiona on this road is the **Virgen de la Roca**, a massive granite image overlooking the sea; it's possible to climb up inside it and onto the boat she holds in her right hand on appropriately solemn religious occasions. Halfway between Baiona and A Guarda is the town of **OIA**, no more than a very tight bend in the coast road, beneath which nestles a remarkable Baroque **monastery**, with its sheer stone facade surviving the constant battering of the Atlantic.

A Guarda

At the mouth of the great Río Minho stands the workaday port of **A GUAR-DA** (La Guardia), largely the modern creation of emigrants returned from Puerto Rico. The main attraction here is the extensive remains of a **celta** (pre-Roman fortified hill settlement), just above the town in the thick woods of Monte Santa Tecla. The ruins are about two-thirds of the way up the mountain, a stiff thirty-minute climb – follow the signs from the Tui side of the town centre. There's also a tarmac road up to the summit.

The *celta* was probably occupied between around 600 and 200 BC, and abandoned when the Romans established control over the north – such settlements were common in this part of Galicia, and even more so in northern Portugal. The site consists of the foundations of well over a hundred circular dwellings, crammed tightly inside an encircling wall. A couple of them have been restored as full-size thatched huts; most are excavated to a few feet, though some are still buried. Set in a thick pine grove on the bleak, seaward hillside, the ancient village forms a striking contrast to the humdrum roofscape of A Guarda below. On the north slope of the mountain there is also a large **cromlech**, or stone circle, while continuing upwards you pass along an avenue of much more recent construction, lined with the Stations of the Cross, and best seen looming out of a mountain mist. Five minutes further on at the top are a church, a small **museum** (March–Nov daily 11am–7pm & 4–7.30pm; free) of Celtic finds, and a hotel (see below) whose café-restaurant has an outdoor balcony with breathtaking views up and down the Portuguese and Spanish coasts, and along the Minho.

A Guarda itself has a couple of small **beaches**, but there's a better stretch of sand at the village of **Camposancos** about 4km away, facing Portugal and a small islet capped by the ruins of a fortified Franciscan monastery. A **ferry** (daily roughly every 30min 9.30am–10.30pm; pedestrians €0.60, car & driver €2.55 one way) links Camposancos with Caminha in Portugal.

Practicalities

ATSA **buses** (every 30min from Tui; 3 daily from Baiona) arrive at the small Praza Avelino Vicente. From here, follow Rúa Concepción Arenal downhill to reach the port, where there's a string of low-key but excellent **seafood restaurants** – none are particularly stylish, but the food's good value and straight out of the sea.

If you want **to stay**, try the *Hostal Martirrey* at Rúa José Antonio 8 (☎986 610 349; ❸) or the *Hostal Fidel Mar* (☎986 610 208; ❹), a fifteen-minute walk from the centre out on the Praia Arena Grande, with wonderful sea views (follow the main Baiona road until you see signs for the *praia*). For real comfort, there's the beautiful *Hotel Convento de San Benito* right by the port at Praza San Benito (☎986 611 166, ⓕ986 611 517; ❼), housed in an old Benedictine convent. Alternatively, the one-star *Hotel Pazo Santa Tecla* (☎986 610 002, ⓕ986 611 072; ❺), right on top of Monte Santa Tecla above the *celta*, has the best views you could wish for, and is pretty good value besides, though things can get a bit windy. There's **camping** out towards the river at *Camping Santa Tecla* (☎986 613 011; open all year), signposted from town.

Along the Minho

The **Río Minho** (Río Miño), the border between Spain and Portugal, so wide
and beautiful upstream, is surprisingly narrow at its mouth. Only about one
hundred metres, mostly of sandbank, separate the two countries, and it's barely navigable – no large ships can make their way inland to **Tui** or **Valença**.
Regular car and passenger ferries do however cross the river right at the mouth
of the *río* between **A Guarda** and Caminha and, a few miles upstream,
between **Goian** (Goyan) and the delightful walled village of Vila Nova da
Cerveira. If you're looking for a beach it's better to head over the river: the
miles of dunes that stretch down the Portuguese coast to Viana make for better bathing than the few around A Guarda on the Spanish side.

Tui

TUI (Tuy, pronounced *twee*), 30km from A Guarda, is the main *gallego* frontier
town on the Minho, staring across to the neat ramparts of Portuguese Valença and
worth a visit even if you don't plan to continue across the border. The old town
stands back from the river, tiered amid trees and stretches of ancient walls above
the fertile riverbank. Sloping lanes, paved with huge slabs of granite, climb to the
imposing fortress-like **Catedral** dedicated to San Telmo, patron saint of fishermen; its military aspect is a distinctive mark of Tui, scene of sporadic skirmishes
with the Portuguese throughout the Middle Ages. There are other churches of
interest, too, such as the Romanesque San Bartolomeo, or Gothic Santo
Domingo with its ivy-shrouded cloisters. More memorable, though, is the lovely rambling quality of the place, coupled with a pair of enticing little river beaches. There's a large **market** on Wednesdays along the main road through town.

Practicalities

Frequent **buses** from Vigo and A Guarda stop opposite the *Hostal La Generosa*
on old Tui's main street, the acacia-lined Paseo Calvo Sotelo. If you're heading
inland by rail towards Ribadavia and Ourense, it's much quicker to catch your
train from Guillarei station, 3km east of town, than to wait for a connection
in Tui itself. The city **turismo** is in front of the *ayuntamiento* (daily 10am–3pm
& 4–9pm, closed Sun pm; no phone).

If you want **to stay**, the *Hostal La Generosa* (✆986 600 055; ❷), at Paseo
Calvo Sotelo 37, is a lovely old-fashioned one-star *hostal*, and excellent value;
even cheaper is the *Habitaciones Otilia*, Rúa Generalísmo 7 (✆986 601 062; ❷),
just up some steps from Paseo Calvo Sotelo – it's rickety and down-at-heel, but
adequate. Other more expensive options include the *Hostal San Telmo*, Avda. de
la Concordia 88 (✆986 603 011; ❺), opposite the train station, and the *parador*
(✆986 600 300, ✆986 602 163, ✉tui@parador.es; ❽). Amongst Tui's **restaurants**, the *Pizzeria di Marco*, just around the corner from *Habitaciones Otilia*, is
surprisingly good and very cheap (pizzas from €4.60), while the *comedor* at the
Hostal Generosa is the place to go for cheap *menús*.

Crossing the border

It's a fifteen-minute walk to the Portuguese border, across an iron bridge
designed by Eiffel; the little town of **VALENÇA**, dwarfed behind its mighty
ramparts, lies a similar distance beyond. There's no border control at the bridge:
just stroll (or drive) across and head up the hill to Valença, past a **turismo**
(Mon–Sat 9.30am–12.30pm & 2.30–6pm, Sun 9.30am–12.30pm; ✆251 823
374) which can provide details about onward Portuguese transport.

North of Tui

There is a road from Tui to Gondomar, and from there to Baiona, which avoids Vigo and makes a spectacular drive through thick virgin forests, but no buses run this way. From Porriño, halfway between Tui and Vigo, the motorway is the most direct route to Ourense, up very steep bleak mountains with not a habitation in sight. On the way, **PONTEAREAS** has a **Corpus Christi** festival (in June) when the streets are spread out with gorgeous patterned "carpets" of bright flowers. Nearby, **MONDARIZ** is a pretty spa town with bathing beaches by a secluded river.

Upstream to Ribadavia and Celanova

Whether you follow the N120 highway or the train line parallel to the Minho, there are numerous rewarding stops along the way. If you want to get away from it all, head for the tiny hamlet of **ALBEOS** where you'll find *La Levada* (℡986 666 413, ℻986 666 413; ❸), an English-run guesthouse situated on an organic farm spilling down the terraces of the valley (if you're arriving by train the owners will pick you up from Albeos station). The views across the Minho are breathtaking from here, and the vegetarian food is good.

One of the best towns to end up in is **RIBADAVIA**. The trip there by train from Tui is a lovely riverside journey, although the valley of the Minho does tend to fill up with freezing mist until midday or so. The town stands among woods and vineyards above the river, looking grander than its size would promise, with several fine churches and a sprawling **Dominican monastery** which was once the residence of the kings of Galicia. There's also an interesting **Barrio Xudeo** (Barrio Judío, or Jewish quarter), dating from the eleventh century when Ribadavia received its first Jewish immigrants; by the fourteenth century these had become half the town's population, and formed one of the most important and prosperous Jewish communities in Spain. Head for the tiny square behind the Iglesia de la Magdalena for a wonderful view of the hillside terraces. Look out too for the remains of the small but quaint **Castillo de los Condes de Ribadavia**, immediately above the Praza Maior.

Buses stop by the river, from where it's a five-minute walk uphill to the Praza Maior; the **train** station is a little further out along the same road. The town's **turismo** is on the Praza Maior (July–Sept daily 10am–3pm & 5–8pm, Oct–June 10am–2.30pm & 4–6.30pm; ℡988 471 275, ⓦwww.ribadavia.com), where you'll also find the only **hostal** in the old town, the *Hostal Plaza* (℡988 470 576; ❹), which has good en-suite rooms. Alternatively, *Hostal Evencio*, Avda. Rodriguex Valcarcel 30 (℡988 471 045; ❹), is rather soulless but has spacious, well-equipped rooms with great views. Several pleasant **bars** around town serve the region's excellent, port-like wine.

The first hydroelectric dam blocks the Minho about 30km below Ribadavia, and it's from then on up that the flooding of the valley makes the river so broad and smooth-flowing, with forests right to the water's edge. The high and winding road along the south bank through Cortegada to the border at São Gregorio makes a good excursion, and can also be used as part of the route to **CELANOVA**. This is hardly more than a village, dominated by a vast and palatial **Benedictine monastery**. It was here that Felipe V retired into monastic life, having spent much of his reign securing the throne in the War of the Spanish Succession (1701–13). The monastery is now a school, but you can borrow the key to explore its two superb cloisters – one Renaissance, the other Baroque – and the cathedral-sized church. Most beautiful of all is the tiny Mozarabic chapel of **San Miguel** in the garden of the monastery. This dates from the tenth century, and is the work of "Arabicized" Christian refugees from *al-Andalus*. **Buses** also come in from Ourense, and the **hotel** *Betanzos* on Castor Elices 12 (℡ 988 451 036; ❹) is excellent.

Ourense

At first sight, **OURENSE** (Orense) is worse than disappointing: a vast clutter of anonymous modern apartment and office blocks which are made to look even drearier by their splendid natural setting on a bend in the expansive River Minho – crossed here by a bewildering number of bridges, including the majestic thirteenth-century **Ponte Romano**. Buried inside the city's depressing outer shell, however, is a personable old quarter; a small but attractive tangle of stepped streets, patrician mansions with escutcheoned doorways and grand little churches squeezed into miniature arcaded squares. The whole area has now been lovingly restored, and with its pedestrianized streets and outdoor cafés is one of urban Galicia's more pleasurable city centres.

At its centre is the dark **Catedral**, an imitation of Compostela's, with a painted (but greatly inferior) copy of the Pórtico de Gloria, and a museum in the cloisters. Other specific sights are few on the ground, though it's worth dropping into the **Museo Arqueolóxico** (Tues–Sun 9.30am–2.30pm & 4–9.30pm, closed Sun pm; €2.40), which has a mildly interesting display of sculptures, ceramics and other finds discovered in the province; it's also housed in one of the city's most interesting buildings, the former Palacio Episcopal, parts of which date back to the twelfth century.

Practicalities

It's a twenty-minute walk into town from the **train station** on the opposite side of the river: cross the road in front of the station and bear right down the road signposted to the Ponte Romano; cross this then turn left up Rua do Concello to reach the Parque San Lázaro, the new town's main square. The **bus station** is five minutes further out past the train station (fairly frequent buses run from both terminals into town). The **turismo** (Mon–Fri 9am–2pm & 4.30–6.30pm; ℡ 988 372 020) is on Rúa M. Curros Enriquez, near the corner of Parque San Lázaro.

There are several *fondas* scattered around the area facing the train station, though you'll do better to head for the pleasant little enclave of **hostales** on the quiet Rúa San Miguel, near the cathedral: the *San Miguel II* at no. 14 (℡ 988 239 203, ℻ 988 242 749; ❸) is a good cheapie, or there's the more upmarket *Hotel Zarampallo* at no. 9 (℡ 988 220 053; ❺). There are several good **restaurants** around here too.

Gorges of the Río Sil

The Minho is more spectacular the further you go upstream; it arrives at Ourense having flowed south from Lugo through the harsh landscape traversed by the Camino de Santiago. Twenty kilometres northeast of Ourense it meets the Río Sil at Los Peares, a crumbling old village on the main train line. You can walk from there along the **Gorges of the Sil**, with precarious farm terraces tumbling down to a chaos of rocks and foam. High above San Esteban is another monastery, the three-cloistered **Monasterio de Ribas do Sil**. On the plain to the north, **MONFORTE DE LEMOS** is a major rail junction. Again, the station is a long way from the town centre, but Monforte is a satisfyingly unspoilt and ancient place. Its **Torre de Lemos** looks out across a featureless expanse from the top of a hill full of tumbledown old houses, and there's a strikingly elegant Renaissance **Colegio** lower down.

To the south of the Sil, **MANZANEDA** is the only *gallego* ski resort, offering most of the necessary facilities but not always the snow, and on the other side of the mountains is **VERÍN**, where a fine castle above the fortified town is now a *parador* (☎988 410 075, ℻988 412 017, ✆verin@parador.es; ➐). The town itself is quite modern, though a few traditional balconied houses remain around the main square, near which Rúa Mayor is a promising area for cheaper accommodation. There's a swimming area, with a few bars and a grassy bank for sunbathing, down beside the Tamega river. Here you're once more within a dozen kilometres of Portugal; buses run alongside the river to the rugged Portuguese frontier town of **Chaves**.

Travel Details

Trains

As well as the FEVE line (see p.32) which journeys along the north coast from Asturias to Ferrol, there are two main lines into and out of Galicia: one from Madrid via Avila, Medina del Campo and Zamora to Ourense; the other from León to Monforte, the junction between Lugo and Ourense. Many of these trains continue to Santiago and A Coruña, but you can usually get about more easily using the *regionales*. Galicia has two regional lines: the first runs from A Coruña to Vigo via Santiago; the second from Vigo to Ourense and on to Monforte. Two further minor lines connect Ferrol with A Coruña, and A Coruña with Lugo and Monforte.

A Coruña to: Barcelona (2 daily; 15hr); Betanzos (4 daily; 30min); Bilbao (1 daily; 12hr); Burgos (3 daily; 8–9hr); Ferrol (2 daily; 1hr 30min); León (3 daily; 5–6hr); Lugo (4 daily; 2hr); Madrid (2 daily; 8hr 30min–10hr 30min); Ourense (3 daily; 2hr 15min–3hr); Santiago de Compostela (17 daily; 1hr–1hr 30min); Vigo (19 daily; 2hr–3hr 30min); Zamora (2 daily; 5hr 20min); Zaragoza (2 daily; 12hr 30min).

Ourense to: Burgos (3 daily; 4–6hr); A Coruña (3 daily; 2hr 30min–3hr 30min); León (4 daily; 4hr);

Madrid (2 daily; 7–8hr); Medina del Campo (2 daily; 3hr 30min–4hr 30min); Monforte (5 daily; 45min); Ponferrada (5 daily; 2hr 30min); Pontevedra (2 daily; 2hr 45min); Ribadavia (6 daily; 25min); Santiago de Compostela (5 daily; 1hr 20min–2hr); Vigo (8 daily; 2hr); Zamora (2 daily; 3hr).

Santiago de Compostela to: Ávila (2 daily; 6hr); A Coruña (18–24 daily; 1hr); Bilbao (1 daily; 10hr 45min); Burgos (1 daily; 8hr); Irún (1 daily; 11hr 30min); León (1 daily; 6hr); Madrid (2 daily; 8–10hr); Medina del Campo (2 daily; 5hr 20min); Ourense (5 daily; 1hr 20min–2hr); Palencia (1 daily; 7hr); Vigo (15–18 daily; 1hr 15min–1hr 45min); Zamora (2 daily; 5hr 30min–6hr 30min).

Vigo to: Ávila (2 daily; 6hr 30min–8hr 30min); Barcelona (2 daily; 15hr–16hr 30min); Burgos (3 daily; 8hr); A Coruña (15–18 daily; 2hr–3hr 30min); Irún (1–9 daily; 11hr 30min); León (3–4 daily; 6hr); Madrid (2 daily; 8–10hr); Medina del Campo (2–9 daily; 6hr 30min); Ourense (7–8 daily; 2hr); Ponferrada (4–5 daily; 4–5hr); Pontevedra (15–18 daily; 30min); Ribadavia (4 daily; 1hr 30min); Santiago de Compostela (15–18 daily; 1hr 15min–1hr 45min); Tui (3 daily; 45min); Zamora (2 daily; 5–6hr); Zaragoza (2 daily; 9–12hr).

Buses

A Coruña to: Betanzos (every 30min; 45min); Camariñas (3 daily; 1hr 45min); Carnota (2 daily; 2hr 40min); Cee (5 daily; 2hr 15min); Corme (3 daily; 1hr 30min); Ferrol (15 daily; 1hr); Finisterre (4 daily; 2hr 30min); Laxe (1 daily; 1hr); Lugo (11 daily; 2hr); Madrid (6 daily; 8hr); Malpica (2 daily; 1hr 15min); Ourense (8 daily; 3hr 30min); Oviedo (4 daily; 5hr); Pontevedra (10 daily; 2hr); Ribadavia (4 daily; 3hr 30min); Santiago de Compostela (hourly; 1hr 30min); Ribadeo (6 daily; 4hr); Vigo (9 daily; 3hr); Viveiro (4 daily; 3hr 30min).

Costa da Morte: Camariñas–Muxia–Cee (3 daily; 30min/1hr 30 min); Finisterre–Corcubión–

Muxia–Camariñas (3 daily; 15min/1hr 15min/2hr); Finisterre–Muros (3 daily; 1hr); Laxe–Muxia (1 daily; 1hr 30min); Muros–Cee (9 daily; 1hr); Muxia–Camariñas (3 daily; 30min).

Lugo to: A Coruña (15 daily; 2hr); Foz (5 daily; 2hr); Ourense (6 daily; 2hr); Pontevedra (6 daily; 2hr); Santiago de Compostela (9 daily; 2hr); Vigo (6 daily; 3hr); Viveiro (6 daily; 2–3hr).

Ourense to: Celanova (1 daily; 1hr 30min); A Coruña (5 daily; 3hr 30min); Lugo (5 daily; 2hr); Oporto (1 daily; 8hr); Santiago de Compostela (9 daily; 2hr 30min); Vigo (13 daily; 2hr).

Pontevedra to: Bueu (16 daily; 30min); Cambados

(11 daily; 1hr); Cangas (21 daily; 1hr); A Coruña (10 daily; 2hr); O Grove (19 daily; 1hr); Isla de Arousa (7 daily; 1hr 30min); Lugo (5 daily; 3hr); Moaña (5 daily; 45min); Noia (1 daily; 1hr 30min); Ourense (8 daily; 2hr); Padrón (hourly; 1 hr); Santiago de Compostela (every 30min; 1hr); Tui (6 daily; 1hr); Vigo (14 daily; 30min–1hr); Vilagarcía (16 daily; 45min).

Santiago de Compostela to: Betanzos (7 daily; 1hr 30min); Camariñas (3 daily; 3hr); Cambados (5 daily; 2hr); Cee (3 daily; 2hr); A Coruña (hourly; 1hr 30min); Ferrol (7 daily; 2hr 30min); Finisterre (3 daily; 2hr 30min); Lugo (6 daily; 2hr); Madrid (3 daily; 9hr 30min); Malpica (2 daily; 2hr); Muros (13

daily; 2hr 30min); Noia (16 daily; 1hr 30min); Ourense (9 daily; 2hr 30min); Padrón (every 30min; 45min); Pontevedra (every 30min; 1hr); Vigo (14 daily; 1hr 30min–2hr); Vilagarcía (9 daily; 1hr).

Vigo to: Baiona (every 30min; 1hr); Barcelona (1 or 2 daily; 14hr); Cangas (2 daily; 1hr); A Coruña (10 daily; 3hr); O Grove (3 daily; 1hr 15min); Lugo (7 daily; 3hr); Madrid (6 daily; 8hr); Noia (1 daily; 3hr); Oporto and Lisbon (4 weekly; 3hr 30min/6hr); Ourense (13 daily; 2hr); Oviedo (2 daily; 8hr); Padrón (13 daily; 2hr); Pontevedra (every 30min; 30min–1hr); Ribadavia (13 daily; 1hr 30min); Santiago de Compostela (every 30min; 2hr 30min); Tui (every 30min; 45min); Vilagarcía (2 daily; 2hr).

GALICIA | Travel Details

Aragón

✱ **Basilica de Nuestra Señora del Pilar, Zaragoza** p.633 A majestic setting for the monumental shrine of the patron saint of Spain.

✱ **Aljafería, Zaragoza** p.634 The most spectacular Moorish monument outside Andalucía.

✱ **El Monasterio de Piedra** p.640 An oasis of waterfalls, grottoes and lakes in the arid landscape of Aragón.

✱ **Teruel** p.641 Visit the old town of this historic town to see some Mudéjar architecture.

✱ **Albarracín** p.644 Wander the streets of the picturesque medieval town.

✱ **Castillo de Loarre** p.651 A spectacular fortress perched dizzily on a rocky outcrop.

✱ **Parque Nacional de Ordesa** p.663 A dramatic Pyrenean backdrop for some of the finest hiking in Spain.

9

Aragón

P olitically and historically Aragón has close links with Catalunya, with which it formed a powerful alliance in medieval times, exerting influence over the Mediterranean as far away as Athens. It is a Castilian rather than Catalan-speaking area though and, locked in on all sides by mountains, has always had its own identity, with traditional *fueros* like the Basques. The modern *autonomía* – containing the provinces of Zaragoza, Teruel and Huesca – is well out of the Spanish political mainstream, especially in the rural south, where Teruel is the least populated region in Spain. Coming from Catalunya or the Basque country, you'll find the Aragonese pace, in general, noticeably slower.

It is the **Pyrenees** that draw most visitors to Aragón, with their stunning valleys, old farming villages, and trekking. The mountains are remarkably unspoilt – and much less commercialized than across the border in France – and they have a stunning focus in the **Parque Nacional de Ordesa**, with its panoply of canyons, waterfalls and peaks. Aragón's Pyrenean villages are also renowned for their Romanesque architecture; **Jaca** has the country's oldest Romanesque cathedral.

The most interesting monuments of central and southern Aragón are, by contrast, **Mudéjar**: a series of churches, towers and mansions built by Muslim workers in the early decades of Christian rule. **Zaragoza**, the Aragonese capital, and the only place of any real size, sets the tone with its remarkable **Aljafería Palace**, the most spectacular Moorish monument outside Andalucía.

ACCOMMODATION PRICE CODES

All the establishments listed in this book have been price-graded according to the following scale. The prices quoted are for the **cheapest available double room in high season**; effectively this means that anything in the ❶ and most places in the ❷ range will be without private bath, though there's usually a washbasin in the room. In the ❹ category and above you will probably be getting private facilities. Remember, though, that many of the budget places will also have more expensive rooms including en-suite facilities. Youth hostels are graded under ❶ as the price per person is less than half of the category's upper limit.

Note that in the more upmarket *hostales* and *pensiones*, and in anything calling itself a hotel, you'll pay a **tax** (IVA) of seven percent on top of the room price.

❶ Under €12   ❹ €27–36   ❼ €60–90
❷ €12–18   ❺ €36–48   ❽ €90–120
❸ €18–27   ❻ €48–60   ❾ Over €120

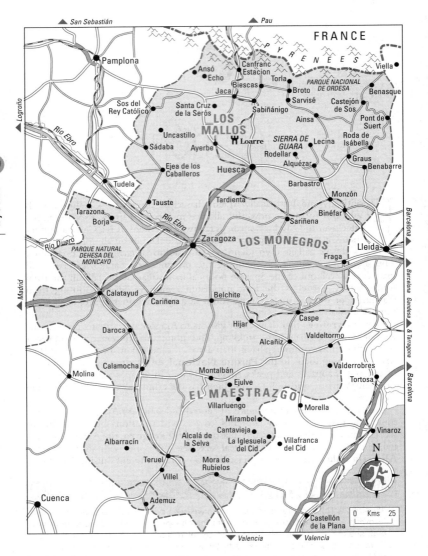

Other examples are to be found in a string of smaller towns, in particular **Tarazona**, **Calatayud** and – above all – the southern provincial capital of **Teruel**.

In southern Aragón, two mountainous regions are also of interest. West of Teruel, the Montes Universales, a frontier with Cuenca province, offer some gorgeous routes and walking, especially around the massively walled village of **Albarracín**. To the east is the isolated region of **El Maestrazgo**, a wild countryside stamped with dark peaks and gorges, whose villages feel extraordinarily remote.

April

8–9 Pilgrimage to the Santuario de Nuestra Señora de la Alegría in Monzón, the journey made in decorated carriages.

Holy Week Small-scale but emotional celebrations at Calatayud and elsewhere. On Maundy Thursday/Good Friday there's the festival of *La Tamborrada* in Calanda, near Alcañiz.

May

First Friday Jaca commemorates the Battle of Vitoria against the Moors with processions and folkloric events.

25 More of the same at Jaca for the *Fiesta de Santa Orosia*.

Monday of Pentecost *Romería Nuestra Señora de Calentuñana* at Sos del Rey Catolico.

June

Nearest Sunday to the 19th Cantavieja celebrates the *Fiesta de los Mozos*: a serious religious event but with dancing and the usual fairground activities.

30 *Ball de Benas*: small festival at Benasque.

July

First Sunday *Romería del Quililay*, pilgrimage and picnic up the mountain above Tarazona.

First–second week Teruel bursts into ten days of festivities for the *Vaquilla del Ángel*, one of Aragón's major festivals.

Late July/early Aug International Folklore Festival of the Pyrenees alternates between France and Spain: it's at Jaca in odd-numbered years, accompanied by a very full programme of traditional music and dance.

August

Early August Fiesta at Huesca in honour of San Lorenzo.

14–15 *Fiestas del Barrio* in Jaca – street markets and mass parties.

16 Patron saint's festival at Biescas – "bigheads" and eats.

27–28 *Encierros* – crazy local bull running – at Cantavieja.

September

Early September Teruel fair.

4–8 Fiesta at Barbastro includes *jota* dancing, bullfights and sports competitions (like pigeon-shooting contests).

8 Virgin's birthday signals fairs at Alcañiz, Hecho, Calatayud, Alcalá de la Selva and Villel.

12–15 Three days of patron saint festivities at Graus including stylized traditional dances and "dawn songs". *Romería* at L'Iglesuela del Cid, with the "Mojiganga", a socially satiric procession, held on the Sunday closest to the 14th.

8–14 Bull running and general celebrations at Albarracín.

October

Second week Aragón's most important festival in honour of the *Virgen del Pilar*. Much of the province closes down around the 12th and at Zaragoza there are floats, bullfights and *jota* dancing.

This chapter is arranged in two sections: **Zaragoza, Teruel and southern Aragón** (covering Zaragoza and Teruel provinces); and **The Aragonese Pyrenees** (covering Huesca province).

Zaragoza, Teruel and Southern Aragón

Zaragoza houses over half of Aragón's 1.5 million population, and most of its industry. It's a big but enjoyable city, with a lively zone of bars and restaurants tucked in among remarkable monuments, and it's a handy transport nexus too, both for Aragón and beyond. Its province includes the Mudéjar towns of **Tarazona, Calatayud** and **Daroca** and, along the border with Navarra, the old **Cinco Villas**, really just ennobled villages, of which the most interesting is **Sos del Rey Católico**. Wine enthusiasts may also want to follow the **Ruta de los Vinos**, south from Zaragoza through Cariñena to Daroca.

Teruel province is a lot more remote, and even the capital doesn't see too many passing visitors. It is unjustly neglected, considering its superb Mudéjar monuments, and if you have transport of your own there are some superb rural routes to explore: especially east, through **Albarracín** to Cuenca, or south through to Valencia. The valleys and villages of the **Maestrazgo**, which border Valencia province, are the most remote of the lot: a region completely untouched by tourism, foreign or Spanish, and where transport of your own is a big help.

Zaragoza

ZARAGOZA is an interesting and inviting place, having managed to absorb its rapid growth with a rare grace, and its centre, at least, reflects an air of prosperity in its wide, modern boulevards, stylish shops and bars. In addition, the city preserves the spectacular Moorish **Aljafería**, and an awesome basilica, devoted to one of Spain's most famous icons, **Nuestra Señora del Pilar**.

The city's **fiestas** in honour of Nuestra Señora del Pilar – which take place throughout the second week of October – are well worth planning a trip around, so long as you can find accommodation. In addition to the religious processions (which focus on the 12th), the local council lays on a brilliant programme of cultural events, featuring top rock, jazz and folk bands, floats, bullfights and traditional *jota* dancing. It's a pretty lively town for the rest of the year too, and if you're anywhere nearby at the weekend, it's well worth spending an evening here just to experience the atmosphere around the old quarter.

Orientation and information

The **old centre** of Zaragoza is bordered to the north by the **Río Ebro**, and on the other sides by a loop of broad *paseos*; bisecting it is the **Avenida de César Augusto**, leading in from the old city gate, Puerta del Carmen. With the exception of the **Aljafería**, most other points of interest are within this loop. Backing onto the river are the two cathedrals, **La Seo** and the **Basílica de Nuestra Señora del Pilar**, flanked on their south side by **Plaza del Pilar**, a huge stone square which is in every sense the heart of the city. Just south of the square, between c/de Alfonso and c/de Don Jaime, is a zone known as **El Tubo**, the hub of Zaragoza's bar and nightlife scene. This leads to the **Plaza de España**, a central terminus for local city buses.

△ Nuestra Señora del Pilar, Zaragoza

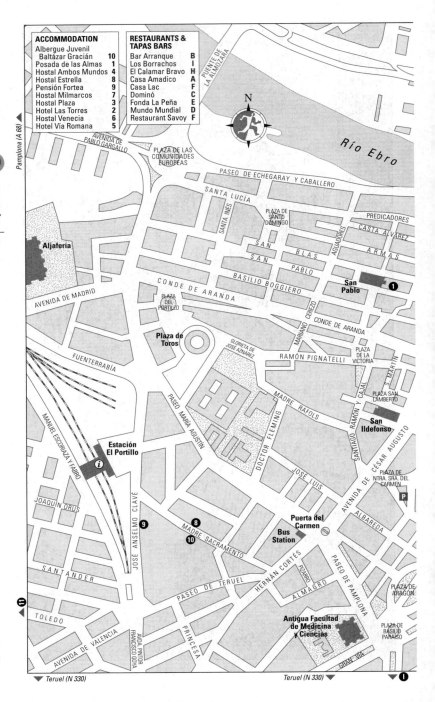

ACCOMMODATION
Albergue Juvenil
 Baltázar Gracián   10
Posada de las Almas   1
Hostal Ambos Mundos   4
Hostal Estrella   8
Pensión Fortea   9
Hostal Milmarcos   7
Hostal Plaza   3
Hotel Las Torres   2
Hostal Venecia   6
Hotel Vía Romana   5

RESTAURANTS & TAPAS BARS
Bar Arranque   B
Los Borrachos   I
El Calamar Bravo   H
Casa Amadico   A
Casa Lac   F
Dominó   C
Fonda La Peña   E
Mundo Mundial   D
Restaurant Savoy   F

N

Río Ebro

Pamplona (A 68)

AVENIDA DE PABLO GARGALLO
PLAZA DE LAS COMUNIDADES EUROPEAS
PASEO DE ECHEGARAY Y CABALLERO
SANTA LUCÍA
SANTA INÉS
PLAZA DE SANTO DOMINGO
PREDICADORES
CASTA ÁLVAREZ
AGUADORES
A R M A S
S A N   B L A S
Aljafería
S A N   P A B L O
BASILIO BOGGIERO
CONDE DE ARANDA
San Pablo ●1
AVENIDA DE MADRID
PLAZA DEL PORTILLO
MARIANO CEREZO
CONDE DE ARANDA
PLAZA DE LA VICTORIA
Plaza de Toros
GLORIETA DE JOSÉ AZNÁREZ
RAMÓN PIGNATELLI
S. MARTÍN
PLAZA SAN LAMBERTO
FUENTERRABÍA
MADRE RÁFOLS
SANTIAGO RAMÓN Y CAJAL
San Ildefonso
MANUEL ESCORIAZA Y FABRO
DOCTOR FLEMING
AVENIDA DE CÉSAR AUGUSTO
Estación El Portillo ℹ
JOSÉ LUIS
PLAZA DE NTRA. SRA. DEL CARMEN
P
JOAQUÍN ORÚS
ALBAREDA
●9
●8
Puerta del Carmen
JOSÉ ANSELMO CLAVÉ
MADRE SACRAMENTO
Bus Station
●10
PASEO MARÍA AGUSTÍN
HERNÁN CORTES
PIZARRO
PASEO DE PAMPLONA
SANTANDER
PLAZA DE ARAGÓN
●11
TOLEDO
PASEO DE TERUEL
ALMAGRO
PLAZA DE BASILIO PARAÍSO
AVDA. PINTOR FRANCISCO GOYA
PRINCESA
Antigua Facultad de Medicina y Ciencias
GRAN VÍA
AVENIDA DE VALENCIA

▼ Teruel (N 330)   Teruel (N 330) ▼   ▼ ●1

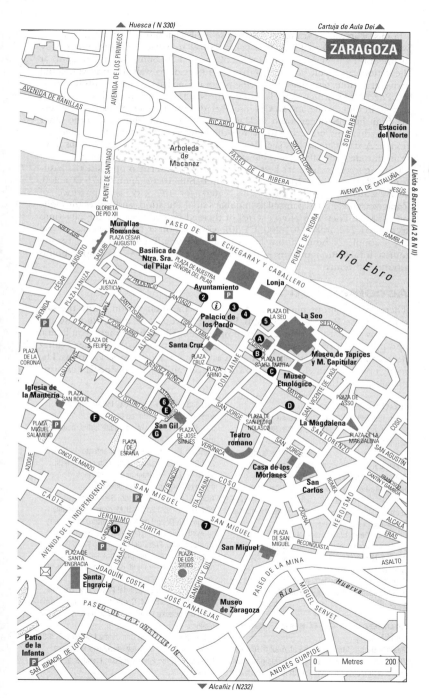

ZARAGOZA

▲ Huesca (N 330)

Cartuja de Aula Dei ▲

Estación
del Norte

AVENIDA DE LOS PIRINEOS

AVENIDA DE RANILLAS

RICARDO DEL ARCO

SOBRARBE

SIXTO CELORRIO

Arboleda
de
Macanaz

PASEO DE LA RIBERA

PUENTE DE SANTIAGO

AVENIDA DE CATALUÑA

JESÚS

► Lleida & Barcelona (A 2 & N II)

GLORIETA
DE PÍO XII

RAMBLA

PUENTE DE PIEDRA

Río Ebro

PASEO DE

ECHEGARAY Y CABALLERO

Murallas
Romanas

PLAZA CÉSAR
AUGUSTO

ABENAIRE

SALDUBA

CÉSAR
AUGUSTO

PLAZA DE NUESTRA
SEÑORA DEL PILAR

Basílica de
Ntra. Sra.
del Pilar

PLAZA
JUSTICIA

C. PRUDENCIO

PLAZA LANUZA

SANTIAGO

Lonja

AVENIDA

O. R. F. E.

SANTA ISABEL

ESPOZ Y MINA

C. CONTAMINA

ALFONSO

Ayuntamiento

P

PLAZA DE
LA SEO

SEPÚTCRO

La Seo

PLAZA
DE S. FELIPE

MÉNDEZ NÚÑEZ

2

3 ⓘ 4

Palacio de
los Pardo

Santa Cruz

PLAZA
CRUZ

5

A

B

C

PLAZA DE
SANTA MARTA

Museo de Tapices
y M. Capitular

PLAZA
DE LA
CORONA

GALILITERTE

PLAZA
DE ARIÑO

DON JAIME I

Museo
Etnológico

MAYOR

SAN VICENTE DE PAÚL

PLAZA DE
ASSO

Iglesia de
la Mantería

PLAZA
SAN ROQUE

C. CUATRO AGOSTO

6 E

SAN JORGE

D

COSO

San Gil

G

PLAZA
DE JOSÉ
SINUÉS

PLAZA DE
SAN PEDRO
NOLASCO

La Magdalena

PLAZA DE LA
MAGDALENA

SAN LORENZO

COSO

SAN AGUSTÍN

PLAZA
MIGUEL
SALAMERO

P

F

PLAZA
DE
ESPAÑA

VERÓNICA

Teatro
romano

SAN JORGE

ROMEA

CANTÍN Y GAMBÓA

FRANCISCO

CINCO DE MARZO

BLANCAS

STA CATALINA

COSO

Casa de los
Morlanes

San
Carlos

ALCALÁ

ERAS

AZOQUE

CADIZ

AVENIDA DE LA INDEPENDENCIA

SAN MIGUEL

P

JERÓNIMO

H

ZURITA

ISAAC PERAL

CAMINO REAL

7

SAN MIGUEL

CÁDIZ

CABÁN

HEROÍSMO

RECONQUISTA

ASALTO

PLAZA DE
SAN
MIGUEL

PASEO DE LA MINA

Huerva

Río

MIGUEL SERVET

PLAZA DE
SANTA
ENGRACIA

P

Santa
Engracia

JOAQUÍN COSTA

San Miguel

SANCHO Y GIL

JOSÉ CANALEJAS

PLAZA
DE LOS
SITIOS

Museo
de Zaragoza

Patio
de la
Infanta

P

SAN IGNACIO DE LOYOLA

PASEO DE LA CONSTITUCIÓN

ANDRÉS GURPIDE

0   Metres   200

▼ Alcañiz (N232)

Points of arrival are scattered. **Trains** use the Estación del Portillo, a 25-minute walk (or bus #22) to Plaza de España; a small **turismo** booth (summer daily 10am–8pm; winter Mon–Sat 11am–2.30pm & 4.30–8pm, Sun 10am–2pm) at the station can supply you with a map if you decide to walk. By **bus**, you could arrive at various terminals. The principal one is at Paseo María Agustín 7, near the Puerta del Carmen; Agreda services for Madrid, Catalunya and several destinations in Old Castile, and La Oscense/Agreda services to Huesca and Jaca, operate from here. Services south to Daroca, Cariñena and Muel, and some other local destinations, use a terminal across the railway tracks (south of the train station) at Avda. Valencia 20. Viajes Viaca buses to many northern destinations leave from outside their offices at c/Pignatelli 120, just opposite the bullring.

Leaving for elsewhere, it's best to check with the **turismo** opposite the basilica on Plaza del Pilar (Mon–Sat 10am–8pm, Sun 10am–2pm; ☏976 201 200, ⓦ www.turismozaragoza.com). This caters for the city and province of Zaragoza, and also has pamphlets and maps on destinations and routes throughout Aragón. They also offer a series of themed guided walks of the city (info ☏902 201 212 or 976 201 200; €1.50), which set off at 11am at weekends and last a couple of hours. From July to October you'll also find up to twenty tourist information officers – dressed in yellow jackets – at various points around the centre.

Accommodation

There are numerous **places to stay** close to the train station, along the side streets off the Paseo María Agustín. However, if you don't mind the noise and company of bars, there's more atmosphere in **El Tubo**, where you'll find upwards of a dozen *pensiones* located in airy mansion blocks; c/Méndez Núñez here, and the smaller streets off it, such as c/Estabañes, are good locations. The more upmarket hotels in Zaragoza are pricey and not very special, catering mainly to a business market.

Budget options

Albergue Juvenil Baltázar Gracián, c/Franco y López 4, off Avda. de Valencia ☏976 551 504. Zaragoza's refurbished youth hostel is on the fifth street on the right as you walk down Avda. de Valencia from Avda. Francisco de Goya. Open Jan–July & Oct–Dec, staffed 8am–3pm. ❶

Hostal Ambos Mundos, Plaza del Pilar 16 ☏976 299 704, Ⓕ976 299 702. Large *hostal* (52 rooms) in an excellent location; spacious rooms with small en-suite baths or showers. ❹

Fonda La Peña, c/de Cinegio 3, 1° ☏976 299 089. Comfortable, clean and inexpensive rooms at this family-run *fonda*. Recommended. ❷–❸

Hostal Venecia, c/Estabañes 7 ☏976 393 661. Don't be put off by the tatty exterior; the rooms are bearably clean, it's inexpensive and the location is great. ❷

Moderate and expensive options

Posada de las Almas, c/San Pablo 22 ☏976 439 700, Ⓕ976 439 143. Soak up the faded grandeur in this well-located old hotel, with its own restaurant and garage (€6 per day for a car). ❺

Hostal Estrella, Avda. de Clave 27 ☏976 283 061. Decent rooms with en-suite baths, near the train station. ❺

Pensión Fortea, c/Madre Sacramento 45 ☏976 282 229. Clean rooms, some with private bath, and handy for the train and bus stations. It's worth trying to bargain the rates down. ❺

Hostal Milmarcos, c/Madre Sacramento 40 ☏976 284 618, Ⓕ 976 284 618. Modern, comfortable rooms with TV and bath. Tends not to get too busy so worth trying to negotiate a cheap deal. ❺

Hostal Plaza, Plaza del Pilar 14 ☏976 294 830. The best choice in this price bracket: decent rooms with showers and, of course, an excellent location. ❹

Hotel Las Torres, Plaza del Pilar 11 ☏976 394 250, Ⓕ976 394 254. Comfortable en-suite rooms in an unbeatable position, looking directly onto the basilica. ❻

Hotel Vía Romana, c/Don Jaime I 54 ☏976 398 215, Ⓕ976 290 511, ⓦ www.husa.es. Smart hotel just off the Plaza del Pilar; cheaper at weekends. ❼

Camping

Camping Casablanca, Valdefierro – 2km from the centre along the Avda. de Madrid ☎ 976 753 870. A rather barren-looking site, but large and well equipped, with a swimming pool. Bus #36 from Plaza del Pilar or Plaza de España runs past. Open April to mid-Oct.

The City

The **Plaza del Pilar** is the obvious point to start exploring Zaragoza. The square, paved in a brilliant, pale stone, was remodelled in 1991, creating a vast, airy expanse from the old cathedral, **La Seo**, past the great **Basilica del Pilar**, and over to the Avenida César Augusto. A look around the square spans the whole extent of the city's history: at one end a patch of Roman wall remains; between the churches is a Renaissance exchange house, **La Lonja**; while at the centre is some modern statuary and a waterfall shaped like a map of South America.

Even if you plan only to change trains or buses in Zaragoza, it is worth coming into the centre to see the square and basilica, and making your way over to **La Aljafería**, either on foot (around 20min) or by taxi.

The Basilica de Nuestra Señora del Pilar

Majestically fronting the Río Ebro, the **Basilica de Nuestra Señora del Pilar** (daily 5.45am–9.30pm) is one of Spain's greatest and most revered religious buildings. It takes its name from a pillar – the centrepiece of the church – on which the Virgin is said to have descended from heaven in an apparition before St James the Apostle. The structure around this shrine is truly monumental, with great corner towers and a central dome surrounded by ten brightly tiled cupolas; it was designed in the late seventeenth century by Francisco Herrera el Mozo and built by Ventura Rodríguez in the 1750s and 1760s.

The **pillar**, topped by a diminutive image of the Virgin, is constantly surrounded by pilgrims, who line up to touch an exposed (and thoroughly worn) section, encased in a marble surround. The main artistic treasure of the cathedral is a magnificent alabaster *reredos* on the high altar, a masterpiece sculpted by Damien Forment in the first decades of the sixteenth century.

Off the north aisle is the **Museo Pilarista** (daily 9am–2pm & 4–6pm; €1.20), where you can inspect at close quarters the original sketches for the decoration of the domes by Francisco de Goya, González Velázquez, and Francisco and Ramón Bayeu. Your ticket also admits you to the **Sacristía Mayor**, off the opposite aisle, with a collection of religious paintings and tapestries. You'll have to pay extra, however, if you want to enjoy the panoramic views from the **Torre**, the tower at the northwest corner of the church (same hours except closed Fri; €1.50).

Around the square

The old cathedral, **La Seo** (summer Tues–Fri 10am–2pm & 5–7pm, Sat 10am–1pm & 5–7pm, Sun 10am–2pm & 5–7pm; winter Tues–Fri 10am–2pm & 4–6pm, Sat & Sun 10am–1pm & 4–6pm; free), recently reopened after extensive restoration work, stands at the far end of the Plaza del Pilar. The now gleaming exterior is essentially Gothic-Mudéjar, with minor Baroque and Plateresque additions, while to the left of the main entrance is a Mudéjar wall with elaborate geometric patterns. Inside, the superb *retablo mayor* contains some recognizably Teutonic figures executed by the German Renaissance sculptor, Hans of Swabia.

Midway between the two cathedrals stands the sixteenth-century **Lonja**, the old exchange building, a Florentine-influenced structure, with an interior of elegant Ionic columns, open periodically for art exhibitions. Over to the other side of the basilica is the **Torreón de la Zuda**, part of Zaragoza's medieval fortifications, and the remains of **Roman walls**, insignificant ruins but a reminder of the city's Roman past. Zaragoza's name derives from that of Caesar Augustus (César Augusto in the Spanish form).

South of the Plaza del Pilar

A block south of the square, in the impeccably restored Palacio de los Pardo at c/Espoz y Mina 23, the **Museo Camón Aznar** (Tues–Fri 9am–2.15pm & 6–9pm, Sat 10am–2pm & 6–9pm, Sun 11am–2pm; €0.60) houses the private collections of José Camón Aznar, one of the most distinguished scholars of Spanish art. Highlights include a permanent display of most of Goya's prints (the artist was born at nearby Fuendetodos, see p.637). At the far end of the street, which becomes c/Mayor, the church of **La Magdalena** has the finest of Zaragoza's several Mudéjar towers.

You can see more works by Goya at the **Museo de Zaragoza** (Tues–Sat 10am–2pm & 5–8pm, Sun 10am–2pm; free), in the Plaza de los Sitios. Other exhibits span the city's Iberian, Roman and Moorish past. Close by the museum are a pair of interesting churches: **San Miguel**, with a minor *retablo* by Forment and a Mudéjar tower, and **Santa Engracia**, with a splendid Plateresque portal and paleo-Christian sarcophagi in its crypt. Two further Mudéjar towers are to be seen at **San Pablo** (daily 9–10am & 8–8.30pm, holidays 8am–1pm; free), over to the west of Plaza del Pilar, with another *retablo* by Damien Forment, and **San Gil**, near the Plaza de España.

The Aljafería

Moorish Spain was never very unified, and from the tenth to the eleventh century Zaragoza was the centre of an independent dynasty, the Beni Kasim. Their palace, the **Aljafería** (mid-April to mid-Oct Tues–Sat 10am–2pm & 4.30–8pm; mid-Oct to mid-April Tues–Sat 10am–2pm & 4–6.30pm, Sun 10am–2pm; closed Thurs & Fri am all year round; €1.80), was built in the heyday of their rule in the mid-eleventh century, and as such predates the Alhambra in Granada and Sevilla's Alcázar. Much, however, was added later, under twelfth- to fifteenth-century Christian rule, when the palace was adapted and used by the *reconquista* kings of Aragón. Since 1987, the Aragonese parliament has met here – a move which adds prestige to both the building and the institution.

From the original design the foremost relic is a tiny and beautiful **mosque**, adjacent to the entrance. Further on is an original and intricately decorated court, the **Patio de Santa Isabella**. Crossing from here, the **Grand Staircase** (added in 1492) leads to a succession of mainly fourteenth-century rooms, remarkable for their carved *artesonado* ceilings; the most beautiful is in the Throne Room, currently under restoration.

Eating, drinking and nightlife

Zaragoza's **bars** are neatly concentrated in the old quarter, along with many of the best-value **restaurants** – no-nonsense *comedores*, often incorporated into the *fondas* and *pensiones*. As you'd expect in a place of this size, there are some very good, more upmarket restaurants, too, scattered all over the city. The old quarter also has a *zona* of **music bars** and **nightclubs** around c/Cantamina and c/Temple, which get unbelievably lively at the weekends, and another, more alternative, *zona* right behind El Corte Inglés at the bottom of Avenida de la

Independencia. The free weekly listings paper *Insomnia* is available at many bars; alternatively, you can look on the website Ⓦ www.zaragoza.lanetro.com.

Tapas bars and restaurants

Bar Arranque, c/Jordan de Urriés 5. A must for Spanish music-lovers, this tapas bar only plays traditional Spanish music, with the record sleeves used to decorate the walls. There are 27 varieties of tapas and an excellent selection of Aragonese wines too.

Los Borrachos, Paseo Sagasta 64 ☏ 976 275 036. A classic Zaragoza restaurant, just south of the Plaza de Aragón, whose specialities are mostly game dishes. It is very expensive: reckon on €30 and up for a meal with wine.

El Calamar Bravo, c/Moneva 5. Hugely popular and inexpensive stand-up seafood tapas bar with outstanding *calamares* sandwiches.

Casa Amadico, c/Jordán de Urriés 3. A popular *cervecería* with a large range of tapas, especially seafood. Closed Mon & Aug.

Casa Lac, c/Mártires. Reputedly the oldest working restaurant in Spain, this place serves pretty good, reasonably priced Aragonese food in its atmospheric dark wood interior.

Dominó, Plaza Santa Marta. Tapas include a fine selection of local cheeses, hams and *chorizo*, and there's a good range of Aragón wines to accompany them.

Fonda La Peña, c/de Cinegio 3. The *comedor* here, open to all, dishes up particularly vast quantities of simple home cooking with its €6 *menú*.

Mundo Mundial, c/San Lorenzo 5. Counterculture eatery serving world food, from Caribbean to Oriental. Tasty *menús* are €6 and €7.20 and there's a vegetarian *menú* for only €5.10.

Restaurant Savoy, Coso 42, facing c/Alfonso. The best place to treat yourself without splashing out. High-class international cuisine and a decent house wine make the €7.80 *menú* a bargain.

Music bars and nightlife

Bar Azul, c/Pizaro 10. Ideal place to get your finger on the pulse of Zaragoza, with art on the walls and up-to-date DJs: big-beats, drum'n'bass, funk, acid jazz and pop all feature, while Sunday features an ambient and trip-hop chill-out.

La Campana de los Perdidos, c/Prudencio 7. Great atmosphere and regular comedy acts and folk music (Thurs–Sat) in the cellar of this bar. Closed Mon, Tues & August.

Chastón, c/Plaza Ariño 4. Pleasant city centre bar with jazz and blues sounds and a summer *terraza*. Starts getting busy after 11pm.

Oasis, c/Boggiero 28. Grand old concert hall transformed into a traditional cabaret – a kind of Aragonese equivalent of the Parisian *Moulin Rouge*, though locals complain it's losing its magic. Open Sat only; closed June–Sept.

Sala Morrisey, Gran Via 33. Irish pub with bogus olde-worlde interior but great alternative DJs Thurs–Sun and occasional live music.

Listings

Bikes You can rent mountain bikes from the Parque Primo de Ribera, at the south end of Gran Vía (bus #30 or #40 from Plaza de España). From the park, paths lead out into forest land on the edge of the city.

Buses Main station on Paseo María Agustín ☏ 976 229 343; terminal at Avda. de Valencia ☏ 976 357 869. Eurolines Julia, at c/Marceliano Isabel 2 ☏ 976 238 373, have the most extensive international services and depart from c/Hernan Cortes 6.

Car rental Hertz ☏ 976 284 460 is at the train station; Avis is at Paseo Fernando el Católico 9 ☏ 976 357 863; Atesa is at Avda. Valencia 3 ☏ 976 352 805.

Cinema The Filmoteca, Plaza de San Carlos, has an arts programme, including original-language movies.

Emergencies For an ambulance call ☏ 976 358 500.

Hospital Miguel Servet, Plaza Isabel la Católica 1 ☏ 976 355 700.

Flea market *El Rastro* takes place near the football stadium, La Romadera, every Sun and Wed morning for clothes, accessories and household objects. The more eclectic *Mercadillo* is held on Sun mornings outside the bullring.

Laundry If you're staying in or around El Tubo there's a self-service launderette at c/San Vicente Paul 25; by the train station, Lavomatique is the nearest, on c/San Antonio María Claret 5, just off Avda. Pintor Francisco Goya.

Post office The *Correos Central* is at Paseo de la Independencia 33 (Mon–Fri 9am–8pm, Sat 9am–2pm). The poste restante is downstairs at window 4.

Shops The big shopping street is Paseo de la Independencia, south of Plaza de España; it is full of fashion shops, and at the end is a large branch of El Corte Inglés – good for English-language books and everything department store-ish. The news stands outside carry foreign newspapers and magazines.

Skiing If you plan to go skiing in the Pyrenees you

are probably better off buying a package deal from a travel agent in Zaragoza than turning up and going your own way. One of the best agents to try is Marsans, Avda. de la Independencia 18 ☎976 236 965 ℱ976 236 974; there are others on Paseo María Agustín.

Swimming pools There's a pleasant open-air pool in the Parque Primo de Ribera, at the south end of Gran Vía (bus #30 or #40 from Plaza de España). It's open 10.30am–1pm, from mid-June to mid-Sept.

Taxis Radio-Taxi Aragón ☎976 383 838; Radio-Taxi Cooperativi ☎976 751 515; Radio-Taxi Zaragoza ☎976 424 242.

Around Zaragoza

Few tourists spend much time exploring the sights and towns around Zaragoza, and with the Pyrenees just a step to the north, it is perhaps no wonder. However, wine buffs heading south might want to follow the **Ruta de los Vinos** south through **Cariñena**, and for Goya enthusiasts there are murals at the monastery of **Aula Dei** and at **Muel**.

Further afield, northwest of the capital, the **Cinco Villas** stretch for some 90km along the border with Navarra. These are really little more than villages, set in delightful, scarcely visited countryside; their title is owed to Felipe V, who awarded it for their services in the War of the Succession (1701–13). The most interesting of the five is the northernmost "town", **Sos del Rey Católico**, on the C127 to Pamplona.

The Cartuja de Aula Dei

At the **Cartuja de Aula Dei**, 12km north of Zaragoza, Goya painted a series of eleven murals depicting the lives of Christ and the Virgin in 1774. They suffered badly after the Napoleonic suppression, when the buildings were more or less abandoned, but subsequent repainting and restoration have revealed enough to show the cycle to be one of the artist's early masterpieces. The monastery is today a strict Carthusian community and visits are currently only possible on the last Saturday of the month by prior arrangement (☎976 714 934). However, this situation may change in the future and it's worth phoning to check, or ask at the turismo in Zaragoza.

To reach Aula Dei, take the Montañana road out of the city, along the east bank of the Río Gallego. The Agreda bus to San Mateo de Gallego runs past the monastery.

The wine route and Goya trail

There are vineyards all over Aragón, but the best wines – strong, throaty reds and good whites – come from the region to the south of Zaragoza, whose towns and villages are accessible from both the road and rail line down to Teruel. The tourist authorities have marked out a **Ruta del Vino** through the area; an alternative route could take you on a brief **Goya trail**, to see further frescoes and his birthplace.

Muel

MUEL marks the northernmost point of the region and was once a renowned pottery centre. It has seen much better days, however, and few trains stop here any more. The town's interest lies in a Roman fountain and a hermitage, **La Ermida de Nuestra Señora del Fuente**, which has some early (1771) frescoes of saints by Goya. The artist, who became court painter to Carlos IV, was in fact born at the village of **FUENDETODOS**, 24km southeast, where a little **Casa Museo** has been done up with period furnishings (Tues–Sun 11am–2pm & 4–7pm; €1.80).

Cariñena

Continuing south from Muel, **CARIÑENA** is a larger, rather ramshackle old town, with a clutch of **wine bodegas**. Out on the main road behind the church (cross the bridge onto the *carretera* and turn left), the Bodega Morte (daily 8am–8pm; free) welcomes visitors to sample its wines, and buy bottles, or fill their own for next to nothing from the huge barrels. If you want **to stay** – and Cariñena, with its open-air swimming pool, is a quiet alternative to Zaragoza – you'll find good rooms at the *Hostal Iliturgis* on the Plaza Ramón, near the church (☎976 620 492; ❸), and *Hotel Cariñena* (☎976 620 837; ❹), on the main Zaragoza road, near the wine *bodegas*. The town also has a Saturday **market**.

Sos del Rey Católico and the Cinco Villas

Moving north from Zaragoza, the **Cinco Villas** comprise **Tauste**, **Ejea de los Caballeros**, **Sádaba**, **Uncastillo** and **Sos del Rey Católico**. They make a pleasant rambling approach to the Pyrenees (the road past Sos continues to Roncal in Navarra) or to Pamplona, though you really need transport to explore more than one of them. Only one bus a day makes it up from Zaragoza to Sos.

Zaragoza to Sos

TAUSTE, closest of the "towns" to Zaragoza, has an interesting parish church built in the Mudéjar style – and accommodation at the central *Hostal Casa Pepe*, c/Santa Clara 7 (☎976 855 832; ❸), and *Hospedaje Nuestra Señora de Sancho Abarca*, c/Sierra de la Virgen (☎976 863 011; ❸ or dorm bed ❶).

Nearby **EJEA DE LOS CABALLEROS** retains elements of Romanesque architecture in its churches, and has a handful of places to stay, including *Fonda Goya*, Plaza Goya 2 (☎976 661 006; ❷), and *Hostal Aragón*, c/Media Villa 21 (☎976 660 630; ❸), which has simple rooms without bath. For a bit more comfort, try *Hostal Cuatro Esquinas*, c/Salvador 4 (☎976 661 003; ❺).

SÁDABA boasts an impressive medieval castle, thirteenth century in origin, as well as the remains of an early synagogue, but no accommodation. **UNCASTILLO**, on a minor road to Sos, through the Sierra de Santo Domingo, also has a castle, as its name suggests, this time dating from the twelfth century, and the remains of an aqueduct. Accommodation is limited to one option, the attractive but expensive *Equestre*, c/Mediavilla 71 (☎976 679 481; ❻), which also has a very good – though fairly pricey – restaurant.

Sos del Rey Católico

SOS DEL REY CATÓLICO is the most interesting town of the five and an excellent place to relax, especially if you're on your way to or from Navarra. The town derives its name from Fernando II, El Rey Católico, born here in 1452 and as powerful a local-boy-made-good as any Aragonese town could hope for. The narrow cobbled streets, like so many in Aragón, are packed with marvellously grand mansions, including the **Palacio de Sada** where Fernando is reputed to have been born, and there's an unusually early parish **church**, with a curious crypt dedicated to the Virgen del Pilar. These are the real attractions of the place, but you could wander up, too, towards the **Castillo de la**

Peña Fernando for lovely views over the village's terracotta rooftops and surrounding countryside, and into the **ayuntamiento**, which displays – as ever – interesting titbits of information about local government in a town whose population scarcely tops a thousand.

There are three **places to stay**: the *Fonda Fernandina*, c/Emilio Alfaro (☎948 888 120; ❷), which is great value and serves inexpensive meals; the modern *Hostal Las Coronas*, opposite the *ayuntamiento* (☎948 888 408; ❺); and the superb *parador* (☎ & ℻948 888 011, ✉sos@parador.es; ❽), whose rooms give sweeping panoramic views across the hills.

Tarazona and around

The Aragonese plains are dotted with reminders of the Moorish occupation, and nowhere more so than **TARAZONA**, which the local tourist authorities promote as "La Ciudad Mudéjar" and even "the Aragonese Toledo". The latter is a bit of an overstatement but Tarazona is a fine-looking place, and if you're en route to Soria or Burgos, it makes a good place to break the journey. Don't miss out, either, on the superb Cistercian monastery of **Veruela**, 15km southeast, off the N122 to Zaragoza.

The Town

It is the **Barrios Altos**, the old "upper quarters" of Tarazona, that are the main attraction here. They stand on a hilly site, overlooking the river, with medieval houses and mansions lining the *callejas* and *pasadizos* – the lanes and alleyways.

At the heart of the quarter, as ever, is a Plaza de España, which is flanked by a truly magnificent **ayuntamiento**, a sixteenth-century town hall, with a facade of coats of arms, sculpted heads and figures in high relief. A one-foot-high frieze, representing the capture of Granada, runs the length of the building. From here, a *ruta turística* directs you up to the church of **Santa Magdalena**, whose Mudéjar tower dominates the town. The *mirador* (viewpoint) here gives a good view of the town, and especially the eighteenth-century **Plaza de Toros** – a circular terrace of houses, with balconies (now filled in) from which spectators could view the *corrida*. Further uphill lies another church, **La Concepción**, again with a slender brick tower.

In the lower town, the main sight is the **Catedral**, built mainly in the fourteenth and fifteenth centuries. It is a typical example of the decorative use of brick in the Gothic-Mudéjar style, with a dome built to the same design as that of the old cathedral in Zaragoza. The interior has been closed for restoration for the last couple of decades, but the Mudéjar inner **cloisters** (July & Aug only: Sat & Sun 10am–1pm; free) have been opened up to the public again, and are well worth a look.

Practicalities

The **turismo**, next door to the cathedral at c/de la Iglesia 5 (Mon–Fri 9am–1.30pm & 4.30–7pm, Sat & Sun 10am–1.30pm & 4.30–6pm; ☎ & ℻976 640 074), will arrange a guided tour of the town if you give them some notice (€3–6; minimum of 5 people). Going your own way, take a look at the **town plan**, showing the principal sights, outside the nearby church of San Francisco.

There are three **accommodation** choices: *Hostal María Cristina*, Ctra de Castilla 3 (☎976 640 084; ❷), on the Soria road, across from the municipal swimming pool; *Hotel Brujas de Becquer*, Ctra de Zaragoza (℡976 640 404, ℱ976 640 198, ⓦwww.brujas.puizt.com; ❺), just out of town on the Zaragoza road; and the upmarket *Hotel Ituri-Asso* (℡976 199 166, ℱ976 199 168; ❼), down by the river near the stone bridge. The *Galeón*, in the lower town at Avda. La Paz 1, is a mid-priced **restaurant**, with good traditional food and a *menú* for €9.

Veruela

El Monasterio de Veruela (Tues–Sun: summer 10am–2pm & 4–7pm; winter 10am–1pm & 3–6pm; €1.80), isolated in a fold of the hills and standing within a massively fortified perimeter, is one of Spain's greatest religious houses. It makes an easy excursion from Tarazona, or a break in the journey to Zaragoza: if you are travelling by bus, you need to get off at **Vera de Moncayo** and then walk uphill for 3km. The monastery is uninhabited now but the great church, built in the severe twelfth-century transitional style of the Carthusians, is kept open. The monastery admission ticket also gives access to the fourteenth-century cloisters and convent buildings, as well as a small and not terribly interesting **Museo del Vino** that sits rather uneasily in the monastic grounds.

Calatayud, Piedra and Daroca

Like Tarazona, **Calatayud** is a town of Moorish foundation, with some stunning Mudéjar towers, and again it offers access to a Cistercian monastery, **Piedra**, set in lush parkland. The town itself, however, is an uninviting, impoverished place, where you wouldn't choose to be stranded, especially with the delightful old town of **Daroca** so close, on the train line and main road southeast to Teruel.

Calatayud

If you are passing, it's worth climbing up to the old upper town of **CALATAYUD**, where amid a maze of alleys are the churches of **San Andrés** and **Santa María**, both of which have ornate Mudéjar towers, reminiscent of Moroccan minarets. Santa María, the collegiate church, also has a beautifully decorative Plateresque doorway, while **San Juan**, towards the river, has frescoes attributed to the young Goya.

Ruins of the Moorish **castle** survive, too, on high ground at the opposite end of town from the train station. The views from here are outstanding, though for a closer view of the towers you'd do best to climb the hill to the hermitage in the centre of the old town.

If you have to **stay** in Calatayud, there are a couple of *fondas* immediately across the square from the train station, the most salubrious being *Fonda Los Ángeles* (℡976 881 133; ❸). In the centre you've got a choice between the recently renovated *Fonda El Comercio* on c/Dato 33 (℡976 881 115; ❸), and the considerably more comfortable *Hotel Fornos*, Paseo Cortes de Aragón 5 (℡976 881 300, ℱ976 883 147; ❺). Check out the website ⓦwww.calatayud .org for more information on the town.

El Monasterio de Piedra

El Monasterio de Piedra – "The Stone Monastery" – lies 20km south of Calatayud, 4km from the village of **NUÉVALOS**. The monastic buildings, once part of a grand Cistercian complex, are a ruin, but they stand amid park-like gardens (daily 9am–7pm; €6), which seem all the more gorgeous in this otherwise harsh, dry landscape.

There are two **routes** through the park. The blue arrows lead around the cloister and shell of the church to the twelfth-century **Torre del Homenaje**, whose *mirador* gives a panoramic view over the park. The red ones take you past a series of romantically labelled waterfalls, grottoes and lakes. If there are crowds, it will be easy enough to escape them, though be warned that you're not allowed to take food into the park; if you've brought a picnic you'll have to eat it before you enter the grounds.

There are two **places to stay** up here; the luxurious *Hotel Monasterio de Piedra*, near the park entrance (☎976 849 011, ⊕976 849 054, ⓦ www.sta.es/monasstpiedra; ❼) and, a little further down the road, the well-equipped and reasonably priced *Hotel Las Truchas* (☎976 849 040, ⊕976 849 137, ⓦ www.encomix.es/users/trucha; ❹), with its own pool, tennis courts and gym. Down in the village, the *Hotel Río Piedra*, at the foot of the road up to the monastery (☎976 849 007, ⊕976 849 087; ❺, has a range of rooms, some with bath. Alternatively, there is a very well-equipped **campsite**, *Lago Park Camping* (☎976 849 038; April–Sept), 3km from Nuévalos (in the other direction from the monastery) on a promontory by a reservoir. There are good fishing opportunities here, if you're an enthusiast.

Just one **bus** daily runs from Zaragoza (from c/Almagro 18) to Nuévalos, leaving at 9am and returning at 7.30pm; note that from November to June, the bus only runs on Tuesdays and Thursdays and at weekends. If you have your own transport, the **roads south** to Cuenca or Albarracín (see p.644) are enjoyable routes.

Daroca

DAROCA, southeast of Calatayud, is a lovely old place, set within an impressive run of **walls** that comprise no fewer than 114 towers and enclose an area far greater than that needed by the present population of 2300. The last major restoration of the walls was in the fifteenth century, but today, though largely in ruins, they are still magnificent.

You enter the town through its original gates, the **Puerta Alta** or stout **Puerta Baja**, the latter endowed with a gallery of arches and decorated with the coat of arms of Carlos I. Within, the Calle Mayor runs between the two gates, past ancient streets dotted with Romanesque, Gothic and Mudéjar churches. The principal church, the **Colegiata de Santa María**, is sixteenth-century Renaissance and has a small museum. But the appeal of Daroca lies more in the whole ensemble rather than any specific monuments.

There are two choices of **accommodation**, the nicer being the fairly central *Hostal-Residencia Agiria*, Carretera Sagunto–Burgos (☎976 800 731; ❹). The *Hostal Legido* (☎976 800 190; ❺) is a characterless modern fallback on the main road outside town. Daroca is on the Calatayud–Teruel **train line**, though the station is 2km outside town and **buses** are easier. There are a couple of daily services each to and from Calatayud, Teruel and Cariñena/Zaragoza.

Teruel

The little provincial capital of **TERUEL** is basically a market town, catering for its remote and sparsely populated rural hinterlands. It is hard to overestimate how much of a backwater this corner of Aragón is: a survey not so long ago found that it was the only part of Spain where deaths outnumbered births. The land is very harsh, and very high, with the coldest winters in the country. If you like back-of-beyond villages, with medieval sights that haven't been prettified, it is a region that merits a fair bit of exploring.

Arrival and information

Teruel doesn't feel quite like a city, despite its capital status, and the separation of the old town from the new reinforces this. Nonetheless, it has most facilities you might need, **trains** from Zaragoza and Valencia, and **buses** from most destinations in the province. The train and bus stations are both close to the city

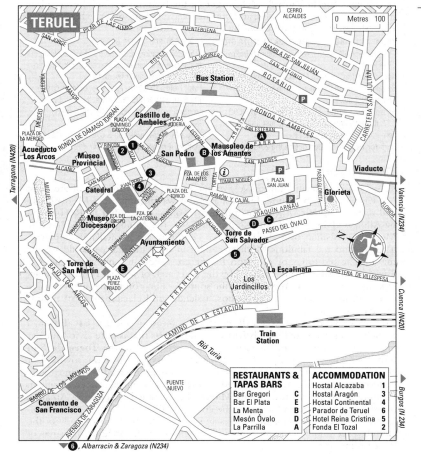

RESTAURANTS & TAPAS BARS

Bar Gregori	C
Bar El Plata	E
La Menta	B
Mesón Óvalo	D
La Parrilla	A

ACCOMMODATION

Hostal Alcazaba	1
Hostal Aragón	3
Hostal Continental	4
Parador de Teruel	6
Hotel Reina Cristina	5
Fonda El Tozal	2

6, Albarracín & Zaragoza (N234)

centre: from the former, cross the ring road and walk north up c/Nueva, and from the latter walk north a short way up the ring road, taking the first left to Plaza Judería. There are no fewer than thirteen bus companies in Teruel, many serving the same destinations, so check the timetables in the windows before buying a ticket on departure, as some buses are considerably slower than others.

You're unlikely to want to stray out of the old quarter, and finding your way around it isn't too difficult, thanks to its size. The city's focal point is Plaza del Torico (shown as Plaza Carlos Castel on some maps); just east of here, at c/Tomás Nogués 1, is the **turismo** (July–Sept Mon–Fri 9am–2pm & 5–7.30pm, Sat 9am–1pm, Sun 10am–2pm & 5–7.30pm; Oct–June Mon–Fri 9am–2.30pm & 5–7.30pm, Sat 9am–7.30pm; ☏978 602 279, ⓦwww.teruel .com or www.teruel.net). To connect to the **internet**, head to *La Red*, c/San Andrés 13 (daily 5–10pm; €3 per hour).

Accommodation

Accommodation is rarely a problem, though be warned that if you're here for the raucous **Fiesta Vaquilla del Ángel** (at the beginning of July) every place in town will be booked solid, and you may have to join other exhausted revellers sleeping in the park down by the train station.

Hostal Alcazaba, c/Joaquin Costa 34 ☏978 610 761. Immaculate rooms, with a restaurant below. ❹–❺

Hostal Aragón, c/Santa María 4 ☏978 601 387. Small but comfortable rooms, with some triples and quadruples. ❹

Hostal Continental, c/Juan Pérez 9 ☏978 602 317. If *Hostal Aragón* is full, this is just around the corner, with similar rooms. ❸

Parador de Teruel, 2km out on the Zaragoza road ☏978 601 800, ⓕ978 608 612, ⒺTeruel@parador.es. This is a modern building but its position is inspired, on a wooded hillside overlooking the town and towers. ❽

Hotel Reina Cristina, Paseo del Óvalo 1 ☏978 606 860, ⓕ978 605 363. Attractive hotel with an excellent restaurant, located by the Torre del Salvador. ❾

Fonda El Tozal, c/Rincón 5 ☏978 601 022. A spotless if rather chilly old *fonda*. ❸

The Town

Teruel is a likeable and impressively monumental place, with some of the finest Mudéjar work to be found. Like Zaragoza, it was an important Moorish city and retained significant Muslim and Jewish communities after its Reconquest by Alfonso II in 1171. Approaching the town, the Mudéjar towers, built by Moorish craftsmen over the next three centuries, are immediately apparent. These – and the fabulous Mudéjar ceiling in the cathedral – should not be missed. The old town, or **el casco histórico**, stands on a hill above the Río Turia: a confusing layout, enclosed by the odd patch of wall, and with a viaduct linking it to the modern quarter to the south. Leading off to the north is a sixteenth-century aqueduct, **Los Arcos**, a slender and elegant piece of monumental engineering.

If you arrive by train, you will see straight ahead of you **La Escalinata**, a flight of steps decorated with bricks, tiles and turrets that is pure civic Mudéjar in style. From the top of the steps c/El Salvador leads to the **Torre de San Salvador** (daily 11am–2pm & 5–8pm; €1.50), the finest of the town's four Mudéjar towers, and the only one you can go up. It's covered with intricately patterned and proportioned coloured tiles, to stunning effect, echoed closely in its more modest sister tower, **San Martín**, best reached via c/de los Amantes (third left off c/El Salvador just at the corner of Plaza del Torico). A common feature of all the towers is that they stand separate from the main body of the church, a technique most probably influenced by the freestanding minarets of the Muslim world.

El Rincón de Ademuz, due south of Teruel, is a strange little region: a Valencian province enclosed within Aragonese territory. It is a very remote corner of Spain, with a bleak kind of grandeur, and scarcely a tourist from one year to the next.

The place to head for – and if you are bussing it, the only realistic place to get to from Teruel – is **ADEMUZ** itself, without doubt Spain's tiniest and least significant provincial capital. Strung along a craggy hill at the confluence of two long rivers, this could make a beautiful base for walking, and there's a fascination just in wandering the streets with their dark stone cottages and occasional Baroque towers. If you want to stay, there's a single, smart *hostal*, *Casa Domingo* (☎978 782 030, ☎978 782 056; ❹), which also serves an €8.50 *menú*.

For energetic trekking, Torre Baja lies to the north along the Río Turia, and beyond it the beautiful village of Castielfabib. The most interesting of these little Ademuz hamlets, Puebla de San Miguel, lies to the east, in the Sierra Tortajada, most easily accessible by road from Valencia, but also from a small route just out of Ademuz in the Teruel direction, east over the Río Turia bridge and signposted to Sabina, Sesga and Mas del Olmo.

The **Catedral** (daily 11am–2pm & 4–8pm; €1.80), built in the twelfth century, but gracefully adapted over subsequent years, boasts another fine Mudéjar tower, incorporating Romanesque windows, and a lantern that combines Renaissance and Mudéjar features. The interior follows a more standard Gothic-Mudéjar pattern and at first sight seems unremarkable, save for its brilliant Renaissance *retablo*. Climb the stairs by the door, however, and put money in the illuminations box, and the fabulous **artesonado ceiling** is revealed. This was completed between 1260 and 1314 by Moorish craftsmen, in a gorgeous and fascinating mix of geometric Islamic motifs and medieval painting of courtly life.

Standing next to the cathedral, the sixteenth-century Palacio Episcopal houses the **Museo Diocesano** (Mon–Sat 10am–2pm; €0.90). Inside, look out for *Calvario*, a beautiful woodcarving of Jesus (whose arms are missing), St John and the Virgin Mary, carved in the fifteenth century but for many years hidden behind a wall in a church in Sarrón, where it was discovered in 1946. Another highlight is the *Arbol de la Vida*, a striking seventeenth-century ivory carving of Christ.

A couple of blocks from the museum is Plaza del Torico (aka Plaza Carlos Castell), the centre of the old quarter, which is flanked by a trio of *modernista* houses. Just beyond here, in another attractive square, is the church of **San Pedro**, once again endowed with a Mudéjar tower. Its fame, however, relates to the adjacent **Mausoleo de los Amantes** (daily 10am–2pm & 5–7.30pm; €0.60), a chapel containing the alabaster tomb of the *Lovers of Teruel*, Isabel de Segura and Juan Diego Martínez de Marcilla. This pair's thirteenth-century tale of thwarted love is a legend throughout Spain. The story goes that Diego, ordered by his lover's family to go away and prove himself worthy, left Teruel for five years, returning only to find that Isabel was to be married that same day. He asked for a last kiss, was refused, and expired, heartbroken; Isabel, not to be outdone, arranged his funeral at San Pedro, kissed the corpse, and died in its arms. The lovers' (reputed) bodies were exhumed in 1955 and now lie illuminated for all to see; it is a macabre and popular pilgrimage for newlyweds.

Lastly, if you intend heading out to the Teruel countryside, a visit to the **Museo Provincial** (Tues–Fri 10am–2pm & 4–7pm, Sat & Sun 10am–2pm; free), close by the cathedral, could be worthwhile. Its range of exhibits include objects of local folklore and traditional rural life.

Eating and drinking

The main *zona* for **food and drink** in Teruel is at the eastern side of the old quarter, principally Plaza Judería, c/Bartolomé Esteban, c/Abadía and c/San Esteban (the first street into the old town from the bus station). The area east of the Mausoleo de los Amantes has a few **bars**, but don't expect much. One laid-back place is *Lennon*, c/San Andres 23, which has occasional live music.

Bar Gregori, Paseo Ovalo, 6. This friendly tapas bar is the locals' choice, complete with sheep's head on the menu. Outside tables, good wine, and sangria for €4.05 a litre all make it a pleasant place to pass the evening.

Bar El Plata, c/Amantes 7. Tapas bar with lots of local treats. Located on the street leading from the Plaza del Torico to the *ayuntamiento*.

La Menta, c/Bartolomé Esteban – behind the Mausoleo de los Amantes. The city's top restaurant

– pricey, with dishes €7.20 and up, but a good choice for a splurge in southern Aragón. Closed Sun, last week of July & first 2 weeks of Aug.

Mesón Óvalo, Paseo del Óvalo 2. Very popular *mesón* with quality cooking (the trout dishes are excellent) and a pretty-good-value €8.40 *menú*. Closed Mon & Jan 8–28.

La Parrilla, c/San Esteban 2. Good-value grill restaurant, with traditional interior, where the meat is flame-grilled on a wood fire.

Albarracín

ALBARRACÍN, 37km west of Teruel, is one of the more accessible targets in rural southern Aragón – and one of the most picturesque towns in the province, poised above the Río Guadalaviar and retaining, virtually intact, its medieval streets and tall, balconied houses. There's a historical curiosity here, too, in that from 1165 to 1333 the town formed the centre of a small independent state, the kingdom of the Azagras.

Over the last few years a small trickle of tourism has begun, and some of the houses have been prettified a bit too much. But Albarracín's dark, enclosed lanes and those buildings that remain unrestored, with their splendid coats of arms, still make for an intriguing wander – reminders of lost and now inexplicably prosperous eras. Approaching from Teruel, you may imagine that you're about to come upon a large town, for the **medieval walls** swoop back over the hillside – protecting, with the loop of the river, a far greater area than the extent of the town, past or present.

The town follows the line of a ridge, above the river, and breaks into two main parts. On the Teruel side, you enter through a gate known as El Túnel, and shortly reach the **Plaza Mayor** and **ayuntamiento**. Follow the c/de Santiago, up towards the walls, and you reach Santiago church and a gateway, the Portal del Molina. If you take instead the c/de la Catedral, a quiet rural lane, you reach a small square (cars can access this from the other side) with the **Catedral** – a medieval building remodelled in the sixteenth and eighteenth centuries – and Palacio Episcopal.

Practicalities

If you want to stay – and you'll have to if you arrive on the daily bus from Teruel – there is a cluster of **hostales and hotels** at the foot of the hill, where the buses stop. These are all pleasant, housed in converted mansions, but tend to be quite pricey. Choices include the *Hotel El Gallo* (☎978 710 032; ❺), the *Hostal Olimpia* (☎978 710 083; ❸) and the *Hostal los Palacios* (☎978 700 307, ℉978 700 358; ❹). There's also a **youth hostel**, the *Albergue Juventud Rosa Bríos* (☎978 710 005; ❶), just past the cathedral at c/Santa María 5. The local

fiesta takes place from September 8 to 17.

Moving on from Albarracín, if you have transport, there's a fabulous route west to Cuenca through beautiful country, by way of **Frías de Albarracín** and the **source of the Río Tajo** (see p.205).

El Maestrazgo

The mountains of **El Maestrazgo**, northeast of Teruel, are an area of great variety and striking, often wild, beauty, with their severe peaks, deep gorges and lush meadows. Tourism isn't a presence here, though you will find at least one simple *fonda* in most of the tiny, scattered villages. The places below are just a small selection and are geared to the more accessible; armed with a decent map, your own transport, or the will to do some walking, the choice is very much your own.

Inevitably **buses** are infrequent (often their main purpose is to deliver the mail) but most villages are connected once a day, with each other and/or Teruel; an alarm clock is useful since they have a nasty habit of leaving before dawn. The main approaches to the region are from Teruel (daily bus to Cantavieja and Villafranca del Cid), or from Morellá in the province of Castellón (see "Valencia" chapter on p.896).

Southern Maestrazgo

Approaching the Maestrazgo from Teruel, you take a minor road off the N420, just a kilometre or so out of town. This passes **Cedrillas**, with its conspicuous, ridge-top castle ruin, and then starts climbing into the hills, over a sequence of *puertos* – gates, or passes. At the **Puerto de Villaroya** (1655m) you cross the highest point of the Maestrazgo, a hair-raising trip on the bus which twists its way down across the valleys, following dried-up rivers, and thundering over narrow, crumbling stone bridges. The first village of any size beyond here is **Cantavieja**.

Cantavieja and El Cid country

CANTAVIEJA, dramatically situated by the edge of an escarpment, at an altitude of 1300m, is a little livelier and larger than most Maestrazgo villages, though its population is still under a thousand. The whitewashed and porticoed **Plaza Mayor** here is typical of the region, and the escutcheoned *ayuntamiento* bears a Latin inscription with suitably lofty sentiments: "This House hates wrongdoing, loves peace, punishes crimes, upholds the laws and honours the upright." It is a useful base for exploring – or walking in – the region, with a **turismo** (June–Sept daily 11am–2pm & 5–8pm; ☎978 185 001), an exceptionally good-value **hotel**, the *Balfagón Alto Maestrazgo* (☎ & ⓕ964 185 076, ⓔmabalgas@arrakis.es; ⓺) near the municipal swimming pool, and a reasonable *fonda*, the *Julián* (☎964 185 005; ❷). There's also an unexpectedly stylish **restaurant**, *Buj* (closed Feb), run by a woman and her two daughters. The food at the *Balfagón* is also good, and it has a €9 *menú*.

MIRAMBEL, 15km northeast of Cantavieja and walkable in about four hours, has a population of a mere 145 and preserves a very ancient atmosphere, with its walls, gateways and stone houses. The village was temporarily thrown into a whirl of excitement when Ken Loach and his team filmed *Land and Freedom* here some years ago, but these days it's back to its usual, sleepy self. The main **bar** offers **accommodation** (though it has no sign to indicate it) and a good atmosphere; there is also an excellent little *fonda*, the *Guimera* (☎964 178 269, ⓕ964 178 293; ❸), with en-suite rooms at bargain rates.

A similar distance to the southeast of Cantavieja, and another fine walk along a rough country road, is **LA IGLESUELA DEL CID**. The village's name bears witness to the exploits of El Cid Campeador, who came charging through the Maestrazgo in his fight against the Infidel. Its ochre-red, dry-stone walls, ubiquitous coats of arms and stream flowing right through the centre are striking enough in this remote countryside, though these features aside, it's a shabby sort of place. There is, however, a characterful **fonda**, *Casa Amada* (☎ & ⓕ964 443 373; ❸), which offers good and substantial country cooking, and a small summer-only **turismo** inside the *ayuntamiento* (summer Tues–Sun 11am–2pm & 4–8pm; winter Mon–Fri 10am–2pm; ☎964 443 325).

Continuing east for 10km brings you to **VILLAFRANCA DEL CID**, across the border in Castellón Province – and at the end of the bus route from either Teruel or Morella. Straddling the hillside, this is a lively, attractive village, and with a population of 3000 it's larger than most places around here. The only **place to stay** in the centre is the *Hostal Prismark*, c/Sagrado Corazón de Jesús (☎964 440 247; ❸), which has good-value en-suite rooms; *L'Om de Llosar* (☎964 441 325; ❺), 2km out of town by a little *ermita*, is more comfortable. If you decide to turn around from here, the **bus** to Teruel departs at 5.45am (Mon–Fri only), passing through La Inglesuela del Cid at 6am.

Northwest from Cantavieja

Another dramatic, almost Alpine route is in store if you head northwest from Cantavieja, past Cañada de Benatanduz, to **VILLARLUENGO**, a beautiful village of ancient houses stacked on a terraced hillside. Just beyond here, you cross a pass, and the Río Pitarque, with a side valley leading to a hamlet of the same name. Here, by the riverside, in isolated and magnificent countryside, is the stylish *Hostal de la Trucha* (☎978 773 008, ⓕ978 773 100; ❼), with a **restaurant** which serves trout caught a few yards away. Back in Villarluengo, *Fonda Villarluengo*, on Plaza Carlos Castell (☎978 773 014; ❷), and *Pensión Josefina*, on c/La Fuente (☎978 773 151; ❸), are rather more affordable. Over another higher pass, the Puerto de Majalinos (1450m), the road drops down to the small village of Ejulve, and just a few more kilometres north you reach the N420 between Montalbán and Alcañiz.

The **bus** runs this way once a day from Cantavieja, taking nearly four hours to cover the ninety-kilometre journey to **Alcorisa** on the N420.

Northern Maestrazgo: Alcañiz and Valderrobres

The northern limits of the Maestrazgo edge into Tarragona Province in Catalunya, and can be approached from Tarragona/Gandesa, or from Zaragoza through Alcañiz. This town also lies at the end of the N420, east of Alcorisa.

Alcañiz

The castle-topped town of **ALCAÑIZ** is quite a sight as you approach, though close up it's a bit of a disappointment. The **Castillo** has been unsympathetically modernized as the *Parador de Alcañiz* (☎978 830 400, ⓕ978 830 366, ⓔalcañiz@ parador.es; ❾), and the best thing about the place is the panorama from its heights. These allow a grand bird's-eye view of the huge Baroque church of **Santa María** which dominates the town below.

The town (and this is a big place in comparison to the Maestrazgo villages, with a population of around 12,000) gives access by bus to Valderrobres (see below) and, by bus or rail, east to Zaragoza and west to the coast at Tortosa or Viñaros via Morella. You probably won't need or want **to stay** but – in addition to the *parador* – there are several cheapish options; try the comfortable *Guadalupe* (☎978 830 750, ℗978 833 233; ❺), on Plaza España near the *castillo* or, for those on a tight budget, the basic *Pensión Santo Domingo* on Plaza Santo Domingo (☎978 831 026; ❷).

Valderrobres

VALDERROBRES is one of the Maestrazgo's most accessible and attractive towns. It stands 36km from Alcañiz, near the border with Catalunya and astride the Río Matarrana, whose crystal waters teem with trout. The old quarter is crowned by a **castle–palace** (July & Aug Tues–Sun 11am–1pm & 5–8pm; Sept–June Sat & Sun 11am–1pm & 4–6pm; €0.90), once occupied by the kings of Aragón, and a Gothic parish church – **Santa María** – which has a fine rose window. In the Plaza Mayor, the unassuming seventeenth-century **ayuntamiento** was considered so characteristic of the region that it was reproduced in Barcelona's *Poble Espanyol* (see p.710) in 1929.

Places to stay include the *Fonda La Plaza* (☎978 850 106; ❹), opposite the *ayuntamiento*, which has an excellent *comedor*, and the newly refurbished *Hostal Querol* (☎ & ℗978 850 192; ❹), across the river in a fourteenth-century inn, which also offers great cooking, and has basic, cheap rooms on the first floor and smart, more expensive, en-suite ones on the second. There's also a tiny *casa rural* at c/Pilar 35, up by the castle (☎978 854 056; ❸). If all else fails the **turismo**, on Plaza España (July & Aug Tues–Fri 10.30am–1pm & 4.30–8pm; Sept–June Tues–Fri 10am–2pm, Sat & Sun 10.30am–1pm & 4.30–7pm; ☎978 850 001), can supply you with a list of alternatives.

The Aragonese Pyrenees

Aragón has the highest and best stretch of the **Pyrenees** on the Spanish side: a fabulous region offering everything from casual day-walks in the high valleys to long-distance treks across the mountains. There are numerous trails, marked out by the Aragón mountain club as either **GR** (*grande recorrido* – long-haul) or **PR** (*pequeño recorrido* – short-haul) trails.

The most popular jumping-off point for the mountains is **Jaca**, an attractive town in its own right, with an important cathedral. From here, most walkers head to the **Parque Nacional de Ordesa** – the most spectacular alpine landscape, with its canyons and waterfall valleys. To the east of Jaca, **Aínsa**, with its picturesque old town, is another pleasant gateway to the mountains, and, further east, **Benasque** offers access to the two loftiest Pyrenean peaks, Aneto (3404m) and Posets (3371m), as well as to the bluff-top cathedral-village of **Roda de Isábena**. There's lighter hiking northwest of Jaca in the valleys of **Ansó** and **Echo**, and in winter there's also **skiing** at the resorts of (from west to east) Astún-Candanchú, Formigal, Panticosa and Cerler; they are reasonably inexpensive and well equipped.

There are a number of possible **routes into the region**. For Jaca and Ordesa, the most obvious way is via **Huesca**, the provincial capital; this is no great shakes in itself but is convenient for visiting the great castle of **Loarre**, the sugarloaf **Los Mallos de Riglos** mountains or the increasingly popular sub-range of the **Sierra de Guara**, whose gorges are among the country's most amazing landscapes. If you're coming from Catalunya (and aiming for Benasque or Aínsa), you could follow a route via **Fraga** and **Barbastro**.

You can **travel by rail** through Huesca, Jaca and up to the Spanish border at Canfranc – though there, sadly, the trains stop. Rail-buses, however, continue **into France** through the new **Somport tunnel**, while drivers can also cross over the pass to the east, the **Puerto del Portalet** or, over towards Benasque, go through the **Bielsa tunnel**. All of these are open year-round, except during periods of exceptionally heavy snow.

From the east: Fraga, Monzón and Barbastro

If you're coming to the Pyrenees from Catalunya, it's possible to approach either Huesca or Benasque via **Monzón** and **Barbastro**; both have regular bus connections with Lleida (Lérida), and interesting sights. If you have time and your own transport, you could approach more slowly from Lleida, following a little-used minor route along the Río Cinca valley from **Fraga**, a pleasant medieval town.

Fraga

It's worth taking a morning to visit **FRAGA**, 25km from Lleida, and just off the *autopista* to Zaragoza. An array of fine brick buildings helps maintain the medieval air of the old town, perched high over the Río Cinca. If you're arriving by bus, cross back over the river from the bus station and strike uphill through the steep and convoluted streets of the old town. The tower of the twelfth-century (restored and restyled) church of San Pedro keeps disappearing and reappearing until you reach a tiny square, dominated entirely by the church. If you want to stay, there are central **rooms** at *Hostal Flavia*, Paseo Barrón 13 (℡974 471 540; ❹), and the more comfortable *Hostal Trébol*, Avda. de Aragón 9 (℡974 471 533; ❹).

North of Fraga, a tiny road follows the east bank of the Río Cinca to Monzón, starting out immediately below Fraga's old town. It is a lovely route: great steppes fall away to the west beyond the river while coarse vegetation and red clay cliffs flank the road. To follow it, however, you will need your own transport. If you don't have transport, Fraga is still a good stop. It has **bus** connections with Lleida (4 daily) and Huesca (leaving Mon–Sat at 6.45am).

Monzón

MONZÓN, 50km from Fraga, stands in a triangle between the rivers Cinca and Sosa (the latter now dry), a strategic position that explains its **Templar castle**, forgotten on the crumbling rock above. Originally a ninth-century Moorish fort, it was later endowed to the Templars by Ramón Berenguer IV and was the residence of Jaime I (king of Aragon 1213–76) in his youth. The ruins (summer only Tues–Sun 11am–1pm & 5–8pm) include a tenth-century

Moorish tower and a group of Romanesque buildings, with a small chapel.

The town below is reasonably substantial – with a population of 15,000 – and has old and (rather grim) new quarters, the former with many fine Aragonese mansions and a Romanesque *colegiata*. Most of the budget **accommodation** is by the train station; try the *Pensión Nueva* at Plaza Cervantes 2 (℡974 400 984; **②**). More comfortable places to stay include the en-suite Hostal Bellomonte, Avda Lérida 87 (℡974 402 044; **③**), and the two-star *Hotel Vianetto*, Avda. Lérida 25 (℡974 401 900, ℗974 404 540, ₩www.mlonzon.net /vianetto; **⑤**), which has an excellent restaurant and a secure garage. Two other very good **restaurants** are *Jairo*, c/Santa Barbara 10 (closed Mon), and *Piscis*, Plaza de Aragón 1; both specialize in fish and are reasonably priced, with *menús* for under €12.

Barbastro

BARBASTRO, 20km from Monzón, straddling the Río Vero before it joins the Cinca, is a historic town of no small importance. It was here that the union of Aragón and Catalunya was declared in 1137, sealed by the marriage of the daughter of Ramiro of Aragón to Ramón Berenguer IV, lord of Barcelona. Although it's now little more than a slightly shabby provincial market town, Barbastro retains an air of importance through its *casco viejo*, or old quarter. Topping a rise just south of the river, the Gothic **Catedral** (Mon–Sat 10am–1.30pm & 4–7.30pm, Sun 10am–noon; €1.80) on a site once occupied by a mosque, has a high altar whose construction was under the authority of Damián Forment: when he died in 1540 only part of the alabaster relief had been completed, and the remainder was finished by his pupils. Just northeast of the cathedral on the Plaza de la Constitución, the facade of the restored fifteenth-century **ayuntamiento**, designed by the Moorish chief architect to Fernando el Católico, is also worth a look. Elsewhere, narrow, pedestrianized shopping streets are lined by faded-pastel houses piled up with their backs towards the river, while the central, tree-lined **Paseo del Coso** at the southwest edge of the old quarter is home to outdoor tables for many of the town's bars and cafés.

Nowadays Babastro is best known for its **wine**, and the town lies at the centre of the Somontano *denominación de origen* vintage district, the most important in Aragón, and one of the most prominent in Spain. Visits can be organized to three of the biggest wineries – Bodega Pirineos, Viñas del Vero and Enate (details from the turismo, see below). Both Hemingway and Orwell tippled in Barbastro during the 1920s and 1930s; unfortunately though, their favourite watering hole, the *Fonda San Ramón*, was recently closed down.

Practicalities

The **bus station** is at the southwest end of the *paseo*; there are regular departures from here for Huesca and Lleida (daily), and Benasque (Mon–Sat). The keen and helpful English-speaking **turismo** (July & Aug daily 10am–2pm & 4.30–8pm; Sept–June Tues–Sat 10am–2pm & 4.30–8pm; ℡974 308 350, ₩www.barbastro-ayto.es) is at Avenida de la Merced 64.

Since the demise of the *Fonda San Ramón*, really appealing budget accommodation is scarce; about as basic as you'd want to be is the *Hostal Goya* (℡974 311 747; **③**) on c/Argensola, a slightly sleazy street just south of the river, at no. 13. More comfort is available at two establishments on c/Corona de Aragón, running parallel to the river at the northeast edge of the *casco viejo*: *Hostal Roxi* at no. 21 (℡974 311 064, ℗974 312 462; **④**), and the *Hotel Clemente* at no. 3 (℡974 310 186; **④**). Several decent restaurants have sprung up to cater to the wine trade, the most central being the *Cenador de San Julián* (closed Mon), just above the turismo, considered one of the town's best, with a €12 menú. Further afield in the new quarter, within walking distance of the centre via the Avenida Pirineos bridge, are three more possibilities: *Flor* at c/Goya 3 and *Cocina Vasca* more or less adjacent, and *L'Arrabal* two blocks west just off Avenida Pirineos. Finally, if you've got transport, the *Hospedería El Pueyo*, 5km west of town, situated within a hilltop monastery dedicated to Barbastro's patroness, *La Virgen del Pueyo*, has a worthwhile comedor.

Huesca and around

HUESCA is the least memorable of the three Aragonese provincial capitals, and if you're heading for the mountains you could bypass it altogether, or stay on the train to Jaca or beyond. However, it does provide a base for exploring the striking **Los Mallos de Riglos** pinnacles and the castle at **Loarre** to the northwest of the town, as well as the **Sierra de Guara** to the northeast.

Huesca also has a reasonably well-preserved **Casco Viejo**, tucked into a loop of *paseos* and the Río Isuela. At the core of this is a late-Gothic **Catedral**, whose unusual facade combines the thirteenth-century portal of an earlier church with a brick Mudéjar gallery, and a pinnacled uppermost section that's Isabelline in style. The great treasure inside is the *retablo* by Damián Forment, a Renaissance masterpiece depicting the Crucifixion and the Deposition.

Next door, the **Museo Diocesano** (summer Mon–Sat 10.30am–1.30pm & 4–7.30pm; winter till 7pm; €1.20) contains a rather mixed collection, gathered from churches in the countryside. Across the way is a Renaissance **ayuntamiento**. These apart, there's little to detain you. The liveliest time to visit is during Huesca's big **fiesta** in honour of San Lorenzo, held over the week of August 10.

Practicalities

Finding your way around Huesca shouldn't be a problem. The **train** station is at the south end of c/Zaragoza, a main thoroughfare, and the **bus station** is nearby on c/del Parque. The **turismo** (daily 9am–2pm & 4–8pm; ☎974 292 100, ⓦwww.huescaturismo.com) is opposite the cathedral in the *ayuntamiento*, and it stocks various pamphlets on the Aragonese mountains.

Accommodation can be hard to find and, during summer, when trekkers from all over are passing through, it is well worth booking ahead. At the budget end of things, there's the *Pensión Augusto*, c/Aínsa 16 (☎974 220 079; ❸), which has tidy rooms above a bar; the similar-standard *Pensión Bandrés* at c/Fatás 5 (☎974 224 782; ❸), on a pedestrianized street near the bus station; and the en-suite *Hostal El Centro*, c/Sancho Ramírez 3 (☎974 226 823, ⓕ974 225 112; ❹), in a grand old building with large, well-renovated rooms, many with balcony. There are more comfortable choices on the central Plaza Lizana, just downhill from the cathedral: the *Hostal Lizana/Lizana 2* (☎974 221 470 or 974 220 792; ❹–❺), and the adjacent three-star *Hotel Sancho Abarca* at no. 13 (☎974 220 650, ⓕ974 225 169; ❼), where most rooms face a quieter side street. The **campsite**, *San Jorge* (☎974 227 416), is at the end of c/Ricardo del Arco.

Restaurants are plentiful enough, typically offering solid mountain fare, including lamb and freshwater fish specialities. *Restaurante Marisquería Navas*, c/Vicente Campo Palacio 3 (closed Sun pm & Mon, late June & late Oct), is

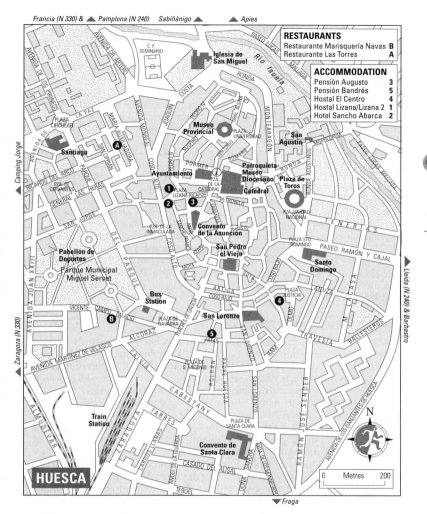

RESTAURANTS

Restaurante Marisquería Navas	**B**
Restaurante Las Torres	**A**

ACCOMMODATION

Pensión Augusto	**3**
Pensión Bandrés	**5**
Hostal El Centro	**4**
Hostal Lizana/Lizana 2	**1**
Hotel Sancho Abarca	**2**

considered Huesca's top restaurant by virtue of its delicious fish or game dishes and home-made desserts; the chef's full works will cost you around €30, but there's also a €12 *menú*. Its only serious rival is the newer *Restaurante Las Torres* at c/María Auxiliadora 3 (closed Sun & Aug 20–Sept ❸), a fancy place offering *nouvelle* Aragonese cuisine (*a la carta* only; allow €30). For excellent **tapas bars** and **nightlife** head for the *zona* around c/San Lorenzo and c/Padre Huesca, between the Coso Bajo and the Plaza de Santa Clara.

Castillo de Loarre

The **Castillo de Loarre** (April–Sept 10am–1.30pm & 4–7pm; Oct–March 11am–2.30pm; closed Mon & Tues except in Aug; free) is Aragón's most spectacular fortress – indeed, there are few that can rival it anywhere in Spain. As you approach, the castle at first seems to blend into the hillside but gradually assumes a breathtaking grandeur: superbly compact, it rises dizzily on a rocky outcrop, commanding the landscape for miles around.

Its builder was Sancho Ramírez, king of Navarra (1000–35), who used it as a base for his resistance to the Moorish occupation. Within the curtain walls is a delicately proportioned Romanesque church, with 84 individually carved capitals. There's also a pair of towers, the Torre de la Reina and the taller Torre del Homenaje, which can be climbed by iron rungs cemented into the wall; if you do go up them, be careful, as the rungs, especially those at the top, are not in the best state of repair.

The castle stands some 40km northwest of Huesca, and 6km beyond the village of **LOARRE**. By **public transport**, it's an awkward trip and you may decide that the views from the road or rail line are sufficient, as bus timetables in particular do their best to conspire against a day-trip. Loarre village has three buses daily from Huesca, all in the afternoon, but there's more than adequate **accommodation** in both Loarre and **AYERBE**, the nearest train station, if you decide to stay the night. Top choice is the *Hospedaria de Loarre*, a restored seventeenth-century mansion on the central plaza in Loarre (☏974 382 706, ☏974 382 713; ➎); this also has the best **restaurant** around (€12 *menú* or about €24 *a la carta*). Failing this, Loarre has one *casa rural*, and Ayerbe a further three, the most characterful being the *Antigua Posada del Pilar* at Plaza Aragón 38 (☏974 380 052; ➌). There's also a good, quiet **campsite** on the road between Ayerbe and Loarre, *La Banera* (☏974 380 242; open all year).

Los Mallos de Riglos

The train line from Huesca to Jaca and the N240 road from Huesca to Pamplona give views not only of Loarre but of the fantastic, pink-tinged sugarloaf mountains known as **Los Mallos de Riglos** – "the ninepins of Riglos". Their majesty, however, may not serve to protect them from partial inundation by a proposed new dam at Biscuarés on the Río Gallego.

If you're travelling by train and want a closer look at the mountains, get off at **Riglos-Concilio** station (you have to ask the conductor to stop) and walk along the road to **RIGLOS** village, tucked high up underneath the most impressive stretch of the peaks. Along the way, you'll be rewarded by a series of superb views of the Mallos and the valley below. At Riglos there's another (unstaffed) station, below the village, from where you can resume your journey.

There's another group of Mallos mountains near **AGÜERO**, a completely isolated village, 5km off the main Huesca–Pamplona road and easily visible from Riglos. The village is a seven-kilometre walk from Riglos-Concilio station, or a five-kilometre walk from Murillo (on the Huesca–Pamplona bus route). The reward, in addition to Mallos views, is an unspoilt village, and a gorgeous, unfinished Romanesque church, the **Iglesia de Santiago** (c. 1200), with portal carvings by the Master of San Juan de la Peña (see p.659); it is reached by following a dirt track up from the main road – ask in the village for the key.

Sierra de Guara

North of the N240 road linking Huesca and Barbastro sprawls the **Sierra de Guara**, a thinly inhabited region protected as a *parque natural* since 1990. The sierra has no dramatic peaks – the highest point is 2078-metre Puntón de Guara – and its low-altitude vegetation often looks distinctly scrubby, but its allure lies lower down, in an unrivalled array of sculpted gorges, painted prehistoric caves and appealing villages. This is the main centre for **canyoning** in Spain, and arguably Europe; it's been known to the French for decades, and French cars match or outnumber local number plates in the popular centres. Many of the adventure outfitters, too, are French-run – there's at least one in every village – though the Spanish are having a go at clawing back some of the trade. Walking opportunities are relatively limited, with poor trail marking, and hiking is best confined to spring or autumn, when the weather is cooler.

The eastern half of the Guara is more popular, and is covered by the Alpina 1:40,000 **map** *Sierra de Guara II*, a must for touring. Due to massive depopulation, there's **no public transport** anywhere in the region; similarly, the only petrol and bank (with an ATM) is at Alquézar (see below).

Alquézar and around

At the far southeastern corner of the range and *parque*, 23km from Barbastro, **ALQUÉZAR** ("Alquezra" in Aragonese) is the Guara's gateway and most developed tourist centre. Lying on the west bank of the Río Vero, it's an atmospheric village, which is packed to the gills most weekends and all summer. Its arcaded lanes culminate in the eighth-century Moorish **citadel** on a pinnacle overlooking the river; the Christians took it in 1064, and by the start of the twelfth century had built the **Colegiata de Santa Maria la Mayor** (daily: summer 11am–1pm & 4.30–7.30pm; winter 11am–1pm & 4–6pm; €1.80, guided visits only) within its fortifications. Only the cloister, its column capitals carved with biblical scenes, remains from the Romanesque era; the Gothic-Renaissance church itself dates from the sixteenth and seventeenth centuries. It's crammed with a miscellany of Baroque art, mostly polychrome wood except for an unpainted pine organ, and a masterly thirteenth-century wooden Crucifixion in the side chapel. From near the citadel paths lead down to the river and the **Puente de Villacantal**, one of several ancient bridges in the *sierra*.

There's a **turismo** at the edge of town on c/Arrabal (Easter & July–Sept Tues–Sun 10.30am–1.30pm & 4–9pm; Oct–June weekends only same hours), which sells the recommended Alpina map. **Accommodation** is fairly abundant but still needs advance booking at busy times. Among several *albergues*, two worth noting are *Tintorero* (☎974 318 354; ❶; April–Sept) in the heart of town at c/San Gregório 18, and the pricier, smaller *Isuala* at c/San Lucas 16, two streets higher (☎974 318 237; ❸; May–Oct). There are also two **campsites** close by: *Alquézar*, 1km downhill by the petrol pump (☎974 318 300, ⓦwww.alquezar.com; open all year), and the slightly lower-standard *Río Vero* (☎974 318 350; April–Oct), down by the river. Representative of six **casas rurales** are the friendly *Casa Jabonero* on c/Pedro Arnal 8 (☎974 318 908; ❷), and *Casa Espartero*, at San Lucas 20 (☎974 318 07; ❸), while the two bona fide **hotels** are the *Villa de Alquézar* on c/Pedro Arnal 12 (☎ & ⓕ974 318 416; ❺) and the *Santa Maria* on c/Arrabal (☎974 318 436, ⓕ974 318 435, ⓦwww.hotel-santamaria.com; ❻), the latter with slick, hi-tech rooms and an in-house adventure centre, Avalancha Deportes, downstairs.

The **bars and restaurants** crowded on Plaza Nueva near the *Santa Maria* are generally mediocre, and pricey to boot; better options are the *comedor* at the *Bar Villacantal* on Plaza Mayor, with its €10.20 *menú*, or (with transport) the *Monclus*, with its own vineyard and winery, on the bypass road 2.5km west of town in **RADIQUERO**. Finally, the village of **BUERA**, 6km southeast across the river, has another lodging/eating possibility in its *Posada de Lalola* (☎974 318 347; ❻), with exquisite designer rooms opening onto a garden and respectable table d'hôte fare (€24).

North: the road to Lecina

The HU340 district road from below Alquézar heads northeast to **COLUN-GO**, 5km away, attractive in a low-key way with its arched doorways and massive buttressed church. The friendly *Hostal Mesón de Colungo* (☎974 318 195; ❸–❹) is your sole option for **staying** and **eating**; you can sample the locally made *aguardiente de anís* at the *A'Olla* bar opposite.

The road continues, in and out of the minor Fornocal gorge, passing two of the four **painted caves** of the Vero valley, which can only be visited on escorted tours (Easter week & mid-July to mid-Sept daily; Easter to early July & mid-Sept to early Oct weekends only; otherwise make arrangements through the Barbastro turismo, see p.649). During peak season, just show up at the signposted lay-bys at 10am or 6pm for the **Covacho de Arpan**, or at 12.15pm or 4.30pm for the **Tozal de Mallata**; for the **Covacho de Barfaluy**, assemble at the turismo in Lecina (see below) at 10am or 5pm. The 4.30pm visits to the remote **Abrigo de Chimiachas** must always be booked through the Alquézar turismo (see above), as a long 4WD transfer is involved.

LECINA itself, some 16km from Colungo, has some imposing houses – it was one of the wealthier Guara villages – and good views northeast to the high peaks. There's a superb place to **stay** and **eat** here: *La Choca* (☎ & ☎974 343 070 or ☎608 633 636; ❺), a restored mansion opposite the church with some of the best food in the Guara (table d'hôte for about €12). There's also a **campsite** down by the river, *Lecina* (☎974 318 386; May–Sept), which doubles as the local canyoning outfitter.

The area around Lecina is one of the few places where **walkers** are actively catered for. The local municipality has waymarked sixteen PR trails, indicated on a sketch map available from the tiny turismo in Lecina or from *La Choca*; a good outing is the three-hour loop Lecina via Almazorre and Betorz.

Northwest: the road to Rodellar

West from Alquézar and Adahuesca, the next significant village is **BIERGE**, with a couple of good **places to stay**: *Casa Rufas*, a *casa rural* in the centre at c/La Cruz 2 (☎974 318 373; ❸), and *Casa Barbara* (☎974 318 060; ❶, but half board at €22.50 per person encouraged), a welcoming *albergue* in the outskirts aimed at canyoners who don't mind being packed nine to a dorm, but with excellent food – including own-baked breads and fruit turnovers – served out in the garden.

North along the ridgetop HU341, the scenery gets grander after about five kilometres, with canyons yawning to either side. After 11km you descend through woods to *Expediciones*, the most pleasant **campsite** of three in the Alcanadre river valley (☎974 343 008, ⓦwww.expediciones.sc.es; open June–Sept); they're also about the most switched-on canyoning operator hereabouts. **LAS ALMUNIAS**, 2km further, is the first proper village, offering the *Hostal Casa Tejedor* (☎ & ☎974 343 015; ❹; March–Oct) with a restaurant, plus the *Albergue Las Almunias* across the road (☎974 343 218; ❶).

RODELLAR, some 4km further and 18km from Bierge at the end of the road, looks achingly photogenic draped along a ridge above the Río Mascún, though the reality close up in peak season is likely to be cars parked nose-to-tail and overstretched **accommodation**. This comprises *Casa Arilla* (☎974 318 343; ❸; April–Oct) and *Casa Regina* (☎974 318 364; ❸), while the *Bar-Restaurante Florentino* opposite *Casa Arilla* is the only spot to eat or drink. Two **campsites**, *Mascún* at the edge of the village (☎974 318 367, ⓦwww.guara-mascun.com; April–Oct), and *El Puente*, 1500m south by the river and the medieval Pedruel bridge (☎974 318 312; April–Oct), also act as canyoning guide centres. If you're not interested in plumbing the deep gorges hereabouts, the most popular activity is the two-and-a-half-hour (one-way) **hike** north to the abandoned hamlet of **Otín**, though path-marking is terrible. It's sobering to reflect that before the current canyoning boom, just two families lived here full time, plus a few pioneering French canyon-explorers who bought old houses here in the 1960s.

Jaca and around

JACA is approached through featureless, traffic-choked suburbs: an unpromising introduction to this early capital and stronghold of Aragón – and the base from which the kingdom was recaptured from the Moors. The old centre, however, is a lot more characterful, overlooked by a huge star-shaped citadel,

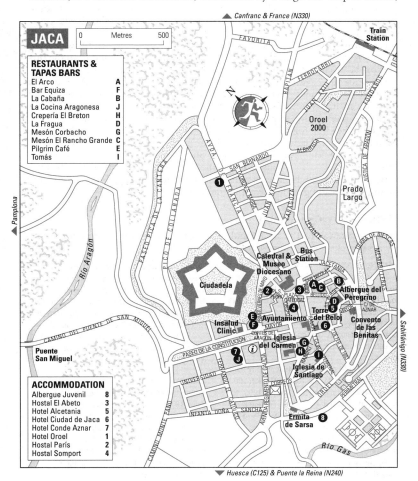

▲ Canfranc & France (N330)

JACA

Metres 0 — 500

RESTAURANTS & TAPAS BARS
El Arco	A
Bar Equiza	F
La Cabaña	B
La Cocina Aragonesa	J
Crepería El Breton	H
La Fragua	D
Mesón Corbacho	G
Mesón El Rancho Grande	C
Pilgrim Café	E
Tomás	I

ACCOMMODATION
Albergue Juvenil	8
Hostal El Abeto	3
Hotel Alcetania	5
Hotel Ciudad de Jaca	6
Hotel Conde Aznar	7
Hotel Oroel	1
Hostal París	2
Hostal Somport	4

▼ Huesca (C125) & Puente la Reina (N240)

retaining patches of Roman and medieval walls, and endowed with a **cathedral** that is one of the high points of Romanesque architecture. This, and the monastery of **San Juan de la Peña**, 20km southeast, are the major local sights, though in winter there is a bonus in the proximity of **Astún-Candanchu**, Aragón's best ski resort. Rail (and, in winter, ski) enthusiasts may be tempted by the trip to **Canfranc**, almost at the French border.

After a spell in the mountains, Jaca's (relatively) "big town" feel and facilities may well be an equal attraction. It can be a lively place – the population is boosted by conscripts at the large military academy and a summer English-language university – and it hosts a terrific week-long **fiesta** (last week of June) with live bands in the main square, lots of traditional costume, and partying in the streets.

Arrival, orientation and information

Central Jaca has two aspects: the northeast side is a little dingy, and shelters all of the budget accommodation and bars; the southwest quarter, abutting Avenida Regimiento de Galicia, is smarter, with a series of sidewalk cafés, restaurants and banks.

The **train station** (ticket office open 10am–noon & 5–7pm) is a fair walk from the centre, so look out for the shuttle bus (€0.45). This runs to and from the **bus station** on Avenida Jacetania, around the back of the cathedral. Useful bus services include those for Pamplona, Biescas via Sabiñánigo, and Echo/Anso, as well as even more frequent services to Zaragoza and Huesca. Although the timetables don't say so, hardly any buses run on Sundays. **Drivers** will find parking easiest in the roomier southwestern quarter, though beware of metered zones.

If you're heading for the mountains, it's worth stopping in at the helpful **turismo**, Avenida Regimiento de Galicia (summer Mon–Fri 9am–2pm & 4.30–8pm, Sat 9am–1.30pm & 5–8pm, Sun 10am–1.30pm; winter Mon–Fri 9am–1.30pm & 4.30–7pm, Sat 10am–1pm & 5–7pm; ☎974 360 098, Ⓦwww.jaca.com), which has a range of leaflets on trekking, skiing, mountain-biking, horse-riding and festival programmes.

Accommodation

Jaca is a gateway to the peaks, and its **accommodation** facilities are almost always stretched, so advance booking is prudent.

Hotels and Hostales

Albergue Juvenil, Avda. Perimetral s/n ☎974 360 536. The local youth hostel, in the south of town by the ice rink, has doubles, triples and five-bed rooms. ❶

Hostal El Abeto, c/Bellido 15 ☎974 361 642. Comfortable enough, with en-suite rooms, though there may be some noise from nearby bars. ❹

Hotel Alcetania, c/Mayor 43–45, but entry from c/Conde Aznar ☎974 356 100, Ⓕ974 356 200. Former *hostal* refurbished as a hotel in 1995. ❺

Hotel Ciudad de Jaca, c/Siete de Febrero 8 ☎974 364 311, Ⓕ974 364 395. Centrally located, but a quiet place with good en-suite rooms. ❺

Hotel Conde Aznar, Paseo de la Constitución 3 ☎974 361 050, Ⓕ974 360 797. An attractive old family-run hotel, with well-renovated rooms and fairly abundant street parking. ❻

Hotel Oroel, Avda. de Francia 37 ☎974 362 411, Ⓕ974 363 804. Modern hotel with its own pool; large rooms with kitchens. ❼

Hostal París, Plaza de San Pedro 5 ☎974 361 020. Best budget *hostal* in town – clean, spacious rooms with washbasin, across from the cathedral. ❸

Hostal Somport, c/Etchegaray 11 ☎ & Ⓕ 974 363 410. Jaca's most affordable en-suite digs, in another renovated old building. ❹

Camping

Camping Peña Oroel, 4km out on the Sabiñánigo road ☎974 360 215. An attractive campsite, set amid woods, with excellent facilities. Open Easter week and mid-June to mid-Sept.

Camping Victoria, 1500m out of town on the Pamplona road ☎974 360 323. An equally shady if cheaper and rather basic site, near the Río Aragón. Open all year.

The Town

Jaca is an ancient town, founded by the Romans and occupied continuously since. It had a very brief period of Moorish rule, after being captured around 716, but in 760 the Christians reconquered the town and held it, save for a few years, from then on. The battle of **Las Tiendas** in 795, when Moorish armies were repulsed, in large part by women, is still commemorated on the first Friday in May, in a mock all-women battle between Christians and Muslims. The town's greatest period, however, came after 1035, when **Ramiro I**, son of Sancho of Navarre, established a court here. It was in this era that the first parliament on record took place, and that the cathedral was rebuilt.

The cathedral

The **Catedral** (daily 8am–2pm & 4–9pm; free) is the main legacy of Jaca's years as the seat of the young Aragonese kingdom, and is one of Spain's most architecturally important monuments. Rebuilt on old foundations during the middle of the eleventh century, it was the first cathedral in Spain to adopt the French Romanesque style of architecture and, as such, exerted considerable stylistic influence on other churches along the Camino de Santiago.

Ramiro's endowment of the cathedral was undoubtedly intended to confirm Jaca's role as a Christian capital, in what was still almost an exclusively Moorish Iberian peninsula. Its design saw the introduction of the classic three-aisled basilica, though unhappily the original Romanesque simplicity has been much obscured by florid decoration over the centuries. It retains some of the original sculpture, however, including realistic carving on the capitals and doorway – a sixteenth-century statue of Santiago looks down from the portal. Inside, the main treasure is the silver shrine of Santa Orosía, Jaca's patron saint; a Czech noble, married into the Aragonese royal family, Orosía was martyred by the Moors for refusing to renounce her faith.

Installed in the dark cathedral cloisters is an unusually good **Museo Diocesano** (June–Sept daily 10am–2pm & 4–8pm; winter Tues–Sun 11am–1.30pm & 4–6.30pm; €1.80), which features frescoes and wooden religious sculpture gathered from village churches in the area and from higher up in the Pyrenees. Highlights include an eerily modern Pantocrastor fresco from a church in Ruesta, a walnut crucified Christ, and the *Flight into Egypt* and *Adoration of the Magi* from Navasa, all from the twelfth century. The Renaissance work is more variable, but features some splendid *retablos*.

The Ciudadela and Puente San Miguel

The **Ciudadela**, a redoubtable sixteenth-century fort, built in the French-style star design, is still part-occupied by the military. You can visit a part of the interior (daily: April–June & Sept–Oct 11am–noon & 5–6pm; July–Aug 11am–noon & 6–8pm; Nov–March 11am–noon & 4–5pm; €1.80), however, on a guided tour. Its walls offer good views of the surrounding peaks, and of the wooded countryside around.

Below the citadel, reached along a rough track from the end of the Paseo de la Constitución, is a remarkable medieval bridge, the **Puente San Miguel**. It was across this bridge, over the Río Aragón, that pilgrims on the Camino Aragonés – a branch of the **Camino de Santiago** (see p.430) – entered Jaca. It must have been a welcome sight, marking the end of the arduous Pyrenean stage for pilgrims following the route from Provence into Spain over the Puerto de Somport. From Jaca, the pilgrims headed on westwards, through Puente la Reina de Jaca, towards Navarra, where they joined up with the more popular route from Roncesvalles. This Aragón section of the Camino de Santiago – like other branches of the route – has experienced quite a revival since the early 1990s, though it's constantly threatened with either inundation by dams or covering over by building projects. In town, there's an **Albergue de Peregrino** (pilgrims' hostel) in the medieval hospital on c/Conde Aznar (daily 9–10am & 3–10pm), while route maps and pilgrimage-related souvenirs are widely available.

Eating and drinking

Jaca has a lively and inviting selection of **restaurants** and **bars** with fairly reasonable prices, and there's a wholesome after-dark atmosphere, especially during the summer months.

El Arco, c/San Nicolás 4. That rare Spanish breed: a vegetarian, no-smoking restaurant. Fresh, filling, international dishes and an inexpensive *menú*. Closed Sun in winter.

Bar Equiza, c/Primer Viernes de Mayo. Scruffy sidewalk tables belie a plush cavernous interior with famously good tapas – especially *gambas* and various *fritos*.

La Cabaña, c/del Pez 10. Reasonable *a la carta* meals (€15–18) in unusually cheerful surroundings.

La Cocina Aragonesa, c/de Cervantes 4. Round the corner from the *Hotel Conde Aznar* – which owns the restaurant – *La Cocina* is reckoned to be the best place in town. The cooking is elaborate and Basque-influenced. Expect to pay €35–45 (the *menú* scarcely costs less than *a la carta*). Closed Wed.

Crepería El Breton, c/Ramiro Primero 10. A passably authentic creperie. Dinner only; closed Mon in winter and last two weeks of June.

La Fragua, c/Gil Berges 4. Generous, reasonably priced grills without any airs or graces. Closed Wed.

Mesón Corbacho, c/Ramiro Primero 2. Regional dishes and grills; costs €10.20 for the *menú*, or €24 *a la carta*.

Mesón El Rancho Grande, c/del Arco 2. Impressive Aragonese cooking, which uses fish, meat and vegetables equally well; skip the dull €9.60 *menú* in favour of the *a la carta* costing around €30.

Pilgrim Café, Avda. Primer Viernes de Mayo 7. Inevitably a bit touristy but a fine old Art Deco building with outdoor tables facing the Ciudadela's lawn, and a variety of breakfasts (including bacon and eggs).

Tomás, c/Ferrenal 8. Hole-in-the-wall, old-fashioned bar with a vast range of tapas and *raciones*; one of several clustered here.

Listings

Adventure activities All sorts of activity expeditions are organized by Jaca Adventura, Avda. Francia 1 ☏974 363 521, Mountain Travel on Avda. Regimiento Galicia ☏974 355 770, and Alcorce-Pireneos Adventura at Avda. Regimiento Galicia 1 ☏974 356 437. All these companies have English-speaking staff.

Car rental Don Auto, c/Correos 2 ☏908 833 227. In high season all cars must be booked at least a day in advance.

Hospital Besides the main one on c/Rapitan, off the map beyond the train station, there's the very central, public Insalud clinic, good for minor ailments.

Laundry There's a self-service *lavandería* next to the supermarket, Superpirineos, on c/Astún.

Trekking maps and gear Maps are available from La Unión bookstore at c/Mayor 34 and at the mountaineering shop, Charli, Avda. Regimiento de Galicia 3. There's another outdoor gear shop, Intersport-Piedrafita, at Avda. de Francia 4.

South to San Juan de la Peña and Santa Cruz de la Serós

San Juan de la Peña, up in the hills to the southwest of Jaca, is the best-known monastery in Aragón. In medieval times San Juan was an important detour on the pilgrim route from Jaca to Pamplona, as it was reputed to hold the Holy Grail – a Roman-era chalice which later found its way to Valencia cathedral. These days, most tourists (and there are many – including school parties) visit for the views and Romanesque cloister.

The most direct **route to the monastery** is from the Jaca–Pamplona (N240) highway. A side road, 11km west of Jaca, leads south 4km to the village of **Santa Cruz de la Serós**, and from here it's a further 7km by road up to San Juan. There is no public transport, although you could take a Puente la Reina/Pamplona bus from Jaca and walk from there – assuming an overnight in Santa Cruz. **Renting a bike** would be easier: reckon on one hour for Jaca to Santa Cruz, then a further hour up the very steep road to San Juan. Returning you could follow the C125 – a gradual descent to Bernués, a slight climb to Puerto de Oroel, then a fierce drop to Jaca – which is very scenic and car-free, but not a leg to do uphill.

Santa Cruz de la Serós

The picturesque village of **SANTA CRUZ DE LA SERÓS**, which comes to life in summer, is dominated by its thick-set but nonetheless stylish Romanesque **church** (daily 10am–2.30pm & 3.30–8pm; €0.90), once part of a large Benedictine monastery which flourished until the sixteenth century. There are a couple of places to **eat** and **drink** in the village: the *Casa d'Ojalatero* in the centre, with plain fare including good house wine, *trigueros con gambas* and grills (two *menús* at €7.20 and €10.80, or €12–18 *a la carta*), and the *Hosteleria Santa Cruz*, with a €9 *menú*, or €24 *a la carta*. The latter also has high-standard **rooms** (℡974 361 975; ❹)

From Santa Cruz, walkers can take the **old path** up to San Juan in about an hour. The path is waymarked as variant 2 of the GR65.3 and is signposted from near the church (where there is also a map-placard). The road takes a more circuitous route around the mountainside, giving wonderful views of the Pyrenean peaks to the north and the distinctive Peña de Oroel to the east.

San Juan de la Peña

SAN JUAN DE LA PEÑA actually comprises two monasteries, 2km apart. Coming from Santa Cruz, you reach the lower (and older) one first.

Built into a hollow under a rocky escarpment, from which various springs seep, the **Lower Monastery** (summer Tues–Sun 10am–2pm & 3.30–8pm; spring & autumn Tues–Sun 10am–1.30pm & 4–6pm; winter Wed–Sun 11am–2.30pm; €2.40) is an unusual and evocative complex, even in its partial state of survival. It was here, in 1071, that the Latin Mass was introduced to the Iberian peninsula by Cluniac monks and here, too, that the Aragonese maintained a stronghold in the early years of the Reconquest. Entering, you pass into the Sala de Concilios – which once served as the refectory – and the adjacent, double-naved, ninth-century Mozarabic chapel. These two chambers were adapted as the crypt of the main Romanesque **church**, built two centuries later, and both retain fragments of Romanesque frescoes. Upstairs, alongside the main church, is a **pantheon** for Aragonese and Navarrese nobles; reliefs on the Gothic nobles' tombs depict events from the early history of Aragón. An adjacent pantheon for the kings of Aragón was remodelled in a cold, Neoclassical style in the eighteenth century and later sacked by Napoleon's troops.

The artistic highlight, however, is the twelfth-century Romanesque **cloisters**. Only two of the bays are complete – another is in a fragmentary state – but the surviving capitals are among the greatest examples of Romanesque carving in Spain. They were the artistry of an anonymous, idiosyncratic craftsman who made his mark on a number of churches in the region. He is now known as the Master of San Juan de la Peña, his work easily recognizable by the unnaturally large eyes on the figures.

The seventeenth-century **Upper Monastery**, a sizeable complex with a flamboyant Baroque facade, can be seen from the outside only, but it is worth the climb, if only for the views of the Pyrenees from a nearby *mirador*. Facing the monastery is a popular picnic-ground in a huge, forest-enclosed meadow; if you arrive by car, this is where you must park – a regular shuttle bus will take you down to the older monastery.

Canfranc-Estación

Since the French railways discontinued their part of the local trans-Pyrenean line, the enormous train station at **CANFRANC-ESTACIÓN**, 30km north of Jaca, has become a white elephant: buildings have been badly vandalized, and tall weeds now grow in the tracks. It's a sad fate for an elegant spot that saw heads of state attend its inauguration in 1928, and that served as a location for the film *Doctor Zhivago*. Spanish undercutting of French ski-resort prices prompted the closure of the line in the first place in 1973, though the last straw was the collapse of a critical bridge, left unrepaired to this day. However, things may improve following the opening of the Somport car tunnel in 2001, and the EU is now committed in principle to rehabilitating the rail line between Oloron-Ste-Marie and Canfranc.

Skiing in Aragón

There are five **ski resorts in the Aragonese Pyrenees** and most of them – following the province's hosting of the 1982 University Winter Olympics – are well equipped, and likely to improve further as the Jaca area bids to host the 2010 Winter Olympics. As in Catalunya, you may find that package deals, bought from any travel agent in northern Spain, work out cheapest, but there are also often mini-packages arranged by the turismos and hotels of each valley. Wherever possible you should take advantage of slow, mid-week periods and thus avoid the busiest weekends and major holidays when all accommodation is booked a month in advance.

Among the best, and certainly the most advanced, option is the twin centre of **ASTÚN-CANDANCHÚ**, north of Canfranc (buses from Jaca). The resorts – smaller Astún dating from 1975, and bigger and higher Candanchú, the first established in these mountains – are just 8km apart, and share a lift pass. Treeless Astún is particularly well organized and better for weak intermediates, with plentiful equipment for hire at modest rates. The only budget accommodation in Candanchú is the *Pensión Somport*, Ctra. de Francia 198 (℡974 373 009; ❷), and two *albergues*, *El Águila* (℡974 373 291; ❶; open ski season & summer) and *Valle de Aragón* (℡974 373 222; ❶; open all year). The hotels *Tobazo*, Ctra de Francia (℡974 373 12, ℻974 373 125; ❼), and *Candanchú*, Ctra de Francia (℡974 373 025, ℻974 373 050, ⊛www.arrakis.es/hotelcan; ❼), reflect the more usual prices for this resort. Astún has just a single, pricey three-star hotel; with a car, you may prefer to stay in Canfranc (see below).

Of the other ski centres, **FORMIGAL** (closest reasonable lodgings at Sallent de Gallego) and **PANTICOSA** (accommodation in the village) are both served by daily buses from Sabiñanigo via Biescas. Formigal nearly rivals Astún-Candanchú for interest and challenge, but Panticosa – despite massive recent investment – remains too low and too limited in its piste plan. The remotest Aragonese resort is **CERLER**, close to Benasque; it too has undergone a recent face-lift, with new snow canons and chairlifts, and it now rates as a good intermediate centre.

The village, such as it is, exists primarily to catch the passing tourist trade (mostly French), with a few gift shops and hotels. It's just about worth the day's trip from Jaca, even if you don't continue into France, for the train ride up the valley. **Accommodation**, all on or just off the through highway, includes the high-quality *Albergue Pepito Grillo* (☎974 373 123; ❶; open all year), the *Hotel Ara* (☎974 373 028; ❹), and the friendly *Hotel Villa Anayet*, Plaza de Aragón (☎974 373 146; ❹). There are also three *casas rurales*, a bit pricier than the norm (❸), near the *Villa Anayet*, as well as a campsite (☎608 731 604; April to mid-Sept) 5km north on the road towards Candanchú. For **meals**, the *comedor* at the *Hotel Villa Anayet* offers by far the best value, with a four-course *menú* for €7.20.

Though there's no train, you can travel on into France several times daily on **buses** run by the SNCF. Up-to-the-minute information can be had from the Canfranc **turismo** (July–Sept Mon–Sat 9am–1.30pm & 4.30–8pm; Oct–June Tues–Sat 9am–1.30pm & 3.30–7pm, closed Nov 1–Nov 15; ☎974 373 141, Ⓦwww.canfranc.com), opposite the station.

Echo and Ansó

Echo and **Ansó** are two of the most attractive valleys in Aragón, their rivers – Aragón Subordan and Veral – joining the Río Aragón to the west of Jaca. Until the 1960s, both valleys felt extremely remote, with villagers wearing traditional dress and speaking a dialect, *Cheso*, descended from medieval Aragonese. These days, they're very much on map for Spanish weekenders and foreign visitors, and the last rural activity seriously engaged in is timber-cutting.

If you don't have transport of your own, renting a **mountain bike** in Jaca would be a good investment for exploring the valleys, as there is only one daily **bus** (Mon–Sat), calling first at Echo and continuing to Ansó; it leaves Jaca at 6.30pm, arriving in Anso at 8.10pm, and begins the journey back from Ansó at 6am, passing Echo 45min later. By bike, reckon on around two and a half hours from Jaca to Echo village, turning off the N240 at Puente la Reina de Jaca, or much the same to Ansó village, turning off at Berdún. For **trekking in the region**, the 1:40,000 Editorial Alpina booklet *Valles de Ansó y Echo* is extremely useful.

Valle de Echo

ECHO is a splendid old village, where whitewash outlines the windows and doors of the massive stone houses. It has a claim to fame in Aragonese history as the seat of the embryonic Aragonese kingdom under Conde Aznar Galíndez in the ninth century, and as the birthplace of the "warrior king", Alfonso I. Although it seems ancient, Echo in its present form is less than two centuries old – like so many villages in these hills, it was burnt and sacked during the Napoleonic wars.

An annual arts festival, which ran from 1975 to 1984, has left a permanent legacy in an open-air **gallery of sculpture**, on the hillside west of the village. Created by a group of artists led by Pedro Tramullas, the 46 pieces are not individually stunning but, taken as a whole, they are quite compelling. Local resistance to the expansion of the venture has been overcome, but unfortunately funds are now lacking to take the project further. Near the enormous central church, there's a more conventional museum, the **Museo Etnológico** (daily 11am–2pm & 6–9pm; €0.90), with interesting collections on Pyrenean rural life and folklore.

The **turismo** is in the *ayuntamiento* (daily June–Sept 10am–2pm & 5–7pm; ☎974 375 329, ✆www.lapagina.de.valledehecho), and has information about much of the surrounding area; if it's shut, ask upstairs and they may open it for you. In summer or at weekends you'd be well advised to book ahead for one of Echo's four **places to stay**. The clear first choice, if you can squeeze in around tour groups, is *Casa Blasquico*, barely marked at Plaza Palacio de la Fuente 1 (☎974 375 007; ❺), with five tastefully converted en-suite rooms. Fallbacks, in descending order of preference, are the *Hostal de la Val* (☎974 375 028; ❺) and *Lo Foratón* (☎974 375 247), the latter comprising a somewhat shabby *hostal* (❸) and a slightly better hotel (❺), both at the north end of the village. There is also a **campsite**, *Valle de Echo* (☎974 375 361; all year), just south of the village, though *Borda Bisáltico* (☎974 375 388), 5km north, is of a much higher standard, offering an *albergue* (❶) and simple rooms (❸) as well.

For **meals**, don't miss a chance to eat at *Casa Blasquico* (Seatings at 1.30 & 8.30pm – reservations mandatory ☎974 375 007; closed part of September), strong on game, duck and decadent sweets and definitely worth a €30 splurge *a la carta* – if money's tight, ask about the cheaper *menú*. Owner-chef Gaby Coarasa was among the first stars of Pyrenean *nouvelle cuisine*, and the walls inside the tiny *comedor* are lined with awards to prove it. If you can't get in, the *Restaurante Serbal* on the east side of the village is very nearly as good, while the friendly *Bar Subordan* next door to the *Casa Blasquico* will fill you up with superb, inexpensive *raciones* of *pimientos de piquillo, longaniza* and *chipirrones*.

Siresa and beyond

Two kilometres north of Echo stands the beautiful, quiet village of **SIRESA**. Keeping watch over riverside pastures is a remarkable ninth-century church, the massive **San Pedro** (daily 11am–1pm & 5–8pm; €1.20), once the core of a monastery. There is a pleasant **hotel** here, the *Castillo d'Acher* (☎974 375 313; ❺), whose owners also operate the *fonda* (❸), over the village bar, and a reasonable **restaurant**.

Walkers may be tempted to continue up the valley from Siresa, along the GR65.3.3, a minor variant of the Camino de Santiago; much of the paved road can be missed out by following the "Via Romana", not Roman but certainly early Christian, signposted 3km above Siresa. Once through the **Boca de Infierno** narrows, you emerge at **SELVA DE OZA**, where there is a pleasant bar. Selva is the jump-off point for climbing **Castillo de Acher** (2390m); the other limestone peaks, including **Bisaurín** (2669m) and **Agüerri** (2449m), are best tackled from the excellent *Refugio de Gabardito* (☎974 375 387 or 676 850 843; ❶; open all year), further down the valley at the end of the track serving Borda Basáltico. The *refugio* is run by the Compañia de Guias Valle de Echo, the best people to see about either summer climbing or wintertime nordic skiing.

North of Selva de Oza, the paved road ends near **La Mina**, trailhead for the two-hour hike up to the **Acherito lake**, one of the local beauty spots. **Laraille/Laraya** peak (2147m) just overhead is another popular target, as is the nearby frontier peak of **Lariste** (2168m). The GR11 long-distance footpath also passes by La Mina, on its way west from Canfranc, heading towards Zuriza in the Ansó valley, a short day's hike distant; at **ZURIZA** there's the well-equipped *Camping Zuriza* (☎974 370 196; all year), with an *albergue* (❶), *hostal* (❹) and restaurant.

On to Ansó

The daily **bus** from Jaca to Echo continues west along 12km of narrow, twisting road, climbing over the Sierra de Vedao before dropping into the **Valle de**

Ansó; the final approaches are guarded by two strangely shaped rocks known locally as "the Monk and the Nun", just above a tunnel.

Non-drivers should use the very enjoyable two-and-a-half-hour **trail** from **Siresa to Ansó**, waymarked as the PR18 and signposted as "Fuen d'a Cruz" by the stream below Siresa.

Valle de Ansó

Once a prosperous, large village, **ANSÓ** fell upon hard times during the depopulation of rural Aragón in the 1950s and 1960s. Today, however, there are signs of revival, with Jaca and Pamplona professionals keeping weekend residences here, and a growing stream of tourists visiting. It's certainly an attractive weekend base, with a little river beach for splashing around in the Río Veral. There are few specific sights, though there's a **Museo Etnológico** (daily 10.30am–1.30pm & 3.30–8pm; €1.20), housed in an ancient church.

Ansó's growing popularity is reflected in several **places to stay**, all filling up quickly in summer. Best is the *Posada Magoria* (☎974 370 049; ❺), in new palatial quarters by the church, with a garden and views; they serve communal vegetarian meals (preference is given to guests). Worthy alternatives include the Peruvian-run *La Posada Veral*, c/Cocorro 6 (☎974 370 119; ❸), or *Hostal Kimboa* (☎974 370 184, ℉974 370 130; ❹) at the north end of town, with modern, comfortable rooms. There's no campsite but tents are tolerated beside the municipal swimming pool, at the south end of the village.

All lodgings have their own **restaurants** – the *Kimboa*'s is reckoned to be the best – and there are various **bars**, the liveliest being the friendly *Zuriza* on the main street and the bar in *La Posada Veral*.

Parque Nacional de Ordesa

The **PARQUE NACIONAL DE ORDESA Y MONTE PERDIDO** was one of Spain's first protected national parks, and is perhaps the most dramatic, with beech and poplar forests, mountain streams, dozens of spring and early summer waterfalls, and a startling backdrop of limestone palisades. The **wildlife**, too, is impressive, including golden eagles, lammergeiers, griffon or Egyptian vultures, and Pyrenean chamois – so numerous that at certain times hunters are allowed to cull the surplus. The park is an increasingly popular destination for walkers, and its foothill villages are becoming more and more commercialized each year. In midsummer, you'll need to book accommodation well in advance, even if you plan to camp. Nevertheless, this is the Aragonese Pyrenees at its most spectacular, and well worth a few days of anyone's time.

The route to Ordesa

Heading for Ordesa from the lowlands, the place to make for is the gateway village of **Torla**, from where the GR15.2 leads into the park. A daily **bus** service from Sabiñánigo to Aínsa stops at Torla and all villages on the way, including Biescas, Linas de Broto, Broto, Sarvisé and Fiscal.

If you're coming **from the southwest**, this leaves Sabiñánigo at 11am, reaches Biescas fifteen minutes later, and gets to Torla at noon. In July and August there's an additional service between Sabiñánigo and Sarvisé, leaving the former at 6.30pm. Sabiñánigo and Biescas receive two daily buses which depart

Jaca at 10.15am and 6.15pm, connecting directly with the onward services cited above.

Coming **from the southeast**, the same bus service leaves Aínsa at 2.30pm, arriving in Torla at 3.30pm, and the summer service leaves Sarvisé at 7.45pm, calling at Torla about fifteen minutes later. Aínsa itself is served by a Mon–Sat evening bus from Barbastro, with an extra morning departure during July and August.

Sabiñánigo, Biescas and Linas de Broto

There's not much to industrial **SABIÑÁNIGO** and you'll probably want to push straight on. The new **bus terminal** is right outside the **train station**. Should you need to stop over, there are a dozen mostly overpriced **places to stay**, mostly on the through road, Avenida de Serrablo. A reasonable choice, near the transport terminals, is *Hostal Laguarta* (☎974 480 004; ❹) at no. 21, above the *Bar Lara*.

If you miss the morning through-service to Torla, there is a year-round 6.30pm service to **BIESCAS**, 17km north, from where you could try your luck hitching the remaining 25km to Torla (or pick up the Torla bus the following morning). If you get stuck (as is likely), Biescas is quite pleasant, with several **places to stay**: *Pensión Las Herras* (☎974 485 027; ❸) offers shared-bath rooms in an old stone house, across the river from the *ayuntamiento*, while *Casa Ruba*, just off the Plaza del Ayuntamiento (☎974 485 001, ⓕ974 485 001; ❹), which has been in the same family since 1884, has a lively bar and a respected *comedor*. There's also a central campsite, *Edelweiss* (☎974 485 084; mid-June to mid-Sept), and a **turismo** (June–Sept 10am–1.30pm & 5–9pm) next to the bridge. The tiny stone hamlet of **LINAS DE BROTO**, 17km east on the way to Torla, with four *hostales* along the through road and a fine position, is also a reasonable spot to base yourself: the *Hostal Jal* (☎ & ⓕ974 486 106, ⓔhostaljal@wanadoo.es; ❹), with a restaurant, has links to a reputable local adventure company.

Torla

The old stone village of **TORLA**, just 8km short of Ordesa, is well encased in ranks of modern hotels, and awash with souvenir stalls. It exists very much as a walkers' base and almost everything is geared to the trade. The **bus** from Sabiñánigo and Aínsa stops at the southern edge of town, by the large car park where all visitors to the park must leave their vehicles (€5.25 per day). The central **turismo** (late June to mid-Sept Mon–Fri 10am–1pm & 6–8pm, Sat & Sun 9.30am–1.30pm & 5–8.30pm; ☎974 229 804) offers free sketch maps showing the main paths in the park. The village also has a bank (with ATM) and shops stocking basic trekking foods and mountain gear.

During July and August, you'll need to book **accommodation** in Torla at least a week ahead; at other times, it's rarely a problem. Top mid-range choices are the *Hostal Alto Aragón* (☎ & ⓕ974 486 172; ❹–❺), with en-suite rooms, and the *Hotel Ballarín* opposite (☎ & ⓕ974 486 155; ❺); the *Ballarín's comedor* is a fine source of sustaining *menús* (€8.40). Among several fancier hotels, the *Villa de Torla* (☎974 486 156, ⓕ974 486 365; ❺) on the village square is the most professionally run, with a pool and an excellent restaurant; the top-floor rooms are best. For budget lodgings, try the two *casas rurales* on c/Fatás, next to the turismo, or one of two *albergues*: the friendly, high-standard *Refugio Lucien Bret* (☎974 486 221; ❶), with most rooms en suite, self-catering facilities and an excellent affiliated restaurant (*Bar Brecha*), or the snootier, cramped *L'Atalaya* (☎974 486 022; ❶), also with a restaurant and basement tapas bar.

Additionally, there are three **campsites** along the road out to Ordesa; closest of these is the riverside *Río Ara* (☎974 486 248), 2km from Torla on the far side of the stream.

Broto, Oto, Sarvisé, Fiscal and Aínsa

If you find Torla full or just too commercialized, you may prefer to stop in one of the villages to the east, along the road to Aínsa. **BROTO**, 4km south of Torla, is a noisy, teeming place, its old quarter hemmed by traffic and new construction. Upriver, just beside the village's collapsed Romanesque bridge, is the quietest place to stay, and one of the last to fill, *Tabierna O Puente* (☎974 486 072; ❹); you could also try the *Hostal Español* (☎974 486 007, ⓕ974 486 423; ❸), nearby on the through road. The **turismo** (June–Sept Tues–Sun 10am–2pm & 4.30–8.30pm; ☎974 486 002) can advise on vacancies in high season. If you're walking, you can follow a well-trodden *camino* to Torla in 45 minutes; marked as the GR15.2, it begins near the ruined bridge.

OTO, 2km southwest, is a more attractive village, with traditional architecture and a pair of medieval towers. It has two **casas rurales**: *Herrero* (☎974 486 093; ❸) and *Pueyo* (☎974 486 371; ❸), and a large if basic **campsite** (☎974 486 075; April to mid-Oct). A further 4km from Broto is **SARVISÉ**, the lowest village of the Valle de Broto. This again has ample high-quality **accommodation**; top two picks are the secluded *Casa Puyuelo* (☎974 486 140; ❹), or the *Hotel Casa Frauca* (☎974 486 182, ⓕ974 486 353; ❹) on the main road, whose famous ground-floor *comedor* draws crowds from near and far (€10.50 *menú*, €18 *a la carta*; reservations required).

Below Sarvisé, the Ara river valley turns east and widens markedly, with evidence of large-scale depopulation; villages just off the road are largely deserted, their fields gone to seed. Aragón in general has the highest proportion of abandoned settlements in Spain, but here the impetus was a never-executed dam at Jánovas. In 1959 local property was expropriated for a pittance by the hydro company, and by 1964 many villagers had been forced to move, their houses dynamited by Franco's Guardia Civil to get the point across.

One village that's found a new lease of life through tourism is **FISCAL**, with a range of **places to stay**: *Saltamontes* (☎974 503 113; ❶), a recently opened *albergue* opposite the church; *Casa del Arco* (☎ & ⓕ974 503 042, ⓦwww.pireneo.com/casadelarco; ❸), in an eighteenth-century building with antique-furnished rooms and engaging management; and the luxurious *Hostal Casa Cadena* near the top of the village (☎ & ⓕ974 503 077; ❺), with an equally posh restaurant (€11.70 *menú* or €30 *a la carta*). There are also two all-year **campsites**, the cosier *El Jabalí Blanco* (☎974 503 074), also with bungalows, having the edge.

The next place of any size is **AÍNSA**, which was prettified in 1994 with stone walkways and boutiques in an attempt to cash in on some of the cross-border trade pouring over from the Bielsa tunnel to the north. Its hilltop **old quarter** remains attractive, centred on an exceptional Romanesque church with a primitive crypt and a climbable belfry, plus a vast, arcaded Plaza Mayor. The only place offering **rooms** in the medieval quarter is *Casa El Hospital* (☎974 500 750; ❹), an old stone house right next to the church; all other accommodation is down in the noisy new town. Old-town **eating** options are more plentiful, the best value being *Bar Restaurante Fes* at c/Mayor 22.

The Ordesa Canyon and central park treks

A tarmac road from Torla leads 4km to the **park information office** (Centro de Visitantes; July–Oct 10am–1pm & 4–8.30pm) just past the Puente de los Navarros, and from here continues another 4km to the former Pradera de Ordesa car park at the entrance to the **Ordesa Canyon**. All private cars are banned during summer beyond Puente de los Navarros; unless you hike in along the GR15.2 from Torla, you must use the regular **shuttle bus** (€2.25 one-way or return) from the car park at the village outskirts. The well-marked GR15.2 **path** starts beside the *Hotel Bella Vista* in Torla, crossing to the east bank of the river; at Puente de la Ereta it links up with the GR11 – the left fork leads to the information office, while the right fork takes you directly to **Pradera de Ordesa**, some 2hr out of Torla and the start of most of the hikes set out below.

At the information office you can buy a range of **maps** of the park; the clearest is the 1:50,000 IGN sheet (which also covers Gavarnie, across the French border), though cheaper ones are perfectly adequate if you're going to stick to the popular, signed paths. All maps mark the park's network of very basic stone **refugios**, where you will need to stay on longer treks, as camping is prohibited in the park (except when the *refugios* are full in the summer months, when you're allowed to camp alongside them). There are no shops beyond Torla, so be sure to bring your own supplies.

Treks in the park

Most day-trippers to Ordesa aim no further than a loop to the *mirador* (viewing point) at the **Cascada del Abanico**, six easy and well-waymarked kilometres from the Pradera de Ordesa, with a return path on the opposite bank of the Río Arazas. However, there are dozens of other trails, encompassing most levels of enthusiasm and expertise. The following is just a selection.

Circo de Soasco

This is one of the most popular and rewarding, if not very difficult, short-distance treks. A steep, 7.5-kilometre walk along a signposted path brings you out at the **Cola de Caballo** (Horsetail Waterfall) in three to four hours (reckon on 6–7hr there and back). The trail begins through beech forest and then climbs past a *mirador*, to emerge into the upper reaches of a startling gorge.

For more solitude in summer, an alternative approach involves climbing the steep **Senda de los Cazadores** (the Hunters' Path) which emerges at the Mirador de Calcilarruego; from here the path levels out along the Faja de Pelay, which joins up with the Circo de Soaso.

Cotatuero Falls and beyond

A shorter walk visits the impressive **Cotatuero Falls**. Starting from Pradera de Ordesa, the Cotatuero route takes you steeply but easily through the woods to a vantage point below the waterfall. An exciting onward route beckons here, if you have a head for heights. With the help of iron pegs, you can climb above the falls to reach the Brecha de Rolando and trek onwards to Gavarnie (see below).

Carriata Falls and beyond

Another waterfall route is signposted from both La Pradera and the information office towards the **Carriata Falls**. You head into the trees and then leave the contour trail to begin a steep zigzag up to the cascade, most impressive in late spring when melted snow keeps it flowing.

If you want to continue, the left-hand route (at a fork on the open mountainside) ascends to the top of the gorge wall via a series of thirteen iron pegs, not so intimidating as those on the Cotatuero route and feasible for any reasonably fit, active walker. The right-hand fork contours spectacularly along the canyon's north wall to meet up with the path up to Cotatuero.

Refugio Góriz and Monte Perdido

A path climbs up from the top of Circo de Soaso to the **Refugio Góriz** (2169m; 99 places; ☎974 341 201; open all year), about an hour's walk away, which is more elaborate than many refuges, equipped as it is with beds and sheets, and an overpriced restaurant. In July and August, it is usually packed to the gills, but you can camp alongside provided you dismount your tent each morning.

For most walkers, the refuge is a starting point for the ascent of **Monte Perdido** (3355m). This is a scramble rather than a climb but a serious expedition nonetheless, for which you should be properly equipped and prepared; the Góriz guardian can advise. It takes around 5hr to get to the summit, which is reached via an alpine lake, Lago Helado.

Torla to Gavarnie

The Ordesa park adjoins the French **Parc National des Pyrénées** and it is possible to trek across to the French border town of **Gavarnie**. This is a fair haul and most easily done from Torla; routes out of the Ordesa park proper are longer and harder.

Leaving Torla, you follow the GR15.2 as far as the indicated left fork for the Puente de los Navarros (just under 1hr), then climb down to the river and follow the GR11 markers up the valley. There's a **campsite**, *Camping Valle Bujaruelo* (☎974 486 348; mid-April to mid-Oct), after another 4km, and, further beyond, the ruined shrine and medieval bridge of San Nicolás. From this bridge the path, now mostly track, heads over the mountains and down to Gavarnie – six to eight hours' walk.

The southern canyons: Escuaín and Añisclo

In the southeast corner of the Ordesa park yawn a pair of **canyons** – the *gargantas* of **Escuaín** and **Añisclo** – every bit the equal of the Ordesa gorge but with far fewer visitors. The lack of transport to the trailheads, and limited accommodation, contribute to this, but the extra effort is amply rewarded.

The Añisclo canyon

The **Garganta de Añisclo** is the more spectacular of the two canyons, and more frequently visited. If you have your own transport, you can reach it on a minor but paved road from Sarvisé to Escalona (10km north of Aínsa) – though a one-way system forces you to park 1km above the canyon. Westbound traffic from Escalona runs through a narrow gorge, the Desfiladero de las Cambras, at the western end of which knots of parked cars announce the mouth of the canyon.

From here, two broad paths – each as good as the other – lead north into this marvellous, wild gorge; it's five hours' round trip through the most spectacular section to La Ripareta. Long-haul trekkers also use the canyon as an alternative approach to the Góriz hut, exiting the main gorge via the Fon Blanca ravine.

If you're doing a day walk, good places to stay locally include **NERÍN**, 45 minutes' walk west of the canyon along the GR15 trail, via the deserted hamlet of Sercué. Nerín has a fine Romanesque **church** – typical of these settlements – and an *albergue* (☎974 489 010; ❶) which serves meals to residents; alternatively there's the *Pensión El Turista* (☎974 489 016; ❹). **FANLO**, 6km west, is the biggest place hereabouts; *Casa Nerin Sese*, La Plaza 1 (☎974 489 009; ❹), has **rooms** and apartments. Attractive **BUERBA**, just south of the canyon, is the closest habitation and offers the relaxed *Casa Marina* (☎698 714 450, ⓦwww.integridad-total.com/marina.htm; ❸), with a young, English-speaking management and home-cooked vegetarian meals.

The Escuaín canyon

The **Garganta de Escuaín,** more properly the valley of the Río Yaga, is reached most easily from **LAFORTUNADA,** 17km northwest of Aínsa and the most convenient overnight base. *Hotel Badain* (☎974 504 006, ⓕ974 405 048, ⓦwww.rci.es/staragon/hhu/hbadain; ❹) has one of the best restaurants in these valleys (*menú* €9.60), while the adjacent *Pensión Casa Sebastian* (☎974 505 120; ❸) offers congenial rooms and filling *menús*. For cheaper accommodation, try the *Albergue de Badaín*, installed in the church tower of the nearby namesake hamlet (☎974 504 075; ❶).

From Lafortunada, the quickest way into the canyon country if you don't have transport is along the **GR15** trail; it's a two-hour climb along the trail to the picturesque village of **TELLA**, with a clutch of Romanesque churches and a park **information office** (daily late June–Oct 9am–2pm & 3–9pm). Beyond, the trail drops to the river at Estaroniello hamlet before climbing through thick woods to **Escuaín,** an abandoned settlement taken over in summer by enthusiasts exploring **the gorge,** which lies just upstream. There's another park information office here (same hours) but the local *albergue* has shut, probably for good, so bring enough food to sustain you further into the water-sculpted ravine. The GR15 continues west, then south to handsome **BESTUÉ** village, where the newly opened *Albergue Tresserols* in the centre (☎646 809 752; ❶) provides meals and makes a good stopoff en route between Lafortunada and Nerín or Buerba (all 4–5hr distant).

Day-hikers, however, should cross the gorge east on a non-GR trail to **Revilla,** a similarly desolate hamlet on the opposite bank. From there you can backtrack to Tella or follow the lovely and little-trodden **PR3** path through Estaroniello to Hospital de Tella, 3km west of Lafortunada. You can complete this figure-of-eight itinerary in a single, long summer's day, taking in the best this limestone Shangri-la has to offer.

Benasque and around

Serious climbers and trekkers gravitate to **Benasque**, in the Ésera river valley, for, above the town, just out of sight, loom the two highest peaks in the Pyrenees – **Aneto** (3404m) and **Posets** (3371m). The town can be reached most easily from Huesca or Barbastro on the one or two daily **buses**.

Over to the west of Benasque, and reachable from it on a variety of low- and high-altitude paths, is the **Valle de Gistau**, a secluded area which should appeal to those wanting to get away from the more commercialized and established Pyrenean valleys. Southeast of Benasque, near the border with Catalunya, the cathedral village of **Roda de Isábena** stands in glorious isolation on its bluff.

Benasque town

Surrounded by hay fields in a wide stretch of its river valley, **BENASQUE** is an agreeable place, good for a rest before or after the rigours of trekking, combining modern amenities with old stone houses, some of them built by the Aragonese nobility of the seventeenth century.

Budget **accommodation** includes *Casa Bardanca*, c/Las Plazas 6 (☎974 551 360; ❷), with shared-bath but pleasant rooms above *Bar Bardanca*; *Casa Gabás-Pichuán*, on quiet c/El Castillo (☎974 551 275; ❹), offering both en-suite rooms and self-catering units; and the somewhat shabby *Fonda Barrabés*, c/Mayor 3 (☎974 551 654; ❸), a mountaineer's hang-out with a cheap *comedor*. For more comfort, try the *Hotel Aragüells* (☎974 551 619, ⑤974 551 664; ❺) at Avda. de los Tilos 1, the main commercial street; the *Hotel Avenida* next door at no. 3 (☎974 551 126, ⑤974 551 515; ❻); or the more institutional *Hotel Aneto* on Ctra. de Anciles (☎974 551 061, ⑤974 551 509, ⓦwww.hoteles-valero.com; ❻), which has a pool, tennis courts, gym, sauna and parking facilities.

Competition for custom means that reasonable *menús* abound at the **bars and restaurants**. Try the *comedores* of the *Bar Bardanca*, or the *Bar Sayó* at c/Mayor 13, which includes quails or sardines on its three-course *menú*. Snackier options include *Pepe and Company* on c/Mayor, or *La Pizzeria*, just off pedestrianized Plaza Mayor. If you fancy a splurge, try *La Parilla* on Ctra. Francia (the bypass road), purveying *nouvelle* Aragonese cooking – stuffed vegetables and such – for €10.20 *menú* or *a la carta* at €24 and up.

Climbs and walks from Benasque

Benasque attracts committed climbers and trekkers, and if you already count yourself among their number you'll be intent on bagging the **peaks of Aneto and Posets**. These ascents require crampons, ice-axe and a rope, and a helmet to guard against falling rocks; if you're not experienced, go with one of the three local group outfitters.

For casual walkers, however, there are plenty of possibilities. The Aragón mountain club has marked out a number of blue-and-white- and yellow-and-white-painted **pequeño recorrido** (PR) paths, and they are documented in a locally available guide prepared by the club. The trails, to surrounding villages and also to all three local refuges, are routed so that you avoid roads as much as possible.

Benasque is a major halt on the **GR11** trail and its variants, hereabouts at their most spectacular. The easiest and most popular **traverse** is northwest, just upstream from town, along the Estós valley and over the Puerto de Gistaín to the *Refugio de Viadós* (☎974 506 082; open Easter & June–Sept), an 8–9hr hike. Seasoned trekkers may prefer the path which heads northwest up the Eriste valley, 4km southwest of Benasque, and then over the high Collado de Eriste on the shoulder of Posets peak, before dropping down to Viadós. This longer route is best broken partway at the recently enlarged *Refugio Ángel Órus* (☎974 344 044; open most of year).

Heading east past Maladeta, use the public shuttle bus (3 times daily) up the Vallivierna, which cuts out a lot of dreary track-tramping; from the unstaffed hut here at the top of the valley, the GR11 cuts east through lonely, lake-spangled country to the *Hospitau Refugi Sant Nicolau* on the Viella road – the better part of two days' hiking, with a tent advised. Another bus (4 daily) brings you to **La Besurta**, near the top of the Ésera valley and just below the *Refugio Renclusa* (☎974 552 106; open Easter & July–Sept). From here the HRP heads southeast over the high Molières pass (crampons always required), giving eye-to-eye views of Aneto, before dropping down another empty valley to the Sant Nicolau refuge – again, tents are useful.

The Valle de Gistau

The **Valle de Gistau**, long beloved of Spaniards but attracting few foreign guests, is the first significant place you'll reach hiking south from the Viadós hut. A mesh of PR and GR trails link the half-dozen villages here – just as well since bus service is very sparse. **PLAN** is the valley "capital", with shops and **accommodation**: try *Casa Ruché* (☎974 506 072; ❸) on the south edge of town, or the more comfortable *Hotel Mediodía* (☎974 506 006; ❹), both with **restaurants**. **SAN JUAN DE PLAN**, 2km north, has more character as a village, with the best-value **place to stay and eat** in the valley: *Hostal Casa la Plaza* (☎ & ⓕ974 506 052; ❹), with wood-decor rooms and an excellent, mountain-style *menú* (€9) downstairs. *Casa Sanches* nearby, also with a *comedor*, is a worthy fallback (☎974 506 050; ❷). *Casas rurales* are the norm for local accommodation, and there are more in **GISTAÍN** just west, including the inexpensive, ebulliently friendly *Casa Zueras* (☎974 506 038; ❷), huge breakfasts extra, or the popular *Casa Fontamil* at the eastern outskirts (☎974 506 192; ❸), with large rooms and table d'hôte suppers.

Heading west from Gistaín, the GR19 trail leads through Sin en route to Salinas and Lafortunada (see "The southern canyons", p.667). The GR19.1 variant peels off at Sin to reach Bielsa, an alternative gateway to the Ordesa country, with plenty of affordable accommodation.

Alternatively, you can descend south from Sin on another PR trail to **SARAVILLO**, near the mouth of the valley. This has a newish *albergue*, *Borda Miguela* (☎974 506 218; ❶), and assorted *casas rurales*, including *Casa Cazcarreta* (☎974 506 273; ❷), with a **restaurant**. Saravillo is also the starting point for excursions southeast to the lakes and *refugios* of the **Circo de Armeña**; the GR15 trail takes you there in just a few hours, the Editorial Alpina *Cotiella* map-pamphlet has all details.

Roda de Isábena

Attractive hill villages are in seemingly endless supply in Aragón, but **RODA DE ISÁBENA**, in the middle of nowhere on a minor road between El Pont de Suert and Graus (80km from Benasque by good roads), is unique for its superb Romanesque **cathedral** at the heart of town. Originally a monastic church, it's a three-aisled affair with Lombard apses and an eighteenth-century, octagonal belfry notable from afar, but there ends any conformity to pattern. The ornate entrance portal, with six series of capitalled columns inside a Renaissance portico, breaches the south wall, because the west end of the nave is occupied by a carved choir and a fine organ, claimed to be one of the best in Europe. Mass is celebrated on the purported sarcophagus of San Ramón, squirming with twelfth-century carvings showing the Nativity and the Flight into Egypt. Immediately below the raised altar area is a vast triple crypt, the central section with worn column capitals but the northerly one graced by brilliant Romanesque frescoes, thought to be painted by the unknown Master of Taüll (see p.841). Admission is only by guided visit (daily every 45min 11.15am–1.30pm & 4.30–6.45pm; €1.50), though you can see the cloister and its colonnade (eroded like the crypt's) by patronizing the excellent restaurant (see below) installed in the former refectory. When you have finished admiring the cathedral, it's enjoyable just to wander the attractive streets and gawp at the views, literally 360-degree from the *mirador*, which make it understandable why the medieval counts of Ribagorça chose Roda as a stronghold.

Roda can – just – be reached by public transport, but most people come with their own transport. It has become a popular weekend retreat, and it's necessary to book accommodation year-round. Top choices include the excellent-value Hospedaría de Roda, right on the multileveled central plaza (☎974 544 554, ℻974 544 500; ❹), for rooms with a view and all mod cons, and the very friendly, English-speaking Casa Simón (☎974 544 528 or enquire at *Bar Mesón de Roda*), with both en-suite rooms (❹) and 4-bed apartments (❺). For food, the Mesón de Roda does decent meals and breakfasts with a ringside seat on the plaza, but the best restaurant here is the Hospedería La Catedral (☎974 544 539) with an *a la carta* so reasonable (€12.60–15.60) that there's little point in taking the €10.20 *menú*.

Travel Details

Trains

Huesca to: Canfranc (2 daily; 2hr 40min); Jaca (2 daily; 2hr); Sabiñánigo (2 daily; 1hr 40min); Zaragoza (4 daily; 1hr).

Zaragoza to: Barcelona (14 daily; 3hr 30min–4hr 30min); Bilbao (4–5 daily; 4hr 30min); Burgos (4–5 daily; 4hr); Cáceres (2 daily; 8hr 30min); Cádiz (1 daily; 9hr); Córdoba (3 daily; 8hr); Gijón (2 daily; 9hr); Girona (3 daily; 5hr); Huesca (1 daily except Sat; 1hr); Irún (2–3 daily; 4hr 30min); Jaca (1 daily except Sat; 3hr 20min); León (3 daily; 6hr); Lleida (10–12 daily; 1hr 40min); Logroño (5–6 daily; 1hr 45min); Lugo (2–3 daily; 10hr 45min); Madrid (12–14 daily; 3hr); Málaga (2 daily; 9hr–10hr 30min); Medina del Campo (1–3 daily; 5hr 30min); Orense (1–2 daily; 10hr 30min); Oviedo (2 daily; 8hr 30min); Palencia (3 daily; 4hr); Pamplona (5–6 daily; 2hr); Sabiñánigo (1 daily; 3hr); Salamanca (3–4 daily; 6hr 30min); San Sebastián (2–3 daily; 4hr 30min); Sevilla (2 daily; 7hr 20min); Tarragona (8–12 daily; 3hr); Teruel (3 daily; 3hr 30min); Valladolid (1–2 daily; 5hr); Vigo (1–2 daily; 12hr 30min); Vitoria (1 daily; 3hr).

Buses

Aínsa to: Bielsa (Mon, Wed & Fri only at 8.45pm, returns 6am next day; 40min); Plan (Mon, Wed & Fri only at 8.45pm, returns 6am next day; 1hr); Sabiñánigo (1 daily; 2hr).

Barbastro to: Benasque (daily 11am, plus Mon–Sat 5.30pm; 2hr); Boltaña via Aínsa (Mon–Sat at 7.45pm, returns next day 6.45am; July 15–Aug 31 also 11am, returning 3pm; Huesca–Barbastro 10am/6.30pm services link with this); Lleida (6 daily; 1hr 15min).

Huesca to: Barbastro (4–7 daily; 50min); Barcelona (2–4 daily; 4hr 20min); Fraga (1 daily; 2hr 15min); Jaca (4–5 daily; 1hr); Lleida (6 daily; 2hr); Loarre (3 daily; 45min); Monzón (4 daily; 1hr 10min); Pamplona (3 daily; 2hr 50min); Sabiñánigo (4–5 Mon–Sat, 3–4 Sun & hols; 55min); Zaragoza (18 Mon–Fri, 10 Sat, Sun & hols; 1hr).

Jaca to: Ansó via Echo (1 daily; 1hr 40min); Astún/Candanchú (5 daily; 45min); Biescas (1–2 daily; 50min); Canfranc-Estación (5 daily; 30min); Huesca (4–5 daily; 1hr); Pamplona (1–2 daily; 1hr 35min); Sabiñánigo (2 daily; 20min); Zaragoza (3–5 daily; 2hr 15min).

Roda de Isábena to: El Pont de Suert (1 daily Mon–Fri at 4.37pm, returns next day at 6.15am; 1 hr); Graus (1 daily at 7.18am, returns at 4pm; 40min).

Teruel to: Albarracín (1 daily; 2hr); Barcelona (2 daily; 5hr); Cantavieja/L'Iglesuela del Cid/Villafranca del Cid (1 daily; 2hr 30min/3hr/3hr 15min); Cuenca (1 daily; 2hr 30min); Valencia (5–6 daily; 2hr). All services reduce dramatically on Sundays.

Zaragoza to: Astorga (2 daily; 8hr); Barcelona (22–25 daily; 3hr 30min–5hr); Bilbao (6–9 daily; 3hr 15min–4hr); Burgos (2 daily; 3hr 45min); Cariñena (2 daily; 1hr 15min); A Coruña (1 daily; 11hr 20min); Huesca (Mon–Sat 19 daily, Sun 7 daily; 1hr 15min); Jaca (3 daily; 2hr 30min); León (2 daily; 8hr); Lleida (5 daily; 2–3hr); Logroño (3 daily; 2hr 30min); Lourdes via Huesca, Jaca, Canfranc, Pau, Oloron (June–Sept Sat 7.30am, Sun 2.30pm; 7hr; passes through Jaca at 9.45am & 5.45pm); Lugo (2–4 daily; 9hr–10hr 30min); Madrid (15–18 daily; 3hr 45min); Palencia (2 daily; 5hr); Ponferrada (2 daily; 9hr); Salamanca (2 daily; 6hr); Santiago de Compostela (1 daily; 12hr 15min); Soria (2–3 daily; 2hr 15min); Sos del Rey Católico (1 daily; 2hr 15min); Tarragona (4–7 daily; 2hr 45min); Valladolid (2–3 daily; 6hr 30min); Zamora (3 daily; 6hr 15min).

more *Spain*

Jerez
Murcia
Gerona

buzzaway.com

buzz™ The low cost airline that gives you more

Budget

Car and Van Rental

Budget goes further with buzz

Get a great deal on car rental! With Budget we offer a price guarantee* exclusive to all buzz flyers.

Reservations made simple

Call **0845 60 60 608** quoting BCD G911300
Or book online at **www.buzzaway.com**

buzz™

car rental with Budget

Barcelona

CHAPTER 10

Highlights

* **Modernisme** p.712 The spectacular *modernista* creations dotted around the city by the architect genius Antoni Gaudí and his contemporaries.

* **Las Ramblas** p.690 The city's famous thoroughfare, bustling with buskers, vendors and street-performers.

* **"La Boqueria" Market** p.692 Wander among a festival of colours and smells of the Mercat Sant Josep in the heart of the city.

* **The Barri Gòtic** p.698 An atmospheric maze of ancient and narrow streets.

* **Santa Maria del Mar** p.703 Pure Catalan-Gothic style in the elegant lines of the pride of medieval Barcelona.

* **The MNAC** p.708 Visit the outstanding collection of Romanesque murals housed on the slopes of Montjuïc.

* **Montserrat** p.722 Catch the cable car up the souring cliff face to the monastery that has drawn pilgrims for a thousand years.

* **El Xampanyet** p.725 Sample Catalan cava and local tapas in the relaxed surroundings of this little neighbourhood bar.

* **La Mercè** p.737 The city's greatest festival, three days of free concerts, fireworks and folklore in September.

* **Sónar** p.737 A weekend-long showcase for the best electronic music the world has to offer.

Barcelona

Barcelona, the self-confident and progressive capital of Catalunya, vibrates with life. A thriving port and prosperous commercial centre, the city is almost impossible to exhaust, and even in a lengthy visit you will likely only scrape the surface: it boasts some superb **museums** – including the world-class Museu d'Art de Catalunya, and individual art museums dedicated to Picasso, Joan Miró and Antoni Tàpies – as well as outstanding Gothic and *modernista* (Art Nouveau) **architecture**, most perfectly and eccentrically expressed in the work of **Antoni Gaudí**, reason in itself for visiting the city. But there's also a multitude of very agreeable ways of doing very little. From midday to long after midnight the city's avenues, from the world-famous **Ramblas** to the broad boulevards of the new town, are choked with people strolling, browsing, listening to buskers or watching street performers. On sunny afternoons, the city's beach beckons thousands of sunbathers and swimmers. The energy of Barcelona is boundless, channelled into its industry and business, art and music, political protest and merrymaking. The city is a pleasure at any time of year, but to see it at its best, come during one of the main **fiestas** (*festes* in Catalan), which include April 23 (*Día de Sant Jordi* or St George's Day), June 24 (*Día de Sant Joan*), September 24 (*Festa de la Mercè*) and many more (see the list on p.747).

Barcelona has long had the reputation of being the avant-garde capital of Spain, especially in design and architecture, though in the 1980s much of the intellectual impetus passed to Madrid. Gaining the 1992 **Olympics** was an important boost: the enormous popular support for sports in Barcelona (especially for

Accommodation price codes

All the establishments listed in this book have been price-graded according to the following scale. The prices quoted are for the **cheapest available double room in high season**; effectively this means that anything in the ❹ and most places in the ❷ range will be without private bath, though there's usually a washbasin in the room. In the ❹ category and above you will probably be getting private facilities. Remember, though, that many of the budget places will also have more expensive rooms including en-suite facilities. Youth hostels are graded under ❶ as the price per person is less than half of the category's upper limit.

Note that in the more upmarket *hostales* and *pensiones*, and in anything calling itself a hotel, you'll pay a **tax** (IVA) of seven percent on top of the room price.

❶ Under €12	❹ €27–36	❼ €60–90
❷ €12–18	❺ €36–48	❽ €90–120
❸ €18–27	❻ €48–60	❾ Over €120

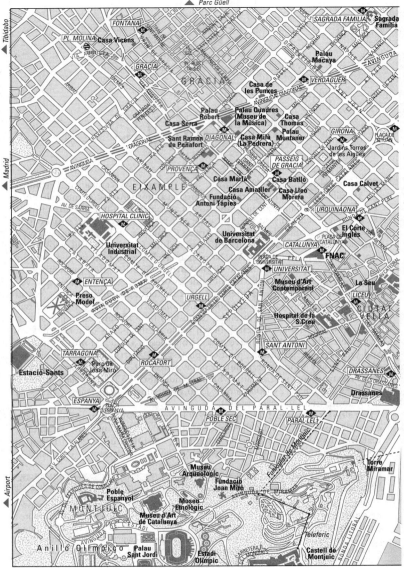

▲ Parc Güell

football, the chief focus of the incessant rivalry with Madrid) helped win the nomination in the first place, and the legacy of the games was an outstanding set of new facilities and a spruced-up city centre. The Olympic Village and **Parc de Mar** development arose from the disintegrating old industrial area of Poble Nou, while the Olympic stadium on Montjuïc, built in 1929 was entirely refitted. Latterly, the harbour area at the foot of the Ramblas has been com-

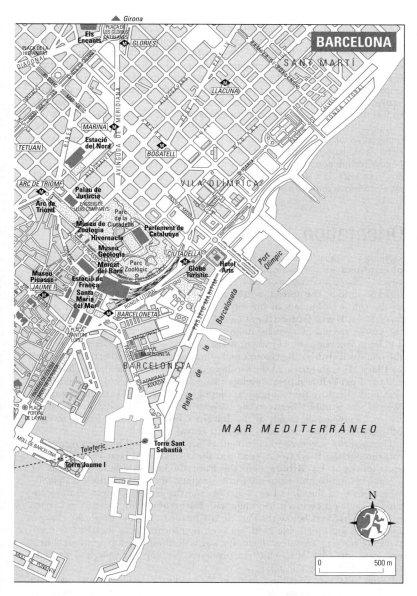

pletely overhauled as part of the **Port Vell** development, and now parts of the Barri Chino/Raval neighbourhood are being rescued from complete decay by an EU-funded renovation programme. And the reforms have not stopped there: new theatres and concert halls have opened and the finishing touches are being added to a World Trade Centre in the city's old port.

But there are darker sides to this prosperity and confidence. As more money is poured into the sleek image, residents of previously poor neighbourhoods are edged out as house prices rocket. Indeed, despite the constant drive for improvement and the high-tech edge to much of the city infrastructure, the old city continues to be disconcertingly dirty and neglected – there is a great deal of poverty here and drug use is evident. The city has also yet to come to grips with integrating an ever-increasing wave of unskilled and illegal immigrants. This all means that **petty crime** is rife and it's not unusual for tourists to feel threatened in their peregrinations around the seedier areas flanking the Ramblas, or around the Arc de Triomf. If you're *very* unlucky you'll be mugged, so take a few precautions: keep passports and tickets locked up in your hotel, leave bags under tables with your feet on them in outdoor cafes, don't be too conspicuous with expensive cameras and, if you are attacked, *never* offer any resistance. If you've brought your car, don't leave anything in view, and always remove the radio and tape deck.

Orientation

Despite a population of over three million, Barcelona is a surprisingly easy place to find your way around. Most sites of historic interest are in the **old town** – the Ciutat Vella, or Casc Antic – which is small enough to master quickly on foot. This spreads northwest from the harbour for about 1.5km up to the southern borders of the city's nineteenth-century grid system. At its heart is the **Barri Gòtic** (*Barrio Gótico* in Castilian), the medieval nucleus of the city – around 500 square metres of gloomy, twisted streets and historic buildings. Bisecting the old town, at the western edge of the Barri Gòtic, are the famous **Ramblas**, Barcelona's main thoroughfare, its northern end marked by **Plaça de Catalunya**. At the southern end of the Ramblas lies the **harbour** and the **Port Vell** (old port) development, where walkways and a swing bridge skip across the harbour to a popular shopping, restaurant and cinema complex. West of the Ramblas, between the harbour and c/de l'Hospital, lies the warren of streets known locally as the **Barrio Chino** (or China Town), though officially the neighbourhood is called **El Raval**.

The medieval streets continue on either side of the Ramblas: reaching northeast through the Barri Gòtic – and past the celebrated **Museu Picasso** in the area known as **La Ribera** – to the **Parc de la Ciutadella** (*Parque de la Ciudadela*); and southwest to the fortress-topped hill of **Montjuïc** (*Montjuïch*), where some of the city's best museums and the main Olympic stadium are sited. A cable car connects Montjuïc with **Barceloneta**, the waterfront district east of the harbour, below the Parc de la Ciutadella. Further northeast, the old industrial suburb of Poble Nou has been transformed over the last few years with the opening of a new university and waterfront developments including the **Parc de Mar** site, which incorporates the Port Olímpic and the Vila Olímpica (Olympic Village).

Beyond Plaça de Catalunya stretches the modern city and commercial centre. Known as the **Eixample** (*Ensanche*), it was conceived in the last century as a breathing space for the congested old town, its simple grid plan split by two huge avenues that lead out of the city; the **Gran Via de les Corts Catalanes** (or simply "Gran Vía") and the **Avinguda Diagonal** ("La Diagonal"). It's in the Eixample that some of Europe's most extraordinary architecture – including Gaudí's **Sagrada Família** – is located.

Beyond the Eixample lie suburbs which were until relatively recently separate villages. The nearest, and the one you're most likely to visit, is trendy **Gràcia**, with its small squares and lively bars. Gaudí left his mark in these areas, too, particularly in the splendid **Parc Güell**, but also in a series of embellished buildings and private suburban houses which the enthusiastic will find simple to track down. **Out of the city**, the mountain-top monastery of **Montserrat** is the most obvious day-trip to make, though the **beaches** on either side of the city also beckon in the summer.

Arrival

Most **points of arrival** are fairly central, with the obvious exception of the airport. If you're aiming to stay on the Ramblas or in the Barri Gòtic – much the best idea – there are fast city transport connections right there from most termini.

By air

Barcelona's **airport** is 12km southwest of the city at El Prat de Llobregat. There's an information office in each terminal (see below), as well as exchange facilities and car rental offices; for details of these and flight information numbers, see "Listings", p.740.

The airport is linked to the city by regular and direct train or bus services. The **train** (6am–10.40pm; journey time 30min; €2 weekdays, €2.25 weekends and public holidays; info on ☎934 811 299) runs every thirty minutes to Sants Estació and – more usefully if you're staying in the Barri Gòtic – continues to the station at Plaça de Catalunya, with the exception of the very last train which terminates in Sants. There's also a very useful **Aerobus** service (Mon–Fri 5.30am–11pm, Sat & Sun 6am–11.30pm; €3) which leaves every fifteen minutes from outside both terminals, stopping in the city at Plaça d'Espanya, Gran Vía (at c/Comte d'Urgell), Plaça Universitat, Plaça de Catalunya and Passeig de Gràcia (at c/de la Diputació) – this takes around thirty minutes to reach Plaça de Catalunya, though allow longer in the rush hour. A **taxi** from the airport costs roughly €20.50 to Estació-Sants, and €21–22 to somewhere more central in the old town.

By train

The main station for national and some international arrivals is **Estació-Sants**, west of the centre. Again, there are exchange, information and car rental offices here, as well as a hotel booking service (see "Accommodation" below). From Sants, metro line 3 runs direct to Liceu for the Ramblas.

The **Estació de França**, next to the Parc de la Ciutadella, east of the centre, handles many of the long-distance arrivals and departures: essentially, this means Talgo services from Madrid, Sevilla and Málaga, Intercity services from other major Spanish cities, and international trains from Paris, Zurich, Milan and Geneva. Some trains stop at both Sants and França – check the timetable first. From França either take metro line 4 from nearby Barceloneta, or simply walk for 5 minutes into the Barri Gòtic, up Vía Laietana and into c/Jaume I.

Other possible arrival points by train are the stations at **Plaça de Catalunya**, at the top of the Ramblas, and **Arc de Triomf**, near the Parc de la Ciutadella (for trains from coastal towns north of the city, the airport, Lleida, and towns on the Puigcerdà–Vic line); **Plaça d'Espanya** (FGC trains from Montserrat and Manresa); and **Passeig de Gràcia** (trains from Port Bou/Girona).

Finding an address

Addresses in Barcelona are all written in Catalan, although some maps still haven't yet caught up and still use Castilian spellings. In this book, the text and maps use Catalan names and addresses.

Addresses are written as: c/Picasso 2, 4° – which means Picasso street (*carrer*) no. 2, fourth floor. You may also see left- (*esquerra*) hand apartment or office; *dreta* is right; *centro* centre. C/Picasso s/n means the building has no number (*sense número*). In the grid of streets of the Eixample, **building numbers** run from south to north (lower numbers at the Plaça de Catalunya end) and from west to east (lower numbers at Plaça d'Espanya).

The other main address **abbreviations** used in Barcelona are: Avgda. (for *Avinguda*, avenue); Pg. (for *Passeig*, more a boulevard than a street); Bxda. (for *Baixada*, alley); Ptge. (for *Passatge*, passage); and Pl. (for *Plaça*, square).

For a full rundown of the Catalan language – and a list of useful words – see the feature on p.750.

By bus

The main bus terminal, used by most international, long-distance and provincial buses, is the **Estació del Nord** on Avinguda Vilanova (main entrance on c/Ali-Bei), three blocks north of the Parc de la Ciutadella (nearest metro is Arc de Triomf, a five-minute walk away). There's a bus information desk on the ground floor, with the ticket offices above at street level. Intercity and international departures also leave from the smaller station just behind Estació Sants at Plaça Joan Peiró (Ⓜ Sants-Estació/Plaça de Sants). When **leaving**, it's a good idea to reserve a seat in advance on the popular long-distance routes; the day before is usually fine. There's a round-up of bus companies and their destinations in "Listings", p.740.

By ferry

Ferries from the Balearics dock at the **Estació Marítima** at the bottom of the Ramblas. There are daily services from Palma (Mallorca) and several times weekly ferries from Ibiza and Menorca. From the ferry terminal you're only a short walk from Plaça Portal de la Pau at the bottom of the Ramblas; nearest metro, Drassanes. Schedules and tickets for departures are available from Transmediterránea, at the Estació Marítima, and from travel agencies; see "Listings", p.740.

By car

Coming into Barcelona along any one of the *autopistes*, head for the Cinturó Littoral, the southern half of the city's ring road, and follow signs for "Port Vell", the main exit for the old town. There are many indoor **car parks** in the city centre; the public ones are linked to display boards which indicate where there are free spaces. Although convenient, these can be expensive (usually €15 for 24 hours). With the exception of the blue meter-zones in the central section of the Eixample, **street parking** is free, but it is not permitted in most of the old town, and it can be tough to find spaces, particularly in older areas like Gràcia. Don't be tempted to double-park or leave your car in loading zones – the cost of being towed can exceed €120, and no mercy is shown to foreign-plated vehicles.

Information

It is a good idea to visit a **turisme** as soon as possible after arrival, where you can pick up a large-scale map of the city (€1.25) and a free public transport map – as well as more detailed pamphlets and brochures on aspects of the city's architecture, history and culture. The tourist offices also sell the **Barcelona Card**, which gives free travel on public transport, reductions of up to fifty percent on entry into many museums and between ten and thirty percent in some shops and restaurants. The card is valid for 24 hours (€15), 48 hours (€18) or 72 hours (€21), and is worth considering if you are only going to be in town for a short time.

The main tourist office is at **Plaça de Catalunya** (daily 9am–9pm; ☎906 301 282 if calling from within Spain, ☎+34 933 043 431 if calling from abroad, or ☎933 043 232, ☎933 043 326 for accommodation information; ⓦwww.barcelonaturisme.com); it's no longer possible to make hotel bookings by phone, but you can use Barcelona Online instead (☎932 473 131, ⓦwww.barcelona-on-line.es/reserves/index.htm). There are also offices at both **airport** terminals (daily 9am–3pm; ☎934 784 704 & 934 780 565), at **Estació-Sants** (June–Sept daily 8am–8pm; Oct–May Mon–Fri 8am–8pm, Sat & Sun 8am–2pm; ☎934 914 431), and inside the **ajuntament** building on Plaça Sant Jaume (Mon–Sat 10am–7pm, Sun 10am–2pm; ☎932 702 429). For information about Catalunya go to **Palau Robert**, Pg. de Gràcia 107 (Mon–Sat 10am–7pm, Sun & holidays 11am–3pm; ☎932 384 000), the tourist office run by the Generalitat (the Catalan government). There is also a summer information **kiosk** (open May–Oct) in front of the Sagrada Familia and wandering tourist information officers in red jackets operating in the old town. The **Municipal Information Office** in Plaça de Sant Miquel (Mon–Fri 8.30am–6pm; ☎932 702 429) is not really for tourists, but is invariably helpful. For the English-speaking **Informació Metropolitana** line (Mon–Sat 8am–10pm), call ☎010.

City transport

Apart from the medieval Barri Gòtic, which is best visited on foot, one of the best ways to get around is by **bicycle**, taking advantage of the city's newly laid-out cycling paths. If you are put off by the volume of traffic, however, you can use Barcelona's excellent transport system to make the most of what the city has to offer. The system comprises the metro, buses, trains and a network of funicular railways and cable cars: to sort it all out, pick up a free **public transport map** (*Guia del Transport Públic de Barcelona*) at any of the tourist offices, or at the city information office in Plaça de Sant Miquel; the map is also posted at bus stops and metro stations. Detailed transport information is also available by telephone (☎010) and online (ⓦwww.tmb.net).

The **metro** starts at 5am (6am on Sun) and shuts down at 11pm – just when most people in Barcelona are thinking of going out. It's extended to 2am on Friday, Saturday, and the evening before a holiday, and to midnight on Sunday. **Bus** routes (4.30am–10.30pm) are far more complicated, but every bus stop displays a comprehensive route map. There's a flat **fare** on both metro and buses of €0.96; if you're staying a couple of days or more it's better to buy a ticket strip or **targeta** (T-10) from metro station ticket offices, which gives you ten journeys at a discounted price. The T-10 costs €5.32 and covers the metro,

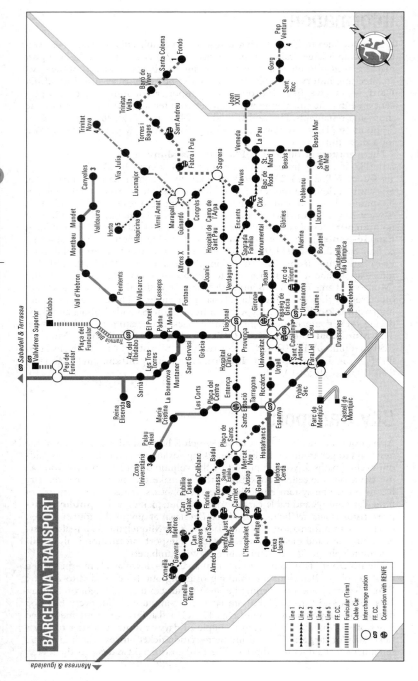

BARCELONA TRANSPORT

◄ *Sabadell & Terrassa*

◄ *Manresa & Igualada*

Line 1
Line 2
Line 3
Line 4
Line 5
FF. CC.
Funicular (Tram)
Cable Car
Interchange station
FF. CC.
Connection with RENFE

buses, and some regional train lines within the city (passes are also available for outlying zones), while a one-day T-Dia costs €4.80. Anyone caught without a valid ticket on the metro is liable to an **on-the-spot fine** of €30. A limited number of yellow **night buses** run from 10.30/11.30pm to 3.30/4.30am, most starting or passing through Plaça de Catalunya; they cost a little more than daytime services. The two routes of the hop-on-and-off **Bus Turístic** link Barcelona's major sights. Tickets (adults: 1 day €13.22, 2 days €16.83; children €7.81) include a booklet of discount coupons for museums, shops and restaurants.

The metro

The quickest way of getting around Barcelona is by the modern and efficient **metro**, which runs on five lines; entrances are marked with a red diamond sign. Its **hours of operation** are Mon–Thurs 5am–11pm; Fri, Sat and the night before a holiday 5am–2am; Sun 6am–midnight; and holidays 6am–11pm.

Buses

Bus routes are easy to master if you get hold of a copy of the transport map and remember that the routes are colour-coded: **city-centre buses** are red and always stop at one of three central squares (Catalunya, Universitat or Urquinaona); **cross-city buses** are yellow; green buses run on all the **peripheral routes** outside the city centre; and **night buses** are blue (and always stop near or in Plaça de Catalunya). In addition, the route is marked at each bus stop, along with a timetable – where relevant, bus routes are detailed in the text. Most buses **operate daily**, roughly from 4–5am until 10.30pm, though some lines stop earlier and some run on until after midnight. The **night buses** fill in the gaps on all the main routes, with services every thirty minutes from around 10pm to 4am.

There's also a **tourist bus**, Bus Turístic (#100; daily 9am–7pm; every 20min), starting at Plaça de Catalunya and linking all the main sights and tourist destinations, including the Sagrada Familia, Parc Güell and the Poble Espanyol. The bus is colour-coded according to its direction: red for northbound and blue for southbound. Tickets cost €12 and are valid for a day, allowing you to get on and off as you please; a two-day ticket costs €15. The ticket also gives discounts at various attractions and on other transport systems, such as the Tibidabo tram.

Trains, funiculars and cable cars

The city has a commuter **train line**, the Ferrocarrils de la Generalitat de Catalunya (FGC), with its main stations at Plaça de Catalunya and Plaça d'Espanya. You'll use this going to Montserrat and Tibidabo.

You may also use the **funicular railway** (€1.50 one-way, €2.25 return) and **cable car** (€3 one-way, €3.75 return) when going to Montjuïc, and there's a tram (€1.65 one-way, €2.40 return) and funicular service (€1.80 one-way, €3 return) to Tibidabo, too – full details in those sections of the text. On these services, the T1 *targeta* is valid only for the Tibidabo tram. You also have to pay separately for the **cross-harbour cable car**, known as the Telefèric, or Transbordador Aéreo de Montjuïc (€6 one-way, €7.20 return, plus €3.60 for the Jaume I lift), which is well worth taking at least once for the views.

Taxis

Black-and-yellow **taxis** (with a green roof light on when available for hire) are inexpensive and plentiful. There's a minimum charge of €1.60 and after that it's around €0.60 per kilometre. But taxis won't take more than four people and charge extra for baggage and on public holidays, for trips to the airport, and for a multitude of other things. Asking for a *recibo* (or *rebut* in Catalan) should ensure that the price is fair. **Cabs** can be called on the following numbers: ☎934 902 222; ☎934 331 020; ☎933 003 811; ☎933 577 755; ☎933 199 268; and ☎933 215 700.

Bikes

Bicycles are the quickest and best way to take in the sights of the city. Although bicycles as city transport is something of a novel concept for Barcelonesos, the city has adapted quickly, laying out rights-of-way along many of the most heavily travelled streets. This said, the population at large has yet to adapt, as the new paths are often ignored by cars or clogged with pedestrians, indignantly reluctant to give way to two-wheelers. Currently, some 30km of cycle paths follow the city's main traffic arteries and the seafront, with more planned to open in coming years. There are a number of rental outfits (see "Listings", p.740), and the tourist office has a free map of bike routes.

Accommodation

You can pick up a list of hotels and *hostales* at any turisme, though these don't usually include the less expensive categories of accommodation. If you don't want to wander the streets when you first arrive, **hotel reservations offices** at the airport and at Sants station (daily 8am–10pm) or the tourist office in Plaça de Catalunya (daily 9am–9pm) will book you a place to stay on arrival, but they don't handle the very cheapest places and, of course, you won't get to see the room beforehand. In high season, be prepared for the worst as far as availability goes; you may want to book ahead in a more expensive place for at least the first night and then shift to cheaper accommodation after arrival.

Hotels and hostales

Most of the **budget accommodation** in Barcelona is to be found in the **Barri Gòtic**, a convenient and atmospheric base. However, what may be atmospheric by day can seem plain threatening after dark, and the further down towards the harbour you get, the less salubrious, and noisier, the surroundings. As a rule, anything above c/Escudellers tends to be acceptable (though not necessarily fancy or modern); anything right on the Ramblas or on the streets above c/Portaferrissa should be reliable and safe. The best hunting ground is between the Ramblas and Plaça de Sant Jaume, in the area bordered by c/Escudellers and c/de la Boqueria, where there are loads of options, from *fondas* to three-star hotels. Beyond, in the wider streets of the **Eixample**, are found most of the city's more expensive places to stay, though you'll also be able to find reasonably priced rooms here. There are more possibilities in the **Gràcia** district, which – though further out – is easily reached by metro.

On (and just off) the Ramblas

The further up the Ramblas you go, towards Plaça de Catalunya, the quieter, more pleasant and more expensive the places become. Alternatively, there are several places on Plaça Reial, halfway down the Ramblas, a nineteenth-century square dotted with palm trees and arcaded walks.

ACCOMMODATION

Residencia Australia	8
Hostal Ciudad Condal	4
Pensión Ciutadella	15
Hotel Claris	6
Hotel Duques de Bergara	11
Hotel Ginebra	9
Hostal Girona	10
Hostal de Joves	13
Hostal Morató	14
Pensión Norma	2
Hostal Orleans	16
Hotel Paseo de Gràcia	3
Hostal de Ribagorza	12
Pensión San Medín	1
Hostal Universal	7
Hostal Windsor	5

RESTAURANTS & TAPAS BARS

Aire	M
Al Diwan	O
Bar Mundial	V
El Berriketa	R
Bice	Q
La Bodegueta	J
Botafumeiro	B
Can-Busto	Z
Can Ganassa	e
Can Ramonet	c
Cantina Mexicana II	a
Cervecería Catalana	L
Comme-Bio II	S
Equinox	D
Euskal Etxea	Y
El Galliner	F
Gargantua & Pantagruel	P
La Gavina	C
L'Hostal de Rita	N
Illa de Gràcia	G
Jai-Ca	b
Laie	T
Lizarran	K
Llar del Filador	U
Lluna Plena	W
El Nou Candanchu	H
Petit Paris	I
Restaurante Carpanta	a
El Rey de la Gamba	E
El Tastavins	E
El Xampanyet	X

Hostal-Pensión El Cantón, c/Nou de Sant Francesc 40 ☎933 173 019, ☎933 022 267, @ hostalcanton@mx4.redestb.es. On a tiny street parallel to the Ramblas, this great-value hotel has good-sized rooms, apartments for families and friendly, professional staff. Disabled access. ❹

Hotel Lloret, Ramblas 125 ☎933 173 366, ☎933 019 283. A grand Ramblas building whose large rooms are better value than most in this category – most have TV and air-conditioning and lots have Ramblas views. Rooms with just washbasins are cheaper. ❼

Hostal Marítima, Ramblas 4 ☎933 023 152. Popular backpackers' choice next to the Wax Museum, offering basic doubles and triples with and without showers; there's a washing machine and luggage storage service too. ❹

Pensión Noya, Ramblas 133 ☎933 014 831. The best choice in this block and a popular stop for young travellers. Nice rooms, separate showers; you might find prices in high season fall into the next category up. ❺

Hotel Oriente, Ramblas 45 ☎933 022 558, ☎934 123 819, @ horiente@husa.es. Appealing, late-nineteenth-century decor in Barcelona's second-oldest hotel and smart, modern rooms, some with Ramblas views; breakfast included. ❽

Hotel Roma Reial, Plaça Reial 11 ☎933 020 366, ☎933 011 839. Lots of airy rooms overlooking the square; others give onto an indoor patio. Although a bit run-down, it's good value for its location – book ahead. ❼

Between Carrer de Ferran and Carrer de la Boqueria

These two streets, and the alleys that run between them, are a good place to start for budget possibilities back from the Ramblas.

Hotel California, c/Rauric 14 ☎933 177 766, ☎933 175 474. Tucked down a side street that crosses c/de Ferran, this friendly hotel is popular with gay travellers. Rooms have TV and air-conditioning, and breakfast is included in the price. ❽

Pensión Europa, c/de la Boqueria 18 ☎933 187 620. A bit on the dingy side but cheap and popular with groups of young travellers. Some rooms have private bath. ❺

Pensión Fernando, c/Ferran 31 ☎ 933 017 993, ⓦ www.barcelona-in-line.es/fernando. Well-kept hotel/hostel with its entrance on the main street. Double rooms have private bath and TV, while dorm accommodation is available for €12 per person. ❺

Plaça de Sant Miquel, Plaça de Sant Jaume and La Ribera

The streets between and around the Barri Gòtic's two central squares are rather more attractive than most in the area and contain several decent budget hotels, while the quieter La Ribera also has a number of good options.

Pensió Alamar, c/Comtessa de Sobradiel 1 ☎933 025 012. An economical old-city option. All the rooms here have balconies onto the street and the *hostal* is clean and well looked after. ❹

Pensión Ciutadela, c/Comerç 33 ☎933 196 203; Ⓜ Barceloneta. Basic six-room *pensión* with minimal facilities and in need of renovation, but friendly and well located – just across from the Estació de França. ❹

Hostal Fontanella, Via Laietana 71 ☎933 175 943; Ⓜ Urquinaona. Spotless and well-decorated *hostal* on a wide avenue in the old town, with a great old-fashioned lift. Prices drop dramatically off-season. ❺

Hostal Levante, Baixada Sant Miquel 2 ☎933 179 565, ☎932 682 042. This welcoming wood-panelled *hostal* is a good first choice. Nice, plain rooms (with and without shower) on two floors in a well-kept building. Recommended. ❺

Pensión Lourdes, c/Princesa 14 ☎933 193 372.

Absolutely basic but cheap and well located for the Barri Gòtic and Pg. Born with clean bathrooms, and a TV room. ❹

Pensión Mari-Luz, c/ de la Palau 4 ☎ & ☎933 173 463. Run by the same people as the *Fernando* (see above), this well-maintained *hostal* is set in an old palace, secluded on a quieter street. Doubles have a sink, and single travellers can share 4- to 6-bed rooms for €9. Kitchen, washing machine and 24-hour entry. ❺

Hostal Marmo, c/Gignás 25 ☎933 105 970; Ⓜ Jaume I. Tucked away behind the central post office near the old port, this clean and basic family-run *hostal* is open all year. No frills, but friendly. ❹

Hostal Orleans, Avgda. Marquès de l'Argentara 13 ☎933 197 382, ☎933 192 219; Ⓜ Barceloneta. Medium-sized family-run *hostal* on the edge of the old town, with good access to the beach and Parc de la Ciutadella. Larger rooms available for groups. ❺

Near the cathedral: Plaça Sant Josep Oriol and Carrer Portaferrissa

Around and beyond the cathedral, from Plaça Sant Josep Oriol northwards, the price and quality of accommodation take a general step up. Carrer Portaferrissa in particular has several decent choices.

Hostal Layetana, Plaça Ramon Berenguer el Gran 2 ⓣ & ⓕ 933 192 012. Close to the cathedral, and with airy rooms, some without showers, for which you'll pay around €9 less. ❹
Hostal Malda, c/del Pi 5 ⓣ 933 173 002. One of the best bargains in the centre. Small, but clean and very well priced. No kitchen facilities, but some rooms with private bath. Single travellers can stay in the tiny tower above the roof for just €6 – book well ahead. ❸

Hostal-Residencia Rembrandt, c/Portaferrissa 23 ⓣ & ⓕ 933 181 011. An excellent place, run by accommodating people. Spotless rooms with shower and balcony; less expensive rooms without, too. ❺
Pensió Vitoria, c/de la Palla 8 ⓣ & ⓕ 933 020 834. Very basic, clean *hostal* in a converted private flat, away from the noise of the Ramblas. Another well-priced option, though the walls are rather thin. Some rooms with private shower available. ❺

West of the Ramblas

There are lots of places to stay on the west side of the Ramblas, though the proximity of the Barrio Chino red-light district doesn't make it the most enticing part of Barcelona. Look especially on c/de Sant Pau and c/Hospital, and c/Junta del Comerç, which runs between these two streets.

Hotel Aneto, c/Carme 38 ⓣ 933 019 989, ⓕ 933 019 862. Small, reasonably priced hotel in a good location, on one of the safer streets in this area. All rooms with bath and air-conditioning – ask for one with a view of the lovely square below. Breakfast included. ❼
Hotel España, c/de Sant Pau 9–11 ⓣ 933 181 758, ⓕ 933 171 134. Designed by Domènech i Montaner; the highlight of this elegant late-nine-teenth-century hotel is the splendid *modernista* dining room. The rooms are spacious and com-fortable, many giving onto delightful interior patios. ❼
Hostal Morató, c/Nou de la Rambla 50 ⓣ 934 423 669, ⓦ www.hostalmorato.com. Newly and attractively renovated, this 32-room *hostal* offers rooms with TV and phone, as well as bicycle park-

ing and a small bar for guests. Rough Guide read-ers get a complimentary breakfast. ❹
Hotel Peninsular, c/de Sant Pau 34 ⓣ & ⓕ 933 023 138. An interesting old building originally belonging to Carmelite nuns, which explains the slightly cell-like quality of the rooms. The main attractions are the attractive covered inner court-yard hung with dozens of plants and the well-restored dining room area; breakfast included. ❼
Hotel Sant Agustí, Plaça Sant Agustí el Nou 3 ⓣ 933 181 658, ⓕ 933 172 928, ⓦ www.hotelsa .com. Barcelona's oldest hotel housed in a seven-teenth-century building on the newly renovated *plaça*. Reservations are practically mandatory at this popular stop for English-speaking travellers. There are 3 rooms outfitted for guests with disabil-ities. ❽

Around Plaça de Catalunya and the Eixample

The top end of the Ramblas, around Plaça de Catalunya, is a central place to stay – with the added advantage of being reached directly from the airport by train or bus. On the whole, the extra money it costs to stay in this part of town is well spent if you're concerned about looks and safety, less so if you're after character and a central position.

Residencia Australia, Ronda Universitat 11, 4° ⓣ 933 174 177, ⓕ 933 025 282; ⓜ Universitat. Good rooms (some with bath), well cared for by a pleasant Antipodean management. You'll need to reserve ahead as this place is always busy – try at least a fortnight in advance in summer. ❺
Hostal Ciudad Condal, c/Mallorca 255 ⓣ 932 151 040; ⓜ Passeig de Gràcia. Plain but comfort-able and one of the few budget options in this

expensive area. All rooms come with bath and TV, some look onto the busy street and those at the back give onto an indoor patio. ❾
Hotel Claris, c/Pau Claris 150 ⓣ 934 876 262, ⓕ 932 157 970, ⓔ claris@derbyhotels.es; ⓜ Passeig de Gràcia. Renovated Eixample *palau* featuring stylish, modern accommodation and up-to-the-minute facilities, including roof terrace, restaurant and pool. ❾

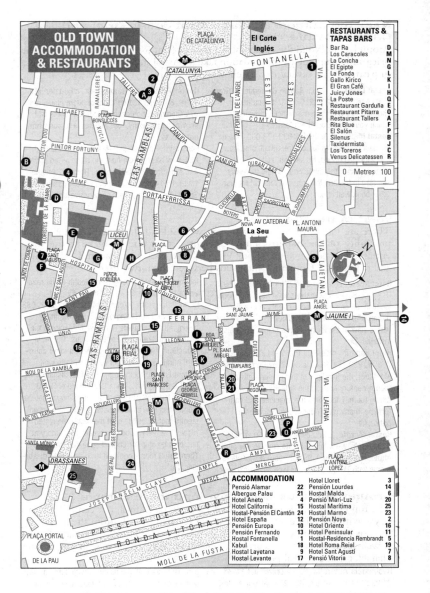

OLD TOWN ACCOMMODATION & RESTAURANTS

RESTAURANTS & TAPAS BARS

Bar Ra	D
Los Caracoles	M
La Concha	N
El Egipte	G
La Fonda	L
Gallo Kirico	K
El Gran Café	I
Juicy Jones	H
La Poste	Q
Restaurant Garduña	E
Restaurant Pitarra	O
Restaurant Tallers	A
Rita Blue	F
El Salón	P
Silenus	B
Taxidermista	J
Los Toreros	C
Venus Delicatessen	R

0 Metres 100

ACCOMMODATION

Pensió Alamar	22	Hotel Lloret	3
Albergue Palau	21	Pensión Lourdes	14
Hotel Aneto	4	Hostal Malda	6
Hotel California	15	Pensió Mari-Luz	20
Hostal-Pensión El Cantón	24	Hostal Marítima	25
Hotel España	12	Hostal Marmo	23
Pensión Europa	10	Pensión Noya	2
Pensión Fernando	13	Hotel Oriente	16
Hostal Fontanella	1	Hotel Peninsular	13
Kabul	18	Hostal-Residencia Rembrandt	5
Hostal Layetana	9	Hotel Roma Reial	19
Hostal Levante	17	Hotel Sant Agustí	7
		Pensió Vitoria	8

Hotel Ducs de Bergara, c/Bergara 11 ☎ 933 015 151, ℱ 933 173 442, ℮ cataloni@hoteles -catalonia.es; Ⓜ Catalunya. Late-nineteenth-century luxury hotel designed by Gaudí's mentor Emili Sala. Set in a small street just off the Plaça de Catalunya behind the new FNAC Triangle shopping centre. ⑨

Hotel Ginebra, Rambla de Catalunya 1 ☎ 933 171 063, ℱ 933 175 565; Ⓜ Catalunya. Small hotel on the third floor of a well-kept building. All rooms come with TV and air-conditioning, and some have impressive views of Plaça de Catalunya. ⑥

Hostal Girona, c/Girona 24 ☎ 932 650 259; Ⓜ Urquinaona. Cosy and beautifully appointed little family-run *pensión*, in a quieter corner of the Eixample, very handy for the *modernista* and Barrí Gótic sights. **⑤**

Hotel Paseo de Gràcia, Pg. de Gràcia 102 ☎932 155 824, ℱ932 153 724; Ⓜ Diagonal. In a good location at the top of Passeig de Gràcia – handy for both the Eixample and Gràcia – this is a comfortable quiet hotel with some stunning views. **⑦**

Hostal de Ribagorza, c/Trafalgar 9 and c/Méndez Núñez 17 ☎933 191 968, ℱ933 191 247; Ⓜ Urquinaona or Arc de Triomf. Right on the edge of the old town near the Arc de Triomf, this functional *hostal* has 11 rooms (many with balconies

and all with TV) and a spacious common room. **④**

Hostal Universal, Aragón 281 ☎934 879 762, ℱ934 874 028; Ⓜ Passeig de Gràcia or Universitat. Very tidy and well-renovated *pensión*. All rooms have private bath and TV, and almost all have balconies on the street. **⑤**

Hostal Windsor, Rambla de Catalunya 84 ☎932 151 198; Ⓜ Passeig de Gràcia. Small *hostal* with English-speaking management, set in a lovely building on the Eixample's nicest avenue. There are only fifteen rooms (some without shower) so book ahead. **⑥**

Gràcia

Staying in Gràcia, you're further away from the old town sights but the trade-off is the pleasant local neighbourhood atmosphere and the proximity to some excellent bars, restaurants and clubs.

Pensión Norma, c/Gran de Gràcia 87 ☎932 374 478; Ⓜ Fontana. Unpromising from the outside and up quite a lot of stairs, this is actually a pleasant place with keenly priced, spotless rooms, with or without shower. **④**

Pensión San Medín, c/Gran de Gràcia 125 ☎932

173 068, ℱ934 154 410; Ⓜ Fontana. Better looking inside than out, this friendly and well-located *pensión* has twelve rooms, some with shower. Situated on the first floor of a nice building but on an extremely busy street, so ask for an interior room. **⑤**

Youth hostels

There are several official (IYHF) and not-so-official **youth hostels** in Barcelona, where accommodation is in multi-bedded dorm rooms. Prices are around €9–12 per person, more in an IYHF hostel if you're over 26 or a non-member. Always ring ahead in summer.

Albergue Palau, c/Palau 6 ☎934 125 080; Ⓜ Liceu. Priority is given to IYHF and ISIC card holders at this small, central hostel. There are no left baggage or laundry facilities but there is a TV room and kitchen (7–10pm). Bed and breakfast is €9.60 per person (sheets €1.20), and the curfew is 3–7am.

Hedy Holiday Hostal, c/Buenaventura Muñoz 4 ☎933 005 785; Ⓜ Arc de Triomf. Also just off of Ciutadella, this brand-new 50-place youth hostel has dorm accommodation. No membership is necessary and there is a TV room and laundry facilities. Also has a great bar. Curfew 2am–7am. Sheets are included with the €15 per-person price.

Albergue Verge de Montserrat, Pg. de la Mare de Déu del Coll 41–51 ☎932 105 151, ℱ934 838 342; Ⓜ Vallcarca and follow the signs, or bus #28 from Plaça de Catalunya. An IYHF hostel (membership essential) a long way out of the city – near

Parc de la Creueta del Coll – but worth the trip for its facilities and setting. Open 7.30am–midnight with breaks in mid-morning and afternoon. Maximum five-night stay; breakfast is included, and there's an optional dinner. It is possible to arrive later than midnight if arranged with the management.

Hostal de Joves, Pg. de Pujades 29 ☎&ℱ933 003 104; Ⓜ Arc de Triomf. An IYHF hostel right by the Parc de la Ciutadella that usually has space. You can stay one night without a card, five nights with. Open 7.30–10am & 3pm–midnight, but opens at regular intervals throughout the night.

Kabul, Plaça Reial 17 ☎933 185 190, ℱ933 014 034, ⓦwww.kabul-hostel.com; Ⓜ Liceu. A budget travellers' haven in the heart of the old town – a great place to meet people. Some rooms (**②**), but mostly dorm accommodation (**①**). A safe hostel with lots of facilities including a big common room/bar, kitchen, laundry and TV; open 24hr.

Campsites

Although there are hundreds of **campsites** on the coast in either direction, none of them is less than 7km from the city. The prices – around €3.75–5 per person, often the same again per tent – do you no favours either, and you'd be better saving your camping for later. Two of the better sites close to the city are:

Cala-Gogo-El Prat, Prat de Llobregat ☎ 933 794 600, Ⓕ 933 794 711. Bus #65 from Plaça d'Espanya. The closest campsite to the city (near the airport). Open mid-March to mid-October.

Masnou, El Masnou ☎ &Ⓕ 935 551 503. RENFE train to El Masnou from Plaça de Catalunya (15min). Clean and well-equipped campsite in the town of El Masnou, 10km from central Barcelona, across the road from a popular sandy beach. Open all year.

The Ramblas and the Old Town

It is a telling comment on Barcelona's character that one can recommend a single street – **the Ramblas** – as a highlight. No day in the city seems complete without a stroll down at least part of what, for Lorca, was "the only street in the world which I wish would never end". Littered with cafés, shops, restaurants and newspaper stalls, it's at the heart of Barcelona's life and self-image – a focal point for locals every bit as much as for tourists, and one to which you'll return again and again.

The Ramblas bisect Barcelona's **old town** (La Ciutat Vella), which spreads north from the harbour in an uneven wedge, and is bordered by the Parc de la Ciutadella to the east, Plaça de Catalunya to the north and the slopes of Montjuïc to the west. Contained within this jumble of streets is a series of neighbourhoods – originally separate medieval parishes and settlements – that retain certain distinct characters even today. Some of these old town neighbourhoods are accessible by diving off the Ramblas into the side streets as you go – such as the **Raval/Barrio Chino**, and the area back from the **harbour** around c/de la Mercè. But by far the greatest concentration of interest is in the cramped **Barri Gòtic**, where you'll find the city's finest medieval buildings and churches tucked into unkempt streets and alleys. East of here, across the broad **Vía Laietana**, the old town streets continue in the area known as **La Ribera** encompassing two of Barcelona's most favoured sights: the graceful church of **Santa María del Mar** and the showpiece **Museu Picasso**.

You could see most of the places and buildings described in this section in a long day's outing. To start your tour, the nearest **metro** stops are Catalunya, Liceu or Drassanes (top, middle and bottom of the Ramblas respectively), or Jaume I for the Barri Gòtic.

Along the Ramblas

Everyone starts with the **RAMBLAS**, no bad thing since they're the city's most famous feature – and deservedly so. The name, derived from the Arabic *ramla* (or "sand"), refers to the bed of the seasonal stream which once flowed here. In the dry season, the channel created by the water was used as a road, and by the fourteenth century this had been paved over in recognition of its use as a link between the harbour and the old town. In the nineteenth century, benches and decorative trees were added, overlooked by stately, balconied buildings, and today – in a city choked with traffic – this wide swathe is still given over to pedestrians, with cars forced up the narrow strip of road on either side.

For the visitor, the first eccentricity is that the tree-lined Ramblas is (or rather, are) **five separate streets** strung head to tail – from north to south, Rambla Canaletes, Estudis, Sant Josep, Caputxins and Santa Mònica – though

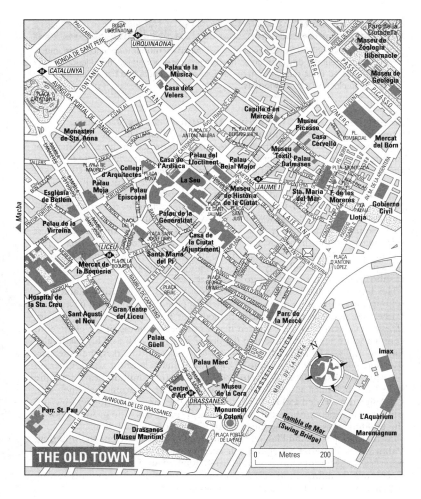

this plurality of names doesn't amount to much more than a subtle change in what's being sold from the kiosks as you head down the street. Here, under the plane trees, you'll find pet canaries, rabbits, tropical fish, flowers, plants, postcards and books. You can buy jewellery and contraband cigarettes, have your palm read and your portrait painted, or just listen to the buskers and watch the pavement and performance artists. If you're around when Barça (FC Barcelona) wins an important match you'll catch the Ramblas at its best: the street erupts with instant and infectious excitement, fans driving up and down with their hands on the horn, cars bedecked with Catalan flags, pedestrians waving champagne bottles.

The following account of the Ramblas runs from **north to south**, from Plaça de Catalunya at the top down to the Columbus monument on the waterfront.

From Plaça de Catalunya to Palau de la Virreina

The huge **Plaça de Catalunya** is many people's first real view of Barcelona. If you've emerged blinking from the metro and train station here, the first few minutes can be a bit bewildering as you try to figure out which way to go for the Ramblas. The square, with its central gardens, seats and fountains, is a focal point for demonstrations, buskers and festivals, and lies right at the heart of the city, with the old town and port below it, the planned Eixample above and beyond. The massive **El Corte Inglés** department store, in the northern corner, has some stupendous views of the city from its ninth-floor cafeteria. The latest addition to the square is the **FNAC** shopping centre on the southwest side, incorporating the renovated *Café Zurich* – a traditional Barcelona meeting place; the **Ramblas** begin at this southern corner. It's a good idea to fix the square in your mind early on, since you'll probably pass through on several subsequent occasions as you go about the city.

Heading down the Ramblas, the first two stretches are **Rambla Canaletes**, with its iron fountain (a drink from which supposedly means you'll never leave Barcelona), and **Rambla Estudis**, named after the city's medieval university (L'Estudi General) that was situated here until the beginning of the eighteenth century, when it was closed down for pro-Catalan subversion. This part is also known locally as Rambla dels Ocells as it contains a bird market, the little captives squawking away from a line of cages on either side of the street. Over on the right, the **Església de Betlem** was begun in 1681, built in heavy Baroque style by the Jesuits; its lavish interior was destroyed during the Civil War. Opposite, the arcaded **Palau Moja** dates from the late eighteenth century and still retains a fine exterior staircase and elegant great hall. The ground floor of the building, restored by the Generalitat, is now an arts bookshop.

Further along the Ramblas, on the corner of c/del Carme, sits the imposing **Palau de la Virreina**, an eighteenth-century palace which now houses temporary art exhibitions (Tues–Sat 11am–8.30pm, Sun 11am–2.30pm; €1.80) and a walk-in information centre and ticket office for cultural events run by the *ajuntament*; drop in and pick up a programme.

Rambla Sant Josep

Beyond the Palau de la Virreina starts **Rambla Sant Josep**, the switch in names marked by the sudden profusion of flower stalls at this point of the Ramblas. The city's most famous produce market – the glorious **Mercat Sant Josep** (Mon–Sat 8am–8pm) – is over to the right, a cavernous hall stretching back from the high wrought-iron entrance arch facing the Ramblas. Built between 1836 and 1840 – though the arch was added 30 years later – and known locally as the Boqueria, it's a riot of noise and colour, with great piles of fruit and vegetables, whole legs of cured ham and an amazing variety of fish and seafood. Across the street, the **Museu de l'Eròtica**, Rambla 96 (daily: July–Sept 10am–midnight; Oct–June 10am–10pm; €6), houses an eclectic collection of erotic art, totems and photographs.

Past the market, c/Hospital leads off to the right to the old Hospital de la

△ La Boqueria market, Las Ramblas

Santa Creu (see "Barrio Chino/El Raval", below). This part of the Ramblas is known as **Plaça de la Boqueria**, and is marked (in the middle of the pavement) by a large round **mosaic** by Joan Miró, just one of a number of the artist's city works.

By now you've reached the Liceu metro station, a little way beyond which is the **Gran Teatre del Liceu**, Barcelona's celebrated opera house, which burned down for the third time in January 1994, but was rebuilt in its former neo-Baroque style to reopen in late 1999. The building has had an unfortunate history, to say the least. Founded in 1847, it was first rebuilt after a fire in 1861 to become Spain's grandest opera house. Regarded as a bastion of the city's late-nineteenth-century commercial and intellectual classes, tragedy struck again in 1893 when an anarchist threw two bombs into the stalls during a production of *William Tell*. He was acting in revenge for the recent execution of a fellow activist – twenty people died in the bombing. If you're not an opera fan, you can still check out the interior, restored by the artist Pere Jaume (Fri–Mon 9.45–11am; €3). Across the way, at Rambla 74, is the famous **Café de l'Opera**, traditional favourite of opera performers and *cognoscenti* for over a century and one of the best places in Barcelona to enjoy a coffee or drink – if you can find a table.

Plaça Reial

A hundred metres or so further down the Ramblas, now the **Rambla de Caputxins**, the elegant nineteenth-century **Plaça Reial** is another good place to call a halt – it's hidden behind an archway on the left and is easy to miss. Laid out in around 1850, the Italianate square is studded with tall palm trees and decorated iron lamps (by the young Gaudí), bordered by arcaded buildings, and centred on a fountain depicting the Three Graces. Just a decade ago this square was a haven of drug addicts and vagabonds, but it's been cleaned up and its terraces now make an ideal spot for a drink while enjoying the jugglers and fire-breathers (though you should still take care late at night). Sunday's **coin and stamp market** (10am–2pm) draws many serious dealers, but its lighter-weight exhibits and frenetic bargaining make it entertaining.

Rambla de Santa Mònica

Continuing down the Ramblas, Gaudí's magnificent Palau Güell stands on c/Nou de la Rambla (see "Barrio Chino/El Raval" below), just over the way from Plaça Reial, beyond which you're on the final stretch, the **Rambla de Santa Mònica**. There's little to see until you reach the bottom of the Ramblas, though at the weekend there's an afternoon street market selling jewellery, ornaments and clothes. On the right-hand side, amidst one of the last and toughest knots of Barcelona's red-light district, sits the plain facade of the former convent **church of Santa Mònica** at no. 7, which has been converted to a **gallery** for temporary art exhibitions (Mon–Sat 11am–2pm & 5–8pm, Sun & holidays 11am–3pm; free). Opposite stands a wax museum, the **Museu de Cera**, down an alley on the left-hand side at nos. 4–6 (July–Sept daily 10am–10pm; Oct–June Mon–Fri 10am–1.30pm & 4–7.30pm, Sat & Sun 11am–2pm & 4.30–8.30pm; €6). An array of displays shows figures from Spanish and Catalan history as well as the usual international wax-figure suspects: politicians, actors and criminals. If the prospect of a wax musuem doesn't thrill you, it's still worth poking into the museum's **bar**, the *Bosc de les Fades* (see p.730), located in a narrow alley to the right of the museum entrance.

The Ramblas end at **Plaça Portal de la Pau**, coming up hard against the teeming traffic that runs along the harbourside road. In the centre stands

BARCELONA | The Ramblas and the Old Town

Columbus, pointing out to sea at the top of a tall and slender iron column built for the Universal Exhibition in 1888: the **Monument a Colom**. You can get inside (June–Sept daily 9am–8.30pm; Oct–May Mon–Sat 10am–1.30pm & 3.30–6.30pm, Sun 10am–6.30pm; €1.50) and take the lift 52m up to his head for aerial views of the city.

The harbour and Port Vell

Columbus is the most obvious landmark down at Barcelona's **harbour**, an area spruced up considerably over the last decade. A harbourside *passeig*, the **Moll de la Fusta** – the city's old timber wharf – is landscaped with benches and trees from the Columbus monument as far as the post office building. Cross the little bridges which span the ring road (built to link Montjuïc with the Olympic Village to the east), and you'll find seats from which you can look out over the marina. There are a few trendy clubs in summer along the promenade, and some bar-restaurants providing meals with pricey views.

PORT VELL (or Old Port), across the harbour from Moll de la Fusta and linked to it by a series of undulating wooden walkways and a swing bridge (called La Rambla del Mar), is the city's most-visited seaside development. The old wharves now accommodate **Maremàgnum**, a attractive modern leisure complex jammed with shops, fast-food outlets, restaurants and bars. Other attractions here include a multiscreen cinema and the Imax Port Vell, showing giant format movies, as well as **L'Aquàrium** (daily 9.30am–8pm, closes 9.30pm July & Aug; €8.75), an impressive series of 21 different aquariums showing off Mediterranean marine life.

To the south of the Columbus monument is a stretch of the port leading to the central cable-car station and the Estació Marítima at the Moll de Barcelona, where the ferries leave for the Balearics. This area is now dominated by the new **World Trade Centre** convention complex.

The Drassanes: Museu Marítim

Opposite Columbus, set back from the road on the western side of the Ramblas, are the **Drassanes**, unique medieval shipyards dating from the thirteenth century. Originally used as a dry dock to fit and arm Catalunya's war fleet in the days when the Catalan-Aragonese crown was vying with Venice and Genoa for control of the Mediterranean, the shipyards – long parallel halls facing the sea – were in continuous use (and frequently refurbished) until well into the eighteenth century.

Nowadays the huge, stone-vaulted buildings make a fitting home for an excellent **Museu Marítim** (daily 10am–7pm, €4.80), whose centrepiece is a copy of the sixteenth-century Royal Galley (*Galera Reial*), a red-and-gold barge rowed by enormous oars. It's surrounded by smaller models, fishing skiffs, sailing boats, old maps and charts, and other nautical bits and pieces – none of which, worthy though they are, can really compete with the soaring building itself. There's also a permanent exhibition about the dangers of the sea, in which you can take a virtual-reality trip in a submarine.

Harbour rides and views

From a couple of points along the Moll de la Fusta, regular sightseeing boats, **Las Golondrinas** (June–Sept daily 11.30am–8pm; Oct–May Mon–Fri noon–1.30pm, Sat & Sun 12.30–5.30pm; departs every 45min Mon–Fri, every 25min Sat & Sun; €3), make the half-hour ride across the harbour through the modern docks to the breakwater. There's also a ninety-minute ride east to the Port Olímpic (daily 11.30am, 1.15pm, 4.30pm & 6pm with an extra trip at

8.15pm on Sat & Sun; €4.20), including a twenty-minute stop at the port.

A more dramatic view of the city is offered by the **cable car** (daily noon–7pm; €6 one-way, €7.20 return, plus €3.60 for the Jaume I lift), which sweeps right across the water from the base of Montjuïc to the middle of the new docks and on to Barceloneta – film buffs may remember Jack Nicholson riding it in Antonioni's film, *The Passenger*. The central **cable-car tower**, Jaume I, is just a few minutes' walk up the Moll de Barcelona from the Columbus monument, and even if you're saving the ride for a full trip from either Barceloneta or Montjuïc, you might consider taking the lift to the top of the tower, as at this point the views over the city are supreme.

The Barrio Chino/El Raval

West of the Ramblas, from the harbour roughly as far north as c/del Hospital, the triangular **BARRIO CHINO** is not the most obvious area of Barcelona in which to sightsee, but it's an interesting place to wander around in the day-time and, as the zone becomes increasingly trendy, the nights are ever livelier too. Officially, the neighbourhood is known as **EL RAVAL** ("the suburb") and historically it has been the city's red-light area. The area's nickname, translated in Catalan as "Barri Xinès" (or more popularly as "Barri Xino", or simply "el Xino"), does not in fact refer to the few Chinese who live here, but comes from an obscure 1920s literary reference.

Like any port town, Barcelona has a long history of thriving prostitution: Orwell relates how after the 1936 Workers' Uprising "in the streets were coloured posters appealing to prostitutes to stop being prostitutes". Franco, for rather different reasons, was equally keen to clear the streets. Neither succeeded, though measured by its former reputation, the Barrio Chino is pretty tame these days; the *ajuntament*'s renovation programme has cleared a wide swathe through the squalid hive of narrow streets, and as the district becomes increasingly fashionable, loft-living yuppies and young bohemians rub shoulders with the area's traditional population of marginalized urban poor and immigrants.

It may be rather hard to credit, given the often shabby surroundings, but the quarter also contains several sights firmly on the tourist map. During the day, don't be unduly concerned as you make your way to the destinations below – which include one of Gaudí's early works. At night, sensible precautions (such as not carrying large wallets down unlit side streets) should see you right: certainly, it would be a shame not to patronize some of the excellent **restaurants** and **bars** that thrive in the area.

Architecturally, most of the *barri* is undistinguished, but the magnificent entryways of many of its buildings attest to its vanished nineteenth-century prosperity. There are also splashes of **modernista** colour among the down-at-heel surroundings; keep an eye out for the **Hotel España** (see p.687) at c/de Sant Pau 9–11 – perhaps the best known of the buildings, with an attractive tiled dining room designed by Domènech i Montaner.

The Palau Güell

Much of Antoni Gaudí's early career was spent constructing elaborate follies for wealthy patrons. The most important was Eusebio Güell, industrialist and aris-tocrat, who in 1885 commissioned the **Palau Güell**, at c/Nou de la Rambla 3, just off the Ramblas (frequent guided tours in English: Mon–Sat 10am–1.30pm & 4–6.30pm; €2.40). The first modern building to be declared a World Heritage building by UNESCO, it is, unusually, open to the public so you can see the interior: most of the Gaudí houses are still privately owned. Here, Gaudí's feel for different materials is remarkable. At a time when architects sought to conceal the iron supports within buildings, Gaudí turned them to his advantage, displaying them as attractive decorative features. The roof terrace, too, makes a virtue of its functionalism, since the chimneys and other outlets are decorated with glazed tiles, while inside, columns, arches and ceilings are all shaped and twisted in an elaborate style that was to become the hallmark of Gaudí's later works – most of which are in the Eixample. The Palau is also one of the places where you can buy your ticket for the **Ruta del modernisme**, which gives discounts on entry to many *modernista* buildings (see p.712).

Sant Pau del Camp

Behind the Gran Teatre del Liceu on the Ramblas, c/de Sant Pau leads down through the heart of the Barrio Chino to the church of **Sant Pau del Camp** (St Paul of the Field; Mon–Sat 10am–12.30pm & 4–7.30pm), its name a reminder that it once stood in open fields beyond the city walls. The oldest church in Barcelona, Sant Pau is laid out in the cruciform Greek style, with a main entrance decorated with faded Romanesque carvings of fish, birds and faces, and a tranquil thirteenth-century cloister.

Hospital de la Santa Creu

On the northern fringes of the Barrio Chino the **Hospital de la Santa Creu** is the district's most substantial relic. The attractive complex of Gothic buildings here, reached down c/de Hospital (from where you get the best views of the building's facade), was founded as the city's main hospital in 1402, a role which it retained until 1930. Today the complex has been converted to cultural and educational use, and its spacious courtyard, punctuated by orange trees, provides airy respite from the Raval's dark streets. Just inside the entrance are some superb seventeenth-century *azulejos* of various religious scenes; note the figure with the word *Iesus* written in mirror image – a formula signifying death. The grand staircase on the left side leads up to the National Library of Catalunya, housed in the spacious fifteenth-century hospital wards. **La Capella** (Tues–Sat noon–2pm & 4–8pm, Sun noon–3pm; free), which is entered separately from c/del Hospital, is a former chapel, now used as an exhibition space featuring a changing programme of works by young Barcelona artists.

The Museu d'Art Contemporani de Barcelona

Carrer de Hospital acts as a sort of frontier for the Barrio Chino, but the Raval itself stretches as far north as c/Pelai and the Ronda Sant Antoni. It's in this area that the city government's ambitious rehabilitation programme for the old city began with the construction in 1995 of the **Museu d'Art Contemporani de Barcelona**, or MACBA (Tues–Fri noon–8pm, Sat 10am–8pm, Sun 10am–2pm; €4.50, Wed €2.25, Articket valid), which you can approach from c/dels Àngels or from the Ramblas (take c/Bon Succés). The contrast between the huge, white, almost luminous structure of the museum and the old apartment buildings around it couldn't be more stark. The museum's rotating collection represents the main movements in twentieth-century art, with an emphasis on Catalunya and Spain. Expect to see paintings by Miró, Tàpies and Joan Brossa, leading light of the Catalan Dau al Set group, as well as a broad collection of abstract and kinetic sculpture.

Adjoining the MACBA is the **Centre de Cultura Contemporània de Barcelona**, or CCCB (Tues–Sat 11am–2pm & 4–8pm, Sun 11am–7pm; €3.60, Articket valid), which hosts temporary art exhibitions as well as films and the Sónar music festival (see p.737). This building is another fine example of the juxtaposition of old and new: built as the Casa de la Caritat in 1714, it was for centuries an infamous workhouse and lunatic asylum and at the entrance you can see the old *azulejos* and facade in a patio presided over by a small statue of Sant Jordi. On the southside of the CCCB, the fifteenth-century **Convent dels Ángels** has also been renovated as a venue for art and design exhibitions.

The Barri Gòtic

A remarkable concentration of beautiful medieval buildings just a couple of blocks northeast of the Ramblas, the **BARRI GÒTIC** forms the very heart of the old town. Once it was entirely enclosed by fourth-century Roman walls, but what you see now dates principally from the fourteenth and fifteenth centuries, when Barcelona reached the height of her commercial prosperity before being absorbed into the burgeoning kingdom of Castile. Renovations continue to bring to light forgotten sections of the ancient walls, and parts of them can still be seen incorporated into later structures, most notably in the towering gates in front of the cathedral.

Plaça de Sant Jaume

The quarter is centred on the **Plaça de Sant Jaume**, a spacious square at the end of the main c/de Ferran. Once the site of Barcelona's Roman forum and marketplace, it's now one venue for the weekly dancing by local people of the Catalan folk dance, the *sardana*, and is also the traditional site of demonstrations and gatherings.

The square contains two of the city's most significant buildings. On the south side stands the town hall, the **ajuntament** – home of the city's socialist government, elected consistently since democracy was introduced in 1977. The most interesting part, the restored fourteenth-century council chamber, the Saló de Cent, is on the first floor and is open to visitors at the weekend (10am–2pm). Otherwise, you get a much better idea of the grandeur of the original structure by nipping around the corner, down c/de la Ciutat, for a view of the former main entrance. It's a typically exuberant Catalan-Gothic facade, but was badly damaged by renovations in the nineteenth century (the same renovations were responsible for the grim Neoclassical facade on Plaça de Sant Jaume).

Right across the square rises the **Palau de la Generalitat**, from where the short-lived Catalan Republic was proclaimed in April 1931. The Palau is the traditional home of the government of Catalunya, which since 1977 has been dominated by Jordi Pujol's right-leaning nationalist party. Begun in 1418, the building presents its best – or at least its oldest – aspect around the side, on c/del Bisbe, where the early fifteenth-century facade by Marc Safont contains a spirited medallion portraying St George (patron saint of Catalunya as well as England) and the Dragon. As you go in through the Renaissance main entrance facing the square, there's a beautiful cloister on the first floor with superb *artesonado* ceilings, while opening off this gallery are the chapel and salon of **Sant Jordi** (St George), also by Safont, and other chambers of the former law courts. The only time you can visit the interior is each year on Sant

Jordi's Day, April 23 (expect a two-hour wait), when the whole square is festooned with bookstalls and flower-sellers. Celebrated as a nationalist holiday in Catalunya, Sant Jordi's Day is also a kind of local Valentine's Day – tradition has it that men give their sweethearts a rose and receive a book in return.

La Seu

La Seu (Mon–Fri 8am–1.30pm & 4–7.30pm, Sat & Sun 8am–1.30pm & 5–7.30pm; free), Barcelona's cathedral, is one of the great Gothic buildings of Spain. Located just behind the Generalitat, on a site previously occupied by a Roman temple, it was begun in 1298 on the foundations of an earlier church and finished in 1448, with one notable exception commented on by Richard Ford in 1845: "The principal facade is unfinished, with a bold front poorly painted in stucco, although the rich chapter have for three centuries received a fee on every marriage for this very purpose of completing it." Perhaps goaded into action, the authorities set to and completed the facade within a ten-year period in the 1880s. Some critics complain that this delay cost the cathedral its architectural harmony, though the facade is Gothic enough for most tastes – and is seen to startling effect at night when it's lit up.

Artificial lighting has transformed the **interior**, replacing the dank mystery with a soaring airiness to echo the grandeur of the exterior. The cathedral is dedicated to Santa Eulàlia, martyred by the Romans for daring to prefer Christianity, and her tomb rests in a crypt beneath the high altar; if you put money in the slot the whole thing lights up to show off its exemplary Catholic kitsch. Look out, too, for the rich altarpieces, the carved tombs of the 29 side chapels and the painted wooden coffins of Ramon Berenguer I (Count of Barcelona from 1018 to 1025), and his wife Almodis, hanging on the wall just to the left of the exit to the cloister.

The most unique part of the cathedral is its magnificent fourteenth-century **cloister** (daily 8.45am–1.15pm & 4–7pm), which looks over a lush garden complete with soaring palm trees and – more unusually – honking white geese. The geese have lived in the cloister's pond for the last five centuries, though no one can recall their origin.

Plaça de la Seu and Plaça Nova

Outside La Seu is the **Museu Diocesà-La Pia Almonia** (Tues–Sat 10am–2pm & 5–8pm, Sun 11am–2pm; €1.80), a small but impressive collection of religious art and artefacts from around Barcelona, housed in a renovated fourth-century Roman tower. Highlights include the frescos of the Apocalypse from a church in Polinyà, and some great *retablos*, including one of St Bartholomew being skinned. Flanking the cathedral, to the west of the **Plaça de la Seu**, are two fifteenth-century buildings closely associated with it. Once the archdeacon's residence and now the city archives, the **Casa de l'Ardiaca** boasts a tiny cloistered and tiled courtyard with a small fountain, while the grander **Palau Episcopal**, just beyond on c/del Bisbe, was the bishop's palace. Though you're not allowed inside either building, you can go as far as both courtyards to see their fine outdoor stairways, a typical feature of Barcelona's palaces; there's also a patio at the top of the Palau Episcopal's stairway with Romanesque wall paintings.

The large **Plaça Nova**, facing the cathedral, marks one of the medieval entrances to the old town – beyond it, you're fast entering the wider streets and more regular contours of the modern city. Even if you're sticking with the Barri Gòtic for now, walk over to study the frieze surmounting the modern **Collegi d'Arquitectes** (College of Architects) building on the other side of the square. Designed in 1960 by Picasso, it has a crude, almost graffiti-like quality at odds with the more stately buildings to the side. The square itself is at its best during the weekly antique market (Thurs 10am–4pm) and the massive Christmas market, the *Fira de Santa Llúcia* (Dec 13–24).

Plaça del Rei and around

The cathedral and its associated buildings aside, the most concentrated batch of historic monuments in the Barri Gòtic is the grouping around the neat **Plaça del Rei**, behind the cathedral apse. The square was once the courtyard of the rambling palace of the counts of Barcelona, and across it stairs climb to the great fourteenth-century **Saló del Tinell** (June–Sept daily 10am–8pm; Oct–May Tues–Sat 10am–2pm & 4–8pm, Sun 10am–2pm; joint ticket with Museu d'Història de la Ciutat Tues–Fri €4.20, Sat & Sun €4.50), the palace's main hall and a fine, spacious example of secular Gothic architecture; the interior arches span seventeen metres. At one time the Spanish Inquisition met here, taking full advantage of the popular belief that the walls would move if a lie was spoken; nowadays it hosts various exhibitions, while concerts are occasionally held in the hall, or outside in the square.

The palace buildings also include the Renaissance, five-storeyed **Torre del Rei Martí** which rises above one corner of the square, as well as the beautiful fourteenth-century **Capella de Santa Agata**, with its tall single nave and unusual stained glass, which is entered via the same monumental staircase as the Saló. The building that closes off the rest of the square, the Casa Clariana-Padellás, is a fifteenth-century mansion moved here brick by brick from nearby c/de Mercaders earlier this century to house the splendid **Museu d'Història de la Ciutat** (June–Sept daily 10am–8pm; Oct–May Tues–Sat 10am–2pm & 4–8pm, Sun 10am–2pm; joint ticket with Saló del Tinell Tues–Fri €4.20, Sat & Sun €4.50); the entrance is on c/del Veguer. Underground, extensive Roman and Visigothic remains (including whole streets and the foundations of a fourth-century Christian basilica) have been preserved where they were discovered during works in the 1930s.

The surrounding streets, between Plaça del Rei and the cathedral, reveal a similar kind of historical cross section. The mid-sixteenth-century **Palau del Lloctinent**, the viceroy's palace, has a facade facing the Plaça del Rei and a fine courtyard with staircase and coffered ceiling (enter on c/dels Comtes). Just one street over, at c/Paradís 10, you'll find a doorway leading down to the four columns which are all that remain of the **Temple of Augustus** (Tues–Sat 10am–2pm & 4–8pm, Sun 10am–2pm; free), which presided over Roman Barchinona in the first century AD.

Perhaps the most engaging sight in the area, however, is the **Museu Frederic Marès** (Tues–Sat 10am–7pm, Sun & holidays 10am–2pm; €1.80, free first Sun of month), which occupies another wing of the old royal palace, behind Plaça del Rei (entrance on c/dels Comtes), and whose large, arcaded courtyard is the most impressive so far. The bulk of this museum consists of an important body of medieval art collected by the sculptor and restorer Frederic Marès, including numerous painted Gothic crucifixes. The upper floors house the **Museu Sentimental** (not always open), an incredibly large – and quickly tedious – jumble gathered during fifty years of the artists' travels, encompassing everything from tarot cards to walking sticks by way of cigarette papers.

Plaça Sant Felip Neri to Plaça Sant Josep Oriol

Heading east back towards the Ramblas from the cathedral, you snake through a series of interconnecting squares and dark streets. Behind the Palau Episcopal,

Barcelona's medieval **Jewish quarter**, El Call, was just to the south of Plaça Sant Josep Oriol, centred on today's c/Sant Domingo del Call (*Call* is the Catalan word for a narrow passage). As elsewhere in Spain, Barcelona's Jewish quarter lay nestled in the shadow of the cathedral – under the Church's careful scrutiny. In the thirteenth and early fourteenth centuries some of the realm's greatest and most powerful administrators hailed from here, but reactionary trends sparked pogroms and led to the closing off of the community in these narrow, dark alleys. Nevertheless a prosperous settlement persisted until the forced conversion of 1391 and exile of 1492. Today little except the street name survives as a reminder of the Jewish presence – after their expulsion, most of the buildings used by the Jews were torn down and used for construction elsewhere in the city. There are still some echoes of the Jewish presence in Barcelona, however: a plaque at c/Sant Domènec del Call 7 marks what may have been the site of the synagogue, and the castle at Montjuïc ("Jewish Mountain") holds thirty of the tombstones recovered from the site of the Jewish cemetery which sat on the eastern side of that hill and which was already a long-established burial place by the eleventh century.

Plaça Sant Felip Neri, scarred by an Italian bomb dropped during the Civil War, is wholly enclosed by buildings and used as a playground by the kids at the square's school. Beyond are three more delightful little squares, with the fourteenth-century **Església de Santa María del Pi** at their heart. Burned out in 1936, and restored in the 1960s, the church boasts a Romanesque door but is mainly Catalan Gothic in style, with just a single nave with chapels between the buttresses. The rather plain interior only serves to set off some marvellous stained glass, the most impressive of which is contained within a huge rose window, often claimed (rather boldly) as the largest in the world.

The church stands on the middle square, **Plaça Sant Josep Oriol**, the prettiest of the three, overhung with balconies and scattered with seats from the *Bar del Pi*, a fine place for a drink in the evening. This whole area becomes an artists' market at the weekend, while buskers and street performers often appear here, too. The squares on either side – Plaça del Pi and Placeta del Pi – are named, like the church, after the pine tree that once stood here.

North towards Plaça de Catalunya

Beyond Plaça Sant Josep Oriol, two or three diversions on the way north to Plaça de Catalunya make it worthwhile to stick to the backstreets, avoiding the Ramblas. Much of the area is devoted to antique shops and art galleries: one of the most famous is at c/Petritxol 5, where the **Sala Pares** was already well established when Picasso and Miró were young; it still deals exclusively in nineteenth- and twentieth-century Catalan art.

The large and rather ugly **Plaça Vila de Madrid** features some well-preserved Roman tombs in its sunken garden, and from here it's a short walk to c/Montsió and **Els Quatre Gats** ("The Four Cats"; see p.730), the bar opened by Pere Romeu and other *modernista* artists in 1897 as a gathering place. Also known as the "Casa Martí", the building itself is gloriously decorated inside – it was the architect Puig i Cadafalch's first commission – and *Els Quatre Gats* soon thrived as the birthplace of *modernista* magazines, the scene of poetry readings and shadow-puppet theatre and, in 1901, the setting for Picasso's first public exhibition.

A small diversion across the nearby Via Laietana takes you to another *modernista* classic, Domènech i Montaner's **Palau de la Música Catalana**, which doesn't seem to have enough breathing space in the tiny c/Sant Pere Més Alt. If you can get a ticket for one of the many fine concerts here, do so, since the building is as fantastic acoustically as it is visually. Alternatively, there are hour-long English-language **guided tours** of the interior which depart hourly (daily 10am–3pm; €4.20).

Vía Laietana to Parc de la Ciutadella

In 1859, as the plans for the Eixample took shape, a wide, new avenue was also constructed to the south, cutting through the old town. This was the **Vía Laietana**, running roughly parallel to the Ramblas. Nowadays it delineates the eastern extent of the Barri Gòtic, but not to push on over the road into the equally dense network of medieval streets beyond would be a mistake. True, there isn't the same concentration of preserved buildings here as in the Barri Gòtic, but there is the major attraction of the **Museu Picasso**, while the street on which it lies (c/de Montcada) and the church at the end of it (Santa María del Mar) encapsulate some of Barcelona's most perfect Catalan-Gothic features.

Carrer de Montcada and the Passeig del Born

Everyone makes the trip to **c/de Montcada** sooner or later, a narrow street lined with leaning, late-medieval mansions. The draw is the Museu Picasso, housed in one of the grander buildings, but the street itself is one of the best-looking in the city. Laid out in the fourteenth century, until the Eixample was planned almost 500 years later, it was home to most of the city's leading citizens who occupied spacious mansions built around central courtyards, from which external staircases climbed to the living rooms on the first floor. The Museu Picasso aside, several of the other mansions are also used as exhibition space today.

Almost opposite the Picasso Museum, at no. 12, the fourteenth-century Palau de Lló and its next-door neighbour contain the extensive collections of the **Museu Textil i d'Indumentaria** (Tues–Sat 10am–8pm, Sun and holidays 10am–3pm; joint ticket with Museu Barbier-Mueller €3, temporary exhibits €4.20, free first Sat of month 3–8pm) – 4000 items altogether, including textiles from the fourth century onwards and costumes from the sixteenth, dolls, shoes, fans and other accessories. Next door at no. 14 there's the **Museu Barbier-Mueller** (Tues–Sat 10am–8pm, Sun and holidays 10am–3pm; joint ticket with Museu Textil i d'Indumentaria €3, temporary exhibits €4.25, free first Sat of month 3–8pm) – a collection of Pre-Columbian art housed in the renovated sixteenth-century Palau Nadal. Close by there's a private gallery at no. 25, the Galeria Maeght, spread across two floors of the former Palau dels Cervelló, and at no. 20, the Palau Dalmasses has been opened as an upmarket bar (see p.741). C/de Montcada ends at the church of Santa María del Mar (see below), fronting which is the fashionable **Passeig del Born**. Once the site of medieval fairs and tournaments, it is now lined with trendy bars, and capped at the far end by the hulking iron skeleton of the **Mercat del Born**, the city's main market from the late 1800s to the 1960s – now awaiting renovation as a cultural venue.

The Museu Picasso

The **Museu Picasso**, c/de Montcada 15–19 (Tues–Sat & holidays 10am–8pm, Sun 10am–3pm; €4.20, free first Sun of month), is Barcelona's biggest tourist attraction, housed in a strikingly beautiful medieval palace converted specifically for the museum. It's one of the most important collections of Picasso's work in the world and certainly the only one of any significance

Picasso in Barcelona

Although born in Málaga, **Pablo Picasso** (1881–1973) spent much of his youth – from the age of 14 to 23 – in Barcelona. He maintained close links with Barcelona and his Catalan friends even when he left for Paris in 1904, and is said to have always thought of himself as Catalan rather than Andaluz. The time Picasso spent in Barcelona contained the whole of his "Blue Period" (1901–04) and many of the formative influences on his art.

Apart from the Museu Picasso, there are echoes of the great artist at various sites throughout the old town. Not too far from the museum, you can still see many of the buildings in which Picasso lived and worked, notably the **Escola de Belles Arts de Llotja** (c/Consolat del Mar, near Estació de França), where his father taught drawing and where Picasso himself absorbed an academic training. The apartments where the family lived when they first arrived in Barcelona – Pg. d'Isabel II 4 and c/Cristina 3, both opposite the Escola – can also be seen, though only from the outside. His first public exhibition was in 1901 at **Els Quatre Gats** (c/Montsió 3). Less tangible is to take a walk down c/d'Avinyó, which cuts south from c/de Ferran to c/Ample. Large houses along here were converted into brothels at the turn of this century, and Picasso used to haunt the street sketching what he saw; women at one of the brothels inspired his seminal Cubist work, **Les Demoiselles d'Avignon**.

in his native country. Even so, some visitors are disappointed: the museum isn't thoroughly representative, it contains none of his best-known works, and few in the Cubist style. But what *is* here provides a unique opportunity to trace Picasso's development from his early paintings as a young boy to the major works of later years.

The museum opened in 1963 with a collection based largely on the donations of Jaume Sabartés, friend and former secretary to the artist. The **early drawings** in which Picasso – still signing with his full name, Pablo Ruíz Picasso – attempted to copy the nature paintings in which his father specialized, and the many studies from his art school days, are fascinating. Indeed, it's the early periods that are the best represented: some works in the style of Toulouse-Lautrec, such as the menu Picasso did for *Els Quatre Gats* restaurant in 1900, reflect his interest in Parisian art at the turn of the twentieth century; other selected works show graphically Picasso's development of his own style – there are paintings here from the famous **Blue Period** (1901–04), the Pink Period (1904–06), and from his Cubist (1907–20) and Neoclassical (1920–25) stages.

The large gaps in the main collection (for example, nothing from 1905 until the celebrated *Harlequin* of 1917) only underline Picasso's extraordinary changes of style and mood. This is best illustrated by the large jump after 1917 – to 1957, a year represented by two rooms on the first floor which contain the fascinating works Picasso himself donated to the museum, his fifty-odd interpretations of Velázquez's masterpiece *Las Meninas*.

Santa María del Mar

At the bottom of c/de Montcada sits the glorious church of **Santa María del Mar** (daily 9am–1.30pm & 4.30–8pm; Sun choral Mass at 1pm), began under orders of King Jaume II in 1324, and built in only five years. Situated on what was then the seashore, at the entrance to the trading district (c/Argentería, named after the silversmiths who worked there, still runs from the church square to the city walls of the Barri Gòtic), the church symbolized the maritime supremacy of the medieval Crown of Aragon, of which Barcelona was capital. The church, with its soaring lines, is an exquisite example of Catalan-Gothic architecture.

Ciutadella to Montjuïc

Recreational space has always been high up the list with every redesign of the city. Recently, peripheral bits of industrial wasteland have benefited from the drive to provide some greenery and relative peace, but the late-nineteenth-century expansion of Barcelona relied instead on transforming previously fortified, and very central, sections of the city. The quickest respite from the centre is still in the **Parc de la Ciutadella**, east of the old town and within easy walking distance of the Barri Gòtic. Once the site of a Bourbon fortress, this is a formal park, with several museums and other attractions spread about its attractive paths and gardens. To the south lies the fishing (and seafood-eating) district of **Barceloneta**, jutting out into Barcelona's central harbour, while a short walk from here, the **Parc de Mar** has totally transformed a previously redundant section of the city's coastline.

You'll probably want to reserve most of a day for the more substantial attraction of **Montjuïc**, the hill that rises over on the other side of the harbour, to the west of the Barrio Chino. This still retains its castle, while the museums, monuments and gardens are connected by an extensive series of paths and viewpoints; some of the attractions are also linked by cable car – a method of transport that also connects Montjuïc with Barceloneta, enabling you to jump fairly swiftly between all the areas described in this chapter. For **transport details**, see the information boxes.

Parc de la Ciutadella

The **PARC DE LA CIUTADELLA** seems to have a peculiar ability to take in far more than would seem possible from its outward dimensions. As well as a lake, a monumental fountain and the city zoo, you'll find here the meeting place of the Catalan parliament and, until 2003 at least, a modern art museum. The last two occupy parts of a fortress-like structure right at the centre of the park, the surviving portion of the star-shaped **citadel** from which the park takes its name. It was erected by Felipe V in 1715, to subdue Barcelona after its spirited resistance to the Bourbons in the War of the Spanish Succession, and a whole city neighbourhood had to be destroyed to make room for the citadel. The Bourbon symbol of authority survived uneasily, until it too was destroyed in 1869 and the surrounding area made into a park. It seems a fitting irony that the main palace structure is once again home to the autonomous Catalan parliament, which first sat here between 1932 and 1939.

Perhaps the most notable of the park's sights is the **Cascada**, the Baroque fountain in the northeast corner. Designed by Josep Fontseré, the architect chosen to oversee the conversion of the former citadel grounds into a park, this was the first of the major projects undertaken here. Fontseré's assistant in the work was the young Antoni Gaudí, then a student, who was also thought to have had a hand in the design of the Ciutadella's iron park gates, at the entrance on Avinguda Marqués de l'Argentera.

The Park and the 1888 Exhibition

In 1888, barely twenty years after it was first created, the park was chosen as the site of the **Universal Exhibition**, which helped start the cultural regeneration of Barcelona. Many of the *modernista* giants called upon to help left their mark here, beginning with Josep Vilaseca i Casanoves's giant brick **Arc de Triomf**, and Josep Domènech's **Palau de la Justicia** outside the main gates at the top of Passeig Lluís Companys.

Just inside the main entrance, Domènech i Montaner designed a castle-like building intended for use as the exhibition's café-restaurant. Dubbed the Castell dels Tres Dragons, it became a centre for *modernista* arts and crafts, and is now the **Museu de Zoologia** (Tues–Sun & holidays 10am–2pm, Thurs 10am–6.30pm; €2.40, free first Sun of month), whose decorated red-brick exterior out-dazzles the rather more mundane interior. The ticket for the museum also includes admission to the adjacent **Museu de Geologia** (same hours). Just beyond is the attractive late-nineteenth-century conservatory – the *hivernacle* – which now houses a pleasant outdoor **bar**.

The Museu d'Art Modern del MNAC

In the centre of the park, the surviving parts of Felipe's citadel – the governor's palace and old arsenal – stand on the Plaça d'Armes. They are now shared by the Catalan parliament and the **Museu d'Art Modern del MNAC** (Tues–Sat 10am–7pm, Sun 10am–2.30pm; €3, Articket valid), though the latter is scheduled to close in 2002, when its collection will be transferred to the main Museu Nacional d'Art de Catalunya (MNAC) on Montjuïc (see p.718).

The museum is devoted to Catalan art dating from the mid-nineteenth century until around 1930 and, as you might expect, it's particularly good on *modernista* and *noucentista* painting and sculpture, the two dominant schools of the period. There are fine examples of the work of Ramon Casas (whose work once hung on the walls of *Els Quatre Gats*) and Santiago Rusiñol, while later *modernista* works include the landscapes of Joaquim Mir and the astonishingly varied output of Isidre Nonell. The museum's latter rooms cover *noucentista* works, a style at once more classical and less consciously flamboyant than *modernisme* – Joaquim Sunyer, perhaps the best-known *noucentista* artist, is among those displayed here, though there are works by a host of others, too, including Xavier Nogués and the sculptor Pau Gargallo.

The Parc Zoològic

For all Ciutadella's cultural appeal, the most popular attraction – apart from the green spaces of the park itself – is the city's zoo, the **Parc Zoològic** (daily: summer 10am–7pm; winter 10am–5pm; €9.35), taking up most of the southeast of the park. There's an entrance on c/de Wellington if you've arrived at Metro Ciutadella, as well as one inside the park. Here the star exhibit is Snowflake, a unique (in captivity at least) and much-gawped-at, pure white albino gorilla. Plans are afoot to move the zoo to the seashore west of the Parc de Mar, which will allow for the expansion of the park and less cramped conditions for the animal inmates.

Barceloneta and Parc de Mar

South of the park, and across the tracks of the Estació de França, the port district of **BARCELONETA** is the closest to the centre of the self-contained village suburbs that used to ring the city and are now part of greater Barcelona. The triangular wedge of development was laid out in 1755 – a classic eighteenth-century grid of streets where previously there had been mud flats – to replace the neighbourhood destroyed to make way for the Ciutadella fortress. The long, narrow streets are still very much as they were planned, broken at intervals by small squares and lined with low-built, multi-windowed houses.

The main reason most people – city inhabitants included – come to Barceloneta is to eat in one of the district's many **fish and seafood restaurants**. It used to be possible to eat right on the beach but the redevelopment of the whole of this waterfront area means that the best restaurants are now

Barceloneta transport

❑ **Metro**: line 4 to Barceloneta, from where it's a short stroll down to the Passeig de Borbó.

❑ **Buses**: #17 and #45 from Vía Laietana, #39 from Arc de Triomf, #59 from the Ramblas, and #57 and #64 from Avgda. Paral·lel and Passeig de Colom, all dropping on Passeig de Borbó. Stay on any bus (except the #45 and #59) until the end of the line in Barceloneta, at the top of Passeig de Borbó, and you're very close to the cable-car station.

❑ **Cable car**: connects Montjuïc (Torre de Miramar) and the Moll de Barcelona (Torre de Jaume I), in the centre of the docks, to Barceloneta (Torre de Sant Sebastià) – daily 10am–7pm; €6 one-way, €7.25 return, plus €3.60 for the Jaume I lift.

found elsewhere – on the main **Passeig de Joan de Borbó**, in the narrow streets of Barceloneta itself, or in the **Palau del Mar**, a renovated warehouse at the northern end of Passeig de Joan de Borbó. The Palau del Mar is also home to the heavily nationalistic **Museu d'Història de Catalunya** (Tues–Thurs 10am–7pm, Fri & Sat 10am–8pm, Sun 10am–2.30pm; €3), which traces the history of the region from the Stone Age to the present time; the best part of the museum, however, is the fourth-floor bar, which has a glorious view of the harbour and city skyline.

It's only a short walk through the Barceloneta streets to the **beach**, much cleaned up recently, furnished with outdoor showers, and backed by the long promenade of the Passeig Marítim. Heading east towards the Vila Olímpica, you can stop for a ride on the **Globus turístic**, Paseo de la Circumval·lació 135, a tethered hot-air balloon in which you can bob 150m above the city for fifteen minutes (Mon–Fri 10am–7pm, Sat & Sun 10am–9pm; €12).

Parc de Mar: the Vila Olímpica and the Port Olímpic

On the beach at Barceloneta you're within walking distance of perhaps the most adventurous urban development project undertaken by the city since the nineteenth-century extension to the north. In preparation for the 1992 Barcelona Olympics, entire blocks of warehouses of the old industrial suburb of Poble Nou were torn apart to make way for the **Parc de Mar**, a huge seafront development that incorporates the **Port Olímpic** and **Vila Olímpica** (Olympic Village), home to the athletes and administrators during the Games. The project was the brainchild of a specialist firm of urban architects led by Josep Martorell, Oriol Bohigas and an Englishman, David Mackay, which planned to turn the 5km of shoreline from Barceloneta to the Río Besòs to the east into a high-tech but user-friendly corridor of apartment blocks, conference and shopping centres, hotels, offices, parks and transport links.

Despite its initial trendiness, however, the Parc de Mar has not proved universally popular, and is viewed as rather sterile by its detractors. The area is usually visited for the restaurants, bars and nightclubs which ring the Port Olímpic, and for its sandy beach. It's easy enough to find at any rate; head for the towers of the Torre Mapfre and the Hotel Arts – the city's two tallest buildings, which are visible from just about anywhere in town.

Montjuïc

Easily visible from Barcelona's harbourside, the steep hill of **MONTJUÏC** is the city's largest green space. The hill took its name from the Jewish commu-

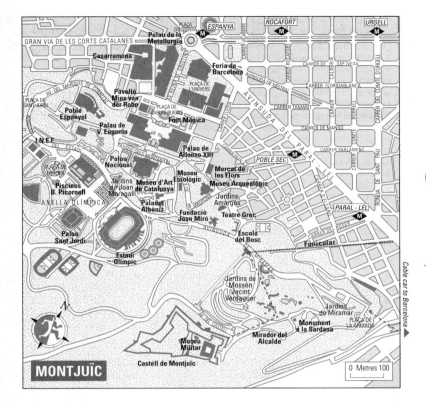

MONTJUÏC

0 Metres 100

nity that once settled on its slopes, and there's been a castle on the heights since the mid-seventeenth century, which says much about the hill's obvious historical defensive role. Since the erection of buildings for the International Exhibition of 1929, however, Montjuïc's prime role has been cultural, and you could easily spend a full day at its varied attractions, which include five museums, various gardens and the famous "Spanish Village". For those short on time, the Museu Nacional d'Arte de Catalunya is undoubtedly the highlight. The architecture on Montjuïc presents a contrast to the remnants from 1888 in the Ciutadella park; *modernisme* was a spent force by 1929 and the stately monumental designs have a heavier, sober air. The obvious highlight architecturally is Mies van der Rohe's German pavilion designed for the 1929 Exhibition and rebuilt in 1986, but more recent building, spurred by the 1992 Olympics, provides an interesting range of architectural styles that make the wooded slopes of Montjuïc intriguing to wander around.

From Plaça d'Espanya to the Palau Nacional

From the **Plaça d'Espanya**, past the square's 47-metre-high twin towers and up the imposing Avinguda de la Reina Maria Cristina, you can either make the stiff climb on foot, or take the long outdoor escalators which were part of the improvements sponsored by the 1992 Olympic Games: either is worth doing at least once for the rewarding views as you go. On either side of the avenue

Montjuïc transport

❑ From **Plaça d'Espanya Metro**, you can **walk** (or take the escalators) up to the Palau Nacional, or take one of four **buses** – #50, which can be picked up on Gran Vía; #61, which runs past most of the sights, stopping at the amusement park (last bus 8.30pm); #13, which links the Plaça to the Poble Espanyol (last bus 10.30pm); or the summer tourist route, #100, which runs past the Poble Espanyol (see p.693 for full details of this service). In the summer there is also a tourist train, the **Tren Turístic de Montjuïc**, which leaves Plaça d'Espanya every half-hour (April–Oct Sat & Sun 10.30am–7.30pm; summer and Easter daily 10.30am–9pm; €2.40 for one complete circuit with unlimited stops).

❑ Starting at the eastern end of the hill, there's a dramatic **cable-car** ride from Barceloneta or from the Moll de Barcelona, near the Columbus statue, to Jardins de Miramar (daily 10am–7pm; €6 one-way, €7.20 return, plus €3.60 for the Jaume I lift). Just beyond, you can then pick up a second cable car to the castle; or simply walk to the nearby museums.

❑ There's also a **funicular** which runs every 15min from Parallel Metro station to the cable-car station for the castle (summer daily 11am–10pm; winter Sat, Sun & holidays 10.45am–8pm; €1.50 one-way, €2.25 return). From here, you're only a few minutes' walk from the Fundació Miró.

and terraces (laid out by Puig i Cadafalch) are various exhibition buildings from 1929, still in use as venues for the city's trade fairs, while the central position in front of the Palau Nacional is given over to the illuminated fountains, the **Font Màgica**, which form part of a spectacular sound and light show (July–Sept Thurs–Sun 8pm–midnight; Oct–June Fri & Sat 8pm–midnight; free).

The Museu Nacional d'Art de Catalunya (MNAC)

The towering **Palau Nacional**, set back at the top of the flight of steps, was the centrepiece of Barcelona's 1929 International Exhibition; it was due to be demolished once the exhibition was over but gained a reprieve and five years later became home to one of Spain's great museums, the **Museu Nacional d'Art de Catalunya** (MNAC; Tues, Wed, Fri & Sat 10am–7pm, Thurs, 10am–9pm, Sun 10am–2.30pm; €4.80). This is by far the best art museum in Barcelona, with a splendid collection of medieval paintings. The museum is currently undergoing a massive long-term refit which will not be completed until 2003 (the collection is open throughout), when the first floor is scheduled to be inaugurated as the new home for the collection, presently at the Museu d'Art Modern (see p.705). With the incorporation of this collection, the museum will span Catalan art from the Middle Ages up to the 1940s. (MACBA – see p.607 – covers the period from the 1950s onward). This massive reorganization will eventually make the museum one of the largest in Europe.

Three of the main sections are already in place: the Romanesque and Gothic collections, and the latest addition, the Baroque and Renaissance gallery. The **Romanesque** collection is superb, without a doubt the best of its kind in the world. From the eleventh century, the Catalan villagers of the high Pyrenees built sturdy stone churches which were then lavishly painted in vibrantly coloured frescoes depicting Christ in majesty, angels and Apostles, martyrs and mythical animals. To save them from robbery and degradation, these were painstakingly removed early in the twentieth century and remounted in mock church interiors within the museum. The collection is laid out chronologically, starting with stone sculptures from the sixth to the tenth century, but the bulk of the work dates from the thirteenth century. The frescoes, still luminescent after eight hundred years, have a vibrant, raw quality, best exemplified by those taken from churches in the Boí valley (see p.840) in the Catalan Pyrenees – like the work of the anonymous "Master of Taüll" on the churches of Sant Climent and Santa Maria; look out for details such as the leper, to the left of the Sant Climent altar, patiently suffering a dog to lick his sores.

The **Gothic** collection is also extensive, ranging over the whole of Spain – particularly good on Catalunya, Valencia and Aragón – and again, laid out chronologically, from the thirteenth to the fifteenth century. The evolution from the Romanesque to the Gothic period was marked by a move from mural painting to painting on wood, and by the depiction of more naturalistic figures showing the lives (and rather gruesome deaths) of the saints and, later, portraits of kings and patrons of the arts.

Renaissance and **Baroque** works are represented in the Colecció Cambó, a collection named after the early-twentieth-century Catalan politician who bequeathed his personal collection to the city of Barcelona. Many of the major European artists from the fifteenth to eighteenth centuries are represented, including Lucas Cranach, Quentin Massys, Rubens, Zubarán and Goya. As 2003 approaches, more works from the museum's own holdings will be added.

The museum also houses a collection of **drawings** and **engravings** (Tues–Thurs 9am–2pm) dominated by Catalan pieces from the last three centuries, and a **photographic** collection, again primarily Catalan. There are usually one or two temporary exhibits on the lower level (separate entry, €3), which turn over every two to four months.

The Museu Etnològic and Museu Arqueològic

Downhill from the Palau Nacional, just to the east, are a couple more collections to find time for – the city's excellent ethnological and archeological museums. The **Museu Etnològic** (Tues & Thurs 10am–7pm, Wed & Fri–Sun 10am–2pm; €2.40, free first Sun of month) boasts extensive cultural collections from Central and South America, Asia, Africa, Australia and the Middle East, housed in a series of glass hexagons.

More compelling, or at least more relevant to Catalunya, is the important **Museu Arqueològic** (Tues–Sat 9.30am–7pm, Sun & holidays 9.30am–2pm; €1.20), lower down the hill. Mostly devoted to the Roman period, the museum also has Carthaginian relics (especially from the Balearics), Etruscan bits and pieces and lots of prehistoric objects; it's of particular interest if you're planning to visit Empúries on the Costa Brava (see p.766), since most of the important finds from that impressive coastal site, and some good maps and photographs, are housed here. Among the more unusual exhibits in the museum is a reconstructed Roman funeral chamber whose walls are divided into small niches for funeral urns – a type of burial known as *columbaria* (literally pigeonholes), which may be seen *in situ* in the south of Spain, at Carmona in Andalucía (see p000).

Over the way, cut into the hillside, is a reproduction of a Greek theatre, the **Teatre Grec**, again built for the 1929 Exhibition and now used during Barcelona's summer cultural festival, the *Grec* season (@ www.grec.bcn.es). The Teatre Grec is part of another ambitious project, La Ciutat del Teatre, a huge arts complex which will eventually also incorporate the nearby Mercat de les Flors, plus two new buildings, the Institut del Teatre and the Teatre Lliure, both currently situated in Gràcia.

From the Poble Espanyol to the Olympic area

A short walk over to the western side of the Palau Nacional brings you to the **Poble Espanyol** or "Spanish Village" (Mon 9am–8pm, Tues–Thurs 9am–2am, Fri & Sat 9am–4am, Sun 9am–midnight; €5.90). This was designed for the International Exhibition and its streets and squares consist of famous or characteristic buildings from all over Spain. If now the site has a rather tacky air, at the time it was an inspired concept and as a crash-course in Spanish vernacular architecture it's still not at all bad. There are also a couple of museums on site (both open daily 9am–2pm), displaying ethnographical and folk items.

Amid the pre-Olympic frenzy, the city authorities brought in Barcelona's hippest designers, Alfredo Arribas and Xavier Mariscal, who installed a club, the *Torres de Ávila*, in the Ávila gate. Other trendy venues followed and, of course, this being Barcelona, the whole complex now stays open until the small hours, a vibrant and exciting centre of Barcelona nightlife.

Just down the road from the village, the 1986 reconstruction by Catalan architects of the **Pavelló Mies van der Rohe** (daily: April–Oct 10am–8pm; Nov–March 10am–6.30pm; €2.40) recalls part of the German contribution to the 1929 Exhibition. Originally designed by Mies van der Rohe, the pavilion has a startlingly beautiful conjunction of hard straight lines with watery surfaces, its dark-green polished onyx alternating with shining glass.

The Olympics on Montjuïc

From the Poble Espanyol, the main road through Montjuïc climbs around the hill and up to the city's principal **Olympic area**, passing on its way a series of buildings all really only of interest to sports or architecture enthusiasts: Ricardo Bofill's **Sports University** (the Institut Nacional d'Educació Física de Catalunya), the **Complex Esportiu Bernat Picornell** (swimming pools and sports complex), and the low-slung, Japanese-designed, steel-and-glass **Palau Sant Jordi**, a sports and concert hall seating 17,000 people.

Overhead looms the **Estadi Olímpic** (daily 10am–6pm; free), a marvellously spacious arena which comfortably holds 65,000. Built originally for the 1929 Exhibition, the stadium was completely refitted by Catalan architects to accommodate the 1992 opening and closing ceremonies. Remarkably, the only part not touched in the rebuilding was the original Neoclassical facade – everything else is new. The **Galeria Olímpica** (Tues–Fri 10am–1pm & 4–6pm, holidays 10am–2pm; €2.40) exhibits items from the opening and closing ceremonies, and displays videos of the Games themselves.

The 1992 Olympics were the second planned for Montjuïc's stadium. The first, in 1936 – the so-called "People's Olympics" – were organized as an alternative to the Nazis' infamous Berlin games of that year, but the day before the official opening Franco's army revolt triggered the Civil War and scuppered the Barcelona games. Some of the 25,000 athletes and spectators who had turned up stayed on to join the Republican forces.

Fundació Joan Miró

Continuing down the main Avinguda l'Estadi, heading towards the cable-car station, you pass what is possibly Barcelona's most adventurous museum, the **Fundació Joan Miró** (Tues–Sat 10am–7pm, Sun & holidays 10.30am–2.30pm, Thurs closes 9.30pm; €4.80, Articket valid), an impressive white structure, opened in 1975 and set among gardens overlooking the city. Joan Miró (1893–1983) was one of the greatest of Catalan artists, establishing an international reputation whilst never severing his links with his homeland. He had his first exhibition in 1918 and after that spent his summers in

Catalunya (and the rest of the time in France) before moving to Mallorca in 1956, where he died. His friend, the architect Josep-Luís Sert, designed the beautiful building that now houses the museum, a permanent collection of paintings, graphics, tapestries and sculptures donated by Miró himself and covering the period from 1914 to 1978.

The **paintings and drawings**, regarded as one of the chief links between Surrealism and abstract art, are instantly recognizable. Perhaps the most affecting pieces in the museum are those of the *Barcelona Series* (1939–44), a set of fifty black-and-white lithographs executed in the immediate post-Civil War period. Other exhibits include his enormous bright **tapestries** (he donated nine to the museum), pencil drawings and **sculpture** outside in the gardens.

As well as the permanent exhibits, excellent temporary exhibitions are a regular feature. There is work by other artists, too, on permanent display, including pieces conceived in **homage to Miró** by the likes of Henri Matisse, Henry Moore, Robert Motherwell and the Basque sculptor Eduardo Chillida (see p.475). The single most compelling exhibit, however, has to be Alexander Calder's **Mercury Fountain**, which he built for the Republican pavilion at the Paris Universal Exhibition of 1936 – the same exhibition for which Picasso painted *Guernica* (see p.106). It is housed in a corridor on the ground floor.

The Castell de Montjuïc

From a point on the main road by the **Jardins de Mossen Jacint Verdaguer**, a cable-car system climbs over Montjuïc's old amusement park – slowly rusting after several years of closure – before coming to rest close to the Montjuïc's final attraction, the eighteenth-century **Castell de Montjuïc**. Built on seventeenth-century ruins, the castle was the scene of a modern martyrdom – the first president of the Generalitat, Lluís Companys, was executed here on Franco's orders on October 15, 1940. Still a military post, the fort today also houses the **Museu Militar** (Tues–Sun 9.30am–8pm; €1.20), which displays models of the most famous Catalan castles and a collection of swords and guns, medals, uniforms, maps and photographs, capped by a collection of suits of armour.

The Eixample

As Barcelona grew more prosperous throughout the nineteenth century, the Barri Gòtic was filled to bursting with an energetic, commercial population. By the 1850s it was clear that the city had to expand beyond the Plaça de Catalunya. A contest was held by the *ajuntament* and the winning plan was that of the engineer Ildefons Cerdà, who drew up a grid-shaped new town marching off to the north, intersected by long, straight streets and cut by broad, angled avenues. Work started in 1859 on what became known as the *Ensanche* in Spanish – in Catalan, the **EIXAMPLE**, or "Extension".

It immediately became the fashionable area in which to live, and the moneyed classes moved from their cramped quarters by the old port to spacious and luxurious apartments along the wide new avenues. As the money in the city moved north, so did a new class of *modernista* architects who, commissioned by the status-conscious bourgeoisie, began to pepper the Eixample with ever more striking examples of their work. The buildings – most notably the work of **Antoni Gaudí, Lluís Domènech i Montaner** and **Josep Puig i Cadafalch**, but others too (see box overleaf) – are still often in private hands,

Modernisme

Modernisme, the Catalan offshoot of Art Nouveau, was the expression of a renewed upsurge in Catalan nationalism in the 1870s. The early-nineteenth-century economic recovery in Catalunya had provided the initial impetus, and the ensuing cultural renaissance in the region – the *Renaixença* – led to the fresh stirrings of a new Catalan awareness and identity after the dark years of Bourbon rule.

Lluís Domènech i Montaner (1850–1923) – perhaps the greatest *modernista* architect – was responsible for giving Catalan aspirations a definite direction with his appeal, in 1878, for a national style of architecture, drawing particularly on the rich Catalan Romanesque and Gothic traditions. The timing was perfect, since Barcelona was undergoing a huge expansion: the medieval walls had been pulled down and the gridded Eixample was giving the city a new shape, with a rather French feel to it, and plenty of new space to work in. By 1874 **Antoni Gaudí** (1852–1926) had begun his architectural career. He was born in Reus (near Tarragona) to a family of artisans, and his work was never strictly modernist in style (it was never strictly anything in style), but the imaginative impetus he gave the movement was incalculable. Fourteen years later the young **Josep Puig i Cadafalch** (1867–1957) would be inspired to become an architect (and later a reforming politician) as he watched the spectacularly rapid round-the-clock construction of Domènech's *Grand Hotel* on the Passeig de Colom. It was in another building by Domènech (the café-restaurant of the Parc de la Ciutadella) that a craft workshop was set up after the Exhibition of 1888, giving Barcelona's *modernista* architects the opportunity to experiment with traditional crafts like ceramic tiles, ironwork, stained glass and decorative stone carving. This combination of traditional crafts with modern technology was to become the hallmark of *modernisme* – a combination which produced some of the most fantastic and exciting modern architecture to be found anywhere in the world.

Most attention is usually focused on the three protagonists mentioned above; certainly they provide the bulk of the most extraordinary buildings that Barcelona has to offer. But keep an eye out for lesser-known architects who also worked in the Eixample; **Josep María Jujol**, renowned as Gaudí's collaborator on several of his most famous projects, can also boast a few complete constructions of his own, or there's the hard-working **Jeroni Granell** (1867–1931), and **Josep Vilaseca i Casanoves** (1848–1910), who was responsible for the brick Arc de Triomf outside the Ciutadella park.

It's Antoni Gaudí, though, that most have heard of – by training a metalworker, by inclination a fervent Catalan nationalist and devout Catholic. His buildings are the most daring creations of all Art Nouveau, apparently lunatic flights of fantasy which at the same time are perfectly functional. His architectural influences were Moorish and Gothic, while he embellished his work with elements from the natural world. Yet Gaudí rarely wrote a word about the theory of his art, preferring its products to speak for themselves. Although he worked throughout Spain, Gaudí has become a symbol of Barcelona and Catalunya; with an enquiry into his beatification announced by the Vatican in early 2000, he may become the first Catalan saint of the twenty-first century.

restricting your viewing to the outside, but turning the Eixample into a huge urban museum around which it's a pleasure to wander.

The most economical way to enjoy Barcelona's modernist heritage is to purchase a ticket for the **Ruta del modernisme**, an itinerary organized by the city which passes most of the main *modernista* sites. The ticket (€3.60, valid for 30 days) is available from the Modernisme Centre in the Casa Amatller (Pg. de Gràcia 41; ☎934 880 139; Mon–Sat 10am–7pm, Sun 10am–2pm), and gives discounts on admission to the Palau Güell, Palau de la Música, Museu Gaudí,

Museu d'Art Modern, Museu de la Música, Museu de Zoologia, La Pedrera, La Sagrada Familia and the Fundació Tàpies. Also in the works is a parallel route which will change annually, focusing each year on a different modernist architect. In 2001 Puig i Cadafalch will be highlighted, in 2002 Gaudí.

The Eixample is still the city's main shopping and business district, spreading out on either side of the two principal (and parallel) thoroughfares, **Passeig de Gràcia** and **Rambla de Catalunya**, both of which cut northwest from the Plaça de Catalunya. The former features several of the best-known examples of Barcelona's *modernista* architecture, including the famous **Manzana de la Discòrdia** and Gaudí's **La Pedrera**. The latter is the district's most attractive avenue, largely pedestrianized and sporting benches and open-air cafés. Almost all the things you're likely to want to see are on the eastern side of the Rambla de Catalunya – an area known as Dreta de l'Eixample – and south of the wide **Avinguda Diagonal**, which slices across the entire Eixample. There's less to get excited about on the west side of Rambla de Catalunya – the so-called Esquerra de l'Eixample – which housed many of the public buildings contained within Cerdà's nineteenth-century plan.

If you're not interested in shopping or architecture, it's not immediately clear why you might spend time in the Eixample, though one bonus is that many of the buildings also contain noteworthy exhibitions and museums; the **Fundació Antoni Tàpies** is Barcelona's latest gallery dedicated to the work of just a single artist. Moreover, the Eixample contains the one building in the city to which a visit is virtually obligatory: Gaudí's extraordinary **Sagrada Familia** church, beyond the Diagonal, in the northeast of the district.

Along Passeig de Gràcia

If you want to walk in the Eixample, the stretch you'll get most out of is the wide **Passeig de Gràcia** which runs northwest from the El Corte Inglés store on the corner of Plaça de Catalunya. Laid out in its present form in 1827, it's a splendid, showy avenue, bisected by the other two main city boulevards, the Gran Vía and Avinguda Diagonal, and continues as far as Gràcia itself – but you're probably not going to walk that far. Stick with it, though, as far as Metro Diagonal for a view of some of the best of the city's *modernista* architecture, flaunted in a series of remarkable buildings on and just off the avenue.

Manzana de la Discòrdia

The most famous grouping of buildings, the so-called **Manzana de la Discòrdia** or "Block of Discord", is just four blocks up from Plaça de Catalunya (Ⓜ Passeig de Gràcia). It gets its name because the adjacent buildings – built by three different architects – are completely different in style and feel.

On the corner of c/de Consell de Cent, at Pg. de Gràcia 35, the privately owned six-storey **Casa Lleó Morera**, completed by Domènech i Montaner in 1906, is perhaps the least appealing of the buildings in the block; it has the least extravagant exterior and has suffered more than the others from "improvements" wrought by subsequent owners, which included removing the ground-floor arches and sculptures. Its semicircular jutting balconies, however, are quite distinctive.

A few doors up at no. 41, Puig i Cadafalch's **Casa Amatller** is more striking, an apartment block from 1900 created largely from the bones of an existing building and paid for by Antoni Amatller, a Catalan chocolate manufacturer. The facade rises in steps to a point, studded with coloured ceramic decoration and with heraldic sculptures over the doors and windows. Step inside the hallway for a peek: the ceramic tiles continue along the walls and there are twisted stone columns, fine stained-glass domes and an interior glass roof. The block contains a Hispanic art institute, the Institute Amatller d'Art Hispànic (library open Sept–June Mon–Fri 10am–1.30pm, also Tues & Thurs 3.30–7pm), located inside the old Amatller family apartments.

Perhaps the most extraordinary creation on the Block of Discord is next door, at no. 43, where Gaudí's **Casa Batlló** (finished in 1907) – designed for the industrialist Josep Batlló – was similarly wrought from an apartment building already in place but considered dull by contemporaries. Gaudí was hired to give it a face-lift and contrived to create a facade which Dalí later compared to "the tranquil waters of a lake". There's an animal aspect at work here, too: the stone facade hangs in folds, like skin and, from below, the twisted balcony railings resemble malevolent eyes. Unfortunately, the mansion's interior now serves as a banquet hall and is closed to the general public – yours to hire for the evening for a mere €3000.

Casa Montaner i Simon: the Fundació Antoni Tàpies

Turn the corner onto c/d'Aragó and at no. 255 (just past Rambla de Catalunya) you'll find Domènech i Montaner's first important building, the **Casa Montaner i Simon**, finished in 1880. The building originally served the publishing firm after which it was named, but, as the enormous aluminium tubular structure on the roof now announces, it's been converted to house the **Fundació Antoni Tàpies** (Tues–Sun 11am–8pm; €4.20, Articket valid).

The third of Barcelona's showpiece single-artist collections is devoted to the life and work of Antoni Tàpies, born in the city in 1923. His first major paintings date from 1945, at which time Tàpies was interested in collage (using newspaper, cardboard, silver wrapping, string and wire) and engraving techniques. Later, coming into contact with Miró among others, he underwent a brief Surrealist period (the fruits of which are displayed in the basement). After a stay in Paris he found his feet with an abstract style that matured during the 1950s, during which time he held his first major exhibitions, including a show in New York. His work became increasingly political during the 1960s and 1970s: the harsh colours of *In Memory of Salvador Puig Antich* commemorate a Catalan anarchist executed by Franco's regime.

La Pedrera and Vinçon

Gaudí's apartment block, the Casa Milà, at Pg. de Gràcia 92 (ⓂDiagonal) is another building not to be missed. Constructed between 1905 and 1911, it was declared a UNESCO World Heritage site in 1984. The rippling facade, which curves around the street corner in one smooth sweep, is said to have been inspired by the mountain of Montserrat, and the apartments themselves, whose balconies of tangled metal drip over the facade, resemble eroded cave dwellings. The building – still split into private apartments – is more popularly known as **La Pedrera**, the "rock pile" or "stone quarry". This was one of Gaudí's last secular commissions – and one of his best – but even here he was injecting religious motifs and sculptures into the building until told to remove them by the building's owners. You can visit **the roof**, to see the enigmatic chimneys at close quarters, as well as a newly opened re-creation of a *modernista*-era bourgeois apartment ("el pis"), and an exhibition about Gaudí's work (daily 10am–8pm; €6, €3.60 for the apartment or the exhibition only, Articket valid). Perhaps the best way to see the building is with the *La Pedrera de Nit* ticket (July–Sept daily 9pm; €9), when you can enjoy the rooftop and night-time cityscape with music and a complimentary *cava*. The building also houses (free) temporary art exhibitions, which are often well worth a look.

Right next to La Pedrera, in the same block, the **Casa Casas** dates from 1899, a huge building designed for the artist Ramon Casas who maintained a home here. In 1941, the **Vinçon** store was established in the building, which emerged in the 1960s as the country's pre-eminent purveyor of furniture and design, a position today's department store (Mon–Sat 10am–2pm & 4.30–8.30pm) still maintains; there are entrances at Pg. de Gràcia 96, c/de Provença 273 and c/Pau Claris 175.

East: between Passeig de Gràcia and Avinguda Diagonal

The buildings along Passeig de Gràcia are perhaps the best known in the Eixample, but the blocks contained within the triangle to the east, formed by the Passeig and **Avinguda Diagonal**, sport their own important, often extraordinary structures. Several are by the two hardest working architects in the Eixample, Domènech i Montaner and Puig i Cadafalch, while Gaudí's first apartment building, the Casa Calvet, is also here. Apart from the Casa Calvet, all the buildings are within a few blocks of each other between the Passeig de Gràcia and Diagonal metro stops.

Just a few blocks from the Plaça de Catalunya, Gaudí's **Casa Calvet** (c/de Casp 48) dates from 1899. This was his first apartment block and, though fairly conventional in style, the Baroque inspiration on display in the main facade was to surface again in his later, more elaborate buildings on the main Passeig de Gràcia. If you need another target, aim for the church and market of **La Concepció**, in between c/de Valencia and c/d'Aragó. The early-fifteenth-century Gothic church and cloister once stood in the old town, part of a convent abandoned in the early nineteenth century and then transferred here brick by brick in the 1870s by Jeroni Granell. The market was added in 1888, its iron-and-glass tram-shed structure reminiscent of others in the city. One block north, the neo-Gothic **Casa Thomas** at c/de Mallorca 291, with its understated pale ceramic tiles, has a ground floor that welcomes visitors into its furniture design showroom. A little way along, set back from the crossroads in a little garden, the **Palau Muntaner** (c/de Mallorca 278) was finished a few years later, in 1893. Now serving as a temporary office for visiting officials, the colourful little building can only be seen from the outside.

From here you can head up to Avinguda Diagonal, and the soaring Casa Terrades at nos. 416–420. More usually known as the **Casa de les Punxes** (House of Spikes) because of its red-tiled turrets and steep gables, it is Puig i Cadafalch's largest work. Further along Avinguda Diagonal, on the other side of the road at no. 373, Puig's almost Gothic **Palau Quadras** from 1904 now houses the **Museu de la Música** (Tues, Thurs–Sun & holidays 10am–2pm, Wed 10am–8pm; €2.40, first Sun of month free). The collection of instruments from all over the world, dating from the sixteenth to the twentieth century, provides an excuse to look inside. Just over the Diagonal, at Pg. de Sant Joan 108, Puig i Cadafalch's palatial **Casa Macaya** contains an impressive Gothic-inspired courtyard and is now a gallery for temporary international art and photography exhibits (Mon–Sat 11am–8pm, Sun & holidays 11am–3pm; free).

La Sagrada Familia

While diverting, and occasionally provocative, the pockets of architectural interest throughout the Eixample hardly command mass appeal. The same is not true, however, of the new town's most famous monument, Antoni Gaudí's great **Temple Expiatori de la Sagrada Familia** (daily: March, Sept & Oct 9am–7pm; April–Aug 9pm–8pm; Nov–Feb 9pm–6pm; €4.80; ⓂSagrada Familia), a good way northeast of the Plaça de Catalunya and just north of the Diagonal. It's an essential stop on any visit to Barcelona, for more than any building in the Barri Gòtic it speaks volumes about the Catalan urge to glorify uniqueness and endeavour.

Begun in 1882 by public subscription, the Sagrada Familia was conceived originally by its progenitor, the Catalan publisher Josep Bocabella, as an expiatory building which would atone for the city's increasingly revolutionary ideas. Bocabella appointed the architect Francesc de Paula Villar to the work, and his plan was for a modest church in an orthodox neo-Gothic style. After arguments between the two men, **Gaudí** took charge two years later and changed the direction and scale of the project almost immediately, seeing in the Sagrada Familia an opportunity to reflect his own deepening spiritual and nationalist feelings. Indeed, after he finished the Parc Güell in 1911, Gaudí vowed never to work again on secular art, but to devote himself solely to the Sagrada Familia (where, by now, he lived in a workshop on site), and he was adapting the plans ceaselessly right up to his death. (He was run over by a tram on the Gran Vía in June 1926 and died in hospital two days later – initially unrecognized, for he had become a virtual recluse, rarely leaving his small studio. His death was treated as a Catalan national disaster, and all of Barcelona turned out for his funeral procession.)

Work restarted in the late 1950s amid great controversy, and in May 2000 the halfway mark of construction was officially reached; completion is projected for 2035. Although the church building survived the Civil War, Gaudí's plans and models were destroyed in 1936 by the anarchists, who regarded Gaudí and his church as conservative religious relics that the new Barcelona could do without. Since no one now knows what Gaudí intended, the arguments continue: some maintain that the Sagrada Familia should be left incomplete as a memorial to Gaudí's untimely death, others that he intended it to be the work of several generations, each continuing in their own style.

The building

The size alone is startling. Eight **spires** rise to over one hundred metres. They have been likened to everything from perforated cigars to celestial billiard cues, but for Gaudí they symbolized the twelve Apostles; he planned to build four more above the main facade and to add a 180-metre tower topped with a lamb (representing Jesus) over the transept, itself to be surrounded by four smaller towers symbolizing the Evangelists.

A precise **symbolism** also pervades the facades, each of which is divided into three porches devoted to Faith, Hope and Charity. The east facade further represents the Nativity and the Mysteries of Joy; the west (currently the main entrance and nearing completion) depicts the Passion and the Mysteries of Affliction. Gaudí meant the south facade, the Gloria, to be the culmination of the Sagrada Familia – designed, he said, to show "the religious realities of present and future life . . . man's origin, his end and the ways he has to follow to achieve it". Everything from the Creation to Heaven and Hell, in short, was to be included in one magnificent ensemble.

Use the **lift** (€1.20) which runs up one of the towers around the rose window, or face the long, steep climb to the top (a vertiginous 400 steps). Either route will reward you with partial views of the city through an extraordinary jumble of latticed stonework, ceramic decoration, carved buttresses and sculpture. You're free to climb still further around the walls and into the other towers, a dizzy experience to say the least.

On site, there's the small **Museu de la Sagrada Familia**, which traces the career of the architect and the history of the Sagrada Familia. Models, sketches and photographs help to make some sense of the work going on around you.

Esquerra de l'Eixample: Plaça de Catalunya to Estació-Sants

The long streets **west of the Passeig de Gràcia** – making up the Esquerra de l'Eixample – are no competition when it comes to planning a route around the Eixample, and most visitors only ever travel this part of the city underground, on their way into the centre by metro. This was the part of the Eixample meant by Cerdà for public buildings, and many of these still stand: the grand **Universitat** (1902) building, at Plaça de la Universitat; the local **Hospital Clínic** (1904); the **Universitat Industrial** (1908), a converted textile complex; the prison – the **Presó Model** (1902) – with its star-shaped cell blocks; and **Les Arenes** bullring, a beautiful structure from 1900 with fine Moorish decoration. However, if you are pressed for time you will probably only venture into this part of the Eixample for a window-shopping stroll along the **Gran Vía de les Corts Catalanes** (usually shortened to just the Gran Vía), which links Plaça d'Espanya with Plaça de les Glòries Catalanes to the east.

However, there is one part of the Esquerra de l'Eixample that it is possible to justify a short walk around, starting at the Plaça d'Espanya. Between here and **Sants** station, several public spaces have been created over the last decade or so in a style known as **nou urbanisme** – typified by a wish to transform former industrial sites into urban parks accessible to local people.

Parc Joan Miró and around Sants station

Built on the site of the nineteenth-century municipal slaughterhouse, the **Parc Joan Miró** (Ⓜ Tarragona) features a raised piazza whose main feature is Miró's gigantic phallic sculpture *Dona i Ocell* (Woman and Bird), towering above a small lake. It's a familiar symbol if you've studied Miró's other works, and was originally entitled "The Cock", until the city authorities suggested otherwise.

Even more controversial are the open park areas created around Sants station, just up the road. Directly in front of the station, the **Plaça dels Països Catalans** features a series of walls, raised meshed roofs and coverings designed by Helio Piñon – a rather comfortless "park" in most people's eyes, more intimidating than welcoming. It's easier to see the attraction of Basque architect Luís Peña Ganchegui's **Parc de l'Espanya Industrial**, two minutes' walk away around the side of the station. Built on an old textile factory site, it has a line of red-and-yellow striped lighthouses at the top of glaring white steps with an incongruously classical Neptune in the water below, seen to best effect at night.

The suburbs

Until the Eixample stretched out across the plain to meet them, a string of small towns ringed the city to the north. Today, they're firmly entrenched as **suburbs** of Barcelona, but most still retain an individual identity worth investigating even on a short visit to the city. **Gràcia**, particularly – the closest to the centre – is still very much the liberal, almost bohemian stronghold it was in the nineteenth century, with an active cultural life and night scene of its own. Apart from mere curiosity, each of the other suburbs also has a specific sight or two that makes it a worthwhile target. Some, like Gaudí's **Parc Güell**, between Gràcia and Horta, and the Gothic monastery at **Pedralbes**, are included in most people's tours of the city, and for good reason. Other sights are more specialized – such as the football museum at FC Barcelona's superb **Camp Nou** stadium or the ceramics collection in the **Palau Reial** – but taken together they do help to counter the notion that Barcelona begins and ends in the Barri Gòtic. Finally, if you're saving yourself for just one aerial view of Barcelona, wait for a clear day and head for **Tibidabo**, way to the northwest; a mountain with an amusement park and a couple of bars with the best views in the city.

Gràcia

GRÀCIA is the most satisfying of Barcelona's peripheral districts, and, given its concentration of bars, clubs and restaurants, the one you're most likely to visit. Beginning at the top of the Passeig de Gràcia, and bordered roughly by c/de Balmes to the west and the streets above the Sagrada Familia to the east, it has been a fully fledged suburb of the city since late nineteenth century. Traditionally the home of a Romany (gypsy) community, it was colonized in the 1970s by arty and political types, students and the intelligentsia, and today still supports a core local population which lends Gràcia an attractive, no-frills, small-town atmosphere. **Getting there** by public transport means taking the FGC railway from Plaça de Catalunya to Gràcia station; bus #22 or #24 from Plaça de Catalunya up c/Gran de Grácia; or taking the metro to either Diagonal, to the south, or Fontana, to the north.

Plaça del Sol is an enjoyable place to sit out during the day at one of the cafés, admiring the solid nineteenth-century buildings that surround the square and the more recent architectural additions by Gabriel Mora and Jaume Bach. At night, especially at the weekend, the square becomes an outdoor meeting place, a base from which to launch yourself at the bars, clubs and restaurants in the vicinity. A couple of blocks down is another pleasant stop, **Plaça Rius i Taulet**, with its thirty-metre-high bell tower. The **Plaça de la Virreina** lies to the north in the heart of the bar district, and is the scene of the *barri's* frequent outdoor celebrations.

Gaudí's first major private commission, the **Casa Vicens** (which he finished in 1885), is at c/de les Carolines 24 (Ⓜ Fontana). Here he took inspiration from the Mudéjar style, covering the facade in linear green-and-white tiles with a flower motif.

Parc Güell

From 1900 to 1914 Gaudí worked for Eusebio Güell (patron of his Palau Güell, off the Ramblas) on the **Parc Güell** (daily 10am–9pm; free), on the outskirts of Gràcia. This was Gaudí's most ambitious project after the Sagrada Familia – which he was engaged on at the same time – commissioned as a private housing estate of sixty dwellings and furnished with paths, recreational areas and decorative monuments. In the end, only two houses were actually built, and the park was opened to the public instead in 1922.

Laid out on a hill which provides fabulous views back across the city, the park is an almost hallucinatory expression of the imagination. Pavilions of contorted stone, giant decorative lizards, a vast Hall of Columns (intended to be the estate's market), the meanderings of a huge ceramic bench – all combine in one manic swirl of ideas and excesses. The mosaics and decorations (many made from broken crockery) found throughout the park were mostly executed by J.M. Jujol, who assisted on several of Gaudí's projects, while one of Gaudí's other collaborators, Francesc Berenguer, designed and built a house in the park in 1904, in which Gaudí was persuaded to live until he left to camp out at the Sagrada Familia for good. The house is now the **Casa Museu Gaudí** (Sun–Fri 10am–2pm & 4–7pm, €1.20), a small but diverting collection of some of the furniture he designed for other projects – a typical mixture of wild originality and brilliant engineering – as well as plans and objects related to the park and to Gaudí's life.

To get to the park, take **bus** #24 from Plaça de Catalunya right to the side gate by the car park, or the **metro** to Vallcarca, from where you walk down Avinguda de l'Hospital until you see the mechanical escalators on your left, then follow the path right to the park entrance. Be warned, however, that the escalators are often not working and the climb up on foot is a particularly stiff one. **Walking from Gràcia**, head straight up the main c/Gran de Gràcia and you'll pass Metro Lesseps, where you should turn right on to the Travessera de Dalt and follow the signs.

Pedralbes and around

Northwest of the city, **PEDRALBES** is a well-to-do, residential neighbourhood of wide avenues and fancy apartment blocks. Allow yourself the best part of a day and you can include the Gothic monastery here in a longer route that takes in the Camp Nou stadium, an early Gaudí creation, and the ceramics museum in the Palau Reial.

Camp Nou: the Museu del Barça

Within the city's Diagonal area, the magnificent **Camp Nou** football stadium of FC Barcelona (Ⓜ Collblanc/María Cristina) will be high on the visiting list of any sports fan. Built in 1957, and enlarged to accommodate the 1982 World Cup semi-final, the comfortable stadium seats a staggering 120,000 people in steep tiers that provide one of the best football-watching experiences in the world – on a par with the famous Maracaña stadium in Brazil. The club is historically one of Spain's most successful teams although in recent years it has suffered on the field at the hands of arch-rival Real Madrid who added insult to injury by poaching star player Figo from the team in 2000. But it's more than just a football club to most people in Barcelona. During the Franco era, it stood as a Catalan symbol, around which people could rally, and perhaps as a consequence FC Barcelona has the world's largest football club membership – currently 106,000 – including the planet's most celebrated clerical goalkeeper, Pope John Paul II, who was persuaded to join on his visit to Spain in 1982.

If you can't get to a game, a visit to the club's **Museu del Barça** (Mon–Sat 10am–6.30pm, Sun 10am–2pm; €3.15) is a pale second-best: a homage to Catalunya's best-known institution. There are team and match photos dating back to 1901, as well as *Futbolart,* an exhibition of paintings and sculpture.

Palau Reial de Pedralbes and the Finca Güell

On the other side of Avinguda Diagonal, the **Palau Reial de Pedralbes** (ⓂPalau Reial) is an Italianate palace set in pleasant, formal **grounds** (daily: winter 10am–6pm; summer 10am–8pm). The interior is open to the public as the **Museu de la Ceràmica** (Tues–Sat 10am–6pm, Sun & holidays 10am–3pm; €2.40, free first Sun of month), where the many exhibits range from the thirteenth to the nineteenth century, and include fine Mudéjar-influenced tiles and plates from the Aragonese town of Teruel, as well as whole rooms of Catalan water spouts (some from the seventeenth century), jars, dishes and bowls. In the modern section, Picasso, Miró and the *modernista* Antoni Serra i Fiter are all represented. Adjoining the Museu de Ceràmica is the **Museu de les Arts Decoratives** (Tues–Sat 10am–6pm, Sun & holidays 10am–3pm; admission included with the Museu de la Ceràmica), a collection of household objects and industrial design from the Middle Ages to the modern day.

From the palace, it's a walk of fifteen minutes or so up Avinguda Pedralbes to the monastery. Just a couple of minutes along the way, you'll pass Gaudí's **Finca Güell** on your left. Built as a stables and riding school for the family of Gaudí's old patron, Eusebio Güell, and now a private residence, you can see no further than its extraordinary metal dragon gateway, with razor teeth snarling at the passers-by.

Monestir de Pedralbes

At the end of Avinguda Pedralbes, the Gothic **Monestir de Santa María de Pedralbes** (Tues–Sun 10am–2pm; €2.40, free first Sun of month, joint ticket with Col·lecció Thyssen-Bornemisza €3) is reached up a cobbled street that passes through a small archway set back from the road. If you're coming from the city centre, the monastery is about a thirty-minute journey by **bus** (#22 from the Passeig de Gràcia, just north of Plaça de Catalunya, to the end of the line); alternatively take the metro to Palau Reial or the FGC to Pedralbes (see above).

Founded in 1326 for the nuns of the Order of St Clare, this is in effect a self-contained religious community, preserved on the outskirts of the city. The harmonious **cloisters** are built on three levels and adorned by the slenderest of columns, and rooms opening off here give the clearest impression of monastic life you're likely to see in Catalunya: there's a large refectory, a fully equipped kitchen, an infirmary (complete with beds and water jugs), a separate infirmary kitchen, and windows overlooking a well-tended kitchen garden. The adjacent **church**, a simple, single-naved structure which retains some of its original stained glass, is also well worth looking in on. In the chancel, to the right of the altar, the foundation's sponsor, Elisenda de Montcada, wife of Jaume II, lies in a superb, carved marble tomb.

After years of negotiations, a selection of religious paintings from the Thyssen-Bornemisza art collection is now on permanent view in one of the monastery's old dormitories. The immense private art collection of Baron Heinrich Thyssen-Bornemisza came to Spain in 1989, and the bulk of it is displayed in Madrid's Villahermosa palace (see p.104), but the promptings of the baron's Catalan wife ensured a cache of paintings found its way to Barcelona. This now forms the **Col·lecció Thyssen-Bornemisza** (Tues–Sun 10am–2pm; €1.80, free first Sun of month, joint ticket with Monestir de Pedralbes €3), a superb body of work which includes priceless pieces from all the major movements in European art from the fourteenth to the eighteenth century.

Tibidabo

If the views from the Castell de Montjuïc are good, those from the 550-metre heights of **Mount Tibidabo** – which forms the northwestern boundary of the city – are legendary. On one of those mythical clear days you can see across to Montserrat and the Pyrenees. The very name is based on this view, taken from the Temptations of Christ in the wilderness, when Satan led him to a high place and offered him everything which could be seen: *Haec omnia tibi dabo si cadens adoraberis me* ("All these things will I give thee, if thou wilt fall down and worship me").

At the summit there's a modern **church** topped with a huge statue of Christ, and – immediately adjacent – a wonderful **Parc d'Atraccions** (mid-April to May Sat & Sun noon–8pm; May Fri 10am–6pm, Sat & Sun noon–8pm; June Thurs & Fri 10am–6pm, Sat & Sun noon–9pm; July & Aug Fri & Sat noon–1am, Sun–Thurs noon–10pm; early Sept Sat & Sun noon–10pm; late Sept & Oct Sat & Sun noon–8pm), founded in 1901. The amusements are scattered around several levels of the mountain-top, connected by landscaped paths and gardens, and comprise a good mix of traditional rides and high-tech attractions, at all of which large queues form at peak times. If you want a real thrill, try the aeroplane ride, a Barcelona icon; it's been spinning since 1928. There are various **admission** charges depending on what you want to do: entry with five ride tickets is €7.20, (additional rides and attractions cost extra, up to €4.50 each); if you want to go on everything, it'll be cheaper to buy an all-inclusive ticket for €14.40.

Take the FGC **train** (Tibidabo line) or **bus** #17 (both from Plaça de Catalunya) to Avinguda Tibidabo (the last stop). From there a regular antique **tram** service (the Tramvia Blau; every 40min or every 20min at weekends, 7am–9.30pm; €1.65 one-way, €2.40 return) runs you up to Plaça Doctor Andreu (there's a bus service when the tram's not running). Here, there are a couple of café-bars, and a **funicular station** with regular connections to the top (Mon–Thurs & Sun noon–10.30pm, Fri & Sat noon–1.30am; €1.80 one-way, €3 return). The special **Tibibús** also runs from Plaça de Catalunya to the foot of the funicular (Mon–Fri hourly from 11am, Sat & Sun every 30min from 10.30am; €1.75, or €15 including park entrance).

Out of the city

Day-trips out of the city are easy and popular, particularly up or down **the coast** to one of the beach resorts that city dwellers have appropriated for themselves. The best coastal destination is Sitges, forty minutes away along the Costa Daurada, dealt with in the "Catalunya" chapter. However, there are plenty of other beaches closer to the city that are worth considering, such as **Castelldefels** to the south, and those of the **Costa Maresme** to the north – all of them are connected to Barcelona by very frequent train services that run throughout the summer. Otherwise, the one essential excursion is to **Montserrat**, the extraordinary mountain and monastery 40km northwest of the city: few visitors are disappointed.

The coast: Castelldefels and the Costa Maresme

All **trains** to the beaches below depart from Estació-Sants, which is where you should go for current timetables. Those heading south to Castelldefels also stop at the station at Passeig de Gràcia; north to the Costa Maresme, you can pick the train up at Plaça de Catalunya.

South, the first coastal stop is at **CASTELLDEFELS**, 20km from Barcelona. Don't get off at the earlier town stop; you want Castelldefels-Platja, where vast numbers alight in summer to descend upon this extremely long beach, which starts just a couple of blocks from the station. **GARRAF**, another five minutes or so south on the train, has a much smaller beach, and more of a family atmosphere, but the town itself is far prettier, with a small port, and uphill by the old highway, **Cava Güell**, a curious *modernista* creation completed by Gaudí in 1901 to house his patron's wine collection.

Immediately **north** of Barcelona, before you reach the Costa Brava, is a stretch of coast known as the **Costa Maresme**. On the whole it's far more industrial and less attractive than the Costa Brava, but its proximity to the city means clogged-up roads and packed trains in the summer, as people head out in search of a change of scenery. Once you get past Badalona, the northeastern part of Barcelona's urban agglomeration, you reach a 10km stretch of pleasant sandy beach connecting **EL MASNOU**, **PREMIÀ DE MAR** and **VILAS-SAR DE MAR**, each served by RENFE trains. Heading east from the grim industrial town of **MATARÓ**, a commuter suburb of Barcelona, the beach continues unbroken to **ARENYS DE MAR**, an hour out of Barcelona. It's the largest fishing port hereabouts and consequently has a harbour that bears investigation and a beach that's serviceable.

SANT POL DE MAR, 45km from Barcelona, is probably your best bet if you're heading for just one spot on the coast. Small, and as unspoiled as these coastal villages get, it offers rocky coves and crowd-free swimming around fifteen minutes' walk from the station, and has several restaurants along the main street. From the train station, cross the tracks and walk to the left, around the corner.

The mountain and monastery of Montserrat

The **mountain of MONTSERRAT**, with its strangely shaped crags of rock, its monastery and ruined hermitage caves, stands just 40km northwest of Barcelona, off the road to Lleida. It is one of the most spectacular of all Spain's natural sights, a saw-toothed outcrop left exposed to erosion when the inland sea that covered this area around 25 million years ago was drained by progressive uplifts of the earth's crust. Legends hang easily upon it. Fifty years after the birth of Christ, St Peter is said to have deposited an image of the Virgin carved by St Luke in one of the mountain caves, and another tale makes this the spot in which the knight Parsifal discovered the Holy Grail. Inevitably the monastery and mountain are no longer remote; in fact they're ruthlessly exploited as a tourist trip from the Costa Brava. But don't be put off – the place itself is still magical and you can avoid the crowds by striking out onto the mountainside, along well-signposted paths, to potent and deserted hermitages. The main **pilgrimages** to Montserrat take place on April 27 and September 8.

Practicalities

The most thrilling approach is by train and cable car from Barcelona. FGC **trains** (line R5: Montserrat–Manresa) leave from beneath Plaça d'Espanya daily from 8.36am–3.36pm at hourly intervals; get off at Montserrat Aeri, just under an hour away. From here, a **cable car** (the Telefèric de Montserrat Aeri; every 15min, daily 10am–1.45pm & 3–6.35pm) completes the journey, an exhilarating five-minute swoop up the sheer mountainside to a spot just below the monastery. Alternatively, buses make the half-hour ride from the train station up to the monastery, departing ten minutes after the trains pull in. A return ticket, including train and cable car, costs €11.40, and there are also two combined tickets: the Transmontserrat, which includes the metro, train, cable car and the two funiculars on the mountain (€17.40 return); and the Totmontserrat, which includes all of this plus museum entry, unlimited use of funiculars, lunch and a five-percent accommodation discount at the monastery's two hotels (€29.40); both tickets are available from any FGC station. **Returning to Barcelona**, the trains back from Montserrat Aeri station are again hourly, this time from 10.35am to 6.35pm.

Otherwise, daily **buses** run from Sants in Barcelona, usually leaving at 9am and returning at around 6pm. These cost €7.40 per person (€8.40 at weekends), and tickets are available from Julia Tours (Plaça Universitat 12; ☎934 904 000), or any travel agent. **Drivers** should take the A2 motorway as far as Martorell, and then follow the N11 and C1411 before zigzagging up to the monastery.

Food at the couple of self-service restaurants is pricey and uninspiring – and the restaurants themselves are crammed at peak times. There's a lot to be said for taking your own picnic and striking off up the mountainside – if you forget to bring supplies, there is a small grocery store right by the monastery. **Staying over** at Montserrat can be an attractive option: it's a very different place once the tour groups have departed. The three-star *Hotel Abat Cisneros* (☎938 777 701, ℱ938 777 724; ❼) has rather pricey rooms, while the *Hotel-Residencia Monestir* (same phone; ❺) is the economical option. The three *refugios* close by are another option: the *Refugio de Santa Cecilia* (reception closes at 10pm), 4km from the main monastery next door to the monastery of the same name, is the most deluxe, with good, clean facilities, while *Sant Benet* and *La Trinitat*, both a short walk from the church of Montserrat, are far more basic. The **campsite** (☎938 777 777; Easter–Oct) is up beyond the Sant Joan funicular, with a clean shower and toilet block and excellent views overlooking the monastery and mountains.

The monastery

It is the "Black Virgin" (*La Moreneta*), the icon supposedly brought here by Saint Peter (but curiously reflecting the style of sixth-century Byzantine carving), which is responsible for the existence of the **monastery of Monserrat**. The legend is loosely wrought, but it appears the icon was lost in the early eighth century after being hidden during the Muslim invasion. It reappeared in 880, accompanied by the customary visions and celestial music and, in the first of its miracles, would not budge when the bishop of Vic attempted to remove it. A chapel was built to house it, and in 976 this was superseded by a Benedictine monastery, set about three-quarters of the way up the mountain at an altitude of nearly 1000m.

Miracles abounded and the Virgin of Montserrat soon became the chief cult image of Catalunya and a pilgrimage centre second in Spain only to Santiago de Compostela. Over 150 churches were dedicated to her in Italy alone, as were the first chapels of Mexico, Chile and Peru; even a Caribbean island bears her name. For centuries, the monastery enjoyed outrageous prosperity, having its own flag and a form of extraterritorial independence along the lines of the

Vatican City. Its fortunes declined only in the nineteenth century; in 1835 the monastery was suppressed for its Carlist sympathies – monks were allowed to return nine years later but by 1882 their numbers had fallen to nineteen. Later, when the Catalan language was suppressed by Franco, the monastery acted to preserve native literature and as a focus of clandestine nationalism. In recent decades Montserrat's popularity has again become established; today there are over 300 brothers and, in addition to the tourists, tens of thousands of newly married couples come here to seek *La Moreneta's* blessing on their union.

The monastery itself is of no particular architectural interest, save perhaps in its monstrous bulk. Only the Renaissance **Basilica** (dating largely from 1560–92) is open to the public. **La Moreneta**, blackened by the smoke of countless candles, stands above the high altar – reached from behind, by way of an entrance to the right of the basilica's main entrance. The best time to be here is at the chanting of Ave Maria, around 1pm, when Montserrat's world-famous **boys' choir** sings.

Near the entrance to the basilica, the **Museu de Montserrat** (Mon–Fri 10am–6pm, Sat, Sun & holidays 9.30am–6.30pm; €3) holds a varied collection of archeological objects brought back by travelling monks, together with painting and sculpture dating from the thirteenth century to the present, including works by Caravaggio, El Greco, Picasso, Dalí, Monet and Degas. Religious items are in surprisingly short supply, as most of the monastery's valuables were carried off by Napoleon's troops.

Walks on the mountain

After you've poked around the monastery grounds, it's the **walks** around the woods and mountainside of Montserrat which are the real attraction. Following the tracks to various caves and the thirteen different hermitages, you can contemplate what Goethe wrote in 1816: "Nowhere but in his own Montserrat will a man find happiness and peace."

Two separate **funiculars** run from points close to the cable-car station. One drops to the **Santa Cova** (Holy Grotto), a seventeenth-century chapel built where the icon is said to have originally been found (every 15–20min, daily 10am–1pm & 3.20–7.30pm; €5.25 return, joint ticket with Sant Joan funicular €6). The other rises to the hermitage of **Sant Joan** (every 15–20min, daily 10am–7.30pm; €2.10 return, joint ticket with Santa Cova funicular €6), from where it's another hour or so's walk to the **Sant Jeroni** hermitage, near the summit of the mountain at 1300m.

Eating

There is a great variety of **food** available in Barcelona and even low-budget travellers can do well for themselves, either by using the excellent markets and filling up on sandwiches and snacks, or eating cheap meals in bars and cafés. Good **restaurants** are easily found all over the city, though you'll probably do most of your eating where you do most of your sightseeing, in the old town, particularly around the **Ramblas** and in the **Barri Gòtic**. Venture into the **Barrio Chino** too, and you'll find some excellent restaurants, some surprisingly expensive, others little more than hole-in-the-wall cafés. In the **Eixample** prices tend to be higher, though you'll find plenty of lunchtime bargains around; **Gràcia**, further out, is a nice place to spend the evening, with plenty of good mid-range restaurants. For the food which Barcelona is really proud of – elaborate *sarsuelas* (fish stews), and all kinds of fish and seafood – you're best off in the **Barceloneta** district, down by the harbour, or in the **Port Olímpic**. Sitting down here for a huge plateful of prawns or mussels and a beer, you'll get away with around €9. A full seafood dinner will be considerably more expensive, even the paellas starting at around €8 a head.

Breakfast, snacks and sandwiches

You can get coffee and bread or croissants almost anywhere, but a few **café-bars** and specialist places – *granjas* and *orxaterias* especially – are worth looking out for. Snacks and sandwiches abound, too, and you'll be tempted by *ensaimadas* (pastry spirals), pizza slices and cakes at any bakery or pastry shop.

Antiga Casa Figueres, Ramblas 83 Ⓜ Liceu. Wonderful *modernista* pastry shop with a few tables outside. Open Mon–Sat 9am–3pm & 5–8.30pm.

Café Torino, Pg. de Gràcia 59 Ⓜ Passeig de Gràcia. Great *modernista*-style wood carved decor and excellent sandwiches. Open Mon–Thurs 8am–11pm, Fri & Sat 8am–1am.

Forn de Sant Jaume, Rambla de Catalunya 50 Ⓜ Passeig de Gràcia. A croissant and sweet specialist, either to take away or eat at the adjacent café. Open Mon–Sat 9am–9pm.

Granja La Pallaresa, c/Petritxol 11 Ⓜ Liceu. Bow-tied waiters glide around this specialist snack

and breakfast stop, dispensing superb *xurros*, pastries, *crema catalana*, croissants, milk shakes and whipped-cream hot chocolates. Open Mon–Sat 9am–1.30pm & 4–9pm, Sun 5–9pm.

Mesón del Café, c/Llibreteria 16 Ⓜ Jaume I. Tiny, off-beat bar where you'll probably have to stand to sample the pastries and the excellent coffee, including a cappuccino laden with fresh cream. Open Mon–Sat 7am–11pm.

Santa Clara, Plaça de Sant Jaume (corner of c/de la Llibreteria) Ⓜ Jaume I. Marvellous coffee and cakes, right on the square; especially busy on Sunday mornings. Open daily 8am–9.30pm.

Tapas bars

For a more substantial snack, you can't beat Barcelona's **tapas bars**. The best (and most famous) concentration in the Barri Gòtic is down by the port, between the Columbus monument and the post office – along c/Ample, c/de la Mercè, c/del Regomir and their offshoots. Jumping from bar to bar, with a bite to eat in each, is as good a way as any to fill up on some of the best food that the city has to offer. Done this way, your evening needn't cost more than a meal in a medium-priced restaurant – say €12–15 a head for enormous amounts to eat and drink.

Ramblas and the Old Town

Bar Mundial, Plaça de Sant Agustí el Vell 1. Simple 70-year-old neighbourhood bar, run by brothers Miguel and Pascual and famous for its seafood tapas and meals. The best option is soup followed by a seafood platter – all washed down with cold white wine. Open Mon & Wed–Sat 10am–11pm, Sun 10am–4pm; closed two weeks in Aug.

Euskal Etxea, Placeta Montcada 1–3 ☎ 933 102 185. A Basque restaurant specializing in *pintxos*, which are served around 12.30pm and 7.30pm. Fight for a place at the bar or join the crowds

spilling onto the street. Open Tues–Sat 9am–midnight, Sun 12.30pm–4.30pm.

Jai-Ca, c/Ginebra 13. Don't let the gruff interior fool you, this is one of the best tapas finds in Barceloneta. In summertime, take your tapas out onto the tiny street-corner patio. Open daily 10am–11pm.

El Xampanyet, c/de Montcada 22. Terrific, bustling, blue-tiled champagne bar with fine seafood tapas, *cava* by the glass or bottle, and local *sidra*. Open Tues–Sat noon–4pm & 6.30–11pm, Sun noon–4pm; closed Aug.

Eixample and Gràcia

El Berriketa, Gran Vía 596 Ⓜ Universitat. New Basque-run establishment with well-crafted and

reasonably priced tapas (€0.90–1.80). Open daily 9am–1am.

Bodega Sepúlveda, c/Sepúlveda 173bis Ⓜ Universitat. An anchovy specialist, which boasts more than a hundred different types of tapas and *torradas*. Open Mon–Sat 9.30am–1am.
La Bodegueta, Rambla Catalunya 98 Ⓜ Passeig de Gràcia. Long-established basement *bodega* with *cava* and a serious range of other wines by the glass or bottle, and cheese and cured meat to soak it all up. It gets very crowded – you may have to stand to snack. Open daily 7am–2am;

closed mornings in Aug.
Cervecería Catalana, c/Mallorca 236 ☎ 932 160 368 Ⓜ Passeig de Gràcia. Excellent tapas lined up along two bars, a good choice of beers and a small terraza. Open daily 7.30am–1am.
Lizarran, c/Mallorca 257 Ⓜ Passeig de Gràcia. The best of the franchised tapas bars, *Lizarran* serves less elaborate *pinxos* than the more upmarket places, but quality and price are good (usually €0.75 per tapa). Open daily 8.30am–1am.

Restaurants

The most common **restaurants** in Barcelona are those serving local **Catalan** food, though more mainstream Spanish dishes are generally available too. There are several speciality **regional Spanish and colonial Spanish** restaurants as well, which are nearly always worth investigating, while the fancier places tend towards a refined Catalan-French style of cooking that's as elegant as it's expensive. The range of **international cuisine** is not as wide as in other European cities, but if you've been in Spain for any length of time, you may be grateful that there's a choice at all – pizzas, Chinese and Indian/Pakistani food provide the main choices, though the cuisines of Mexico, North Africa, the Middle East and Japan are represented, too.

Restaurants are generally **open** approximately 1 to 4pm and 8 to 11pm. A lot of restaurants **close on Sundays, on public holidays and throughout August** – check the listings for specific details but expect changes since many places imaginatively interpret their own posted opening days and times. At the more expensive restaurants, it's recommended that you **reserve a table** in advance; either ring the number provided, or call in earlier in the day.

We have divided the restaurants into areas and listed the closest **metro** station for that part of the city at the start of the section; any exceptions are stated in individual accounts.

Ramblas and the Barri Gòtic

Ⓜ Liceu or Jaume I

Los Caracoles, c/Escudellers 14 ☎ 933 023 185. Reasonably priced, cavernous Barcelona landmark whose name means "snails", so it would be churlish not to have them, or the fine spit-roast chicken on display in the street outside. Around €21 a head if you include both as part of a big meal. Reserve ahead. Open daily 1pm–midnight. Moderate.
La Concha, c/Escudellers 40 ☎ 933 171 283. One of the best deals in the old town; plentiful and cheap Spanish cuisine – paella and *parallada* are house specialities. Open daily 1–5pm & 8pm–midnight; closed second week of Aug. Inexpensive to moderate.
La Dolce Herminía, c/Magdalenes 27 ☎ 933 170 676. Newly opened venue specializing in Catalan cuisine. The chic interior and impeccable service are contrasted by economical prices both on the *menú* and à la carte. Good place to try *fideuà*, a paella-type dish from Valencia made with noodles. Open daily 1–3.45pm & 8.30–11.30pm. Moderate.

El Egipte, La Rambla 79 ☎ 933 179 545. Market-fresh cooking in this opera singers' favourite right next to the Boqueria. The lunchtime *menú* has a huge range of choices and is good value (€7.20, going up to €12.60 at night). Moderate.
La Fonda, c/Escudellers 10. Modern, spacious, rattan-decorated restaurant on two floors that serves good-value Catalan dishes, including paella. Be prepared to queue, as this place is incredibly popular and they do not accept reservations. Open Tues–Sun 1–3.30pm & 8.30–11.30pm. Inexpensive.
Gallo Kirico, c/d'Avinyó 19. Pakistani-run joint with bargain rice and couscous combinations (around €3.60 a plate) served at the long bar or at tables in a dining room hacked out of the old Roman wall. Open noon–1.30am. Inexpensive.
El Gran Café, Baixada de Sant Miquel 1 ☎ 933 187 196. Catalan restaurant set in a great, old café. The high-ceilinged, wood-panelled dining room exudes European sophistication. Just off c/Avinyó, south of Ferran. Open 1–4.30pm & 8.30pm–12.30am. Moderate.

Restaurant prices in Barcelona

As a rough guide, you'll be able to get a three-course meal with drinks in Barcelona for:

Inexpensive under €12 a head
Moderate €12–24 a head
Expensive €24 and upwards.

But bear in mind that the lunchtime *menú del día* often allows you to eat for much less than the price category might lead you to expect; check the listings for details.

Juicy Jones, c/Cardenal Casañas 7. Bright restaurant/juice bar with a good-value *menú del día* and other dishes served all day. One of Barcelona's few true vegan options. Open Tues–Sun noon–midnight. Inexpensive.

Restaurant Pitarra, c/d'Avinyó 58 ☎933 011 647. A renowned Catalan cookery in operation since 1890, lined with paintings and serving good, reasonably priced local food from around €15 a head and a very good-value *menú del día*. Open Mon–Sat 1.15–4pm & 8.30pm–11pm. Moderate.

Taxidermista, Plaça Reial 8 ☎934 124 536. This late addition to the Barcelona scene offers inventive cuisine with French and Magribian touches in a modern sophisticated environment. Plans are afoot for live jazz sessions on Tues & Sun nights. Open Tues–Sun 10am–2.30am. Moderate.

Venus Delicatessen, c/Avinyó 25. A hip eatery which gets crowded after 10pm. At meal times there is a *menú* for €7; otherwise select from international Mediterranean sandwiches, salads and snacks. Good option for vegetarians. Inexpensive.

C/de Montcada and the Born

ⓜ Jaume I or Barceloneta

Bar-Restaurant Can-Busto, Pg. del Born 4. Basic dining room with a limited menu, quick service and budget-priced food. Open daily except Tues 12.30–4pm & 8–11.30pm. Inexpensive.

Llar del Filador, c/Cortines 13 ☎933 192 690. Tucked away in a dark lane in the Ribera, this renovated workshop is the place to enjoy meat, cheese and dessert fondues in a subdued and romantic atmosphere. Open evenings 7.30pm–1.30am and lunch by reservation. Moderate.

Lluna Plena, c/Montcada 2 ☎933 105 429. Traditional Catalan fare – particularly roasted meats with *alioli* – in a renovated old building. The very popular (reserve ahead) lunchtime *menú* is a deal at €6; otherwise a meal will run to around €15. Moderate.

La Poste, c/Gignás 23. One of the best deals

around for variety, quantity and price. The 4-course €5.75 *menú* is available daily for lunch and dinner. Open Mon–Fri noon–12.30am, Sat & Sun noon–4.30pm. Inexpensive.

Restaurante Carpanta, c/Sombrerers 13 ☎933 199 999. Intimate restaurant housed in a candlelit Gothic house around the back of Santa María del Mar; a great place to sample *arroz negre* (€9), though other meals will set you back €24 and up. Reserve a table in advance. Open Tues–Sat 1–5pm & 8.30pm–midnight, Sun 1–5pm. Expensive.

El Salón, c/L'Hostal d'en Sol 6–8. Renovated old building serving imaginative dishes and British-style desserts in a relaxed laid-back atmosphere with terribly slow service. You can stay late and drink at the bar, too. Open Mon–Sat 1pm–midnight, Sun 7pm–midnight. Inexpensive.

Barrio Chino/El Raval

ⓜ Liceu

Bar Ra, Plaça de la Garduña (behind the Boqueria market). Extremely hip restaurant/bar, very popular with the student set, serving up eclectic world cuisine on a sunny patio. Open daily 9am–2am. Inexpensive.

Restaurant España, c/de Sant Pau 9–11 ☎933 181 758. Eat in *modernista* splendour in the hotel of the same name designed by Domènech i Montaner, though the décor is more memorable than the food. However, the *menú del día* is good value at €7.20 (€9 at night). Open daily 1–4pm & 8.30pm–midnight. Moderate.

Restaurant Garduña, c/Morera 17–19. Tucked away at the back of La Boqueria market, off the Ramblas, this recommended restaurant (busiest at lunch, when there's a €6 *menú del día*) offers excellent paellas and good, fresh market produce. Around €15. Closed Sun. Moderate.

Restaurant Tallers, c/dels Tallers 6–8 ⓜ Catalunya. A good-value *menú del día* (you pay a bit more if you opt for the fine baked chicken). Open Tues–Sun 1–3pm and 8–10pm; closed Aug. Inexpensive.

Rita Blue, Plaça Sant Agusti el Nou s/n ☎934 123 438. New-generation gastro-bar specializing in Mediterranean-style cooking in a sleekly modern establishment. Occasional jam sessions and other events on the lower floor. Lunch *menú* €6.60. Open Mon–Fri 11am–2am, Sat & Sun 7pm–3am. Moderate.

Silenus, c/dels Àngels 8. A pleasant airy place near the MACBA frequented by young, arty types. The *menú del día* is good value at €7.20. Open 1–4pm & 9–11.30pm, closed Sun and Mon evening. Moderate.

Los Toreros, c/Xuclà 5 ⓣ 933 182 325. Just off of the Ramblas, a long-established bar/restaurant with kitschy bullfighting decor. Lunch *menú* at €5.70, dinner features all you can drink and all you can eat tapas for groups of 6 or more. Book ahead for dinner. Closed Mon & Aug. Inexpensive to moderate.

The harbour, Port Vell, Barceloneta and Port Olímpic

ⓜ **Barceloneta**

Can Ganassa, Plaça de Barceloneta 4–6. An extensive range of tapas, snacks and *torradas* on Barceloneta's central square, a cheap and filling €5.70 *menú del día* at lunchtime, and more expensive seafood if you want it. Open daily except Wed 12.30–11pm; closed Nov. Moderate.

Can Ramonet, c/Maquinista 17 ⓣ 933 193 064. Reputedly the oldest restaurant in the port area, this restaurant now has the added attraction of a terraza on a newly opened square in the heart of Barceloneta. Good seafood and *jamón* (*pernil* in Catalan) and charming service. Open daily noon–midnight. Moderate.

Can Ros, c/Almirall Aixada 7, off Pg. de Borbó ⓣ 932 214 579. Intimate, wood-panelled seafood restaurant with superb appetizers and a rich paella or *arroz negre*, both of which cost just €7.20. Open daily except Wed 1–5pm & 8pm–midnight. Moderate.

El Rey de la Gamba, Pg. de Borbó 46–48, 49 & 53 ⓣ 932 217 598. Much-promoted restaurant, whose various extensions now occupy half the street and whose outdoor tables are always busy. It's popular for its prawns and dried meats, but the food is overpriced. Open daily noon–midnight. Expensive.

TapasBar, Avgda. Littoral 12–14, Marina Village ⓣ 932 215 717 ⓜ Vila Olímpica. Slick new tapas bar and restaurant. Pick at an impressive range of traditional and inventive tapas, or enjoy a *fideuà*, washing down the food with throat-burning *anise*. Open Mon–Thurs 8pm–1am, Fri 8pm–3am, Sat 11am–3am & Sun 11am–1am. Moderate.

Eixample

Aire, c/Eric Granados 48 ⓣ 934 518 462 ⓜ Passeig de Gràcia. Gay-run restaurant serving imaginative French-Catalan dishes in roomy civilized surroundings. Open daily 1–4pm and 9.30pm–midnight. Moderate.

Al Diwan, València 204 ⓣ 933 234 651 ⓜ Universitat. Traditional Lebanese cuisine, with all of the usual *tabbouleh*, *hummus*, and *kofta* dishes. Things liven up in the evening with traditional belly-dancing (Thurs, Fri & Sat). Open daily 1–4pm & 8.30pm–midnight; closed Sat lunch & Sun. Moderate.

Bice, c/Consell de Cent 333 ⓣ 934 880 050 ⓜ Catalunya. This Barcelona branch office of the famous Milanese restaurant of the same name offers the best Italian cuisine in the city. Its two levels are sumptuously decorated with Tàpies originals and there is a summertime patio. Open daily 1–4pm & 8–11.30pm. Expensive.

Comme-Bio II, Gran Vía 603 (corner Rambla de Catalunya) ⓜ Catalunya. Vegetarian restaurant that doubles as a health-food store. There's another branch in Via Layetana. Open Mon–Sat 9am–midnight, Sun noon–midnight. Moderate.

Gargantua & Pantagruel, c/Aragó 215 ⓣ 934 532 020 ⓜ Passeig de Gràcia. Dining in Rabelaisian surroundings. Specializing in Catalan food, especially meats grilled on their open hearth and accompanied by *alioli*. Open Mon–Fri 1–4pm & 9pm–midnight, Sun 9pm–midnight. Expensive.

L'Hostal de Rita, c/Aragó 279 ⓜ Passeig de Gràcia. Good Catalan cooking at reasonable prices in a very attractive dining room. Always packed and you can't book in advance so be prepared to queue. Open daily 1–3.45pm & 8.30–11.30pm. Inexpensive.

Laie, c/Pau Claris 85 ⓜ Urquinaona. Restaurant, café, book emporium and jazz venue. Pleasant airy atmosphere with laid-back staff. *Menú* is €11.25; Cajun food and live jazz Tues nights (*menú* includes a whiskey sour). Open daily 9am–2am, with kitchen open till 1am. Moderate.

Petit Paris, c/Paris 196 ⓣ 932 182 678 ⓜ Diagonal. Sophisticated club-like atmosphere in this restaurant specializing in game fowl cooked *à la française*. Open daily 1–4pm & 8.45pm–midnight. Expensive.

Gràcia

Botafumeiro, Gran de Gràcia 81 ⓣ 932 184 230 ⓜ Fontana. Justly famous for both its food and sophisticated atmosphere, this is perhaps Barcelona's best *gallego marisceria* (seafood restaurant). Open daily 1pm–1am, closed part Aug. Expensive.

Cantina Mexicana II, c/Torrent de Flors 53 ⓣ 932 131 018 Ⓜ Joanic. Authentic Mexican cooking in this friendly *cantina*. If you can't decide what to order or want to try everything, your waiter will throw together a selection of various small portions. Closed Aug. Moderate.

Equinox, c/Torrent de l'Olla 143 Ⓜ Fontana and Equinox Sol, Plaça del Sol 14 and c/Verdi 21–23. By far the best falafels and *shawarma* in town, plus other delicious Lebanese dishes, and wicked baklava. Eat your fill for under €6. Open Mon–Thurs 6pm–2.30am, Fri–Sun 6pm–3.30am. Inexpensive.

El Galliner, c/Martínez de la Rosa 71 Ⓜ Diagonal. Intimate restaurant in an old house offering cod cooked in over forty different ways. Between €12 and €18 a head. Open 1.30–3.30pm & 8pm–1am; closed Tues & Sun nights. Moderate.

La Gavina, c/Ros de Olano 17 Ⓜ Fontana. This wacky pizzeria – known locally as "Els Ángels" due to the fact that the only sign is a series of *putti* pasted over the door – is a Gràcia secret. Possibly the best and cheapest pizzeria around. Arrive before 8pm or you will have a long wait (no reservations are accepted). Open Tues–Sun noon–1am. Inexpensive.

El Glop, c/Sant Lluís 24 Ⓜ Joanic. Authentic Catalan taverna, with enough *torradas* and salads to satisfy vegetarians, as well as grilled meats. Lively and popular; around €12 a head, less if you're careful. There are also branches at Rambla de Catalunya 65 and c/Casp 21. Open Tues–Sun 1–4pm & 7pm–1am. Moderate.

Illa de Gràcia, c/Sant Domènec 19 Ⓜ Fontana. Bright vegetarian restaurant serving decent salads, pasta, rice dishes, omelettes and crepes – all around €4.80. Open Tues–Fri 1–4pm & 9pm–midnight, Sat & Sun 2pm–midnight; closed mid-Aug to mid-Sept. Inexpensive.

El Nou Candanchu, Plaça Rius i Taulet 9 Ⓜ Fontana. Sit beneath the clock tower in summer and enjoy a sandwich, or choose from the wide selection of local dishes. Now managed by an affable bunch of young guys, the service has improved but the food is still cheap. Open daily 7am–3am, Fri & Sat until 3am; closed Tues. Inexpensive.

El Tastavins, c/Ramon y Cajals 12 Ⓜ Fontana. Under new management, the *Tastavins* offers food of exceptional quality and good prices, with warm service. Perhaps the best choice is the "Entrecôt Café de Paris" with a 38-ingredient sauce. Also open on Sunday afternoons for tapas and vermouth. Open Tues–Sat 1.30–3.30pm & 9pm–12.30am, Sun 1–4pm. Moderate.

Buying your own food: markets, super-markets, delis

If you want to buy fresh food, or make up your own snacks and meals, use the city's **markets**. There's less choice in the **supermarkets**, though they're worth trying for tinned products, as are the **delicatessens** and small central shops which specialize in tinned fish and meat, cheeses and cooked meats. The best-value food and provisions shops are those in the Barrio Chino, particularly down c/de Sant Pau.

Champion, Rambla 113. Department store with food department. Open Mon–Thurs 9am–8pm, Fri & Sat 9am–9pm.

El Corte Inglés, Plaça de Catalunya 14. The main-floor grocery section of this department store stocks lots of hard-to-find goodies from home. Pricey. Open Mon–Sat 10am–9.30pm.

Día, c/del Carme; c/Comtessa de Sobradiel; and many other locations. The cheapest supermarket chain in town, with the first branch just around the corner from the pricier Champion (see above).

La Fuente, c/de Ferran 20 Ⓜ Liceu. A *xarcuteria*, but better visited for its wide selection of tinned and preserved food, wines and cheeses. Open Mon–Fri 9am–1pm & 4–8pm, Sat 9am–1pm; closed Aug.

Mauri, Rambla de Catalunya 100 Ⓜ Passeig de Gràcia. Superb deli specializing in cakes and pastries, with an attached café. Open Mon–Sat 9am–9pm, Sun 9am–3pm.

Mercat Sant Josep/La Boqueria, Rambla Sant Josep 89 Ⓜ Liceu. The best place in the city for fresh fruit, vegetables, meat, fish and dried foods. Open Mon–Sat 8am–8pm.

Drinking and nightlife

There are lively **bars and cafés** throughout the centre – in the Barri Gòtic as well as the Eixample and Gràcia – catering for all types and styles. One of the city's great pleasures is to pull up a pavement seat outside a bar, sip a coffee or a beer, and watch the world go by. There's little difference between a bar and café (indeed, many places incorporate both words in their name), but some of the other names you'll see do actually mean something – a *bodega* specializes in wine; a *cervesería* in beer; and a *xampanyería* in champagne and *cava*. Alongside the regular bars and cafés, Barcelona also has a range of **designer bars** geared towards late-night drinking, and there's a disco and club **nightlife** that is one of Europe's most enjoyable.

For **listings** of bars and clubs, get the weekly *Guía del Ocio* from newsstands, or SexTienda's map of **gay** Barcelona with a list of bars, clubs, and contacts (see p.751 for SexTienda's address). It's worth noting, that – unlike restaurants – most bars and cafés stay open throughout August.

Bars and cafés

Generally, the bars in the **old town** are a mixture of traditional tourist haunts, local drinking places or trendy downbeat bars. The area around the Museu Picasso is currently one of the places to be at night – **Passeig del Born**, the square at the end of c/de Montcada behind Santa María del Mar, is the main focus, while the streets around c/d'Avinyó and c/Escudellers also have their share of the action. The **Port Olímpic** and the Maremàgnum complex have become more mainstream summer night-time playgrounds for locals and tourists alike. Barcelona is also known for its *bars modernos* or *bars musicals*: hi-tech, music-filled places concentrated mainly (though not exclusively) in the **Eixample** and the streets in the western part of **Gràcia** around c/Santaló and c/Marià Cubí. The "in" places change rapidly, with new ones opening up all the time; the decor is often astounding, the drinks always expensive. For more low-key, late drinking (though still pricey), the centre of Gràcia itself is the place, full of little squares bordered by busy café-terraces.

Ramblas and the Barri Gòtic

Ⓜ **Catalunya/Liceu/Jaime I**

Bar 13, c/Lleona 13. Unpretentious new alternative music bar, packing out with twenty-somethings at weekends and playing the hits of the 90s. Open Mon–Thurs 10pm–2am, Fri & Sat 10pm–3am.

El Bosc de les Fades, Rambla de Santa Mónica 6. Tucked away in an alley beside the entrance to the wax museum, this dark little bar, "The Forest of the Fairies", is sculpted with gnarled plaster tree trunks and populated by plastic gnomes. Frequent jazz and modern music shows. Open Sun–Thurs 10.30am–1am, Fri & Sat 10.30am–3am.

Café de l'Opera, Rambla Caputxins 74. Morning coffee, afternoon tea or late-night brandies in this fashionable, late-nineteenth-century bar which retains its original decor. Busy with tourists, locals and post-show opera fans. Open daily 9am–3am.

Cerería, Baixada de Sant Miquel 3–5, just off c/Avinyó. New hip café, filled with literary student types and pseudo-intellectual hipsters. Open daily 9am–10pm.

Glaciar, Plaça Reial 3. Traditional Barcelona meeting point and the first and best of the patios on the Plaça Reial. Packs out at weekends. Open Mon–Thurs 4pm–2am, Fri & Sat 4pm–3am, Sun 9am–2am.

La Palma, c/Palma de Sant Just 7. Comfortable, traditional *bodega*, with large wooden tables and antiques on display. The house red wine is deadly. Open Mon–Sat 8am–4pm & 7–10pm.

Parnasse, c/Gignás 21. Laid-back and friendly atmosphere in this hip bar, where you can listen to jazz over a single-malt whisky or the legendary absinthe, *à la française*. Open Tues–Sat 6pm–3am.

Els Quatre Gats, c/Montsió 3. *Modernista* haunt of Picasso and his contemporaries (see p.703), and still an interesting, arty place for a drink or meal. Open 10am–2am; closed Sun lunch.

Salero, c/del Rec 60. The name in English means salt cellar, which may explain the all-white decor of this stylish new bar which attracts a chic clientele. The kitchen runs from 1.30–4pm & 9pm–midnight (closed for Sat lunch). Open 2pm–2.30am; closed Sun night and Mon morning.

Schilling, c/Ferran 23. Fashionable café-bar packed all day with a mixture of locals and tourists; shout for your drink over the music and be prepared to wait for it. Open daily 10am–2.30pm.

Tarkus, c/ Avinyó 32. Grungy rock-and-roll bar in the heart of the old town, and a good jumping off point for after-hours clubs. Open Tues–Thurs 9pm–1am, Fri & Sat 9pm–3am.

Thiossan, c/Vidre 5. African reggae bar, popular at weekends. Come here for the music, the Senegalese food or to try imported African drinks like Ginger juice or Bissap. Open Tues–Thurs & Sun 8pm–2am, Fri & Sat 8pm–3am.

C/de Montcada and the Born
Ⓜ **Jaume I/Barceloneta**

Bar del Born, c/Rec 49. Downmarket hipness in this popular drinking hole, just off the main drag of the Born. Open Tues–Sat 7pm–3am.

Cocktel, Pg. del Born 18. Tiny bar with eclectic popular music and an exhaustive range of traditional cocktails and mixologist Andy's own inventions. Open Tues–Sun 6pm–3am.

Idea, Plaça Comercial 2 Ⓦ www.ideaborn.com. Trendy café/bookshop/cybercafé across from the old Mercat del Born. Have a drink or snack on comfortable couches while leafing through Spanish and foreign newspapers, or surf the net. Weekly classical music and opera recitals round out this incredibly eclectic establishment. Open Sun–Thurs 10am–midnight, Fri & Sat 10am–2am.

Palau Dalmasses, c/Montcada 8. Expensive and slightly snooty, the interior of this renovated palace looks like it may have served as a Peter Greenaway film set. Sip champagne or cognac, and on Thurs (8pm) and Sun (7pm) nights enjoy live Baroque and chamber music (€15, drink included). Open Tues–Sat 8pm–2am, Sun 6–10pm.

Pas del Born, c/Calders 8. A tiny and wacky haunt of musicians, artists and acrobats. Often hosts frenetic and interactive flamenco shows, as well as circus trapeze acts (check the listings on the bar's window). Open Wed–Sun 6pm–3am.

Suborn, c/Ribera 18. A tapas place by day and a restaurant/music bar by night. A nightly rotation of DJs spin just about everything except techno or house while you dine on imaginative Mediterranean cuisine, or just have a drink. Open

Mon–Thurs 10am–5pm & 7.30pm–2.30am, Fri 10am–2.30am, Sat noon–3am, Sun noon–2.30am.

Barrio Chino/El Raval
Ⓜ **Catalunya/Liceu/Universitat**

El Almirall, Joaquim Costa 33. Dating from 1860, Barcelona's oldest bar – a venerated leftist hangout – is a great place to chat or to kick off an evening of more intense bar-hopping. Open daily 7pm–3am.

Bar Fortuny, c/Pintor Fortuny 31. A good place for a quiet drink, attracting a mixture of people from the *barrio*, and popular with local lesbians. Food available at lunchtime. Open Tues–Sun 10am–12.30pm.

Bar Pastis, c/Santa Mònica 4 (just behind Centre d'Art Santa Mònica). Tiny, dark French bar, right in the red-light district, awash with artistic and theatrical memorabilia, and soothed by wheezy French music. Open 7.30pm–2.30am, Fri & Sat until 3.30am; closed Tues.

Café Galería Nou 3, c/Doctor Dou, 12. Eccentric atmosphere in this gay-run establishment which attracts a very mixed crowd. Sunday night's (8pm) show is full of surprises. Daily 7pm–1am.

El Café Que Pone "Muebles Navarro", c/Riera Alta 4–6. Big, airy café-bar in a converted furniture store (hence the name) which is a friendly comfortable place to have a drink or a snack. Open Mon–Sat 11am–midnight, Sun 5pm–midnight.

London Bar, c/Nou de la Rambla 34. Opened in 1910, this well-known *modernista* bar today attracts a mostly tourist clientele, puts on live jazz and hosts fortune-telling sessions. Open Wed–Sun 5pm–4am.

Marsella, c/de Sant Pau 65. Late-nineteenth-century bar now frequented by a spirited mix of local characters and young trendies. Occasional live music and performances. Open Mon–Thur & Sun 9am–2.30am, Fri & Sat 6pm–3.30am.

The harbour, Port Vell and Port Olímpic
Ⓜ **Drassanes/Barceloneta**

Café Café, Moll de Mestral 30, Port Olímpic. One of the neighbourhood's more relaxed and better-decorated bars, serving lots more besides coffee. Open daily noon–3am, 5am at weekends.

Distrito Marítimo, Moll de la Fusta 1. Large terraza overlooking the harbour, playing techno and house to a trendy pre-club gay crowd. Open Fri & Sat 11pm–3am.

Insólit, Local 111, Maremàgnum/Port Vell. A multi-space venue which doubles as restaurant and internet café during the week, only to turn into a big dance floor after 1am at weekends, where a mixed crowd dance to 60s' and 70s' sounds or enter cyberspace on the computers upstairs. Open daily 1pm–midnight (until 5am at weekends).

Jugolandia, Moll de Mestral 6, Port Olímpic. Huge range of tropical fruit juices, some laced with alcohol, served on a terrace overlooking the marina. Open daily 3pm–3am.

Octopussy, Moll de la Fusta 4. Hip, happening club with a big terraza overlooking the port with guest DJs playing soul, dub, drum and bass, with live music as well. Packed at weekends in the summer. Open Thurs, Fri and Sat midnight–3am.

Eixample

L'Arquer, Gran Vía 454 Ⓜ Universitat. Bar with good tapas and – believe it or not – an archery range where you can have a go under the careful supervision of someone more sober than you. Open daily 6pm–2.30am, weekends till 3.30am.

Café Dietrich, c/Consell de Cent 255 (between c/Muntaner and c/Aribau). This popular gay hang-out serves food until midnight and becomes a disco with drag shows after that. Open daily 6pm–3am.

Dry Martini, c/Aribau 166 Ⓜ Hospital Clínic. Legendary Barcelona cocktail bar, with a rich dark wood and brass interior. Business types dominate in the early evening, while a younger set moves in on weekend nights. Open daily 6.30pm–2.30am, Fri & Sat to 3am.

El Velòdrom, c/Muntaner 213 Ⓜ Diagonal. Old-style bar and pool hall, with an Art Deco interior dating to before the Civil War. A great spot to relax and kick back. Open Mon–Sat 6pm–1.30am; closed Aug.

Velvet, c/Balmes 161 Ⓜ Diagonal. The creation of designer Alfredo Arribas, this was inspired by the velveteen excesses of film-maker David Lynch. Slightly cosier and smoother than others, with an older clientele which appreciates the mainly 60s' and 70s' sounds. Open daily until 5am.

Gràcia

Bahia, c/Séneca 12 Ⓜ Diagonal. Relaxed and attractive bar with gay, lesbian and straight pun-

ters. Open daily 7pm–2.30am.

Café del Sol, Plaça del Sol 16 Ⓜ Fontana. Popular, split-level neighbourhood bar attracting the local cool types. Seats outside in the square make this pleasant at any time of the day or night. Open daily except Mon 1pm–3am.

El Canigó, Plaça de la Liberació 10 Ⓜ Fontana. Family-run neighbourhood bar now entering its third generation. Weekend evenings it packs out with a young, hip and largely local crowd. Open Tues–Sun 11am–midnight.

El Galpon Sur, c/Guilleries 16 Ⓜ Fontana. A refuge for homesick Andalucians, the *Galpon* is popular both for drinks and for southern Spanish food. There are also monthly art exhibitions on its walls. Better to come during the week when things are quieter. Open Tues–Sun 4pm–1am.

Mi Bar, c/Guilleries 6 Ⓜ Fontana. Tiny neighbourhood bar for Gràcia's alternative music set. Bartender/DJ Felipe spins a mix of everything from punk to flamenco. Open Tues–Sat 11pm–3am.

Roma, c/Alfons XII 4 FGC Plaça Molina. Spacious relaxed gay bar with friendly staff, which gets full around midnight with a pre-club crowd. Open daily 8pm–3am.

Universal, c/Marià Cubí 184 FGC Plaça Molina. A classic designer bar that's been at the cutting edge of Barcelona style since 1985 and there are still queues to get in. Be warned, they operate a strict door policy here and if your face doesn't fit you won't get in. Open 11pm–4.30am.

Virreina, Plaça de la Virreina 1. Popular bar with seats outside in one of Gràcia's loveliest squares. A great place to enjoy hard-to-find Trappist beers from Belgium. Open daily except Wed noon–2am.

Zig Zag, c/de Plató 13 FGC Muntaner. This long-established place (open since 1980) was designed by Alicia Nuñez and Guillem Bonet (creators of *Otto Zutz*; see "Discos and Clubs" below). It has all the minimalist designer accoutrements – chrome and video – but better, quieter music than usual, and a young, rich clientele. Open daily 10pm–3am.

Discos and clubs

Quite why Barcelona is one of Europe's hippest nightspots is something of a mystery to everyone except the Catalans, who knew all along. There aren't, in fact, too many places which are *that* good – but gripped by Friday and Saturday night fever it's eminently possible to suspend disbelief.

Be warned that clubbing in Barcelona is extremely expensive and that in the most exclusive places a beer is going to cost you roughly ten times what it costs in the bar next door. If there is free entry, don't be surprised to find that there's a minimum drinks charge of anything between €3 and €6 – if you're given a card as you go in and it's punched at the bar, be prepared to pay a minimum charge. Also note that the distinction between a music-bar and a disco is between a closing time of 2 or 3am and 5am – with a corresponding price rise. Barcelona stays open **very late** at the weekends, if you can take it; some of the places listed below feature a second session of action some time between 5am and 9am.

Arena, c/Balmes 32. Popular club catering to a mainly gay male crowd with a black room. Entry €3.60 (drink included). Open daily midnight–5am.

Bikini, c/Deu i Mata 105, off Avgda. Diagonal, behind the shopping centre L'Illa Ⓜ Maria Cristina. This traditional landmark of Barcelona nightlife offers regular live music and a popular disco, specializing in salsa and tangos on Sundays. Open Tues–Sun 11pm–5am.

Carpe Diem, Avgda. Dr Gregorio Marañón 17 Ⓜ Palau Reial. Near the university campus and Camp Nou stadium, *Carpe Diem* is a huge tent containing various bars, restaurants and dance floors. Open all year, but best and most packed in summer. Open daily 6pm–5am.

Firestiu, Plaça Univers y Palau 4 de la Fira Ⓜ Espanya. Multispace entertainment in a series of tents and awnings in the exhibition centre zone. Inside are dozens of bars set up by well-known city venues, as well as dance floors, fairground rides, minigolf and even bungee-jumping. Open June–Aug Thurs–Sat 10pm–5am.

Jamboree, Plaça Reial 17 Ⓜ Liceu. Live music every night followed by a disco with great jazz, funk and dance, attracting a very mixed crowd. Open daily 9pm–5am.

Metro, c/Sepúlveda 158 Ⓜ Universitat. A gay institution in Barcelona, extremely crowded at weekends. €6 cover. Open daily midnight–5am.

Moog, Arc del Teatre 3. Lively disco playing techno and house to a young trendy crowd. Open daily 11pm–5am.

The Music Box, c/ Beethoven 15 and c/Diagonal 618 Ⓜ Hospital Clinic. Lavish two-room disco specializing in 60s and 70s sounds. No cover charge.

Wed–Mon 11pm–5am.

Otto Zutz, c/de Lincoln 15. Still one of the most fashionable places in the city, a three-storey warehouse converted by architects Núñez and Bonet into a nocturnal shop window for everything that's for sale or hire in Barcelona. With the right clothes and face you're in (you may or may not have to pay – around €12 – depending on how impressive you are, the day of the week, etc); the serious dancing is 2–5.30am. Open Tues–Sat midnight–5.30am.

Paradís, c/Paradís 4. Underground club playing reggae, African and Latin sounds in the heart of the Barri Gòtic. Open daily till late.

Sotto Voce, Bori i Fontestà 25, Sarrià. The hot place for the young, swish 18 to 25-year-old set. Featuring chart-toppers of the 70s, 80s and 90s. Open Mon–Sat 11pm–3am.

La Terrazza, Avgda. Marquès de Comillas s/n (behind Poble Espanyol). Non-stop techno, and the place to be in summer, though don't get there until at least 4am. Open midnight–7am weekends.

Torres de Ávila, Avgda. Marqués de Comillas, Poble Espanyol, Montjuïc. The creation of Mariscal and Arribas, located inside the mock twelfth-century gateway in the "Spanish Village" built for the 1929 fair. It's a stunning fantasy, with a fabulous panoramic terrace. Beware that the dress code is strict (no sports shoes) and drinks are very expensive. Open Thurs–Sat 10pm–5am.

Wateke, Gran Via 390, Eixample. Barcelona meets Havana in this Cuban-oriented club. Heavy on the salsa, with live performance and other special events. Open Mon–Sat 8pm–3am, Sun 5pm–1am.

Music, the arts and festivals

Quite apart from the city's countless bars, restaurants and clubs, there's a full **cultural life** worth sampling. Barcelona hosts a wide range of **live music** events throughout the year and **film** and **theatre** are also well represented, as you'd expect in a city this size. Even if you don't speak Catalan or Spanish there's no need to miss out, since several cinemas show films in their original language, while Barcelona also boasts a series of old-time music hall/**cabaret** venues putting on largely visual shows, appealing in any language. Catalan performers have always steered away from the classics and gone for the innovative, and so the city also boasts a long tradition of **street and performance art**. Finally, if you're lucky (or you've planned ahead), you'll coincide with one of the city's excellent **festivals** and open-air events, in which case you'll be able to immerse yourself in what Barcelona does best: enjoying itself.

The most important ticket office is the **Centre d'Informació** in the Palau de la Virreina, Rambla Sant Josep 99 (☎933 017 775; mid-June to mid-Sept Mon–Sat 10am–7pm; mid-Sept to mid-June Mon–Fri 10am–2pm & 4–8pm, Sat 10am–2pm; Ⓜ Liceu), which dispenses programmes, advance information and tickets for all the *ajuntament*-sponsored productions, performances and exhibitions, including the *Grec* season events. The booth on the corner of c/Aribau and the Gran Vía, close to Plaça Universitat (Mon–Sat 10.30am–1.30pm & 4–7.30pm) sells **tickets** for major rock and pop concerts and for most theatre productions; record shops also carry concert tickets; or go straight to the relevant box office at the venue. With a credit card you can use the ServiCaixa automatic dispensing machines in many branches of La Caixa to obtain tickets for many events. Theatre and some concert tickets can be bought through Tel-Entrada (☎902 101 212, Ⓦ www.telendtrada.com).

For **listings** of almost anything you could want in the way of culture and entertainment, buy a copy of the weekly *Guía del Ocio* from any newspaper stand. This has full details of film, theatre and musical events (free and otherwise), as well as extensive sections on bars, restaurants and nightlife. It's in Spanish but easy enough to decipher. There are similar listings in *El País*, and there's also a free monthly guide published by the *ajuntament*, available from tourist offices. For listings in English look for *Barcelona Metropolitan*, available free in hotels and bars.

Live music

Many major **bands** now include Barcelona on their tours at a variety of venues, including the huge Palau d'Esports, the Veldromo and larger nightclubs like *Zeleste* and *Bikini*. Tickets for these are every bit as pricey as they are elsewhere in the world. However, lots of the city's smaller clubs and discos regularly feature bands, too; the more reliable places are listed below, and entrance to these is usually reasonably priced and often includes a complimentary drink. Look out also for the free or cheap **experimental music** concerts sponsored year-round by the Gràcia collective, Gràcia Territori Bonor (Ⓦ www.gracia-territori.com), which often feature international guests.

Most of Barcelona's **classical music** concerts take place in Domènech i Montaner's Palau de la Música Catalana, a splendid *modernista* creation (for more on which see p.701) or at the newly opened 2000-seat L'Auditori at c/Lepant 150. **Opera** has returned to its traditional home, the Gran Teatre del Liceu on the Ramblas, which burned down in 1994 and reopened five years later (see p.694 for more), and performances are also held at the Teatre Victòria, Avgda. del Paral·lel 67 (☎934 432 929).

For details of Barcelona's live music **festivals**, see p.736.

Rock, pop, folk and jazz

Barcelona Pipa Club, Plaça Reial 3 ☎933 024 732; Ⓜ Liceu. Small club with jazz most nights; admission around €3–4.

Centre Artesà Tradicionàrius, Trav. de Sant Antoni 6–8, Gràcia ☎932 184 485; Ⓜ Fontana Folk. recitals by local performers on Thurs and Fri around 10pm. Watch out for the festival organized here in the spring.

La Cova del Drac, c/Vallmajor 33, Gràcia ☎932 007 032 FGC Muntaner. One of Barcelona's best

jazz clubs serves up live music Tues–Sat 11pm–5am. Cover charge €9–18 depending on the act. Closed Aug.

Garatge Club, c/Pallars 195, Poble Nou ☎933 091 438; Ⓜ Poble Nou. Local rock and pop bands, never on much before midnight. Open Thurs–Sun only.

Harlem Jazz Club, c/Comtessa de Sobradiel 8 ☎933 100 755; Ⓜ Jaume I. Small, central venue for mixed jazz styles; live music most nights from around 9–10pm. Usually no cover charge, and reasonably priced drinks. Closed Aug.

El Heliogàbel, c/Ramon i Cajals 80; Ⓜ Joanic or Fontana. After-hours club for Gràcia's hardcore bohemia, with frequent experimental music concerts and poetry readings. Open Wed–Sat 10pm–late.

Luz de Gas, c/Muntaner 246, Eixample ☎ 932 097 711; Ⓜ Diagonal. Smart venue popular with a slightly older suit-and-tie crowd; live music every night around midnight.

Magic, Pg. Picasso 40, Born ☎ 933 107 267; Ⓜ Barceloneta. Live rock music and DJs. Open Tues–Sun 11pm–5am.

Sidecar, c/Heures 4–6, Barri Gòtic ☎ 933 021 586; Ⓜ Liceu. Hip bar – pronounced "See-day-car" – with a pool table, downstairs concert space and nightly DJs. On Tuesday nights from 11pm (Oct–June only) the bar hosts **G's Club** – alternative music and performance art from Barcelona and abroad (€4.80; drink included). Open daily 10pm–3am.

Zeleste, c/Almogàvers 122 ☎ 933 091 204; Ⓜ Llacuna. Foreign rock and pop bands play regularly at the warehouse-style club.

Classical music and opera

Auditori Winterthur, L'Illa, Avgda. Diagonal 547 ☎ 932 184 800. Privately owned concert hall in the Illa shopping centre.

Centre Cultural de la Fundació La Caixa, Pg. Sant Joan 108 ☎ 934 588 905; Ⓜ Verdaguer. Regular concerts and recitals.

L'Espai, Trav. de Gràcia 63, Gràcia ☎ 934 143 133; Ⓜ Diagonal. Performances by a variety of soloists and groups especially good for dance.

Fundació Joan Miró, Parc de Montjuïc s/n ☎ 934 439 470 (see also p.710). Regular contemporary music concerts especially during the summer when the venue puts on its *Nits de Música* sessions, usually on Thursdays.

Palau de la Música Catalana, c/Sant Francesc de Paula 2, off c/Sant Pere Més Alt ☎ 932 681 000; Ⓜ Urquinaona. Home of the Orfeó Català choral group, and venue for concerts by the Orquestra Ciutat de Barcelona among others. Concert season runs Oct–June. Box office open Mon–Fri 10am–9pm, Sat 3–9pm.

Sala Cultural Caja de Madrid, Plaça de Catalunya 9 ☎ 933 014 494. Regular, free concerts and recitals.

Saló del Tinell, Plaça del Rei ☎ 933 151 111; Ⓜ Jaume I. Choral music in the Gothic hall of the Palau Reial; usually free entry.

Teatre Grec, Pg. Santa Madrona s/n, Montjuïc ☎ 933 017 775; Ⓜ Espanya. Impressive open-air summer venue for concerts and recitals. The amphitheatre is used extensively during the summer *Grec* season.

Theatre and cabaret

Barcelona has nothing like the **theatrical life** of Madrid, but it does have some worthy venues and happenings. Ninety-nine percent of the regular theatre productions, however, are in Catalan and you'll rarely see a Spanish classic. The centre for commercial theatre is on Avinguda. Paral·lel and the streets immediately around. Some theatres draw on the city's strong **cabaret** tradition – more music-hall entertainment than stand-up comedy, and thus a little more accessible to non-Catalan/Spanish speakers.

Tickets for most theatres are available from the kiosk on the corner of c/Aribau and the Gran Vía, and from the Centro de Localidades at Rambla Catalunya 2. For advance tickets for the Mercat de les Flors productions, you have to go to the Palau de la Virreina (Ramblas 99). Theatre tickets can also be bought through Tel-Entrada (☎ 902 101 212, ✆ www.telentrada.com).

Café Concert Llantiol, c/Riereta 7 ☎ 933 299 009; Ⓜ Parallel. Daily cabaret featuring curious bits of mime, song, clowns, magic and dance. Shows normally begin at 10pm.

El Cangrejo, c/Montserrat 9; Ⓜ Drassanes. Friday and Saturday nights at 11.30pm this infamous club hosts outrageous transvestite cabarets – come early to get a seat. Free.

Conservas, c/Sant Pau 58 ☎ 933 020 630; Ⓜ Liceu. True underground venue for occasional

fringe theatre, experimental music and poetry readings.

Mercat de les Flors, c/de Lleida 59 ☎ 934 251 875; Ⓜ Poble Sec. A nineteenth-century building worth visiting for the architecture alone. Hosts visiting fringe theatre and dance companies.

Teatre Lliure, c/Montseny 47, Gràcia ☎ 932 189 251; Ⓜ Fontana. The "Free Theatre" is the home of a progressive Catalan company, due for an eventual move to a new home in the Ciutat del

Teatre on Montjuïc. Also hosts visiting dance companies, concerts and recitals.

Teatre Malic, c/Fusina 3 ⓣ 933 107 035; Ⓜ Jaume I. Tiny theatre with offbeat productions and the occasional concert or performance artist.

Teatre Nacional de Catalunya, Plaça de les Arts 1 ⓣ 933 065 700, tickets by credit card ⓣ 903 332 211. Designed by Ricardo Bofill, and intended to foster Catalan works, this new theatre built as a modern emulation of an ancient Greek temple features native and European companies.

Teatre Romea, c/Hospital 51 ⓣ 933 017 189. Built in 1863, the theatre was forced to use Castilian under Franco, but has now come back as the Centre Dramàtic de la Generalitat de Catalunya with an emphasis on Catalan-language productions.

Film

All the latest international films reach Barcelona fairly quickly (though they're usually shown dubbed into Spanish) – central **main screens** include those at Rambla de Canaletes 138, Rambla Catalunya 140, Plaça de Catalunya 3, Pg. de Gràcia 13 and Maremàgnum at Port Vell. More accessibly, the cinemas listed below show mostly **original-language** ("V.O.") foreign films. Tickets cost €3.90–4.80, and most cinemas have one night (usually Mon or Wed) – *el día del espectador* – when entry is **discounted**, usually to around €3.60.

Cines Icaria-Yelmo, c/de Salvador Espriu 61, Vila Olímpica ⓣ 932 217 585; Ⓜ Ciutadella. No fewer than fifteen screens showing "V.O." movies; late-night screenings on Fri and Sat; discount night Mon.

Filmoteca, Avgda. de Sarrià 33, Eixample ⓣ 934 107 590; Ⓜ Hospital Clínic. Run by the Generalitat, the Filmoteca has an excellent programme, showing three or four different films (often foreign, and usually in "V.O.") every night; €2.40 per film, or buy a pass for €15 allowing entry to 10 films.

Maldá, c/de Pi 5 ⓣ 933 178 529; Ⓜ Liceu.

Repertory cinema featuring two different shows per day (usually English "V.O.") on a weekly rotation. Late-night sessions on Fri & Sat, matinees Sat & Sun; reduced price Wed.

Renoir-Les Corts, c/ugeni d'Ors 12 ⓣ 934 905 510; Ⓜ Les Corts. Six screens showing good "V.O" films. Late-night sessions on Fri & Sat; discount night Mon.

Verdi, c/Verdi 32, Gràcia ⓣ 932 370 516; Ⓜ Fontana. Nine screens showing quality "V.O." movies. Late-night films on Fri & Sat; discount night Mon.

Festivals, open-air events and the sardana

Best of the annual arts events is the Generalitat's summer *Grec* season, when theatre, music and dance can be seen at various venues around the city, including the Teatre Grec at Montjuïc. But there are plenty of other times when Barcelona lets its hair down. Catalunya's national **folk dance**, the *sardana*, can be seen for free at several places in the city: in front of the cathedral (Sat 6.30pm and Sun noon) and Plaça Sant Jaume (Sun 6pm). Mocked in the rest of Spain, the Catalans claim theirs is a very democratic dance. Participants (there's no limit on numbers) all hold hands in a circle, each puts something in the middle as a sign of community and sharing, and since it is not overly energetic (hence the jibes) old and young can join in equally.

A more dramatic custom, occasionally performed at *festes*, is the **castell**, in which huge neighbourhood teams compete making human towers up to ten persons high. The **correfoc**, an incredibly frenetic and interactive parade of fireworks and drumming, is a feature of most of the *festes* listed below. Cultural events such as these are listed in the pink section of Friday's *La Vanguardia* newspaper (in Spanish).

January The *Cabalgata de los Reyes Magos*, on the afternoon of January 5, is when the Three Kings (who distribute Christmas gifts to Spanish children) ride into town.

March Barcelona's *Festes de Carnaval* are not as famous as those of nearby Sitges, but there are colourful parades and nearly everyone dresses up in costume.

April *Sant Jordi* and the International Day of the Book both fall on April 23 (coinciding with Cervantes' and Shakespeare's birthday). The city fills with roses and books and sweethearts exchange them as gifts.

May In the first two weeks of the month the *Festival de Música Antiga* brings medieval and baroque groups from around the world. Paying concerts are held in larger venues, but free shows can be seen outdoors in the *plaças* of the Casc Antic. Also in May, the *Marató de l'Espectacle* (Entertainment Marathon) takes place at the Mercat de les Flors theatre, a nonstop, two days' worth of local theatre, dance, cabaret, music and children's shows. Late in May and early June, *La Fira del Llibre*, a massive outdoor book fair, clogs the Passeig de Gràcia.

June The *Grec* season starts in the last week (and runs throughout July and into August), a summer festival incorporating a wide variety of events, some of which are free. Information and booking is at the Palau de la Virreina. There's also a *Festival de Jazz Ciutat Vella* and a European jazz festival, as well as *Sónar* (Ⓦ www.sonar.es) a cutting-edge electronic music festival. The *Verbena de Sant Joan* celebrations on the 23rd involve bonfires, fireworks, dancing and music throughout the city. The *Caixa Flamenco Festival* takes place in the same month; while the *Barcelona Film Festival* starts at the end of the month and continues throughout July.

August The *Festa Major* in mid-August is in Gràcia; bands and events in the streets and squares.

September *Festa de la Mercè* is the city's biggest festival. The parades, free concerts of international stature, fireworks and general mayhem last from the 22nd to the 25th.

October/November The *Festival de Jazz* highlights visiting bands in the clubs, and hosts street concerts and events.

Shopping and markets

While not on a par with Paris or the world's other style capitals, Barcelona is head and shoulders above the rest of Spain when it comes to **shopping**. It's the country's fashion and publishing capital, and there's a long tradition of innovative design which is perhaps expressed best in the city's fabulous architecture but which is also revealed in a series of shops and malls selling the very latest in designer clothes and household accoutrements. Shop **opening hours** are typically Monday–Friday 10am–1.30/2pm and 4.30–7.30/8pm, Saturday 10am–1.30/2pm, although various markets, department stores and shopping centres open right through lunch.

As well as the places picked out below, visit one of the city's **department stores and shopping arcades**: Bulevard Rosa, at Pg. de Gràcia 55 and Avgda. Diagonal 609–615, Barcelona's first shopping mall, both arcades featuring around 100 shops; El Corte Inglés, Plaça de Catalunya 14, and Avgda. Diagonal 617, the city's biggest department store; the FNAC Triangle, also on Plaça de Catalunya; and Centre Comercial Barcelona Glòries, Plaça de les Glòries 1 (ⓂGlòries), a shopping, restaurant and cinema complex. El Mercadillo, c/Portaferrissa 17 (ⓂLiceu), is a small complex of clothes and shoe shops, together with a restaurant and nice patio garden.

Antiques, arts and crafts

There are lots of antiques stores in the old town; perhaps the best area for browsing is around c/de Palla, between the cathedral and the Plaça del Pí.

Art Escudellers, c/Escudellers 23–25 Ⓜ Liceu. An enormous shop selling ceramics from different regions of Spain. Not cheap – better deals can be had outside Barcelona – but a good selection. Open daily 11am–11pm.

La Caixa de Fang, c/Freneria 1 Ⓜ Jaume I. Off Baixada de la Llibretaria, behind the cathedral, this has very good-value ceramics and recycled glass.
Cereria Subirà, Baixada Llibertaria 7. Barcelona's oldest shop (since 1760), selling handcrafted candles.

La **Cubana**, c/de la Boqueria 26 Ⓜ Liceu. Old shop selling fans and mantillas.
La Manual Alpargatera, c/Avinyó 7 Ⓜ Liceu. Workshop making and selling *alpargatas* (espadrilles) to order, as well as other straw and rope work.
Populart, c/de Montcada 22 Ⓜ Jaume I. Delightful shop filled with antiques and crafts.
1748, Plaça de Montcada 2 Ⓜ Jaume I. Good ceramic shop with one of the widest selections.

Books

You'll find English-language books, newspapers and magazines at the stalls along the Ramblas, and a good selection of English-language books (novels and general unless otherwise stated) at the following shops:

The Book Store, c/la Granja 13, Gràcia Ⓜ Fontana. Secondhand English-language books. Closed Aug.
Casa del Llibre, Pg. de Gràcia 62, Eixample Ⓜ Passeig de Gràcia. Barcelona's newest book emporium, strong on literature and humanities with lots of English titles.
Crisol, Rambla de Catalunya 81, Eixample Ⓜ Passeig de Gràcia. Magazines, books and music – open until 1am.
Happy Books, c/Pelai 32 and Pg. de Gràcia 77, Eixample Ⓜ Universitat or Catalunya, Passeig de Gràcia. Good travel and dictionary sections as well as some other English-language titles. Generally the best prices and some very good sales.
Laie, Pau Claris 85. Bookstore with excellent selection of humanities and literature and lots of English-language titles. Café/restaurant and jazz venue upstairs (see p.728).
Llibreria Mallorca, Rambla de Catalunya 86, Eixample Ⓜ Passeig de Gràcia. Big selection of British and American newspapers and magazines.
Llibreria Pròleg, c/Dagueria 13, just off c/Jaume I. A women's/feminist bookshop, though with most works in Spanish/Catalan. Closed Aug.
Llibreria Quera, c/Petritxol 2 Ⓜ Liceu. Maps and trekking guides in a cramped little Barri Gòtic store. Closed Sat in Aug.

Clothes, shoes and accessories

Adolfo Domínguez, Pg. de Gràcia 89 Ⓜ Passeig de Gràcia. Men's and women's designs from the well-known *gallego* designer.
Camper, c/Muntaner 248; c/València 249; Avgda. Pau Casals 5; Bd. Rosa Pedralbes. These are the four branches of Spain's most stylish value-for-money shoe-shop chain.
Contribucions, c/Riera de Sant Miquel 30 Ⓜ Diagonal. Discount outlet for designer fashion.
Groc, Rambla Catalunya 100; c/Muntaner 385 Ⓜ Passeig de Gràcia. The shops of one of Barcelona's most innovative designers, Antoni Miró; the first is for men, the second for women.
Jean Pierre Bua, Avgda. Diagonal 469 Ⓜ Diagonal. The city's temple for fashion victims: a postmodern shrine for Yamamoto, Gaultier, Miyake, Westwood, Miró and other international stars.
Joaquín Berao, c/Rosselló 277, Eixample Ⓜ Diagonal. Avant-garde jewellery in a stunningly designed shop.
Lailo, c/Riera Baixa 20 Ⓜ Liceu. Off the west side of the Ramblas, this secondhand clothes shop is usually worth a look.
Obach Sombrería, c/del Call 2 Ⓜ Liceu. An excellent selection of hats of all types.
Pedro Morago, Avgda. Diagonal 520 Ⓜ Diagonal. Morago is a classic Barcelona designer, producing everything from suits to sports shirts for men and women.
Preu Bo, c/Comtal 22 Ⓜ Plaça de Catalunya. A bargain-hunter's dream. Top-name *haute couture* and substantial discounts.

Design and decorative art

BD Ediciones de Diseño, c/Mallorca 291, Eixample Ⓜ Diagonal. The building is by Domènech i Montaner, the interior filled with the very latest in furniture and household design.
D. Barcelona, Avgda. Diagonal 367, Eixample Ⓜ Diagonal. Up the road from Dos i Una, and with a similar but much bigger selection.
Dom, Pg. de Gràcia 76, Eixample Ⓜ Passeig de Gràcia. Original, amusing household and personal items at accessible prices.
Dos i Una, c/Rosselló 275, Eixample Ⓜ Diagonal. Contemporary, imaginative household and personal items.
Vinçon, Pg. de Gràcia 96, Eixample Ⓜ Passeig de Gràcia. This palace of design houses stylish and original items, pioneered since the 1960s by Fernando Amat, and with logo and carrier bags by the ubiquitous Mariscal. Temporary art and design exhibitions are held here, too.

△ Antigua Casa Figueres, Las Ramblas

Markets

Barcelona's **daily food markets**, all in covered halls, are open Monday–Saturday 8am–3pm and 5–8pm, though the most famous, La Boqueria on the Ramblas, opens right through the day (although it is at its best before 1.30pm). Other **specialist markets** are open only on certain days. Good ones to try include:

Antiques: every Thurs (Sept–June only) in Plaça del Pi (Ⓜ Liceu) and Plaça Nova (Ⓜ Jaume I) from 9am.

Christmas items: The *Fira de Nadal* or *de Santa Llúcia* which chokes alleys around the cathedral is held Dec 13–24.

Coins, books and postcards: every Sun outside Mercat Sant Antoni 10am–2pm.

Crafts: first Sun of the month at Avgda. Pau Casals, Eixample (Ⓜ Hospital Clinic), from 10am – ceramics, textiles, glassware, wrought iron.

Flea market: Els Encants, every Mon, Wed, Fri and Sat 8am–1.30pm, is currently held on the northwest side of Plaça de les Glòries Catalanes (Ⓜ Glòries), but is due to be moved in 2002/3 (destination as yet undetermined) – clothes, jewellery, junk and furniture.

Food: Mercat Abaceria Central, c/de Puigmartí, Gràcia (Ⓜ Diagonal); Mercat Sant Antoni, Ronda de Sant Pau (Ⓜ Sant Antoni); Mercat Sant Josep/La Boqueria, Ramblas (Ⓜ Liceu); Mercat Santa Catarina, Pg. Lluis Companys (Ⓜ Arc de Triomf).

Listings

Airlines Almost all are located on Pg. de Gràcia or around the corner on the Gran Vía. The main ones include: Air France, Pg. de Gràcia 56 ☏ 901 112 266; British Airways, Pg. de Gràcia 85 ☏ 932 156 900; Easyjet ☏ 902 299 992; Iberia, Diputació 258 ☏ 902 400 500.

Airport information ☏ 932 983 838, Ⓦ www.aena.es/ae/bcn/homepage.htm.

Banks and exchange Main bank branches are in Plaça de Catalunya and Pg. de Gràcia. El Corte Inglés department store in Plaça de Catalunya also has efficient and competitive exchange facilities. Banco de Santander on c/de Ferran (corner Plaça de Sant Jaume) and Caja de Madrid on Plaça de Catalunya both have ATMs. Exchange offices include: Plaça de Catalunya tourist office (daily 9am–9pm); airport (daily 7.30am–10.45pm); Estació-Sants (daily 8am–10pm); and El Corte Inglés, Plaça de Catalunya 14 (Mon–Sat 10am–9.30pm).

Bicycles Several rental places cluster around the Estació de França, including two unnamed establishments at Pg. Picasso 40 and 46, and Bici-rent, Avgda. Marqués de l'Argentera 15 (☏ 933 106 540). Hours are unpredictable, but they are generally open July & Aug daily 10am–7pm and the rest of the year daily 10am–1pm & 5–7pm. Die-hard cyclists can find fellow enthusiasts through the Federació Catalana de Ciclisme at c/Fontanella 11 (☏ 933 012 444).

Buses The main bus terminal is the Estació del Nord on Avgda. Vilanova (☏ 932 656 508; Ⓜ Arc de Triomf), but there are also many departures from the smaller station behind Estació-Sants at Plaça Joan Peiró (☏ 934 904 000). Bus companies include: Alsa ☏ 902 422 242, Ⓦ www.alsa.es (Valencia & South); Alsina Graells ☏ 932 656 866 (Andorra, Lleida, La Pobla de Segur and Vall d'Aran); Autocares Julia ☏ 934 904 000 (London and Europe, Montserrat, Zaragoza); Bacoma ☏ 932 313 801 (Córdoba, Granada, Sevilla); Barcelona Bus ☏ 932 320 459 (Girona); Empresa Sarfa ☏ 932 651 077 (Costa Brava); Enatcar ☏ 932 452 528 (Madrid, Palencia, Valencia); Eurolines ☏ 932 476 047 at Nord, ☏ 934 904 000 at Sants (All of Spain, France, London, Prague, Morocco, Andorra); Iberbus ☏ 932 650 700 (London, Rome, Paris and Amsterdam); Linebus ☏ 932 650 700 at Nord, ☏ 934 904 405 at Sants (France, London, Morocco); Viacarsa ☏ 934 904 000 (Bilbao, Vitoria); Vibassa ☏ 934 911 010 (Vigo, Galicia); Zatrans ☏ 932 310 401 (Burgos, Logroño, Valladolid, Zamora).

Car rental Atesa, c/Muntaner 45 ☏ 933 230 701, & at the airport ☏ 933 983 433; Avis, c/Casanova 209 ☏ 932 099 533, c/Aragó 235 ☏ 934 878 754, and at the airport ☏ 932 983 601; Budget, Josep Tarradellas 35 ☏ 934 102 508, and at the airport ☏ 932 983 500; Europcar, c/Viladomat 214 & at the airport ☏ 934 398 401; Hertz, c/Tuset 10 ☏ 932 178 076, at the airport ☏ 932 983 636 & at Estació-Sants ☏ 934 908 662; Totcar, Berlin 97 ☏ 934 192 294, Ⓦ www.totcarpncsa.es; Vanguard, c/Londres 31 ☏ 934 393 880.

Consulates Australia, Gran Vía Carlos III 98 ☎ 933 309 496; Britain, Avgda. Diagonal 477 ☎ 934 199 044; Canada, c/Elisenda de Pinós 10 ☎ 932 042 700; Ireland, Gran Vía Carlos III 94 ☎ 934 915 021; New Zealand, Trav. de Gràcia 64 ☎ 932 090 399; USA, Pg. de la Reina Elisenda 23 ☎ 932 802 227.

Cultural institutes The British Council at c/Amigó 83 (☎ 932 096 090 or 934 146 888) has an English-language library, lists of language schools and a good noticeboard advertising lessons and accommodation. The North American Institute, Vía Augusta 123 (☎ 932 405 110), has newspapers, magazines and a reference library.

Emergencies For an ambulance or emergency doctor, dial ☎ 061 or go to the accident and emergency departments of the Hospital Clinic or Hospital Sant Pau (see below).

Ferries Departures to the Balearics are from the Estació Marítima (☎ 932 986 000; Ⓜ Drassanes) at the bottom of the Ramblas. Buy tickets at travel agencies, at the Transmediterránea office (☎ 932 454 645, ⓦ www.trasmediterranea.es) or from Buquebús (☎ 902 414 242). The ferries get very crowded in July and August – book ahead.

Gay and lesbian Barcelona There's a lesbian and gay city telephone hotline on ☎ 900 601 601 (6–10pm only) whose operators can answer questions ranging from health through to entertainment. Cómplices, c/Cervantes 2, and Antinovs, c/Josep Anselm Clavé 6, are gay bookshops with useful contacts and information. For a map of gay Barcelona, detailing bars, clubs, hotels and restaurants, contact either SexTienda, c/Raurich 11 (Mon–Sat 10am–9pm), or Zeus, c/Riera Alta 11 (Mon–Sat 10am–9pm; ☎ 934 429 795). Look out also for a free magazine called Nois which carries an up-to-date list of the scene. Most of the city's lesbian groups meet at Ca la Dona: c/Caspe 38 (☎ 984 127 161): these include the Grup de Lesbianes Feministes de Barcelona, which meets on Thurs at 8pm, and L'Eix Violeta, a young lesbian group. Other contacts include Casal Lambda, c/Ample 5 (☎ 934 127 272; Mon–Thurs 5–9pm, Fri 5–11pm, Sat & Sun noon–9pm), a gay and lesbian group with a wide range of social, cultural and educational events; the Front d'Alliberament Gai (FAG) de Catalunya, c/Verdi 88 (☎ 932 172 669), an association for gay men, with a library, meetings and video shows, and a gay youth group at the same address; and the Col·lectiu Gai de Barcelona, c/Paloma 12 (☎ 933 181 665), a gay men's organization with a magazine, Infogai. Finally, the city's annual lesbian and gay pride march is on June 28, starting in the evening at Plaça Universitat. Establishments which attract primarily gay clientele are qualified as de ambiente ("with atmosphere").

Hospitals Ciutat Sanitària Vall d'Hebron, Pg. Vall d'Hebron 119–129 ☎ 934 183 400; Hospital Clinic, c/Villaroel 170 ☎ 934 546 000; Hospital de Sant Pau, c/Sant Antoni Mari Claret 167 ☎ 932 919 000; Centro Diagnostic Malalties Sexuales (Sexually Transmitted Disease Clinic), Avgda. Drassanes 17–19 ☎ 933 294 495.

Internet access Cybercafés are springing up all over the city, and many telephone kiosks and trendy bars now also have terminals. Two central Internet places are Cibercafé, Ramblas 42 Psje. (Mon–Sat 10am–8pm), and Cibermundo, c/Bergara 3 (Mon–Fri 10am–11pm, Sat 11am–1pm & Sun noon–11pm).

Language schools The cheapest Spanish classes in Barcelona are at the Escola Oficial d'Idiomes, Avgda. Drassanes (☎ 933 292 458), where a lottery system is in force – queue up for a ticket, then see if you've won a place to sit the exam that day. Expect big queues at the start of term. Or try International House, c/Trafalgar 14 ☎ 932 680 239, ⓦ www.ihes.com/bcn; Ⓜ Urquinaona. The Generalitat offers low-cost Catalan classes to Spaniards and foreigners through the Centre per a la Normalització Lingüística, c/Quintana 11 ☎ 934 127 224; Ⓜ Liceu.

Laundry Self-service launderettes (lavanderías automáticas) are rare – you normally have to leave your clothes for the full works (usually around €7.20). Try Martin, c/Carme 65 (off the Ramblas) – and have a coffee or drink next door in the old neighbourhood bar, Muy Buenas, while you wait. Note that by a law much ignored in the old city you're forbidden from leaving laundry hanging out of windows over a street, and some hostales can get shirty if you're found doing excessive washing in your bedroom sink.

Left luggage At Estació-Sants the consigna is open daily from 4am–midnight and costs €2.40–3.60 a day. There are lockers at the Estació de França (6am–11.30pm), Pg. de Gràcia and the Estació del Nort for €2.40.

Libraries The Biblioteca Nacional de Catalunya and the Biblioteca Popular de Sant Pau are at c/de Hospital 56, inside the Hospital de la Santa Creu (Mon–Fri 9am–8pm, Sat 9am–2pm); for the BNC a letter of reference may be required. The public library of the Universitat de Barcelona is at Gran Vía 585 (Mon–Fri 8am–8.30pm, also Oct–June Sat 9am–2pm).

Lost property If you lose anything, try the ajuntament (objetos perdidos) at c/de la Ciutat 9 (Mon–Fri 9.30am–1.30pm; ☎ 934 023 161), or the transport office in the Universitat metro station.

Newspapers You can buy foreign newspapers, magazines and trade papers at the stalls down the Ramblas, around Plaça de Catalunya and at Estació-Sants.

Noticeboards For apartment sharing, lifts, lessons and other services check the noticeboards at the cultural institutes (see above); at International House (c/Trafalgar 14); at the university (in the main building; take door on far left and, inside, bear left and then right); at Escola Oficial d'Idiomes (see "Language schools"), and at Llibreria Pròleg (see "Books", p.1061).

Police The main police station is at Vía Laietana 49 (☎ 932 903 000) where there is also a department for women who've suffered violent crime. The tourist police – the Centro Atencíon Policial – are at Rambla 43 (open 24hr in summer; ☎ 933 019 060). If you are the victim of robbery you will have to go to the Comisería Drassanes of the Policía Nacional at c/Nou de la Rambla 62; keep a copy of the report for your insurance claim. The various police bodies in the city can be contacted on the following numbers: Guàrdia Civil ☎062; Policía Nacional ☎091; Guàrdia Urbana ☎092.

Post office The main post office (Correus) in Barcelona is at Plaça d'Antoni López, facing the water at the end of Pg. de Colom (Mon–Sat 8am–8pm). Poste restante (llista de correus) is at window 17 (Mon–Fri 9am–8pm, Sat 9am–2pm). There is another post office at c/Aragó 282 (Mon–Fri 8am–9pm, Sat 9am–2am).

Residence permits In Barcelona, residence permits for EU nationals are issued by the Servicio de Extranjeros at Avgda. Marqués de l'Argentera 4 (Mon–Fri 9am–1pm; ☎ 934 820 544 or 934 820 530) – queue up before 9am. You will be required to show a Spanish bank statement in your name, typically with a balance of at least €4000.

Swimming pools To swim at one of Barcelona's pools, take your passport along; you may need to show it before being allowed in. Central pools include Club Natació at Pg. Marítím (daily 6.30am–10pm; €6), Piscina Municipal Floch i Torres at Reina Amelia 31 (Ⓜ Sant Antoni; daily 7.30am–9pm; €5.40) and, best of all, the Olympic Piscines Bernat Picornell, Avgda. de l'Estadi 30–40, Montjuïc (Mon–Fri 7am–midnight, Sat 7am–9pm, Sun 7.30am–2.30pm; summer €7.20, winter €3.90).

Telephone offices There are Telefónica offices at c/Fontanella 4, off Plaça de Catalunya (Mon–Sat 8.30am–9pm), and at Estació-Sants (daily 8am–10pm). There are also very well-priced private long-distance phone stands on the Ramblas and scattered about the Barri Gòtic.

Trains For train information, call RENFE ☎ 934 900 202; international routes on ☎ 934 901 122, 10am–2pm. You can buy train tickets at the RENFE office in the underground foyer at Pg. de Gràcia (corner of c/Aragó). Otherwise, at Sants-Estació (☎ 934 903 851) there's both a RENFE information office (daily 6.30am–10.30pm; English-speaking) and an International Train Information Office (daily 7am–10pm), where you can reserve seats and couchettes on international trains. This is recommended in high season, compulsory on some trains, and should be done in advance – at least a couple of hours before departure, the day before if possible. Certain routes in Catalunya are operated by FGC; for information call ☎ 932 051 515 or 933 663 361, or check out their website ⓦ www.fgc.catalunya.net.

Travel agencies General travel agencies are found on the Gran Vía, Pg. de Gràcia, Vía Laietana and the Ramblas. For city tours, Catalunya holidays and trips try Julia Tours, Plaça Universitat 12 (☎ 933 176 454 or 933 176 209). For deals (including student specials) on flights, the best places are Viatgi, Ronda Universitat 1 (☎ 933 011 629, ⓔ viatgi@grupoeuropa.com) or, if you can brave the hours-long wait, USIT, Ronda Universitat 16 (☎ 934 120 104, ⓦ www.unlimited.es). For youth train tickets head to Wasteels, inside Estació-Sants.

Travel details

Trains

Barcelona to: Cerbère, France (18 daily; 2hr 55min); Figueres (29 daily; 1hr 30min); Girona (30 daily; 1hr 20min); Lleida via Manresa (6 daily; 4hr); Lleida via Valls or Tarragona/Reus (16 daily; 2–3hr); Madrid (8 daily; 12hr); Paris (7 daily; 11–15hr); Portbou (16 daily; 2hr 50min); Puigcerdà (7 daily; 3hr 30min); Ripoll (12 daily; 2hr); Sitges (every 30min; 25–40min); Tarragona (every 15–30min; 1hr 30min); Valencia (16 daily; 4–5hr); Vic (6 daily; 1hr); Zaragoza (14 daily; 4hr 30min–6hr 30min).

Buses

Barcelona to: Alicante (4 daily; 9hr); Andorra (2 daily; 4hr 30min); Banyoles (2–3 daily; 1hr 30min); Besalú (2–3 daily; 1hr 45min); Cadaqués (2–5 daily; 2hr 20min); Girona (Mon–Sat 6–9 daily, Sun 3 daily; 1hr 30min); Lleida (12 daily, Sun 4 daily; 2hr 15min); Lloret de Mar (July–mid-Sept 10 daily; 1hr 15min); Madrid (6 daily; 10hr); Olot (2–3 daily; 2hr 10min); Palafrugell (8 daily; 2hr); Perpignan, France (2 daily; 4hr); La Pobla de Segur (1 daily; 3hr 30min); La Seu d'Urgell (2 daily; 4hr); Tarragona (18 daily; 1hr 30min); Torroella (3 daily; 4hr 30min); Tossa de Mar (July–mid-Sept 12 daily; 1hr 35min); Valencia (9 daily; 6hr); Vall d'Aran (1 daily; 7hr); Viella (June–Nov 1 daily; 7hr); Zaragoza (6 daily; 5hr).

Ferries

Barcelona to: Palma, Mallorca (1–4 daily; 4–9hr); Ibiza (2 weekly; 9hr); Maó, (2 weekly; 7hr).

Catalunya

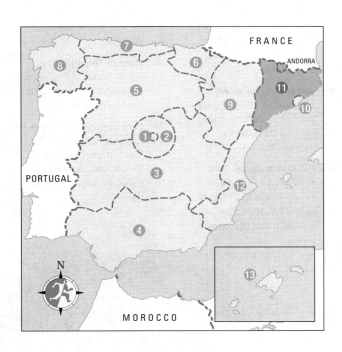

CHAPTER 11   # Highlights

Catalunya

Y ou can't think of visiting Barcelona without seeing something of its surroundings. Although the city is fast becoming international, the wider
area of Catalunya (Cataluña in Castilian Spanish, traditionally Catalonia
in English) retains a distinct regional identity that borrows little from the
rest of Spain, let alone from the world at large. Out of the city – and especially
in rural areas – you'll hear Catalan spoken more often and be confronted with
better Catalan food, which is often highly specialized, varying even from village
to village. Towns and villages are surprisingly prosperous, a relic of the early
industrial era, when Catalunya developed far more rapidly than most of Spain;
and the people are enterprising and open, celebrating a unique range of festivals (see the list on p.752–753) in almost obsessive fashion. There's a confidence
in being Catalan that traces right back to the fourteenth-century Golden Age,
when what was then a kingdom ruled the Balearics, Valencia, the French border regions, Sardinia, parts of Greece and Corsica, too. Today, Catalunya is officially a semi-autonomous province, but it can still feel like a separate country –
cross the borders into Valencia or Aragón and you soon pick up the differences.

Catalunya is also a very satisfying region to tour, since two or three hours in
any direction puts you in the midst of varying landscapes of great beauty; from
rocky coastlines to long, flat beaches, from the mountains to the plain, and from
marshlands to forest. There are some considerable distances to cover, especially
in the interior, but on the whole everything is easily reached from Barcelona,
which is linked to most main centres by excellent bus and train services. The

---

Accommodation price codes

All the establishments listed in this book have been price-graded according to the
following scale. The prices quoted are for the **cheapest available double room in
high season**; effectively this means that anything in the ❶ and most places in the
❷ range will be without private bath, though there's usually a washbasin in the
room. In the ❹ category and above you will probably be getting private facilities.
Remember, though, that many of the budget places will also have more expensive
rooms including en-suite facilities. Youth hostels are graded under ❶ as the price
per person is less than half of the category's upper limit.

Note that in the more upmarket *hostales* and *pensiones*, and in anything calling
itself a hotel, you'll pay a **tax** (IVA) of seven percent on top of the room price.

❶ Under €12	❹ €27–36	❼ €60–90
❷ €12–18	❺ €36–48	❽ €90–120
❸ €18–27	❻ €48–60	❾ Over €120

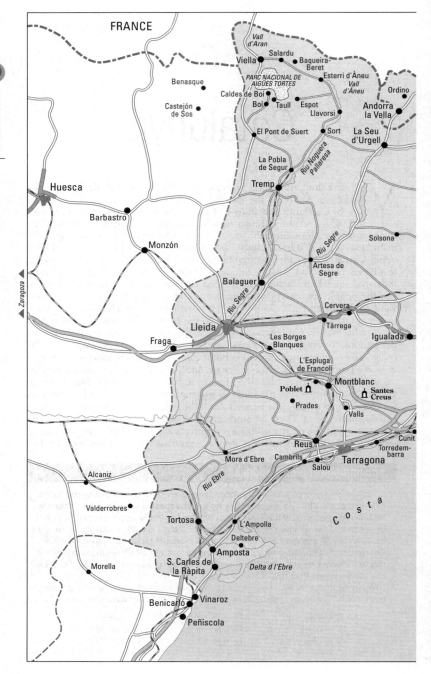

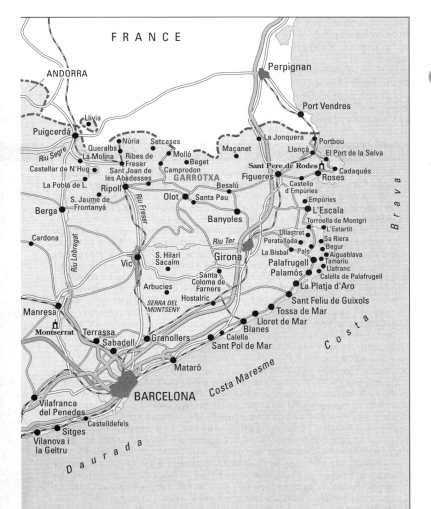

FRANCE

ANDORRA

Perpignan

Port Vendres

Llívia

Puigcerdá

La Jonquera   Portbou

Núria   Setcases

Queralbs

Maçanet   Llançá   El Port de la Selva

La Molina   Ribes de

Molló

Castellar de N'Hug   Freser   Beget   Sant Pere de Rodes   Cadaqués

Sant Joan de   Camprodon   GARROTXA   Figueres   Roses

La Pobla de L.   les Abadesses   Besalú   Castello   B

Ripoll   Olot   Santa Pau   d'Empúries   r

S. Jaume de   Empúries   a

Berga   Frontanyá   Banyoles   L'Escala   v

Torroella de Montgri   a

Cardona   Riu Ter   Ullastret   L'Estartit

Peratallada   Sa Riera

S. Hilari   La Bisbal   Pals   Begur

Vic   Sacalm   Girona   Palafrugell   Aiguablava

Tamariu

Santa   Palamós   Llafranc

Arbucies   Coloma de   Calella de Palafrugell

Farners   La Platja d'Aro

Hostalric   C

SERRA DEL   Sant Feliu de Guixols   o

MONTSENY   Tossa de Mar   s

Manresa   Lloret de Mar   t

Blanes   a

Montserrat   Terrassa   Calella

Sabadell   Granollers   Sant Pol de Mar   Costa Maresme

Mataró

BARCELONA

Vilafranca

del Penedes   Castelldefels

Sitges   D a u r a d a

Vilanova i

la Geltru

MAR   MEDITERRANEO

N

Riu Segre

Riu Llobregat

Riu Freser

0   Kilometres   50

easiest targets are the **coasts** north and south of the city, and the various **provincial capitals** – Girona, Tarragona and Lleida – all destinations that make a series of day-trips or can be linked together in a loop through the region.

The best of the beach towns lie on the famous **Costa Brava**, which runs up to the French border. This was one of the first stretches of Spanish coast to be developed for mass tourism, and though that's no great recommendation, the large, brash resorts to the south are tempered by some more isolated beaches and lower-key holiday and fishing villages further north. Just inland from the

Català

The traveller's main problem throughout the province is likely to be **language** – *Català* (Catalan) has more or less taken over from Castilian and you might not realize that *Dilluns Tancat*, for example, is the same as *Cerrado Lunes* (closed Monday). On paper it looks like a cross between French and Spanish and is generally easy to understand if you know those two but, spoken, it has a very harsh sound and is far harder to come to grips with, especially away from Barcelona where accents are stronger. Few visitors realize how ingrained and widespread *Català* is, and this can lead to resentment because people won't "speak Spanish" for you. Increasingly, though, *Català* is replacing Castilian rather than cohabiting with it, a phenomenon known as the *venganza* (revenge). Never commit the error of calling it a dialect!

When Franco came to power, publishing houses, bookshops and libraries were raided and *Català* books destroyed. While this was followed by a let-up in the mid-1940s, the language was still banned from the radio, TV, daily press and, most importantly, schools, which is why many older people today cannot read or write *Català* (even if they speak it all the time). Conversely, in the capital virtually everyone *can* speak Castilian, even if they don't, while in country areas, many people can only understand, not speak it.

Català is spoken in Catalunya proper, part of Aragón, most of Valencia, the Balearic islands, the Principality of Andorra, and in parts of the French Pyrenees, albeit with variations of dialect (it is thus much more widely spoken than several better-known languages such as Danish, Finnish and Norwegian). It is a Romance language, stemming from Latin and more directly from medieval Provençal and *lemosí*, the literary French of Occitania. Spaniards in the rest of the country belittle it by saying that to get a *Català* word you just cut a Castilian one in half. In fact, the grammar is much more complicated than Castilian and it has eight vowel sounds (three diphthongs). There is a deliberate tendency at present in the media to dig up old words not used for centuries, even when a more common, Castilian-sounding one exists. In Barcelona, because of the mixture of people, there is much bad *Català* and much bad Castilian spoken, mongrel words being invented unconsciously.

In the text we've tried to keep to *Català* names (with Castilian in parentheses where necessary) – not least because street signs and turisme maps are in *Català*. Either way, you're unlikely to get confused as the difference is usually only slight: ie Girona (Gerona) and Lleida (Lérida).

Català glossary

Most **Català** words are similar to Castilian, but some are completely unrecognizable. The criteria for the following words and phrases which you might encounter are either that they are very common or that they are very different from Castilian.

One	*Un(a)*	Five	*Cinc*
Two	*Dos (dues)*	Six	*Sis*
Three	*Tres*	Seven	*Set*
Four	*Quatre*	Eight	*Vuit*

coast, the small town of **Figueres** contains another reason to visit the area: the Museu Dalí, Catalunya's biggest tourist attraction. South of Barcelona, the **Costa Daurada** is less enticing, though it has at least one fine beach at **Sitges** and the attractive coastal town of **Tarragona** to recommend it; inland, the romantic monastery of Poblet figures as one approach to the enjoyable provincial capital of **Lleida**.

Travels in inland Catalunya depend on the time available, but even on a short trip you can take in the medieval city of **Girona** and the surrounding area, which includes the isolated Montseny hills and the extraordinary volcanic

Nine	*Nou*	In	*Dins*
Ten	*Deu*	With	*Amb*
Eleven	*Onze*	Still/yet/even	*Encara*
Twelve	*Dotze*	A lot, very	*Força*
		A little	*Una mica*
Monday	*Dilluns*	Near	*(a) Prop*
Tuesday	*Dimarts*	Far	*Lluny*
Wednesday	*Dimecres*	(Six) years ago	*Fa (sis) anys*
Thursday	*Dijous*	Self/same	*Mateix*
Friday	*Divendres*	Half/middle	*Mig/mitja*
Saturday	*Dissabte*	Stop, enough!	*Prou!*
Sunday	*Diumenge*	Too much/too	*Massa*
		many	
Day before	*Abans d'ahir*		
yesterday		To work	*Treballar*
Yesterday	*Ahir*	To go	*Anar*
Today	*Avui*	To call, phone	*Trucar*
Tomorrow	*Demà*	To have dinner	*Sopar*
Day after	*Demà passat*	(evening)	
tomorrow		To eat	*Menjar*
Left, Right	*Esquerre*		
	(a),Dret(a)	Girl	*Una noia*
Ladies, Gents	*Dones, Homes*	Boy	*Un noi*
(WC)	*(Serveis)*	Child/term of	*Nen(a)*
Open, Closed	*Obert(a), Tancat*	affection	
Good morning/	*Bon dia*	Dog	*Gos*
Hello			
Good evening/	*Bona nit/Adéu*	Place	*Lloc*
Goodbye		Light	*Llum*
Very well	*Molt bé*	Chief, head	*Cap*
Bad	*Malament*	Time, occasion	*Vegada*
Got a light?	*Tens foc?*		
I like	*M'agrada*	Drinking glass	*Got*
Well, then	*Sisplau*	Table	*Taula*
What do you	*Que vols?*	Milk	*Llet*
want?		Egg	*Ou*
Where is?	*On és?*	Strawberry	*Maduixa*
Sometimes	*A vegades*	Orange	*Taronge*
Never, ever	*Mai*	Carrot	*Pastanaga*
More	*Més*	Lettuce	*Enciam*
Nothing	*Res*	Salad	*Amanida*
None, some, any,	*Cap*	Apple	*Poma*
towards			

Fiestas

In some cases, dates may vary slightly from year to year.

January
20–22 Traditional pilgrimage in Tossa de Mar, the *Pelegri de Tossa*, followed by a lively fiesta. Annual festival at Llança.

February/March
Carnaval Sitges has Catalunya's best celebrations (see p.848). Celebrations also at Solsona, Sort, Rialp and La Molina.

Easter
The *Patum* festival in Berga (see p.809) is the biggest and best Easter festival in Catalunya; Holy Week celebrations at Besalú, Girona and La Pobla de Segur.

April
23 *Semana Medieval de Sant Jordi* in Montblanc – a week of exhibitions, games, dances and medieval music to celebrate the legend of St George.

May
11–12 Annual festival in Lleida; and the annual wool fair, *Festa de la Lana*, in Ripoll. *Festa de Corpus Christi* in Sitges – big processions and streets decorated with flowers.
Third week *Fires i Festes de la Santa Creu* in Figueres; processions and music.

June
21–23 Festival in Camprodon.
24 *Día de Sant Joan* celebrated everywhere; watch out for things shutting down for a day on either side.
29 Annual festival at Tossa de Mar.
Last week The *Raiers* (rafters) festival and river racing in Sort.

July
First Sunday Annual festival at Puigcerdà.

Garrotxa region. With more time you can head for the **Catalan Pyrenees**, with their magnificent and relatively isolated hiking territory, particularly in and around the **Parc Nacional de Aigüestortes**. East of here is **Andorra**, a combination of tax-free hellhole and mountain retreat set amidst quieter, generally neglected border towns, all offering great hiking and, in winter, good skiing.

Catalanisme

The **Catalan people** have an individual and deeply felt historical and cultural identity, seen most clearly in the language, which takes precedence over Castilian on street names and signs. Despite being banned for over thirty years during the Franco dictatorship, Catalan survived behind closed doors and has staged a dramatic comeback since the Generalísimo's death. As in the Basque country, though, regionalism goes back much further than this. On the expulsion of the Moors in 874, Guifré el Pelós (Wilfred the Hairy) established himself as the first independent **Count of Barcelona**; his kingdom flourished and the region became famous for its seafaring, mercantile and commercial skills, characteristics which to some extent still set the region apart. In the twelfth century came union with Aragón, though the Catalans kept many of their tra-

10 *Sant Cristobal* festival in Olot, with traditional dances and processions.
Third week *Festa de Santa Cristina* at Lloret de Mar. Also, annual festival at Palafrugell.
25 Festival at Portbou in honour of St James.
26 Annual festival at Blanes.

August
First week *Festa Major* at Andorra la Vella; annual festival at Sant Feliu de Guixols.
10–12 Annual festival at Castelló d'Empúries.
15 Festival at La Bisbal and Palafrugell.
19 Festa de Sant Magi in Tarragona.
Last week *Festa Major* in Sitges, to honour the town's patron saint, Sant Bartolomeu.

September
First week Festival at Cadaqués and at L'Escala.
8 Religious celebrations in Cadaqués, Núria and Queralbs. Processions of *gigantes* at Solsona. Festivals at Sort and Esterri d'Àneu.
22 Annual festival at Espot.
23 *Festa de Santa Tecla* in Tarragona, with processions of *gigantes* and human castles.
24 Annual festival at Besalú.

October
8 Annual fair at Viella.
Last week Fires i Festes de Sant Narcis in Girona, and Festa de Sant Martirià in Banyoles.

November
1 *Sant Ermengol* celebrations in La Seu d'Urgell.

December
18 Festival at Cadaqués.

ditional, hard-won rights (*usatges*), and from then until the fourteenth century marked Catalunya's **Golden Age**. By the end of that time the kingdom ruled the Balearic islands, the city and region of Valencia, Sardinia, Corsica and much of present-day Greece. In 1359 the Catalan Generalitat formed Europe's first parliamentary government.

In 1469, through the marriage of Fernando V (of Aragón) to Isabel I (of Castile), the region was added on to the rest of the emergent Spanish state. Throughout the following centuries the Catalans made various attempts to secede and to escape from the stifling grasp of the central bureaucracy, which saw Catalan enterprise as merely another means of filling the state coffers. Early industrialization, which was centred here and in the Basque country, only intensified political disaffection. In the 1920s and 1930s, anarchist, communist and socialist parties all established major power bases in Catalunya. In 1931, after the fall of the dictator General Primo de Rivera, a **Catalan Republic** was proclaimed and its autonomous powers guaranteed by the new Republican government. Any incipient separatism collapsed, however, with the outbreak of the Civil War, during which Catalunya was a bastion of the Republican cause, Barcelona holding out until January 1939.

In return, Franco pursued a policy of harsh suppression, attempting to wipe out all evidence of the Catalan cultural and economic set-up and finally to establish the dominance of Madrid. Among his more subtle methods – employed also in Euskal Herria – was the encouragement of immigration from other parts of Spain in order to dilute regional identity. Even so, Catalunya remained obstinate, the scene of protests and demonstrations throughout the dictatorship. After Franco's death there was massive and immediate pressure – not long in paying dividends – for the reinstatement of a **Catalan government**. This, the semi-autonomous Generalitat, enjoys a very high profile, whatever the complaints about its lack of real power. It controls education, health and social security, with a budget based on taxes collected by central government and then returned proportionally. The province's official title is the Comunitat Autonoma de Catalunya and it is also known internally as the Principalitat. Since autonomy was granted, the region has consistently elected centre-right governments, which may be difficult to understand in view of the recent past, but which might be explained by the fact that such regimes are seen to be better able to protect Catalan business interests.

The Costa Brava

The **Costa Brava** (Rugged Coast), stretching from Blanes, 60km north of Barcelona, to Portbou and the French border, was once the most beautiful part of the Spanish coast with its wooded coves, high cliffs, pretty beaches and deep blue water. In many parts it's still like this: the northern section of the coast retains its handsome natural attractions and boasts a string of small towns and villages, which – while hardly undiscovered – are at least frequented only by locals and passing French motorists. In the south part of the coast, though, thirty-five years of package-holiday saturation have taken their inevitable toll, and the concrete development in some towns has been ruthless.

Although the development appears all-encompassing at first glance, the Costa Brava splits into two distinct parts. The southern string of resorts, beginning at **Blanes**, *is* fairly horrible, though it's redeemed in a couple of places: the old town and medieval walls of **Tossa de Mar** are as attractive as anything you'll see in Catalunya, and **Sant Feliu de Guixols** further north has more going for it than most towns along the coast. Even the area's most notorious resort, **Lloret de Mar**, is a matter of taste: a brash, tacky concrete pile it may be, but if you like your nightlife loud, late and libidinous, you'll have few complaints.

Beyond **Palamós** the main road runs inland and the coastal development here is relatively low-key; the beaches and villages close to the small inland town of **Palafrugell**, in particular, are still wonderfully scenic. An added attraction is the ancient Greek site of **Empúries**, within walking distance of **L'Escala**, itself a resort on an eminently reasonable scale. Beyond here, the hinterland of the large bay, the **Golf de Roses**, is rural and fairly isolated, crossed by only a few minor roads and encompassing a nature reserve, the Parc Natural dels Aiguamolls de l'Empordá. Around the bay, **Roses** is the last of the Costa Brava's massive tourist developments; nearby **Cadaqués** is becoming more

Getting around the Costa Brava

Driving is the easiest way to get around, though you can expect the smaller coastal roads to be very busy in summer and parking to be tricky in the major resorts. **Buses** in the region are almost all operated by the SARFA company, but although they are reasonably efficient, it can be a frustrating business trying to get to some of the smaller coastal villages. Consider using Figueres, or even Girona, as a base for lateral trips to the coast; both are big bus termini and within an hour of the beach. The **train** from Barcelona to Portbou and the French border runs inland most of the time, serving Blanes, Girona and Figueres, but emerging on the coast itself only at Llançà.

There are also daily **boat services** (*cruceros*) which operate along the coast for most of the year. From June to September boats run from Calella (south of Blanes and not to be confused with the one near Palafrugell) to Palamós, calling chiefly at Blanes, Lloret, Tossa, Sant Feliu and Platja d'Aro; in March, April, May and October they run only as far as Tossa. The Lloret–Tossa trip costs around €7.20 return, and it's worth taking at least once as the rugged coastline makes for an extremely beautiful ride. There are several operators, but the main one is Crucetours, whose central office for information and reservations – with English-speaking staff – is on the beach in Lloret (☎972 372 692).

popular by the year, though you can find quieter coastal fishing villages right the way up to the French border, including the likeable small resort of **Portbou**, last stop before France. Inland, the town of **Figueres** is the birthplace of Salvador Dalí and home to his superb, surreal museum.

There's more accommodation along the Costa Brava than anywhere else in Catalunya, but that doesn't necessarily make **rooms** any easier to find. In the large resorts, block-booking by tour operators reduces the supply considerably and if you're heading independently to Lloret or Tossa, for example, in the summer, you'd be wise to book well in advance. You *will* generally find something if you arrive on spec, but you'll almost certainly pay over the odds for it. There are few problems with **camping**, provided you can put up with enormous, crowded sites often some way out of the towns and villages.

Blanes

Just over an hour from Barcelona, **BLANES** is the first town of the Costa Brava, though in parts there's little to distinguish it from the other resort towns back down the coast towards the city. With its industrial base and heavy-duty fishing port, it's a largely uninspiring stop, though its pine-sheltered, sandy **beach** is one of the coast's longest, and the clifftop **Mar i Murtra botanical gardens** at Pg. Karl Faust 9 (April–Oct daily 9am–6pm; Nov–March Mon–Fri 10am–5pm, Sat–Sun 10am–2pm; €2.10) are worth the visit for the coastal views and for the amazing variety of plants and trees from all over the world.

Blanes at least has the advantage over many similar places of being a real town rather than just a tourist settlement. There are dozens of largely indistinguishable **hotels and hostales** here, and no fewer than twelve local **campsites** as well. The **turisme** in Plaça de Catalunya (June–Sept Mon–Sat 9am–8pm, July & Aug also Sun 9am–2pm; May & Oct Mon–Fri 9am–2pm & 4–7pm; Nov–April Mon–Fri 9am–3pm; ☎972 330 348, ⓦwww.blanes.net) can help you find a room should you decide to stay. There's an excellent Catalan **restaurant**, *Les Brases*, with a delicious €6.60 *menú*, about ten minutes' walk from Plaça de Catalunya at c/Antiga 40 – left off Rambla Joaquim Ruyra, while *Casa Oliveras* at Pg. Cortils i Vieta 12 serves an imaginative blend of Catalan and Latin American dishes for around €18 a head.

The **train** station is inland, a little way out of town; there's a half-hourly service to Barcelona and several trains daily to Girona and Figueres. Regular buses run from the station to the beach, and **buses** also connect Blanes with Lloret every twenty minutes until 9.35pm.

Lloret de Mar

Despite the increasingly developed character of the coast as you head north, nothing will prepare you for **LLORET DE MAR**, one of the most extreme resorts in Spain and the one place on the Costa Brava that most people have heard of. On the surface, it's a mess: high-rise concrete tower blocks, a tawdry mile or so of sand and alongside it the most prosaic, unimaginative display of cafés, restaurants and bars you'll ever see. But to see the town in this way is misguided, since Lloret makes no pretence that it's anything other than an out-and-out holiday resort and, as these go, it is as accommodating as they come. During the day, the central **beach** is packed with oily bodies, but it's flanked by attractive little coves and lookout points which you can either reach by footpath or view from the coastal boat service that calls at Lloret. Budget meals abound, while there are plenty of more expensive, and more impressive, Catalan and Spanish **restaurants** too. Beer and *sangría* flow ceaselessly, mopped up in the loud bars, pubs and discos along c/de la Riera and the surrounding streets.

Practicalities

Cruceros and other coastal **boats** dock at the beach, which is where the ticket offices are too; there are around a dozen daily services to Tossa de Mar, thirty minutes away, though fewer outside the summer months. The **bus station** is north of the town centre, on Carretera de Blanes, in front of the football ground. As well as regular services from nearby Blanes and Tossa, there are seven daily buses from Barcelona. There's a **turisme** (May–Oct Mon–Sat 9.30am–1pm & 4–8pm; Nov–April closes 7pm; ☎972 365 788) just outside the bus station if you want to pick up a map and hotel listings, and another one in the centre close to the seafront at Plaça de la Vila 1 (June–Sept Mon–Sat 9am–9pm, Sun 9.30am–2pm; March–May & Oct Mon–Sat 9.30am–1pm & 4–8pm; ☎972 364 735, ✉lloretpmt@versin.com).

Accommodation

If you're intending **to stay**, arm yourself with a list of hotels and *hostales* and start looking early in the day. As you'd expect, there are a lot of high-rise hotels, but there are also some very good places in the old part of town not far from the beach or on the outskirts.

Hostal Residencia Astor, c/Venecia 51 ☎972 364 216, ☎972 344 435. Small, economical *hostal* well away from the bustle of the centre. ❹
Hostal La Habana, c/Les Taronges 11 ☎972 367 707, ☎972 372 074. Smart, family-run *pensió* with a good restaurant on a narrow street leading from the beach to the old town. ❹
Pensió María del Mar II, Apartado de Correos 98 ☎972 364 437, ☎972 368 365. Friendly establishment near the post office with clean, quiet rooms. June–Sept. ❹

Pensió Reina Isabel, c/Vall de Venecia 12 ☎972 364 121, ☎972 369 978. Very quirky and friendly *pensió* in the heart of the old town just one block from the beach. March–Oct. ❹
Hostal Santa Cristina, Ermita de Santa Cristina ☎972 364 934. An antiquated and charming *hostal* next to the Church of Santa Cristina perched on a headland between the beaches at Santa Cristina and Cala Treumal. March–Oct. ❸
Pensió Tropicana, Avgda. Joan Llaverias 19 ☎972 364 130. A reasonably priced small *pensió*

in the old town, which is clean and has sea views. June–Sept. **④**

Hotel Vila del Mar, c/de la Vila 55 ☏ 972 349 292, ⓕ 972 371 168, ⓦ www.6tems.com/viladelmar. A

small and stylish hotel whose comfortable rooms are surprisingly quiet in the midst of the old town's bustle. Feb–Nov. **⑧**

Eating and drinking

If you're determined to eat Spanish **food** – a heretical choice in Lloret – then the heavily Catalan *Ca l'Avi*, at Avgda. Vidreres 30, should satisfy you for around €18 a head, while a more modern variation on Catalan cuisine can be found at *Can Tarrades* at Plaça d'Espanya 7, although expect to pay a good €24. Kids – and adults – will love shaking to a 7.8 earthquake at *Disaster Café*, at c/Layret 5–7 in Fenals beach, which will set you back around €24 each for upmarket fast food.

Tossa de Mar

Arriving by boat at **TOSSA DE MAR**, 13km north of Lloret, is one of the Costa Brava's highlights, the medieval walls and turrets pale and shimmering on the hill above the modern town. Although an unashamed resort, Tossa is still very attractive and – if you have the choice – infinitely preferable to Lloret as a base.

Arrival and information

There are plenty of day-trippers in Tossa, which is linked to Lloret by half-hourly **buses**. *Cruceros* **boats** (see box, p.755) stop right at the centre of the beach, with the ticket offices nearby. If you're going to stay, pick up a free map and accommodation lists from the efficient **turisme** (March & Nov Mon–Sat 10am–1pm & 4–7pm; April, May & Oct Mon–Sat 10am–2pm & 4–8pm, Sun 10.30am–1.30pm; June–Sept Mon–Sat 9am–9pm, Sun 10am–2pm & 4–8pm; Dec–Feb Mon–Fri 10am–1pm & 4–7pm, Sat 10am–1pm; ☏ 972 340 108, ⓦ www.tossademar.com), located in the same building as the bus station. To reach the centre, and the beaches, head straight down the road opposite the bus station.

Accommodation

There is plenty of **accommodation** to be had in the warren of tiny streets around the church and below the old city walls; in summer, the more obscure streets away from the front are the ones to check. There are five local **campsites**, all within a two- to four-kilometre walk of the centre: *Cala Llevadó* (☏ 972 340 314, ⓕ 972 341 187, ⓔ calalleva@grn.es; May–Sept) is 3km out, off the road to Lloret, and costs around €5.80 per person and per tent – the bus to Lloret should drop you close by if you ask.

Pensió Can Lluna, c/Roqueta 20 ☏ 972 340 365, ⓕ 972 340 757. Comfortable, reasonably priced *pensió*. Open March–Sept. **③**

Pensió Can Tort, Trav. del Portal 1 ☏ 972 341 185. Clean and friendly option; breakfast included. April–Oct. **⑤**

Pensió Cap d'Or, Pg. del Mar 1 ☏ 972 340 081. Very friendly seafront *pensió* nestling under the walls of the old town. Open April–Oct. **⑤**

Hotel Capri, Pg. del Mar 17 ☏ 972 340 358, ⓕ 972 341 552, ⓦ www.tossa.com/capri. Good-value, comfortable hotel on the seafront. Open April–Oct. **⑥**

Hotel Diana, Plaça d'Espanya 6 ☏ 972 341 886, ☏ 972 341 103. Nicely located hotel in a *modernista* mansion in an attractive square. Prices drop dramatically outside summer. Late March to mid-Nov. **⑦**

Hotel Mar Blau, Avgda. de la Costa Brava 16 ⊤972 340 282. Pleasant hotel on the edge of the old town where the weekly market is held. Open June–Sept. ⑤

Hotel Tonet, Plaça de l'Església 1 ⊤972 340 237, ⊕972 343 096. Pleasantly located family-run hotel with comfortable, good-value rooms. The only place in town open all year. ⑥

The Town

Founded originally by the Romans, Tossa has twelfth-century walls surrounding an old quarter, the **Vila Vella**, which is all cobbled streets, whitewashed houses and flower boxes, offering terrific views over beach and bay. Within the quarter you'll eventually happen upon the **Museu de la Vila Vella** at Plaça Roig i Soler 1 (Tues–Sun June–Sept 10am–10pm; Oct–May 10am–1pm & 3–6pm; €1.80), which features some Chagall paintings, a Roman mosaic and remnants from a nearby excavated Roman villa.

Tossa's best **beach** (there are four) is the Mar Menuda, around the headland away from the old town. The main central beach, though pleasant and clean enough, gets crowded even on the gloomiest of days. Booths here sell tickets for **boat trips** around the surrounding coastline, a reasonable way to blow €6.60 or so if you're not going to take the *cruceros* coastline service beyond Tossa. Fonda Crystal, with a booth amongst the others on the beach, run glass-bottomed boat trips (⊤972 342 229; April–Oct; €7.20).

Out of season, Tossa's attraction is even greater, simply because there are fewer people to disturb the tranquil old town streets. It's in winter, too, that you'll see something of the Costa Brava's previous, more traditional, life. This is best represented by the annual *Pelegri de Tossa* on January 20 and 21, a **pilgrimage** from Tossa to the inland town of Santa Coloma in honour of St Sebastian, followed by a winter fair.

Eating

Most of Tossa's **restaurants** feature *menús del día* of varying quality, while there are endless "Full English Breakfast" bargains offered in places on the way out to the bus station – *Bar Lluís*, c/de la Guàrdia 22, is friendly and at least has a few Catalan dishes and a €6 *menú*. More atmospherically, there is a whole host of excellent restaurants up in the old quarter and just outside the walls, where you'll require big money or a credit card. For local specialities, three well-known places are *Bahía*, Passeig del Mar (⊤972 340 322), whose swish interior is the setting for tasty seafood meals, *Es Molí*, c/Tarull 3 (⊤972 341 414; closed Tues & Oct–April), expensive but with a garden patio and fine local cooking, and *Castell Vell*, c/Pintor Roig i Soler s/n (⊤972 341 030; closed Nov–Feb), also expensive but serving excellent fish and seafood on a shaded terrace. A less exclusive place, with reliable Catalan food and an €11.40 *menú del día* is *Tito's*, at c/Sant Telm 6. The *Roqueta Mar*, c/de la Roqueta 2, is similarly priced and has a lovely setting, with a creeper-shaded terrace in a rambling corner of the old town. For tapas, the atmospheric *La Lluna* at c/Abad Oliva s/n has an excellent selection for around €12 a head.

Sant Feliu to Palamós

Tossa is something of an aberration and the coast immediately to the north is again heavily developed and often thoroughly spoiled. Fairly regular buses ply the route, though, and the ride isn't bad in parts, particularly the winding section between Tossa and Sant Feliu. Even nicer is to use the **boat service** (see box, p.755), which continues up the coast via Sant Feliu to Palamós – another lovely ride, and really the only reason to be stopping in most of the towns below. Incidentally, many of the buses on this coastal route originate in Girona or Palafrugell, so it's easy enough to see the various towns on day-trips from either of those places, too.

Sant Feliu de Guixols

SANT FELIU DE GUIXOLS is probably the best stop between Tossa and the beaches of Palafrugell. It's another full-blown resort, but at least a reasonably pleasant one with only low-rise hotels, a decent sweep of coarse sand, a yacht harbour, and an attractive seafront, Passeig del Mar, decked out with pavement cafés and plane trees. Back from the beach, the narrow streets of the old town – thick with café-bars – are commercial but undeniably appealing, while a weekly market in the central Plaça de Mercat adds a bit of local colour. Sant Feliu owes its handsome buildings and air of prosperity to the nineteenth-century cork industry which was based here, but the origins of the town go back as far as the tenth century, when a town grew up around the Benedictine **monastery**, whose ruins still stand in Plaça Monestir. The squat round tower and tenth-century arched gateway, the Porta Ferrada, sit back from the square, and if you want to look inside, the complex is usually open from 8am Mass until noon, and again at 8pm Mass. A **museum** around the back houses a permanent display of work by local artist Josep Albertí, who died in April 1993.

Practicalities

Cruceros **boats** dock on the main beach, where you'll also find the various ticket offices. There are two **bus terminals**: Teisa services to and from Girona stop opposite the monastery, next to which is the **turisme**, at Plaça Monestir (June–Sept Mon–Sat 10am–2pm & 4–8pm, Sun 10am–2pm; Oct–May Mon–Sat 10am–1pm & 4–7pm, Sun 10am–2pm; ☎972 820 051, ✉otsfg@ddgi.es); the SARFA bus station (for buses to and from Palafrugell, Girona and Barcelona) is five minutes' walk north of the centre on the main Carretera de Girona, at the junction with c/Llibertat.

A score of family-run **pensiones and hotels** can be found in the old town streets, all within a five-minute walk of each other and the sea; pick up a list and current prices from the turisme. Just opposite the turisme at Avgda. Juli Garreta 43–45, just off Plaça Monestir, is the *Hostal Zürich* (☎972 321 054; ❹); while a favourite budget choice is the *Gas Vell*, c/Santa Magdalena 29 (☎972 321 024, ☏972 321 024, ❸), though it's a long way from the sea. Set back from the seafront in the market square is the friendly, family-run *Hotel Plaça*, Plaça Mercat 22 (☎972 325 155, ☏972 821 321; ❼), while the very laid-back *Hotel Tulipán*, c/Joan Maragall 28 (☎972 323 251, ❺www.hotel.tulipan.com; ❻) offers good value for money. The understated luxury of the Costa Brava's only five-star hotel, *Hostal de La Gavina* (☎972 321 000, ☏972 321 573, ✉gavina@iponet.es; ❾) sits on a headland in neighbouring S'Agaró, immediately to the north of Sant Feliu. Of the two **campsites**, *Camping Sant Pol*, c/Doctor Fleming (☎972 327 269; March–Nov), is more expensive but only 1km from the seafront.

There are **restaurants** everywhere, although those on the Passeig del Mar are overpriced, certainly if you're eating fish. Probably the best-value *menú del día*, at €9.60, is at *Optimus II*, c/Major 23. Otherwise, try the *Club Nautic*, at the far end of the harbour in among the yachts, less for the food than for the unimpeded sea views; *Amura*, Placeta Sant Pere 7, for fish; or the Art Deco setting of the expensive *El Dorado Petit*, Rambla Vidal 23, for seafood. For tapas, *El Gallo*, down the backstreets at c/Especiers 13, is very popular with locals.

The *modernista*-influenced *Nou Casino de la Constancia*, which faces the water on Passeig dels Guixols, is also worth a visit at some point. It's open daily from 8am to 1am (11pm in winter), and you can get a beer here and watch the old-timers fleecing each other at cards. During July and August there's also live music on the terrace in the evenings.

La Platja d'Aro, Calonge and around

There's another immense concrete concentration a few kilometres to the north, in the area around **LA PLATJA D'ARO** (Playa de Aro), whose only recommendation is its three-kilometre beach and nightlife to equal Lloret's – though as it recommends itself to thousands of others, too, you may as well give it a miss.

Beyond Platja d'Aro, buildings are still going up, and around **Sant Antoni de Calonge** the main road traffic kicks up swirls of concrete dust. Four times daily the Palafrugell bus detours to **CALONGE** itself, just 2km inland but hardly visited by the beach hordes. It has a closely packed medieval centre with a church and castle, and there's a **restaurant**, *Can Muni*, at c/Major 5, whose speciality mussel recipes and €12 *menú del día* are alone worth the trip. The village also has several upmarket *hostales*, though you'd be better off moving back to the coast for the night.

Eleven kilometres west of Calonge, along a minor road (no public transport), the ancient, megalithic stone of **Cova d'en Daina** at **ROMANYÀ DE LA SELVA** is one of the very few surviving examples in Catalunya. If you're driving, the diversion is warranted, though under your own steam getting there involves taking the bus between Sant Feliu and Girona and asking to be put off at the turning outside Llagostera, from where it's a tiring seven-kilometre walk.

Palamós

Heading for Palafrugell, the only other realistic stop is at **PALAMÓS**, a modern-looking resort set around a harbour full of yachts, and last stop on the *cruceros* boat run. The town was originally founded in 1277, and the old part is set apart from the new, on a promontory at the eastern end of the bay. Palamós still retains its fishing industry, the day's catch being auctioned off on the busy quayside in the late afternoon. You can kill time until then on the town's good beach. Don't bother with the small Museu de la Pesca, signposted from various points in the town; you'll spend more time finding it than you will inside.

The **bus station** (for services to and from Sant Feliu, Palafrugell and Girona) is one block back from the **turisme** (daily: June–Sept 8am–9pm; Oct–May 8am–3pm; ☎972 600 550, ✆info@palamos.org) at Passeig de Mar 22.

Palafrugell and around

The small town of **PALAFRUGELL**, 4km inland from a delightful coastline, has managed somehow to remain almost oblivious to its tourist-dominated surroundings. An old town at its liveliest during the morning market, Palafrugell maintains a cluster of old streets and shops around its sixteenth-century church that aren't entirely devoted to the whims and wants of foreigners. The central square, it's true, is ringed with pavement cafés, but you're as likely to fetch up next to a local as to a tourist, and elsewhere in town there are only five or six hotels, and a similar number of restaurants. All of which means that Palafrugell is still a very pleasant place to visit, while it's also a convenient place to base yourself if you're aiming for the nearby coastline – and considerably less expensive than staying at the beach.

The coast, too, makes a marked change from what's gone before. With no true coastal road, this stretch boasts quiet, pine-covered slopes backing the little coves of Calella, Llafranc and Tamariu, all with scintillatingly turquoise waters. The beach development here has been generally mild – low-rise, whitewashed apartments and hotels – and although a fair number of foreign visitors come in season, it's also where many of the better-off Barcelonans have a villa for weekend and August escapes. All this makes for one of the nicest (though hardly undiscovered) stretches of the Costa Brava.

Practicalities

Buses arrive at Palafrugell's SARFA **bus terminal** at c/Torres Jonama 67: the town centre is a ten-minute walk away to the right; you turn left from the terminal and left again at the roundabout to find the **turisme**, c/Carrilet 2 (April–June & Sept Mon–Sat 10am–1pm & 5–8pm, Sun 10am–1pm; July & Aug Mon–Sat 10am–9pm, Sun 10am–1pm; Oct–March Mon–Sat 10am–1pm & 4–7pm; ☎972 300 228, ✉turisme@palafrugell.net), which supplies a map (including a useful plan of the local coastline) and accommodation lists. A second turisme lies in the more central Plaça de l'Església s/n (same times as above; ☎972 611 820, ℗972 611 756), offering the same services. **Drivers** should be warned that finding a metered parking space in the narrow central streets can take hours.

Places to stay can be found at any of the nearby beaches (see "Around Palafrugell" below), though rooms here are expensive and zealously sought after. It's easier and cheaper to stay in Palafrugell itself and get the bus to the beach with everyone else: in summer it's wise to try and book ahead. The best budget choice is *Fonda L'Estrella*, c/de les Quatre Cases 13 (☎972 300 005; ❹), on a little street near the main Plaça Nova. The rooms are simple and cool, arranged around a cloistered courtyard with tables and potted plants. On the other side of the square but not nearly so charming is *Pensió Familiar*, c/Sant Sebastià 29 (mobile ☎689 268 538; ❸), which has clean rooms with separate baths and showers. Further down the same street, the **Hostal Plaja** at c/Sant Sebastià 34 (☎ & ℗972 300 526; ❹) is slightly pricier and more comfortable. It also has a secure garage.

If you stay in Palafrugell, you'll have to **eat** there as well since the last bus back from the beaches is at around 8.30pm. There's not a great deal of choice, but what there is is generally good value. The friendly *La Taverna*, just off c/de la Verge Maria on the narrow c/de Gilalt I Subirós, has a decent €6 *menú del día*, and substantial *platos del día* for much less. Up a few steps from Plaça Nova, *Restaurant l'Arc* is recommended for inexpensive pizzas and other main dishes. Pricier are *La Xicra*, c/de Sant Antoni 17, a very pleasant Catalan restaurant where a meal will run to €18 a head, and the similarly priced and highly praised *Mas Olivier* (☎972 301 041), on Avinguda d'Espanya. The town **market** runs daily (not Mon) from 7am till 1pm; it's on c/Pi i Margall, leading north from Plaça Nova.

Drinking and entertainment revolve entirely around Plaça Nova, where the café-bars are reasonably priced and well placed for idling the time away. In July and August on Tuesday and Thursday nights from around 10pm, there's dancing to a piano-and-drum-machine combo, while Friday nights at the same time see a more traditional *sardana* in the square.

Around Palafrugell

Such is the popularity of the **nearby beaches** that an almost nonstop summer shuttle service runs from the bus terminal at Palafrugell to Calella and then on to Llafranc (8am–9pm: July and Aug every 30min, June & Sept roughly hourly). You might as well get off at Calella, the first stop, since Llafranc is only a twenty-minute coastal walk away and you can get a return bus from there. Other less frequent services run to the more distant beach at Tamariu (June–Sept 3–4 daily), and **inland** to Begur (June–Sept 3–4 daily). Note that all **bus services** are drastically reduced before June and after September when they generally only run on weekdays. However, it's also reasonably inexpensive to make the trip to the coast from Palafrugell by **taxi** – around €6.60 to Calella.

Calella and Llafranc

CALELLA is still (just) a fishing port. Its gloriously rocky coastline is punctuated by several tiny sand beaches which are always packed, but the water is inviting and the village's whitewashed villas and narrow streets are very attractive. If you want to do more than lounge about, a 45-minute walk south leads to the **Castell i Jardins de Cap Roig** (daily: June–Sept 8am–8pm; Oct–May 9am–6pm; €2.10), a cliff-top botanical garden which took fifty years to lay out. **Bars**, **hotels** and **restaurants** line the coastline at Calella; one to look out for is *La Gavina*, c/Gravina 7, where you can enjoy excellent traditional Catalan cooking and a superb selection of fish and seafood every day for around €15.

A gentle, hilly, twenty-minute walk high above the rocks brings you to **LLAFRANC**, tucked into the next bay, with one goodish stretch of beach and a glittering marina. Llafranc seems a little more upmarket, with expensive beachside restaurants and hillside villas glinting in the sun, but essentially the development in both places remains on a human scale. While you're here, try *cremat*, a typical drink of the fishing villages in this region, reputedly brought over by sailors from the Antilles. The concoction contains rum, sugar, lemon peel, coffee grounds and sometimes a cinnamon stick; it will be brought out in an earthenware bowl and you have to set fire to it, occasionally stirring until (after a few minutes) it's ready to drink.

The **bus back to Palafrugell** leaves from the roundabout on the main road outside Llafranc. If you want to stay in either village, pick up a **hotel** list in Palafrugell and ring from there: good places in Calella are the *Hotel Sant Roc* at Plaça Atlàntic 2 (℡972 614 250, ℻972 614 068, ✉santroc@grn.es; ❽), a plush hotel with superb views over the coves, and the friendly *Hotel Port-Bo*, c/August Pi i Sunyer 6 (℡972 614 962, ℻972 614 065; ❼), set a few streets back from the beach. In Llafranc, the *Hotel Casamar*, c/del Nero 3 (℡972 300 104, ℻972 610 651; ❼), is up 113 steps from the seafront, a climb well worth making for the view of the bay from the hotel's balconies. There's probably more chance of a space at one of the villages' **campsites**, which are open only from mid-April to September: *Moby Dick* (℡972 614 307) and the less good *La Siesta* (℡972 615 116) in Calella, or *Camping Kim's* (℡972 301 156) in Llafranc.

Tamariu

TAMARIU, 4km north of Llafranc, is even lovelier, and although it has a smaller beach than either of the other two villages, there are fewer buses and consequently fewer people. You could just about walk through the woods from Llafranc (around ninety minutes), although the last part of the winding road, with its speeding traffic, is rather dangerous. In any case, walk at least as far as the **lighthouse** above Llafranc, with grand views over the beach villages and Palafrugell set in the plain behind. There's a **campsite** in Tamariu, 200m from the beach (☏972 620 422; March–Nov), and several *hostales* and **hotels**, though only the relatively basic *Hotel Sol d'Or*, Reieri 16 (☏972 300 424; ❺) costs less than €45 a night in July and August. The *Hotel Tamariu* (☏972 620 031; March–Nov; ❼) is small and friendly, and has a mid-priced restaurant that faces the sea.

Begur, Aiguablava and other nearby beaches

For something other than just beaches, and for fewer people, head instead for **BEGUR**, about 8km from Palafrugell and slightly inland. It's a crumbling hill town, and the remnants of its seventeenth-century castle command extensive views of the central Costa Brava. The peeling medieval streets harbour a squat church and a couple of empty restaurants – and nothing but peace and quiet in the heat of the day. *Hotel Plaja* (☏972 622 197; ❺), opposite the church, has decent rooms, and serves a remarkably good-value *menú del día*.

With a little energetic walking from Begur, you can reach the beaches at **Aiguafreda** and **Fornells** or, if you have transport, the tranquil hamlets of **SA RIERA** and **SA TUNA** to the north. There are *hostales* at several of these beaches, open only in summer, and Sa Riera also has a selection of bars and restaurants for lunch. Drivers can also detour to **AIGUABLAVA** where the views are even more scenic than from Begur. The magnificent *Parador Nacional de la Costa Brava* (☏972 622 162, 📠972 622 112; ❾) is the best place to soak up the scenery; non-guests can fork out for a couple of drinks at the bar just for the sheer luxury of enjoying the pool and getting a look at the marble and mosaic opulence within.

Inland: La Bisbal, Pals and Torroella

Inland from Palafrugell there are several towns and villages that can provide an afternoon's escape from the beaches. A couple would even serve as overnight stops if you prefer tranquil medieval streets to the teeming coastal promenades.

La Bisbal and around

LA BISBAL, 12km northwest of Palafrugell and on the bus route to Girona, is a medieval market town in an attractive river setting. Since the seventeenth century, La Bisbal has specialized in the production of **ceramics**, and pottery shops line the main road through town, where – with a bit of browsing – you can pick up some terrific local pieces. Ceramics apart, La Bisbal makes a pleasant stop anyway, as its handsome old centre retains many impressive mansions, the architectural remnants of a once thriving Jewish quarter and parts of a medieval castle built for the bishops of Girona. If you fancy a luxurious **stay** or **meal** locally, the newly opened *Hotel Castell d'Empordà* (☏972 646 254, 📠972 645 550, 🌐www.castelldemporda.com; ❾), perched atop a hill 3km north of the town in an 800-year-old castle that once belonged to one of Columbus's captains, is a most rewarding detour.

From La Bisbal, a couple of tiny medieval villages to the northeast – now undergoing restoration work – are worth visiting, though you'll need your own transport. At **ULLASTRET** there was an Iberian settlement, whose ruins can be seen a little way outside the village. Nearby **PERATALLADA** is especially beautiful, with a ruined castle whose origins have been dated back to pre-Roman times, a fortified church and a number of houses embellished with coats of arms and arches. There's good local food and wine at *Can Nau*, c/d'en Bas 12 (closed Wed).

Pals

The bus journey north to L'Escala can be broken 8km north of Palafrugell at **PALS**. This fortified medieval village was long neglected until it recently received rather an alarming new sheen at the hands of enthusiastic restorers. It's inevitably attracting an increasing number of day-trippers, and ceramic and pottery shops are proliferating in the old quarter, whose buildings date largely from the fourteenth century. However, the commercialization can't detract from the beauty of Pals's quiet hilltop setting: golden-brown buildings cluster around a stark tower, all that remains of the town's Romanesque castle. Below is the beautifully vaulted Gothic parish church, while you could also look into the town **museum** (June–Sept Mon–Sat 10am–2pm & 4–8pm, Sun 10am–2pm; Oct–May opening hours vary; €1.80), an eclectic collection housed in a restored mansion. Exhibits here include odds and ends retrieved from an English warship sunk in the siege of Roses in the 1808 War of Independence, and there's a steady turnover of art exhibitions, too.

Pals has a regular programme of dances and concerts throughout the summer, including a **wine festival** in mid-August, for which you might be tempted to stay. There are a couple of newish hotels, but the best budget **accommodation** is at the *Hostal Barris* at c/Enginyer Algarra 51 (℡972 636 702; ❺) in the nondescript new quarter of town, which also does meals. **Buses** stop right in front of the post office, while the **turisme** (June & Sept Mon–Sat 10am–2pm & 5–8pm; July & Aug daily 9am–2pm & 3–8pm; ℡972 667 857) is at c/Aniceta Figueres 6.

Torroella de Montgrí and L'Estartit

TORROELLA DE MONTGRÍ, 9km beyond Pals on the Ter River, was once an important medieval port but today has been left high and dry by a receding Mediterranean. It now stands 5km inland, beneath the shell of a huge, battlemented thirteenth-century castle (a stiff thirty-minute walk away), and remains distinctly medieval in appearance with its narrow streets, fine mansions and fourteenth-century parish church. Oddly, only a couple of coachloads of tourists a day come to look round, and hardly anyone stays. If you do decide to **stay**, the *Fonda Mitja*, at c/d'Església 10 (℡972 758 003; ❸ half board, ❹ full board), just off the arcaded Plaça de la Vila, is excellent, and there are several other *hostales* scattered about town; for a list head over to the **turisme** (July & Aug Mon–Fri 9am–1pm & 4–8pm; ℡972 758 300, ℻972 751 749) at Avgda. Lluis Companys 51. The town is probably best known for its annual **classical music festival**, held over July and August in the main square and church. Advance bookings can be made from early June at the Festival Internacional de Música, Apt 70, Codina 28 (℡972 760 605, ℻972 760 648, ⓦwww.ddgi.es/tdm/fimtdm).

The nearest beach is 6km to the east at **L'ESTARTIT**, a typical Costa Brava resort, though one with a quieter, more family-oriented atmosphere than many. There's a wide, though not particularly stunning, beach, and boat services to the nearby **Illes Medes**, Catalunya's only offshore islands. These form a protected nature reserve, hosting the most important colony of herring gulls in the Mediterranean, numbering some 8000 pairs. There are hourly **buses** from Torroella to L'Estartit.

L'Escala and Empúries

From either Palafrugell or Figueres you're only 45 minutes by bus from **L'ESCALA**, a small holiday resort at the southern end of the Golf de Roses. On nothing like the same scale as the resorts to the south, it caters mainly for local tourists, which means that the steeply sloping streets and rocky coastline are genuinely appealing. L'Escala's proximity to the archeological site of **Empúries** (Ampurias), which lies just a couple of kilometres out of town, is a further attraction. One of Spain's most interesting sites, Empúries's fascination derives from the fact that it was occupied continuously for nearly 1500 years. You can see the ruins in a leisurely afternoon, spending the rest of your time either on the crowded little sandy **beach** in L'Escala or on the more pleasant duned stretch in front of the ruins. The wooded shores around here hide a series of lovely cove beaches with terrific, shallow water and soft sand. At weekends the woods are full of picnicking families, setting up tables, fridges and gas stoves from the backs of their cars. L'Escala is also widely known for its canning factories where Catalunya's best **anchovies** are packaged. You can sample them in any bar or restaurant, or buy small jars to take home from shops around town.

L'Escala practicalities

Buses all stop on Avinguda Girona, just down the road from the **turisme** at Plaça de las Escoles 1 (July & Aug Mon–Sat 9am–8.30pm, Sun 10am–1pm; Sept–June Mon–Sat 9am–1pm & 4–7pm, Sun 10am–1pm; ☎972 770 603, ⓦwww.lescala.org). Here, you can pick up a map, local bus timetables – for Figueres, Palafrugell, Girona and Barcelona – and an up-to-date list of hotels. Drivers can find **free parking** at the football stadium on Cami Ample, around the corner from the bus stop, near the campsite.

Accommodation

L'Escala usually has plenty of **rooms** available, mostly in the streets sloping back from the sea, around the central Plaça Victor Català. Of these streets, c/de Gràcia has the most choice. There are **campsites** at each of the little bays that surround L'Escala, or – in the centre of town – at *Cami Ample*, c/Cami Ample 21 (☎972 770 084; mid-April to Sept), which is down the hill and right from the bus stop.

Hotel Ampurias, La Platja Portitxol ☎ & ⓕ 972 770 207. Located practically on the beach near the archeological sites. Open mid-May to Sept. ❼
Hostal Garbi, c/Sta. Maxima 7 ☎ & ⓕ972 770 165. Very friendly *hostal* with renovated rooms in a lovely old building near the seafront. Closed Feb. ❺
Hotel Mediterrà, c/Riera 22–24 ☎972 770 028, ⓕ972 774 593. Relaxed and comfortable hotel;

prices drop outside July and Aug. ❹
Hostal Torrent, c/Riera 28 ☎972 770 278. Friendly, clean and good value. Open July–Sept only. ❸
Hotel Voramar, Pg. Lluis Albert 2 ☎972 770 108, ⓕ972 770 377. Comfortable hotel with good sea views from most rooms. Open April–Dec. ❼

Eating, drinking and entertainment

The best deals for food are in the **restaurants** attached to the small hotels and *hostales*. Both the *Poch* and *Mediterrà* have decent menus, while the restaurant at the *Hostal Garbi*, just back from the beach at c/Sant Maxima 7, is more formal, but still affordable. If you're missing tapas, you can get a wide choice at the *Taberna Gallego*, c/Gràcia 77.

Otherwise, there are sea views with the food at any of the bars and restaurants overlooking the town beach, but bear in mind that you'll often pay through the nose for the privilege, particularly if you occupy one of the appealing cliff-top seats. As for **entertainments** other than beach-going, a *sardana* (Catalan folk dance) is held on the seafront every Wednesday night in July and August.

Empúries: the site

Empúries was the ancient Greek *Emporion* (literally "Trading Station"), founded in 550 BC by merchants who, for three centuries, conducted a vigorous trade throughout the Mediterranean. In the early third century BC, their settlement was taken by Scipio, and a Roman city – more splendid than the Greek, with an amphitheatre, fine villas and a broad marketplace – grew up above the old Greek town. The Romans were replaced in turn by the Visigoths, who built several basilicas, and *Emporion* disappears from the records only in the ninth century when, it is assumed, it was wrecked by either Saracen or Norman pirates.

The **site** (June–Sept Tues–Sun 10am–8pm; Oct–May 10am–6pm; €2.40) lies behind a sandy bay about 2km north of L'Escala. The remains of the original **Greek colony**, destroyed by a Frankish raid in the third century AD – at which stage all moved to the Roman city – occupy the lower part of the site. Among the ruins of several temples, to the left on raised ground is one dedicated to Asklepios, the Greek healing god whose cult was centred on Epidavros and the island of Kos. The temple is marked by a replica of a fine third-century BC statue of the god, the original of which (along with many finds from

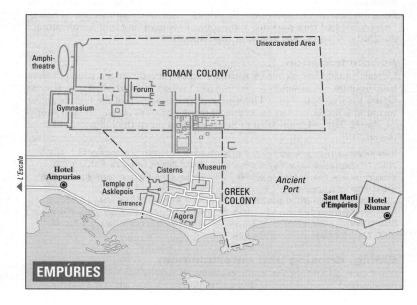

EMPÚRIES

the site) is in the Museu Arqueològic in Barcelona. Nearby are several large cisterns: *Emporion* had no aqueduct so water was stored here, to be filtered and purified and then supplied to the town by means of long pipes, one of which has been reconstructed. Remains of the town gate, the **agora** (or marketplace, in the centre) and several streets can easily be made out, along with a mass of house foundations, some with mosaics, and the ruins of Visigoth basilicas. A small **museum** (€1.80) stands above, with helpful models and diagrams of the excavations as well as some of the lesser finds and an excellent audiovisual display giving a brief history of the settlement. Beyond this stretches the vast but only partially excavated **Roman town**. Here, two luxurious villas have been uncovered, and you can see their entrance halls, porticoed gardens and magnificent mosaic floors. Further on are the remains of the **forum**, **amphitheatre** and outer walls.

Sant Marti d'Empúries

A short walk along the shore from the site brings you to the tiny walled hamlet of **SANT MARTI D'EMPÚRIES**. What was once a lovely, decaying place has been entirely taken over by visiting tourists who descend upon the shaded bar-restaurants in the square for lengthy lunches. Though it's still undeniably pretty, there are usually too many people around for comfort; generally, it's less oppressive in the evenings, when Sant Marti can still be perfect for a drink amid the light-strung trees. From the walls outside the village you can see the whole of the Golf de Roses, with kilometre after kilometre of beach stretching right the way round to Roses itself, glinting in the distance. The only place to stay is *Hotel Riomar* (☎972 770 362, ℉972 770 358; May–Sept; ❼ half board), next to the beach.

Figueres and around

The northernmost resorts of the Costa Brava are reached via **FIGUERES**, a provincial town with a population of some 30,000. Although it's the capital of Alt Empordà – the upper part of the massive alluvial plain formed by the Muga and Fluvià rivers – it would pass almost unnoticed were it not for the **Museu Dalí**, installed by Salvador Dalí in a building as surreal as the exhibits within. As it is, Figueres itself tends to be overshadowed by the museum, which is the only reason most people come here. Stay longer and you'll find a pleasing town with a lively central *rambla* and a reasonable amount of cheap food and accommodation. It's also a decent starting point for excursions into the little-visited **Serra d'Albera mountains** to the north, which form part of the border with France.

Arrival, information and accommodation

Arriving at the **train station**, you reach the centre of town by simply following the "Museu Dalí" signs. The **bus station** is just a couple of minutes' walk up on the left, at the top of Plaça Estació above the train station. There's a small **tourist information booth** just outside the bus station (July–Sept Mon–Sat 9.30am–1pm & 4–7pm), another on the Plaça de Museu Dalí (same hours) and a full-blown **turisme** at the other end of town, on Plaça del Sol, in front of the post office (Easter–June & Oct Mon–Fri 8.30am–3pm & 4.30–8pm, Sat 9.30am–1.30pm & 3.30–6.30pm; July–Sept Mon–Sat 8.30am–8.30pm, Sun

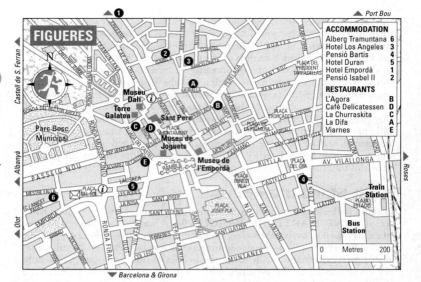

9am–3pm; Nov–Easter Mon–Fri 8.30am–3pm; Ⓦ www.figueres.org). All three dish out a town map, handy hotel lists, and timetables for all onward transport. There's an **Internet café**, *Pizz@fono*, near the bus station at c/Antonio 27 (June–Aug daily 9.30am–1pm & 4–11pm; Sept–May Tues–Sun 4–11pm; €3 per hour, first 10min free).

Accommodation

There's a good choice of **places to stay**, ranging from the most basic to the more upmarket, though many of the better hotels and *hostales* lie on the main roads out of town. The best-value budget accommodation is *Pensió Bartis*, c/Méndez Núñez 2 (Ⓣ972 501 473; ❷), not far from the train and bus stations; if you want to be more central, *Pensió Isabel II*, c/Isabel II 16 (Ⓣ972 504 735; ❸) and the friendly *Hotel Los Angeles*, c/Barceloneta 10 (Ⓣ972 510 661, Ⓔ hangeles@olemail.com; ❺) are both handy for the museums. For more comfort, try the old-style *Hotel Duran*, c/Lasauca 5 (Ⓣ972 501 250, Ⓕ972 502 609; ❼), just off La Rambla, or the plush *Hotel Empordà*, CN-II s/n (Ⓣ972 500 562, Ⓕ972 509 358, Ⓦ www.hotelemporda.com; ❼) on the main road out of town, which is famous locally for its excellent restaurant. There's a good **youth hostel** off the Plaça del Sol, *Alberg Tramuntana*, c/Anicet Pagès 2 (Ⓣ972 501 213; closed Sept; ❶) and a clean, good-value **campsite**, *Pous* (Ⓣ972 675 496; open April–Oct), 2km out on the road to France.

The Museu Dalí

The **Museu Dalí** (July–Sept daily 9am–7.45pm, plus 10.30pm–12.30am in Aug; Oct–June Tues–Sun 10.30am–5.45pm; €7.20; Ⓦ www.dali-estate.org), the most visited museum in Spain after the Prado and Bilbao's Guggenheim, is a real treat. Dalí was born in Figueres in 1904 and gave his first exhibition here when he was just fourteen. In 1974, in a reconstruction of the town's old municipal theatre, the artist inaugurated his Museu Dalí, which he then set about fashioning into an inspired repository for some of his most bizarre works.

△ Dalí museum, Figueres

Dalí: whose life is it anyway?

Controversy surrounds **Salvador Dalí's** final years, with some observers believing that he didn't so much choose to live as a recluse as find himself imprisoned by his three guardians. Dalí suffered severe burns in a fire at his house in Púbol (see p.787) in 1984, after which he moved into the Torre Galatea in Figueres, the tower adjacent to the museum. Fitted with a pacemaker and suffering psychological problems, Dalí became increasingly depressed, and several Spanish government officals and friends fear that, in his senile condition, he was being manipulated. In particular, it's alleged that he was made to sign blank canvases – and this has inevitably led to the questioning of the authenticity of some of his later works. Since the mid-1980s, there has been a series of trials in the US based on charges that various individuals have exploited bogus prints and lithographs. In 1990, two Americans, William Mett and Marvin Wiseman, were found guilty of art fraud – in particular of promoting spurious Dalí reproductions – and were fined nearly $2 million and sentenced to three years in prison.

The divison of his legacy of (genuine or otherwise) paintings was made yet more complicated by the fact that Dalí, by the terms of his last will made in 1982, left his entire estate, valued at $130 million, to the Spanish state, with the works of art to be divided between Madrid and Figueres. The Catalan art world was outraged, and battled successfully to keep the canvases from being removed – plans are currently under way to exhibit over a hundred of the paintings in an as yet undecided location in Catalunya.

Having moved back to Figueres at the end of his life, Dalí died here on January 23, 1989; his body now lies behind a simple granite slab inside the museum. Although it does contain paintings (some by other artists) and sculpture, the thematically arranged display is not a collection of Dalí's "greatest hits" – those are scattered far and wide. Nonetheless, what you do get beggars description and is not to be missed.

The very building (signposted from just about everywhere, on Plaça Gala i Salvador Dalí, a couple of minutes' walk off the *rambla*) is an exhibit in itself, as it was designed to be. Topped by a huge metallic dome and decorated with luminous egg shapes, it gets even crazier inside. Here, the walls of the circular central well are adorned with stylized figures preparing to dive from the heights, while you can water the snail-infested occupants of a steamy Cadillac by feeding it with coins. There's also a soaring totem pole of car tyres topped with a boat and an umbrella. Climb inside to the main building and one of the rooms contains an unnerving portrait of Mae West, viewed by peering through a mirror at giant nostrils, red lips and hanging tresses. Other galleries on various levels contain a complete life-sized orchestra, skeletal figures, adapted furniture (a bed with fish tails), sculpture and ranks of surreal paintings.

The rest of town

After the museum, the main sight in town is the huge eighteenth-century **Castell de Sant Ferran** (daily: June–Sept 10.30am–7pm; Oct–May 10.30am–2pm; free), 1km northwest of the centre – follow Pujada del Castell from just beyond the Dalí museum, going straight on at the roundabout along c/Al Castell de Sant Ferran. This was the last bastion of the Republicans in the Civil War, when the town became their capital after the fall of Barcelona. Earlier in the war, it had been used as a barracks for newly arrived members of the International Brigade before they moved on to Barcelona and the front.

The castle is still in use by the military, but the circuit around the outside of the star-shaped walls makes a good walk.

Back in the centre, pavement cafés line the *rambla*, and you can browse around the art galleries and gift shops in the streets and squares surrounding the church of Sant Pere. There are two more museums, too. The **Museu de l'Empordà** at Rambla 2 (Tues–Sat 11am–7pm, Sun 10am–2pm; €1.80), has some local Roman finds and work by local artists, and the **Museu de Joguets** (June–Sept Mon–Sat 10am–1pm & 4–7pm, Sun 11am–1.30pm & 5–7.30pm; Oct–May closed Mon & Sun pm; €3.90) further up the *rambla* on the same side, is a toy museum with over 3000 exhibits from all over Catalunya. The statue at the bottom of the *rambla* is a monument to Narcis Monturiol, a local who distinguished himself by inventing the submarine.

Eating and drinking

A gaggle of tourist **restaurants** cram into the narrow streets around the Dalí museum, particularly along c/Jonquera. More stylish, but still reasonably priced, is *L'Agora* in the old casino building, on the corner of c/Ample and c/Peralada, a spacious, modern bar-restaurant with excellent *menús* (€8.10–16.20) including Catalan specialities, and *La Churraskita* at c/Magre 5, serving imaginative Argentinian and Italian dishes for above €15 a head. *La Difa*, c/Muralla 17 (closed Sun, Mon evening & Sat lunch) is slightly pricier but has vegetarian main courses, while *Viernes*, Pujada del Castell 23, serves up generous portions of traditional Spanish fare at around €14 a time. If money's no object, head for the *Hotel Duran*, where they serve generous regional dishes with a modern touch. The *rambla* has several popular pavement **cafés**, though the ones on Plaça de l'Ajuntament and Plaça Pius XII, near the Dalí museum, are quieter and less cramped; *Café Dalicatessen* at c/Sant Pere 17–19 offers good juices, pots of Earl Grey tea and fresh croissants. Eating aside, Figueres is generally fairly comatose **at night** with the exception of an odd hotchpotch of new bars on Plaça del Sol opposite the turisme: even so, most weekend evenings find traffic jams on the road to Roses as everyone heads out to the coast.

North of Figueres: the Serra d'Albera mountains

The most interesting inland outings **west from Figueres** visit large villages to either side of the forest-fringed **Pantà (Reservoir) de Boadella**, a focus for local water-sports enthusiasts. During World War II the region **north of Figueres** was so deserted that there were no Guardia Civil stationed between the Castell de Requesens and Portbou, which made the eastern Serra d'Albera a favoured escape route from France. Of late, numbers of foreigners – mainly Dutch and German – have moved in to convert the crumbling farms to second homes, and Catalan trippers scour the countryside at weekends, replenishing their cellars at the many wineries that dot the area.

Sant Llorenç de la Muga

There's a single midday bus from Figueres to **SANT LLORENÇ DE LA MUGA**; driving yourself, follow signs out of town for the N-11 to La Jonquera, and then keep an eye out for the poorly marked turning for Llers, and thence to Sant Llorenç itself, about 17km west of the town. This large, fortified village, nestled in greenery along the Riu Muga, makes an excellent excursion; it's linked to Maçanet de Cabrenys (see below) by a marked but rough track (hikers or 4WD only) skirting wetlands on the reservoir's west shore. The sole **eatery** is *Sa Muga* on the central *rambla*, or you can have a drink at either *El Lluro* on Plaça Baixa or the *Societat La Fraternitat* on the *rambla*. As yet there's no place to **stay** in the old quarter, though you'll find a **campsite**, *La Fradera* (☎972 542 054), 1.5km west of the village, and a **casa rural**, *Can Carreras* (☎972 569 199; ❺), 4km away overlooking the river.

Darnius and Maçanet de Cabrenys

North of the Pantà de Boadella – accessible from the Muga valley by a road below the dam, or directly off the N11 – lies **DARNIUS**, which has regular bus links to Figueres. It's not exactly a thriving place and if you're going to **stay** nearby, far better to do so at *La Central* (☎972 535 053, ℱ972 550 431, ⓦwww.lacentral.com; ❹–❼), a *modernista* chalet set in idyllic surroundings 6km southwest along a well-marked track. The in-house **restaurant** is renowned for its seafood; budget €24 per head.

Culture buffs may prefer to stay on the same bus or point their car/bicycle towards livelier and more atmospheric **MAÇANET (MASSANET) DE CABRENYS** 26km from Figueres. Cars (and the **bus**) stop south of this densely packed, oval-shaped medieval ensemble. There are two recommended places to **stay** and **eat**: *Hostal La Quadra* at the northwest edge of town (☎972 544 032; ❸), with a vaulted cellar restaurant serving regional specialities (closed Tues except July–Sept); and the *Hotel Pirineos* (☎972 544 000, ℱ972 544 000; ❺), set in a 400-year-old baronial mansion in the centre.

The Espolla region

Northeast of Figueres, a daily bus heads for **ESPOLLA**, which boasts at least ten prehistoric sites in the immediate area. Easiest to find is the **Dolmen de la Cabana Arqueta**, nearly five thousand years old; from Espolla take the **Sant Climent** road, and at the rising bend 1km beyond the village turn down the farm track to the right – the dolmen is ten minutes' walk on. The most important, however, is the **Dolmen del Barranc**, the only carved tomb yet found in the area; it lies 3km from the village off the track leading north to the Col de Banyuls.

Espolla itself is a typical Alt Empordà village, its shuttered houses crammed into a labyrinth of streets that come to life each year with the flurry of the grape harvest. The only **accommodation** here is the friendly, family-run *La Manela*, at Plaça del Carmé 7 (☎972 563 065; ❸), which also cooks good, inexpensive meals. It's always fully booked during July and August. Four kilometres south there's more hearty country fare at *Ca La Maria* (closed Mon night, Tues & Sun), a big barn of a place (it was previously a wine warehouse) in the centre of **MOLLET DE PERALADA** – it's an Alt Empordà institution and highly recommended.

The Golf de Roses

The **Golf de Roses** stretches between L'Escala and Roses, a wide bay backed for the most part by flat, rural land, well watered by the Muga and Fluvià rivers. Left to its own quiet devices for centuries, this coast is distinct from the otherwise rocky and touristy Costa Brava, and has really only suffered the attention of the developers in towns at either end of the bay, most notably in the few kilometres between the marina-cum-resort of Ampuriabrava and Roses.

Probably the most you'll do is cross the attractive farmlands on your way to or from Figueres, but there are a couple of specific targets if you want to avoid the beach for a while, as well as the excellent beach itself at the resort of Roses.

Parc Natural dels Aiguamolls de l'Empordà

Halfway around the bay in two parcels of land on either side of the Ampuriabrava is one of Spain's more accessible nature reserves, the **PARC NATURAL DELS AIGUAMOLLS DE L'EMPORDÀ** (open daily; free), an important wetland reserve created by the Catalan government in 1983 to save what remained of the Empordà marshland, which once covered the entire plain here, but has gradually disappeared over the centuries as a result of agricultural developments and cattle-raising. Relying heavily on the natural history students of Barcelona University and volunteers, the park looks a little raw in places, but attracts a wonderful selection of birds to both its coastal terrain and the paddy fields typical of the area. There are several easy paths around lagoons and marshes, and hides have been created along the way: morning and early evening are the best times for bird-watching in the marshes and you'll see the largest number of species during the migration periods (March–May & Aug–Oct). You'll almost certainly see marsh harriers and various waterfowl, and might spot bee-eaters, kingfishers and the rare glossy ibis.

Without your own transport, access is by one of the numerous daily **buses** of the SARFA company plying the Figueres–Roses road; get off the bus at Castelló d'Empúries and take the turning south in the direction of Sant Pere Pescador. After about 4km, you'll see a sign on the left pointing the way to the **visitors' centre** at El Cortalet (daily: March–Sept 9.30am–2pm & 4.30–7pm; Oct–Feb 9.30am–2pm & 3.30–6pm; ☎972 454 222), where you can pick up a brochure marking recommended routes. You can cut out the walk to the centre by using the twice-daily Roses–Girona bus via Sant Pere Pescador; buses en route from Figueres to Palafrugell also stop at Sant Pere Pescador. To get the most out of the park, take a pair of binoculars – and in summer and autumn you'll need mosquito repellent. The only **camping** allowed within the park is at either the massive *Nàutic Almatà* (☎972 454 477, ⓦ www.almata.com; mid-May to Sept), or the smaller *La Laguna* (☎972 450 553, ⓦ www.campinglaguna.com; April–Oct).

Sant Pere Pescador

The nearest village to the park is **SANT PERE PESCADOR**, 3km south of the information centre. The village is easily reached by bus from Figueres and there are also services from Palafrugell, L'Escala and Girona. Despite being a drab place in the middle of nowhere, Sant Pere is relatively developed, and this does at least mean that there's plenty of choice if you need to spend the night here: there are half a dozen *hostales* and hotels (most open only June–Sept), and several bars and restaurants. There's also a bike rental shop.

Castelló d'Empúries

The delightful small town of **CASTELLÓ D'EMPÚRIES**, halfway between Roses and Figueres, makes a much more attractive base for the park – and indeed is worth a stop in passing anyway. A five-minute walk from the outskirts where the bus halts (and where cars should be parked), transports you into a little medieval conglomeration that's lost little of its genteel charm despite being so close to the beach-bound hordes. Formerly the capital of the counts of Empúries, the town's narrow alleys and streets conceal some fine preserved buildings, a medieval bridge, and a thirteenth-century battlemented church, **Santa María**, whose ornate doorway alone is reward enough for the trip.

The nature reserve lies around 5km south, reached on the minor road to Sant Pere Pescador, and the beach at Roses is also close by – only fifteen minutes away by bus. There are several **places to stay** and while prices are a little higher here than usual, it's a price worth paying for the peace and quiet when the day-trippers have all gone home. There are two places next to each other south of the centre at the corner of Avgda. Generalitat and c/Santa Clara, near where the bus stops, which are much nicer than their position suggests. The *Hostal Ca L'Anton* (☎972 250 509; ❹) has an attached restaurant with a fine *menú* and plenty of local cuisine, while the adjacent *Pensió Serratosa* (☎972 250 508; ❹) is better appointed and better value, with off-street parking and its own *menjador*. At the heart of the old quarter, the *Hotel Canet* (☎972 250 340, ℉972 250 607, ⓦwww.hotelcanet.com; ❺) enjoys a fine position at Plaça Joc de la Pilota 2, with a good terrace restaurant.

Finally there are a couple of **cases rurals** in the area worth considering. *La Caputxeta* is just across the river from Castelló (☎972 250 310 or 972 250 646; ❹), and is owned by a French-speaking sculptor couple who run art seminars but welcome all-comers; there's also a self-catering kitchen. The other, in the remoter village of **SIURANA D'EMPORDÀ** between Figueres and Sant Pere Pescador, is *El Molí* (☎972 525 139, ℮casaelmoli@teleline.es; ❺), an award-winning premises set amongst vast gardens.

Roses

ROSES itself enjoys a brilliant situation, beneath medieval fortress walls at the head of the grand, sweeping bay. It's a site that's been inhabited for over three thousand years – the Greeks called the place *Rhoda*, when they set up a trading colony around the excellent natural harbour in the ninth century BC – but apart from the castle, the extensive ruined citadel and the surviving sections of the city wall, there's little in present-day Roses to hint at its long history. Instead, the town trades exclusively on its four kilometres of sandy beach, which have fostered a large and popular water-sports industry. Roses is a full-blown package resort, with the usual supermarkets, discos and English breakfasts; if you're staying, worthwhile escapes include the bus ride across the plain to more attractive Cadaqués (see below), which gives superb views back over the resort and bay, or the **boat excursions** around the cape to Cadaqués or out to the Illes Medes.

Buses stop at the corner of c/Gran Vía Pau Casals and c/Riera Ginjolas. There's a **turisme** (daily: June–Sept 9am–9pm; Oct–May 9am–6pm; ☎972 257 331, ℮otroses@ddgi.es) on the seafront promenade, which should be able to help if you show up in mid-season without an **accommodation** reservation. At slower times you could try *Hotel Univers*, c/Josep Pla (☎972 256 150, ℉972 150 961; ❼). There are also several huge **campsites** on the road between Roses and Figueres.

Cadaqués and around

CADAQUÉS is a far more pleasant place to stay, reached only by the winding road over the hills from either Roses or Port de la Selva and consequently retaining an air of isolation. With box-like, whitewashed houses lining narrow, hilly streets, a tree-lined promenade and craggy headlands on either side of a harbour that is still a working fishing port, it's genuinely picturesque. Already by the 1920s and 1930s the place had begun to attract the likes of Picasso, Man Ray, Lorca, Buñuel, Thomas Mann and Einstein; Norman Lewis used it as the partial basis for his fictional village Farol in *Voices of the Old Sea* (see "Books", p.1061). But Cadaqués really "arrived" as an **artistic-literary colony** after World War II when Surrealist painter Salvador Dalí and his wife Gala settled at nearby Port Lligat, attracting for some years a floating bohemian community. Post-"discovery" Cadaqués no longer gets the sort of hippie crowd that once flocked here in the 1960s and 1970s, and is now a bit too hedonistic and trendy for its own good, with beautiful people all around and more than a few Mercedes. Nonetheless, if you can bear the dense company and the high prices, you'll probably have fun.

Local **beaches** are all tiny and pebbly, but there are some enjoyable walks around the harbour and nearby coves, while the town itself makes for an interesting stroll, clambering around the streets below the church. The number of private art galleries here has mushroomed since the moneyed set began stopping by, and a couple of good museums soak up browsers, too. The **Museu Perrot-Moore**, in the middle of town at c/Vigilant 1 (daily 10.30am–1.30pm & 5–9pm; €4.20), has paintings, drawings and graphics by Dalí and Picasso, although it is temporarily closed while a forgery scandal is being investigated, and the **Museu Municipal d'Art** on c/Monturiol 15 (daily 10am–1.30pm & 4–8pm; €3.60) features work by local artists whose efforts are mostly inspired by the spectacular local coastline.

Practicalities

Buses arrive at the little SARFA bus office on c/Sant Vicens, on the edge of town. It's less than ten minutes from here, following c/Unió and c/Vigilant, to the central beachside Plaça Frederic Rahola. Just off the square, the **turisme** is at c/des Cotxe 2 (July–Sept Mon–Sat 10am–2pm & 4–9pm, Sun 10.30am–1pm; Oct–June Mon–Sat 10am–2pm & 4–7pm, closed Wed pm; ☎972 258 315).

Finding **rooms** is likely to be a big problem unless you're here outside peak season: a town plan posted at the bus stop marks all the possibilities. The cheapest rooms are at one of three *fondas* scattered about the town: *Fonda Vehí*, c/de l'Església 5 (☎972 258 470; ❹), has the best position, just below the church, but is open only from June to September. Just back from the main square, very close to the seafront, the *Hostal Marina* (☎972 258 199; ❺) and *Hostal Cristina* (☎972 258 138; ❺), the latter with parking facilities, are the next step up – similarly priced, with more expensive en-suite rooms, too, and discounts out of season. *Hotel Ubaldo*, on the way into town from the bus stop at c/Unió 13 (☎972 258 125, ☏972 258 324; ❻), is quite good value, with all rooms en suite, while the *Hotel Playa Sol* at c/Pianc 3 (☎972 258 100, ☏972 258 054, ✉playasol@playasol.com; ❾) is sheer seafront luxury with prices to match. There's a noisy, though well-equipped **campsite** (☎972 258 126; mid-April to late-Sept) on the road to Port Lligat, a steep 1km out of town; it also rents out cabins for around €30 a double.

The harbourside esplanade is lined with pizzerias and **restaurants**, all fairly indistinguishable. If you're not sick of it yet, Cadaqués is a nice place to sit outside and dive into a paella, which most places offer as part of a *menú del día*. Elsewhere, the restaurant attached to the *Fonda Vehí* has seafood *menús* at €9.60–10.80 and a seaview terrace; *El Pescador*, 150m off to the right as you face the water, has dining both inside and out and offers an authentic Catalan paella (with seafood, sausage and spare ribs), plus *menús* at €12.60; or there's *Casa Anita* on c/Miquel Rosells, a long-running institution where queues form early in the evening during high season. Calle Miquell Rosells, one block inland from the esplanade, is also home to most of Cadaqués' **nightlife**.

Around Cadaqués: the Casa-Museu Salvador Dalí

A well-signposted twenty-minute walk north of Cadaqués is the tiny harbour of **PORT LLIGAT**, former home of Salvador Dalí. The artist lived here for much of his childhood and youth, and later with his wife and muse, Gala, having converted a series of waterside fishermen's cottages into a sumptuous home that has all the quirks you would expect of the couple, such as speckled rooftop eggs and a giant fish painted on the ground outside. The house is now open to the public as the **Casa-Museu Salvador Dalí** (mid-March to mid-June Tues–Sun 10.30am–6pm; mid-June to mid-Sept daily 10.30am–9pm; mid-Sept to early Jan Tues–Sun 10.30am–6pm; €7.80; ☎972 251 015), and although there's not much in the way of artworks, it's worth the visit to see firsthand how the bizarre couple lived until Gala's death in 1982, after which Dalí moved to Figueres. Visitor numbers are strictly controlled and you have to book a visit by ringing the museum beforehand.

Tours take in most of the house, and include Dalí's studio, the exotically draped model's room, the couple's master bedroom and bathroom and, perhaps best of all, the oval-shaped sitting room that Dalí designed for Gala, which, apparently by accident, boasts stunning acoustics. Upstairs you can see the garden and swimming pool where the couple entertained guests – they didn't like too many strangers trooping through their living quarters. The phallic swimming pool and its various decorative features, including a giant snake and a stuffed lion, are a treat.

El Port de la Selva and Sant Pere de Rodes

If you miss the single daily bus connection along the coast north of Cadaqués you'll have to backtrack to Figueres for onward transport. Alternatively, you can attempt the relatively easy 13-kilometre walk/hitch across the base of the **Cap de Creus**, from Cadaqués to **EL PORT DE LA SELVA**, a fishing port set on the eastern side of a large bay. Primarily a locals' family resort, this is also the last place, heading north, that you'll see other foreigners (mostly Germans) in any numbers. It's not especially picturesque (though rather more so than neighbouring Llança), and rather dull by night, but makes a good base for visiting Sant Pere de Rodes, the most important monastery in the region.

If you need to **stay** there are a few choices: the *Pensió Solisombra*, c/Nou 5 (☎972 387 060; ❺, half board – obligatory in July & August – ❻); the *Hostal La Tina*, c/Major 15 (☎972 387 149, ⓦwww.gna.es/hostallatina/; ❼), is comfortable and central; or there's the more expensive *Hotel Porto Cristo*, c/Major 59 (☎972 387 062; ❾), currently being upgraded to four stars, which is expensive in August (❾, but drops drastically the rest of the year (❼), and has an attached diving centre (March–Dec) – one of the most active on the Costa

Brava. You may as well take up any offers of half board, as there are few recommendable independent eateries in the resort. There are also a few **campsites** within 2km of the beach, the best being *Port de la Vall*, Ctra. de Llanca km 6 (T972 387 186, F972 387 186; Easter-Sept) and *Port de la Selva*, Ctra. Cadaques km 1 (T972 387 287, F972 387 548; June-Sept).

Sant Pere de Rodes

Just below the 670-metre-high summit of the Serra de Roda stands the Benedictine monastery of **Sant Pere de Rodes** (Tues-Sun June-Sept 10am-8pm; Oct-May 10am-5.30pm; €3.60, plus €1.20 per car). It's 8km up the paved **road** from El Port, via Selva de Mar; approaching **by foot**, use the marked trail (90min) through the Vall de Santa Creu, which begins at Molí de la Vall.

The monastery was one of the many religious institutions founded in this area after the departure of the Moors. The first written record dates back to 879, and in 934 the monastery became independent, answerable only to Rome: in these early years, and thanks especially to the Roman connection, the monks became tremendously rich and powerful. As the monastery was enlarged it was also fortified against attack, starting a period of splendour that lasted four hundred years before terminal decline set in. Many fine treasures were looted when it was finally abandoned in 1789, and it was also pillaged by the French during the Peninsular War; some of the rescued silver can be seen in Girona's Museu d'Art.

Sant Pere used to be one of the most romantic ruins in all of Catalunya, its central church universally recognized to be the precursor of the Catalan Romanesque style. But following a brutal 1996-99 restoration job, the monastery now unhappily ranks as a tourist trap of the first order. No original columns or capitals remain in the cloister, and only the lofty, well-lit **cathedral** retains its original stonework from the tenth to fourteenth centuries, including eleventh-century column capitals carved with wolves' and dogs' heads.

Nearby is the peaceful pre-Romanesque church of **Santa Elena**, all that remains of the small rural community which grew up around the monastery. Above the monastery (and contemporary with it) stands the ruined **Castell de Sant Salvador**, a twenty-minute walk up a steep, narrow path. This provided the perfect lookout site for the frequent invasions (French or Moorish), which normally came from the sea; in the event of attack, fires were lit on the hill to warn the whole surrounding area.

Llançà, Colera and Portbou

The train line from Barcelona finally joins the coast at Llançà, 8km north of El Port de la Selva and a handier base for touring. Here you can pick up trains heading for the pretty town of Portbou, just a few kilometres from the French border. At several, usually inconvenient, times throughout the day, these trains will also stop at Colera, a small village that makes a pleasant lunchtime break.

Llançà

Once a small fishing town, **LLANÇÀ** has been opened up to the passing tourist trade by the road and rail route to France – and is shameless in its attempts to cash in. Unlike many such towns, however, it does have compensatory attractions. The beach is a good 2km from the train station, but the **old**

town is much closer, just off to the right – set back so far from the water to escape the attentions of pirates. A tiny café-ringed Plaça Major houses an outsize fifteenth-century episcopal palace attached to a later parish church, as well as the renovated remains of a fourteenth-century defensive tower, which houses an exhibition (summer daily 10am–1pm & 6–9pm; winter Sat & Sun 4–6pm) of photographs of bygone Llançà.

The road down to the **port**, where there's a clothes market every Wednesday morning, is lined with restaurants, souvenir shops and miniature golf courses. At the end you'll find a coarse sandy beach backed by a concrete esplanade. For better, more secluded **beaches**, you'll need to head 2–3km north to **Cap Ras**, a promontory covered by a forested nature reserve crisscrossed by trails: north-facing **Borró** is the main sandy bay here, near the parking area. Beyond Borró, accessible by path only, lie more protected coves popular with nudists.

Practicalities

There are nine **buses** a day to Llançà from El Port de la Selva in July and Aug (only two Sept–June); they stop opposite the **turisme** (July & Aug Mon–Sat 9.30am–9pm, Sun 10am–1pm; Sept–June Mon–Fri 9.30am–2pm & 4.30–8pm, Sat 10am–1pm & 5–7pm, Sun 10am–1pm; ☎972 380 855, ⓦwww.llanca.net) on Avinguda de Europa. For **accommodation**, there are some cheap *habitaciones* and *hostales* in the old town, or you can stay down at the harbour. Try the pleasant *Habitaciones Can Pau*, c/Puig d'Esquer 4 (☎972 380 270; ❸); the *Hotel La Goleta* (☎972 380 125, ⓕ972 120 686, ⓦwww.hotelgoleta.com; ❻); or *Hotel Carbonell* around the corner on c/Major 19 (☎972 380 209; ❺). Alternatively you can stay down by the water at either the *Pensió Miramar*, Passeig Marítim 7 (☎972 380 132; ❺), or out at the pink, kitsch *Hotel Grifeu* (☎972 380 050; Easter–Sept; ❻) at the beach.

A couple of recommended **restaurants** are the pricey *La Brasa*, Plaça Catalunya 6 (open March–Nov), which specializes in grilled meat, and a seafood restaurant, *Can Manel*, Paseo Marítimo 4 (closed Thurs in winter), which is slightly cheaper. At the southeast end of the esplanade, *La Finestra* is a snack bar good for crepes, salads and roast chicken: open through the afternoon and an unrivalled people-watching spot.

Colera

One of the smallest villages left on this coast, **COLERA** (offically known as Sant Miquel) is used mainly by Spanish holiday-makers. It's a rather shabby, down-at-heel place, with numerous high-rise blocks and very pebbly beaches, but the water is clean and clear (despite the town's name), and quite safe for children to splash about in. If you want to **stay**, *Pensió Mont Mercè*, by the sea at Pg. del Mar 107 (☎972 389 126; ❺), is an adequate place to sleep and eat. Alternatively, there are a few more upmarket *hostales* by the two small beaches, including the well-kept *Hostal La Gambina* (☎972 389 172; ❼), which discounts its rooms out of season. There's also a good **campsite**, *Sant Miquel* (☎972 389 018; April–Sept), set well back from the beach, just off the main road. A couple of pricey **restaurants** overlook the water, or there are some more reasonable, equally congenial, alternatives inland on the village square, Plaça Pi i Margall.

For cheaper lodging – and a better beach – head 2km south to **Platja de Garbet**, where the *Pensió Garbet* (☎972 389 001, ⓕ972 128 059; ❹) is perfectly adequate, as are two adjacent **restaurants** facing the scenic, gravel-and-sand bay.

Portbou

PORTBOU, 7km farther north, and only 3km from the French border, is a fine place to approach by road, over the hill and around the bay. It's even worth walking from Colera (it takes around two-and-a-half hours) and suffering the initial steep climb to enjoy the view down over the green hills, deep blue water and small, pebbled beach. Close up, it's still a very pretty place, with a natural harbour and stone beach used by the local fishermen to mend their nets. There are some excellent outdoor **restaurants**, both in the backstreets of the old town and lining the quay, none of them outrageously expensive; you can get an excellent meal here for €7.20–9. And you can spend the rest of your day pottering around the little coves nearby, reached on footpaths scratched out of the rocks and all clean and relatively uncrowded.

If you arrive on the **train** the massive station with its souvenir stalls creates a poor impression, although it is true that the railway has transformed the place. Before the Barcelona–Cerbère line came into operation, Portbou was a small fishing village; now it's a stop on the dash in and out of Spain, getting much of its trade from French tourists who come to stock up on booze and souvenirs before crossing straight back into France. Other visitors include those killing the afternoon hours before the night train from Cerbère to Paris, certainly a better way to pass the time than sitting in the Cerbère station bar.

Practicalities

There's a friendly **turisme** (June–Sept daily 9am–8pm; ☎972 390 284) right at the harbour on Passeig Lluis Companys, which has a map and list of **hotels** to give away. Out of season you're on your own, with very little choice. The best of the very few places to stay are the *Hotel Comodoro*, c/Mendez Nuñez 1 (☎972 390 187; ❺), near the harbour, or the *Hostal Costa Blava,* c/Cervera 20 (☎972 390 386; June–Sept; ❼).

Of the **restaurants** along the seafront promenade, Passeig de la Sardana, *L'Ancora* serves a fabulous seafood paella, and also has a €9 *menú*. The adjacent *Espanya* might also be worth trying, as well as the *Tauro* (open summer only) on Avinguda de Barcelona (the Figueres road). For snacks, head for *Casa David* in the main Plaça del Mercat, which has popular outdoor seating; over the road is the little **market** hall itself, open in the mornings for picnic fixings.

Girona and around

Just an hour inland from the coast, the city of **Girona** with its medieval core provides a startling and likeable contrast to the wilder excesses of the Costa Brava. It's easy to make the day-trip here from the coast, or from Barcelona (to which it's connected by regular trains and buses), but it really warrants more time than that – two or three nights in Girona would show you the best of the city and let you enjoy some of the striking surrounding countryside. The quickest trip is to the lakeside town of **Banyoles**, only half an hour from Girona, and it's not much further on to beautiful **Besalú**, one of the oldest and most attractive of Catalan towns.

To see more of the province of which Girona is capital you have to head for **Olot**, an hour and a half west of the city, at the heart of the **Garrotxa** region. Much of this is an ancient volcanic area, now established as the **Parc Natural de la Zona Volcanica**, whose rolling, fertile countryside is pitted with spent craters. Some of these are within the town boundaries of Olot itself, but the best of the scenery is around the village of **Santa Pau**, just to the east. North of here, and also close to Olot, **Castellfollit de la Roca** is the starting point for several good excursions which take you into the foothills of the nearby Pyrenees.

In the other direction, south towards Barcelona, those with a little more time can veer off into the mountainous **Serra del Montseny**, whose spa towns make for a restful diversion – though one you'll find easiest to see if you have your own transport, since buses are infrequent.

Girona

The ancient, walled city of **GIRONA** stands on a fortified hill, high above the Riu Onyar. It's been fought over in almost every century since it was the Roman fortress of *Gerunda* on the Vía Augusta and, perhaps more than any other place in Catalunya, it retains the distinct flavour of its erstwhile inhabitants. Following the Moorish conquest of Spain, Girona was an Arab town for over two hundred years, a fact apparent in the maze of narrow streets in the centre, and there was also a continuous Jewish presence here for six hundred years. By the eighteenth century, Girona had been besieged on 21 occasions, and in the nineteenth it earned itself the nickname "Immortal" by surviving five attacks, of which the longest was a seven-month assault by the French in 1809. Not surprisingly, all this attention has left Girona a hotchpotch of architectural styles, from Roman classicism to *modernisme*, yet the overall impression for the visitor is of an overwhelmingly beautiful medieval city, whose attraction is heightened by its river setting.

Girona's airport serves most of the Costa Brava's resorts, so by day the old quarter gets plenty of attention from day-tripping tour groups and passing French motorists. After dark, however, the streets empty and Girona's character reasserts itself. It's a fine place, full of historical and cultural interest, and one where you can easily end up spending longer than you'd planned. There are two or three excellent museums and a cathedral that's the equal of anything in the region. Even if these leave you unmoved it's hard to resist the lure of simply wandering the superbly preserved medieval streets, fetching up now and again at the river, above which high blocks of pastel-coloured houses lean precipitously over the banks.

Arrival and information

Girona's **airport** (☎972 186 600), 13km south of the city, is used mainly by Costa Brava package charters, whose clientele are transferred to their resorts by special buses; accordingly, there's no bus into town, so you'll have no choice but to take a taxi which will cost around €12–15. The **train station** is at Plaça d'Espanya, across the river in the new part of the city; from here, it's a twenty-minute walk into the old centre, where you're most likely to want to stay. The **bus station** is around the back of the train station. If you **drive** in, be aware that the old town is a controlled-access zone for residents only; use the car park at Plaça Catalunya or the underground car park at Plaça Constitució. Girona's

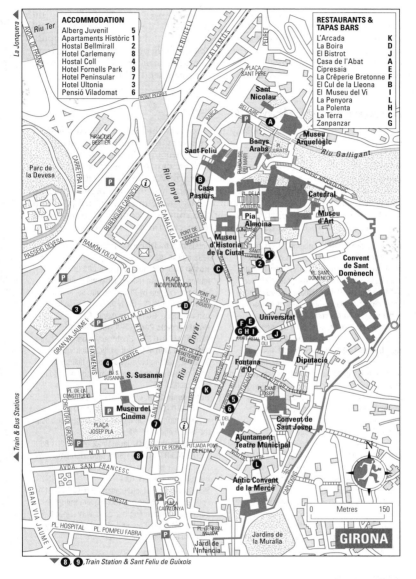

ACCOMMODATION
Alberg Juvenil **5**
Apartaments Històric **1**
Hostal Bellmirall **2**
Hotel Carlemany **8**
Hostal Coll **4**
Hotel Fornells Park **9**
Hotel Peninsular **7**
Hotel Ultonia **3**
Pensió Viladomat **6**

RESTAURANTS & TAPAS BARS
L'Arcada **K**
La Boira **D**
El Bistrot **J**
Casa de l'Abat **A**
Cipresaia **E**
La Crêperie Bretonne **F**
El Cul de la Lleona **B**
El Museu del Vi **I**
La Penyora **L**
La Polenta **H**
La Terra **C**
Zanpanzar **G**

GIRONA

8 , 9 , Train Station & Sant Feliu de Guíxols

old town area is compact and easily explored on foot. Buses cover the greater city, but you're more likely to use a **taxi** for short hops – there are ranks at the train station, Plaça Catalunya and Plaça Independencia.

There's a **turisme** inside the train station (July to mid-Sept Mon–Sat 9am–2pm & 4–8pm), while the main office is at Rambla de la Llibertat 1 (April–Sept Mon–Sat 9am–8pm, Sun 9am–2pm; Oct–March Mon–Sat

9am–5pm, Sun 9am–2pm; ☎972 226 575, Ⓦwww.girona-net.com), right on the river at the southern end of the old town. Both offices have well-informed English-speaking staff who can supply you with useful maps and accommodation lists, as well as bus and train timetables for all onward services. A third office, the Punt de Benvinguda, at c/Berenguer Carnicer 3 (☎972 211 678), will reserve hotels and restaurants and you can send and receive emails at €1.20/30 mins.

Accommodation

There are plenty of **places to stay** in Girona, including one or two *hostales* near the train station, though if you arrive at any reasonable time during the day it's much better to look for a place in or near the old town, which is also where you'll find the youth hostel. The nearest **campsite** is at Fornells de la Selva, 8km south of town and open all year (☎972 476 117), with excellent amenities and an English-speaking proprietor, though you might prefer to camp at livelier Banyoles, half an hour by bus to the northwest (see p.787). If you have your own transport, you might also consider a couple of *turisme rurales* between Girona and Banyoles, within easy reach of both (see p.789).

Alberg Juvenil, c/dels Ciutadans 9, off Plaça del Vi ☎972 218 003. Girona's youth hostel has a good old-town location and smart new facilities, including laundry, TV and video; reception open 8–11am and 6–10pm; breakfast included in the price, dinner available. But note that it's hardly any better value than the very cheapest of the *hostales*, and if you're over 25 it's actually more expensive. Open July–Sept only. **❷**

Apartaments Històric, c/Bellmirall 4/A ☎972 223 583, Ⓦwww.meridian.es/historic. In a restored building, these superb 2-, 4- or 6-person flats with fully equipped kitchens are currently the best value in Girona at €21 per person. Management is voluble, friendly and English-speaking.

Hostal Bellmirall, c/Bellmirall 3 ☎972 204 009. Attractive *pensió*, close to the cathedral and nicely turned out, with stone walls, artefacts and paintings. There are only seven rooms (with and without bath), so book ahead. The price includes an excellent, filling breakfast. **❺**

Hotel Carlemany, Plaça Miquel Santaló ☎972 211 212, Ⓕ972 214 994, Ⓦwww.carlemany.es. Luxurious rooms in a new hotel in the modern part of the city about twenty minutes walk from the old town. A rapidly becoming famous restaurant in the

hotel offers traditional and innovative cooking at €36 a head. **❽**

Hostal Coll, c/Hortes 24 ☎972 203 086. Inexpensive, clean rooms, some with balconies, in a central location by Plaça Constitució. Enquire next door at *Bar Coll* (daily 7am–10pm), where you can also get a €6 midday *menú*. **❸**

Hotel Fornells Park, CN-II, km 719 ☎972 476 125, Ⓕ972 476 579. Bright, airy rooms in a rambling hotel 3km outside the city, which would be an ideal, relaxing base for a touring holiday. A very good restaurant and large swimming pool add to its attraction. **❼**

Hotel Peninsular, c/Nou 3 ☎972 203 800, Ⓕ972 210 492. Well-located and pleasant (if rather bland) hotel on a busy shopping street, near the bridge and river. **❺**

Hotel Ultonia, Avgda. Jaume I 22 ☎972 203 850, Ⓕ972 203 334. Comfortable, modern rooms in a very friendly hotel on a busy street leading into Plaça Independencia. **❼**

Pensió Viladomat, c/Ciutadans 5 ☎972 203 176. Popular place whose airy rooms (with bath) fill quickly in July and Aug due to its very central location. At the bottom end of its price category. Breakfast available for €2. **❹**

The City

Although the bulk of modern Girona lies on the west side of the Riu Onyar, bordered to the north by the large riverside Parc de la Devesa, most visitors spend nearly all their time in the **old city**, over the river. This thin wedge of land, tucked under the hillside, contains all the sights and monuments, and as it takes only half an hour or so to walk from end to end it's easy to explore thoroughly. A zone of high walls, stepped streets, closed gates and hidden court-yards, the old city has been zealously preserved. Recent restorations mean that many of the oldest buildings and arcades now house trendy galleries, exclusive shops, restaurants and bars – Girona and its province have the highest per capita income in Spain – but stringent local regulations mean that the changes have managed to preserve the spirit of the old city.

The cathedral

The centrepiece of the old city is Girona's **Catedral** (summer Tues–Sat 10am–8pm, Sun 10am–2pm; winter Tue–Sat 10am–2pm & 4–7pm, Sun 10am–2pm), a mighty Gothic structure built onto the hillside and approached by a magnificent flight of seventeenth-century Baroque steps. This area has been a place of worship since Roman times, and a Moorish mosque stood on the site before the foundation of the cathedral in 1038. Much of the present building dates from the fourteenth and fifteenth centuries, though parts are four hundred years older, notably the five-storey Torre de Carlemany, and the Romanesque cloisters with their exquisite sculpted capitals.

The main facade, remodelled in the eighteenth century, bursts with exuberant decoration: faces, bodies, coats of arms, and with saints Peter and Paul flanking the door. Inside, the cathedral is awesome – there are no aisles, just one tremendous single-naved Gothic vault with a span of 22m, the largest in the world. Contemporary sceptics declared the vault to be unsafe, and building went ahead only after an appeal by its designer, Guillermo Bofill, to a panel of architects. The huge sweep of stone rises to bright stained glass, the only thing obstructing the grand sense of space being the enormous organ, installed late in the nineteenth century.

You can visit the cloisters by buying a ticket to the **Museu Capitular** (same times as cathedral; €3) inside the cathedral, which in this case is certainly a good idea. The museum is rich in religious art, including a perfect *Beatus* illuminated by Mozarabic miniaturists in 975, and the famous eleventh- to twelfth-century *Creation Tapestry* in the end room – the best piece of Romanesque textile in existence, depicting in strong colours the months and seasons, and elements of the earth. The irregularly shaped **cloisters** themselves (1180–1210) boast minutely carved figures and scenes on double columns, while steps lead up to a chamber above full of ecclesiastical garb and adornments.

The Museu d'Art

If you find the collection in the cathedral's museum remotely interesting, the large **Museu d'Art** (March–Sept Tues–Sat 10am–7pm, Sun 10am–2pm; Oct–Feb Tues–Sat closes 6pm; €1.80) is well worth a visit; it's housed on the eastern side of the cathedral in the restored Episcopal Palace. Early wings highlight Romanesque art, particularly rare manuscripts such as an eleventh-century copy of Bede and an amazing martyrology from the Monastery of Poblet, and impressive *Majestats* (wooden images of Christ garbed in a tunic) rescued from the province's country churches. You then progress through Renaissance works – including a room full of fifteenth-century *retablos* – to the collection of nineteenth- and twentieth-century Catalan art on the top two floors. Here you'll find some fine nineteenth-century Realist works, as well as pieces by the so-called Olot School of artists (better represented in the museum at Olot itself; p.794, and even examples of local *modernista* and *noucentista* art.

Around Sant Feliu

Climb back down the cathedral steps for a view of one of Girona's best-known landmarks, the blunt tower of the large church of **Sant Feliu**, whose huge bulk backs onto the narrow main street. Shortened by a lightning strike in 1581 and never rebuilt, the belfry tops a hemmed-in church that happily combines Romanesque, Gothic and Baroque styles; massive restoration works are under way at present, as well as some "urban clearance" on the river side of the church.

The streets behind the church by the river are a bit more down-at-heel than most in the neighbourhood: **c/de la Barça** is typical, with its bare bars and grocery stores. Historically a red-light district, the area is being steadily gentrified; doubtless it will soon receive the sort of attention visited on c/de la Barça's southern continuations, c/Calderers and c/Ballesteries, now lined with lively bars and exclusive shops.

The Banys Arabs

Close to Sant Feliu, through the twin-towered Portal de Sobreportes below the cathedral, are Girona's so-called **Banys Arabs** (April–Sept Mon–Sat 10am–7pm, Sun 10am–2pm; Oct–March Tues–Sun 10am–2pm; €1.20), probably designed by Moorish craftsmen in the thirteenth century, a couple of hundred years after the Moors' occupation of Girona had ended. They are the best preserved baths in Spain after those at Granada and show a curious mixture of Arab and Romanesque styles. The layout, a series of three principal rooms for different temperatures, with an underfloor heating system, is influenced ultimately by the Romans. The cooling room (the *frigidarium*) is the most interesting; niches (for your clothes) and a stone bench provide seats for relaxation after the steam bath, while the room is lit, most unusually, by a central skylight vault supported by octagonally arranged columns.

The Museu Arqueològic and the city walls

From the cathedral square, the main street, Pujada Rei Marti, leads downhill to the Riu Galligants, a small tributary of the Onyar. The **Museu Arqueològic** (summer Tues–Sat 10.30am–1.30pm & 4–7pm, Sun 10am–2pm; winter Tues–Sat 10am–2pm & 4–6pm, Sun 10am–2pm; €1.80) stands on the far bank in the former church of Sant Pere de Galligans, a harmonious setting for the varied exhibits. The church itself contains Roman artefacts, while the fine **cloisters** shelter medieval relics, including nearly a dozen inscribed stones from the former Jewish cemetery. The Romanesque architecture is perhaps the most memorable feature of a visit, reinforced by the inclusion of a full-size replica of the west rose window in the transept. Extensive galleries above the cloisters methodically outline the region's history from Paleolithic to Roman times, but unless you read Catalan or Spanish you'll get little out of these exhibits.

From the museum you can gain access to the **Passeig Arqueològic**, where steps and landscaped grounds lead up to the walls of the old city. Once onto the **ramparts** (daily 8am–10pm), there are fine views out over the rooftops and the cathedral, and endless little diversions into old watchtowers, down blind dead ends and around crumpled sections of masonry. The walls and the little paths lead right around the perimeter of the city, with several other points of access along the way: by the Banys Arabs, behind the Sant Domènec convent, and down by Plaça Catalunya at the southern end of the old city.

Carrer de la Força and the Call

Quite apart from its Roman remains and Arab influences, Girona also contains the best-preserved **Jewish quarter** in western Europe. There is evidence that Jews settled in Girona before the Moorish invasion, although the first mention of a real settlement – based in the streets around the cathedral – dates from the end of the ninth century. Gradually, the settlement spread, having as its main street the **c/de la Força**, which in turn followed the course of the old Roman road, Vía Augusta. The area was known as the **Call** and at its height was home to almost a thousand people who formed a sort of independent town within Girona, protected by the king in return for payment. From the eleventh century onwards, however, the Jewish community suffered systematic and escalating persecution, with attacks on them and their homes by local people: in 1391 a mob killed forty of the Call's residents, while the rest were locked up in a Roman fortress until the fury had subsided. For the next hundred years, until the expulsion of the Jews from Spain in 1492, the Call was effectively a ghetto, its residents restricted to its limits, forced to wear distinguishing clothing if they did leave, and prevented from having doors or windows opening onto c/de la Força.

For an idea of the layout of this sector of tall, narrow houses and maze-like interconnecting passages, visit the **Centre Bonastruc Ça Porta** (May–Oct Mon–Sat 10am–8pm, Sun 10am–3pm; Nov–April Tues–Sat 10am–6pm, Sun 10am–3pm; €1.20), which is signposted (to "Call Jueu") up the skinniest of stepped streets off c/de la Força. Opened to the public in 1975, the complex of rooms, staircases, a courtyard and adjoining buildings off c/de Sant Llorenç was the site of the synagogue, the butcher's shop and the community baths. Work is still going on here, with other nearby alleys currently sealed off but awaiting reopening, and there's a museum, an information office, a café and a small library (Mon–Fri 10am–3pm & 5–8pm, Sun 10am–2pm) if you want to find out more (books in English available).

The Museu d'Historia de la Ciutat

A little way back up c/de la Força, at no. 27, the **Museu d'Historia de la Ciutat** (Tues–Sat 10am–2pm & 5–7pm, Sun 10am–2pm; €1.20) completes Girona's set of museums in the old city. For casual, nonspecialist browsing it's the most rewarding of the lot, housed in an eighteenth-century convent. Remains of the convent's cemetery are visible as you enter, with niches reserved for the preserved bodies of the inhabitants. The rest of the collection is fascinating, less for the insights into how Girona developed as a city – though this is explained efficiently through text, exhibits and photos – than for the strange, miscellaneous bits and pieces displayed. A circuit of the rooms shows you old radios from the 1930s, a 1925 Olivetti typewriter, a 1970 IBM computer, a printing press, cameras, machine tools, engines and a dozen other mechanical and electrical delights. On the top floor you'll find a modern art exhibition, including a few works by Dalí and Miró.

Museu del Cinema

Tucked away in a sidestreet near the Plaça Independencia at c/Sequia 1, the **Museu del Cinema** (Tues–Sat 10am-8pm, Sun 11am–3pm; €3) is a fascinating and fun interactive museum detailing the history of the cinema from the first moving images to the present day. Based on a private collection belonging to Tomás Mallol, an award-winning local director, the museum has exactly the right mix of hands-on exhibits and informative displays to please kids and adults. Most interesting are the attempts by the most diverse cultures at creating animated images and some surprisingly sophisticated examples of early experiments in recording pictures. A shop on the ground floor is full of cinema memorabilia, ranging from posters and models to experiment packs for children.

Eating and drinking

Girona's chic **bars** and **restaurants** are grouped on c/de la Força, on and around the riverside Rambla Llibertat and on the parallel Plaça del Vi; the last two places are also where you'll find the best daytime cafés with outdoor seating. Another little enclave of restaurants with good *menús* is over the river in Plaça de la Independencia. A five-minute taxi ride from the centre will take you to the Pedret area on the road out to Palamos, where you'll find a wide variety of eateries and late-night bars.

Nightlife in Girona has undergone a transformation in recent years, with a number of very lively and fashionable bars opening in and around Plaça Independencia and in Pedret, while the old city is gradually re-emerging as a late-night venue. During the summer there are also some pricey open-air bars – collectively known as *Les Carpes* – in the Parc de la Devesa, which have live music or dancing from Wednesday to Saturday.

Restaurants

Boira, Plaça de la Independencia 17. The best food on the square, very popular with locals and visitors alike. €6–7.20 buys a very Catalan *menú*.

El Bistrot, Pujada de Sant Domènec. Delicious pizzas, pasta, crepes and drinks either outside on the steps below the church, or inside in cool, jazzy surroundings. Live classical music on Tues and Wed.

Cipresaia, c/General Fournàs 2. Superb creative Catalan cuisine, specialising in fish dishes, in plush surroundings. Expect to pay around €24. Closed Mon.

La Crêperie Bretonne, Cort Reial 14. A piece of France in Girona. Delicious savoury crepes for €4.10–4.70, excellent salads and while you wait for your food you can use the crayons provided to draw on the tablecloths. Closed Mon & Wed lunchtime in winter.

El Cul de la Lleona, Calderers 8. An imaginative fusion of Catalan and Moroccan cuisine in a tiny restaurant near the Sant Feliu church. The €1.20 *menú* is very reasonable but eating *a la carta* can get expensive. Closed Mon.

El Museu del Vi, Cort Reial 14. Conspicuously Catalan bar-restaurant serving up typical dishes in its pebble-dashed *comedor*. Plenty of filling *plats combinats* for around €4.20, plus a €6.90 *menú* and excellent *torrades* (toasts). Closed Mon.

La Penyora, c/Nou del Teatre 3. Staunchly Catalan restaurant hidden away and worth seeking out. There are two €9 *menús del día* – one vegetarian and one non-vegetarian – and a reasonable if limited *a la carta* choice. Closed Tues.

La Polenta, c/Cort Reial I6. This tiny vegetarian restaurant serves delicious organic grub – the *menú* is €7.80 – and is always busy. Open lunchtimes only; closed Sat, Sun and Aug.

Bars and cafés

Aleshores, Plaça Independencia 4. House music in a long, narrow bar with a dance floor at the far end – if you can get to it. Open daily until 3am.

L'Arcada, Rambla Llibertat 38. Bar-restaurant situated underneath the arcade, serving good breakfast pastries and outstanding pizzas. Outdoor tables are a nice place to relax in summer – though you'll pay for the privilege.

La Casa de l'Abat, Galligants. Atmospheric bar in the sixteenth-century guest rooms of the Bishop's House, opposite the Museu Arqueològic, where you can also get good light snacks. Live music plus tango and jazz nights. Closed Mon.

Excalibur, Plaça de l'Oli 1. Friendly bar, frequented by both expats and locals, and decorated in the Spanish idea of traditional English style – they've even got a bell to call time. Guinness and bitter on tap, and a fine international selection of bottled beers. Open daily till 3am.

Nummulit, c/Nord 7. Very lively bar near Plaça Independencia, where half Girona's young seems to fetch up after midnight. Open daily till 3am.

Sala del Cel, c/Pedret 118. Enormous club built on various levels in an old mansion, playing mainly house music from resident and visiting DJs, but with some quieter areas and terraces. Open 11pm–6am.

La Terra, c/Ballesteries 23. Colourful tiled-wall bar with window seats overlooking the river, ideal for a relaxing early-evening snack or late-evening drink. Open daily until 2am.

Zanpanzar, c/Cort Reial. Newly opened and best of Girona's tapas bars serving delicious and reasonably priced Basque *pinos* as well as a superb €8.40 lunchtime *menú*.

Listings

Banks and exchange There's an exchange office at the train station, and you'll find banks along the Rambla Llibertat.

Books English-language books available at the friendly and reasonably well-stocked Girona Books, c/Rutlla 22 (☎972 224 612)

Buses From the bus station (☎972 212 319), there are Rafael Mas services (☎972 213 227) to Lloret de Mar; SARFA (☎972 201 796) to Tossa, Palafrugell and Sant Feliu; Teisa (☎972 200 275) to Olot; and Barcelona Bus (☎972 202 432) express services to Barcelona and Figueres. International bus services are run by Eurolines, Via and Julia (all on ☎972 211 654).

Car rental Most agencies are close to the train station on c/Barcelona: Avis ☎972 206 933 and Hertz ☎972 210 108. Local companies such as Cabeza, c/Barcelona 30 (☎972 218 208), are

much cheaper, though all cars have to be returned to Girona.

Emergencies Dial ☎092 or contact the Cruz Roja on ☎972 222 222.

Hospital Doctor Trueta, Avgda. França 60 ☎972 202 700.

Internet access Teranyina, c/Bonaventura Carreras Peralta 2, near c/Força, is a computer shop with Internet facilities (€4.80 per hour) and friendly, knowledgeable staff.

Newspapers British and American newspapers available at the kiosks in Plaça de la Independencia and Plaça de Catalunya.

Police Policia Municipal at c/Bacià 4 ☎972 419 090 or 972 419 092; Mossos d'Esquadra (Catalan police: ☎972 213 450).

Post office At Avgda. Ramón Folch 2; Mon–Fri 8.30am–8.30pm, Sat 8.30am–2pm.

Around Girona: Púbol

If you're interested in Salvador Dalí, you might want to make the effort to travel the 22km to the tiny village of **PÚBOL**, site of the medieval castle Dalí bought – and decorated – for his wife Gala in 1970. The castle has now been opened to the public as the **Casa–Museu Castell Gala Dalí** (mid-March to mid-June & mid-Sept to Nov Tues–Sun 10.30am–6pm; mid-June to mid-Sept daily 10.30am–8pm; €7.20) and, as at Port Lligat (see p.776), it gives a fascinating glimpse of the painter's lifestyle. Contained within are a host of artworks Dalí gave his wife to decorate the house, as well as various pieces of furniture and other bizarre objects the couple bought. Particularly interesting are the elephant sculptures and Richard Wagner swimming pool in the garden, and Gala's collection of *haute couture* dresses. Dalí lived permanently at the castle after his wife's death in 1982 (Gala is buried in the grounds), writing extensively and painting his last authenticated work (*Kite's Tale and Guitar*) until a fire broke out in 1984, injuring Dalí and causing him to move to Figueres.

Getting to Púbol is tricky without your own transport; you're best off catching the train (every 90min; 30min) from Girona to Flaçà (also on the C255 to La Bisbal), and then taking a taxi for the remaining 5km (around €4.80). There's not much else in the village, and unless you've already organized a taxi on the way out, you'll have to ask to phone for one (☎972 488 107) from the village bar, as there's no phone box.

Banyoles

For an escape into the countryside around Girona, take a bus to **BANYOLES**, half an hour (18km) north of the city. Here, the Pyrenees are on the horizon and the town basks around its greatest attraction – the **lake**, famed for its enormous carp. The lake has been under state protection since 1951, something that kept Banyoles little developed until it was announced that the 1992 Olympic rowing events would be held here. Most of the lakeside closest to town was consequently redeveloped, with tourist boats, new hotels and fancy restaurants much in evidence. Even so, it remains an attractive place to visit, with an old town which has escaped much of the recent building and plenty of opportunities for walking around the lake on shaded footpaths, beyond the new development.

The Town

Banyoles grew up around a monastery originally founded by Benedictines in 812. This, the **Monestir de Sant Esteve** at the eastern end of town, is still easily the biggest structure in old Banyoles, and though it's usually locked, you might try asking around for the key holder who lives nearby. If you do get in, don't miss the magnificent fifteenth-century *retablo* by Joan Antigo. The medieval streets which lead back into town from here are full of other ancient buildings, including an almshouse and a dye market. In the end, all streets lead to the central **Plaça Major**, a lovely tree-lined, arcaded space with several café-bars and a Wednesday market that has been held here since the eleventh century.

From the square, signs point the way to the **Museu Arqueològic Comarcal** (July & Aug Tues–Sat 11am–1.30pm & 4–8pm, Sun 10.30am–2pm; Sept–June Tues–Sat 10.30am–1.30pm & 4–6.30pm, Sun 10.30am–2pm; combined ticket with Museu Municipal Darder d'Historia Natural €3), installed in a fourteenth-century poorhouse in Plaça de la Font. The museum used to contain the famous jawbone of a pre-Neanderthal man found in the nearby Serinya caves, but nowadays you have to make do with a replica; authentic specimens include Paleolithic tools, and bison, elephant and lion bones, all found locally. The **Museu Municipal Darder d'Historia Natural** (same hours as Museu Arqueològic; combined ticket €3), in nearby Plaça dels Estudis, has a display of (mainly non-native) flora and fauna.

The lake itself – the **Estany de Banyoles** – is a fifteen-minute walk from Plaça Major. It's long been used for water sports, so the Olympic choice wasn't surprising, and although there's little that's distinctive or attractive about the area nearest the centre, a thirty-minute walk through the woods around the southern edge takes you to the tiny hamlet of **PORQUERES**, where the water is at its deepest (63m). Here the elegant Romanesque church of **Santa María** was consecrated in 1182 and has a barrel-vaulted interior, and unusual capitals with plant and animal designs. The lake itself boasts a whole series of **boating** options – cruises, rowing boats and pedaloes – for fooling about on the water.

Practicalities

Buses all stop on c/Álvarez de Castro, with the bus office (where you buy onward tickets) nearby at the corner of Passeig de la Industria. Cross this road and signs point you down to Plaça Major, two minutes' away. The **turisme** is at Passeig de la Industria 25 (summer Mon–Sat 10am–2pm & 4–8pm, Sun 10am–1pm; winter Mon–Fri 10am–2pm & 5–7pm, Sat 10am–1pm; ☎972 575 573, ✉turisme@ajbanyoles.org). For local **trekking information**, the Centre Excursionista de Banyoles, c/del Puig 6 (☎972 572 551), near Sant Esteve, seems to be open most evenings and has a wide range of maps available and tips on local routes.

With Girona so close, there is no advantage in staying in Banyoles, whose **hotels** are expensive anyway. If you do want to stay, the most pleasant old-town hotel is *Fonda Comas*, c/del Canal 19 (☏972 570 127; closed Sat in winter; ❺), off Plaça dels Estudis, near the Darder museum: this immaculate building, with stone staircases and its own courtyard and restaurant, has nice rooms with and without bath. **Camping** is perhaps a more attractive proposition here than in most places. There's a large site, *El Llac* (☏972 570 305), which you'll pass on the walk to Porqueres, just before the church, and a few more in the vicinity – ask at the tourist office. Alternatively, if you've a car or bike, there are two good local **turismes rurales**: *Can Ribes*, 6km south of Banyoles beyond the hamlet of Camós (☏972 573 211, ℻972 581 073, ✉can.ribes@retemail.es; ❺), has simple, tiled-floor rooms and a roof terrace; even better is *Can Fabrica* (☏ & ℻972 594 629; closed Jan 7–Easter; ❻), a restored seventeenth-century farmhouse 1km beyond the hamlet of Santa Llogaia del Terri.

There are a few places to **eat and drink** in the old town. The *menú del día* at the *Fonda Comas* is €7.80, and usually very good, while cheaper meals are served at *Les Olles*, Plaça dels Estudis 6. Eating in the hotel-restaurants over-looking the lake is more expensive, though the four-star *Mirallac*, Passeig Darder 50, won't break the bank as long as you eat meat rather than fish or go for the €12 *menú*. Another good place nearby with an inexpensive *menú* is the *Fonda la Paz*, c/Ponent 18 (closed Sun), whose chef has made quite a name for himself locally in recent years. The best place for an evening drink or just a sandwich is Plaça Major, whose café-bars spill under the medieval arcades.

Besalú

From the road, the imposing eleventh-century bridge by the confluence of the Fluvià and Capellada rivers is the only sign that there is anything remarkable about **BESALÚ**, 14km north of Banyoles (and connected by regular daily buses). But walk a couple of minutes into the town and you enter a medieval settlement that provides one of the most interesting half-day outings from Girona. Steep narrow streets, sunbaked squares and cave-like arcaded shops bear silent witness to an illustrious history out of proportion to its current humble status. Besalú was an important town before the medieval period – Roman, Visigothic, Frankish and Moorish rulers came and went – but all the surviving monuments date from the eleventh century and after, when it briefly became the seat of a small, independent principality. Despite a total population of just eight hundred it prospered and remained a place of importance well into the fourteenth century.

The Town

The most striking reminder of Besalú's grandeur is the splendid eleventh-century **Pont Fortificat** – fortified bridge – over the river Fluvià. In the middle stands a fortified gatehouse complete with portcullis. Down to the left beyond the bridge the **Miqwé**, or Jewish bathhouse (key from tourist office; €0.60), was originally attached to a synagogue positioned in the old Jewish quarter in the heart of the lower town, along the riverbank.

Plaça Llibertat, in the centre of Besalú, is entirely enclosed by medieval buildings, including the elegant thirteenth-century Casa de la Vila, which now houses the *ajuntament* and the turisme. There's a weekly **market** in the square each Tuesday. The majestically porticoed c/Tallaferro leads up from here to the ruined shell of **Santa María** (you can't get inside), which for just two years (1018–20) was designated Cathedral of the Bishopric of Besalú; union with Barcelona meant the end of its short-lived episcopal independence.

Further west, the twelfth-century monastery church of **Sant Pere** is the sole remnant of the town's Benedictine community, which was founded in 977. It stands in its own square, El Prat de Sant Pere, from where the most eye-catching feature is the window in the otherwise severe main facade, flanked by a pair of grotesque stone lions. Elsewhere in the web of cobbled streets radiating from Plaça Llibertat, you'll come across other attractive buildings – many sporting stone flourishes, ornate windows and columns. Finally, you can work your way around to the delightful little church of **Sant Vicenç**, close to the main Olot–Banyoles road in a plant-decked square with a café-restaurant and outdoor seating. The church (its entrance arches decorated with mythical monsters) is a lovely example of Catalan Romanesque.

Practicalities

The **bus** stop is on the main Olot–Banyoles road, from where it's a short walk south to the central Plaça de la Llibertat. Here you'll find the **turisme** (daily 10am–2pm & 4–7pm; ☎972 591 240), where you can pick up a map and plan your tour.

The town has three very comfortable and quite reasonable **places to stay**, a very attractive proposition, as in the daytime Besalú is prey to whirlwind coach parties, while by early evening it has settled down to its own infinitely preferable pace of life. The *Hotel Siqués* (☎972 590 110, ⓕ972 591 243; ❺) is at Avgda. Lluís Companys 6, on the main road just down from the bus stop; the atmospheric *Residencia María* (☎ & ⓕ972 590 106; ❹) is better positioned, right on Plaça Llibertat; while the best budget choice is the spick-and-span *Fonda Venència*, c/Major 6 (☎972 591 257; ❹).

For **meals**, the *Hotel Siqués* has an enormous *menú del día* for around €9 (closed Mon Nov–Easter), while at the *Curia Reial* (closed Tues and Feb), you can sit on the outdoor terrace next to the square, or on the beautiful patio at the rear overlooking the bridge. Eating at both places can lead to rather large bills if you don't have the *menú*. Cheaper meals can be found at the *Can Quei*, Plaça Sant Vicenç 4, outside the church of the same name, which has good-value sandwiches, *platos combinados* and *menús* for €8.40 and €12. *Pont Vell*, c/Pont Vell 28, is much more expensive (around €24 a head), but beautifully situated, with outdoor tables more or less under the bridge, while if you want to really splash out, the new *Els Fogons de Can Llaudes* on Prat de San Pere, serves the best nosh in town for around €30 per person.

The Garrotxa region

Besalú is on the eastern edge of the lush and beautiful **GARROTXA REGION**, bisected by the Fluvià River and the main C150 road. The northernmost part – the **Alta Garrotxa** – is a thinly populated area of isolated farms set amidst low mountains, with just a handful of villages. The C150, and buses along it, skirt the lower edge of the Alta Garrotxa on its way from Besalú to Olot – the main town of the Garrotxa region, described on p.795 – and in parts the route is spectacular, as at **Castellfollit de la Roca**, where the houses peer over a sheer basalt cliff. South of the Fluvià lies volcanic **Baixa Garrotxa**,

The Garrotxa region's flora and fauna

The lower slopes of the Garrotxa region's distinctive hills are clothed with **forest** of evergreen oak, yielding higher up into deciduous oak and beech woods, with sub-alpine meadows and pastures at the highest altitudes. More than 1500 species of vascular plant have been recorded within the park, ranging from typical forest floor dwellers like snowdrops, yellow wood anemones and rue-leaved isopyrum to high-altitude specialities like ramonda and Pyrenean saxifrage. In addition, the Garrotxa contains a number of Iberian rarities, several of which are found nowhere else in the world: the white-flowered *Allium pyrenaicum*, typical of rocky limestone cliffs, Pyrenean milkwort (*Polygala vayredae*), a woody species with large pinkish-purple flowers, and shrubby gromwell (*Lithodora oleifolia*), a creeping plant with pale pink flowers that turn blue with age.

A phenomenal 143 species of **bird** have been observed in the region. Since three-quarters of the park is covered with forest, goshawks, tawny owls, short-toed treecreepers, great spotted woodpeckers and nuthatches are common. Flocks of bramblings and hawfinches take refuge in the beech woods during winter, while the more barren volcanic summits support alpine choughs and alpine accentors. Summer visitors include short-toed eagles, hobbies, wrynecks, red-backed shrikes and Bonelli's warblers, along with Mediterranean species such as subalpine warblers, golden orioles and bee-eaters.

Forest-dwelling **mammals** include beech martens, wildcats, genets, badgers and the acorn-loving wild boar, as well as a number of small insectivores – common, pygmy and Etruscan shrews – and the noctural oak dormouse, characterized by its "Lone Ranger" mask and long, black-tufted tail. Otters are also sighted along the rivers from time to time.

where over ten thousand years of erosion have moulded the dormant cones into rounded and fertile hills. The narrow C524, from Banyoles to Olot via **Santa Pau** (an infrequent bus route), takes in the terrific walking in the **Parc Natural de la Zona Volcanica** and the remnants of the great beech wood known as **La Fageda d'en Jorda**.

Alta Garrotxa

The **Alta Garrotxa** stretches north from the main Besalú–Olot road as far as the peaks along the French border. For speleologists, the region is almost inexhaustible, with more than a hundred catalogued caves, and for walkers it's a fabulous area as well; the Editorial Alpina *Garrotxa* map is a useful aid.

Castellfollit de la Roca

Fourteen kilometres west of Besalú, just off the C150, **CASTELLFOLLIT DE LA ROCA** presents its best aspect as you climb up from the main road to the village. It's built on the edge of a precipice that falls sixty metres sheer to the Fluvià river, with the church crowded by houses onto the very rim of the cliff. It's an impressive sight from a distance (even more so at night, when spotlights play on the natural basalt columns), but close to it's another story, with grubby brown buildings that give no hint of anything out of the ordinary. Despite the opening of a new bypass around the village, Castellfollit still hasn't recovered from being on the main road for so long.

You might leave your vehicle, however, to take in the view from the top of the village over the edge of the cliff: head south from the prominent clock-tower to the church and the viewing platform behind. On the through road, 100m downhill from the clocktower, Castellfollit's **Museum of Sausages**

(Mon–Sat 9.30am–1.30pm & 4–8pm, Sun 9.30am–2pm & 4.30–8pm), run by the Sala family to celebrate a century and a half in the skin-stuffing business, is almost certainly unique, as claimed.

Castellfollit is the starting point for some of the region's best **treks**, heading north and northeast through the Alta Garrotxa. You could easily enough **stay** in Olot, but if you want an early start then the *Ca la Paula*, Plaça de Sant Roc 3 (☎972 294 032; ❹), in the centre of Castellfollit, is very reasonable and has a restaurant and decent bar attached.

North to France

It's 8km from Castellfollit up the **Llierca valley** past Montagut de Fluvià to **SADERNES** (minor road all the way), taking in en route the photogenic **Pont de Llierca**, a Roman bridge which today carries the GR1 over it, on its way to Besalú (3hr distant). In Sadernes – barely a hamlet – the popular *Hostal de Sadernes* (Fri–Sun) serves up hearty **meals** (€13.20 for three courses) served on the arcaded ground floor of an old farmhouse. Upstream from Sadernes, you can continue on the trail to the *Refugi de Santa Aniol*, right on the northern edge of the Garrotxa. From here, the Col de Massanes (1126m) border-crossing can be reached by continuing north on the footpath from the refuge, spending the next night at Coustouges or Saint-Laurent-de-Cerdans, both French villages in the Tech valley.

Oix, Beget and Rocabruna

Staying in Spain, a more populated route heads **northwest** into the Ripoll region. From Castellfollit de la Roca, take the paved but narrow road 9km northwest to the attractive village of **OIX**. Right opposite the Romanesque church of Sant Llorenç on Plaça Major, you can **stay** at the *Hostal de la Rovira* (☎ & ☏972 294 347; ❻ half board), a well-restored mansion with a ground-floor **restaurant**. Alternatively, there are two **campsites** 1km west, on opposite sides of the valley, both with pools: *Els Alous* (☎972 294 173) and *Masia Can Vila* (☎972 294 232).

Twelve kilometres northwest, a wide, comfortable dirt road leads to the showcase village of **BEGET**, done up by lowlanders as a weekend retreat veering perilously close to tweeness. The graceful twelfth-century church of **Sant Cristòfor**, standing at the entrance to the village, is celebrated for its particularly solemn and serene *Majestat*. All but a dozen or so of these Catalan wooden images of a fully dressed Christ were destroyed in 1936; this example is one of the very few that can be seen in its intended context (keys available from the souvenir shop at no. 15 when the church is closed). Beget has a couple of **places to stay**, both with their own restaurant: *Can Joanic*, by the church (☎972 741 241; ❺), and the pricier *El Forn* (☎972 741 230; ❼ half board) near the top of the village. The GR11 passes through here, and these are the only places to stay on this stretch of the trail.

Some 7km west on either the GR11 or the now-paved road, **ROCABRUNA**, with its ruined castle and handsome Romanesque church, stands just below the watershed dividing the Garrotxa from El Ripollès, the county of Ripoll. The only place to **stay**, 2km west on the main road and then 1km down a dirt track, right astride the GR11, is the friendly, English-speaking *turisme rural Exalde* (☎972 130 317; ❺, a working dairy farm; self-catering kitchens make it ideal for trekkers or cyclists en route. Surprisingly for such a tiny place, Rocabruna itself has two good **restaurants** which draw crowds on weekend nights from far afield. Particularly noteworthy is *Can Po*, one of the best eateries in El Ripollès (reserve on ☎972 741 045) – reckon on between €18 and €30.

Sant Joan les Fonts

SANT JOAN LES FONTS lies 3km west of Castellfollit, along the alternate, but equally busy, route to Olot. You'll soon glimpse its enormous monastery-church in the distance, high above the river, though this vies for prominence with smokestacks of obsolete industries, and a modern paper mill. From the lower end of the village, cross the restored medieval bridge, which spreads beneath the massive twelfth-century walls of Romanesque Sant Esteve, and take the path (signposted "Ruta de les Tres Colades") which passes below and to the right of the church. This leads within 250m of the so-called "Molí Fondo", massive waterfalls spilling from a dam on the Fluvià, next to which is the mill (*molí*) of the name. You might have a dip in the pool above or splash about under the falls, or continue another 250m along the route to "Boscarró", basalt columns twisted into a variety of shapes. Afterwards, you can drive, walk or take public transport the remaining 4km to Olot – all buses coming from Besalú go through Sant Joan.

Baixa Garrotxa: along the C524

Most of the **Baixa Garrotxa** region – accessible on the minor C524 which runs between Banyoles and Olot – is volcanic in origin, and has been within the **Parc Natural de la Zona Volcanica de la Garrotxa**, which covers almost 120 square kilometres, since 1985. It's one of the most interesting such areas in Europe, the road passing through a beautiful wooded landscape, climbing and dipping around the craters, offering some lovely valley views. It's not, however, a zone of belching steam and boiling mud; it's been almost 12,000 years since the last eruption, during which time the ash and lava have weathered into a fertile soil whose luxuriant vegetation masks the contours of the dormant volcanoes. There are thirty cones in all in the area, the largest of them some 160m high and 1500m across the base.

If you don't have your own transport, you'll find **access** a little problematic, since the only bus is the three-times-weekly Olot–Santa Pau–Banyoles service (Mon, Wed & Sat) to Santa Pau, the central village of the volcanic zone. Alternatively, you might consider **staying in Olot** (see p.807) and walking to Santa Pau from there – it's three hours by track and trail, with the added bonus of passing through the beautiful Fageda d'en Jordà beech forest.

Santa Pau

The central village of the volcanic zone, medieval **SANTA PAU**, 9km southeast of Olot, makes a great base for some gentle local walking. To the outside world it presents a defensive perimeter of continuous and almost windowless house walls; inside the village, balconies drip with flowers, steps and walls are tufted with grass and huge potted plants line the pavement arcades. Slightly less discovered than Besalú, it's even more atmospheric, though again verging on the twee. The cobbled alleys converge on the thirteenth-century arcaded Plaça Major, with its dark Romanesque church of Santa María and an **information centre** (summer Mon–Sat 10.30am–2pm & 4.30–7pm, Sun 10.30am–2pm) that's good for trekking information. The more adventurous can book a hot-air balloon ride over the volcanoes setting off from Santa Pau (℡972 680 255, Ⓦwww.garrotxa.com/voldecoloms), with *cava* and a hearty breakfast thrown in, for around €120.

In the square adjacent to Plaça Major, Plaçeta dels Balls, you'll find pricey but tasty **meals** at *Cal Sastre* (open Fri–Sat only in winter, closed Sun night & Mon year-round); they also offer highly regarded **accommodation** in a renovated old building with beamed ceilings and antique furnishings at the edge of town, at c/de les Cases Noves 1 (☎972 680 049, ⓕ972 680 481, Ⓔsastre@agtat.es; ⓺). Two kilometres up the road towards Olot, *Mas Collelldemunt* (☎972 680 523, ⓕ972 270 101, ⓦwww.turismerural.net/collelldemunt; ⓸, half board ⓺) is a *casa rural* co-run by Gonzalo, the only officially certified **guide** for the park (organized hikes offered); facilities are basic, but there's wheelchair access and it's open all year except Christmas and New Year. One kilometre further there's *Lava* (☎972 680 358; open all year), a large, well-positioned **campsite** in the shadow of two cones.

A loop walk

An excellent way to get acquainted with the Baixa Garrotxa is to take a **loop walk** out of Olot which almost totally avoids paved roads and can easily be completed by any reasonably fit person in a single day. If you're not up for the full distance, you could arrange to be fetched at Santa Pau, roughly halfway.

Begin in Olot by following the multiple signposts directing you across the Riu Fluvià, from where it's an hour south along surfaced country lanes, equal-ly suited to horse-riding or mountain-biking (as is most of this circuit), to the **Fageda d'en Jordà**. Although much reduced, this beech forest is still a treat in the autumn when the leaves are turning; it takes about half an hour more to emerge on the far side of the spooky, maze-like groves, deserted except for the tourist *carruatges* (horsecarts) visiting from Santa Pau.

Turn left when you meet the helpfully marked **GR2** long-distance trail, then right twice in succession when you encounter the track to Sa Cot. Follow the signposts to stay on the GR2, which soon becomes a proper path as it heads east for thirty minutes to the medieval chapel of **Sant Miquel de Sa Cot**, a popular weekend picnic spot. The **Volcà Santa Margarida** is visible just behind and, within forty minutes more, you should be up on its rim and then down into its grassy caldera, where another tiny chapel sits at the bottom. From the turn-off to the cone – just fifteen minutes from Sant Miquel – you descend to the **Font de Can Roure**, source of the only water en route, before skirt-ing Roca Negra with its disused quarry, then entering Santa Pau 45 minutes from the shoulder of Santa Margarida, and some three hours from Olot (not counting the detour to the caldera).

From Santa Pau the GR2 continues north towards the scenic **Serra de Sant Julià del Mont**, just east of which are two superb places to stay in the tran-quil **LA MIANA** hamlet (also reachable by a signposted, six-kilometre track from the Besalú–Olot road): the English-run *Can Jou* (☎972 190 263, ⓕ972 190 444, Ⓔcanjou@turismerural.net; ⓸, half board ⓹), which also organizes horse-riding; and the amazing *Rectoria de la Miana* (☎972 190 190 or 972 223 059; half board €30 per person), a medieval manor complete with crumbling twelfth-century Romanesque chapel.

However, for day-trekkers, this would inconveniently lengthen the circuit, so you're best advised to bear west at **Can Mascou** and approach **Volcà Croscat** via the *Lava* campsite (see "Santa Pau" above). You skirt the northeast flank of Croscat, badly scarred by quarrying, and from the campsite it's another hour, along a progressively narrowing track unsigned except for "BATET" painted on hunting-zone signs, to the high (720m) plateau of **Batet de la Serra**, scat-tered with handsome farms. Here you meet a marked path and track coming west from the Serra de Sant Julià, turning west yourself to follow the road briefly before adopting the well-marked *camí* – beautiful and partly cobbled in basalt – which passes the hamlet of Santa María de Batet on its way down to Olot. It takes just under another hour of downhill progress, or a total of something less than seven hours, to emerge at the top of c/Sant Cristòfor, which runs right down to the main boulevard through Olot.

Olot

OLOT, the main town of the Garrotxa, makes a good base for the region, with frequent bus connections and a fair choice of food and accommodation. It's a far nicer place than first impressions suggest – as you penetrate towards the centre, the industrial outskirts and snarling through roads give way to a series of narrow, old-town streets and a pleasant *rambla*. The centre is largely made up of attractive eighteenth- and nineteenth-century buildings, evidence of the destructive geological forces that surround the town: successive fifteenth-century earthquakes levelled the medieval town, and – thankfully dormant but easily accessible – three small volcanoes can be seen just to the north, reminders of the volcanic zone beyond.

Arrival and information

The **bus station** is on the main road through town and there's a **turisme** right opposite at c/Bisbe Lorenzana 15 (summer Mon–Fri 9am–3pm & 4–8pm, Sat 10am–2pm & 5–8pm, Sun 10am–2pm; winter Mon–Fri 9am–2pm & 3–7pm, Sat 10am–2pm & 5–7pm, Sun 11am–2pm; ☎972 260 141, ✉impc@olot.org), which has English-speaking staff and contains a good stock of local brochures, maps and timetables, as well as accommodation lists. More local **trekking information** can be had from the Centre Excursionista d'Olot (daily 7.30–9pm; ☎972 260 675) next to the theatre on the Passeig d'en Blay; maps and guides are sold at the DRAC bookshop, at the bottom of the *passeig*. Although there are no **Internet** cafés in Olot, you can connect at the local *biblioteca* at c/del Pati 2 (Mon–Fri 9.30am–1.30pm & 4–8.30pm, Sat 9.30am–1.30pm; €3 per hour).

Accommodation

Olot has a reasonable range of **places to stay**, and if you've got transport there are also a few good *turismes rurals* in neighbouring hamlets. The closest **campsites** are the slightly noisy *Les Tries* (☎972 262 405; May–Oct), 1km east of town on the way to Girona, and *La Fageda* (☎972 271 239; open all year), 4km out on the minor road to Santa Pau (no bus).

Alberg Torre Malagrida, Passeig de Barcelona 15 ☎972 264 200, ⓦwww.gencat.es/catalunya.jove. Youth hostel southwest of the centre overlooking the river, about halfway to the Casal dels Volcans. It's open 8–10am and 1pm–midnight and is closed Sept and Sun & Mon Oct–May. ❷

Mas La Garganta, La Pinya hamlet (follow signs west out of Olot toward Riudaura) ☎972 271 289, ✉garganta@agtat.es. *Casa de pagès* set in a rambling farmhouse looking southwest over the fertile Vall d'en Bas towards the Collsecabra volcano. Rooms are tasteful and en suite, and breakfast is served on a balcony. The cooking draws on the family's *charcuterie* shop in town, though veg-

etarian options are available, plus a kitchen for self-catering. ❼ half board.

Mas El Guitart, above Sant Andreu de Socarrats village ☎972 292 140, ✉guitart@agtat.es. Perched just above the Romanesque *ermita* of Santa Margarida, this *casa de pagès* has mock-antique-furnished wood-floor rooms; there are also self-catering apartments available. A minimum stay of 2 days is required. ❺

Pensió Narmar, c/Sant Roc 1 ☎972 269 807. Very pleasant and well-located (off Plaça Major) *pensió*, with clean, modern rooms with sinks, and its own restaurant-patisserie downstairs. ❸

Hostal Sant Bernat, Ctra. de les Feixes 31 ☎972 261 919, ℻972 268 844, ✉bernat@agtat.es.

Although it's a bit out of the way towards the north-east end of town, this *hostal* is quiet and friendly and its garage makes it the best choice if you've got a car or a bike. Some rooms have bath. ❸ **La Torra de Santa Margarida**, above Sant

Andreu de Socarrats village ☎ 972 291 321. More old-fashioned and homey than *Mas El Guitart*, set on a working cattle farm where roaring fires heat common areas during colder months (vital on this north-facing slope). ❼ half board.

The Town

If you arrived by bus on the busy main through road, the older streets nearby – between Plaça Major and Sant Esteve church – are a revelation. Filled with fashionable shops, art galleries and smart patisseries, they tell of a continuing wealth, historically based on textiles and the production of religious statuary. **Sant Esteve** lies right at the heart of town, built high above the streets on a platform, its tower a useful landmark. Beyond the church, the central **rambla**, Passeig d'en Blay, is lined with pavement cafés and benches, and adorned by the delightful nineteenth-century Teatre Principal. Between 6 and 8pm, this whole area teems with life as the well-dressed *passeig* swings into action.

Museu Comarcal de la Garrotxa

The substantial cotton industry that flourished here in the eighteenth century led indirectly to the emergence of Olot as an artistic centre: the finished cotton fabrics were printed with coloured drawings, a process that provided the impetus for the foundation of a Public School of Drawing in 1783. Joaquim Vayreda i Vila (1843–94), one of the founders of the so-called **Olot School** of painters, was a pupil of the school, but it was his trip to Paris in 1871 that was the true formative experience. There he came under the spell of Millet's paintings of rural life and scenery, and must have been aware of the work of the Impressionists. From these twin influences, and the strange Garrotxa scenery, evolved the distinctive and eclectic style of the Olot artists.

Some of the best pieces produced by the Olot School can be seen in the town's excellent museum, the **Museu Comarcal de la Garrotxa** (11am–2pm & 4–7pm, closed Sun afternoon & Tues; €1.80), which occupies the third floor of a converted eighteenth-century hospital at c/Hospici 8, a side street off c/Mulleras. The first part of the museum traces the development of Olot through photos and models of its industries. The bulk of the collection, though, is work by local artists and sculptors, and it's an interesting and diverse set of paintings and figures. There's characteristic work by Ramón Amadeu, whose sculpted rural figures are particularly touching; Miquel Blay's work is more monumental, powerfully influenced by Rodin, while Joaquim Vayreda's *Les Falgueres* is typical of the paintings in its re-creation of the Garrotxa light. By way of contrast – and indicative of a continuing artistic tradition in the town – there's also a room of modern ironwork sculpture and a few striking postwar paintings.

Jardí Botànic and the Casal dels Volcans

A twenty-minute walk from the centre are the town's landscaped botanical gardens, the **Jardí Botànic** (daily: April–Sept 9am–9pm, Oct–March 9am–7pm; free); follow the signs for Casal dels Volcans. They're worth walking out to, not least because they contain the fascinating **Casal dels Volcans** itself (July–Sept 10am–2pm & 5–7pm; Oct–June 10am–2pm & 4–6pm; closed Tues & Sun pm; €1.80 or free with Museu Comarcal ticket), a small museum devoted to the local volcanic region and housed in a Palladian building. Even if you don't speak Catalan or Castilian, you'll get a pretty good idea of the displays: there are pho-

tos and maps of the local craters, rock chunks and a seismograph, and even a
"what to do in an earthquake" series of explanatory drawings (the answer
appears to be run like hell). The building also houses an information centre on
activities in the Garrotxa volcanic zone.

Eating, drinking and nightlife

Olot's attractive historical centre boasts numerous lively **bars** and **restaurants**,
where you'll find the grilled meat specialities of the region, as well as a surprisingly wide range of non-regional dishes. If you want to try some of the
region's outstanding local produce, there's a farmers' market every morning
along c/del Rengle.

Can Guix, c/Mulleras 3. Cheerful bar-restaurant
where queues form for large servings. Eat heartily
for €8.40 – the local wine is served in a *porrón*,
but you get a glass to decant it into if you chicken
out. Closed Sun.

La Dolce Vita, Passeig de Barcelona 2. Smart and
trendy pizzeria serving the best pizza in town for
around €9 a head.

Font de l'Ángel, Plaça Móra 3. Snack bar/café
with garden seating and inexpensive *menús* and
platos combinados. Closes Sundays after characteristically lively Saturday nights.

Pensió Narmar, c/Sant Roc 1. The restaurant
attached to the *pensió* has reasonably priced, well-
cooked food and a *menú* for €6.60. Especially
good is the free-range – *de montaña* – chicken
and rabbit.

Ramón, Plaça Clara 11. Bar serving mid-priced
Catalan tapas and *platos combinados* – also a
good vantage point if you just want a drink.

La Terra, c/Bonaire 22 ☎ 972 274 151.
Macrobiotic veggie restaurant that serves a very
tasty lunchtime *menú* for €7.80. Closed evenings
and weekends, though will open by prior arrangement for groups of six or more.

Nightlife

More than a dozen **bars and cafés** are scattered between the bullring and
Plaça Carmé at the eastern end of the Barri Antic. Aside from some obvious
ones on the Passeig d'en Blay (itself the best place for an outdoor drink), try
the genteel *Cocodrilo* on c/Sant Roc, the youthful *Bar 6T7* at c/dels Sastres 35,
or the Senegalese-run *Bar-Restaurant Malem*, c/Pare Antoni Soler 6, a spacious
converted clothing factory decorated with original artworks that also serves a
good Catalan *menú*. For something a little alternative, there's also the raucous
Bar del Carme, Plaça del Carme 3, which plays all sorts of music and hosts
impromptu jam sessions. There are even two **cinemas**: Colom, on the *passeig*,
is classier than Núria, near Plaça Carmé. Most events of the **summer festival**
take place in the Plaça del Mig, behind the museum.

The Montseny region

South of Girona, the train line and main road to Barcelona both give a wide
berth to the province's other great natural attraction, the **Serra del
Montseny**, a chain of mountains that rises in parts to 1700m. It's a well-forest-
ed region, and from it comes the bulk of Catalunya's mineral water, which is
bottled in small spa villages. You can approach from either Girona or Barcelona,
though if you're using public transport you'll have to be prepared to stay the
night in whichever village you aim for, since the infrequent services rarely
allow for day-trips. The company which operates most of the routes below is
La Hispano Hilariense, whose buses leave from the bus station in Girona or
from the *Bar La Bolsa*, c/Consolat 45, in Barcelona's Plaça de Palau.

Breda and Riells

The bus route from Girona into the region passes through **HOSTALRIC**, an old walled village in the heart of a cork-oak growing district, but **BREDA**, about 6km farther on, is a better place to call a halt – known for its ceramic shops, and adorned by a Gothic church with an eleventh-century tower.

There's a fork at Breda, with a minor road (and occasional local bus) running the 7km up to **RIELLS**, which provides your first real glimpse of the hills. There's not much to Riells, and little to do except stroll around the pretty surroundings, but there is a good **place to stay** just before the village: *Hostal Marlet* (☎972 870 943; ❸), with a garden and restaurant. It's open July and August, and weekends throughout the year, and you have to take full board.

Sant Hilari Sacalm

The main bus route continues up the other road, past Arbúcies, with the views getting ever more impressive as you approach **SANT HILARI SACALM** (1hr 20min from Girona, 2hr from Barcelona). Perched at around 850m above sea level, Sant Hilari is a pleasant spa town that could make an enjoyable base for a couple of days. It's famous for its *Via Crucis Vivent*, or Eastertime Passion stagings, the most full-blown of several such in Catalunya. Many of its hotels and **hostales** cater for people taking the curative local waters, and consequently open only during the summer (July–Sept); one option that seems to stay open most of the year is the central *Hostal Torras*, Plaça del Dr Gravalosa 13 (☎972 868 096, ☎972 872 234; ❺), which also serves good food. A **turisme** (July–Sept Mon–Sat 10am–2pm & 4–8pm, Sun 11am–2pm; ☎972 868 826, ✉pijhil@ddgi.es), at the junction of the main roads through town, has details of all bus connections in the area.

Viladrau

If you're driving, it's a splendid, winding seventeen-kilometre ride southwest to **VILADRAU**, another mountain spa town, though not as large as Sant Hilari. By public transport, you have to approach from the other side of the range, by taking the train from Barcelona to Balenyá (on the line to Vic) and connecting with the local bus from there for a twenty-kilometre journey to Viladrau. Even this is not easy, as there are currently only two services a week from Balenyá; check first in Barcelona.

Being more difficult to reach, Viladrau manages to preserve a very tranquil feel within its old streets and attractive surrounding countryside. There are plenty of local wooded walks – ask at the sporadically functioning turisme on the Plaça Major – and a handful of places to stay should the area appeal to you: the *Hotel La Coromina*, Ctra. Vic (☎972 884 926; ❼), is a romantic hideaway among the trees, or there's the *Hostal Bofill* (☎938 849 012; ❺), a vast *belle epoque* period piece with a reasonable restaurant attached.

The Catalan Pyrenees

Away from the coast and Catalunya's three largest cities you don't have to travel very far before you reach the foothills of the **Catalan Pyrenees**, the easternmost stretch of the mountain chain that divides Spain and France. From Barcelona, you can reach **Ripoll** by train in just a couple of hours. The area north of here has been extensively developed with a number of **skiing stations**: during summer it's also increasingly busy, particularly in the valleys leading to **Camprodon**. Following the Freser valley north from Ripoll brings you to **Ribes de Freser**, start of the private train line up to **Núria** (combination shrine and ski centre), one of the most stunning rides in Catalunya. Further north, by the French border, **Puigcerdà** has the only surviving train link with France over the Pyrenees, while the odd Spanish enclave of **Llívia** lies wholly enclosed within France.

For serious Pyrenean walking – and a wider range of scenery, flora and fauna – you need to head further west, beyond **La Seu d'Urgell** and the adjacent duty-free principality of **Andorra**, which approximately mark the middle of the Catalan Pyrenees. Although more interfered with (by hydroelectric projects in particular) than, say, the Aragonese peaks to the west, the mountains here offer some of the best trekking in the whole Pyrenees. The **Noguera Pallaresa** valley, the **Vall d'Aran** and the superbly scenic **Parc Nacional d'Aigüestortes i Estany de Sant Maurici** are all reasonably accessible, offering routes and hikes that novices will be able to follow, as well as more specialist terrain. A further lure is the **Vall de Boí** on the western edge of the national park, which has a magnificent concentration of **Romanesque churches**.

One complication for anyone intent upon seeing more than a small part of the Catalan Pyrenees in one go, even with their own transport, is the geographical layout of the region. The central Vall d'Aran, in the northwestern corner of Catalunya, has an east–west orientation, as does the Cerdanya upland, but most of the other valleys run north–south, with few lateral roads, which means that connecting between them on two or four wheels is not always easy. Determined hikers can follow various passes between the valleys, but visitors without transport or walking ability will have to content themselves with **approaching** from the towns and villages to the south of the range, and backtracking a bit out of the mountains each time before they venture up a new valley.

This section is arranged accordingly, starting in the east, closest to Barcelona, and moving west; it details the easiest approaches and the routes that can be followed by public transport, as well as useful, time-saving side roads and tunnels for those with a bike or car.

Vic

The quickest approach to the mountains from Barcelona is to take the train north to Ripoll. About an hour out of the city, the route passes through the handsome town of **VIC**, whose few well-preserved relics are just about worth stopping to see. Capital of an ancient Iberian tribe, Vic was later a Roman settlement (part

Skiing in the Pyrenees

If you want to go **skiing** in the Catalan Pyrenees – which remain marginally less developed and pricey than the French side – it will usually prove cheapest to buy an inclusive **package**, and in any case will work out at up to a third less than in the Alps. The main destination promoted **overseas** in Britain is Andorra (p.821), though some agents (and ski websites) offer Núria and Baqueira-Beret in Spain, too. If you're already in Spain you'll get most choice if you go through a travel agency in Barcelona or any of the largest Catalan towns, though an increasing number of resorts are offering the possibility of arranging **on-the-spot** "mini-packages". The local tourist office will usually keep literature detailing valley hotels which offer all-in deals of half board and lift pass, which save a good 25 percent compared to doing it "à la carte", even more if you show up on weekdays. Full kit (skis, boots, poles) typically **rents** for about €12 per day, less for multi-day periods, whilst lift passes bought on their own **cost** €18–24 daily (again, less for longer periods), depending on day of the week and complexity/quality of the lift scheme.

The best Spanish Catalan **downhill** resorts for beginners or families are considered to be Port-Ainé above the Noguera Palleresa, Núria, and Super Espot at the east edge of the Parc Nacional de Aigüestortes i Estany de Sant Maurici; intermediate and advanced skiers might prefer La Masella at the south edge of the Cerdanya, Boí-Taüll at the west edge of Aigüestortes, and Baqueira-Beret at the head of the Vall d'Aran. For **cross-country skiing**, the north margin of the Cerdanya (p.817) and much of the Cadí (p.810) are covered with trails.

Pyrenean skiing tends to cost less because the range lacks international cachet (and really convenient airports – Barcelona and Toulouse are the choices), and the **clientele** is almost totally Spanish and family oriented. There's none of the snootiness or nocturnal excess occasionally met with in the Alps, and as a foreigner you'll be the object of benign curiosity or outright friendliness – though you may have trouble finding English-speaking instruction. **Infrastructure** is adequate – certainly better than Romania or Bulgaria – and improving as large sums are spent on snow canons or new lifts. The downside is that, canons or not, snow can be thin and/or mushy, since Catalunya gets its weather from the Mediterranean rather than the damper Atlantic; don't set out specially for a week's holiday without checking conditions first.

The system for **grading pistes** used in local ski literature is based on a universal colour code: green for beginners, blue for easy, red for intermediate and black for difficult. It's not a completely dependable system – a red run in one resort might rate only as blue in another – but it does give a fair idea of what to expect.

of a second-century temple survives in town) and then a wealthy medieval market centre. The **market** continues to thrive here, taking place twice weekly (Tuesday and Saturday) in the enormous arcaded main square. Vic is also renowned for its excellent sausages, which you'll see on sale in the market and throughout the town.

The old quarter of town is dominated by a rather dull, Neoclassical **Catedral**, containing some impressive wall paintings by Josep María Sert. Next door in Plaça del Bisbe Oliba is the more interesting **Museu Episcopal** (daily: mid-May to mid-Oct 10am–1pm & 4–6pm, closed Sun afternoon; mid-Oct to mid-May 10am–1pm; €2.10), which houses a wealth of eleventh- and twelfth-century frescoes and wooden sculptures rescued from local Pyrenean churches – the second most important collection of Romanesque art outside Barcelona's Museu d'Art de Catalunya. As with the Barcelona collection, you don't need to be a specialist to appreciate the craft that went into these objects, and the work here is likely to set you off on the trail of other similar pieces scattered throughout the region.

All this said, however, the best reason to come to Vic is for one of its two annual **music festivals**: the *Mercat de Música Viva* (Live Music Market), four days of live events in mid-September spanning genres from jazz to rock by way of Catalan *cançó*; and the mid-March *Festival de Jazz*, mostly centred on the club *Vic Bang Jazz Cava* on Rambla dels Moncada.

Practicalities

From the **train station**, walk east straight along the road opposite to reach the main market square, Plaça Major. **Drivers** will need to park in the outskirts, as traffic is highly restricted (and parking virtually impossible) in the centre. The **turisme** (Mon–Fri 9am–8pm, Sat 9am–2pm & 4–7pm, Sun 10am–1pm; ☎938 862 091, ⓦwww.ajvic.es) is based here, along with a handful of small **hotels** should you want to stay – though you're close enough to either Barcelona or the Pyrenees proper to make it unnecessary. A good place for **lunch** or dinner is the renowned *La Taula*, Plaça Don Miquel de Clariana 4 (☎938 863 229; closed Sun night, Mon & Feb), a restaurant in an old mansion, with fine local food at around €24 a head, and exceedingly slow service.

If you have transport (and plenty of cash), you might be tempted to drive the 14km north to the Embassament de Sau reservoir, overlooking which is the grand **Parador Nacional de Vic** (☎938 122 323, Ⓕ938 122 368, Ⓔvic@parador.es; ❼). This converted country house has all the upmarket facilities you'd expect, including a good Catalan restaurant.

Ripoll

RIPOLL, an hour's journey from Vic, occupies so prominent a place in Catalunya's history that it's impossible not to be initially disappointed by this rather shabby place, buzzed by traffic and divided by the manifestly polluted Riu Ter. The inhabitants seem to agree, resigned to working here but deserting it in droves at weekends when Ripoll assumes the air of a ghost town. But just ten minutes' walk from the southeast corner of town – where trains and buses stop – lies one of the most remarkable monuments in the Catalan Pyrenees, the **Monestir de Santa María**, founded in 888 by Guifré el Pelós (Wilfred the Hairy) to spur Christian resettlement of the surrounding valleys following the expulsion of the Moors.

The Town

Following an 1835 fire, the landmark Benedictine **Monestir de Santa María** lay in ruins; today's barrel-vaulted **nave** (daily 8am–1pm & 3–8pm) is a copy of the original structure erected over Guifré's tomb by Abbot Oliba, a cousin of the counts of Besalú, in the early eleventh century. The magnificent Romanesque **west portal**, however, survived the fire, and is now protected by a glass conservatory against the elements. Erected in the twelfth century, and now the main entrance, this portal squirms with carvings of religious and astro-logical subjects: the Apocalypse (across the top), the Book of Kings (to the left), Exodus (to the right), scenes from the lives of David, St Peter and St Paul (at the bottom), and the months of the year (around the inner side of the pillars).

The adjacent, double-columned **cloister** (daily 10am–1pm & 3–7pm; €0.60), far less damaged in the succession of earthquakes, sackings and fires vis-ited on the monastery, is particularly beautiful. The **capitals** of the lower colonnade, dating from the twelfth-century Romanesque "Golden Age", portray monks and nuns, beasts mundane and mythical, plus secular characters of the period. They completely overshadow the nominal **Museu Lapidari** here, which displays assorted stonework, sarcophagi and funerary art along the walls.

Adjacent to the monastery on Plaça Abat Oliba stands the fourteenth-century church of **Sant Pere**, part of which houses the **Museu dels Pireneus** (Tues–Sun: late June–late Sept 9.30am–7pm; late Sept–late June 9.30am–1.30pm & 3.30–6pm; €2.40), with a whole room of pistols and rifles, along with exhibits ranging from old coins through to ancient clothing, church art, archeology and folkloric items. You're only likely to get into the church itself if it serves as a venue for Ripoll's **music festival**, staged on successive weekends during July and August.

Besides the monastery and museum there's little to detain you, though it's worth climbing around the back of Sant Pere to a **terrace** from where you can overlook Santa María. A nearby bar has tables here, too, certainly the nicest seats in town. Down in the modern district, two *modernista* specimens may claim your attention: the spouting stone flourishes and battlements of **Can Bonada**, c/del Progrés 14, on the way to the bus and train stations, and the tiny church of **Sant Miquel de la Roqueta** (1912), a couple of blocks up the hill, looking like a pixie's house with a witch's cap on top – and designed by Antoni Gaudí's contemporary Joan Rubió.

Practicalities

The **train and bus stations** stand within sight of each other, a ten-minute walk from the heart of town, over the Pont d'Olot to the Plaça de l'Ajuntament. On adjacent Plaça d'Abat Oliba, the **turisme** (daily 9.30am–1.30pm & 4–7pm, Sun 10am–1pm; ☎972 702 351) is found under the sundial, near the monastery and the Museu dels Pireneus, stocking plenty of maps, pamphlets and local transport timetables. Aside from this helpful spot, conventional tourism in Ripoll marches resolutely backwards: places to stay tend to be overpriced, noisy and uninspiring, and there are very few places for a sit-down meal. Taken together, these factors make it highly advisable to base yourself somewhere nearby (for example Ribes de Freser, see p.807) and make a flying visit.

If you do decide **to stay**, the least expensive option is the recently refurbished *Habitacions Paula*, Plaça de l'Abat Arnulf 6 (☎972 700 011; ❺), 70m west of the tourist office. Next niche up is occupied by the *Hostal del Ripollès* on Plaça Nova (☎972 700 215; ❹), entered through its ground-floor pizzeria. The overpriced *Pensió La Trobada*, Passeig Honorat Vilamanyà 4 (☎972 714 353; ❻), across the river, represents the highest standard in town. There's also a large **campsite**, the *Solana de Ter* (☎972 701 062; open all year), 2km south of town on the Barcelona road.

If you have transport, it's worth foregoing all of the above in favour of *La Font* (☎972 198 087; ❺), a **casa de pagès** in the hamlet of **LES LLOSSES**, 18km away on the road to Berga. The triples and quad (most with shared bath) here are particularly well suited for families or groups, and the price includes breakfast; supper is also served in the fine upstairs common area, with views over the adjacent wooded hillside.

Eating and drinking options in Ripoll are far from plentiful. *Restaurant Perla*, Plaça Gran 4, features rather expensive *a la carta* food along with humdrum *menús*, though the *Pizzeria Piazzetta* on the ground floor of the *Hostal del Ripollès* is more reasonable and appetizing. These are the only full-service restaurants in the centre; for excellent tapas and crepes, head for *Bar El Punt* at

Plaça de l'Ajuntament 10, which has tables both outside and in the air-conditioned premises.

Northeast: the Romanesque Trail

From Ripoll an important "**Romanesque Trail**" of beautiful churches and monasteries leads northeast into the mountains. To follow the whole route by public transport you'll have to be prepared to wait (sometimes overnight) for buses, which get scarcer the further north you go. The first two towns, Sant Joan de les Abadesses and Camprodon, are easy to reach on day-trips from Ripoll or from Olot (see p.794). The other, more distant villages take more time and effort but are correspondingly less developed, except in the vicinity of the Vallter 2000 ski resort.

Sant Joan de les Abadesses

The small town of **SANT JOAN DE LES ABADESSES**, 11km northeast of Ripoll, owes its existence to the eponymous **monastery** (daily: March–April & Oct 10am–2pm & 4–6pm; May–June & Sept 10am–2pm & 4–7pm; July–Aug 10am–7pm; Nov–Feb 10am–2pm, also 4–6pm weekends; €1.20) founded in 887 by Guifré el Pelós, apparently for the benefit of his daughter Emma, the first abbess. However, the institution was closed temporarily in 1017 by Pope Benedict III as a result of politically motivated accusations of immorality by Count Bernat Tallaferro, to whom devolved – not coincidentally – all the prior feudal privileges of the convent. The present church, consecrated in 1150, is a single-nave structure of impressive austerity, built to a Latin-cross plan with five apses, and housing a curious thirteenth-century wooden sculpture depicting Christ's Deposition, the *Santíssim Misteri*, in its main chapel. According to the printed handouts, the figure of Christ retains on his forehead "a piece of Holy Bread . . . preserved untouched for seven hundred years". Admission to the monastery also includes entry to the Gothic **cloisters** and the **Museu del Monestir**, whose well-presented exhibits include ornate chalices, curiosities such as a crucifix in rock crystal, and a fine series of late-medieval altarpieces.

Other than the monastery, there are few specific sights in Sant Joan, but the old quarter boasts a fair-sized grid of ancient houses along streets almost shorter than their names, all leading to a small but appealingly arcaded **Plaça Major**. The slender twelfth-century bridge down in the well-tilled valley was only restored in 1976, after being destroyed in fierce fighting of February 1939, during the final Republican retreat of the Civil War.

Practicalities

Buses arrive at a shelter behind the monastery church apse; the well-stocked **turisme** (Mon–Sat 10am–2pm & 4–7pm, Sun 10am–2pm; ☎972 720 599), occupies the cloistered, fifteenth-century Palau de Abadia, just fifty paces left from the Museu del Monestir's entrance.

In theory Sant Joan would make a far more pleasant base than Ripoll, with frequent bus links in each direction; in practice, however, many places have closed down in recent years and finding somewhere **to stay** may prove difficult. The sole surviving options are both in the new district near the bus stop: *Pensió Nati* at c/Pere Rovira 3 (☎972 720 114; ❸), with large shared-bath rooms, and *Hostal Fonda Can Janpere*, around the corner at c/del Mestre Josep

Andreu 3 (☎972 720 077; ❺), which offers comfortable en-suite rooms with heating and TV.

Preferable to either, if you have a car, is the **turisme rural** property *Mas Mitjavila* (☎972 722 020; ❻), 11km northwest of Sant Joan in the hamlet of **OGASSA**. From the north side of the new bridge, follow the asphalt road 4km to Surroca village, and then continue the remaining distance on a cement driveway. Along with the adjacent tenth-century church of Sant Martí de Ogassa, *Mas Mitjavila* was once a dependency of the monastery of Sant Joan, and enjoys a superb eyrie-like setting 1300m up, overlooking the valleys of Ripoll. There are easy hikes in the surrounding mountains, and half board and farm produce are both available.

Back in town, both surviving *hostales* have attached **restaurants**, Can Janpere in particular with economical *menús* and a more adventurous *carta*. Otherwise you can sit outside at the pleasant cafés on Passeig Comte Guifré, the main *rambla*, one of which – *Cafeteria La Rambla* – offers a menú and *platos combinados*.

Camprodon

Climbing gradually along the lively Riu Ter from Ripoll and Sant Joan, the first place with the character of a real mountain town is **CAMPRODON** (950m), a fact exploited in the nineteenth century by the Catalan gentry who arrived by a (now defunct) rail line to spend summer in the hills. The town, 14km from Sant Joan, still retains the prosperous air of those times, with shops full of leather goods, outdoor gear, cheese and sausages. Ornate villas front a *rambla* clogged with towering trees, and other town houses are occasionally embellished with *modernista* flourishes.

Like Ripoll, Camprodon straddles the confluence of two rivers, here the Ter and the Ritort, and is knit together by little bridges. The principal one, the sixteenth-century **Pont Nou**, still has a defensive tower. From here you can follow the narrow main commercial street, pedestrianized c/València, to the restored Romanesque monastic church of **Sant Pere** (consecrated in 904), near the northeast end of town next to the larger parish church of Santa María. There is also a small castle overhead, but no apparent way up.

Camprodon was the birthplace of the composer **Isaac Albéniz** (1860–1909), a fact which neither the town nor the region made much of until recently – probably because there is little distinctively Catalan in the music he produced during his wanderings through Spain. However, the great man now has a street, and a **café** on c/València (recommended for croissants and coffee), named for him, a bust near Sant Pere, an eponymous summer **music festival**, and a less worthwhile **museum** near the bridge commemorating his life and times (daily 11am–2pm & 4–7pm; €2.40).

Practicalities

Buses from Ripoll stop at the TEISA depot, well south of the main Plaça d'Espanya, where you'll find the **turisme** (July–Sept Mon–Sat 10am–1.30pm & 4.30–8pm, Sun 10am–2pm; Oct–June Mon–Fri 10am–2pm & 4–7pm, Sat 10am–2pm & 4–8pm, Sun 10am–2pm; ☎972 740 010) in the *ajuntament* building.

Accommodation tends to be expensive, given the town's role as a minor ski resort, and advance reservations are advisable throughout the year. On often noisy c/Josep Morer there's *Can Ganansi* at no. 9 (☎972 740 134; ❺) and *Hostal Sayola* at no. 4 (☎972 740 142; ❺), both with en-suite rooms. The overpriced *Hotel Sant Roc* (☎972 740 119; ❼) and the better-value *Hostal La Placeta* (☎972 740 807; ❸) overlook Plaça del Carmé, just east of c/Josep Morer and the first square you reach as you come into town from Sant Joan. Finally, the well-appointed rooms and on-site parking of the dead-central *Hotel Güell*, Plaça d'Espanya 8 (☎972 740 011; ❻), justify a mild splurge. Some 3km up the road to Molló there's a less-than-brilliant **campsite**, *Els Solans* (☎972 740 012).

Can Ganansi's **restaurant** offers several different *menús* plus local dishes such as duck and trout, while *Hotel La Placeta* also has an attached diner (dinner only). Otherwise *Bar-Restaurant Núria*, at Plaça d'Espanya 11, is a characterful place and features a good-value lunch *menú* (at night it's *a la carta* only, featuring such delights as "prog legs"). Local specialities, besides the ubiquitous *ànec amb peres* or duck with pears, include *pinyes*, extremely rich and dense pine-nut sweets, which you can find on sale at bakeries throughout the town.

Beyond Camprodon: the Ter and Ritort valleys

Beyond Camprodon you're increasingly dependent on your own transport and ultimately your own legs. The majority of people who venture this way are either hikers, or skiers driving northwest up the **Ter valley** to the runs of Vallter 2000, with comparatively little traffic moving northeast up the **Ritort** that isn't bound for France. The construction of holiday flats for lowlanders, and of more short-term tourist facilities, now reigns supreme, but you still catch a glimpse of the area's former agricultural economy in the herds of grazing horses, and cattle ambling home at dusk.

The first settlement that might tempt you to stop is rather ordinary **VILALLONGA DE TER**, 5km from Camprodon. Opposite the standard-issue Romanesque church of **San Martín** on the main *plaça* are two **accommodation** possibilities: *Hostal Pastoret* (☎972 740 319; ❼ half board) at Constitució 10, and the unstaffed *Habitacions Cal Mestre* around the corner at c/del Pou 1 (information at c/Major 3; ☎972 740 407; ❺). There's also an all-year **campsite**, *Conca de Ter* (☎972 740 629) in the outskirts, better equipped than Camprodon's but still pitched mainly at well-anchored caravanners. Just one bus daily from Camprodon passes through here on its way to Setcases (see below).

Alternatively, you can bear left 1km past Vilallonga for the steep detour to **TREGURÀ**, 4km from the main road. Perched on a sunny hillside at 1400m, with sweeping views east over the valley, the upper part of this double village has a church dating from about 980. There are also two places to **stay**: the welcoming *Fonda Rigà* (☎972 136 000; ❺, ❼ half board), with its popular **restaurant**, and the rather more institutional *Hotel El Serrat* (☎972 136 019; ❼ half board).

From Tregurà, it's possible to **hike west** in a day to Queralbs, where you can pick up the rack-and-pinion railway down to Ribes or up to Núria. This route provides a lower-altitude, far more scenic alternative to the GR11 long-distance trail, which crosses the Ter valley much higher up. Using the lower path, you can break the journey after four hours or so at the **Refugi Coma de Vaca** (2000m; staffed Easter & mid-June to Sept or by arrangement on ☎936 824 237) at the top of the Gorges del Freser. Another path connects Coma de Vaca with the **Refugi Ulldeter** (2220m; open July–Sept and weekends all year) on the slopes of the Vallter ski resort.

Setcases and Vallter 2000

SETCASES, 6km northwest of Vilallonga in the Ter valley, has been completely gentrified. Once an important agricultural village, it was almost totally abandoned until the nearby ski station began to attract hoteliers, chalet developers and second-home owners. The ski trade ensures that short-term beds and food are relatively pricey, but if you need to **stay**, the most affordable accommodation stands adjacent on the riverbank road: the *Hostal Ter* (☎972 136 096; ❺) or the *Nueva Can Tiranda* (☎972 136 037; ❹), though you may be required to take half board – as you definitely are in the village centre at *Hostal El Molí* (☎972 136 049; ❼ half board). At those rates, the relative luxury of *Hotel La Coma* (☎972 136 073; ❻), at the very entrance to the village, might be worth considering; the price includes breakfast. Local trippers flock here to **eat** at weekends, most notably at the independent restaurant *Can Jepet* (reserve on ☎972 136 104). The food – well-presented salads, grilled quail with artichoke and roast peppers, home-made *flan* – is excellent value at under €18 a head.

Situated at the head of the valley, below the frontier summits of Bastiments (2874m) and Pic de la Dona (2702m), compact **VALLTER 2000** (no public transport) is the most easterly downhill ski resort in the Pyrenees. While south-facing, the glacial bowl here has a chilly microclimate that lets snow linger into April most years – though the runs remain heavily dependent on canons. The range of *pistes* are enough to keep you interested for the duration of a weekend, when Barcelonans flood the place.

The Ritort valley

From Camprodon, the road up to the **Col d'Ares** (1513m) and down into France initially follows the relatively treeless **Ritort valley**. The main, slight attraction of **MOLLÓ**, 8km from Camprodon, is the Romanesque church of Santa Cecília, with its four-storey bell-tower; one daily bus (not Sun) makes the trip from Camprodon. There are a couple of overpriced places to stay here, but give these a miss in favour of an excellent **casa de pagès**, *Can Illa* (☎972 740 512; ❼ half board), 3km north in Ginestosa district and accessible by road or a half-hour, yellow-and-white-marked spur path. A working cattle ranch with sweeping views, *Can Illa* has mostly en-suite rooms, a self-catering kitchen, a common room with wood stove, and a refuge-type dorm for groups. Your final chance of food and a place to stay before the border is the *Habitacions El Quintà* (☎972 741 374; ❻) in the attractive hillside hamlet of **ESPINAVELL**, 2km northeast of the main road (turn off before Ginestosa); half board is also available through the affiliated *Restaurant Les Planes* next door.

The Upper Freser valley and Núria

From Ripoll, the **Freser valley** rises to Ribes de Freser (912m) and then climbs steeply to Queralbs, where it swings eastwards through a gorge of awesome beauty. Just above Queralbs, to the north, the Riu Núria has scoured out a second gorge, beyond which lie the ski station and valley sanctuary of Núria. You can take the **train** all the way from Barcelona on this route, one of Catalunya's most extraordinary rides. The first stretch is by RENFE to Ribes de Freser, about a two-and-a-half-hour ride (or just twenty minutes from Ripoll). From there, the *Cremallera* (Zip) rack-and-pinion railway takes over; the small carriages of this private line take another 45 minutes to reach Núria.

Ribes de Freser

Generally bypassed in the rush up to Núria, dull but unobjectionable **RIBES DE FRESER** offers little to the traveller except hotels – more plentiful and better value than anything in Ripoll – and, out of season, its integrity as a real town. Local shops sell sacks of grain, seeds, oils and other agricultural and domestic paraphernalia, and there's a much-used *petanca* (boules) court in the centre, as well as a lively weekly market and an annual sheepdog contest every September.

Regular **trains** on the Barcelona–Puigcerdà line serve Ribes in either direction. Alight at "Ribes de Freser-RENFE" for the ten-minute walk into town, or just cross the platform to "Ribes-Enllaç" and take the *Cremallera* train (see box, overleaf), which makes a stop in the centre of town (Ribes-Vila) to pick up more passengers before trundling off into the mountains.

Practicalities

If the idea of **staying** appeals, pick of the bunch is *Mas Ventaiola* (booking essential on ☎972 727 948), a *casa de pagès* 1km from the centre, reached via the cemetery track taking off from the Pardines road. Perched on the hillside and recently refurbished, this offers both en-suite rooms (❹) and several 4-bed apartments (€60). Otherwise, in the town itself, very close to the *Cremallera* station, quietest choices are *Hotel Caçadors, c/*Balandrau 24–26 (☎972 727 006, ☎972 728 001; ❺–❻), which has a range of en-suite rooms, or the *Pensió Traces* just around the corner at c/de N. S. de Gràcia 3 (☎972 727 137; ❹). If you're still stuck, there's a helpful **turisme** at Plaça de l'Ajuntament 3 (Tues–Sat 10am–2pm & 5–8pm, Sun 11am–1pm). **Eating** out, the restaurant at the *Caçadors* is pleasant if slightly overpriced – count on €15 for three courses – while the *menjador* in the *Hotel Prats* out on the main through road is a little cheaper and generally features a number of fish dishes.

Along the Cremallera Line

The *Cremallera* makes a fabulous introduction to the mountains. After a leisurely start through the lower valley, the tiny, three-car train lurches up into the mountains, following the river between great crags before starting to climb high above both river and forests. Occasionally it slows down, leaving you poised between a sheer drop into the valley and an equally precipitous rockface soaring overhead.

Queralbs and Fustanyà

The only intermediate stop on the *Cremallera*, **QUERALBS** (1220m) is an attractive stone-built village, though now being dwarfed by apartment complexes on its outskirts, and suffering from the attentions of too many tourists in peak season. Near the highest point, beside the GR11 trail which passes through the village, stands the tenth-century church of **Sant Jaume**, adorned with a fine colonnaded porch. Reasonable en-suite **accommodation** is provided by the co-managed *Fonda Sierco/Hostal L'Avet*, on the main street (☎972 727 377; open weekends only in low season; ❹, half board at €36 per person mandatory in summer); the *hostal* rooms are small but wood-trimmed, with a cosy lounge on the ground floor, while the refurbished *fonda* units are directly over the restaurant *Ca La Mary*, which has all keys. other **restaurants** in the village include the recommended *Masia Constants*, 1km north on the Fontalba road, perched right above the *cremallera* tracks; they too serve country fare daily in summer but are only open weekends and holidays otherwise.

The Cremallera railway

The **Cremallera** ("Zip" in Catalan) railway, built in 1931, is the last private rack-and-pinion line operating in Catalunya. Services **depart** Ribes-Enllaç daily year-round except November, when it's closed. "Low season" (weekdays Dec–June except Christmas, New Year and Easter, plus mid-Sept to Oct) sees 6 daily departures between 7.30am and 5.30pm; there's an additional, final departure around 8.55pm Fridays and Saturdays, plus an extra train daily at 10.35am whenever the ski station is functioning. "High season" (winter holidays, plus July to mid-Sept) features a minimum of 9 daily trains from about 7.30am until 5.30pm, plus up to four extra departures on holiday dates. Trains pass through Ribes-Vila – where there's a weather report posted – eight minutes later, though note that the day's first train often starts at Ribes-Vila, not Ribes-Enllaç. The **journey time** up or down is 45 minutes; return adult **tickets** to Núria from Ribes cost around €13.20 (one-way is forty percent less than this). Rail passes of any kind are not valid. For the latest information see ⓦ www.valldenuria.com/valldenuria/crem.htm or phone ☎ 972 732 020.

For more reliable, year-round board and lodging, head 3km out of Queralbs to the well-signposted *Mas La Casanova* on the opposite side of the valley (☎ 972 198 077; ❺), in **FUSTANYÀ** hamlet. This recently opened **casa de pagès** is a superbly restored manor house; the outgoing proprietress provides reasonable table d'hôte evening meals, and there are also large family suites available.

Núria

Beyond Queralbs, the *Cremallera* hauls itself up the precipitous valley to **NÚRIA**, twenty minutes further on. Once the train passes the entrance to the Gorges del Freser, seen tantalizingly to the right, and enters the Gorges de Núria, the views are dramatic. Having passed through a final tunnel, you emerge into a south-facing bowl, with a small lake at the bottom and – at the far end – the hideously monolithic, coffee-coloured **Santuari de Nostra Senyora de Núria**, founded in the eleventh century on the spot where an image of the Virgin was said to have been found. The Virgin of Núria is believed to bestow fertility on female pilgrims, and many Catalan girls – presumably the result of successful supernatural intervention – are named after her.

The sanctuary building combines a dull church, tourist office (which posts weather reports), bar, restaurants, ski centre and **hotel** all in one. Rates at the *Hotel Vall de Núria* (☎ 972 732 000, ⓕ 972 732 001; ❺–❻) vary by season and its **restaurant**, open for lunch and dinner, offers cheap *menús*. The only indoor budget lodging is the youth hostel *Pic de L'Àliga* (☎ 972 732 048; ❶), marvellously poised at the top of the ski centre's cable-car line (free ride up with return train ticket). **Camping** is permitted only at a designated site behind the sanctuary complex.

Besides the hotel, **eating** options include *La Cabana dels Pastors*, behind the complex, offering expensive bistro fare at lunchtime only; the *Bar Finestrelles*, downstairs in the sanctuary building, with typical bar snacks; and, best value of all, the lunchtime-only *Autoservei* self-service restaurant in the west wing, where you can eat reasonably well for €10.80–13.20.

Activities laid on in the valley include an archery range, horse-riding programme (high summer only) and boating on the lake. The entire resort has a dedicated **website** at ⓦ www.valldenuria.com.

Walking and skiing

Despite the day-trippers and hordes of kids, solitude is easily found amidst the bleak, treeless scenery. Serious **climbers** can move on from Núria to the summit of **Puigmal** (2909m), a four-to-five-hour hike: the 1:25,000 *Puigmal-Núria* Editorial Alpina contoured map/guide booklet is recommended. Most people, however, aren't this committed, so the **return to Queralbs** on foot along the river gorge (2hr 30min) ranks as the most popular hike out of Núria. The GR11 threads the gorge on a high-quality, well-marked path, but you'll still want good shoes and a water bottle.

Downhill **skiing** at Núria – best for beginners and weak intermediates – is surprisingly popular, given that the piste plan is very limited, the chair lift only reaches 2262m, and the maximum altitude difference is a paltry 288m. Lift passes are accordingly cheap by Pyrenean standards, though equipment hire is much the same as elsewhere.

Berguedà

An alternative approach to this eastern section of the Catalan Pyrenees is to aim initially for the *comarca* (county) of **Berguedà**, west of Ripoll. It's easiest with your own transport: from Barcelona, the fast, improved C1411 road runs through Manresa and then heads due north to Puigcerdà, via the **Túnel del Cadí**, Spain's longest tunnel. You can come this way by bus, too – heading first for **Berga**, the region's main town, from Barcelona – though this approach is much slower than the rail trip to Puigcerdà, via Ripoll.

In this region there's nothing as immediately spectacular as the Núria train journey, though northeast of Berga villages and hamlets like Sant Jaume de Frontanyà and Castellar de N'Hug lend monumental interest. To the northwest, the vast **Serra del Cadí** offers the best local walking, including treks around (and a possible ascent of) the twin peaks of that most recognizable of Catalan mountains, **Pedraforca**.

Berga

Served twice daily by bus from Barcelona (2hr), the capital of the *comarca* is **BERGA**, where the Pyrenees seem to arrive with a startling abruptness. The town itself is fairly dull, bearing ample traces of its long history as an industrial centre, but it does have a ruined castle, a well-preserved medieval core and – as capital of Berguedà *comarca* – onward connections to higher settlements in the county, provided by the ATSA bus company at the top of Passeig de la Pau.

There's just one other reason to come to Berga, and that's at Corpus Christi when the town hosts the **Festa de la Patum**, one of the most famous of Catalunya's festivals. For three days, huge figures of giants and dwarfs process to hornpipe music along streets packed with red-hatted Catalans intent on a good time. A dragon attacks onlookers in the course of a symbolic battle between good and evil, firecrackers blazing from its mouth, while the climax comes on the Saturday night, with a dance performed by masked men covered in grass.

Not surprisingly, **accommodation** is impossible to find during the festival unless you've booked weeks in advance; at other times you should have few problems. Try the small but well-appointed *Hotel Passasserres*, c/La Valldan (☎938 210 645; ❾), with sauna, gym and off-street parking; *Pensió Passeig*, Passeig de la Pau 12 (☎938 210 415; ❹); or the very central two-star *Hotel*

Queralt, Plaça de la Creu 4 (☎938 210 611; ❺), whose en-suite rooms have all mod cons. There's also a **campsite**, out of town on the C1411 (☎938 211 250; open all year). The **turisme** is just behind it (June–Sept daily 9am–1pm & 4–8 pm; Oct–May reduced hours; ☎938 221 500). The best **restaurant** in town is the *Sala* at Passeig de la Pau 27 (closed Sun evening and Mon) – count on about €30 a head for a full gourmet meal, less if you opt for the *menú*. If your budget doesn't stretch to that, there's the *menjador* of the *Hostal Guiu*, Ctra de Queralt, offering regional specialities.

Northwest of Berga: the Serra del Cadí

If you're a fully equipped and experienced trekker, the **Serra del Cadí** range to the northwest of Berga offers three or four days' trekking through wild, lonely areas. A number of paths and tracks cross the range, though the favourite excursion remains the ascent of Pedraforca. As in other limestone massifs, finding fresh water can be problematic, and that – combined with intense summer heat at this relatively low altitude – means the peak visitors' season is during May–June and September. In recognition of its unique landscape, the Cadí was declared a natural reserve some years ago, and it maintains several fairly well-placed, staffed refuges, accessible from a number of foothill villages which are themselves served poorly, or not at all, by bus, so you may have to drive, walk or hitch to them from the larger towns down-valley. For extended explorations of this region, you'll need the Editorial Alpina 1:25,000 *Serra del Cadí/Pedraforca* and *Moixeró* maps and guide.

From the Llobregat valley extending north of Berga there are two major routes west into the Cadí. **From Bagà**, a partly paved road follows the Riu Bastareny to the hamlet of Gisclareny. A much busier paved road highway beginning just south of **Guardiola de Berguedà** runs parallel to the Saldes river valley to Gòsol village, via Saldes village, the closest habitation to Pedraforca.

Bagà and Gisclareny

BAGÀ, the second town in the *comarca* after Berga, has something going for it in the form of a tiny old quarter with an arcaded *plaça* and several **accommodation** options. Choose between *Hotel La Pineda*, c/Raval 50 (☎938 244 515; ❹), at the eastern end of the main shopping street, and the *Hostal Ca L'Amagat* (☎938 244 032; ❹), quietly placed in the heart of the old town. On the southeast edge of town, *Hostal Cal Batista* (☎938 244 126; ❹) occupies two unexciting modern buildings, but staying here does solve parking problems, plus they've a well-regarded **restaurant** with a nice line in local trout and rabbit *all-i-olli*. A **campsite**, the *Bastareny* (☎938 244 420; open all year), 1km west of town, caters mostly to caravans.

The fourteen-kilometre road up the **Bastareny valley** begins at the campsite by the river, climbing steeply through dense forest before emerging through the **Coll de l'Escriga** (1360m) onto the south side of the mountain. **GISCLARENY**, 3km beyond the pass, is merely a handful of spread-out farms and two **campsites**, one of which – *Cal Tasconet* (☎608 493 317 or 937 441 016), 1500m west of the hamlet centre – also operates a **refuge** (❶). Beyond Gisclareny, trails or tracks give handy access to the heart of the Cadí within a few hours. Arriving on foot, it's possible to skip the Bastareny valley-floor track in favour of the direct Bagà–Gisclareny **path**, shown more or less correctly on the Editorial Alpina *Moixeró* map.

Guardiola de Berguedà, Saldes and Gòsol

Strung out grimly along the old course of the C1411 (a new bypass avoids the town), **GUARDIOLA DE BERGUEDÀ** is on the bus routes from Berga (21km south) or Ripoll, and only 1.5km north of the turning for Saldes and Gòsol (see below). Sole **accommodation** option is *Pensió Guardiola* (☎938 227 048; ❸), on the main street at the south end of town, which also does meals; the *menú* is €7.20. There's just one daily (5.35pm) bus to Saldes and Gòsol – note that it doesn't enter town, but turns at the junction 1500m south.

The first significant habitation, after 18km, is the small village of **SALDES**, set dramatically at the foot of Pedraforca and the usual starting point for explorations of the peak. Here you'll find two stores with trekking provisions, plus two inexpensive **inns** where reservations are virtually mandatory in season: the *Fonda Carinyena* (☎938 258 025; ❸) near the church, and the pricier *Cal Manuel* (☎938 258 041; ❹), on Plaça Pedraforca (where cars park) serving meals. Better value than either of these, however, is *Cal Xic* (☎938 258 081; ❹), a **casa de pagès** 1.5km west of the village in Cardina hamlet, at the start of the road up towards Pedraforca. Although a somewhat sterile building, the en-suite rooms are heated, clean and cheerful, and asking for a *desayuno salado* gets you ham, sausages, cheese and a *porrón* to wash it all down with.

The old stone village of **GÒSOL**, 10km beyond Saldes, is an altogether more substantial place, spilling appealingly off a castellated hill. Pablo Picasso came here from Paris during the summer of 1906 and stayed for several weeks in fairly primitive conditions, inspired to paint by the striking countryside; one of the streets off the Plaça Major is named after him. Gòsol makes a good alternative base to Saldes for explorations of the entire Cadí, with well-trodden trails up towards the less spectacular backside of Pedraforca. There are two **hostals**, both with decent attached restaurants: *Cal Franciscó*, on the little roundabout as you come into town (☎ & ℱ973 370 075; ❹,❺ half board), and the smaller, central *Can Triuet*, Plaça Major 4 (☎973 370 072; ❹). There's also a **campsite**, *Cadí de Gòsol* (☎973 370 134; open all year), southwest of the village, reached by dirt road from beside *Cal Franciscó*.

Up Pedraforca – and beyond

Most people tackle **Pedraforca** (the "stone pitchfork") from Saldes: a good ninety-minute path short-cuts the road up, which passes fifteen minutes below the **Refugi Lluís Estasen** (1640m; advance booking recommended on ☎908 315 312 or 938 220 079; open all year; ❶). From here the ascent of the 2491-metre peak is a popular outing, steep but not technically demanding if you approach clockwise via the scree-clogged *couloir* heading up the "fork"; at the divide between the two summits you'll meet a proper path coming up from Gòsol. The anticlockwise climb from the refuge via the Canal de Verdet is harder; descent that way is almost impossible, and however you do it count on a round trip of five to six hours.

From the *Estasen* refuge, a day's walk separates you from the Segre valley to the north. The easiest traverse route, on a mixture of 4WD tracks and paths, goes through the Pas dels Gosolans, a notch in the imposing, steeply dropping north face of the Cadí watershed. An hour's steep descent below, the *Refugi Cesar Torres* at **Prat d'Aguiló** (2037m; ☎934 120 777; open all year, in summer staffed with a fee) is well placed near one of the few springs in these mountains. From the refuge it's best to arrange a ride along the 15km of track north via Montellà to Martinet, on the main valley road linking La Seu d'Urgell with Puigcerdà.

Northeast of Berga

From Berga a daily bus heads northeast to **LA POBLA DE LILLET**, an hour away; you can also get here by the afternoon bus from Ripoll, 28km to the east. Here two ancient bridges arch over the infant Llobregat river, with a well-stocked **turisme** (daily summer and Easter 10am–2pm & 5–8pm) beside the smaller one; the old districts to either side of the stream make for a pleasant half-hour stroll, but there's little else to see. **Accommodation** and **eating** are both overpriced and restricted to the central *Hostal Can Pericas*, c/Furrioles Altes 3 (☎938 236 162; ❺), and the slightly shabbier *Hostal Cerdanya* at Plaça del Fort 5 (☎938 236 083; ❺).

North: Castellar de N'Hug

From La Pobla there's a steady 11km ascent northeast towards Castellar de N'Hug and, since you can leave the road only for a short section at the beginning and at the end, without transport you miss little by hitching – or waiting for the evening **bus** (not Sun) up from Berga via La Pobla. Three kilometres out of La Pobla on the left stands a disused cement factory, a flamboyant *modernista* building designed by Rafael Guastavino in 1901. Approaching Castellar, you'll come to the **Fonts de Llobregat**, source of the river that divides Catalunya in two. Every year hundreds of Catalans come here as if on a pilgrimage – summer droughts cause many local rivers to dwindle to nothing, so there's great pride in any durable water source, and this one has never stopped in living memory, even during the driest year.

Heaped up against the rise of the Serra de Montgrony, **CASTELLAR DE N'HUG** makes a good if slightly touristy base for the Moixeró section of the natural reserve, or (in winter) for snow sports at Alp 2500 (see p.814). High seasons here are September and October – when people come mushroom-hunting in the surrounding forests – and the skiing season of January and February. There's a fair amount of inexpensive **accommodation**: first choices are the friendly *Hostal La Muntanya* (☎938 257 065; ❹) at Plaça Major 4, with excellent, copious dinners, and the *Pensió Fanxicó* (☎938 257 015; ❹) across the way, which also does meals. One to avoid is the unwelcoming, overpriced *Pensió Peremiquel*. For slightly more luxury, there's the *Hostal Alt Llobregat* (☎938 257 074; ❺), at the southeast edge of the village on the road down towards the Santuari de Montgrony.

North from Castellar, the paved road, sporadically snowploughed in winter, continues over the range to La Molina and the Collada de Toses via the **Coll de la Creueta**. There are paths in this direction as well, but they're not marked; it's best to ask advice in the village for the five-hour walks to Toses or Planoles and equip yourself with the Editorial Alpina map *Montgrony/Fonts de Llobregat*.

Sant Jaume de Frontanyà and beyond

The eleventh-century church at **SANT JAUME DE FRONTANYÀ**, unquestionably the finest Romanesque church in the region, lies 12km southeast of La Pobla, easily accessible by a newly paved road not yet shown on commercial or tourist office maps; the turning south from the B402, 2km east of La Pobla, is well marked. Set at the foot of a naturally terraced cliff, the church is built in the shape of a Latin cross with three apses and a twelve-sided lantern. Sets of the church keys are kept by both of the hamlet's two excellent, characterful **restaurants**: "*Hostal*" *Sant Jaume* and *Fonda Cal Marxandó*, the latter also with inexpensive, shared-bath **rooms** (☎938 239 002; ❼) above its beam-ceilinged *menjador*.

To the French border: the Cerdanya

The train from Barcelona, via Ripoll and Ribes de Freser, ends its run on the Spanish side of the border at Puigcerdà, having cut through the Spanish portion of the **Cerdanya**. This wide agricultural plain, ringed by mountains to the north and south, shares a past and a culture with French Cerdagne over the border. The division of the area followed the 1659 Treaty of the Pyrenees, which also gave France control of neighbouring Roussillon, but left Llívia as a Spanish enclave just inside France. Today, the **train** continues over the border into France (the only surviving trans-Pyrenean summer rail route), providing a good alternative method of leaving or entering Spain. Note that if you're heading to France by train, via Puigcerdà, it's wise to reserve a seat in advance in Barcelona – otherwise you may find yourself turfed out at La Tour de Carol, the first French station, to fight for space with holiday-makers on their way back to Toulouse and Paris.

Spanish Cerdanya remains marginally more rural and traditional than the French side, though it began to be a popular summer holiday area for wealthy Barcelonans during the nineteenth century. Since the early 1990s this trend has accelerated, with blocks of second-home flats dwarfing nearly every village. Besides skiing – the main impetus for all this construction – golf, horse-riding, glider-piloting and even hot-air ballooning are growing in popularity, with the gently rolling countryside ideal for such activities.

Ripoll to Puigcerdà

All routes **from Ripoll** initially follow the Freser river north to Ribes de Freser (p.807), and then veer west, climbing steadily up the Rigart river valley. The train line to Puigcerdà sticks to the bottom of the valley, while the N152 road takes a higher course, allowing a good look south over the Serra Montgrony. Beyond the Collada de Toses, technically in the Cerdanya, the ski resort of **Alp 2500** is one of the more serious winter-sports areas in the Catalan Pyrenees.

Planoles, Fornells and Toses

PLANOLES, 7km from Ribes, is nothing extrordinary as a village but it makes a good base for the ski slopes to the west. There's an outstanding **casa de pagès**, *Mas Cal Sadurní* (☎972 736 135; ❻–❼ half board), set on a natural terrace just uphill from the train station. This superbly restored farmhouse is packed out most weekends and offers a mix of doubles and family-size quads, most en suite, plus an eight-bunk "refuge" for groups. The in-house restaurant closes Tuesday and Wednesday, when your best local **eating** option is the widely acclaimed *Restaurant-Casino* (lunch only, closed Mon) behind the church; the *menú* costs €7.80. The nearby hamlet of **FORNELLS DE LA MUNTANYA**, 8.5km beyond Planoles, also has a noteworthy restaurant, *Can Casanova* (closed Tues), which offers hearty mountain cuisine at reasonable prices.

TOSES, 3.5km beyond Fornells, is the last village in the Rigart valley and, at 1450m altitude, is one of the highest permanently inhabited villages in Spain. The only **accommodation**, 100m from the train station, is the welcoming, good-value *Cal Santpare* (☎972 736 226; ❼ half board), with a good restaurant (closed Wed) and comfortable en-suite rooms; they also have a ten-person "*refugi*" (€24 per person half board), and a self-catering kitchen is planned. The glory of Toses is its tenth-to-twelfth-century church of **San**

Cristófol, at the highest, southeast end of the village, with a simple barrel-vaulted nave and a so-called "Lombard" belfry, rectangular and gable-roofed. The ancient key (obtain from *Cal Pep* on the square) allows you inside to see the **frescoes**, skilful copies of the originals in the Museu d'Art de Catalunya in Barcelona. The main theme, Christ's Ascension, is half-obliterated, but well preserved around the lancet window is an image of a lad hefting a sheep – highly apt for this pastoral community.

Beyond Toses, road and train enter Cerdanya respectively over and under the Collada de Toses – the railway by the amazing **Cargol tunnel**, where the line executes a complete spiral to gain altitude. The pass affords excellent views west, the bare rolling mountains of the Montgrony range relieved by swathes of deep green forest.

Alp 2500 – and Alp village

The broad meadows of Tosa d'Alp (2537m) and Puigllançcada (2406m) form the pistes of **LA MOLINA** and **MASELLA**, adjacent ski resorts linked via lifts and runs and marketed together as "**ALP 2500**", claimed to be the largest ski area in the Pyrenees. Both have their own websites – www.lamolina.com and *www.masella.com* respectively – and by Spanish Pyrenean standards the skiing is impressive. Publicly run La Molina is probably more suitable for beginners; larger, private Masella is better managed, with more scenic runs.

Getting to the slopes, it's really best to have your **own car**, though during winter an infrequent "**Bus Blanc**" is provided, with one early-morning departure up from the Cerdanya flatlands, and two well-spaced returns in the afternoon. With few exceptions, **accommodation** at the foot of the slopes is overpriced and sterile; you're far better off staying in the villages of the Cerdanya to the north (see "Villages around Puigcerda", p.816). Closest of these is **ALP**, 6km northwest, where the friendliest of the three lodgings is the *Aero Hotel Cerdanya*, Passeig Agnès Fabra 4 (T972 890 033, F972 890 862; ●), which also has a well-regarded gourmet **restaurant**, *Ca l'Eudald*, in the basement.

Puigcerdà

Although it was founded by King Alfonso I of Aragón in 1177 as a new capital for then-unified Cerdanya, **PUIGCERDÀ** (pronounced "Poocherdah") retains no compelling medieval monuments, partly owing to heavy bombing during the Civil War. The church of Santa María was one of these wartime casualties, but its forty-metre-high **belltower** still stands in the namesake *plaça*. The east end of town, down the pleasant, tree-lined Passeig Deu d'Abril, escaped more lightly; here, you can see medieval murals in the gloomy parish church of **Sant Domènec**. Dwelling morbidly on the saint's martyrdom, surviving fragments show Dominic's head being cloven in two by a sabre. The renovated thirteenth-century **convent** next door is now used as a local cultural and youth centre; work continues to restore what's left of the medieval cloisters behind.

The greatest attraction of the town, however, is its atmosphere – if you've just arrived from France, the attractive streets and squares, with their busy pavement **cafés** and well-stocked shops, present a marked contrast to moribund Bourg-Madame just over the border. Allow at least enough time for a meal or an evening in a bar; enjoyable outdoor cafés crowd the merged *plaças* of Santa María and dels Herois. Between drinks, you can explore the older quarter between Plaça de l'Ajuntament and Passeig Deu d'Abril, or amble up to the small recreational **lake**, five minutes' walk to the north.

Arrival and accommodation

From the **train station** (outside which buses also stop) in Plaça de l'Estació, wearyingly steep steps lead ten minutes up to Plaça de l'Ajuntament in the heart of town, with reviving views far west over the Cerdanya. At the top of the steps, to the right, stands the newish Casa de la Vila, with the central **turisme** alongside at c/Querol 1 (June to mid-Sept daily 9am–2pm & 3–8pm; mid-Sept to May Mon 9am–1pm, Tues–Sat 10am–1pm & 4–7pm; ☎972 880 542). The giant **regional branch**, 1.5km southwest of town near the *Puigcerdà Park Hotel* (May to mid-Sept same hours; mid-Sept to May Mon–Sat 9am–1pm & 4–7pm, Sun 10am–2pm), is particularly well stocked with leaflets and more convenient with your own transport.

There's not a great selection of **places to stay** in Puigcerdà, and you might consider staying in one of the nearby villages instead (see overleaf). Acceptable options in town include the fairly quiet and good-value *Hostal La Muntanya*, c/Coronel Molera 1 (☎972 880 202; ❹), close to Plaça Barcelona; the very central, friendly *Hostal Alfonso*, c/d'Espanya 5 (☎972 880 246; ❹); and the *Hostal Residència Rita Belvedere* at c/Carmelites 6–8 (☎972 880 356; ❹–❺), which offers excellent views and a choice of rooms old-style or modern. For a mild splurge, there's none better than the garden-set *Hostal del Lago*, Avenguda Dr Piguillém (☎972 881 000, ℻972 141 511; ❼), just off Plaça Barcelona towards the lake.

Eating and drinking

Passing French tourists are responsible for the relatively high prices and bland menus in Puigcerdà, but there are still a number of reasonable places to **eat**. At the budget end of the scale, *Sant Remo* at c/Ramon Cosp 9 is a straightforward if slightly divey bar offering large *menús* at €6.60 and €8.40. *La Cantonada* at c/Major 46, beyond the bell tower, has acceptable €7.80 *menús* and more attractive surroundings; the *Carmen* nearby on Plaça de Santa María, with an upstairs *menjador*, is similar. For a jump in standards in the same area, head for the fancier *La Cachimba* at Rambla Josep Martí 12, which features pizzas as well. If the locals want to splash out they head for *Casa Clemente* at Avgda. Dr Piguillém 6.

The **bars** with outdoor seating on Plaça dels Herois and the adjoining Plaça de Santa María – in particular the adjacent *Kennedy* and *Miami Dos* – are usually busy, and while their full-on food service is tourist pap to be avoided, they're okay for a drink and tapas. If these don't suit, then just round the corner you will find *Bar Arenas* on Rambla Josep Martí, which is quieter, considerably cheaper and also has outdoor seating. The atmospheric *Bodega* at c/Miguel Bernades 4, has a clientele of locals and French tourists and the wine is served and sold from the barrels that line the walls: enjoy a glass or two in its intimate interior or take in your own bottle and you can buy a litre of pretty good wine for under €1.20. The *Cerveseria Claude* on arcaded Plaça Cabrinetty styles itself as an international beer specialist, and if you're so inclined you can sit indoors or out, tippling your way around the world's breweries.

Moving on: west to Andorra and north to France

If you're heading **west towards Andorra** on public transport, you may have to spend the night in Puigcerdà as there are only three buses a day to La Seu d'Urgell, via Bellver de Cerdanya (see below). Heading into **France**, several **trains** daily cross the border, bearing northwest to Latour-de-Carol, six minutes away, but only three of these have connections for Toulouse (4hr), and just one for Paris (12hr). If you're **driving**, you enter France via the adjacent small town of Bourg-Madame; it's also a simple matter to walk across to Bourg-Madame, 2km from the centre of Puigcerdà. The frontier is open 24 hours, year-round, and controls are now nonexistent, with the customs/immigration booths typically unstaffed.

Villages around Puigcerdà

You'll find better-value accommodation, and often food, in the hamlets and villages immediately south of Puigcerdà, home to some of the more distinguished members of Girona province's *turisme rural* scheme.

Top billing goes to the superb *Residència Sant Marc*, 1.5km south of the edge of town on the road to **Les Pareres** hamlet (☎972 880 007 or 936 322 260; ❼, ❽ half board). Set on a 150-hectare stud farm, this elegant *belle époque* mansion offers wood-floored rooms with antique furniture, and is managed by friendly Bolivians; reservations are recommended in summer. Two kilometres east of Puigcerdà in **AGE**, the *Cal Marrufès/Hipica Age* (☎972 141 174, ⓦwww.calmarrufes.com; ❻) is a brand-new, tasteful restoration of an old stone-built farm in the village centre, recently expanded to include 4-person suites (€70).

In sleepy **URTX**, 5km south of Puigcerdà, the friendly *Cal Mateu* (☎972 890 495; ❺) is part of a working dairy farm; the good-value en-suite rooms are bland modern rather than rustic and the breakfasts are nothing special, but self-catering is available; booking is advised for summer and Christmas/New Year. Urtx hasn't any other facilities; the closest good **eats** are 1.5km downhill inside the converted but still-functioning Queixans RENFE station, where *L'Estació* (closed Wed) has cheap lunch *menús* or *a la carta* at €12–15 per head.

Finally, in resolutely rural **SANAVASTRE**, *Can Simó* (☎972 890 240; ❺, ❼ half board), at the edge of the village, is another engagingly rustic cow farm which hasn't been overly restored, though most units are en suite; despite map appearances, Sanavastre is accessible *only* from Alp (not from the main highway to La Seu).

Llívia

The Spanish town of **LLÍVIA**, 6km from Puigcerdà but totally surrounded by French territory, is a curious place indeed, worth visiting not least so you can say you've been there. There are several **buses** daily from Puigcerdà (the Alsina Graells bus stops in front of the train station and again in Plaça Barcelona), but the ninety-minute walk out isn't too strenuous: bear left at the junction 1km outside town, just before the border at Bourg-Madame, and keep to the main road.

French **history** books claim that Llívia's anomalous position is the result of an oversight. According to the traditional version of events, in the exchanges that followed the Treaty of the Pyrenees the French delegates insisted on possession of the 33 Cerdan villages between the Ariège and newly acquired Roussillon. The Spanish agreed, and then pointed out that Llívia was technically a town rather than a village, and was thus excluded from the terms of the handover. Llívia had in fact been capital of the valley until the foundation of Puigcerdà, and Spain had every intention of retaining it at the negotiations, which were held in Llívia itself.

There's a strong medieval feel to the centre of town, not least in the fifteenth-century fortified **church** (June–Sept daily 10am–1pm & 3–7pm; Oct–May Tues–Sun 10am–1pm & 3–6pm), which boasts a curious nail-reinforced door and carved stone floor. Since 1982, an increasingly popular **music festival** has been held in and around the church on August weekends. Opposite the church, the unusual **Museu Municipal** (April–Sept Tues–Sat 10am–1pm & 3–7pm, Sun 10am–2pm; Oct–March Tues–Sat 10am–1pm & 3–6pm, Sun 10am–2pm; €1.20) contains the interior of the oldest pharmacy in Europe, functioning in Llívia from 1594 until 1918. Displays feature apothecarial pots and hand-painted boxes of herbs, as well as local Bronze Age relics, old maps and even the eighteenth-century bell mechanism from the church. The entry ticket also gets you into the fifteenth-century **Tour Bernat de So**, adjoining the church. This also serves as the home to the sporadically functioning **turisme**.

Practicalities

Most visitors just stay long enough for a **meal** – not a bad idea given the limited choice of accommodation. In the main Plaça Major at no. 1, there's the attractive *Can Ventura* restaurant (closed Mon evening & Tues), with flower-filled balconies; Cerdanyan cuisine with the freshest ingredients weighs in at a mildly extravagant €24 (there's no *menú*). *Can Marcel-li*, visible just up the hill at c/Frederic Bernades 7, has a pleasant dining room above the bar with a €9.60 *menú*. Still further up the slope near the church, the good-value *Can Francesc* at c/dels Forns 7–15 has courtyard dining in summer and a €9.90 *menú*.

The few places to **stay** tend to fill quickly. Least expensive is *Can Marcel-li* (☎972 146 096; ❺), with a few en-suite doubles, plus bathless singles – ask at the bar. There seems little point in staying at the pair of much more expensive hotels on the busy main road – you'll do much better for the money in the *cases rurals* around Puigcerdà.

Bellver de Cerdanya and Martinet

The second largest village in the Cerdanya and a possible halting point on the road between Puigcerdà and La Seu d'Urgell, **BELLVER DE CERDANYA**, stands on a low hill on the left bank of the trout-laden Segre, 18km west of Puigcerdà. With a ruined castle and its sprinkling of old balconied houses, it's a much-visited example of a typical mountain village, made doubly attractive by the Romanesque church of **Santa María de Talló**, a short stroll south of the town. Known locally as the "Cathedral of Cerdanya", this is a rather plain building, but has a few nice decorative touches in the nave and apse, and retains a wooden statue of the Virgin that's as old as the building itself.

The **turisme** is at Plaça Sant Roc 9 (June–Sept Mon–Sat 11am–1pm & 6–8pm, Sun 11am–1pm; rest of year hours vary). The best **place to stay** is the *Fonda Biayna*, c/Sant Roc 11 (☎973 510 475, ☎973 510 853; ❺), an atmospheric, rambling old mansion with creaky wood-floored rooms with small bathrooms and antique furnishings, a lively downstairs bar and an adjacent *menjador*. Other **eating** options are *Jou Vell* (closed Thurs & Oct) across the *plaça* from the turisme, and *Mas Marti*, about 3km east in the hamlet of **BEDERS** (open weekends, Easter, Dec 24– Jan 6 & daily late July–late August; ☎973 510 022 for reservations), which mixes French and local cuisine to good effect for about €21 per person. Bellver has a pleasant **campsite** on the outskirts, *Solana del Segre* (☎973 510 310; open all year).

Continuing downstream along the Riu Segre towards La Seu on the C1313/N260, the next place you're likely to stop is **MARTINET**. Tracks from Estana village and the refuge at Prat d'Aguilo, in the Cadí foothills to the south, also emerge here. Martinet is mostly strung uninspiringly along the through road, c/El Segre, but there are a couple of good **places to stay**: *Fonda Pluvinet* at c/El Segre 13 (℡973 515 075;❸), with a few en-suite rooms, and the quieter *Fonda Miravet*, north of the highway on c/de les Arenes (℡973 515 016; ❹), with views across a little stream. A meal stop in Martinet is positively recommended: both listed accommodations have ground-floor **restaurants**, the *Pluvinet's* (closed Sun eve & Mon) in particular excellent value.

The road to Andorra

The semi-autonomous principality of Andorra (p.821) is not much of a goal in itself, and you'll get immeasurably better trekking (if that's what you're after) in the Pyrenees to either side. However, if you're curious – or in transit back towards France – the route there is a reasonably interesting one, covered regularly by buses **from Barcelona**. These end their run in La Seu d'Urgell, the last Spanish town before Andorra. You can also approach Andorra **from Puigcerdà**, by taking the bus west along the C1313 to La Seu d'Urgell.

The bus service from Barcelona to La Seu d'Urgell is run by the Alsina Graells company (Ronda Universitat 4), and takes four to four-and-a-half hours. Whether travelling by public transport or driving yourself, the most interesting route is via Cardona and Solsona on the C1410 (see below); this eventually joins the C1313 for the final run up the Segre valley to La Seu. This route is the quickest if you're driving towards Andorra or the western Pyrenees, though less attractive than the roads further east.

Cardona

CARDONA lies about halfway between Barcelona and Andorra, and is dominated by a medieval hillside castle, whose eleventh-century chapel contains the tombs of the counts of Cardona. The castle has been converted into a *parador* (℡938 691 275, ℻938 691 636;❾), which as a luxurious overnight stop would be hard to beat, particularly since it also contains an excellent Catalan restaurant, where dinner runs to around €30 a head. Perhaps the most remarkable thing about Cardona, however, is its salt "mountain", the *Salina*, close to the river – a massive saline deposit which has been in existence since ancient times.

Solsona

Twenty kilometres further on, **SOLSONA** is a smallish, ramshackle town of considerable charm, with medieval walls and gates, and a ruined castle. The **Catedral** here is gloomy and mysterious, in the best traditions of Catalan Gothic, and has fine stained glass and a diminutive twelfth-century image of the Virgin, reminiscent of the Montserrat icon. Inside the adjacent seventeenth-century Bishop's Palace is the **Museu Diocesà** (June–Sept Tues–Sat 10am–1pm & 4.30–7pm, Sun 10am–2pm; Oct–May Tues–Sat 10am–1pm & 4–6pm, Sun 10am–2pm; €0.60), a collection of Romanesque frescoes, altar panels and sculpture taken from local churches.

If you want to break the journey to Andorra without splashing out on Cardona's *parador*, Solsona is probably the best place. The most central **accommodation** is the *Pensió Pilar* near the cathedral square (℡973 480 156;❸), with a *comedor* attached, and the *Pensió Sant Roc*, Plaça de Sant Roc 2 (℡973 480 827;❺), just off the road to La Seu opposite the *Bar San Fermín* (where most buses stop).

The Segre valley and Organyà

Once you've left Solsona, and joined the main highway from Lleida (the C1313), the drama begins. Amid tremendous mountain vistas the road plunges through the impressive gorge of Tresponts, lined with terraces of rock jutting to over 600m above. This journey upstream through the **Segre valley** alone makes the trip worthwhile, and Andorra starts to seem an alluring prospect by the time you reach La Seu d'Urgell.

Only one spot – **ORGANYÀ** – might induce a brief stop en route. A small, round building (summer Mon–Sat 10am–2pm & 6–9pm, Sun 10am–2pm; winter Mon–Sat 11am–2pm & 5–7pm, Sun 11am–2pm) on the main road contains both the local **turisme**, and what is possibly the oldest document in the Catalan language, the twelfth-century *Homilies d'Organyà* – annotations to some Latin sermons, discovered in a local presbytery at the beginning of the twentieth century. If you get stranded here, there are two **hostals** almost opposite: *La Cabana* (☎973 383 000; ❹), and *Els Tres Ponts* (☎973 383 092; ❹), both with **restaurants**.

La Seu d'Urgell

The capital of Alt Urgell, **LA SEU D'URGELL** lies beside the Riu Segre 23km upstream from Organyà. For years a rather sleepy place with a neglected medieval core, La Seu has undergone a mild transformation since the 1992 Olympic canoeing competitions were held nearby. There are two or three fancy new hotels, as well as the purpose-built canoe facilities by the Segre, but as most new development has fallen outside the old quarter, you should still be able to enjoy a fairly relaxed stay before sampling the excesses of Andorra.

The Town

Named after the imposing cathedral at the end of c/Major, La Seu has always had a dual function as episcopal seat and commercial centre – there's still a street farmers' market each Tuesday and Saturday, attracting vendors from throughout the *comarca*. A bishopric was established here as early as 820, and it was squabbling between the bishops of La Seu d'Urgell and the counts of Foix over local land rights that led directly to the independence of Andorra in the thirteenth century.

The original cathedral and city, on the hill where Castellciutat (see below) now stands, was destroyed in the eighth century by Moorish invaders. The present **cathedral** (summer Mon–Sat 10am–1pm & 4–7pm, Sun 10am–1pm; winter Mon–Fri noon–1pm & 4–6pm, Sat & Sun 11am–1pm) was consecrated in 839 but completely rebuilt in 1175, and restored several times since. Nonetheless, it retains some graceful interior decoration and fine cloisters with droll capitals, which you can see by buying an inclusive ticket around the back of the church – €2.10 gets you into the cloisters, the adjacent eleventh-century church of Sant Miquel and the **Museu Diocesà** (same hours as cathedral), containing a brilliantly coloured tenth-century Mozarabic manuscript with miniatures, the *Beatus*. To see only the cloister and church costs €0.90.

Other than these few sights, time is most agreeably spent strolling the dark, cobbled and arcaded streets west of the cathedral, which is where you'll find many of La Seu's best bars and restaurants. A strong medieval feel is accentuated by the fine buildings lining c/dels Canonges (parallel to c/Major); the town's fourteenth-century stone corn measures still stand under the arcade on c/Major.

Castellciutat

Fine views of the Segre valley can be enjoyed from the village of **CASTELL-CIUTAT**, just 1km west of town, and its nearby ruined castle (now a luxury hotel). Follow c/Sant Ermengol, cross the river and climb up to the village; there's a *pensió* on this road and another on Castellciutat's square (see "Accommodation" below) – either makes a nice retreat from La Seu. From Castellciutat, follow a path around the base of the castle and cross the main road for the nearby Torre Solsona; the scanty remains of the old fortifications are crumbling away here, assisted by quarrying below – take care near the edges. You can vary your route to Castellciutat or back by following the walkways through the pleasant, post-Olympic riverside **Valira** park: from La Seu, head west from Avinguda de Pau Claris (north of c/Sant Ot) to intercept it.

Practicalities

The **bus station** is on c/Joan Garriga Massó, just north of the old town; local services include the thrice-daily Alsina Graells buses to Puigcerdà and much more frequent La Hispano-Andorrana departures to Andorra (for details of which see p.822 below). The **turisme** (Mon–Sat 10am–2pm & 5–8pm; ☎973 351 511) is on Avinguda de les Valls d'Andorra, the main road into town from the north; in July and August, there may also be a supplementary office behind the cathedral in the *ajuntament*, supplying maps and hotel information.

Accommodation

In the wake of the Olympic facelift, very little decent **budget accommodation** remains in La Seu. The standard seems set by *Pensió Palomares*, c/dels Canonges 38–40 (☎973 352 178; ❸), a warren of windowless chipboard closets, tolerable only if you can obtain one of the multi-bedded front rooms with balcony. Otherwise there's only *La Valira* **youth hostel** (☎973 353 897; closed Sept; ❶), at the western end of c/Joaquim Viola la Fuerza beyond the *petanca* court, by the Valira park. The colossal **campsite**, *En Valira* (☎973 351 035; open all year), is 300m northeast of the hostel, at Avgda. del Valira 10.

Under the circumstances, you're probably better off at one of the **hotels** on the main roads through town. Best placed of these is the *Andría*, Passeig Joan Brudieu 24 (☎973 350 300; ❺–❼), an elegant if faded establishment with a range of rooms offering all mod cons. Less attractive, but friendly and adequate, is the *Pensió Cadí* (☎973 350 150; ❺) at c/Josep de Zulueta 4, close to Plaça de Catalunya. Top-of-the-range places include the elegant *parador*, converted from a former monastery, at c/Sant Domènec 6 (☎973 352 000; ❼), and the exclusive *El Castell* (☎973 350 704; ❾), incorporated within the castle at Castellciutat. Or consider staying in the village of **Castellciutat** itself: the friendly, family-run *Pensió Fransol* in the central Plaça de l'Arbre (☎973 350 219; ❹) is quiet, though without views; or the plusher *Hotel La Glorieta* (☎973 351 045, ☎973 354 261; ❺), with a pool and restaurant, gets an eyeful of the valley, perched above the river on the road up to the village.

Eating and drinking

Lively **tapas bars** are plentiful in La Seu's old town: try *Bar Eugenio*, c/Major 20, or *Bodega Fabrega*, c/Major 81. For good-value **restaurant** meals, *Cal Pacho*, in a quiet corner on c/la Font (at the southern end of c/Major, then east), has a €6.60 lunch *menú*, and *a la carta* dishes in the evening – cod-stuffed peppers and roast goat will set you back around €15. For coffee and cakes, the *Blau Arts Café* on c/dels Estudis makes a good choice.

Outside of the old quarter there's more choice. *Les Tres Portes* at c/Joan Garriga Massó 7 offers a good-value *menú* (€8.40) in a quaint chalet-style house with a summer patio. The *menjador* of the *Hotel Andria* also has a good *menú* for €10.20, together with gourmet dishes *a la carta*, featuring own-reared chicken and mushrooms in season. Moving towards the snackier end of things, *Restaurant Canigó*, c/Sant Ot 3 (at the north end of the *passeig*) does mostly pizzas, while east of the main *passeig*, there's the *Bambola Pizzeria-Creperia* at c/Andreu Capella 4.

Andorra

After seven hundred years of feudalism, the twentieth century has finally forced itself upon the **PRINCIPALITY OF ANDORRA**, 450 square kilometres of mountainous land between France and Spain. A referendum held on March 14, 1993 (henceforth the big national holiday) produced an overwhelming vote in favour of a democratic constitution, replacing a system in effect since 1278, when the Spanish bishops of La Seu d'Urgell and the French counts of Foix settled a long-standing quarrel by granting Andorra semi-autonomous status under joint sovereignty.

Despite a certain devolution of powers – the counts' sovereignty passed successively to the French king and then the French president – the principality largely managed to maintain its independence over the centuries. The Spanish and French *co-seigneurs* appointed regents who took little interest in the day-to-day life of the principality. The country was run instead by the Consell General de les Valls (General Council of the Valleys), made up of appointed representatives from Andorra's seven valley communes, who ensured that the principality remained well out of the European mainstream – it even managed to maintain neutrality during the Spanish Civil War and World War II.

It was during these conflicts that Andorra began its meteoric economic rise, as locals first smuggled goods from France into Spain during the Civil War and, a few years later, goods from Spain into France under German occupation. After World War II, this trade was largely replaced by legitimate duty-free business in alcohol, tobacco and electronics, and by the huge demand for winter skiing. Much of the principality became little more than an unsightly, drive-in megastore, with the main road through the country clogged with French and Spanish visitors. Seasoned Spain-watcher John Hooper has called Andorra "a kind of cross between Shangri-La and Heathrow Duty-Free", while the Spanish daily broadsheet *El Pais* once dismissed it as a "high-altitude Kuwait".

Ironically, though, this **tax-free status** held the seeds of Andorra's belated conversion to democracy. Although the inhabitants enjoyed one of Europe's highest standards of living, twelve million visitors a year began to cause serious logistical problems: the country's infrastructure was sorely stretched and the valleys increasingly blighted by speculators' building sites, while the budget deficit grew alarmingly since little entrepreneurial wealth went towards the public sector. Spanish entry to the EC in 1986 only exacerbated the situation, diminishing the difference in price of imported goods between Spain and Andorra (which now typically measures about twenty percent). However, the damage has long since been done; Andorra's cancerous commercial growth has killed off any significant trade in the nearest French or Spanish towns.

Andorra practicalities

Getting there

From Spain, there are four daily direct buses from Barcelona (6am, 7am, 2.30pm & 7pm; 4hr 30min), and regular services from **La Seu d'Urgell** which depart at 8am, 9.30am, 12.15pm, 2pm, 3.20pm, 6pm and 7.15pm (Sun 8am, 9.30am, 12.15pm, 2pm, 4.15pm and 7.15pm), taking forty minutes to reach the capital of Andorra la Vella.

From France, Saturday buses leave **L'Hospitalet** at 7.35am, 10.30am, 1.15pm, 5pm (summer only: 4.20pm from Ax-les-Thermes) and 7.45pm, arriving at Pas de la Casa twenty to thirty minutes later; on weekdays you may find that only the 7.35am and 7.45pm departures function. From Pas de la Casa the onward bus journey to Andorra la Vella takes one hour ten minutes. Services also leave La Tour de Carol at 10.30am and 1.15pm, taking 45 minutes to Pas de la Casa.

Even if you're **driving** you might as well leave the car behind and take the bus – in high season (summer or winter) the traffic is so bad that the bus isn't much slower, and parking in Andorra la Vella is an ordeal. On the plus side, **petrol** is famously cheap – about 12–15 percent cheaper than in Spain – so fill up before leaving.

Leaving Andorra

Buses back to **La Seu d'Urgell** leave from Plaça Guillemó in Andorra la Vella, parallel to the main road. Departures are Monday to Saturday at 8.05am, 9.05am, 11.30am, 1.30pm, 4.05pm, 6pm and 8pm; Sunday 9.05am, 11.30am, 1.30pm, 4.05pm and 8.05pm. **To France**, La Hispano-Andorrana company (☏376/82 13 72 or 82 13 27) runs at least 2 buses a day from Andorra la Vella to Pas de la Casa (1hr 20min) and L'Hospitalet (1hr 45min), one leaving in the morning and one in the afternoon, with an extra departure in summer and usually 5 on Saturdays. Towards La Tour de Carol, Autos Pujol Juguet provide two daily services, at 7.30am and 10.30am (2hr 15min).

Getting around

Internal **bus services** are cheap and frequent. The following routes run between about 7.30am and 9pm: Andorra la Vella–Sant Julià de Lòria, Andorra la Vella–Encamp–Canillo, and Andorra la Vella–La Massana–Ordino. Buses leave from Plaça Guillemó.

Currency, mail and phones

Andorra has never had **money** of its own, so both pesetas and French francs were historically accepted; the euro is naturally, now the common currency. There's also a shared postal system, with both a French and Spanish **post office** in Andorra la Vella and Canillo, for example. Andorra has its own **phone system** and phone code – ☏376 – applicable to the whole republic.

Language

Catalan is the official **language**, but Spanish and, to a slightly lesser extent, French are widely understood.

The 1993 referendum was an attempt to come to terms with the economic realities of twentieth-century Europe. Or rather, some of the economic realities, since none of the parties involved in the negotiations and arguments seriously suggested that the solution would be to introduce direct taxation: there is still no income tax in Andorra, and barely any indirect taxes either. Instead, the idea is to transform Andorra into a kind of "offshore" banking centre, to rival the likes of Gibraltar, Lichtenstein and Luxembourg.

Following the referendum, the state's first **constitutional election** was held in December 1993. Only the ten thousand native Andorrans were entitled to vote (out of a total population then of sixty thousand) and an eighty percent turnout gave Oscar Ribas Reig, outgoing head of the Consell General, the biggest share of the vote. His Agrupament Nacional Democratic took eight seats in the new 28-seat parliament – also dubbed the **Consell General** – and formed a coalition with other right-wing parties to usher in the new democratic era. Since then, Andorran citizens (those born there, or who have lived there for over twenty years) can vote freely, and join trade unions or political parties, while their government now has the right to run its own foreign policy and establish its own judicial system; Andorra has been accepted as a full member of the United Nations and the Council of Europe.

Given all this, it's useful to remember that as recently as 1950 Andorra was virtually cut off from the rest of the world – an archaic region which, romantically, happened also to be a separate country. There are still no planes and no trains, but the rest of the development has been all-encompassing: it can take an hour in bumper-to-bumper traffic to drive the few kilometres from La Seu d'Urgell to Andorra la Vella, the main town, while the large-scale ski resorts have already monopolized the most attractive corners of the state, with enlargements of existing ones mooted and a new resort planned for the beautiful Prat Primer upland. If you're curious, it can be worth a day or so for the cheap shopping and eating, and it's worth getting at least a little way out of the capital to see some of the scenery that attracted early visitors. Don't expect to find an unspoiled spot anywhere, though, unless you're prepared to strike off up the mountains on foot – and if you are, there are much more rewarding places on either side of Andorra where you could shoulder a rucksack.

Andorra La Vella

At just over 1000m, **ANDORRA LA VELLA**, with its stone church, river and enclosing hills, must once have been an attractive little town. Today the main street is a seething mass of tourist restaurants (specializing in six-language menus), tacky discos and brightly lit shops crammed with everything from electricals, perfumes and watches to cars and kitchenware. There's a partial respite in the old quarter, the **Barri Antic**, which lies on the heights above the river Valira, to the south of the main through road, Avinguda Princep Benlloch. But even here, the sole monument is the sixteenth-century stone **Casa de la Vall** in c/de la Vall (free guided tours Mon–Fri 10am–1pm & 3–7pm), which houses the Sala de Sessions of Andorra's parliament, and a small museum on the top floor.

Practicalities

Buses leave passengers on Avenguda Princep Benlloch, very near the church of Sant Esteve. There are about half a dozen public **car parks** scattered around town, should you bring your own vehicle – count on walking up to a kilometre from any space you happen to find. The **turisme**, on c/Dr Vilanova (Mon–Sat 10am–1pm & 3–7pm, Sun 10am–1pm; ☏376 820 214), east of the Barri Antic, has lists of local accommodation, restaurants and bus timetables.

There are several reasonable places if you decide to **stay**: the friendly, basic *Hostal del Sol*, at Plaça Guillemó 3 (☏376 823 701;❸); the slightly larger *Hotel Les Arcades* on the same square at no. 5 (☏376 821 355;❸); and the *Hotel Racó d'en Joan*, in the old quarter at c/de la Vall 20 (☏376 820 811;❸), which also has a ground-floor restaurant.

A better plan, perhaps, is to linger just long enough for something to **eat**; intense competition fosters low prices. Best value in the Barri Antic is *Minim's*, tucked away in the tiny Placeta de la Consorcia (closed Wed Oct–June), a small, stylish place with hearty French cuisine and a lunch *menú* for €6.60. Other fairly central and characterful places include *Pizzeria Primavera*, c/Dr Nequi 4, near the *Barri Antic*, *Restaurant Macary*, c/Mossèn Tremosa 6, just northeast of the Plaça Princep Benlloch, and *Les Arcades* at Plaça Guillemó 5, which has a bargain €5.90 *menú*.

If you do stay the night, there are two **cinemas** (at Avgda. Meritxell 26 and Avgda. Meritxell 44) and a live jazz **club**, *Àngel Blau*, in c/de la Borda.

Up the Valira d'Ordino

It's hard to convince yourself that not all of Andorra is like this (sadly, much of it is) but with a bit of effort you can effect a partial escape by heading up the **Valira d'Ordino**. At **LA MASSANA**, 7km out of Andorra La Vella, the road splits, the left-hand fork climbing up to the ski resorts of **ARINSAL** and **PAL**. The former is the most developed – with three daily buses from Andorra La Vella, 23 runs and a lively nightlife – while the latter is a pretty, stone-built village with a fine belfried Romanesque church (the ski centre is 5km beyond the village).

The right fork at La Massana is for **ORDINO** itself, a quiet, agreeable place with a handful of old stone edifices amongst the new chalets and apartment buildings. There are a few good **eating** options along the main street, including the *Granja Patisseria 1930*, with delicious cakes and snacks, or the bar-restaurant *Babi* next door, for more substantial meals. *Hotel Santa Barbara* on the *plaça* (☎376 837 100, 🖷376 837 092; ❺) is a reasonable **place to stay** here, or just 2km beyond Ordino, there's a pleasant riverside campsite, the *Borda d'Ansalonga* (☎376 850 374, 🖷376 850 445; closed May & Oct).

You'll have more choice, however, in the little villages of the valley proper, along the 8km or so north of Ordino; the landscape becomes more appealing here, with far fewer tower-cranes and high rises. **Accommodation** en route includes *Hotel Sucarà* in unspoilt La Cortinada, 2.5km north of Ordino (☎376 850 151; ❹); the *Hotel Arans* in Arans hamlet, 500m beyond (☎376 850 111; ❹); and *Hostal Vilaró* (☎376 850 225; ❹), slightly isolated just below the village of **LLORTS**, some 5km from Ordino. Llorts also offers one of the better rural **restaurants** in Andorra, *L'Era del Jaume* (reservations on ☎376 850 667), which specializes in grills (€18 *a la carta*, plus a lunchtime *menú*).

El Serrat and Ordino-Arcalis

Eighteen kilometres (and three daily bus departures) from Andorra la Vella, **EL SERRAT** stands at the head of the valley, graced by some tumbling waterfalls. Here you'll find the last **accommodation** before the ski centre of Ordino-Arcalis: the fairly basic *Hotel Tristaina* (☎376/850 081, 🖷376 850 730; ❸) and the recently refurbished *Hostal del Serrat* (☎376 735 735, 🖷376 735 740; ❺), the latter with a well-regarded restaurant. From El Serrat the road climbs steeply to the ski resort of **ORDINO-ARCALIS**, which retains snow well into April and is probably the most pleasant place to ski at intermediate level in Andorra, with a mostly Spanish, French and local clientele, and appealing views north over the Tristaina lakes and border ridge beyond.

The road to France: the Valira del Orient

It's around 35km from Andorra La Vella to the French border at Pas de la Casa, a route served as far as Soldeu by hourly buses from the capital. You're unlikely to be tempted to get off anywhere for casual touring, though there are a few possibilities.

Just 2km northeast of Andorra La Vella, **ESCALDES** is little more than a continuation of the capital – cars, coaches, hotels and restaurants – though it does have an excellent spa complex to unwind at. On a shelf of land just to the north is **Sant Miquel d'Engolasters**, one of Andorra's most attractive Romanesque churches, though its frescoes, like those of many Andorran churches, have been taken to the Museu d'Art de Catalunya in Barcelona. To get there, take the road that climbs to the dammed lake of Engolasters, passing the church after 4km.

Canillo

CANILLO, 14km from Andorra, makes one of the best compromise bases in Andorra: along the main road (and bus route) between Andorra la Vella and the nearby ski resort of Soldeu-El Tarter, but far enough away from both to retain some dignity and character. On the eastern fringe of the town, most of the belfried Romanesque church of **Sant Joan de Caselles** is originally eleventh century, but the porch is a fifteenth-century addition; back in the centre, a warren of old streets north of the highway leads to **Sant Sadurní**, nearly as ancient. When snow levels are sufficient, a bubble-lift rises south up to **El Forn**, a sub-area of El Tarter ski centre (see below).

Hotels line c/General, the main through road, with a couple of budget choices: the rock-bottom *Comerç* (☎376 851 020; ❸) and the friendly *Casa Nostra* (☎376 851 023; ❷–❸), with both en-suite and shared-bath rooms. The better-value *Canigó* (☎376 851 024; ❹) is opposite, or there's the *Hotel Pic Blanc*, at the west, lower end of the street (☎376 851 054; ❹). Among several local **campsites**, best is the tree-shaded *Camping Santa Creu* (☎376 851 462; mid-June to Sept) near the centre, on the south bank of the river. The restaurants at the *Comerç* and *Casa Nostra* are both very pleasant; alternatively, there's the *Molí del Peano* (closed mid-May to mid-June & mid-Oct to mid-Nov), where under €15 will get you grilled *conill* (rabbit) *all-i-oli*, goat's cheese salad, home-made mousse and a beer or two.

Soldeu-El Tarter

Development at **SOLDEU** village, 3km on, is surprisingly restrained considering that the adjacent ski centre is the largest in Andorra, with ample skiing for all ability levels amongst 47 pistes – it's the best place in Andorra for beginners, a fact appreciated by the British and Spanish families who seem to make up the main clientele. Once over the **Port d'Envalira** (though a tunnel is being prepared), the road tumbles down to the ghastly high-rise **PAS DE LA CASA**, a combination of duty-free bazaar and winter sports station and of not more than passing interest.

The Noguera Pallaresa valley

The **Noguera Pallaresa**, the most powerful river in the Pyrenees, was once used to float logs down from the mountains to the sawmills at La Pobla de Segur, a job now done by truck. These days, the river is known for its river-rafting opportunities, while for those with less specialized enthusiasms, its valley provides an efficient way of getting into the high Pyrenees, particularly to the Vall d'Aran and the east flank of the Parc Nacional d'Aigüestortes i Estany de Sant Maurici.

Access to the valley is easiest through La Pobla de Segur (see below), which can be reached directly from Barcelona or Lleida. Approaching from the east, there's a road (2 buses daily) from La Seu d'Urgell to Sort, in the middle of the valley (see below), through 53km of gorgeous scenery. Alsina Graells buses leave Barcelona (from Plaça de la Universitat) for La Pobla de Segur, a three-and-a-half-hour ride via dismal Artesa de Segre (on the C1313). Much better to take the regular **train** from Lleida to La Pobla – a spectacular ride behind a steam locomotive, with glimpses of cliff and water between spells in the many tunnels.

Tremp, Talarn and Santa Engràcia

However you approach, the first major halt in the Noguera Pallaresa valley itself is at **TREMP**, poised between two hydroelectric dams that supply much of Catalunya's power. There's accommodation here, a pleasant central square, and even a tourist office, but if you're going to be overnighting locally, far better spots to **stay** and **eat** – with or without your own transport – are found just outside of town.

Two kilometres northwest is the large, fortified hill town of **TALARN**, where the *Casa Lola*, c/Soldevila 2, shines as a beacon of country cuisine, attracting clientele from near and far; proprietress "Lola" (Glorieta) is a character, giving free *pa amb tomàquet*-making lessons to the uninitiated. She also has a few apartments (☎973 650 814; ❺). Alternatively, if you have your own transport, you can head out from just below Talarn along a narrow but paved 10km road west to **SANTA ENGRÀCIA**, one of the most spectacularly located villages in Catalunya, tumbling off the south flank of a rock monolith. Here *Casa Guilla* (☎973 252 080, ⓦ www.ctv.es/USERS/casaguilla; closed Dec–Feb; ❺ half board), a restored rambling farmhouse with sweeping views, offers simple, rustic rooms – many with shared bath – plus a pool, restaurant and bar; reservations are advised.

La Pobla de Segur

Thirteen kilometres north of Tremp, **LA POBLA DE SEGUR** is a lively enough town if you want to break your journey, although most people only come here for onward connections. La Pobla is served by a twice-daily Alsina Graells **bus** from Barcelona (departs 7.30am and 2.30pm from Plaça de la Universitat, labelled *Pont de Rei*), and by three daily **trains** from Lleida which terminate here. The bus from Barcelona continues up the Noguera Pallaresa through Sort and Llavorsí, passing within 7km of Espot, a major entry point to the Aigüestortes national park (see p.833). Arriving from Lleida, morning train and bus services should connect with this bus, which departs La Pobla at 11.35am; there's another service at 6.35pm. From June to mid-November, the first of these two bus services continues over the pass into the Vall d'Aran.

As well as these buses along the Noguera Pallaresa, local services also journey west to El Pont de Suert, Boí and Capdella for the western margins of the Aigüestortes region, and to Viella through its namesake tunnel for the Vall d'Aran.

Trains arrive in the new town, from where you walk up the road, cross the bridge and head along the main street towards the terminal of the Alsina Graells **bus** company at c/de la Font 8. Should you get stranded, there is just one *hostal*, the bunker-ugly *Torrentet* at Plaça Pedrera 5 (☎973 680 352; ❹).

Rafting on the Noguera Pallaresa

The main **rafting season** on the Noguera Pallaresa lasts from April until September, though some organizations offer programmes from March to October if snowmelt (and the power company) are amenable. The original rafts – used for the journey downstream to the sawmills of La Pobla de Segur – were logs lashed together ten-wide. Today's water-sport versions are reinforced **inflatables**, up to six and a half metres long. If you sign on for a trip – which guarantees a soaking and about as much excitement as any well-balanced person would want – you'll usually share a boat with seven others, including your guide/pilot, who sits in the rear.

The 14km between Llavorsí and Rialp is the easiest and thus most commonly rafted sector of the river, while the 18km from Sort to Desfiladero de Collegats is advanced and even more scenic. Daily **departures** are typically at 11am and noon; in the former case you'll be in the water by 11.20am, and clambering into the return-shuttle van at Rialp by 12.40pm. **Prices** start at about €27 for a two-hour rafting trip, either Llavorsi-Rialp or Sort-Collegats, or €48 for the entire 35-kilometre distance (a full afternoon's outing, packed lunch €12 extra).

Gerri de la Sal and around

From La Pobla de Segur the C147 road threads through the **Desfiladero de Collegats**, an impressive gorge hewn by the Noguera Pallaresa through three-hundred-metre-high cliffs. Unfortunately, since a series of tunnels was blasted through much of the defile, drivers see little of the spectacular valley, though the narrow, abandoned old road is still open to cyclists and pedestrians. The Catalan intelligentsia have been coming here to admire the scenery for over a century, and the portion of the canyon labelled as **L'Argenteria**, with its sculpted, papier-mâché-like rockface streaked with rivulets, was apparently the natural inspiration for Antoní Gaudí's La Pedrera apartment building in Barcelona.

As the gorge opens out, you emerge at the rickety village of **GERRI DE LA SAL** – "de la Sal" because of the local salt-making industry. You'll see still-functioning salt pans by the riverside as you pass by, but the most obvious landmark is the Benedictine monastery of **Santa María** (€1.20), originally founded in 807. The present twelfth-century structure, with its huge and dilapidated bell-wall, faces the village on the far side of a beautiful old bridge.

If you have a vehicle this is a fine place for a short break. In Gerri itself there's a **restaurant** and a bar, but for **accommodation** you have to continue 4km north to the tiny village of **BARO**, where there are rooms and food at the *Bar Restaurant Cal Mariano* (☎973 680 550; ❷), plus a large riverbank **campsite**, the *Pallars Sobirà* (☎973 662 030; open all year), and a supermarket.

Sort, Rialp and Port-Ainé

SORT, 30km north of La Pobla, retains an old centre of tall, narrow houses, though it's now hemmed in by apartment buildings. This rapid development is owed mainly to the fact that Sort and neighbouring villages have suddenly found themselves among the premier **river-running spots** in Europe (see box, above). Every year during late June/early July, the communities of the valley stage the festival of the *Raiers* (Rafters), re-enacting the exploits of the old-time timber pilots who could still put the slick new daredevils to shame.

Because of the upmarket sports clientele it attracts, Sort has priced itself out of any casual trade, and in any case it's not a place to linger unless you're here for the action. Its main street is almost exclusively devoted to rafting and adventure shops – among these, Rubber River (℡973 620 220, ℻973 620 237, ⓦwww.rubber-river.com) is reputable – and there's nowhere inexpensive to stay or eat, though there is a **turisme** (summer Mon–Fri 9am–2pm & 5–9pm, Sat 10am–1pm & 5–8pm) on the main street. The bus stops at an obvious shelter on Plaça Catalina Albert, at the north end of town where the two through roads join up.

RIALP, 3km north, is a marginally more appealing mix of old houses and new boutiques; the bus stop/ticket office here is the bar under the *Hotel Victor* (℡973 620 379; ❺), the most reasonable if somewhat unexciting place to stay. Fourteen kilometres northeast, the ski station at **PORT-AINÉ** offers some of the best beginners' and intermediates' skiing in the Catalan Pyrenees on its 28 longish runs.

Llavorsí

Probably the most attractive place to stay along this stretch of the valley is **LLAVORSÍ**, 10km above Rialp at the meeting of the Noguera Pallaresa and the Cardós rivers. Despite extensive renovation, a rash of new bar/restaurants and rafting outfitters on the main road, plus a mammoth power substation across the way, this tight huddle of stone-built houses and slate roofs still retains much of its character. There are two good riverside **campsites**, both with pools and bars – the *Aigües Braves* 1km north of town (℡973 622 153; March–Sept), and the smaller *Riberies* east of the centre in the Cardós valley (℡973 622 151; mid-June to mid-Sept) – plus ample **accommodation** catering for the river trade. In rafting season, reserve in advance; try the *Hotel Lamoga* (℡973 622 006; May–Sept only; ❺, half board preferred) on the riverfront, with a good *menú* for under €12; the quieter, adjacent *Hostal de Rey* (℡973 622 011; ❹); or the *Hostal Noguera* (℡973 622 012; ❹) on the opposite bank, whose restaurant has river-view seating and a reasonable if rather limited *menú*.

Two local **sports/adventure operators** offering rafting, canyoning, hydrospeed, mountain-biking and rock-climbing are Yeti Emotions (℡973 622 201, ℻973 622 260, ⓦwww.yetiemotions.com), some 500m south of Llavorsí, on the west bank of the river opposite a road tunnel, and the central, friendly Rafting Llavorsi (℡973 622 158, ℻973 622 134, ⓦwww.raftingllavorsi.com).

The Vall d'Àneu

From Llavorsí the road continues upstream along the Noguera Pallaresa, past the turning for Espot (see p.838) and the placid, artificial lake of Pantà de la Torrasa, to **LA GUINGUETA D'ÀNEU** at the head of the reservoir. This is the first of three villages incorporating the name of the local valley, the **Vall d'Àneu**.

ESTERRI D'ÀNEU, 4km further beyond the lake and, from late November to May, end of the line for the bus from Barcelona, was transformed virtually overnight during the early 1990s from somnolent farming community to chic resort. Parts of town still form as graceful an ensemble as you'll see in the Catalan Pyrenees – the few huddled houses between the road and the river, an arched bridge and slender-towered Sant Vicenç church – but the new apartment buildings and fancy hotels to the south are another matter. At the moment Esterri's growth has stalled, tied to the overflow of the Super Espot ski clientele (see p.838) for its trade, but the mooted expansion of the closer Baqueira-Beret resort (see p.830) could set off another spasm of construction. Nonetheless, there are worse places to end up in the evening. The best-value

place to stay has historically been the delightful and recently renovated *Pensió Agustí* (☎973 626 034; ❺), in a quiet location behind the church in Plaça de l'Església, with an old-fashioned *menjador*. *Pensió Costa* at c/Major 14 (☎973 626 061; ❹) is rather grim; ask instead for their plusher, second premises, *Costa 2* (☎973 626 401; ❺). The closest **campsite**, *La Presalla* (☎973 626 031; April–Sept), is 1.5km south of the village and has chalet huts available to rent.

València d'Àneu and the Port de la Bonaigua

Three kilometres further up the main road, **VALÈNCIA D'ÀNEU**, with its traditional stone houses and small Romanesque church, has been far less disrupted by development than Esterri d'Àneu, and should remain pretty rural – unless the proposed extension of the Baqueira-Beret resort over the hill takes place. València was much more important at one time than its current sleepy profile suggests; an ongoing archeological dig on the outskirts has brought to light the remains of a tenth-century **castle**, apparently the power base of counts who ruled over many of the surrounding valleys. When the volunteer excavators are present in summer, visitors are welcome to have a look around.

Best choice for **accommodation** here is the exceptionally good-value *Hotel La Morera* (☎973 626 124; ❺), with enormous balconied rooms, a valley-side pool and wonderful breakfasts; runners-up are the *habitacions* (❹) above the recommended **restaurant** *La Bonaigua* (☎973 626 110; usually closed Jan 7–end March & mid-Oct to Nov), which features local game and trout on its affordable *menús*. Another worthwhile spot to eat, in the village centre off the through road, is *Felip*, with a €8.10 *menú* or an ample *carta*.

Beyond València, the road quits the Noguera Pallaresa as it climbs above the quilt of green and brown fields around Esterri; the Riu de la Bonaigua takes over as the roadside stream, lined by forests of silver birch, pine and fir. The views get ever more impressive as you approach the treeline, above which is perched the **restaurant-bar** of *Mare de Déu de les Ares*, next to the eponymous *ermita*. Near the top of the bleak **Port de la Bonaigua** (2072m; usually closed in winter), snow patches persist year-round, half-wild horses graze and you get simultaneous panoramas of the valleys you've just left and the Vall d'Aran to come. There's a fine full-day circuit south from here via Estany Gerber through the Circ de Saborèdo with its half-dozen lakes and staffed **refuge** (2310m; ☎973 253 015), then back to the pass; drive or arrange a ride to the starting point, as bus timings are unhelpful.

The Vall d'Aran

The **Vall d'Aran**, with its luxuriantly alpine feel, is completely encircled by the main Pyrenean watershed and its various spur-ridges. Although it has belonged to Aragón or Catalunya – later unified Spain – since 1192, the valley, with the Garona river cleaving down the middle, eventually opens to the north, and is actually much more accessible from France. Like Andorra, it was virtually independent for much of its history, and for centuries it was sealed off from the rest of Spain by snow for seven months of the year, but in 1948 the Viella tunnel was finally finished (through slave labour provided by Republican POWs) to provide a year-round link with the provincial capital of Lleida along the N230 highway.

Since the early 1980s, life in the valley has changed beyond recognition. The old scythe-wielding hay-reapers of summer have been replaced by Massey

Ferguson balers, overlooked by holiday chalets for city folk, which have sprouted at the edge of each and every village. Although the development is undeniably sympathetic – the new Aranese-style stone buildings fit closely with the originals – the vast numbers of chi-chi restaurants and sports shops sit incongruously with the little medieval villages they surround. By getting off the perennially congested main road through the valley it's still possible to get some idea of the region as it was fifty years ago, but even there don't expect virgin rural expanses. Aran is best regarded as a comfortable overnight or two en route to more spectacular destinations, and overall the valley is one of the most expensive, overdeveloped and (unless you're skiing) overrated corners of alpine Catalunya.

The valley's legendary greenness derives from the streams that drain into it – mostly from the lakes of Aigüestortes on the south slope – rather than particularly high rainfall. When the weather *is* wet, black and yellow fire salamanders move with unconcerned slowness on the damp footpaths; before and after the rain, equally brilliant butterflies, for which the Vall d'Aran and the Aigüestortes park are both famous, flutter about.

Among themselves the inhabitants speak Aranés, a **language** (not a dialect, as a glance at the bizarre road signs will tell you) based on elements of Catalan and Gascon with a generous sprinkling of Basque vocabulary. *Aran*, in this language, means "valley": *Nautaran*, (High Valley) is the most scenic eastern portion. The Aranese spelling of local place names is given in parentheses below.

Baqueira-Beret

The ride down from Port de la Bonaigua isn't for the acrophobic or those with dodgy brakes, with its hairpins and sharp drop into the Ruda valley on one side. The first place you encounter coming down from the pass is **BAQUEIRA-BERET**, a mammoth skiing development that has served as the biggest engine of change in the region. The resort core itself is modern, posey (the Spanish royal family frequents it) and has little to offer other than four- or five-star hotels, but it's no trouble to stay nearby at Salardú or Tredòs (see below) and show up for the **skiing**, some of the best in these mountains – at least until March, when the snow can start to get mushy. Day lift passes are among the priciest in the Pyrenees at about €28, but you are being pampered with a preponderance of chair lifts and an interlinked domain of 47 runs – the full story is at ⓦ www.baqueira.es.

Salardú

SALARDÚ, a few kilometres further west, is in effect the capital of *Nautaran* and the most logical base for explorations: large enough to offer a reasonable choice of accommodation and food, but small enough to feel pleasantly isolated (except in August, or peak ski season). With steeply pitched roofs clustered around the church, it retains some traditional character, though the main attraction in staying is to explore the surrounding villages, all centred on beautiful Romanesque churches.

Salardú's is the roomy, thirteenth-century church of **Sant Andreu**, set in its own pleasant grounds. The doors are flanked by the most ornate portal in the valley, whose carved column capitals feature birds feeding their young and four eerie little human faces peeping out; once inside, you can enjoy some fine sixteenth-century fresco patches, restored in 1994, including Christ Enthroned, the Assumption, various saints and smudged panels of the Four Virtues personified.

Practicalities

There's a wooden **turisme** hut (summer only Mon–Fri 10.30am–1.30pm & 4.30–8pm, Sat 10am–1pm & 4–7pm, Sun 10am–1pm) just off the main road at the turning for Bagergue. The one **bank** in the village has normal opening hours, plus an ATM. There is also a **swimming pool** (mid-June to Aug daily 11am–7pm) if you fancy a dip.

Even at the height of the summer you should be able to find a **bed** (if not a room) easily enough in Salardú. The YHA hostel at the east edge of town is perennially full of Spanish school groups; more dependable options aimed at trekkers are the *Refugi Rosti*, Plaça Major 1 (☎973 645 308, ℉973 645 814; closed May, June, Oct & Nov; ➍ , dorms €13.20 per person), in a 300-year-old building on the main square, and the *Refugi Juli Soler Santaló* (☎973 645 016; ➊), 200m east of the tourist booth next to the pool. For conventional accommodation, try the wood-decor **rooms** – some en suite – above the *Bar Montanha* (☎973 644 108; ➌), or those at *Residència Aiguamòg* (☎973 645 996; ➎). A more upmarket choice is the *Hotel deth Pais* in Plaça dera Pica (☎973 645 836, ℉973 644 500; ➏).

Most of the places to stay in the village serve good-value **meals**: non-guests can eat excellent *menús* at the highly recommended *Refugi Juli Soler Santaló*, or spend about €18 *a la carta* at *Aloy*, offshoot of the *Hotel deth Pais*. Alternatives are scarce, especially as the handful of village restaurants are overpriced for what you get. While the restaurant at the *Refugi Rosti* is decent enough, its main appeal is the nicest **bar** in town: *Delicatesen*.

Villages around Salardú

The bus from La Pobla de Segur gets into Salardú at around 2pm, leaving plenty of time to find accommodation and then strike off into the surrounding villages. Houses here are traditionally built of stone, with slate roofs, and there's surprisingly little to distinguish a 400-year-old home from a four-year-old one. Many display dates on the lintels – not of the same vintage as the churches but respectable enough, with some going back as far as the sixteenth century.

UNYA (Unha), 700m up the hill into the Unyola valley, boasts a shrine of the same age as the church in Salardú, though you're more likely to be interested in the half-dozen **restaurants** here, the most economical of which is the *Casa Restaurante Perez*. **BAGERGUE**, 2km higher up the road (or reached via the marked GR211 path from Unya) remains the most countrified of the *Nautaran* settlements, and offers yet another handsome church – plus three more **restaurants**. Most famous of these is *Casa Peru* (reserve on ☎973 645 437), which deserves the plaudits adorning its entrance: an *olha aranesa* (hot-pot) to die for, venison meatballs in wild mushroom sauce, wild-fruit flan with merengue plus good house wine for €27 – far less than the more pretentious places in Salardú or Arties.

Across the river from Salardú, and about twenty minutes' walk upstream along the country lane signposted as the *Camin Reaiu* (King's Road), **TREDÒS** was once the prettiest of the *Nautaran* villages but has had its old core overwhelmed by a rash of new ski chalets. Still, in the centre, the *Restaurante Saburedo* is a find, with a hearty four-course *menú* for about €18. They also have en-suite and shared-bath **rooms** (☎973 645 089; ➌ –➍) if you want **to stay**, as does the *Casa Micalot* (☎973 645 326; ➌) on the same lane. Otherwise, after taking a look at the massive church with its free-standing belfry, there's nothing to stop you from walking back to Salardú.

Arties

ARTIES, 3km west of Salardú, features the usual complement of recent holiday homes, with more under construction. Nevertheless, if you're driving, and Salardú is full up, it has considerable appeal, particularly in its old village core straddling the Garona, and its two **churches**: Santa María, with Templar fortifications, and deconsecrated Sant Joan on the main road, now home to a small **museum** of changing exhibits (Tues–Fri 5–8pm, Sat 10am–1pm & 5–8pm, Sun 10am–1pm; €1.20). Arties is also known for its high-quality food and lodging (see below), and for its **hot springs**, long shut down but recently sold and undergoing renovation. The *camí* leading past them (marked as the GR211.1) cuts out 3km of the busy main highway, rejoining it at Casarilh village, a boon if you're cycling.

Practicalities

The best budget **accommodation** in Arties is the quiet *Pensió Barrie*, alias *Casa Portolá* (☎973 640 828; ④) at c/Mayor 21, three floors of wood-and-tile decor en-suite rooms. For more comfort, try either the friendly *Hotel Besiberri* by the stream at c/Deth Fòrt 4 (☎ & ⓕ973 640 829; closed Nov; ⑦), with smallish but well-appointed rooms and lovely common areas; or the *Hotel Valarties* at c/Major 3 (☎973 644 364; closed May to mid-June & mid-Oct to Nov; ⑦), where many of the wood-floored rooms overlook the enormous rear garden. There's also a **campsite**, *Era Yerla d'Arties* (☎973 641 602; open all year), just below the village on the main road to Viella, considered the best in the valley.

Arties' half-a-dozen **restaurants** also represent better value for money than those in Salardú, though many hike up their prices during ski season. Tried and tested options include *Montagut* (closed Tues) up on the highway, with three *menús* (€9–19), and *Casa Irene*, inside the *Hotel Valarties*, one of the most innovative – and expensive – restaurants in the valley. The friendly South African-run *El Pollo Loco* (open Dec–April only), in the same building as *Montagut*, offers four *menús* (€8–17), including a vegetarian one, featuring local pâtés, duck, game and of course the chicken of the name, all washed down by organic cider.

Viella

From *Nautaran*, the highest of the three divisions of the Vall d'Aran, you move west into *Mijaran* (Mid-Aran), whose major town is **VIELLA** (Vielha), administrative centre for the whole valley and end of the line for the bus from Barcelona/La Pobla de Segur in summer. This arrives at 2.30pm, with the daily service in the opposite direction leaving at about 11.45am. You may also reach Viella from Lleida, via El Pont de Suert, a spectacular route in its final stages that culminates in the awesome **Túnel de Viella**, nearly 6km long and scheduled to be enlarged in the near future.

In truth, the ride to Viella from either direction is more attractive than the town itself, and there's little reason to stay, particularly if you have your own wheels or can make a bus connection onwards. Viella has become intensely developed and smartened up since 1990, a trend aggravated by the French customers of the numerous supermarkets, boutiques and restaurants. If you have time to kill, pop into the parish church of **Sant Miquèu**, right in the centre on the east bank of the Riu Nere; its twelfth-century wooden bust, the *Cristo de Mijaran* – probably part of a *Descent from the Cross* – is reckoned the finest specimen of Romanesque art in this part of the Pyrenees. The **Museu deth**

Val (Mon–Sat 10am–1pm & 5–8pm, Sun 10am–1pm; €1.20), at c/Major 26, west of the church and across the Nere, is also worth a look for its coverage of Aranese history and folklore. The only other potential diversion is the mammoth **Palai de Gèu** (Ice Palace) across the Garona, a combination swimming pool, ice rink and gymnasium (€8.40 admission to all facilities including skate hire).

Practicalities

Buses stop just downhill from the major roundabout at the west end of town. The **turisme** (June–Sept Mon–Sat 9am–1pm & 4–8pm, Sun 10am–1pm & 4.30–7.30pm; Oct–May opening times vary; ☎976 640 110), is near the post office at c/Sarriulera 6, just off the church square, and offers maps and complete valley accommodation lists.

As you might expect there's no shortage of **accommodation** in Viella, but most of it is aimed at ski clientele, with little of outstanding value. Coming from the church, you'll find the best of the inexpensive places by turning left along the main street and then right down the lane just across the bridge. Just off to the left, at Plaça Sant Orenç 3, there's the *Hostal El Ciervo* (☎973 640 165, ℱ973 642 072; ❹); the often full *Pensió Puig*, c/Camin Reiau 4 (☎973 640 031; ❷); and the tiny *Pensió Casa Vicenta* across the way at no. 3 (☎973 640 819; ❹).

Least expensive and most central of Viella's **restaurants** is the *Basteret*, c/Major 6a, with an €10.80 *menú*. With a bit more outlay, try *Eth Hurat* at Passeig dera Llibertat 14, a supper-only creperie, or *Eth Cornèr* on Passeig dera Llibertat 7, with *a la carta* fare.

Baixaran

You can continue from Viella by bus, car or bike through **ARRÒS** (6km) and **ES BÒRDES** (Era Bordeta; 9km), two places that play a key role in Aranese domestic architecture. Es Bòrdes supplies the granite for the walls and Arròs the slates for the slightly concave roofs that are generally demanded in *Nautaran* and *Mijaran*. Arròs itself, though, is almost in the lower **Baixaran** (Low Aran) region, and the balconied houses here, around the octagonal bell tower, have rendered white walls and red-tiled roofs. There are two mammoth **campsites** at Arròs – the *Artigané* (☎973 640 189; June–Sept) and the *Verneda* (☎973 641 024; June–Sept) – plus two smaller ones just past Es Bòrdes.

The focus of *Baixaran* is the large village of **BOSSÒST**, 16km from Viella, where the houses are strung out along the main road, alternating with tacky shops. There's no real reason to stop: it's only 4km to **LES**, with a spa and less expensive accommodation; 9km to the **French border** at Eth Pònt de Rei, and 20km to the first significant French town, Saint-Béat.

Parc Nacional d'Aigüestortes i Estany de Sant Maurici

The deservedly most popular target for trekkers in the Catalan Pyrenees is the **PARC NACIONAL D'AIGÜESTORTES I ESTANY DE SANT MAURICI**, a vast and beautiful mountainous area constituting Catalunya's only national park (albeit not recognized as such by international bodies owing to its intrusive hydroelectric works). Established in 1955, and considerably

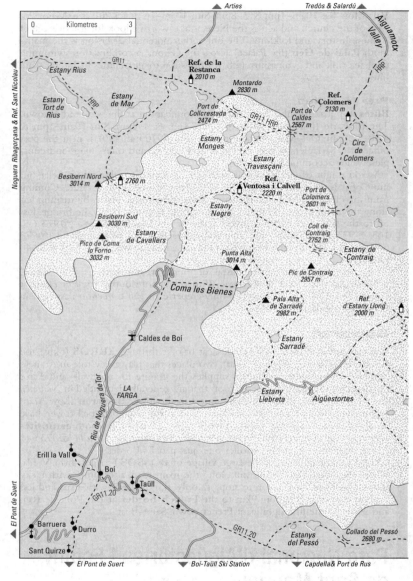

enlarged between 1986 and 1996 to over 140 square kilometres, it's a rock- and forest-strewn landscape of harsh beauty, including spectacular snow-spotted peaks of up to 3000m, nearly four hundred lakes and dramatic V-shaped valleys. For the less adventurous, there are any number of mid-altitude rambles to be made through some lovely scenery. The Sant Nicolau valley and its tributaries (in the west) have many glacially formed lakes and cirques, as well as the

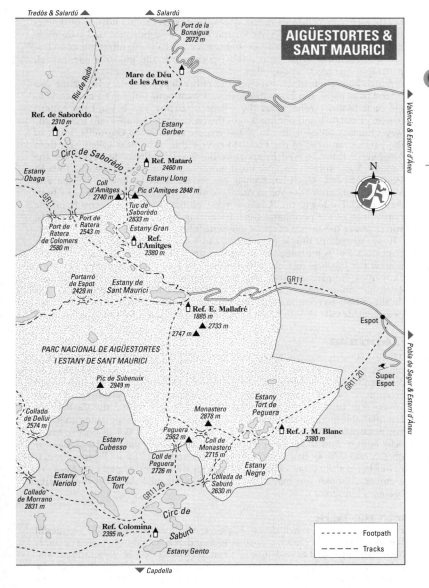

AIGÜESTORTES & SANT MAURICI

Tredòs & Salardú ▲▲   ▲ Salardú

Port de la Bonaigua 2072 m

Mare de Déu de les Ares

Riu de Ruda

Ref. de Saborèdo 2310 m

Estany Gerber

Circ de Saborèdo

Ref. Mataró 2460 m

Estany Obaga

Estany Llong

Coll d'Amitges 2740 m

Pic d'Amitges 2848 m

Tuc de Saborèdo 2833 m

GR11

Port de Ratera 2543 m

Estany Gran

Port de Ratera de Colomers 2580 m

Ref. d'Amitges 2380 m

Portarró de Espot 2429 m

Estany de Sant Maurici

GR11

N

Ref. E. Mallafré 1885 m

Espot

2747 m ▲   ▲ 2733 m

PARC NACIONAL DE AIGÜESTORTES I ESTANY DE SANT MAURICI

GR11.20

Super Espot

Pic de Subenuix 2949 m

Estany Tort de Peguera

Collada de Dellui 2574 m

Monastero 2878 m

Peguera 2982 m

Ref. J. M. Blanc 2380 m

Estany Cubesso

Coll de Monastero 2715 m

Coll de Peguera 2726 m

Estany Negre

Estany Neriolo

Estany Tort

Collada de Saburó 2630 m

Collado de Morrano 2831 m

GR11.20

Circ de

Ref. Colomina 2395 m

Saburó

Estany Gento

- - - - - Footpath
— — — Tracks

▼ Capdella

water meadows of Aigüestortes (Twisted Waters) themselves. In the eastern sector, highlights include the Circ de Saborèdo and the Peguera valley, as well as the Estany de Sant Maurici, at the head of the Escrita valley. Just outside the park, in the so-called "peripheral zone of protection" of 270 square kilometres, are even more lake-spangled cirques.

The most common **trees** are fir and Scotch pine, along with silver birch and

835

beech, especially on north-facing slopes. There's also an abundance of flowers in spring and early summer. As for the **fauna**, wild boar, fox and hare roam here and at the very least you should see *isards* (chamois); otters are considerably more elusive. **Birds** you might spot include the golden eagle, kestrel, ptarmigan and black woodpecker.

Which **approach** to the park you use rather depends upon which zone you intend to explore, and how strenuous you want your walking to be. Access to the Sant Maurici zone is via the village of **Espot**, just beyond the eastern fringes of the park and within 7km of the La Pobla de Segur–Viella main highway. Quickest access to the high and remote peaks is via **Capdella**, south of the park at the head of the Flamisell river – this is the next valley west from Noguera Pallaresa, served by sporadic bus from La Pobla de Segur. For the western Aigüestortes zone, the usual entrance is from **Boí**, approached via **El Pont de Suert**, which has regular bus service from La Pobla de Segur and Viella. Finally, from the Vall d'Aran, narrow roads, then trails, lead up from **Arties** and **Tredòs** to the Restanca and Colomers refuges respectively, on the north flank of the peripheral zone. It's boring hiking up to these, but at least you're not at the mercy of sparse bus schedules.

If you can afford only a day or two, and are strictly reliant on public transport, then Boí is probably the best place for which to aim. It's easy to reach, just off the bus line to Caldes de Boí, and though the village itself lies some 7km from the park entrance, the public bus past the La Farga trailhead or a 4WD-taxi up to Aigüestortes will solve this problem. All the approaches – and details of how to move on into the park – are dealt with fully below, while for **practical details** about the park itself check the boxed feature opposite.

Capdella

There are fairly regular buses (Alsina Graells; 5.15pm; Oct–May Mon–Fri; June–Sept Mon, Wed & Fri only) from La Pobla de Segur to **CAPDELLA**, 30km upstream. The village, the highest of half a dozen in the little-known Vall Fosca, is in two quite distinct parts: the upper part has no facilities, while the lower, 2km below – where the bus stops – is based around the Central (de Energia), the oldest hydroelectric power plants in these parts, dating to 1914. For **accommodation** here, *Hostal Leo* (☎973 663 157; ❼ half board), originally built to host the power company workers, is fairly elegant; *Hotel Monseny* (☎973 663 079; ❼ half board), 800m south and officially in Espui village, is newer but equally good value. Both lodgings are currently open only Easter to October, although this may change when the planned ski resort for the area becomes a reality.

Into the park

From Capdella it's a half-day trek, past the Sallente dam, to the wonderful **Refugi Colomina** (2395m; open year-round, but staffed only early Feb, mid-March to mid-April & mid-June to Sept; ☎973 252 000, ⓦwww.luthiers.net/colomina/colomc.htm), an old wooden chalet ceded to mountaineers by the power company and set among superb high mountain lakes on the southern perimeter of the park. You can cut out much of the trek by taking the *teléferic* (cable car) from the back of the Sallente reservoir to within 45 minutes' walk of the refuge (July–Sept only, daily up at 9am & 3pm, down at 1pm & 6pm; €3.60 one-way).

The immediate surroundings of the refuge have several short outings suitable for any remaining daylight. The more adventurous will set out the following

Park rules and practicalities

❑ **Entry** to the park is free, but private cars are completely prohibited. The only means of vehicle access is via the reasonably priced 4WD-taxis which ply from both Espot and Boí. Driving yourself, the closest you can get are the 200-vehicle-capacity car parks 4km west of Espot, at the east boundary, or at La Farga north of Boí in the west, by the edge of the peripheral zone.

❑ **Accommodation in the park** is limited to five mountain refuges (staffed with wardens during the summer – you'll need sleeping bags at all of them), but there are five more in nearly as impressive alpine areas just outside the park boundaries. Each refuge has bunk beds (about €6 per head), a meal service and a telephone or emergency transmitter. FEEC-managed places allow you to self-cater inside; CEC-managed ones do not. More information is available at Ⓦ www.rotativo.com/refugios/. **Camping** in the park is officially forbidden, and technically restricted within the peripheral zone – for which you're supposed to secure a permit from the nearest village – but as long as you pitch your tent well away from refuges and paths, nobody will bother you. There are managed campsites at Taüll in the west, and at Espot in the east. All the approach villages have *hostales*, *cases de pagès* and hotels.

❑ The region is covered by several Editorial Alpina **map/booklets**: the two you'll need for walking any of the routes described below are *Sant Maurici* for the east, and *Montardo/Vall de Boí* for the west, both 1:25,000 and available in Boí, Espot and good bookshops throughout the Pyrenees and in Barcelona. You can also buy the two-for-the-price-of-one *Parc Nacional d'Aigüestortes I Estany de Sant Maurici*, without the booklet. If you intend to approach from the north, you'll need the 1:40,000 *Vall d'Aran* Alpina map. Sketched handouts available at the various park information offices generally prove insufficient for route-finding – get a proper commercial map if you intend to leave the most popular paths.

❑ Be aware of, and prepared for, **bad weather**, which, as everywhere in the Pyrenees, can arrive rapidly and without warning. In midsummer many rivers are passable which are otherwise not so, but temperature contrasts between day and night are still very marked. Local climatic patterns in recent years have alternated between daily rain showers throughout July and August, or prolonged drought, with a general trend towards warmer, drier summers. The best time to see the wonderful colour contrasts here are in autumn or early summer. Many passes, even those mapped with a bona fide trail over them, will be difficult or impossible without special equipment after a harsh winter owing to snowpack. If you're going to do a less common traverse, tell the warden of the refuge you'll be leaving, who should be able to give current **route pointers** and, if there's any cause for concern, phone or radio ahead to your destination to give an estimated time of arrival – and perhaps make you a reservation.

❑ In **winter**, the park is excellent for cross-country and high-mountain **skiing**, though there are no marked routes. The refuges usually open around Christmas and Easter, as well as on selected weekends and school holidays in between. There are currently two ski resorts on the fringes of the park: Boí-Taüll in the west and Super Espot in the east – with another planned for the Sallente area above Capdella.

day to Estany Llong and its refuge, via Estany Tort and Collada (Pass) de Dellui (2570m). Alternatively, there's the classic (if difficult) traverse due north into the national park via the Coll (Pass) de Peguera (2726m), taking six hours. You end up near the base of the Sant Maurici dam at the **Refugi Ernest Mallafré** (1885m; mid–June to end Sept; ☎973 250 118), poised for further walks. If it's full, the comfortable **Refugi d'Amitges** is just ninety minutes away (2380m; open late Feb, Easter, mid–June to end Sept; ☎973 250 109). If you enter the park this way, there's a seasonal **information post** (Easter & July–Sept daily 9.30am–2pm & 4–6.30pm) by the Sant Maurici dam.

Espot and Super Espot

The approach from Espot is less strenuous, though purists (and people with heavy backpacks) will object to the possible necessity of road walking both the very steep 7km up from the turning on the main road where the Barcelona–Viella bus drops you, and the similar distance beyond the village to the usual park entrance. Wait for a 4WD-taxi at the turn-off and save your legs for later; it costs €3.60 per person for the short run up to Espot.

ESPOT (1320m) itself is still surprisingly unspoiled, despite decades of exploitation as a tourist centre. There remain four or five places to stay in the predominantly rural village, and there's a **park information office** (April–Oct daily 9am–1pm & 3.30–6.45pm; Nov–March Mon–Sat 9am–2pm & 3.30–6pm, Sun 9am–2pm; ☎973 624 036) at the edge of Espot, where you can pick up **maps** of the park and check conditions if you intend to stay and trek for some time.

Two kilometres above the village is the ski centre of **SUPER ESPOT** (information at *www.espotesqui.com*) which, despite a northeast orientation, has a snow record which isn't up to most neighbouring resorts; many runs may be closed by March, and the whole place can shut for the day at 3pm.

Practicalities

The best-value **accommodation** in Espot village is at *Casa Felip* (☎973 624 093; ❸–❹), simple but very clean with most rooms en suite. Other possibilities include the *Pensió La Palmira* (☎973 624 072; ❹) and the *Hotel Roya* (☎973 624 040, ☏973 624 041; ❺). There are three **campsites** close by: the smallish *Sol i Neu* (☎973 624 001; Easter, June–Sept) has excellent facilities including a pool, and lies just a few hundred metres from the village; *De La Mola* (☎973

Classic traverses

One of the classic hikes – accessible to anyone in reasonable shape – is right across the park from east to west, starting at the Sant Maurici reservoir and climbing over the Portarró d'Espot (2429m). To reach the other jeep-taxi terminus at Aigüestortes it's about six hours' walking; if you have to hoof it all the way to Boí, allow ten hours. The **Refugi d'Estany Llong** (2000m; open late Feb, Easter, June to mid-Oct; ☎629 374 652) is at **Estany Llong**, four hours along this wide track; there are some excellent day-treks to be enjoyed from the refuge.

If you're very committed to trekking, and proficient and well equipped, there are better traverses to undertake from the east side of the park. Heading northeast from Sant Maurici on the GR11 path, you can reach the **Refugi de Colomers** (2130m; open Feb/March weekends, Easter, mid-June to late Sept; ☎973 253 008), at the base of its lake-swollen cirque, within five to six hours via the east Port de Ratèra (2580m). From there most will continue along the GR11 for an easy but scenic day, partly in the park, to the **Refugi de Restanca** (2010m; open weekends most of the year plus mid-June to late Sept; ☎608 036 559), a 1990s construction perched near its namesake reservoir; from here the **Hospitau Refugi Sant Nicolau** (1630m; open most of the year; ☎973 697 052) right by the main Viella-bound road at the southern mouth of the tunnel, is another four hours away along the GR11.

The fourth of the park's refuges, **Refugi Josep Maríá Blanc** (2380m; staffed mid-June to Sept; ☎973 250 108), in the Peguera valley, is reached by a direct trail from Espot in around three and a half hours. You can continue to the Colomina refuge in another three and a half to four hours from here: this is a well-travelled route, marked as the GR11.20 variant trail.

624 024; Easter, July–Sept), 2km farther down the hill, also has a pool; and at the far (upstream) edge of Espot, beyond the old bridge, the tiny *Solau* (☎973 624 068), in the *barrio* of that name, also rents out rooms (€30) – a good fall-back if the village centre is full.

Quality **eating** opportunies are limited, with few economical *menús*, although the *menjador* of the *Pensió La Palmira* is an honourable exception. Most of the bars serve sandwiches and *platos combinados*; the pub *La Coveta* provides some semblance of **nightlife**. There are also two well-stocked **supermarkets** and another shop selling maps, camping gas cartridges, and the like.

Into the park

From Espot, another road leads 3.5km to the park boundary and from there a further 3.5km to the end of the tarmac at the **Estany de Sant Maurici**. The GR11 trail avoids most of the road, or alternatively take 4WD-taxis – at €3.60 per passenger they're a not terribly expensive way to miss out some fairly dull road walking. Once at the lake, the classic postcard view is south, dominated by the 2700-metre-plus spires of **Els Encatats** ("The Enchanted Ones"), in legend two hunters and their dog, who snuck off to go hunting instead of to church on the day of the patron saint's festival, were lured heavenward by a spectral stag, and then forthwith turned to stone by a divine lightning bolt.

El Pont de Suert and the route to Boí

The route into the western area of the Aigüestortes park begins just past **EL PONT DE SUERT**, a small town 41km northwest of La Pobla de Segur: currently, there's an Alsina Graells **bus** daily in summer at 9.30am from La Pobla, as well as two daily services each direction from Viella and Lleida. The buses all stop on the main road, opposite the unmissably hideous modern church, erected in 1955 as a sort of perverse homage to the real Romanesque churches further up the valley.

Otherwise, El Pont de Suert is pleasant enough if you have to spend the night before catching the bus north to Boí the next day (11.15am, daily June–Sept only), though you shouldn't need to, as the morning buses from Viella, Lleida and La Pobla are all designed to dovetail with the Boí service. The only **accommodation** in the centre is *Can Mestre* at Plaça Major 8 (☎973 690 306; ❹), with a pleasant river-view **restaurant**.

Up the Vall de Boí

Some 2km northwest of El Pont de Suert, a good sideroad turns off to the thread north along the **Vall de Boí**, following the Noguera de Tor towards Caldes de Boí, and passing the turn-offs for several villages on the way. It's an area crammed with **Romanesque churches**, the finest such specimens in Catalunya. The only disappointments are that most of their frescoes are reproductions, the originals having long since been whisked away to the Museu d'Art de Catalunya in Barcelona, and that certain churches open only for Mass, or guided tours offered by the local tourist office.

After about 8km there's a turn-off left to the village of **CÓLL** up on the hillside, with its twelfth-century **Santa María de l'Assumpció**; the church's west portal and masonry is particularly fine, but the grounds are usually locked. Cóll is also where you'll find the family-run *Hotel Casa Peyró* (☎973 297 002; ❺, ❼ half board), with one of the best **restaurants** in the area. It isn't cheap, but the food is worth it, especially the *entrantes*.

BARRUERA, 5km farther on and much larger, has several places to **stay**, the best value being *Casa Coll* (☎973 694 005, or contact the Besiberri Sports shop on the main road; ❸), an echoing old mansion near the top of c/Major in the old town. Barruera supports the main **turisme** for the entire valley (most of year Mon–Sat 10am–2pm & 5–7pm; ☎973 694 000), right opposite the petrol station. Just opposite the cramped campsite stands Barruera's Romanesque church, the riverside **Sant Feliu**, with its engaging thirteenth-century portal and creaking interior (Tues–Sat 11am–2pm & 4–7pm, Sun noon–2pm & 4–7pm, also Mon in Aug; €0.60). There's another 3km away in relatively unspoilt **DURRO**: **La Nativitat de la Mare de Déu**, with a massive bell tower and Lombard brickwork. You can stay here at *Can Marquès* in the centre (☎973 694 054; ❸) and eat at *Casa Xuqúin*, which does a reasonable *menú* or tapas in the bar.

Further on, just before the turn-off for Boí, a 1km side road leads west to **ERILL LA VALL**, whose twelfth-century church of **Santa Eulàlia** (same hours as Sant Feliu above; €0.90) sports an unusual arcaded porch, and a six-storey belfry which rivals Sant Climent's in Taüll (see opposite). In high season it's a relatively quiet base, more likely to have a vacancy than either Boí or Taüll. Choice **accommodation** includes the *Casa Pernallé* (☎973 696 049; ❸–❺), just before the entrance to the village, with off-street parking and a choice of rooms, or the *Hostal La Plaça* (☎973 696 026, ℗973 696 128; ❺), right opposite the belfry, with a decent restaurant.

Boí

BOÍ stands 1km above the main road, which continues up to Caldes de Boí; buses usually take you up into the centre. On arrival, the village may prove something of an anticlimax: a minuscule medieval core swamped by a mess of car parks, modern buildings, old houses defaced with new brick repairs, and – in common with almost every village in the valley – various adventure-travel outfits offering guided hikes, mountain-bike tours and special-interest safaris. Even the twelfth-century church of **Sant Joan** (same hours as Santa Eulàlia; €0.90) has been extensively renovated, the only original parts being the squat belfry and part of the apse; the interior mural (again a copy) shows the stoning of St Stephen.

One compensation for being based in Boí is that you're well poised to visit other local villages and their churches **on foot**. The non-GR path to Erill la Vall from Boí, across the valley, takes half an hour; the hiking route to Durro is the well-signposted GR11.20 path which you can pick up behind Boí village – it starts just over the little bridge at the back of the village and takes around an hour to follow. In the other direction, the GR11.20 up to Taüll takes about forty minutes, greatly shortcutting the steep 3km road.

Practicalities

Although Boí is certainly the least prepossessing of local villages, you may want or need to **stay** at the beginning of or conclusion to a visit to the park. Despite being out of the way, one good choice is the *Hostal Pascual*, down by the junction and bridge, equidistant from Erill (☎973 696 014; ❹), with helpful owners and a decent *menú* in the dining room. In the village itself, the central *Hostal Beneria* (☎973 696 030; ❺) and the *Casa Pey* (☎973 696 036; ❹) are more expensive for roughly the same facilities. There are also some clean modern **rooms** just through the stone archway in the old quarter – look for the *habitacions* sign.

Eating out, you'll not do better than at the *Casa Higinio*, 200m up the road to Taüll, above the village centre. Its wood-fired range produces excellent grilled meat dishes, or try the fine *escudella* (minestrone soup) and trout – a big meal accompanied by the local wine will come to just under €12. None of the other diners attached to the various central *hostals* are anywhere near as good value, though the *Pey* offers *a la carta* fare for well under €18, served on its popular terrace overlooking the main Plaça del Treio.

The **national park office** (April–Oct daily 9am–1pm & 3.30–6.45pm; ☎973 696 189) is on the main square; you can buy Alpina maps here, as well as book 4WD-taxis into the park (see below). The **bank** behind the supermarket has an ATM.

Into the park

It's 3.5km from Boí to the national **park entrance**, and another 3.5km to the scenic waterfalls of **Aigüestortes**, tumbling from their eponymous water meadows to feed the Estany Llebreta. A final kilometre above the falls – passed closely by both road and trail "#5" (see below) – there's another park **information booth** (July–Sept daily 9.30am–2pm & 4–7pm), next to which is a map-placard with various suggested **day hikes**; the most popular leads east to Estany Llong (1hr one-way).

4WD-taxis from Boí's village square make the trip as far as the information booth; as in Espot, this costs €3.60 one-way, €7.20 round trip. Vehicles wait to depart until they're full; the last downhill return from Aigüestortes is at 7pm in midsummer, 6pm in spring and autumn. The closest you can get to the park boundary with your **own vehicle** is the car park at La Farga, or another, smaller one 1.5km east right at the boundary. If you leave your car at either, and arrange for a 4WD-taxi to meet you and take you further uphill, at day's end you can follow marked trail "#5" from the infomation booth ("Aparcament") which shortcuts the road by a good 45 minutes.

Alternatively, you can flag down the one midday bus from the junction of the Boí side road up to the spa complex of **Caldes de Boí**, 5km upstream, where the bus line ends. Nearby, the conspicuously high dam at the south end of Estany de Cavallers marks the trailhead for walks towards the beautiful natural lakes northwest of the park, just below Besiberri and Montarto peaks; the closest refuge is **Joan Ventosa i Calvell**, at Estany Negre (2220m; open mid-June to late Sept & some winter weekends; ☎973 297 090), just over an hour away and itself within easy reach of the Colomèrs or Restanca huts.

Taüll and Boí-Taüll

The character of **TAÜLL** has been altered considerably by the ski resort of Boí-Taüll, established on the mountainside a few kilometres to the southeast. There's an enormous holiday complex 1500m beyond the village at Pla de l'Ermita, en route to the ski station, and even in summer Taüll is a target for tour coaches and family cars seeking out panoramic picnic spots. But once away from the peripheral ski chalets, the village centre retains considerable character, and is certainly preferable to Boí as a long-term base.

Moreover, two of the best local Romanesque churches stand in the village. **Sant Climent de Taüll** (summer daily 10.30am–2pm & 4–8pm; winter Mon–Sat 10.30am–2pm & 4–7pm, Sun 10.30am–2pm; €0.90) is the more immediately impressive by virtue of its famous six-storey belfry and original triple apse. Your admission ticket entitles you to climb the rickety wooden steps to the top of the bell tower for sweeping views through the delicately arched windows. At the heart of the village, **Santa María** (daily 10am–8pm; free) is very similar in design, though after a millennium of subsidence, there's not one

△ Sant Climent de Taüll, Catalunya

right angle remaining in the building, with the four-storey belfry in particular at an engaging list.

Some 11km southeast of Taüll, the ski centre at **BOÍ-TAÜLL** is the newest in the Catalan Pyrenees (inaugurated in 1990) and the only rival to Baqueira-Beret for really serious skiing, with 41 pistes, more than half of them red-rated; accordingly it's not the best resort for beginners or weak intermediates. More information is available from the resort's website – ⓦwww.boitaullresort.es.

Practicalities

Accommodation options, many under the *cases de pagès* programme, include the en-suite *Pensió La Coma* (☎973 696 025; ❹) at the village entrance; the *Pensió Sant Climent*, across the lane from *La Coma* (☎973 696 052; ❹), with its own restaurant; and *Casa Plano Minguero* (☎973 696 117; ❹), well located in the upper part of the village, with its own parking (a problem here). *Ca de Corral* (☎973 696 004 or 973 696 028; ❸), run by the *Bar Mallador* (see below), offers shared-bath rooms in an old house well situated in the lower part of the village. Other inexpensive rooms – with self-catering facilities – can be found at the friendly *Casa Llovet*, Plaça Franch 5 (☎973 696 032; ❸), and at *Casa Xep* (☎973 696 054; ❸), just below Plaça Santa María – ask at the adjacent super-market. A **campsite** (☎973 696 082; open all year), also offering bungalows, spreads attractively on the slope below Sant Climent.

La Coma's **restaurant** is justly popular for its local fare (wild boar and quail) and good service; the *menú* costs €9.60, *a la carta* around €13.20. *El Caliu*, at the top of Taüll, is also well regarded and just about affordable. Last but not least, just beside Sant Climent, *Mallador* (closed May–23 June & 15 Oct–end Nov) is run by nice folk with good taste in music, and combines the virtues of being the most popular village **bar** (garden seating in summer) with an excellent upstairs restaurant.

The South

The great triangle of land **south** of Barcelona is not the first place you think of going when you visit Catalunya. It's made up of the province of Tarragona and part of the province of Lleida (the rest of which takes in the western Pyrenees) and, with the exception of the obvious attractions of the coast and one medieval monastery, almost all the interest lies in the provincial capitals themselves.

The main target is the **Costa Daurada** – the coastline that stretches from Barcelona to Tarragona and beyond – which is far less exploited than the Costa Brava. Although this might seem reason in itself to visit, it is easy enough to see why it has been so neglected. All too often the shoreline is drab, with beaches that are narrow and characterless, backed by sparse villages overwhelmed by pockets of villas. There are exceptions, though, notably vibrant **Sitges**, which is just forty minutes from Barcelona. This is one of the great Spanish resorts, bolstered by its reputation as a major gay summer destination. If all you want to do is relax by a beach for a while, there are several other less trendy and perfectly functional possibilities, ranging from tiny **Cunit** to the region's biggest holiday resorts at **Salou** and **Cambrils**.

The Costa Daurada really begins to pay dividends, however, if you can forget about the beaches temporarily and plan to spend a couple of days in **Tarragona**, the provincial capital. It's a city with a solid Roman past – reflected in an array of impressive ruins and monuments – and it makes a handy springboard for trips inland into Lleida province. South of Tarragona, Catalunya peters out in the lagoons and marshes of the **Delta de l'Ebre**, a riverine wetland that's rich in bird life – perfect for slow boat trips, fishing and sampling the local seafood.

Inland attractions are fewer, and many travelling this way are inclined to head on out of Catalunya altogether, not stopping until they reach Zaragoza. It's true that much of the region is flat, rural and dull, but nonetheless it would be a mistake to miss the outstanding monastery at **Poblet**, only an hour or so inland from Tarragona. A couple of other nearby towns and monasteries – notably medieval **Montblanc** and **Santa Creus** – add a bit more interest to the region, while by the time you've rattled across the huge plain that encircles the provincial capital of **Lleida** you've earned a night's rest. Pretty much off the tourist trail, Lleida makes a very pleasant overnight stop: from here, it's only two and a half hours to Zaragoza, or you're at the start of dramatic road and train routes into the western foothills of the Catalan Pyrenees.

Sitges

SITGES, 40km from Barcelona, is definitely the highlight of the Costa Daurada. Established in the 1960s as a holiday town whose loose attitudes openly challenged the rigidity of Franco's Spain, it has now become the great weekend escape for young Barcelonans, who have created a resort very much in their own image. It's also a noted **gay** holiday destination, with a nightlife to match: indeed, if you don't like vigorous action of all kinds, you'd be wise to avoid Sitges in the summer – staid it isn't. As well as a certain style, the Barcelona trippers have brought with them the high prices from the Catalan capital – the bars, particularly, can empty the deepest wallets – while finding anywhere to stay (at any price) can be a problem unless you arrive early in the day or book well in advance. None of this deters the varied and generally well-heeled visitors, however, and nor should it, since Sitges as a sort of Barcelona-on-Sea is definitely worth experiencing for at least one night.

The town itself is reasonably attractive – a former fishing village whose pleasing houses and narrow streets have attracted artists and opted-out intellectuals for a century or so. The beaches, though crowded, are far from oppressive, and Sitges even has a smattering of cultural interest – though no one is seriously suggesting you come here just for that.

Arrival and information

Trains to Sitges leave Barcelona-Sants every ten to twenty minutes throughout the day; the station is about ten minutes' walk from the town centre and seafront. **Buses** stop in front of the train station, except those to and from Barcelona which stop outside the main turisme. If you're driving, it's probably best to pay for a **car park** rather than leave your vehicle on the street: car parks are marked on the map.

On arrival you may as well drop in at the **turisme** (July to mid-Sept daily

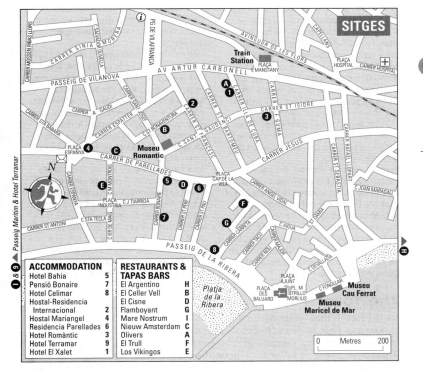

ACCOMMODATION		RESTAURANTS & TAPAS BARS	
Hotel Bahia	5	El Argentino	H
Pensió Bonaire	7	El Celler Vell	B
Hotel Celimar	8	El Cisne	D
Hostal-Residencia		Flamboyant	G
Internacional	2	Mare Nostrum	I
Hostal Mariangel	4	Nieuw Amsterdam	C
Residencia Parellades	6	Olivers	A
Hotel Romàntic	3	El Trull	F
Hotel Terramar	9	Los Vikingos	E
Hotel El Xalet	1		

9am–9pm; mid-Sept to June Mon–Fri 9am–2pm & 4–6.30pm, Sat 10am–1pm; ℡938 945 004 or 938 944 251, ⓦwww.sitgestur.com) at the Oasis shopping mall, which is a right turn out of the train station and then right again up Passeig Vilafranca. It has a useful map (€0.60) with local listings on the back, and all sorts of English-language information about the town. From July to September, there's also tourist information available from a building on Plaça de l'Ajuntament (daily 10am–1pm & 5–9pm).

Accommodation

If you're offered a **room** by someone as you get off the train, take it: if it's substandard, you can always look for a better one later. Otherwise, try one of the places listed below, though note that in July and August they are all liable to be full; it's always best to book ahead. If you arrive without a reservation, a short walk through the central streets and along the front (particularly Passeig de la Ribera) reveals most of the possibilities – places near the station are not exactly glamorous, but are more likely to have space. Come **out of season** (after October and before May) and the high prices tend to soften a little, though in midwinter you may have real difficulty finding anywhere that's open, especially at the budget end of the scale.

The nearest local **campsite** is *El Rocà* (℡938 940 043; late March–Aug), well signposted north of the turisme under the railway bridge.

Hotel Bahia, c/de les Parellades 27 ☎ & ⓕ938 940 012, ⓔmadisonbahia@infomail.lacaixa.es. Not far from the beach, though on a fairly noisy street, this comfortable hotel-restaurant drops its prices out of season. Closed Nov. Price includes breakfast. ❼

Pensió Bonaire, c/Bonaire 31 ☎938 945 326. Just back from the sea, this tiny *pensió* is one of the least expensive around. Open April–Sept. ❹

Hotel Celimar, Passeig de la Ribera 20 ☎938 110 170, ⓕ938 110 403. Seafront hotel at the bottom end of this range, worth trying early on for a balconied room with a view. Prices fall a category outside high season. ❽

Hostal-Residencia Internacional, c/Sant Francesc 52 ☎938 942 690. Clean and simple place where the family owners have made a bit of effort with the decor; the rooms are light and crisp. Nearer the station than the beach, but not massively inconvenient. Open all year. ❺

Hostal Mariangel, c/de les Parellades 78 ☎938 941 357. One of the town's most popular budget places, so it fills quickly. There's a small lounge. Closed mid-Sept to mid-Nov. ❹

Residencia Parellades, c/de les Parellades 11 ☎938 940 801. The large airy rooms and decent location make this a good first choice. Open April–Sept. ❹

Hotel Romàntic, c/Sant Isidre 33 ☎938 948 375, ⓕ938 948 167. Attractive, old converted nineteenth-century villa in the quiet streets away from the front, not far from the train station. It's a favourite with gay visitors. Many rooms have a terrace overlooking the gardens; those with showers are in the next category. Open April to mid-Oct. The similar *La Renaixença*, owned by the same management (same telephone number and prices), is open all year. ❼

Hotel Terramar, Passeig Marítim 80 ☎938 940 050, ⓕ938 945 604. Superb position at the end of the long promenade, and splendid views from its large, balconied rooms, but a bit dated in style and decor. Open April–Dec. ❽

Hotel El Xalet, c/Illa de Cuba 35 ☎938 110 070, ⓕ938 945 579. Charming, discreet hotel in a beautiful *modernista* house near the train station. There are only ten rooms – booking ahead is a necessity in summer. Price includes breakfast. ❽

The Town

It's the **beach** that brings most people to Sitges, and it's not hard to find, with two strands right in town, to the west of the church. From here, a succession of beaches of varying quality and crowdedness stretches west as far as the *Hotel Terramar*, a couple of kilometres down the coast. A long seafront promenade, the **Passeig Marítim**, runs all the way there, and all along there are beach bars, restaurants, showers and watersports facilities. Beyond the hotel, following the train line, you eventually reach the more notorious nudist beaches, a couple of which are exclusively gay. It's worth noting that as the town's popularity has increased, petty crime seems to have been exported from Barcelona to Sitges. Watch your possessions on the beaches and exercise care at night.

Back in town, make the effort at some stage to climb up the knoll overlooking the beaches, topped by the Baroque parish church – known as *La Punta* – and a street of old whitewashed mansions. One contains the **Museu Cau Ferrat**, an art gallery for want of a better description. Home and workshop to the artist and writer Santiago Rusiñol (1861–1931), its two floors contain a massive jumble of his own paintings, as well as sculpture, painted tiles, drawings and various collected odds and ends, such as the decorative ironwork Rusiñol brought back in bulk from the Pyrenees. Two of his better buys were the minor El Grecos at the top of the stairs on either side of a crucifix. The museum also contains works by the artist's friends (including Picasso) who used to meet in the *Els Quatre Gats* bar in Barcelona.

All **museums** in Sitges have the same opening hours and prices: mid-June to mid-Oct daily 9am–9pm; mid-Oct to mid-June Tues–Fri 10am–1.30pm & 4–9pm, Sat 10am–7pm, Sun 10am–3pm; €3 each (free first Wed of month) or €4.80 for a **combined ticket** for all the museums, valid for a month.

Two other museums are worth giving a whirl on a rainy day. The **Museu Maricel de Mar**, next door to the Museu Cau Ferrat, has more minor artworks, medieval to modern, and maintains an impressive collection of Catalan ceramics and sculpture. More entertaining is the **Museu Romàntic** (guided tour every hour), which aims to show the lifestyle of a rich Sitges family in the eighteenth and nineteenth centuries by displaying some of their furniture and possessions. It's full of nineteenth-century knick-knacks, including a set of working music boxes and a collection of antique dolls. The museum is right in the centre of town, at c/Sant Gaudenci 1, off c/Bonaire.

Eating

International tourism has left its mark on Sitges: multilingual menus and "English breakfasts" are everywhere. Fortunately there are reasonable **restaurants** among them, and though you're unlikely to be sampling Catalan cuisine at its finest you'll find plenty of good *menús del día*. Some suggestions appear below, but good general areas to explore are the side streets around the church, or the beachfront for more expensive seafood restaurants. For picnic supplies, the town's **market** – the Mercat Nou – is very close to the train station, on Avinguda Artur Carbonell. **Ice-cream** fiends should check out *Ribera*, Passeig de la Ribera 5, *Italiana*, c/Jesús, or *Heladería* and *Il Gelatieri*, both on c/Parellades.

El Argentino, Passeig Aiguadolç 22. If you're sick of seafood this is the place for serious charcoal-grilled meat – especially beef – though a meal here will set you back €21 upwards.

El Celler Vell, c/Sant Bonaventura 21. Very good Catalan food served up in rural-chic surroundings. Around €15 a head or there's a very good-value €7.20 *menú*.

El Cisne, c/Sant Pere 4 (junction with c/de les Parellades). Nothing adventurous here, but you'll get well-cooked food in a dining room at the back of the bar – around €10.50 for the *menú del día*.

Flamboyant, c/Pau Barrabeig, off c/Carreta. Rather expensive, but with a beautiful garden setting. Around €24–30 a head unless you go for the €16.20 *menú*. Open daily from 8.30pm.

Mare Nostrum, Passeig de Ribeira 60. Long-established fish restaurant situated on the seafront, with a menu that changes according to the catch and season. Around €21 a head, unless you stick to the *platos del día*.

Nieuw Amsterdam, c/de les Parellades 70. Medium-priced Indonesian and Dutch specialities.

Olivers, c/Illa de Cuba 39. A mid-priced Spanish, rather than Catalan, restaurant, but the menu has some interesting flourishes that make the food memorable. Meals from around €18 a head. Open daily from 8.30pm.

El Trull, c/Mossèn Félix Clarà 3, off c/Major. Fairly pricey French-style restaurant in the old town, though with careful selection you could get away with around €12 for a meal.

Los Vikingos, c/Marqués de Mont Roig 18. Good, cheap restaurant right on the main tourist drag serving anything and everything (including fresh fish) accompanied by loud music.

Bars and nightlife

The main part of the action in Sitges is concentrated in a block of streets just back from the sea in the centre of town. Late-opening bars started to spring up here in the late-1950s: today, **c/1er (Primer) de Maig** (marked as c/Dos de Mayo on some old maps) and its continuation, **c/Marqués de Montroig**, are fully pedestrianized, while c/de les Parellades and c/Bonaire complete the block – not somewhere to come if you're looking for a quiet drink. This is basically one long run of disco-bars, pumping music out into the late evening, interspersed with the odd restaurant or fancier cocktail bar, all with outdoor tables vying for your custom. The bars are all loud and their clientele predominantly young, and you can choose from just about any style you care to imagine. The best policy is to browse and sluice your way around until you find a favourite, though a few are picked out below. More **genteel bars** are not so easy to come by, though the places right on the seafront are generally quieter.

Afrika, c/1er de Maig. One of the best of the music bars.
Atlántida, Sector Terramar, 3km out of town. The town's favourite club, the cliff-top *Atlántida* can be reached on regular buses which run there and back all night from the bottom of c/1er de Maig.
Bar Bodega Talino, c/de les Parellades 72. That rare thing in Sitges – a real tapas bar.

Café-Bar Roy, c/de les Parellades 9. An old-fashioned café with dressed-up waiters and marble tables. It's good for breakfast, or for a glass of *cava* and a fancy snack.
Parrots Pub, Plaça de la Industria. Stylish bar at the top of c/1er de Maig that's a required stop at some point of the day; it's just one place you can pick up the free gay map of Sitges (see below).

The gay scene and Carnaval

The **gay scene** in Sitges is frenetic and ever-changing, but chronicled on a gay map of town available from *Parrots Pub* in Plaça de la Industria, as well as from several other bars and clubs.

During the day, a current favourite hang-out is the *Picnic Bar* on Passeig de la Ribera (opposite *Les Anfores* restaurant in the *Calipolis* hotel), popular for its sandwiches. By early **evening**, everyone's moved on to *Parrots Pub* for cocktails. The best concentration of bars and discos is in c/Bonaire and c/Sant Buenaventura: at *Bourbons*, c/Sant Buenaventura 9, gay women are especially welcome, as they are in the *Bar Azul* (at no. 10), where happy hour is 9–10.30pm. The best gay disco is at *Trailer* at c/Àngel Vidal 14, in the old town. *Bar Seven*, at c/Nou 7, is a bar serving late breakfasts before an afternoon on the beach.

Carnaval

Carnaval in Sitges (Feb/March) is outrageous, thanks largely to the gay populace. The official programme of parades and masked balls is complemented by an unwritten but widely recognized schedule of events. The climax is the Tuesday late-night parade, in which exquisitely dressed drag queens swan about the streets in high heels, twirling lacy parasols and coyly fanning themselves. Bar doors stand wide open, bands play, and processions and celebrations go on until four in the morning; *Bar Seven* has photos of parades from days gone by if you miss the action.

Listings

Banks Banco Español de Credito, Plaça Cap de Vila 9; Banco de Sabadell, Plaça Cap de Vila 7; La Caixa, c/de les Parellades 16.
Cinema Casino Prado, c/Francesc Gumà 4, and El Retiro, c/Àngel Vidal 13.
Hospital Hospital Sant Camil, c/de Puigmolte ☎938 960 025; in emergencies, call Ambulancis Urgències ☎904 100 904.
Pharmacist Two central *farmacias* are Ferret de Querol, c/de les Parellades 1, and Planas, c/Artur Carbonell 30.

Police Plaça de l'Ajuntament ☎938 117 625.
Post office Plaça Espanya (Mon–Fri 8am–2.30pm, Sat 9.30am–1pm).
Taxis There's a rank outside the train station (☎938 941 329), and you should find someone prepared to take you to/from Barcelona airport, which is 30km away.
Train information Call ☎934 900 202.
Travel agencies Viajes Sitges, c/Marquès de Montroig 21; Viajes Playa de Oro, c/de les Parellades 22.

Vilanova i la Geltrú

Eight kilometres south down the coast is the large fishing port of **VILANO-VA I LA GELTRÚ**. Sitges gets most of its fish from here, but Vilanova borrows little in return – this is a real working port, whose quayside is lined with great trucks waiting to load the catches from the hundreds of boats moored alongside. Although the town itself is nothing special, it's fascinating to wander along the docks through the scattered fishing nets, and when you tire of this there's a tourist side to Vilanova which is a pleasant contrast to the excesses of Sitges. There are two **beaches**: one beyond the port, the second – better – at the end of the seafront promenade.

You might be tempted by Vilanova's fair smattering of **museums**, two of which are found straight out of the train station door: one of Spain's few railway museums to the right (July & Aug Tues–Fri 5–9pm, Sat & Sun 10am–2pm; Sept–June Tues–Fri 10am–2pm & 5–7pm, Sat & Sun 10am–2pm; €1.80), probably best left to the specialists, and the **Biblioteca Museu Balaguer** (June–Sept Tues–Sat 10am–1.30pm & 4.30–7pm, Sun 10am–1.30pm, Wed closes 8.30pm; Oct–May Tues–Sat 10am–1.30pm & 4–6.30pm, Sun 10am–1.30pm, Wed closes 8.30pm; €1.80) to the left, founded by a local nineteenth-century politician. This is actually a quite rewarding stop, featuring pieces loaned from the Prado alongside a hoard of Catalan nineteenth- and twentieth-century paintings. Best of all, though, is the town's **Museu Romàntic Can Papiol**, on c/Major 32, behind the church at the very top of the Rambla Principal (Tues–Sat 10am–1pm & 4–6pm, Sun 10am–2pm; €1.80). It's the sister museum to the one in Sitges, and the entrance fee includes a guided tour around the lavishly furnished eighteenth-century town house in which the collection is housed.

Practicalities

Trains and **buses** run about every twenty to thirty minutes from Sitges, and there are daily bus connections between Vilanova and Vilafranca del Penedés if you want to take an inland loop back to Barcelona. The bus might drop you off on the seafront; otherwise the main stop is in front of the train station – from here, cross the tracks under the tunnel and keep heading straight on to the seafront. The port is on the left, while to the right is the Passeig Maritím where you'll find the **turisme** (July & Aug Mon–Sat 10am–8pm, Sun 10am–2pm; Sept–July Mon–Sat 10am–2pm & 5–8pm, Sun 10am–2pm; ☎938 154 517, ✆turismevng@readysoft.es).

There are a few **hotels** opposite the tourist office – and the town's best beach just beyond – though a less expensive *hostal*, the *Costa d'Or*, is at Passeig Maritím 49 (☎938 155 542; ❼ full board). If you don't mind being away from the beach, there's a budget choice near the station, *Bar Restaurant Central* (☎938 155 469; ❸), at Rambla Ventosa 13. Vilanova also has three **campsites**, including the friendly beach-based *Platja Vilanova* (☎938 950 767; April–Sept). There are a dozen or so **restaurants** along the seafront *passeig*, which on the whole are better value than the equivalents in Sitges. All have outdoor seating and while the views may not be quite so special as further up the coast, the atmosphere is a lot more down to earth. A good choice is the *Daviana*, at no. 104, which offers a hearty *menú del día* for around €9 or a terrific paella for the same price. If you fancy a snack there is also the *L'Orient Express*, opposite the port at Passeig de Carme 48, which serves Eastern Mediterranean tapas, some of which are **vegetarian**, from €1.80.

Cunit, Puerta Romana and Torredembarra

If the Costa Daurada beaches so far seem too crowded and frenetic – a distinct possibility in high season – there are a couple of other possible stops before Tarragona. Travelling by train, make sure you catch a local and not an express which will run straight through.

CUNIT, about 15km south of Sitges, is the first stop inside Tarragona province. Rather soulless – more a collection of villas than a village – nonetheless it has a good, long beach. There's a **campsite**, *Mar de Cunit* (☎977 674 058; June–Sept), behind the beach and a few good places **to stay**: *Los Almendros* (☎977 675 437; ❹), at the top of the village, but cut off from it by the highway, or the more pricey *Hostal La Diligencia* at Plaça Major 4 (☎977 674 081; ❼ half board), opposite the church in the centre. The former has an outdoor grill and a decent €7.20 *menú del día*, while *La Diligencia* has a particularly good restaurant, with a €7.80 *menú*.

Again little more than a few streets of villas, the hamlet of **PUERTA ROMANA**, 15km before Tarragona, has perhaps the best swimming and sunbathing on this stretch of coast, with clean sand and clear water. It's not on the map or signposted from the main road, and the nearest train station is at the small resort of **TORREDEMBARRA** (where there are a few hotels), from where you could walk the 4km north. Coming by bus, ask to be put down at *Camping Sirena Dorada* (☎977 801 303) by the main road; this is open all year, changes money and has huts to rent. From there walk straight towards the sea, across the railway line, and you'll reach Puerta Romana, where there's another campsite – *Gavina* (☎977 801 903; late March–Oct) – slap-bang on the beach.

Tarragona

Majestically sited on a rocky hill, sheer above the sea, **TARRAGONA** is an ancient place. Settled originally by Iberians and then Carthaginians, it was later used as the base for the Roman conquest of the peninsula, which began in 218 BC with Scipio's march south against Hannibal. The fortified city became an imperial resort and, under Augustus, *Tarraco* became capital of Rome's eastern Iberian province – the most elegant and cultured city of Roman Spain, boasting at its peak a quarter of a million inhabitants. Temples and monuments were built in and around the city and, despite a history of seemingly constant sacking and looting since Roman times, it's this distinguished past which still asserts itself throughout modern Tarragona.

Time spent in the handsome upper town quickly shows what attracted the emperors to the city: strategically – and beautifully – placed, it's a fine setting for some splendid Roman remains and a few excellent museums. There's an attractive medieval part, too, while the rocky coastline below conceals a couple of reasonable beaches. If there's a downside, it's that Tarragona is today the second largest port in Catalunya, so the views aren't always unencumbered – though the fish in the Serrallo fishing quarter is always good and fresh. Also, the city's ugly outskirts to the south have been steadily degraded by new industries which do little for Tarragona's character as a resort: chemical and oil refineries, and a nuclear power station.

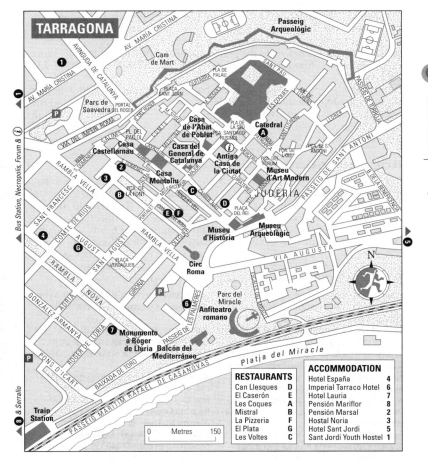

RESTAURANTS

Can Llesques	D
El Caserón	E
Les Coques	A
Mistral	B
La Pizzeria	F
El Plata	G
Les Voltes	C

ACCOMMODATION

Hotel España	4
Imperial Tarraco Hotel	6
Hotel Lauria	7
Pensión Mariflor	8
Pensión Marsal	2
Hostal Noria	3
Hotel Sant Jordi	5
Sant Jordi Youth Hostel	1

Arrival and information

The city divides clearly into two parts, on two levels: a predominantly medieval, walled upper town (where you'll spend most time), and a prosperous modern extension below. Heart of the upper town is the sweeping **Rambla Nova**, a sturdy provincial rival to Barcelona's, lined with fashionable cafés and restaurants. Parallel, and to the east, lies the **Rambla Vella**, marking – as its name suggests – the start of the old town. To either side of the *rambles* are scattered a profusion of relics from Tarragona's Roman past, including various temples, and parts of the forum, theatre and amphitheatre.

The **train station** is in the lower town: when you arrive, turn right and climb the steps ahead of you and you'll emerge at the top of the Rambla Nova, from where everything is a short walk away. The **bus terminal** is at the other end of the Rambla Nova, at Plaça Imperial Tarraco. The **turisme** is at c/Major 39 (July–Sept Mon–Fri 9.30am–8.30pm, Sat 9.30am–2pm & 4–8.30pm, Sun

10am–2pm; Oct–June Mon–Fri 10am–2pm & 4.30–7pm, Sat 10am–2pm, Sun 10am–2pm; ☎977 250 795, ⓦwww.fut.es/~turisme), and there is also a seasonal information booth (July–Sept same hours) at Plaça Imperial Tarraco. If you're travelling further afield the regional tourist office is near Rambla Nova at c/Fortuny 4 (Mon–Fri 9am–2pm & 4–6.30pm, Sat 9am–2pm; ☎977 233 415).

You're unlikely to use the city's **local bus** network, other than for trips out to the campsite or to the aqueduct (details are given below), but the turisme can let you know the routes if you're interested. They can also provide you with the excellent *Guia d'Accessibilitat*, which lists all **wheelchair accessible** buildings in the city.

Accommodation

Tarragona makes a great stopover, and is certainly less exhausting than Sitges. The nicest **rooms** in town, or at least the ones in the best location, are in the pedestrianized Plaça de la Font, just in the old town off Rambla Vella. If these are full, there are a couple of less desirable places near the train station. Cheapest lodgings are at the *Sant Jordi* youth hostel (see list below for details), while down towards the beach, Platja Arrabassada, a few kilometres out of town, are some more small hotels and **campsites**: to get to *Camping Tarraco* (☎977 239 989; April–Sept) take bus #1, #3 or #9 (every twenty minutes) from Plaça de Corsini, near the market and local forum.

Hotel España, Rambla Nova 49 ☎977 232 712, ⓕ977 232 712. Affordable mid-range hotel on the *rambla*, with bath in every room. ❺

Imperial Tarraco Hotel, Plaça Imperial Tarraco 5 ☎977 233 040, ⓕ977 216 566, ⓔimperial@tinet.fut.es. The city's best and most expensive hotel, modern but beautifully positioned, sitting on top of the cliff and facing out to sea. ❽

Hotel Lauria, Rambla Nova 20 ☎977 236 712, ⓕ977 236 700. Posh three-star hotel on the main *rambla*. Outside July and Aug, room prices become eminently reasonable. ❼

Pensió Mariflor, c/General Contreras 29 ☎977 238 231. Only two blocks from the train station, and much less shifty than its location suggests. Housed in a modern apartment block, this has fairly large rooms and is clean and friendly; hot showers cost €0.60 extra. ❸

Pensió Marsal, Plaça de la Font 26 ☎977 224 069. This is the square's best-value choice, with modern, well-kept rooms; ask for one with a view of the square. Bathrooms are separate and spotless. ❹

Hostal Noria, Plaça de la Font 53 ☎977 238 717. Smarter and more upmarket than most around the *plaça*, but good value out of season. Ask inside the bar/cafetería. ❺

Hotel Sant Jordi, Vía Augusta 185 ☎977 207 515, ⓕ977 207 632. Old-time favourite moved from its previous berth in Plaça de la Font into these more roomy premises. Well run and friendly; all rooms have bath. ❼

Sant Jordi Youth Hostel, Avgda. President Companys 5 ☎ & ⓕ977 240 195. An IYHF hostel with four- or six-bedded rooms (over-26s pay fifty percent more) and sports facilities; breakfast included in the price. Reception open 7–10am & 2–8pm; reservations advised in July & Aug; closed Sept. ❷

The City

Much of the attraction of Tarragona lies in the **Roman remains** dotted around the city. Some of the most impressive monuments are a fair way out (see "Out of the centre" p.867), but there's enough within walking distance to occupy a good day's sightseeing and to provide a vivid impression of life in Tarragona in imperial Roman times. It's worth noting in advance that all Tarragona's sights and museums except for the cathedral are **closed on Mondays**, and unless otherwise stated cost €1.80.

Passeig Arqueològic

For an overview of the city and its history, start at the **Passeig Arqueològic** (April & May Tues–Sat 10am–1.30pm & 3.30–6.30pm, Sun 10am–2pm; June–Sept Tues–Sat 9am–9pm, Sun 10am–2pm; Oct–March Tues–Sat 10am–1.30pm & 3.30–6.30pm, Sun 10am–2pm), a promenade which encircles the northernmost half of the old town. From the entrance at the Portal del Roser, a path runs between **Roman walls** of the third century BC and the sloping, **outer fortifications** erected by the British in 1707 to secure the city during the War of the Spanish Succession. Megalithic walls built by the Iberians are excellently preserved in places, too, particularly two awesome gateways; the huge blocks used in their construction are quite distinct from the more refined Roman additions. Vantage points (and occasional telescopes) give views across the plain behind the city and around to the sea, while various objects are displayed within the Passeig – several Roman columns, a fine bronze statue of Augustus, and eighteenth-century cannons still defending the city's heights.

Roman Tarragona: the Necropolis, Forum and Amphitheatre

The most interesting remains in town are those of the ancient Necropolis, a twenty-minute walk out of the centre down Avinguda Ramón i Cajal, which runs west off Rambla Nova. Here, both pagan and Christian tombs have been uncovered, spanning a period from the third to the sixth century AD. They're now contained within the fascinating **Museu i Necropolis Paleocristians** (June–Sept Tues–Sat 10am–8pm, Sun 10am–2pm; Oct–May Tues–Sat 10am–1pm & 4–7pm, Sun 10am–2pm), whose entrance is on Passeig de la Independencia. The museum is lined with sarcophagi and displays a few fragmented mosaics and photographs of the site, but it's outside in the covered trenches and stone foundations that you get most sense of Tarragona's erstwhile importance. Scattered about are amphorae, inscribed tablets and plinths, rare examples of later Visigothic sculpture, and even the sketchy remains of a mausoleum. Most of the relics attest to Tarragona's enthusiastically Christian status: St Paul preached here, and the city became an important Visigothic bishopric after the break-up of Roman power. Back in the centre, the Roman forum has survived too. Or rather forums, since – as provincial capital – Tarragona sustained both a ceremonial **provincial forum** (the scant remnants of which are close to the cathedral) and a **local forum**, whose more substantial remains are on the western side of Rambla Nova, near the market hall and square. Located on the flat land near the port, this was the commercial centre of imperial *Tarraco* and the main meeting place for locals for three centuries. The site (April & May Tues–Sat 10am–1.30pm & 3.30–6.30pm, Sun 10am–2pm; June–Sept Tues–Sat 9am–9pm, Sun 10am–2pm; Oct–March Tues–Sat 10am–1.30pm & 3.30–5.30pm, Sun 10am–2pm), which contained temples and small shops ranged around a porticoed square, has been split by a main road: a footbridge now connects the two halves where you can see a water cistern, house foundations, fragments of stone inscriptions and four elegant columns.

Tarragona's other tangible Roman remains lie close to each other at the seaward end of the Rambla Vella. Most rewarding is the **Amfiteatre** (same opening hours as forum site), built into the green slopes of the hill beneath the *Imperial Tarraco* hotel. The tiered seats backing onto the sea are original, and from the top you can look north, up the coast, to the headland; the rest of the seating was reconstructed in 1969–70, along with the surviving tunnels and structural buildings.

Above here, on the Rambla Vella itself, are the visible remains of the Roman Circus, the **Circ Roma**, also known as Les Voltes del Circ, whose vaults disappear back from the street into the gloom and under many of the surrounding buildings. If you want a closer look, the Circ now forms part of the **Museu de la Romanitat** (June–Sept Tues–Sat 10am–8pm, Sun 10am–3pm; Oct–May Tues–Sat 10am–5.30pm, Sun 10am–3pm). Built at the end of the first century AD to hold chariot races, the Circ has been restored and presented to spectacular effect. The rest of the museum contains computer-generated pictures of Roman Tarragona's buildings, and an lift cuts right through the building and onto the roof for the best views in Tarragona.

The old town

For all its individual Roman monuments, the heart of Tarragona is still the steep and intricate streets of the medieval **old town** which spreads east of the Rambla Vella. Here and there the towering mansions in the side streets incorporate Roman fragments, while the central c/Major climbs to the quarter's focal point, the **Catedral** (mid-March to June Mon–Sat 10am–1pm 4–7pm; July to mid-Oct Mon–Sat 10am–7pm; mid-Oct to mid-Nov Mon–Sat 10am–12.30pm & 3–6pm; mid-Nov to mid-March Mon–Sat 10am–2pm), which sits at the top of a broad flight of steps. This, quite apart from its own grand beauty, is a perfect example of the transition from Romanesque to Gothic forms. You'll see the change highlighted in the main facade, where a soaring Gothic portal is framed by Romanesque doors, surmounted by a cross and an elaborate rose window. Except for services, entrance to the cathedral is through the **cloisters** (*claustre*; signposted up a street to the left of the facade), themselves superbly executed with pointed Gothic arches softened by smaller round divisions. The cloister also has several oddly sculpted capitals, one of which represents a cat's funeral being directed by rats. The ticket lets you proceed into the cathedral, and into its chapterhouse and sacristy, which together make up the **Museu Diocesa**, piled high with ecclesiastical treasures.

Strolling the old town's streets will also enable you to track down Tarragona's excellent clutch of museums. The least obvious – but worth seeing for the setting inside one of the city's finest medieval mansions – is the **Casa Museu de Castellarnau** on c/Cavallers 14 (June–Sept Tues–Sat 9am–9pm, Sun 10am–2pm; Oct–May Tues–Sat 10am–1.30pm & 4–6.30pm, Sun 10am–2pm). The interior courtyard alone rewards a visit, with its arches and stone coats of arms built over Roman vaults. Otherwise, the small-scale collections are largely archeological and historical (coins and jars), rescued from banality by some rich eighteenth-century Catalan furniture and furnishings.

Museums of archeology and history

The most stimulating exhibitions in town are in adjacent buildings off Plaça del Rei at the edge of the old town. The splendid **Museu Nacional Arqueològic** (June–Sept Tues–Sat 10am–8pm, Sun 10am–2pm; Oct–May Tues–Sat 10am–1.30pm & 4–7pm, Sun 10am–2pm; €2.40) is a marvellous reflection of the richness of imperial *Tarraco*. Its huge collection is admirably laid out, starting in the basement with a section of the old Roman wall preserved *in situ*. On other floors are thematic displays on the various remains and buildings around the city, accompanied by pictures, text and relics, as well as whole rooms devoted to inscriptions, sculpture, ceramics, jewellery – even a series of anchors retrieved from the sea. More importantly, there's an unusually complete collection of mosaics, exemplifying the stages of development from the plain black-and-white patterns of the first century AD to the elaborate polychrome pictures of the second and third centuries.

Out of the centre

Tarragona is compact enough not only to be able to walk everywhere in the city, but to reach most of the outlying districts on foot, too. It's less than half an hour to either the port area of **Serrallo** or, across town, to the best local beach at **Arrabassada**. The Roman **Aqueduct**, 4km inland, is best reached by bus, but for most of the other Roman remains dotted around the surrounding countryside you'll need transport of your own.

Other Roman remains

Perhaps the most remarkable (and least visited) of Tarragona's monuments stands outside the original city walls. This is the **Roman Aqueduct**, which brought water from the Riu Gayo, some 32km distant. The most impressive extant section, nearly 220 metres long and 26 metres high, lies in an overgrown valley, off the main road in the middle of nowhere: take bus #5, marked "Sant Salvador" (every twenty minutes from the stop outside Avgda. Prat de la Riba 11, off Avinguda Ramón i Cajal; last bus back at around 10.45pm) – a ten-minute ride. The trip is undoubtedly worthwhile; the utilitarian beauty of the aqueduct is surpassed only by those at Segovia and the Pont du Gard, in the south of France. Popularly, it is known as El Pont del Diable (Devil's Bridge) because, remarked Richard Ford, of the Spanish habit of "giving all praise to 'the Devil', as Pontifex Maximus".

Other local Roman monuments of similar grandeur are more difficult to reach: in fact, without your own transport, almost impossible. If you're determined, keep a wary eye out for signs, and expect to have to ask directions locally from time to time. The square, three-storeyed **Torre dels Escipions**, a funerary monument built in the second century AD and nearly ten metres high, stands just off the main Barcelona road, the N340, 6km northeast up the coast. A couple of kilometres farther north, the **Pedrera del Medol** is the excavated quarry that provided much of the stone used in Tarragona's constructions, while 20km from the city, after the turn-off for Altafulla, is the triumphal **Arc de Bera**, built over the great Via Maxima in the second century AD.

Serrallo

A fifteen-minute walk west along the industrial harbour front from the train station (or the same distance south from the Necropolis) takes you right into the working port of **SERRALLO**, Tarragona's so-called "fisherman's quarter". Built a century ago, the harbour here is authentic enough – fishing smacks tied up, nets laid out on the ground for mending – but the real interest for visitors is the line of **fish and seafood restaurants** which fronts the main Moll dels Pescadors. You'll get something to eat, somewhere, on most days, though the weekend is when the locals descend and then you'll need to arrive early to grab a table. None of the restaurants is designed for budget eaters, but there are a couple of more basic joints hidden in the parallel backstreet, and it's also worth checking the *menús del día*. Where these are available you should be able to eat for around €9 a head; otherwise, commit yourself to the higher *a la carta* prices in the knowledge that the fish is as fresh as can be. *La Puda* (no. 25), at the far end, has tables overlooking the harbour inside and out, a short selection of seafood tapas, and a main menu that's overpriced but very good – the full three-course seafood works for two, plus wine, will cost around €48.

After your meal, you can walk back to Tarragona through the tangle of boats and nets, following the rail lines – or wait on the main road for city bus #2 back up to the old town. Alternatively, if you fancy a bop, you could stay in Serrallo and head to *La Vacaría*, c/de Rebolledo 11, a **music-bar** which also has occasional live rock and jazz.

Tarragona's beaches

The closest beach to town is the long **Platja del Miracle**, over the rail lines below the amphitheatre. The nicest, though, is a couple of kilometres farther up the coast, reached by taking Vía Augusta (off the end of Rambla Vella) and turning right at the *Hotel Astari*. Don't despair upon the way: the main road and railway bridge eventually give way to a road which winds around the headland and down to **Platja Arrabassada**, an ultimately pleasant walk with gradually unfolding views of the beach. There are regular buses in summer (#1, #3 or #9) from various points throughout town.

Arrabassada isn't anything very special, though it's roomy enough and has a few other diversions that make it worthwhile. Top of the list is the *Brasilmos* beach **bar-restaurant**, at the far end by the headland, which features seafood tapas, Latin American sounds, a pool table and occasional live music on summer evenings. There are a couple of other beach bars, too, and under the railway line, by *Brasilmos*, tiny **ARRABASSADA** village itself, which boasts two or three restaurants, a couple of hotels and *hostales*, a supermarket and two **campsites**, including *Camping Tarraco* (see "Accommodation", p.852). A bit further along the coast at **Platja Llarga**, a cluster of restaurants offer good food at low prices and stay open late. There's also a very lively Cuban **disco**, the *Corason*, where you'll find local familes – including grandparents – dancing the night away, fuelled by potent cocktails. Entrance is free, but you'll be expected to buy at least one drink.

Eating and drinking

There are plenty of good **restaurants** in the centre of Tarragona, as well as the fish and seafood places down in Serrallo. Many – particularly in and around Plaça de la Font – have outdoor seating in the summer. *Pescado romesco* (fish with *romesco* sauce) is the regional **speciality** and you'll find it on several *menús del día* around town: *romesco* sauce has a base of dry pepper, almonds and/or hazelnuts, olive oil, garlic and a glass of Priorato wine. Beyond this, there are many variations, as cooks tend to add their own secret ingredients. Good **bars** are less in evidence in Tarragona, though there are a few recommended ones listed below. Instead, you can join the locals in their nocturnal search for **cakes and ice cream**: Rambla Nova particularly is groaning with pavement cafés, all doing a roaring trade.

Restaurants

Can Llesques, c/Natzaret 6, on Plaça del Rei. Cramped, atmospheric restaurant with low stone arches serving endless variations of *Pa amb tomaquet*, accompanied by drinks dished up in ceramic pitchers. It's amazingly popular; go early or prepare to hang around for a table. Sitting outside attracts a ten-percent surcharge.

El Caseron, c/de Cos del Bou 9. Small restaurant just off Plaça de la Font, with a decent menu of staples – rabbit, paella, grills and fries – and a very good-value *menú del día*. Closed Mon after 5pm, Sat & Sun.

Les Coques, c/Nou del Patriarca 2. Fine dining in an upmarket Catalan restaurant, just off Plaça de la Seu near the cathedral. Upwards of €18 a head. Closed Sun.

Mistral, Plaça de la Font 19. Pizzas for around €3.60–6, plus the usual (Spanish) menu, including pricey *pescado romesco*. Tables on the square in summer are its main attraction, though.

La Pizzeria, c/Cos del Bou 8. There are cheaper pizzerias, but this family-run place has a relaxed and friendly atmosphere. Closed Mon lunch & Sun.

El Plata, c/August 20. Summer outdoor dining in the pedestrian zone between the two *ramblas*. There's a decent *menú del día* at €8.40 and a wide tapas selection.

Restaurant Les Voltes, c/Trinquet Vell 12. One of the best restaurants in the Cathedral area, recommended for its hearty *pa amb tomàquet* meals and grilled meats. Around €12. Closed Sun.

Bars and cafés

Bar Frankfurt el Balcon, Rambla Nova 3. Outdoor tables in the best spot on the *rambla*, on the balcony of land next to the statue of Roger de Lluria. Sandwiches and tapas.

Bar Musical El Cau, c/Trinquet Vell 2. Situated in an underground Roman vault in the old town, this dark venue has live indie-pop or rock every Saturday night. Open daily 10pm–4am.

Café L'Antiquari, c/Santa Anna 3. Laid-back café-bar with funk and rock sounds and a liberal use of borrowed religious artefacts and statues, including a confessional box converted into a telephone cabin. A noticeboard at the entrance has details of events around town.

Café Cantonada, c/Fortuny 23. Civilized café-bar whose roomy interior and pool table encourage extended visits. Breakfast served from 8.30am to midday; closed Mon.

El Candil, Plaça de la Font 13. Fashionable, friendly bar with tapas, a wide selection of herbal teas and coffees as well as alcohol. Open late at weekends.

Frankfurt, c/Canyelles (off Rambla Nova, on the left before the fountain). A bar with good hot and cold sandwiches prepared in front of you – a wide selection for €1.50–3 a go.

La Geladeria, Plaça del Rei 6. Popular ice-cream parlour outside the archeological museum.

Kennedy, c/Vilarroma 24. Busy Irish bar with a good selection of beers and Irish whiskeys. Occasional live music. Open daily until 3am.

Moto Club Tarragona, Rambla Nova 53. Busy *rambla* bar with televised soccer if it's on. Open daily from 7am to midnight for drinks and snacks.

Patisseria Granta, c/Major 32. Cakes and pastries in a swish, modern *patisseria*. Counter or table service; popular on Sundays.

La Penya, Plaça de la Font 35. Friendly, hippyish bar offering hearty Catalan cuisine, with generous shots of *vermouth de la casa* (at €0.90 a go) and, if you ask a couple of days beforehand, excellent Mexican food too.

Listings

Airlines Iberia, Rambla Nova 116 ☎977 240 751.

Banks and exchange Many banks have offices along Rambla Nova. Outside banking hours you can exchange money and travellers' cheques at Viajes Eurojet, Rambla Nova 42 (Mon–Fri 9am–1.30pm & 4.30–8.30pm, Sat 9am–1pm). This agency also handles American Express matters, and will exchange cheques and hold mail.

Bus information Local bus information is available from the tourist offices or the cabin on c/Cristòfor Colom ☎977 549 480. Bus station information on ☎977 229 126.

Car rental Atesa, at Viatgens Marsans, c/Lleida 11 ☎977 219 867; Racc, Rambla Nova 114 ☎977 211 962; Avis, c/Pinisoler 10 ☎977 219 156; Hertz, Vía Augusta 91 ☎977 384 137.

Cinemas Movies are shown at Oscars, c/Ramón i Cajal 15; Lauren Multicines, c/Vidal I Barraquer 15–17; and Catalunya, Rambla Vella 9. Listings from the tourist offices or in the local newspaper.

Emergencies Call ☎092 or ☎977 222 222 for an ambulance.

Hospitals Hospital de Sant Pau i Santa Tecla, Rambla Vella 14 ☎977 259 900.

Markets Daily food market (not Sun) on and around Plaça Cosini, near the provincial forum; indoor food market at Plaça de Corsini (Mon–Fri 9am–1pm & 4–8pm, Sat 7am–1pm). On Sundays, there's an antiques market at the top of the cathedral steps, with jewellery, bric-a-brac, ornaments and antiques spilling over into the arcades along c/Mercería.

Post office At Plaça de Corsini (Mon–Fri 8am–8.30pm, Sat 8am–2pm).

Taxis There are ranks on Rambla Nova (at the Moto Club), in Plaça del Font, and at the bus and train stations. Or call ☎977 221 414, 977 236 064 or 977 215 656.

Train information RENFE has an office at Rambla Nova 40 for tickets and enquiries (Mon–Fri 9am–1pm & 4–7pm; ☎977 232 534).

Travel agencies For local tours, train and bus information, and tickets, contact Viajes Eurojet, Rambla Nova 42; Viatgens Marsans, c/Comte de Rius 26; Vibus, Rambla Nova 125; or Wagon Lits, c/Cristòfor Colom 8.

Salou-Cambrils

The coast south of Tarragona is an uninspiring prospect. The occasional beaches are not easily reached by public transport, and few of them have anything to encourage a stop: long, thin strips of sand, they are almost universally backed by gargantuan caravan-camping grounds, packed full and miles from anywhere. This part of the Costa Daurada also boasts one of Catalunya's biggest tourist developments, the extended coastal stretch that is the resort of **Salou-Cambrils**. It's actually two separate towns, but the few kilometres between them have long been filled and stacked with holiday apartments, bars and restaurants. You may wish to give them a miss altogether – understandable in high summer when every inch is block-booked and smothered in sunscreen – though Cambrils does have its good points, especially out of season.

Salou

The ten-minute train ride from Tarragona to **SALOU** makes an unpromising start, passing through a mesh of petrochemical pipes and tanks before rounding on the resort itself – an almost entirely unrelieved gash of apartment blocks and hotels spilling down towards the sea. There are three or four separate beaches here, ringed around a sweeping bay and backed by a promenade studded with palms. From the seafront it's quite an attractive prospect, but the town is resolutely downmarket and stuffed to the gills in summer, the streets back from the sea teeming with "English pubs" and poor restaurants serving overpriced food and beer. Just outside town lies **Port Aventura** (daily: mid-June to mid-Sept 10am–midnight; mid-Sept to mid-June 10am–8pm; information ☎902 202 220; €28.90). This massive theme park, with its own RENFE station, boasts five themed "lands" including China and the Wild West, each offering death-defying rides, garish restaurants and live entertainment. If it's your bag, you might want to buy a two-day pass (€43.30) and stay in Salou, which is packed with hotels and *pensiones*. Otherwise, you're much better off heading for Cambrils, 7km south. Buses regularly ply the coastal road between the two, or it's one more stop on the train.

Cambrils

Smaller **CAMBRILS** is nicer in every way, the town set back from a large harbour which still has working boats and fishing nets interspersed among the restaurants and hotels. In summer it's as full as anywhere along the Catalan coast, and Cambrils is probably better seen as a day-trip from Tarragona, only fifteen minutes to the north. Out of season, though, it's more relaxed and while inexpensive accommodation isn't easy to come by, it might be worth persevering for a night to eat in the good fish restaurants and amble around the harbour and nearby beaches. There's a **market** in town every Wednesday (the one in Salou is on Monday).

Practicalities

Arriving by bus from Tarragona, you'll pass through Salou and can ask to be dropped in Cambrils on the harbour front. By **train**, you're faced with a fifteen-minute walk from the inland part of town down to Cambrils-Port and the harbour: from the station, turn right and then right again at the main road, heading for the sea. Across the bridge on your left is the main **turisme** (daily 10am–1pm & 5–8pm; ☎977 794 579, ℗977 794 572, ✉ptur.cambrils@altanet.org), which has free maps, local bus and train timetables posted on the door, and may be able to help find a room. From here, Cambrils-Port is straight ahead, down any of the roads in front of you.

Finding rooms can be a problem, since **accommodation** in town is mainly in apartments. The hotels that exist are pricey, and not inclined to reduce their rates out of season. On the square outside the train station, and on the way to the harbour, a few places advertise *habitaciones*: you'd probably do best to take whatever's going in summer, even though here you're fifteen minutes or so from all the action. Down at the harbour, hotels mingle with places just offering rooms. Try the *Hostal Moncusi*, c/Roger de Llúria 16 (☎977 360 029; ❹), whose clean, bright rooms (without bath) are about the best value in town; ask at the *Restaurant Playa* (see below) for directions – the *hostal* is marked CH. The *Hotel-Restaurant Miramar*, Passeig Miramar 30 (☎977 360 063; ❼), is a deal more expensive, but nicely positioned overlooking the sea. There are also eight **campsites** in and around Cambrils, and the turisme has a free map showing where they all are. Closest to the centre is *Camping Horta* (☎977 361 243; April–Sept), north of the harbour at the top of Rambla Regueral; the others are spread up and down the coast in both directions.

Food prices in Cambrils are on the steep side, but there's plenty of choice and some splendid fish **restaurants** along the harbour if you're prepared to dust off your wallet. The *Restaurant Playa* makes a good start, with three variously priced *menús del día*, the most expensive of which – at around €9 a head – guarantees you a fine feast. Elsewhere, you're looking at a *menú* for around €7.20 in most of the restaurants, though *a la carta* seafood at one of the harbour-front restaurants comes in at considerably more than that. Less expensive meals are found at several places along c/Pau Casals, or go for the modestly priced *platos combinados* at *Cafetería La Sirena*, c/Sant Pere 2 (entrance on c/Roger de Llúria; closed Thurs). The bar opposite the train station has seafood tapas and the usual *comedor* standbys.

Tortosa

The only town of any size in Catalunya's deep south is **TORTOSA**, slightly inland astride the Riu Ebre. In the Civil War the front was outside Tortosa for several months until the Nationalists eventually took the town in April 1938. The battle cost 35,000 lives – a traumatic event that is commemorated by a gaunt metal monument standing on a huge stone plinth in the middle of the river in town. The fighting took its toll in other ways, too: there's little left of the medieval quarter in the few old streets around the **cathedral**, though the building itself is worth a look. Founded originally in the twelfth century on the site of an earlier mosque, it was rebuilt in the fourteenth century, and its Gothic interior and quiet cloister – although much worn – are very fine. Several *modernista* houses around town (marked on the turisme map) also add a bit of interest.

Tortosa's brightest point is also its highest. **La Suda**, the old castle, sits perched above the cathedral, glowering from behind its battlements at the Ebre valley below and the mountains beyond. Like so many in Spain, the castle has been converted into a luxury *parador* (see below), but there's nothing to stop you climbing up for a magnificent view from the walls, or even from marching into the plush bar and having a drink. From the cathedral, c/de la Suda takes you straight there. On the other side of La Suda, a garden beneath the castle houses a collection of **sculptures** (April to mid-Sept Tues–Sat

10am–1pm & 4.30–7.30pm, Sun 10am–2pm; mid-Sept to March Tues–Sat 10am–1pm & 3.30–5.30pm, Sun 10am–2pm; €2.40) of the human figure by Santiago de Santiago.

Practicalities

Tortosa is the main transport terminus for the region: in particular, regular buses run from here out to the principal towns and villages of the Delta de l'Ebre (see below). This, really, is the main reason to come, since the town is otherwise hardly an inspirational stopover, unless you stay at the *parador*. Moving on **out of Catalunya**, regular **buses** run from Tortosa to Vinaròs (in Castellón province to the south), from where you can reach the wonderful inland mountain town of Morella; and less regularly west to Alcañiz (in Aragón). **Trains** head south, passing through Vinaròs, on their way to Valencia.

The main **turisme** (Mon–Fri 10am–1pm & 4–7pm, Sat 10am–1pm; ☎977 510 822, 🖷977 585 852, 🖃aj.tortosa@altanet.org) is in the Plaça del Bimil.lenari, to the south of the town, and there's a more central summer turisme (April–Sept Tues–Sat 10am–1pm & 4–8pm, Sun 10am–1pm) on the main road into town, Avinguda de la Generalitat, in the park on the left-hand side. To get there from the bus or train stations, follow the train tracks towards the river and turn left – away from the centre – under the bridge. Further out of town along here is the *Pensió Virginia*, at no. 133 (☎977 444 186; ❸), a good place to stay if your budget doesn't run to the **parador** (☎977 444 450, 🖷977 444 458; ❽) at La Suda. If you do stay at the *parador* you should eat there as well, since it has the best **restaurant** in town, open to non-guests. The *Virginia* also has a decent restaurant, but other good places to eat are thin on the ground in Tortosa.

The Delta de l'Ebre

In the bottom corner of Catalunya is the **Delta de l'Ebre** (Ebro Delta), 320 square kilometres of sandy delta constituting the biggest wetland in Catalunya and one of the most important aquatic habitats in the western Mediterranean. Designated a natural park, its brackish lagoons, marshes, dunes and reed beds are home to thousands of wintering birds and provide excellent fishing; around fifteen percent of the total Catalan catch comes from this area.

Since much of the area of the **Parc Natural de Delta de l'Ebre** is a protected zone, access is limited. It's also difficult to visit without your own transport, though the effort of doing so is rewarded by tranquillity and space. If you're relying on buses, aim for one of the three main towns – Amposta, Sant Carles de la Ràpita or Deltebre – where you'll find accommodation and boat services on into the delta. Outside the towns, camping is allowed in certain areas.

Amposta

AMPOSTA, at the far western edge of the delta, is the largest and least attractive of the towns in the region, and not really somewhere you need to stay long. There are a couple of places to stay on the edge of town and a **turisme** at Sant Jaume 1 (April to mid-Sept Mon–Sat 10am–1pm & 4–7pm, Sun 10am–2pm; mid-Sept to March Mon–Fri 11am–1pm; ☎977 703 453, 🖷977 704 132, 🖃otur.amposta@altanet.org), which can advise you about the possibility of renting a boat to take you down to the river mouth: with costs shared between a group of people, this is not too expensive.

Sant Carles de la Ràpita

SANT CARLES DE LA RÀPITA, to the south, is a more inviting place, with regular daily buses from Tortosa – though few at the weekend – and a **turisme** (June–Sept Mon–Fri 9am–2pm & 4–6pm, Sat & Sun 11am–1pm & 5–7pm; Oct–May Mon–Sat morning only, closed Sun; ⓣ977 740 100, ⓕ977 744 387, ⓔturisme@larapita.com) in the *ajuntament*. It's quite a busy town in summer, drawing families to the several campsites stretching away down the coast – prepare to fend off swarms of mosquitoes if you stay at them – and to the dozens of restaurants which are said to serve the best prawns in the Med. Unless you've access to a car, though, you'll be able to explore only the immediate surroundings.

For **rooms** in town, try the large *Hotel Roca Mar*, Avgda. Constitucío 8 (ⓣ & ⓕ977 740 458; ❸), whose rooms without bath are fine, or *Casa Ramon*, c/Arsenal 16 (ⓣ977 740 361, ⓕ977 744 397; ❹), which has very good-value full- and half-board deals. An excellent **restaurant**, much frequented by locals, is the *Can Victor*, signposted from all over town, whose position right beneath the market guarantees the freshest of produce.

Deltebre, Sant Jaume d'Enveja and around

From Amposta, road and river run to **DELTEBRE** (buses from Tortosa), at the centre of the delta. The **park information office** here, on the edge of town on Plaça Vint de Maig and well signposted (Mon–Fri 10am–2pm & 3–6pm, Sat 10am–1pm & 3–6pm, Sun 10am–1pm; ⓣ977 489 679), can provide you with a map of the delta, and has information about tours and local walks. At the same place there's an interesting **Ecomuseum** (Tues–Sun 9am–1pm; €0.60), which has an aquarium displaying species from the delta, and also maintains hides for bird-watchers which overlook a pond. There are three or four places to stay in Deltebre, all reasonably priced, as well as a **youth hostel** (ⓣ977 480 136, ⓕ977 481 284; ❶) at Avinguda de les Goles del Ebre, and a ferry across to **SANT JAUME D'ENVEJA** on the opposite shore. The local restaurants serve wonderful fish dishes, the speciality being *arròz a banda*, similar to paella except that the rice is brought before the seafood itself.

Three islands lie between Amposta and the open sea, the biggest being the **Illa de Buda** just by the river mouth. It's covered with rice fields (the main local crop) and you can reach it on excursion boats from Deltebre or by scheduled ferry from Sant Jaume. The road which runs along the south bank of the river leads to the so-called Eucaliptus **beach**, where there's a campsite, *Mediterrani Blau* (ⓣ977 479 046; April–Sept).

Inland: the route to Lleida

The train line from Barcelona forks at Tarragona, and the choice is either south towards Tortosa or **inland** for the fairly monotonous three-hour ride northwest across the flat lands to Lleida. The Tarragona–Lleida bus is a slightly more attractive proposition than the train, if only because it climbs the odd bluff and ridge on the way for good views over the plain. The bus also takes you directly to the region's only major attraction, the monastery of Poblet, which you could see in half a day and then move on to Lleida. Access to the monastery by train is possible, but means walking some of the way – not an unpleasant task by any means if the weather's fine since the surroundings are lovely.

Montblanc

The walled medieval town of **MONTBLANC**, 8km before the turning to the monastery at Poblet, is also on the train line to Lleida, so it's easy enough to see both on the same trip. It's a surprisingly beautiful place to discover in the middle of nowhere, and astonishingly lively during the evening *passeig* around the picturesque Plaça Major. There are many fine little Romanesque and Gothic monuments contained within a tight circle of old streets; all are marked on a map attached to the town's medieval gateway, the **Portal de Boue**, which is just a hundred metres or so up from the train station.

The grand Gothic parish church of **Santa María**, just above the central square, is perhaps the first thing to look out for: its elaborate facade has lions' faces on either side of the main doorway and cherubs swarming up the pillars. There's a fine view from the once-fortified mound that rises behind the church – over the rooftops, defensive towers and walls, and away across the plain. A couple of other churches to track down are Romanesque Sant Miquel (usually locked) and Sant Marcel, on the other side of the mound, which contains the **Museu Marès** (June–Sept Tues–Sat 10am–2pm & 4–8pm, Sun 10am–2pm; Oct–May Sat & Sun only; free). Like the one in Barcelona (p.700), it's an eclectic collection of religious sculpture and art. Montblanc also has a fine local history museum, the **Museu Comarcal de la Conca de Barberà** (June–Sept Tues–Sat 10am–2pm & 5–8pm, Sun 10am–2pm; Oct–May Tues–Sat 10am–1pm & 4–7pm, Sun 10am–2pm; €2.40), just off Plaça Major below the church, which is bright and informative, although all annotated in Catalan.

Practicalities

There's a tiny, very helpful **turisme** (opening hours vary) inside the Casa de la Vila building in the arcaded Plaça Major. When it's closed, the policeman on the door should hand over a map. If you're driving, Montblanc would make a fine base for visiting Poblet – even on foot, it's only 8km to the monastery. The friendliest place to stay is the *Fonda Cal Blasi*, c/Alenyà 11–13 (℡977 861 336, ℻977 861 329, ⓦwww.infonegocio.com/fondacalblasi; ❺), a restored nineteenth-century farmhouse a short distance from the bus station; it also serves meals.

The Monestir de Poblet

There are few ruins more stirring than the **MONESTIR DE POBLET**. It lies in glorious open country, vast and sprawling within massive battlemented walls and towered gateways. Once *the* great monastery of Catalunya, it was in effect a complete manorial village and enjoyed scarcely credible rights, powers and wealth. Founded in 1151 by Ramón Berenguer IV, who united the kingdoms of Catalunya and Aragón, it was planned from the beginning on an immensely grand scale. The kings of Aragón-Catalunya chose to be buried in its chapel and for three centuries diverted huge sums for its endowment, a munificence that was inevitably corrupting. By the late Middle Ages Poblet had become a byword for decadence – there are lewder stories about this than any other Cistercian monastery – and so it continued, hated by the local peasantry, until the Carlist revolution of 1835 when a mob burned and tore it apart.

The monastery was repopulated by Italian Cistercians in 1940 and over the past decades a superb job of restoration has been undertaken. Much remains delightfully ruined but, inside the main gates, you are now proudly escorted around the principal complex of buildings. As so often, the **cloisters**, focus of monastic life, are the most evocative and beautiful part. Late Romanesque, and sporting a pavilion and fountain, they open onto a series of rooms: a splendid Gothic **chapterhouse** (with the former abbots' tombs set in the floor), wine cellars, a parlour, a **kitchen** equipped with ranges and copper pots, and a sombre, wood-panelled **refectory**.

Beyond, you enter the **chapel** in which the twelfth- and thirteenth-century tombs of the kings of Aragón have been meticulously restored by Frederico Marès, the manic collector of Barcelona. They lie in marble sarcophagi on either side of the nave, focusing attention on the central sixteenth-century altarpiece. You'll also be shown the vast old **dormitory**, to which there's direct access from the chapel choir, a poignant reminder of Cistercian discipline. From the dormitory (half of which is sealed off since it's still in use), a door leads out onto the cloister roof for views down into the cloister itself and up the chapel towers.

Entry to the monastery costs €3, and it's open daily from 10am to 12.30pm and from 3 to 6pm (closing half an hour earlier in the winter). Officially, it can be toured only by members of a **guided group**. The tours take an hour and depart roughly every half-hour (every fifteen minutes Sunday and holidays). However, the porter may let you in to walk around alone if there aren't enough people within a reasonable period of time. There's a **turisme**, on the left as you enter (daily 10am–1.30pm & 3–5.30pm; ☎977 871 247).

Getting there by bus

Three **buses** a day (Mon–Sat only) run to Poblet from Tarragona or Lleida, passing right by the monastery. It's an easy day-trip from either city, or can be seen on the way between the two – the gap between buses is roughly three hours, which is enough time to get around the complex. You could also **stay overnight** at Poblet, an even more attractive proposition if you have your own transport, since there are several pleasant excursion targets in the surrounding countryside (see below). The solitary *Hostal Fonoll* outside the main gate of the monastery (☎977 870 333; closed mid-Dec to mid-Jan;❸) has a decent restaurant and bar, functional standard rooms and more expensive rooms with bath; while 1km up the road, around the walls, the hamlet of **LES MASIES** has a couple more hotels and restaurants, including the *Villa Engràcia* (☎977 870 308, ℱ977 870 326;❺), which has a pool, tennis courts and parking facilities.

Getting there by train: L'Espluga de Francolí

The approach by **train** is much more atmospheric. You get off at the ruined station of **L'ESPLUGA DE FRANCOLÍ**, from where it's a beautiful three-kilometre walk to the monastery. L'Espluga itself is a bit of a one-horse town and there's no baggage *consigna* at the station, but there are a couple of places **to stay**, including the *Hotel del Senglar* (☎977 870 121, ℱ977 871 012;❻), a very comfortable set-up – with a decent restaurant, pool, tennis courts and parking – on the main road through town that leads to Poblet.

You can of course vary your approach to the monastery, taking the bus one way and choosing to walk to or from L'Espluga (3km), Montblanc (8km) or even Vimbodi (5km), at all of which the Tarragona–Lleida train stops.

Around Poblet: excursions

If you have time and transport, a couple of excursions into the countryside surrounding Poblet are well worth making. The red-stone walled village of **PRADES**, in the Serra de Prades, 20km from the monastery, is a beautifully sited and tranquil place that needs no other excuse for a visit. The *Pensió*

Espasa, c/Sant Roc 1 (℡977 868 023; ❹), offers simple accommodation if you decide you like it enough to stay on. Prades is also the place to be during the second weekend of July, when they replace the water in the fountain with *cava*, and for a mere €7.20 you can join in and help yourself.

The other option is to take in two more twelfth-century Cistercian monasteries. **Santes Creus** (summer daily 10am–1.30pm & 3–7pm; winter Tues–Sun 10am–1.30pm & 3–6pm; €3.60) is the easier to reach, northeast of **VALLS** on the other side of the Tarragona–Lleida highway. It's built in Transitional style, with a grand Gothic cloister and some Romanesque traces, and you can explore the dormitory, chapterhouse and royal palace. There's a once-daily bus from Tarragona to Valls, which connects with a local service to Santa Creus, but check on return times because you don't want to get stranded in these parts. Trickier to find, though worth the drive, is the monastery of **Vallbona de les Monges** (summer Mon–Sat 10.30am–1.30pm & 4.30–6.45pm, Sun noon–1.30pm & 4.30–6.45pm; winter daily closes 5.45pm; free), north of Poblet, reached up the C240 from Montblanc. This has been occupied continuously for over 800 years, and the church is particularly fine.

Lleida

LLEIDA (Lérida), at the heart of a fertile plain near the Aragonese border, has a rich history. First a *municipium* under the Roman empire and later the centre of a small Arab kingdom, it was reconquered by the Catalans and became the seat of a bishopric in 1149. Little of those periods survives in today's pleasant city but there is one building of outstanding interest, the old cathedral, which is sufficient justification in itself to find the time for a visit. If you have to spend the night in Lleida – and you will if you're heading north to the Pyrenees by train or bus – there are a couple of museums and a steep set of old-town streets to occupy any remaining time. Rooms are easy to come by, and the students at the local university fill the streets and bars on weekend evenings in good-natured throngs.

Arrival and information

Plaça de Sant Joan is a fifteen- to twenty-minute walk east of the **train station**, with the **bus station** a similar distance in the other direction, down Avinguda de Blondel. The very informative **turisme** (Mon–Sat 11am–8pm, Sun 11am–1.30pm; ℡902 250 050, ⓦwww.paeria.es/turisme) is at Plaça Espanya 1 and includes a shop and free hotel and restaurant reservation service. There's also a provincial/national office (June–Sept Mon–Fri 9am–8pm, Sat 9am–2pm; Oct–May Mon–Fri 9am–7pm, Sat 9am–2pm; ℡973 270 997) at Avgda. Madrid 36, overlooking the river. You can connect to the **internet** at *Café d'Internet*, c/Bonaire 8 (Mon–Sat 9am–2pm & 3.30pm–2am, Sun 7pm–midnight; €3 per hour).

Accommodation

There are a couple of **places to stay** right outside the train station, and more along the road straight ahead – Rambla Ferrán – which leads into the centre. Otherwise, press on to the central Plaça Sant Joan, around which there are several possibilities. There's a **campsite**, *Les Basses* (℡973 235 954; mid-May to Sept), a couple of kilometres out of town on the Huesca road, though at the time of writing it had just changed hands, so phone before setting off to check it's still open. Take the bus labelled "BS" or "Les Basses" (every 45min from Rambla Ferrán).

Alberg Sant Anastasi, Rambla d'Aragó 11 ☎973 266 099. Lleida's youth hostel, newly renovated and centrally located but only open in July and Aug. ❷

Pensió Alex, c/Tallada 33 ☎973 275 629. Good *pensió* on a quiet street near the market. ❹

Hostal España, Rambla Ferrán 20 ☎973 236 440. More upmarket than either of the neighbouring *habitaciones*, this *hostal* offers some rooms with a shower, but it's a busy road – so ask to see the room first. ❸

Residencia Mundial, Plaça de Sant Joan 4 ☎973 242 700. Central and friendly *residencia*, with a breakfast bar and parking facilities. Some of the rooms (with and without bath) overlook the square. ❸

Hotel Principal, Plaça de la Paeria 8 ☎973 230 800) Just off the Plaça de Sant Joan, a more luxurious and, inevitably, more expensive option. ❺

Hotel Sansi Park, c/Alcade Porqueras ☎973 244 000, ☎973 243 138. The most characterful of the mid-priced options in the centre. ❻

Hotel Ramon Berenguer, Plaça Ramon Berenguer IV 2 ☎973 237 345. Good value for money and well-equipped rooms in a renovated building near the train station. ❺

The City

The **Seu Vella** (Tues–Sat 10am–1.30pm & 4–7.30pm, closes 5.30pm in winter, Sun 9.30am–1.30pm; €2.40), or old cathedral, is entirely enclosed within the walls of the ruined castle (La Suda), high above the Riu Segre, a twenty-minute climb from the centre of town – or you can take the lift from Plaça de Sant Joan (same hours; €0.40). It's a peculiar fortified building, which in 1707 was deconsecrated and taken over by the military, remaining in military hands until 1940. Enormous damage was inflicted over the years (documented by photos in a side chapel) but the church remains a notable example of the Transitional style, similar in many respects to the cathedral of Tarragona. Once again the Gothic cloisters are masterful, each walk comprising arches different in size and shape but sharing delicate stone tracery. They served the military as a canteen and kitchen. Outside, the views from the walls away over the plain, are stupendous.

You can climb back down towards the river by way of the aforementioned new cathedral, the **Seu Nova**, a grimy eighteenth-century building only enlivened inside by a series of minuscule, high stained-glass windows. Nearby, halfway up the steep c/Cavallers at no. 15, is the **Museu de Arte Jaume Morera** (Tues–Sat 11am–2pm & 5–8pm, Sun 11am–2pm; free), a permanent display of contemporary art by local artists, housed on the second floor of an old monastery building. On the other side of the cathedral, on Avinguda de Blondel, the **Museu Arqueològic** (June–Sept Tues–Fri 10am–2pm & 6–9pm, Sat 11am–2pm & 7–9pm, Sun 11am–2pm; Oct–May Tues–Fri 10am–2pm & 5–8.30pm, Sat noon–2pm & 5.30–8.30pm, Sun noon–2pm; free) is a fairly negligible collection, but again is housed in an interesting building, this time the fifteenth-century Santa María hospital.

Once you've seen the cathedral and museums, you've just about seen the lot that Lleida has to offer, though its central pedestrianized shopping streets are good for a browse, and you can wind up in the newly renovated **Plaça de Sant Joan** for a drink in one of the outdoor cafés.

Eating and drinking

Finding anything to **eat** or **drink** can be surprisingly difficult in the evening in Lleida, particularly on Sunday when many places are closed (including most of those detailed below). For breakfast and *platos combinados*, *Café Triunfo* on the

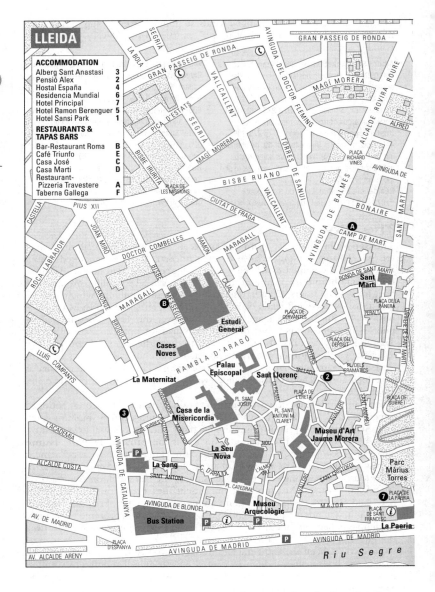

edge of Plaça de Sant Joan is good – step inside anyway for a look at the photographs of old Lleida. The cheapest and best meals are at the unpretentious *Casa José*, c/Botera 17 (near the Auditori, off c/Magdalena; closed Sun & mid-Aug), which is very popular with the locals – especially for the *mariscos* – so it's best to arrive before 9pm when it really starts filling up. Nearby *Casa Marti*, c/Magdalena 37, is much smarter: the restaurant above the bar serves fine,

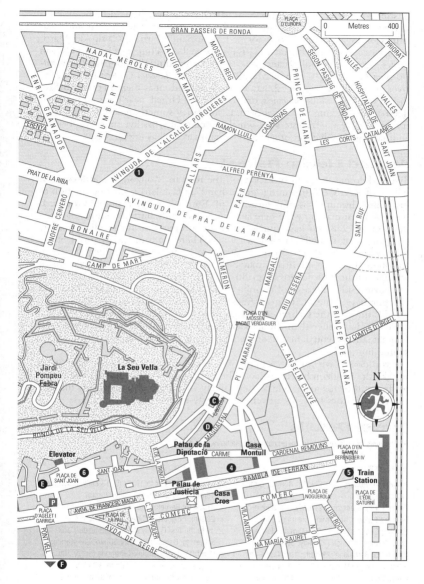

locally inspired food at mid-range prices €9–12 for a full meal or €7.20 for the *menú del dia*. You'll find more budget dining up the hill in the streets around the university: *Bar-Restaurant Roma*, c/Bisbe Messeguer 1, is an inexpensive student hang-out here with good tapas. The **market** is just at the top of c/Cavallers (Mon–Sat 9am–2pm), in Plaça dels Gramàtics.

If you're looking for more variety and better restaurants, head for the block of streets north of the church of Sant Marti. The university is close by, and this is where the students come to eat and hang out, in the restaurants and loud **music-bars** along the block formed by c/Sant Marti, c/Camp de Marti, c/Balmes and Avinguda Prat de la Riba. As well as a couple of budget Catalan places, there are several pricier pizzerias here, including the popular *Restaurant-Pizzeria Travestere*, c/Camp de Mart 27. Finally, the *Taberna Gallega,* south of the river at Avgda. Garrigues 52, has a strong seafood tapas menu. For **nightlife**, there's only one club, *Brownie's*, on c/Comtes d'Urgell, near the station, but it doesn't start kicking until after 3am. If you fancy something a little mellower, try *Antares Jazz*, c/Ballesters 15, which is open daily, has live music on Fridays and has a wide selection of alchoholic drinks as well as herbal teas.

Around Lleida: Raimat

Twelve kilometres north of Lleida, off the road to Monzon, the little-known village of **RAIMAT** (meaning "grape-hand" in Catalan), with a population of just three hundred, is the location of Europe's biggest single **vineyard**. They've been making wine here since 1627 but only started commercial production in 1978 and have quickly built up a reputation for producing some of Spain's best, though least-known wines. There are tours (in Spanish) of the factory at weekends (10.30am, 11.30am & 12.30pm; ☎973 724 000; free), although, if you phone first, it may be possible to visit during the week or to arrange a tour with Carlos Negrillo, who speaks excellent English. The tour, of course, ends with a small tasting (€1.20) and a visit to the shop, where you can purchase some of Raimat's finest for very reasonable prices. Particularly good is the *cava*, the Cabernet Sauvignon, especially the 1994 vintage, and the 1998 Abadia. Other than the factory, there's not a lot else to occupy you in Raimat, unless you fancy a drink at the bar of the village's summer-only swimming pool.

If you don't have your own transport, the only way to get to the vineyard is to take the Monzon bus from Lleida bus station (3–4 daily) and ask the driver to stop at the crossroads, which they usually will if you don't have any luggage in the hold; from here, it's a twenty- to thirty-minute walk.

Travel Details

For services from Barcelona to destinations in Catalunya, see p.742.

Trains

Blanes to: Figueres (2 daily; 1hr 30min); Girona (10 daily; 45min).

Figueres to: Barcelona (21 daily; 1hr 30min–2hr); Blanes (2 daily; 1hr 30min); Colera (8 daily; 25min); Girona (21 daily; 25–35min); Llançà (12 daily; 20min); Portbou (12 daily; 30min).

Girona to: Barcelona (29 daily; 1hr 10min–1hr 30min); Blanes (10 daily; 45min); Figueres (21 daily; 35min); Portbou (12 daily; 1hr 10min).

Lleida to: Barcelona via Valls or Reus/Tarragona (17 daily; 2hr–4hr 15min); La Pobla de Segur (4 daily; 2hr); Tarragona (8 daily; 1hr 30min–2hr); Zaragoza (11 daily; 1hr 50min).

Puigcerdà to: La Tour de Carol (6 daily; 5min).

Ribes de Freser to: Núria (9–13 daily in summer; 45min); Queralbs (9–13 daily; 25min).

Ripoll to: Barcelona (8–12 daily; 1hr 45min–2hr 20min); Puigcerdà (6 daily; 1hr 10min; 4–5 continue to the first French station, Latour-de-Carol).

Sitges to: Barcelona (every 30min; 25–40min); Cunit (12 daily; 15min); Tarragona (every 30min; 1hr); Vilanova (every 10–20min; 10min).

Tarragona to Barcelona (every 30min; 1hr 30min); Cambrils (10 daily; 20min); Cunit (10 daily; 50min); Lleida (3 daily; 2hr); Salou (11 daily; 10min); Sitges (direct every 30min; 1hr); Tortosa (8 daily; 1hr); Valencia (8 daily; 4hr); Vilanova i la Geltrú (17 daily; 50min); Zaragoza (6 daily; 3hr 30min).

Buses

Banyoles to: Besalú (Mon–Sat 8 daily, Sun 4; 15min); Girona (Mon–Sat 11–16 daily, Sun 6; 30min); Olot (Mon–Sat 8 daily, Sun 4; 50min).

Cadaqués to: Barcelona (2–4 daily; 2hr 20min); Castelló d'Empúries (4 daily; 1hr); Figueres (3 daily; 1hr 5min); Roses (4 daily; 30min).

Camprodon to: Molló (Mon–Sat 1 daily; 15min); Setcases (Mon–Sat 1 daily; 30min).

L'Escala to: Barcelona (July–Sept 3 daily; 2hr 40min); Figueres (5 daily; 45min); Girona (1 daily; 1hr); Palafrugell (4 daily; 45min); Pals (3 daily; 35min); Sant Pere Pescador (5 daily; 20min); Torroella de Montgrí (4 daily; 20min).

Figueres to: Barcelona (3–8 daily; 1hr 30min); Cadaqués (3 daily; 1hr 5min); Castelló d'Empúries (hourly; 15min); El Port de la Selva (2 daily; 40min); L'Escala (5 daily; 45min); Espolla (1 daily; 35min); Girona (Mon–Sat 4–8 daily, Sun 3; 1hr); Llançà (2 daily; 25min); Olot (2–3 daily; 1hr 30min); Palafrugell (4 daily; 1hr 30min); Pals (4 daily; 1hr 20min); Roses (every 30min; 40min); Sant Pere Pescador (5 daily; 35min); Torroella de Montgrí (4 daily; 1hr 10min).

Girona to: Banyoles (Mon–Sat 11–16 daily, Sun 6; 30min); Barcelona (Mon–Fri 7 daily, Sat & Sun 3; 1hr 30min); Besalú (Mon–Sat 8 daily, Sun 4; 50min); L'Escala (Mon–Fri 2 daily; 1hr); Figueres (Mon–Sat 4–8 daily, Sun 3; 1hr); Olot (Mon–Sat 14 daily, Sun 9; 1hr 15min); Palafrugell (hourly; 1hr 15min); Palamós (14 daily; 1hr); Platja d'Oro (12–13 daily; 45min); Sant Feliu (Mon–Sat 11–14 daily, Sun 7; 2hr); Sant Hilari Sacalm (Mon–Fri 3 daily, Sat 1; 1hr 15min); Tossa de Mar (July–Sept 2 daily; 1hr).

Lleida to: Artesa de Segre (3 daily; 1hr); Barcelona (Mon–Sat 9 daily, Sun 3; 2hr 15min); Huesca (5 daily; 2hr 30min); La Seu d'Urgell (2 daily; 3hr 30min); Montblanc (6 daily; 1hr 30min); Pobla de Segur (1 daily; 2hr); Poblet (3 daily except Sun; 1hr 15min); Tarragona (3 daily; 2hr); Viella, via Túnel de Viella (Mon–Sat 2 daily; 3hr); Zaragoza (Mon–Sat 4 daily, Sun 1; 2hr 30min).

Lloret de Mar to: Barcelona (July to mid-Sept 10 daily; 1hr 15min); Blanes (every 15min; 15min); Girona (5 daily; 1hr 20min); Palafrugell (2 daily; 1hr 30min); Palamós (2–4 daily; 1hr); Platja d'Oro (2–4 daily; 50min); Sant Feliu (2–4 daily; 40min); Tossa de Mar (every 30min; 15min).

Olot to: Banyoles (Mon–Sat 9–10 daily, Sun 6; 50min); Barcelona (Mon–Sat 7–8 daily, Sun 4; 2hr 15min); Besalú (Mon–Sat 9–10 daily, Sun 6; 30min); Camprodon (1–2 daily; 45min); Figueres (2–3 daily; 1hr); Girona (11 daily Mon–Sat, Sun 4; 1hr 15min); Ripoll (5 daily; 50min–1hr); Santa Pau (Wed & Sat am, plus Mon 2; 15min); Sant Joan de

les Abadesses (2–3 daily; 50min).

Palafrugell to: Barcelona (8 daily; 2hr); L'Escala (4 daily; 45min); Figueres (3 daily; 1hr 30min); Girona (15 daily; 1hr 15min); Lloret de Mar (2 daily; 1hr 30min); Palamos (12 daily; 15min); Pals (4 daily; 10min); Sant Feliu (hourly; 45min); Sant Pere Pescador (4 daily; 1hr); Torroella de Montgrí (4 daily; 25min).

La Pobla de Segur to: Barcelona (1 daily; 3hr 45min); Capdella (Sept–May Mon–Fri 1 daily, June–Aug Mon/Wed/Fri 1 daily; 1hr); Esterri d'Aneu (2 daily Mon–Sat; 1hr 15min); Lleida (1 daily; 2hr); El Pont de Suert (Mon–Sat 1 daily; 1hr 30min); Viella (May–Nov Mon–Sat 1 daily; 3hr).

El Port de la Selva to Figueres (4 daily; 40min); Llançà (July to mid-Sept 9 daily, rest of the year 2–4 daily; 25min).

Puigcerdà to: Alp (4 daily; 5min); Bagà/Berga (4 daily; 35min–1hr); Llívia (5 daily; 5min); La Molina (1 daily; 30min); La Seu d'Urgell (3 daily; 1hr).

Ripoll to: Camprodon (6–8 daily; 45min); Guardiola de Berguedà (Mon–Fri 1 daily; 2hr); La Pobla de Lillet (Mon–Fri 1 daily; 1hr 45min); Olot (3–4 daily; 50min); Sant Joan de les Abadesses (6–8 daily; 20min).

Sant Feliu to: Barcelona (8 daily; 1hr 30min); Girona (July–Sept 11 daily; 2hr); Lloret de Mar (July & Aug 2 daily; 40min); Palafrugell (hourly; 45min); Palamós (hourly; 30min); Platja d'Oro (hourly; 15min).

La Seu d'Urgell to: Andorra la Vella (6–7 daily; 30min); Barcelona (4 daily; 3hr 30min); Lleida (2 daily; 2hr 30min); Puigcerdà (3 daily; 1hr); Sort (2 daily; 1hr 15min).

Tarragona to: Andorra (1–2 daily; 4hr 30min); Barcelona (18 daily; 1hr 30min); Berga (July & Aug 1 daily, rest of the year Sat & Sun only; 3hr 10min); L'Espluga (3 daily; 1hr); La Pobla de Lillet (July & Aug 1 daily, rest of the year Sat & Sun only; 4hr 15min); La Seu d'Urgell (daily at 8am; 3hr 45min); Lleida (3 daily; 2hr); Montblanc (3 daily; 50min); Poblet (3 daily; 1hr 5min); Salou-Cambrils (every 30min; 20min); Tortosa (Mon–Fri 1 daily; 1hr 30min); Valencia (7 daily; 3hr 30min); Zaragoza (4 daily; 4hr).

Tortosa to: Deltebre (Mon–Fri 5 daily, Sat 2; 1hr); Sant Carles de la Ràpita (Mon–Sat 5 daily, Sun 1; 40min); Tarragona (Mon–Fri 1 daily; 1hr 30min).

Tossa de Mar to: Barcelona (July–Sept 12 daily; 1hr 35min); Girona (July–Sept 2 daily, Oct–June 1; 1hr); Lloret de Mar (every 30min; 15min).

Viella to: Lleida (Mon–Sat 2 daily; 3hr); La Pobla de Segur (May–Nov Mon–Sat 1 daily; 3hr 10min); Salardú (Mon–Sat 1 daily; 20min).

Cruceros boats

Blanes to: Lloret de Mar/Tossa de Mar (June–Sept 5 daily; 20min/45min).

Tossa de Mar to: Sant Feliu (June–Sept 5 daily; 45mins); Platja d'Aro/Sant Antoni de Calonge/Palamós (June–Sept 4 daily; 1hr 15min/1hr 25min/1hr 45min).

CATALUNYA | Travel Details

Valencia and Murcia

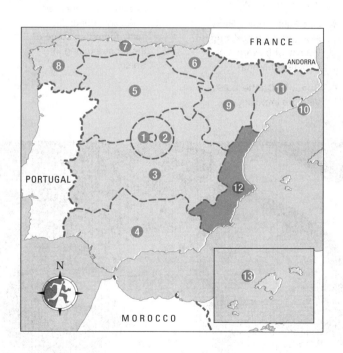

CHAPTER 12 **Highlights**

* **Horchata** p.885 Sample a cool glass of Valencia's own tiger-nut shake; strange but refreshing.

* **Paella** p.884 Try Spain's most famous dish in its home setting – ideal for a beachside meal.

* **Las Fallas** p.881 Party along at the week-long festival of fireworks and bonfires in March.

* **Sagunto Castle** p.891 Visit the imposing Moorish fortress presiding over Sagunto's medieval centre.

* **Benicàssim** p.893 Home to a huge annual music festival featuring the biggest names in 'alternative' pop.

* **Beaches** Experience Valencia's beach life – justly famed as some of the most exciting in Spain.

Valencia and Murcia

The area known as the Levante (the East), combining the provinces of Valencia and Murcia, is a bizarre mixture of ancient and modern, of beauty and beastliness. The rich *huerta* of **Valencia** is said to be the most fertile slab of land in Europe, crowded with orange, lemon and peach groves, and with rice fields still irrigated by systems devised by the Moors. Unsurprisingly, the farmhouse is the most characteristic building of the Valencian *huerta*: called a *barraca*, its most striking feature is its steeply pitched thatched roof. *Valenciano*, a dialect of Catalan, is spoken in some parts of the province and, as it's been recently revived in schools, it now receives a higher profile in the capital. There's even an extreme nationalist group who deny the dialect's Catalan origins, but they haven't managed to convince anyone else. Evidence of the lengthy Moorish occupation can be seen throughout the province, in the castles, irrigation systems, crops and place names – Benidorm, Alicante, Alcoy all come from Arabic.

Murcia is quite distinct, a *comunidad autónoma* in its own right, and there could hardly be a more severe contrast with the richness of the Valencian *huerta*. This southeastern corner of Spain is virtually a desert and is some of the driest territory in Europe. It was fought over for centuries by Phoenicians, Greeks, Carthaginians and Romans, but there survives almost no physical evidence of their presence – or of five hundred years of Moorish rule, beyond an Arabic feel to some of the small towns and the odd date palm here and there.

Much of the region's **coast**, despite some fine beaches, is marred by the highway to the south, the industrial development which has sprouted all around it (with consequent pollution), and of course the heavy overdevelopment of villas and vacation homes. The coves around **Denia** and **Xábia** (Jávea) in Valencia are the prettiest beach areas, but access and accommodation are difficult. The resorts of the **Mar Menor** in Murcia are similarly attractive, but again don't even think of turning up in season if you don't have a reservation. For the "wild" beaches of **southern Murcia**, transport is the major hurdle, but crowds won't be a problem. **Valencia** and **Alicante** are the major urban centres, and there are several historic small towns and villages a short way inland, such as **Xátiva**, **Orihuela** and **Lorca**. Throughout the region, trains are usually less expensive and faster than buses on shorter journeys.

There's no shortage of **culinary pleasures** in the region. Gourmets tend to agree that the best paellas are to be found around (but not *in*) Valencia, the city where the dish originated. It should be prepared fresh, and cooked over wood (*leña*), not scooped from some vast, sticky vat; most places will make it for a minimum of two people, with advance notice. Of the region's other rice-based dishes, the most famous is *arròs a banda*, which is served in two stages: first the

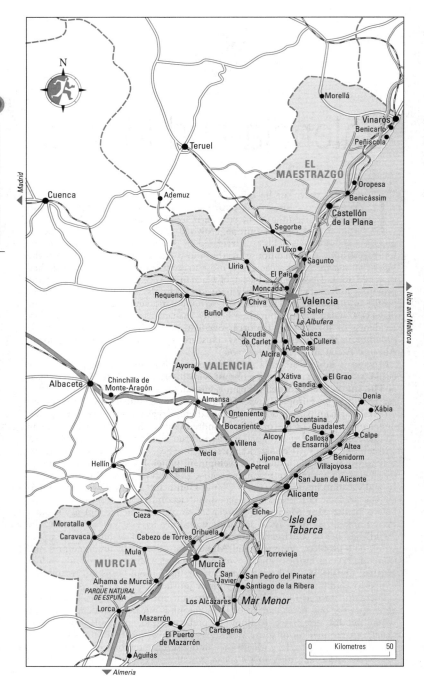

rice, then the fish. Another speciality is eels served with piquant *all i pebre* (garlic and pepper) sauce. The sweet-toothed should try *turrón*; made of nuts and honey, it traditionally comes in a soft, flaky variety or very hard like a nougat (the *turrón* from Jijona is the finest). You could follow it with an *horchata* (or *orxata*), a dense drink made from tiger nuts (*chufas*) or almonds (*almendras*).

The Valencia area has a powerful tradition of **fiestas** and there are a couple of elements unique to this part of the country. Above all, throughout the year and more or less wherever you go, there are mock battles between Muslims and Christians (*Moros y Cristianos*). Recalling the Christian Reconquest of the country – whether through symbolic processions or re-creations of specific battles – they're some of the most elaborate and colourful festivities to be seen anywhere. The other recurring feature is the *fallas* (bonfires) in which giant carnival floats and figures are paraded through the streets before being ceremoniously burned.

Valencia

Valencia, the third largest city in Spain, may not approach the cosmopolitan vitality of Barcelona or the cultural variety of Madrid, but it does boast some of the best nightlife to be found in mainland Spain. *Vivir Sin Dormir* (Live Without Sleep) is the name of one of its bars, and it could be taken as the Valencian motto. The city is alive with noise and colour throughout the year, with unexpected explosions of gunpowder, fireworks and festivities. Although in summer the air becomes heavy with pollution, the clear Levante light, special to the area, flatters the city and, while the traffic is still a problem, four metro lines are reducing the congestion in the centre.

Always an important city, Valencia was fought over for the agricultural wealth of its surrounding *huerta*. After Romans and Visigoths, it was occupied by the Moors for over four centuries with only a brief interruption (1094–1101) when El Cid recaptured it. He died here in 1099 but his body, propped up and led out through the gates, was still enough to cause the Moorish armies – previously encouraged by news of his death – to flee in terror. It wasn't until 1238 that Jaime I of Aragón permanently wrested Valencia back. It has remained one of Spain's largest, richest and most stylish cities ever since. Despite its size, however, Valencia retains a strong feeling of *pueblo*. You won't hear much English spoken here and there are as yet few tourists outside *Fallas* time.

Valencia's **fiestas** are some of the most riotous in Spain. The best is *Las Fallas*, March 12–19 (see box overleaf), which culminates in a massive bonfire in which all the processional floats are burned. In July the city celebrates the *Feria de Julio* with bullfights, concerts, the "Battle of the Flowers" and fireworks. In September, there's a spectacular fireworks competition held in the riverbed park.

Arrival and information

Arriving by train at Valencia's beautifully tiled **Estación del Nord**, you're very close to the town centre; walk north along Avenida Marqués de Sotelo to the Plaza del Ayuntamiento, the central square. The **bus station** is some way out on the north side of the river, take local bus #8, or allow 25 minutes if you decide to walk. The **Balearic ferry terminal** connects with the central plaza via bus #4 and with the train station via the #19.

Fiestas

February

2–5 Moors and Christians battle for the castle in Bocariente, with wild firework displays at night.

Week before Lent *Carnaval* in Águilas is one of the wildest in the country after Tenerife and Cádiz. Good carnival celebrations also in Cabezo de Torres and Vinaròs.

March

12–19 *Las Fallas de San José* in Valencia is by far the biggest of the bonfire festivals, and indeed one of the most important fiestas in all Spain. The whole thing costs as much as €1,200,000, most of which goes up in smoke (literally) on the final *Nit de Foc* when the grotesque cardboard and wooden caricatures are burned. These *fallas* may be politicians, film stars or professional athletes, and anyone else who is a popular target for satirical treatment. Throughout, there are bullfights, music and stupendous fireworks.

The middle of the month, especially around the **19th** (*San José*), also sees smaller *fallas* festivals in Xátiva, Benidorm and Denia.

Third Sun of Lent *Fiesta de la Magdalena* in Castellón de la Plana is marked by major processions and pilgrimages.

April

Holy Week is celebrated everywhere. In Elche there are, naturally, big Palm Sunday celebrations making use of the local palms, while throughout the week there are also religious processions in Cartagena, Lorca, Orihuela, Moncada and Valencia. The **Easter processions** in Murcia are particularly famous and they continue into the following week with, on the Tuesday, the *Bando de la Huerta*, a huge parade of floats celebrating local agriculture and, on the Saturday evening, the riotous "Burial of the Sardine" which marks the end of these spring festivals.

22–24 Famous *Moros y Cristianos* in Alcoy. After a colourful procession, battle commences between the two sides.

25 Morella holds the traditional fiesta of *Las Primes*.

May

1–5 *Fiestas de los Mayos* in Alhama de Murcia, and *Moros y Cristianos* in Caravaca de la Cruz.

Second Sun *La Virgen de los Desamparados* in Valencia. The climax of this celebration is when the statue of the Virgin is transferred from her basilica to the cathedral.

Third Sun Moors and Christians battle in Altea.

June

23–24 *Día de San Juan*. Magnificent *hogueras* festival around this date on the beaches of San Juan de Alicante. Similar to the March *fallas* of Valencia, with pro-

---

On the **Plaza del Ayuntamiento**, you'll find the **post office** crowned with trumpeting angels, and on the other side of the plaza the **turismo** (Mon–Fri 8.30am–2.15pm & 4.15–6.15pm, Sat 9.15am–12.45pm; ☎963 510 417), which gives out an excellent map. There's a regional turismo at c/de la Paz 48 (Mon–Fri 10am–6pm, Sat 10am–2pm; ⓦwww.comunitat-valenciana.com) and other municipal offices on the corner of c/Poeta Querol and c/Barcos (Mon–Fri 10am–2.30pm & 4.30–7pm, Sat 10am–2pm, Sun 11am–2pm), and at the train station (Mon–Fri 9am–6.30pm).

cessions and fireworks, and celebrated on a smaller scale on the beaches of Valencia (Malvarossa, Cabanyal and Aloboraya) with bonfire-jumping.

July
Early July *Fiestas de la Santísima Sangre* in Denia with dancing in the steets, music and mock battles.
15–20 *Moros y Cristianos* in Orihuela.
16 In San Pedro del Pinatar a maritime *Romería* in which an image of the Virgin is carried in procession around the Mar Menor.
Second week *Feria de Julio* in Valencia with much music and above all fireworks, ending with the Battle of the Flowers in the Alameda. Festival of music in Valencia throughout the month, featuring open-air concerts in Viveros park.
25–31 *Moros y Cristianos* battle in Villajoyosa by both land and sea.

August
4 Festival in El Palmar with processions by boat into the lake.
First week Local fiesta in Segorbe.
First weekend Benicàssim's international music festival, a massive party bringing together the major names in 'alternative' music.
15 Local festivities in Denia, Jumilla, and Requena.
21–23 Local festivities in Jijona.
Last week *La Tomatina* a riotous free-for-all of tomato-throwing takes place in Buñol usually on the last Wednesday of the month (though this is subject to change). See the box on p.889
Last Wed Local fiesta in Sagunto and at the same time the great Moors and Christians and a mystery play in Elche.

September
4–9 *Moros y Cristianos* in Villena.
8 *Mare de Deu de la Salut* – colourful folkloric processions in Algemesi.
10–13 International Mediterranean Folk Festival in Murcia.
13 Rice festival in Sueca includes a national paella contest.
22 Fiesta of *Santo Tomás* in Benicàssim with bands and a "blazing bull".

October
Second Sun Benidorm celebrates its patron saint's day.
18–22 Moors and Christians in Calpe.

November
1 *Fiesta de Todos los Santos*; All Saints' festival in Cocentaina.

December
6–8 *La Fiesta de la Virgen* in Yecla when the effigy of Mary is carried down from the sanctuary on top of the hill amid much partying.
14 The weekend after this date sees four days of Moors and Christians in Petrel.

Accommodation

Valencia's budget **accommodation** is centred around the train station, in c/Bailén and c/Pelayo, parallel to the tracks off c/Játiva. C/Pelayo is the quieter of the two streets, but most of the *hostales* in this area tend to be a bit grubby; for nicer – and not necessarily much pricier – places, head for the centre of town, around the market and out near the beach. There are **campsites** all along the coast, but none less than 20km from the city.

VALENCIA

ACCOMMODATION

Albergue Juvenil Colegio Mayor	13
Albergue Juvenil Las Arenas	11
Hotel Alkazar	10
Hotel Astoria Palace	5
Hotel Inglés	4
Hotel La Marcelina	1
Hotel Melia Plaza	8
Hostal Moratín	7
Hotel La Pepica	2
Hospedería del Pilar	3
Hostal Residencia Lyon	12
Hostal Venecia	6
Hotel Reina Victoria	9

RESTAURANTS & TAPAS BARS

Albacarar	M
Bar Almudín	D
Bar Amorós	J
El Asador de Aranda	O
Barbacoa	B
Bar Cánovas	N
Civera	A
Gargantua	L
Bar Gaviota	P
Bar Glorieta	I
La Hacienda	K
La Lluna	C
Restaurante Patos	H
Bar Pilar	E
La Riua	F
Rotunda	G
Bar Todo a Cien	Q

0 Metres 90

▲ A

▼ 13

▼ Alicante & Albacete

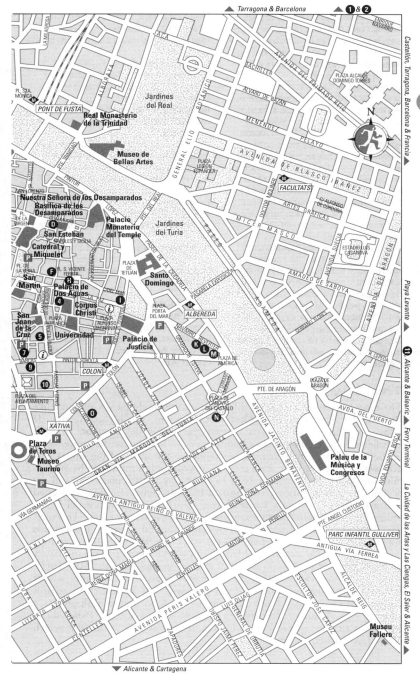

12

VALENCIA AND MURCIA | Valencia

PL. STA. MÓNICA

PONT DE FUSTA

LA MALAGROSA

ALBEREDA

JACA

BOTÁNICO

BACHILLER

AVENIDA DEL PRIMADO REIG

ENRIQUE NAVARRO

PLAZA ALCALDE DOMINGO TORRES

Jardines del Real

ÁLVARO DE BAZÁN

MENÉNDEZ

PELAYO

AVENIDA DE BLASCO IBÁÑEZ

Real Monasterio de la Trinidad

GENERAL ELIO

PINTOR

PI. BENLLIURE

BILBAO

Museo de Bellas Artes

PLAZA LEGIÓN ESPAÑOLA

FACULTATS

DOCTOR MOLINER

C/ ALFONSO DE CÓRDOBA

ARTES GRÁFICAS

MICER MASCÓ

AVENIDA SUECIA

ESTADIO LUIS CASANOVA

SAN LORENZO

LÓPEZ

PTE. DEL REAL

Jardines del Turia

PASEO DE LA CIUDADELA

PASEO DE LA EXPOSICIÓN

AMADEO DE SABOYA

DOCTOR SERRANO

R. CEPEDA

AVENIDA DE ARAGÓN

Nuestra Señora de los Desamparados

Basílica de los Desamparados

PL. DE LA VIRGEN

D

San Esteban

NÁPOLES Y SICILIA

Catedral y Miquelet

PLAZA DE TETUÁN

Santo Domingo

PLAZA PORTA DEL MAR

San Martín

PL. S. VICENTE FERRER

F

H

Palacio de Dos Aguas

4

CIDELLMAR

Corpus Christi

PLAZA DE LA REINA

P

Palacio Monaterio del Temple

GUARDIA

i

AVENIDA DE ACEQUIA

M

ALBEREDA

NAVARRO REVERTER

i

PLAZA PORTA DEL MAR

PLAZA ALFONSO MAGNÁNIMO

PL. DE LA PATRIARCA

San Juan de la Cruz

5

Universidad

i

7

BARCAS

9

PINTOR SOROLLA

Palacio de Justicia

SORNI

K

L

M

PLAZA DE AMÉRICA

ESTRE

JATIVA

P

XÁTIVA

P

O

COLÓN

COLON

M

P

PLAZA DE CÁNOVAS DEL CASTILLO

N

AMBROS

CIRILO

CONDE DE ALTEA

PLAZA DE ARAGÓN

PTE. DE ARAGÓN

AVDA. DEL PUERTO

AVENIDA JACINTO BENAVENTE

AVDA. EDUARDO BOSCA

Plaza de Toros

Museo Taurino

P

GRAN VÍA MARQUÉS DEL TURIA

REINA DOÑA GERMANA

RUZAFA

Palau de la Música y Congresos

VÍA GERMANÍAS

AVENIDA ANTIGUO REINO DE VALENCIA

BURRIANA

PTE. ÁNGEL CUSTODIO

DENIA

XÁTIVA

REINA DOÑA MARÍA

PEDRO III EL GRANDE

MATÍAS

CENTELLES

PARC INFANTIL GULLIVER

ANTIGUA VÍA FÉRREA

LITERATO AZORÍN

AVENIDA PERIS VALERO

ZAPADORES

CENTELLES

REINA DOÑA MARÍA

LUIS OLIAG

OBISPO JAIME PÉREZ

GENERAL DE URRUTIA

LUIS QUIAG

ESCULTOR JOSÉ CAPUZ

ALCALDE REIG

SCULTOR JOSÉ CAPUZ

Museu Fallero

879

Albergue Juvenil Colegio Mayor "La Paz", Avda. del Puerto 69 ☎ 963 617 459. This youth hostel is out of town halfway to the port. Inexpensive but not too attractive, with a midnight curfew. Open July–Sept only. Bus #4 or #19 from Plaza del Ayuntamiento. ❷

Albergue Juvenil "Las Arenas", c/Egenia Viñes 24 ☎ 963 564 288, ⓦ www.ran.es/personal/hostel. Excellent, old-school backpackers' hostel, situated right by the southern end of Malvarossa beach at the end of bus line #32. Very sociable, with kichen facilities, laundry and no curfew. However, to some it may seem a bit grubby and you'll definitely need the mosquito repellent. Price includes half-hour internet connection. ❷ (❶ for RG readers, who receive fifty-percent discount)

Hotel Alkázar, c/Mosén Femades 11 ☎ 963 529 575, ⓕ 963 512 568. Dependable and well-cared-for town centre hotel, near the post office. All rooms with shower. ❹

Hotel Astoria Palace, Plaza Rodrigo Botet 5 ☎ 963 981 000, ⓕ 963 981 010. Luxurious accommodation in this traditional and upmarket hotel, located in a quiet square. ❾ (❻ in August)

Hotel Inglés, Marqués de Dos Aguas 6 ☎ 963 516 426, ⓕ 963 940 251. Old-fashioned, stylish hotel next to the Palacio Dos Aguas. ❾ (❽ in August)

Hostal-Residencia Lyon, c/Xátiva 10 ☎ 963 517 247. About the nicest of the cheapies round the station; clean enough, with reasonably friendly staff. ❸

Hotel La Marcelina, Paseo de Neptuno 72, near the sea ☎ 963 725 135. Pleasant, recently renovated place offering comfortable rooms with baths. ❹

Hotel Meliá Plaza, Plaza del Ayuntamiento 4 ☎ 963 520 612, ⓕ 963 520 426. Modern upmarket hotel in a central location. All rooms are en suite with satellite TV. ❼

Hostal Moratín, c/Moratín 15 ☎ 963 521 220. Good-value, central *hostal* with clean and comfortable rooms. ❺

Hotel La Pepica, Avda. Neptuno 2, near the beach ☎ 963 714 111, ⓕ 963 714 200. Comfortable hotel offering good-value rooms with bath. ❸

Hospedería del Pilar, Plaza Mercado 19 ☎ 963 916 600. Crumbling, safe and central. ❹

Hotel Reina Victoria, Barcas 4 ☎ 963 520 487, ⓕ 963 522 721. Upmarket, centrally located hotel near the *ayuntamiento*, with off-season discounts. ❼

Hostel Venecia, c/en Llop 5 ☎ 963 524 267, ⓕ 963 524 421. The best-value *hostal* in a street full of budget accommodation; all rooms are en suite with TV. ❻

Camping

Devesa Gardens, Nazaret-Oliva ☎ 961 611 136. 20km out, near the golf course of the same name by La Albufera; take the hourly bus from the junction of Gran Vía and c/Sueca to El Saler-Perelló. Open all year.

The City

The most interesting area for wandering around is undoubtedly the mazelike **Barrio del Carmen** (the oldest part of town), roughly between c/de Caballeros and the Río Turia around the Torres de Serranos. In c/de Caballeros, look for the old door knockers placed high up for the convenience of the horse-borne gentlemen residents (hence the name of the street). The **city walls**, which judging from the two surviving gates must have been magnificent, were pulled down in 1871 to make way for a roundabout, and the beautiful church of **Santo Domingo**, in Plaza de Tétuan, has been converted into a barracks – the very barracks from which General Milans del Bosch ordered his tanks onto the streets during the abortive coup of 1981. This incident, however, isn't representative of the city's political inclination, which has always been to the left – Valencia was the seat of the Republican government during the Civil War after it fled Madrid, and was the last city to fall to Franco.

The oldest part of the city is almost entirely encircled by the **Río Turia**, which is now a **riverbed park**. The river was diverted in 1956 after serious flooding which damaged much of the old town. The ancient stone bridges remain, and the riverbed houses cycle paths and footpaths, football pitches, a stadium, a giant Gulliver for children to climb on and also the **Palau de la Música**, a striking, greenhouse-style glass concert hall, built in 1987, which offers daily classical and jazz concerts.

Las Fallas

From March 12 to 19, around the saint's day of San José, Valencia erupts in a blaze of colour and noise for the **Fiesta de las Fallas**. During the year, each *barrio* or neighbourhood builds a satirical caricature or **falla**. These begin to appear in the plazas of each *barrio* at the beginning of March and are judged and awarded prizes before being set alight at midnight on March 19, the *Nit de Foc*. The festival takes its name from the Valencian word for torch. Traditionally, carpenters celebrated the day of San José and the beginning of spring with a ritual burning of spare wood. They would decorate the torches used over the winter and add them to the bonfire. This simple rite of spring has become an international tourist attraction, and it's an extraordinary sight to watch these painstakingly constructed models, some as tall as buildings, some big enough to walk inside, be strung with firecrackers and literally go up in smoke. The *fallas* are ignited in succession; the last to go up are the prizewinners. Each *falla* has a small model or **ninot** beside it, usually created by the children of the *barrio*. The *ninots* are exhibited in La Lonja before the fiesta begins, and the best is added to the Museu Faller; the rest are burnt with the *fallas*. Finally, around one o'clock, the *falla* of the Plaza del Ayuntamiento goes up in flames, set off by a string of firecrackers, followed by the last thunderous firework display of the fiesta.

During the fiesta, processions of *falleros*, dressed in traditional costume and accompanied by bands, carry flowers to the Plaza de la Virgen, where the flowers are massed to create the skirt of a huge statue of La Virgen. The daily **Las Mascaletas** firecracker display takes place at 2pm in the Plaza del Ayuntamiento – for a reputedly unpunctual race, the Valencians observe the timing of this celebration religiously. Traffic comes to a standstill, streets are blocked and the whole city races to the central square for a ten-minute series of body-shuddering explosions. There are nightly fireworks, bullfights, paella contests in the streets and *chocolate y buñuelos* stalls selling fresh doughnuts. On March 20, Valencia returns to normality – the streets are cleaned overnight, and the planning begins for the next year's *Fallas*.

Around the Plaza del Ayuntamiento

Within the **Plaza del Ayuntamiento** is a central square lined with flower stalls, and an impressive floodlit fountain. The *ayuntamiento* houses the **Museo Historico Municipal** (Mon–Fri 8.30am–2.30pm; free) whose library has an impressive eighteenth-century map of Valencia showing the city walls intact.

The distinctive feature of Valencian architecture is its wealth of elaborate Baroque facades – you'll see them on almost every old building in town, but none so extraordinary or rich as the **Palacio del Marqués de Dos Aguas**. Hipólito Rovira, who designed its amazing alabaster doorway, died insane in 1740, which should come as no surprise to anyone who's seen it. Inside is the **Museo Nacional de Cerámica** (Tues–Sat 10am–2pm & 4–8pm, Sun 10am–2pm; €2.40, free Sat pm & Sun) with a vast collection of ceramics from all over Spain. Valencia itself was a major ceramics centre, largely owing to the size of its *morisco* population. Apart from an impressive display of *azulejos*, the collection contains some stunning plates with gold and copper varnishes (*reflejos*), a trio of evocatively ornate eighteenth-century carriages and, on the top floor, a reconstruction of a traditional Valencian kitchen. In the same decorative vein as the *palacio* is the church of **San Juan de la Cruz** (or San Andrés) next door.

Nearby, in the Plaza Patriarca, is the Neoclassical former **university** with lovely cloisters where free classical concerts are held throughout July, and the beautiful Renaissance **Colegio del Patriarca**, whose small **art museum** (daily 11am–1.30pm; €0.60) includes excellent works by El Greco, Morales and Ribalta. Another Ribalta, *The Last Supper*, hangs above the altar in the college's **chapel**; in the middle of the *Miserere* service at 10am on Friday mornings it's whisked aside to reveal a series of curtains. The last of these, drawn at the climactic moment, conceals a giant illuminated crucifix. The whole performance is amazingly dramatic, and typical of the aura of miracle and mystery which the Spanish church still cultivates. The university **library** contains the first book printed in Spain, *Les Trobes*, in 1474.

The cathedral

North from the university, along c/de la Paz, is the **Plaza de la Reina** and Valencia's **Catedral** (Mon–Sat 7.15am–1pm & 4.30–8.30pm, Sun 7.30am–1pm & 5–8.30pm). The plaza is dominated by two octagonal towers, the florid spire of the church of **Santa Catalina** and the fourteenth- to fifteenth-century **Miguelete**, the unfinished tower of the cathedral itself. You can make the long climb up to the roof for a fantastic view over the city with its many blue-domed churches. Entrance to the tower from inside the cathedral costs €1.20; hours are not fixed but it's usually open in the morning until about 1pm and again from about 5 to 8pm, closing earlier in the winter. The church's most attractive and unusual feature is the lantern above the crossing, its windows glazed with sheets of alabaster, a popular material in the region as it lets in the Valencian light.

In the **Museu de la Seu**, the cathedral museum (Mon–Sat: March–Nov 10am–1pm & 4.30–8pm; June–Sept 10am–1pm & 4.30–7pm; Dec–Feb 10am–1pm; €1.20), is a gold and agate cup (the Santo Cáliz) said to be the one used by Christ at the Last Supper – the Holy Grail itself. It's certainly old and, hidden away throughout the Dark Ages in a monastery in northern Aragón, it really did inspire many of the legends associated with the Grail. Other treasures include two Goyas, one of which depicts an exorcism (the corpse was originally naked, but after Goya's death a sheet was painted over it), and a 2300-kilo tabernacle made from gold, silver and jewels donated by the Valencian people. Made in 1939, it is paraded through the streets at Corpus Christi. The bells actually ring, and the silver figures of saints have removable clothes.

Leaving the cathedral through the **Puerta de los Apóstoles**, you enter the **Plaza de la Virgen**. Here the Tribunal de las Aguas, the black-clad regulatory body of Valencia's water users meets at noon every Thursday to judge grievances about the water irrigation system of the *huertas*. The practice dates back to Moorish times and Blasco Ibáñez (1867–1928) describes their workings in detail in his novel *La Barraca*, which is about peasant life in the Valencian *huerta* and remains the best guide to the life of the region at that time.

Two footbridges allow the clergy (only) to go straight from the cathedral into the Archbishop's Palace and the tiny chapel of **Nuestra Señora de los Desamparados**, also on the Plaza de la Virgen, where thousands of candles constantly burn in front of the image of the Virgin, patron of Valencia.

From the plaza, c/Caballeros leads to the **Palau de la Generalitat**, built in 1510, and today the seat of the Valencian autonomous government. The courtyard can be visited on weekdays (9am–8pm; free), but to see inside you need to make an appointment (☎963 866 100; English-speaking guide available). It's worth the phone call to see the beautifully painted ceilings and frescoes depicting a meeting of the assembly (1592) in the Salón Dorado and Salón de Cortes.

Silk exchange and markets

If you tire of Baroque excesses, visit the beautifully elegant Gothic **Lonja de los Mercaderes** (also known as Lonja de la Seda, or the Silk Exchange; Tues–Sat 9.30am–2pm & 5–9pm, Sun 9.30am–2pm; free) in the Plaza del Mercado. On weekdays it still operates as a commercial exchange. Opposite is the enormous **Mercado Central**, a modernist iron, girder and glass structure built at the beginning of the twentieth century and crowned with swordfish and parrot weathervanes. It's one of the biggest markets in Europe – fitting for *huerta* country – with amazing local fruit and vegetables, as well as hard-to-find herbs, health foods and dried goods. It closes around 2pm every day. Valencia's other spectacular market is the Mercado Colón on c/Cirilo Amoros.

Museums and galleries

The **Museu de Belles Artes** (Mon–Sat 9am–2.15pm & 4–7.30pm, Sun 10am–7.30pm; free) on the far side of the river has one of the best general collections in Spain with works by Bosch, El Greco, Goya, Velázquez, Ribera and Ribalta as well as quantities of modern Valencian art. Outside is the largest of Valencia's parks – the **Jardines del Real** (also called the Viveros) – in the centre of which is a small **zoo** (daily 10am–9pm; €3). The gardens are the site of various events during the summer: a book fair in May and a music fair in July with open-air concerts.

As you head back into town don't miss the fourteenth-century **Torres Serranos** (Tues–Sat 9am–1.45pm & 4.30–7.45pm, Sun 9am–1.45pm; free), an impressive gateway defending the entrance to the town across the Río Turia, with panoramic views from the top. The other gateway, guarding the western approach, is the **Torres de Quart**, a simpler structure but equally awesome in scale.

A couple of minutes' walk east of here is IVAM, the **Instituto Valenciano de Arte Moderno** (Tues–Sun 10am–10pm; €2.10, free Sun), whose main gallery at c/Guillém de Castro 118 has a permanent display of works by Julio González as well as many excellent temporary exhibitions by mainly Spanish contemporary artists. It also has a smaller gallery near Plaza de Carmen at c/Museu 2 (Tues–Sat 10am–2.15pm & 4–7.30pm, Sun 10am–7.30pm; free), currently devoted to temporary shows.

If you're interested in bullfighting, the **Museu Taurino** is behind the bull ring on Pasaje Doctor Serra (Mon 10am–2pm, Tues–Sun 10am–8pm; free). If on the other hand you want to gain insight into Valencia's *Fiesta de las Fallas* (see box on p.881), head for the **Museu Fallero**, Plaza de Monteolivete (Tues–Sat 9am–1.30pm & 4–7.30pm, Sun 10am–2pm; €1.80), near the riverbed park (bus #13 from Plaza del Ayuntamiento). Here you'll find a fascinating array of *ninots* which have been voted the best and consequently saved from the flames. For a more hands-on experience, the **Museo del Artista Fallero** (Tues–Fri 9.15am–2pm & 5.30–9pm, Sun 9.15am–2pm; €1.80), at c/del Ninot 24 (bus #27 from behind the *ayuntamiento*) reveals exactly how the *fallas* are made.

La Ciudad de las Artes y las Ciencias

In its bid to attract tourists to the city outside *Fallas* time, the city's Generalitat has undertaken an ambitious new project – **La Ciudad de las Artes y las Ciencias** (City of Arts and Sciences; Ⓦ www.cac.es) – a giant complex set by the Turia between Autopista del Saler and Calle Moreras, consisting of gigantic futuristic edifices designed by Valencian architect, Santiago Calatrava.

The bulk of the project is due to open in late 2002, but for the moment you can visit the **Puente Mirador** and the **L'Hemisfèric** (daily 10am–11.30pm; €6), a striking eye-shaped building with a huge concave screen used for films, laser shows and a planetarium. Although at first all its nuts and bolts were not quite in place (the fire brigade declared it a safety hazard), it is now a resounding success and already ranks as the fourth most-visited building in Spain.

The other edifices will be the **Palacio de las Artes**, a multifunctional centre with a 2500-seater open-air auditorium, which will host plays, operas and concerts; the **Museo de las Ciencias**, with interactive exhibits; and the **Parque Oceanográfico** (designed by Félix Candela), an underwater city with an aquarium housing dolphins, killer whales and an underwater restaurant.

Eating

Although it's the home of **paella**, the city of Valencia doesn't offer the best opportunities for sampling this most Spanish of dishes. The finest places to eat are, in fact, out of town in Perellonet or El Palmar (see p.889), or along the city beach, **Playa Levante**; Paseo Neptuno is lined with small hotels all with their own paella and *marisco* restaurants. For tapas and budget eating, you're best off heading for the area around the train station.

Albacarar, c/Sorní 35 ☎963 951 005. Stylish restaurant near Plaza de America serving modern Mediterranean cuisine. Closed Sat lunchtime, Sun & Aug 7–Sept 7.

El Asador de Aranda, c/Félix Pizcheta 9 ☎963 529 791. Fine Aragonese delicacies, including *lechazo asado*. Closed Sun evenings during July & Aug.

Bar Almudín, c/Almudín 14. Situated just behind the cathedral and renowned for its good seafood tapas.

Bar Amorós, c/en Llop 3, just off Plaza del Ayuntamiento. Inexpensive tapas bar which has specialized in seafood tapas for seventy years. Closed Sun and mid-Aug.

Bar Cánovas, Plaza Cánovas Castillo. One of the city's best tapas bars, which also serves full meals including a €5.40 *menú*.

Bar Gaviota, c/Pelayo 21. Good tapas, friendly, and has one of the best inexpensive *menús* in the area near the train station.

Bar Glorieta, Plaza Alfonso Magnánimo. Large old bar serving tapas and excellent coffee (closes about 9pm). Closed Sun and Easter.

Bar Pilar, on the corner of c/Moro Zeit, just off Plaza del Esparto. Traditional place for *mejillones* (mussels) – they serve them in a piquant sauce and you throw the shells into buckets under the bar. Closed Wed.

Bar Todo a Cien, c/Bailen 42. Great budget eats beside the train station; most tapas cost just €0.65, and they also serve a €4.80 *menú* during the week. Closed Sun.

Barbacoa, Plaza del Carmen 6 ☎963 922 448. Serves a wonderful *menú del día* including barbecued meat for €11.40. Although recently expanded,

Horchata

Valencia is also known for its **horchata** – a drink made from *chufas* (tiger nuts) served either liquid or *granizada* (slightly frozen). It is accompanied by *fartóns* (long, thin cakes). Legend has it that the name "horchata" was coined by Jaume I, shortly after he conquered Valencia. He was admiring the *huerta* one hot afternoon, and an Arab girl offered him a drink so refreshing that he exclaimed, "*Això es or, xata*" (this is gold, girl).

You can get *horchata* all over the city but the best traditionally comes from **Alboraya**, formerly a village in the Valencian suburbs, now absorbed into the city. The oldest *horchatería* in town is the *Santa Catalina* on the bottom corner of Plaza de la Reina. The various *horchaterías* and *heladerías* on Plaza San Lorenzo, just in from the Torres de Serranos, are excellent and very good value. To get to Alboraya, take bus #70 or metro line #3 to Metro Alboraya from Estación Pont de Fusta (across the river from Torres de Serranos). The most renowned *horchatería* is *Daniel*, Avda. de la Horchata 41, where you can sit on the terrace and escape from the summer heat of the city.

reservation is recommended at weekends as it's popular.

Civera, c/Lérida 11 & 13 ☏963 475 917. Valencia's best seafood restaurant, situated across the river from the Torres de Serranos. Expensive.

Escuela de Hostelería y Turismo, c/ Correjería 28 ☏963 155 250. Set in a beautiful seventeenth-century mansion, enjoy excellent food and service at moderate prices from Valencia's future restaurateurs and maitres d'. Closed Sun & July–Aug.

Gargantua, c/Navarro Reverter 18 ☏963 346 849. Good Valencian restaurant serving regional specialities. Closed Sat lunchtime, Sun, late Aug and Easter.

La Hacienda, c/Navarro Reverter 12 ☏963 340 644. Best and most expensive restaurant in town where the speciality is bull's tail Cordoban-style.

Note that you won't even get past the doorman unless fully suited and booted. Closed Sat lunch time, Sun & Easter.

La Lluna, c/San Ramón 23 ☏963 922 146. Good and inexpensive vegetarian restaurant right in the heart of the Barrio del Carmen wih a €5.40 *menú*. Closed Sun, Aug and Easter.

Restaurante Patos, c/de la Mar 28 ☏963 921 522. Handy if you're staying in c/Conde Montornes, this small, quiet restaurant has reasonably priced, interesting international dishes.

La Riua, c/del Mar 27. Good restaurant serving up home-made paella and *fideuá*.

Rotunda, Plaza Redonda. Moderately priced restaurant, superbly situated on Valencia's distinctive round plaza. Closed evenings.

Bars and nightlife

Valencia takes its **nightlife** very seriously and has one of the liveliest bar scenes in mainland Spain. However, the action is widely dispersed, with many locations across the Turia, and if you don't know where to go, the city can seem dead at night. To get across the Turia, or go from one zone to another as the Spanish do, you'll either have to do a lot of walking or take taxis. Surprisingly, the area where you would expect at least some action, around the cathedral, is quite dead after dark.

There are three weekly **listings guides**, *Qué y Dónde, Cartelera Turia* and the high-brow *Valencia Semanal* – all available from news kiosks for around €1.20.

Barrio del Carmen

In town, the **Barrio del Carmen** (in Valenciano "de Carme") is one of the liveliest areas at night, especially around Plaza San Jaime, with scores of small cafés, music-bars and restaurants. The whole area between Plaza de Reina, Plaza Santa Ursula and Plaza Portal Nueva is heaving at the weekend. It's a peculiar mix of the *pijo* (posh) and *grunge* (grungy), and more or less everything shuts at

> ## Combinados Valencianos
>
> The *valencianos* really seem to like *combinados*, or **cocktails**, which don't necessarily have the upmarket connotation they have elsewhere. The *Rincón Latino*, c/Gobernador Viejo 10, off c/Conde Montornes, near Plaza San Vicente Ferrer, is a smoky cellar where the speciality is inexpensive Nicaraguan drinks – order a rum and pineapple cocktail and you'll get a tiny glass of each, the idea being to toss back all the rum in one go, quickly followed by the juice. A classic cocktail goes under the name of *Agua de Valencia* and is served by the jug in a series of old bars. The *Cervecería de Madrid*, just below Plaza de la Reina at c/de la Abadía de San Martín 10, is a popular old-fashioned bar with walls crammed full of paintings, where they serve the orthodox *Agua de Valencia* made with orange juice, champagne and vodka – in fact they claim to have invented it. The *Café Malvarrosa*, c/Ruíz de Lihoro, off c/de la Paz, has its own *Agua de Malvarrosa*, made with lemon instead of orange.

3 or 4am. Of the former, *Slavia,* on Plaza San Jaime, is one of the friendlier places and serves reasonably priced jars of *Agua de Valencia* (see box above), while *Ghecko*, in Plaza del Negrito, has outdoor seating. One of the best *pijo* discos in the area is *Calcutta*, in a converted old house in c/Reloj Viejo off c/Caballeros. Otherwise, there are a host of themed designer bars around, though they tend to be fairly sterile and expensive. Of the grungy bars, *Café del Temps*, c/Obispo Jerónimo 4, is intimate, attracts a varied crowd and plays an interesting mix of good music, while *Radio City Bar*, c/Santa Teresa 19, is larger and has a mainly young ex-pat clientele; *Immortal*, c/San Dionisio 3, offers heavy metal and rock and exceedingly cheap beer. Brazilian music – live on Saturdays – with well-mixed *caipirinha* can be had at *Café Bahiano*, c/Calatrava 12. You'll find plenty of other lively options along c/Serranos, c/de Quart (running into c/de Caballeros), c/Alta and c/Baja, c/Beneficiencia, and the four parallel streets of Na Jordana, San Ramón, de Ripalda and Dr Chiarri.

Across the Río Turia

You'll also find plenty of bars on the **other side of the river** beyond the Barrio (around c/Ruaya, c/Visitación and c/Orihuela), and behind the Gran Vía de Fernando el Católico (along c/Juan Llorens and c/Calixto). In the latter area, the *Café Carioca* and *Café La Habana*, at c/Juan Llorens 52 and 41, and *La Torna*, at c/Carmen 12, are currently in favour.

Most of the "in" places are in the new **university** region. The trendiest bars are on Avenida Blasco Ibáñez – try *Picasso* at no. 109. The bars of Plaza Xuquer, just off the Blasco Ibáñez, are popular meeting places – *Kubalitro*, in the corner, serves litre plastic cups of *combinados* (see box above). Wherever you look around here there's a bar worth calling in at – they're particularly thick on the ground in c/Artes Gráficas, c/Rodrigo Poros, c/Alfonso de Córdoba (the town side of Blasco Ibáñez, towards the Jardín del Real) and c/Menéndez Pelayo (on the opposite side).

Malvarrosa beach

In summer, the bars lining the **Malvarrosa beach** are the places to be, especially the *Genaro, Tropical, ACTV* and *Casablanca*, large bar-discos on c/Eugenio Vines (the beach road). To get there, take bus #1 or #2 from the bus station, or #19 from Plaza del Ayuntamiento. All three buses go along the Avenida del Puerto and turn into c/Dr Lluch; get off about halfway along and go down to the beach along c/Virgen del Sufragio – *Genaro* is on your right, *Tropical* is along on the left. The stop for the return bus is one road back from where you got off, though you'll probably need a taxi late at night. There are also several bars between Paseo Neptuno and the new Paseo Marítimo next to the port which are less rowdy. *Vivir Sin Dormir* is the local hangout of the *Las Arenas* hostel, and there is always the odd traveller or two playing pool or sitting at the candle-lit tables. Also very popular is the open-air *La Floridita* which serves up Latin sounds to an older crowd.

Plaza Cánovas Castillo

At the end of Gran Vía Marqués del Turia lies the fashionable area in and around **Plaza Cánovas Castillo**, which is full of *pubs* (music bars) where people go to see and be seen. The bars along c/Serrano Morales (especially *Champán*) and c/Grabador Esteve are yuppie haunts (the cars outside are a good indicator), but those off the opposite side, down c/Salamanca, c/Conde de Altea and c/Burriana are more mixed. In both cases, each bar has its own particular age group and style – there's something for everyone, from salsa to flamenco to *bacalao* (see below). In many of the bars around Plaza Cánovas you can ask the waiters for discount/free entrance cards for discos, but these will be available only early in the evening.

Discos and clubs

Most **discos** play exclusively rave techno music. Known as **bacalao** or *makina* (machine) music, this scene has ruled in Valencia since the late 1980s, though can be a bit much for some. There's plenty of **alternative music** around, however; try *La Marxa* off c/Caballeros, *Un Sur* in c/Maestro Gozalbo, *Época* in c/Cuba or *Jerusalem*, c/Jerusalem off Plaza de España, all in or near the city centre.

There are also lots of good discos in the **university area**: the slick *Jardines del Real*, off c/General Elio in Plaza Legión Española 13, just over the Puente del Real; *Acción* at Blasco Ibáñez no. 111, playing *makina*; the more poppy (and popular) *Warhol* next door; the teenage *Woody*, c/Menéndez Pelayo; and *Arena*, c/Emilio Baró, which as well as a disco is a venue for visiting bands. Be prepared to pay €6 and upwards for entrance to any of these.

The rest of the discos are **out of town** on the main road heading south along the coast. The *Rockola* – for twenty-somethings who want to re-live the 1990s – and *The Face* – which plays *bacalao* – are near each other on the Playa de Pinedo, Camino Montañares. Further out on the Nazaret–Oliva road in El Perelló, you'll find *Heaven* and *Puzzle* which are both big *bacalao* spots. In Les Palmeretes, *La Barraca* is a pop disco and *Chocolate* is also pure 1990s.

For **jazz**, the current favourite is the *Black Note Club* at c/Polo y Peyrolón 15, off Avenida Blasco Ibáñez near the football stadium, which offers quality jazz, blues, soul and Latin rhythms nightly.

Gay scene

Valencia has a thriving **gay scene**, and there are scores of bars and discos, varying from "mixed" to a heavier, gay male-only scene. Most of the gay bars/discos are found around Central Market and c/Quart. *Venial*, c/Quart 26, is young, trendy, open at midnight and you pay to get in only at weekends (€7.80). Or try the very popular *North Dakota*, Plaza Margarita Valldaura, just off c/de la Paz, a bar with a Wild West theme. A full listing of gay Valencia is produced by the Collectiu Lambada de Gais i Lesbianes, available free at most venues or from their offices at c/Salvador Giner 9 (Mon–Sat 5–10pm).

Listings

Airlines Iberia, c/de la Paz 14 ☎963 520 677, or their telephone information line ☎902 400 500.

Airport Manises, 8km away (☎961 598 515); bus #15 from bus station (5am–11.40pm; 2–6 hourly).

Banks Main branches of most banks are around the Plaza del Ayuntamiento or along c/Las Barcas. There's a Barclays at c/Barcos 4, with nine other branches throughout the city. Outside banking hours, the branch of the Caja de Ahorros at c/Játiva 14, to the left as you come out of the train station, is open Mon–Sat 9am–8pm.

Beaches The city beach, Malvarrosa, is polluted, but is being cleaned up and does have an elegant promenade. Buses #30 and #32 run from the Plaza del Ayuntamiento to Passeig Marítim, supplemented during the summer by buses #20, #21 and #22, which go from various points in the centre (9am–8.30pm; every 10–15mins). It's best to go to El Salér, a long, wide stretch with pine trees behind. A bus leaves from the corner of Gran Vía Marqués del Turia and c/Sueca (May–Sept every half-hour; Oct–April every hour). The ride takes 20min and it stops in the village before heading down to the beach and then turning back.

Bookstores English books are available from the ABC International Bookshop on c/Ruzafa, the English Book Centre on c/Pascual y Genis and Crisol, c/Antic Regne de Valencia.

Bus information Main station is at Avda. Menéndez Pidal 3, across the Turia (☎963 497 222). Regular services to northern Europe and to London leave from here – offices in the station.

Car rental Best value is probably Cuñauto Car Hire, c/Burriana 51 (☎963 748 561). Otherwise, there's Avis at the airport and at c/Isabel la Católica 17 ☎963 510 734, Hertz at the airport and c/Segorbe 7 ☎963 415 036, Atesa at the airport and c/Joaquín Costa 57 ☎963 953 605, and many more.

Cinema Original-language films are shown regularly at the subsidized municipal Filmoteca, Plaza del Ayuntamiento, and are sometimes also shown at Albatros Mini-Cines, Plaza Fray Luís Colomer, and Babel, c/Vincente Sancho Tello 10.

Consulates UK Consulate in Alicante ☎965 216 022; USA, c/Romagosa 1 ☎963 516 973.

Cycling There are various cycle paths (marked in green) running through the city; watch out for straying pedestrians. Turyciclo, c/Dr Sanchis Sivera 28 ☎963 854 284, and Cicloturismo, c/Museu 7 ☎963 923 239, both rent bicycles and organize tours.

Ferries Information and tickets from Trasmediterránea, Avda. Manuel Soto 15 (☎902 454 645, ◉www. trasmediterranea.es), or from any of the half-dozen travel agents on Plaza del Ayuntamiento. Note that if you are going to Ibiza outside of the summer months, it's far better to go from Denia, with more services that take 10 hours less and cost only a little more.

Hospital Avda. Cid, at the Tres Cruces junction, ☎963 862 900; ◉Avda. del Cid.

Internet access An hour of internet daily can be had for free on the fifth floor of the Centro Cultural Bancaja, Plaza de Tekuán (Mon–Fri 9am–2pm & 4–9pm, Sat 9am–2pm) on production of your passport – though it's fairly slow. Otherwise one of the cheapest places is *Confederation*, near the train station at c/Ribera 8 (daily 11am–11pm; €3 per hr, minimum 1hr, though you can use it up as you like). An up-to-date list of cyber-cafés is available from the tourist office.

Laundry El Mercat, Plaza Mercado 12.

Left luggage Self-store lockers at RENFE; 24hr access, €1.80–3.60 a day.

Markets Check out the crowded Sunday flea market, next to the football stadium on c/Sucia. Otherwise, there are markets selling clothes and general goods in a different location daily – ask at the tourist office for details. For food, the Mercado Central is a treat.

Police Headquarters are on Gran Vía Ramón y Cajal 40 ☎963 539 539.

Post office Main *Correos* is at Plaza del Ayuntamiento 1 (Mon–Fri 8.30am–8.30pm, Sat 9.30am–2pm). There is a *poste restante* on the first floor.

Telephones Pasaje Rex 7, just off Avda. Marques de Sotelo, close to Plaza del Ayuntamiento (Mon–Fri 9am–3pm & 4–9pm, Sat 9am–2pm) or inside the RENFE station (daily 10am–10pm).

Train information RENFE is on c/Játiva 24 ☎902 240 202. Several trains depart daily for Barcelona, Madrid and Málaga. For destinations around Valencia, there's the FGV (metro) from Plaza España (lines 1 & 2) and Puente de Madera (line 3).

Trekking Treks through various mountain areas in the region are organized year-round. You can either join a guided group or, if you want to go it alone, they'll provide route maps and info. Details from Centro Excursionista de Valencia, Plaza Tabernes de Valldigna 4 ☎963 911 643.

Around Valencia

There are a number of good **day-trips** to be made from Valencia, including visits to the region's very best paella restaurants at El Palmar, El Perelló and Perellonet. The city can get extremely hot in the summer and the cool mountains of the Alto Turia are an enticing option.

La Albufera and the paella villages

La Albufera is a vast lagoon separated from the sea by a sandbank and surrounded by rice fields. Being one of the largest bodies of freshwater in Spain it constitutes an important wetland, and attracts tens of thousands of migratory birds – a throng composed of 250 species, of which ninety breed here regularly. In the Middle Ages it was ten times its present size but the surrounding paddies have gradually reduced it. After growing contamination by industrial waste, domestic sewage and insecticide, the area was turned into a natural park.

Whether you're into bird-watching or not, the lagoon area makes a relaxing change from the city, and you can eat paella and local speciality eels with *all i pebre* (piquant sauce) in the nearby villages of El Palmar and El Perelló. **EL PALMAR**, the prettier of the two, was once a settlement of fishing huts; today it's packed with **restaurants**, as struggling fishing families turn to the catering

---

All pulped out: la Tomatina

La Tomatina – the tomato-throwing festival of Buñol – is about as wild and excessive as Spanish fiestas get. Picture this: 30,000 people descend on a small provincial town, at the same time as a fleet of municipal trucks, carrying 120,000 tonnes of tomatoes. Tension builds. 'To-ma-te, to-ma-te' yell the crowds. And then the truckers let them have it, hurling the ripe, pulpy fruit at everyone present. And everyone goes crazy, hurling the pulp back at the trucks, at each other, in the air... for two hours. It is a fantasy battle made flesh: exhausting, not pretty, and not to everyone's taste. But it is Buñol's contribution to fiesta culture, and most participants will tell you that it is just about as much fun as it is possible to have with your clothes on. Not that you should wear a great deal.

The 'Tomatina' has been going since 1944, but it has got a lot bigger in recent years, following a string of articles in the press in Spain and abroad. The novelist Louis de Bernières was one of the first foreign writers to cover the event: he wrote a superb account that is reprinted in *Spain: Travelers Tales*, and concluded that, if he planned his life well and kept his health, he could attend another 19 tomatinas, before he would be too enfeebled for the occasion.

If the idea of a tomato fight appeals, then you will need to visit Buñol on the last Wednesday of August (but call the Valencia Tourist Office just to check, as some years it takes place a week or two early). You can get there by train or bus and you will need to arrive early, with a spare set of clothing that you should leave at a bar (Buñol having no hotel). The tomato trucks appear on the central Plaza del Ayuntament at 11am and battle commences on the dot: this is no spectator sport – everyone is considered fair game. At 1pm an explosion signals the end of the battle and nobody hurls another speck of tomato for the next twelve months. Instead, the local fire brigade arrive, hose down the combatants, buildings and streets, and a lull comes over the town. And then, miraculously, within the hour, everyone arrives back on the street, perfectly turned out, to enjoy the rest of the fiesta, which, oddly enough, includes such refined pursuits as orchestral concerts in the town's open-air auditorium.

As Buñol has no accommodation options – and indeed no reason to visit outside Tomatina time – most people take in the fiesta as a day-trip from Valencia.

business. One of the better restaurants is *Mateu*, on the main street, c/Vincente Baldovi, at no. 17 (☎961 620 270). On August 4 El Palmar celebrates its **fiesta**; the image of Christ on the Cross is taken out onto the lake in a procession of boats to the *illuent*, or centre, of the lake, where hymns are sung.

Further along the road to El Perelló is the small – and otherwise unexceptional – village of **PERELLONET**, where you can eat some of the best paella around. Try *Blayet*, Avda. Gariotas 17 – which is also a **hostal** (☎961 777 454, Ⓕ961 177 366; ❺) – or *Gaviotas*, next door (☎961 777 575; booking required), which also does good *mariscos* and *all i pebre*. Also worth a visit is *Vert i Blau*, further down Avenida Gariotas at no. 72, for *patatas Amparín* – a potato *tapa* with a kick. The nearest **campsite** is *Devesa Gardens* (☎961 611 136; open all year) 2km out on the Carretera El Salér, near the golf course of the same name. Regular hourly **buses** run from the city via El Salér and on to the lagoon, El Palmar and El Perelló.

Manises

Fifteen kilometres southwest of the city at **MANISES**, where Valencia's airport is located, is the centre of the region's ceramics business. The **Museo de Cerámica**, c/Sagrario 22 (Tues–Sat 10am–1pm & 4–7pm, Sun 11am–2pm; free), has displays of ceramics from medieval blue and metallic varnishes to award-winning modern examples, and a demonstration of the traditional process of ceramics-making.

North of Valencia – the Costa del Alzahar

The best **beaches** along the Costa del Alzahar are around **Benicàssim**, north of the provincial capital, **Castellón de la Plana**. Further north still, **Peñíscola**, a historic town with good beaches and seafood restaurants, is worth a visit, and **Benicarló** is pleasant too. Perhaps the best place to stop en route to Catalunya or Morella is **Vinaròs** at the mouth of the tiny Río Servol – a real town, not developed exclusively for tourists.

Real Monasterio del Puig de Santa Maria

Eighteen kilometres north of Valencia on the road to Sagunto is the small town of **EL PUIG**, where it's well worth spending a couple of hours visiting the impressive **Real Monasterio del Puig de Santa Maria** (Tues–Sun 10.30am–1pm & 4–6.30pm; €1.80), a huge building flanked by four towers, which dominates the town and surrounding countryside. The Orden de la Merced – the order who act as guardians of the sanctuary – was founded by Pedro Nalaso in 1237 after he'd seen a vision of the Virgin Mary on the nearby hill. It is a favourite pilgrimage for Valencians and royalty alike, from Jaime I to the present monarchs Juan Carlos I and Doña Sofia, although in Franco's time, it was put to a rather different use – as a prison.

In the lower cloister, the **Museum of Print and Graphics** (one of the most important in Europe) contains a wealth of artefacts, including the smallest book in the world – the size of your thumbnail. Looking at it through a magnifying glass reveals the Padre Nuestro (Lord's Prayer) in half a dozen languages. Other star exhibits include a copy of the Gutenberg Bible and a wonderful pictorial atlas of natural history, both from the sixteenth century. In the upper cloister, the ceramics room houses various Roman pieces, but its real treasures are the fourteenth-century plates, bowls and jars recovered from the seabed close to El Puig. Keep an eye out too throughout the monastery for the neck manacles which the monks use as candle holders.

El Puig is served by **train** (14 daily; 20min) and **bus** (half-hourly daily; 25min) from Valencia.

Sagunto and around

Twenty-four kilometres north of Valencia are the fine Roman remains of **SAGUNTO** (Sagunt). This town passed into Spanish legend when, in 219 BC, it was attacked by Hannibal in one of the first acts of the war waged by Carthage on the Roman Empire. Its citizens withstood a nine-month siege before burning the city and themselves rather than surrendering. When belated help from Rome arrived, the city was recaptured and rebuilding eventually got under way. Chief among the ruins is the second-century Roman amphitheatre, the **Teatro Romano** (May–Sept Tues–Sat 10am–8pm, Sun 10am–2pm; Oct–April Tues–Sat 10am–6pm, Sun 10am–2pm; free), the basic shape of which survives intact. Debate continues about its recent restoration: it's now functional and plays are performed here during the summer, but for many people it has lost its authenticity. However, the views from its seats are wonderful, taking in a vast span of history – Roman stones all around, a ramshackle Moorish castle on the hill behind, medieval churches in the town below and, across the plain towards the sea, the black smoke of modern industry. Further Roman remains are being excavated within the walls of the huge **acropolis–castle** (summer Tues–Sat 10am–2pm & 5–8pm, Sun & festivals 10am–2pm; winter Tues–Sat 10am–2pm & 5–6pm, Sun & festivals 10am–2pm; free). Also worth a look is Sagunto's well-preserved Jewish quarter, where you'll find medieval houses among the cobbled alleyways. For programme information, contact the local tourist office on ☎962 662 213.

Twenty-eight kilometres north of Sagunto, at **VALL D'UIXO**, is the underground river of San José, featuring caves with wonderful stalactites – you can tour the river by boat with Río Subterranio de San José, based on the road leading to the caves (daily 10.30am–1.30pm & 3.30–8pm; €5.70).

Practicalities

The main road passes below the town – with frequent **buses** from Valencia – as do the main Valencia–Barcelona (7 daily) and Valencia–Zaragoza (4 daily) **train** lines. If you want to **stay** near Sagunto, try the inexpensive *La Pinada* (☎962 660 850, ⓕ962 650 543, ⓦwww.serbit.com/lapinada; ④), which has a swimming pool and sauna; it's 3km out of town on the CN234, the road to Teruel. Alternatively, *Hostal Carlos*, near the station on the busy Avenida País Valenciá at no. 43 (☎962 660 902; ④), is slightly more expensive but conveniently located.

Segorbe and Montanejos

About 30km inland from Sagunto is **SEGORBE**, the Roman Segóbriga, which is worth a visit more for its tranquillity and surrounding scenery than its sights, though part of the old city wall remains. It lies in the valley of the Río Palancia, among medlar and lemon orchards.

Segorbe's **cathedral** was begun in the thirteenth century, but suffered in the Neoclassical reforms, and only the cloister is original. Its **museum** (Tues–Sun 10.30am–1.30pm, closed beginning of Sept; €2.40) contains a few pieces of

Gothic Valencian art, with a *retablo* by Vicente Maçip. One kilometre outside town on the road to Jérica, you'll find the "fountain of the provinces" which has fifty spouts, one for each province of Spain, each labelled with the coat of arms.

Segorbe lies on the main **train** line from Valencia to Teruel and Zaragoza and there are three trains a day. If you want **to stay**, the only options are the *Pensión Millan* (☎964 135 225; ❹), at the north of the town at the beginning of Carretera Teruel, or for a bit more luxury the more central *Hospederia el Palen* (☎964 710 740; ❼), at c/Franco Ricart 9. Segorbe has its **fiestas** at the beginning of September, when *La Entrada* takes place, and bulls are run through the town by horses.

From Segorbe, it's an easy trip to **MONTANEJOS** (not to be mistaken for Montan, the village just before). Turn off at Jérica for the road to Montanejos, or catch the bus in Segorbe. This tiny village has two hotels and three *hostales*, and is popular with visitors to the hot springs, **Fuente de Baños**, where the water emerges at 25°C and has medicinal properties. Walks around the village join up with the *Gran Recorrido* route. If you want to **stay** here, there's the spa, *Hotel Rosaleda del Mijares*, Carretera de Tales 28 (☎964 131 079, ☎964 131 466; ❼), *Hostal La Valenciana*, c/San Jaume 40 in the centre (☎964 131 062; ❻), or *Hostal Gil*, Avda. Fuente de Baños 25 (☎964 131 063; ❸).

Castellón de la Plana

Continuing north along the coast, **CASTELLÓN DE LA PLANA** is a pleasant enough place to stop off; it's also one of the least expensive places to stay along this stretch of coast, and there are some surprisingly good **beaches** within easy reach.

In the old part of town, there's a fine seventeenth-century **ayuntamiento** (Mon–Fri 7.45am–1.15pm) with a collection of works by local artists and a painting of San Roque attributed to Francisco Ribalta. Nearby is the sixteenth-century bell tower **El Fadrí** and the striking, neo-Gothic **Concatedral de Santa Mariá** (daily 9–10.30am, 11.30am–1pm & 7–8pm; free) – the original eleventh-century building was destroyed in the Civil War. Crossing the square, the **Convento de Capuchinas** (daily 4–8pm; free) has some valuable works by Francisco Zurbarán. Also worth a visit is the **Museo de Bellas Artes** on c/Caballeros 25, between Plaza Mayor and Plaza de Aulas (Mon–Fri 10am–8pm, Sat 10am–2pm; €2.10), with displays of ceramics, pictures and sculptures by local artists.

The beaches are at the Grao (port) with others along the coast to Benicàssim. **Buses** for the former leave regularly from Plaza Borrull, while for the latter departures are from the nearby Plaza Farrell more frequently.

Practicalities

Arriving by **bus** or **train**, you'll find yourself at the new combined station on Avenida Pintor Oliet. To get to the centre either walk the twenty minutes or so down Paseo Morella, or catch the frequent bus #9, which also stops at Plaza María Agustina. Here there is a helpful **turismo** (July & Aug Mon–Fri 9am–7pm, Sat 10am–2pm; Sept–June Mon–Fri 9am–2pm & 4–7pm, Sat 10am–2pm; ☎964 358 688, ✉touristinfo.castellon@turisme.m400.gva.es) which has a wealth of information about the city and the whole province. If you decide to **stay the night** you have several options. The basic but clean *Hostal Residencia Marti*, c/Herrero 19 (☎964 224 566; ❷), is good value and central, while the *Hostal La Esperanza*, c/Trinidad 37 (☎964 222 031; ❸), has immaculate rooms and a good restaurant, with a *menú* for €5.40. For a beach base, *Pensión Los Herreros*, Avda. del Puerto 28 (☎964 284 264; ❹), is a good bet; more upmarket is *Hotel del Golf* at Playa del Pinar (☎964 280 180, ℻964 281 123; ❸), with a pool and tennis courts.

There are plenty of **places to eat**, especially around the Grao: *Club Nautico*, Escollera de Poniente, serves good *arroz* and *pescado al horno*, while *Casa Juanito*, Paseo Buenavista 11, offers an excellent selection of seafood. For the best *arroz negro* (rice cooked with squid), head for *Tasca del Puerto* at Avda. del Puerto 13.

For **nightlife**, local folk generally start off with a few tapas and a spot of convivial drinking in the many bars and cafés on and around Plaza Santa Cruz – you'll also find plenty of *tascas* and pubs on c/Poeta Guimerá y Alloza. At around midnight people head off to the bars around c/Lagasca and c/Tenerías. For **discos**, there are two *zonas* that come to life at about 3am: Polígono "Los Cipréses", way out on the main Valencia road, which has something for everyone, and the north of the town around c/Cuadra de Borriolenc, which attracts a younger, alternative crowd. To get to either, you'll need to take a taxi from the centre.

During the **summer**, everyone heads to the beach at night, with Plaza del Mar the starting point, moving on later to the many temporary bars and parties on the beach going up towards Benicàssim – keep walking and you're bound to find something to your taste.

Villafamés

VILLAFAMÉS, 24km inland from Castellón, is an attractive hill town which successfully mixes the medieval, Renaissance and modern. In the highest part of the town there's an ancient ruined castle, conquered by Jaime I in 1233. The fifteenth-century Palau del Batle houses the **Museo de Arte Contemporáneo** (summer Mon–Fri 11am–1pm & 5–8pm, Sat & Sun 11am–2pm & 5–8pm; winter Mon–Fri 11am–1pm & 4–7pm, Sat & Sun 11am–2pm & 5–8pm; €1.80), a collection of over five hundred sculptures and paintings including works by Miró, Lozano and Mompó. There are good **rooms** at *El Rullo*, c/de la Fuente (☎964 329 384; ❸), which also has a restaurant.

Benicàssim and around

BENICÀSSIM, a few kilometres north of Castellón, is famed for its Moscatel wine, and was once well known as a wine-producing area, although today very few vineyards remain and the town is better known as a tourist resort. Wine-tasting visits are on offer at *Bodegas Carmelito* on Avenida Castellón (summer 10am–8pm; winter 10am–5pm; free).

FIB

The annual **Benicàssim** (🌐www.fiberfib.com) international festival on the first weekend of August (Thurs to Sun) draws tens of thousands of young people to hear the world's biggest names in alternative music. In 2001 the line-up of the three-day multi-stage event featured dozens of groups, headlined by the likes of P.J Harvey, Pulp, Tricky and the Manic Street Preachers, all for the price of €90. In addition to the music there are chill-out areas, discos and the ubiquitous festival carnival of henna tattooists, trinket sellers and jugglers. A massive campsite handles the overflow as the *pensiones* in Benicàssim and around pack out.

△ Palm trees at Santa Pola, Alicante

Though Benicàssim is heavily developed, budget accommodation is scarce – the **turismo**, Médico Segura 4 (summer daily 9am–3pm & 5–7pm; winter Mon–Sat 9am–3pm; ☏964 300 962), has a list of **hostales** and will provide a free map of the town. Among the better-value *fondas* in the old village near the train station *Fonda Garamar*, c/Queipo de Llano 3 (☏964 304 953; ❹) is a good bet – or try your luck along c/Santo Tomas for the real cheapies. The *Buenavista*, c/San Antonio 13 (☏964 300 905; ❹; closed Oct–March), is large and inexpensive for rooms with bath. More upmarket is the *Hostal Montreal 76*, in the town at c/Barracas 5 (☏964 300 681, ℉964 393 717; ❺), which has lots of facilities including a swimming pool. There's also a year-round **youth hostel**, *Argentina*, on Avenida de Ferrandis Salvador (☏964 300 949; ❷), and at least seven **campsites** in the area; *Camping Florida*, Sigalero 34 (☏964 392 385; April–Sept), is close to the beach, with a pool and tennis courts.

Six kilometres inland from Benicàssim is the **Desierto de las Palmas**, a Carmelite monastery in an idyllic setting which dates from 1694. The Carmelites run meditation courses here (☏964 300 950) and there is also a museum of religious history (daily 10.30am–1pm & 4.30–7pm; free), though at the time of writing it was closed for restoration. Nearby is **Monte Bartolo**, which is worth climbing for a great view across the plains; unfortunately parts of the mountain were stripped of trees by a forest fire in 1992 – a serious problem throughout the whole of Valencia and often caused by arsonists.

In summer there is a regular **bus** service from Benicàssim to Castellón (buses leave from c/Santo Tomàs every 15min in summer, every 30min in winter).

Peñíscola

There's not much else along the stretch of coast north of Benicàssim until you reach Peñíscola 60km away, although the resort of **OROPESA** just beyond Benicàssim does have reasonable beaches, good campsites and a lively atmosphere in the summer.

PEÑÍSCOLA occupies a heavily fortified promontory jutting out into the Mediterranean. There was once a Phoenician settlement here, and later it saw Greek, Carthaginian, Roman and Moorish rulers, but the present castle was built by the Knights Templar with alterations by Pedro de la Luna. Pope Benedict XIII (Papa Luna) lived here for six years after he had been deposed from the papacy during the fifteenth-century Church schisms. The **castle** today (daily: summer 9.30am–2pm & 4.30–9.30pm; winter 9am–1pm & 3.15–6pm; €1.20), where part of *El Cid* was filmed, is heavily restored and largely a museum to Papa Luna, but it's impressive from a distance and the old town that clusters around its base is extremely picturesque, if heavily commercialized. There are small **beaches** on either side of the castle but the best one is on the town side, even though it's accordingly more crowded.

Practicalities

You'll find a **turismo** on Paseo Marítimo (summer Mon–Sat 9am–8pm, Sun 10am–1pm; winter Mon–Fri 9.30am–1.30pm & 4–7pm; ☏964 480 208, ℮touristinfo.penyiscola@turisme.m400.gva.es), which will provide a free map that marks all the town's **accommodation** and the eleven campsites dotted around the town. Peñíscola is best visited off-season to avoid the crowds and to make sure of finding a place to stay in the old town: for sea views, try any of the many places along Avenida Papa Luna – *Hostal-Residencia Bodegon 2000*, at no. 77 (☏964 480 330, ❺), is the least expensive, while the *Hostería del Mar*, at no. 18 (☏964 480 600, ℉964 480 363; ❼), offers more luxury and also specializes in medieval banquets every Saturday, with music and dancing. There are several reasonably priced *hostales* near the base of the castle and along the beach road; *Simo*, Porteta 5 (☎ & ☏ 964 480 620; ❹), is right on the beach, while the no-frills *Hostal-Residencia El Torcio*, c/Jose Antonio 18 (☎ 964 480 202; ❺), is just 100m from the sea. Around here you'll find the town's many **restaurants**, serving local dishes, such as *susquet de peix* (fish stew), and *all i pebre de polpet* (small octopus with garlic and pepper sauce). **Buses** run down the coast from Vinaròs (7am–10pm) and Benicarló (8.15am–1pm & 6–8pm) every half-hour.

Benicarló

BENICARLÓ, seven kilometres farther along the coast, boasts a church with a fine octagonal tower and blue-tiled dome and a small but tranquil beach. Also worth a look are its docks, which are important for shipbuilding. There are several inexpensive **places to stay** right in the centre – *Pensión Las Palomas*, Hernán Cortés 14 (☎ 964 474 771; ❸), is decent, while *Hostal Residencia Mateu*, Ferreras Breto 8 (☎ 964 471 085; ❺), has good views of the church. For more luxury, head for the modern *Parador de Benicarló*, Avda. Papa Luna 3 (☎ 964 470 100, ☏ 964 470 934; ❽), with pool, garden and a good restaurant. There's a **youth hostel** at Avda. de Yecla 29 (☎ 964 470 500; ❶) and **campsites** on the coast nearby, including *Camping Alegria del Mar* (☎ 964 470 871; open all year), 1.5km north on the Carretera Valencia–Barcelona.

Vinaròs

The **beaches** of **VINARÒS**, next along the coast, are small but rarely packed, and in town there's an elaborate Baroque church, with an excellent local produce market nearby. Unfortunately accommodation options here are scarce; try the recently renovated *Hotel Roca*, on Avenida San Roque (☎ 964 401 312; ❺). The decidely unhelpful **turismo** (daily 10am–2pm & 5–9pm; ☎ 964 453 334), close to the church on Paseo Colón, should be able to help you with more options, but don't count on it.

The **fish** is locally caught and excellent; the *langostinos* are reputedly the best in Spain. Go down to the dockside market in the early evenings to watch the day's catch being auctioned and packed off to restaurants all over the region. *Bar Neus* (which makes excellent iced coffee), opposite the bus terminal, is the main source of information for all timetables or routes from the town; there is currently one morning and one afternoon **bus** to Morella. The town's **train station** is a good 2km from the centre.

Morella

MORELLA, 62km inland on the road from the coast to Zaragoza, is the most attractive town in the province of Castellón and one of the most remarkable in the entire area. A medieval fortress town, it rises from the plain around a small hill crowned by a tall, rocky spur and a virtually impregnable **castle** which dominates the countryside for miles around. A perfectly preserved ring of ancient walls defends its lower reaches. The city was recovered from the Moors in the thirteenth century by the steward of Jaime I. He was reluctant to hand it over to the crown, and it is said that the king came to blows with him over the possession of the city.

Chief among the monuments, apart from the castle, is the church of **Santa María la Mayor** (*Iglesia Arciprestal*; summer daily 11am–2pm & 4–7pm; winter Mon–Fri noon–2pm & 4–6pm, Sat and Sun 11am–2pm), a fourteenth-century Gothic construction with beautifully carved doorways (*dels Apòstols*) and an unusual raised *coro* reached by a marble spiral stairway. A few minutes' walk to the left, at the foot of the castle, is the restored **Monasterio de San Francisco** (summer daily 10.30am–7.30pm, winter 11am–2pm & 4–6pm), worth visiting for its elegant Gothic cloister and chapterhouse. The **fortress** itself (daily 10.30am–7.30pm; €1.20) is in ruins but is still impressive. It's a tiring climb but there are tremendous views in every direction from the crumbling courtyard at the top – down over the monastery, bullring and town walls to the plains. In the distance are the remains of the weird Gothic **aqueduct** which once supplied the town's water.

Not far from the monastery is the curious **Museo Tiempo de los Dinosaurios** (Tues–Sun 11am–2pm & 4–7pm; Oct–April closes 6pm; €1.80), containing fossils of dinosaurs found in the area. Also of interest is the house on c/de la Virgen de Villavana where San Vicente Ferrer performed the prodigious miracle of resurrecting a child who had been chopped up and stewed by its mother – she could find nothing else fit for a saint to eat. Annually in the last week of August Morella hosts a **festival of classical music**.

Practicalities

Be prepared for lower temperatures in Morella than elsewhere in the province, and for snow in winter. The **turismo** (daily 10am–2pm & 4–7pm; ☎964 173 032, 📧touristinfo.morella@turisme.m400.gva.es) is a five-minute walk from the bus station, in Plaza de San Miguel, and has useful maps and leaflets on town sights.

Budget **accommodation** can be found at *La Muralla*, c/Muralla 12 (☎964 160 243; ❸), and at *Hostal El Cid*, Puerta San Mateo 2 (☎964 160 125; ❹), right by the bus stop and town gate, with views of the hills from its balconied rooms (but it can be noisy). During fiestas and national holidays, you should book rooms in advance, as Morella is very popular with Spanish holidaymakers. If you are stuck without accommodation, the neighbouring village of **FORCALL** has a good *hostal*, *Alguilar*, at Avda. III Centario 1 (☎964 129 047; ❹), as well as a comfortable hotel, *Palau dels Osset*, Playa Major 16 (☎964 177 524, 📠964 177 556; ❸).

Morella's main porticoed street, **Els Porxos**, bisected by steep steps leading down to the lower walls, is the place to focus on for **food**, with its bars, bakeries and cafés – *Vinatea* and *Rourera* are both excellent for tapas. Below the monastery are a couple of small plazas where you can sit at outdoor cafés – especially pleasant in the evening.

Morella is one possible approach to the Maestrazgo region of southern Aragón. **Buses** leave for Alcañiz (3–5 weekly at 10am) and Cantavieja/Villafranca del Cid (1 daily Mon–Fri), as well as to Vinaròs (2 daily Mon–Fri) and Castellón (2 daily Mon–Fri).

The Costa Blanca

South of Valencia stretches a long strip of country with some of the **best beaches** on this coast, especially between Gandía and Benidorm. Much of it, though, suffers from the worst excesses of **package tourism** and in the summer it's hard to get a room anywhere if you just turn up on spec – in August it's virtually impossible. Campers have it somewhat easier – there are hundreds of campsites – but driving can be a nightmare unless you stick to the toll roads.

Leaving Valencia, both road and rail pass the vast **Ford factory**, one of the Spanish government's earliest successes in persuading multinational companies to invest in the country's cheap labour and favourable tax measures. If you're taking the inland route as far as Gandía, you'll get the opportunity to see the historic town of **Xátiva**.

Xátiva and around

The ancient town of **XÁTIVA** (Játiva), 50km south of Valencia, was probably founded by the Phoenicians and certainly inhabited by the Romans. Today it's a scenic, tranquil place to kill a few hours in the relative coolness of the hills, and makes a good day-trip from the capital. Medieval Xátiva was the birthplace of Alfonso de Borja, who became Pope Calixtus III, and his nephew Rodrigo, father of the infamous Lucrezia and Cesare Borgia. When Rodrigo became Pope Alexander VI, the family moved to Italy.

Xátiva has a fine collection of mansions scattered around town, but most are private and cannot be entered. Many of the churches have been recently renovated, and the **old town** is a pleasant place to wander.

From the old town, it's a long and tiring walk up a steep hill to the plain but sturdy **castle** (Tues–Sun 10am–7pm; Nov–Feb till 6pm; €1.80) – follow signposts from the main square, the Plaza del Españoleto, or take a taxi from outside the turismo. On the way, you'll pass the thirteenth-century **Iglesia de San Feliu** (April–Sept Mon–Sat 10am–1pm & 4–7pm, Sun 10am–1pm; Oct–March Mon–Sat 10am–1pm & 3–6pm, Sun 10am–1pm), a hermitage built in transitional Romanesque-Gothic style; ancient pillars, fine capitals and a magnificent Gothic *retablo* are the chief attractions of the interior.

Back in the centre of town, the **Museo del Almudín** (Tues–Fri 10am–7pm, Sat & Sun 10am–2pm; €1.80) consists of two separate sections, one an archeological collection, the other an art museum. The latter includes several pictures by José Ribera (who was born here in 1591) and engravings by Goya – *Caprichos* and *Los Proverbios*. A portrait of Felipe V is hung upside down in retribution for his having set fire to the city in the War of Succession and for changing its name.

Fiestas are held during Holy Week and in the second half of August when the *Feria de Agosto* is celebrated with bullfights and livestock fairs, but beware, it can get unbearably hot at this time of year.

Practicalities

If you arrive by **train**, follow c/Baixada Estación up towards the central tree-lined c/Alameda Jaume I, where you'll find the **turismo** at no. 50 (Mon–Sat 10am–2.30pm; ☎962 273 346, ✉touristinfo.xativa@turisme.m400.gva.es). If you're enjoying Xátiva's peace and quiet and want to **stay**, the best place for price and location is the *Hostal Margallonero*, Plaça del Mercat 42 (☎962 276 677;❸) – they also serve food. If you can afford to splash out, head for the wonderful *Hostería de Mont Sant* (☎962 275 081, ✆962 281 905, ⓦwww.seridex.com/montsant; ❽), on the way up to the castle. Another excellent place is *Calixto III* (☎902 120 691; closed winter) at Plaza Calixte III 8, though rooms are rented on a weekly basis only. Flanked by the impressive Basilica La Seu on one side and the fifteenth-century hospital on the other, this *hostal* has spotlessly clean en-suite rooms with TV and kitchenette, and with a day's notice they will knock you up a meal of paella and pumpkin pie. Prices for a three-bed room are around €300 a week. For shorter stays you might also try the comfortable hotel *Murta* at c/Angel Lacalle s/n (☎962 276 611;❻).

Keep an eye open for *arnadí* in the **bakeries** – it's a local speciality of Moorish origin, a rich (and expensive) sweet made with pumpkin, cinnamon, almonds, eggs, sugar and pine nuts. For a good **restaurant** head for the mid-priced *Casa La Abuela*, c/Reina 17 (☎962 281 085; closed Sun & mid-June to mid-Aug); many Valencians drive out here to savour its traditional fare. For something less expensive, there are a host of *cafeterias* with cheap *menús* around the train station, or *Don Pepe*, Avda. de Selgas 12 (the continuation of c/Alameda Jaume I), has great tapas and pleasant outdoor seating.

Xátiva is served by **buses** and **trains** from Valencia; the train (1hr) is half the price of the bus and leaves every half-hour. There are also connections to Gandía by bus and to Alicante by train.

Llosa de Ranes

Five kilometres from Xátiva lies the small town of **LLOSA DE RANES**, of little note other than for its fourteenth-century hermitage, **Santa Maria**, which sits astride the mountain where James I first set eyes on Xátiva. The turismo in Xátiva will lend you the ancient and only keys. Aside from a decorative arched ceiling and an amazing echo, the hermitage's real highlight is the spectacular view, which during the summer is a favourite local pilgrimage at sunset. Llosa de Ranes is served erratically by bus from Xátiva.

Gandía

There's not much along the coast south of Valencia until you get to **GANDÍA**, the first of the big resorts. A few kilometres inland from the modern seafront development, the old town is quiet and provincial, with one sight that's well worth seeing, and some good, inexpensive accommodation.

Gandía was once important enough to have its own university but the only real testimony to its heyday is the **Palacio Ducal de los Borja**, built in the fourteenth century but with Renaissance and Baroque additions and modifications. There are regular guided tours throughout the year (summer Tues–Sat 10am–1.30pm & 5.30–8.30pm & Fri 9–10pm, Sun 10am–1.30pm; winter Mon–Fri 11am–noon & 5–6pm; €1.50). Tours are in Spanish, but photocopied translations are available at the reception (☎962 871 204). The lifetime of Duke Francisco de Borja coincided with the golden age of the town (late fifteenth to early sixteenth century) in terms of urban and cultural development, a process in which he played an important part; learned and pious, the duke opened colleges all over Spain and Europe, and was eventually canonized. The palace contains his paintings, tapestries and books, but parts of the building itself are of equal interest, such as the *artesonado* ceilings and the pine window shutters, so perfectly preserved by prolonged burial in soil and manure that resin still oozes from them when the hot sun beats down. There are also several beautiful sets of *azulejos*, but these are outshone by the fourteenth-century Arabesque wall tiles, whose brilliant lustre is now unattainable as it was derived from pigments of plants that became extinct soon after the Muslims left.

Practicalities

Both **buses** and **trains** arrive on Marqués de Campo. The **turismo** (Mon–Fri 9.30am–1.30pm & 4–7pm, Sat 10am–1pm; ☎962 877 788, ✉touristinfo.gandia @turisme.m4000.gva.es) occupies a brown hut, cleverly camouflaged behind some trees opposite the train station. There is a handful of **places to stay** in town; good bets include *Hotel Los Naranjos*, c/Pío XI 57 (☎962 873 143, ⊕962

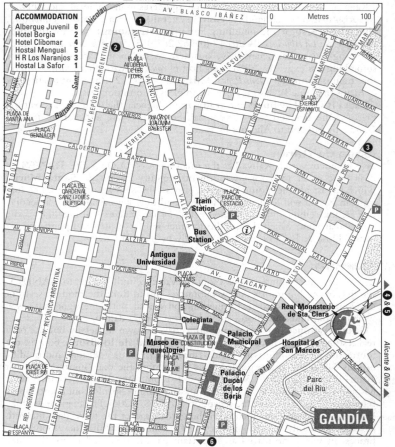

ACCOMMODATION
Albergue Juvenil 6
Hotel Borgia 2
Hotel Clibomar 4
Hostal Mengual 5
H R Los Naranjos 3
Hostal La Safor 1

GANDÍA

873 144; ❹), and the nearby *Hotel La Safor*, Avda. de Valencia 40 (☎962 864 011, ℱ962 864 179; ❹), with phone and TV in all rooms. More luxurious is *Hotel Borgia*, Avda. República Argentina 5 (☎962 878 109, ℱ962 878 031; ❻). For a base on the beach, there's *Hotel Clibomar* (☎962 840 237; ❺), in c/Alcoy by the Playa de Gandía, or the cheaper *Hostal Mengual* at Plaza de Mediterráneo 4 (☎962 842 102; ❹) – though both are closed during the winter. The exceptionally pleasant **youth hostel** (☎962 831 748; ❶; closed Feb) is on the beachfront at **Playa de Piles**, 5km down the coast, and there are four buses there from outside the train station (Mon–Sat 10am, 11.45am, 4.45pm & 6.45pm). Gandía's economical **restaurants** are along the Paseo and around the *ayuntamiento*, while the best are ten minutes from town at the beach along with most of the **bars**. One recommendable place – that isn't overly expensive – is the popular *La Tasca Gallega*, between the two on Avenida de la Paz, which serves well-cooked Galician fare. Two popular **discos** – *Flash* and *Fakata* – are also out of town on the Carretera de Valencia.

Gandía beach

Buses run every fifteen to twenty minutes (6am–11.30pm) from the turismo down to the enormous **beach**, Gandía Playa. The beach is packed in summer (especially with Spanish families) and lined with high-rise apartments which out of season can be remarkably good value. You'll find the town's second **turismo** at Paseo Neptuno 45 (mid-March to mid-Oct Mon–Sat 10am–2pm & 5–8pm, Sun 10am–1.30pm). The beach zone is a good place for **seafood** and paellas; don't miss *fideuà*, a local speciality with a strong seafood flavour, cooked with vermicelli instead of rice, and freshly made *cocques* (similar to pizzas) from Taro bakery on Passeig de los Germaines. *La Gamba* (☎962 841 310), on Carretera Nazaret-Oliva, a few blocks back from the beach, is one of the best places to eat around here.

Gandía to Altea – around the cape

A string of lovely little towns and beaches stretches from Gandía to Altea before you reach the developments of Benidorm and Alicante, but your own transport is essential to enjoy the best of them and accommodation can be pricey. The most inexpensive option along this coast is to camp. There are scores of decent **campsites**, and a useful booklet listing them is available from local turismos. Try *La Merced* 12km northwest of Altea in Calpe, Urb La Merced 1a (☎965 830 097; open all year), and *El Naranjal*, 1.5km out of Xábia on the Carreterra de Cabo (☎965 792 989; open March to Sept).

Oliva

OLIVA, 8km south beyond Gandía, is a much lower-key development. Again the village is set back from the coast and, although the main road charges through its centre, it's relatively unspoiled and there are a number of **hostales and fondas**. *La Tropical* is a rather upmarket *hostal* on Avda. del Mar 9 (☎962 850 602; ❹), with seasonal reductions and a variety of rooms. There's a **turismo** on Passeig Luís Vives (Sept–June Mon–Fri 9.30am–1.30pm & 4.30–7pm, Sat 10am–1pm; July & Aug Mon–Fri 10am–2pm & 5–7.30pm, Sat 10am–1pm; ☎962 855 528), who can provide you with a map of the town. Oliva's **beach** is served by frequent buses, and stretches a long way to the south, almost as far as Denia, so if you're prepared to walk, or better still if you've got transport, you can escape the crowds altogether. Playa de Oliva itself has hundreds of villas and apartments (booked up throughout July and Aug) but is refreshingly free of concrete and tackiness. A good **place to eat** is *Restaurante El Rebollet*, near the filling station at the entrance of the village.

Denia

DENIA, at the foot of the Montgó Natural Park, is a far bigger place, a sizeable town even without its summer visitors. There is a combined train and bus service to Alicante airport throughout the day, and a rattling narrow-gauge railway (FGV; ⓦwww.cop.gva.es/fgv/) runs down the coast from Denia to Alicante, with seven trains a day from 6.25am to 7.25pm. There are also boat services to Mallorca and Ibiza which run daily: contact Balearia Lines (☎902 160 180, ⓦwww.balearia.com) or Trasmediterránea (☎902 454 645, ⓦwww.trasmediterranea.es) for more information. Beneath the wooded capes beyond, bypassed by the main road, stretch probably the most beautiful **beaches** on this coastline – but you'll need a car to get to most of them, and there's little inexpensive accommodation. If you want to **stay**, try the *Hostal Residencial Llacer*, Avda. del Mar 37 (☎965 785 104; ❺), or *Hostal Residencial Cristina*, Avda.

del Cid 5 (☎965 786 100; ❹). Slightly more upmarket is *Hotel Costa Blanca*, Pinto Llorens 3 (☎965 780 336, ⓕ965 783 027; ❼) – handy for the centre and train station. If you want to stay on the beach, *Hostal Noguera*, Ptda Estanyo, Las Marinas (☎966 474 107; ❹), is a good option.

Xábia

At the heart of this area, very near the easternmost Cabo de la Nau, is **XÁBIA** (Jávea), an attractive village surrounded by hillside villas, and with two smallish beaches hemmed in by hotels, and a very pleasant old town. In summer both Denia and Xábia are lively in the evenings, especially at weekends, as they're popular with young people from Valencia. One of Xábia's best-value *hostales* is the *Hostal Residencia Portichol*, Partida Portichol 157 (☎966 461 050; ❹); alternatively, there's *Hostal Jávea*, Pío X 5 (☎965 795 461, ⓦwww.javea.net; ❻). There is also a *parador*, the modern *Parador de Jávea* (☎965 790 200, ⓕ965 790 308; ❾) on Avenida del Mediteraneo, which has good low-season rates at around €90 for two nights' half board. **Nightlife** is centred around the beach; good bars include *Mongo di Bongo* and *Terra*. Later in the evening, the crowds move to the out-of-town discos or *Moli Blanc* in Xábia itself.

Calpe

If you have a car, you could make a detour to the busy family resort of **CALPE** (Calp) and the dramatic rocky outcrop known as the **Peñón de Ifach**. The Peñón has been declared a national park to prevent encroaching tourist development; you can reach the top via a pathway through the rock and, on a clear day, the island of Ibiza is visible. The harbour at its foot is used by a small fleet of fishing vessels. There is a helpful **turismo** on Avenida de los Ejércitos Españoles (summer Mon–Sat 9am–9pm, Sun 10am–2pm; winter Mon–Sat 9am–2pm & 4–6pm; ☎965 837 413), who can provide you with a free map of the town.

Calpe has plenty of **accommodation** on offer; good bets include *Hostal Centrica*, Plaza Ifach 20 (☎965 835 528; ❷), the basic but clean *Hostal le Vieux Bruxelles*, near the beach at Avda. Isla Formentera 18 (☎965 834 357; ❹), and the slightly pricier *Hotel Porto Calpe*, Avda. Puerto 7 (☎965 837 322; ❺). If you feel like splashing out, *Hotel Galetamar*, c/Urb la Caleta 28 (☎965 832 311, ⓕ965 832 328; ❼), has en-suite rooms with TV and a swimming pool. For a good set *menú* for €9–15 (around €18 a head à la carte), try out *Restaurante Real Club Nautico*, on Puerto Pesquero.

There is a daily **bus** service (run by Ubesa) between Alicante and Valencia (nearly every hour in summer), which can be caught in Calpe from Capitán Pérez Jorda in front of the Centro de Salud.

Altea

Back on the main road again is **ALTEA**, set on a small hill overlooking this whole stretch of coastline. Restrained tourist development is centred on the seafront, and the town has retained its character and charm. The old village up the hill is picturesquely attractive with its white houses, blue-domed church and profuse blossoms. For **accommodation**, try *Hostal Fornet*, c/Beniards 1 (☎965 843 005; ❺ with bath), high up on the northern edge of the old village with shared bathroom, or *Hostal Paco* on Avenida Alt Rei en Jaime I (☎965 840 541; ❻). **Eating** is best done down on the seafront, which is lined with pizza and pasta joints – *L'Obrador*, at c/Concepción 8, serves some of the best pasta in the whole area at around €18 a head. The best places to **drink**, however, are to be found on the main square of the old village, which has a host of atmospheric bars.

Benidorm

Hugely high-rise, vaguely Vegas and definitely dodgy, **BENIDORM** is the king when it comes to package tourism. Just over forty years ago Rose Macaulay could describe Benidorm as a small village "crowded very beautifully round its domed and tiled church on a rocky peninsula". The old part's still here, but it's so overshadowed by the miles of towering concrete that you'll be hard-pressed to find it. If you want hordes of British and Scandinavian sun-seekers, scores of "English" pubs, almost two hundred discos and disco-bars, and bacon and eggs for breakfast, then this is the place to come. The **Playa de la Levante**, Benidorm's biggest highlight, with its 2km of golden sand, is undeniably pleasant when you can see it through the hordes of roasting corpses. A little further from the centre is the slightly more relaxed and less exposed **Playa de Ponienete**.

Arrival and information

Trains arrive at the top of town, off Avenida de Beniarda, while the main **bus stop** (there isn't a station) is at the junction of Avenida de Europa and c/Gerona, with the ticket offices in the shopping centre there. You'll find Benidorm's helpful **turismo** in the old town, at Avda. Martínez Alejos 16 (Mon–Sat 10am–2pm & 4–8pm; July–Sept Mon–Fri 9am–9pm, Sat 10am–1pm & 5.30–8.30pm; ☎965 868 189, Ⓦwww.benidorm.org), which provides a useful list of accommodation and a free map – kindly sponsored by the British newspaper *The Sun*. Other turismos can be found on Avenida Europa (daily 10am–1pm & 5.30–8.30pm) and on Avenida del Derramoor (Mon–Sat 10am–1pm & 5.30–8.30pm). **Getting to Alicante** you can either take the bus or the train – both leave every half-hour and are similarly priced, but the bus is much quicker and more convenient. There is a night train, *Trensnochador*, that runs along the coast in July and August.

Accommodation

With over 40,000 hotel beds and hundreds of apartments, finding a **place to stay** isn't a problem (except perhaps in August). Budget places are clustered around the old town and out of season many of the giant hotels slash their prices drastically, making Benidorm a cheap base from which to explore the surrounding area. One of the best *hostals* in town is the comfortable *Hostal Santa Faz*, c/Santa Faz 18 (☎965 854 063, Ⓕ965 859 134; ❼), while *Hostal El Primo*, c/Antonio Ramos Carratalá 1 (☎965 866 943; ❹), is basic but clean, and not far from the beach. For more comfort, and a swimming pool, head for the very central *Hostal Nacional*, c/Verano 9 (☎ & Ⓕ965 850 432; ❹); nearby *Hotel Don José*, c/Alt 2 (☎965 855 050, Ⓕ965 855 054; ❻), is an attractive alternative. For real luxury, *Hotel Cimbel*, Avda. Europa 1 (☎965 852 100, Ⓕ965 860 661; ❾), is the last word in luxury, with two pools and plenty of comfort. Benidorm has no fewer than nine **campsites**, the closest – and least expensive – being the basic *Don Quijote* (☎965 855 065), at the end of c/Esperanto.

Eating

Fish and chips dominate, and if you're after a fry-up, you'll be spoilt for choice. For authentic **Spanish food**, head for the pleasant and reasonably priced *Casa Enrique*, near the main turismo on Carrer de Ricardo, with its set *menú* for €7.80, or *La Palmera*, on Avenida Severo Ochoa, which specializes in rice dishes – allow €18 per person. *Tiffany's*, at Avda. Mediterráneo 51, offers great, if pricey, international cuisine, while *The Vagabond*, hidden away in the old town

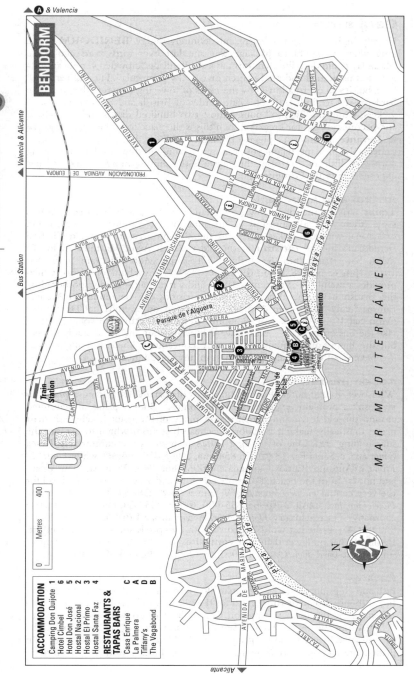

BENIDORM

A & Valencia

▲ Valencia & Alicante
◄ Bus Station

Train Station

MAR MEDITERRÁNEO

Parque de l'Alguera

Parque de l'Elche

N

Metres
0 · · · · 400

ACCOMMODATION
Camping Don Quijote · · · · · · 1
Hotel Cimbel · · · · · · · · · · · · · 6
Hotel Don José · · · · · · · · · · · · 5
Hostal Nacional · · · · · · · · · · · 2
Hostal El Primo · · · · · · · · · · · · 3
Hostal Santa Faz · · · · · · · · · · 4

RESTAURANTS & TAPAS BARS
Casa Enrique · · · · · · · · · · · · · C
La Palmera · · · · · · · · · · · · · · · A
Tiffany's · · · · · · · · · · · · · · · · · D
The Vagabond · · · · · · · · · · · · B

Ayuntamiento

Playa de Levante

Playa de Poniente

▼ Alicante

at c/Retiro 4, is a less expensive English-run restaurant that serves Greek and Indian specialities and always has **vegetarian** dishes.

Guadalest and around

An hour inland from Benidorm, accessible by three daily buses, is **GUADALEST**, justifiably one of the most popular tourist attractions in Valencia. The sixteenth-century Moorish castle town is built into the surrounding rock and you enter the town through a gateway tunnelled into the mountain. If you can put up with the hordes of tourists and gift shops, it's worth visiting for the view down to the reservoir and across the mountains. In the main street you'll find the **Casa Típica**, an eighteenth-century house-museum (Mon–Fri & Sun 10am–9pm; €1.80), with exhibitions of antique tools and agricultural methods. The modern **turismo**, c/Avenida de Alicante (Apr–Sept Mon–Fri & Sun 10am–2pm & 3–6pm & Sun 10am–7pm; Oct–Mar Mon–Fri & Sun 11am–2pm & 3–7pm; ☎965 885 298), is very helpful and will provide you with a map. There's no accommodation in Guadalest, but if you have your own transport it can be done as a day-trip from Benidorm or Alicante. Alternatively, there are two **pensiones** close by in **CALLOSA D'EN SARRIÀ**, including *Pensión Avenida* on Ctra d'Alacant 9 (☎965 880 053; ❸). Just 3km away from here, you'll find the **Fuentes del Algar**, a series of very pretty waterfalls in a secluded spot, where you can swim.

Alicante

There is little to see in the industrial town of Villajoyosa, or anywhere else along the coast south of Benidorm before you reach **ALICANTE**. This thoroughly Spanish city has an elegant Mediterranean air; its wide esplanades, such as the Rambla de Méndez Núñez and the Avenida Alfonso Sabio, and its seafront *paseos*, full of terrace cafés, are perfect for stylish relaxation. Founded by the Romans, who named it "Lucentum" (City of Light), and dominated by the Arabs in the second half of the eighth century, the city was finally reconquered by Alfonso X in 1246, for the Castilian crown. In 1308 Jaime III incorporated Alicante in the kingdom of Valencia.

Today Alicante is Valencia's second largest city, and receives millions of visitors through its airport each year. With its long sandy beaches, mild and pleasant climate, recently renovated old town and lively nocturnal offerings, this is definitely a city to spend at least one night in. The main **fiesta**, *Las Hogueras*, is at the end of June, and ignites a series of cracking celebrations second only to the *Fallas* in Valencia.

Arrival and information

The main **train station**, Estación de Madrid, on Avenida Salamanca, has direct connections to Madrid, Albacete, Murcia and Valencia, but trains on the FGV line to Benidorm and Denia leave from the far end of the Playa del Postiguet. The **bus station** for local and international services is on c/Portugal. Arriving by air, the **airport** is 12km west from the centre of Alicante, in El Altet. Airport buses into town operate between 6.30am and 11.35pm (€4) and stop outside the bus station and on the central Avenida Rambla Mendez Nuñez.

You'll find Alicante's enormous and brand new regional **turismo** at Avda. Rambla Mendez Nuñez 23 (summer Mon–Sat 10am–8pm; winter Mon–Fri

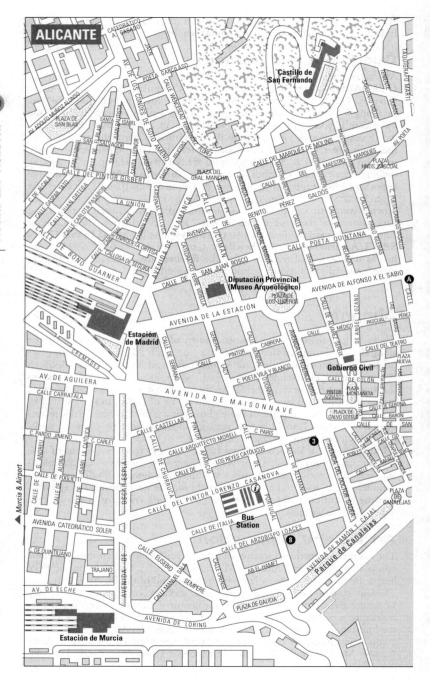

ALICANTE

Castillo de
San Fernando

Estación
de Madrid

Diputación Provincial
(Museo Arqueológico)

PLAZA DE
LOS LUCEROS

Gobierno Civil

Murcia & Airport

Bus
Station

Parque de Canalejas

Estación de Murcia

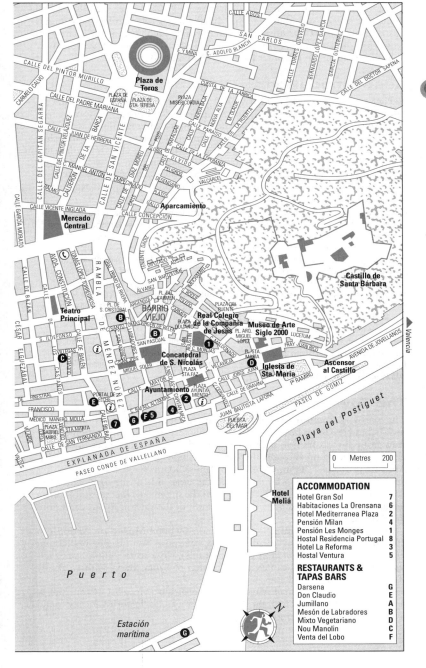

▶ Valencia

ACCOMMODATION

Hotel Gran Sol	7
Habitaciones La Orensana	6
Hotel Mediterranea Plaza	2
Pensión Milan	4
Pensión Les Monges	1
Hostal Residencia Portugal	8
Hotel La Reforma	3
Hostal Ventura	5

RESTAURANTS & TAPAS BARS

Darsena	G
Don Claudio	E
Jumillano	A
Mesón de Labradores	B
Mixto Vegetariano	D
Nou Manolin	C
Venta del Lobo	F

10am–7pm, Sat 10am–2pm & 3–7pm; ☎965 200 000). There are also several municipal offices, including one on the Plaza del Ayuntamiento (Mon–Fri 10am–2pm; ☎965 149 290), another on Portal de Elche (Mon–Fri 10am–2pm & 4–7pm) and a third in the bus station (summer Mon–Fri 9am–2pm & 4–8pm, Sat 10am–2pm; winter Mon–Sat 9am–2pm & 5–8pm).

Accommodation

Except in August, you should have little problem finding a **room**, with the bulk of the possibilities concentrated at the lower end of the old town, above the Explanada de España (a weirdly tiled seafront walk seen on all local postcards), on c/San Fernando and c/San Francisco. Among several **campsites** along the coast, *El Molino* on the Playa de San Juan (☎965 652 480) is the closest and is accessible by the frequent bus #21. Otherwise, *Internacional La Marina* (☎965 419 051), 29km out on the Ctra Alicante–Cartagena and served by Costa Azul buses, is pleasantly located in some woods, near a good beach. Both are open all year.

Hotel Gran Sol, Rambla Mendez Núñez 3 ☎965 203 000, ✆965 211 439, ✉gransol@trypnet.com. Old 1970s-style residence; the rooms have TV, and some have sea views. Well placed for the old town. **❽**
Hotel Mediterranea Plaza, Plaza del Ayuntamiento 6 ☎965 210 188, ✆965 206 750. Newly opened four-star hotel, with all mod cons and a location at the heart of the town. **❾**
Pensión Milán, c/San Fernando 6 ☎965 204 515. Large rooms with balconies and shared facilities. Not as clean as it could be. **❷**
Pensión les Monges, c/Monges 2 ☎965 215 046. Friendly and recently refurbished *pensión* with comfortable rooms, some en suite. **❹**

Habitaciones La Orensana, c/San Fernando 10 ☎965 207 820. Five simple rooms with shared bath beside *Café Bolero*. Useful for old town and nightlife. **❸**
Hostal Residencia Portugal, c/Portugal 26 ☎965 929 244. Light, airy rooms near the bus station in this clean and convenient *hostal*. **❹**
Hotel La Reforma, c/Reyes Católicos 7 ☎965 928 147, ✆965 923 950. Clean, modern and functional rooms with air conditioning, TV and phone. **❼**
Hostal Ventura, c/San Fernando 10 ☎965 208 337. Simple, clean double rooms with bath, in this *hostal* on the fifth floor of the building. **❸**

The Town

The rambling **Castillo de Santa Bárbara**, an imposing fortress on the bare rock behind the town beach, is Alicante's only real "sight" – with a tremendous view from the top. It's best approached from the seaward side where a shaft has been cut straight up through the hill to get you to the top. The lift (daily: April–Sept 10am–7.30pm; Oct–March 9am–6.30pm; €2.40 in coins only) is directly opposite Meeting Point Five on the other side of the road from Playa Postiguet. Drivers can reach the castle from the other side. Iberian and Roman remains have been found on the site, but most of the present layout dates from the sixteenth century.

Alicante's other main attraction is a remarkably good **Museo de Arte Siglo 20** (June–Sept Tues–Sat 10am–2pm & 5–9pm, Sun 10.30am–2.30pm; Oct–May Tues–Sat 10am–2pm & 4–8pm; free), close to the impressive *ayuntamiento* and opposite Alicante's oldest church of Santa María, with works by Picasso, Tàpies, Miró and Dalí.

The town also has a small **Museo Arqueológico** (Mon–Sat 10am–2pm & 4–8pm, Sun 10am–2pm; free) on Plaza Dr Gómez Ulla, featuring locally found relics from the Iberian to medieval periods.

Fiestas de Moros y Cristianos

One of the most important fiestas in the region and the most important of its kind is the three-day **Fiesta de Moros y Cristianos** in **Alcoy**, about 60km from Alicante. It happens the three days around St George's Day (*San Jorge*, April 23), but the date varies slightly according to when Easter falls. Magnificent processions and mock battles for the castle culminate in the decisive intervention of St George himself –- a legend that originated in the Battle of Alcoy (1276) when the town was attacked by a Muslim army. New costumes are made each year and prizes are awarded for the best which then go into the local museum, Museu de la Festa Casal de San Jordi, at c/San Miguel 60 (Mon–Fri 11am–1pm & 5.30–7.30pm, Sat & Sun 10.30am–2pm; free).

On day one the Christians make their entrance in the morning, the Moors in the afternoon; day two is dedicated to St George, with several religious processions; day three sees a gunpowder battle, leading to the saint's appearance on the battlements. Access from Alicante is easy, with five buses a day. You may have to commute since reasonably priced accommodation in Alcoy is not plentiful; if you do stay though try *Hostal Savoy*, c/Casablanca 5 (℡965 547 272; ❹ with bath, ❼ during fiestas), or the more expensive *Hotel Reconquista*, Puente San Jorge 1 (℡965 330 900, ℻965 330 955; ❼, ❾ during fiestas). After Alcoy's fiesta, the *Moros y Cristianos* fiestas in **Villena** (beginning of Sept) and **Elche** (August) are two of the best.

Beaches

For the best local **beaches** head for **San Juan de Alicante**, about 6km out, reached either by bus #21 (every 15–20min) from the Plaza del Mar or on the FEVE Alicante–Denia railway. The town beach – **Playa del Postiguet** – is crowded and none too clean. Between Urbanova and Playa del Saladar, there's a *playa libre* (nudist beach); take bus #C-7 for Urbanova which leaves from Avenida de la Constitucion (by the theatre), and ask the driver to drop you off. You can also take a day-trip to the **island of Tabarca** (a marine reserve), to the south – boats leave, weather permitting, from the Explanada de España (June–Sept 3–4 daily; €12 return; Oct–May Sat & Sun 1 daily; ℡965 216 396) – but the rock tends to get very cramped and crowded during the summer.

Eating, drinking and nightlife

There are dozens of **restaurants** clustered around the *ayuntamiento* – including a couple of places on c/Miquel Saler where you can eat couscous, and a couple of excellent *churrerías* – though most tend to be overpriced. Over on the other side of town, c/San Francisco, leading off a square near the bottom end of the *rambla*, has a group of restaurant/*tabernas* with seats outside and *menús* for under €6 – *Don Claudio* has the cheapest. On c/San Fernando the *Venta del Lobo* does reasonably priced *carnes a la brasa* (barbecued meats), and in Plaza Santa María, opposite the Gothic portico of the church, you'll find a good **vegetarian** restaurant, *Mixto Vegetariano*, which also serves meat dishes. For the best of Alicante's culinary delights, try one of the three most renowned places and expect a hefty bill of around €24 a head: the posh *mesón*-style *Restaurante Jumillano*, c/César Elguezábal 64 (℡965 212 964), which serves a mean *perdices escabechadas* (pickled partridge); *Nou Manolin*, c/Villegas 3 (℡965 200 368), which is a bit more *moderno*, with a tapas bar downstairs and a €12 *menú* at lunchtime; and the daddy, the classy *Restaurant Darsena* out in the Marina Deportivo at c/Muelle 6 (℡965 200 368). For **tapas** try the atmospheric *Mesón de Labradores*, c/Labradores 19, and sample their *montaditos* (tiny bread rolls) or seafood specialities – if you can't squeeze in here there's another smaller branch at c/San Pasuel 3.

If you want to buy your own food, visit the enormous **Mercado Central**, housed in a wonderful old *modernista* building on Avenida Alfonso X el Sabio. Near here there are plenty of good places to buy Alicante's famous nougat-like *turrón*, with many shops on c/Capital Serralla, and in the centre on c/Mayor – Turrón 1880 is the best. Another market (a major outdoor event) is held by the Plaza de Toros on Thursdays and Saturdays (9am–2pm).

Bars and nightlife

For **drinking** and the best **nightlife**, head into the Barrio Santa Cruz, whose narrow streets lie roughly between the cathedral, Plaza Carmen and Plaza San Cristóbal. At night El Barrio, as it's called, covers the old town area, and there are so many bars here that you can easily steer clear of the questionable places. If you enter via the Plaza San Cristóbal or c/Santo Tomás below it, you'll quickly hit the main area. An excellent starting point is *Desden*, c/Labradores 22, which plays jazz in the afternoon and house, dance and funk through the night till 4am. For a late-night bop, *Cien Fuegos*, on the street of the same name, plays uplifting trance and techno. Both the *Armstrong* bar, c/Carrer de Carmen 3, and *Desafinado*, Santo Tomás 6, have great jazz.

Another area to check out for nightlife is on the other side of town, in particular along c/Italia, c/Alemania and c/Loaces, which tends to be a bit smarter than Santa Cruz with a corresponding difference in prices – most places don't allow trainers. For trendy cafés and upmarket restaurants, head for Explanada de España, which also has lively *mesones* and noisy bars. In summer the bars along Playa San Juan are always packed, especially along Avenida de Niza, beside the sea.

Listings

Airlines Iberia's offices are at Avda. Dr Gadea 12 ☎965 217 982 and British Airways' at the airport ☎966 919 472.

Airport Located in El Altet, 12km from Alicante city centre (☎966 919 100 or 966 919 400).

Banks There are banks throughout the centre, especially along Avda. Rambla Mendez Nuñez, Avda. Alfonso X el Sabio and Explanada. The latter is where you'll find *bureaux de change* offices open daily.

Bus information ☎965 130 700.

Cinema The Cine Astoria, in the middle of El Barrio (pl. del Carmen, 16), sometimes has original-language films (€4.20).

Consulates British Consulate, Plaza Calvo Sotelo 1–2 ☎965 216 022.

Doctor Centro de Salud, c/Gerona 24 ☎965 143 587.

Internet *Yazzgo Internet*, Explanada de España 3; *Up Internet*, c/ Ángel Lozano, 3; *Zipposbar*, c/Labradores, 1.

Police The *Commisaría* is at c/Médico Pascual Pérez ☎965 148 888.

Post office There are many *Correos* in the town including one near the bus station at the junction of c/Alemania with c/Arzobispo Loaces (Mon–Fri 8am–8.30pm).

Telephones There are many *locutorios* throughout the centre, especially along c/San Francisco and c/San Fernando and around. Telefónica has one inside the bus station (Mon–Fri 10am–2pm & 5–9pm).

Train information Estación de Madrid ☎902 240 202. For FGV trains call ☎965 262 233.

Inland – Elche and Orihuela

ELCHE, 20km inland and south from Alicante, is famed throughout Spain for its exotic **palm forest** and for the ancient stone bust known as La Dama de Elche discovered here in 1897 (and now in the Museo Arqueológico in Madrid, see p.109). The palm trees, originally planted by the Moors, are still the town's chief industry – not only do they attract tourists, but the female trees produce dates, and the fronds from the males are in demand all over the country for use in Palm Sunday processions and as charms against lightning. You can see the forest, unique in Europe, almost anywhere around the outskirts of the city; the finest trees are those in the specially cultivated **Huerto del Cura** on c/Federico García Sánchez.

Elche is also the home of a remarkable **fiesta** in the first two weeks of August which culminates in a centuries-old mystery play – *Misteri*, held in the eighteenth-century **Basilica Menor de Santa María** over August 14–15. Additional celebrations include one of the best examples of the mock battles between Christians and Muslims. Over several days the elaborately costumed warriors fight it out before the Moors are eventually driven from the city and the Christian king enters in triumph.

There are **buses** more or less hourly from Alicante to Elche. Outside fiesta time you should have no problem finding somewhere to **stay**, though there are few budget options: try *Pensión Juan*, c/Pont dels Ortissos 15 (T965 458 609; ❸), for basic but clean rooms with shared bathroom. Elche also has a smart *parador*, *Hotel Huerto del Cura*, Porta de la Morera 14 (T966 610 011, F965 421 910, Wwww.huertodelcura.com; ❽). The *Bar Águila* on c/Dr Coro 31 is highly recommended for convivial drinking and good **tapas**, while the restaurant in the park, *Parque Municipal*, serves *arroz con costra*, the delicious local rice dish. If you want the very best of local cuisine, however, you'll need to go to *El Granaíno*, c/José Maria Buck 40 (closed Sun and mid-Aug) – though you'll pay through the nose for it.

Elche is also regularly connected with **SANTA POLA** on the coast – previously a village but now quite developed, with good rooms to let, clean beaches, and ferries to the tiny **island of Tabarca** that are slightly faster than those from Alicante. Inland, the road continues to Orihuela.

Orihuela

Just over 50km southwest of Alicante lies the capital of the Vega Baja district, **ORIHUELA**, where in 1488 los Reyes Católicos held court. The town's aristocratic past is reflected in the restored old quarter, and the impressive renovation of the **Teatro Circo**. Despite its proximity to the coast, Orihuela retains its provincial charm and is worth wandering around. Though it doesn't take long to see the monuments, it's worth spending a whole day (and maybe even a night) to enjoy its pace of life – you're unlikely to run into other tourists here. Orihuela also has a natural attraction in **El Palmeral**, the second largest palm forest in Spain – walk out beyond Colegio de Santo Domingo or take the Alicante bus (from the centre) and ask to be dropped off. Many of the town's seventeenth- and eighteenth-century mansions are closed to the public; however, you can roam around the one occupied by the turismo (see "Practicalities" below) and parts of the Palacío Marqués de Arneva, which now houses the *ayuntamiento*.

Opposite the turismo is the **Iglesia de Santiago** (Mon–Fri 10am–1pm & 4–6.30pm, Sat 10am–1pm), one of the town's three medieval churches – all of which are Catalan Gothic (subsequently altered), a style you won't find any further south. The oldest part of the church is the front portal, the Puerta de Santiago, a spectacular example of late fifteenth-century Isabelline style. Inside, the furniture is Baroque, and there is a *retablo* by Francisco Salzillo. Heading back down towards the town centre, just past the *ayuntamiento*, you'll see the second medieval church, the **Iglesia de Santas Justa y Rufina** – its tower is the oldest construction in the parish and has excellent gargoyle sculptures.

Just round the corner, on c/Salesas Marques Arneva, is one of Orihuela's hidden treasures, the Baroque **Monestario de la Visitacion Salesas** (Tues only 10am–2pm, 4–5.30pm & 6.30–7pm; €0.60), whose cloisters contain several paintings by the nineteenth-century artist Vincente Lopez – a monk will show you around.

Right in the centre of the old town is the medieval **Catedral** (summer Mon–Fri 10.30am–1.30pm & 5–7.30pm, Sat 10.30am–1.30pm; winter Mon–Fri 10.30am–1.30pm & 4–6.30pm, Sat 10.30am–1.30pm), no bigger than the average parish church, built with spiralling, twisted pillars and vaulting. A painting by Velázquez, *The Temptation of St Thomas,* hangs in a small museum in the nave – and don't overlook the Mudéjar-influenced, fourteenth-century Puerta de las Cadenas. The **Museo Diocesano de Arte Sacro** (same hours as cathedral; €0.60), above the cloister, contains an unexpectedly rich collection of art and religious treasures (including a painting by Ribera), many of which are brought out during *Semana Santa,* the town's most important fiesta. There's also a **Museo Semana Santa** (Mon–Fri 10am–1pm & 4–6pm, Sat 10am–1pm; €0.60), not far from the cathedral, containing religious artefacts, photos and costumes particular to the Easter celebrations.

Orihuela's other main sight is the Baroque **Colegio de Santo Domingo** (Tues–Fri 10am–2pm & 5–8pm; reduced hours in winter; free), out towards the palm forest. Originally a Dominican monastery, it was converted into a university in 1569 by Pope Pío V, then closed down by Fernando VII in 1824. The two cloisters are well worth seeing, along with the fine eighteenth-century Valencian tiles in the refectory. For a view of the town and surrounding plains, walk up to the seminary on top of the hill. From Plaza Caturla in the centre of town, take the road leading up on the right; not far from the top, there are a couple of steeper short cuts to the right.

Practicalities

Arriving by **bus** or **train**, you'll find yourself at the combined station at the bottom of Avenida de Teodomiro. The helpful tourist information desk here (Mon–Sat 9am–2pm & 4–8pm, Sun 10am–1.30pm) can provide you with a map and glossy brochure. Otherwise, the main **turismo** is located in the impressive Palacio Rubalcara, c/Francisco Die 25 (Mon–Fri 8am–2.30pm; ☎965 302 747). The only **accommodation** in the town, *Hostal Rey Teodomiro* (☎966 743 348; ●), is at the top of the long avenue from the train station – it's clean, and there are plenty of rooms, all with bath. Out by El Palmeral, *Casa Corro* (☎965 302 963; ●) and *Hostal El Palmeral* (☎966 743 500; ●) are two more options, but neither is very convenient.

If you cross over the road from the *Hostal Rey Teodomiro* and take the first right, you'll come to the best **place to eat**, *Mesón Don Pepe* at c/Valencia 3; it has great tapas and a good lunch menu during the week – try the *consomé al Jerez* (soup with sherry) or the region's speciality, *arroz con costra* (literally "rice and crust", made with rice, eggs, *embutidos*, chicken and rabbit). For something a bit more economical, *Mesón Ramon,* just off Avenida Duque de Tamamas on c/Luis Bacala, has a well-priced *menú*, and there are several outdoor **cafés** along Avenida de Teodomiro. Orihuela's **nightlife** is surprisingly good. In the early evening, head for the bars along c/Duque de Tamames, and later on try c/Castellón, c/Valencia and the surrounding area. There are also a lot of big *bacalao* discos just outside town, but you'll need a car to get to them – they include *Metro* in Bigastro and *Blue Sky* in Benijófar.

Murcia

MURCIA, according to the nineteenth-century writer Augustus Hare, would "from the stagnation of its long existence, be the only place Adam would recognize if he returned to Earth". Things have changed slightly – there is industrial development on the outskirts and a gathering movement to spruce up the centre – but it remains basically a slow-moving city. Founded in the ninth century on the banks of the Río Segura (no more than a trickle now), by the Moors, Murcia soon became an important trading centre and, four centuries later, the regional capital. It was extensively rebuilt in the eighteenth century, and the buildings in the old quarter are still mostly of this era.

Today it's the commercial centre of the region and most of the industry is connected with the surrounding agriculture. There are very few tourists and a refreshing lack of tawdry souvenir and postcard stands. Surrounded by mountains, Murcia has a tranquillity and unspoilt air impossible to find in most modern cities.

Arrival, information and accommodation

Both bus and train stations are on the edge of town. If you're arriving by **bus**, either walk down to the Plano de San Francisco, then follow the river until you see the cathedral, or buses #5 or #17 will take you there. The **train station** is across the river at the southern edge of town – take bus #9, #11 or #17 to the centre. Murcia's regional **turismo** is on c/San Cristóbal (summer Mon–Fri 8.30am–2.30pm; winter Mon–Fri 9am–2pm & 5–9pm; ☎968 277 676, ⓦ www.murcia-turismo.com). Murcians seem to know it's hard to find and will tell you the way; it's an unusually helpful office, full of ideas and generous with their posters, pamphlets and postcards. Two other **municipal offices** can be found at Plano de San Franscisco 8 (Mon–Sat 10am–2pm & 5.30–9.30pm, Sun 10am–2pm; ☎968 358 720) and by the theatre on c/Santa Clara (same hours).

Accommodation

Albergue Juvenil, Albergue del Valle ☎968 607 185. Beautiful youth hostel in a *parque natural* in La Alberca, 5km outside Murcia. Catch bus #29 from the Jardín de Floridablanca over the bridge on the south side of town. The YH is signposted about 1km beyond the last stop. ❶

Pensión Avenida, c/Canalejas 10 ☎968 215 294. Basic budget *pensión* on the other side of the river across Puente Viejo, offering rooms without baths. ❸

Pensión Desvío-Rincón de Paco, c/Cortés 27 ☎968 218 436. Basic rooms near bus station. ❷

Pensión Hispano I, c/Trapería 8 ☎968 216 152, ⓕ968 216 859. Comfortable and convenient spot in the pedestrianized zone with easy access to surrounding sights. ❹

Hotel Hispano II, c/Radio Murcia 3 ☎968 216 152, ⓕ968 216 859. Upmarket hotel with good restaurant. ❺

Pensión Perro Azul, c/Simon Garcia 19 ☎968 221 700. Practically at the centre of the action and ideal for party animals, with clean, comfortable rooms and a pleasant bar downstairs. ❻

Hotel Rincón de Pepe, c/Apósteles 34 ☎968 212 239, ⓕ968 221 744. One of the best hotels in Murcia with a famous restaurant downstairs. ❽

Hotel Siete Coronas, Ronda de Garay 5 ☎968 217 771, ⓕ968 221 294. Expensive hotel overlooking the river, especially popular for Spanish weddings, but not as central as *Rincón de Pepe*. ❾

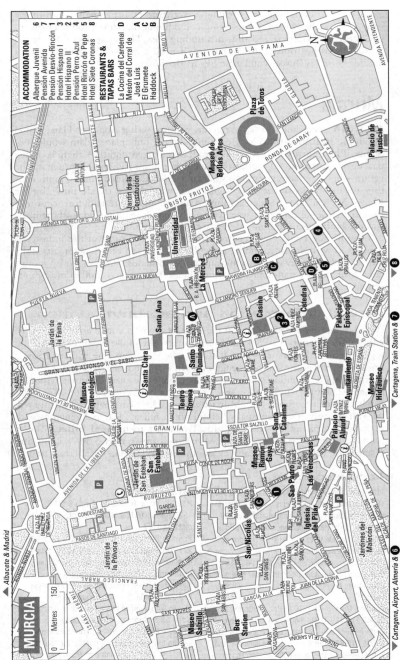

MURCIA

Metres
0 ——— 150

ACCOMMODATION

Albergue Juvenil	6
Pensión Avenida	7
Pensión Desvío-Rincón	1
Pensión Hispano I	3
Hotel Hispano II	2
Pensión Perro Azul	4
Hotel Rincón de Pepe	5
Hotel Siete Coronas	8

RESTAURANTS & TAPAS BARS

La Cocina del Cardenal	D
Mesón del Corral de José Luis	A
El Grumete	C
Haddock	B

◀ Albacete & Madrid

◀ Cartagena, Airport, Almería & 6

▼ Cartagena, Train Station & 7

▲ Albacete & Madrid

The City

The **Catedral** (closed for restoration at the time of writing; daily 10am–1pm & 5–7pm) towers over the mansions and plazas of the centre. Begun in the fourteenth century and finally completed in the eighteenth, it's a strange mix of styles, known as "Mediterranean Gothic" because of the relations between the crown of Aragón and the kingdom of Murcia. The outside is more interesting architecturally, particularly the west side with its Baroque facade, and the tower rising on the north, which you can climb for great views of the city. Inside, the most remarkable aspect is the florid Plateresque decoration of the chapels – particularly the **Capilla de los Vélez** (1491–1505). Originally designed as a funeral area, but never completed, it's one of the finest examples of medieval art in Murcia and one of the most interesting pieces of Hispanic Gothic in Spain; an urn in the niche of the main altar contains the heart of Alfonso the Wise. The **museum** (closed for restoration at the time of writing; daily 10am–1pm & 5–7pm; July & Aug till 8pm; €1.20) has some fine primitive sculptures and, above all, a giant processional monstrance – 600 kilos of gold and silver twirling like a musical box on its revolving stand.

Across the Plaza Cardenal Belluga stands the newest addition to Murcia's architectural heritage. Rafael Moneo's extension to the *ayuntamiento* closes the square with a strict regular building that faces the cathedral facade with a rhythmic twentieth century version of the Baroque *retablo*.

The **Museo Salzillo**, west of the centre in Plaza San Agustín, near the bus station (summer Tues–Sat 9.30am–1pm & 4–7pm, Sun 11am–1pm; July and Aug closed Sat & Sun; winter Tues–Sat 9.30am–1pm & 4–7pm, Sun 11am–2pm; €3), has an extraordinary collection of the figures carried in Murcia's renowned Holy Week procession (which is when they are seen at their best). They were carved in the eighteenth century by Francisco Salzillo and they display all the cloying sentimentality and delight in the "rustic" of that age. Other museums include the **Museo de Bellas Artes** at c/Obispo Frutos 12 (Tues–Fri 9.30am–2pm & 4–8.30pm, Sat & Sun 10am–2pm; €1.80, free to EU citizens), with a representative collection of local art from medieval to contemporary, some of it good; and the **Museo Arqueológico**, Paseo Alfonso X 5 (Mon–Fri 9am–2pm & 4–8pm, Sat 10am–1.30pm; free), which has an extensive collection of potsherds (broken fragments of pottery).

The **Casino** (daily 9.30am–9pm; free), at c/Trapería 22, dates from 1847 and eclectically combines an Arabic-style patio and vestibule, an English-style library reading room, a Pompeiian patio with Ionic columns, a billiard room and French ballroom. Most extraordinary of all, perhaps, is the neo-Baroque ladies' powder room (open to all) whose ceiling depicts angelic ladies among the clouds, powdering their noses and tidying their hair.

Eating, drinking and nightlife

Murcia is known as *la huerta de Europa* (the orchard of Europe), and although this might be a slight exaggeration, you'll find local produce in all the city's restaurants. Murcia is an important rice-growing region, and the local variety, *Calasparra*, is renowned in Spain. It's the vegetables, though, that the area is really known for, and you'll find that vegetable soups, grills and paellas are a speciality.

Restaurants and tapas bars

Just before **lunchtime** the whole of the Gran Vía Alfonso X and the Plaza de las Flores (towards the river end of Gran Vía Salzillo) is packed with people drinking aperitifs and picking at tapas. If you're on a budget, any one of the *mesones* in the Plaza de Julián Romea (beside the theatre) and Plaza San Juan is a safe bet. For an excellent *menú del día* for €9, head for *Mesón del Corral de José Luís*, Plaza de Santo Domingo 23. You'll find the best **tapas** at *Barra del Rincón* (which shares the same chef as *Hotel Rincón de Pepe*), which also has a superb *menú* for €7.20 and is easily one of the liveliest places to eat in town. If you fancy **seafood**, *El Grumete* serves tasty, fresh *mariscos* by weight, and has two branches at c/Vara de Rey 6 and Plaza San Nicolas 3. For **dinner**, *La Cocina del Cardenal* in Plaza Belluga is very good, but for the ultimate gastronomic experience, visit the famous *Hotel Rincón de Pepe*, at c/Apósteles 34 (☎968 212 239), and try their *leche frita* for dessert.

Bars and nightlife

As a university town, Murcia has a good **nightlife** during semesters. The liveliest area is around the university, near the Museo de Bellas Artes, in particular c/Dr Fleming, c/de Saavedra Fajardo and the side streets off them. There is also a sizeable gay scene in Murcia, unusual for a provincial Spanish town.

A good place to start the evening is by the university on Plaza Beato A. Hibermón in the intimate bar *Icaro*, or on the terrace of *El Refugio* on the nearby Plaza de Bolsas, which is more or less at the centre of the action. Most bars offer the same mix of happy Spanish pop and mainstream techno tunes, though there are exceptions: *B12*, c/Trinidad 17, plays excellent funk, hip-hop and reggae; *Boca de Lobo*, on c/Luisa Aledo, is the best for rock and metal; *El Perro Azul* (of the *pensión* of the same name) is a bit more relaxed with reggae and 1960s rock; and *Yesería* plays anything alternative, from Bob Dylan to punk. At 3am the action disperses to various discos throughout the city with *Centro*, in Plaza Julián Romea, and *De Nai Clu*, on c/Puerta Nueva, both current favourites. Should you require solid nourishment before moving on, *Haddock*, c/Vara del Rey 17, makes excellent toasted sandwiches and serves drinks till the small hours.

If none of these tickle your fancy, *La Puerta Falsa*, on the other side of the university at c/San Martin de Porres 5, is an outstanding **jazz** bar with live music every night and a quality selection of drinks. For **salsa** and Latin grooves, *La Codiga,* on Gran Vía Alfonso X, and *Cha Cha Cha*, just round the corner, are your best bets and stay open till late. *Maricoco*, on c/Vitorio, is a mainly **gay bar**, with the crowd moving on to *On* (aka *Metropol Max Music Hall*), near the bus station on c/San Andrés, which plays rave and techno until the early hours.

Listings

Airlines Iberia, Avda. Alfonso X el Sabio 11 ☎968 240 050. Most of the others are represented by travel agencies.

Airport Located 45km away at San Javier on the Mar Menor (☎968 172 000). There are limited internal flights to Almería, Barcelona and Madrid. To get to the airport, bus #70 goes to San Javier, from where it's a 3km walk or taxi-ride.

Banks All the big ones, with foreign exchange desks, are on both the Gran Vías.

Bookshops Antaño, on c/Puerta Nueva, sells a good selection of English books.

Bus information The bus station is on c/Sierra de la Pila ☎968 292 211.

Car rental Hertz, next to the train station on Plaza Condestable ☎968 299 015; Eurocar, Avda. Miguel de Cervantes 9 ☎968 283 086; Sol Mar, Avda. Juan de Borbón 36 ☎968 239 387; and Atessa, Juan Carlos I 2 ☎902 100 101.

Hospitals While the General Hospital is being rebuilt, the main centre is Hospital José Maria Morales Meseguer (☎968 360 900) near Plaza Circular at Avda. Marqués de los Vélez 22; Red Cross (☎968 222 222).

Internet L@ Red, c/Antonio Puig 1, just north of the university (Mon–Sat 10.30am–2pm & 5–10pm; €2.25 per hour).

Market The Mercado Municipal, c/Verónicas, has

stacks of wonderful local produce including kiwi fruit, dates, bananas and, of course, citrus fruit.

Police Avda. San Juan de la Cruz ☎968 266 600.

Post office The *Correos* is at Plaza Circular (Mon–Fri 9am–2pm & 5–8pm, Sat 9am–2pm).

Shopping El Corte Inglés has two buildings either side of Gran Vía Salzillo. The main shopping area is around the Gran Vías.

Train information RENFE, Plaza de la Industria ☎968 252 154.

Telephones The *Telefónica* is on c/Jerónimo de Roda, off Gran Vía Salzillo.

The coast south of Torrevieja

The stretch of coast around the south of **Torrevieja** has been developed at an alarming rate, and is now home to a mix of Europeans, Russians and Spaniards. Just to the south is a series of pleasant beaches, known collectively as **Las Playas de Orihuela** (as they come within Orihuela's provincial boundary). Both Playa La Zenía and Playa Cabo Roig are good, clean options with car parks and cafés (the restaurant at Cabo Roig is also exceptionally good and enjoys wide views over the harbour).

The Murcian Costa Cálida starts at the **Mar Menor** (Lesser Sea), a broad lagoon whose shallow waters (ideal for kids) warm up early in the year, making this a good out-of-season destination. With its high-rise hotels, the "sleeve" (*la manga*) looks like a diminutive Miami Beach; the upmarket resorts on the land side of the lagoon are more appealing, and they do have a few *hostales*. The main problem is getting a room in season – the area is immensely popular with Spaniards and by April all the cheaper places are often booked up for the summer.

San Pedro del Pinatar

SAN PEDRO DEL PINATAR, the first resort, is probably your best bet in season as it's not as polished-looking as the others, and is actually more pleasant as a result. The **bus station** is up in the old town, but it's not worth spending much time here. Head down the town's main avenue – about a twenty- minute walk – or take a bus straight to the seafront. On Monday there's a big market (on the inland side of the main road) with a large selection of food, clothes and shoes.

Much of the town **beach** area, called Lo Pagán, was reconstructed after terrible floods in 1986. Year after year people return to La Puntica beach to coat themselves in its **therapeutic mud**, a product of the salt pools behind, which reputedly relieves rheumatism and is good for the skin. The best beach near here is Playa de las Llanas, the other side of the salt pool area; it's a long way to walk though – from town, go down Emilio Castelar and turn off into Avenida Salinera Española (*puerto* direction).

Practicalities

There is no accommodation up in the old town but there are plenty of *hostales* by the beach, including *Pensión Alas Playa*, Bartolomé Gil 3 (☎968 181 017; ❹), very good value and virtually on the beach but only open May to September, and the clean and friendly *Hostal Casa Lucrecia*, Caserío de los Sáez (☎968 181 928; ❹), half a kilometre out of town towards Cartagena, with a good and inexpensive restaurant. Should you have any problems finding a place to stay, the **turismo** on the front by the Parque de los Reyes de España (summer Mon–Fri 9.30am–1.30pm & 5–7.30pm, Sat 10.30am–1pm; winter Mon–Fri 9.30am–1.30pm & 4–8pm, Sat 10.30am–1pm; ☎968 183 706,

Ⓦwww.sanpedrodelpinatar.net) can help, as well as supplying the usual bumph.

Places to eat are in good supply – the *Hogar del Pescador* is an inexpensive seafood restaurant at c/Lorenzo Morales 2, near the main square; *Mesón La Panocha*, c/Muñoz Delgado, near the seafront, has excellent tapas; *El Venezuela* is a high-quality if rather expensive seafood place virtually on the beach; and for budget food *Los Madroños*, off Avda. de Generalísimo at c/Asturia 6, serves a well-cooked and generous €6 *menú* as well as offering cheap rooms (no phone; ❷). Most of San Pedro's bars and discos are along Avenida de Generalísimo.

There are daily **buses** from San Pedro to Cartagena (8 daily) and Murcia (hourly).

Santiago de la Ribera

The next town on the Mar Menor, and within walking distance, is **SANTIAGO DE LA RIBERA**, a fancy resort that's popular with *murcianos*. There's an important sailing club here, as the calm sea is perfect for novices.

One of the best budget **pensiones** is *Manida*, near the sea at c/Muñoz 11 (Ⓣ & Ⓕ968 570 011; ❹), with a range of rooms and good full-board deals. Alternatively, *Pensión K Hito*, c/Maestre 9 (Ⓣ968 570 002; ❹ with bath; open July–Sept only), and *Hotel Trabuco*, Avda. Mar Menor 1 (Ⓣ968 570 051, Ⓕ968 570 638; ❺), are close together at the back of the town. More expensive is *Hotel Don Juan*, Avda. Nuestra Señora de Loreto 2 (Ⓣ968 571 043; ❺). Also worth trying on c/Zarandona are *Pensión La Obrera*, at no. 7 (Ⓣ968 570 042; ❹ with bath), and *Hotel Madrid* at no. 18 (Ⓣ968 570 504; ❺). If you're looking for seafood, you'll get the best in town at *Mesón El Pescador* on Explanada Barnuevo. There are two **campsites** in the area, both open all year: *Alcázares* (Ⓣ968 575 100) in Los Alcázares, with a pool, and *Mar Menor* (Ⓣ968 570 133) on the Alicante–Cartagena road.

The nearest **train station** for this area is Balsicas (connected with San Pedro and Santiago by 3–4 buses daily). Trains run direct from here to Barcelona, Valencia and Madrid.

Cartagena

Whether you're approaching **CARTAGENA** from one of the numerous resorts along Mar Menor, inland from Murcia, or from Almería to the south, it's not a pretty sight. Scrub and semi-desert give way to a ring of hills littered with disused factories and mines, eventually merging into the newer suburbs. It's only when you reach the old part of town down by the port, with its narrow medieval streets, packed with bars and restaurants, that the city's real character emerges.

Cartagena was Hannibal's capital city on the Iberian peninsula, named after his Carthage in North Africa, and a strategic port and administrative centre for the Romans. International Nautical Week is celebrated here in June, in July the Mar de Músicas festival (Ⓦwww.lamardemusicas.org) presents some of the best in world music, and in November the city hosts an International Festival of Nautical Cinema. The **fiestas** of *Semana Santa* are some of the most elaborate in Spain with processions leaving from the church of Santa María de Gracia in the early hours of Good Friday morning.

Arrival, information and accommodation

Cartagena has a new **bus station** on c/Trovero Marín, and you'll find the FEVE **train station** (with trains running to Los Nietos on the Mar Menor) almost next door and the RENFE station nearby at the end of Avenida America. The city's **turismo** is across the Plaza del Almirante Basterreche on the corner of c/Lealtad (Mon–Fri 10am–1pm & 5–7pm, Sat 10.30am–7pm; ☎968 506 483); they can provide a free map of the town.

Places to stay are somewhat thin on the ground, and not particularly low in price. For good value and a central location, head for *Hotel Peninsular*, c/Cuatro Santos 3 (☎ & ⓕ968 500 033; ❹), just off c/Mayor. *Pensión Isabelita*, Plaza María José Artes 7 (☎968 507 735; ❸), adjacent to Plaza del Ayuntamiento, is clean and fairly decent, while *Hostal Cartagenera* at c/Jara 32 (☎968 502 500; ❺) is also good. For a more upmarket choice, try the nearby *Hotel Los Habaneros*, c/San Diego 60 (☎968 505 250, ⓕ968 509 104, ⓦwww.forodigital.es/habaneros; ❼), which also has a quality, but expensive, restaurant.

The City

Cartagena does not have an excess of sights and much of what it does have is in ruins or not open to the public. The vast military **Arsenal** that dominates the old part of the city dates from the mid-eighteenth century and, like the Captaincy General building, is still in use, heavily guarded and not open to the public. However, you can visit the **Naval Museum**, c/Menéndez Pelayo 6 (Tues–Sun 10am–1.30pm; free), set in the walls of the Arsenal, and the **National Museum for Underwater Archeology** (Tues–Sun 10am–3pm; free), which is a long walk round the outer walls of the Arsenal on the way to the lighthouse, and has a reconstructed Roman galley and a lot of interesting exhibits salvaged from shipwrecks. The **Museo Archeológico**, c/Ramón y Cajal 45 (Tues–Fri 10am–2pm & 5–8pm, Sat & Sun 11am–2pm; free), in the new part of town, is built on a Roman burial ground and has an excellent collection of Roman artefacts and a good introduction to the ancient history of the city.

The best of Cartagena's churches is **Santa María de Gracia**, on c/San Miguel, which contains various works by Salzillo, including the figures on the high altar. There are more works by Salzillo and a fine art collection in the Neoclassical church **La Caridad** on c/la Caridad. You'll see a large number of *modernista* buildings around the city. Most of these are the work of former Cartagenian and disciple of Gaudí, Victor Beltri (1865–1935). In particular, have a look at Casa Maestre in Plaza San Francisco, Casa Cervantes, c/Mayor 15, and the old *Hotel Zapata*, Plaza de España.

To get a feel of the city's distinguished past, wander along the sea wall towards the old military hospital. It's a huge, empty, but evocative building, now falling into disrepair, and no one will mind you looking around. From the lighthouse there are great views of the harbour and city, but perhaps the best **city views** are from Torres Park, reached along c/Gisbert. Past the ruins of the old cathedral, the road winds down back into Plaza del Ayuntamiento.

Eating, drinking and nightlife

There are plenty of unexploited **bars** and **restaurants** in the old town with Spanish-only menus and uninflated prices. The best places to look for food are Plaza del Ayuntamiento and Plaza María José Artes – best value is *Casa Pedrero* on the corner of Plaza María José Artes with very low-priced *platos combinados* and an €4.80 *menú del día*. *Mesón Artes*, opposite, has a vast range of tapas, and the popular *El Mejillonería*, c/Mayor 4, just off Plaza del Ayuntamiento, is definitely worth trying to squeeze your way into. The side streets around the squares also contain plenty of good places: on c/Escorial, *El Bahia* is a tiny seafood restaurant with meals cooked straight from its tanks of live fish, and the more expensive *Mare Nostrum*, down by the port, also offers excellent seafood dishes as well as tapas.

In the evening, try *El Macho*, on the corner of c/Aire and c/del Cañon, which specializes in *pulpo* and *patatas bravas*; *La Uva Jumillana*, on c/Jara, which serves extremely strong wines from the barrel; and the more modern *Cervecaría-Restaurante Principal*, c/Príncipe de Vergara 2, which serves fine tapas and has art exhibitions and notice boards detailing cultural events. You'll find Cartagena's **discos** and late-night bars on c/del Cañon, on the streets of Plaza de San Agustín and along c/Jiménez de la Espada.

The Golfo de Mazarrón

South of Cartagena, on the coast of the **Golfo de Mazarrón**, only Mazarrón and Águila are easily accessible. Very little building has been allowed around the beaches between these two towns, because the area is a breeding ground for **tortoises** and a species of **eagle** – for the last decade there have been plans to make it a nature reserve. The few roads that lead down to the better beaches usually end up as tracks.

Mazarrón and around

The inland village of **MAZARRÓN** is small and peaceful with an attractive plaza and a few **places to stay**; both *Pensión Calventus II*, Avda. de la Constitución 60 (☎968 590 094; ❸), and the fancier *Guillermo II*, c/Carmen 3 (☎968 590 436, ☎968 590 609; ❻), are worth trying. Puerto de Mazarrón resort is 6km away, served by three daily buses from Cartagena.

Despite a fair amount of development, **PUERTO DE MAZARRÓN** is pretty quiet even in season, but most of the **accommodation** is in expensive resort hotels. If you're looking for something a little less pricey, *Pensión Delfín*, by the beach at Caudillo 13 (☎968 594 639; ❸), and *La Línea*, c/San Isidro (☎968 594 350; ❸), are both clean and reasonable. For more comfort, head for *Hotel Bahía*, Playa de la Reya (☎968 594 000, ☎968 154 023; ❻), or *Hotel Playa Grande*, Ctra Bolnuevo (☎968 594 684, ☎968 153 430; ❽). The massive **campsite**, *Garoa Playa de Mazarrón* (☎968 150 660), on Crta Bolnuevo, is open year round. You'll find a useful **turismo** at c/Doctor Meca 20 (summer Mon–Sat 9am–2pm & 6–10pm, Sun 10am–1pm; winter Mon–Sat 9am–2pm; ☎968 594 426). The better **beaches**, Cabo Tiñoso to the north and Punta Calnegre to the south, are not served by public transport, but the best one, Bolnuevo, is just about walkable from Puerto de Mazarrón. Nearby is the "Enchanted City of Bolnuevo", a small area of weird, eroded rocks. If you get tired of sunbathing, the nature reserve at **La Rambla de Moreras** has a lagoon which attracts a variety of migratory birds.

For **food** the best place to head for is *Virgen del Mar* on Paseo de la Sal, which serves excellent *arroz con bogavante* (rice with lobster). Slightly cheaper is the seafood restaurant *Beldemar*, Avda. Costa Cálida, where you buy fresh fish and have it cooked for you on the spot. In summer, the **nightlife** is centred along Vía Axial.

Totana and Aledo

Inland from Mazarrón is the town of **TOTANA**, at the foot of the Sierra Espuña, home to wild boars and royal eagles. The strange stone domes dotted around in the mountains are "snow wells", used to store snow before the thaw. The sanctuary La Santa, 7km outside the town, has a beautifully carved wooden ceiling, and houses a collection of sixteenth- and seventeenth-century paintings. Totana is served by hourly buses and trains from Murcia, and buses continue on to **ALEDO**, another ancient mountain town with Arabic walls and a tower. Medieval traditions are still strong here and on January 6 it hosts the **Auto Sacramental** (mystery play). Just outside the town is the *Hotel El Pinito del Oro* (T968 484 590, F968 484 436; ●) with magnificent views.

Águilas

ÁGUILAS lies at the southern end of the Golfo de Mazarrón, bordered inland by fields of tomatoes, one of the few things that can grow in this hot, arid region. Fishing, along with the cultivation of tomatoes, is the mainstay of the economy here, and a fish auction is held at around 5pm every day in the port's large warehouse. **Carnaval** is especially wild in Águilas, and for three days and nights in February the entire population lets its hair down with processions, floats and general fancy-dress mayhem.

Arrival and information

You'll find the **turismo** (summer Mon–Fri 9am–2pm & 5–9pm, Sat 10am–2pm & 5–9pm, Sun 11am–2pm; winter Mon–Fri 9am–2pm & 5–7pm; T968 493 285, Wwww.aguilas.org) on Plaza de Antonio Cortijos, near the port; they can provide free maps of the town. **Buses** stop at the *Bar Peña Aguileña*, with services to Almería, Cartagena, Murcia (all 6 daily) and Lorca (Mon–Fri 17, Sat & Sun 6). There are also three **trains** daily to both Murcia and Lorca. If you plan on exploring the surrounding beaches, hiring a car or bike is a good idea; **car rental** is available from Auriga, c/Iberia 65 (T968 447 046), and **mountain bikes** can be found along c/Julián Hernández Zaragoza for around €9 a day.

Accommodation

Pensiones tend to be full from mid-July to mid-August. In the centre of town, *Hostal La Aguileña*, at c/Isabel la Católica 8 (T968 410 303; ● without bath), is a good bet, as is *Pensión Rodríguez*, Ramón y Cajal 3 (T968 410 615; ●). For more comfort, head for *Hotel Carlos III*, near the pretty Plaza de España, at c/Rey Carlos III 22 (T968 411 650, F968 411 658; ●). The *Albergue Juvenil* (T968 413 029; ●) is 4km out of town at Calarreona along the Carretera Almería, and there is no bus out this way. There are two **campsites** in the area, both open all year: *Águilas* (T968 419 205) is 2km from the beach, and *Bellavista* (T968 449 151) is on the Vera–Almería road in a quiet green spot.

The town and its beaches

Águilas is a popular spot as the beaches are plentiful, reasonably served by public transport and the area has a superb year-round climate. The town itself has managed to escape the excesses of tourism, and retains much of its rural charm and character.

You'll find two fine **beaches**, and over thirty small *calas* (coves) in the vicinity. Those to the north are rockier and more often backed by low cliffs; to the south they are grittier and more open. The main attraction, however, is the lack of surrounding development – some are totally wild, others have a smattering of villas, others have just one bar. The beaches are cleaned daily from May onwards, as a lot of seaweed is washed up.

Heading north from Águilas, Playa Hornillo (on the summer-only Calabardina bus route) is a nice beach with a couple of bars nearby. From here, it's possible to walk round to Playa Amarillo, probably the most secluded and beautiful of the beaches. A string of beaches are served by the Calabardina bus in summer; Playa Arroz, La Cola and Calabardina itself (7km from town). If you feel energetic you could walk across Cabo Cope to yet another chain of beaches beginning at Ruinas Torre Cope, but there's really no need to go so far.

South of Águilas, the Las Lomas bus serves the rocky Playa Las Lomas, from where you can walk to Playa Matalentisco with shallow stretches ideal for kids. The Las Palomas beach (known locally as La Cabaña) has the added attraction of a restaurant; beside it is Calarreona beach, then comes La Higuérica, 5km from town. Further south, Playa Cuatro Calas has a drinks stall, but no other unnatural presence, and by the time you get to La Carolina, on the border of Andalucía, the shore is completely wild.

Eating and drinking

You won't go hungry in this part of the world as **fresh fish** is always in supply. For a fine selection of fish and *arroz a la piedra* (a tasty rice dish), head for *Las Brisas* on Explanada del Puerto (closed Mon), or the excellent *El Puerto*, Plaza Robles 18 (closed Wed), which specializes in *pulpo* (octopus). Good choices at the lower end of the price scale include *Mesón Maribel* at c/Rambla 22 (closed Wed), which is good for meat dishes, and *Frankfurt Marmar* and *El Oriente*, at Carretera de Vera 50 and 52, which both specialize in fish dishes and have inexpensive *menús*.

Inland to Lorca

Many of the historic villages of inland Murcia are accessible only with your own transport, but one place you can reach easily is **Lorca**, a beautiful former frontier town. The villages around all have their share of Renaissance and Baroque architecture and are surrounded by stunning countryside.

Lorca

Despite being slowly shaken to pieces by the traffic that hammers straight through its centre, **LORCA** still has a distinct aura of the past. For a time it was part of the caliphate, but it was retaken by the Christians in 1243, after which Muslim raids were a feature of life until the fall of Granada, the last Muslim stronghold. Most of the town's notable buildings – churches and ancestral homes – date from the sixteenth century onwards.

Arrival, information and accommodation

Arriving by **train**, get off at Lorca Sutullera; **buses** will also drop you at the station, but the bus stop before is closer to town. The **turismo**, on c/Lópe Gisbert (daily: Mon–Fri 9.30am–2pm & 5.30–7.30pm, Sat 11am–2pm; winter Mon–Fri 9.30am–1.30pm & 4.30–7.30pm, Sat 11am–1.30pm; ☎968 466 157), can provide a good map and an excellent guided architectural walk of about an hour around the town – though not much else. Both trains and buses connect Lorca with Murcia; the train is cheaper and quicker. Heading south to

Granada there are two buses daily, at 10.40am and 4pm.

Even though it really only takes an hour or two to look around Lorca, it's still a good place to stop overnight, with inexpensive **rooms** all along the highway. *Pensión del Carmen*, c/Rincón de los Valientes 3 (☎968 466 459; ❹), and *Casa Juan*, c/Guerra 10 (☎968 468 006; ❹, with air conditioning ❺), are decent and reasonably priced, while *Hotel Félix*, Avda. Fuerzas Armadas 141 (☎968 467 654, ☎968 467 650; ❸), is an old-fashioned place and very good value. If you have trouble finding a room, the enormous *La Alberca*, Plaza Juan Moreno 1 (☎968 468 850; ❸), is shabby but friendly and is likely to have space. If you're coming for Holy Week you'll have to book at least a month in advance, or stay in Murcia or Águilas.

The Town

Before heading up to the old town it's worth popping into the **Centro de Artesanía**, next door to the turismo, which displays and sells work combining traditional crafts with avant-garde design (Mon–Fri 10am–2pm & 5–7.30pm; free).

The old part of town lies up the hill from c/López Gisbert. The **Casa de los Guevara**, above the turismo, is an excellent example of civic Baroque architecture from the end of the seventeenth century and is the best mansion in town. On the corner of Plaza San Vicente and c/Corredera, the main shopping artery, is the **Columna Milenaria**, a Roman column dating from around 10 BC: it marked the distance between Lorca and Cartagena on the *Vía Heraclea*, the Roman road from the Pyrenees to Cádiz. The Gothic **Porche de San Antonio**, the only gate remaining from the old city walls, lies at the far end of the Corredera. On Plaza de España, the focal point of the town, and seemingly out of proportion with the rest, you'll find the imposing **Colegiata de San Patricio** (Mon–Fri 11am–1pm & 4.30–6.30pm, Sat & Sun 11am–1pm; free), with its enormous proto-Baroque facade, built between the sixteenth and eighteenth centuries – there's a marked contrast between the outside and the sober, refined interior, which is largely Renaissance. Nearby is the **ayuntamiento**, with its seventeenth- to eighteenth-century facade. An equally impressive front is presented by the sixteenth-century **Posito**, down a nearby side street – originally an old grain storehouse, it's now the municipal archive.

The thirteenth- to fourteenth-century **Castillo** overlooking the town seems an obvious destination but it's a very hot walk and not really worth it, as the two towers of interest are open only on November 23, the day the fortress was recovered from the Moors. The impoverished *barrio antiguo*, huddled below the castle, can be a little dangerous at night, but it's worth wandering around in daylight.

Lorca is famed for its **Semana Santa** celebrations which out-do those of Murcia and Cartagena, the next best in the region. There's a distinctly operatic splendour about the dramatization of the triumph of Christianity, with characters such as Cleopatra, Julius Caesar and the royalty of Persia and Babylon attired in embroidered costumes of velvet and silk. The high point is the afternoon and evening of Good Friday.

Eating and drinking

A good **place to eat** is the *Restaurante El Teatro*, Plaza Colón 12 (closed Sun) – the square is on the same road as the turismo. Also try the *Restaurante Barcas Casa Cándido*, c/Santo Domingo 13, for their very good *menús*. Up the road from here in c/Tintes, on the corner of Est. Cava, is a great, seedy **bodega**, where they serve powerful shots of port-like *vino tinto* for next to nothing.

Caravaca de la Cruz and Moratalla

CARAVACA DE LA CRUZ, an important border town, can be reached from Lorca by daily bus, although there are more direct buses from Murcia (hourly; 1hr 30min). The town is dominated by the **Castillo**, which contains a beautiful marble and sandstone church, **El Santuario de Vera Cruz**. The church houses the cross used in the Easter celebrations, and on May 3 the cross is "bathed" in the temple at the bottom of town to commemorate the apparition of a cross to the Moorish king of Valencia, Zayd Abu Zayd, in 1231. Just outside the church, cloisters lead to the **museum** (guided visit: Aug daily every hour 10am–1pm & 5–8pm, otherwise Tues–Sun 11am–1pm & 5–7pm; €2.40) which concentrates on religious art and history. The churches that tower over the rest of the town, **La Iglesia del Salvador** and **La Iglesia de la Concepción**, are also worth a visit; the latter contains some excellent examples of carved Mudéjar wood. **Accommodation** is limited, but good bets include *Pensión Victoria*, c/María Girón 1 (℡968 708 624; ❸), *Pensión Patio Andaluz*, Gran Vía 28 (℡968 707 682; ❸), and *Hotel Central*, Gran Vía 18 (℡968 707 055, ℱ968 707 369; ❺), which also has a decent restaurant.

Moratalla

Fourteen kilometres on is **MORATALLA**, a pretty village spread around the foot of a fortress. The steep, winding streets of the old town lead up to the **castle** from where there are stunning views of the surrounding countryside and its vast forests.

Moratalla is a lovely place to **stay** if you want to relax: *Pensión Levante*, Carretera del Canal 21 (℡968 730 454; ❹), although slightly out of town has comfortable rooms and modern bathrooms, while *Pensión Reyes*, c/Tomas el Cura 7 (℡968 730 377; ❷), is simple but clean. There is a **campsite** 8km out of town in La Puerta (℡968 730 008, ⓔlapuerta@forodigital.es; open all year). If you're driving, you might head out to *Hotel Cenajo* (℡968 721 011, ℱ 968 720 645; ❺), hidden away in the hills (but signposted), overlooking a beautiful reservoir. Moratalla is full of little **bars**; the *Alhameda* is one of the best for food. For **tapas**, head for *Bar Luquillas*, c/Ctra San Juan 34, which serves delicious ham-filled *croquetas*.

Travel details

Trains

Alicante to: Albacete (10 daily; 1hr 30min); Benidorm (hourly; 1hr 10min); Denia (7 daily; 2hr 15min); Madrid (10 daily; 3hr 45min); Murcia (5 daily; 1hr 15min); Valencia (10 daily; 1hr 30min–2hr 15min); Xátiva (5 daily; 1hr 20min).
Murcia to: Águilas (4 daily, 1 Sun; 2hr); Barcelona (3 daily; 7hr); Cartagena (14 daily; 50min); Granada (2 daily; 8hr); Lorca (10–16 daily; 1hr); Madrid (4 daily; 3hr 50min).

Valencia to: Alicante (10 daily; 1hr 35min–2hr 10min); Barcelona (14 daily; 2hr 50min–5hr); Benicàssim (7 daily; 50min); Castellón (17 daily; 30min–1hr); Gandía (every 15min; 50min); Madrid (8 daily; 3hr 30min); Málaga (2 daily; 10hr); Murcia (5 daily; 3hr 25min); Orihuela (5 daily; 3hr); Peniscola (8 daily; 1hr 20min); El Puig (every 15min; 20min); Sagunto (10 daily; 20min); Segorbe (3 daily; 1hr); Xátiva (16 daily; 1hr); Zaragoza (3 daily; 5hr–6hr 45min).

Buses

Alicante to: Albacete (2 daily; 2hr 30min); Almería (2 daily; 7hr); Barcelona (7 daily; 8hr); Cartagena (10 daily; 2hr); Granada (5 daily; 5hr); Madrid (3 daily;

6hr); Málaga (6 daily; 9hr); Murcia (9 daily; 2hr); Orihuela (8 daily; 1hr 20min); San Pedro del Pinatar (11 daily; 1hr 15min); Torrevieja (10 daily; 1hr).

Murcia to: Águilas (6 daily; 2hr); Albacete (2–6 daily; 2hr 30min); Alicante (8 daily; 2hr); Almería (8 daily; 4hr); Barcelona (5–7 daily; 8hr); Cartagena (hourly; 1hr); Granada (5 daily; 6hr); Lorca (5–12 daily; 1hr 15min); Madrid (9 daily; 8hr); Málaga (5 daily; 8hr); Mazarrón (2–4 daily; 1hr 30min); Orihuela (6 daily; 1hr); Valencia (7 daily; 4hr 30min).

Valencia to: Alicante (17–19 daily; 4hr); Barcelona (14–17 daily; 4hr 15min–5hr); Benidorm (17–19 daily; 3hr 15min); Castellón (5–7 daily; 1hr 30min); Cuenca (3 daily; 4hr); Denia (7 daily; 1hr 45min); Gandía (8 daily, 12 in summer; 1hr); Madrid (13 daily; 4hr); Murcia (5–7 daily, 10 in summer; 4hr 45min); Oliva (12 daily, 18 in summer; 1hr 30min); Orihuela (2 daily; 3hr); El Puig (14 daily; 20min); Sagunto (30 daily; 30min); Segorbe (7 daily; 1hr); Sevilla (3 daily; 11hr).

Balearic connections

From Alicante Air Nostrum 3 daily summer flights to Ibiza. **From Denia** Trasmediterránea sailings to: Sant Antoni de Portmany, Ibiza (2–3 daily; 4hr).

From Valencia Trasmediterránea sailings to: Palma de Mallorca (3–6 weekly; 9hr); Ibiza (1 weekly, 7 weekly June–Sept; 9hr). At least 4 flights daily to Palma (40min), at least 2 daily to Ibiza (30min).

The Balearic Islands

Highlights

The Balearic Islands

Comprising an archipelago to the east of the Spanish mainland, the four chief Balearic islands – Ibiza, Formentera, Mallorca and Menorca – maintain a character distinct from the rest of Spain and from each other. **Ibiza**, firmly established among Europe's trendiest resorts, is wholly unique with an intense, outrageous street life and a floating summer population that seems to include every club-going Spaniard from Sevilla to Barcelona. It can be fun, if this sounds like your idea of a good time, and above all if you're gay – Ibiza is a very tolerant place. **Formentera**, small and a little desolate, is something of a beach-annexe to Ibiza, though it struggles to present its own alternative image of reclusive artists and "in the know" tourists. **Mallorca**, the largest and best-known Balearic, also battles with its image, popularly reckoned as little more than sun, booze and high-rise hotels. In reality you'll find all the clichés, most of them crammed into the mega-resorts of the Bay of Palma and the east coast, but there's lots more besides: mountains, lovely old towns, some beautiful coves and the Balearics' one real city, Palma. Mallorca is in fact the one island in the group you might come to other than for beaches and nightlife, with scope to explore, walk and travel about. And last, to the east, there's **Menorca** – more subdued in its clientele, and here, at least, the grim modern resorts are kept at a safe distance from the two main towns, the capital Maó, and the highly scenic, pocket-sized port of Ciutadella.

Access to the islands is easy from Britain and the rest of northern Europe, with charter **flights** and complete package deals dropping to absurd prices out

Accommodation price codes

All the establishments listed in this book have been price-graded according to the following scale. The prices quoted are for the **cheapest available double room in high season**; effectively this means that anything in the ❶ and most places in the ❷ range will be without private bath, though there's usually a washbasin in the room. In the ❹ category and above you will probably be getting private facilities. Remember, though, that many of the budget places will also have more expensive rooms including en-suite facilities. Youth hostels are graded under ❶ as the price per person is less than half of the category's upper limit.

Note that in the more upmarket *hostales* and *pensiones*, and in anything calling itself a hotel, you'll pay a **tax** (IVA) of seven percent on top of the room price.

❶ Under €12	❹ €27–36	❼ €60–90
❷ €12–18	❺ €36–48	❽ €90–120
❸ €18–27	❻ €48–60	❾ Over €120

Fiestas

January

16 *Revetla de Sant Antoni Abat* (Eve of St Antony's Day) is celebrated by the lighting of bonfires (*foguerons*) in Palma and several of Mallorca's villages – especially Sa Pobla and Muro, where the inhabitants move from fire to fire, dancing round in fancy dress. Also observed in Sant Antoni (Ibiza).

17 *Beneides de Sant Antoni* (Blessing of St Antony). St Antony's feast day is marked by processions in many of the Balearics' country towns, notably Sa Pobla and Artà on Mallorca.

17 *Processó d'els Tres Tocs* (Procession of the Three Knocks). Held in Ciutadella, Menorca, this procession commemorates the victory of Alfonso III over the Muslims here on January 17, 1287.

19 *Revetla de Sant Sebastià.* Palma, Mallorca, has bonfires, singing and dancing for St Sebastian.

20 *Festa de Sant Sebastià.* Celebrated in Pollença, Mallorca, with a religious procession accompanied by *Cavallets* (literally "merry-go-rounds"), two young dancers each wearing a cardboard horse and imitating the animal's walk. Of medieval origin, you'll see *Cavallets* at many of the islands' festivals.

21 *Festa de Santa Agnès de Corona,* Ibiza. Traditional dances, live music and fireworks.

February

Carnaval Towns and villages throughout the islands live it up during the week before Lent with marches and fancy-dress parades.

March/April

Semana Santa (Holy Week) is as widely observed here as everywhere else in Spain. On Maundy Thursday in Palma, Mallorca, there's a religious procession through the streets. There are also Good Friday (*Divendres Sant*) processions in many towns and villages, especially in Palma, Sineu (Mallorca) and Maó. Most holy of all, however, is the Good Friday *Davallament* (the Lowering), the culmination of Holy Week in Pollença, Mallorca.

March

19 *Festa de Sant Josep* in Ibiza features live classical music followed by a fireworks display.

April

5 *Festa de Sant Vicent,* Ibiza. Tiny village fiesta.

23 *Festa de Sant Jordi,* Ibiza. Traditional dances (*ball pagès*) in Sant Jordi, and book-giving throughout the Balearics.

---

of season or with last-minute bookings. From mainland Spain, too, there are charters, though believe it or not these can often cost as much or even more. **Ferries** – from Barcelona, Valencia and Dénia – are slightly less expensive: the single passenger fare from Barcelona to Ibiza will, for example, set you back around €34, with vehicle rates starting at around €113 one-way. **Catamarans**, which run from the same mainland ports in the period mid-June to mid-September, are even more expensive – Valencia to Palma, for instance, costs €50. Likewise, rates for **inter-island** ferries are also high, and for journeys such as Ibiza–Mallorca or even Mallorca–Menorca it can actually be better value to fly. The catch here is availability: in the high season tickets are snapped up fast, so it's a good idea to book ahead of time – a few days beforehand is usually suffi-

May

Mid-May *Festa de Nostra Senyora de la Victòria* in Port de Sóller, Mallorca, features mock battles between Christians and infidels in commemoration of the thrashing of Turkish pirates here in 1561. Lots of booze and firing of antique rifles (in the air).
30 *Festa de Sant Ferran* in Sant Ferran, Formentera.

June

23–25 In Ciutadella, Menorca, the midsummer *Festa de Sant Joan* features jousting competitions, folk music, dancing, and processions. Also wildly celebrated in Sant Joan, Ibiza, with bonfires and fireworks.

July

15–16 Día de Virgen de Carmen. The patron saint of seafarers and fishermen is honoured with parades and the blessing of boats, especially in Ibiza Town and La Savina, Formentera.

August

2 *Mare de Déu dels Àngels*. Moors and Christians battle it out in Pollença, Mallorca.
8 *Sant Ciriac*. Small ceremony in Dalt Vila, Ibiza, to commemorate the Reconquest of 1235, plus a mass watermelon fight in Es Soto below the walls, and a huge firework display in the harbour.
Second weekend *Festa de Sant Llorenç*, in Alaior, Menorca; high jinks on horseback through the streets of the town. Also a small fiesta in Sant Llorenç, Ibiza.
20 *Cavallet* Week-long festival in Felanitx, Mallorca.
24 *Día de Sant Bartomeu*. Concerts, cultural events and a large firework display in the harbour area of Sant Antoni de Portmany
Throughout August International Festival at Pollença, Mallorca, including art and sculpture exhibitions and chamber music.

September

Second week *Nativitat de Nostra Senyora* (Nativity of the Virgin) in Alaró, Mallorca, with a pilgrimage to a hilltop shrine near the Castell d'Alaró.

November

16 *Festa de Santa Gertrudis*, Ibiza. Folk dancing and live music in the village square.

December

3 *Día de Sant Francesc* celebrated in Sant Francesc Xavier, Formentera, with fireworks, dancing and bonfires.
Christmas (*Nadal*) is especially picturesque in Palma, Mallorca, where there are Nativity plays in the days leading up to the 25th.

cient. For fuller details on **routes** see "Travel details" at the end of this chapter.

Expense and **over-demand** can be crippling in other areas, too. As "holiday islands", each with a buoyant international tourist trade, the Balearics charge considerably above mainland prices for **rooms** – which from mid-June to mid-September can double in cost, and are in very short supply. If you go at these times, it's sensible to try to fix up some kind of reservation in advance or at least get a bag of small change and phone round before tramping the streets (though many places accept only agency bookings). If you plan to rent a **car**, note that these can also be in short supply in season. **Mopeds, scooters and bicycles** are a good option on the islands but be sure to check your insurance policy: it should definitely include theft as well as accident. To avoid

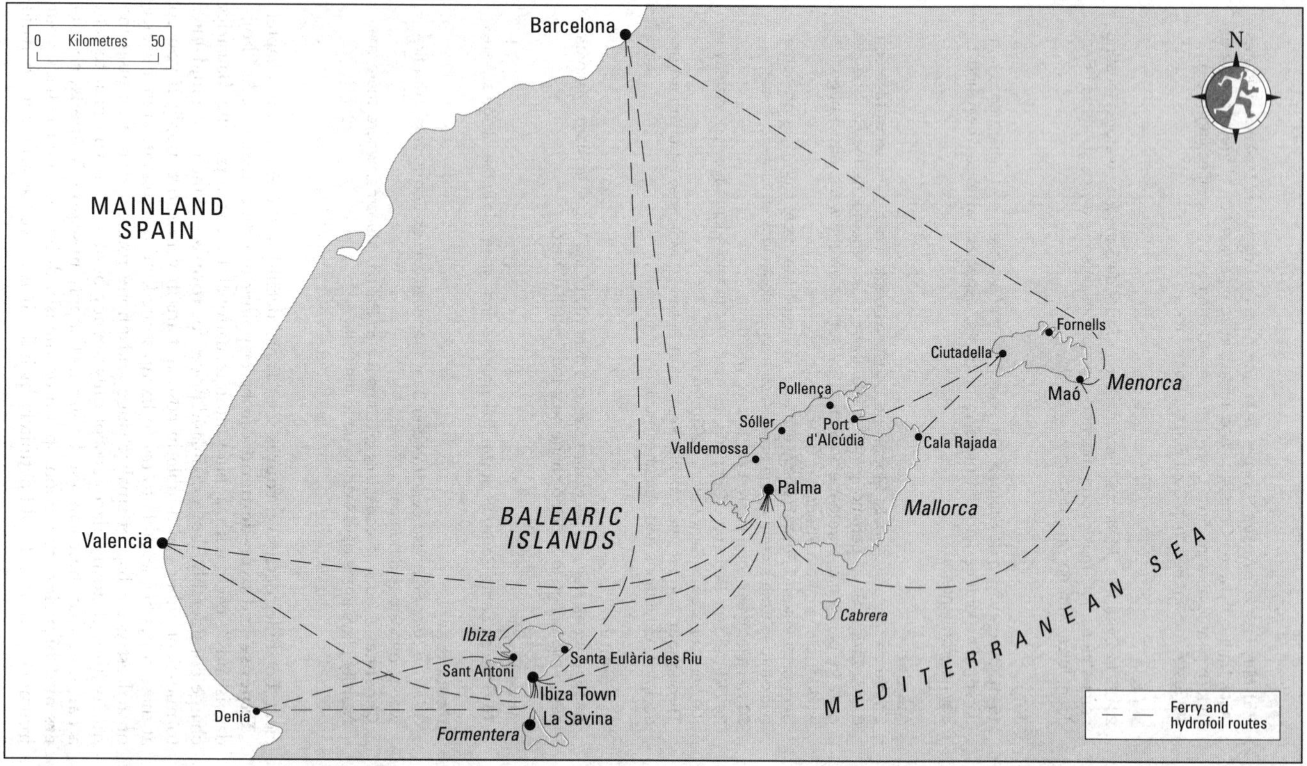

MAINLAND
SPAIN

0   Kilometres   50

N

Barcelona

Valencia

Denia

MEDITERRANEAN SEA

Menorca

Fornells
Maó
Ciutadella
Cala Rajada

Mallorca

Cabrera

Pollença
Port d'Alcúdia
Sóller
Valldemossa
Palma

BALEARIC
ISLANDS

Santa Eulària des Riu
Ibiza Town
La Savina
Ibiza
Sant Antoni
Formentera

Ferry and
hydrofoil routes

the latter, store most of your baggage somewhere before setting out – riding with a pack is both exhausting and dangerous. Without your own transport, the **bus** network is reasonably comprehensive – and services are detailed in "Travel Details" as well as the text for the specific islands.

As elsewhere in Spain, the Balearics have revived their own **dialects** since the death of Franco. Throughout the islands a dialect of **Catalan** is spoken, a result of their capture from the Moors by the thirteenth-century king of Catalunya and Aragón, Jaume I. Each of the three main islands has a different sub-dialect, and indeed many inhabitants object to their language being called Catalan at all, though generally the islanders speak their native language and Castilian (Spanish) with equal fluency. For the visitor, confusion arises from the difference between the islands' road signs and street names – which are almost exclusively in Catalan – and many of the maps on sale, which are in Castilian. In particular, note that Menorca now calls its capital Maó rather than Mahón, while both the island and town of Ibiza are usually referred to as Eivissa. The influx of tourists also means that you'll find no shortage of people with fluent English, German or sometimes French. In this chapter we give the Catalan name for towns, beaches and streets with the Castilian name in brackets where helpful, except for Ibiza and Ibiza Town which are not widely known by their Catalan names outside Spain.

Ibiza

IBIZA (*Eivissa* in Catalan) is an island of excess. Beautiful, and blessed with scores of stunning cove beaches, towering cliffs and dense pine forests it's nevertheless the islanders (*ibicencos*) and their visitors who make it special. However outrageous you may want to be (and outrageousness is the norm here) the locals have seen it all before – and remain determinedly blasé about the thousands of lotion-smeared tourists preening themselves on the beaches during the day, in preparation for an all-night session in the bars and clubs.

For years Ibiza was *the* European hippie escape, but nowadays it's the extraordinary clubbing scene that most are here to experience. Home to seven of the most famous venues in Europe, the island can lay a strong claim to be the globe's clubbing capital, with virtually all of the world's top house DJs, and many more minor players performing during the summer season. Visit the island between October and May and you'll find a very different, much more peaceful island – just one club (Pacha) and a few funky bars remain open through the winter months. **Ibiza Town**, the capital, is the obvious place to base yourself: only a short bus ride from two great beaches – **Ses Salines** and **Es Cavellet** – and rammed with bars, restaurants and boutiques. **Sant Antoni de Portmany**, a large, high-rise resort on the western coast, is far less cosmopolitan in character – largely catering to young British clubbers – but can almost match Ibiza Town in the hedonism stakes, its wide bay and "sunset strip" lined with groovy chill-out bars. **Santa Eulària des Riu**, the only other real town, is a mundane little place that's popular with holidaying families – fairly featureless except for a pretty hilltop church. Around the entire shoreline of the

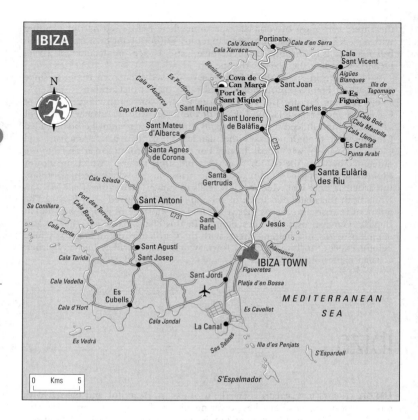

island, you'll find dozens of exquisite cove **beaches** (*calas*), many all but deserted even in high season, though you'll need your own transport to reach the best spots. **Inland** the scenery is hilly and thickly wooded, dotted by a series of tiny hamlets, each boasting a stunning whitewashed village church, and an atmospheric local bar or two.

Salt attracted the Greeks, and after them the Phoenicians and **Carthaginians**, who made the island a regular stop on their Mediterranean cruises – to such an extent that Ibiza has hundreds of Punic burial sites. Under Roman rule the island continued to prosper until dropping into the familiar pattern of Spanish history, occupied successively by Goths and Moors before being liberated by the Catalans early in the thirteenth century. Thereafter decline set in and, despite occasional imperialist incursions, Ibiza was effectively an abandoned and impoverished backwater until the middle of the twentieth century, when it began to acquire status as the most chic of the Balearics.

Ibiza practicalities

Getting around the island is relatively easy. There is a good **bus service** between Ibiza Town, Sant Antoni de Portmany, Santa Eulària des Riu, Portinatx, the airport and a few of the larger beaches, and local **boats** from the three main towns serve various destinations along the coast; however, renting some form of **vehicle** will widen your options no end (see p.940). The main problem – and expense – on the island is **accommodation**, which is difficult, sometimes impossible, to find in high season; Ibiza Town is generally your best bet. For information on the island's airport, see below.

Ibiza Town

In physical terms as well as in its atmosphere and adventure, **IBIZA TOWN** (*Ciutat d'Eivissa*) is easily the most attractive place on the island. Most people stay in rented apartments or small *hostales* which means there are fewer ugly hotels. Approach by sea and you'll get the full frontal effect of the old medieval walls rising like a natural extension of the rocky cliffs which protect the harbour. Within the walls, the ancient quarter is topped by a sturdy cathedral, whose illuminated, but often inaccurate, clock shines out across the harbour throughout the night.

Daylight hours are usually spent on the **beaches** at Ses Salines and Es Cavellet or the nearer (but not so nice) Figueretes. In summer, the streets are packed with people exploring the whitewashed, warren-like port area, where many of the fashionable boutiques stay open until 2am in summer, and stalls line the pavements, selling everything from jewellery and sarongs to Ibiza-mix CDs. **Bars** stay open until 4am or later, and afterwards the action moves to the **clubs** until daylight, and for the serious hedonists, there are yet more after-hours bar-clubs. As a break from the stress of sunbathing and the simple pleasures of wandering the streets, there are a couple of modest museums and fancy modern art galleries with prices that will amaze you even if the displays don't.

Arrival, information and orientation

Ibiza's international **airport** is situated 6km southwest of Ibiza Town. In the airport, the efficient **turisme** (May–Sept daily 10am–midnight) can provide maps and lists of the island's accommodation as well as details of vehicle rental. Several car rental firms have desks in the Arrivals lounge too (see "Listings", p.950). From the airport you can take a bus (hourly 7.30am–10.30pm; €1.10, or a taxi (€10.20), into Ibiza Town.

Ibiza Town has two **ferry terminals**: one near the foot of Avgda. Sta Eulària for local boats along the Ibiza coast and to Formentera, and the other on Passeig des Moll for the Spanish mainland and Mallorca.

The waterfront is just a stone's throw from the **lower town** – the old port area – which divides into two quarters, La Marina and Sa Penya. From here, it's a brief walk straight ahead to the walls of the **Dalt Vila**, literally "High Town". The unattractive, concrete-clad **new town** is round to the west, beyond the Passeig Vara de Rey. The **bus station** is in the new town on Avgda. Isidor Macabich, but most services – including those from the airport – pass close to the harbour front.

Ibiza's main **turisme** is on the harbour front on Passeig des Moll (June–Sept Mon–Fri 8.30am–2.30pm & 5–7pm, Sat 9.30am–1.30pm; Oct–May Mon–Fri 8.30am–2.30pm; ☎971 301 900).

Talamanca ▲   ▲ Talamanca & ❶

Plaça de Toros

0 Metres 100

MEDITERRANEAN SEA

Ferries:
local & to
Formentera

Port d'Eivissa

Estació
Marítim

Ferries:
mainland &
inter-island

N

PASSEIG DES MOLL

LA MARINA

SA PENYA

BARTOLOMEU DE ROSELLÓ

Teatro
Pereira

Mercat ❶

Baluard de
Sant Joan

Portal de
ses Taules

Museu
d'Art
Contemporani

Baluard de
Santa Llúcia

Sant
Domingo

**RESTAURANTS &
TAPAS BARS**

La Brasa	I
C'an Alfredo	F
C'an Costa	C
Croissant Show	H
Macao	D
Madagascar	G
La Marina	B
El Olivio	J
Los Pasajeros	E
Sa Torreta	K
La Victoria	A

Baluard des
Portal Nou

Seminari

DALT VILA

Museu
d'Arqueològic

Baluard de
Sant Jaume

Catedral

Ajuntament

Baluard de
Santa Tecla

ACCOMMODATION

Hostal Bimbi	12
Hostal Residencia Juanito	4
Hostal Residencia Las Nieves	5
Hotel Residencia Montesol	3
Ocean Drive	1
Hostal Residencia Parque	8
Hostal El Puerto	2
Apartamentos Roselló	11
Hostal Residencia Sol y Brisa	6
La Torre del Canónigo	10
Casa de Huéspedes Vara de Rey	7
Hostal Residencia La Ventana	9

Baluard de
Sant Bernat

Baluard
de Sant Jordi

ES SOTO

IBIZA TOWN

▼ ❶ & ❷

Accommodation

Most of the **budget accommodation** is in the lower town within easy striking distance of the waterfront, and half a dozen establishments are clustered in
the mundane side streets around the Passeig de Vara de Rey. If you're confident
with Spanish telephones, it's obviously easier to phone around, but fortunately the town is small and compact enough to make finding a place on foot perfectly feasible. Even if you stay to the west of the centre in Figueretes, you're
not that far removed from the action. The turisme has a comprehensive list of
Ibiza Town accommodation – indeed they have lists that cover the whole island
– with details of **hotels** and **hostales** as well as **apartments** for stays of a week
or more, but remember that in the height of the season last-minute vacancies
are very hard to come by. If you haven't booked ahead, you may well be
reduced to one of the island's four **campsites**, two of which are in the vicinity of Santa Eulària des Riu and two are close to Sant Antoni.

Hostal Bimbi c/Ramón Munaner 55, Figueretes ☎971 305 396, ⓕ971 305 396. Comfortable family-run *hostal*, just above Figueretes beach and a ten-minute walk from the centre of Ibiza Town. Popular with backpackers, the nineteen rooms – singles, doubles and triples – are all tastefully decorated and kept spotlessly clean. Open Easter–October only. ❸

Hostal Residencia Juanito & **Hostal Residencia Las Nieves**, c/Joan d'Austria 18 ☎971 315 822. These two *hostales* have clean rooms, some en suite. Same management and prices for both. Two blocks north of the Passeig de Vara de Rey. ❸

Hotel Residencia Montesol, Passeig de Vara de Rey 2 ☎971 310 161. Set on the corner of the Vara de Rey, looking across to the marina, this established hotel offers decidedly old-fashioned but very central accommodation. All rooms are air-conditioned and have bath, TV and telephone. ❻

Ocean Drive Port d'Eivissa ☎ 971 661 738, ⓕ971 312 228, ⓦwww.oceandrive.de. Commanding a fine position overlooking the north side of the harbour and a short stumble from Talamanca beach, the clubs Pacha and El Divino. Art Deco-inspired decor, rooms (air-conditioned) here are all surprisingly reasonable in low season, when doubles are priced from €90. ❽

Hostal Residencia Parque, Caieta Soler s/n ☎971 301 358. Modern *hostal* overlooking a pleasant square, with its own café-bar. Very good value single rooms, but some doubles are a little on the small side. ❻

Hostal El Puerto, c/Carles III 22 ☎971 313 827, ⓕ971 317452. Motel-style modern block, with choice of either hotel rooms or spacious apartments. Somewhat soulless twin bedrooms are at least well equipped with full cooking facilities, televisions and many have big sun terraces. ❽

Apartamentos Roselló c/General Juli Cirer i Vela, Puig des Molins ☎ & ⓕ971 302 790. Exceptionally located apartments, positioned right above the Mediterranean, but just five minutes' walk from Figueretes beach and Ibiza Town. Very tranquil, comfortable accommodation, with simply decorated living areas – most have wonderful sun terraces. Tricky to find, but best reached through the tunnel (*el túnel*) behind Dalt Vila. ❺

Hostal Residencia Sol y Brisa, Bartomeu Vicente Ramón 15 ☎971 310 818. Family-run *hostal* with small, very clean and fairly comfortable rooms close to the port area, though it can be a little noisy at night. Shared bathrooms. ❸

La Torre del Canónigo Carrer Major 8, Dalt Vila ☎ 971 303 884, ⓕ 971 307 843, ⓔhotelcanonigo@ ctv.es. Stupendous apartment-hotel, magnificently located next to the Cathedral in Dalt Vila. The rooms – all are suite size – are much more spacious than most luxury hotels in Ibiza Town and also the best appointed, fitted with air-conditioning, satellite TV, video and private Jacuzzi, with either harbour or city views. The most extravagantly luxurious address in the island, but also good value considering the exceptional quality of accommodation. No restaurant, but breakfast available. Open April–Nov & New Year. ❾

Casa de Huéspedes Vara de Rey, Passeig de Vara de Rey 7 ☎971 301 376. Set on the third floor of an old building, this clean and friendly guesthouse offers reasonably priced rooms with fans, some decorated with original driftwood sculptures. Good, central location. ❹

Hostal Residencia La Ventana, Sa Carrossa 13 ☎971 390 857, ⓕ971 390 145. High-quality accommodation inside the walls of Dalt Vila, where all rooms, though smallish for the price, come with four poster beds. Immaculately furnished with Asian fabrics, with superb views of the old city from the terraces. Has a stylish, outdoor restaurant and all mod cons. ❽

The Town

The city's stone walls reach a dramatic climax at the imposing main entrance, the **Portal de ses Taules**, a triple gateway designed to withstand the heaviest artillery barrage. Inside this monumental entrance you enter a UNESCO world heritage site – the entire historic enclave of Dalt Vila was bestowed the honour in December 1999. Just beyond the main gate is the Plaça de Vila, packed with restaurants and cafés. Here too, above the arch of the Portal de ses Taules, is the **Museu d'Art Contemporani** (summer Tues–Fri 10am–2pm & 5–8pm, Sat 10am–2pm; winter Tues–Fri 10am–2pm & 4–6pm, Sat 10am–1.30pm; €2.40); the large stone premises house good contemporary art exhibitions and cultural events.

Heading east uphill along Sa Carrossa, you'll pass a strip of fine restaurants, and have easy access to the top of the walls, which provide great views down over the town. You'll soon reach c/General Balanzat, where the sixteenth-century church of **Sant Domingo** (also known as the Església de Sant Pere) stands next to its former monastery, converted in 1838 into the *ajuntament*, which overlooks the pretty, palm-lined Plaça d'Espanya. Across the square a long tunnel leads through the walls; a five-minute walk around their exterior will take you back into the old town at the Baluard de Santa Tecla above Plaça de la Catedral.

Some 90m above sea level, the site of the **Catedral** (Tues–Sun: June–Sept 9am–4pm; Oct–May 10am–2pm; free) has been a place of worship for over 2000 years. Originally a Carthaginian temple graced this pivotal position above the harbour, then a Roman replacement was constructed, dedicated to the god Mercury, and later a mosque. Today's thirteenth-century cathedral is pleasingly austere, its sombre, sturdy Gothic lines supported by giant buttresses. Inside, the decor is far less attractive: whitewashed throughout, with somewhat trite Baroque embellishments. A plaque commemorates the massacre of over a hundred churchmen, soldiers and ordinary islanders at the hands of anarchists during the Civil War. The cathedral's **museum** is closed for renovation at the time of writing but is scheduled to reopen in late 2002 with displays of ecclesiastical regalia: bishops' mitres, sandals, gloves, cloaks and so on.

Across the square is the **Museu Arqueològic d'Eivissa i Formentera** (April–Sept Tues–Sat 10am–2pm & 5pm–8pm, Sun 10am–2pm; Oct–March Tues–Sat 10am–1pm & 4pm–6pm, Sun 10am–2pm; €1.80 with a collection of local archeological finds. The majority of the objects on display are from Phoenician and Carthaginian (Punic) sites, but there are also some bones from Formentera that date back to 1600 BC, and various Arab and Roman curiosities. If this whets your appetite, check with the turisme to see if the museum on Via Romana, on the slopes of Puig des Molins – a hill just west of Dalt Vila – has reopened, as this contains many finds from a huge Punic necropolis that was excavated here. Among the objects unearthed were some decorative terracotta pieces, clay figurines, amphoras and amulets depicting Egyptian gods. Ibiza, the sacred island of the goddess Tanit, functioned as a A-list burial site, with wealthy Carthaginians paying by special minted currency for the shipment of their bodies to the island upon death, in anticipation of a fast-track passage to heaven.

Outside the walls

Not quite as grand, nor as ancient as the Dalt Vila, the **Sa Penya** quarter of the lower town snuggles between the harbour and the ramparts, a maze of raked passages and narrow streets crimped by balconied, whitewashed houses. Here, especially along the waterside promenade and c/d'Enmig, the evening *passeig* reaches its exuberant peak and everyone – local and visitor alike – gravitates towards the bars and restaurants. This is where many of the shops are too, occupying almost every doorway that isn't a bar.

Finally, and further to the west, the **new town** is generally of less interest, but there's activity here as well, centred on the boulevard-like Passeig de Vara de Rey and the leafy, traffic-free Plaça des Parc just to the south. Both places have scores of cafés and restaurants and are popular meeting places.

Eating

Ibiza Town has plenty of **cafés** and **restaurants** to cater for the crowds. Many of the pricier places are up in Dalt Vila – mostly on Plaça de Vila and Sa Carrossa – or down by the waterfront, while the less expensive establishments are dotted round the lower town in between. Opening hours are fairly elastic, with many places staying open from the morning until very late at night. For an **early breakfast**, head for *Madagascar*, on Plaça des Parc, or the *Croissant Show* on Plaça de sa Constitució.

If you plan to prepare your own meal, or want to gather ingredients for a picnic, be warned that the covered **market** in Plaça de sa Constitució sells vastly overpriced fruit and vegetables, so you're better heading to the Supermercado Spar, on the east side of Plaça des Parc, or the SYP store at the southern end of Avgda. d'Ignasi Wallis.

Restaurants

C'an Alfredo, Passeig de Vara de Rey ☎971 311 274. Classy restaurant catering for any wallet, with main courses from €5–15. International dishes set the tone, but there are Balearic specialities too, and the seafood is outstanding.

La Brasa, c/Pere Sala 3, ☎971 301 202. Elegant Mediterranean restaurant with a delightful garden terrace and a simple, but pretty pricey, fish and meat-based menu. Service manages to be relaxed and efficient.

C'an Costa, c/Crue 19 ☎971 310 866. Smoky, moderately priced restaurant in the lower town serving good, fresh Spanish dishes, plus plenty of hearty Ibizan specials. Closed Sun.

Macao, Paseig des Moll s/n ☎971 314 707. Set at the extreme eastern end of the port, this smart Italian restaurant is very popular with the celebrity crowd and offers a suprisingly reasonably priced menu with fine fresh pasta.

La Marina c/Barcelona 7 ☎971 310 172. Venerable, top-notch seafood restaurant down by the harbour. On the pricey side, but a good place for a splurge.

El Olivio, Plaça de Vila. First-class international cuisine with prices to match; open until 1.30am.

Los Pasajeros, c/Vicent Soler s/n. First-floor restaurant that's one of the hippest places to dine, with unpretentious, plain decor and a tasty Spanish *menú* and cheap wine. A good place to find out what's happening, and open until 2am.

Sa Torreta Plaça de Vila s/n. ☎971 300 411. Excellent, expensive French-inspired menu and sublime, atmospheric setting inside the walled city. Closed Nov–March.

La Victoria, c/Riambau 1. ☎971 310 622. Popular and well-established Ibizan restaurant in the lower town, offering generous portions of basic but tasty local specialities – excellent value.

Drinking and nightlife

However good the restaurant scene in Ibiza Town, it's something of a sideshow compared with the bars and clubs which have made the island internationally famous – you come to Ibiza to party. Together they keep the place going pretty much twenty-four hours a day, and with money, mobility and stamina the night is yours, never mind the morning. The town's **bars** throng the streets of the lower town, where unsuspecting visitors are herded into terrace bars around Plaça de sa Tertulia by teams of hustlers and fleeced for as much as €6 for a beer. Better to start the night in Plaça des Parc in *Sunset* or *Madagascar,* where prices are more reasonable, and then head for the stylish bars of Sa Penya – *Bar Zuka* on c/de la Verge, *Base Bar* and *Rock Bar* at the eastern end of c/Garijo – all attract a seriously funky, clubby clientele. The gay scene is centred on c/de la Verge, perhaps the wildest street in the western Mediterranean, where dozens of bars, and myriad shops cater for an almost exclusively (male) gay crowd; *Caprichio* and *Teatro* are both fashionable spots, but the *Dôme* bar close by at c/d'Alfonso XII is the really *über*-hip gay destination bar. Meanwhile, **clubs** – some of the globe's most spectacular venues – are spread across the southern half of the island, but primarily in Sant Antoni, Sant Rafel, Platja d'en Bossa, and of course, Ibiza Town itself. It's actually quite easy to hop from one club to the other courtesy of the *Disco Bus* (nightly 0.30am–6.30am; €1.80 per journey; details from the tourist office). Neither is there much difficulty in finding out what's happening: each club employs PR people, who descend on Ibiza Town to parade through the streets in a competitive frenzy of night hype. Processions of stilt-walkers, silver- and gold-painted angels, devils and dwarfs strut through the streets, drumming up custom. Many of the happening bars also hand out free club entry tickets in return for your custom, which represent a significant saving. None of the clubs open until midnight, but there again they do carry on until at least 7am. Most have a policy of a free drink with the admission price and the majority accept credit cards.

For **live music**, the prime spot is *Teatro Pereira*, c/Comte de Rosselló 3, housed in the old municipal theatre near the Passeig de Vara de Rey. This splendid old building, has a great atmosphere and showcases live acts each night – blues, R&B, reggae, rock and jazz. Open 8pm–5am all year, it has no admission fee but the drinks are expensive.

Clubs

Amnesia , Ibiza Town/Sant Antoni road, km6 ☎971 198 041, ⓦwww.amnesiaibiza.com. Cavernous, 5000-capacity club, historically the island's most innovative venue, where resident DJs helped kickstart the acid house revolution. Today the club is split in two halves: a dark, moody club ideal for trance and hard house and an airy, verdant atrium-topped terrace where the music has more of a Balearic flavour. Booked by British promoters Cream and God's Kitchen in the summer, but also showcases the club's own foam parties. Daily mid-June to end-September. Admission: €30–42; drinks from €5.40.

Anfora , c/Sant Carles 7, Dalt Vila ☎971 302 893. Set in the heart of Dalt Vila, this is a men-only gay club built into a natural cave in the old town. Attracts a very international, mixed-age crowd with a combination of hard house and camp anthems. Daily May to late-September. Admission around €15.

El Divino , Port d'Eivissa ☎971 190 176, ⓦwww.eldivino-ibiza.com. Across the bay from La Marina, jutting into the harbour waters with superb views of the marina and Ibiza Town from its luxuriant outdoor terrace. Comparatively small – with a capacity of 1000 – El Divino attracts an older, moneyed crowd with garage and US house mixes. Daily mid-June to late-September. Admission €30–45; drinks from €6.

Pacha , Avgda. 8 d'Agost ☎971 313 600, ⓦwww.pacha.com. On the edge of Ibiza Town, around the marina on the Santa Eulària road. The *grand dame* of the Ibiza clubs, set superbly in a converted white farmhouse, with house and garage in the main room, a techno chamber, a funky room and a salsa salon. Beautiful terrace overlooks the city, there's also a fine restaurant and a new sushi bar. Used by the UK club Ministry of Sound in the summer season. Daily April–end-Sept; Oct–March weekends only. Admission: €30–42; drinks from €6.

Privilege , off the Ibiza Town/Sant Antoni de Portmany road at Sant Rafel ☎971 198 160, ⓦwww.privilege-ibiza.com. Formerly known as Ku, this club was the forerunner of the Ibiza scene and is the sole reason why some people come to the island. High up in the hills, this huge, glass-sided and -roofed building has splendid views over the interior. Inside, the club resembles a movie set, with a huge swimming pool in the centre of the dance floor, fountains, fourteen bars, a capacity of around 10,000, an outdoor terrace garden, a chill-out dome, a café and a main room bedecked with futuristic scaffolding in silver, black and gold. Home to Manumission and Renaissance and used by MTV in the 2001 summer season. Daily mid-June to late September, midnight–7am, and later on special party nights. Admission: €30–48; drinks from €6.

Space Platja d'en Bossa ⓦwww.space-ibiza.com. Uniquely, this vast club-cum-bunker on the beach is essentially a day club, (opening its doors around 9am) though it's also now starting to promote some night-time dance sessions. Split into two distinct parts: a shadowy, moody interior with pounding techno and trance, and a delightful open-air terrace where DJs play Balearic, and funky house mixes. The most cosmopolitan clubbing crowd in Ibiza gathers for the legendary Sunday session, extended in recent years into a 22 hour carry-on-clubbing marathon. Only for the hardcore. Admission €30–48.

Listings

Airport information ☎971 302 200. The Iberia office is at Passeig de Vara de Rey 15 ☎971 302 580.

Car rental Avis ☎971 809 176; Atesa-Eurodollar ☎971 395 393; Hertz ☎971 809 178 – all at the airport.

Consulates Britain, Avgda. d'Isidor Macabich 45 ☎971 301 818 (Mon–Fri 9am–3pm); Netherlands, Via Punica 2B ☎971 300 450 (Mon–Fri 9am–1.30pm).

Ferries Mainland and Mallorca sailings with Trasmediterránea (☎971 315 050, www.trasmediterranea.es) and Baleària (☎971 971 314 005, www.balearia.com); local boats along the Ibiza coast and to Formentera operated by several companies, including Transmapi (☎971 310 711) and Umafisa (☎971 314 513).

Hospital Hospital Can Misses, on the way to the airport ☎971 397 000.

Internet access There are several places to go online in Ibiza Town, with two on Avgda. D'Ignasi Wallis alone, but the best is *Chill*, at Via Púnica 49 (☎971 399 736, ⏻ www.chillibiza.com, Mon–Sat 10am–midnight, Sun 5pm–midnight), where you'll find delicious, healthy snacks like bagels and salads.

Laundry The best place is Wash & Dry, Avgda. d'Espanya 53 where you can surf the web while waiting for your wash. Otherwise Masterclean, close to *Hostal El Puerto* on c/Felip II is efficient.

Moped rental Motos Valentín, Bartomeu Vicent Ramón 19 ☎971 310 822; Motosud, Avgda. d'Espanya s/n ☎971 302 442 – a 1km walk west of the centre.

Post office The main *Correu* is 1km from the centre of town at the eastern end of Avgda. d'Isidor Macabich (Mon–Fri 8.30am–2pm).

Around Ibiza Town: the beaches

There's sea and sand close to Ibiza Town at **Figueretes**, **Platja d'en Bossa** and **Talamanca**, but the first two of these are built-up continuations of the capital with over-exploited beaches, and only at the third is there any peace and quiet. All are accessible by short and inexpensive ferry rides from the terminal near the foot of Avinguda Santa Eulària.

Ses Salines and Es Cavallet

To the **south of Ibiza Town**, stretching from the airport to the sea, are thousands of acres of **salt flats**. Ibiza's history, and its powerful presence on ancient trade routes, was based on these salt fields (*salines*), a trade that was vital, above all, to the ancient Carthaginians. Indeed, salt remained an important economic resource until comparatively recently; the island's only rail line ran from the middle of the marshes to **La Canal**, a dock where an enormous container ship would arrive weekly to be loaded with the bright, pinky-white sea salt. Even now, though tourism brings in far more money and the rail line has been torn up, salt production continues.

There are two beaches around here and buses from Ibiza Town leave regularly for the more westerly, **SES SALINES**, whose fine white sand arcs around a bay, the crystal clear waters fringed by pines and dunes. The beach also has a handful of beach bars, with supremely cool chill-out sounds at *Sa Trincha* at the southern end of the sands. From Ses Salines, it's a brief walk around the rocks or along the paths that maze the sand dunes to **ES CAVALLET**, a quieter if broadly similar beach that's long been a favourite of gay visitors – the dunes behind the beach are a well-known cruising area. The southern ends of both beaches are reserved for nude sunbathing.

The east coast

Heading northeast from Ibiza Town, it's just 15km to **SANTA EULÀRIA DES RIU**, a somewhat bland little town pushed tight against the seashore and situated beside the only river in the Balearics. It does boast an attractive hilltop **church** however, a fortified whitewashed sixteenth-century construction with a beautifully shady, arched entrance porch. Just below the church the little ethnological **museum** (Mon–Fri 11am–1pm & 4–7pm) set in an ancient farmhouse, is not a wildly exciting affair, with a collection of old tools, ploughs and an olive press. There's nothing else to see in Santa Eulària, so it's best to press on to **SANT CARLES**, 7km to the north, an agreeable one-horse vil-

△ Sunset from Benirràs, Ibiza

lage. Here you can refuel at bar-café *Las Dalias*, just before you reach the village, where there's a "hippie market" every Saturday, or the legendary *Anita's* bar, opposite the whitewashed church which attracts islanders and resident bohemians in roughly equal proportion.

East of Sant Carles the road passes through burnt-red fields of olive, almond and carob trees to several almost untouched beaches. **CALA LLENYA**, 4km from Sant Carles, a 200m-wide sandy cove, with sparkling waters, a snack bar and shade and sunbeds for hire, is the nearest; it's popular with families. Tiny **CALA MASTELLA**, 2km farther north is a supremely peaceful spot, with a diminutive sandy beach, crystal clear sheltered, water and two simple fish restaurants, *Sa Seni*, and *Cala Mastella*, some 50m around the shoreline (both summer only). Just 1km to the north of Cala Mastella, **CALA BOIX** is another stunning sandy cove, a little larger and more exposed, where you'll find fine, moderately priced seafood at the *Restaurant La Noria* (☎971 335 397), which is open all year, and also spacious excellent-value rooms at the *Hostal Cala Boix* (☎971 335 224, ❸) on the cliffs above the shore. North of Cala Boix, the coastal road follows an exhilarating, serpentine route above the shore, through thick pine forests, via the lonely nudist beach of **AIGÜES BIANCAS** to **CALA DE SANT VICENT** where the developers have dumped huge concrete hotels on a once-breathtaking beach.

The North

From Cala de Sant Vicent it's a tortuous ascent up over the spine of the Serra de la Mala Costa, to the pretty hilltop village of **SANT JOAN**, home to a typically minimalist, whitewashed Ibizan village church, the *Eco Centre* internet caff, and very, cheap clean, rooms at the *hostal Can Pla Roig* (☎ & ☎971 333 012; ❷). There are more stunning beaches north of Sant Joan, especially remote **CALA D'EN SERRA**, a tiny, exquisite sandy cove, with turquoise waters perfect for snorkelling and a first-class *chiringuito* bar-café. From Sant Joan a road also wriggles through a beautiful, fertile valley, past olive-terraces down to **PORTINATX**, an inoffensive but somewhat banal resort, which sprawls around three bays, where you'll find the two-star *Hostal Cas Mallorqui* (☎971 333 082, ☎971 333 159; ❼), whose comfortable and commodious rooms overlook the resort's Es Port beach.

West of Sant Joan, 3km along the Sant Miguel road, there's a turn-off for **BENIRRÀS**, another beautiful cove, backed by high wooded cliffs and all but untouched except for a few unobtrusive villas and three beachside café-restaurants. Benirràs is Ibiza's premier hippie-centric beach – dozens gather here to burn herbs and pound drums to the setting sun, especially on Sundays. The next village to the west is **SANT MIQUEL**, where there's another fine hilltop church, and a number of simple tapas bars, try *Es Pi Ver* or *Bar March* for a simple inexpensive feed. The once astonishingly beautiful, almost fjord-like inlet, **PORT DE SANT MIQUEL**, 3km north of the village, has been badly mauled by the developers, – unenticing surroundings for the modest cave complex **Cova de Can Marça** (daily 11am–1.30pm & 3pm–5.30pm, guided tours every half-hour; €4.50), which is well signposted on the twisting road above the bay. The cave features some spectacular lighting effects, including a very kitsch artificial waterfall that cascades over fossil-rich rocks to a soundtrack of 1970s band Tangerine Dream. There's also an excellent **view** of the coastline from outside.

The west coast: Sant Antoni

For years unchallenged at the top of Europe's *costa hoolgania* league, **SANT ANTONI** is trying hard to shake off a tarnished, boozing'n'brawling image. The untidy, high-rise skyline remains as unappealing as ever, the nauseous pubs of the West End district haven't changed, but an attractive "sunset strip" of funky new chill-out bars, spread around the north end of the bay now provide a tranquil environment for a drink and a snack, and both the town's two clubs are superb. Virtually everyone in Sant Antoni is here on a package tour, with beds very hard to come by in high season, but try the helpful **turisme** (Mon–Fri 9.30am–8.30pm, Sat & Sun 9.30am–1pm; ☎971 343 363), at the beginning of the waterfront Passeig de ses Fonts, for information on **places to stay**. Reasonably priced, downtown options include *Hostal Residencia Roig*, c/Progres 44 (☎971 340 483; ❸), where all the rooms have good-sized bathrooms and pleasant pine furniture, and *Hotel Residencia Vedra*, c/De La Mar 7 (☎971 340 150, ℻971 342 656; April–Oct; ❹), a family-run affair with balconied bedrooms, some of which (on the upper floors) have sea views. Alternatively, there's a pricier-than-average **campsite**, *Camping San Antonio* (mobile only, ☎617 835 845); April–Oct), just outside town beside the main road to Ibiza Town. It occupies a surprisingly quiet and palm-shaded area, and comes equipped with a swimming pool, bar and laundry. Pitches cost €4.20, plus €4.20 per person, and there are also bungalows (❸).

There are plenty of **cafés** and restaurants to choose from, but you will find good global grub at the northern end of the sunset strip at the *Kasbah* (☎971 348 364) in Caló des Moro, and tasty Spanish food at *Rias Baixes*, c/d'Ignasi Riquer 4 (☎971 340 480) in the centre of the town. There are now a dozen or so groovy "sunset" bars, all offering prime views, but the best are still probably the veteran *Café del Mar* at the west end of c/Vara de Rey, the original chill-out bar, and *Mambo* just next door. A little further north from here, the spectacular new *Coastline* bar-restaurant is a striking new addition to the scene, with three pools and a huge sun terrace. San An has two huge **clubs**: *Es Paradis* (Ⓦwww.esparadisibiza.com) topped by a huge glass pyramid and *Eden* (Ⓦwww.edenibiza.com) which looks like a psychedelic mosque, complete with electric blue domes and minarets, both just off Avgda. Dr. Fleming in the centre of town. Both clubs are open May–October with entrance typically costing €24–33, and they book big-name DJs like Judge Jules and Ibiza's own Alfredo and DJ Gee.

To escape the town, **car rental** is available from Avis, down by the harbour on Passeig de la Mar (☎971 342 715), and from Ibiza-Betacar, just behind the waterfront on c/General Balanzat (☎971 345 068). **Bicycle rental** outlets include Autos Reco, c/Ramón i Cajal (☎971 340 388), a few minutes' walk from the harbour front on the east side of the town centre. Sant Antoni offers a wide range of **boat trips**, from glass-bottomed tours of the harbour and a shuttle service west across the bay to the undeveloped but busy, broad sandy beach of Cala Bassa, through to trips round the island. **Buses** leave for Ibiza Town every half-hour, four times daily to Santa Eulària and frequently to the southwest *calas* Vedella, Conta and Tarida. **Timetables** are available at the turisme, all buses leave from the Passeig de la Mar.

Around Sant Antoni

Heading **north** out of Sant Antoni, you'll find another attractive beach, and glorious countryside within easy striking distance. From here the road climbs steeply through thick aromatic pine forests, passing a turn–off, 3km from Sant Antoni, to the small cove of **CALA SALADA**, where the beach is of fine sand and the sea excellent for swimming. There's a small and cheerful restaurant here, a beach bar and epic sunsets. Further north, and inland, the sleepy hamlet of **SANTA AGNÉS DE CORONA** drapes over a hillside surrounded by picturesque fields dotted with hundreds of almond and fruit trees. The village has a wonderful whitewashed church, and a superb village bar, *Can Cosmi*, which serves excellent tapas and the finest tortilla in Ibiza. From the village, a rough but paved country road continues east across the hilly interior of the island via diminutive Sant Mateu to Sant Miquel (see p.953).

South of Sant Antoni de Portmany is the ugly, sprawling package ghetto zone known as "San An bay" which stretches to the small resort of Port des Torrent, but travel a few kilometres further and there are several exquisite coves. Of the first two beaches, sheltered **CALA BASSA** gets packed with holidaying families in high season but it does have a campsite (☎971 344 599), while the more exposed, blue flag beach of **CALA CONTA** is less crowded, with three simple fish restaurants above the shore and pole postion for sunsets over the ocean. The most beguiling beach in the Balearics, **CALA D'HORT**, is in the extreme southwest of the island, with a lovely quiet sand-and-pebble shoreline plus three good, moderately priced seafood restaurants. What really sets the beach apart however are the mesmeric vistas of **Es Vedrà**, a canine tooth of rock stabbing through the bay just offshore. The jagged, 378-metre-high islet is revered by islanders and island hippies alike, and starred in the film *South Pacific* as the mysterious island of Bali Hai.

Sant Antoni de Portmany to Ibiza Town

It's just 15km from Sant Antoni de Portmany to Ibiza Town east along the main road, but you can detour taking the southern, more scenic route via **SANT JOSEP**, a pretty village with a magnificently minimalist village church, and a selection of good places to stop for a drink or a snack; *El Destino* (☎971 800 341), opposite the church, serves superb healthy dishes, with plenty of choice for vegetarians. Some 5km further east from Sant Josep, a side road turns south through fields of melons and grapes to **CALA JONDAL**, a popular spot where you can get delicious seafood and juices at the bar *Tropicana* or dance under the stars at the *Jockey Club* (midnight–7am, €12), where leading Ibizan DJs like Pippi and Reche play soulful house and garage throughout the summer months – Sundays are busiest. The drawback is the beach – an uncomfortable, pebbly affair – though recent dollops of imported sand have changed matters somewhat, while the shallow waters make it safe for swimmers.

Formentera

Just eleven nautical miles south of Ibiza Town, **FORMENTERA** (population 5600) is the smallest of the inhabited Balearics. It's actually two small islets joined together by a narrow sandy isthmus and is just 20km long from east to west. It's a short ferry crossing from Ibiza, but strong currents ensure that it's slow – around an hour – and can be rough. Return fares are about €14; €23 on the hydrofoil, which is quicker (35 min) but less enjoyable. There are usually rival sailings to choose from: check the return times before deciding.

Formentera's history more or less parallels that of Ibiza, though for nearly three hundred years – from the early fifteenth century to the end of the seventeenth – it was left uninhabited for lack of water and fear of Turkish pirate raids. Under the Romans it had been an agricultural centre (some historians think its name could derive from *frumentaria*, "granary"), and when repopulated in 1697 the island was again divided up for cultivation. It never regained its original level of productivity, however, and nowadays is largely barren, the few crops having to be protected, as on Menorca, against the lashing of winter winds. Indeed, most of the island is now covered in rosemary, growing wild everywhere, and crawling with thousands of brilliant green lizards – the **Ibiza wall lizard** (*Podarcis pityusensis*) which flourishes in arid scrubland.

Modern income is derived from tourism (especially German, Italian and British), taking advantage of some of Spain's longest, whitest and least-crowded beaches. The shortage of freshwater continues to keep development within acceptable limits – there are only around forty *hostales* and hotels on the whole island – and for the most part visitors here are seeking escape with little in the way of sophistication. Nevertheless, Formentera has become increasingly popular with day-trippers from neighbouring Ibiza, and is certainly not the "unspoilt paradise" it once was, especially in high season. Nude sunbathing is tolerated – indeed the norm – just about everywhere.

Arrival, information and accommodation

There is a basic **bus** service from the **port of arrival**, La Savina, but buses connect only the settlements that string out along the main island road, plus a few of the larger resorts, leaving you long, hot walks to any of the more isolated beaches. **Taxis** are cheap and are the most popular form of island transport. You'll find ranks at La Savina, Sant Francesc and Es Pujols (see box, p.948). Fares are about €7.20 for 5km but as the distances involved are small, the cost is never extortionate. It's best to book a taxi the day before you need it in August. For **car rental**, reckon on €36 per day (see box, p.948). **Renting a bicycle** is a popular option too; apart from some of its coastal extremities, the island is extremely flat. You'll find a strip of bike rental places at La Savina by the ferry dock, and in Es Pujols. A day's hire will set you back around €4.50.

The island's main **turisme** (Mon–Fri 10am–2pm & 5–7pm, Sat 10am–2pm; ☎971 322 057), is at the ferry port in La Savina, and can provide information on all aspects of the island, including accommodation. If you're staying on the island, consider buying the IGN 1:25,000 **maps** which show the dirt tracks as well as the tarmac roads.

Accommodation

Most visitors treat Formentera as a **day-trip** from Ibiza, and if you want to be one of the few who **stay** you'd be well advised to make an advance reservation – the bulk of the island's limited supply of beds is snapped up early by the tour operators. Bear in mind also that almost all the hotels and *hostales* close down for the winter – from November to March. Neither does Formentera have a campsite and although people do doss down behind the beaches, it's not encouraged and has, in the past, damaged the delicate ecology of the dunes.

Hostal Bellavista, Passeig de la Marina s/n, La Savina ☎ & ⓕ 971 322 255 Large formal hotel, next to the harbour, with forty rooms all with sea view. There's a waterside restaurant and terrace bar here as well. Open all year. ⑥

Hostal Residencia Illes Pitiüses Sant Ferran ☎ 971 328 189, ⓕ 971 328 017, ⑩ hostalillespitiuses@cempresarial.com. Twenty-six very comfortable, tasteful rooms, all equipped with satellite TV and air-conditioning. On the main road, with a café-restaurant downstairs. Open all year. ⑤

Hostal Residencia Mar Blau Caló de Sant Agustí ☎ & ⓕ 971 327 030. Small attractive hotel next to a tiny fishing harbour a short stroll from Ses Platgetes beach. The bright modern rooms all have panoramic sea views, and there are also good apartments next door run by the same owners. April–Oct only. ⑥

Hostal Residencia Mayans, Es Pujols ☎ & ⓕ 971 328 724. Pleasant, one-star hostal, 100m from the beach, in a quiet spot away from the main resort area. The 23 modern, pleasantly decorated rooms either with sea or island views all have private bathrooms. There's a terrace café downstairs. Open April–Oct. ⑤

Hostal La Savina, La Savina ☎ & ⓕ 971 322 279. Large blue and white hostal about 50m from the harbour front on the road out of town. Open mid-April to Oct. ⑤

Pensión Bon Sol, Sant Ferran ☎ 971 328 882. Eight simple but clean and fairly spacious rooms, with shared bathrooms. Just about the cheapest accommodation in Formentera. ⑥

Around the island

Sailing out of Ibiza Town harbour, there's a stupendous view of the citadel astride its cliff and soon the sand-fringed islets which herald Formentera hove into view – one of the tiniest being the Illa d'es Penjats ("Hanged Men's Island"), once the last stop for Ibiza's criminals. Ferries and hydrofoils then proceed to Formentera's one and only ferry dock at **LA SAVINA**. There's nothing much to the place, apart from a taxi rank and rows of rental cars, bicycles and mopeds, all racked up for a quick getaway, and a couple of places to stay. The island capital, **SANT FRANCESC XAVIER** is a few kilometres inland from the port and is easily reached on foot or by bike, bus or taxi if you're not planning to rent a vehicle. The town is something of a crossroads and serves as the island's commercial and shopping centre with restaurants, cafés, bars, banks, supermarkets, a health-food shop, a pharmacist and open-air markets – but it's an insignificant place all the same, its only real sight being the mighty fortified **church**, now stripped of its defensive cannons, sitting in a large square at the top of the town.

Heading east from the capital, it's just 3km along the main island road to tiny **SANT FERRAN**, the island's second town and home to *Pepe*, c/Major, a long-established and laid-back bar-cum-restaurant, that's something of an island institution. You can also stay here, though most rooms are block booked by tour operators in high season.

From Sant Ferran, a side road leads to the north coast at **ES PUJOLS**, Formentera's largest resort development – though it's still tiny, and tame by mainland (and Mallorcan) standards. Originally a fishing village, the resort centres on two smallish sandy beaches which nestle in amongst craggy rocks, backed by pines. The islet-studded bay is very pretty, the sand is bright white and the sea is clear and shallow, but behind the shore lurk tasteless hotels, which will probably prompt an early departure. If you do hang around, there's windsurfing and other water sports, plenty of good seafood restaurants and some late-night bars.

Northwest of Es Pujols, the **Es Trucadors peninsula** pokes a flat and sandy finger out towards Ibiza. There are more long and slender beaches here – notably **Platja de ses Illetes** on the west shore – and at the peninsula's end, across a narrow channel, lies the uninhabited island of **S'Espalmador**.

Back in Sant Ferran, the main island road travels east, passing the rough, dirt turnings which twist south through arable farmland and acres of sand dunes to the middle portion of the **Platja de Migjorn**, whose fine white sands and turquoise waters extend for some 5km. There's some development at either end of the beach – in the west at **Es Ca Mari** and to the east around the equally unenticing **Maryland** – but the centre remains largely untouched and it's here in the dunes you'll find the superb *Blue Bar*, one of the finest beach cafés in the Balearics, with languid, chill-out tunes and tasty snacks.

Beyond the Maryland turning, the main road leaves the flatlands to snake up through pine forests, passing a first-rate restaurant, *El Mirador* (⊕971 327 037) – where the views of Formentera are exceptional – as it skirts the northern flanks of **La Mola**, at 192m the island's highest point. Soon you reach the drowsy little town of El Pilar, where the road straightens for the final 2km

---

Formentera: useful numbers

Car rental Autos Betacar ⊕971 322 031; Avis ⊕971 322 123; Hertz ⊕971 322 242.

Emergencies For the police, fire brigade or an ambulance call ⊕112.

Ferries Umafisa ⊕971 323 007; Transmapi ⊕971 322 703; Trasmediterrànea ⊕971 315 050.

Post office Plaça de sa Constitució 1, Sant Francesc.

Taxis Taxis La Savina ⊕971 328 016; Taxis Sant Francesc ⊕971 322 243; Taxis Es Pujols ⊕971 322 016.

dash to the **Far de La Mola** (lighthouse), which stands on the cliffs high above the blueness of the ocean. It was here that Jules Verne was inspired to write his *Journey Round the Solar System* as he gazed into the clear night sky – hence the large stone block with the bronze plaque. Before you head back, you can soak up the scene at the tiny bar-café, *Es Puig*, next to the lighthouse, where they serve up tremendous plates of cheese and ham.

Eating and drinking

Es Pujols, the principal resort, has a plethora of seafront **bars and restaurants**, with menus to suit most wallets, and excellent seafood on offer. Good options include the busy little *Bar Pupit*, and *Can Vent*, which serves great seafood. For breakfast, try the café at *Hostal Residencia Mayans*. Here also is where you'll find the island's **nightlife**, with a strip of late bars including the trendy *Moon Bar* and two small clubs: *Tipik* and *Magoo*. Elsewhere on the island, you'll find the best pizza at the Italian-owned *Es Pla* (☎971 322 903) by the turning for Cala Saona, while *Restaurant Rafalet* (☎971 327 077), in Caló de Sant Agustí, boasts a lovely seafront setting for delicous fish and seafood. Sant Ferran has several good bars around its plaza where you can enjoy a languid drink. Most of Formentera's *hostales* serve meals, or you can get your own supplies from the market and supermarket in Sant Francesc.

Mallorca

Few Mediterranean holiday spots are as often and as unfairly maligned as **MALLORCA**. The island is commonly perceived as little more than sun, sex, booze and high-rise hotels – so much so that there's a long-standing Spanish joke about a mythical fifth Balearic island called *Majorca* (the English spelling), inhabited by an estimated eight million tourists a year. However, this image, spawned by the helter-skelter development of the 1960s, takes no account of Mallorca's beguiling diversity. It's true that there are sections of coast where high-rise hotels and shopping centres are continuous, wedged beside and upon one another and broken only by a dual carriageway down to more of the same. But the spread of development, even after 50 years, is surprisingly limited, essentially confined to the Badia de Palma (Bay of Palma), a thirty-kilometre strip flanking the island capital, and a handful of mega-resorts notching the east coast. Elsewhere, things are very different. **Palma** itself, the Balearics' one real city, is a bustling, historic place whose grand mansions and magnificent Gothic cathedral defy the expectations of many visitors. And so does the northwest coast, where the rearing peaks of the rugged **Serra de Tramuntana** harbour beautiful cove beaches, a pair of intriguing monasteries at Valldemossa and Lluc, and a string of delightful old towns – Deià, Sóller and Pollença – as well as the picturesque villages of Biniaraix and Fornalutx. There's a startling variety and physical beauty to the land, too, which, along with the mildness of the climate, has drawn tourists to visit and well-heeled expatriates to settle here since the nineteenth century, including artists and writers of many descriptions, from Robert Graves to Roger McGough.

Mallorca practicalities

Palma, the site of the only airport and the island's principal ferry port, is, for all the aesthetic disasters of its bay, an excellent initial base, especially as it's the hub of an extensive public transport system, with bus services linking the capital to all of Mallorca's principal settlements. There are even a couple of train lines running out of Palma – one, a beautiful ride up through the mountains to Sóller (see p.960), is an attraction in itself – while by car Palma is within three hours' drive of the island's furthest corner. When you feel you've exhausted Palma's possibilities, your best bet is to move across to the **Serra de Tramuntana** for a few days in the mountains, preferably working your way up the coast to the handsome town of **Pollença** – and perhaps squeezing in a visit to the bird-rich marshlands of the **Parc Natural de S'Albufera** as well.

The main constraint for travellers is **accommodation**. From mid-June to mid-September rooms are in short supply and, if you do go at this time, you're well advised to make a reservation several months in advance or to book a package. Out of season, things ease up and you can idle round, staying pretty much where you want. Bear in mind also that five of Mallorca's **monasteries** rent out renovated cells at exceptionally inexpensive rates – reckon on €18–24 per double room per night. The Monastir de Nostra Senyora at Lluc (see p.964) and the Ermita de Nostra Senyora del Puig outside Pollença (see p.965) are both reachable via public transport, while those with their own transport could also try the Ermita de Sant Salvador at Felanitx (℡971 827 282), the very basic

Ermita de Nostra Sra. de Bonany at Petra (℡971 561 101), and the rather more comfortable Ermita de Nostra Sra. de Cura in Algaida Randa (℡971 120 260).

Palma

In 1983 **PALMA** became the capital of one of Spain's newly established autonomous regions, the Balearic Islands, and since then it's shed the dusty provincialism of yesteryear, developing into a go-ahead and cosmopolitan commercial hub of 325,000 people. The new self-confidence is plain to see in the city centre, a vibrant and urbane place which is akin to the big cities of the Spanish mainland – and a world away from the heaving tourist enclaves of the surrounding bay. There's still a long way to go – much of suburban Palma remains obdurately dull and somewhat dilapidated – but the centre now presents a splendid ensemble of lively shopping areas, mazy lanes and refurbished old buildings, all enclosed by what remains of the old city walls and their replacement boulevards. This geography encourages downtown Palma to look into itself and away from the sea, even though its **harbour** – now quarantined by the main highway – has always been the city's economic lifeline. Indeed, arriving here by sea, Palma is still beautiful and impressive, with the grand bulk of the cathedral towering above the old town and the remnants of the medieval walls. In these are encapsulated much of the city's and island's history: Moorish control from the ninth to the thirteenth century, reconquest by Jaume I of Aragón and a meteoric rise to wealth and prominence in the fifteenth century as the main port of call between Europe and Africa.

Arrival and information

Mallorca's ultramodern international **airport** is 11km east of Palma, immediately behind the resort of Ca'n Pastilla. It has one enormous terminal, which handles both scheduled and charter flights with separate floors for Arrivals and Departures. The Arrivals floor has 24-hour **ATMs**, **car rental** and **currency exchange** facilities as well as a provincial **turisme** (Mon–Sat 9am–2pm & 3–8pm, Sun 9am–2pm), which has lists of hotels and *hostales*, public transport timetables, taxi rates, maps and general island information. The turisme will not, however, help arrange **accommodation** and neither will most of the package-tour travel agents scattered around the Arrivals hall. An exception is Prima Travel (℡971 789 322), who have a good selection of places, or you can, of course telephone hotels and *hostales* direct.

The airport is linked to the city and the Bay of Palma resorts by a busy highway (*autopista*), which shadows the shoreline from S'Arenal in the east to Magaluf in the west. The least expensive way to reach Palma from the airport is by **bus** #17 (daily, every 15min from 6am to 9.30pm & every 30min 9.30pm–1.30am; €1.80). This leaves from the main entrance of the terminal building just behind the taxi rank, and goes to Plaça Espanya, on the north side of the city centre. A **taxi** from the airport to the city centre will set you back about €12; taxi rates are controlled and a list of island-wide destinations along with the cost of the taxi fare is displayed in the window of the tourist office.

Palma **ferry terminal** is about 4km west of the city centre. There are two passenger terminals, about 160m apart. Bus #1 runs from Terminal 2 to the centre (Mon–Sat 8am to 9pm; reduced service on Sun and holidays; €1.05), pausing at Plaça de la Reina and Plaça Rei Joan Carles I, before continuing on to Plaça Espanya. There's also a taxi rank outside the terminal building.

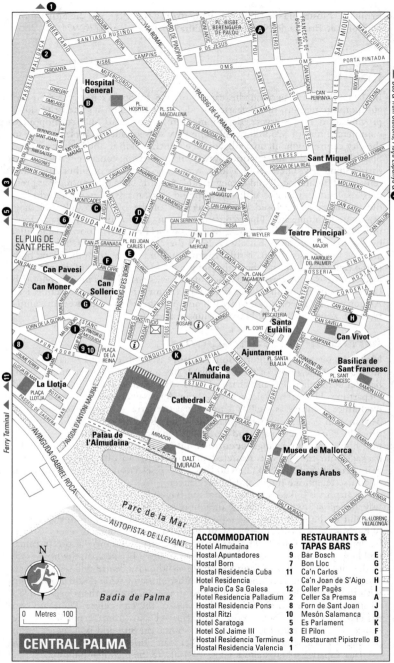

ACCOMMODATION

Hotel Almudaina	6
Hostal Apuntadores	9
Hostal Born	7
Hostal Residencia Cuba	11
Hotel Residencia Palacio Ca Sa Galesa	12
Hotel Residencia Palladium	2
Hostal Residencia Pons	8
Hostal Ritzi	10
Hotel Saratoga	5
Hotel Sol Jaime III	3
Hostal Residencia Terminus	4
Hostal Residencia Valencia	1

RESTAURANTS & TAPAS BARS

Bar Bosch	E
Bon Lloc	G
Ca'n Carlos	C
Ca'n Joan de S'Aigo	H
Celler Pagès	I
Celler Sa Premsa	A
Forn de Sant Joan	J
Mesón Salamanca	D
Es Parlament	K
El Pilon	F
Restaurant Pipistrello	B

CENTRAL PALMA

The provincial **turisme** is just off the Passeig d'es Born at Plaça de la Reina 2 (daily 9am–8pm; ☎971 712 216), while the main municipal office is at c/Sant Domingo 11, in the subway at the end of c/Conquistador (Mon–Fri 9am–8pm, Sat 9am–2pm; ☎971 724 090). Both provide city and island-wide information, dispensing free maps, accommodation lists, bus and ferry schedules, lists of car rental firms, boat trip details and all sorts of special interest leaflets.

Accommodation

There are around twenty *hostales* and thirty hotels dotted around Palma, and if you haven't got a reservation, your first move in the summer should be to pick up the official list from the tourist office. The bulk of Palma's **budget accommodation** is in the city centre – fortunately so, as this is by far the most diverting part of town. In particular, there's a cluster of places among the side streets off the Passeig d'es Born and around the Plaça Espanya. Alternatively, several of the **fancier hotels** are grouped together on the Passeig Mallorca and to the west of the centre along Avinguda Gabriel Roca, overlooking the waterfront.

Hotel Almudaina, Avgda. Jaume III 9 ☎971 727 340, ℉ 971 722 599, ✉almudaina@bitel.es. Smart, modern rooms above a noisy street right in the centre. ❾

Hostal Apuntadores, c/Apuntadors 8 ☎971 713 491, ✉apuntadores@jet.es. Appealingly laid-back *hostal* in an old house off the Passeig d'es Born. Rooms are simple but adequate, and there's a café downstairs. ❸

Hostal Born, c/Sant Jaume 3 ☎971 712 942, ℉971 718 618, ✉hborn@bitel.es. Comfortable and justifiably popular *hostal* in excellent downtown location. Set in an old, refurbished mansion with its own courtyard café. ❼

Hostal Residencia Cuba, c/Sant Magí 1 ☎971 738 159, ℉971 403 131. Pleasant, functional rooms in an attractively refurbished stone house, complete with its own tower and balustrade; overlooks the bottom of busy Avgda. Argentina. ❺

Hotel Residencia Palacio Ca Sa Galesa, c/Miramar 8 ☎971 715 400, ℉971 721 579, ⓦwww.palaciocasagalesa.com. Charmingly renovated seventeenth-century mansion amongst the narrow alleys of the oldest part of town, a couple of minutes' walk from the cathedral. Small indoor pool, and a wonderful rooftop terrace, with fine views of the city. Just a dozen luxurious rooms and suites. Very expensive. ❾

Hotel Residencia Palladium, Passeig Mallorca 40 ☎971 713 945, ℉971 714 665. Clean, trim and tidy rooms in a modern high-rise. No dining room. ❼

Hostal Residencia Pons, c/Vi 8 ☎971 722 658. Simple rooms in a lovely old house with a courtyard and house plants. In the old part of town, near the Passeig d'es Born. ❸

Hostal Ritzi, c/Apuntadors 6 ☎971 714 610. Basic, one-star rooms in an ancient, five-storey house off the Passeig d'es Born; can get noisy at night. ❸

Hotel Saratoga, Passeig Mallorca 6 ☎971 727 240, ℉971 727 312. Excellent, newly refurbished hotel with swimming pool. Most rooms have balconies overlooking the boulevard. ❾.

Hotel Sol Jaime III, Passeig Mallorca 14 ☎971 725 943, ℉971 725 946. Agreeable three-star hotel with spacious, modern twin-bed rooms, most with balconies. Discounts possible outside high season. ❽

Hostal Residencia Terminus, c/Eusebi Estada 2 ☎971 750 014, ✉terminus@mail.cinet.es. Decent hotel next to the train station, with a quirkily old-fashioned foyer and fairly large bedrooms. ❹

Hostal Residencia Valencia, c/Ramón i Cajal 21 ☎971 733 147. Modern, thirty-room *hostal* on the northern edge of the city centre. Spruce, almost antiseptic rooms, some with balconies overlooking the boulevard. ❺

The City

Finding your way around Palma is fairly straightforward once you're in the centre. The obvious landmark is the **cathedral** – *La Seu* in Catalan – which dominates the waterfront and backs onto the oldest part of the city, a cluster of alleys and narrow lanes whose northern and eastern limits are marked by the zigzag of avenues built beside – or in place of – the city walls. On the west side of the cathedral, Avinguda d'Antoni Maura/Passeig d'es Born cuts up from the seafront to intersect with Avinguda Jaume III/Unio at Plaça Rei Joan Carles. These busy thoroughfares form the centre of the modern town.

The cathedral

Palma's **cathedral** (April–Oct Mon–Fri 10am–5.30pm, Sat 10am–1.30pm; Nov–March Mon–Fri 10am–3pm, Sat 10am–2pm; €3), five hundred years in the making, is a magnificent building – the equal of almost any on the mainland – and a surprising one, too, with *modernista* interior features designed by Antoni Gaudí. The original foundation came with the Christian Reconquest of the city, and the site taken, in fulfilment of a vow by Jaume I, was that of the Moorish Great Mosque. Essentially Gothic, with massive exterior buttresses to take the weight off the pillars within, the church derives its effect through its sheer height, impressive from any angle but startling when glimpsed from the waterside esplanade.

In the central nave, fourteen beautifully aligned, pencil-thin pillars rise to 21 metres before their ribs branch out – like fronded palm trees – to support the single-span, vaulted roof. The nave, at 44 metres high, is one of the tallest Gothic structures in Europe and its length – 121 metres – is of matching grandeur. This open, hangar-like construction, typical of Catalan Gothic architecture, was designed to make the high altar visible to the entire congregation, and to express the mystery of the Christian faith, with kaleidoscopic floods of light filtering in through the **stained-glass windows**. For once the light isn't trapped by the central *coro* (choir) that normally blocks the centre of Spanish cathedrals. The innovative sidelining of the *coro*, and the fantastic forms of the lighting system above the altar, were Gaudí's work, undertaken between 1904 and 1914. At the time, these measures were deeply controversial; no *coro* had ever before been removed in Spain. The artistic success of the project, however, was undeniable, and it was immediately popular. Compared with Gaudí's designs in Barcelona (see p.716), everything here is simple and restrained but there are touches of his characteristic flamboyance, notably in the wrought-iron contraption (baldachin) above the altar that symbolizes the Crown of Thorns.

On the way into the church, you pass through the three rooms of assorted ecclesiastical bric-a-brac that comprise the **Museu de la Catedral**. The first room's most valuable exhibit, in the glass case in the middle, is a gilded silver monstrance of extraordinary delicacy, its fairy-tale decoration dating from the late sixteenth century. On display around the walls are assorted chalices and reliquaries and a real curiosity, the portable altar of Jaume I, a wood and silver chessboard with each square containing a bag of relics. The second room is mainly devoted to the Gothic works of the **Mallorcan Primitives**, a school of painters who flourished on the island in the fourteenth and fifteenth centuries, producing strikingly naive devotional works of bold colours and cartoon-like detail.

The Palau de l'Almudaina and Sa Llotja

Opposite the cathedral entrance stands the **Palau de l'Almudaina** (April–Sept Mon–Fri 10am–6.30pm, Sat 10am–2pm; Oct–March Mon–Fri 10am–2pm & 4–6pm; €2.70, but free on Wed to EU citizens), originally the palace of the Moorish *walis* (governors) and later of the Mallorcan kings. The interior has been painstakingly restored, but its rabbit warren of rooms and corridors has been left comparatively bare, the only decorative highlight being a handful of admirable Flemish tapestries, each devoted to classical themes.

A steep flight of steps leads down from the Palau de l'Almudaina through some pleasant gardens and a restored section of the old city walls to the fifteenth-century **Llotja** (Tues–Sat 11am–2pm & 5–9pm, Sun 11am–2pm; free), the city's former stock exchange. This carefully composed building, with its octagonal turrets and tall windows, now hosts frequent and often excellent exhibitions.

The rest of the city

Even more engaging is the medina-like maze of streets at the back of the cathedral, and here, at c/Can Serra 7, you'll come upon the **Banys Àrabs** (daily: April–Nov 9.30am–8pm; Dec–March 9.30am–7pm; €1.20). One of the few genuine reminders of the Moorish presence, this small brick *hammam* (bath-house) contains an elegant, horseshoe-arched and domed chamber, though if you've been to the ones in Girona or Granada, the impact can be anticlimactic; the garden outside, with tables where you can picnic, is perhaps nicer. Nearby, on c/Portella, the **Museu de Mallorca** (April–Sept Tues–Sat 10am–2pm & 5–8pm, Sun 10am–2pm; Oct–March Tues–Sat 10am–1pm & 4–6pm, Sun 10am–2pm; €1.80, but free on Sat afternoon and Sun), occupying one of the many fifteenth- and sixteenth-century patrician mansions that dot this part of town, has extensive local archeology exhibits and some exceptionally fine medieval religious paintings – further examples of the work of the Mallorcan Primitives.

A five-minute walk away along Pont i Vich and Pare Nadal, and occupying, oddly enough, the site of the old Moorish soap factory, the **Basílica de Sant Francesc** (Mon–Sat 9.30am–12.30pm & 3.30–6pm, Sun 9.30am–12.30pm; €0.60) is the finest among a host of worthy medieval churches. A substantial building founded towards the end of the thirteenth century, the church's main facade displays a stunning severity of style, with a great sheet of dressed sandstone stretching up to an arcaded balcony and pierced by a gigantic rose window. Entered via a trim Gothic cloister and a grassy quadrant, the cavernous interior is a little disappointing, but you can't miss the monumental **high altar**, a gaudy, gold leaf affair illustrative of the High Baroque. Incidentally, the strange statue outside the church – of a Franciscan monk and an loin-clothed native American – celebrates the missionary work of **Junipero Serra**, a Mallorcan priest dispatched to California in 1768, who subsequently founded San Diego, Los Angeles and San Francisco.

From the basilica, it's a couple of minutes' walk west to **Santa Eulàlia** (Mon–Fri 7am–12.30pm & 5.45–8.30pm, Sat 7am–1pm & 4.30–8.45pm, Sun 8am–1pm & 6.30–8.30pm; free), the first church to be built after Jaume's arrival, a typically Gothic construction with a yawning nave originally designed – as in the cathedral – to give the entire congregation a view of the high altar. Close by, the **ajuntament** (town hall) is a debonair example of the late-Renaissance style with a grand and self-assured foyer.

Eating

Eating in Palma is less pricey – or can be – than anywhere else in the Balearics. Inexpensive **cafés** and **tapas bars** are liberally distributed around the city centre, with a particular concentration in the side streets off the Passeig d'es Born and Avinguda Antoni Maura. In central Palma, especially along the harbour front and around Plaça Llotja, many **restaurants** are unashamedly geared to the tourist trade, with menus in a babble of Euro-tongues. Most serve perfectly reasonable food, mainly grilled meats and fish, but away from these enclaves you'll find that prices are a little lower and menus more exclusively Catalan and Spanish. At all but the most expensive of places, €18 will cover the cost of a starter, main course, and half a bottle of wine.

Cafés and tapas bars

Bar Bosch, Plaça Rei Joan Carles I. One of the most popular and inexpensive tapas bars in town, the traditional haunt of intellectuals and usually humming with conversation. At peak times you'll need to be assertive to get served.

Bon Lloc, c/Sant Feliu 7. One of the few vegetarian café-restaurants on the island, centrally situated off the Passeig d'es Born. Informal atmosphere and good food at low prices. Open Mon–Sat 1–4pm and the odd evening, usually Fri, till 9pm.

Ca'n Joan de S'Aigo, c/Can Sanç 10. Long-established coffee house with wonderful, freshly baked *ensaimadas* (cinnamon-flavoured spiral pastry buns) for just €0.70 and fruit-flavoured mousses to die for. Charmingly formal, period-piece decor. c/Can Sanç is a tiny alley near Plaça Santa Eulàlia. Closed Tues.

Mesón Salamanca, c/Sant Jaume 3. Mostly Castilian cuisine in a tastefully refurbished, warren-like mansion off Avgda. Jaume III. Delicious tapas on the ground floor (avoid the overpriced, stuffy restaurant upstairs).

El Pilon, c/Can Cifre 4, off the north end of Passeig d'es Born. Vibrant, cramped and crowded tapas bar serving all manner of Spanish and Mallorcan dishes at very reasonable prices.

Restaurants

Ca'n Carlos, c/de S'Aigua 5, off Avgda. Jaume III ☎971 713 869. Charming, family-run restaurant featuring exquisite Mallorcan cuisine – grilled meats and squid, snails, and stuffed aubergine. The menu isn't extensive, but everything is beauti-

fully prepared and there's a daily special. Main courses average around €12.

Celler Pagès, off c/Apuntadors at c/Felip Bauza 2 ☎971 726 036. Traditional Mallorcan food in a tiny, inexpensive restaurant near Passeig d'es Born. Easy-going atmosphere, but can be stifling in the summer. Closed Sun.

Celler Sa Premsa, Plaça Bisbe Berenguer de Palou 8 ☎971 723 529. Justly popular restaurant with delicious seafood, a five-minute walk west of the Plaça Espanya. Old bullfighting photos and posters adorn the walls amidst a pot-pourri of dusty bygones; you'll probably share a table with other diners. Prices are surprisingly low – as little as €11 per person for a three-course meal.

Forn de Sant Joan, c/Sant Joan 4 ☎971 728 422. Extremely popular Catalan restaurant near Sa Llotja, one of several busy spots on this narrow alley. Fine fish dishes for around €13.30, tapas from €5.70.

Es Parlament, c/Conquistador 11 ☎971 726 026. All gilt-wood mirrors and chandeliers, this old and polished restaurant specializes in paella. The tasty and reasonably priced *menú del día* is recommended too. A favourite hang-out of local politicians and lawyers.

Restaurant Pipistrello, c/Concepció 34 ☎971 715 601. Atmospheric restaurant set in a 500-year-old stable block, with vaulted ceiling. The cuisine matches the location – a simple, creative and very well-priced menu of salads (around €4.80), fresh pasta (around €9) and sublime meat and fish dishes (around €13.80).

Drinking and nightlife

There's a cluster of lively **late-night bars** – mostly with music as the backdrop rather than the main event – amongst the narrow side streets backing onto Plaça Llotja. A second concentration of slightly more upmarket bars embellishes the bayside modernity of Avinguda Gabriel Roca, about 3km west of the city centre. The grimy suburb of El Terreno, also west of the centre, once accommodated Palma's best late-night bars. The district has gone downhill, and now features topless "entertainment" and porn shops, but it's here you'll find the occasional offbeat bar, as well as several gay bars.

The **club scene** in Palma is small but improving. More and more leading European DJs are playing here, but note that the city's clubs are never worth investigating until around midnight and entry charges will cost you anything between €6 and €24, depending on the night and what's happening.

Late-night bars

Abaco, just off c/Apuntadors at c/Sant Joan 1. Inhabiting a charming Renaissance mansion, this is easily Palma's most unusual bar, with an interior straight out of a Busby Berkeley musical: fruits cascading down its stairway, caged birds hidden amid patio foliage, elegant music and a daily flower bill you could live on for a month. Drinks, as you might imagine, are extremely expensive (beers €6, cocktails from €12) but you're never hurried into buying one. The clientele is less than hip but it's a good place to start an evening out.
Barcelona Jazz Café Club, c/Apuntadors 9. Groovy little spot on one of the busiest streets in town. Jazz, blues and Latin sounds. Metres from the corner of c/Sant Joan.
La Bóveda, c/Boteria 3, off Plaça Llotja. Classy, bustling bar, one of several on this short alley, with long, wide windows and wine stacked high along the back wall. Be prepared to queue to get in – or come early.

Box Office, Avgda. Gabriel Roca 31. Hip and popular bar near the Jardins La Quarentena, about 3km west of the centre along the waterfront.
Gotic, Plaça Llotja 4. Cramped bar redeemed by its stylish, often candle-lit patio, and pavement tables which nudge out across the piazza.
Latitud, c/Felip Bauza 8, off c/Apuntadors. Tiny, upbeat bar, playing jazz, blues and sometimes classical music.
La Lonja, opposite Sa Llotja. Gregarious, vaguely pub-like haunt, with revolving doors, chessboard tiled floors and darkwood panelling and furnishings. Good mix of locals, backpackers and tourists. Reasonable prices.
Made in Brasil, Avgda. Gabriel Roca 27. Alarming tropical decor in this pocket-sized club-cum-bar, some 3km west of the centre along the waterfront. Great Latin sounds and cocktails.

Clubs

Pacha, Avgda. Gabriel Roca 42 ☏971 455 908. Raucous, happening club with guest DJs from Ibiza, the mainland and the UK. Funky, soulful house, plus a little trance and R&B. Garden bar. Some 3.5km west of the centre along the waterfront.
Tito's, Plaça Gomila 3 ☏971 730 017. With its stainless steel and glass exterior, this long-estab-

lished nightspot looks a bit like something from a sci-fi film set. Outdoor lifts carry you up from the back entrance on the waterfront Avgda. Gabriel Roca – about 2.5km west of the centre – to the dance floor, which pulls in huge crowds from many countries. Mainstream, vocal-driven house and garage mixes.

Listings

Banks Many banks are on and around the Passeig d'es Born and Avgda. Jaume III. There are 24-hour cash card and credit card machines dotted round the city too.
Bookshops The biggest department store in town, El Corte Inglés, at Avgda Jaume III, 15 (Mon–Sat 10am–10pm), sells a small and rather eccentric assortment of English-language books – from Ken Follett to Anne Frank. It also has a modest selection of Mallorca guidebooks and maps. Libreria Fondevila, near the Teatre Principal at Costa de Sa Pols 18 (Mon–Fri 9.45am–1.30pm & 4.30–8pm, Sat 9.45am–1.30pm; ☏971 725 616), doesn't do much better when it comes to novels and guide books, but it does have a fairly good selection of general maps of Mallorca. In addition, it has a reasonably comprehensive selection of IGN hiking maps. Also see "Maps" below.
Car rental Mallorca's airport heaves with car rental companies and so does Palma, where there's a concentration – including many small concerns – along Avgda. Gabriel Roca. Amongst

the big companies, there's Atesa-National at Avgda. Gabriel Roca 25 ☏971 456762 & at the airport ☏971 789 896; Avis at Avgda Gabriel Roca 16 ☏971 730 720 & at the airport ☏971 789187; Betacar, at Avgda. Gabriel Roca 20 ☏971 455 144 & at the airport ☏971 789 135; and Hertz, at Avgda. Gabriel Roca 13 ☏971 734 737 & at the airport ☏971 789 670. The tourist office will supply a complete list of rental companies.
Consulates Ireland, c/Sant Miquel 68A ☏971 719 244; United Kingdom, Plaça Major 3 ☏971 712 445; USA, Avgda. Jaume III, 26 ☏971 725 051.
Emergencies General emergency number ☏112.
Ferries Palma's tourist offices have ferry schedules and tariffs. Tickets can be purchased at travel agents or direct from the two ferry lines concerned down at the ferry port, about 4km west of the city centre along Avgda. Gabriel Roca. At Terminal 2 is Trasmediterránea (☏902 454 645), who operate ferries to Maó on Menorca, Ibiza, Barcelona and Valencia; and a couple of minutes' walk away at Terminal 3 is Balearia (☏902 160 180), with

services to Valencia, Ibiza and Dénia. For details of routes see "Travel details" at the end of this chapter.

Hospital Hospital General, Plaça Hospital 3 ☎971 212 000.

Internet access *La Red cybercafé*, c/Concepció 5, just off Avgda Jaume III ☎971 713 574, ⓦwww.laredcafe.com. Easily the best cyber café in town, La Red has fifteen PCs with internet access as well as fax machines and scanners. Good sounds, plus snacks and drinks too. Open Mon–Fri 11am–1am, Sat & Sun 4–12pm; €5.10 per hour.

Laundry There's a downtown self-service laundry, Lavandería Self Press at c/Annibal 14, off Avgda. Argentina ☎971 730643.

Maps Palma has one specialist map shop, the Casa del Mapa, c/Sant Domingo 11 ☎971 225 945 (Mon–Fri 9am–2pm), with a fairly comprehensive selection of IGN hiking maps as well as various maps of the island and Palma. See also "Bookshops" above.

Mopeds RTR Rental, Avgda. Joan Miró 340 ☎971 702 775.

Post office The old central *correu*, at c/Constitució 5, is currently being refurbished. In the meantime, its services have been transferred to the post office at Passeig d'es Born 15 (Mon–Fri 8.30am–8.30pm, Sat 9.30am–2pm).

Trains The tourist office has train timetable details or you can phone direct: Palma to Inca ☎971 752 245; Palma to Sóller ☎971 752 051.

Around Palma

For a **day out** from Palma, anywhere in the west or centre of the island is readily accessible, but if you're after a quick **swim** the most convenient option is to stick to the resorts strung along the neighbouring **Badia de Palma** (Bay of Palma). Locals tend to go east on the #15 bus (every 10min; 30min) from Plaça Espanya to the individual *balneario* (beach bar) sections of **S'Arenal**, where there's an enormously long, if crowded, sandy beach.

Alternatively, you might be tempted by the **Castell de Bellver** (April–Sept Mon–Sat 8am–8pm, Sun 10am–7pm; Oct–March Mon–Sat 8am–7pm, Sun 10am–5pm; €1.65, free Sun), a strikingly well-preserved fortress of canny circular design built for Jaume II at the beginning of the fourteenth century. The castle perches on a wooded hilltop some 3km west of the city centre and offers superb views of Palma and its harbour.

Andratx, Sant Elm and Illa Dragonera

Inland from Palma bay, you could certainly find worse ways to spend an afternoon than hopping on a bus to **ANDRATX**, a small, undeveloped town huddled among the hills to the west. From here, it's another short bus ride through a pretty, orchard-covered landscape to the dishevelled, low-key resort of **SANT ELM**. There are plans to expand the resort, but at present it's a relatively quiet spot where there's a reasonable chance of a **room** in high season, either at the conspicuous *Hotel Aquamarín* (☎971 239 105, ⓕ971 239 125; May–Oct; ⑤) or, preferably, at the *Hostal Dragonera* (☎971 239 086, ⓕ971 239 013; ⑥), a simple, modern building with clean and neat rooms, most of which offer sea views. For such a small place, there's also a surprisingly wide choice of **cafés and restaurants**, the best being *Na Caragola,* which specializes in seafood and has a charming terrace and ocean views – reckon on €36 for a complete meal, including house wine.

From May to October, **buses** ply between Sant Elm and Andratx seven times a day Monday to Saturday, and once on Sundays (in winter, once daily). With more time to spare, boats shuttle across from Sant Elm's minuscule harbour to the austere offshore islet of **Illa Dragonera**, an uninhabited chunk of rock, some 4km long and 700m wide, with an imposing ridge of sea cliffs dominating its northwestern shore.

Northwest Mallorca

Mallorca is at its scenic best in the gnarled ridge of the **Serra de Tramuntana**, the imposing mountain range which stretches the length of the island's western shore, its rearing peaks and plunging sea cliffs intermittently intercepted by valleys of olive and citrus groves and dotted with the most beguiling of the island's towns and villages. There are several possible routes which take in the best of the region, but perhaps the most straightforward if you're reliant on public transport is to travel up from Palma to **Sóller**, in the middle of the coast, and use this town as a base, making selected forays along the coastal road, the C710; not far away to the **southwest** lie the mountain village of **Deià** and the monastery of **Valldemossa**, while within easy striking distance to the **northeast** are the monastery of **Lluc**, the quaint town of **Pollença** and the relaxing resort of **Port de Pollença**.

The Serra de Tramuntana also provides the best walking on Mallorca, with scores of **hiking trails** latticing the mountains. Generally speaking, paths are well marked, though apt to be clogged with thornbushes. There are trails to suit all aptitudes and all levels of enthusiasm, from the easiest of strolls to the most gruelling of long-distance treks, but in all cases you should come properly equipped – certainly with an appropriate hiking map (these are available in Sóller and Palma) and, for the more difficult routes, with a compass. Also available locally are a variety of **hiking books**, the best of which are those by Herbert Heinrich (*12 Classic Hikes through Majorca*), while the *Rough Guide to Mallorca* details several of the island's most famous hiking routes, too. Spring and autumn are the best times to embark on the longer trails; in midsummer the heat can be enervating and water is scarce. Bear in mind also that the mountains are prone to mists, though they usually lift at some point in the day. For obvious safety reasons, lone mountain walking is not recommended.

As far as **beaches** are concerned, most of the region's coastal villages have a tiny, shingly strip, and only around the bays of Pollença and Alcúdia are there more substantial offerings. The resorts edging these bays have the greatest number of hotel and *hostal* rooms, but from June to early September, and sometimes beyond, vacancies are extremely thin on the ground. Indeed, **accommodation** – especially if you have a tight itinerary and are travelling in the summertime – requires some forethought, though there's a reasonable chance of getting a room on spec in Sóller, and in the monasteries at Lluc and just outside Pollença. To compensate, distances are small, the roads are good and the **bus** network is perfectly adequate for most destinations. One of the most useful buses is the twice-every-weekday service (May–Oct) along the C710 from Port de Sóller to Port de Pollença, and on to Port d'Alcúdia. **Taxis** can work out a reasonable deal too, if you're travelling in a group: for instance, the fare for the thirty-kilometre trip from Palma to Sóller is about €28.80.

The train from Palma to Sóller

Easily the best way to get to the Serra de Tramuntana is to take the **train from Palma to Sóller**, a 28-kilometre journey that takes about one hour and twenty minutes on antique rolling stock that seems straight out of an Agatha Christie novel. The rail line, constructed on the profits of the nineteenth-century orange and lemon trade, dips and twists through the mountains and across fertile valleys, offering magnificent views. There are five departures daily from Palma station throughout the year (sometimes six from Sóller); a return costs €4.60 (€2.30 one-way), though the mid-morning *Turist* train – with air-conditioning and a brief photo-stop in the mountains – will set you back €9 return (€4.50 one-way).

Sóller

Arriving by train at **SÓLLER**, the obvious option is to continue by **tram** (every 30min or 1hr from 7am–9pm; 15min; €0.70) down to the seashore, a rumbling, 5km-journey ending at **Port de Sóller**. If you pass straight through, however, you'll miss one of the most laid-back and enjoyable towns on Mallorca, an ideal and fairly inexpensive base for exploring the surrounding mountains. Rather than any specific sight, it's the general flavour that appeals, the town's narrow, sloping lanes cramped by eighteenth- and nineteenth-century stone houses, whose fancy grilles and big wooden doors once hid the region's fruit-rich merchants. All streets lead to the main square, **Plaça Constitució**, an informal, pint-sized affair of crowded cafés just down the hill from the train station. The square is dominated by the hulking mass of the church of **Sant Bartomeu**, a crude neo-Gothic remodelling of the medieval original, its only saving grace the enormous rose window cut high in the main facade. Inside, the cavernous nave is suitably dark and gloomy, the penitential home of a string of gaudy Baroque altarpieces.

Although the options are very limited, there's a good chance of finding a vacant **room** in Sóller during the high season. Options include the *Hotel El Guía*, c/Castanyer 2 (℡ & ℻971 630 227; April–Oct; ❺), a lovely, old-fashioned one-star hotel just down the steps from the train station platform and turn right; *Casa de Huéspedes Margarita Trías Vives*, c/Reial 3 (℡971 634 214; April–Oct. ❹), in an attractive old terraced house also close to the train station; and *Hostal Residencia Nadal*, c/Romaguera 27 (℡ & ℻971 631 180; ❹), a simple, central two-star, in a neatly decorated and well-kept house about five minutes' walk north of Plaça Constitució. The best place to **eat** is at the *Hotel El Guía*. It may be a little formal for some, but the prices are very reasonable, with a delicious *menú del día* for around €15. Closed Mondays and limited opening hours from November to March. Alternatively, *Restaurante Es Carrete*, c/Cetre s/n (℡971 633 996) is a great neighbourhood spot done out in rustic style. Chicken for as little as €5.50, but the swordfish is more of a treat even if it does cost twice as much.

Port de Sóller

PORT DE SÓLLER is one of the most popular resorts on the west coast, and its horseshoe-shaped bay must be the most photographed spot on the island after the package resorts around Palma. The high jinks of the Badia de Palma are about the last thing imaginable down here, though – the place is almost stiflingly staid. There's no point in staying just for the swimming either, since, although the water is warm and calm, it's often surprisingly murky (courtesy of the yachts at anchor), and the two sandy beaches are overlooked on all sides – by the road, hotels and restaurants. Probably the best option is to make the fifty-minute stroll out to the lighthouse, which guards the cliffs above the entrance to Port de Sóller's inlet. From here, the views out over the wild and rocky coast are spectacular, especially at sunset. Directions couldn't be easier as there's a tarmac road all the way: from the centre of the resort, walk round the southern side of the bay past the beach and keep going along the seashore.

As for practicalities, trams from Sóller clank to a full stop beside the waterfront, bang in the centre of town and a couple of minutes' walk from **turisme**, beside the church on c/Canonge Oliver (March–Oct Mon–Fri 10am–1pm & 3–6.30pm, Sat 10am–1pm; also March–June Sun 10am–1pm; ℡971 633 042), which has a full list of local hotels and *hostales*. Outside peak season there's a chance of a reasonably priced room at the mundane *Hotel Miramar*, c/Marina

THE BALEARIC ISLANDS | Mallorca

12 (☎971 631 350, ⓕ971 632 671; ❺), a standard-issue sky-rise down by the waterfront in the centre, and at the equally unexciting, 100-room *Hotel Generoso*, nearby at c/Marina 4 (☎971 631 450, ⓕ971 632 200; ❻). The string of one- and two-star hotels and *hostales* behind the Platja den Repic on the south side of the bay are worth considering too: the pleasant *Los Geranios*, Passeig sa Platja 15 (☎971 631 440, ⓕ971 631 651; ❺), is as good as any.

Port de Sóller heaves with **cafés** and **restaurants**, but standards are very variable: some serve up mediocre food with the package tourist in mind, others are more authentically Mallorquín – or at least Spanish. The majority are dotted along the bay shore with a cluster of better restaurants on c/Santa Caterina d'Alexandria, a short side street that cuts up from the waterfront close to the naval base. Two appealing options are the *Celler d'es Port*, c/Antoni Montis 17A (closed Wed), an unassuming neighbourhood café-bar where the food is inexpensive and the emphasis is on traditional Mallorcan dishes; and *Restaurante El Pirata*, c/Santa Caterina d'Alexandria 7 (☎971 631 497), where the seafood is first-rate. Consider also the *Cafeteria Es Faro* (☎971 633 752), which perches high up on the cliffs at the entrance to the harbour offering spectacular views and great food – reservations are recommended.

Southwest from Sóller: Deià

It's a dramatic 10km journey **southwest from Sóller** along the C710 to the beautiful village of **DEIÀ**. The mighty Puig des Teix meets the coast here, and, although its lower slopes are now gentrified by the villas of the well-to-do, the mountain retains a formidable, almost mysterious presence. Doubling as the coastal highway, Deià's main street skirts the base of the Teix, showing off most of the village's hotels and restaurants. At times, this main street is too congested to be much fun, but the tiny heart of the village, tumbling over a high and narrow ridge on the seaward side of the road, still manages a surprising tranquillity. Labyrinthine alleys of old peasant houses curl up to a pretty country **church**, in the precincts of which stands the **grave of Robert Graves**, the village's most famous resident – marked simply "Robert Graves: Poeta, E.P.D." (*En Paz Descanse*: "Rest In Peace"). From the graveyard, the views out over the coast are truly memorable.

Graves put Deià on the international map, and nowadays the village is the haunt of long-term expatriates. These inhabitants congregate at the **Cala de Deià**, the nearest thing the village has to a beach – some 200m of shingle at the back of a handsome rocky cove of jagged cliffs, boulders and white-crested surf. It's a great place for a swim, the water clean, deep and cool, and there's a ramshackle beach bar, but in summer the cove often gets crowded, especially when the day-trippers arrive by boat from Port de Sóller. It takes about twenty minutes to walk from the village to the *cala*, a delightful stroll down a wooded ravine; from the bus stop, walk in the Palma direction to a sharp right bend in the main road, then turn right down the shallow steps and continue downhill, taking a right fork after a few minutes. When the lane ends a signposted footpath continues in the same direction; after about five minutes turn right by a white painted sign and follow the path until it joins a surfaced road about 500m from the cove. Alternatively, driving there takes about ten minutes: head north along the main road out of Deià and watch for the sign.

Practicalities

The Palma–Port de Sóller **bus** scoots through Deià five times daily in each direction (Nov–March reduced service on Sun). There's no tourist office, but

Robert Graves in Deià

Robert Graves lived in Deià from after the end of World War II until his death in 1985. This was his second stay; during the first – in the 1930s – he shared his house at the edge of the village with **Laura Riding**, an American poet and dabbler in the mystical. Riding came to England in 1926 and, after she became Graves's secretary and literary collaborator, the two of them had an affair. The tumultuous course of their relationship created sufficient furore for them to decide to leave England and they supposedly chose Mallorca on the advice of Gertrude Stein. Graves and Riding were forced to leave Mallorca in 1936 at the onset of the Spanish Civil War, and back in England Laura ditched Graves, who subsequently took up with a mutual friend, **Beryl Hodge**. Graves returned to Mallorca in 1946, Beryl joined him and they were married in Palma in 1950. But they didn't live happily ever after; Graves had a predilection for young women muses, claiming the need for female muses to inspire his poetic vision; outwardly Beryl accepted this waywardness, but without much enthusiasm. Furthermore, while Graves' novels – *Goodbye to All That*; *I, Claudius*; *Claudius the God* – became increasingly well known and profitable, his romantic poetry – of which he was particularly proud – fell out of fashion, and his last anthology, *Poems 1965–1968*, was widely snubbed.

the village's hotels and *hostales* will gladly provide local advice on walks and weather, and can fix you up with a **taxi** – or do it yourself on ☎971 630 571. Of the two places where there's a good chance of a reasonably priced **room** in high season, the *Fonda Villa Verde*, c/Ramón Llull 19 (☎971 639 037; ⓕ971 639 485; ❻) has lovely premises near the village church, while the *Hotel d'es Puig* (☎971 639 409, ⓕ971 639 210; March to mid-Nov; ❽) occupies a tastefully converted old stone house close by. Deià also possesses two of the finest hotels on Mallorca, both overlooking the main road: *Es Moli* (☎971 639 000, ⓕ971 639 333; April–Oct; ❾) and *La Residencia* (☎971 639 011, ⓕ971 639 370; ⓔlaresidencia@atlas-iap.es; ❾), each of which occupies a gracious and beautifully maintained mansion.

As for **eating** in Deià, you're spoiled for choice. There's a concentration of cafés and restaurants along the main street towards the west end of the village. These include *Café La Fábrica*, which offers reasonably priced tapas, *bocadillos* and the traditional *pa amb oli* (bread rubbed with olive oil), and the *Bar-Restaurante Deià*, where you'll pay a little more for a light meal, but with the compensation of a terrace overlooking the valley. Moving up the price range, the *Restaurant Jaime* (☎971 639 029), which is also at the west end of the village, offers mouthwatering Mallorcan cuisine.

Valldemossa

Some 10km **southwest of Deià** along the C710, the ancient and intriguing hill town of **VALLDEMOSSA** is actually best approached from the south, where, after squeezing through a narrow, wooded defile, the road from Palma enters a lovely valley, whose tiered and terraced fields ascend to the town, a sloping jumble of rusticated houses and monastic buildings backclothed by the mountains. The origins of Valldemossa date to the early fourteenth century, when the asthmatic King Sancho built a royal palace here in the hills where the air was easier to breathe. Later, in 1399, the palace was given to Carthusian monks from Tarragona, who converted and extended the original buildings into a **monastery**, which is now the island's most visited building after Palma cathedral.

Remodelled on several occasions, most of the present complex – formally, the **Real Cartuja de Jesús de Nazaret** (Mon–Sat 9.30am–6pm, Sun 10am–1pm; Nov–Feb Mon–Sat closes 4.30pm; €7.80) – is of seventeenth- and eighteenth-century construction, its square and heavy church leading to the shadowy corridors of the cloisters beyond. The monastery owes its present fame almost entirely to the novelist and republican polemicist **George Sand**, who, with her companion, the composer **Frédéric Chopin**, lived here for four months in 1838–39. Just three years earlier the last monks had been evicted during the liberal-inspired suppression of the monasteries, so the pair were able to rent a commodious set of vacant cells. Their stay is commemorated in Sand's *A Winter in Majorca*, a stodgy, self-important book that is considerably overplayed hereabouts, being available in just about every European language.

A visit begins in the gloomy, aisleless **church**, which is distinguished by its fanciful bishop's throne, though the lines of the nave are spoiled by the clumsy wooden stalls of the choir. In the adjoining cloisters, the first port of call is the **pharmacy**, which survived the expulsion of the monks to serve the town's medicinal needs well into the twentieth century. Its shelves are crammed with a host of beautifully decorated majolica jars, antique glass receptacles and painted wood boxes, each carefully inscribed with the name of the potion or drug. The nearby **prior's cell** is, despite its name, a comfortable suite of bright, sizeable rooms with splendid views down the valley. It's also, together with the adjoining library and audience room, the proud possessor of a wide assortment of religious *objets d'art*. Further along the corridor, **cell no. 2** exhibits miscellaneous curios relating to Chopin and Sand, from portraits and a lock of hair to musical scores and letters (it was in this cell that the composer wrote the *Raindrop Prelude*). There's more of the same next door in **cell no. 4**, plus Chopin's piano, which arrived only after three months of unbelievable complications – and just three weeks before the couple left for Paris. Considering the hype, these incidental mementoes are something of an anticlimax, but persevere: upstairs, there's a small but outstanding collection of **modern art**, including work by Miró and Picasso, not to mention Francis Bacon and Henry Moore. And be sure also to take the doorway beside the prior's cell, which leads outside the cloisters to the enjoyable **Palace of King Sancho**. It's not the original palace at all – that disappeared long ago – but it is the oldest part of the complex and its fortified walls, mostly dating from the sixteenth century, accommodate a string of handsome period rooms.

Practicalities

Easily reached from Deià and Palma, **buses** to Valldemossa stop at the west end of town beside one of the several car parks that edge the bypass. Services from Palma, 18km away, pause here before continuing to Deià and Sóller; four days a week a bus also comes from Andratx and points west along the coast. From the bus stop, it's just a couple of minutes' walk to the monastery – cross the bypass and keep going straight on.

Downtown **accommodation** is limited to the *Ca'n Mario*, c/Uetam 8 (☎971 612 122, ℱ971 616 029; ❺), an attractive *hostal* where an elegant, curio-cluttered foyer leads to comfortably old-fashioned rooms; it's situated just a couple of minutes' walk from the monastery – from the pedestrianized area between the church and the palace, go downhill and take the first turning on the right.

The centre of Valldemossa is packed with **restaurants and cafés**, mostly geared up for day-trippers – and many offer dire fast food at inflated prices. Nonetheless, amongst the dross there are one or two quality places, in particular *Ca'n Pedro*, a large café-restaurant beside the car park next to the bus stop.

Northeast from Sóller to Lluc

Beyond doubt, the most interesting approach to the northernmost tip of the island is the continuation of the **C710** northeast from Sóller, slipping through the highest and harshest section of the **Serra de Tramuntana**. For the most part, the mountains drop straight into the sea, precipitous and largely unapproachable cliffs with barely a cove in sight. The accessible exceptions are the comely beach at **Cala Tuent** and the horribly commercial hamlet of **Sa Calobra** next door. But easily the best place to break your journey is at **LLUC**, tucked away in a remote mountain valley about 35km from Sóller. Mallorca's most important place of pilgrimage since the middle of the thirteenth century, supposedly after a shepherd boy named Lluc (Luke) stumbled across a tiny, brightly painted statue here in the woods, Lluc is dominated by the austere, high-sided dormitories of the **Monestir de Nostra Senyora** (daily 10am–5.30pm; free). At the centre of the monastery is the main shrine and architectural highlight, the **Basílica de la Mare de Déu de Lluc**, a dark and gaudily decorated church dominated by heavy jasper columns, whose stolidness is relieved by a dome over the crossing. On either side of the nave, stone steps extend the aisles round the back of the Baroque high altar to a modest chapel. This is the holy of holies, built to display the much-venerated statue of the Virgin, which has been commonly known as **La Moreneta** ("the Dark-Skinned One") ever since the original paintwork peeled off in the fifteenth century to reveal brown stone underneath.

From the information desk close to the basilica, a stairway climbs up one floor to the enjoyable **Museu de Lluc** (daily: April–Sept 10am–5.30pm, Oct–March 10am–1.30pm & 2.30–5.30pm; €1.80). After a modest section devoted to archeological finds from the Talayotic and Roman periods, come cabinets of intricate old vestments, medieval religious paintings, and an intriguing assortment of votive offerings – folkloric bits and bobs brought here to honour La Moreneta. The museum also boasts an extensive collection of **majolica**, tin-glazed earthenware whose characteristic shapes are two-handled drug jars and show dishes or plates, of which some two or three hundred are on display. Allow time, too, for a stroll along the **Camí dels Misteris del Rosari** (Way of the Mysteries of the Rosary), a broad pilgrims' footpath that winds its way up the rocky hillside behind the monastery.

Practicalities

Buses to Lluc, which is situated 700m off the C710, stop right outside the monastery. In addition to the Port de Sóller–Port de Pollença–Port d'Alcúdia service, buses run to Lluc at least once a day from Palma via Inca. **Accommodation** at the monastery is highly organized, with simple, self-contained apartment-cells. In summer phone ahead if you want to be sure of space, but at other times simply book at the monastery's information office on arrival (℡971 871 525, ℻971 517 096, ✉info@lluc.net; ❸). For **food**, there's a café-bar and a restaurant beside the car park, but far preferable, even though it has become a little pricey, is the monks' former dining room, where the food is traditional Spanish – and the meat dishes are much better than the fish.

Pollença

Northeast of Lluc, the C710 twists through the mountains to travel the 20km to **POLLENÇA**, a tranquil and ancient little town which nestles among a trio of hillocks where the Serra de Tramuntana fades into coastal flatland. Following standard Mallorcan practice, the town was established a few kilometres from the seashore to militate against sudden pirate attack, with its harbour, Port de Pollença (see below), left an unprotected outpost. For once the stratagem worked. Unlike most of Mallorca's old towns, Pollença avoided destruction, but nevertheless little of the medieval town survives today, and the austere stone houses that cramp the twisting lanes of the centre mostly date from the eighteenth century. In the middle, **Plaça Major**, the main square, accommodates a cluster of laid-back cafés and the dour facade of the church of **Nostra Senyora dels Àngels**, a sheer clifface of sun-bleached stone pierced by a rose window. Pollença's pride and joy is, however, its **Via Crucis** (Way of the Cross), a long, steep and beautiful stone stairway, graced by ancient cypress trees, which ascends **El Calvari** (Calvary hill) directly north of the principal square. At the top, a much-revered statue of **Mare de Déu del Peu de la Creu** (Mother of God at the Foot of the Cross) is lodged in a simple, court-yarded **Oratori** (chapel), whose whitewashed walls sport some of the worst religious paintings imaginable. However, the views out over coast and town are sumptuous. On Good Friday, a figure of Jesus is slowly carried by torchlight down from the Oratori to the church of Nostra Senyora dels Àngels, in the **Davallament** (Lowering), one of the most moving religious celebrations on the island.

There are further magnificent views from the **Ermita de Nostra Senyora del Puig**, a rambling, mostly eighteenth-century monastery which occupies an extraordinarily serene and beautiful spot on top of the Puig de Maria, a 320-metre-high hump facing the south end of town. The monastic complex, with its fortified walls, courtyard, chapel, refectory and cells, has had a chequered history, alternately abandoned and restored by both monks and nuns. The Benedictines now own the place, but the monks are gone and today a custodian supplements the order's income by renting out cells to tourists (see below). To get to the monastery, take the signposted turning left off the main Pollença–Inca road just south of town; head up this steep, 1500-metre-long lane until it fizzles out, to be replaced by a cobbled footpath which winds up to the monastery entrance. It's possible to drive to the top of the lane, but unless you've got nerves of steel, you're better off leaving your vehicle by the turning near the foot of the hill. Allow just over an hour each way if you're walking from the centre of town.

Practicalities

Regular **buses** from Palma, Lluc and Port de Pollença halt immediately to the south of Pollença's Plaça Major and across the street from the **turisme** (Tues–Sat 9am–1pm & 5–8pm, Sun 9am–1pm; ☎971 865 467). There is one central place to **stay**, the excellent *Hotel Juma*, Plaça Major 9 (☎971 535 002, ⓕ971 534 155, ⓦ www.hoteljuma.com; March–Oct; ❼), a medium-sized hotel with comfortable, air-conditioned, modern bedrooms. There are, however, cheaper lodgings at the *Ermita de Nostra Senyora del Puig* (☎971 184 132; ❶) – see above for directions – where the original monks' cells have been renovated to provide simple accommodation. Be warned, though, that it can get cold and windy at night, and the refectory food is mediocre.

Pollença does well for **cafés** and **restaurants**. On Plaça Major, the *Café Espanyol* offers snacks and a good strong cup of coffee, the *Juma* serves up first-rate tapas and the *Restaurante Il Giardino* provides superb French-style cuisine. On c/Montisión, in between the main square and El Calvari, you'll also find the upbeat and fashionable *Restaurante Cantonet*, where the seafood is delicious.

Port de Pollença

Over at **PORT DE POLLENÇA** things are a little more touristy, though still pleasantly low-key. With the mountains as a backcloth, the resort arches through the flatlands behind the Badia de Pollença, a deeply indented bay whose sheltered waters are ideal for swimming. The **beach** is the focus of attention, a narrow, elongated sliver of sand that's easily long enough to accommodate the crowds, though as a general rule you'll have more space the further southeast (towards Alcúdia) you walk. A rash of apartment buildings and hotels blights the edge of town, and the noisy main road to Alcúdia runs close to most of the seashore, but all in all the place is very appealing, especially in the centre behind the marina, where old narrow streets hint at the resort's origins as a small port and fishing harbour.

For a change of scene, **water taxis** shuttle between the marina and the Platja de Formentor, one of Mallorca's most attractive beaches (April–Oct 5–7 daily; 30min; €5.40 one-way). Also, **boat trips** cruise the bay (June to mid-Oct Mon–Sat 1 daily; 2hr 30min; €12), or work their way along to Cap de Formentor (same times & price). There's also the option of making a delightful three-kilometre (each way) **hike** across the neck of the Península de Formentor to **Cala Boquer**. On the seafront north of the marina, take a left up **Avinguda Bocchoris**. Proceed over the Formentor road and keep straight along a wide footpath fringed with pine trees and tamarisk. Beyond the end of the footpath is an untidy area, whose tarmac marks the lay-out of a proposed housing development. Ahead, at a sign saying "Predio Bóquer Propriedad Privada Camin Particular", take the wide path north with the ridge of Serra del Cavall Bernat straight ahead and you'll soon reach an iron gate, beyond which is Bóquer farmhouse. The trail leads on through the mountain-sheltered **Vall de Boquer** (Boquer Valley), a favourite of ornithologists, especially for its migrant birds, and of botanists for its wild flowers and shrubs. After about 45 minutes' walking you reach a small, shingly **beach** offering good swimming in clean water (though the shore is sometimes rubbish-strewn).

Practicalities

Buses to Port de Pollença from Palma, Alcúdia, Port d'Alcúdia and Port de Sóller stop by the marina right in the town centre. Just inland, a couple of minutes' walk away, is the **turisme**, at c/Joan XXIII 46 (June–Sept Mon–Fri 9am–1.30pm & 4–7pm, Sat 9am–1pm; Oct–May Mon–Fri 8am–3.30pm, Sat 9am–1pm; ☎971 865 467). The flatlands edging the Badia de Pollença and stretching as far as Alcúdia and Pollença make for easy, scenic cycling. **Mountain bikes** can be rented for €7.20 a day from a shop called March at c/Joan XXIII 89 (☎971 864 784), as can **mopeds** and **motorcycles**. The walking holiday specialist Globespan has a waterfront office at Passeig Saralegui 114 (☎971 864 711, ✉globespan@atlas-iap.es), where you can pay to join one of its day-long guided walks (from €10–€21 per person). The office will provide all the details; you should book a minimum of 24 hours beforehand.

There are several reasonably priced and convenient **accommodation** options, though getting a room in season may be difficult. Overlooking the tiny main square stands the pleasant *Hostal Residencia Borrás*, Plaça Miquel Capllonch 16 (☎971 866 447, ☎971 865 093; ❺), where most of the rooms are comfortably spacious and you can eat breakfast in the pretty little courtyard. On the seafront, the *Hotel Miramar*, Passeig Anglada Camarasa 39 (☎971 866 400, ☎971 864 075; April–Oct; ❼), is an attractive three-star hotel, with balconied rooms set behind a grand facade; also by the water is the friendly, unpretentious *Hostal Residencia Eolo* at Plaça Enginyer Gabriel Roca 2 (☎971 866 550, ⓕ971 866 301; ⓺), a hikers' favourite, where breakfast is included.

Among a plethora of **restaurants**, an excellent choice is the *Restaurant Stay* (☎971 864 013) on the marina's Moll Vell jetty, a chic little place which features the freshest of seafood and charges under €36 for a full à la carte meal; it is a popular (and romantic) spot, so reservations are advised. There's also *Restaurante El Pozo*, c/Joan XXIII, 25 (☎971 866 777), an informal, laid-back café-bar-cum-restaurant that offers a good range of local dishes and is less expensive than its seafront rivals; and the outstanding *Restaurante Ivy Garden*, c/Llevant 14 (☎971 866 271), which features an inventive modern menu at reasonable prices. Dishes change, but examples of present offerings include fillet of salmon with pesto and lemon dressing for €10.85, duck with ginger sauce €13.25.

The Península de Formentor

Heading northeast out of Port de Pollença, the road clears the military zone at the far end of the resort, before weaving up into the craggy hills of the 20km-long **Península de Formentor**, the final spur of the Serra de Tramuntana. At first, the road (which suffers a surfeit of tourists from mid-morning to mid-afternoon) travels inland, out of sight of the true grandeur of the scenery, but after about 4km the **Mirador de Mal Pas** rectifies matters with a string of lookout points perched on the edge of plunging, north-facing sea cliffs. From here, it's another couple of kilometres to the woods backing onto the **Platja de Formentor**, a pine-clad beach of golden sand in a pretty cove. It's a beautiful spot, with views over to the mountains on the far side of the bay. From May to October, you can get here from Palma and Port de Pollença on a once-daily **bus** service, Monday to Saturday. At the end of the cove, opposite a tiny islet, stands the *Hotel Formentor* (☎971 899 100, ⓕ971 865 155; ⓺). Opened in 1930, this wonderful hotel – arguably the island's best – lies low against the forested hillside, its hacienda-style architecture enhanced by Neoclassical and Art Deco features and exquisite terraced gardens. Stay here if you can afford it – there's a surprisingly good chance of a vacant room, even in high summer. Beyond the turn-off for the beach, the main peninsula road runs along a wooded ridge, before tunnelling through Mont Fumat to emerge on the rocky mass of **Cap de Formentor**, a tapered promontory of bleak seacliffs and scrub-covered hills which offers spectacular views.

Alcúdia

Moving south from Port de Pollença, it's just 10km round the bay to the pint-sized town of **ALCÚDIA**, whose main claim to fame is its imitation medieval wall. Indeed, the whole place is overly spick and span, a poor reflection of the town's historical importance. Situated on a neck of land separating two large, sheltered bays, the site's strategic value was first recognized by the Phoenicians, and later by the Romans, who built their island capital, Pollentia, here in the first century AD, on top of the earlier settlement. In 426, the place was destroyed by the Vandals and lay neglected until the Moors built a fortress in about 800, naming it *Al Kudia* (On the Hill). After the Reconquest, Alcúdia prospered as a major trading centre, a role it performed well into the nineteenth century, when the town slipped into a long and gentle decline – until tourism refloated its economy.

It only takes an hour or so to walk around the antique lanes of Alcúdia's compact centre, and to explore the town walls and their fortified gates. This pleasant stroll can be extended by a visit to the meagre remains of Roman **Pollentia** (April–Sept Tues–Fri 10am–1.30pm & 5–7pm, Sat & Sun 10.30am–1pm; Oct–March Tues–Fri 10am–1.30pm & 3.30–5.30pm, Sat & Sun 10.30am–1pm; €1.20), whose broken pillars and mashed-up walls lie just outside the walls.

Buses to Alcúdia halt beside the town walls on Plaça Carles V; there's no tourist office. For **food**, there are several good cafés on Plaça Constitució, but it's hard to beat the cosy café-bar of *Ca's Capella*, just east of the church of Sant Jaume along c/Rectoria.

Port d'Alcúdia

PORT D'ALCÚDIA, 2km south of Alcúdia, is easily the biggest and busiest of the resorts on the Badia d'Alcúdia, its clutch of restaurants and café-bars attracting crowds from a seemingly interminable string of high-rise hotels and apartment buildings. The tower blocks are, however, relatively well distributed and the streets neat and tidy. Predictably, the daytime focus is the **beach**, a superb arc of pine-studded golden sand, which stretches south for 10km from the combined marina and fishing harbour.

Port d'Alcúdia acts as northern Mallorca's summertime transport hub, with frequent **bus** services to and from Palma, Port de Sóller, Port de Pollença, Pollença and Artà, as well as other neighbouring towns and resorts. Most local and long-distance bus services travel the length of **Carretera d'Artà**, the main drag, which slices right through the resort, running broadly parallel to the bay and punctuated by a series of clearly signed bus stops (there is no bus station). The main **turisme** (Easter to Oct Mon–Sat 9am–7pm; ☎971 892 615) is situated on Carretera d'Artà, about 2km south round the bay from the marina. The office can supply all sorts of information, most usefully free maps marked with all the resort's hotels and apartments, but bear in mind that in season vacant rooms are few and far between, and in winter almost everywhere is closed. In addition, a superabundance of **car, moped and bicycle rental** companies are strung out along Carretera d'Artà. Mountain bikes will cost you around €7.25 per day, €20 for three days.

Parc Natural de S'Albufera

Heading south around the bay from Port d'Alcúdia on the C712, it's about 6km to the **Parc Natural de S'Albufera** (daily: April–Sept 9am–7pm; Oct–March 9am–6pm; free), an eight-square-kilometre segment of pristine wetland. This is all that remains of the marshes that once extended round most of the bay – the rest has been developed to take advantage of the enormous pine-studded sandy beach. The signposted entrance to the park is on the C712, but access is only on foot or cycle – so if you're driving you'll need to park up on the main road. About 1km from the entrance, you come to the park's **reception centre**, from where footpaths radiate out into the reedy, watery tract beyond. It's a superb habitat, with ten well-appointed hides allowing excellent **bird-watching**. Over two hundred species have been spotted: resident wetland-loving birds, autumn and/or springtime migrants, and wintering species and birds of prey in their scores. There's no problem getting here by public transport – **buses** from Port d'Alcúdia to Ca'n Picafort stop beside the entrance.

Eastern Mallorca

Mallorca's **east coast**, stretching for about 60km north from Cala Figuera to Cala Rajada, is fretted by narrow **coves**, the remnants of prehistoric river valleys created when the level of the Mediterranean was much lower. Of great natural beauty, all but the least accessible of these coves has, however, been engulfed by a tide of development and, frankly, you're better off staying away, especially if you haven't got your own transport. That said, if you do decide to pass this way, there are one or two incidental attractions, not least the attractive minor road which links the resorts, running, for the most part, a few kilometres inland along the edge of the **Serres de Llevant**, a slim and benign band of grassy hills which rises to over 500m at its two extremities – south outside Felanitx and north around Artà.

Porto Cristo

Halfway up the east coast, **PORTO CRISTO** is the largest town hereabouts, a busy and slightly old-fashioned place near the two sets of caves that are the area's most popular tourist attractions. These are the **Coves des Hams** (daily 10.30am–5/6pm; €9) and the **Coves del Drac** (daily: April–Oct 10am–5pm; Nov–March 10.30am–3.30pm; €6.65), each of which can only be visited on a guided tour. The cave complexes are very similar – and both feature classical musicians sailing around on a subterranean lake – so you'd hardly want to visit them both; opt for the Drac (Dragon) caverns, which are located about fifteen minutes' walk from the centre of Porto Cristo.

Artà and around

Heading north from Porto Cristo, it's about 20km to **ARTÀ**, an ancient hill town of sun-bleached roofs clustered beneath a castellated chapel-shrine, with the bunching peaks of the Serres de Llevant providing a dramatic backdrop. It's a delightful scene, though at close quarters the town is something of an anti-climax – the cobweb of cramped and twisted alleys doesn't quite match the setting. Nonetheless, the ten-minute trek to the **Santuari de Sant Salvador**, the shrine at the top of Artà, is a must for the views out over eastern Mallorca. Also make time to visit the substantial remains of the prehistoric settlement of **Ses Paisses** (April–Sept daily 9am–1pm & 3–7pm; Oct–March Mon–Fri 9am–1pm & 2.30–5pm, Sat 9am–1pm; €1.20), tucked away in a grove of olive, carob and holm oak trees about 1km to the south of the town.

Buses to Artà stop on the edge of the town centre, beside the C715. From the bus stop, it's a couple of hundred metres west to the short main street, c/Ciutat, where there are several **cafés**. The best is *Café Parisien*, at no. 18, a trendy little place with an outside terrace, that offers tasty tapas and salads at reasonable prices. The *Ca'n Balague*, at no. 19, is a more traditional café-bar also serving light meals.

Artà is a major crossroads: to the **east**, the main road cuts through the village of **CAPDEPERA** – a dusty, elongated village, crouched below a fine crenellated castle – before descending to the coast at the massive resort of **CALA RAJADA**, whose excellent beaches are a favourite haunt of German package tourists. Twice-daily, passenger-only **catamarans** connect the resort with Ciutadella in Menorca (see p.979) throughout the year. To the **west**, the C712 weaves through the hills to Ca'n Picafort and the Badia d'Alcúdia (see opposite).

Menorca

Often and unfairly maligned as an overdeveloped, package-tourist nightmare, boomerang-shaped **Menorca** is, in fact, the least developed – and second largest – member of the Balearic Islands. Unlike its neighbours, Menorca remains essentially rural, its rolling fields, wooded ravines and humpy hills filling out the interior in between its two main – but still small – towns of **Maó** and **Ciutadella**. Much of this landscape looks pretty much as it did at the turn of the twentieth century and only on the edge of the island, and then only in parts, have its rocky coves been colonized by sprawling villa complexes. Neither is the development likely to spread: the resorts have been kept at a discreet distance from the two main towns, and this is how the Menorcans like it. Furthermore, determined to protect their island from the worst excesses of the tourist industry, the Menorcans have clearly demarcated development areas and are meanwhile pushing ahead with a variety of environmental schemes.

Menorca is littered with prehistoric monuments, weatherworn stone remains that are evidence of a sophisticated culture. Little is known for sure of the island's prehistory, but the monuments are thought to be linked to those of Sardinia and are classified as part of the second-millennium BC **Talayot culture**. *Talayots* are the rock mounds found all over the island – popular belief has it that they functioned as watchtowers, but it's a theory few experts accept. They have no interior stairway, and only a few are found on the coast. Even so, no one has come up with a much more convincing explanation. The megalithic *taulas* – huge stones topped with another to form a T, around 4m high and unique to Menorca – are even more puzzling. They have no obvious function, and they are almost always found alongside a *talayot*. Some of the best-preserved *talayot* and *taula* remains are on the edge of Maó at the **Trepucó** site. Then there are *navetas* (dating from 1400 to 800 BC), stone-slab constructions shaped like an inverted loaf tin. Many have false ceilings, and although you can stand up inside they were clearly not living spaces – communal pantries, perhaps, or more probably tombs.

In more recent history, the long and slender, deep-water channel of the port of Maó promoted Menorca to an important position in European affairs. The British saw its potential as a naval base during the War of the Spanish Succession and achieved their aim by having the island ceded to them through the Treaty of Utrecht (1713). Spain regained possession in 1783, but with the threat of Napoleon in the Mediterranean, a new British base was temporarily established under admirals Nelson and Collingwood. The British influence is still considerable, especially in architecture: the sash windows so popular in Georgian design are still sometimes referred to as *winderes*, locals often part with a fond *bye-bye*, and there's a substantial expatriate community. The British also moved the capital from Ciutadella to Maó and constructed the main island road. More importantly they introduced the art of distilling juniper berries: Menorcan **gin** (Xoriguer, Beltran or Nelson) is renowned.

Before much of it was killed off by tourism, Menorcan **agriculture** had become highly advanced. A dry stone wall protected every field from the *tramóntana* (the vicious north wind), which ripped away the topsoil, and even olive trees had their roots individually protected in little stone wells. Nowadays, apart from a few acres of rape and corn, many of the fields are barren, but the walls survive. Any vegetation that dares to emerge above their safety is soon swept away by the gusts.

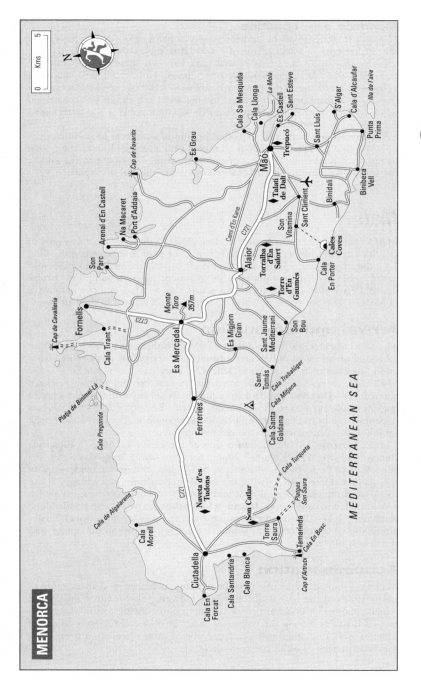

MENORCA

MEDITERRANEAN SEA

N

0   Kms   5

Cap de Cavalleria

Cala Pregonda

Platja de Binimel-Là

Fornells

Cala Tirant

Son Parc

Arenal d'En Castell

Na Macaret

Port d'Addaia

Cap de Favàritx

Es Grau

Cala Sa Mesquida

Cala Llonga

La Mola

Es Castell

Sant Esteve

Maó

Trepucó

Sant Lluís

S'Algar

Cala d'Alcaufar

Illa de l'aire

Punta Prima

Binibeca Vell

Binidalí

Talatí de Dalt

Sant Climent

Son Vitamina

Camí d'En Kane

C721

Alaior

Torralba d'En Salort

Torre d'En Gaumés

Cala En Porter

Cales Coves

Monte Toro 357m

Es Mercadal

C723

Es Migjorn Gran

Sant Jaume Mediterrani

Son Bou

Sant Tomàs

Cala Trebalúger

Cala Mitjana

Cala Santa Galdana

Ferreries

Cala Turqueta

Naveta d'es Tudons

Son Catlar

C721

Plàtges Son Saura

Torre Saura

Tamarinda

Cala En Bosc

Cap d'Artrutx

Cala de Algaiarens

Cala Morell

Ciutadella

Cala En Forcat

Cala Santandría

Cala Blanca

Menorca practicalities

Menorca stretches from the enormous natural harbour of Maó in the east to the smaller port of Ciutadella in the west. **Bus** routes are distinctly limited, adhering mostly to the main central road between these two, occasionally branching off to the larger coastal resorts. Consequently, you'll need your own **vehicle** to reach any of the emptier **beaches** – which are sometimes down a track fit only for four-wheel-drive – and the wind, which can be very helpful when it's blowing behind you, is distinctly uncomfortable if you're trying to ride into it on a **moped**.

Accommodation is at an exploited premium, with little of anything outside Maó and Ciutadella – and you can count on all the beds in all the resorts being block-booked by the tour operators from the beginning to the end of the season (May to October). Advance booking is essential in August.

Maó

MAÓ (*Mahón* in Castilian), the island capital, is likely to be your first port of call. It's a respectable, almost dull little town, the people restrained and polite. So is the architecture – an unusual hybrid of classical Georgian sash-windowed town houses and tall, gloomy Spanish apartment blocks shading the narrow streets. Port it may be, but there's no seamy side to Maó, and the harbour is home to a string of restaurants and cafés that attract tourists in their droves.

Arrival and information

Menorca's **airport**, just 5km southwest of Maó, is short on amenities, with just a handful of car rental outlets and a **tourist information desk**, which has a good selection of free literature (May–Oct daily 8.30am–11pm; ☎971 157 115). There are no buses into the town, but the taxi fare will only set you back about €7.50. **Ferries** from Barcelona and Palma sail right up the inlet to Maó harbour, mooring next to the Trasmediterránea offices (☎902 454 645) directly beneath the town centre. From behind the ferry dock, it's a five-minute walk up the wide stone stairway to the old part of town.

Maó's **turisme,** on the landward side of the centre on Plaça S'Esplanada (June–Aug Mon–Fri 8.30am–7.30pm, Sat 9am–2pm; Sept–May Mon–Fri 9am–1.30pm & 5–7pm, Sat 9am–1pm ☎971 363 790), will provide maps of the island and free leaflets giving the lowdown on almost everything you can think of, from archeological sites and beaches to bus timetables, car rental, accommodation and banks. **Island-wide buses** arrive at the stands along Avinguda Quadrado, round the corner from the tourist office; **local buses**, which shuttle up and down the southeast coast, stop just across the square from the tourist office.

Accommodation

Maó has a limited supply of **accommodation** and excessive demand tends to inflate prices at the height of the season. However, along with Ciutadella, it remains the best Menorcan bet for bargain lodgings, with a small concentration of **hostales** among the workaday streets near Plaça Princep, a couple of minutes' walk east of the town centre. None of these places are inspiring, but they're reasonable enough and convenient.

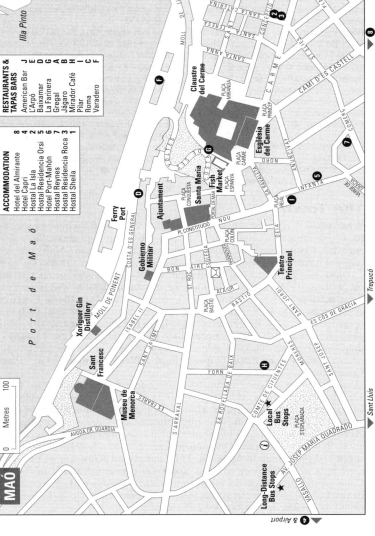

MAÓ

Port de Maó

Illa Pinto

Naval Base

ACCOMMODATION

Hotel del Almirante	8
Hotel Capri	4
Hostal La Isla	2
Hostal Residencia Orsi	5
Hotel Port-Mahón	6
Hostal Reynes	7
Hostal Residencia Roca	3
Hostal Sheila	1

RESTAURANTS & TAPAS BARS

American Bar	J
L'Arpó	E
Baixamar	D
La Farinera	G
Gregal	A
Jágaro	B
Mirador Café	H
Pilar	I
Roma	C
Varadero	F

Xoriguer Gin Distillery

Sant Francesc

Museu de Menorca

Ferry Port

Gobierno Militar

Ajuntament

Santa Maria

Fish Market

Claustre del Carme

Església del Carme

Teatre Principal

Local Bus Stops

Long-Distance Bus Stops

Metres 0 100

▲ Ⓐ Ⓑ & Ⓒ   ▲ ❻

► ❽

► Trepucó

► Sant Lluís

◄ ❹ & Airport

Budget options

Hostal La Isla, c/Santa Caterina 4, at the corner of c/Concepció ☎971 366 492 or 971 364 358. Recently refurbished, this an excellent, comfortable one-star run by a very friendly couple. The 25 attractive rooms may be on the small side, but all have private baths and TV. Popular bar and restaurant downstairs. ❹

Hostal Residencia Orsi, c/Infanta 19 ☎ & ℱ 971 364 751. Nicest *hostal* in town. Frugal rooms, most with shared bath, with large windows and green shutters. Scottish-American owners are a mine of local information. Simple help-yourself breakfast included. ❺

Hostal Reynes, c/Comerç 26, just off c/Infanta ☎971 364 059. Undistinguished modern block with stark but clean shared-bath rooms – 12 doubles and 12 singles. Breakfast extra. ❸

Hostal Residencia Roca, c/Carme 137, at the corner of c/Santa Caterina ☎971 350 839. Very basic, no-frills rooms, none with private bath, in a plain but quite cheerful modern block with a ground-floor café. ❸

Moderate and expensive options

Hotel del Almirante, Carretera de Maó, nearly 2km from Maó by the coastal road to Es Castell ☎971 362 700, ℱ 971 362 704. Once the residence of British admiral Lord Collingwood, this maroon and cream Georgian house has a delightful, antique-crammed interior, though some of the bedrooms are modern affairs overlooking the swimming pool round the back. The package-tour operators Thomson use the place, but there are often vacancies. ❼

Hotel Capri, c/Sant Esteve 8 ☎971 361 400, ℱ 971 350 853, ℮capri@rtmhotels.com. Large, proficiently modern three-star hotel in the centre of Maó, popular with business people. A brief walk west of the tourist office along Avgda. Quadrado. ❼

Hotel Port-Mahón, Avgda. Fort de l'Eau s/n ☎971 362 600, ℱ 971 351 050. Elegant colonial-style hotel of columns, pediments and circular windows, in a superb location overlooking the Maó inlet. There's a swimming pool and all mod cons. Room prices vary enormously, with the top whack a hefty €192. The hotel is a twenty-minute walk east of the town centre along via c/Carme. ❾

Hotel Sheila, c/Santa Cecília 41, at the corner of c/Sant Nicolau ☎971 364 855. This old terraced house has been tastefully refurbished in ultra-modern style, with eleven neat and tidy rooms. Car parking and café. ❼

The Town

While you'll need transport to get around the island, **Maó** itself is best seen on **foot** – its compact centre, with its deep streets rising high above the water's edge, is no more than ten minutes' walk from top to bottom. Maó's fine setting and its crowded old mansions are its charm, rather than any specific sight, and you can explore the place thoroughly in a day. From near the ferry terminal, set beneath the cliff that supports the remains of the city wall, a generous stone stairway leads up to four small squares. The first, the **Plaça Espanya**, offers views right across the port and bay and houses Maó's fish market, in operation since 1927. Immediately to the left is the **Plaça Carme**, with a simple Carmelite church whose cloisters have been adapted to house a variety of shops and fruit and vegetable stalls plus a supermarket in the basement. In the other direction from Plaça d'Espanya lie the **Plaça Conquesta** and **Plaça Constitució**.

Plaça Constitució boasts the town's main church, **Santa María**. Founded in 1287 by Alfonso III to celebrate the island's Reconquest and remodelled on several subsequent occasions, the church is a pleasing architectural hybrid and inside a particular highlight is the **high altar**, whose larger-than-life Baroque excesses shoot up to the roof flanked by spiral columns. The church's pride and joy is, however, its **organ**, a monumental piece of woodwork, all trumpeting angels and pipes, built in Austria in 1810 and lugged across half of Europe at the height of the Napoleonic wars under the concerned charge of Admiral Collingwood. Next door, the eighteenth-century **ajuntament** benefited from British largesse too, its attractive arcaded facade graced by a clock that was presented to the islanders by the first British governor.

A short walk away, at the end of c/Isabel II, the Baroque facade of **Sant Francesc** appears as a cliff face of pale golden stone set above the rounded, Romanesque-style arches of its doorway. The church was a long time in the making, its construction spread over the seventeenth and eighteenth centuries, following the razing of the town by Barbarossa in 1535. The nave is poorly lit, but it's still possible to pick out the pinkish tint in much of the stone and the unusual spiral decoration of the pillars. In contrast, the **Chapel of the Immaculate Conception**, tucked away off the north side of the nave, is flooded with light; this octagonal wonderland of garlanded vines and roses is an exquisite example of the Churrigueresque style. The chapel is attributed to Francesc Herrara, who trained in Rome and worked in both Menorca and Mallorca.

The adjacent monastic buildings now house the **Museu de Menorca** (Tues–Sat 10am–1pm & 4–6pm, Sun 10am–2pm; free) easily the island's biggest and best museum. Entry to the collection is through the **cloister** of Sant Francesc, whose sturdy pillars and vaulted aisles represent the high point of Menorcan Baroque. Beyond, up the stairs, the museum's **first floor** holds a wide sample of prehistoric artefacts, beginning with bits and pieces left by the Neolithic pastoralists who settled here about 4000 BC; there's also an extensive range of material from the Talayotic period. Most of the exhibits carry multilingual labels.

From the museum, it's a brisk five-minute walk up through the town to the flowerbeds and fountains of the undistinguished main square, the **Plaça S'Esplanada**. South from Plaça S'Esplanada a thirty-minute walk will take you to the prehistoric remains of **Trepucó** (open access; free). To get there, follow c/Moreres from the northeast corner of the square, take the first right down c/Cós de Gràcia and then go straight on down c/Verge de Gràcia to the ring road. Here, go straight over the traffic island and follow the twisting lane directly ahead, past the cemetery. Thereafter the route is not, at present, clearly signed. After 200m, go straight at the fork, and then – 500m later – veer left at the fork and, after a further 100m, turn right. Surrounded by olive trees and dry-stone walls, the tiny site's focal point is a 4.2-metre-high and 2.75-metre-wide **taula**, one of the largest and best preserved of these T-shaped monoliths on the island. The *taula* stands inside a circular compound which is edged by the remains of several broadly circular buildings. These were thoroughly excavated by a team of archeologists from Cambridge University in the late 1920s, but even they couldn't work out how the complex was structured. There are two cone-shaped **talayots** close by, the larger one accessible, the other not. The shape of the larger *talayot* is, however, not entirely authentic as, during the invasion of 1781, the French increased its width to mount their guns.

Back near the ferry terminal, the **Xoriguer gin distillery** (June–Aug Mon–Fri 8am–7pm, Sat 9am–1pm; Sept–May Mon–Fri 9am–1pm & 4–7pm; free) is where you should go to help yourself to free samples of gin, various liqueurs and other spirits. From here, you can stroll the entire length of the **quayside** to the southeast edge of town, a half-hour trip that will take you past a long string of restaurants, bars and cafés as well as the town's bulging marinas. By day, this makes a relaxing stroll; at night it's slightly more animated, but not much.

Eating, drinking and nightlife

Maó has a place in culinary history as the eighteenth-century birthplace of **mayonnaise** (*mahonesa*). Various legends, all of them involving the French, claim to identify its inventor: take your pick from the chef of the French commander besieging Maó; a peasant woman dressing a salad for another French general; or a housekeeper disguising rancid meat from the taste buds of a French officer. The French also changed the way the Menorcans bake their bread, while the British started the dairy industry and encouraged the roasting of meat. Unfortunately, traditional Balearic food is not very much in evidence these days, as most of Maó's **restaurants** specialize in Spanish, Catalan or Italian dishes. These tourist-oriented establishments are mainly spread out along the harbourside – the Moll de Ponent west of the main stairway, the Moll de Llevant to the east. There's also a smattering of cheaper restaurants and **coffee bars** in the centre of town, though surprisingly few **tapas bars**.

Nightlife is not Maó's forte, but some fairly lively **bars** dot the harbourfront, staying open till around 2am on summer weekends.

Cafés and tapas bars

Café Baixamar, Moll de Ponent 17. Attractively decorated little café-bar, with old-fashioned mirrors and soft-hued paintwork, serving tasty traditional Menorcan snacks and tapas – island cheese and sausage, for example, costing just €3.

Café-bar La Farinera, Moll de Llevant 84. Spruce and modern café-bar offering tasty snacks near the ferry port. Usually open from 6am. Also has a selection of interesting photographs of old Menorca stuck on the walls.

Mirador Café, Plaça Espanya s/n. Tasty snacks and great views over the harbour from this little café-bar with a terrace. Footsteps from the fish market, at the top of the main stairway leading from the harbour to the town centre. Jazz is the favoured background music.

Varadero, Moll de Llevant 4. Close to the ferry terminal, this smart, modern place has a restaurant on one side and a café-bar on the other. The café-bar is the place to aim for – a stylish spot to nurse a drink and sample a small range of tapas. Very popular with tourists in the summer.

Restaurants

L'Arpó, Moll de Llevant 124 ☎971 369 844. Cosy and intimate restaurant featuring a superb selection of fish dishes from €11. Try the paella.

Gregal, Moll de Llevant 306 ☎971 366 606. The decor is uninspired – just run-of-the-mill modern and comfortable – but the food is outstanding, with mouthwatering seafood dishes prepared in all sorts of delicious (and often traditional) ways. Try, for instance, the John Dory in leek sauce at €27 or the sea anemone fritters at €10. Near the east end of the harbour front.

Jàgaro, Moll de Llevant 334 ☎971 362 390. Ambitious restaurant with a smart, traditional interior and a terrace packed with greenery. The menu

is perhaps a little too wide-ranging for its own good, featuring everything from hamburgers to paella. Stick to the fish at €12–18 per main course. At the east end of the waterfront.

Pilar, c/Forn 61 ☎971 366 817. A very intimate and cosy family-run place featuring traditional Menorcan cuisine, with main courses costing around €12. It's near Plaça S'Esplanada: leave the square along c/Pi, a short pedestrianized alley on its north side, take the first right and then the first left. Closed Mon, sometimes Sun too. Recommended.

Roma, Moll de Llevant 295. Popular, fast-service eatery specializing in well-prepared Italian food at bargain prices, with pasta and pizzas from €5.50. The decor is a tad old-fashioned, but that seems to suit the clientele. Closed in winter.

Bars and nightclubs

Bar Akelarre, Moll de Ponent 41. Probably the best – and certainly the most fashionable – bar in town, down on the waterfront near the ferry terminal. Occupies an attractively renovated ground-floor vault with stone walls and a miniature garden-cum-terrace at the back, right at the foot of the old city walls. Jazz and smooth modern sounds are the backcloth with occasional live acts.

Café Marès, Plaça Conquesta s/n. Down a narrow alley off Plaça Conquesta and with fine views over the port, this smart café-bar, with its lean modern furnishings and pastel-painted walls, is one of Maó's chicest spots.

Nou Bar, c/Nou 1. The ground-floor café here, with its ancient armchairs and gloomy lighting, is a dog-eared old place much favoured by locals. At the corner of Costa de Sa Plaça.

Sí, c/Verge de Gràcia 16. Low-key, locals' late-night bar south of Plaça Reial. Usually open from 11.30pm to around 3am.

Listings

Banks Banco de Credito Balear, Plaça S'Esplanada 2; Banca March, c/Sa Ravaleta 7; Banco de Santander, c/Moreres 46 and 69.

Bicycle rental VRB, c/S'Arraval 52 ☎ 971 353 798, rents ordinary and mountain bikes at reasonable rates. Advance booking recommended.

Bookshops Llibrería Fundació, facing Plaça Colón at Costa de Sa Plaça 14 ☎ 971 363 543 (Mon–Fri 9.30am–1.30pm & 5–8pm, Sat 9.30am–1.30pm), has a fair selection of English-language guidebooks and is strong on bird-watching guides. It also has general maps of Menorca – including the pick of the bunch, the Distrimapas Telstar (1:75000) – plus a reasonable, though far from exhaustive, assortment of IGN walking maps.

Car rental Amongst several companies, both Avis (☎ 971 361 576) and Atesa (☎ 971 366 213) have branches at the airport, while downtown there's another Avis outlet at Plaça S'Esplanada 53

(☎ 971 364 778), plus many smaller concerns – the tourist office has an exhaustive list.

Emergencies General emergency number (fire, police and ambulance) ☎ 112. Local Police ☎ 092.

Ferries Schedules, tariffs and tickets direct from the ferry line, Trasmediterránea (☎ 902 454 645), next to the ferry port.

Internet access *Webera*, opposite the Església de Santa Maria at c/ Església 1B (Mon–Fri 10am–2pm & 4–9pm, Sat 6–10pm; €3/hr; ☎ 971 356 873).

Maps See Bookshops above

Mopeds Motos Gelabert, Avgda J. A. Clavé 12 ☎ 971 360 614.

Post office The central *correu* is at c/Bon Aire 11–13, near Plaça Bastió (Mon–Fri 9am–5pm, Sat 9am–1pm).

Taxis There's a taxi rank on Plaça S'Esplanada. Alternatively, telephone Radio Taxis ☎ 971 367 111.

Northwest to Fornells

Northwest of Maó, the road to Fornells runs through some of Menorca's finest scenery – the fields are cultivated and protected by great stands of trees, and the land rises as the road approaches Monte Toro (see p.989) and skirts round it to the north. At the end of the road, just 25km from the capital, **FORNELLS** is a low-rise, classically pretty fishing village at the mouth of a long and chubby bay. Despite the lack of a decent beach, it has been popular with tourists for years, above all for its **seafood restaurants**, whose speciality, *caldereta de llagosta* (*langosta* in Castilian), is a fabulously tasty – and wincingly expensive – lobster stew. Nevertheless, there's been little development, just a slim trail of holiday homes extending north from the village in a suitably unobtrusive style.

The wild and rocky coastline west of Fornells boasts several **cove beaches** of outstanding beauty. Getting to them, however, can be a problem: this portion of the island has barely been touched by the developers, so the coast is often poorly signposted and the access roads are of very variable quality – some are just dirt tracks. These access roads branch off from the narrow, asphalted country lanes which criss-cross the lovely pastoral hinterland. Two excellent beaches to head for are **Binimel-Là** and **Cala Pregonda**. Public transport around here is, as you might expect, nonexistent, and the nearest car rental is back in Maó (see above).

As regards **food**, Fornells boasts several fine waterfront **restaurants** to either side of the minuscule main square, Plaça S'Algaret. Such is their reputation that King Juan Carlos regularly drops by on his yacht, and many people phone up days in advance with their orders. The royal favourite is the harbourside *Es Pla* (☎ 971 376 655), which offers a superb paella for two for €50 as well as the traditional lobster stew. More relaxed alternatives include *Sibaris*, Plaça S'Algaret 1 (☎ 971 376 619), which concentrates on a magnificent *caldereta de llagosta* – as does the *Es Port*, nearby at c/Riera 5 (☎ 971 376 403). As a general rule, reckon on about €12–15 for a seafood main course, twice that for paella or lobster stew.

Fornells has three reasonably priced, comfortable **hostales**. The two-star *S'Algaret*, Plaça S'Algaret 7, is a neat little place, with slightly old-fashioned furnishings and plain but cheerful rooms (May–Oct; ☎971 376 674, ℱ971 376 666; ⑤), and the nearby *Hostal Residencia La Palma* is very similar (April–Oct; ☎971 376 634; ⑤). The *Hostal Fornells*, c/Major 17 (☎971 376 676, ℱ971 376 688; ⑦), is slightly smarter, a sprucely modern three-star with a swimming pool.

Across the island

The road from Maó to Ciutadella, the **C721**, forms the backbone of Menorca, and what little industry the island enjoys – a few shoe factories and producers of the island's famous cheeses – is concentrated along it.

Alaior

Just 4km out of Maó, you pass the short and clearly signposted country lane leading to **Talatí de Dalt**, another illuminating Talayotic remnant. Much larger than Trepucó, the site is enclosed by a Cyclopean wall and features an imposing *taula*, which is adjacent to the heaped stones of the main *talayot*. All around are the scant remains of prehistoric dwellings. The exact functions of these are not known, but there's no doubt that the *taula* was the village centrepiece, and probably the focus of religious ceremonies. The rustic setting is charming – olive and carob trees abound and a tribe of boar roots around the undergrowth.

Cheese is a good reason to stop at **ALAIOR**, 12km from Maó, an old market town which has long been the nucleus of the island's dairy industry. There are two major companies, both of which have factory shops near to – and clearly signposted from – the old main road, as it cuts across the southern periphery of the town centre: come off the new bypass at the most easterly of the three Alaior exits and follow the signs. Approaching from Maó, the first shop is owned by **La Payesa** (Mon–Fri 9am–1pm & 5–8pm), while the second is the bigger and better outlet of **Coinga** (Mon–Fri 9am–1pm & 5–8pm, Sat 9am–1pm). Both companies sell a similar product, known generically as *queso Mahon*, after the port from which it was traditionally exported. It's a richly textured, white, semi-fat cheese made from pasteurized cow's milk with a touch of ewe's milk added for extra flavour. The cheese is sold at four different stages of maturity, either *tierno* (young), *semi-curado* (semi-mature), *curado* (mature) or *añejo* (very mature). Both shops have the full range and, although quite expensive, their prices are the best you'll see.

On the hill above the cheese shops, the old centre of Alaior is a tangle of narrow streets and bright white houses set beneath the imposing church of **Santa Eulàlia**. Apart, however, from a quick gambol up and down the hill, there's not much reason to hang around – unless you happen to be here the second weekend of August when Alaior lets loose during the **Festa de Sant Llorenç**.

Es Mercadal and Monte Toro

Nine kilometres northwest of Alaior you arrive at **ES MERCADAL**, squatting amongst the hills at the very centre of the island. Another old market town, it's an amiable little place of whitewashed houses and trim allotments whose antique centre straddles a quaint watercourse. The town also boasts a top-notch **restaurant**, the *Can Aguedet*, at c/Lepanto 30 (☏971 375 391), which serves up traditional Menorcan cuisine, and a simple, one-star **hostal residencia**, the spick-and-span *Jeni*, in a modern building at c/Miranda del Toro 81 (☏971 375 059; ❼). To get there, leave the main square – Sa Plaça – along c/Nou and take the first left and then the first right. **Buses** from Maó and Ciutadella stop just off the C721 on Avinguda Metge Camps, which leads on to c/Nou.

From Es Mercadal you can set off on the ascent of **Monte Toro**, a steep 3.2-kilometre climb along a serpentine road. At 357m, the summit is the island's highest point and offers wonderful vistas: on a good day you can see almost the whole island, on a bad one to Fornells, at least. From this lofty vantage point, Menorca's geological division becomes apparent: to the north, Devonian rock (mostly reddish sandstone) supports a rolling, sparsely populated landscape edged by a ragged coastline; to the south, limestone predominates in a rippling plain that boasts both the island's best farmland and, as it approaches the south coast, its deepest valleys.

Monte Toro has been a place of pilgrimage since medieval times, and the Augustinians plonked a monastery on the summit in the seventeenth century. Bits of the original construction survive in the **convent**, which shares the site today with an army outpost and a monumentally ugly statue of Christ. Much of the convent is out of bounds, but the public part, approached across a handsome courtyard, encompasses a couple of gift shops, a delightful terrace café and a cosy church.

Ferreries

The next town along the C721 is **FERRERIES**, an appealing little place, no more than a village really. There's little to detain you here, though one definite plus is the *Vimpi* bar on the plaza at the entrance to town, which serves some of the tastiest tapas on the island. Heading on from Ferreries, you'll find one of the best examples of a *naveta* – the **Naveta d'es Tudons** – beside the main road some 6km short of Ciutadella. Seven metres high and fourteen long, the structure is made of massive stone blocks slotted together in a sophisticated dry-stone technique. The narrow entrance leads into a small antechamber, which was once sealed off by a stone slab; beyond lies the main chamber where the bones of the dead were stashed away after the flesh had been removed. Folkloric memories of the *navetas*' original purpose survived into modern times, for the Menorcans were loathe to go near these odd-looking and solitary monuments well into the eighteenth century.

Ciutadella and around

Like Maó, **CIUTADELLA** sits high above its harbour. Here, though, navigation is far more difficult, up a narrow channel too slender for all but the smallest of cargo ships. Despite this nautical inconvenience, Ciutadella has been the island's capital for most of its history. The Romans chose it, the Moors adopted it as *Medina Minurka*, and the Catalans of *la reconquista* flattened the place and began all over again. In 1558, the Catalan-built town was, in its turn, razed by Turkish corsairs. Several thousand captives were carted off to the slave markets of Istanbul, but the survivors determinedly rebuilt Ciutadella in grand style, its compact, fortified centre brimming with the mansions of the rich. To the colonial powers of the eighteenth century, however, Ciutadella's feeble port had no appeal when compared with Maó's magnificent inlet. In 1722 the British moved the capital to Maó, which has flourished as a trading centre ever since, and Ciutadella stagnated – a long-lasting economic reverie that has, fortunately, preserved its old and beautiful centre as if in aspic. The bulk of the Menorcan aristocracy remained in Ciutadella, where the colonial powers pretty much left them to stew – an increasingly redundant, landowning class far from the wheels of mercantile power. Consequently, there's very little British or French influence in Ciutadella's **architecture**; instead, the narrow, cobbled streets boast fine old palaces, hidden away behind high walls, and a set of Baroque and Gothic churches very much in the Spanish tradition.

Essentially, it's the whole architectural ensemble that gives Ciutadella its appeal rather than any specific sight, and that, together with some excellent restaurants and an adequate supply of *hostales* and hotels, makes this a lovely place to stay. Allow at least a couple of days, more if you seek out one of the beguiling cove beaches within easy striking distance of town: **Cala Turqueta** is the pick of the bunch.

Arrival and information

Ciutadella's compact centre could hardly be more convenient. **Buses** from Maó and points east arrive at the station on c/Barcelona, just south off the end of the Camí de Maó, an extension of the main island highway, the C721. **Local buses** shuttle up and down the west coast from Plaça dels Pins, on the west side of the town centre next to the main square, Plaça d'es Born. **Catamarans** from Cala Rajada and **car ferries** from Port d'Alcúdia, both on Mallorca, dock in the harbour below the Plaça d'es Born.

The **turisme** (May–Oct Mon–Fri 9am–1.30pm & 6–8pm, Sat 9am–1pm; Nov–April Mon–Fri 9am–1.30pm & 5–7pm, Sat 9am–1pm; ☎971 382 693) has buckets of information on Menorca as a whole and Ciutadella in particular. It's opposite the cathedral on Plaça Catedral, bang in the middle of the old town, which can only be explored on foot.

Accommodation

There's hardly a plethora of **accommodation** in Ciutadella, but the town does have two quality hotels that aren't booked up by package-tour operators and a handful of fairly comfortable and reasonably priced *hostales* dotted in and around the centre, with a concentration in the vicinity of Plaça Alfons III and Plaça Artrutx.

Hotel Residencia Alfonso III, Camí de Maó 53 ☎971 380 150, ⓕ 971 481 529. Brashly modern but fairly well-maintained hotel with fifty simple one-star rooms. Located beside the main road from Maó, a couple of minutes' walk from the ring road; try to get a room at the back away from the noisy road. ⑥

Hostal Residencia Ciutadella, c/Sant Eloi 10 ☎ & ⓕ 971 383 462). Unassuming yet comfortable two-star, in an old terraced house down a narrow side street off Plaça Alfons III. Breakfast included. ⑥

Hotel Residencia Geminis, c/Josepa Rossinyol 4 ☎971 384 644, ⓕ 971 383 683. Painted pink

and white, with blue awnings to add to the effect, this well-tended, central and comfortable one-star certainly has comfortable rooms decorated in bright modern style. Closed Jan. ⑥

Hotel Madrid, c/Madrid s/n ☎971 380 328. Fourteen quite comfortable rooms in a villa-style building with its own ground-floor café-bar. Located near the sea a fifteen-minute walk west of the town centre, halfway along c/Madrid: follow Passeig Sant Nicolau from the Plaça dels Pins, take the third turning on the left (c/Saragossa) and you'll hit c/Madrid just east of the hotel at the first major intersection. ⑤

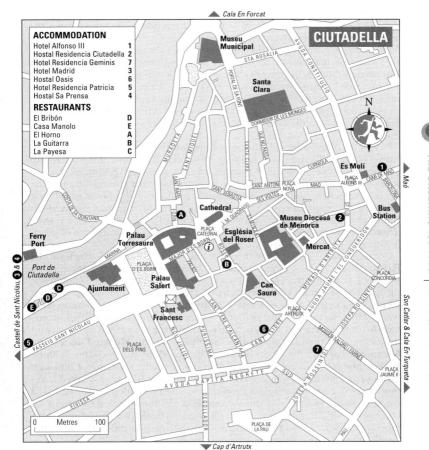

ACCOMMODATION

Hotel Alfonso III	1
Hostal Residencia Ciutadella	2
Hotel Residencia Geminis	7
Hotel Madrid	3
Hostal Oasis	6
Hotel Residencia Patricia	5
Hostal Sa Prensa	4

RESTAURANTS

El Bribón	D
Casa Manolo	E
El Horno	A
La Guitarra	B
La Payesa	C

CIUTADELLA

Hostal Residencia Oasis, c/Sant Isidre 33, footsteps away from Plaça Artrutx ☎971 382 197. Attractive one-star with nine simple rooms set around a courtyard-restaurant. Breakfast is included. ❹

Hotel Residencia Patricia, Passeig Sant Nicolau 90 ☎971 385 511, ℻ 971 481 120. The best hotel in town, popular with business folk and handy for the centre. Extremely comfortable, ultramodern rooms with all facilities, the only down point being the lack of a sea view – though the

best rooms have rooftop balconies with panoramic vistas. ❽

Hostal Sa Prensa, Plaça Madrid s/n ☎971 382 698. Villa-like, one-star *hostal* with six spartan rooms above a café-bar. It's a fifteen-minute walk west of the centre, close to the rocky seashore at the end of c/Madrid. To get there, follow Passeig Sant Nicolau from the Plaça dels Pins, take the fifth turning on the left (c/Joan Ramis i Ramis) and you'll hit c/Madrid just beside the *hostal*. ❹

The Town

Ciutadella's compact centre crowds around the fortified cliff face shadowing the south side of the harbour. The main *plazas* and points of interest are within a few strides of each other, on and around the main square, **Plaça d'es Born**, in the middle of which is a soaring **obelisk** commemorating the futile

981

defence against the Turks in 1558. On the western side of the square stands the **ajuntament**, whose nineteenth-century arches and crenellations mimic Moorish style, purposely recalling the time when the site was occupied by the wali's Alcázar (palace). In the square's northeast corner, the massive **Palau Torresaura**, built in the nineteenth century but looking far older, is the grandest of several aristocratic mansions edging the plaza. Embellished by self-important loggias, its frontage proclaims the family coat of arms above a large wooden door giving onto an expansive courtyard. The antique interior, however, is off limits, as the house is still owner-occupied – like most of its neighbours.

From Palau Torresaura, c/Major d'es Born leads to the **Cathedral** (Mon–Sat 8am–1pm & 6.30–9pm; free), built by Alfonso III at the end of the thirteenth century on the site of the chief mosque. So soon after the Reconquest, its construction is fortress-like, with windows set high above the ground – though the effect is somewhat disturbed by the flashy columns of the Neoclassical west doorway, the principal entrance. Inside, light from the narrow, lofty windows bathes the high altar in an ethereal glow, the hallmark of the Gothic style. There's also a wonderfully kitschy, pointed altar arch, and a sequence of glitzily Baroque side chapels.

Cutting down c/Roser from the cathedral, you'll pass the tiny **Església del Roser**, whose striking Churrigueresque facade, dating from the seventeenth century, boasts a quartet of pillars engulfed by intricate tracery. The church was the subject of bitter controversy when the British commandeered it for Church of England services – not at all to the liking of the Dominican friars who owned the place. At the end of c/Roser, turn left past the palatial, seventeenth-century mansion of **Can Saura**, which is distinguished by its elegant stonework, and then left again for c/Seminari and the **Museu Diocesà de Menorca** (Tues–Sat 10.30am–1.30pm, plus May–Sept Sun 10.30am–1.30pm; €1.80), housed in an old and dignified convent. Inside, the convent buildings surround an immaculately preserved Baroque cloister, whose vaulted aisles sport coats of arms and religious motifs. The museum's collection is distributed chronologically, and the first three rooms hold the most interesting pieces – a hotchpotch of Talayotic and early Classical archeological finds, notably a superbly crafted, miniature bull and a similarly exquisite little mermaid, both Greek bronzes dating from the fifth century BC.

Behind the museum lies the **mercat** (market), on Plaça Llibertat, another delightful corner of the old town, where fresh fruit, vegetable and fish stalls mingle with lively and inexpensive cafés selling the freshest of *ensaimadas*. Alternatively, c/Seminari proceeds north to intersect with the narrow, pedestrianized main street that runs through the old town – here **c/J.M. Quadrado** though it goes under various names along its route. To the east of this intersection, it boasts a block of whitewashed, vaulted arches, **Ses Voltes**, distinctly Moorish in inspiration and a suitable setting for several attractive shops and busy cafés. Carrer J.M. Quadrado then leads into **Plaça Nova**, a minuscule square edged by some of the most popular pavement cafés in town. Continuing east along c/Maó, you leave the cramped alleys of the old town at Plaça Alfons III.

Retracing your steps along c/J. M. Quadrado, turn north down c/Santa Clara for the five-minute walk to the **Museu Municipal** (mid-April to Oct Tues–Sat 11am–2pm & 7–10pm, Sun 7–10pm; Nov–April Tues–Sat 10am–2pm; €1.80), inhabiting part of the old city fortifications at the end of c/Portal de Sa Font. Inside the museum, a long vaulted chamber is given over to a wide range of archeological finds, amongst which there's a substantial collection of Talayotic remains, featuring artefacts garnered from all over the island and covering the several phases of Talayotic civilization. A leaflet detailing the exhibits in English is available free at reception.

Eating and drinking

For an early **breakfast** make your way to the market (*mercat*) on Plaça Llibertat, where a couple of simple cafés serve coffee and fresh pastries. Later in the day, round **lunchtime**, aim for c/J. M. Quadrado, Plaça Nova and Plaça Alfons III, which together hold a good selection of inexpensive café-bars, offering tapas and light meals. In the **evening**, more ambitious and expensive food is available at a string of excellent restaurants down by the harbourside, or at a couple of good places tucked away near Plaça d'es Born. Almost all the harbourside places have the advantage of an outside terrace, but note that – unlike those restaurants near the Plaça d'es Born – they usually close down in winter.

Cafés and café-bars

Café-bar Sa Llesca, Plaça Nova 4. One of several pleasant, and largely indistinguishable, café-bars on this tiny square. The ground-floor terrace café is one of the more popular spots in the old town and there's a first-floor dining room inside too.

Café-bar Ulises, Plaça Llibertat. Amenable, low-key café-bar next to the market. A locals' favourite, their *ensaimadas*, a snip at €1.20 each, are probably the best in town.

Cafeteria Sa Barreta, c/J. M. Quadrado 16. In the vaulted arches – Ses Voltes – bang in the middle of the old town, this unassuming family-run café is great for fresh *pa amb oli* and other traditional Menorcan snacks – sausage and so forth.

Pa amb oli, c/Nou de Julio s/n. Kitted out in vaguely rustic style, this excellent café-bar specializes in all things *menorquín*, with bowls of peppers and olives liberally distributed along the counter and smoked sausages hanging from the ceiling. The food is filling, delicious and traditional – and inexpensive too. Just off Plaça d'es Born. Highly recommended.

Unger Madison, c/Sant Joan 8. The chicest bar in town with angular wooden tables, soft lighting and modern paintings on the wall. First-rate selection of domestic and imported wines. Open Mon–Fri from 6pm till early in the morning, Sat from 8pm; closed Sun. Near Plaça Artrutx.

Restaurants

Casa Manolo, c/Marina 109 ☎971 380 003. Fabulous seafood, with main courses averaging around €15. At the end of the long line of restaurants flanking the south side of the harbour.

El Bribón, c/Marina 107 ☎971 385 050. Superb harbourside restaurant specializing in seafood, often prepared in traditional Menorcan style. Reckon on around €11 for the *menú del día*, €12–15 for a main course. Next door to *Casa Manolo*.

El Horno, c/Forn 12 ☎971 380 767. French-style basement restaurant, with good and reasonably priced food. Near the northeast corner of Plaça d'es Born. Evenings only.

La Guitarra, c/Dolors 1 ☎971 381 355. Arguably the best restaurant in town, this superb spot features the very best of Menorcan cuisine with main courses – anything from seafood to lamb – averaging a very reasonable €9. The restaurant occupies an old cellar, whose stone walls sport a scattering of agricultural antiques. It is located a short walk from the cathedral. Open Mon–Sat 12.30–3.30pm & 7.30–11pm; closed Sun. Highly recommended.

La Payesa, c/Marina 65 ☎971 380 021. Popular tourist restaurant with a wide-ranging menu, featuring everything from pizzas through omelettes to seafood. Very child-friendly.

Listings

Banks Banca March, Plaça d'es Born 10 and Plaça Alfons III, 5; Sa Nostra, c/Maó 2, on Plaça Nova.

Bicycle and moped rental Bicicletas Tolo, c/Sant Isidre 32, off Plaça Artrutx ☎971 381 576.

Car rental Ciutadella has half a dozen car rental companies. Amongst them, there's an Avis outlet on the ring road at Avgda Jaume I El Conqueridor

81 (☎971 381 174) and a Betacar along the street at no. 59 (☎971 382 998).

Catamarans and ferries Two ferry companies link Ciutadella and Mallorca. The first, **Cape Balear de Cruceros** (☎ & ⓕ 971 818 668), operates a passenger-only catamaran service from Cala Rajada between one and three times daily. It is a 75-

minute journey, which costs €48 return, a single half that. The second is **Iscomar** (☎ 902 119 128), whose car ferries run from Port d'Alcúdia once or twice daily in three and a half hours. The single fare is €26 and vehicles up to 4.5m in length cost an additional €47. Remember, however, that car hire firms on the Balearics do not allow their vehicles off their home island. In Ciutadella, the tourist office has information on sailings – as does Menorca's daily newspaper, the *Menorca – Diario Insular*. Both ferry companies have a kiosk down on the harbourside, but these are only open around departure times. You can buy tickets at the kiosk, or (if they aren't open) on the boat.

Internet access Café Internet, Plaça dels Pins 37 (€1.20/hr).

Emergencies General emergency number (fire, police and ambulance) ☎ 112. Local Police ☎ 092.

Maps and books Both Punt i Apart, c/Roser 14, and Libreria Pau, c/Nou de Juliol 23, have a reasonably good selection of travel books, general maps and Menorcan walking maps from the IGN series.

Post office The main *correu* is handily located at Plaça d'es Born 8 (Mon–Fri 8.30am–2.30pm, Sat 9.30am–1pm).

Taxis There are taxi ranks on Plaça dels Pins and Avgda. Constitució, round the corner from Plaça Alfons III. The fare from Ciutadella to the airport is, for example, €33.

Southeast of Ciutadella: Cala Turqueta

Beginning at the traffic island on c/Alfons V, the cross-country **Camí de Sant Joan de Missa** runs southeast from Ciutadella to the remote coves of the south coast. The one to head for is **Cala Turqueta**, a lovely cove flanked by wooded limestone cliffs. About 3km from town, you reach the clearly marked farmhouse of **Son Vivó**, where the road branches into two with the more easterly (signposted) road leading to the **Ermita de St Joan de Missa**, a squat, brightly whitewashed church with a dinky little bell tower. There's a fork here too, but the signs are easy to follow and you keep straight with the road slicing across the countryside before swerving round the **Marjal Vella farmhouse**. Shortly afterwards, about 4.3km from the church, you reach the start of the 1km-long, private lane that leads down to the little dell behind **Cala Turqueta**. The beach, a sheltered horseshoe of white sand, slopes gently into the sea, making ideal conditions for bathing, and because there are no facilities it's most unusual to find a crowd. Admission costs €4.20 per person.

Travel details

Mallorca

Trains

Palma to: Binissalem (hourly; 30min); Inca (hourly; 40min); Sóller (5 daily; 1hr 20min).

Buses

Ca'n Picafort to: Palma (2–5 daily; 1hr); Port d'Alcúdia (May–Oct every 15min; Nov–April 11 daily; 20min); Porto Cristo (May–Oct Mon–Sat 3 daily; 1hr).

Palma to: Alcúdia (May–Oct Mon–Sat hourly, 5 on Sun; Nov–April 3 daily; 1hr); Andratx (hourly; 45min); Artà (Mon–Sat 4 daily, 1 on Sun; 1hr 25min); Ca'n Picafort (2–5 daily; 1hr); Coves del Drac (May–Oct Mon–Sat 4 daily, 1 on Sun; 1hr); Deià (5 daily; 45min); Inca (Mon–Sat 9 daily, 4 on Sat, 2 on Sun; 30min); Lluc (1–2 daily; 1hr); Platja de Formentor (May–Oct Mon–Sat 1 daily; 1hr

15min); Pollença (3–5 daily; 1hr); Port d'Alcúdia (May–Oct Mon–Sat hourly, 5 on Sun; Nov–April 3–5 daily; 1hr 10min); Port de Pollença (3–5 daily; 1hr 10min); Port de Sóller (via the tunnel: Mon–Fri 5 daily, 2 on Sat, no Sun service; 35min; via Valldemossa: 5 daily; 55min); Sóller (via the tunnel: Mon–Fri 5 daily, 2 on Sat, no Sun service; 30min); Valldemossa (5 daily; 30min).

Port d'Alcúdia to: Alcúdia (May–Oct every 15min; Nov–April 11 daily; 15min); Cala Rajada (May–Oct Mon–Sat 2 daily; 40min); Ca'n Picafort (May–Oct every 15min, Nov–April 11 daily; 20min); Lluc (May–Oct Mon–Sat 2 daily; 1hr 15min); Palma (May–Oct Mon–Sat hourly, 5 on Sun; Nov–April 3–5 daily; 1hr 10min); Platja de Formentor (May–Oct 2 daily; 25min); Pollença (May–Oct every 15min, Nov–April 11 daily; 20min); Port de

Pollença (May–Oct every 15min; Nov–April 11 daily; 20min); Port de Sóller (May–Oct Mon–Sat 2 daily; 2hr).

Port de Pollença to: Alcúdia (May–Oct every 15min; Nov–April 11 daily; 20min); Ca'n Picafort (May–Oct every 15min; Nov–April 11 daily; 1hr); Palma (3–5 daily; 1hr 10min); Platja de Formentor (May–Oct 2 daily; 20min); Pollença (6–16 daily; 10min); Port d'Alcúdia (May–Oct every 15min; Nov–April 11 daily; 20min); Port de Sóller (May–Oct Mon–Sat 2 daily; 1hr 55min); Sóller (May–Oct Mon–Sat 2 daily; 2hr).

Port de Sóller to: Deià (5 daily; 20min); Palma

(via the tunnel: Mon–Fri 5 daily, 2 on Sat, no Sun service; 35min; via Valldemossa: 5 daily; 55min); Pollença (May–Oct Mon–Sat 2 daily; 1hr 45min); Port d'Alcúdia (May–Oct Mon–Sat 2 daily; 2hr); Port de Pollença (May–Oct Mon–Sat 2 daily; 1hr 50min); Sóller (5 daily; 5min); Valldemossa (5 daily; 30min).

Porto Cristo to: Ca'n Picafort (May–Oct Mon–Sat 3 daily; 1hr); Port d'Alcúdia (May–Oct Mon–Sat 3 daily; 1hr).

Valldemossa to: Andratx (Mon–Sat 1 daily; 1hr); Deià (5 daily; 15min); Palma (5 daily; 30min); Peguera (Mon–Sat 1 daily; 1hr 10min).

Menorca

Buses

Ciutadella to: Alaior (Mon–Sat 7 daily, 4 on Sun; 40min); Es Mercadal (Mon–Sat 7 daily, 4 on Sun; 30min); Ferreries (Mon–Sat 8 daily, 5 on Sun; 20min); Maó (Mon–Sat 6 daily, 4 on Sun; 1hr).
Ferreries to: Alaior (Mon–Sat 6 daily, 4 on Sun; 20min); Cala Santa Galdana (May–Oct 10 daily; 20min); Ciutadella (Mon–Sat 6 daily, 4 on Sun; 20min); Es Mercadal (Mon–Sat 6 daily, 4 on Sun; 10min); Maó (Mon–Sat 6 daily, 4 on Sun; 40min).

Fornells to: Es Mercadal (May–Oct 1–2 daily except on Sun; Nov–April 1 daily on 4 days a week; 15min); Maó (May–Oct 1–2 daily except on Sun; Nov–April 1 daily on 4 days a week; 35min).
Maó to: Alaior (Mon–Sat 11 daily, 9 on Sun; 20min); Ciutadella (Mon–Sat 6 daily, 4 on Sun; 1hr); Es Mercadal (Mon–Sat 6 daily, 4 on Sun; 30min); Ferreries (Mon–Sat 6 daily, 4 on Sun; 40min); Fornells (May–Oct 1–2 daily except on Sun; Nov–April 1 daily on 4 days a week; 35min).

Ibiza

Buses

Ibiza Town to: Figueretes (every 30min; 5min); Platja d'en Bossa (every 30min; 10min); Airport (hourly, 20mins); Portinatx (2–3 daily; 45min); Sant Antoni (every 30min; 30min); Ses Salines (hourly; 20min); Santa Eulària des Riu (hourly; 25min); Sant Joan (2–6 daily; 35min); Sant Miquel (2–4 daily; 30min); Sant Josep (5 daily, 20mins).

Boats

Ibiza Town to: Es Canar (7 daily; 1hr 10min); Platja d'en Bossa (6 daily; 20min); Santa Eulària des Riu (7 daily; 50min), Talamanca (every 20mins, 10mins).

Inter-island flights, ferries and hydrofoils

Flights are operated by Iberia (☎ 902 400 500, ⓦ www.iberia.com) and Air Europa (☎ 902 401 501, ⓦ www.aireuropa.com). Inter-island ferries and hydrofoils are operated by Trasmediterránea (☎ 902 454 645, ⓦ www.trasmediterranea.es) Baleària (☎ 902 191 068, ⓦ www.balearia.com) plus two other small operators that link Ibiza and Formentera.

Formentera to: Ibiza (9 ferries daily in summer, 5 in winter 1hr; 12 passenger-only hydrofoils daily in

summer, 4 daily in winter, 35min).
Ibiza to: Palma (12 daily flights, 30min; 2 daily ferries (5hrs) and one daily summer-only hydrofoil (2hr 15min)
Palma to: Maó (8 flights daily, 30min; 1–2 Trasmediterránea car ferries weekly, 6hr).
Cala Rajada to: Ciutadella (1–3 Cape Balear catamarans daily; 1hr 15min).
Port d'Alcúdia to: Ciutadella (1–2 Iscomar car ferries daily; 3hr 30min).

Mainland car ferry connections

Car ferries to the Balearics from the Spanish mainland are operated by Trasmediterránea (☎ 902 454 645, ⓦ www.trasmediterranea.es) and Balearia

(☎ 902 160 180, ⓦ www.balearia.com).
Barcelona to: Ibiza (2–4 weekly with Trasmediterránea; 9hr); Maó (3–8 weekly with

Trasmediterránea; 9hr); Palma (2–4 daily with Trasmediterránea; 8hr).
Dénia to: Ibiza (daily; 5hr); Palma via Sant Antoni with Balearia (1 daily; 8hr).

Valencia to: Ibiza (daily in summer, 2 weekly in winter; 8hr); Maó via Palma with Trasmediterránea (1 weekly; 17hr); Palma with Trasmediterránea (6–7 weekly; 9hr); Palma with Balearia (1 daily; 8hr).

Mainland Catamaran connections

Catamaran services to the Balearics from the Spanish mainland are operated by Trasmediterránea (☎902 454 645, ⓦwww.trasmediterranea.es) and Balearia (☎902 160 180, ⓦwww.balearia.com).

Barcelona to: Palma with Trasmediterránea (mid-June to mid-Sept 1 daily; 4hr 30min).
Valencia to: Ibiza with Trasmediterránea (mid-June to mid-Sept 1 daily; 2hr 30min); Palma with Trasmediterránea (mid-June to mid-Sept 1 daily; 6hr 15min).

contexts

contexts

CONTEXTS

The Historical Framework

Early Civilizations

The first identifiably Iberian peoples arrived on the peninsula from southern France towards the close of the Paleolithic age. They were cave dwellers and hunter-gatherers and seem to have been heavily concentrated in the north of the country, around the modern province of Santander. Here survive the most remarkable traces of their culture (which peaked around 15,000 BC), the deftly stylized cave murals of the animals that they hunted. The finest examples are at Altamira – now closed for general visits, though you can see similar paintings at Puente Viesgo, also near Santander.

Subsequent prehistory is more complex and confused. There does not appear to have been any great development in the cave cultures of the north. Instead the focus shifts south to Almería, which was settled around 5000–4000 BC by the "Iberians", **Neolithic** colonists from North Africa. They had already assimilated into their culture many of the changes that had developed in Egypt and the Near East. Settling in villages, they introduced pastoral and agricultural ways of life and exploited the plentiful supply of copper. Around 1500 BC, with the onset of the **Bronze Age**, they began to spread outwards into fortified villages on the central Meseta, the high plateau of modern Castile. At the turn of the millennium they were joined by numerous waves of **Celtic** and **Germanic** peoples. Here, Spain's divisive physical make-up – with its network of mountain ranges – determined its social nature. The incoming tribes formed distinct and isolated groups, conquering and sometimes absorbing each other but only on a very limited and local scale. Hence the Celtic "urnfield people" established themselves in Catalunya, the **Vascones** in the Basque country and, near them along the Atlantic coast, the **Astures**. Pockets of earlier cultures survived, too, particularly in Galicia with its *citanias* of beehive huts.

First Colonies

The Spanish coast meanwhile attracted colonists from different regions of the Mediterranean. The **Phoenicians** founded the port of Gadir (Cádiz) around 1100 BC and traded intensively in the metals of the Guadalquivir valley. Their wealth and success gave rise to a Spanish "Atlantis" myth, based on the lost kingdom of Tartessus, mentioned in the Bible and probably sited near Huelva; the sophisticated jewellery it produced is on display in Sevilla's archeological museum. Market rivalry later brought the **Greeks**, who established their trading colonies along the eastern coast – the modern Costa Brava. There's a fine surviving site at Empúries, near Barcelona.

More significant, however, was the arrival of the **Carthaginians** in the third century BC. Expelled from Sicily by the Romans, they saw in Spain a new base for their empire, from which to regain strength and strike back at their rivals. Although making little impact inland, they occupied most of Andalucía and expanded along the Mediterranean seaboard to establish a new capital at Cartagena. Under Hannibal they prepared to invade Italy and in 219 BC attacked Saguntum, a strategic outpost of the Roman Empire. It was a disastrous move, precipitating the **Second Punic War**; by 210 BC only Cádiz remained in their control and they were forced to accept terms. A new and very different age had begun.

Romans and Visigoths

The **Roman colonization** of the peninsula was far more intense than anything previously experienced and met with great resistance from the Celtiberian tribes of the north and centre. It was almost two centuries before the conquest was complete and indeed the Basques, although defeated, were never fully Romanized.

Nonetheless, Spain became the most important centre of the Roman Empire after Italy itself, producing no fewer than three emperors, along with the writers Seneca, Lucan, Martial and Quintilian. Again, geography dictated an uneven spread of influence, as it was strongest in Andalucía, southern Portugal and on the Catalan coast around Tarragona. In the first two centuries AD the Spanish mines and the granaries of Andalucía brought unprecedented wealth and Roman Spain enjoyed a brief "**Golden Age**". The finest monuments were built in the great provincial capitals – Córdoba, Mérida (which boasts the finest remains) and Tarragona – but across the country more practical construction was undertaken: roads, bridges and aqueducts. Many were still used well into recent centuries – perhaps the most remarkable being the aqueducts of Segovia and Tarragona – and quite a few bridges remain in use even today.

Towards the third century, however, the Roman political framework began to show signs of decadence and corruption. Although it didn't totally collapse until the Muslim invasions of the early eighth century, it became increasingly vulnerable to **barbarian invasions** from northern Europe. The Franks and the Suevi (Swabians) swept across the Pyrenees between 264 and 276, leaving devastation in their wake. They were followed two centuries later by further waves of Suevi, Alans and Vandals. Internal strife was heightened by the arrival of the **Visigoths** from Gaul, allies of Rome and already Romanized to a large degree. The triumph of Visigothic strength in the fifth century resulted in a period of spurious unity, based upon an exclusive military rule from their capital at Toledo, but their numbers were never great and their order was often fragmentary and nominal, with the bulk of the subject people kept in a state of disconsolate servility, and the military elite divided by constant plots and factions – exacerbated by the Visigothic system of elected monarchy and by their adherence to the heretical Arian philosophy. In 589 **King Recared** converted to Catholicism but religious strife was only multiplied: forced conversions, especially within the Jewish enclaves, maintained a constant simmering of discontent.

Moorish Spain

In contrast to the long-drawn-out Roman campaigns, **Moorish conquest** of the peninsula was effected with extraordinary speed. This was a characteristic phenomenon of the spread of Islam – Muhammad left Mecca in 622 and by 705 his followers had established control over all of North Africa. Spain, with its political instability, its wealth and its fertile climate, was an inevitable extension of their aims. In 711 Tariq, governor of Tangier, led a force of 7000 Berbers across the straits and routed the Visigoth army of King Roderic; two years later the Visigoths made a last desperate stand at Mérida and within a decade the Moors had conquered all but the wild mountains of Asturias. The land under their authority was dubbed "**al–Andalus**", a fluid term which expanded and shrunk with the intermittent gains and losses of the Reconquest. According to region, the Moors were to remain in control for the next three to eight centuries.

It was not simply a military conquest. The Moors (a collective term for the numerous waves of Arab and Berber settlers from North Africa) were often content to grant a limited autonomy in exchange for payment of tribute; their administrative system was tolerant and easily absorbed both Jews and Christians, those who retained their religion being known as "Mozarabs". And al-Andalus was a distinctly Spanish state of Islam. Though at first politically subject to the Eastern Caliphate (or empire) of Baghdad, it was soon virtually independent. In the tenth century, at the peak of its power and expansion, Abd ar-Rahman III asserted total independence, proclaiming himself caliph of a new **Western Islamic Empire**. Its capital was Córdoba – the largest, most prosperous and most civilized city in Europe. This was the great age of Muslim Spain: its scholarship, philosophy, architecture and craftsmanship were without rival and there was an unparalleled growth in urban life, in trade, and in agriculture aided by magnificent irrigation projects. These and other engineering feats were not, on the whole, instigated by the Moors, who instead took basic Roman models and adapted them to a new level of sophistication. In **architecture** and the **decorative arts**, however, their contribution was original and unique – as may be seen in the fabulous monuments of Sevilla, Córdoba and Granada.

The Córdoban caliphate for a while created a remarkable degree of unity. But its rulers were to become decadent and out of touch, prompting the brilliant but dictatorial **al-Mansur** to usurp control. Under this extraordinary ruler Moorish power actually reached new heights, pushing the Christian kingdom of Asturias-León back into the Cantabrian mountains and sacking its most holy shrine, Santiago de Compostela. However, after his death the caliphate quickly lost its authority and in 1031 disintegrated into a series of small independent kingdoms or *taifas*, the strongest of which was Sevilla.

Internal divisions amongst the *taifas* weakened their resistance to the Christian kingdoms which were rallying in the north, and twice North Africa had to be turned to for reinforcement. This resulted in two distinct new waves of Moorish invasion – first by the fanatically Islamic **Almoravids** (1086) and later by the **Almohads** (1147), who restored effective Muslim authority until their defeat at the battle of Las Navas de Tolosa in 1212.

The Christian Reconquest

The **reconquest** of land and influence from the Moors was a slow and inter-mittent process. It began with a symbolic victory by a small force of Christians at Covadonga in the Asturias (727) and was not completed until 1492 with the conquest of Granada by Fernando and Isabel.

Covadonga resulted in the formation of the tiny Christian **Kingdom of the Asturias**. Initially just 65 by 50km in area, it had by 914 reclaimed León and most of Galicia and northern Portugal. At this point, progress was temporarily halted by the devastating campaigns of al-Mansur. However, with the fall of the Córdoban caliphate and the divine aid of Spain's Moor-slaying patron, St James the Apostle (see "Santiago de Compostela"), the Reconquest moved into a new and powerful phase.

The frontier castles built against Arab attack gave name to **Castile**, founded in the tenth century as a county of León-Asturias. Under Fernando I (1037–65) it achieved the status of a kingdom and became the main thrust and focus of the Reconquest. Other kingdoms were being defined in the north at the same time: the Basques founded Navarra (Navarre), while dynastic mar-riage merged Catalunya with Aragón. In 1085 this period of confident Christian expansion reached its zenith with the capture of the great Moorish city of Toledo. The following year, however, the Almoravids arrived on invita-tion from Sevilla, and military activity was effectively frozen – except, that is, for the exploits of the legendary **El Cid**, a Castilian nobleman who won con-siderable lands around Valencia in 1095.

The next concerted phase of the Reconquest really began as a response to the threat imposed by the Almohads. The kings of León, Castile, Aragón and Navarra united in a general crusade which resulted in the great victory at **Las Navas de Tolosa** (1212). Thereafter Muslim power was effectively paralysed and the Christian armies moved on to take most of al-Andalus. Fernando III ("El Santo", the saint) led Castilian soldiers into Córdoba in 1236 and twelve years later into Sevilla. Meanwhile, the kingdom of Portugal had expanded to more or less its present size, while Jaime I of Aragón was to conquer Valencia, Alicante, Murcia and the Balearic Islands. By the end of the thirteenth centu-ry only the kingdom of Granada remained under Muslim authority and for much of the following two centuries it was forced to pay tribute to the mon-archs of Castile.

Two factors should be stressed regarding the Reconquest. First, its unifying religious nature – the **spirit of crusade**, intensified by the religious zeal of the Almoravids and Almohads, and by the wider European climate (which in 1085 gave rise to the First Crusade). This powerful religious motivation is well illus-trated by the subsequent canonization of Fernando III, and found solid expres-sion in the part played by the military orders of Christian knights, the most important of which were the **Knights Templar** and the Order of Santiago. At the same time the Reconquest was a movement of **recolonization**. The fact that the country had been in arms for so long meant that the nobility had a major and clearly visible social role, a trend perpetuated by the redistribution of captured land in huge packages, or *latifundia*. Heirs to this tradition still remain as landlords of the great estates, most conspicuously in Andalucía. Men from the ranks were also awarded land, forming a lower, larger stratum of nobility, the *hidalgos*. It was their particular social code that provided the mate-rial for Cervantes in *Don Quixote*.

Any spirit of mutual co-operation that had temporarily united the Christian kingdoms disintegrated during the fourteenth century, and independent lines of development were once again pursued. Attempts to merge **Portugal** with Castile foundered at the battle of Aljubarrota (1385), and Portuguese attention turned away from Spain towards the Atlantic. Aragón experienced a similar pull towards the markets of the Mediterranean, although pre-eminence in this area was soon passed to the Genoese. It was **Castile** that emerged the strongest over this period: self-sufficiency in agriculture and a flourishing wool trade with the Netherlands enabled the state to build upon the prominent military role played under Fernando III. Politically, Castilian history was a tale of dynastic conflict until the accession of the Catholic monarchs.

Los Reyes Católicos

Los Reyes Católicos – the **Catholic Monarchs** – was the joint title given to **Fernando V of Aragón and Isabel I of Castile**, whose marriage in 1479 united the two largest kingdoms in Spain. Unity was in practice more symbolic than real: Castile had underlined its rights in the marriage vows and Aragón retained its old administrative structure. So, in the beginning at least, the growth of any national unity or Spanish – as opposed to local – sentiment was very much dependent on the head of state. Nevertheless, from this time on it begins to be realistic to consider Spain as a single political entity.

At the heart of Fernando and Isabel's popular appeal lay a **religious bigotry** that they shared with most of their Christian subjects. The **Inquisition** was instituted in Castile in 1480 and in Aragón seven years later. Aiming to establish the purity of the Catholic faith by rooting out heresy, it was directed mainly at Jews – resented for their enterprise and influence in high places, as well as for their faith. Expression had already been given to these feelings in a pogrom in 1391; it was reinforced by an edict issued in 1492 which forced up to 400,000 Jews to flee the country. A similar spirit was embodied in the reconquest of the **Kingdom of Granada**, also in 1492. As the last stronghold of Muslim authority, the religious rights of its citizens were guaranteed under the treaty of surrender. Within a decade, though, those Muslims under Christian rule had been given the choice between conversion or expulsion.

The year 1492 was symbolic of a fresh start in another way: it was in this year that Columbus discovered America, and the papal bull that followed, entrusting Spain with the conversion of the American Indians, further entrenched Spain's sense of a mission to bring the world to the "True Faith". The next ten years saw the systematic conquest, colonization and exploitation of the **New World** as it was discovered, with new territory stretching from Labrador to Brazil, and new-found wealth pouring into the royal coffers. Important as this was for Fernando and Isabel, and especially for their prestige, priorities remained in Europe and strategic marriage alliances were made with Portugal, England and the Holy Roman Empire. It was not until the accession of the Habsburg dynasty that Spain could look to the activities of Cortés, Magellan and Pizarro and claim to be the world's leading power.

Habsburg Spain

Carlos I, a Habsburg, came to the throne in 1516 as a beneficiary of the marriage alliances of the Catholic monarchs. Five years later, he was elected emperor of the Holy Roman Empire as Carlos V (**Charles V**), inheriting not only Castile and Aragón, but Flanders, the Netherlands, Artois, the Franche-Comté and all the American colonies to boot. With such responsibilities it was inevitable that attention would be diverted from Spain, whose chief function became to sustain the Holy Roman Empire with gold and silver from the Americas. It was only with the accession of **Felipe II** in 1556 that Spanish politics became more centralized. The notion of an absentee king was reversed. Felipe lived in the centre of Castile near Madrid, creating a monument to the values of medieval Spain in his palace, El Escorial.

Two main themes run through his reign: the preservation of his own inheritance, and the revival of the crusade in the name of the Catholic Church. In pursuit of the former, Felipe successfully claimed the Portuguese throne (through the marriage of his mother), gaining access to the additional wealth of its empire. Plots were also woven in support of Mary Queen of Scots' claim to the throne of England, and to that end the ill-fated Armada sailed in 1588, its sinking a triumph for English naval strength and for Protestantism.

This was a period of unusual religious intensity: the **Inquisition** was enforced with renewed vigour, and a rising of *Moriscos* (subject Moors) in the Alpujarras was fiercely suppressed. Felipe III later ordered the expulsion of half the total number of *Moriscos* in Spain – allowing only two families to remain in each village in order to maintain irrigation techniques. The **exodus** of both Muslim and Jew created a large gulf in the labour force and in the higher echelons of commercial life – and in trying to uphold the Catholic cause, an enormous strain was put upon resources without any clear-cut victory.

By the middle of the seventeenth century, Spain was losing international credibility. Domestically, the disparity between the wealth surrounding Crown and Court and the poverty and suffering of the mass of the population was a source of perpetual tension. Discontent fuelled regional revolts in Catalunya and Portugal in 1640, and the latter had finally to be acknowledged as an independent state in 1668.

Bourbons and the Peninsular War

The **Bourbon dynasty** succeeded to the Spanish throne in the person of **Felipe V** (1700); with him began the War of the Spanish Succession against the rival claim of Archduke Charles of Austria, assisted by British forces. As a result of the Treaty of Utrecht which ended the war (1713), Spain was stripped of all territory in Belgium, Luxembourg, Italy and Sardinia, but Felipe V was recognized as king. Gibraltar was seized by the British in the course of the war. For the rest of the century Spain fell very much under the French sphere of influence, an influence that was given political definition by an alliance with the French Bourbons in 1762.

Contact with France made involvement in the **Napoleonic Wars** inevitable and led eventually to the defeat of the Spanish fleet at Trafalgar in 1805.

Popular outrage was such that the powerful prime minister, Godoy, was overthrown and King Carlos IV forced to abdicate (1808). Napoleon seized the opportunity to install his brother, Joseph, on the throne.

Fierce local resistance was eventually backed by the muscle of a British army, first under Sir John Moore, later under the Duke of Wellington, and the French were at last driven out in the course of the Peninsular War. Meanwhile, however, the **American colonies** had been successfully asserting their independence from a preoccupied centre and with them went Spain's last real claim of significance on the world stage. The entire nineteenth century was dominated by the struggle between an often reactionary monarchy and the aspirations of liberal constitutional reformers.

Seeds of Civil War

Between 1810 and 1813 an ad hoc Cortes (parliament) had set up a **liberal constitution** with ministers responsible to a democratically elected chamber. The first act of Fernando VII on being returned to the throne was to abolish this, and until his death in 1833 he continued to stamp out the least hint of liberalism. On his death, the right of succession was contested between his brother, Don Carlos, backed by the Church, conservatives and Basques, and his infant daughter, Isabel, who had the support of the liberals and the army. So began the **First Carlist War**, a civil war that lasted six years. Isabel II was eventually declared of age in 1843, her reign a long record of scandal, political crisis and constitutional compromise. Liberal army generals under the leadership of General Prim effected a coup in 1868 and the queen was forced to abdicate, but attempts to maintain a republican government foundered. The Cortes was again dissolved and the throne returned to Isabel's son, Alfonso XII. A new constitution was declared in 1876, limiting the power of the Crown through the institution of bicameral government, but again progress was halted by the lack of any tradition on which to base the constitutional theory.

The years preceding World War I merely heightened the discontent, which found expression in the growing **political movements** of the working class. The Socialist Workers' Party was founded in Madrid after the restoration of Alfonso XII, and spawned its own trade union, the UGT (1888), successful predominantly in areas of high industrial concentration such as the Basque region and Asturias. Its anarchist counterpart, the CNT, was founded in 1911, gaining substantial support among the peasantry of Andalucía.

The loss of **Cuba** in 1898 emphasized the growing isolation of Spain in international affairs and added to economic problems with the return of soldiers seeking employment where there was none. A call-up for army reserves to fight in **Morocco** in 1909 provoked a general strike and the "Tragic Week" of rioting in Barcelona. Between 1914 and 1918, Spain was outwardly neutral but inwardly turbulent; inflated prices made the postwar recession harder to bear.

The general disillusionment with parliamentary government, together with the fears of employers and businessmen for their own security, gave **General Primo de Rivera** sufficient support for a military coup in 1923 in which the king, Alfonso XIII, was pushed into the background. Dictatorship did result in an increase in material prosperity, but the death of the dictator in 1930 revealed the apparent stability as a facade. New political factions were taking shape: the Liberal Republican Right was founded by Alcalá Zamora, while the Socialist Party was given definition under the leadership of Largo Caballero. The victory of antimonarchist parties in the 1931 municipal elections forced the abdication of the king, who went into exile, and the **Second Republic** was declared.

The Second Republic

Catalunya declared itself a republic independent of the central government and was conceded control of internal affairs by a statute of 1932. **Separatist movements** were powerful too in the Basque provinces and Galicia, each with their own demands for autonomy. Meanwhile, the government, set up on a tidal wave of hope, was hopelessly divided internally and too scared of right-wing reaction to carry out the massive tax and agrarian reforms that the left demanded, and that might have provided the resources for thoroughgoing regeneration of the economy.

The result was the increasing polarization of Spanish politics. **Anarchism**, in particular, was gaining strength among the frustrated middle classes as well as among the workers and peasantry. The **Communist Party** and left-wing **Socialists**, driven into alliance by their mutual distrust of the "moderate" socialists in government, were also forming a growing bloc. On the right the **Falangists**, basically a youth party founded in 1923 by **José Antonio Primo de Rivera** (son of the dictator), made uneasy bedfellows with conservative traditionalists and dissident elements in the army upset by modernizing reforms.

In an atmosphere of growing confusion, the left-wing Popular Front alliance won the general election of **February 1936** by a narrow margin. Normal life, though, became increasingly impossible: the economy was crippled by strikes, peasants took agrarian reform into their own hands, and the government failed to exert its authority over anyone. Finally, on July 17, 1936, the military garrison in Morocco rebelled under **General Franco**'s leadership, to be followed by risings at military garrisons throughout the country. It was the culmination of years of scheming in the army, but in the event far from the overnight success its leaders almost certainly expected. The south and west quickly fell into Nationalist hands, but Madrid and the industrialized north and east remained loyal to the Republican government.

Civil War

The ensuing **Civil War** was undoubtedly one of the most bitter and bloody the world has seen. Violent reprisals were taken on their enemies by both sides – the Republicans shooting priests and local landowners wholesale, the Nationalists carrying out mass slaughter of the population of almost every town they took. Contradictions were legion in the way the Spanish populations found themselves divided from each other. Perhaps the greatest irony was that Franco's troops, on their "holy" mission to ensure a Catholic Spain, comprised a core of Moroccan troops from Spain's North African colony.

It was, too, the first modern war – Franco's German allies demonstrated their ability to wipe out entire civilian populations with their bombing raids on Gernika and Durango, and radio proved an important weapon, as Nationalist propagandists offered the starving Republicans "the white bread of Franco".

Despite sporadic help from Russia and thousands of volunteers in the International Brigade, the Republic could never compete with the professional armies and the massive assistance from Fascist Italy and Nazi Germany enjoyed by the Nationalists. In addition, the left was torn by internal divisions which at times led almost to civil war within its own ranks. Nevertheless, the Republicans held out in slowly dwindling territories for nearly three years, with **Catalunya** falling in January 1939 and armed resistance in **Madrid** – which never formally surrendered – petering out over the following few months. As hundreds of thousands of refugees flooded into France, General Francisco Franco, who had long before proclaimed himself head of state, took up the reins of power.

Franco's Spain

The early reprisals taken by the victors were on a massive and terrifying scale. Executions were commonplace and upwards of two million people were put in concentration camps until "order" had been established by authoritarian means. Only one party, the Falange, was permitted, and censorship was rigidly enforced. By the end of World War II, during which Spain was too weak to be anything but neutral, **Franco** was the only fascist head of state left in Europe, one responsible for sanctioning more deaths than any other in Spanish history. Spain was economically and politically isolated and, bereft of markets, suffered – almost half the population were still tilling the soil for little or no return. When General Eisenhower visited Madrid in 1953 with the offer of huge loans, it came as water to the desert, and the price, the establishment of American nuclear bases, was one Franco was more than willing to pay. However belated, economic development was incredibly rapid, with Spain enjoying a growth rate second only to that of Japan for much of the 1960s, a boom fuelled by the tourist industry and the remittances of Spanish workers abroad.

Increased **prosperity**, however, only underlined the political bankruptcy of Franco's regime and its inability to cope with popular demands. Higher incomes, the need for better education and a creeping invasion of Western culture made the anachronism of Franco ever clearer. His only reaction was to attempt to withdraw what few signs of increased liberalism had crept through, and his last years mirrored the repression of the postwar period. Trade unions remained outlawed, and the rampant inflation of the early 1970s saw striking workers across Spain hauled out of occupied mines and factories and imprisoned, or even shot in the streets. Attempts to report these events by the liberal press resulted in suspensions, fines and censorship. **Basque nationalists**, whose assassination of Admiral Carrero Blanco had effectively destroyed Franco's last hope of a like-minded successor, were singled out for particularly harsh treatment. Hundreds of so-called terrorists were tortured, and the Burgos trials of 1970, together with the executions of August 1975, provoked worldwide protest.

Franco finally died in November 1975, nominating **King Juan Carlos** as his successor. Groomed for the job and very much in with the army – of which he remains official commander in chief – the king's initial moves were cautious in the extreme, appointing a government dominated by loyal Francoists who had little sympathy for the growing opposition demands for "democracy without adjectives". In the summer of 1976 demonstrations in Madrid ended in violence, with the police upholding the old authoritarian ways.

The Return of Democracy

The violent events leading up to and following his mentor's death seem to have persuaded Juan Carlos that some real break with the past and a move towards **democratization** was now urgent and inevitable. Using the almost

ister, Carlos Arias Navarro, and replaced him with **Adolfo Suárez**, an ambitious lawyer and former head of Spanish TV. In 1976 Suárez pushed a **Law of Political Reform** through the Cortes, reforming the legislature into two chambers elected by universal suffrage – a move massively endorsed by the Spanish people in a referendum. Suárez also passed legislation allowing the setting up of free trade unions, as well as legitimizing the Socialist Party (PSOE) and, controversially, the Communists. Several cabinet ministers resigned in

opposite is more likely. The weaknesses of the *autonomía* system were further highlighted in Spain's **BSE crisis** when, in attempting to deal with a widespread mad cow outbreak, the central government issued edicts – concerning the testing of herds and disposal of carcases – which were often simply ignored by the regional authorities who have sole responsibility for their own agricultural affairs. Nor is there any forum in which the leaders of the *autonomías* can meet to co-ordinate policies – the only time they ever gather together in the same place is for a royal wedding. Some regional leaders have suggested that the moribund Spanish Senate should be reformed to resemble Germany's Bundesrat, or upper house, where the German Länder (the equivalent of Spain's autonomous regions) are represented.

The violence by the Basque terrorist group **ETA** remains a threat and although it has claimed over 800 lives since 1968 there are signs that support both for its methods and its political wing, Euskal Herritarok, is waning, as more Basques openly condemn the violence and voice their protests at frequent demonstrations. However, a substantial number of Basques (perhaps as many as 60 percent) support the aims, if not always the actions, of ETA and this has made a solution hard to come by. Influenced by the emerging peace settlement in Northern Ireland (ETA and the IRA have long had close links), in the summer of 1998 ETA announced an **indefinite ceasefire**, somewhat catching the hardline Aznar administration on the hop. Aznar's subsequent inflexibility, when he categorically refused to allow the referendum on "self-determination" demanded by the Basque nationalists, and rejected any talks with the terrorists until they permanently renounced violence, resulted in a stagnant deadlock. Apparently convinced that Aznar would never agree to serious negotiations, in November 1999 ETA **called off its ceasefire** and a series of car bombs and assassinations of Partido Popular and non-nationalist politicians throughout the Basque country followed. Recent murders of journalists and newspaper executives who have voiced criticism of ETA's strategy have plunged both the nation and the Basque country back into the darkest days of the 1980s with little apparent hope of any solution in the foreseeable future, and the more pessimistic commentators predicting the possibility of a civil war in the region. The **regional elections** in the Basque country in May 2001 saw a victory for the Basque Nationalist Party (PNV) and a fifty-percent fall in seats (14 down to seven) for Euskal Herritarok, ETA's political wing, a clear message from the Basque voters that they want an end to the violence. However, there seems little chance that this rebuff will influence the terrorist group's strategy of bombings and assassinations until some new initiative emerges from the central government in Madrid.

Meanwhile, the **sovereignty of Gibraltar** (see box, p.274) continues to be an important issue in Spanish politics, though it is viewed less urgently in London. However, the British – at Spain's bidding – have begun to pressurize the Gibraltar authorities into clamping down on the scourges of drug and tobacco smuggling and money laundering which have exploded in the colony over the last decade. A proposal by the Spanish government to share sovereignty over Gibraltar for one hundred years, after which the colony would revert to Spain, received a blast of abuse from the inhabitants of the Rock and an inscrutable silence from Whitehall. Gibraltar's current leadership remains uninterested in any deals with Spain except on its own narrowly defined terms – such as opening the colony's airport to international flights – and there is currently no sign of the deadlock being broken.

protest and an outraged military began planning their *coup d'état*.

When elections were held in June 1977, Suárez's own hastily formed centre-right party, the Unión del Centro Democrático (UCD), was rewarded with a 34 percent share of the vote, the Socialists coming in second with 28 percent, and the Communists and Francoist **Alianza Popular** marginalized at 9 percent and 8 percent respectively. Despite the overwhelming victories in Catalunya and the Basque Country of parties appealing to regional sentiment, this was almost certainly a vote for democratic stability rather than for ideology, something reflected in the course of the parliament, with Suárez governing through "consensus politics", negotiating settlements on all important issues with the major parties.

The first parliament of the "New Spain" now embarked on the formidable task of drawing up a **constitution**, whilst the Suárez government applied for membership of the then EEC. On December 6, 1978, the new constitution was overwhelmingly endorsed in a national referendum and, remarkably, only three years after the death of Franco, Spain had become a full democracy.

Elections in March 1979 almost exactly duplicated the 1977 result but when the UCD, a fractious coalition of moderates and extremists, started to crack at the seams, Suárez resigned in January 1981. This provided the trigger for a **military coup**, launched by a contingent of Civil Guards loyal to Franco's memory and commanded by the tragi-comic, moustachioed Colonel Antonio Tejero. They stormed into the Cortes with Tejero brandishing a revolver, and sub-machine-gunned the ceiling as diputados (MPs) dived for cover. The crisis, for a while, was real; tanks were brought out on to the streets of Valencia, and only three of the army's ten regional commanders remained unreservedly loyal to the government. But as it became clear that the king would not support the plotters, most of the rest then affirmed their support. Juan Carlos had taken the decision of his life and emerged with immensely enhanced prestige in the eyes of most Spaniards.

The González Era

On October 28, 1982, the Socialist PSOE, led by charismatic **Felipe González**, was elected with the biggest landslide victory in Spanish electoral history to rule a country that had been firmly in the hands of the right for 43 years. The Socialists captured the imagination and the votes of nearly ten million Spaniards with the simplest of appeals: "for change".

Once in power, however, the Socialist Party chose the path of pragmatism, and a relentless drift to the right followed. Four successive election victories kept the party in power for fourteen years and by the mid-1990s the PSOE government's policies had become indistinguishable from the conservative administrations of Britain or Germany. The party's abandonment of many of its core principles in favour of a more blatant opportunism was neatly encapsulated in a popular witticism, which redefined the "changes" (*cambios*) promised by González as the "three Cs": *casa* (a new house), *coche* (a new car), and *compañera* (a new girlfriend).

González himself, meanwhile, had been equally transformed, from a radical young labour lawyer into a careworn elder statesman. Control of inflation had become a more urgent target than reducing unemployment, whilst loss-making heavy industries (steel and shipbuilding especially) were ruthlessly overhauled and other industries privatized. European Community (now **European Union**) membership came in 1986, and the pride which most Spanish people felt at this tangible proof of their acceptance by the rest of Europe bought the Socialists more valuable time.

The issue of **NATO** (or OTAN as the Spaniards know it), perhaps more than any other, demonstrated how much González had sacrificed to pragmatism. During the 1982 election campaign he had made an impassioned speech at a rally against Spain remaining a member of NATO, which the dying UCD administration had rushed into joining at the behest of the military. When the promised referendum was finally held four years later – which surprisingly turned out marginally in favour of staying in – his was one of the main voices in favour of continued membership. González finally buried the question of NATO as a political issue for the mainstream left when in 1995 he agreed to and supported the elevation of his foreign secretary and close colleague, Javier Solana, to the post of secretary general of the organization he had spent most of his political life reviling.

After long years of being hopelessly divided, in the late 1980s the **Spanish right** realigned itself when former prime minister Adolfo Suárez's UCD Christian Democrats merged with the Alianza Popular to form the new right-of-centre **Partido Popular** (PP) which came a respectable second in the 1989 elections; a new far-left coalition, **Izquierda Unida** (United Left), composed of the Communists and smaller leftist parties, came third, albeit with the same number of seats (18) in the Congress of Deputies as the Catalan Nationalists, barely a tenth of the PSOE's representation.

The nation's progressive disillusionment with Felipe González's government in the early 1990s saw the rise to prominence of **José María Aznar** as leader of the PP. A former tax inspector and devoid of charisma, Aznar was dogged in his criticism of government incompetence in dealing with its own sleaze and the growing economic crisis. This debilitated the PSOE's position still further in the build-up to the **1993 elections**. However, the PSOE confounded the pundits and the opinion polls to hang on to power by the skin of its teeth, albeit with the help of a coalition with Pujol's Catalan Nationalists. But González's victory was a poisoned chalice, for he had no new ideas to deal with urgent economic problems, whilst his past now began to catch up with him. As illegal financing of the PSOE and corruption and commission-taking on government projects by party officials and ministers were being exposed, the director of the Guardia Civil (appointed by González) jumped the country with millions of dollars of secret service funds, and the governor of the Bank of Spain was caught out making a private (and illegal) fortune. But the most serious of all the scandals to beset González was the **GAL affair** (Grupo Antiterrorista de Liberación), when it was discovered that a semi-autonomous antiterrorist unit had been carrying out a dirty war against the ETA terrorists in the 1980s, which included kidnapping and wholesale assassinations of suspected ETA members. The press – and a later judicial investigation – exposed police participation in these crimes and a clear chain of command reaching up to the highest echelons of the PSOE government. González's attempts to muzzle journalists' investigations only poisoned further relations between the government and the media and feeling grew that the truth would never come out. However, in the summer of 1998, the legal system confounded the cynics by convicting two senior ex-ministers of sponsoring kidnapping and misappropriating public funds whilst co-ordinating GAL activities. They were each sentenced to ten years' imprisonment (later rescinded on appeal) for covering up the plot, and stiff prison terms were given to chiefs in the Guardia Civil, as well as several officers.

Contemporary Politics

The PSOE administration limped on towards what looked likely to be a crushing defeat in the **1996 elections**. The surprise result, however, was another **hung parliament**, making everyone a loser. Aznar, the narrow victor, was denied the "absolute majority" he had believed to be his throughout the campaign, which meant that he would be forced to do a deal with the nationalist parties (whom he had described as "greedy parasites" on the hustings) to have a workable parliamentary majority. Meanwhile, the PSOE's avoidance of the expected overwhelming defeat was proclaimed as a vindication by González, who hastily dismissed ideas of retirement. This merely delayed the inevitable and, unable to make any significant impact on changing public opinion, and with the PSOE still in turmoil, early in 1998 **González** finally **resigned** the leadership of the party he had dominated for 23 years.

The reasons for Aznar's failure to win an outright majority are equally significant. When Felipe González told the king after the PSOE's first election victory in 1982 that his party's success had completed the transition from dictatorship to democracy, the monarch sagely advised him that the end of the transition would be when the Socialists lost an election to the right. The long and repressive Franco period still casts a heavy shadow across the Spanish political scene, and many voters seemed to have become nervous at the prospect of a right-wing party with a big majority curtailing their new-found liberties and dismantling the social security system – a vital lifeline in poorer regions such as Extremadura and Andalucía. Thus it was that **Andalucía**, one of the largest *autonomías*, performed its traditional role as the *sartenilla* or frying pan of Spanish politics – traditionally frying the votes of the right-leaning north – by confounding the opinion polls and turning out to vote for the discredited government, effectively denying Aznar a majority.

Elected on a centre-right platform, during his first term in office following his narrow 1996 victory, Aznar progressively moved his party to the centre, shifting aside the government's remaining hardliners in the hope of gaining the electorate's confidence and a working majority not dependent on alliances with the northern nationalists. In tandem with this realignment, he frequently declared his admiration for the ideas of British Prime Minister Tony Blair.

Following the resignation of Felipe González in 1998, a PSOE leadership election replaced him with **José Borrell**, a former transport minister in González's government, but not the former leader's preferred choice of successor. González hovered constantly in the background, making it impossible for Borrell to stamp his own mark on the party or the leadership. The following year, when a financial scandal involving Borrell while he had been a minister was unearthed, he opted to resign, and was replaced by the party hierarchy's – and González's – original nominee, **Joaquín Almunia**. With a general election now on the horizon and the PSOE still trailing in the polls, Almunia set up an electoral pact with the ex-communist Izquierda Unida (United Left), thinking that their combined votes could overturn a likely Aznar victory.

The outcome of the March 2000 **general election** was a stunning **triumph for Aznar** and the PP, and for the first time since the death of Franco the right was in power with an overall majority. Naturally, this was a disaster for the left: apparently the electorate had been unconvinced by the "shotgun marriage" between the PSOE and the IU (bitter enemies since the Civil War), which smacked more of political opportunism than a government in waiting. Moreover, large numbers of voters seemed unwilling to risk the undoubted economic gains of Aznar's period in office while many of the left's traditional supporters didn't bother to vote at all. On election night, when the scale of the PSOE/IU defeat became clear, Joaquín Almunia **resigned** from the leadership of the PSOE. At the party convention which followed, the old guard and its candidates were swept aside and delegates elected a relatively unknown young politician, **José Luis Rodríguez Zapatero** – a member of the moderate socialist "Nueva Via" (new way) group within the PSOE – as their **new leader**. The party clearly hopes that a charismatic new torchbearer will sweep them back to power in the same way that Tony Blair did for New Labour in Britain.

In hindsight, a defeat for the left always appeared to be the most likely outcome, if only because the lacklustre Aznar (when asked for the main achievement of his government he replied "normality") had nevertheless kept the **economy** on course with an economic growth rate among the highest in Europe, causing a majority of Spaniards – according to a pre-election poll – to feel extremely satisfied with life. Unemployment, though still the highest in the EU, has fallen to below 20 percent for the first time in over a decade and looks set to fall further, whilst new jobs are being created faster than in any other European economy. The main thrust of economic policy has been to accelerate progress along the path opened up by the previous PSOE regime, with subsidies being withdrawn from ailing industries such as shipbuilding, and former state-owned concerns like the steel industry being sold off into the private sector. The privatization programme has since been accelerated, taxes on earnings have been reduced and greater flexibility has been introduced into labour laws. However, after years in opposition spent hounding the González government's record on sleaze, Aznar also stands accused of cronyism and corruption with many of his personal and the PP's political friends accused of making vast fortunes on the back of government goodwill and lucrative contracts.

The main political failure of Aznar's period in power has been his **inability to curb ETA terrorism**. During the 2000 general election campaign and following his election victory he threatened to smash the gunmen with tough policing and kick the moderate nonviolent Basque Nationalist Party (the PNV, whom Aznar regards as ETA apologists) out of office in the Basque autonomous region. The central plank in this strategy was to place his hardline interior minister, Jaime Mayor Oreja, in charge of the PP's campaign in the Basque regional elections of 2001. The result was a resounding defeat for the PP and an increased vote for the PNV which left Aznar's Basque policy in ruins. It remains to be seen whether he will now pull back from his previously uncompromising stance and go along with the PNV's demand for all-party peace talks (which would include Euskal Herritarok, ETA's political wing) based on Northern Ireland's Good Friday agreement.

When he announced the day after the general election victory that, despite having won a majority, he would seek to make a governmental **alliance** with the nationalist parties (excepting the troublesome Basques), Aznar was also signalling his intention not to endanger the delicate consensus which has maintained stability in the post-Franco period. This softly, softly approach in government seems to have won over many in the electorate who appeared unconvinced by the warnings from the left during the election campaign that, once in power with an overall majority, the PP's social-democratic mask would come off and there would be a wholesale dismantling of the health, welfare and pensions systems, together with attacks on the trade unions. An acknowledgement of the previous PSOE administration's role in modernizing Spain, coupled with a recent declaration that the PP is now a party of the "reforming centre" rather than the "centre right", suggests that Aznar intends to continue this policy during the remainder of his second term.

The consensus across Spanish politics on Spain's role in **Europe** means that while the nation is no longer as starry-eyed about the EU as it was a decade ago, most citizens are acutely aware of the benefits flooding into the country as a result of huge EU grants funding important infrastructure projects as well as subsidies channelled to the pivotal farming sector under the Common Agricultural Policy. Ideologically, a significant majority of Spaniards still identify strongly with European integration and see their participation at the launch of a **single currency** and the replacement of the peseta with the **euro** in 2002 as a landmark in the country's move into the European mainstream.

Architecture

Spain's architectural legacy is a highly distinctive one, made up of a mixture of styles quite unlike anything else in Europe. The country was usually slow to pick up on the main currents of European architecture, and when a new style was adopted it was often in an extreme or stylized form. There are French, Dutch, German and Italian currents, but all were synthesized into something uniquely Spanish. Centuries of Moorish occupation have left an indelible mark, too, manifested both in the handful of wonderful buildings which represent the highpoint of Moorish civilization in Andalucía, and in a powerful influence on Christian and secular architecture, including the layout of entire towns.

There has been less of the wanton destruction of old buildings in Spain than in most other countries, and in general the architecture here is astonishingly well preserved. There's perhaps less purity of form than elsewhere in Europe – additions over the years have left many buildings with a medley of different styles – but no other country can boast quite as many old churches, castles and unspoiled towns and villages.

At the risk of making generalizations, it's possible to identify a number of **trends** in the buildings of Spain. As a rule, there is an emphasis on the longitudinal, and on solidity of construction. A heavy use of surface ornament is often popular, with elaborate doorways and rich decoration. Because of the warm climate there is an interest in outdoor living and a need for cool and open space, which accounts for the prevalence of patios in civic buildings and cloisters in religious edifices, including those which were not monastic. There is also a tendency to break up long vistas by various means, creating a variety of compartments within a large space.

The Roman Period

Although fragments of earlier civilizations do exist, Spain's architectural history (in terms of surviving buildings) begins in the **Roman** period, from which there remain a number of remarkable structures. These have no particular Spanish flavour, nor were they to prove as influential on subsequent developments as in some other countries, but nonetheless the aqueduct at **Segovia**, the bridge at **Alcántara** (the highest in the Roman world and still in use), and the theatre and associated remains at **Mérida** belong among the first rank of Roman survivals anywhere. There's another fine group in and around **Tarragona**, with walls, a necropolis, an arena, a forum and a praetorium in the city itself, and more notably an aqueduct, the Centcelles Mausoleum, the Arco de Bar and the Torre de Scipio all within a radius of a few kilometres.

Other Roman monuments worthy of special note include the walls of Lugo, the amphitheatre and castle at Sagunto, and the three-span triumphal arch at Medinaceli. Excavations of complete towns can be seen at Empúries, Itálica, Numancia and Bilbilis.

Visigothic and Asturian Periods

The **Visigothic** period, which succeeded the Roman, bequeathed a small number of buildings of uncertain date. Visigothic buildings have simple exteriors, and were the first in Spain to adopt the horseshoe arch (later to be altered and used widely by the Moors). They also developed elements from Roman buildings, the most refined example of which is at **Quintanilla de las Viñas** in Old Castile, a church whose exterior is enlivened by delicately carved stone friezes set in bands; inside there's a triumphal arch over the apse, carved with the earliest surviving representation of Christ in Spain. Other remnants of the era survive at the modern industrial town of **Tarrasa** in Catalunya, formerly Egara, in the shape of three churches, one of which − the Baptistry of San Miguel − dates from the fifth or sixth century; the other two have apses that are probably of ninth-century construction. Other Visigothic buildings include part of the crypt of Palencia Cathedral, and the nearby basilica of San Juan at Baños de Cerrato, documented as seventh century.

Hard on the heels of the Visigothic epoch was the **Asturian** period, named after the small kingdom on the northern coast, which developed its own style during the ninth century. This retained Visigothic elements alongside technical developments that anticipated the general European trends still to come. A little group of buildings centred around **Oviedo** − the Cámara Santa, the church of Santulano in the city itself, San Miguel de Lillo and Santa María de Naranco on the slopes of Monte Naranco nearby − are, unusually in Spanish history, clearly superior to and more highly developed than any contemporaneous work in Europe. The last represents the pinnacle of the style, a perfectly proportioned little building with barrel vaulting and arches supported on pilasters, as well as delicate decoration using Roman and Byzantine elements. The isolated surrounding countryside holds a few similar buildings from the succeeding century, but the Asturian style was soon to be swallowed up by the new Romanesque movement which swept across the north of Spain from France and Italy.

The Moorish Period

By this time most of Spain was under Muslim domination. It remained so, at least in part, until the final defeat of the Moors in 1492. During this period Moorish architecture did not develop in the way we understand the word, and it is best to consider the different epochs of building separately.

The first real style was the **Caliphate**, centred around Córdoba, whose great surviving monument − the **Mezquita** − was built and added to over a period from the eighth to the tenth century. The Caliphate style demonstrates most of the vocabulary used by Moorish builders over the years − horseshoe, cusped and multifoil arches, the contrasting use of courses of stone and brick, the use of interlacing as a particular feature of design, doors surmounted by blind arcades, stuccowork, and the ornamental use of calligraphy along with geometric and plant motifs. Various technical innovations, too, were introduced in the construction of the Mezquita, from the original solution of two-tiered arches to give greater height, to the ribbed dome vaults in front of the *mihrab* (prayer-niche).

Another example of the Caliphate style, the (now ruined) palace-city of **Medina Azahara**, just outside Córdoba, was no less splendid than the Mezquita. Many of its buildings were produced according to the descriptions of Solomon's temple. In **Toledo**, El Cristo de la Luz is a small-scale Caliphate mosque, and the old Bisagra Gate was part of the fortifications of that time. As the Reconquest progressed, other fortifications went up. Gormaz was begun in around 965. Only part of the original Moorish building has survived, including two gateways. Calatayud, in the north, holds more fortifications of the period, probably of an even earlier date.

With the fall of the caliphate at the end of the eleventh century, Moorish Spain was divided into independent kingdoms or **taifas**, giving rise to the *alcazabas* or castles at Granada, Málaga, Guadix, Almería, Tarifa and Carmona. The Aljafería palace in Zaragoza also dates from this period, much altered over the years but preserving its mosque and a tower. The strongest *taifa* was at Sevilla, where later the **Almohad** dynasty created an art of refined brickwork and left behind the Patio de Yeso in the Alcázar, the Torre del Oro, which originally formed part of the city's fortifications, and the Giralda – former minaret of the mosque and arguably the finest tower ever built in the Arab world.

The apotheosis of pure Muslim art came, however, with the **Nasrid** dynasty in Granada, the last city to fall to the Christians. The gorgeously opulent palace of the **Alhambra** went up between the thirteenth and fifteenth centuries. Built on a hill against the romantic backdrop of the Sierra Nevada, this structure provided the necessary partner in the union between art and nature sought by the Moorish architects, especially in the lush gardens of the more modest Generalife section. As for the palace itself, the buildings are structurally very poor, with no exterior features of note; yet the interior, around the two great courtyards, is one of the most intoxicating creations in the world, the culminating ideal of Moorish civilization, built when it was already in irreversible decline.

Mozarabic and Mudéjar

The Moorish occupation had an indelible influence on the architecture of Spain, and led directly to two hybrid architectural styles unique to the country – **Mozarabic** and Mudéjar. The former was the style of Christians subjugated by the Moors who retained their old religion but built in the Arabic style. Their churches are mostly in isolated situations – San Miguel de Escalada east of León, Santa María de Lebena near the Picos de Europa and San Baudelio near Berlanga de Duero in Soria Province are the finest examples.

Mudéjar is far more common, the style of the Arabs who stayed on after their homelands had been conquered, or who had migrated to the Christian kingdoms. Often they proved to be both the most skilful builders and the cheapest workforce, and they left their mark on almost all of the country over a period of several centuries. They continued to build predominantly in brick, mainly working on the construction of parish churches, resulting in an odd – though unmistakeably Moorish – Christian-Islamic hybrid that some claim is barely a distinct architectural style at all. There are details of Mudéjar buildings under the relevant European headings below, although a number deserve inclusion here as being more firmly within the Arab tradition. Among these are the palaces of Tordesillas and the Alcázar in Sevilla; various secular buildings in Toledo; the Chapel of the Assumption of Santiago at Las Huelgas; and the synagogues of Toledo and Córdoba.

The Romanesque

Back in the mainstream of European architecture, the **Romanesque** style in Spain is most associated with the churches, bridges and hospices built along the **pilgrim road** to Santiago de Compostela. None of the hospices has survived, but the Puente la Reina in Navarra is the most famous of a number of Romanesque-era bridges. The churches come in various shapes and forms, but all include beautiful sculpture. The cathedral of Jaca, the monasteries of Santa Cruz de la Seros, San Juan de la Peña and Leyre, and the churches of Santa María la Real at Sanguesa, San Miguel at Estella, San Martín at Fromista and San Isidoro at León are the most notable examples, but the climax, of the style as of the pilgrimage, came with the great **Cathedral of Santiago** itself. This is now almost entirely encased by Baroque additions, but preserves the original shape of the interior. Begun around 1070, it was built to allow as much space as possible for the pilgrims to circulate – hence the large triforium gallery, and the ambulatory with radiating chapels. Santiago's cathedral also served as a model for many contemporary derivations, particularly the nearby cathedrals of Lugo, Orense and Tuy.

Elsewhere, the influence of the great Burgundian abbey of Cluny, which so influenced the development of the pilgrimage, can be seen most clearly at **San Vicente** in Ávila. Another building closely related to the pilgrimage churches is the monastery of **Santo Domingo de Silos**, where the architecture and superb bas-reliefs of the cloisters, the only surviving part of the original building, are clearly derived from French models. There's an additional ingredient, too: most of the capitals here show an unmisteakable Moorish influence – a very early example of the mix of East and West to be found in Spain.

Other Romanesque buildings tend towards regional variants. In **Catalunya**, whose architectural history so often diverges from that of the rest of Spain, the influence was more from Lombardy than France, with tall, square bell towers, prominent apses, blind arcading and little sculptural detail – although this last was later to become important, for example in the cloisters of the cathedral and San Pedro in Girona.

Belfries were a dominant feature in **Segovia**, where the main innovation was the construction of covered arcades in the manner of cloisters built against the sides of the building, making the parish churches of this city amongst the most distinctive in Spain. **Soria**'s churches, particularly San Domingo, recall those of Poitiers, although the fantastic cloister of San Juan de Duero defies classification in its combination of the round-headed Romanesque, early pointed Gothic, and Moorish horseshoe and intersecting arches in one extraordinarily capricious composition. **Zamora** was unusual in having a Byzantine influence; also its portals tended to lack tympana, but had richly carved archivolts. Finally, there are a number of churches in a crossover **Mudéjar**/Romanesque style in such places as Toledo, Sahagún, Cúellar and Arévalo.

Military architecture of this period is dominated by the complete walls of Ávila, the best preserved in Europe, and by the castle at Loarre, the most spectacular of the early Christian castles built to defend the conquered lands.

Survivors of civil buildings are few and far between, but there are precious examples in the form of the palaces of Estella and Huesca.

The Transitional Style

With the advent of the Cistercian reforms, the **Transitional** style was introduced to Spain in the middle of the twelfth century, first in a series of monasteries – La Oliva, Veruela, Poblet, Santes Creus, Las Huelgas and Santa María la Huerta – that are notable for massiveness of construction combined with the introduction of such Gothic characteristics as the pointed arch and the ribbed vault.

In some ways, **La Oliva** can claim to be the first Gothic building in Spain, although in both its solidity and ground plan it is still Romanesque in spirit. The severe, unadorned style of the Cistercians was to have a great impact at a time when the rest of Europe was moving towards an appreciation of the structural advantages of Gothic, not quickly realized in Spain. The late twelfth and early thirteenth centuries saw the construction of a number of cathedrals in the Transitional style – Siguenza, Ávila, Santo Domingo de la Calzada, Tarragona and Lleida – all of which had fortress-like features and were indeed at times used for defensive purposes. Similar is the Collegiate church at Tudela, although the sculpture here, in direct contravention of Cistercian rules, is among the richest in Spain.

A few buildings of the same period show clear **Byzantine** influence – the Old Cathedral of Salamanca, Zamora Cathedral and the Colegiata at Toro – each with a distinctive central dome, although their design otherwise shows normal Transitional elements. Closely related are the cathedral of Ciudad Rodrigo and the often octagonally shaped buildings associated with the Knights Templar: La Vera Cruz in Segovia, and two mysterious buildings on the Pilgrim Route whose exact nature is uncertain – Eunate and Torres de Río.

The Gothic Style

Examples of the early **Gothic** style in Spain are rare, and those that there are seem to derive from French and English sources. The refectory of Santa María la Huerta is as pure and elegant as the best in France; Cuenca Cathedral, begun about 1200, seems to derive from a Norman or English model. Later, buildings began to develop a more specifically Spanish style, eschewing any notions of purity of form.

Three great cathedrals commenced in the 1220s best exemplify the increasingly Spanish features of the churches of the time. Of these, the overall plans and building of **Burgos** and **Toledo** are obviously indebted to French models, but they are far from the grace and lightness of the great French Gothic cathedrals. The windows are much smaller – partly, perhaps, to cut down on excessive sunlight, partly to preserve a greater sense of mystery than their French equivalents did. Both were also given the rich interior decoration that soon became the norm for Spanish cathedrals, most characteristic of which was the *coro*, an elaborate set of choir stalls often enclosed by a *trascoro* or retrochoir, situated in the nave – a feature that looks odd to those used to the chancel-based choirs of northern Europe. The reasons for this are unclear, but it seems it was associated with the predominance of the choir services of the clergy, which meant that the construction of the *coro* made the best use of the space; it may also have been felt that the chancel should be reserved solely for the Holy Sacrament, and not downgraded for any other purpose.

Equally typical are the giant *retablos*, the most important of which are situated over the high altar, again masking the architecture. Generally these were carved and multicoloured, and contained a series of scenes from the life of Christ and of the Virgin, perhaps along with statues of saints. Basically their function was similar to that of stained-glass windows in the cathedrals of France, providing pictorial representation of the Bible to an illiterate population. Smaller *retablos*, either painted or carved, were placed over smaller altars. In addition, tombs of monarchs, aristocratic families, bishops and saints were often placed in specially built chapels, and sometimes enclosed by iron gates or grilles (*rejas*) which were often of a highly elaborate workmanship and would enclose the entrances to the *coro* and the chancel too. The overall effect of all this decoration can appear over-sumptuous to the modern eye, but it gives a better impression of a medieval cathedral than anything that can be found in northern Europe, where reformation, revolution, war and restoration have combined to leave buildings that are architecturally far purer but spiritually far less authentic.

The third great cathedral of the 1200s, **León**, was the only one to adopt the normal French system of triple portal, prominent flying buttresses and large windows filled with brilliantly coloured stained glass. Even here, however, there were Spanish touches, such as the cloister and its dependencies, and the later construction of a *coro*.

All the other cathedrals followed the model of Burgos and Toledo. **El Burgo de Osma** is in a way a miniature version of them, although it's purer Gothic in form. **Palencia**, built in the fourteenth and fifteenth centuries, is unusual in that most of its decoration is roughly contemporary with the architecture, with very few later additions. At **Pamplona** and **Huesca**, the architects built in the knowledge that there would be a *coro* in the nave – though ironically these were removed relatively recently by restorers. Pamplona's cloister, the earliest part of the building, is perhaps the most beautiful Gothic cloister in Spain. It has several fine doorways and a chapel with an exquisite star vault, a feature that was to be Spain's main contribution to the vocabulary of Gothic architecture, as characteristic as fan vaulting in England, although far more common – and with an obvious debt to Moorish models. There are other, equally grand examples of the national Gothic style: **Murcia** and **Oviedo** are two, **Sevilla** a more spectacular one, its vast size determined by the ground plan of the mosque that preceded it.

Regional Styles

Regional forms of Gothic are found in Catalunya and Aragón. In **Catalunya**, churches were built with huge arcades, omitting the triforium and including only a small clerestory. Long spans were also common; aisles, if there were any, were very nearly the same height as the nave; buttresses were internalized by the construction of tall, straight-walled chapels built between them, lending a rather sober appearance to the outside. Barcelona's **Cathedral of Santa María del Mar** is a good example of all these features, as is **Palma Cathedral**, although the most spectacular of the Catalan cathedrals is **Girona** – so daring structurally as to be admired more for its engineering than its aesthetic appeal.

In **Aragón** there was strong Mudéjar influence, which extended even to the cathedrals of **Zaragoza**, **Tarazona** and **Teruel**. The towers of these cities, and of **Calatayud**, tend to be either square in shape and decorated with ceramic tiles that glisten in the sun, or else octagonal and of brick only. Both show a virtuoso skill in decoration with what appear to be very basic and unpromising materials. Each of the cathedrals has a central cupola, while Tarazona has an amazing cloister filled with Mudéjar ornament. There's another unusual cloister far away in Guadalupe, while more orthodox Mudéjar Gothic churches are all over, though there's a fine concentration in **Toledo**.

Military Architecture

Turning to **military architecture**, a number of fortified towns from the Gothic period still survive. Toledo has several gateways and two bridges of the era, and there are fine examples of walls at Albarracín, Daroca, Morella, Berlanga de Duero, Madrigal de las Altes Torres and Montblanch. Spain's castles of this period are without parallel in Europe. However, those that had a genuine function in the Reconquest are as a rule in the poorest condition, while those that look most impressive today often had little if any defensive purpose. It should be remembered that there is no Spanish equivalent at any time to the English or French country house. Where great houses were built by the nobility in Spain, they often resembled castles, even if they were never used for military purposes.

Perhaps the finest fourteenth-century castle is that of **Bellver** near Palma, a circular structure built as a summer residence by the kings of Mallorca. The great fifteenth-century castle at **Olite** is a palace in the pastiche form on a grand scale. For all the monumentality of its towers, many are wholly ornamental and would have been quite useless in time of war. Unfortunately, what you see today gives little hint of the richness of the former interior decoration.

Along the banks of the Duero are castles which were genuinely in action at the time of the Reconquest. **Gormaz** is particularly interesting, showing how an originally Moorish building was adapted by the Christians after its capture. **Peñafiel**'s fifteenth-century castle is actually the successor to the one that was built as protection against the Moors; apart from its own severe beauty, it clearly shows the importance of a strong strategic location. The many brick castles in the **area of Segovia and Valladolid** should be thought of more as expressions of the wealth and power of the nobility than as genuine military constructions of the time. These often incorporated Mudéjar features, and their construction was often in reality rather delicate: **Coca** is the best example of this.

Civil Buildings and Late Gothic

The legacy of **Gothic civil architecture** is also impressive. Large numbers of towns preserve their medieval character in layout and design, even if many of the houses are not, strictly speaking, original. Important town mansions survive all over the country, often characterized by the carving of a coat of arms on the facade. **Cáceres**, in Extremadura, is probably the richest place for seigneurial houses, although most of the other towns in this province are also notable for vernacular architecture of this, and later dates. Elsewhere, the shipyards of **Barcelona** constitute a unique survival from the Gothic period, as do parts of the Barri Gòtic, which contains a number of original municipal buildings. Barcelona also has the earliest *lonja*, or exchange – later and more exotic examples of which can be found in Valencia, Palma and Zaragoza.

Spanish **late–Gothic** architecture is particularly spectacular, the increasing ornamentation partly the result of the mid-fifteenth-century influx of artists from Germany and the Netherlands to Spain. **Burgos** and **Toledo** were the centre of the developing style. Juan de Colonia built the superb openwork spires of Burgos Cathedral, modelled on those of his native Cologne – which themselves, ironically, existed only on paper until the nineteenth century. His son, Simon, was responsible for other work on the same building, particularly the Capilla del Condestable at the east end, and worked with his father on the Cartuja de Miraflores. At the same time, Anequin de Egas from Brussels began a series of additions to Toledo Cathedral.

A little later the focus shifted to **Valladolid** and became increasingly florid – the **Isabelline** style – reaching its most extreme in the facades of San Pablo and the Colegio San Gregorio. It's not known who was responsible for these, or for the equally ornate facade of Santa María in Aranda de Duero, though a variety of people have been suggested, not least Juan Guas, who is known to have built San Juan de los Reyes in Toledo, the gallery of the castle at **Manzanares el Real** and perhaps the Palacio del Infantado in **Guadalajara**. The Isabelline style, at its best, combined the Moorish penchant for hanging decoration with standard European motifs, and has been seen by some commentators as the one chance Spain had to create its own special, unified architectural style. However, Isabelline had a very short life. The queen after whom it was named became more enchanted by the Italians before long, and encouraged the adoption of the Renaissance in Spain.

There was also a countermovement towards a purer Gothic form. The New Cathedral of **Salamanca** and the cathedral of **Segovia** were both begun in the sixteenth century in what was then a wholly archaic language by Juan Gil de Ontañón, and continued by his son Rodrigo. Juan de Álava also built a number of monuments in this style – San Esteban in Salamanca, part of the cathedral at Plasencia, and the cloisters at Santiago. **Segovia Cathedral** too – unusually for Spain – displays a remarkable unity of form, using the traditional Gothic elements rejected by earlier builders.

The Renaissance

Oddly enough, the **Renaissance** was introduced to Spain with the **Collegio Santa Cruz** in Valladolid, just a few hundred metres from the simultaneous construction of two Isabelline facades. The architect, Lorenzo Vázquez, for all his historical importance, remains a rather shadowy figure. (Later, he was to build an Italian Renaissance palace at La Calahorra in Andalucía.) Enrique de Egas, who built the hospitals at Toledo (Santa Cruz), Granada and Santiago, and who also worked in a late-Gothic style, as witnessed by his Capilla Real in Granada and his design for the adjoining cathedral, is much better documented.

Much early Spanish Renaissance architecture is termed **Plateresque**, from the profusion of carving which allegedly resembled the work of silversmiths. The term is now applied rather loosely, but it is most associated with **Salamanca**, which is built of an extremely delicate rose-coloured sandstone. The supreme masterpiece of the style is the facade of the **University** here, where instead of the wild and irregular carvings of Valladolid, a generation before, all is order and symmetry while equally ornate. The motifs used in Plateresque carving are wholly Italianate – figures in medallions, *putti*, candelabra, grotesques, garlands of flowers and fruit, scrollwork and coats of arms. No convincing attribution has been made for the university facade, but one Plateresque architect whose work can be traced is **Alonso de Covarrubias**. He built the Capilla de los Reyes Nuevos in Toledo Cathedral, part of the Alcázar and probably the Hospital de Tavera in the same city, and worked on Sigüenza Cathedral, particularly the amazing sacristy. The facade of the University of Alcalá de Henares is a more severe Plateresque masterpiece by Rodrigo Gil de Ontañón; other important works are San Marcos in León by Juan de Badajoz, and the Hospital del Rey near Burgos.

The **High Renaissance**, by contrast, centred around **Andalucía**, the part of the country that was most lacking in Christian architecture following its liberation from the Muslim powers. The real masterpiece of the style is the **Palace of Carlos V** in Granada – incongruously located in the Alhambra, but a superbly pure piece of architecture. It is rare in being based on a round courtyard, and is the only surviving building by Pedro Machuca. As for churches, the leading architect of the Andalucian Renaissance in this field was Diego de Siloé, who began his career as a sculptor in Burgos under his father, Gil, and built the marvellous Plateresque Escalera Dorada in the cathedral there. Following study in Italy, he worked as an architect, devising an ingenious east end for the cathedral at Granada, and designing Guadix Cathedral and El Salvador at Úbeda. The last-named was actually built by his pupil, Andrés de Vandelvira, whose own main work is the monumental cathedral of Jaén. All these buildings show a strongly classical influence.

The severest, purest and greatest Spanish Renaissance architect was **Juan de Herrera**, who succeeded Juan Bautista de Toledo as architect of **El Escorial**, to which he devoted much of his working life. To many, this vast building is excessively sober, particularly in a country where ornamentation has so often reigned supreme. However, it does have a unique grandeur, and illustrates the Spanish penchant for taking any style to its extremes. Herrera's other main building is the **Cathedral of Valladolid**, though sadly only half of this was ever built, and some of that well after Herrera. In this truncated form it can appear rather cold and sombre, although the model for the complete building shows what a well-proportioned, harmonious and majestic edifice it might have become.

The Baroque

For a time, Herrera's style was to spawn a number of imitations, and early **Baroque** architecture was remarkably restrained – Madrid's early seventeenth-century **Plaza Mayor** by Juan Gomez de Mora being a case in point. In the east, Neapolitan influence was paramount, and led to the building of a large number of dignified churches.

Before long, however, this early phase gave way to an exuberant, playful and confident style that is perhaps Spain's most singular contribution to European architecture, the **Churrigueresque** – taken from the name of the family of architects, the Churrigueras, with whom the style was most associated. Ironically, their own work in architecture was far less ornate than that of many of their successors, although they also designed **retablos**, which are as embellished as anything that followed, so large as to seem almost pieces of architecture in themselves. These were typically of carved wood, painted and gilded, with twisted columns populated by saints in visionary or ecstatic mood and swirling processions of angels. *Retablos* of this type were soon to be found in churches all over Spain. Often the work of far cruder imitators, they raised the ire of visiting Protestant travellers, who used the term "Churrigueresque" to signify all that was basest in art. It's still a pejorative term, although the Churrigueras did actually create a number of masterpieces.

José, the eldest brother, created a complete planned town in **Nuevo Baztán**, not far from Madrid. Alberto, the youngest and most talented, laid out the **Plaza Mayor** in Salamanca in collaboration with Andrés García de Quiñones – a superb and harmonious piece of town planning, integrated wonderfully with the town's older buildings, and with the plain sides enlivened by carvings deriving from Plateresque work, and the rhythmic facade of the *ayuntamiento* providing a central focus on the north side.

The Churrigueras' contemporaries were more profusely ornate, often imitating the form of the *retablos* in their portals, perhaps the finest example of which is the **Hospicio San Fernando** in Madrid by Pedro de Ribera. Another new architectural feature was the *transparente*, in which a lavish altarpiece is lit from above by a window cut in the vault, giving a highly theatrical effect. The most famous example is that in **Toledo Cathedral** by Narciso Tomé, a brilliant piece of illusionism when the sun shines through, though in an utterly incongruous setting.

The Baroque style was also, of course, used when making additions to existing buildings, something you see all over Spain. Sometimes the merging of Baroque and medieval was triumphantly successful, as in the mid-eighteenth-century Obradoiro facade of **Santiago Cathedral** by Fernando Casas y Novoa, the climax of about a century's work, encasing the old Romanesque building in a lively Baroque exterior. While the loss of the Romanesque exterior is regrettable, particularly as some of the Baroque building is mediocre, the facade ranks as one of the most joyous creations in all architecture, and the ultimate triumph of Spanish Baroque. Other notably successful Baroque additions are the towers of the cathedrals of El Burgo de Osma, Santo Domingo de la Calzada and Murcia, which all harmonize surprisingly well with the existing structures, and give them a dimension they previously lacked. Many other additions, however, were far less fortunate: much of the time Baroque builders paid insufficient attention to the scale, style and materials of the existing work, and even when each is a competent piece of work in its own right, old and new scream at each other in horror.

Because of the trend towards enlivening old buildings, only one complete Baroque cathedral was built in Spain, at **Cádiz**. Nor are there many notable Baroque monasteries, although a number of charterhouses (*cartujas*) were built, not least at **Granada**, which became more and more extreme as construction progressed, culminating in the outrageous *sagrario* (sacristy) by Francesco Hurtado Izquiero. However, Spanish Baroque never found favour at court, where Italian and French models were preferred, and architects and decorators were imported from these countries, producing the Bourbon palaces of

Aranjuez, La Granja de San Ildefonso and Madrid, which stand apart from Spanish buildings of the period. Filippo Juvara, the famous architect of Turin, was summoned to Spain in the penultimate year of his life to design the garden front of La Granja and the overall plan for Madrid, although both were executed by his pupil, Giovanni Battista Sachetti.

Neoclassicism

In time, the court taste changed to **Neoclassical**, enforced by the mid-century establishment of academies, and the presiding architectural style became heavy and monumental in scale. The dominant figure was **Ventura Rodríguez**, a technically competent architect who built a lavish Augustinian church in **Valladolid** and completed the **Basílica del Pilar** in Zaragoza – a colossal building with elements drawn from a variety of styles that is more notable for its grandiose outline than for any other feature. But Rodríguez's talents were not put to their best use: his facade for **Pamplona Cathedral** would look fine on a bank but is wholly incongruous for a church, and a serious distraction in what is otherwise a fine building; and his plain, rather nondescript church at **Santo Domingo de Silos** is a similarly poor partner for the great cloister there. Another leading Neoclassical architect was **Juan de Villaneuva**, who built the **Prado** (actually as a natural history museum) and the two **Casitas** at El Escorial.

Spain's subsequent provincial history is mirrored in the paucity of buildings of much consequence. The slow process of industrial and social change meant that there were few of the self-confident expressions of prosperity found all over northern Europe. There were a host of imitative styles, but it is really only on the small scale that they give much pleasure. **Neo-Gothic**, also, was nowhere near as vital or as prevalent as elsewhere: the cathedrals built in this style, at **San Sebastián** and **Vitoria**, are not especially notable, and the most satisfying work was probably the completion of **Barcelona Cathedral**, which was actually accomplished according to a fifteenth-century plan.

The Twentieth Century

Spain's architecture in the twentieth century was characterized by four distinct epochs: the tail-end of the Modernisme movement in Catalunya, which flourished between 1880 and 1910; the early modernism of the Second Republic in the 1930s; the imperialism of the fascist years; and the resurgent contemporary architecture of the socialist era at the end of the twentieth century.

Modernisme

The Catalan **Modernisme** (or *modernista*) movement – characterized by organic form, structural daring and sculptural expression – sprang up in Barcelona at the end of the nineteenth century, fuelled by the city's economic prosperity and its subsequent radical growth (developed within the strict grid of the Eixample, planned by Ildefons Cerdà in 1859). At the forefront of the movement was **Antoni Gaudí**, one of the most distinctive voices of the age. His main architectural influences were Moorish and Gothic, which he considered the greatest European styles. From the former he took towers, *trompe l'oeil* effects, repeated elements, ceramics, cornices, dragons and the use of water, all employed, like his Gothic influences, in a free and fantastic way. He was also influenced by the natural world – trees, rocks, embankments, animals, birds, eroded and organic forms – and captivated by the potential of industrial technologies. He combined all these elements in an amazing – and distinctive – architectural vocabulary.

Some of his projects were almost impossibly ambitious. He worked for over forty years on the **Sagrada Familia**, yet only built a small portion. The **Parc Güell** was another vast project for a complete garden city, a commercial failure that has become a successful public park. Still, many less grandiose plans in a variety of forms were completed in Barcelona, and his work can also be seen in Astorga, León and Comillas.

Although Gaudi stands out amongst his **contemporaries**, a number of other architects of the time were instrumental in the *modernista* movement and produced schemes of great significance, both in terms of their visual impact on the city and in the influence they exert on Catalan architects today. Buildings worthy of particular note are Francesc Berenguer's Garraf Wine Cellar (1890); Josep Puig i Cadafalch's Casa Macaya (1901); Lluís Domènech i Montaner's sumptuous Palau de la Musica Catalana (1908, brilliantly refurbished by Oscar Tusquets in 1990); and J.M. Jujol's Casa Planells (1923) on the Avenida Diagonal.

Modernism

The advent of **modernism** (the International Style) in Spain is inextricably linked to the rise of socialism. In 1929 the International Exposition in Barcelona saw the construction of one of the twentieth century's masterpieces, the **German Pavilion**, designed by Mies van der Rohe (and rebuilt in 1986). Its rigorous geometry, pared down yet luxurious palette of materials and sensitive exploitation of natural light precede the very best of the world's contemporary architecture, and its impact on the young modernists of Spain was instrumental in the formation of **GATEPAC** (Grupo de Arquitectos y Tecnicos Españoles para una Arquitectura Contemporanea) in 1930 – a movement which promoted the adoption of new technologies and functional design. The group's best buildings were constructed in Barcelona; key amongst these was Sert, Torres and Subirana's Dispensario Antituberculoso (1934–38), which managed to be both modern in expression and traditional in planning, and thus paved the way for Spain's contemporary fusion of modernism with traditional idioms.

Imperialism

The outbreak of civil war in 1936 brought a sudden end to socialist ideals and dramatically ushered in the **iconoclastic** and **imperial style** of the **fascists**. The early years of the Falange regime were characterized by cultural introversion, centralization and retrogressive pastiche. Overscaled buildings blighted city centres, none worse than the vast, overbearing Air Ministry at Moncloa in Madrid (1957). The majority of Spain, however, was saved from total desecration by a severe shortage of cash preventing any significant building programme. The period even threw up one or two individual gems which have proved influential to the modern day: Cabrero and Aburto's brick-clad gridded Casa Sindical (1949; now the Ministry of Work and Social Affairs) opposite the Prado in Madrid, acted as a precursor to much of the city's rationalist social housing of the 1980s, while in Barcelona, Coderch's Casa de la Marina, with its inflected facades and fragmented plan, stands as a key reference to influential contemporary Catalan architects such as MBMP, Garces and Sorria, and Torres Martínez-Lapeña.

By the end of the 1950s introverted politics had brought Spain close to bankruptcy and the fascists were forced to turn to America for economic salvation. The country opened its doors to the **internationalism** which was spreading through the rest of the developed world. In contrast with its more prosperous neighbours, Spain's construction had limited technical capacity, and the majority of new buildings from this era were built in brick with concrete floors, softening the lines of the tough reinforced concrete, steel and glass buildings mushrooming all over northern Europe. Nonetheless, the advent of international intervention did bring with it some catastrophic development which, with little thought to urban planning, marred much of Spain's coastline and cities. Amongst this unchecked destruction, three architects stand out for high quality and hugely influential work: Alejandro de la Sota (architect of the Maravillas Gymnasium in Madrid, 1962), Javier Sáenz de Oiza (architect of the Torres Blancas in Madrid, 1968) and Oriel Bohigas (architect of the Thau School in Barcelona, 1970). Each, through their emblematic buildings and teaching, heralded the dramatic architectural change of the late twentieth century.

Contemporary Architecture

With the death of Franco in 1975, the socialists swept into power on a wave of optimism – proclaiming change and using architecture to prove it. Planning legislation was reformed to save the nation's heritage and encourage considered building. Investment poured in and throughout the country there was a massive construction programme of social housing, schools, libraries, medical centres and small urban spaces. These projects, geared towards **community regeneration**, were intended to foster public confidence in the new regime. Representative of this regeneration are the vast number of new housing projects in Vallecas in Madrid and the numerous public spaces instigated by Oriel Bohigas in Barcelona.

The massive building programme culminated in the **1992 Barcelona Olympics** and **Sevilla World Expo**. These events acted as major catalysts of urban regeneration in each city, and opened the world's eyes to Spain's emergent modern architecture – and Spain's doors to the world's best architects. In **Barcelona** vast arrays of redundant warehousing were ripped down to make way for the Olympic Village and Port, master-planned by Martorell, Bohigas, Mackay, Puigdomenec (MBMP), with buildings by the best of Catalunya's new wave of young architects, including Viaplana and Piñon, Bach and Mora, Torres Martínez-Lapeña, Enric Miralles, Garces and Sorria. The hilltop of Montjuic was taken over for the sporting arenas. To facilitate the developments a whole new infrastructure was required; fast dual carriageways were constructed and the airport was doubled in size by Ricardo Bofill. Architects from around the world designed complementary monuments, eminent among them Norman Foster's Torre de Collserola communications tower and Arato Isozaki's Palau Saint Jordi indoor stadium on Montjuic. The impact of the Expo on **Sevilla** was less significant, although Santiago Calatrava's Alamillo bridge over the Guadalquivir and MBMP's Pabellon de Exposiciones stand out as structural *tours de force.* More significant was the construction of the AVE high-speed train link between two of Europe's most elegant modern stations – Rafael Moneo's Atocha in Madrid and Cruz and Ortiz's Santa Justa in Sevilla.

The recession which enveloped the rest of the world left Spain with a particularly harsh hangover after the euphoria of 1992, though it also enabled a younger generation to explore new ideas and technologies. As the recession passed, Spain's regional authorities returned to architecture to express optimism in the future, this time recruiting **international architects** to add glamour and prestige to the projects. Among these key buildings are Norman Foster's Palacio de Congresos in Valencia, Jean Nouvel's extension to the Centro de Arte Reina Sofía in Madrid, and, most fantastic of all, Frank O. Gehry's spectacular titanium-clad **Guggenheim** in Bilbao – one of the great buildings of the twentieth century. Spain's own architects have also increasingly won significant commissions around the world. Notable projects by **Spanish architects abroad** include Rafael Moneo's art gallery in Stockholm and cathedral in Los Angeles; Navarro Baldeweg's work in Princetown; and the late Enric Miralles' School of Architecture in Venice and Scottish Parliament in Edinburgh.

Alongside its flagship schemes, Spain continues to invest in both public and private projects, creating modern architecture that is amongst the best in the world. Such buildings include Mansilla & Tuñon's Castellón Museo de Bellas Artes, Alberto Campo Baeza's CIT building in Inca, Mallorca and Fraile and Revillo's Trade Fair Centre in Zamorra. Allied with a healthy respect for the conservation of its historical inheritance, this new wave of construction places Spain at the forefront of European architecture and makes it one of the most exciting architectural destinations in the world.

Gordon McLachlan and Hugh Broughton

Spanish Painting

From the Middle Ages to the present day, the history of Spanish painting is one of fits and starts, a process of development marked on one hand by extreme originality and on the other by near-fatal injections of foreign influence. Nevertheless, the highpoints are high, from Catalan Romanesque art and the monastic manuscript tradition through giants such as El Greco, Velázquez, Goya, Picasso and Dalí. Spanish art is at its best when its roots are deepest in Iberian soil: from the ecstatic agony of Castile and Andalucia in Zubarán, or the darkness and satire of Aragonese Goya, to the irreverent subversiveness of Catalan Surrealism.

Early examples of this strength of expression can be found in the **illuminated manuscripts** and **mural paintings** of the eleventh and twelfth centuries. Dominant among the manuscripts are the many versions of Beatus's *Commentaries on the Apocalypse*, the original text of which, written by an eighth-century Spanish monk, inspired a whole series of versions illuminating the text with brilliantly coloured miniatures. These books have found their way into libraries all over the world, but many still remain in Spain, with those in Girona, El Burgo de Osma and La Seu d'Urgell particularly worthy of note.

The great decorated interiors of village churches are also characteristic of the period, especially in Catalunya, though for the most part these are no longer *in situ*; many were saved just in time to prevent them from deteriorating irrevocably, and have been removed to museums, of which Barcelona's have by far the finest collection. The most imposing example of this style is by the so-called **Master of Taüll**, whose decoration of the apse of the church of Sant Climent combines a Byzantine hierarchical composition with the vibrant colours and strong outlines of the manuscript illuminators. His overall rawness and monumentality seem strangely anticipatory of much of the best modern art.

Amazingly, two other highly talented painters also worked in the village of Taüll in the 1120s: art historians have christened them the **Master of Maderuelo** and the **Master of the Last Judgement**. Another notable artist of the period is the **Master of Pedret**, who incorporated scenes of everyday and natural life into his paintings.

Catalan studios also produced painted wooden altar frontals, often based on a central figure of a saint, surrounded by scenes from his life. In time, this grew in scale into the large *retablo* over the high altar – a key feature of Spanish churches for centuries. The most remarkable frescoes outside Catalunya are those of the Panteón de los Reyes in San Isidoro in León. These date from the second half of the twelfth century, and show a softer, more courtly style, perhaps influenced by French models.

The Catalan School

In the Gothic period, Catalunya's predominance continued, rivalled only by Valencia. The leader of the school was **Ferrer Bassa** (c. 1285–1348), court painter to Pedro IV (king of Aragón and count of Barcelona) and a manuscript illuminator. Unfortunately, his only certain surviving work comes from late in his long career – a series of murals in the Convent of Pedralbes in Barcelona. These are charming, notable for their colouring and descriptive qualities, along with a sense of movement and skilled draughtsmanship, and are clearly influenced by the paintings of the Sienese school, though they're freer and less refined. Bassa may also have been influenced by the rounder qualities of Giotto and the Florentine school – Italian currents that are also found in the work of the artist's followers, along with various French trends.

The most notable names of this school were **Jaume Serra** (d. 1395), his brother, **Pere Serra** (d. 1408), **Ramon Destorrents** (1346–91), **Lluís Borrassa** (d. 1424) and **Ramon de Mur** (d. 1435). **Bernat Martorell** (d. 1452) is perhaps the most appealing of the group, a notable draughtsman who worked very carefully and deliberately, striving to give character to faces in his paintings. **Lluís Daimau** (d. 1460) came strongly under the influence of contemporary Flemish painting, in particular that of Jan van Eyck, and no other foreign currents are discernible in his work. **Jaume Huguet** (c. 1414–92) applied this new realism to the traditional forms of the Catalan school, and can thus be seen as a representative of the International Gothic style of painting.

The Valencian School

The Valencian school tended towards a more purely Italian influence, although one of its main painters, **Andrés Marzal de Sax** (d. 1410), may have been German. Other notable names are **Pedro Nicolau** (d. 1410), **Jaime Baco** ("Jacomart") (d. 1461), **Juan Rexach** (1431–92), and **Rodrigo de Osona** (d. 1510), the last of whom was influenced by the Renaissance. The greatest of all the Spanish Primitives, however, was **Bartolomé Bermejo** (d. 1495/8), originally from Córdoba, who worked in both Valencia and Barcelona. He seems to have had a fairly long career but only a few works, of a consistently high quality, survive. His earlier paintings, of which the Prado's *Santo Domingo de Silos* is a good example, are sumptuous; the later works, particularly the *Pietà* in Barcelona Cathedral, are altogether more complex, with a haunting sense of mystery and a Flemish and French influence that marks the introduction of oil painting to Spain.

The Castilian School

In Castile, artists of foreign origin predominated – **Deillo Delli** ("Nicolas Florentino"; d. 1470) in Salamanca, **Nicolás Francés** (1425–68) in León, **Jorge Inglés** (dates unknown) in Valladolid, and **Juan de Flandes** (d. 1514) in Salamanca and Valencia. The last became court painter to Isabel la Católica and introduced a Renaissance sense of space along with the beautiful modelling and colouring typical of the Flemish school. There was a rustic local school active in Ávila, however, and towards the end of the century native artists came increasingly to the fore. Particularly notable is **Fernando Gallego** (c. 1440–1507), who worked in Zamora and Extremadura. Superficially, his paintings seem strongly reminiscent of Flemish types, but his exaggerated sense of drama – manifested in distorted expressions, strange postures and movements frozen in mid-course – is far removed from these models. Nonetheless, the garments are correctly drawn, and landscape is often a feature of the backgrounds.

Pedro Berruguete (c. 1450–1504) was originally trained in the Flemish style, but spent an extended period in Italy at the court of Urbino. His productions from this period are so close to those of the Fleming Justus van Gent that art historians have frequently been unable to distinguish between them. On his return to Spain in 1482, Berruguete worked in a hybrid style: although his drawing was precise and he introduced chiaroscuro to Spanish art, he persisted in using the traditional gold backgrounds – an anachronistic mixture that is surprisingly satisfying. Berruguete was never a slavish imitator of Italian models, like too many of his successors, and his most impressive works are those with crowd scenes, where the differentiation of types and attitudes is remarkable. **Alonso Berruguete** (1486–1561), his son, also went to Italy, and his paintings are heavily Mannerist in style, with strong drawing and harsh colours. His work as a sculptor is more significant: uneven in quality but sometimes truly inspired, with many powerful and intensely personal images. Certainly, he was the most distinctive and arguably the greatest native Spanish artist of the Renaissance.

The Late Renaissance

Too often the quality of Italian art was diluted in Spain: neither nudes nor mythological subjects – both of crucial importance in Italy – had any attraction here, and there is barely an example of either. Instead, there was a sweetening and sentimentalization of religious models. In Valencia, **Fernando Yáñez** (d. 1531) and his collaborator **Fernando de los Llanos** (dates unknown) adopted this facet of the art of Leonardo da Vinci, while **Juan Vicente Masip** (c. 1475–1550) and his son of the same name, usually referred to as **Juan de Juanes** (1523–79), drew more from Raphael, becoming ever more saccharine as time went on.

Sevilla also had a school of painters, beginning with **Alejo Fernández** (d. 1543), but although less slavishly imitative of Italian models than the Valencian, it also failed to produce an artist of the very first rank. The Extremaduran **Luís Morales** (c. 1509–86) is more notable: he was revered by the common people, who referred to him as "El Divino", but he never found favour with authority, and much of his work is still in village churches. He is at his best with such small-scale subjects as the Madonna and Child, which he repeated many times with slight variations. Strongly Mannerist in outlook, his drawing is rather stiff and his colours often cold, but he has a genuine religious feeling.

Ironically enough, it took a foreigner, Domenico Theotocopoulos (1540–1614), universally known as **El Greco**, to forge a truly great and quintessentially Spanish art in the late-Renaissance period. He arrived in Toledo in 1575, having come from his native Crete via Italy. Presumably he hoped to find favour at court, particularly in the decoration of El Escorial, but was soon disappointed, and spent the rest of his life painting portraits of the nobility, along with a host of religious works for the many churches and monasteries of Spain's ecclesiastical capital. Having shown himself adept at both the Byzantine and Venetian styles of painting, he drew from both to create a highly idiosyncratic art that was ideally suited to the mood of Spain at the time. Distinguished features of his style include elongated faces and bodies, together with a sense of spiritual ecstasy that gives a strong feeling of the union of the terrestrial and the celestial. El Greco's gift for portraiture, too, is shown not only in his paintings of real-life sitters, but also in those of historical subjects, most notably in the several series of Apostles he was required to produce. His greatest work, *The Burial of the Count of Orgaz*, in Santo Tomás in Toledo, displays all the facets of his genius in a single canvas. Later, El Greco's style became increasingly abstract, with a freeing of his brushwork that anticipates many subsequent developments in the history of art. Sadly, although he maintained a flourishing studio which produced many replicas, none of El Greco's followers picked up much of his master's style. Most talented was **Luís Tristán** (1586–1624), whose own output was very uneven.

At court, a school of portraiture was founded by a Dutchman, **Antonio Moro** (1517–76), who emphasized the dignity of his sitters in their facial expressions and by giving prominence to clothes and jewellery – a style that was followed by two native artists, **Alonso Sánchez Coello** (1531–88) and **Juan Pantoja de la Cruz** (1553–1608). At El Escorial, minor Italian Mannerists were imported in preference to native artists. An exception was the deaf-mute **Juan Navarret** (1526–79).

In Valencia, **Francisco Ribalta** (1565–1628) began working in a similar Mannerist style, but soon came under the influence of Caravaggio and introduced naturalism and the sharp contrasts of light associated with tenebrism into Spain. He was followed by a yet more significant painter, **Jusepe (José) de Ribera** (1591–1652). Ribera spent nearly all his career in Naples under the protection of the Spanish viceroys, who sent many of his works back to his native land. He had two distinctive periods: early on in his career he used heavy chiaroscuro and small, thick brushstrokes; later he brightened his palette considerably. Above all he was interested in the dignity of human beings, and whether he painted ancient philosophers in contemplation, saints in solace, or martyrs resigned to their fate, his art is a concentrated one, with the spotlight very much on the main subject. His subjects at times can appear gruesome, but they are very much of their period in that respect, and the treatment is never mere sensationalism. For a long time out of critical favour, Ribera now appears as one of the most accomplished artists of European Baroque.

The Seventeenth Century

In the early seventeenth century, Sevilla and Madrid replaced Valencia and Toledo as the main artistic centres of Spain. **Francisco Pacheco** (1564–1654) was the father figure of the Sevillan school, although nowadays his work as a theorist is considered more significant than his paintings. He adopted a naturalistic approach as a reaction against Mannerism, and was followed in this by **Francisco Herrera** (c. 1590–1656) and his son of the same name (1622–85), who painted in an increasingly bombastic and theatrical manner.

Towering high above these, Pacheco's son-in-law, **Diego Velázquez** (1599–1660), is probably the artist the Spanish people take most pride in. Velázquez was a stunning technician. His genre scenes of Sevillan life, painted while he was still in his teens, have a naturalistic quality that is almost photographic. In contrast with many of his fellow countrymen, Velázquez was a slow and meticulous worker: he probably painted fewer than 200 works in his entire career, some 120 of which survive, almost half of them in the Prado.

In 1623 Velázquez went to Madrid to work for the court, a position he retained for the rest of his life. As well as the many royal portraits, he portrayed the jesters and dwarfs of the palace, giving them a Spanish sense of dignity. In *The Surrender of Breda* he revolutionized history painting, ridding it of supernatural overtones. His greatest masterpieces, *Las Hilanderas* and *Las Meninas*, date from near the end of his life, and are remarkable for the way they immortalize fleeting moments, as well as for their absolute technical mastery, particularly of aerial perspective.

Juan Bautista del Marzo (c. 1615–67), son-in-law and assistant to Velázquez, was so adept at imitating his style that it is often difficult to determine which works are the originals and which are copies. His independent work, however, is altogether of inferior quality. **Juan Carreno de Miranda** (1614–85) also followed Velázquez's portrait style closely, and was very active as a painter of religious subjects, a field largely abandoned by Velázquez in his maturity.

In Sevilla, the greatest painter was **Francisco de Zurbarán** (1598–1664), who is best known as an illustrator of monastic life of the times. He painted mainly for the more austere orders, such as Carthusians and Hieronymites, and many of his portraits of saints are modelled on real-life monks, some of them single figures of an almost sculptural quality. Zurbarán's palette was a bright one, his lighting effects are subtle rather than dramatic, and he ranks as one of the supreme masters of still lifes, which have a frequent presence in his larger paintings as well as in a few independent compositions. A complete example of one of his decorative schemes is still extant at Guadalupe, but sadly his later work sometimes shows a fall-off in quality: to pay off his debts he was forced to produce a large number of works for export to religious foundations in Latin America.

Zurbarán also sentimentalized his style in order to meet the competition of his highly successful younger contemporary, **Bartolomé Esteban Murillo** (1618–82), who spent his entire career in Sevilla. Murillo's light, airy style was in perfect accord with the mood of the Counter-Reformation, and he was to have an important impact on Catholic imagery. His versions of subjects such as the Immaculate Conception, Madonna and Child, and the Good Shepherd, became the norm in terms of the portrayal of traditional dogma. His genre scenes of street urchins and portraits in the manner of van Dyck made him popular in northern Europe, too, and for a long time he was considered one of the greatest artists of all time. His reputation slumped considerably in the nineteenth century, and it is only in the last few years that critical opinion has turned again in his favour. Certainly his subject matter can seem cloying to modern tastes, but Murillo nearly always painted beautifully, and he was a marvellous storyteller. His later works were particularly successful, employing the *vaporoso* technique of delicate brushwork and diffuse forms, and there's no doubt that he was a substantial influence on much subsequent eighteenth- and nineteenth-century painting in Spain, France and England.

In complete contrast to Murillo, **Juan Valdés Leal** (1622–90) preferred the violent and macabre side of the Baroque. His work was very uneven in quality; the paintings in the Hospital de la Caridad in Sevilla are the most celebrated. **Alonso Cano** (1601–67) was the leading painter of Granada and also active as an architect and sculptor. He led a rather dissolute life, and changed his working style abruptly several times. Perhaps the most successful of his paintings are the mature, pale-coloured religious works, which reveal debts to van Dyck and Velázquez.

A large number of artists can be grouped together under the **Madrid school**. One of the earliest was the Florentine-born **Vicente Carducho**

(1576–1638), who painted large-scale works in sombre colours for the Carthusians and other orders. **Fra Juan Rizi** (1600–81) illustrated contemporary monastic life in a different and less mystical way than Zurbarán. His brother, **Francisco Rizi** (1614–85), favoured full-blown canvases of Baroque pomp. **Fra Juan Bautista Maino** (1578–1649) was more influenced by the classical aspects of seventeenth-century art; he painted some notable religious and historical canvases with strong colouring, but with little interest in lighting effects. **Juan de Arellano** (1614–76) and **Bartolomé Pérez** (1634–93) worked mainly with landscape and historical religious works, while **José Antolínez** (1635–75) was particularly renowned for his versions of the Immaculate Conception. **Mateo Cerezo** (1626–66) painted fluid religious canvases under the influence of the works by Titian and van Dyck in the royal collections. The last major figure was probably also the most accomplished: **Claudio Coello** (1642–93), who was a master of the large-scale decorative style, using techniques of spatial illusion and very complicated arrangements of figures. His work at El Escorial shows his style at its best.

The Eighteenth and Nineteenth Centuries

The late seventeenth century and the first half of the eighteenth century was a very thin time in the history of Spanish painting: even the French and Italian artists imported by the Bourbon court were seldom of great merit. One native artist worthy of mention, however, is **Luís Meléndez** (1716–80), a master of still-life subjects. **Anton Raphael Mengs** (1728–79) came to Spain from Bohemia in 1761 as court painter, and in this capacity was a virtual dictator of style for a while, spearheading the adoption of an academic, Neoclassical tone, particularly in portraiture. His assistant, **Francisco Bayeu** (1734–95), was a prolific fresco painter for both royal and religious patrons, and was also in charge of the cartoons for the Royal Tapestry Factory. His brother, **Ramón Bayeu** (1746–93), worked on similar projects but was far less accomplished.

It was the Bayeus' brother-in-law, however, **Francisco Goya** (1746–1828), who was the overwhelmingly dominant personality of the period. Goya's output was prolific and his range of subject matter and style so immense that it is hard to believe one man was responsible for so much. Interestingly, he was no prodigy. In his twenties he became a highly competent painter of religious murals, his work at Zaragoza and Aula Dei already surpassing that of his contemporaries. After moving to Madrid, he worked for many years on tapestry cartoons (preparatory drawings), which in their graceful handling and skilful grouping made the most of their rather frivolous subject matter and gave Goya an entry into court circles, after which he became a fashionable portrait painter. It was in this role that his originality began to show through: his portraits eschew any attempt at flattery, and it's clear that he was less than impressed by his sitters. A serious illness in the early 1790s left him deaf and led to a more bitter and sarcastic art; his increasingly fantastic style may have emerged from his developing interest in witchcraft, which resulted in many paintings and two series of etchings: *Los Caprichos* and, later, *Los Disparates*. The marvellous frescoes in San Antonio de la Florida in Madrid are the exception here, among his most beautiful creations ever and containing a remarkable representation of the various social types of the day. But the Peninsular War further darkened Goya's mood, as shown by *The Second fof May* and especially *The Third of May*, and by the engravings *The Disasters of War*. The last paintings are probably his most remarkable, especially those of bullfights, in which he showed an extraordinary visual perception, the exactness of which was proved only with the development of the slow-motion camera. Finally, there were the despairing "black paintings" made on the walls of his own house, the Quinta del Sordo, now detached and hung in the Prado.

Of Goya's contemporaries, the most interesting are **Luís Paret y Alcázar** (1746–99), who painted Rococo scenes under French and Italian influence, and **Vicente López** (1772–1850), an academic portrait painter in the manner of Mengs whose severe portrait of Goya hangs in the Prado. The nearest artist to Goya in style was **Eugenio Lucas** (1824–70), who followed his interest in bullfighting and Inquisition scenes, but made little stylistic advance. Indeed, most of the nineteenth century was extremely barren in terms of Spanish art, a period of imitation, largely of French models, at least twenty years late. The most gifted painter was perhaps **Mariano Fortuny** (1838–74), who specialized in small, very highly finished canvases, often of exotic subjects. Other artists worthy of mention are **Dario de Regoyos y Valdés** (1857–1913), the nearest thing to an Impressionist working in Spain at the time; **Joaquín Sorolla** (1863–1923), who was noted for his beach scenes; and **Ignacio Zuloaga** (1870–1945), who painted portraits against landscape backgrounds.

The Twentieth Century

As with architecture, it was Catalunya that took the lead in painting towards the end of the nineteenth century. **Isidoro Nonell** (1873–1911) was best known as a naturalistic painter of the poor. In contrast, **José María Sert** (1874–1945) was at his best in large-scale mural decorations, particularly in the powerful sepia and grey frescoes he produced for Vic Cathedral, replacements for two earlier sets.

Although born in Málaga, **Pablo Picasso** (1881–1973), the overwhelmingly dominant figure in twentieth-century art, spent many of his formative years in Barcelona, achieving great technical facility at a very early age, and creating many accomplished works in a representational style before the age of twenty. In 1900 he first visited Paris, where the influence of Toulouse-Lautrec made itself felt in the "blue period" of 1901–4, during which he depicted many of society's victims in Paris and Barcelona, following the lead of Nonell. The "rose period" of 1904–6 was perhaps Picasso's most Spanish phase (although by now he was living in Paris). Actors, clowns and models featured among his subjects, and his interest turned to the work of El Greco and ancient Iberian sculpture. The following "negro period" of 1907–9 marked the break with traditional forms, as manifested in the key work, *Les Demoiselles d'Avignon*. After this Picasso returned to representational painting only for a short time in the 1920s, and from 1910 onwards developed Cubism in association with Frenchman Georges Braque.

The movement's first phase, analytical Cubism, was largely concerned with form, with being able to depict objects as if seen from different angles at the same time. This was followed by synthetic Cubism, which showed a revival of interest in colour and handling. For a time in the 1920s and 1930s, Picasso combined Cubism with Surrealism, inventing a new anatomy for the human form, and eventually becoming noted as a painter of protest, most markedly in *Guernica*, a cry of despair about the Civil War in his native land (which he had by then left for good). Until his death, Picasso worked in a variety of styles, active in sculpture and ceramics as well. He was prolific to an almost unimaginable degree – in 1969 alone he produced almost as many canvases as Velázquez did in his lifetime, among the most notable of which were variations on well-known paintings such as *Las Meninas*.

One of the most faithful Cubists was **Juan Gris** (1887–1927), who favoured stronger colours and softer forms than others in the group. In **Surrealism**, two Catalans were among the leading figures: **Joan Miró** (1893–1983) and **Salvador Dalí** (1904–89). Miró created the most poetic and whimsical works of the movement, showing a childlike delight in colours and shapes, and developing a highly personal language that was freer in form and more highly decorative than that of the other Surrealists. One of his favourite techniques during the 1930s was to spill paint on the canvas and move his brush around in it. He was also active in a variety of artistic media besides paint and canvas: collage, murals, book illustrations, sculpture and ceramics. Aside from an early period as a Futurist and Cubist, Dalí was more concerned with creating his own vision of a dream world. He was particularly interested in infantile obsessions and in paranoia, and his works often showed wholly unrelated objects grouped together, the distortion of solid forms, and unrealistic perspectives. He also worked on book illustrations, some of them his own texts, and on films. In later years he looked for other stimuli and painted a number of religious subjects. Few other artists in history have shown such talent for self-publicity. There are few artists, either, who have been so easily forged: in his later years Dalí reputedly made millions by signing thousands of blank pieces of paper.

Artists of the same generation include **Óscar Domínguez** (1906–57), who used both the Cubist and Surrealist idioms, at times combining the two in a wholly individualistic way. Another isolated figure of note was **José Gutiérrez Solana** (1885–1945), whose impoverished background led him to seek out his subjects amongst the lowlife of Madrid he knew so well, adopting a realist approach with strong use of colour.

Spanish art of the late twentieth century was dominated by the "abstract generation", many of whom are still living, and who run a museum at Cuenca devoted solely to their works. By far the most individual figure of the group was **Antonio Saura** (1930–1999), whose violently expressive canvases, the earlier of which are painted in black and white only, are overtly political in tone, showing Man oppressed but unbowed. He used religious themes in a deliberately humanist or even blasphemous way in his triptychs of crowd scenes, and transformation of the Crucifixion into a parable of secular oppression. The Catalans **Joan Brossa** (b. 1919) and **Antoni Tàpies** (b. 1923) are abstractionists in the tradition of the Dada movement. Brossa, primarily a sculptor, is also famous as a dramatist and poet; while Tàpies, who is better known, began by making collages out of newspaper, cardboard, silver wrapping, string and wire. For a period he turned to graffiti-type work with deformed letters, before returning to experiments with unusual materials, particularly oil paint mixed with crushed marble.

For those who despair of the theoretical and iconoclastic side of the modern movement, **Antonio López García** (b. 1936) comes as a refreshing change – a hyperrealist painter of landscapes, cityscapes, and sculptor of still lifes and nudes with an unsettling photographic clarity to his work. **Eduardo Arroyo**

(b. 1937) is a follower of the Pop Art movement, with its emphasis on large-scale depictions of familiar everyday faces and objects.

The political changes of the 1970s injected a frenetic optimism into Spanish art, and the end of censorship provoked a brash and sensational reaction featuring much concept art – a rejection of painting itself by the generation of this period, which the Mallorcan **Miquel Barceló** (b. 1957), whose "Action Painting" follows the tradition of Pollock and Tàpies characterized as having produced more junkies than artists. The 1980s saw the pendulum swing back towards traditional Spanish painting before the "Post-Enthusiast" 90s, which neither rejected nor glorified painting, but incorporated it with other media, including sculpture, photography and video. Spanish art is now globalizing, and is ever more susceptible to foreign currents and trends. Typical of the tendency to cross-media are young artists like **Pedro G. Romero** (b. 1961) who is an artist and rock musician, or **Rogelio Lopez Cuenca** (b. 1959) whose pop art and video is heavily influenced by the Russian avant-garde. Other new lights include the Duchamp-influenced **Federico Guzmán** (b. 1964), **José Espaliu** (b. 1955) and **Fermín García** (b. 1961), a self-taught painter whose city- and landscapes blend realism with impressionistic touches.

Gordon McLachlan

Wildlife

Despite its reputation as the land of the package holiday, you can't beat Spain for sheer diversity of landscape and wildlife. When the Pyrenees were squeezed from the earth's crust they created an almost impenetrable barrier stretching from the Bay of Biscay to the Mediterranean Sea. Those animals and plants already present in Spain were cut off from the rest of Europe, and have been evolving independently ever since. In the same way, the breach of the land bridge at what is now the Strait of Gibraltar, and the subsequent reflooding of the Mediterranean basin, stranded typical African species on the peninsula. The outcome was an assortment of wildlife originating from two continents, resulting in modern-day Iberia's unique flora and fauna.

Spain is the second most **mountainous** country in Europe after Switzerland. The central plateau – the Meseta – averages 600–700m in elevation, slopes gently westwards and is surrounded and traversed by imposing sierras and *cordilleras*. To the north, the plateau is divided from the coast by the extensive ranges of the Cordillera Cantábrica, and in the south the towering Sierra Nevada and several lesser ranges such as the Serranía de Ronda run along the Mediterranean shores (where these southern sierras continue across the Mediterranean basin, the unsubmerged peaks are today known as the Balearic Islands). The Pyrenean chain marks the border with France, and even along Spain's eastern shores the narrow coastal plain soon rises into the foothills of the Sierras of Montseny, Espuña and los Filabres, among others. The ancient Sierras de Guadarrama and Gredos cross the Meseta just north of Madrid, and the Sierra Morena and the Montes de Toledo rise out of the dusty southern plains. So it is not surprising to find that both flora and fauna of Spain possess a distinctly alpine element, with many species adapted to high levels of ultraviolet light and prolonged winter snow-cover.

The centre of Spain lies many kilometres from the coast, and thus the **climate** is almost continental in character. The summers are scorching, the winters bitter, and what rain there is falls only in spring and autumn. Moving eastwards, the Mediterranean Sea has a moderating effect on this weather pattern, favouring the coastal lands with mild winters and summers which become progressively hotter as you move south towards Africa. What most people tend to forget, however, is that the northern and western parts of the country are endowed with a climate that, if anything, is even worse than that of Britain. Depressions coming in from the Atlantic Ocean are responsible for almost continual cloud cover, high rainfall and persistent mists along the appropriately named Costa Verde; when the sun does show its face the high humidity can make life very uncomfortable.

These climatic variations have produced a corresponding diversity in Spanish wildlife. The wet, humid **north** is populated by species common throughout Atlantic Europe, especially Ireland, whilst the **southern** foothills of the Sierra Nevada, situated only a stone's throw from Africa, have an almost subtropical vegetation. The continental weather pattern of much of the **interior** has given rise to a community of drought-resistant shrubs, together with annual herbs which flower and set seed in the brief spring and autumn rains, or more long-lived plants which possess underground bulbs or tubers to withstand the prolonged summer drought and winter cold.

Landscape

The Iberian peninsula was once heavily forested, although it is estimated that today only about ten percent of the original **woodland** remains, mostly in the north. Much of the Meseta was covered with evergreen oaks and associated shrubs such as laurustinus and strawberry tree (*el madroño* – the tree in the symbol of Madrid), but the clearance of land for arable and pastoral purposes has taken its toll, as have the ravages of war. Today tracts of Mediterranean woodland persist only in the sierras and some parts of Extremadura. When it was realized that much of the plateau was unsuitable for permanent agricultural use, the land was abandoned, and is now covered with low-growing, aromatic scrub vegetation, known as *matorral* (maquis). The southeastern corner of the Meseta is the only part of Spain which probably never supported woodland; here the arid steppe **grasslands** – *calvero* – remain basically untouched by man. In northern Spain, where vast areas are still forested, the typical tree species are more familiar: oak, beech, ash and lime on the lower slopes, grading into pine and fir at higher levels.

Much of the Meseta is flat, arid and predominantly brown. Indeed, in Almería, Europe's only true **desert** is to be found, such is the lack of rainfall. But the presence of subterranean water supplies gives rise to occasional **oases**: flashes of green and blue, teeming with wildlife. The numerous tree-lined **watercourses** of the peninsula also attract birds and animals from the surrounding dusty plains. The great Ebro and Duero rivers of the north, and the Tajo and Guadiana in the south, have been dammed at intervals, creating **reservoirs** which attract wildfowl in winter.

The Spanish **coastline** has a little of everything: dune systems, shingle banks, rocky cliffs, salt marshes and sweeping sandy beaches. In Galicia, submerged river valleys, or *rías*, are reminiscent of the Norwegian fjords, and the offshore islands are home to noisy sea-bird colonies; the north Atlantic coast is characterized by limestone promontories and tiny, sandy coves; the Mediterranean coast, despite its reputation for wall-to-wall hotels and beach towels, still boasts many undeveloped lagoons and marshes; and west of Gibraltar lies perhaps the greatest of all coastal marshlands: the Coto Doñana.

The Spanish **landscape** has changed little since the early disappearance of the forests. While the rest of Europe strives for agricultural supremacy, in Spain the land is still **farmed** by traditional methods. The olive groves of the south, the extensive livestock-rearing lands of the north and even the cereal-growing and wine-producing regions of the plains are still havens for the indigenous wildlife of the country. It is only since Spain joined the European Community that artificial pesticides and fertilizers and huge machines have made much impact. Even so, Spain is still essentially a wild country compared with much of Europe. Apart from a few industrial areas around Madrid and in the northeast, the landscape reflects the absence of modern technology, and the low population density means that few demands are made on the wilderness areas that remain.

Flowers

With such a broad range of habitats, Spain's **flora** is nothing less than superb. Excluding the Canary Islands, about 8000 species occur on Spanish soil, approximately ten percent of which are endemic: that is, they are found nowhere else in the world. Due to the plethora of high **mountains**, an alpine flora persists in Spain well beyond its normal north European distribution, and because of the relative geographical isolation of the mountain ranges, plants have evolved which are specific to each (there are about 180 plants which occur only in the Pyrenees, and over forty species endemic to the Sierra Nevada).

The **buttercup** family makes a good example. In the Pyrenees, endemic species include the pheasant's-eye *Adonis pyrenaica* and the meadow-rue *Thalictrum macrocarpum*; the Sierra Nevada has *Delphinium nevadense* and the monkshood *Aconitum nevadense*, and of the columbines *Aquilegia nevadensis* occurs here alone. *A. discolor* is endemic to the Picos de Europa, *A. cazorlensis* is found only in the Sierra de Cazorla and *A. pyrenaica* is unique to the Pyrenees. Other handsome montane members of this family include alpine pasque flowers, hepatica, hellebores, clematis and a host of more obvious buttercups.

The dry Mediterranean grasslands of Spain are excellent hunting grounds for **orchids**. In spring, in the meadows of the Cordillera Cantábrica, early purple, elder-flowered, woodcock, pink butterfly, green-winged, lizard and tongue orchids are ten a penny, and a little searching will turn up sombre bee, sawfly and Provence orchids. Further into the Mediterranean zone, exotic species to look for include Bertoloni's bee, bumblebee and mirror orchids. Lax-flowered orchids are common on the Costa Brava and high limestone areas will reveal black vanilla orchids, frog orchids and summer lady's tresses a bit later in the year.

The Mediterranean **maquis** is a delight to the eye and nose in early summer, as the cistus bushes and heaths come into flower, with wild rosemary, thyme, clary and French lavender adding to the profusion of colour. The *dehesa* grasslands of southwest Spain are carpeted with the flowers of *Dipcadi serotinum* (resembling brown bluebells), pink gladioli and twenty or so different trefoils in May. In the shade of the ancient evergreen oaks grow birthworts, with their pitcher-shaped flowers, bladder senna and a species of lupin known locally as "devil's chickpea".

Even a trip across the **northern Meseta**, although apparently through endless cereal fields, is by no means a dull experience: arable weeds such as cornflowers, poppies, corncockle, chicory and shrubby pimpernel are sometimes more abundant than the crops themselves. Where the coastal **sand dunes** have escaped the ravages of the tourist industry you can find sea daffodils, sea holly, sea bindweed, sea squill and the large violet flowers of *Romulea clusiana*.

Mammals

Spain's mammalian fauna has changed little since the Middle Ages: only the beaver has been lost since that time. Unfortunately, that doesn't mean that the remaining creatures are easy to see. Although still quite common in the mountains of the north and west, **wolves** (*lobo*) keep out of man's way as much as possible (they're sporadically protected in Spain, but are widely regarded as a threat to livestock; the shepherds complain that wolves seem to know when a man is carrying a rifle and react accordingly). Neither are you likely to come across any of the few remaining brown **bears** (*oso pardo*). In fact, of Spain's enormous wealth of mammals, only a few species are active during the day and present in sufficient numbers for regular sightings to be made.

In the **northern mountains** – the Pyrenees and the Cordillera Cantábrica – you should get at least a glimpse of chamois, roe and red deer, and possibly **wild boar** (*jabalí*), which can be seen at dusk during the winter when they conduct nightly raids on village potato patches. Wildcats sometimes cross the road in front of you, and red squirrels are quite common, especially in the pine forests. The **ibex** (*cabra montés*), Spain's amazingly agile wild goat with robust scimitar-shaped horns, was nearly hunted out of existence early in the last century but is now a protected species and an increasingly common sight in the Sierras de Cazorla, Grazalema (both Andalucía), and Gredos (Castilla-León). **Marmots** can occasionally be seen in the Pyrenees.

The typical mammals of **southern Spain** are seldom seen, but include the **pardel lynx** (*lincé iberico*, which is paler than the north European one), whose dwindling numbers are now mainly confined to the Coto Doñana national park; the Egyptian mongoose; the Mediterranean or blind mole; and fallow deer, also to be found among the umbrella pine woods of Doñana. No fewer than 27 species of **bat** occupy caves and woodlands throughout Spain, including four types of horseshoe bat. Over a score of **whale** and **dolphin** species frequent Spanish waters (prompting numerous boating companies to run trips out to see them) and the Mediterranean shores are still home to some of the last remaining Mediterranean **monk seals**.

Birds

If you care to spend your vacation with binoculars trained on the sky, trees or marshes, then Spain is one of the best venues in Europe for **bird-watching**. Most people head for the Coto Doñana National Park if it's birds they're after, but other parts of the country are just as rewarding, even if the list of sightings isn't quite so long at the end of the day.

If you have the patience to search out and identify **birds of prey**, Spain is an ideal destination, especially in **summer**, as about 25 species breed here. Some, such as red kites, goshawks, Bonelli's and golden eagles, griffon vultures, peregrine falcons and marsh harriers can be seen at all times of year in almost any part of the country. Others are confined to certain parts of the peninsula, where climate, landscape and vegetation combine to provide the right environment in which to raise their young. You will see the rare black-shouldered kite, for example, only in the southwest, or the majestic lammergeier in the high Pyrenees (and sometimes in the peaks behind the eastern coast), while black vultures (about 240 pairs) and the rare Spanish race of the imperial eagle are restricted to the southern half of the country.

Some of these raptors visit Spain only in the **winter**; these are best seen in late autumn or early spring on migration, and include the kestrel-like red-footed falcon and magnificent spotted eagle. By contrast, when these birds are leaving for their African and Asian nesting sites, others, like Montagu's harriers, short-toed and booted eagles, Eleonora's falcons and Egyptian vultures are coming the other way, having spent the winter in warmer climes, but returning to breed in Spanish territory.

There is no less variety in other types of birds; the **white stork** (*cigüeña blanca*) is a summer visitor that has endeared itself to Andalucía and south central Spain and few conurbations are without the unkempt nest atop a bell tower, electricity pylon or war monument. Woodpeckers are most abundant in the extensive forests of the **northern mountain ranges.** White-backed woodpeckers are confined to the Pyrenees, other such rarities as black and middle-spotted woodpeckers may also be seen in the Cordillera Cantábrica, and the well-camouflaged wryneck breeds in the north and winters in the south of the country. Other typical breeding birds of these northern mountains are the turkey-like capercaillie, tree pipits, wood warblers, pied flycatchers, ring ouzels, alpine accentors, citril and snow finches, ptarmigan in the Pyrenees, and that most sought-after of all montane birds: the wallcreeper.

In the open **grasslands** and cereal fields of the Meseta, larks are particularly common. Look out for the Calandra lark, easily identified by the trailing white edge to the wing, although loads of patience and good binoculars are needed to distinguish between short-toed, lesser short-toed, crested and Thekla larks. Other small brown birds of the plains are rock sparrows and corn buntings, but more rewarding, and a lot easier to identify, are great and little bustards – majestic at any time of year, but especially the males when they fan out their plumage during the springtime courtship display. Look out also for the exotically patterned pin-tailed sandgrouse, the only European member of a family of **desert-dwelling birds**, as well as stone curlews and red-necked nightjars, the latter seen (and heard) mainly at dusk.

If you come across an ancient olive grove, or an area of southern Spain where the evergreen oak **forests** are still standing, then stop! A colourful assemblage of birds is typical of such oases of natural vegetation: hoopoes, azure-winged magpies, golden orioles, great grey and woodchat shrikes, bee-eaters, rollers, greater-spotted cuckoos, redstarts and black-eared wheatears. On a sunny summer's day, these birds are active and easy to spot.

Natural inland bodies of **water** often have wide marshy borders owing to the fluctuating water level. In these rushy margins look out for water rail and purple gallinule, as well as the diminutive Baillon's crake, and scrutinize reed beds carefully for signs of penduline and bearded tits. The airspace above the water is usually occupied by hundreds of swifts and swallows; you should be able to pick out alpine, pallid and white-rumped swifts and red-rumped swallows if you are in the southern half of the country, as well as collared pratincoles. These lakes are also frequented by wintering waterfowl (although Spain has no breeding swans or geese), European cranes and sometimes by migrating flamingos.

The **coastal wetlands** are certainly a must for any serious bird-watcher, with common summer occupants including black-winged stilts, avocets and most members of the heron family: cattle and little egrets, purple, squacco and night herons, bitterns and little bitterns. On the Mediterranean coast, especially in low-growing scrub, keep an eye out for a small quail-like bird called the Andalucian hemipode: strangely enough, it is closely related to the graceful crane. Wintering waders are not outstandingly distinctive, though wherever you go, even on the Atlantic coast, spoonbills are frequently encountered. Grey phalaropes visit the northwest corner, as do whimbrel, godwits, skuas and ruff, taking a break from their northern breeding grounds.

The **Balearic Islands** can provide you with a few more exotic cliff-nesting species, such as Cory's shearwater and storm petrels; and the Islas Cíes, off the Galician coast, provide breeding grounds for shags, the rare Iberian race of guillemot and the southernmost colony in the world of lesser black-backed gulls.

Hundreds more birds could be listed: with a good field guide you should find many of them for yourself.

Reptiles and Amphibians

As with other types of wildlife, Spain is especially rich in amphibians and reptiles, with about sixty species in total. Some of the easiest to see are **fire salamanders**, which occur throughout Spain, albeit with colouration varying from yellow stripes on a black background to vice versa, depending on the exact locality. The best time to see them is in cool, misty weather in the mountains, or immediately after rain.

Three other species of **salamander** live in Spain. The golden-striped salamander (a slender, rather nondescript beast, despite its name) is endemic to northwest Iberia; the large sharp-ribbed salamander is found only in the south west of the peninsula; and the Pyrenean brook salamander is confined to the Pyrenees.

Closely related to the salamanders are the **newts**, of which there are only four species in Spain. If you take a trip into the high mountain pastures of the Cordillera Cantábrica, where water is present in small, peaty ponds all year round, you should see the blackish alpine newt; marbled newts can be seen round the edges of many of Spain's inland lakes, and reservoirs. Midwife **toads** strike up their chorus at dusk, and can often be heard well away from water, sometimes causing confusion with the call of the Scops owl. If you search through tall waterside vegetation you may be rewarded by the sight of a tiny, lurid-green tree-frog: striped in the north and west, but stripeless along the Mediterranean coast.

Two species of **tortoise** occur in Spain; spur-thighed tortoises can still be found along the southern coast and on the Balearic Islands, which are also the only Spanish locality for Hermann's tortoise. European pond terrapins and stripe-necked terrapins are more widely distributed, but only in freshwater habitats.

Perhaps the most exotic reptilian species to occur in Spain is the **chameleon**, although again this swivel-eyed creature is confined to the extreme southern shores. **Lizards** are numerous, with the most handsome species being the ocellated or eyed lizard – green with blue spots along the flank. Some species are very restricted in their range, such as Ibizan, Italian and Lilford's wall lizards, which live only in the Balearic Islands.

Similarly, **snakes** are common, although few are venomous, and in any case it's sometimes quite difficult to spot them before they spot you and take evasive action themselves. Asps and western whip snakes occur in the Pyrenees, but you are likely to see horseshoe whip snakes and false smooth snakes only in the extreme south.

Protecting the environment of a country which encourages well over forty million tourists to leave their footprints in the sand each year could easily be perceived as a lost cause. But since most of these visitors flock to, and stay on, a comparatively narrow coastal strip, the damage is contained.

The environmental impact of "**costa**" tourism, with its pressures on water supply, sewage disposal and landscape, is a specialist subject in its own right, and one in which the battles are by no means over. According to the Barcelona-based environment group DEPANA, there is cause for worry over the second boom in coastal tourism as foreigners start to buy holiday homes. Meanwhile in inland, rural areas encroachment is fostered by domestic second-home buyers.

Concerned people in Spain have a common complaint: while there may be lip service paid to environmental matters, actually goading bureaucracy into action is a different matter. The only language understood by all sides is an economic one, the good news being that the value of the environment to tourism is becoming increasingly evident and important in bargaining terms.

Protection, then, is the name of a game increasingly played in the political arena, in which environmental benefit becomes almost incidental. Spain is still one of the wilder places of Europe, and wilderness can be found surprisingly close to some of the major urban and tourist centres. There are about eight **Parques Nacionales** (national parks) covering some 17,000 square kilometres, and a much larger number of **Parques Naturales** (natural parks) and hunting reserves, adding up to a total protected area of around 40,000 square kilometres. Representing nine percent of Spain's total land area, this is, of course, chicken feed compared with the level of ecological threat, but protection of the environment isn't yet on the worry list of the average Spaniard, and doesn't attract priority spending.

The stirrings of a movement towards environmental education can be seen in the creation of the regionally nominated and managed **Parques Naturales**, the majority of which are in Catalunya, Galicia and Andalucía, though they now exist in every part of the country; with their fairly comprehensive protection, they cover an area significantly larger than that of the national parks.

The contradictions in Spain's environmental policy were highlighted by a disaster in 1998 which hit the country's highest-profile national park, the **Coto Doñana**. An upstream mining dam used for storing toxic waste just outside the park burst, unleashing five million cubic litres of heavy metals into the Guadiamar river which carried it towards the park. The unfolding calamity grabbed the world's headlines and threatened to become one of the worst ecological catastrophes in Spanish history. A series of emergency dykes stopped the deadly tide just 2km from the park's boundary, but grave damage was done to farmland surrounding Doñana, devastating nesting birds and poisoning fish, which provide a vital food source for much of the park's wildlife. Scientists have said that these areas should recover over time, and that the spill should have no long-term effects on the park itself, but it was a very close shave and many environmentalists question whether any lessons have been learned. The **Parc Nacional d'Aigüestortes**, too, has lost international recognition as a national park because of continuing hydroelectric exploitation of its lakes.

Wetlands

In 1980 Spain had 10,852 square kilometres of wetlands, six times more than France. It has not been so ready as some other nations to condemn wetland out of hand and rush to get it drained. Spain was an early signatory of the Ramsar Convention, an international agreement (the only one of its kind) to protect wetland. Three Spanish sites of international importance had been nominated by 1985. None of this, however, has prevented the steady decline of wetland areas, either by pollution or indirect draining.

The **Coto Doñana**, perhaps the most important wetland, is facing chronic drought and is suffering both from chemical run-off pollution (which caused the disaster mentioned above) and from detrimental agricultural practices. Just across the Río Guadalquivir from the Doñana, the last remaining unprotected wetland of the region has been drained and converted into farms.

The **Tablas de Daimiel** in La Mancha, too, are well known in conservationist circles for their deteriorated condition. Once recognized as being one of Europe's most important wetlands, and designated Reserva Nacional in 1966, then Parque Nacional in 1973, the area has nonetheless suffered terribly. Most blame is put on local viniculture upstream (in what is now one of Spain's major wine-producing zones), with its irrigation and resultant heavy demand on artesian water. The Río Guadiana dried up in 1982 and the nearby Cigüela is heavily polluted. In the summer months particularly, the region can hardly support wildlife at all and certainly no longer attracts the once fabulous amounts of waterfowl which earned it worldwide fame.

There is some comfort in knowing that the plight of the Tablas has been officially recognized, with the launch of a project aimed at restoring former water levels. Naturalists are certain that if the water returns, so will the birds and ditto the visitors. **La Albufera de Valencia** was once one of the largest bodies of freshwater in Spain, but it too is shrinking rapidly and is now ten times smaller than it was in the Middle Ages. On a more positive note, the most accessible wetland of the lot, **Aiguamolls de l'Empordà**, just behind the tourist beaches of the Costa Brava, has very recently been established as a Parque Natural.

Hunting

The greatest confrontation over environmental issues in Spain involves hunting and farming groups. Many middle-aged and older men in Spain believe a shotgun is an accessory that they shouldn't be seen without in the countryside, and feel personally threatened at the news of the establishment or expansion of protected areas. One of the most emotive subjects is the protection of **wolves**. In areas where they have been protected, in the north especially, numbers have grown rapidly. Over recent years, outraged farmers have taken to increasingly militant demonstrations in an attempt to "protect" their land.

The figures speak for themselves. Although national parks protect more than 1700 square kilometres, **hunting reserves** (*reservas nacionales de caza*) cover a vastly greater area – almost four million acres to date. Largest is Saja in Cantabria, which is larger than all the mainland national parks put together. And although more species than ever before are protected and now forbidden to the hunter (ibex, bears, capercaillie and most of the major birds of prey, for instance), there is no shortage of demand for other hunting trophies such as wild boar, deer and chamois. Supermarkets stock all hunting gear, including shotgun cartridges, and walkers have to take care not to look shootable at weekends in season, when the hills are alive with the sound of double barrels.

Exceeding quotas or **poaching** is considered virtually normal procedure, especially in areas where shooting and trapping provide an extra source of income for the poor. **Waterfowl** are a popular target, with huge numbers being killed each year.

The shooting and netting of **common birds** is also a major problem, as it is in much of southern Europe and North Africa. The annual slaughter of migrating birds in the Pyrenees, for a start, contributes substantially to the overall global figure of 900 million bird deaths each year. Latest European estimates for Spain are that about 30 million birds, often accused of being agricultural pests, are caught each year.

Insects

Almost 100,000 insects have been named and described in Europe and an untold number await discovery. In Spain, with areas where no one knows for sure how many bears there are, insects have barely begun to be explored.

From early spring to late autumn, as long as the sun is shining, you will see **butterflies**: there are few European species which do not occur in Spain, but by contrast there are many Spanish butterflies which are not found north of the Pyrenees. These seem to be named mostly after obscure entomologists: Lorquin's blue, Carswell's little blue, Forster's furry blue, Oberthur's anomalous blue, Lefèbvre's ringlet, Zapater's ringlet, Chapman's ringlet, Zeller's skipper, and many others. You need to be an expert to identify most of these, but the more exciting butterflies are in any case better-known ones: the Camberwell beauty, almost black and bordered with gold and blue; swallowtails, yellow and black or striped like zebras, depending on the species, but always with the distinctive "tails"; the lovely two-tailed pasha, which is often seen feeding on the ripe fruit of the strawberry tree; and the apollo (papery white wings with distinctive red and black eyespots), of which there are almost as many varieties as there are mountains in Spain. Other favourites include the small, bejewelled blues, coppers, fritillaries and hairstreaks that inhabit the hay meadows.

Aside from the butterflies, keep an eye open for the largest **moth** in Europe, the giant peacock, which flies by night but is often attracted to outside lights, or the rare, green-tinted Spanish moon moth, a close relative of tropical silk moths. During the day, take a closer look at that hovering bumble bee, as it may be a hummingbird hawkmoth, or a broad-bordered bee-hawk, flying clumsily from flower to flower. Oleander and elephant hawkmoths (resplendent in their pink and green livery) are often seen around flowering honeysuckle bushes at dusk. Many moths have bizarre caterpillars, for example the lobster moth, which feeds on beech, or the pussmoth, found on willows and poplars, although the adults may be quite nondescript in appearance.

Grasslands and arid scrub areas are usually good hunting grounds for **grasshoppers and crickets**, which you can locate by following their calls. Mole crickets and field crickets live in burrows they have excavated themselves, but look to the trees for the adult great green bush cricket, about 7–8cm long. French lavender bushes in the maquis are a favourite haunt of the green mantis *Empusa pennata*, identified by a large crest on the back of the head (the nymphs are brown, with a distinctive curled-up abdomen). **Stick insects** are harder to spot, as they tend to sit parallel with the stems of grasses, where they are well camouflaged.

Members of the *Arachnidae* (**spiders**) to be found include two species of **scorpion** in the dry lands of southern Spain. Look out also for long-legged *Gyas*, the largest harvest-spider in Europe, which can be about 10cm in diameter, although the body is little larger than a pea. Spanish **centipedes** can grow to quite a size too: *Scutigera coleopatra*, for example, often live indoors – they have fifteen pairs of incredibly long, striped legs, which create a wonderful rippling effect when they move across walls.

Where and When to Go

Virtually anywhere in Spain, outside the cities and most popular tourist resorts, rewards scrutiny in terms of wildlife. Perhaps the best thing about this country is that so much wilderness remains to be discovered on your own, without guidebooks to tell you where to go.

The main drawback, however, is getting anywhere on public transport, which often doesn't stop between departure point and destination. There is rarely any problem getting off a bus when you feel the urge, but you may have problems stopping the next one, which in any case may not arrive until the following day.

The following suggestions, then, are largely limited to those which are easily accessible by public transport. Inevitably this means that other people will be there, too: you'll have to head off into the hills on foot in order to experience the best of Spanish wildlife.

Southern Spain is a good choice for any **time of year**, since even in the depths of winter the climate is mild and many plants will be in full bloom. If you decide on the **northern mountain ranges**, spring and early summer are best. The weather can be temperamental, but for the combination of snowy peaks and flower-filled meadows, it's worth taking the risk. The **interior** of Spain is freezing in winter and almost too hot to bear in midsummer, so spring or autumn – to coincide with the occasional rains and the flowering of the maquis and steppe grasslands – are best. Again, if your real interest is the **coastal bird life** of Spain, visit in spring or autumn, not only to catch the phenomenal migrations of birds between Africa and northern Europe, but also because accommodation in the resorts can be incredibly low-priced outside the tourist season.

The Pyrenees

The Moors called these mountains El Hadjiz – the barricade – which is effectively what they are, isolating Spain from the rest of Europe. The Spanish flanks of the Pyrenees are somewhat hotter and drier than their northern counterparts, but the high passes are nevertheless snowbound for several months in the winter.

If you avoid the ski resorts there are still many unspoiled valleys to explore, with their colourful alpine meadows studded with Pyrenean hyacinths and horned pansy, and some of the highest forests in Europe, extending up to 2500m in places. The **Vall d'Aran**, close to Pico de Aneto (the highest point of the chain, at 3408m), is a botanical paradise at any time of year. Go in spring and you will find alpine pasque flowers, trumpet gentians and sheets of daffodils, among them pale Lent lilies and pheasant's-eye narcissi. A little later in the year sees the flowering of Turks'-cap lilies, dusky cranesbill and Pyrenean fritillaries, sheltering among the low-growing shrubs on the hillsides; while in autumn, following the annual haymaking, the denuded meadows shimmer with a pink-purple haze of merendera and autumn crocuses.

Further west, the **Parque Nacional de Ordesa y Monte Perdido** in the Aragonese Pyrenees shelters valleys clothed in primeval pine, fir and beech forests which are home to pine martens, wildcats, genets, red squirrels, polecats and wild boar among the 32 mammal species that live within the park boundaries. Dominating the forests are sheer cliffs with spectacular waterfalls and towering rock formations, the haunt of the sprightly chamois which thrive here in profusion. Although these antelope-like creatures are easily spotted, you will need to have your sights set firmly on the heavens to see the most renowned occupant of Ordesa: the lammergeier. A vulture of splendid proportions, it is now almost completely confined to the Pyrenees and a few eastern ranges in Spain. Its Spanish name – *quebrantahuesos*, or "bone-breaker" – refers to its habit of dropping animal bones from great heights to smash on the rocks below, exposing the tender marrow.

The second national park in the Spanish Pyrenees is that of **Aigüestortes**, centred on the glacial hanging valleys and impressive cirques of northern Catalunya. The extensive coniferous forests of Scots pine and common silver fir are populated by capercaillie and black woodpeckers. Just above the timberline, early purple orchids and alpine and southern gentians flourish in the superb alpine meadows, and the rocky screes conceal pale, delicate edelweiss and yellow mountain saxifrage. The fast-flowing mountain rivers are home to otters; and the tiny secretive Pyrenean desman, Pyrenean brook salamanders and alpine newts live in the clear waters of the glacial lake of San Mauricio. In the airspace above the peaks look out for honey buzzards and golden eagles soaring on the thermals, and if you scrutinize the cliff faces you might be rewarded with the sight of a wallcreeper.

Cordillera Cantábrica

This mountain chain runs more or less parallel to the north coast from the Portuguese border eastwards into the Basque country. It has long formed a barrier between the northern coast and the rest of Spain since there are few crossing points, and a good proportion are impassable during the winter. The vegetation is clearly affected by the rain-laden clouds which constantly sweep in from the Atlantic, as can be seen by the extensive oak and beech forests that shroud the slopes. Extensive beef and dairy farming is the traditional way of life, and the majority of the flower-filled meadows have never been subjected to artificial fertilizers and pesticides. One of the most fascinating aspects is the abundance of meadow flowers now rarely found in northern Europe: lizard orchids, heath lobelia, greater yellow rattle, moon carrot, Cambridge milk-parsley, galingal and summer lady's-tresses – a delicate, white-flowered orchid.

The high point of the Cordillera Cantábrica is the small limestone mountain range of the **Picos de Europa**, visible from miles offshore in the Bay of Biscay. Over sixty species of mammal have been recorded here, ranging from such typical wilderness creatures as brown bears and wolves to snow voles, tiny denizens of the high peaks. Red squirrels, roe deer and chamois are easy to see, but many of the mammals that haunt these mountains, such as genets, beech martens and wildcats, are secretive nocturnal beasts.

One of the most outstanding landscape features of the Picos de Europa is the **Cares gorge**, where the riverbed lies almost 2000m below the peaks on either side. The sheltered depths of the gorge are home to a number of shrubs more typical of Mediterranean Spain – figs, strawberry trees, wild jasmine and barberry – and the sheer rock faces are home to the exotic wallcreeper, a small ash-grey bird with splashes of crimson under the wings, the sight of which is highly coveted by bird-watchers.

The **Covadonga National Park** covers much of the western massif of the Picos de Europa, its focal point being the glacial lakes of Enol and Ercina. In spring the verdant pastures which surround the lakes are studded with pale yellow hoop-petticoat daffodils and tiny dog's-tooth violets, but a visit later in the year will be amply rewarded by the discovery of hundreds of purple spikes of monkshood and the steel-blue flowers of Pyrenean eryngo. A few hours scrambling across the limestone crags away from the lake should be sufficient for excellent views of griffon and Egyptian vultures, or you don't even have to leave the small café in the car park to see alpine choughs scavenging among the litter-bins.

For those who prefer more gentle scenery, **Galicia**, with its green rolling hills and constant mists, is hard to beat. Few people live in the countryside, which as a consequence is teeming with wildlife. The oak and beech woods of Ancares provide shelter for deer and wild boar; although the chamois were hunted to extinction for food during the Civil War. The meadows benefit from the frequent rains and you can find all manner of wet-loving plants, such as large-flowered butterwort, bog pimpernel, globe flowers, marsh helleborines, whorled caraway and early marsh orchids.

The Interior

If you believed everything you read you'd be tempted to regard inland Spain as a flat, barren plain covered with mile after mile of bleached cornfields. But the wildlife is there – if you know where to look.

A good place to start is the **central sierras**. Just to the north of Madrid, almost bisecting the vast plain of the Meseta, run several contiguous mountain ranges which are well worth a visit. They may not have the rugged grandeur of the Pyrenees but there is plenty of wildlife to be found on the rocky, scrub-covered slopes. Venture into the extensive pine forests of the **Sierra de Guadarrama** to see Spanish bluebells and an unmistakeable toadflax, *Linaria triornithophora*, which has large snapdragon-like flowers each with a long tail, sometimes pink, sometimes white. Birds of prey are abundant, and not too difficult to tell apart; both red and black kites can be seen, easily distinguished from other raptors by their distinctly forked tails (the red kite has clear white patches under its wings). Booted eagles are identified by the black trailing edge to their wings, and the Spanish short-toed eagle, here known as *águila culebrera*, the "snake eagle", is almost pure white below, with a broad, dark head.

Further west the granite bulk of the **Sierra de Gredos** boasts some of the highest peaks in Spain after the Sierra Nevada and the Pyrenees. Scots and maritime pines occur at the higher levels, sweet chestnut and Pyrenean and cork oaks on the southern slopes. The springtime flora is superb, including lily-of-the-valley, conspicuous St Bernard's and martagon lilies, and several species of brightly coloured peonies. On some of the drier slopes, where the trees have been cleared, the aromatic gum cistus forms a dense layer up to 2m high. There is no need to fight your way through their sticky branches to discover the delights of the flora here: even the edges of the shepherds' tracks are ablaze with asphodels, French lavender, a strange-looking plant called the tassel hyacinth and the closely related grape hyacinth. But best of all in the Gredos are the ibex, very common in the pine zones between the cirques of Laguna Grande and Cinco Lagunas. Look out also for Egyptian and griffon vultures, red and black kites and Bonelli's eagles overhead, crossbills and firecrests in the coniferous forests, and rock buntings, identified by their striped heads, almost everywhere.

Moving away from the mountains there are still sights to be seen in the plains. *Dehesa* parkland is the best habitat, especially for birds: **Monfragüe Natural Park**, in Extremadura, contains some excellent areas of *dehesa*. Golden orioles, woodchat and great grey shrikes, hoopoes and bee-eaters are impossible to miss, and you might even see a roller. In winter about 7000 common cranes descend on the Monfragüe grasslands, and the flooded river valleys which are an integral part of this park are good viewing points for red-rumped swallows and collared pratincoles in summer.

Monfragüe is perhaps best known for its breeding population of the endangered Spanish **imperial eagle**, easily identified by the distinct white shoulder markings. The central reserve where this raptor nests is open only to permit holders, but you may see them soaring over the *dehesa*. The same can be said for the rare black vulture: a huge bird which is impossible to miss. Monfragüe has the largest known breeding colony (about sixty pairs). Most people head for the huge rock outcrop known as Peñafalcón, where black storks, now extremely rare as a breeding bird in Spain, can be seen perched up on the cliff face, and the sky is constantly filled with griffon vultures coming and going. And look out for a smallish, light-coloured hovering bird – it might be a rare black-shouldered kite, which you certainly won't see elsewhere in Europe.

Heading in the other direction, towards Zaragoza in the northeastern corner of the plains, you might consider visiting the **Laguna de Gallocanta**. This is Spain's largest natural inland lake, and has a lot to recommend it. Look out for birds more typical of the arid plains – pin-tailed sandgrouse and stone curlews – as well as those usually associated with freshwater. Gallocanta is a national stronghold for red-crested pochard.

Mediterranean Coast

Spain's Mediterranean coast conjures up visions of sandy beaches packed with oiled bodies and a concrete wall of hotels stretching from the French border to Gibraltar. Even in the heart of the Costa Brava, though, there's rich wildlife to be found. The **Parc Natural dels Aiguamolls de l'Empordà** in Catalunya is a salt marsh and wetland reserve sandwiched between the A7 motorway and the hotel developments in the Gulf of Roses. It is the nearest thing in Spain to a British nature reserve, with signposted nature trails, a well-equipped information centre and several bird hides. This rather detracts from the wilderness aspect of the site, but it is nevertheless a good place to watch out for the 300 species of birds that have been observed here. Apart from the more typical water birds, look out for little bittern, black-winged stilt, bearded tit and purple heron, all of which breed here. Spring is perhaps the best time, when flamingos, glossy ibis and spoonbills drop in on migration.

If you can't stand the mosquitos from the marshes, try the drier, Mediterranean scrub areas nearby, which are ideal for spotting red-footed falcons on migration, breeding lesser grey shrikes (the only Spanish locality), stone curlews, great spotted cuckoos and moustached and Marmora's warblers in summer. And of course, marsh and Montagu's harriers are always present.

Other promising wildlife locations include the fan-like **Delta de l'Ebre** (Ebro Delta), with up to 100,000 wintering birds and a large colony of purple herons. Again isolated from the mainland by the A7 motorway, the lagoons and reed beds here attract squacco and night herons, avocets and red-crested pochard, with isolated islands providing nesting areas for the rare Audouin's and slender-billed gulls. Look out, too, for lesser short-toed larks, and a multitude of terns, including gull-billed, whiskered, roseate and Sandwich.

Further south again lies a smaller coastal wetland known as the **Albufera de Valencia**. It is so close to the city of Valencia that to learn it supports a breeding colony of the rare ferruginous duck is quite a surprise. Other water birds to look out for are red-crested pochard and, during the winter, the extremely rare crested coot, as well as cattle and little egrets, breeding night, purple and squacco herons, little bitterns, black-necked grebes and bearded and penduline tits.

Southern Spanish Sierras

Stretching for miles behind the coastal metropolises of the Costa del Sol, these lofty mountains are a complete contrast from the sun-and-sea image of southern Spain. Perhaps the best-known is the **Sierra Nevada** at the eastern end of the range, which was upgraded to **national park** status in 1999. The range's highest peak is Mulhacén (3482m), also the highest mountain in mainland Spain, and snow persists for much of the year at the highest levels, but the south-facing foothills are only about 150km from Africa. Environmental conditions thus range from alpine to almost tropical. Not surprisingly there is an incredible range of plant and animal life. If you are equipped to visit the high mountains when the snow is starting to melt you should see such attractive endemic plants as glacier eryngo, looking not unlike its Pyrenean counterpart, and Nevada daffodils, saxifrages and crocuses. Later on in the year there is still plenty to see, including the strange, spiny mountain tragacanth, wild tulips, peonies, pinks, alpine gentians, the Nevada monkshood and columbine, and the white-flowered rockrose *Helianthemeum apenniunum*.

Owing to the extreme altitude of the Sierra Nevada, birds more commonly found further north – crossbills, alpine accentors and choughs – have a final European outpost here. You should also see many of the smaller birds which favour dry, rocky hillsides. Perhaps the most distinguished of these is the black wheatear, the males identified by their funereal plumage and white rump. Further north, in the limestone **Sierras de Cazorla y Segura**, raptor-watching will be amply rewarded. Cazorla is the only Spanish locality outside the Pyrenees where lammergeiers regularly breed, and the smaller Egyptian vultures are common here. Small numbers of golden and Bonelli's eagles nest in the peaks and goshawks frequent the extensive forests (black, maritime and Aleppo pines at high levels and holly, holm and Lusitanian oaks, with narrow-leaved ash and strawberry trees, on the lower slopes).

These mountain ranges, birthplace of the great Río Guadalquivir, are rather unusual in Spain in that they run approximately north–south rather than east–west. They also have a flora of some 1300 unique species including such handsome rock-dwelling plants as the crimson-flowered Cazorla violet (*Viola cazorlensis*), the columbine *Aquilegia cazorlensis*, a relict carnivorous butterwort (*Pinguicula vallisneriifolia*) and several endemic narcissi.

To the west lie some extraordinary Jurassic limestone ranges, eroded over centuries into formations known collectively as *torcales*. One of the more famous of these is at **Grazalema**, renowned for its Spanish fir forest. This tree (*Abies pinsapo*) is a unique pre-Ice Age survivor, now restricted to just a handful of localities in southern Spain, including the **Serranía de Ronda**, and a specialized flora has evolved to cope with the dense shade that the trees cast. You should be able to find the colourful peonies *Paeonia coriacea* and *P. broteri*, as well as paper-white daffodils and the winter-flowering *Iris planifolia*, with a large, solitary flower on a ridiculously short stem. A whole range of typical Mediterranean shrub species grow here, including laurustinus, grey-leaved and poplar-leaved cistus, Spanish barberry, Etruscan honeysuckle, the nettle tree (*Celtis australis*) and *Acer granatense*, a maple species confined to the mountains of southern Spain. Also, in these woods the **eagle owl** breeds: the largest and most powerful in Europe, it even preys on roe deer and capercaillie.

As a break from the mountains you might consider a visit to **Fuente de Piedra**, the largest inland lagoon in Andalucía (about 15 square kilometres). Partly because the water is never more than 1.5m deep (the level being further reduced by intense evaporation in summer) and also due to the lack of pollution, large numbers of flamingos construct their conical mud nests here every year. Fuente de Piedra is thus one of only two regular breeding places for greater flamingos in Europe, and has been designated a *Reserva Integral*, the most strictly protected type of nature reserve in Spain. Altogether about 120 species of bird, 18 mammals and 21 reptiles and amphibians have been recorded here.

Southern Atlantic Coast

The more or less tideless Mediterranean ends at Gibraltar, so the coast stretching westwards up to the Portuguese border is washed by the Atlantic Ocean. Here, the low-lying basin formed by the Río Guadalquivir contains one of Europe's finest wetlands: the **Coto Doñana**, Spain's most famous national park.

Perhaps the most renowned spectacles are the breeding colonies of spoonbills and herons in the cork oaks which border the marshes, but equally impressive are the huge flocks of **waterfowl** which descend on the lagoons during the winter. As for breeding ducks, Doñana is the European stronghold for the marbled teal, a smallish, mottled-brown dabbling duck which rarely breeds in Europe outside Spain. Ruddy shelduck – large, gooselike birds, generally confined to the eastern Mediterranean – are also present throughout the year, but breeding has not yet been proved. White-headed ducks definitely nest and rear their young here, although the more renowned nursery for this is at the Lagunas de Córdoba in central Andalucía. One of Europe's rarest birds is the crested coot, distinguished from the common coot only at close range by two small red knobs on its forehead, or in flight by the absence of a white wingbar. It breeds in Morocco, migrating northwards into southern Spain for the winter; Doñana is the only Spanish locality where this species is resident all year round, although again no one is quite sure whether it breeds here or not.

Water birds aside, keep an eye out for large flocks of pin-tailed sandgrouse, which perform prodigious aerobatics in perfect time, rather like a shoal of fish;

and, at ground level, cattle egrets in the grasslands, usually in the company of some of the renowned black bulls of the region. Cattle egrets are most easily distinguished from other egrets by their pinkish legs (black or yellow in all other species). A smaller bird to watch out for is the Spanish sparrow, which commonly makes its home in the nether regions of the large, untidy nests of the white stork. Doñana also boasts an impressive roll call of birds of prey, including the imperial eagle and black vulture.

Some large **mammals** are relatively easy to see in Doñana: red and fallow deer and wild boar display an inordinate lack of fear when approached by people, despite the fact that this area was a Royal Hunting Reserve until quite recently. The same, unfortunately, cannot be said for Doñana's pardel lynxes, of which there are some 25 pairs, estimated to represent about half the total Spanish population. Egyptian mongooses also frequent the dry, scrubby areas, and genets are occasionally seen by day in the more remote, forested parts of the national park. If you can drag your eyes from the veritable feast of bird life you might spot a curious creature known as Bedriaga's skink. Endemic to Iberia, this small lizard has only rudimentary legs; you are most likely to see it burrowing rapidly into the sand in an effort to escape detection.

The nearby **Marismas de Odiel**, which lie within the boundaries of the city of Huelva, a little to the west, are also very worthwhile. Apart from the flamingos, which are increasingly preferring these saline coastal marshes as breeding grounds to the nearby Doñana, you will also be rewarded by the sight of large numbers of spoonbills, purple herons and other typical southern Spanish water birds.

The Balearic Islands

Despite the sun-seeker image of the Balearic Islands, there are many remote spots which have escaped the ravages of the tourist industry. Even on the big ones you can escape easily enough, and in total there are fifteen islands (most uninhabited).

One of the wilder regions is the **Sierra de Tramuntana**, which runs along the northern coast of Mallorca, dropping abruptly into the sea for much of its length. It is a good place to see the diminutive Eleonora's falcon and enormous black vulture. Around your feet you can feast your eyes on an array of exotic plants such as *Cyclamen balearicum*, an autumn-flowering crocus (*Crocus cambessedesii*), *Helleborus lividus* (a rare member of the buttercup family), the pink-flowered *Senecio rodriguezii,* and many other endemic species of peony, birthwort and hare's ear. Even in January many plants are in flower, but the best time of year to see the blossoming of the islands is from March to May.

Away from the mountains, other wildlife refuges are the low-lying coastal marshes which have to date defied the hotel trade. **S'Albufera**, on Mallorca, is a bird-watcher's paradise. The maze of tamarisk-lined creeks and lagoons is the summer haunt of water rail, spotted crake and little egrets, and a little careful scrutiny may reveal more secretive denizens: Savi's, Cetti's, Sardinian, moustached, fan-tailed and great reed warblers. Also easy to get to are the saltpans known as **C'an Pastilla**, close to the airport at Palma, where whiskered and white-winged black terns, as well as Mediterranean and Audouins's gulls (this latter bird is the rarest breeding gull in Europe), are frequently seen.

The Balearics are also ideal places for watching the endemic races of lizards; they are usually quite undeterred by your presence, and make excellent subjects for portrait photography. If you are keen on marine life, don't forget your flippers and snorkel, as the underwater scenario is superb.

Teresa Farino

Music

The Spanish music scene in the year 2002 contrasts sharply with that of the 1960s and 1970s when Spain was starting to emerge from many dark years of dictatorship. Music at the time was either a challenge to the dictatorial regime or a cliché. In the former camp there were singers such as Raímon, Joan Manuel Serrat, Luís Eduardo Aute and Lluís Llach, who dared with the strength of their voices and lyrics, filling many venues and selling thousands of records; in the latter camp there was the easy listening music about love and romantic passion from Julio Iglesias, Raphael and Camilo Sesto. There was relatively little space for experimentation, and such that there was came from jazz (groups such as Pegasus) and avant-garde rock (groups such as Rock Laieta).

The **1980s** were a time of explosive creativity, with the urban music scene opening up fully to foreign influences, mainly Latin American and Anglo-Saxon, and everyone finally free to experiment: folk musicians incorporated electric sounds and crossed over into other genres; pop and rock musicians looked to the UK's new wave and punk movements; flamenco performers mixed in elements of pop, rock and blues. The beginning of the current scene was taking shape. Pop and rock bands such as El Ultimo de la Fila, Radio Futura, Gabinete Caligari, La Union, Loquillo y los Trogloditas, Los Secretos, Rebeldes, Heroes del Silencio, Nacha Pop and the massive Mecano defined the soundtrack for a new generation.

Flamenco

Flamenco – one of the most emblematic musics of Spain and its richest musical heritage – has recently enjoyed huge exposure and today is more popular than ever before. Twenty-five years or so ago it looked like a music on the decline, preserved only in the clubs or *peñas* of its *aficionados*, or in travestied castanet-clicking form for tourists. However, prejudice vanished as flamenco went through a tremendous period of innovation in the 1980s and 1990s, incorporating elements of pop, rock, jazz and Latin, and today there's a new respect for the old "pure flamenco" artists and a huge joy in the new.

The initial impetus for flamenco's new-found energy came at the end of the 1960s, with the innovations of guitarist **Paco de Lucia** and, especially, the late, great singer **El Camarón de la Isla**. These were musicians who had grown up learning flamenco but whose own musical tastes embraced international rock, jazz and blues.

They have been followed by groups such as **Ketama, Raimundo Amador** (ex Pata Negra), **La Barbería del Sur, Navajita Platea** and **Niña Pastori**, who have all reached massive audiences that neither Paco de Lucia nor the great Camarón de la Isla could have dreamt of decades before. At the end of the 1990s there were even successful comebacks from such established artists as **Enrique Morente** and **José Merce**. Morente – the established king of flamenco – experimentally revisited old styles and combined them with new moves, releasing a spectacular new album, *Omega*, in 1996, with **Lagartija Nick**, one of the most emblematic bands of the Spanish indie rock scene. José Merce collaborated with **Vicente Amigo** – recognized as the most gifted player of the moment, notably for his sense of syncopation – on *Del Amanecer*. Paco de Lucia acknowledges Amigo as his successor in the innovation of flamenco guitar.

Young flamenco musicians to look out for include **Miguel Poveda, Duquende** and **Ginesa Ortega** (who all hail from the Catalan–Barcelona flamenco scene – it's no coincidence that Barcelona hosted the XXVIII Convention of Flamenco Art in 2000), as well as **Juan Manuel Canizares**.

Origins

Flamenco evolved in southern Spain from many sources: Morocco, Egypt, India, Pakistan, Greece, and other parts of the Near and Far East. Most authorities believe the roots of the music were brought to Spain by gypsies arriving in the fifteenth century. In the following century it was fused with elements of Arab and Jewish music in the Andalucian mountains, where Jews, Muslims and "pagan" gypsies had taken refuge from the forced conversions and clearances effected by the Catholic kings and Church. Important flamenco centres and families are still found today in quarters and towns of *gitano* and refugee origin, such as Alcalá, Jerez, Cádiz, Utrera and the Triana *barrio* of Sevilla. Although flamenco is linked fundamentally to **Andalucía**, emigration from that province has long meant that flamenco thrives not only there but also in Madrid, Extremadura, the Levante and even Barcelona – wherever Andalucían migrants have settled.

Flamenco *aficionados* enjoy heated debate about the purity of their art and whether it is more validly performed by a **gitano** (gypsy) or a **payo** (non-gypsy). Certainly during dark times flamenco thrived preserved by the oral tradition of the closed *gitano* clans. Its power too, and the despair which its creation overcomes, seem to have emerged from the vulnerable life of a people surviving for centuries at the margins of society. These days though, there are as many acclaimed *payo* as *gitano* flamenco artists, and the arrival on the scene of singers from Barcelona like Vicente Amigo – who has no Andalucian blood but grew up in a neighbourhood full of flamenco music – has de-centred the debate.

The concept of dynasty, however, remains fundamental for many. The veteran singer **Fernanda de Utrera**, one of the great voices of "pure flamenco", was born in 1923 into a *gitano* family in Utrera, one of the *cantaora* (flamenco singer) centres. The granddaughter of the legendary singer "Pinini", she and her younger sister Bernarda, also a notable singer, both inherited their flamenco with their genes. This concept of an active inheritance is crucial, and has not been lost in contemporary developments: the members of Ketama, for example, the Madrid-based flamenco-rock group, come from two *gitano* clans – the Sotos and Carmonas.

While flamenco's exact origins are debated, it is generally agreed that its "laws" were established in the nineteenth century. Indeed, from the mid-nineteenth into the early twentieth century flamenco enjoyed a Golden Age, the tail-end of which is preserved on some of the earliest 1930s recordings. The musicians found a first home in the **café cantantes**, traditional bars which had their own groups of performers (*cuadros*). One of the most famous was the *Café de Chinitas* in Málaga, immortalized by the poet Gabriel Garciá Lorca in his poem *A las cinco de la tarde* (At five in the afternoon), in which he intimates the relationship between flamenco and bullfighting, both sharing root emotions and flashes of erratic genius, and both also being a way to break out of social and economic marginality.

The Art of Flamenco

Flamenco is played at *tablaos* and fiestas, in bars and at *juergas* (informal, more or less private parties). The fact that the Andalucian public are so knowledgeable and demanding about flamenco means that musicians, singers and dancers found at even a local club or village festival are usually very good indeed.

Flamenco songs often express pain. Generally, the voice closely interacts with improvising guitar, which keeps the *compás* (rhythm), the two inspiring each other, aided by the **jaleo** – the hand-clapping *palmas*, finger-snapping *palillos* and shouts from participants at certain points in the song. *Aficionados* will shout encouragement, most commonly *¡olé!* when an artist is getting deep into a song, but also a variety of other less obvious phrases. A stunning piece of dancing may, for example, be greeted with *¡Viva la maquina escribir!* (long live the typewriter), as the heels of the dancer move so fast they sound like a clicking machine; or the cry may be *¡agua!* (water), for the scarcity of water in Andalucía has given the word a kind of glory.

The encouragement of the audience is essential for an artist, as it lets them know they are reaching deep into the emotional psyche of their listeners. They may achieve the rare quality of **duende** – total communication with their audience, and the mark of great flamenco of any style or generation. Latterly the word *duende* has been used to describe "innovation" which, while it is significant, does not always capture the real depth of the word.

Flamenco Songs

There is a classical repertoire of more than sixty flamenco **songs** (*cantes*) and dances (*danzas*) – some solos, some group numbers, some with instrumental accompaniment, others *a cappella*. These different styles (or *palos*) of flamenco singing are grouped in families according to more or less common melodic themes, establishing three basic types of cante flamenco: **cante grande** (comprising songs of the *jondo* type), **cante chico**, and **cante intermedio** between the two. Roughly speaking the *jondo* and *chico* represent the most and the least difficult *cantes* respectively in terms of their technical and emotional interpretation, although any form, however simple, can be sung with the maximum of complexity and depth. **Cante jondo** (deep song) comprises the oldest and "purest" songs of the flamenco tradition, and is the profound flamenco of the great artists, whose *cantes* are outpourings of the soul, delivered with an intense passion, expressed through elaborate vocal ornamentation. To a large extent however, such categories are largely arbitrary, and few flamenco musicians talk about flamenco in this way; what matters to them is whether the flamenco is good or bad.

The basic *palos* include **soleares**, **siguiriyas**, **tangos** and **fandangos**, but the variations are endless and often referred to by their place of origin: *malagueñas* (from Málaga), for example, *granaínos* (from Granada), or *fandangos de Huelva*. *Siguiriyas*, which date from the Golden Age, and whose theme is usually death, have been described as cries of despair in the form of a funeral psalm. In contrast there are many songs and dances such as tangos, *sevillanas*, *fandangos* and *alegrías* (literally "happinesses") which capture great joy for fiestas. The **sevillana** originated in medieval Sevilla as a spring country dance, with verses improvised and sung to the accompaniment of guitar and castanets (rarely used in other forms of flamenco). In the last few years, dancing *sevillanas* has become popular in bars and clubs throughout Spain, but their great natural habitats are Sevilla's April *Fería* and the annual *romería* or pilgrimage to El Rocio. Each year wonderful new *sevillanas* come onto the market in time for the fiestas.

Another powerful and more seasonal form are the **saetas**. These are songs in honour of the Virgins carried on great floats in the processions of *Semana Santa* (Easter Week), and traditionally they are quite spontaneous – as the float is passing, a singer will launch into a *saeta*, a sung prayer for which silence is necessary and for which the procession will therefore come to a halt while it is sung.

Camarón – or more fully **El Camarón de la Isla** – was by far the most popular and commercially successful singer of modern flamenco. Collaborating with the guitarists and brothers Paco de Lucía and Ramón de Algeciras, and latterly, Tomatito, Camarón raised *cante jondo* to a new art. He died in 1992, having almost singlehandedly revitalized flamenco song, inspiring and opening the way for the current generation of flamenco artists.

Flamenco Guitar

The guitar used to be simply an accompanying instrument – originally the singers themselves played – but in the early decades of this century it began developing as a solo instrument, absorbing influences from classical and Latin American traditions. The greatest of these early guitarists was **Ramón Montoya**, who revolutionized flamenco guitar with his harmonizations and introduced a whole variety of arpeggios – techniques of right-hand playing adapted from classical guitar playing. Along with Niño Ricardo and Sabicas, he established flamenco guitar as a solo medium, an art extended from the 1960s on by **Manolo Sanlucar**, whom most *aficionados* reckon the most technically accomplished player of his generation. Sanlucar has kept within a "pure flamenco" orbit, and not strayed into jazz or rock, experimenting instead with orchestral backing and composing for ballet.

The best known of all contemporary flamenco guitarists, however, is undoubtedly **Paco de Lucía**, who made the first moves towards "new" or "fusion" flamenco. A *payo*, he won his first flamenco prize at the age of 14, and went on to accompany many of the great singers, including a long partnership with Camarón de la Isla. He started forging new rhythms for flamenco following a trip to Brazil, where he was influenced by *bossa nova*, and in the 1970s established a sextet with electric bass, Latin percussion, flute and saxophone. Over the past twenty years he has worked with jazz-rock guitarists like John McLaughlin and Chick Corea, while his own regular band, featuring his other brother, the singer Pepe de Lucía, remains one of the most original and distinctive sounds on the flamenco scene.

Other modern-day guitarists have equally identifiable sounds and rhythms, and fall broadly into two camps, being known either as accompanists or soloists. The former include **Tomatito** (Camarón's last accompanist), Manolo Franco and Paco Cortés, while among the leading soloists are the brothers Pepe and Juan Habichuela; Rafael Riqueni, an astonishing player who is breaking new ground with classical influences; Enrique de Melchor; Gerardo Nuñez; and Vicente Amigo. Jerónimo Maya was acclaimed by the Spanish press as the "Mozart of Flamenco" when he gave his first solo performance, aged seven, in 1984.

Nuevo Flamenco

The **reinvention of flamenco** in the 1980s was initially disliked by purists, but soon gained a completely new young public. Paco de Lucía set the new parameters of innovation and commercial success, and following in his footsteps came **Lolé y Manuel** and others, updating the flamenco sound with original songs and huge success. **Jorge Pardo**, Paco de Lucía's sax and flute player, originally a jazz musician, has continued to work at the cutting edge. **Enrique Morente** and **Juan Peña El Lebrijano** were two of the first to work with Andalucian orchestras from Morocco, and the Mediterranean sound remains important today, together with influences from southern India.

Paco Peña's 1991 *Missa Flamenca* recording, a setting of the Catholic Mass to flamenco, with the participation of established singers like Rafael Montilla "El Chaparro" from Peña's native Córdoba and a classical academy chorus from London, has stayed a bestseller since its first appearance, remaining a benchmark for such compositions.

The encounter with rock and blues was pioneered at the end of the 1980s by Ketama and Pata Negra. **Ketáma** (named after a Moroccan village famed for its hashish) were hailed by the Spanish press as creators of the music of the "New Spain" after their first album, which fused flamenco with rock and Latin salsa, adding a kind of rock–jazz sensibility, a "flamenco cool" as they put it. They then pushed the frontiers of flamenco still further by recording the two *Songhai* albums in collaboration with Malian kora-player Toumani Diabate and British bassist Danny Thompson. The group **Pata Negra**, a band led by two brothers, Raímundo and Rafael Amador, introduced a more direct rock sound with a bluesy electric guitar lead, giving a radical edge to traditional styles like *bulerías*. Their *Blues de la Frontera* album caused an equal sensation. After splitting, Raimundo Amador has continued as a solo artist.

Collectively, these young and iconoclastic musicians became known, in the 1990s, as **nuevo flamenco** – a movement associated in particular with the Madrid label Nuevos Medios. They form a challenging, versatile and at times musically incestuous scene in Madrid and Andalucía, with musicians guesting at each others' gigs and on each others' records. Ketáma have gone on to have massive hits nationally, bringing flamenco fully into the mainstream.

In the 1980s and '90s, the music became the regular sound of **nightclubs**, through the appeal of young singers like **Aurora** – whose salsa-rumba song *Besos de Caramelo*, written by Antonio Carmona of Ketama, was the first 1980s number to crack the pop charts. Pop singer **Martirio** (Isabel Quiñones Gutierrez) is one of the most flamboyant personalities on the scene, appearing dressed in lace mantilla and shades like a cameo from a Pedro Almodóvar film, recording songs with ironic, contemporary lyrics, full of local slang, about life in the cities. Martirio's producer, **Kiko Veneno**, who wrote Camarón's most popular song, *Volando Voy*, is another key artist who helped open up the scene. A rock musician originally, he has a strongly defined sense of flamenco. **Rosario**, one of Spain's top woman singers, has also brought a flamenco sensibility to Spanish rock music.

Other more identifiably *nuevo flamenco* bands and singers to look out for include La Barbería del Sur (who add a dash of salsa); Wili Gimenez and Raimundo Amador; and José El Frances. In the mid-1990s **Radio Tarifa** emerged as an exciting group, leading the exploration of a flamenco–Mediterranean sound with a mix of Arabic and medieval sounds on a flamenco base. They started out as a trio, later expanding to include African musicians.

Discography

Various Arte Flamenco: Excerpts from the collection (Mandala).

Various Arte Flamenco: Vol. 7 La Nina de los Peines (Mandala).

Various Arte Flamenco: Vol. 9 El cante en Sevilla (Mandala).

Various Concurso de Cante Jondo (Sonifolk).

Various Duende: The Passion and Dazzling Virtuosity of Flamenco (Ellipsis Arts; 3CDs).

Various Magna Antología del Cante Flamenco (Hispavox; 10 volumes).
Various Early Cante Flamenco: Classic Recordings from the 1930s (Arhoolie).
Various Fiesta: Flamenco Vivo (Auvidis).
Various Flamenco: Grande Figures (Chant du Monde).
Various Flamenco: The Rough Guide (World Music Network).
Various Noches Gitanas (EPM; 4CDs).
Various Sevillanas: the soundtrack of Carlos Saura's film (Polydor).
Escudero & Ramos de Almaden Flamenco de Triana (Tradition).
Remedios Amaya Me voy contigo (Hemisphere).
Agustín Carbonell Bola Carmen (Messidor).
Duquende Duquende y la guitarra de Tomatito (Nuevos Medios).
Federico García Lorca De Granada a la luna (Sombra).
Federico García Lorca & La Argentina Colección de Canciones Populares Españolas (Sonifolk).
El Indio Gitano Nací gitano por la gracia de dios (Nuevos Medios).
Camarón con tomatito Paris 1987 (Universal).
Camarón de la Isla Potro de rabia y miel (Polygram), Calle Real (Polygram) and Una leyenda flamenca, Vivire and Autorretrato (Philips).
Carmen Linares Cantaora (Riverboat).
Paco de Lucía Luzía (Polygram) and Siroco (Philips).
Enrique de Melchor Cuchichi (Fonodisc).
José Menese El viente solano (Nuevos Medios).
José Mercé & Vicente Amigo Del Amanecer (Virgin).

Moraíto Morao y oro (Auvidis).
Enrique Morente Negra, si tú supieras (Nuevos Medios) and Omage (Karonte).
Niña Pastora Cañailla (Aviola/BMG).
Paco Peña Flamenco Guitar Music of Ramon Montoya and Niño Ricardo (Nimbus Records).
Ramón el Portugués Gitanos de la Plaza (Nuevos Medios).
Saetas Cante de la Semana Santa Andaluza (Auvidis).
Tomatito Barrío Negro (Nuevos Medios).
Various Los Jóvenes Flamencos Vol 1–5 (Nuevos Medios).
Amalgama y Karnataka College of Percussion (Nuba).
La Barbería del Sur (Nuevos Medios).
Chano Domínguez Chano (Nuba).
Ray Heredía Quien no corre, vuela (Nuevos Medios).
Jazzpaña (Nuevos Medios).
Ketama Canciones hondas (Nuevos Medios) and Ketama (Hannibal).
Lolé . . . y Manuel (Gong Fonomusic).
Paco de Lucía Sextet Solo quiero caminar and Live in America (Philips), Live . . . One Summer Night (Phonogram).
Pata Negra Blues de la Frontera (Nuevos Medios/Hannibal).
Radio Tarifa Rumba Argelina and Temporal (both World Circuit).
Songhai (Ketama/Toumani Diabate/Danny Thompson) Songhai and Songhai 2 (Nuevos Medios/Hannibal).
Juan Peña Lebrijano y Orquestra Andalusi de Tanger Encuentros (Ariola/Globestyle).

Folk and regional music

Spain has a centuries-long tradition of folk song and dance. At the beginning of the twentieth century certain dances became emblematic of certain regions and their communities – for example, the *muiñeira* in Galicia, the *zortziko* in the Basque country and the *sardana* for Catalunya. As with many other totalitarian regimes, the Franco dictatorship exploited folklore as a way of promoting nationalism, with the women's section of the Falange party collecting folk songs. As a result, what became known as "folklorism" was somewhat discredited, particularly among those most opposed to the regime.

The inspiration of the 1970s, '80s and '90s was therefore to give new value to folk music and rescue it from patriotic cliché and Francoesque kitsch. While the restoration of democracy was crucial, great impetus also came from the fact that Spain is composed of several different autonomies, each with their own financial support and official nurturing from regional government. Today a new generation of folk musicians have also reclaimed the music and made it their own, creating music with elements drawn from all parts of the country.

The Key Musicians

Currently, folk and regional music is at its most developed in the northwest, from Galicia to Euskadi – Celtic Spain. The *Fiesta del Mundo Celta* at Ortigueira has played a leading role in this revival, and there is a regular summer scene of local festivals in the Basque country, Asturias and Galicia.

Galician music is in particularly fine fettle, rooted in pipes, bagpipes and drums and now heard all over the country, with groups such as **Milladoiro** regulars on the European festival scene. The music of Galician bagpiper **Carlos Nuñez** exemplifies that of a new generation who have grown up steeped in tradition, with classical training and a passion for many other musics. Nuñez, who served a kind of touring apprenticeship with Irish group The Chieftains, constantly searches out collaborations which bring out different aspects of Galician music, such as the inspiring *pandereta* (tambourine) group and singers of Cantegueiras Xiradella, from Martezo, near A Coruña, who have learnt traditional spirited work songs and *jotas* from older women in the countryside. Nuñez has also collaborated with North American guitarist Ry Cooder and Cuba's Vieja Trova Santiaguera, while his 1999 project, *Os Amores Libres*, explores the rhythmic connections between Celtic and flamenco music, with contributions from Irish and Scottish musicians. Other Galician musicians who have helped revitalize the scene include Na Lua (who combine saxophone with bagpipe); Doa, Citania, Trisquell, Fía Na Roca and Xorima (all traditional and acoustic); Palla Mallada (hyper-traditional); and Alecrín, Brath and Matto Congrio (electric folk). Emilio Cao switches back and forth between traditional folk and more modern singer-songwriting.

The Basque country, **Euskadi**, is home to a wild accordion music called *trikitrixa* (meaning the devil's bellows). *Trikitrixa* maestro, **Josepa Tapia**, who plays with *pandereta* player Leturia in the Tapia et Leturia band, is one of the stars. **Kepa Junkera** has taken *trikitrixa* further afield playing with Carlos Núñez. Other key Basque musicians include **Ruper Ordorika**, whose music has a rock edge to it, **Benito Lertxundi**, whose energies generally go into traditional Basque music but who has also recently experimented with the Celtic sounds of the northern coast, and **Oskorri**, a fine, politicized electro-acoustic group, who were instrumental in keeping Basque music publicly alive in the latter years of Franco and who have since gone from strength to strength. Also impressive are Ganbara and Azala. Younger artists include Txomin Artola, his former companion Amaia Zubiría, and Imanol.

A Celtic movement exists in **Asturias** centring on two festivals in Oviedo (the Oviedo Folk Festival and the *Noche Celta*). Most groups are fairly traditional, particularly Ubiña and Lliberdón, though Llan de Cubel are adventurous and challenging.

Turning to the **Balearics**, Mallorcan **María del Mar Bonet** has brought the rich treasury of her own island to huge acclaim at home and abroad. Starting in the 1960s, Bonet was part of the Catalan singer-composer group Els Setge Jutges, and the movement of *nova cançó* (new song) which incurred the displeasure of Franco's censors by singing in Catalan. Key Bonet songs include Mallorca's unofficial hymn, *La Balanguera*, ballads like *La Mort de la Margalida* as well as lively dances like *La Jota Marinera* and the apocalyptic medieval *La Sybilla,* sung only on Christmas Eve in certain churches in Mallorca. Other Balearic musicians of interest include the groups Musica Nostra, Sis Som,

Calitja and Aliorna, who play traditional styles; Coanegra and Siurell Electric, with a more progressive sound; and Calabruix, an electro-acoustic duo.

In **Catalunya**, Maria del Mar Bonet's colleague and friend in Els Setge Jutges, **Lluís Llach**, has enjoyed a long career, as has fellow Catalan **Joan Manuel Serrat**. Serrat, one of the big record sellers in Spain, sings both in Catalan and Spanish and enjoys a huge reputation in Latin America. The early songs of Llach (from the period when Franco censored Catalan song), such as *El Bandoler* and *L'Estaca,* are still highly esteemed and sung today. For Llach they resulted in four years' exile in France, when his seminal recording at the Paris Olympia with its classic version of *País Petit* (My Small Country) circulated clandestinely. Returning as Franco died, to great celebration, Llach is now a Spanish superstar, touring with a superb group of musicians, and mixing jazz and rock in his arrangements. Another member of Els Setge Jutges who celebrated thirty years singing in 1997, is **Raimon**, composer of many key songs including *Al Vent,* a song about being free in the wind, which conjured up images of liberty during the 1960s and '70s. Other interesting Catalan groups, mostly playing folk music, include La Murga and the newer Tradivarius.

Catalunya also has a number of **orchestras** playing traditional dance music – some closer to salsa like the Orquesta Platería and the Salseta del Poble Sec, others more traditional like Tercet Treset and the Orquesta Galana. The emblematic *sardana* dance remains important too in every local festival, as does a tradition of popular singing linking Catalunya with Cuba, known as *habanera*, which thrives today in summer festivals on the Costa Brava coast, particularly in Calella de Palafrugell. With maritime connections strong in the nineteenth and twentieth centuries, the music of *ida y vuelta,* coming and going, of greeting and farewell, has endured in fishermen's choirs and small groups, and has now been taken up again by young people.

Andalucía is home not only to flamenco but also other musics: Almadraba from Tarifa explore the highly traditional, while Lombarda from Granada are more revivalist. Andalucía is also where you'll find **Sephardic** (Iberian Jewish) music, often a cross between folk and traditional styles. Rosa Zaragoza and Aurora Moreno are two female singers who have produced interesting work in this field; Moreno is also involved in Mozarabic *jarchas* (Arabic verse set to music). Els Trobadors and Cálamus have both also successfully revived medieval traditions, while the outstanding Luís Delgado works with Sephardic, medieval and Spanish Arabic music.

Other Spanish musicians to take note of include Al Tall, an interesting band from Valencia, whose last major project was a joint effort with Muluk El Hwa; Alimara, a group from Marrakesh who are involved with both music and traditional dance; Salpicao, who have experimented with flamenco-based fusions; and La Vella Banda, an innovative horn band. Joaquín Díaz has for many years dominated the musical life of Castile, as have the prolific Nuevo Mester de Juglaría, a distinguished group who established an alternative roots music to Franco's folkloristic ventures. Manuel Luna and La Musgaña have created fine sounds, as has the singer María Salgado, who has made recordings of the *habanera* tradition found outside Catalunya, and who worked on *La sal de la vida* (The Salt of Life), with two other women musicians, Uxía from Galicia and Rasha from the Sudan – together they explore the similarities and differences, rhythms and cadence, of each other's cultures, including largely unheard-of songs from Galicia and Asturias. Other musicians to listen out for include the Segovian group, Rebolada, who include eight *dulzainas* (flutes) in their line-up, and Habas Verdes from Zamora, who produce spirited, vivid versions of traditional tunes on instruments such as the hurdy-gurdy and the *dulzaina,* as well as the cello, organ and guitar.

Singer-songwriters

In the 1990s the scene of **cantautores**, or singer-songwriters, underwent a revival, with new talent following in the footsteps of the heroes of the 1970s and '80s and gaining a younger audience. **Pedro Guerra** developed his own mellow style, influenced by sounds from the Canary Islands, Brazil and classic Latin American singers and poets. **Ismael Serrano** used his melodies to make open social commitment, while **Javier Alvarez**, with his disc *Tres*, shifted away from the classic voice-guitar structure by diving into drum programming and sampling. **Rosana** brought singer-songwriters to the front covers of newspapers with her soft, melodic style and whispering voice, seducing a million Spanish people with her first album.

The most impact, however, has been made by **Joaquín Sabina**, a man who began in the Franco years and whose cult following has made him the most talked-about artist not only in Spain but in much of South and Central America too. His recent album, *19 dias y 500 noches*, has been acclaimed worldwide by critics and the public as one of his best works.

Discography

Various El gusto es nuestro (Ariola).

Various Magna Antología del Folklore Musical de España (Hispavox; 17LPs).

Various La sal de la vida (NubeNegra).

Various Voice of Spain: Spanish regional music (Heritage).

Rafael Alberti y Paco Ibañez A galopar (PDI).

Javier Alvarez Tres (EMI).

Bernardo Atxaga Nueva Etiopia (Colleccion Lcd el Europeo).

Luís Eduardo Aute y Silvio Rodríguez Mano a mano (Ariola).

María del Mar Bonet Salmaia (Ariola) and El cor del temps (Picap, Spain, 2CDs).

Andres Calamaro Honestidad brutal (Gaza/DRU).

Carlos Cano Quedate con la Copla (CBS).

Charo Centenera No soy la Piquer (RNE).

Llan de Cubel L'otru llaou de la mar (Fono Astur).

Vainica Doble 1970 (RNE).

Fía na Roca (Arpafolk).

Pedro Guerra Raíz (BMG).

Pablo Guerrero Todo la vida es ahora (Polygram).

Habas Verdes En el jardin de la yerba buena (Gam).

Imanol Alfonsina, viaje de mar y luna (Ediciones Cúbicas).

Kepa Junkera Bilbao 00.00 (Resistencia) and Trikitixa zoom (Nuba).

Kepa, Zabaleta & Imanol Triki Up (Elkar).

Mikel Laboa Lau-Bost (Elkar).

Leilía Leilía (Discmedi Blau).

Benito Lertxundi Hyunkidura kuttunak (Elkar).

Lluís Llach Lluis Llach A L'Olympia (Fonomusic), Ara 25 anys in directe (Picap) and Mon porrera (Picap).

Manuel Luna Como hablan las sabinas (RNE).

Rosana Lunas Rotas (Universal).

Luar Na Cubre Cabo do Mundo (WEA).

La Musgaña El Diablo Cojuelo (Sonifolk).

Mestisay El cantar viene de lejos (Manzana).

Milladoiro Galicia no temp (Discmedi).

Nuevo Mester De Juglaría 25 Aniversario (Polygram).

Aurora Moreno Aynadamar (Saga).

Carlos Núñez A Irmandade das Estrelas (Ariola) and Os Amores Libres (BMG).

Ruper Ordorika Ez da posible (Gasa), Hiru truku (Nuevos Medios) and Bilduma Bat (Elkar).

Oskorri Badok hamahiru (Elkar).

La Paloma One Song For All Worlds (Indigo).

Albert Pla No solo de rumba vive el hombre (Ariola).

Port-Bo Arrel de tres and Canela y ron (both Picap).

Radio Tarifa Rumba Argelina and Temporai (both World Circuit).

Raimon Cancons (Auvidis).

Marina Rossell Marina (PDI).

Bleizi Ruz, Leilía, La Musgaña Hent Sant Jakez (Shamrock Records).

Joaquín Sabina 19 dias u 500 noches (BMG).

María Salgado Mirandote (NubeNegra).

Salpicão (RNE).

Joan Manuel Serrat Utopia, Mediteraneo, Serrat en directo and Sombras de la China (all Ariola).

Al Tall y Muluk el Hwa Xarq al-Andalus (RNE).

Tapia Eta Leturia Dultzemenoea (Elkar).

Els Trobadors Et ades sera l'Alba (Lyricon).

Uxía Estou vivindo no ceo (NubeNegra).

Rock, Pop and Hip-Hop

In the 1970s Anglo-American rock inspired the first rock groups, including **Miguel Ríos** and **Los Bravos,** as well as the progressive proto-rock of Los Canarios, Maquina and Música Dispersa, pioneers of the musical underground. Madrid was dominated by **heavy rock**, with a series of groups like Burning, Mermelada and Indiana, whose fans lived in the working-class districts of the capital and in the dormitory towns of the outskirts. Meanwhile, in Barcelona, the scene was split between musicians who were producing a very cool **jazz-rock**, and those into a warmer **Catalan salsa**, or Barcelona's own *gitano* music – **Catalan rumba**, popularized first by Peret, a Barcelona musician. On the fringes were the singer-songwriters and the Latin American groups who, despite Franco, managed to tour Spain.

At the end of the 1970s, a **punk** reaction began to take hold among teenagers, just as it did in Britain and the US. Some older rockers, like Ramoncín, attempted to take punk on board, but punk challenged and broke up the old order, setting the scene for the future, with an explosion of diverse groups.

Since then, straight **pop** has been the main area of activity, but there have been various phases in which punks, technos, *garajistas*, *siniestros*, Romantics and rockabillies have had success, crossing over between genres. Today the goddess of the Spanish pop scene is **Monica Naranjo**, her success based on her unique kitsch look, passionate lyrics and extraordinary voice. The current king of Spanish pop is **Alejandro Sanz,** who became a teenage idol in the early 1990s and has gone on to prove his brilliance with compositions ranging from flamenco to Latin pop. His groundbreaking album *Más* is already a classic for Spanish audiences of all ages.

A key figure in Madrid from punk days was **Alaska**, a club owner and one-time muse of modernity, whose records are less significant than her brilliant live performances. Female singer **Mecano**, accompanied by two male musicians, became one of the most successful Spanish pop groups ever, popular in Latin America, France and Italy, as well as Spain. Established bands today include the country-influenced Los Secretos; the futuristic Aviador Dro; Miguel Ríos and Ramoncín, both of whom stick to classic rock; and the heavy-metal groups, Rosendo, Obús and Barón Rojo. A slightly younger generation includes Gabinete Caligari (macho Hispano-pop), Los Coyotes (Latin rockabilly) and La Frontera (cowboy), while Luz, and Rosario, an interesting and original singer from a flamenco dynasty (the daughter of Rosa Flores), have become big stars. Look out too for Radio Futura, who brought the Latin and Cuban touch onto the scene in the late 1980s with their album *Semilla negra*; Jarabe de Palo, whose *La Flaca* is a classic of the pop scene; Juan Pero (ex Radio Futura); and Enrique Bunbury (ex Heores del Silencio).

In **Barcelona** one of the most innovative bands has been El Ultimo de la Fila, a duo with engaging lyrics and a sophisticated Mediterranean sound; Manolo Garcia has now gone solo. Equally enjoyable are Los Rebeldes, former rockabilly heroes, who have been exploring new directions.

Euskadi has witnessed a two-part musical scene: radical rock has been represented by Negu Gorriak, Potato, Hertzainak and La Polla Records, who use hot rhythms, reggae and ska as a base for a message with a political conscience. On a more straightforward rock level, 21 Japonesas and La Dama se Esconde have demanded attention.

From **Galicia** (especially Vigo) a surprising number and diversity of bands have emerged, including Siniestro Total and Os Resentidos in the 1980s, with Os Diplomaticos an interesting new arrival of the 1990s. Los Ilegales, powerful rockers with a strong live set, have emerged in **Asturias**, as well as Hevia, an electronic pop bagpiper, while in **Aragón**, Heroes del Silencio have been one of the major chart rock groups in the 1990s.

In **Andalucía**, the *malagueño* combo Danza Invisible have had some unforgettable catchy hits, and the long list of artists from Sevilla include the astonishing Martirio (who combines pop and traditional songs with a playful, witty sense of challenging Spanish stereotypes), Arrajatabla and Kiko Veneno. Veneno's sporadic albums are clever, literate, utterly Spanish rock songs and come highly recommended.

The **indie scene** proved to be one of the most interesting in the 1990s, with the creation of new record companies allowing the exposure of new talent. Pop rock, hip-hop and electronic music have all been at the forefront. In the late 1990s the powerful guitar sound and clear melodies of **Dover** from Madrid became a massive success with *Devil Came To Me* while **Los Planetas**, from Granada, mix acid guitars and subtle melodies with lyrics on post-teenage love, pain and drugs.

Electronic music emerged in Spain in the 1970s and 1980s. Barcelona was the vanguard city, with groups such as Macromassa, La Fura dels Baus and Gringos making the most impact. Many labels have emerged since then and electronic music has developed into dance sounds. The Sónar **festival** started up in the 1990s, boasting more than 50,000 festival-goers in the year 2001 (see p.737). Some of the top names to look out for are the house DJ Toni Rox, drum'n'bass-leaning Oscar Mulero, from the Ibiza scene, the techno tunes of Angel Molina and the more experimental, conceptual sounds of Sandro Bianchi.

Spanish **hip-hop** emerged towards the end of 1996 and is now an industry in itself, acknowledged as one of the most creative musical scenes, with distribution through its own specialized record labels. An urban street genre, it has flourished among teenagers living in working-class areas of big cities, focusing as it does on key political issues including fascism, racism, drugs, immigration and xenophobia. One of the most popular and respected rappers is **Mala Rodriguez**, from Sevilla, whose flamenco-tinted songs are fronted by feminist lyrics. Three big **festivals** celebrate hip-hop: Festimad in Madrid, Benicàssim on the Valencian coast (see p.893) and Sónar in Barcelona (see p.737).

Discography

7 Notas 7 Colores Hecho es simple (BCA).
Ari Glancho perfecto (Zona Bruta).
Arrajatabla Sevilla blues (Fonomusic).
Ana Belen, Miguel Rios, Víctor Manuel, Joan Manuel Serrat El gusto es nuestro (Ariola).
Ana Belen Veneno para el corazón (Ariola).
Camela Simplemente amor (EMI).
Celtas Cortos Cuentame un cuento and Tranquilo majete (both DRO).
Ciudad Jardín Ojos mas que ojos (Hispavox).
Corcobado Tormenta de tormento (Triquinoise).
Dover Devil came to me (Subterfuge).
Estopa Estopa (BMG).
Fangoria Una ola cualquiera en Vulcano (Gasa).
Manolo Garcia Arena en los bolsillos (BMG).

Héroes del Silencio El espíritu del vino (Hispavox).
Hevia Tierra de nadie (Hispavox).
Illegales Regreso al sexo químicamente puro (Hispavox).
Jarabe De palo la flaca (Virgin).
Luz A contraluz (Hispavox).
Los Planetas Una semana en el motor de un autobus (BMG).
Monica Naranjo Palabra de mujer (Sony).
Negu Gorriak Borreroak baditu milaka aurpegi (Esan Ozanki).
Presuntos Implicados Alma de blues (WEA).
Radio Futura Tierra para bailar (Ariola).
Los Rebeldes La rosa y la cruz (Epic).
Os Resentidos Están aqui (Gasa).

Miguel Ríos Así que pasen 30 años (Polydor).
Los Rodríguez Sin documentos (Gasa).
Rosario De Ley (Epic).
Alejandro Sanz Más (WEA).
Los Secretos Cambio de planes (Dro).
Seguridad Social Furia Latina (Gasa).
Sólo Los Solo Retorno al principio (BCA).

Tam Tam Go! Vida y color (Hispavox).
Manolo Tena Sangre Española (Epic).
El Ultimo de la Fila Astronomía razonable (EMI).
Antonio Vega El sitio de mi recreo (Polygram).
Kiko Veneno La Pequeña Salvaje (Nuevos Medios)
and Échate un cantecito (BMG).

Jazz

Jazz in Spain has always had loyal fans tucked away in small clubs, but since the end of the 1970s it has really taken off. Many jazz musicians have become internationally acclaimed not only through their jazz music, but also through their ability to merge jazz with local genres such as flamenco and Mediterranean sounds.

In the 1970s, when the great pianist **Tete Montonliu** was already a figure on the international scene, **Pegasus** started introducing experimental fusion sounds, and guitarist **Joan Bibiloni** a very Mediterranean one. Then in the 1980s, the flamenco-influenced generation – many of whom had played with Paco de Lucia and El Camaron, including the bass player **Carlos Benavent**, saxophonists **Jorge Pardo**, **Pedro Iturralde** and **Perico Sambeat**, and pianist **Chano Dominguez** – discovered ways of creating and expressing something that was both local and global in its appeal, reaching audiences all over the world with their innovative flamenco-influenced jazz, which embraced influences from Brazil, Peru and other parts of the world.

Names to watch for today include **Baldo Martínez**, whose recent album *No pais dos ananos* was much acclaimed, and **Angel Blanco**. The **Orquesta Nacional de Jazz de España** – created in 2000 by Chano Dominguez – explores a rich Spanish and Latin repertoire. The country's biggest **jazz festival** is held at San Sebastián in July. Vitoria holds one in the same month, and there are two in Madrid: one in May (*Fiestas de San Isidro*), the other in November. There's also a November festival in Barcelona. Other worthwhile events are the *Fiesta de Jazz* in Murcia and the *Muestra de Jazz* in Ibiza.

Discography
Chano Domiguez Iman (Nuba/Karonte).
Fangoria Una temporada en el infierno (Diablo).
Alex Martin Join the band (Coconar).

Jan Fairley, David Loscos and Manuel Dominguez

Cinema

It has not always been easy for cinema to take root in Spain. The lack of a proper infrastructure, the devastation of the Civil War, and the restrictions of the Franco regime all meant that Spanish film-makers had to struggle to get films made, and then often struggle again to get them released.

The vast majority of Spanish films remain unseen outside Spain. From the 1950s onwards, Spanish films would periodically appear on the film festival circuit and, on occasion, be taken up by an art-house cinema. One director in particular, **Carlos Saura**, achieved international prestige even while working under the restrictions of the Franco regime. From an earlier generation, **Luis Buñuel** has long been accepted as one of the major figures in the history of cinema. But Saura was something of an exception, while Buñuel made almost all of his films in either France or Mexico.

The end of the dictatorship, however, was followed by a remarkable degree of film-making activity, and today the films of Spanish directors, **Pedro Almodóvar** in particular, are capable of filling cinemas within and beyond Spain. The garishly modern Madrid of *Women on the Edge of a Nervous Breakdown*, the dusty Los Monegros plains of *Jamón Jamón*, the magical-realist Basque landscape of *Vacas* – these have all helped to establish Spain on the world cinema map.

The Early Decades

The history of Spanish film goes back to the last century, when Spain produced one of the pioneers of early cinema, **Segundo de Chomón**, a man whose use of trick photography rivalled that of the French director, Georges Méliès. Overall, however, Spanish cinema developed slowly. Spain entered the twentieth century lacking the technology, the capital and the urban audiences that produced a thriving film industry in neighbouring France. "In my own village of Calanda," wrote Luis Buñuel in his autobiography, ". . . the Middle Ages lasted until World War I." Like Buñuel, Segundo de Chomón spent most of his career abroad, and ended up producing special effects for other directors in Italy and France. By the 1920s, a Spanish film industry had been established, but its modest scale and pretensions are indicated in the slogan used to promote one film made in 1925 – "It's so good that it doesn't seem Spanish."

Without a strong production base, cinema in Spain was particularly susceptible to the rapidly developing power of **America**. In the early 1930s "Spanish" films were being produced, but often in Hollywood rather than Madrid, as the major American film companies dealt with the coming of sound (and the threat that an active Spanish film industry might have provided) by producing Spanish versions of their English-language product. In the process they deprived Spain of a number of its film-makers.

However, in 1934, a major production and distribution company, **CIFAS**, was founded in Madrid. With a degree of support from the Republican government, and with the native product proving more popular than subtitled American movies (though dubbing was gradually adopted as a standard practice), the Spanish film industry began to appear relatively healthy. Luis Buñuel returned to Spain from France – where, with fellow Spaniard Salvador Dalí, he had directed a couple of Surrealist classics, *Un Chien Andalou* (1928) and *L'Age* *d'Or* (1930) – to make *Land Without Bread* (1932). This film, an unremitting documentary about rural poverty, was promptly banned, but Buñuel stayed on, dubbing films for Warner Bros, and working as executive producer (and reputedly occasional director) on four more mainstream projects.

The **Civil War** and the eventual Nationalist victory drove Buñuel into exile. It also ended the brief flowering of popular Spanish cinema that had been exhibited in films such as *Paloma Fair* (1935) and *Clara the Brunette* (1936), the latter featuring the first "star" of Spanish cinema, Imperio Argentina.

During the war, the communists and the anarcho-syndicalists produced numerous short works extolling their cause; there were also appeals for international support for the Republican cause in films such as Joris Ivens' *The Spanish Earth* (1937). Some **propagandist** films were produced by the victorious Nationalist regime, including *Madrid Front* (1939) and *Race* (1941), the latter an adaptation of Franco's own novel. More significant was the establishment of the **Supreme Board of Film Censorship**, inaugurating four decades in which censorship became the strongest force in Spanish cinema.

The Franco Years

Under Franco, both scripts and completed films had to be submitted for approval, and films had to be dubbed into the "official" Castilian dialect. No actual code of censorship was laid down until 1963, but this only gave greater freedom to the censors. Film-makers also needed to placate the Catholic Church, which in 1950 established the **National Board of Classification of Spectacles** which made its own "recommendations".

Some efforts were made to support an indigenous Spanish film industry. In 1947 a **film school** was established in Madrid (where students were able to see foreign films banned from public exhibition), and in 1952 state **subsidy** regulations were changed to allow for the award of fifty percent of the costs of films deemed to be of "national interest". In practice this did little to vary the diet of epics, dramas, musicals and comedies which glorified the Spanish past and presented **idealized images** of the state, the Church and the family.

It was against this background that a group of **left-wing film-makers** met in 1955, declaring contemporary Spanish cinema to be "1 – Politically futile. 2 – Socially false. 3 – Intellectually worthless. 4 – Aesthetically valueless. 5 – Industrially paralytic." Inspired by the example of Italian neo-realism, such film-makers were, in fact, already beginning to present a less idealized picture of Spanish society. Films such as Luis Berlanga's *Welcome Mr Marshall* (1952), a satire about the effect of America's Marshall Plan on a Spanish village, and Antonio Bardem's *Death of a Cyclist* (1956), suggested that there was some room for alternative voices in the Spanish film industry.

The restrictions continued (in 1956 Bardem was briefly imprisoned for his political views), but the Spanish government did institute a slightly more flexible policy, if largely to attract international support and investment. While American film companies were being persuaded to use relatively inexpensive **Spanish locations** for films such as *Alexander the Great* (1955), the prestige offered by the international film festival circuit meant that even films offering a critical view of Spanish institutions could be used as a means of "selling" Spain abroad.

The contradictions inherent in this policy were shown up most blatantly when Buñuel was invited back to Spain to make a film for the production company **UNINCI**, which had been formed by a group of film-makers including Bardem, Berlanga and Carlos Saura. The resulting film, *Viridiana*

(1961), revealed that the director of *L'Age d'Or* could be as uncompromising as ever. Astonishingly, the film was initially passed by the censor despite scenes including a parody of The Last Supper, acted out by an assortment of drunks and beggars – and was only banned after it had been attacked in the Vatican newspaper. The result was that Buñuel resumed his career in Mexico and France, and the promise and short life of UNINCI was brought to a close. Buñuel returned to Spain to make *Tristana* in 1970 and *That Obscure Object of Desire* in 1977, though both were French–Spanish co-productions rather than exclusively Spanish. *Viridiana* was not publicly shown in Spain until 1977.

In the slightly liberalized but still restrictive atmosphere of the 1960s and 1970s, some directors managed to develop the problem of getting round the censor into something of a fine art. **Carlos Saura**, in particular, who had quickly left behind the naturalism of his earliest films, used the power of suggestion, allegory and symbol to attack Francoist pretensions in films such as *The Hunt* (1965) and *The Garden of Delights* (1970). Working with the actress Geraldine Chaplin and the producer Elías Querejeta, he used his developing international prestige to retain a remarkable degree of control over his own films.

Other directors lacked Saura's prestige, though the loose movement known as the **Barcelona School** attempted to challenge the dominance of Madrid and the lack of adventure in mainstream Spanish cinema. Meanwhile, another side of Spanish cinema was revealed in the developing market for **low-budget horror films**, capitalizing on the fact that violence was less heavily censored than the directly sexual or political.

In the last years of the Franco regime, Saura continued to maintain his independence, exploring the scars of the Civil War in *Cousin Angelica* (1973), and the consequences of repression in *Raise Ravens* (1975). The aftermath of the Civil War also provided the theme for Victor Erice's remarkable debut feature, *The Spirit of the Beehive* (1973), a lyrical film set in a bleak Castilian village and featuring, like *Raise Ravens*, the young **Ana Torrént**.

A more violent picture of rural Spain was presented in Ricardo Franco's *Pascuale Duarte* (1975) and José Luis Borau's *Poachers* (1975). In its story of **disintegrating authority**, the latter film, released shortly before Franco's death, seemed almost to anticipate the demise of the dictatorship: it was shown despite objections from the censor, and drew large crowds at the box office.

After Franco

In 1977 censorship was formally abolished, and though a none too sympathetic portrayal of the Civil Guard in **Pilar Miró**'s *The Cuenca Crime* (1980) initially led to that film being seized by the police, Miró's film also went on to break box-office records. In 1982 Miró herself – whose *Gary Cooper, Who Art in Heaven* (1980) told of the difficulties of a woman working in a male-dominated industry – was appointed Director General of Cinema by the incoming Socialist government. After her appointment, she continued to direct, including *Beltenebros* (1991), a *film-noir* treatment of Franco-era Spain, starring Terence Stamp and Patsy Kensit.

With the **death of Franco**, and the **lifting of censorship**, Spanish filmmakers were able to engage with politics more directly: *Black Brood* (1977), directed by Manuel Gutiérrez Aragón, dealt with right-wing terrorists; *The Truth About the Salvatore Affair* (1978), directed by Antonio Drove, returned to history (Barcelona between 1917 and 1923) to examine the economic roots of political change; while Juan Bardem mixed thriller and documentary in his *Seven Days in May* (1978).

Liberalization brought its own problems. Under Franco the Spanish film industry had been restricted but also cushioned; now film-makers found themselves competing against an influx of American imports for a share of a declining audience. As Director General of Cinema, Miró set out to halt this trend by reintroducing **protectionist measures** and government subsidies. Efforts were also made to decentralize the film industry, and to move away from Franco's exclusive emphasis on Spain's Castilian heritage. For the first time, films using the Catalan language became possible following the establishment in 1975 of the **Institute of Catalan Film**, while the Basque government also financed a number of projects. National and regional subsidies have continued, although since the Socialists' fall from power they have been significantly reduced.

For directors who had mastered the art of indirect statement under Franco, the end of the dictatorship necessitated a change of direction. For **Carlos Saura** this change bore fruit in the form of *Blood Wedding* (1981), which showed Antonio Gades and his troupe rehearsing and performing a ballet version of the Federico García Lorca play; his collaboration with Gades continued with *Carmen* (1983) and *Love the Magician* (1986). Saura returned to the Civil War with the tragi-comic *Ay, Carmela* (1990), and has continued to explore subjects from dance to neo-fascism in films such as *Flamenco* (1995) and *Taxi* (1996).

Since *The Spirit of the Beehive*, **Victor Erice** has directed just two films. In *The South* (1983), he gave a further poetic and unsentimental exploration of a father-daughter relationship under the shadow of the Civil War. *The Quince Tree Sun* (1991) – a slow but ultimately rewarding study of an artist at work – recorded the meticulous preparations made by the Spanish artist Antonio López while he waited to capture the exact light needed for his painting.

Julio Medem, one of a number of Basque directors to emerge in recent years, has carved an individual, sometimes mystifying, but also striking path with *Vacas* (1991) – four interrelated stories about a feud between two families as seen through bovine eyes – *The Red Squirrel* (1993), *Earth* (1996) and *Lovers of the Arctic Circle* (1998). His most recent film, *Lucía and Sex* (2001) maintains the surreal tone of his earlier work.

Vicente Aranda, who directed his first film in 1964, achieved his international breakthrough with *The Lovers* (1991), a highly charged story of fatal attraction in 1950s Madrid starring **Victoria Abril**, who had made her debut in Aranda's *Change of Sex* (1976). More recently Aranda has had commercial if not critical successes with both *Turkish Passion* (1994) and the big-budget Civil War drama *Libertarians* (1996).

The past has continued to figure prominently in Spanish films, though most directors have avoided directly confronting the Civil War. Pedro Olea's *The Fencing Master* (1993) returned to nineteenth-century Madrid for its narrative of love, fate and death; **Fernando Trueba**'s *Belle Epoque* (1993), set in a nostalgic re-creation of the Republican 1930s, became the second Spanish film to win the Best Foreign Film Oscar (the first being *Begin the Beguin* in 1982, directed by José Luis Garci); while before her death in 1997, Pilar Miró had a box-office success with *The Dog in the Manger* (1996), an adaptation of Lope de Vega's seventeenth-century comedy.

Other directors who came to prominence after the dictatorship seemed intent on turning their back on history. The cinema of **Pedro Almodóvar**, in particular, represents a break with both the idealized films that toed the Franco line, and the social commitment of directors such as Bardem and Berlanga. "I never speak of Franco," he has stated. "I hardly acknowledge his existence. I start after Franco."

Almodóvar made his feature film debut in 1980 with the cheap and transgressive *Pepi, Lucy, Bom and a Whole Load of Other Girls*. His prodigious output during the 1980s included *What Have I Done to Deserve This?* (1982), a black comedy about drugs, prostitution and the forging of Hitler's diaries; *Matador* (1986), a dark thriller linking sexual excitement with the violence of the bullfight; *The Law of Desire* (1987), a story involving a gay film director, his transsexual brother/sister, murder and incest; as well as the internationally successful *Women on the Edge of a Nervous Breakdown* (1988). Almodóvar's films have benefited from the performances of actors such as Carmen Maura, Victoria Abril, Rosy de Palma and Antonio Banderas, and over time they have gained in narrative coherence and production values while retaining the capacity to offend – notably with *Tie Me Up, Tie Me Down* (1990). One of the very few directors able to attract audiences across the globe with films in a language other than English, Almodóvar's 1995 *Flower of My Secret* pushed him more into the mainstream, while *All About My Mother* (1999), which marks a return to his trademark obsession with transsexuals, won him an Oscar for Best Foreign Film.

Bigas Luna is another director capable of simultaneously offending and delighting audiences within and beyond Spain. He achieved notoriety with *Jamón Jamón* (1992), and has continued his relentless preoccupation with sex, food and machismo in films such as *Golden Balls* (1993) and *The Tit and the Moon* (1994). **Alex de la Inglesia**'s *Mutant Action* (1993) imagined (in gruesome detail) a future in which the disabled wage war on the beautiful, while **Juanma Bajo Ulloa**, director of the disturbing psychological thriller, *The Dead Mother* (1993), had a hit at the Spanish box office with *Airbag* (1995), a gleefully tasteless comedy about three men searching for a missing wedding ring through a succession of brothels.

New directors have continued to emerge. **Iciar Bollaín**, after acting roles that included the daughter in Erice's *The South* and a fiery freedom fighter in Ken Loach's Civil War drama, *Land and Freedom* (1995), wrote and directed *Hi, Are You Alone?* (1996), a sympathetic portrait of a pair of young women travelling through Spain with an uncertain destination. **Alejandro Amerábar** made his directorial debut with *Thesis* (1995), an intelligent thriller about a student researching violence in the media, which collected a handful of awards at the Goya ceremony (the Spanish version of the Oscars); Ana Torrént, now a veteran of Spanish cinema, played the student. Amerábar, aged 23 when he made the film, and who has gone on to make *Open Your Eyes* (1998) belongs to a generation with barely a memory of Spain under Franco. His most recent release, *The Others* (2001), starring Nicole Kidman, has wowed audiences in the USA and at the Venice Film Festival alike. Among his more notable contemporaries is **Fernando Trueba**, whose *Child of Your Eyes* (1998), another Franco-era period piece, was impressively successful abroad.

In the late 1990s Spanish **actors** have also gained ground abroad, though some of the country's greatest performers, such as **Fernando Ferran Gómez**, remain little known beyond the Pyrenees. **Antonio Banderas**, once the star of Almodóvar's stable, is now successfully installed in Hollywood as both an actor and director, while **Penelope Cruz**, a favourite of Trueba, has become an a-list star and respected actress on both sides of the Atlantic. Another Spanish favourite currently being feted internationally is **Javier Bardem**, who won critical acclaim and an Oscar nomination for his role in the Mexican film *Perdito Durango* (2001).

Guy Barefoot

Books

Listings below represent a highly selective reading list on Spain and matters Spanish, especially in the sections on history. Most titles are in print, although we've included a few older classics, many of them easy enough to find in secondhand bookshops and libraries. For all books in print, publishing details are in the form (UK publisher; US publisher), where both exist; if books are published in one country only, this follows the publisher's name (eg Serpent's Tail, UK). University Press has been abbreviated as UP, o/p signifies out of print.

If you have difficulty finding any title, an excellent source for books about Spain – new, used, and out of print – is Books On Spain, PO Box 207, Twickenham, TW2 5BQ, UK (☎ & ℻020/8898-7789, ⓦwww.books-on-spain.com).

Impressions, travel and general accounts

The best introductions

⭐ **John Hooper** *The New Spaniards* (Penguin, UK/US). This excellent, authoritative portrait of post-Franco Spain was written by the *Guardian*'s former Spanish correspondent in 1986 and published in a revised edition (now ageing) in 1995. It is one of the best possible introductions to contemporary Spain.

Lucy McCauley (ed) *Spain: Travelers' Tales* (Travelers' Tales, US).

It would be hard to better this anthology of writing on Spain, which gathers its stories and journalism predominantly from the last ten years. Featured authors include Gabriel García Márquez, Colm Tóibín and Louis de Bernières, whose "Seeing Red", on the tomato-throwing festival of Buñol, is worth the purchase price on its own.

Recent travels/accounts

Carrie B. Douglass *Bulls, Bullfighting and Spanish Identities* (Arizona UP, US). Anthropologist Douglass delves into the symbolism of the bull in the Spanish national psyche, and then goes on to examine the bullfight's role in some of the thousands of fiestas countrywide that support it.

Nina Epton *Grapes and Granite* (o/p). One of the few English books on Galicia – full of folklore and rural

life in the 1960s – and well worth hunting down in libraries or secondhand bookshops.

David Gilmour *Cities of Spain* (Ivan R Dee, US). A modern cultural portrait of Spain, but very much in the old tradition; it is a little fogeyish at times but excellent, nonetheless, in its evocation of history, especially on the Moorish cities of Andalucía.

△ Cervantes statue, Plaza de España, Madrid

Robert Hughes *Barcelona* (Harvill/Vintage). This is the best of the 1992 books on the Olympic city: a text that, in the author's stated ambition, "explains the zeitgeist of the place and the connective tissue between the cultural icons".

Michael Jacobs *Between Hopes and Memories: a Spanish Journey* (o/p). The thorough and entertaining account of a journey through Spain in 1992 with lively digressions on food, art, literature and the characters met along the way. *Andalucía* (Pallas Athene, UK/US), by the same author, is an outstanding introduction to the region.

A.L. Kennedy *On Bullfighting* (Yellow Jersey Press; Knopf). Curious book by a Scottish fiction author who starts out – knowing nothing of bullfighting – by comparing the dicing with death of the *matadores* in the ring to her own attempted suicide. She travels to Spain, meets the experts, hears the anecdotes and – despite tortured misgivings – becomes an *aficionada*.

Peter B. Meyer *A True Story About Doing Business in Spain* (Avon Books, UK). This quirkily written insider's view of Spanish business life features encounters with corrupt bureaucracy, shifty lawyers, crooked business partners and a parade of police and politicos straight out of central casting. Sometimes skewed, but always fascinating.

Cees Nooteboom *Roads to Santiago: Detours and Riddles in the Land and History of Spain* (Harvill; Harcourt Brace). This is one of the most literary travel books of recent decades: an almost Shandyesque tale (few of the roads travelled lead anywhere near Santiago), garnished from the notebooks of this quirky, architecture-obsessed Dutch writer. Very highly recommended.

Paul Richardson *Our Lady of the Sewers* (Abacus/Little Brown, UK). An articulate and kaleidoscopic series of insights into rural Spain's customs and cultures, fast disappearing.

Chris Stewart *Driving Over Lemons – An Optimist in Andalucía* (Sort Of/Penguin; Pantheon). A funny, insightful and very charming account of life on a remote peasant farm in the Alpujarras. The author, oddly enough, was the original drummer in *Genesis*.

Robert White *A River in Spain* (I.B. Tauris UK/US). Well-written account of an American's love affair with the Duero valley; strong on towns, history, architecture and local folklore.

Earlier twentieth-century writers

Gerald Brenan *South From Granada* (Penguin, UK). An enduring classic. Brenan lived in a small village in the Alpujarras in the 1920s, and records this and the visits of his Bloomsbury contemporaries Virginia Woolf, Lytton Strachey and Bertrand Russell.

Camilo José Cela *Journey to the Alcarria* (Granta Books; Wisconsin UP). A Nobel Prize-winner for literature, Cela explored a hidden corner of New Castile in 1946 – a study of a rural world that no longer exists.

Laurie Lee *As I Walked Out One Midsummer Morning* (Penguin, UK), *A Rose For Winter*

(Penguin, UK), *A Moment of War* (Penguin; New Press). *One Midsummer Morning* is the irresistibly romantic account of Lee's walk through Spain – from Vigo to Málaga – and his gradual awareness of the forces moving the country towards Civil War. As an autobiographical novel, of living rough and busking his way from the Cotswolds with a violin, it's a delight; as a piece of social observation, painfully sharp. In *A Rose For Winter* he describes his return, twenty years later, to Andalucía, while in *A Moment of War* he looks back again to describe a winter fighting with the International Brigade in the Civil War – by turns moving, comic and tragic.

James A. Michener *Iberia* (Corgi; Crest). A bestselling, idiosyncratic and encyclopedic compendium of interviews and impressions of Spain on the brink – in 1968 – looking

forward to the post-Franco years. Fascinating, still.

★ **Jan Morris** *Spain* (Penguin; Prentice-Hall). Morris wrote this in six months in 1960, on her (or, at the time, his) first visit to the country. It is an impressionistic account – good in its sweeping control of place and history, though prone to see everything as symbolic. The updated edition is plain bizarre in its ideas on Franco and dictatorship – a condition for which Morris seems to believe Spaniards were naturally inclined.

★ **George Orwell** *Homage to Catalonia* (Penguin; Harvest Books). Stirring account of Orwell's participation in the early exhilaration of revolution in Barcelona, and his growing disillusionment with the factional fighting among the Republican forces during the ensuing Civil War.

Older classics

George Borrow *The Bible in Spain* and *The Zincali* (both o/p). On first publication in 1842, Borrow subtitled *The Bible in Spain* "Journeys, Adventures and Imprisonments of an English-man"; it is one of the most famous books on Spain – slow in places but with some very amusing stories. *Zincali* is an account of the Spanish gypsies, whom Borrow got to know pretty well.

★ **Richard Ford** *A Handbook for Travellers in Spain and Readers at Home* (Centaur Press; Gordon Press); *Gatherings from Spain* (Pallas Athene, UK). *The Handbook* (1845) must be the best guide ever written to any country and stayed in print as a *Murray's Handbook* (one of the earliest series of guides) well into the twentieth century. Massively opinionated, it is an extremely witty book in its British, nineteenth-cen-

tury manner, and worth flicking through for the proverbs alone. *The Gatherings* is a rather timid – but no less entertaining – abridgement of the general pieces, intended for a female audience who wouldn't have the taste for the more cerebral stuff.

Washington Irving *Tales of the Alhambra* (originally published 1832; abridged editions are on sale in Granada). Half of Irving's book consists of oriental stories, set in the Alhambra; the rest of accounts of his own residence there and the local characters of his time. A perfect read *in situ*.

George Sand *A Winter in Majorca* (Academy Press, US). Sand and Chopin spent their winter at the monastery of Valldemossa. They weren't entirely appreciated by the locals, in which lies much of the book's appeal. Local editions, including a translation by late Mallorcan resident Robert Graves, are on sale around the island.

Anthologies

Jimmy Burns (ed) *Spain: A Literary Companion* (John Murray, UK). A good anthology, including nuggets of most authors recommended here, amid a whole host of others.

David Mitchell *Travellers in Spain: An Illustrated Anthology* (Cassell, UK).

A well-told story of how four centuries of travellers – and most often travel-writers – saw Spain. It's interesting to see Ford, Brenan, Laurie Lee and the rest set in context. Also published as *Here in Spain* (Lookout, Spain), widely available at bookshops in tourist areas.

History

General

Juan Lalaguna *A Traveller's History of Spain* (Windrush; Interlink). A lucid – and pocketable – background history to the country, which spans the Phoenicians to the 1990s and the maturing of democratic Spain.

M. Vincent & R.A. Stradling *Cultural Atlas of Spain and Portugal* (Andromeda, UK). A formidable survey of the Iberian peninsula from ancient times to the present, in coffee-table format, with excellent colour maps and well-chosen photographs.

Prehistoric and Roman Spain

★ **James M. Anderson** *Spain: 1001 Sights, An Archeological and Historical Guide* (Hale; Calgary UP). A good guide and gazetteer to 95 percent of Spain's archeological sites, with detailed instructions of how to get there.

María Cruz Fernandez Castro *Iberia in Prehistory* (Blackwells, UK). A major study of the Iberian peninsula prior to the arrival of the Romans which surveys recent archeological evidence relating to the remarkable technical, economic and artistic progress of the early Iberians.

Roger Collins *Spain: An Archeological Guide* (Oxford UP, UK).

Covering just 130 sites, this book's more detailed coverage makes it a more useful guide to the major sites than Anderson's work (above).

S.J. Keay *Roman Spain* (British Museum Publications; California UP). Definitive survey of a neglected subject, well illustrated and highly readable.

John Richardson *Roman Spain* (Blackwells, UK). This new assessment of the period, which includes recent discoveries and excavations, is part of a fourteen-volume history of Spain, covering prehistoric times to the present.

Early, medieval and beyond

J.M. Cohen *The Four Voyages of Christopher Columbus* (Cresset Library, UK). The man behind the myth; one of the best books on Columbus in English.

Roger Collins *The Arab Conquest of Spain 710–97* (Blackwells, UK). Controversial study which documents the Moorish invasion and the significant influence that the conquered Visigoths had on early Muslim rule. Collins's earlier *Early Medieval Spain 400–1000* (Macmillan, UK), takes a broader overview of the same subject.

John A. Crow *Spain: The Root and the Flower* (California UP, UK/US). Cultural/social history from Roman Spain to the present.

★ **J.H. Elliott** *Imperial Spain 1469–1716* (Penguin, UK/US). The best introduction to "the Golden Age" – academically respected and a gripping tale.

★ **Richard Fletcher** *The Quest for El Cid* (OUP, UK) and *Moorish Spain* (Orion–Phoenix/California UP). Two of the best studies of their kind – fascinating and highly readable narratives. The latter is a masterly introduction to the story of the Moors in Spain.

L.P. Harvey *Islamic Spain 1250–1500* (Chicago UP, UK/US). Comprehensive account of its period – both the Islamic kingdoms and the Muslims living beyond their protection.

David Howarth *The Voyage of the Armada* (Penguin, US). An account from the Spanish perspective of the personalities, from king to sailors, involved in the Armada.

★ **Henry Kamen** *The Spanish Inquisition* (Mentor, US). Highly respected examination of the causes and effects of the Inquisition and the long shadow it cast across Spanish history. *The Spanish Inquisition: An Historical Revision* (Weidenfeld & Nicolson, UK), by the same author, returns to the subject in the light of more recent evidence, while his *Philip of Spain* (Yale UP, UK/US) is the first fully researched biography of Felipe II, the ruler most associated with the Inquisition.

Elie Kedourie *Spain and the Jews: the Sephardi Experience, 1492 and After* (Thames & Hudson, UK/US). A collection of essays on the three million Spanish Jews of the Middle Ages and their expulsion by the Catholic kings.

John Lynch *Spain 1598–1700* and *Bourbon Spain: 1700–1808* (Blackwells, UK). Two further volumes in the Blackwells project, written by the General Editor, dealing with Spain's rise to Empire and the critical Bourbon period.

Colin Smith, Charles Melville & Ahmad Ubaydli *Christians and Moors in Spain* (Aris & Phillips, UK; 3 vols). A fascinating collection of documents by Spanish and Arabic writers from the Muslim conquest to the Christian supremacy, which are intended for the lay reader as well as the academic.

The twentieth century

⭐ **Gerald Brenan** *The Spanish Labyrinth* (CUP, UK/US). First published in 1943, Brenan's account of the background to the Civil War is tinged by personal experience, yet still an impressively rounded account.

⭐ **Raymond Carr** *Modern Spain 1875–1980* (OUP, UK/US) and *The Spanish Tragedy: the Civil War in Perspective* (Weidenfeld, UK). Two of the best books available on modern Spanish history – concise and well-told narratives.

Ronald Fraser *Blood of Spain* (Pimlico; Pantheon). Subtitled "The Experience of Civil War, 1936–39", this is an equally impressive piece of research, constructed entirely from oral accounts.

⭐ **Ian Gibson** *Federico García Lorca* (Faber & Faber; Pantheon), *The Assassination of Federico García Lorca* (Penguin, UK) and *Lorca's Granada* (Faber & Faber, UK/US). The biography is a compelling book and *The Assassination* a brilliant reconstruction of the events at the end of his life, with an examination of fascist corruption and of the shaping influences on Lorca, twentieth-century Spain and the Civil War. *Granada* contains a series of walking tours around parts of the town familiar to the poet.

⭐ **Gerald Howson** *Arms for Spain: the Untold Story of the Spanish Civil War* (John Murray, UK). This important book uses Russian and Polish archives to reveal how the Republicans were double-crossed by almost every foreign government they attempted to purchase arms from (including the Nazis) during the war – with their avowed ally Moscow one of the major culprits.

⭐ **Paul Preston** *Franco* (Fontana, UK), *Concise History of the Spanish Civil War* (Fontana, UK). *Franco* is a penetrating – and monumental – biography of Franco and his regime, which provides as clear a picture as any yet published of how he won the Civil War and survived in power so long. *Civil War* is a compelling introduction to the subject and more accessible for the general reader than Thomas's work (below).

Adrian Shubert *A Social History of Spain* (Routledge, UK). Comprehensive and highly readable analysis of social development in Spain from 1800 to the 1980s.

⭐ **Hugh Thomas** *The Spanish Civil War* (Penguin; Touchstone). This exhaustive 1000-page study is regarded (both in Spain and abroad) as the definitive history of the Civil War.

Art, architecture, photography, film and design

Marianne Barrucand and Achim Bednoz *Moorish Architecture* (Taschen, Germany). A beautifully illustrated guide to the major Moorish monuments.

Bernard Bevan *History of Spanish Architecture* (o/p). Classic study of Iberian and Ibero-American archi-tecture which includes extensive coverage of the Mudéjar, Plateresque and Baroque periods.

Hugh Broughton *Madrid: A Guide to Recent Architecture* (Ellipsis, UK). Modern Spanish architecture is at the cutting edge of world design and this is a fluent and pocketable guide to a hundred of the best examples in Madrid, each with its own photo and directions on how to get there.

Jerrilyn D. Dodds *Al-Andalus* (Abrams, UK/US). An in-depth study of the arts and monuments of Moorish Andalucía, put together as a catalogue for a major exhibition at the Alhambra.

Godfrey Goodwin *Islamic Spain* (Chronicle Books, US). Portable architectural guide with descriptions of virtually every significant Islamic building in Spain, and a fair amount of background.

Michael Jacobs *Alhambra* (Frances Lincoln; Rizzoli). Sumptuously produced volume with outstanding photographs and expert commentary. Authoritatively guides you through the history and architecture of the Alhambra, and concludes with a fascinating essay on the hold that the palace has had on later artists, travellers and writers, from Irving and Ford to de Falla and Lorca.

★ **Cristina García Rodero** *Festivals and Rituals of Spain* (Abrams, US), *España Oculta* (Smithsonian Institute, US). *Festival and Rituals* is a mesmerizing photographic record of the exuberance

and colour of Spain's many fiestas by Spain's most astonishing contemporary photographer. *Oculta* is an equally atmospheric collection of black and white pictures celebrating the country's religion and mysticism.

Gabriel Ruiz Cabrero *The Modern in Spain* (MIT Press). This readable book is a clear, comprehensive study of post-war Spanish architecture. The author is an architect and professor in the renowned Faculty of Architecture at Madrid's *Politécnica*.

Suzanne Slesin et al *Spanish Style* (Thames & Hudson; Clarkson N. Potter). A gorgeous photographic compendium of Spanish style, old and new, in everything from its statuary and *azulejo* tilework to modern furniture and interiors.

Fréderic Strauss *Almodóvar on Almodóvar* (Faber & Faber, UK). Frank conversations between Strauss (co-editor of *Cahiers du Cinéma*) and the Spanish film director concentrate on the work rather than the hype, punctuated by Almodóvar's contagious humour.

Numerous individual studies of Picasso, Miró, Dalí and Gaudí, as well as the classic Spanish painters, are, of course, also available.

Fiction and poetry

Spanish classics

Pedro de Alarcón *The Three-Cornered Hat* (Dover, UK). Ironic nineteenth-century tales of the previous century's corruption, bureaucracy and absolutism.

Leopoldo Alas *La Regenta* (European Schoolbook). Alas's nineteenth-century novel, with its sweeping vision of the disintegrating

social fabric of the period, is a kind of Spanish *Madame Bovary* (a book that it was in fact accused of plagiarizing at time of publication).

Ramón Pérez de Ayala *Belarmino and Apolonio* (California UP, US) and *Honeymoon, Bittermoon* (California UP, US). A pair of tragi-comic picaresque novels written around the turn of the twentieth century.

Emilia Pardo Bazán *The House of Ulloa* (Georgia UP, US). Bazán was an early feminist intellectual and in this, her best-known book, she charts the decline of the old aristocracy in the time of the Glorious Revolution of 1868.

Miguel de Cervantes *Don Quixote* (Penguin; Signet) and *Exemplary Stories* (Oxford, UK). *Quixote* is of course *the* classic of Spanish literature and still an excellent read. If you want to try Cervantes in a more modest dose, the *Stories* are a good place to start.

Benito Pérez Galdós *Fortunata and Jacinta* (Penguin, UK/US). Galdós wrote in the last decades of the nineteenth century and his novels of life in Madrid combine comic scenes and social realism; he is often characterized as a "Spanish Balzac". Other Galdós novels available in translation include *Misericordia* (Dedalus, UK), *Nazarín* (Oxford, UK), and the epic *"I"* (Columbia, US).

Saint Teresa of Ávila *The Life of Saint Teresa of Ávila* (Penguin, UK/US). Saint Teresa's autobiography is said to be the most widely read Spanish classic after *Don Quixote*. It takes some wading through but it's fascinating in parts. Various translations are available.

Modern fiction

Felipe Alfau *Locos: A Comedy of Gestures* (Illinois UP, US). Though Alfau emigrated to New York and wrote in English (in the 1930s and 1940s), his novels are very Spanish; also well ahead of their time in terms of style, so perhaps not the easiest of reads.

Bernardo Atxaga *Obabakoak* (Espasa Calpe, SA). This challenging novel by a Basque writer won major prizes on its Spanish publication. It is a sequence of tales of life in a Basque village and the narrator's search to give them meaning.

Arturo Barea *The Forging of a Rebel* (o/p). Superb autobiographical trilogy, taking in the Spanish war in Morocco in the 1920s, and Barea's own part in the Civil War. The books have been published in UK paperback editions under the individual titles *The Forge*, *The Track* and *The Clash*.

Michel del Castillo *The Disinherited* (Red Fox; Consort). Gripping tale of Madrid during the Civil War, written in 1959.

Victor Català (Caterina Albert i Paradís) *Solitude* (o/p). This tragic tale of a woman's life and sexual passions in a Catalan mountain village is regarded as the most important pre-Civil War Catalan novel.

Juan Luís Cebrián *Red Doll* (Grove-Atlantic, US). Easy-to-read thriller set in post-Franco years, involving Basque terrorists, the KGB, right-wing backlash and, of course, romance.

Camilo José Cela *The Family of Pascual Duarte* (Little Brown, US). Cela should be the grand old man of Spanish fiction – a Nobel Prize-winner and integral to the revival of Spanish literature after the Civil War – though his reputation in Spain is compromised by his past involvement with Franco's government. *Pascual Duarte*, his first and best-known novel, portrays the brutal story of a peasant murderer from Extremadura, set against the backdrop of the fratricidal Civil War.

★ **Juan Goytisolo** *Marks of Identity* (Serpent's Tail; Consort), *Count Julian* (Serpent's Tail, UK/US), *Juan the Landless* (Serpent's Tail, UK/US), *Landscapes after the Battle* (Serpent's Tail/Seaver Books), *Quarantine* (Illinois UP, US). Born in Barcelona in 1931, Goytisolo became a bitter enemy of the Franco regime, and has spent most of his life in self-exile, in Paris and in Morocco. He is perhaps the most important modern Spanish novelist, confronting, above all in his great trilogy (comprising the first three titles listed above), the whole ambivalent idea of Spain and Spanishness, as well as being one of the first writers to deal openly with homosexuality. The more recent *Quarantine* documents a journey into a Dante-esque netherworld in which the torments of hell are set against reportage of the Gulf War. Goytisolo has also written an autobiography, *Forbidden Territory* (Serpent's Tail, UK).

Montserrat Lunati (ed) *Rainy Days: Short Stories by Contemporary Spanish Women Writers* (Aris & Phillips, UK). This impressive collection (with Spanish parallel text) has work by celebrated literary lights such as Rosa Montero and Maruja Torres.

★ **Javier Marias** *Tomorrow in the Battle Think on Me* (Harvill, UK). There are many who rate Marias as Spain's finest contemporary novelist – and the evidence is here in this searching, psychological thriller, with its study of the human capacity for concealment and confession. Harvill also publishes two other Marias novels, *A Heart So White* and *All Souls*.
Ana María Matute *School of the Sun* (Columbia UP, US). The loss of childhood innocence on a Balearic island, where old enmities are redefined during the Civil War.

Manuel Vázquez Montalban *Murder in the Central Committee*, *Southern Seas*, *An Olympic Death*, *The Angst Ridden Executive* and *Off Side* (all Serpent's Tail, UK). Montalban is one of Spain's most influential writers. A long-time member of the Communist Party, he lives in Barcelona, like his great creation, the gourmand private detective Pepe Carvalho, who stars in all of his wry and racy crime thrillers. The one to begin with – indeed, a bit of a classic – is *Murder in the Central Committee*.

★ **Arturo Pérez Reverte** *The Seville Communion* (Harvill Press, UK). Entertaining crime yarn by one of Spain's leading writers, involving a hacker in the pope's computer, a stubborn old local priest up against rapacious bankers eager to bulldoze his church, a number of corpses, and an investigator dispatched by the Vatican. All is played out against the colourfully described backdrop of Sevilla.

Julián Ríos *Larva* (Dalkey Archive, US). Subtitled *Midsummer Night's Babel*, *Larva* is a large, complex, postmodern novel by a leading Spanish literary figure, originally published to huge acclaim in Spain.

Javier Tomo *The Coded Letter* and *Dear Monster* (Carcanet, UK). A pair of Kafkaesque tales from one of Spain's leading post-Franco-era novelists.

If you can read **Spanish**, the following modern novelists are also of interest: **Luís Martín Santos** (*Tiempo de Silencio*); **Alfonso Grosso** (*Con Flores a María*); **Mariano Antolín** (*Wham!*, *Hombre Arañal* – the Spanish William Burroughs); **Montserrat Roig** (best of contemporary feminist writers); **Rafael Sánchez Ferlosio** (*El Jarama*, *Alfanhuí*); **Pío Baroja** (*El Arbol de la Ciencia*); and **Miguel Delibes** (*El Camino*, or any others).

Plays and poetry

Pedro Calderón de la Barca *Life is a Dream and other Spanish Classics* (Nick Hern Books; Players Press), *The Mayor of Zalamea* (Absolute Press; Dramatic Publications). Some of the best works of the great dramatist of Spain's "Golden Age".

Federico García Lorca *Five Plays: Comedies and Tragicomedies* (Penguin; New Directions). The great pre-Civil War playwright and poet. Arturo Barea's *Lorca: the Poet and His People* is also of interest.

Lope de Vega. The nation's first important playwright (b. 1562) wrote literally hundreds of plays, many of which, including *Lo Cierto por lo Dudoso* (A Certainty for a Doubt) and *Fuenteobvejuna* (The Sheep Well), remain standards of classic Spanish theatre.

J.M. Cohen (ed.) *The Penguin Book of Spanish Verse* (Penguin, UK/US). Spanish poetry from the twelfth century to the modern age, with (parallel text) translations from all the major names.

Spain in foreign fiction

Harry Chapman *Spanish Drums* (Bethany, US). An engaging thriller, telling of an Englishwoman outsider's entry into the life of a family in Teruel – and her discovery of all the terrible baggage of its Civil War past.

Graham Greene *Monsignor Quixote* (Penguin; Pocket Books). The journey of a small-town priest around modern Spain; Greene at his comic best.

Kathryn Harrison *A Thousand Orange Trees* (Fourth Estate, UK). A complex and intense novel set during the Inquisition in the seventeenth century.

Ernest Hemingway *The Sun Also Rises* and *For Whom the Bell Tolls* (both Vintage/Arrow; Scribner). Hemingway remains a big part of the American myth of Spain – *The Sun Also Rises* contains some lyrically beautiful writing, while the latter is a good deal more laboured. He also published an enthusiastic and not very good account of bullfighting, *Death in the Afternoon*.

Arthur Koestler *Dialogue with Death* (o/p). Koestler was reporting the Civil War in 1937 when he was captured and imprisoned by Franco's troops – this is essentially his prison diary.

Matthew Lewis *The Monk* (Penguin, UK/US). You'd be hard-pressed to find a more gripping holiday read than this thriller, set in a Capuchin monastery in Madrid, with its tale of lustful monks, evil abbesses, rape, incest and murder. And oddly enough it's a classic novel, the most gothic of the genre, first published in 1796.

Norman Lewis *Voices of the Old Sea* (Picador, UK). Lewis lived in Catalunya from 1948 to 1952, just as tourism was starting to arrive. This book is an ingenious blend of novel and social record, charting the breakdown of the old ways in the face of the "new revolution".

Amin Malouf *Leo the African* (Abacus, UK). A wonderful historical novel, re-creating the life of Leo Africanus, the fifteenth-century Moorish geographer, in the last years of the kingdom of Granada, and on his subsequent exile in Morocco and world travels.

Colm Tóibín *The South* (Picador, UK). First novel by the Irish writer, who spent the early 1990s in Barcelona. The city is the setting for his tale of an Irish woman looking for a new life.

Specialist guidebooks

★ **Phil Ball** *Morbo – The Story of Spanish Football* (When Saturday Comes Books, UK). Excellent and well-written account of the history of Spanish football from its nineteenth-century beginnings with the British workers at the mines of Río Tinto in Huelva to the golden years of Real Madrid and the dark days of Franco, with the ever present backdrop of the ferocious rivalry or *morbo* – political, historical, regional and linguistic – which has driven the Spanish game since its birth. Essential reading for every football aficionado visiting Spain.

Bob Carrick *Ventas Within a Short Drive of the Costa del Sol* (Santana, Málaga). Useful guide to some of the best *ventas* – Spain's bargain roadside restaurants – within easy reach of the Málaga coast. Widely available at bookshops in major resorts.

Trekking and cycling

David and Ros Brawn *Alpujarras: A Walking Guide to the Poqueira and Trevelez Valleys* (Discovery, UK; order via email at Ⓔwiwg@walking.demon.co.uk). Walking guide to this outstandingly picturesque corner of the Alpujarras; fifteen walks are covered, ranging from half an hour to a full day. The same authors have produced twenty similar format trekking guides covering the Balearic and Canary islands; check out their website (Ⓦwww.walking.demon.co.uk) for details.

Robin Collomb *Picos de Europa, Sierra de Gredos* and *Sierra Nevada*, plus others (West Col, UK). Detailed guides aimed primarily at serious trekkers and climbers.

Valerie Crespi-Green *Landscapes of Mallorca* (Sunflower Books, UK). Aimed at fairly casual walkers and picnickers. Sunflower Books also publish reliable and well-researched walking and trekking guides on the Picos de Europa, the Canary Islands, Menorca, Catalunya and the Costa Blanca.

★ **Teresa Farino** *Picos de Europa* (Sunflower, UK). An excellent walking and touring guide to this spectacularly beautiful mountain wilderness in northern Spain. Written by the Picos-resident author of the wildlife section for this guide (see.p1044).

Paul Lucia *Through the Spanish Pyrenees: GR11 Long Distance Footpath* (Cicerone Press, UK). New guide to the GR11, a high-level and recently waymarked trail which crosses the Spanish Pyrenees from coast to coast.

Jacqueline Oglesby *The Mountains of Central Spain* (Cicerone Press, UK). Walking and scrambling guide to the magnificent Sierras de Gredos and Guadarrama by resident author.

★ **John & Christine Oldfield** *Andalucía and the Costa del Sol* (Sunflower Books, UK). This addition to the popular *Landscapes* walking guide series has 23 clearly described walks (with maps) ranging from 5km to 22km in Las Alpujarras,

Sierra Nevada, Axarquía and Grazalema, as well as the areas bordering the Costa del Sol.

June Parker *Walking in Mallorca* (Cicerone Press, UK). This popular guide is now in its third edition, with many new treks.

Kev Reynolds *Walks and Climbs in the Pyrenees* (Cicerone Press, UK). User-friendly guide for trekkers and walkers, though half devoted to the French side of the frontier.

Bob Stansfield *Costa Blanca Mountain Walks* (Cicerone Press, UK). Walks within this little-known, but spectacular, area near Alicante. **Robin Walker** *Walks and Climbs in the Picos de Europa* (Cicerone Press, UK). New guide by experienced resident mountaineer.

Andy Walmsley *Walking in the Sierra Nevada* (Cicerone Press, UK).

Reliable coverage of 45 routes, with details of flora and fauna – from easy short walks in the Alpujarras to ascents of the highest peaks.

In Spanish, look out for the excellent series of guides published by **Sua Edizioak** of Bilbao. These include *Topoguias* and *Rutas y Paseos* covering most of the individual **Spanish sierras and mountain regions**, and a superb range of **regional guides for cyclists,** *En Bici,* functionally ring-bound, with detailed maps and route contours. The Barcelona-based map publisher **Editorial Alpina** (Ⓦwww.editorial alpina.com) has an equally good range of 1:25,000 to 1:40,000 walking maps and guides covering Andalucía, Catalunya, the Pyrenees, the Picos de Europa and other parts of Spain. The reliable **Penthalon** guides, available from major bookshops in Spain, detail walks in various regions throughout the country.

The pilgrim route to Santiago

La Ruta de Plata a Pie y en Bicicleta (El País/Aguilar, Spain). Spanish guide to the alternative (and lesser-known) pilgrim route to Santiago, the Vía (or Ruta) de Plata – from Sevilla via Mérida, Cáceres and Salamanca. Also has detailed itinerary for the same route for cyclists.

John Higginson *Le Puy to Santiago – A Cyclist's Guide* (Cicerone Press, UK). A cyclist's guide to the pilgrim route which follows as closely as possible (on tarmac) the walker's path, visiting all the major sites en route.

Edwin Mullins *The Pilgrimage to Santiago* (o/p). This is a travelogue rather than a guide, but is by far the best book on the Santiago legend and its fascinating medieval pilgrimage industry.

Alison Raju *Le Puy to Santiago – A Walker's Guide* (Cicerone Press, UK). The first guide in English to cover the whole route, written by an experienced Iberian hiker. In *The Vía de Plata* (available from the Confraternity of Saint James, see below) she also describes the lesser-known pilgrim route, described above.

Pilgrim Guide to Spain (Confraternity of Saint James, UK). A pamphlet, revised annually, with information on the routes and places to stay and eat. The confraternity can also supply many other relevant publications, as well as pilgrim accreditation. Their address is: c/o Marian Marples, Confraternity of St James, 1st floor, 1 Talbot Yard, Borough High St, London SE1 1YP, UK (Ⓣ020/7404 4500, Ⓕ7407 1468).

Wildlife

★ **Frederic Grunfeld and Teresa Farino** *Wild Spain* (Sheldrake Press; Prentice Hall). A knowledgeable and practical guide to Spain's national parks, ecology and wildlife.

Heinzel, Fitter and Parslow *Collins Guide to the Birds of Britain and Europe* (Collins, UK). Alternative to the other Collins guide below.

Peterson, Mountfort and Hollom *Collins Field Guide to the*

Birds of Britain and Europe (Collins Reference; Houghton Mifflin). Standard reference book – covers most birds in Spain.

Oleg Polunin and Anthony Huxley *Flowers of the Mediterranean* (Chatto, UK). Useful if by no means exhaustive field guide.

K.J. Stoba *Bird Watching in Mallorca* (Cicerone Press, UK). Island guide listing 282 species and where and when to see them.

Food and wine

Coleman Andrews *Catalan Cuisine* (Grub Street, UK). Best available English-language book dealing with Spain's most adventurous regional cuisine.

Nicholas Butcher *The Spanish Kitchen* (Macmillan, UK). A practical and knowledgeable guide to creating Spanish dishes when you get back. Lots of informative detail on tapas, olive oil, *jamón serrano* and herbs.

Penelope Casas *The Foods and Wines of Spain* (Knopf, US). Superb Spanish cookbook, covering classic and regional dishes with equal, authoritative aplomb. By the same author is the useful *Tapas: the little dishes of Spain*. (Knopf, US).

Alan Davidson *The Tio Pepe Guide to the Seafood of Spain and Portugal* (Anness, UK). An indispensible pocket book that details and illustrates every fish and crustacean you're likely to meet in restaurants and bars along the Spanish costas.

★ **Julian Jeffs**, *Sherry* (Faber, UK). The story of sherry – history, production, blending and brands. Rightly a classic and the best introduction to Andalucía's great wine.

Mark and Kim Millon *Wine Roads of Spain* (HarperCollins, UK/US). Everything you ever wanted to know about Spanish wine and sherry: when, how and where it's made, with a good array of useful maps.

John Radford *The New Spain* (Mitchell Beazley, UK). Lavish coffee table format disguises this book's serious content – a detailed region-by-region guide to Spanish wine with colour maps, *bodega* and vintage evaluations and fine illustrations.

Jan Read *Guide to the Wines of Spain* (Mitchell Beazley, UK). Encyclopedic (yet pocketable) guide to the classic and emerging wines of Spain by a leading authority. Includes maps, vintages and vineyards.

Language

Once you get into it, Spanish is the easiest language there is – and you'll be helped everywhere by people who are eager to try and understand even the most faltering attempt. English is spoken, but only to any extent in the main tourist areas, and wherever you are you'll get a far better reception if you at least try communicating with Spaniards in their own tongue. Being understood, of course, is only half the problem – getting the gist of the reply, often rattled out at a furious pace, may prove far more difficult. Nevertheless, you'll be getting there.

The rules of **pronunciation** are pretty straightforward and, once you get to know them, strictly observed. Unless there's an accent, words ending in d, l, r, and z are **stressed** on the last syllable, all others on the second last. All **vowels** are pure and short; combinations have predictable results.

A somewhere between the "A" sound of back and that of father.

E as in get.

I as in police.

O as in hot.

U as in rule.

C is lisped before E and I, hard otherwise: *cerca* is pronounced "thairka" (though in Andalucía many natives pronounce the soft "c" as an "s").

G works the same way, a guttural "H" sound (like the ch in loch) before E or I, a hard G elsewhere – *gigante* becomes "higante".

H is always silent.

J the same sound as a guttural G: *jamón* is pronounced "hamon".

LL sounds like an English Y or LY: *tortilla* is pronounced "torteeya/tor-teelya".

N is as in English unless it has a tilde (accent) over it, when it becomes NY: *mañana* sounds like "manyana".

QU is pronounced like an English K.

R is rolled, RR doubly so.

V sounds more like B, *vino* becoming "beano".

X has an S sound before consonants, normal X before vowels. More common in Basque, Gallego or Catalan words where it's sh or zh.

Z is the same as a soft C, so *cerveza* becomes "thairvaitha" (but again much of the south prefers the "s" sound).

The list of a few essential words and phrases opposite and overleaf should be enough to get you started, though if you're travelling for any length of time a dictionary or phrasebook is obviously a worthwhile investment. If you're using a **dictionary**, bear in mind that in Spanish CH, LL, and Ñ count as separate letters and are listed after the Cs, Ls and Ns respectively.

Spanish words and phrases

Basics

Yes, No, OK	Sí, No, Vale
Please, Thank you	Por favor, Gracias
Where, When	Dónde, Cuando
What, How much	Qué, Cuánto
Here, There	Aquí, Allí
This, That	Esto, Eso
Now, Later	Ahora, Más tarde
Open, Closed	Abierto/a, Cerrado/a
With, Without	Con, Sin
Good, Bad	Buen(o)/a, Mal(o)/a
Big, Small	Gran(de), Pequeño/a
Cheap, Expensive	Barato, Caro
Hot, Cold	Caliente, Frío
More, Less	Más, Menos
Today, Tomorrow	Hoy, Mañana
Yesterday	Ayer

Greetings and responses

Hello, Goodbye	Hola, Adiós
Good morning	Buenos días
Good afternoon/ night	Buenas tardes/ noches
See you later	Hasta luego
Sorry	Lo siento/ disculpéme
Excuse me	Con permiso/ perdón
How are you? (usted)?	¿Como está
I (don't) understand	(No) Entiendo
Not at all/ You're welcome	De nada
Do you speak English?	¿Habla (usted) inglés?
I (don't) speak Spanish	(No) Hablo español
My name is...	Me llamo. . .

What's your name?	¿Como se llama usted?
I am English/ Australian/ Canadian/ American/ Irish	Soy inglés(a)/ australiano(a)/ canadiense(a)/ americano(a)/ irlandés(a)

Hotels and transport

I want	Quiero
I'd like	Quisiera
Do you know...?	¿Sabe...?
I don't know	No sé
There is (is there)?	(¿)Hay(?)
Give me... (one like that)	Deme...(uno así)
Do you have...?	¿Tiene...?
the time	la hora
a room	una habitación
...with two beds/ double bed	...con dos camas/cama matrimonial
...with shower/bath	...con ducha/ baño
It's for one person	Es para una persona
(two people)	(dos personas)
for one night	para una noche
(one week)	(una semana)
It's fine, how much is it?	¿Está bien, cuánto es?
It's too expensive	Es demasiado caro
Don't you have anything cheaper?	No tiene algo más barato?
Can one...?	¿Se puede....?
camp (near) here?	¿...acampar aquí (cerca)?
Is there a hostel nearby?	¿Hay un hostal aquí cerca?

How do I get to...?	¿Por donde se va a...?	ten	diez
		eleven	once
Left, right, straight on	Izquierda, derecha, todo recto	twelve	doce
		thirteen	trece
		fourteen	catorce
Where is...?	¿Dónde está....?	fifteen	quince
the bus station	la estación de autobuses	sixteen	diez y seis
		twenty	veinte
the train station	la estación de station ferro-carril	twenty one	veintiuno
		thirty	treinta
the nearest bank	el banco mas cercano	forty	cuarenta
		fifty	cincuenta
the post office	el correos/la oficina de correos	sixty	sesenta
		seventy	setenta
the toilet	el baño/aseo/ servicio	eighty	ochenta
		ninety	noventa
		one hundred	cien(to)
Where does the bus to...leave from?	¿De dónde sale el autobús para...?	one hundred and one	cien-to uno
		two hundred	doscientos
Is this the train for Mérida?	¿Es este el tren para Mérida?	two hundred and one doscientos uno	
		five hundred	quinientos
I'd like a (return) ticket to...	Quisiera un billete (de ida y vuelta) para...	one thousand	mil
		two thousand	dos mil
		two thousand and one	dos mil un
What time does it leave (arrive in...)?	¿A qué hora sale (llega a...)?	two thousand and two	dos mil dos
What is there to eat?	¿Qué hay para comer?	two thousand and three	dos mil tres
What's that?	¿Qué es eso?	first	primero/a
What's this called in Spanish?	¿Como se llama este en español?	second	segundo/a
		third	tercero/a
		fifth	quinto/a

Numbers and days

one	un/uno/una	tenth	décimo/a
two	dos	Monday	lunes
three	tres	Tuesday	martes
four	cuatro	Wednesday	miércoles
five	cinco	Thursday	jueves
six	seis	Friday	viernes
seven	siete	Saturday	sábado
eight	ocho	Sunday	domingo
nine	nueve		

For a food and drink vocabulary, see pp.48–49.

Phrasebooks, dictionaries and teaching yourself

Spanish

Numerous Spanish phrasebooks are available, not least the *Spanish Rough Guide Phrasebook*, laid out dictionary-style for instant access. For teaching yourself the language, the BBC tape series *España Viva* and *Dígame* are excellent, as is their two-week crash-course *Get By in Spanish*. *Breakthrough Spanish* (Macmillan) is probably the best of the tape-and-book home study courses.

Many of the books available in North America are geared to Latin American usage – more old-fashioned publications may be better for Spain itself. Langenscheidt, Cassells, Collins and others all produce useful dictionaries; Berlitz and others publish separate Spanish and Latin American phrasebooks.

Català

The best book for learning Català is a total immersion course called *Digui Digui* (published by the Generalitat de Catalunya), a series of books and tapes that's presented entirely in Catalan; you'll need to speak Spanish to take this on. In Britain, the best place to find it is Grant & Cutler, 55 Great Marlborough St, London W1 (☎020/7734 2012). *Teach Yourself Catalan* (Hodder & Stoughton) is less ambitious (and presented in English); while if you're serious you'll also need *Catalan Grammar* (Dolphin Book Company) and *Parla Català* (Pia), the only available English–Catalan phrasebook.

Spanish and architectural Terms: a Glossary

Alameda Park or grassy promenade.
Alcazaba Moorish castle.
Alcázar Moorish fortified palace.
Apse Semicircular recess at the altar (usually eastern) end of a church.
Ayuntamiento/ajuntament Town hall.
Azulejo Glazed ceramic tilework.
Barrio Suburb or quarter.
Bodega Cellar, wine bar or warehouse.
Calle Street.
Capilla Mayor Chapel containing the high altar.
Capilla Real Royal Chapel.
Capital Top of a column.
Cartuja Carthusian monastery.
Castillo Castle.
Chancel Part of a church containing the altar, usually at the east end.
Churrigueresque Extreme form of Baroque art named after José Churriguera (1650–1723) and his extended family, its main exponents.
Colegiata Collegiate (large parish) church.
Convento Monastery or convent.
Coro Central part of church built for the choir.
Coro Alto Raised choir, often above west door of a church.
Correos Post office.
Corrida de Toros Bullfight.
Crypt Burial place in a church, usually under the choir.
Custodia Large receptacle for Eucharist wafers.
Dueño/a Proprietor, landlord/lady.
Ermita Hermitage.
Gitano Gypsy or Romany.
Iglesia Church.
Isabelline Ornamental form of late Gothic developed during the reign of Isabel and Fernando.
Loggia Covered area on the side of a building, usually arcaded.
Lonja Stock exchange building.
Mercado Market.
Mihrab Prayer niche of Moorish mosque.

Mirador Viewing point.
Modernisme (Modernista) Catalan/Spanish form of Art Nouveau, whose most famous exponent was Antoni Gaudí.
Monasterio Monastery or convent.
Morisco Muslim Spaniard subject to medieval Christian rule – and nominally baptized.
Mozárabe Christian subject to medieval Moorish rule; normally allowed freedom of worship, they built churches in an Arab-influenced manner (Mozarabic).
Mudéjar Muslim Spaniard subject to medieval Christian rule, but retaining Islamic worship; most commonly a term applied to architecture which includes buildings built by Moorish craftsmen for the Christian rulers and later designs influenced by the Moors. The 1890s to 1930s saw a Mudéjar revival, blended with Art Nouveau and Art Deco forms.
Narthex Entrance hall of church.
Nave Central space in a church, usually flanked by aisles.
Palacio Aristocratic mansion.
Parador Luxury hotel, often converted from minor monument.
Paseo Promenade; also the evening stroll thereon.
Patio Inner courtyard.
Plateresque Elaborately decorative Renaissance style, the sixteenth-century successor of Isabelline forms. Named for its resemblance to silversmiths' work (*platería*).
Plaza Square.
Plaza de Toros Bullring.
Portico Covered entrance to a building.
Posada Old name for an inn.
Puerta Gateway, also mountain pass.
Puerto Port.
Reja Iron screen or grille, often fronting a window.

Reliquary Receptacle for a saint's relics, usually bones. Often highly decorated.

Reredos Wall or screen behind an altar.

Retablo Altarpiece.

Ría River estuary in Galicia.

Río River.

Romería Religious procession to a rural shrine.

Sacristía, Sagrario Sacristy or sanctuary of church – room for sacred vessels and vestments.

Sardana Catalan folk dance.

Seo, Seu, la Se Ancient/regional names for cathedrals.

Sierra Mountain range.

Sillería Choir stall.

Solar Aristocratic town mansion.

Taifa Small Moorish kingdom, many of which emerged after the disintegration of the Córdoba caliphate.

Telefónica The phone company; also used for its offices in any town.

Transepts The wings of a cruciform church, placed at right angles to the nave and chancel.

Tympanum Area between lintel of a doorway and the arch above it.

Turismo Tourist office.

Vault Arched ceiling.

Political parties and acronyms

CNT Anarchist trade union.

Convergencia I Unio Conservative party in power in Catalunya.

ETA Basque terrorist organization. Its political wing is Euskal Herritarrok.

Falange Franco's old fascist party; now officially defunct.

Fuerza Nueva Descendants of the above, also on the way out.

IU Izquierda Unida, broad-left alliance of communists and others.

MC Movimiento Comunista (Communist Movement), small radical offshoot of the PCE.

MOC Movimiento de Objeción de Conciencia, peace group, concerned with NATO and conscription.

OTAN NATO.

PCE Partido Comunista de España (Spanish Communist Party).

PNV Basque Nationalist Party – in control of the right-wing autonomous government.

PP Partido Popular, the centre-right alliance formed by Alianza Popular and the Christian Democrats. The PP is currently Spain's government, under José María Aznar.

PSOE Partido Socialista Obrero Español, the Spanish Socialist Workers' Party, and the main opposition party, led by José Luis Rodríguez, elected in July 2000.

UGT Unión General de Trabajadores, the Spanish TUC.

index

and small print

Index

Map entries are in colour.

INDEX

1083

INDEX

1085

INDEX

Twenty Years of Rough Guides

In the summer of 1981, Mark Ellingham, Rough Guides' founder, knocked out the first guide on a typewriter, with a group of friends. Mark had been travelling in Greece after university, and couldn't find a guidebook that really answered his needs.There were heavyweight cultural guides on the one hand – good on museums and classical sites but not on beaches and tavernas – and on the other hand student manuals that were so caught up with how to save money that they lost sight of the country's significance beyond its role as a place for a cool vacation. None of the guides began to address Greece as a country, with its natural and human environment, its politics and its contemporary life.

Having no urgent reason to return home, Mark decided to write his own guide. It was a guide to Greece that tried to combine some erudition and insight with a thoroughly practical approach to travellers' needs. Scrupulously researched listings of places to stay, eat and drink were matched by careful attention to detail on everything from Homer to Greek music, from classical sites to national parks and from nudist beaches to monasteries. Back in London, Mark and his friends got their Rough Guide accepted by a farsighted commissioning editor at the publisher Routledge and it came out in 1982.

The Rough Guide to Greece was a student scheme that became a publishing phenomenon. The immediate success of the book – shortlisted for the Thomas Cook award – spawned a series that rapidly covered dozens of countries. The Rough Guides found a ready market among backpackers and budget travellers, but soon acquired a much broader readership that included older and less impecunious visitors. Readers relished the guides' wit and inquisitiveness as much as the enthusiastic, critical approach that acknowledges everyone wants value for money – but not at any price.

Rough Guides soon began supplementing the "rougher" information – the hostel and low-budget listings – with the kind of detail that independent-minded travellers on any budget might expect. These days, the guides – distributed worldwide by the Penguin group – include recommendations spanning the range from shoestring to luxury, and cover more than 200 destinations around the globe. Our growing team of authors, many of whom come to Rough Guides initially as outstandingly good letter-writers telling us about their travels, are spread all over the world, particularly in Europe, the USA and Australia. As well as the travel guides, Rough Guides publishes a series of dictionary phrasebooks covering two dozen major languages, an acclaimed series of music guides running the gamut from Classical to World Music, a series of music CDs in association with World Music Network, and a range of reference books on topics as diverse as the Internet, Pregnancy and Unexplained Phenomena. Visit **www.roughguides.com** to see what's cooking.

Rough Guide Credits

Text editor: Lucy Ratcliffe
Series editor: Mark Ellingham
Editorial: Martin Dunford, Jonathan Buckley,
Jo Mead, Kate Berens, Ann-Marie Shaw,
Helena Smith, Judith Bamber, Orla Duane,
Olivia Eccleshall, Ruth Blackmore, Geoff
Howard, Claire Saunders, Gavin Thomas,
Alexander Mark Rogers, Polly Thomas, Joe
Staines, Richard Lim, Duncan Clark, Peter
Buckley, Clifton Wilkinson, Alison Murchie,
Matthew Teller, Andrew Dickson (UK);
Andrew Rosenberg, Stephen Timblin, Yuki
Takagaki, Richard Koss, Hunter Slaton (US)
Production: Susanne Hillen, Andy Hilliard,
Link Hall, Helen Prior, Julia Bovis, Michelle
Draycott, Katie Pringle, Mike Hancock, Zoë

Nobes, Rachel Holmes, Andy Turner
Cartography: Melissa Baker, Maxine Repath,
Ed Wright, Katie Lloyd-Jones
Picture research: Louise Boulton, Sharon
Martins, Mark Thomas
Online: Kelly Cross, Anja Mutic-Blessing,
Jennifer Gold, Audra Epstein, Suzanne
Welles, Cree Lawson (US)
Finance: John Fisher, Gary Singh, Edward
Downey, Mark Hall, Tim Bill
Marketing & Publicity: Richard Trillo, Niki
Smith, David Wearn, Chloë Roberts, Demelza
Dallow, Claire Southern (UK); Simon Carloss,
David Wechsler, Kathleen Rushforth (US)
Administration: Tania Hummel, Julie
Sanderson

Publishing Information

This tenth edition published January 2002 by
Rough Guides Ltd,
62–70 Shorts Gardens, London WC2H 9AH.
Penguin Putnam, Inc. 375 Hudson Street,
NY 10014, USA.
Distributed by the Penguin Group
Penguin Books Ltd,
80 Strand, London WC2R ORL
Penguin Putnam, Inc.
375 Hudson Street, NY 10014, USA
Penguin Books Australia Ltd,
487 Maroondah Highway, PO Box 257,
Ringwood, Victoria 3134, Australia
Penguin Books Canada Ltd,
10 Alcorn Avenue, Toronto, Ontario,
Canada M4V 1E4
Penguin Books (NZ) Ltd,
182–190 Wairau Road, Auckland 10,
New Zealand
Typeset in Bembo and Helvetica to an
original design by Henry Iles.

Printed in Italy by LegoPrint S.p.A

© Mark Ellingham and John Fisher 2002

No part of this book may be reproduced in
any form without permission from the
publisher except for the quotation of brief
passages in reviews.

1128pp includes index
A catalogue record for this book is available
from the British Library

ISBN 1-85828-870-3

The publishers and authors have done their
best to ensure the accuracy and currency of
all the information in **The Rough Guide to
Spain**. However, they can accept no
responsibility for any loss, injury, or
inconvenience sustained by any traveller as a
result of information or advice contained in
the guide.

Help us update

We've gone to a lot of effort to ensure that
the tenth edition of **The Rough Guide to
Spain** is accurate and up to date. However,
things change – places get "discovered",
opening hours are notoriously fickle,
restaurants and rooms raise prices or lower
standards. If you feel we've got it wrong or
left something out, we'd like to know, and if
you can remember the address, the price,
the time, the phone number, so much the
better.

We'll credit all contributions, and send a
copy of the next edition (or any other Rough
Guide if you prefer) for the best letters.
Everyone who writes to us and isn't already a
subscriber will receive a copy of our full-
colour thrice-yearly newsletter. Please mark
letters: "**Rough Guide Spain Update**" and
send to: Rough Guides, 62–70 Shorts
Gardens, London WC2H 9AH, or Rough
Guides, 4th Floor, 345 Hudson St, New York,
NY 10014. Or send an email to:
mail@roughguides.co.uk or
mail@roughguides.com

Acknowledgements

Robert Alcock thanks Almu for everything, Martin Robiette for introducing him to Vitorian lasai, and the People's Republic of Zorrozaurre for being there.

Simon Baskett thanks Trinidad López for all her hard work, patience and invaluable help with the research, to James and Penny for their kindness and generosity and Lucy for her inside knowledge and tips on Madrid.

Brian Catlos would like to thank Núria Silleras Fernández, Mike Lane and Mari Carmen Guitierrez

Chris Lloyd would like to thank all the tourist offices in Catalunya plus Liz Armitage, Concepcio Bascompte, Isabel Goday and Anna Suades

Iain Stewart thanks Martin Davies, José Saché, Roberta, Andy and Chrissie, and Fiona for coming along.

The editor would like to thank Ruth Blackmore and Pau Sandham for Basics, Rachel Holmes for typesetting, Katie Pringle for picture layout, Julie Sanderson for her help with the readers' letters, Mark Thomas for picture research, Ed Wright for cartography, and David Price for proofreading.

Readers letters

Our continued thanks to everyone who has contributed letters, comments, accounts and suggestions over the years, and especially to this 2002 edition. In particular: Sheila Adam, Lynne Adams, Mohammad Ahmad, Jo Alexander, Avril Allan, John Andree, Gabriela Avendano, Michael & Valerie Bacon, Laurel Baden, Jatinder Bahia, Martin Bates, Bas Berwers, Andrea Bethell, Magda Biesemans, J.A. Briffett, Euan Bowater, Connie Brim, W.D. Brookes, Daniel Burns, Mr & Mrs J. Patrick Byrne, Anna Campbell & Nick Hulton, Chris Carter, George & Emily Cassedy, Rita Chandhuri, Andrew Charity, Joseph Chouinard, Aidan Coleman, Rachel Coll & Ed Shinton, Bernadette Colley, Mike Constantine, Jim and Angela Cook, Dr J. Cox, Denis Cros, Gwenno Dafydd, Andrew Davidson, Mrs J.M. Davies, Steve Deegan, Raymond Campbell Paterson, Ms F. Dickin, Maarten van de Donk, Lynn Dunlop & Peter Northcott, Tony Dyer, Mel Eastburn, Gary Elflett, Mark English & Marian Hobbs, David Evans & Susannah Temple, Colin Fisher, Imogen Forster, Christine Gilmour, Rusfad Hansen, Diane Graham. W.G. Green, Christopher Hanson-Smith, Michael Hart, Stephen Hayward, Louise Heal, Rodney & Dorothy Heap, Edward James, Paul Henriquez & Diederik van Elst, Alex Hetwer, Ken Hillman, Annie Hills, John Hipwood, Stephen Hrynczak, Lavinia Hyde, Kemal Ibrahim, Mrs Diana Jacob, Kelly Jacob, Michael L. Johnson, Sara Jones, Analia Kandal, Vanessa Kingwell, Lucien Lahaye, Carole Le Brun, Ruth Johnson & Michael Lewis, Kevin, David Lilley, Mr D. Lockwood, Dr Louisa Lam, Adrian Legge, Brian Levinson, Catrin Lloyd Jones, Chris M. Lobley, A. Logan, Jonathan Long, Anna K. Lyon, Jenny Major, Mrs D. Marsland, Claire Martin & Gerard Kennedy, Colin MacInnes, Peter MacLeod, David Mather, Thomas McBeth Dougan, Kate McLachlan, W.J. McLintic, J. McManus, Cathleen Medwick, Sue Mercer, Michele Mildenhall, Joshua Miller, Liz Moore, Sandy Moritz & Ad van Veen, Ken & Sue Napier, Robin Newberg, Massimo Noro, Paul Oakes, Rosamund O'Daly, Sheila Openshaw, Linda Orton, Carol Pardy, G.A Parkinson, Lynne Parkinson, Georgina Peake, Steve Perkins, Rosie Phipson, Richard Posner, Alostal Pinariega, Dori Pinku, Vic Poole, Sarah Alexander & Adam Porter, Gill & Kev Preece, Matthew Preston, Rupert Price, Jessica Reed, Mrs Gill Rees, M.J. Reeves, Madeleine Riley, John Roberts, Sheila Roberts, Sam Robson, Karen Roden, Mike & Tanya Rome, Jeff & Caroline Rowlands, Dermot Ryan, Sarah & Pepe, L. Sanchez, Ann Sargent, Caroline Scott, J.P Scott, Mrs C.J. Scovell, Miss Phillippa Scriven, Lesley Sevitt, Liz Shaw & Andrew Wood, Heather Shenton, Isobel Sidebottom, Mrs G.S. Skelt, Theo Smeele, Diana Smith, Jenny & Andrew Smith, Judith Smith, John Spoor, Fiona Stenhouse, Christine M. Strand, Olga Szuba, Anna Taranko, Kate Taylor, Sarah Taylor, Deirdre Timoney, Amelia & Dimitri Tishler, Anne Towner, Jenn Toynbee, Jill Tulloch, Bruno Turner, Joanna Vallely, Gijs van Soest, A.R Varachhia, James Venables, Ann Viera, Beatriz Villaverde, N.C. Walker, Robert Warburton, Hazel Wallis, David Watson, John Waugh, Sam Webb, L.W.J. Webster, Cara Weisman, Ewa Werenowska, Lucy Williams, Tom Williams, Neil Wingrove, Roger de Wolf, Geoff Woollen and Ian Young.

SMALL PRINT

Photo Credits

SMALL PRINT

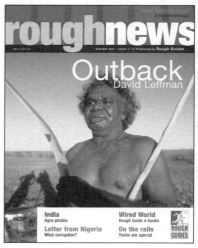

The ideas expressed in this code were developed by and for independent travellers.

Learn About The Country You're Visiting

Start enjoying your travels before you leave by tapping into as many sources of information as you can.

The Cost Of Your Holiday

Think about where your money goes - be fair and realistic about how cheaply you travel. Try and put money into local peoples' hands; drink local beer or fruit juice rather than imported brands and stay in locally owned accommodation. Haggle with humour and not aggressively. Pay what something is worth to you and remember how wealthy you are compared to local people.

Embrace The Local Culture

Open your mind to new cultures and traditions - it will transform your experience. Think carefully about what's appropriate in terms of your clothes and the way you behave. You'll earn respect and be more readily welcomed by local people. Respect local laws and attitudes towards drugs and alcohol that vary in different countries and communities. Think about the impact you could have on them.

Exploring The World – The Travellers' Code

Being sensitive to these ideas means getting more out of your travels - and giving more back to the people you meet and the places you visit.

Minimise Your Environmental Impact

Think about what happens to your rubbish - take biodegradable products and a water filter bottle. Be sensitive to limited resources like water, fuel and electricity. Help preserve local wildlife and habitats by respecting local rules and regulations, such as sticking to footpaths and not standing on coral.

Don't Rely On Guidebooks

Use your guidebook as a starting point, not the only source of information. Talk to local people, then discover your own adventure!

Be Discreet With Photography

Don't treat people as part of the landscape, they may not want their picture taken. Ask first and respect their wishes.

We work with people the world over to promote tourism that benefits their communities, but we can only carry on our work with the support of people like you. For membership details or to find out how to make your travels work for local people and the environment, visit our website.

www.tourismconcern.org.uk

Tourism Concern
Campaigning for Ethical and Fairly Traded Tourism

Don't bury your h___d!

T___ __!

worldwide www.roughguides.com/insurance

ROUGH GUIDES

Insurance organized by Torribles Insurance Brokers Ltd, 21 Prince Street, Bristol, BS1 4PH, England